Mastering
Windows XP Home Edition

Mastering™
Windows® XP Home Edition

Guy Hart-Davis

San Francisco   London

Associate Publisher: Joel Fugazzotto

Acquisitions and Developmental Editor: Ellen Dendy

Editor: Susan Berge

Production Editor: Leslie H. Light

Technical Editor: Mark L. Chambers

Book Designer: Maureen Forys, Happenstance Type-O-Rama

Graphic Illustrator: Tony Jonick

Electronic Publishing Specialist: Interactive Composition Corporation - Rozi Harris

Proofreaders: Dave Nash, Nancy Riddiough, Emily Hsuan, Laurie O'Connell, Amey Garber, Nelson Kim, Yariv Rabinovich

Indexer: Ted Laux

Cover Designer: Design Site

Cover Illustrator/Photographer: Tania Kac, Design Site

This book is dedicated to Rhonda.

Acknowledgments

MY THANKS GO TO the following people for their help with this book:

- Joel Fugazzotto for getting the book approved

- Ellen Dendy for developing the book

- Susan Berge for editing the book carefully and lightly

- Mark Chambers for reviewing the manuscript for technical accuracy and offering both helpful suggestions and encouragement

- Leslie Light for coordinating the book project

- Interactive Composition Corporation and Rozi Harris for typesetting the book

- Dave Nash, Nancy Riddiough, Emily Hsuan, Laurie O'Connell, Amey Garber, Nelson Kim, and Yariv Rabinovich for proofreading the book

- Ted Laux for creating the index

Contents at a Glance

Contents

Chapter 19 • Surfing the Web with Internet Explorer **573**

Introduction

WINDOWS XP HOME EDITION is a huge operating system—huge both in terms of its 40 million–odd lines of programming code and the number of features it offers. Windows XP Home Edition is also huge in that it's a huge improvement on its predecessors: Windows 95, Windows 98, and Windows Me. Not only does it offer features that can simplify your computing life, but it's extremely stable: It crashes seldom, and then only under extreme provocation.

Microsoft has worked hard to make Windows XP Home Edition easier to use than the earlier versions of Windows. But there's still a huge amount you need to know about XP Home Edition in order to use it most effectively.

This book gives you that information.

Who Is This Book For?

This book is for beginning, intermediate, and advanced users who want to get the most out of Windows XP Home Edition with the minimum effort.

Beginning, intermediate, *and* advanced—that's a wide brief. Because any book that covered absolutely everything to do with XP Home in detail would be several thousand pages long, and this book isn't that long, it assumes that you want to get things done with XP Home rather than know everything about it. Instead of presenting arcane trivia or every single way of doing something, the book presents useful information and the easiest and most effective ways of getting something done. (There *is* some arcane information in the book, but it's there because you may find it useful or interesting.) This book also presents the background that you need to know in order to make important decisions about how you configure and use XP Home. But it doesn't hold your hand every step of the way.

NOTE   *To present the information you need within its limited number of pages, this book assumes that you have basic knowledge of Windows already. If you're new to Windows, see Appendix A, "Windows Basics," and the first few sections of the* Essential Skills *section for a quick orientation on the XP Desktop and graphical user interface.*

What Does This Book Cover?

Glad you asked. Here's an overview of what the book covers:

The *Essential Skills* section at the beginning of the book gives you a visual guide to some of the most important procedures you'll need to take with XP Home. These procedures are also explained in full in the main text of the book, so you may want to flip between the visual treatment and the detailed text treatment of a topic.

Chapter 1, "Introducing Windows XP Home Edition," discusses what Windows XP Home Edition is, what's new in it, whether you should upgrade to Windows XP from your current version of Windows, and whether (if you decide to upgrade) you should go to Windows XP Professional rather than Windows XP Home.

Chapter 2, "Installing Windows XP Home Edition," discusses how to install XP Home in each of the three ways you're likely to want to install it: as an upgrade to Windows 98 or Windows Me, as a dual-booting new installation alongside your current version of Windows, or as a clean installation on a computer with no other operating system installed. The chapter starts by discussing how to establish whether your computer is up to running XP Home, and finishes by showing you how to install XP Home automatically.

Chapter 3, "Getting Started with Windows XP Home Edition," discusses how to log on and log off, how to switch from one user session to another, and how to exit XP. It also discusses how you can find out who else is logged on to the computer when you're working at it and how you can get an idea of which programs the other users are running.

Chapter 4, "Customizing Your Desktop," discusses how to get your Desktop into shape so that you can work comfortably, effectively, and enjoyably. These changes range from those you should make immediately (such as choosing the best display resolution, configuring the keyboard and mouse, and setting any accessibility options you need) to changes you may want to make before too long (such as choosing a screen saver, changing your Desktop background, customizing the Start menu, and creating custom toolbars).

Chapter 5, "Installing, Removing, and Running Programs," discusses how to install, configure, remove, and run programs—and how to shut them down when they fail to respond to conventional stimuli.

Chapter 6, "Managing Your Files and Folders," discusses how to manage files and folders—everything from what files and folders actually are to what you can do with them and the tools that XP provides for manipulating them.

Chapter 7, "Making the Most of the Bundled Programs," discusses the bundled programs that come with XP: WordPad, Notepad, Character Map, Paint, Calculator, Windows Picture and Fax Viewer, ClipBook Viewer, and Command Prompt. These programs are deliberately limited—Microsoft would like you to buy extra programs, preferably Microsoft programs—but they're useful for a variety of tasks. This chapter points out the most important features of the bundled programs, including features that most users miss.

Chapter 8, "Finding Help to Solve Your Windows XP Problems," discusses how to find the help you need to use XP most effectively—both the new Help and Support Center and other resources that you may need to turn to for difficult problems.

Chapter 9, "Managing Users and Accounts," discusses how to manage users and accounts to give each user their own Desktop and folders and to maintain security. The chapter covers what user accounts are, what they're for, and why you should use them; the three different types of user account in XP Home; how to create, delete, and modify user accounts; and how to perform some advanced maneuvers using command-line account-management tools.

Chapter 10, "Sharing and File Types," shows you how to use XP Home's sharing and security features to share folders you want to share and keep private those you don't want to share. It also discusses the complex but essential topic of file extensions, file types, and file associations, which allow you to control what happens when you double-click different types of files in Explorer.

Chapter 11, "Managing Your Disks and Drives," discusses how to manage your disks and drives, showing you how to take actions such as formatting a disk, converting a disk's file system to NTFS, using compression to free up disk space, using quotas to allot disk space to users, and creating and deleting partitions.

Chapter 12, "Working with the Registry," discusses the Registry, the configuration database that contains most of XP's settings, and how you can use the Registry Editor to examine it and change it. The chapter starts by detailing the step you *must* take before you make any changes to the Registry and concludes by showing you how to change the Registry so that you can crash your computer with two keystrokes—for testing purposes only, of course.

Chapter 13, "Installing, Configuring, and Managing Printers and Fonts," shows you how to install printers, configure them, and manage print jobs, including printing offline and printing to a file when necessary. This chapter also covers how to install, remove, and use fonts.

Chapter 14, "Managing Hardware, Drivers, and Power," discusses how to install hardware on your computer and how to install, update, and roll back device drivers, the software that makes hardware function. It also covers how to configure power management on your computer and install an uninterruptible power supply.

Chapter 15, "Using Windows XP Home Edition on a Portable Computer," outlines the considerations for using XP Home on a portable computer. Many of these considerations (such as the basics of power management) apply to desktop computers as well and so are covered in other chapters, but this chapter discusses using portable-specific power-management features, using PC Cards, using hardware profiles, and using different locations for dial-up networking. It also shows you how to use XP's Briefcase feature to synchronize files between two computers.

Chapter 16, "Optimizing Windows XP Home Edition," shows you how to deal with program hangs and crashes and how to use Event Viewer to identify problems with your software. It discusses how to use the Windows Update feature and Windows Update website to keep XP up-to-date, how to optimize and monitor performance, how to enable and disable error reporting, and how to set start-up and recovery options.

Chapter 17, "Backup, Troubleshooting, and Disaster Recovery," covers a variety of topics related to when things go wrong. This chapter starts by discussing how to protect your data against disaster by backing it up, and how to restore it when necessary. It talks briefly about XP's Windows File Protection feature, which does its best to prevent you (or malware) from deleting vital system files. It discusses how to use System Restore to save snapshots of your system state, and how to return XP to one of those snapshots. Then the chapter moves on to heavy-duty recovery, discussing how to restore the Last Known Good Configuration (which you can use to recover when XP won't start successfully), how to use the Recovery Console to recover from severe problems, and how to troubleshoot boot problems (which can be the most troublesome problems of all).

Chapter 18, "Connecting to the Internet," covers how to connect to the Internet with XP Home and how to secure your Internet connection. You'll learn about the different types of Internet connection and the benefits they offer; what dial-up networking is, how it works, and how to configure and troubleshoot it; and how to work with digital certificates to verify the authenticity of a document or transaction.

Chapter 19, "Surfing the Web with Internet Explorer," discusses how to browse the Web with Internet Explorer and how to configure Internet Explorer to deliver the performance and security you should be demanding. Among many other things, this chapter covers how to control your browsing history and use the Content Advisor to screen out objectionable content. At the end of the chapter, you'll find a brief introduction to MSN Explorer, the user-friendly client for Microsoft's Internet service.

Chapter 20, "Using Address Book," shows you how to make the most of the Address Book program that comes built into XP. Address Book is an unassuming program, but it's capable enough to be useful for home (and some home-office) contact management.

Chapter 21, "E-mail with Outlook Express," shows you how to use Outlook Express, the powerful e-mail and newsreader program built into XP and Internet Explorer, for e-mail. The chapter covers setting up e-mail accounts; configuring Outlook Express' many options; creating, sending, reading, and replying to messages; filtering your messages; and working with both multiple e-mail accounts and multiple identities. This is a long chapter, but the topic is almost guaranteed to be of interest to you.

Chapter 22, "Reading News with Outlook Express," is a much shorter chapter. It shows you how to use Outlook Express's newsreader features to read messages posted to Internet newsgroups and to post messages yourself. It also covers configuring Outlook Express to access your news server.

Chapter 23, "Instant Messaging with Windows Messenger," shows you how to get started with Microsoft's entry into the IM arena: Windows Messenger. At this writing, Windows Messenger still can't exchange messages with AOL Instant Messenger, but apart from this severe drawback, it offers a full set of features, including voice calls, video calls, file transfer, whiteboarding and program-sharing, and making PC-to-phone calls. This chapter shows you how to use these features and more.

Chapter 24, "Giving and Getting Remote Assistance," shows you how to use XP's innovative Remote Assistance feature. Remote Assistance lets you request assistance securely across the Internet to solve computer problems—or supply such assistance to someone else.

Chapter 25, "Publishing Information to the Web," discusses the considerations to keep in mind when publishing information to the Web: the legalities of what you can publish, the options of where to publish it, and the most satisfactory methods for getting it there.

Chapter 26, "Windows Media Player," covers Windows Media Player, the powerful multimedia player incorporated in XP. You'll learn how to configure Windows Media Player for optimum performance, copy CDs to your hard drive, tune into Internet radio, play DVDs, and deal with digital rights management. The chapter also shows you how to use Volume Control to control audio output and input, and how to use Sound Recorder to record sounds and convert audio files from one format to another.

Chapter 27, "Working with Pictures and Videos," shows you how to use image-manipulation tools that XP Home provides. Coverage includes installing scanners and digital cameras, scanning documents, and retrieving images from a digital camera.

Chapter 28, "Burning CDs on XP," walks you through XP's features for burning both audio CDs and data CDs. This chapter also discusses how to choose recordable CD media and how to choose a CD recorder drive.

Chapter 29, "Playing Games on XP Home Edition," starts with a brief introduction to the single-player and multiplayer games included with XP Home Edition. It then discusses the hardware you need for serious gaming, how to add and configure games controllers, and how to get the best performance on games.

Chapter 30, "Understanding Windows Networking," discusses what a network is, why you might want to implement one in your home or home office, and what hardware you'll need to get in order to implement a network. It covers what you need to know about network architectures, network topologies, and network equipment in order to choose a network that's right for your situation.

Chapter 31, "Building a Home or Home-Office Network," discusses how to build an effective network for your home or your home office. It starts with the simplest type of network—a direct connection between two computers—before moving on to cover setting up wired and wireless networks by using the Home Networking Wizard.

Chapter 32, "Sharing Resources on Your Network," shows you how to go beyond what the Home Networking Wizard does and configure your network manually if necessary. You'll learn how to connect your network to the Internet, share your Internet connection with other computers, share folders, and share printers. You'll also learn how to configure networking components manually and how to connect two networks via a network bridge.

Chapter 33, "Securing Your Network," discusses the points of weakness on most networks and the ways of securing them. It touches on backing up your network, securing your Internet connection, securing other aspects of your network, and troubleshooting both wired and wireless networks. It includes a special section on the threats to the security of a wireless network and how you can counter them most effectively.

Chapter 34, "Connecting to a Remote Computer or Network," discusses the technologies that XP offers for controlling a remote computer and for connecting to a remote network. It first covers Remote Desktop Connection, which lets you take control of a computer running XP Professional and work on it as if you were sitting in front of it. (For example, you might access your work PC from home.) It then moves on to creating a dial-up connection to a remote network before discussing how to use virtual private network (VPN) connections to connect securely to a remote network across an insecure connection. It finishes by discussing how to troubleshoot VPNs.

Appendix A, "Windows XP Basics," provides a quick introduction to the XP Desktop and the main elements of the graphical user interface.

Appendix B, "Faxing and Telephony," discusses how to send faxes and make telephone calls in XP Home by using Fax Services and their various helper applications (for faxing) and Phone Dialer and HyperTerminal (for telephony).

In addition to the 1100-odd pages in the book, we've put more than 100 pages of extra content on the Web. For details, see the section after the next.

NOTE *This book concentrates on XP Home as you'll typically see it—either as the operating system preinstalled on a computer you buy or the operating system you install manually after buying the software in some kind of store. It discusses how to get the most out of XP's built-in features, and it touches briefly on some other software you may want to use in order to keep XP working in tip-top condition. It doesn't discuss software that you may want to run on XP—office applications, music programs, genealogy programs, and so on. (For those, you need other books.) But it does assume that there's one type of software you're likely enough to be interested in that you'll probably download and install it: the XP PowerToys add-on items that you can download from the Microsoft Windows XP Downloads page. The PowerToys have a strange status— they're provided by Microsoft, but Microsoft doesn't stand behind them in the way that it stands behind XP (or Office, or the other software packages it sells), and Microsoft certainly doesn't support them. But they seem pretty solid and stable, and most people find at least some of them well worth trying.*

What's New in the Second Edition?

This second edition of *Mastering Windows XP Home Edition* contains three new chapters (Chapters 17, 33, and 34) plus new material added right the way through the book. Because Sybex preferred not to turn the book into an expensive and unwieldy 1400-page monster, I've condensed much of the material from the first edition to make space for extra material. So while the second edition appears to have "only" 150 pages more than the first (1100 pages compared to 950 pages), it in fact contains nearly 400 pages of new material. Much of the new material covers advanced topics and troubleshooting.

When condensation occurs, something usually drops out. In this case, I've sacrificed a number of illustrations that seemed less useful than other illustrations. For example, XP includes many wizards—automated series of dialog boxes ("pages") that walk you through the steps of a procedure (for example, setting up a network connection). When describing how to use a wizard, this book shows only the pages that need extra attention. It doesn't show every single page of the wizard, because that would take up a lot of space that's better occupied with text.

Apart from the figures, three lengthy topics have dropped out—but only as far as the Sybex website (www.sybex.com), so that you can access them easily if you're interested in them without their taking up a large amount of space in the book. For details of these topics, see the next section.

The book still has what some readers have called a pedantic approach in its instructions: It tells you exactly what you need to do in order to accomplish a task, in most cases starting from the Desktop but sometimes starting from another established point of reference (for example, the Network Connections screen). This pedantry—step-by-step instructions: putting one foot in front of the other and repeating the process—is to avoid any possible confusion in the face of a multitude of screen elements. I'm assuming that you'd sometimes rather skim the easy steps of instructions that tell you how to do things you happen to know than struggle to follow condensed instructions that elide vital steps.

Extra Content on the Web

To supplement the content in the book, we've made three chapters available on the Sybex website (www.sybex.com). The easiest way to access these chapters is to search for this book's four-digit book number, 4133, follow the resulting link to the book's home page, and then click the Bonus Material link.

Web Chapter 1, "Installation Walkthroughs," presents a detailed walkthrough of the three different ways of installing XP Home: an upgrade installation from Windows 98 or Windows Me, a new installation on a computer that already has another version of Windows installed (but which you don't want to upgrade to XP), and a clean installation on a computer that doesn't have another operating system installed (or whose operating system you want to overwrite with XP). Designed to be a supplement to Chapter 2, this web chapter takes a step-by-step, graphical approach to the installation procedures. It's recommended if you don't have experience of installing Windows.

Web Chapter 2, "Making Movies with Windows Movie Maker," discusses how to use Windows Movie Maker to capture and edit your own movies.

Web Chapter 3, "Sharing and Conferencing with NetMeeting," shows you how to make the most of NetMeeting, the collaboration, file-sharing, and videoconferencing package built into Windows. You'll also learn how to use NetMeeting's Remote Desktop Sharing feature to take control of your computer from a remote location, which is useful for computers that use XP Home rather than XP Professional. (For accessing a computer that runs XP Professional, Remote Desktop Connection is better than Remote Desktop Sharing.)

Terminology and Conventions Used in This Book

To keep its waistline under control while presenting information concisely and accurately, this book uses a number of conventions:

- The menu arrow, ➤, indicates selecting a choice from a menu or submenu. For example, "choose Edit ➤ Preferences" means that you should pull down the Edit menu and select the Preferences item from it.

- + signs indicate key combinations. For example, "press Ctrl+P" means that you should hold down the Ctrl key and press the P key. Likewise, "Ctrl+click" and "Shift+click" indicate that you should hold down the key involved and then click.

- *Italics* mostly indicate new terms being introduced, but sometimes they simply indicate emphasis.

- **Boldface** indicates text that you may need to type letter for letter.

- URLs: The book leaves off the `http://` from each URL for brevity (and to prevent bad line breaks). For example, the URL `http://www.sybex.com` appears in the book as `www.sybex.com`. So you'll need to add the `http://` to each URL you use, or have Internet Explorer (or another browser) add it for you.

Mastering™
Windows XP Home Edition
Essential Skills

The Essential Skills for Windows XP Home Edition

Welcome to the *Windows XP Home Edition Essential Skills* section! This visual section teaches you 37 of the most important Windows XP Home Edition skills through a series of easy-to-follow screens with step-by-step instructions. These numbered steps show you exactly what you'll see on your screen at every step along the way as you learn, hands-on, the skills that will enable you to take control of your computer quickly and effectively. In minutes, you'll learn how to perform important tasks ranging from logging on to Windows XP, to sharing folders on the network and changing hardware drivers. Each screen highlights the elements you'll need to click.

These step-by-step directions are so easy to follow that you may want to simply sit at your computer and walk through all the procedures at once to get up and running with Windows XP quickly. Or you may prefer to flip to the *Essential Skills* section each time you need to perform a key task. You'll find references in the main text of the book to indicate when a step-by-step process is covered in the *Essential Skills* section, so that you can easily move from the detailed discussion of a topic to the graphical coverage of the steps involved.

None of the procedures covered in this section involve long textual explanations, background information, or troubleshooting. Those discussions occur in later sections of the book, when you have the background to understand them. In this section, you'll learn the important tasks that empower you to use Windows XP most efficiently. So sit yourself down at your PC with this section and master the most important Windows XP Home Edition skills hands-on!

Contents

LOGGING ON TO WINDOWS XP

To begin using Windows XP, log on under your user account.

XP is designed to be used by multiple users—for example, the members of a family. The XP setup routine encourages you to create a user account for each user, so that each person can keep their programs and files separate and protect them if necessary.

By default, XP displays the Welcome screen. If someone has turned off the Welcome screen, XP displays the Log On to Windows dialog box instead.

1. Click your username on the Welcome screen.

If you don't have an account on this computer, and the Guest account is available, log on as the Guest user.

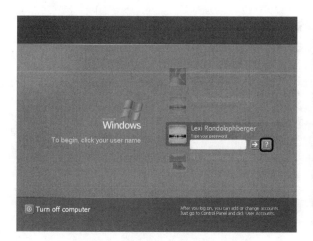

2. If you need to enter a password to log on, XP displays the Type Your Password text box.

To see your password hint (if you have one), click the Password Hint button.

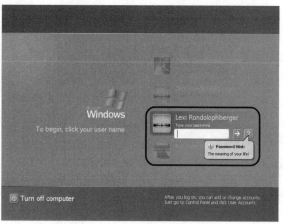

3. XP displays the password hint.

Type the password and press Enter.

XP logs you on and displays the Desktop.

LOGGING OFF FROM WINDOWS XP

The counterpart to logging on is (as you'd expect) logging off. When you've finished working in XP, you can log off to end your user session.

When you log off, XP closes any programs and files you've left open. If the files contain unsaved changes, XP prompts you to save them. It's a good idea to close programs and files manually before logging off because it's easier to see which application you're working with than when XP prompts you during logoff.

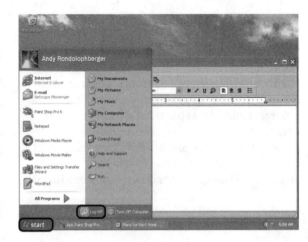

1. Click the Start button.

Click the Log Off button.

2. XP displays the Log Off Windows screen.

Click the Log Off button.

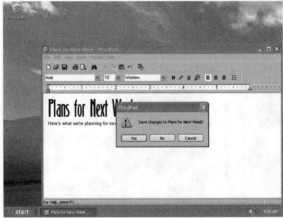

3. If an open file contains unsaved information, XP prompts you to save it. Choose Yes or No.

XP then displays the Welcome screen, from which you (or other users) can log on.

SWITCHING FROM ONE USER TO ANOTHER

Instead of logging off and closing all the programs and files you were using, you can *switch user* and leave the programs running and the files open.

Switching user has several advantages over logging off. The main advantage is that when you log back on, you can resume your work from where you left off without needing to reopen programs and files. Another advantage is that you can leave tasks running. For example, you could switch user and leave a large download happening in the background.

Switching user also has disadvantages. Other users can't see which files you're using, so they may try to use the same files. They may even shut down the computer, which loses you any work you haven't saved. Also, leaving user sessions running in the background uses memory and processor power. This can slow down the computer for the active user.

1. Click the Start button.

Click the Log Off button.

2. XP displays the Log Off Windows screen.

Click the Switch User button.

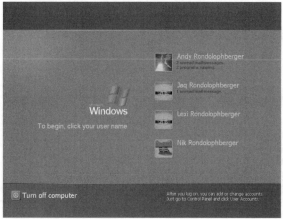

3. XP displays the Welcome screen, from which other users can log on or you can resume your XP session by clicking your username.

Your session keeps running, and the programs and files you were using remain open.

SHUTTING DOWN WINDOWS XP

When you've finished using your computer for the day, week, or month, shut down XP and power down your computer.

Before shutting down XP, close any open programs and files and make sure that no other users have left sessions running. (See the section "Seeing Which Programs the Other Users Are Running" in Chapter 3.) If you shut down XP while other users are still using it, they will lose any unsaved work in the programs they were using.

1. Click the Start button. XP displays the Start menu.

Click the Turn Off Computer button. XP displays the Turn Off Computer screen.

2. Click the Turn Off button.

XP closes itself and turns off your computer.

Expert Advice

◆ You can also display the Turn Off Computer screen by pressing the power button on many computers.

◆ XP automatically powers off most computers. If you have an older computer, you may need to power it off manually.

◆ If you're not sure whether other users are still logged on to the computer, use Task Manager to find out. (See Chapter 3.)

◆ From the Turn Off Computer screen, you can restart your computer by clicking the Restart button.

◆ If your computer supports hibernation, you can put it into hibernation by clicking the Hibernate button. If your computer supports standby, you can put it into standby by clicking the Stand By button.

USING THE START MENU

The Start menu and its submenus provide quick access to programs, settings, files, and help.

The Start menu's basic shape remains more or less the same, but its content changes. The current user's name appears at the top of the Start menu. One section of the Start menu automatically changes to display programs you've used recently. You can fix programs manually to this section of the Start menu so that they're always available. You can also perform some customization on the other parts of the Start menu.

When you install a program, its setup routine usually adds an entry for the program to the Start menu's All Programs submenu.

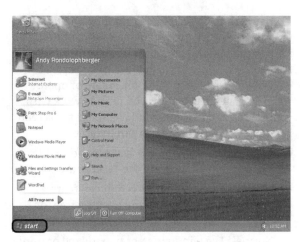

1. Click the Start button.

XP displays the Start menu.

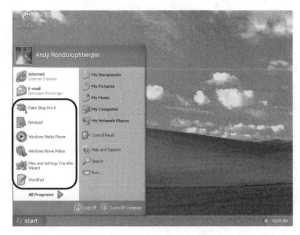

2. Click one of the items on the Start menu to open it.

The marked area of the left panel contains recently used programs.

The other items on the menu remain there unless you customize the menu.

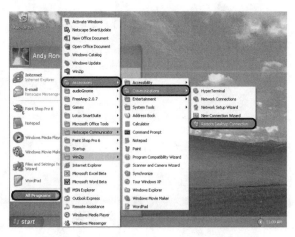

3. If the program or item doesn't appear on the first part of the Start menu, click the All Programs button.

Choose an item to open it, or open a submenu (indicated by an arrow) to access further items.

Highlights indicate new items.

RESIZING, MOVING, AND CLOSING A WINDOW

Each program displays one or more windows—rectangular (or nearly rectangular) areas containing information. Many programs use several windows. For example, Word for Windows uses a separate window for each document you create or open.

To display the programs you need to work with, you can resize and move windows about the screen. Most windows can appear in three states:

♦ Maximized: The window is expanded to fill the Desktop (apart from the Taskbar area).

♦ Minimized: The window is reduced to its Taskbar button, leaving the Desktop free for other windows.

♦ Normal: The window is not maximized or minimized, but is some size in between.

1. Open one or more program windows. To maximize a window, click the Maximize button.

XP maximizes the window and replaces its Maximize button with the Restore Down button.

2. To restore a maximized window to the normal state, click the Restore Down button.

XP restores the window to its previous size and replaces its Restore Down button with the Maximize button.

3. To minimize a window, click the Minimize button.

XP reduces the window to its button on the Taskbar.

RESIZING, MOVING, AND CLOSING A WINDOW *(continued)*

4. To restore a minimized window, click its Taskbar button.

XP restores the window to its previous state—maximized or normal.

5. To resize a window, move the mouse pointer over an edge or corner of the window so that the pointer changes into a double-headed arrow.

Click and drag the window edge or corner to the size you want.

6. To move a window, click the title bar and drag the window to its new location.

7. To close a window, click its Close button.

XP closes the window.

If the window contains unsaved information, the program may prompt you to save it.

ARRANGING WINDOWS BY USING THE TASKBAR

XP provides the following automated commands for arranging windows easily:

- **Cascade Windows:** Displays the nonminimized windows overlapping each other so that you can see the title bar of each
- **Undo Cascade:** Restores the windows to the positions they were in before cascading
- **Tile Windows Horizontally:** Implements a horizontal tiling scheme for all nonminimized windows
- **Tile Windows Vertically:** Implements a vertical tiling scheme for all nonminimized windows
- **Undo Tile:** Restores the windows to the positions they were in before tiling
- **Show the Desktop:** Displays the Desktop by minimizing all nonminimized windows.
- **Show Open Windows:** Restores the windows to the positions they were in before minimization via the Show the Desktop command

1. Right-click the notification area or open space in the Taskbar. XP displays the context menu.

Choose the appropriate command for the action you want to take.

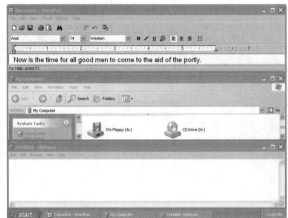

2. Issuing a Show the Desktop command minimizes all windows.

To restore the windows to their previous positions, issue the Show Open Windows command.

3. Issuing a Tile Windows Horizontally command tiles the windows in a horizontal pattern.

To restore the windows to their previous positions, issue the Undo Tile command.

ARRANGING WINDOWS BY USING THE TASKBAR *(continued)*

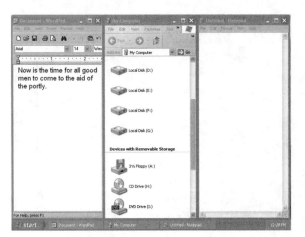

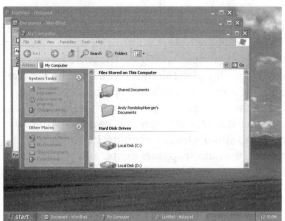

4. Issuing a Tile Windows Vertically command tiles the windows in a vertical pattern.

To restore the windows to their previous positions, issue the Undo Tile command.

5. Issuing a Cascade Windows command arranges the windows in an overlapping pattern with their title bars visible.

To restore the windows to their previous positions, issue the Undo Cascade command.

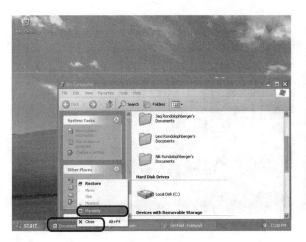

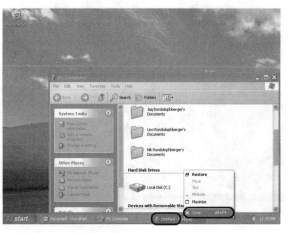

6. To maximize a window, right-click its Taskbar button and choose Maximize from the context menu.

7. To close a window, right-click its Taskbar button and choose Close from the context menu.

USING THE TASKBAR TO ACCESS A WINDOW

The Taskbar lets you quickly access and manage the windows you have open.

The Taskbar displays a button for each open window or group of windows. The window you're working in is called the *active* window. The Taskbar button for the active window or group is visually highlighted in some way. For example, in the Windows XP theme, the button for the active window or group appears in a darker blue. In the Classic theme, the button appears lighter and pushed-in.

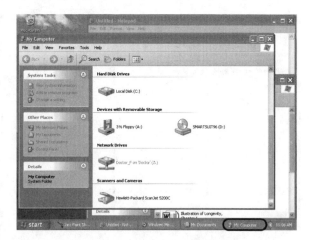

1. Click the Taskbar button once to display the window. Click the button again to minimize the window to its Taskbar button.

2. When the first row of the Taskbar is full, XP groups the buttons for similar windows.

Click the group button to display a menu of the window buttons it contains.

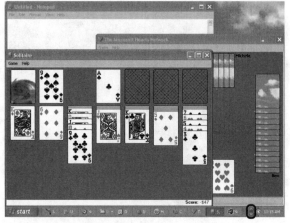

3. When the buttons for open windows and groups won't fit on one row, the Taskbar displays scroll buttons for accessing subsequent rows.

Click the scroll buttons to scroll up or down a row of buttons.

UNLOCKING, RESIZING, AND MOVING THE TASKBAR

By default, the Taskbar is locked so that it cannot be resized or moved, and so that you cannot display any Desktop toolbars.

By unlocking the Taskbar, you can resize it, move it to another edge of the screen, and display and use the Desktop toolbars.

1. To unlock the Taskbar, right-click the notification area. XP displays the context menu.

Choose the Lock the Taskbar item. XP unlocks the Taskbar and removes the check mark from the context menu item.

2. To resize the Taskbar, move the mouse pointer over its border so that the pointer becomes a double-headed arrow.

Drag the border to enlarge or reduce the Taskbar.

3. To move the Taskbar to another edge of the screen, click open space in it and drag it to the edge you want. XP moves the Taskbar.

To lock the Taskbar at its new size or position, right-click the notification area and choose Lock the Taskbar.

NAVIGATING IN EXPLORER

Windows Explorer is a program for viewing and manipulating the contents of the drives and folders on your computer.

You can use Explorer for a wide variety of tasks including creating, deleting, and renaming files and folders; copying and moving files and folders; and finding files and folders you've lost.

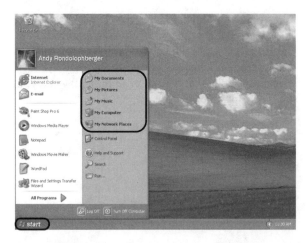

1. Click the Start button. XP displays the Start menu.

Choose one of the five circled links from it. If your computer isn't connected to a network, you won't have a My Network Places link.

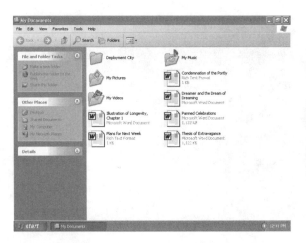

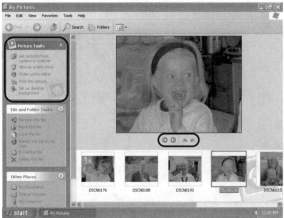

2. The My Documents link displays the \My Documents\ folder, in which XP automatically places files you create other than graphics, music, or video files. This folder contains the \My Pictures\ folder, the \My Music\ folder, and the \My Videos\ folder.

3. The My Pictures link displays the \My Pictures\ folder, in which XP automatically places picture files you create and download. This folder contains features and links for manipulating pictures.

NAVIGATING IN EXPLORER *(continued)*

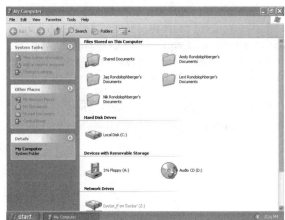

4. The My Music link displays the \My Music\ folder, in which XP automatically places music files you create and download. This folder contains features and links for working with music files.

5. The My Computer link displays a list of document folders and drives on the computer.

6. To perform a task on a file or folder, select it and use the File and Folder Tasks list.

7. To navigate to other frequently used places and folders, use the Other Places list.

To open a folder or file, double-click it.

USING VIEWS IN EXPLORER

Explorer provides five different views for looking at the contents of most files and folders, together with a specialized view for folders containing graphics. The different views are designed to make it easy to work with different types of folder contents.

Some custom folders also have other views. You can apply these views from the View menu.

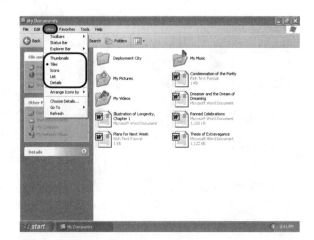

1. Display the View menu, then choose one of the views from it.

2. Thumbnails view displays a large icon for each file or folder. For graphics files, Thumbnails view displays a miniature version of each graphic.

3. Tiles view displays a medium-sized icon for each file or folder. It's good for viewing folders that contain relatively few files or folders.

USING VIEWS IN EXPLORER *(continued)*

4. Icons view displays a smallish icon for each file or folder. It's good for viewing folders that contain a moderate number of files or folders.

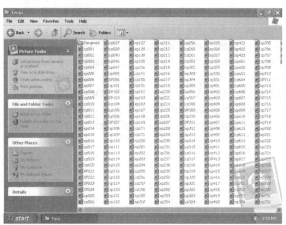

5. List view displays a list of folders and files, showing only the filename or folder name and a small icon for each. It's good for viewing folders that contain a large number of files or folders.

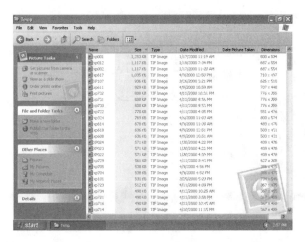

6. Details view displays a list of files and folders, including the filename or folder name, a small icon, the file size, the file type, and the date on which it was modified. You can sort by any of the columns displayed.

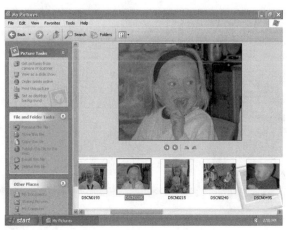

7. The \My Pictures\ folder and the \Shared Pictures\ folder also have a Filmstrip view designed for scrolling through a folder of images.

SELECTING AND DESELECTING FILES

In order to manipulate files and folders in Explorer, you need to select them first.

The easiest selection techniques use the mouse and the keyboard together. (You can also select files by using only the keyboard.) These selection techniques work the same on the Desktop, in most common dialog boxes in Windows applications, and in some Windows applications.

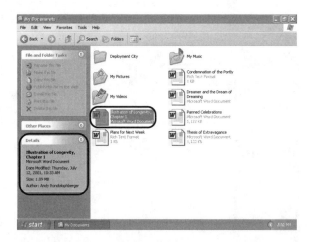

1. To select a file or folder, click it. The Details pane displays information about the file or folder.

To deselect a selected file or folder, click in empty space in the window.

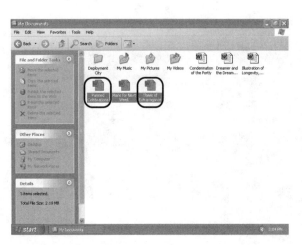

2. To select a group of adjacent files, click the first file, then hold down Shift and click the last file in the group.

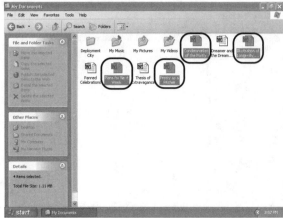

3. To select a group of nonadjacent files, select the first file, hold down Ctrl, and click each of the other files.

To deselect a file in a selected group, hold down Ctrl and click the file.

CREATING A FOLDER

XP lets you create an almost unlimited number of folders in which to store your files. By using separate folders, you can group your files by category such as subject, type, or date, keeping the files organized and making it easy to find the ones you need.

You can create folders on your Desktop as well by using the technique shown here.

1. Open an Explorer window to the folder in which you want to create the new folder. For example, choose Start ➤ My Documents if you want to create the new folder in the \My Documents\ folder.

2. Click the Make a New Folder link.

XP creates a new folder named New Folder or a similar name (New Folder 1, New Folder 2, and so on) and displays an edit box around the name.

3. Type the name for the folder and press Enter. XP renames the folder.

RENAMING A FILE OR FOLDER

Often, you'll need to rename a file or folder, to make its name shorter, longer, more explicit, or simply different from the names of other files or folders in the same folder. Including the drive and folder path to it, a filename can be up to 255 characters long, so you can get verbose if necessary.

Filenames can't contain the following characters: forward slashes (/), backslashes (\), colons (:), asterisks (*), question marks (?), double quotation marks ("), less-than (<) and greater-than (>) signs, or pipe characters (|).

To rename a file or folder, open an Explorer window to the appropriate folder. If the file or folder is on the Desktop, you can work directly on the Desktop using the same technique.

1. Select the file or folder you want to rename.

Click the Rename This File link or the Rename This Folder Link.

XP displays an edit box around the name.

2. Type the name you want, and then press Enter.

XP applies the new name to the file or folder.

Expert Advice

◆ Instead of clicking the Rename This File link or the Rename This Folder link, you can display an edit box around the filename or folder name by clicking it again a moment or two after selecting it.

◆ This two-click technique works on the Desktop and in common dialog boxes as well as in Explorer windows.

◆ If you can't get the hang of clicking twice slowly enough, select the file or folder and press F2, or right-click it and choose Rename from the context menu.

COPYING OR MOVING A FILE OR FOLDER

Often, you'll need to copy files or folders—for example, so that you can store copies in a safe location, or so that you can share the files or folders with someone else.

Similarly, you'll frequently need to move files or folders from their current location to a different location. For example, you might need to move a folder of files from your \My Documents\ folder to the \Shared Documents\ folder so that other users can work with it.

XP provides several ways to copy or move a file or folder. This page shows you the easiest and most consistent way of performing each operation.

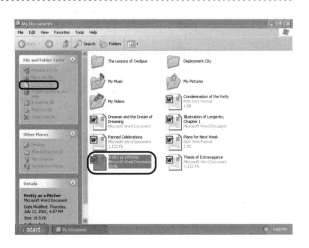

1. Select the file or folder.

To copy it, click the Copy This File link or the Copy This Folder link. Proceed to step 2.

To move it, click the Move This File link or the Move This Folder link. Proceed to step 3.

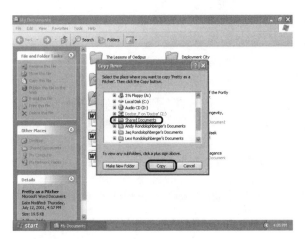

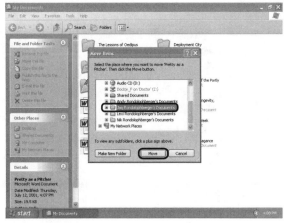

2. Navigate to the folder in which you want XP to place the copy of the file or folder.

Click the Copy button. XP closes the Copy Items dialog box and copies the file or folder.

3. Navigate to the folder to which you want XP to move the file or folder.

Click the Move button. XP closes the Move Items dialog box and moves the file or folder.

COPYING OR MOVING BY USING COPY, CUT, AND PASTE

You can also copy a file or folder by using the Copy and Paste commands, and move a file or folder by using the Cut and Paste commands.

The Copy, Cut, and Paste commands are most useful for copying and moving files and folders when you have two Explorer windows open, one showing the source folder and the other the destination folder. You can then quickly copy or move files or folders from the source folder to the destination folder. But you can also use the Copy, Cut, and Paste commands in a single window if you find them easy or convenient.

1. Open two Explorer windows and arrange them so that you can see both.

In one Explorer window, navigate to the source folder.

In the other Explorer window, navigate to the destination folder.

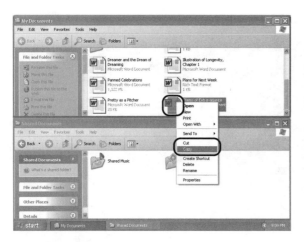

2. In the source folder, right-click the file or folder you want to copy or move.

From the context menu, choose Copy (to copy the item) or Cut (to move it).

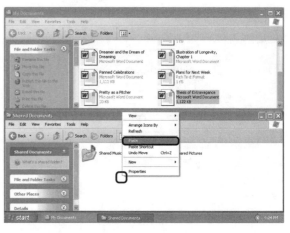

3. Right-click in open space in the destination folder.

From the context menu, choose Paste.

XP pastes the copy of the file or folder, or the file or folder itself, into the destination folder.

COPYING FILES TO A FLOPPY DISK OR REMOVABLE DISK

Because you'll often need to copy files to a floppy disk or another removable disk (such as a Zip drive), XP provides a convenient way of doing so.

You can also use a similar technique for creating a shortcut located on the Desktop that refers to an item in the current folder.

1. Open an Explorer window to the folder that contains the file or folder you want to copy.

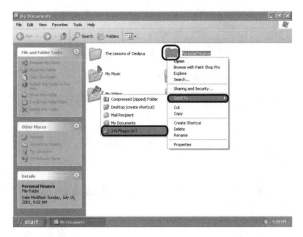

2. Right-click the file or folder. XP displays the context menu.

Choose Send To. XP displays the submenu.

Select the item for the floppy disk or removable disk. XP copies the file or folder.

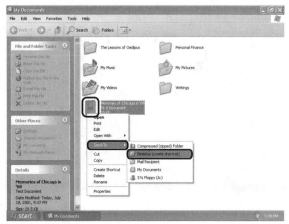

3. You can also create a shortcut on the Desktop to the file or folder by using a similar technique.

Right-click the file or folder and choose Send To ➢ Desktop (Create Shortcut).

XP creates a shortcut on the Desktop.

COPYING FILES OR FOLDERS TO A RECORDABLE CD

If you have a recordable CD (CD-R) drive, you can copy files or folders to a recordable CD.

Because recordable CDs are capacious, inexpensive, durable, and (at least in theory) relatively long lasting, they're good for backup and archiving. Even if the CDs turn out not to last, they're good for transferring files from point A to point B in the short term, because most computers have CD drives.

XP also provides features for recording an audio CD that you can play on most CD players—audio CD players as well as computer CD drives.

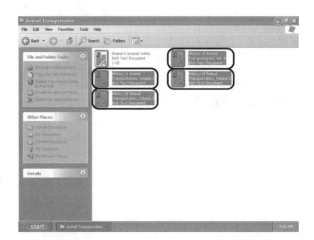

1. Load a blank CD in your recordable CD drive.

Open an Explorer window to the appropriate folder.

Select the files or folders you want to copy to the CD.

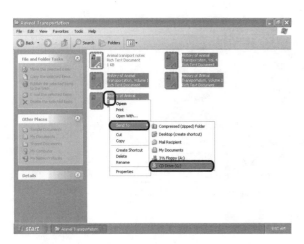

2. Right-click one of the selected files or folders and choose Send To ➤ CD Drive.

XP copies the files or folders to a queue for writing to the CD drive and displays a notification-area icon and pop-up.

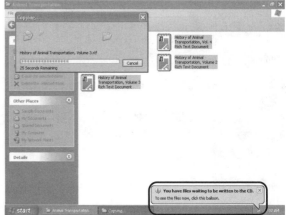

3. Add further files or folders to the CD list as necessary.

Click the notification-area pop-up to open an Explorer window showing the CD drive. (If the pop-up disappears, choose Start ➤ My Computer, then double-click the CD drive.)

COPYING FILES OR FOLDERS TO A RECORDABLE CD *(continued)*

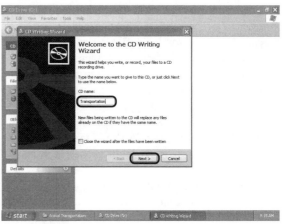

4. Click the Write These Files to CD link.
XP starts the CD Writing Wizard.

5. Change or improve the name for the CD. (The wizard suggests the current date for the CD's name.)

Click the Next button. The wizard starts writing the files to the CD.

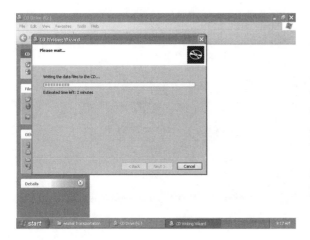

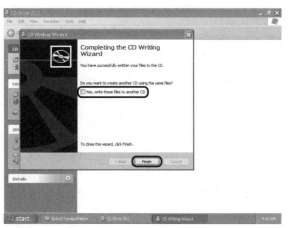

6. When the wizard has finished writing the CD, it ejects the CD and displays the Completing the CD Writing Wizard page.

7. If you want to create another CD containing the same files, select the Yes, Write These Files to Another CD check box.

Click the Finish button. The wizard closes or restarts, as appropriate.

DELETING A FILE OR FOLDER

When you no longer need a file, you can delete it to remove it from your disk. By default, deleting a file on your hard disk sends the file to the Recycle Bin, from which you can retrieve it if necessary. Deleting a file on a removable disk, a floppy disk, or a network drive gets rid of the file immediately.

Don't try to delete any of XP's system files. Doing so can prevent XP from running. Usually, though, XP simply reinstalls the files when it discovers they're missing, so deleting them achieves nothing.

Similarly, it's best not to delete any program files manually. Instead, use XP's Remove Programs feature to remove the program, as discussed on page 49.

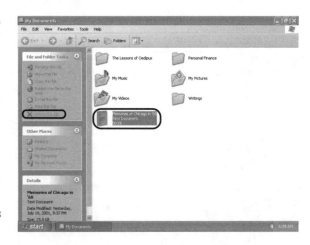

1. Select a file that you're sure you don't need.

Click the Delete This File link.

XP displays the Confirm File Delete dialog box.

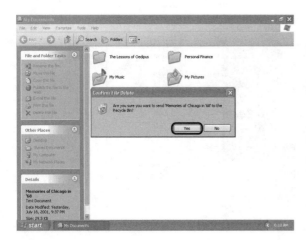

2. Click the Yes button.

Depending on where the file is stored, XP moves the file to the Recycle Bin or deletes it.

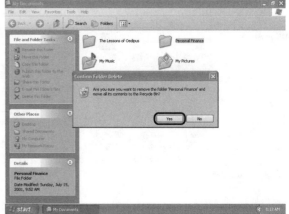

3. To delete a folder, select it and click the Delete This Folder link.

XP displays the Confirm Folder Delete dialog box, asking if you want to remove the folder and all its contents.

Click the Yes button.

RECOVERING A DELETED FILE OR FOLDER FROM THE RECYCLE BIN

If you move a file or folder to the Recycle Bin and subsequently wish you hadn't, you may be able to recover the file or folder.

Files or folders stay in the Recycle Bin until the Recycle Bin gets full or you empty it manually. When the Recycle Bin gets full, XP discards the oldest files or folders to make space for new files or folders you delete.

Once XP has deleted a file or folder from the Recycle Bin, you may be able to recover it using a specialized undelete utility, but there's no guarantee that this will work. So when you delete a file or folder by mistake, it's best to recover it immediately. When you recover a file or folder, XP removes it from the Recycle Bin and restores it to the folder that previously contained it.

1. Double-click the Recycle Bin icon on the Desktop.

XP opens an Explorer window showing the contents of the Recycle Bin.

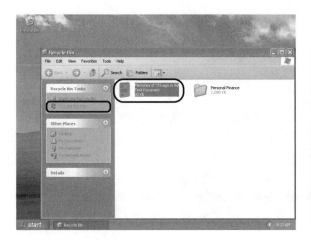

2. Select the file or folder.

Click the Restore This Item link.

To restore all the files and folders in the Recycle Bin, click the Restore All Items link without selecting a file or folder.

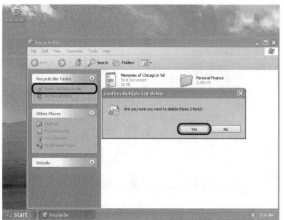

3. To get rid of the files and folders in the Recycle Bin, click the Empty the Recycle Bin link.

XP displays the Confirm Multiple File Delete dialog box.

Click the Yes button.

CREATING A SHORTCUT ON YOUR DESKTOP

If you need quick access to a program or file, place a shortcut to it on your Desktop or in another convenient place. The shortcut acts as a pointer, making it easy to access the program or file. You can create any number of shortcuts to any given program or file.

You can create a shortcut in several different ways. This section shows two of the easiest ways to create a shortcut.

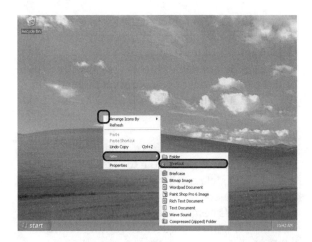

1. Right-click open space on the Desktop. XP displays the context menu.

Choose New ➢ Shortcut.

XP starts the Create Shortcut Wizard.

2. Click the Browse button.

XP displays the Browse for Folder dialog box.

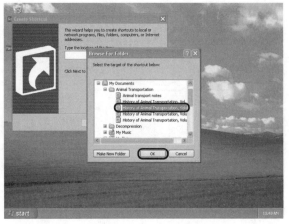

3. Navigate to the program or file and select it.

Click the OK button. XP closes the Browse for Folder dialog box and enters the path and filename in the Create Shortcut Wizard.

CREATING A SHORTCUT ON YOUR DESKTOP *(continued)*

4. Click the Next button.

The wizard displays the Select a Title for The Program page and suggests the file or program's name as the name for the shortcut.

5. Change the name if necessary.

Click the Finish button.

The wizard creates the shortcut, names it, and places it on your Desktop.

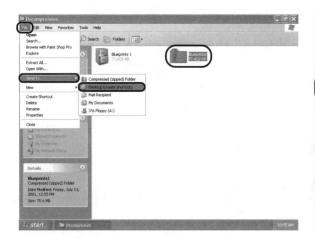

6. You can also create a shortcut from an Explorer window.

Select the file. Then choose File ➤ Send To ➤ Desktop (Create Shortcut).

XP creates a shortcut on the Desktop.

7. Change the name of the shortcut if necessary (see page 22 for details of how to rename a file).

XP names shortcuts created this way *Shortcut to* and the filename.

SHARING FILES OR FOLDERS WITH OTHER USERS OF THE COMPUTER

To share a file or folder with other users of your computer, copy or move it to the \Shared Documents\ folder or one of its subfolders. XP provides the \Shared Documents\ folder for shared documents, the \Shared Music\ folder for shared music files, the \Shared Pictures\ folder for shared pictures, and the \Shared Videos\ folder (when you start working with video) for shared video files.

If you copy the file or folder (as described here), you can keep the original to yourself. If you move the file or folder, anyone can change the original.

1. Open an Explorer window to the folder that contains the file or folder.

2. Select the file or folder.

Click the Copy This File link or the Copy This Folder link. XP displays the Copy Items dialog box.

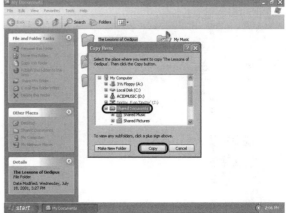

3. Select the Shared Documents icon.

Click the Copy button.

XP copies the file or folder to the \Shared Documents\ folder.

KEEPING A FOLDER PRIVATE

Even if you don't share a folder under your \My Documents\ folder, other Computer Administrator users of your computer can access it. To prevent them from doing so, you need to mark the folder as private.

If you don't have a password on your user account, you need to set one. (Otherwise, other users can log on as you and see your folders.)

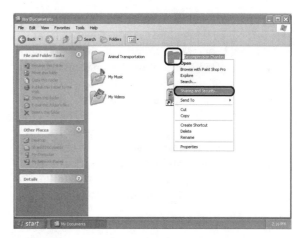

1. Right-click the folder and choose Sharing and Security from the context menu. XP displays the Sharing page of the Properties dialog box.

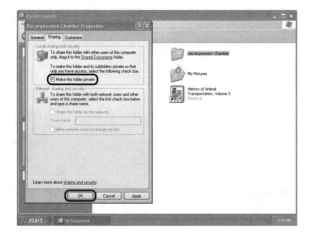

2. Select the Make This Folder Private check box. Click the OK button. XP closes the Properties dialog box and makes the folder private.

Expert Advice

◆ If you don't have a password on your user account, XP displays the Sharing dialog box warning you that because you don't have a password, anyone can log in as you and then access the folder you've made private.

◆ Click the Yes button in the Sharing dialog box. XP displays the Create a Password for Your Account screen of User Accounts.

◆ Enter the password in the top two text boxes.

◆ If you want, enter a cryptic word or phrase for a password hint.

◆ Click the Create Password button. XP applies the password to your account. The folder is then securely private.

SEARCHING FOR FILES

If you create a lot of files, you'll probably forget before too long where one or more files are located.

XP provides a feature called Search Companion for searching for files. You can search by all or part of a file's name, by its approximate size, by the date it was created, or even by a word or phrase contained in the body of the file.

Search Companion offers different features for searching for specific types of files such as document files or files containing pictures, music, or video. This example shows how to search for all file types, because this gives the most flexible search.

1.   Choose Start ➤ Search.

XP displays a Search Results window.

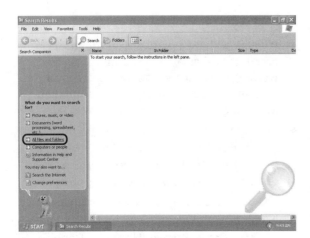

2.   Click the All Files and Folders link.

Search Companion displays a panel of search options.

3.   To search by filename, enter a distinctive part of the filename in the All or Part of the Filename text box.

SEARCHING FOR FILES *(continued)*

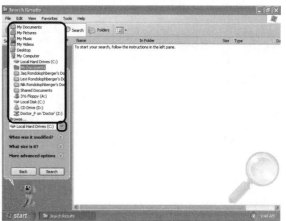

4. To search by contents, or to narrow a search by other criteria, you can enter a distinctive word or phrase in the A Word or Phrase in the File text box.

5. Specify the drives or folders to search.

6. To specify a range of dates when the file was modified, click the When Was It Modified? heading.

Use the options for specifying a time period.

7. To search only for files of a specified size, click the What Size Is It? heading.

Use the options for specifying an approximate size.

SEARCHING FOR FILES (continued)

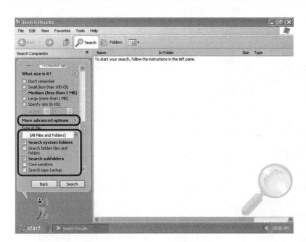

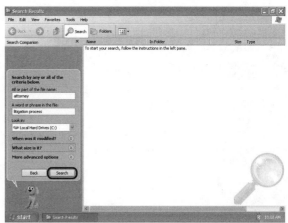

8. To specify advanced options, such as searching hidden files or folders or tape backup, click the More Advanced Options heading.

By default, Search Companion searches system folders and subfolders.

9. Click the Search button. Search Companion performs the search and returns a list containing any matches it finds.

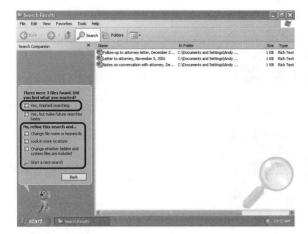

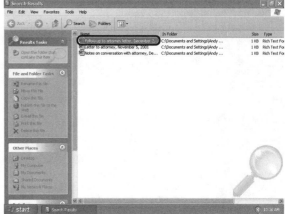

10. If Search Companion didn't find the right match, use the No, Refine This Search And... links to search again.

Otherwise, click the Yes, Finished Searching link to close Search Companion.

11. Select a file to display its details.

Double-click a file to open it.

Select a file and click the Open the Folder That Contains This Item link to open the folder.

BROWSING THE WEB

Windows XP includes Internet Explorer, a powerful program for browsing the Web. Internet Explorer can display many different types of web content, including text, forms, graphics, and various kinds of animations.

Once you're connected to the Internet, you can access any available web page by entering its address. A web address is called a Uniform Resource Locator, or URL. Many web pages contain hyperlinks (jumps) to other URLs. You can access these URLs by clicking the hyperlinks.

1. Choose Start ➤ Internet. XP starts Internet Explorer, which displays your home page.

If you're not connected to the Internet, XP prompts you to connect.

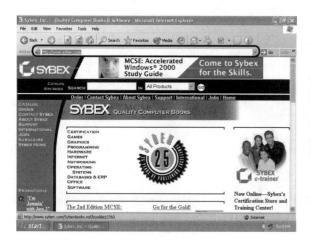

2. To open a web page, click in the Address bar.

Internet Explorer highlights the current contents of the Address bar.

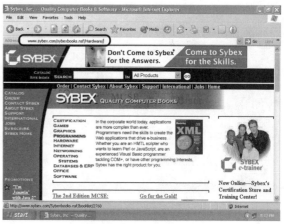

3. Type the URL for the website you want to display. You can omit the http:// that appears at the beginning of many URLs. Internet Explorer adds this automatically.

BROWSING THE WEB *(continued)*

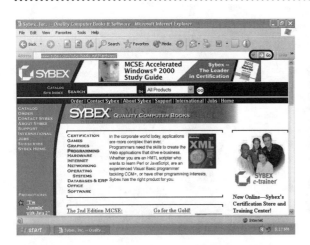

4. Press the Enter key or click the Go button.

Internet Explorer displays the web page.

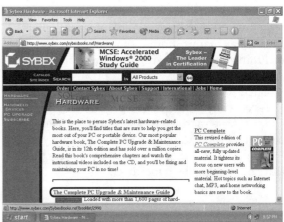

5. To follow a hyperlink, click it.

Most hyperlinks appear underlined, in a different color, or both.

The mouse pointer changes to a different shape when it's over a hyperlink. The status bar shows the linked URL.

6. To move back to the last web page you visited, click the Back button.

To move forward again after moving back, click the Forward button.

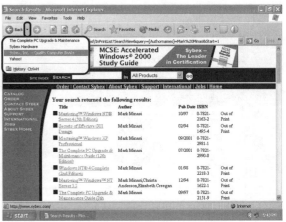

7. To move back or forward several pages, click the arrow button on the Back button or the Forward button and choose the page from the list.

BROWSING THE WEB *(continued)*

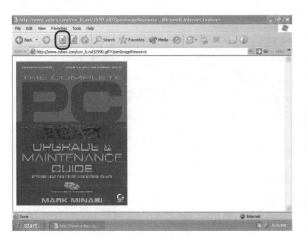

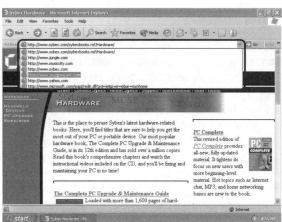

8. To stop a page being displayed (for example, if it's taking too long), click the Stop button.

9. To return to an URL you've visited recently, click the arrow button on the Address bar and select the URL from the list.

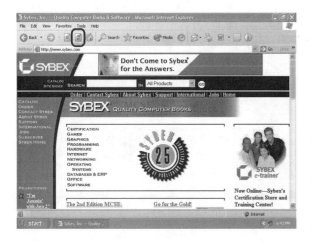

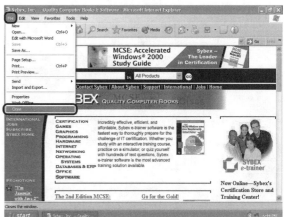

10. To refresh the current web page with the latest information, click the Refresh button or press the F5 key.

11. To exit Internet Explorer, choose File ➢ Close or click the Close button.

CHANGING YOUR HOME PAGE

Your home page is the page that Internet Explorer automatically opens when you start it. You can also display your home page at any time by clicking the Home button on the toolbar or pressing Alt+Home.

Internet Explorer uses MSN as its default home page. You'll probably want to change this to a site of your choosing, so that you see information that interests you when you start Internet Explorer. You can use any valid URL for your home page. Alternatively, you can use a local file or folder as your home page. For example, you can create an HTML file that contains links to the sites you're most interested in, and use that file as your home page to give you quick access to those sites.

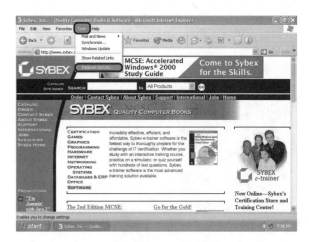

1. Navigate to the web page, local file, or folder that you want to use as your home page.

Choose Tools ➤ Internet Options.

Internet Explorer displays the General page of the Internet Options dialog box.

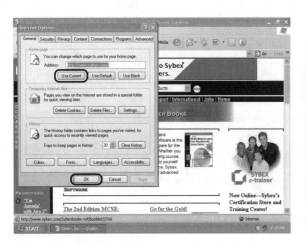

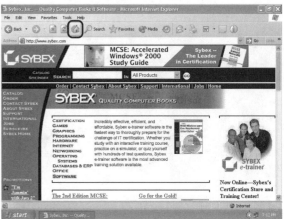

2. Click the Use Current button.

Click the OK button. Internet Explorer closes the Internet Options dialog box.

3. To access your home page, click the Home button.

SEARCHING THE WEB

With more pages being added every microsecond, the Web can seem an unnavigable maelstrom of information. But by using searching, you can usually produce some order out of the chaos—or at least find some pages containing the information you need.

Like Explorer, Internet Explorer uses Search Companion to present its search capabilities. For Internet Explorer, Search Companion uses a natural-language interface that lets you phrase your query as a full sentence if you prefer rather than boiling it down to the essential words.

1. Click the Search button. Internet Explorer displays Search Companion.

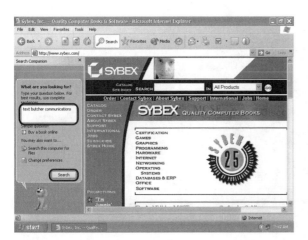

2. Enter your query in the What Are You Looking For? text box.

Press the Enter key or click the Search button. Internet Explorer performs the search and displays search results.

3. Click a result to display its page.

Alternatively, follow one of the search links in Search Companion.

Click the Search button again to hide Search Companion.

CREATING AND ACCESSING FAVORITES

Internet Explorer's favorites feature lets you keep a list of web pages (or local files or folders) that you want to be able to access quickly. You can divide your favorites into folders to keep them organized, and you can export your list of favorites for backup or for use on another computer.

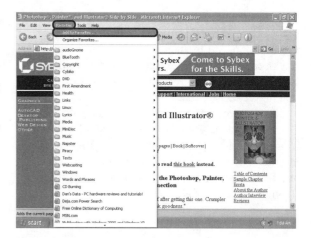

1. Open the web page, file, or folder for which you want to create a favorite.

Choose Favorites ➤ Add to Favorites. Internet Explorer displays the Add Favorite dialog box.

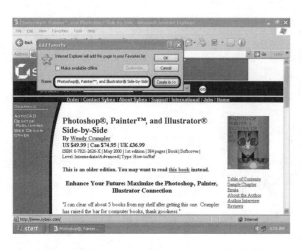

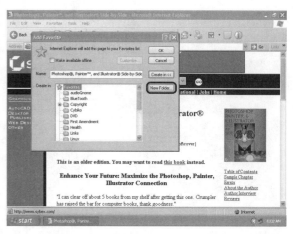

2. Check the name for the favorite. Change it if you want.

Click the Create In button. Internet Explorer expands the Add Favorite dialog box.

3. Select the existing folder in which to store the favorite.

To create a new folder, click the New Folder button. Internet Explorer displays the Create New Folder dialog box.

CREATING AND ACCESSING FAVORITES *(continued)*

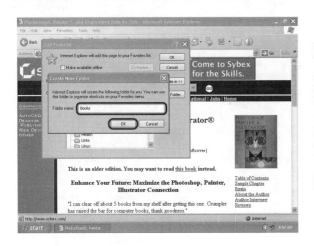

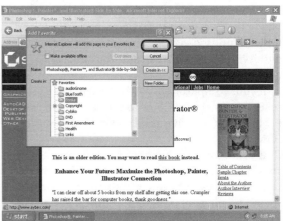

4. Enter the name for the folder.

Click the OK button. Internet Explorer closes the dialog box, creates the folder, and selects it in the Add Favorite dialog box.

5. Click the OK button. Internet Explorer closes the dialog box and creates the favorite.

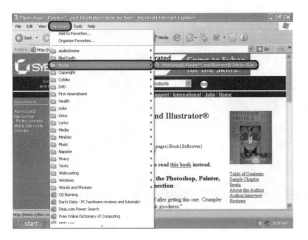

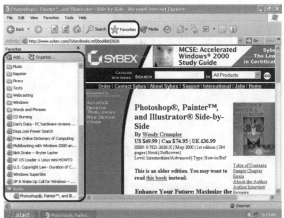

6. To access a favorite, select it from the Favorites menu.

7. To browse and access favorites, use the Favorites Explorer bar.

Click the Favorites button on the toolbar. Internet Explorer displays the Favorites Explorer bar.

LISTENING TO AN AUDIO CD

Windows Media Player is a capable multimedia player that you can use for listening to music and for watching video files. You can also watch DVDs with Windows Media Player if you add a DVD decoder to XP.

If your computer has a CD drive, you can use it to listen to an audio CD or to copy the audio from a CD to your hard drive as Windows Media Audio (WMA) files.

If your computer has a sound card, connect the speakers or headphones to the output jack. If your computer doesn't have a sound card, connect the speakers or headphones to the output jack on your CD drive.

If AutoPlay is disabled on your computer, the CD won't start playing automatically. Instead, start Windows Media Player manually by choosing Start ➢ All Programs ➢ Windows Media Player.

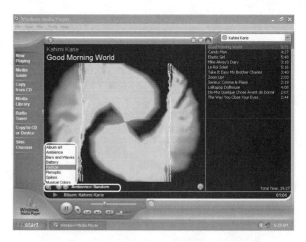

1. Load the CD in your CD drive. Windows Media Player opens automatically, starts playing the CD, and displays a visualization on the Now Playing page.

Use the visualization buttons to change the visualization.

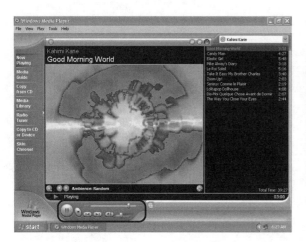

2. Use the play controls to control the play.

Drag the Volume slider to control the volume.

Click the Mute/Sound button to mute and unmute the sound.

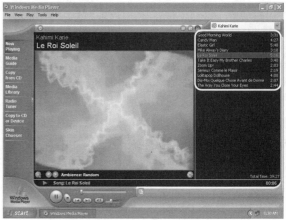

3. To jump to a track, double-click it in the playlist.

COPYING A CD TO YOUR HARD DRIVE

Windows Media Player lets you "copy" an audio CD to your hard disk by extracting the audio data from the CD and encoding it to a compressed format called Windows Media Audio (WMA).

By storing tracks from your CDs as music files on your hard disk, you can create a jukebox-like selection of tracks that you can play back in Windows Media Player or another audio player (for example, Winamp or MusicMatch Jukebox). You can also use WMA files with some portable audio players.

The first time you copy a CD, choose quality settings as described here. After that, change quality settings only when necessary.

1. Load the CD.

 If Windows Media Player doesn't start automatically, choose Start ➢ All Programs ➢ Windows Media Player.

2. Click the Copy from CD tab. Windows Media Player displays information for the CD.

 If Windows Media Player doesn't display CD information, start your Internet connection and click the Get Names button.

3. Choose Tools ➢ Options. Windows Media Player displays the Options dialog box.

COPYING A CD TO YOUR HARD DRIVE (continued)

4. Click the Copy Music tab. Windows Media Player displays the Copy Music page of the Options dialog box.

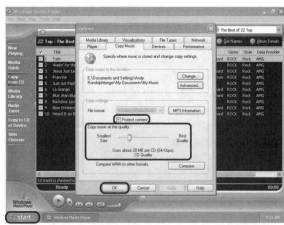

5. Drag the slider to select the encoding quality.

Clear the Protect Content check box if you will need to transfer the tracks to another computer or device.

Click the OK button.

6. Select the tracks to copy by selecting and clearing the check boxes. Clicking the top-most check box selects or clears all the check boxes.

Click the Copy Music button.

7. Windows Media Player copies the tracks. It creates a folder with the CD's name inside a folder with the artist's name and names each track with the track number and name shown on the Copy from CD page.

INSTALLING A PROGRAM

XP comes with a modest selection of mostly limited programs (such as Notepad, WordPad, and Paint, all discussed in Chapter 7), but you'll probably want to add various programs to supplement them.

If you have the program on a physical medium, such as a floppy disk, a CD-ROM, a DVD, or a removable disk, load the disk in the appropriate drive. If you downloaded the file, you need only know where you saved it.

Before installing a program, it's a good idea to close all open programs. This isn't always necessary, but it's possible for the files you're installing to conflict with files that are being used by open programs.

1. Choose Start ➢ Control Panel. XP displays Control Panel.

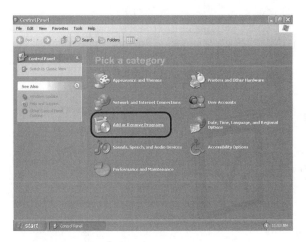

2. Click the Add or Remove Programs link. XP displays the Add or Remove Programs window.

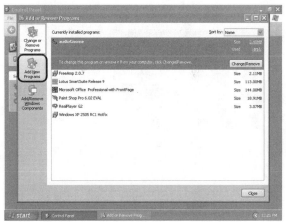

3. Click the Add New Programs button. XP displays the Add New Programs page.

INSTALLING A PROGRAM *(continued)*

4. Click the CD or Floppy button. XP displays the Install Program from Floppy Disk or CD-ROM page.

5. If the program is on a CD or a floppy, and you haven't inserted the disk already, do so now.

Click the Next button. XP searches your floppy drives and CD drives for a setup file and displays the Run Installation Program dialog box.

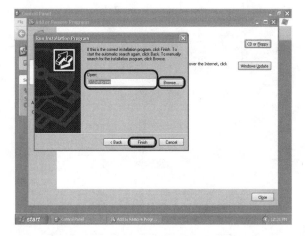

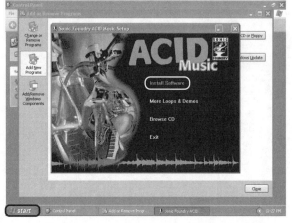

6. If XP found a setup file, it lists it in the Open text box. Make sure this is the right file. If not, or if XP didn't find the file, click the Browse button and use the Browse dialog box to locate the setup file.

Click the Finish button. XP starts the setup routine for the program.

7. Follow the prompts, supplying decisions and information as necessary.

REMOVING A PROGRAM

If you cease to find a program useful, or if you replace it with a better program, you can remove the program to reclaim the space it occupied on disk.

To remove a program, always use the procedure shown on this page. If you try to remove a program by deleting its files, you'll usually be able to remove only part of it, so it'll still take up some space on the disk. Worse, XP won't know that you've disabled the program, which may cause problems.

Before you remove a program, make sure that no other user still needs it. Make doubly sure that no other user is currently using it.

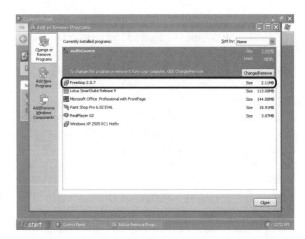

1. Take steps 1 and 2 of the previous item to display the Change or Remove Programs page of the Add or Remove Programs window.

Select the program. The window displays information about the program and buttons for changing it or removing it.

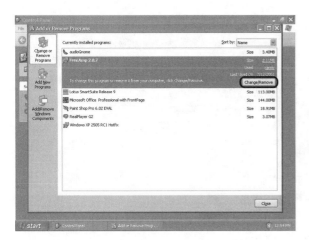

2. Click the Remove button or the Change/Remove button. XP starts the uninstall routine for the program.

Most uninstall routines display some kind of confirmation dialog box.

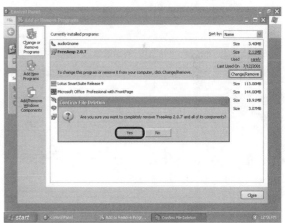

3. Choose the confirmation button in any confirmation message box.

You may also need to choose uninstall options and confirm the removal of some files.

KEEPING XP UP-TO-DATE WITH WINDOWS UPDATE

Windows Update keeps your copy of XP up-to-date and secure by downloading and installing the latest updates, additions, and security patches that Microsoft releases. In order to use Windows Update, your computer needs to be connected to the Internet.

By default, Windows Update runs itself periodically, downloads update files you might want to install, and prompts you to install them. If you prefer, you can run Windows Update manually as described in this section. You can also run Windows Update from Help and Support Center.

Because Windows Update is implemented via the Microsoft website, the interface may have changed from the screens shown here.

1. Choose Start ➢ All Programs ➢ Windows Update. XP opens an Internet Explorer window to the Windows Update website.

2. Click the Scan for Updates link. XP scans the available updates and presents a list.

If you see a Security Warning dialog box asking you to install controls signed by Microsoft Corporation, choose the Yes button.

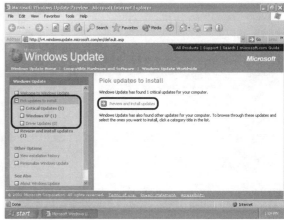

3. Click the Review and Install Updates link. XP displays information on the updates.

If there are no critical updates, you can choose other updates in the Pick Updates to Install area.

KEEPING XP UP-TO-DATE WITH WINDOWS UPDATE *(continued)*

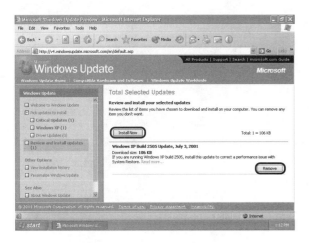

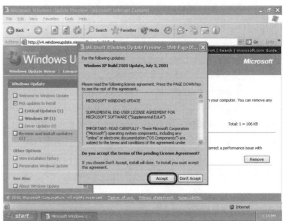

4. Click the Remove button to remove any update you don't want to install.

Click the Install Now button. XP may display a license agreement.

5. Click the Accept button if the license is acceptable.

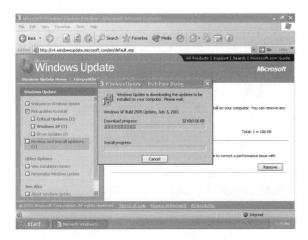

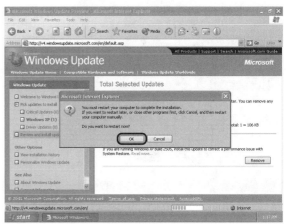

6. Wait while XP downloads and installs the updates. When it has finished, it may display the Installation Complete screen or may require you to shut down your computer (as shown here).

7. Click the OK button to restart your computer. XP restarts your computer and finishes installing the update.

CONFIGURING AUTOPLAY

XP includes an AutoPlay feature that's set by default to spring into action when you insert a removable storage item such as a CD, a DVD, a removable disk (for example, a Zip disk), or a CompactFlash card or SmartMedia card.

AutoPlay is designed to take different actions for different types of content: audio files (for example, MP3 files), picture files (for example, digital photos), video files, and mixed content. By configuring AutoPlay, you can make XP take the actions you want for a given type of content.

1. Choose Start ➤ My Computer. XP opens an Explorer window showing your drives.

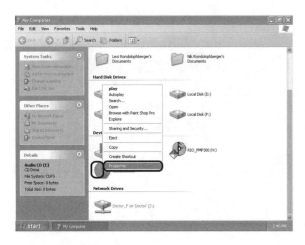

2. Right-click the removable drive and choose Properties from the context menu. XP displays the Properties dialog box for the drive—in this example, a CD drive.

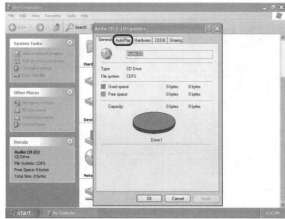

3. Click the AutoPlay tab. XP displays the AutoPlay page.

CONFIGURING AUTOPLAY *(continued)*

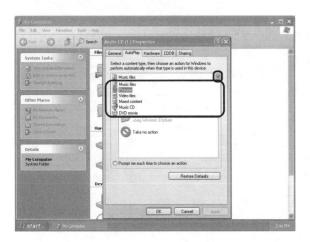

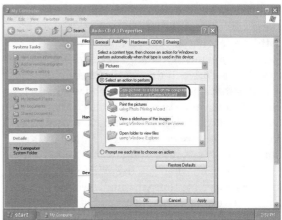

4. In the drop-down list, select the type of content you want to set AutoPlay for.

The Actions group box displays actions for that type of content.

5. To have XP perform an action, select the Select an Action to Perform option button, then select the action in the list box.

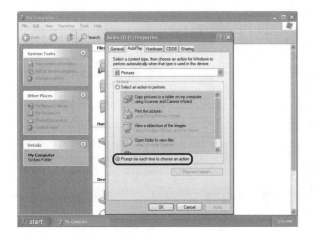

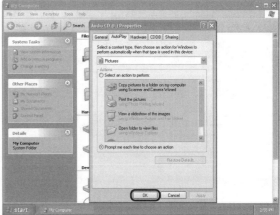

6. To have XP prompt you for an action each time, select the Prompt Me Each Time to Choose an Action option button.

7. Set AutoPlay options for other content types.

Click the OK button. XP closes the Properties dialog box and applies your settings.

SETTING SYSTEM RESTORE POINTS

The System Restore feature lets you roll back your computer's software state following a change of software that doesn't turn out satisfactorily. For example, you might update a device driver but find that the new driver didn't work correctly. Or you might install a program that doesn't work as it should—and which won't uninstall correctly.

System Restore lets you return your computer to a system restore point created in the past. XP automatically creates system restore points both periodically and when you use Windows Update, and you can create them manually whenever you want—for example, before installing or updating software or changing configuration settings. With typical settings, XP retains two to three weeks' worth of restore points, giving you good flexibility in recovering from software and hardware mishaps.

1. Choose Start ➤ All Programs ➤ Accessories ➤ System Tools ➤ System Restore. XP starts System Restore.

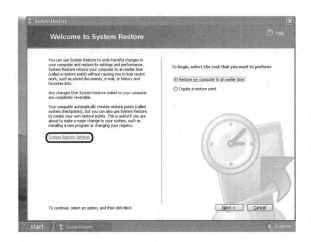

2. Click the System Restore Settings link. System Restore displays the System Restore page of the System Properties dialog box.

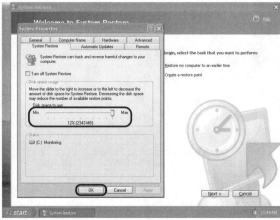

3. If necessary, use the Disk Space to Use slider to adjust the amount of space System Restore uses. (If your system has multiple drives, click the Settings button and use the Settings dialog box.)

Click the OK button.

SETTING SYSTEM RESTORE POINTS *(continued)*

• •

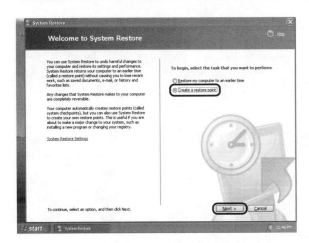

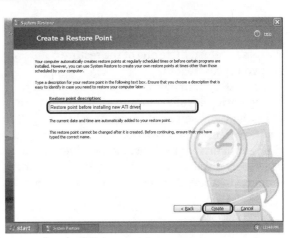

4. Select the Create a Restore Point option button.

Click the Next button. System Restore displays the Create a Restore Point screen.

5. Enter the name for the restore point.

Click the Create button. System Restore creates the restore point and displays the Restore Point Created screen.

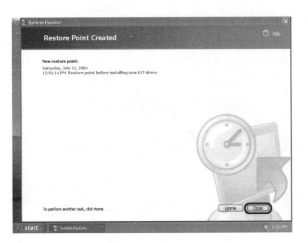

6. Click the Close button. System Restore closes.

Expert Advice

◆ You can turn off System Restore by selecting the Turn Off System Restore check box (or the Turn Off System Restore on All Drives check box, if you have multiple drives) on the System Restore page of the System Properties dialog box, but doing so isn't a good idea: Although XP is reliable and stable, badly written software or drivers can still prevent it from running. But you may be able to save disk space by reducing the amount of space System Restore can take up. System Restore needs at least 200MB of space on your system drive.

◆ If you have multiple hard drives, you can save disk space by turning off System Restore for data-only drives. Keep System Restore turned on for the drive that contains your XP files and your program files.

RESTORING YOUR SYSTEM

When a software installation or a driver upgrade doesn't work as planned, you can use System Restore to return XP to one of the restore points that you or XP created.

Because System Restore changes the software configuration of your computer, it's best to use it only when your software goes seriously wrong. If you experience a problem that you can solve by changing a driver or rolling back a driver to the previously installed driver, it's better to solve the problem that way than by using System Restore.

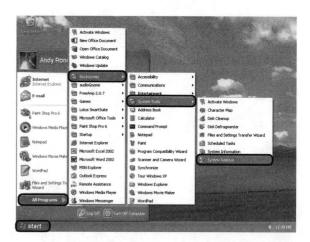

1. Choose Start ➤ All Programs ➤ Accessories ➤ System Tools ➤ System Restore. XP starts System Restore.

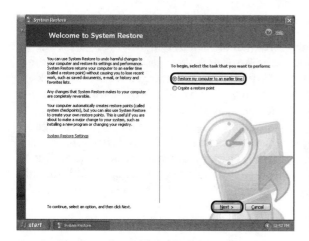

2. Make sure the Restore My Computer to an Earlier Time option button is selected.

Click the Next button. System Restore displays the Select a Restore Point screen.

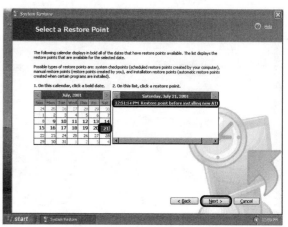

3. Use the calendar to select the date to which you want to restore the computer. Bold dates indicate restore points.

Select a restore point in the list for the date.

Click the Next button. System Restore displays the Confirm Restore Point Selection screen.

RESTORING YOUR SYSTEM *(continued)*

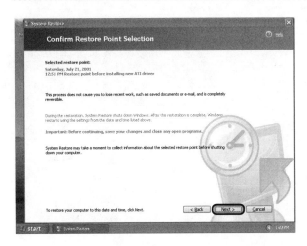

4. Close any other open programs.

Click the Next button. System Restore restores your system to the restore point you chose, then restarts XP and displays the Restoration Complete page after you log on.

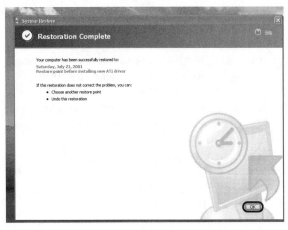

5. Click the OK button. System Restore closes. Check your system to see if it's running properly.

Expert Advice

◆ System Restore stores several weeks' worth of restore points, depending on how much space you've allocated to it.

◆ Restoring your system affects only your system files—it doesn't affect your data files. So any data files that you've created since the restore point to which you're restoring XP will still be there after the restoration.

◆ Conversely, this also means that you can't use System Restore to rescue a data file that you've deleted or damaged. For example, if you delete the contents of an Excel workbook and then save it, you can't recover an earlier version of the file by using System Restore.

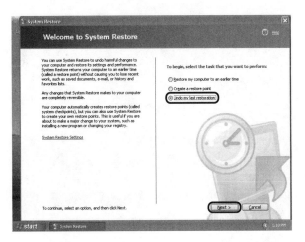

6. If the restoration didn't produce the effect you wanted, run System Restore again. You can either choose a restore point further in the past or undo your last restoration.

RUNNING DISK CLEANUP

XP's Disk Cleanup feature lets you keep your hard disk in order by removing temporary files, emptying the Recycle Bin, and compressing old files. By getting rid of old files, you can reclaim disk space.

It's a good idea to run Disk Cleanup once every few weeks. If you find it hard to remember to run Disk Cleanup, you can schedule it to run automatically at a convenient time, as described in the next section.

See "Cleaning Up Your Disks with Disk Cleanup" in Chapter 11 for a discussion of the pros and cons of removing the various types of files that Disk Cleanup rounds up for deletion.

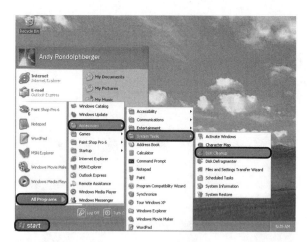

1. Choose Start ➢ All Programs ➢ Accessories ➢ System Tools ➢ Disk Cleanup. XP starts Disk Cleanup, which displays the Select Drive dialog box.

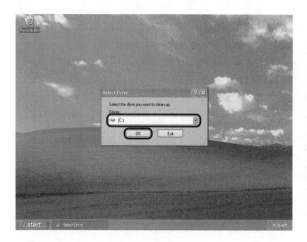

2. Select the drive to clean up.

Click the OK button. Disk Cleanup scans the drive and displays the Disk Cleanup dialog box.

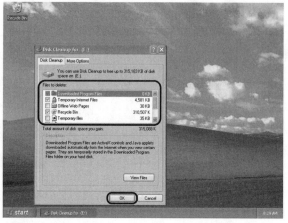

3. Select the items you want to delete.

Click the OK button. XP removes the items and closes the Disk Cleanup dialog box.

Part I

Up and Running with Windows XP Home Edition

Chapter 1

Introducing Windows XP Home Edition

THIS CHAPTER DISCUSSES WHAT Windows XP Home Edition is, what it does, and who it's for. It covers in some detail the features and improvements in XP Home (as I'll refer to it), so that you'll know what the operating system offers, and mentions which chapter of the book covers which feature.

The chapter then discusses whether you should upgrade from your current version of Windows. As you might imagine, the answer depends on which version of Windows you're currently running, what you're trying to do with it, and what degrees of success and satisfaction you're experiencing. But for most people who have adequate hardware, XP offers significant improvements over all previous versions of Windows.

At the end of the chapter, you'll find a discussion of the main ways in which XP Professional differs from XP Home, because you may want to consider Professional rather than Home if you need any of the additional features that Professional offers.

If you're already up to speed on all of XP's features, skip straight ahead to the next chapter and get started on installing XP.

This chapter covers the following topics:

- ◆ What is Windows XP Home Edition?
- ◆ What's new in Windows XP Home Edition?
- ◆ Should you upgrade to Windows XP Home Edition?
- ◆ Should you upgrade to Windows XP Professional Edition instead?

What Is Windows XP Home Edition?

Windows XP Home Edition is the latest version of Windows aimed at the consumer market. XP Home comprises a feature set designed for home users, while its more powerful (and more expensive) sibling Windows XP Professional offers features designed for professional and corporate users.

If you've used Windows before, or if you're currently using Windows, you may wonder what the big deal is. The good news is that XP *is* a big deal, especially if you've had less than satisfactory experiences with Windows in the past. XP isn't the be-all and end-all of operating systems, but it's a great improvement on its predecessors.

As you probably know, through the second half of the 1990s and up until 2001, Microsoft offered two main categories of Windows versions for personal computers: the Windows 95 family and the Windows NT family. In the Windows 95 family were Windows 95 itself, naturally enough; Windows 98; Windows 98 Second Edition, which (despite its unassuming name) was a major upgrade to Windows 98; and Windows Millennium Edition, also known as Windows Me. In the Windows NT family were Windows NT versions 3.1, 3.5, 3.51, and 4, each of which came in a Workstation version and a Server version, and then Windows 2000, which came in a Professional version and several Server versions.

The Windows 95 family, widely referred to as Windows 9*x* in a brave attempt to simplify Microsoft's inconsistent naming, offered impressive compatibility with older hardware (*legacy hardware*, as it's sometimes politely termed) and software (*legacy software*), including full (or full-ish) DOS capabilities for running games and character-based programs. These versions of Windows kept their hardware demands to a reasonable minimum. They were aimed at the consumer market. When things went wrong (which happened regrettably often), they became unstable. And they crashed. Frequently.

Many of those people—both professionals and home users—who couldn't stand or afford to lose their work because of Windows 9*x*'s frequent crashes migrated to Windows NT instead. (Others tried OS/2 while it lasted, then returned disconsolately to Windows. Others went to Linux, and mostly stayed with it.) NT, which stands for New Technology, had a completely different underpinning of code than Windows 9*x*. NT was designed for stability, and as a result, it crashed much less frequently than Windows 9*x*. Unfortunately, though, NT wasn't nearly as compatible as Windows 9*x* with legacy hardware and software. Most games and much audio and video software wouldn't run on NT, and it was picky about the hardware on which it would run. (Actually, this wasn't unfortunate at all—it was deliberate on Microsoft's part, and probably wise. But the result was far from great for many users.)

So for the last half-dozen years, users have essentially had to decide between stability and compatibility. This led to a lot of unhappy users, some of whom couldn't run the software they wanted, and others who kept losing work or at least having to reboot their computers more than they should have had to.

The Windows 9*x* line culminated in Windows Me, which tacked some stability and restoration features onto the Windows 9*x* code base. NT culminated in Windows 2000 Professional, which featured increased compatibility with programs over NT (which wasn't saying all that much), a smooth user interface, and usability enhancements.

Windows 2000 Professional was arguably the most stable operating system that Microsoft had produced until XP came along. (Some old-timers reckon Windows NT 3.51 was more stable.) But Windows 2000 Professional's stability came at a price: It had no interest in running any games or other demanding software that wouldn't conform to its stringent requirements. And while it was compatible with quite an impressive range of legacy hardware, many items still wouldn't work. Even up-to-date hardware could be problematic, especially if it connected via universal serial bus (USB).

Since the late 1990s, Microsoft had been promising to deliver a consumer version of Windows that melded the stability of NT and the compatibility of Windows 9x. In Windows XP Home Edition, that version of Windows is finally here.

What's New in Windows XP Home Edition?

This section outlines the most striking and appealing new features in XP Home, starting with installation and upgrading, moving through the user interface and visible features, and ending up with the features hidden under the hood.

Some of these new features fall into convenient categories, and this section presents them in categories. Others don't; this section presents these features individually.

Easier Installation and Updating

XP includes several features designed to make it easier to install and keep up-to-date. These include Dynamic Update and Windows Update; the Files and Settings Transfer Wizard; more wizards for a variety of tasks; a wider selection of device drivers; simplified installation for multifunction devices; and effective uninstall back to Windows 98 and Windows Me.

DYNAMIC UPDATE AND WINDOWS UPDATE

If you're installing XP, one of the first new features you'll notice is Dynamic Update, which runs during setup from an existing installation of Windows and offers to download the latest patches, packages, and fixes so that they can be installed during the setup process. Getting these latest items gives you the best chance of getting all your hardware and software to work on XP.

After installation, Windows Update runs periodically and offers to download the latest patches, packages, and fixes and install them so that your copy of XP is as up-to-date, secure, and compatible as possible. (You can also run Windows Update manually whenever you want to.) Windows Update is a compelling feature—and you can turn it off if you don't like it.

Chapter 2 discusses Dynamic Update. Chapter 16 discusses Windows Update.

FILES AND SETTINGS TRANSFER WIZARD

Making its debut in XP is the Files and Settings Transfer Wizard, a feature that Windows users have been demanding for a good 10 years. The Files and Settings Transfer Wizard provides a way of transferring designated files and settings from one computer to another, or from one installation of Windows to another on the same computer. You'll still need to reinstall all your programs on the new computer or new installation of XP, but you can transfer your data and a good amount of information about your work environment easily.

If you're migrating from an old computer to a new computer, or if you're installing XP as a dual-boot with an existing version of Windows, you can use the Files and Settings Transfer Wizard to clone your existing Desktop and files and transfer them to the new computer or new version of XP.

Chapter 2 discusses how to use the Files and Settings Transfer Wizard.

MORE WIZARDS TO MAKE TASKS EASIER

XP includes a slew of wizards designed to walk you through complicated processes (and some that aren't so complicated). Perhaps most welcome are the improvements to the Network Setup Wizard (discussed in Chapter 31), which provides effective configuration of simple networks and Internet connection sharing, and the two Hardware Wizards, the Add Hardware Wizard and the Found New Hardware Wizard (discussed in various chapters, but primarily in Chapter 14).

Other wizards are less useful. For example, the Desktop Cleanup Wizard pops out periodically like the neighborhood dog and tries to persuade you to let it herd the stray icons on your Desktop into a folder where they'll be available but less obtrusive. If you refuse, it wags its virtual tail and goes away for a while. If you don't like this wizard, you can disable it.

MORE DEVICE DRIVERS

XP comes complete with drivers for a large number of devices, including scanners, digital still cameras, digital video cameras, printers, and so on. So there's a better chance than with another version of Windows (say Windows Me or Windows 2000) that, when you plug in a new device, XP will be able to load a driver for it and get it working without any fuss. That said, you may still need to download a driver for the device, either from the manufacturer or from Windows Update.

Like hardware, drivers pop up in various places throughout the book, but most of the action is in Chapter 14.

SIMPLIFIED INSTALLATION FOR MULTIFUNCTION DEVICES

Apart from having more drivers (as described in the previous section), XP makes it easier to install multifunction devices—for example, a multifunction printer/scanner/fax device (the kind that people sometimes call *hydra* machines or *all-in-one* machines), a PC Card that combines a network interface card with a modem, or a sound board with extra features.

Previous versions of Windows tended to recognize the component pieces of multifunction devices separately in sequence. If you installed a hydra, Windows would recognize the printer and demand the installation software for it. Once that was done, Windows would recognize the fax and demand the software for *that*. After that, it would recognize the scanner and suggest you might want to install yet more software. XP improves on this social ineptitude by recognizing multifunction devices as such the first time you introduce it to them, and so it demands the installation software only once.

EFFECTIVE UNINSTALL BACK TO WINDOWS 98 AND WINDOWS ME

XP Home provides an effective uninstall feature for rolling back the XP installation to your previous installation of Windows 98 or Windows Me. You can't uninstall XP Home and revert to an operating system other than these two. (XP Professional supports upgrading from and uninstalling back to a different set of previous versions of Windows, as you'll see later in this chapter.)

Effective Multiuser Capabilities

XP provides far better multiuser capabilities than Windows 9x. You'll notice this at once when you start XP, because by default the Welcome screen that's displayed when XP starts lists each user who has an account on the computer.

While Windows 9x let anybody log on to the computer by creating a new account, XP requires an existing account in order to log on. By default, no account has a password in XP Home, though, so in effect anybody can log on using one of the existing accounts until you require passwords—and you ought to require passwords immediately to protect your data.

Windows 9x let you create a profile for each separate user, so that each user could have their own Desktop, Start menu, and set of programs; but it didn't offer any features for preventing one user from seeing another user's files. By contrast, XP takes the approach of NT and Windows 2000, which keep each user's files separate, letting you set Windows up so that no user can see another user's files unless they have been shared deliberately.

XP goes further than NT and Windows 2000, though, in that it lets multiple users be logged on at the same time, each with programs running and files open. Only one user can be actually *using* the computer, or *active* in XP parlance, at any one time, but the other user sessions continue running in the background (*disconnected*, in XP parlance). When you've finished with the computer for the time being, you can log off XP, just as you did in previous versions of Windows. Logging off closes all the programs you were using and frees up the memory they took up. But if you stop using the computer only temporarily, you may prefer to *switch user*, which leaves your programs running but lets someone else use the computer in the interim. Further encouraging you to switch user, XP's default screen saver setting is to display the Welcome screen after 10 minutes of inactivity, performing the equivalent of a Switch User command as it disconnects the user but leaves their session running hidden in the background.

As you might imagine, having multiple user sessions running like this can cause some problems. For example, what happens when one user has a shared file open for editing in their (disconnected) session, and along comes another user who logs on, opens the same file, and starts editing it? And what happens if a disconnected session has the Internet connection open, preventing the currently active user from using the phone line?

Turn to Chapter 5 to find out the answer to the first question, and Chapter 32 to learn the answer to the second question.

Enhanced User Interface

XP has a completely revamped user interface with a large number of visual enhancements and improved functionality. Some of the visual enhancements improve usability, while others are mere eye candy. But the overall effect is mostly easy to use and mostly looks good—and if you don't like the look, you can restore the "classic" Windows look with minimal effort.

The following sections discuss the main changes to the user interface.

REDESIGNED START MENU

XP sports a redesigned Start menu that's supposedly easier and quicker to use than the old-style Start menu found in Windows 9x and Windows 2000. Whether you find XP's Start menu easier and quicker depends on your previous experience. But don't worry if you like the "classic" Start menu—you can restore it easily enough with a few clicks of the mouse, as discussed in Chapter 4.

The Start menu appears as a panel containing two columns (shown in Figure 1.1). The right-hand column remains the same unless you customize it. The lower section of the left-hand column starts off with items Microsoft thinks you ought to know about immediately after installation. It then automatically reconfigures itself to show your most used programs. You can pin an item to the Start menu to prevent it from moving and keep it available.

FIGURE 1.1

The redesigned Start menu contains a static column of choices on the right and a variable column of choices on the left.

As you can see in the figure, the current user's name appears in a bar across the top of the Start menu, and the Log Off button and Turn Off Computer button appear at the bottom of the menu.

REDESIGNED EXPLORER

Explorer windows use a pair of technologies called WebView and ListView to present context-sensitive lists of tasks you may want to perform or other locations you may want to access.

For example, when you select a file (as in Figure 1.2), you see a list of File and Folder Tasks (including links for Rename This File, Move This File, and Delete This File), a list of Other Places (other folders you may want to access from this folder), and a list of Details (which contains information about the file selected and is off the screen in the figure). When you select a folder, Explorer displays a list of File and Folder Tasks (including links for Rename This Folder, Copy This Folder, and Publish This Folder to the Web). When you select your My Network Places folder, you get a Network Tasks list (including links for View Network Connections and Set Up a Home or Small Office Network).

Context menus (right-click menus) in Explorer are also improved, with more context-sensitive commands added where appropriate. But most of the action takes place in the Tasks list for the selected item. That's because some 80 percent of users apparently weren't using the context menus successfully—an impressive and frightening statistic thrown up by Microsoft's research on Windows users.

REDESIGNED CONTROL PANEL

XP also has a redesigned Control Panel (shown in Figure 1.3) that uses WebView and ListView technology to present Control Panel as categories of items and actions you can take with them. (If you regard Control Panel as an oddly behaved Explorer window, it should come as no surprise after reading the previous section that Control Panel uses WebView and ListView.)

New users will likely find the Category view of Control Panel easy to use. Users comfortable with the regular manifestation of Control Panel in Windows 9x, Windows NT 4, and Windows 2000 will probably prefer to use the Classic view.

FIGURE 1.2

Explorer windows use the new Web-View and ListView technologies to present lists of tasks associated with the selected item.

FIGURE 1.3

Control Panel also uses WebView and ListView by default, dividing its bevy of icons into categories. You can use the Classic view to see all the icons at once.

EYE CANDY

To complement its highly graphical interface, XP includes a dangerous amount of eye candy. Most people will like at least some of it. Some people will love it all. And no doubt some people will claim to detest every subtly shaded pixel of it.

The prime example of eye candy is the My Pictures Slideshow screen saver, which lets you set up an automated (or mouse-controlled) slideshow of designated pictures instead of a regular screen saver. This feature seems destined to be widely popular.

Less assured of a rapturous welcome are the staggering amounts of adornment in the interface, such as shadows under the mouse pointer and under menus; the color gradient in the title bar of windows; and the effect of sliding icons, controls, and Taskbar buttons. This overbearing emphasis on graphics places heavy demands on your graphics card and processor, and if your computer's hardware tends to the lukewarm rather than the hot, you may find that the eye candy exacts an unacceptable performance penalty. Microsoft has had the sense to let you set performance options to balance the demands of appearance against your need for performance, so you can turn off the least necessary effects and speed up your computer. (Chapter 11 discusses how to set performance options.)

Taskbar Changes and Enhancements

XP includes a number of tweaks to the Taskbar. These seem designed for beginners, so if you're an experienced Windows user, you may find some good and others bad. Fortunately, you can change the Taskbar's behavior back to how it was in previous versions of Windows. You'll find the details in Chapter 4.

TASKBAR LOCKING

By default, the Taskbar is locked in XP Home so that you cannot resize it or move it. Presumably this is intended to help prevent users from dragging their Taskbar to an inaccessible line at the edge of the screen, but it will annoy experienced users who want to be able to resize and move their Taskbar freely. (You can unlock it easily enough.) In XP Professional, the Taskbar is *not* locked by default.

TASKBAR SCROLLING

If you read the previous paragraph, you probably started raising objections: If the Taskbar is a fixed size, the buttons for the running programs must become tiny and useless as soon as you've got 10 or more programs running.

Two other changes come into play here, of which the first is Taskbar scrolling. When the Taskbar is locked, XP keeps the buttons bigger than a minimum size. To accommodate the buttons, XP increases the depth of the Taskbar, but displays only its top row. On the displayed portion of the Taskbar, XP puts scroll buttons so that you can scroll the Taskbar up and down one row of buttons at a time.

TASKBAR BUTTON GROUPING

The second change that makes Taskbar locking reasonable is Taskbar button grouping.

By default, XP groups related Taskbar buttons once you've opened enough windows to more or less fill the Taskbar. Whereas other versions of Windows displayed one Taskbar button for each program window, XP groups them onto a pop-up menu from a single Taskbar button. For example, if you open nine Internet Explorer windows in Windows 98, Windows displays nine Internet

Explorer buttons on the Taskbar. Having all these buttons can make it easy to find the window you want, but the buttons take up a lot of space (or each button on the Taskbar gets shrunk to a tiny size to fit them all in).

In XP, if the program has multiple open windows, the Taskbar button displays the number of windows, the title of the current active window or last active window, and a drop-down arrow. To access one of the other open windows, click the Taskbar button. XP displays a list of the windows by title (shown in Figure 1.4). Select the window you want, and XP displays it.

FIGURE 1.4

Unlike previous versions of Windows, XP can group related Taskbar buttons onto a single button.

NOTIFICATION AREA

By default, XP Home collapses the notification area (also known as the System Tray) so that only the icons you've used most recently are displayed. To display the other icons in the notification area, click the < button at the left end of the notification area.

Better Audio and Video Features

XP includes a slew of new features and improvements for audio and video. These include a new version of Windows Media Player; better features for grabbing and handling images from digital input devices such as scanners and cameras; and Windows Movie Maker, a modest video-editing program.

WINDOWS MEDIA PLAYER VERSION 8

Front and center among the improved audio and video features of XP is Windows Media Player version 8, which combines a video and DVD player, a CD player, an Internet radio tuner, and a jukebox for playing and organizing digital-audio files such as Windows Media Audio (WMA) files and MP3 files. Windows Media Player 8 comes with several visually interesting *skins* (graphical looks) that you can apply at will. You can even create your own skins if you have the time and talent to invest.

All in all, Windows Media Player 8 is a huge improvement over the 98-pound weakling version of Windows Media Player shipped with all previous versions of Windows except Windows Me. (Windows Me included Windows Media Player 7, which offered many of the features of version 8.) Windows Media Player 8 can even burn audio CDs at the full speed of your CD-R or CD-RW drive.

Windows Media Player 8 is a strong program, but two missing features will disappoint many users:

- Windows Media Player 8 has no codec (coder/decoder) for playing back DVDs. If you want to watch DVDs, you'll have to add a codec of your own—and almost certainly pay for the privilege.
- Windows Media Player 8 can encode audio to the universally popular MP3 format—but only if you add a third-party encoder. You'll probably have to pay for this too.

Chapter 26 discusses Windows Media Player 8.

MY MUSIC FOLDER AND MY PICTURES FOLDER

Like several of its predecessors, XP uses custom folders for music (the My Music folder) and pictures (the My Pictures folder). Again like its predecessors, it tries none too subtly to persuade you to save your music in these folders. But XP goes further, making these folders much more useful than they were in earlier versions of Windows.

As you'd expect, the My Music folder and the My Pictures folder use WebView and ListView to present customized lists of actions you can take with music files and picture files. Some of these actions tend to the commercial—for example, the Order Prints Online link in the Picture Tasks list, and the Shop for Music Online link in the Music Tasks list. But others are solidly useful—for example, the Play All link in the Music Tasks list, which lets you play all the music in a folder without spelunking into it, or the View As a Slide Show link in the Picture Tasks list, which lets you set a whole folder of pictures running as a slideshow with a single click.

Not surprisingly, the My Music folder works closely with Windows Media Player. Windows Media Player is definitely happy for you to keep your music in the My Music folder, though it will let you keep your music elsewhere as well. Better yet, Windows Media Player's features for cataloging music tracks are flexible enough to keep track of music files even when you move them from one folder to another.

The My Pictures folder works closely with Windows Image Acquisition, Windows Picture and Fax Viewer, and Paint (all three of which are discussed in the next section). The folder includes a slideshow applet and a filmstrip view, and it can publish your pictures to the Web.

BETTER IMAGE ACQUISITION AND HANDLING

XP provides strong features for capturing images from scanners, still cameras, and video cameras. It also provides better throughput for video streams, although unless you have a duplicate computer running an older version of Windows to use as a benchmark, you could be forgiven for failing to go into raptures over the improvement. Less cynically, the improvement in throughput is unquestionably a good thing, and on decent hardware, XP delivers adequate to impressive video performance.

One of the central tools for image acquisition and handling is the Scanner and Camera Wizard. This wizard has a variety of duties, including transferring image files from still cameras and digital media (for example, CompactFlash cards and SmartMedia cards) to the computer. Most of its capabilities stay on the useful side of the esoteric. For example, you can scan multiple pages into a single image file, an ability that can come in handy in both home and business settings.

XP provides some basic tools for handling still images. As mentioned in the previous section, the My Pictures folder acts as a default repository for images and provides some basic image-handling abilities, such as rotating an image. Windows Picture and Fax Viewer feature lets you examine an image (and annotate a fax). And Paint, the basic image-manipulation and drawing package that's been included with Windows since Windows 3.*x*, has been beefed up as well. Paint can now open—and save—JPEG, GIF, TIFF, and PNG images as well as Windows bitmap (BMP) files, making it about five times as useful as before.

WINDOWS MOVIE MAKER

XP includes Windows Movie Maker, a basic package for capturing video, editing video and audio, and creating video files in the Windows Media format. You won't find yourself making the next *Timecode* or *Traffic* with Windows Movie Maker, but it's good enough for home-video editing. You can also create video slideshows with still images for those family occasions on rainy weekends or holidays.

Web Chapter 2, available from this book's web page at www.sybex.com, discusses how to get started with Windows Movie Maker.

CD Burning

XP comes with built-in CD-burning capabilities. You can burn CDs from an Explorer window with minimal effort. You can also burn CDs directly from Windows Media Player, which lets you easily create audio CDs that you can play in regular CD players.

Chapter 28 discusses how to burn CDs.

Compressed Folders

XP has built-in support for compressed folders in both the ubiquitous ZIP format and the Microsoft Cabinet (CAB) format. You can create ZIP folders containing one or more files or folders. Better still, you can view the contents of a ZIP or CAB folder seamlessly in Explorer as if it were a regular folder.

Chapter 6 discusses how to work with compressed folders.

Improved Features for Sending Attachments

XP includes improved features for sending files and folders as attachments to e-mail messages. Instead of blindly attaching the files and folders identified by the user, XP offers to optimize the file size and display size of the pictures so that they transfer faster and fit onto the recipient's screen when they arrive. If the recipient is using XP, they get to choose whether to open the file or files at the original size or at the optimized size.

Because this feature can actually change the files sent, it seems suspect. But if it reduces the number of multimegabyte digital pictures landing on your ISP's mail server, you may well find it a positive feature—even if you choose never to use it yourself.

Chapter 21 discusses how to use Outlook Express for e-mail, including attachments.

Search Companion

XP includes Search Companion, an enhanced search feature for finding information both on your PC and in the wider world. You can use Search Companion to search for files, for computers or people online, or for information in Help and Support Center. Search Companion brokers the search requests that you enter and farms them out to the appropriate search mechanisms.

You can choose between having Search Companion appear in a straightforward and unexceptionable window and having it manifest itself using one of various animated characters reminiscent of the Microsoft Office Assistant.

Chapter 6 discusses how to use Search Companion.

Easy Publishing to the Web

XP makes it easier to publish files or folders to a website by using a web-hosting service. XP includes a feature called Web Digital Authoring and Versioning (WebDAV for short) that lets you save information to the Web from any program rather than having to use the regular web-publishing protocols.

Chapter 25 discusses how to publish information to the Web.

A Sane Implementation of Autoplay

If you've used Windows 9x, NT 4, or 2000, you'll know all about the Autoplay feature and how it used to drive people crazy. You remember Autoplay—the moment you insert a CD, it starts playing the music from it or installing any software it contains. By default, Autoplay was enabled, so you had to switch it off (or override it by holding down the Shift key while closing the CD tray) to prevent this from occurring.

XP includes a new version of Autoplay that's improved in several ways. First, you can customize it. Second, you can configure it to take different actions depending on what the CD (or other medium) contains. For example, you might want XP to play your audio CDs automatically when you insert them (okay, you don't—but you *might*), or you might want XP to display a slideshow automatically when you insert a CD containing nothing but pictures.

What's that about *other medium*? That's the third thing: In XP, Autoplay works for CDs, DVDs, assorted flashcards (including CompactFlash, Memory Stick, and SmartMedia), PC Cards, Zip and other removable disk drives, and FireWire hot-plug external drives.

Chapter 6 discusses how to configure Autoplay.

More Games

XP includes more games than previous versions of Windows. Some of these are single-player games (for example, Spider Solitaire). Others are multiplayer games that you can play across the Internet via MSN's Zone.com website.

Chapter 29 discusses the games that XP includes and how to configure XP for playing more demanding games.

Remote Desktop Connection

XP Home includes Remote Desktop Connection, a technology that lets you use your computer to access a remote computer (for example, your computer at the office) that's running XP Professional. Once you've connected to the remote computer, you can control it as if you were sitting at it.

Chapter 34 discusses how to use Remote Desktop Connection.

More Windows-Key Shortcuts

XP includes more shortcuts for the Windows key (sometimes called the *Winkey*). You can still press the Windows key to open or close the Start menu, but you can also use it in 15 or so key combinations. For example, pressing Windows key+M issues a Minimize All command (showing the Desktop), and pressing Windows key+Shift+M issues an Undo Minimize All command.

For the full list of Windows key combinations, see the section "Using the Windows Key" in Chapter 3. You'll also find Windows key combinations throughout the book when you may want to take a Windows key action.

Improvements for Portable Computers

XP includes several improvements for portable computers.

First, XP supports processor power control, which lets the computer make use of features in chips such as Intel's SpeedStep, in which the processor runs at full speed when the computer is plugged into the main power supply (or told that it's plugged in) but at a lower speed to save power when it's running on battery power (or told that it is).

Throttling back the processor like this reduces the computer's power usage a bit, improving battery life, but in most portables, the screen consumes far more power than the processor. XP also targets the screen, providing a couple of features designed to reduce power use when the computer is running on battery power. First, XP turns off the display when the user closes the computer's lid, on the basis that the user probably isn't looking at the display. Second, it runs the screen at a dimmer brightness when the computer is running off the battery. The cynical among you will point out that the better-designed portables implement both these functions already in hardware. Still, it shouldn't do any harm to have XP help out for the manufacturers who design their machines a little less carefully. Anyway, Chapter 15 discusses these features.

XP also includes some other less obvious visual enhancements, such as support for ClearType, a Microsoft text-display technology that improves the look of fonts on LCD screens that have digital interfaces. While these screens aren't strictly confined to portables, that's where the bulk of the market is.

Faxing

XP Home contains a built-in fax client that's more than adequate for most home needs and many home-office needs. You can send faxes from any program that supports printing, and you can specify whether to print out incoming faxes automatically or store them in a folder. You can even configure different fax/modems to take different roles. For example, if you use faxes extensively, you might want to keep separate incoming and outgoing fax lines. You'll need a modem for each of the phone lines involved, but that's about as difficult as it gets.

Appendix B discusses faxing and telephony.

More Help

XP delivers more help—and more different types of help—than any other version of Windows.

If you've searched fruitlessly for information in the past, you'll be aware that Windows' Help files have never exactly delivered the ultimate in user satisfaction. Digging information out of help often felt so difficult that if you knew Windows well enough to find help on the right topic, you could probably solve the problem without help's assistance.

XP takes a new approach to help. There are Help files on your hard drive still, but they're integrated into a program called Help and Support Center. Help and Support Center not only works with the Help files but also with the Microsoft Knowledge Base (a database of support queries) and other online sources of information. For example, if you run a query within Help and Support Center to find information on hardware, it might return some information from local files, some information from the Microsoft website, and some information from hardware manufacturers' websites, all packaged into one window so that you can access the information conveniently.

Help and Support Center also provides a gateway to other areas of support, including Microsoft Assisted Support and Microsoft Communities, and to programs that you can use to get help from other users (such as Remote Assistance) and troubleshoot your computer (such as System Configuration Utility and System Restore).

The following sections discuss some of the Help and Support Center features. Chapter 8 discusses how to use Help and Support Center.

MICROSOFT ASSISTED SUPPORT

XP's Microsoft Assisted Support feature lets you automatically collect information on a problem you're having and submit it to Microsoft electronically. A Microsoft technician then sends a solution, which appears as a pop-up in your System Tray. You can read the response in the Help and Support Center window and apply the wisdom it contains to fix the problem.

Microsoft Assisted Support is designed to bypass the problems inherent with tech support via phone call, namely that it's difficult for the user to tell the help technician what's wrong with their computer; it's even harder for the technician to get a good idea of what's going wrong without knowing a fair bit of technical information about the computer; and waiting on hold for tech support is nobody's idea of fun, especially if you're paying for a long-distance call as well as for the support.

WINDOWS NEWSGROUPS

Instead of contacting a Microsoft technician via Microsoft Assisted Support, you can try to get support from the Windows Newsgroups, which are Microsoft-hosted newsgroups dedicated to Windows. Your mileage *will* vary in the Windows Newsgroups depending on whether helpful users answer your query soon and whether the stars have decided to shine on your horoscope for the day.

REMOTE ASSISTANCE

Remote Assistance is an ingenious feature by which you can get assistance from a friend or other knowledgeable person remotely by computer.

Here's the brief version of how Remote Assistance works. You send out an invitation file via e-mail, via Windows Messenger instant messaging, or via a file saved to the network (for example, in a business environment) or floppy disk. Your helper receives the invitation and responds to it. Remote Assistance sets up a secure connection between their computer and yours, using a password to verify their identity. Your helper can then view your screen remotely and chat with you (via text chat and voice). If you trust your helper, you can even let them control your computer so that they can take actions directly.

Chapter 24 discusses how to use Remote Assistance.

HELP QUERIES: ERRORS, EVENTS, AND COMPATIBILITY

You can use Help queries to search for information on error messages, event messages, and compatibility. Help and Support Center's integrated approach lets you search seamlessly across multiple websites (for example, the Microsoft Knowledge Base and the hardware manufacturer's website) to find the information you need.

TOOLS CENTER

Help and Support Center includes a Tools Center that gives you quick access to information about your computer (My Computer Information and Advanced System Information) and its configuration (System Configuration Utility), network diagnostic tools (Network Diagnostics), the System Restore feature, and more. In addition to the tools that Microsoft makes available in the Tools Center, OEMs (original equipment manufacturers) can add tools of their own, so you may also find custom tools provided by your computer manufacturer.

Many of the tools accessible through the Tools Center are also accessible in other ways through the XP interface. For example, XP includes an improved version of Disk Defragmenter, which you can use to keep your hard disk from becoming fragmented (fragmentation decreases performance). You can run Disk Defragmenter from Tools Center, but you can also run it from the System Tools submenu of the Start menu (Start ➢ All Programs ➢ Accessories ➢ System Tools ➢ Disk Defragmenter). Similarly, you can run Windows Update from inside Help and Support Center. This can be convenient, but it offers no great advantage over running Windows Update from the Start menu.

FIXING A PROBLEM TOOL

Help and Support Center includes an area called Fixing a Problem that contains several troubleshooters for walking you through the steps of diagnosing and curing various common problems. Fixing a Problem isn't a panacea, but it's a good place to start, and it can save you a call to a guru or even a trip to your local computer shop.

DEVICE DRIVER REFERRAL SITE

Help and Support Center contains a system for referring searches for drivers that don't come with XP or with the hardware device. When you plug in a new hardware device, and XP finds that it doesn't have a driver for it and you can't supply a driver, XP invites you to send information about the hardware to Microsoft. Once you've sent the information, you can take a variety of actions depending on what information is available. For example, you might be able to view a list of compatible devices (if any), search for information on compatible devices or Knowledge Base articles about the hardware, or find a link to the vendor's website.

OTHER HELP IMPROVEMENTS

Help and Support Center includes assorted other help improvements that can save you time. For example, you can print out a whole chapter of help information at once instead of having to slog through it screen by screen. And you can open multiple Help and Support Center windows at the same time. This makes it easier to pursue different avenues of exploration for the information you need. When you find useful information, you can create a favorite for it so that you can access it quickly again when you need it.

Network Connectivity

XP Home provides various improvements in network connectivity, from creating a home or home-office network to joining a computer to two separate networks. There are also great improvements in Internet connectivity, discussed in the next section.

NETWORK SETUP WIZARD

The Network Setup Wizard simplifies the process of creating a network; sharing printers, Internet connections, and other resources; and configuring protocols and security.

Chapter 31 discusses how to use the Network Setup Wizard to set up a network.

ALL-USER REMOTE ACCESS SERVICE

The All-User Remote Access Service lets you create a credential for all users of the computer so that they can share a connection. For example, you can make your high-speed Internet connection available to all the users of the computer without divulging the account password to them. The name is a bit intimidating and the acronym (AURAS) is nonsensical, but the process is easy.

Chapter 18 discusses how to do this.

ALTERNATIVE TCP/IP CONFIGURATION

XP provides an alternative TCP/IP configuration that allows you to connect to a network that has a DHCP server and to a network that doesn't without changing your TCP/IP settings. For example, you might use a laptop at work (where the network has a DHCP server) and at home (where your network doesn't).

This feature is (jargon alert) *transparent to the user*—in other words, you won't usually notice it. Nevertheless, Chapter 32 discusses it briefly.

NETWORK BRIDGING

XP's network-bridging capability lets you use a computer with two or more network adapters to join two separate networks. Even at home or in a small office, you may well find that you need to bridge two networks. For example, you might need to bridge a FireWire network to an Ethernet network, or you might need to bridge a wireless network to a wired network. Chapter 32 discusses how to bridge networks.

Internet Connectivity and Web Browsing

XP provides many enhanced features for Internet connectivity and web browsing, from Internet connection sharing and a firewall to a new version of Internet Explorer.

INTERNET CONNECTION SHARING AND INTERNET CONNECTION FIREWALL

Like Windows 98 Second Edition, Windows Me, and Windows 2000, XP includes an Internet Connection Sharing (ICS) feature that lets you share an Internet connection on one computer with one or more networked computers. XP's version of Internet Connection Sharing has some tweaks, such as that you can disconnect the shared Internet connection from another PC if necessary—for example, if you need to use the phone line that the connection is using. XP includes a Quality of Service Packet Scheduler that works to optimize the utilization of a shared Internet connection.

Internet Connection Sharing is a great convenience, particularly if you have a high-speed connection such as a DSL or a cable modem—but it lays your network open to assault from the Internet. XP goes one better than its predecessors by including a software firewall (called Internet Connection Firewall) to protect the Internet connection (whether shared or not).

Chapter 18 discusses Internet Connection Firewall, and Chapter 33 discusses Internet Connection Sharing.

New Version of Internet Explorer

XP includes Internet Explorer 6, the latest version of Internet Explorer. Even if you feel you've already had it up to here with new versions of Internet Explorer, stifle your impatience, because Internet Explorer 6 offers several welcome innovations, including the following:

◆ You can save images, music, and videos more easily to your computer.

◆ The new Media bar lets you listen to streaming audio directly in Internet Explorer and (perhaps a less welcome feature) access WindowsMedia.com easily.

◆ Internet Explorer provides better handling of cookies and digital certificates for securing information transfer and authenticating content.

◆ Internet Explorer can automatically resize an image you've displayed directly. If you've ever used Internet Explorer to open a digital photo, and found it displayed bigger than your screen so that you could see only part of it, you may appreciate this feature. (But you'd be better off opening the photo in Paint in the first place.)

◆ Internet Explorer 6 has more integrated functionality for handling different file types. This won't strike you over the head; you'll simply find that more file types open without your being prodded to download and install extra components. For example, Internet Explorer 6 has built-in support for some animations, and support for Cascading Style Sheet (CSS) Level 1. The net result is that more animations will play without your needing to add software, and documents formatted with CSS1 style sheets will be displayed as their authors intended. (They may still look horrible, but at least you'll know that they're meant to look that way.)

Chapter 19 discusses how to configure and use Internet Explorer.

MSN Explorer

XP includes MSN Explorer, an Internet client dedicated to MSN. If you don't have an ISP, you may want to use MSN Explorer to connect to the Internet.

Chapter 18 provides a brief introduction to MSN Explorer.

.NET Passport Integration

To implement many of its Internet services, XP relies heavily on Microsoft's .NET Passport feature. For example, you need to get a .NET Passport in order to use Windows Messenger for instant messaging, to use Hotmail (Microsoft's web-based e-mail service), to create web pages on MSN, or to visit a website that requires a Passport sign-in (for instance, to download certain files from the Microsoft website).

.NET Passport (or, more simply, just *Passport*) is an electronic identifier that's associated with your user account on your PC. (If you use the same Passport with multiple PCs, it can be associated with multiple user accounts.) You can sign up for a Passport by using an existing e-mail account. If you don't have an e-mail account, Microsoft encourages you to base your Passport on a Hotmail account or an MSN account.

Passport enables many cool features—but it also locks you into using Microsoft technologies when you may not want to use them. Worse, it can (or *could*) give Microsoft a way to track some of your actions online. Microsoft protests that it is committed to your online privacy, and does give you the choice of opting out of some of the tracking features, but you don't need to be paranoid to find Passport's possibilities frightening—especially as Microsoft has had to patch a handful of high-profile holes in Passport's security.

You can use Passport Wallet features to (in Microsoft's words) "simplify your online shopping experience"—in other words, spend money faster online and with less effort. You get to decide whether this is a good idea. (Hint: Evaluate Passport Wallet carefully. Don't rush into anything.)

What's Hiding under the Hood

The features mentioned so far catch the eye—some even on a cursory scan of the XP Desktop and interface.

Less glamorous, but more important in the long run, are the enhancements hiding under XP's hood. This section discusses the major enhancements that you probably *won't* see.

PROTECTED MEMORY MANAGEMENT

XP improves on Windows 9*x* (Windows 95, 98, and Me) by offering fully protected memory management. Windows 9*x* didn't protect the areas of memory used by the operating system. This meant that if a program tried to store information in memory already used by another program or by the operating system, the program could crash not only itself but also the operating system. If you've used any version of Windows 9*x* for any length of time, you're probably familiar with these crashes. Typically, you see a succession of instances of the Blue Screen of Death with assorted error messages, and eventually have to perform a warm reboot (Ctrl+Alt+Delete) or a hard reboot (by powering the computer down and back up again). In the meantime, you lose any unsaved work in the programs you're using.

With protected memory management, XP can handle memory errors with more aplomb. When a program tries to access memory that doesn't belong to it, XP can close the program without affecting any other running program. You still lose any unsaved work in the guilty program, but all your other programs continue running.

While XP is dealing with the misbehaving program, you can move the program's window so that it doesn't obstruct your view of any other programs you have open.

WINDOWS FILE PROTECTION

XP offers a feature called Windows File Protection that protects your system files from ill-advised actions on your part.

XP tries to persuade you not to view the contents of folders that you probably shouldn't be messing with, by refusing to show them to you until you demand it show them. You can then delete system files if you want (except for any file that's actively in use, which is locked automatically). But the next time XP boots, or if it catches the damage you've done before you reboot it, it replaces the files you deleted without notifying you.

Chapter 14 discusses Windows File Protection.

SYSTEM RESTORE

XP offers a System Restore feature similar to but more effective than the System Restore feature in Windows Me. System Restore automatically creates restore points both periodically and each time you make a change to the system—for example, by installing a program or a driver. You can also create system restore points manually. When one of your changes leads to an unwelcome result, such as your computer failing to work as well as it did before, you can use System Restore to roll back the change to an earlier point at which the system was working properly.

Chapter 17 discusses how to use System Restore.

DEVICE DRIVER ROLLBACK

Device drivers have long been the bane of Windows—okay, *one* of the banes of Windows. By installing the wrong driver, or a buggy driver, you could render your computer useless until you reinstalled Windows (or turned in frustration to another operating system).

XP tracks the drivers you install and lets you roll back the installation of the driver—in other words, you can revert to the driver you were using before.

Better yet, XP stores details of the previous driver in what's called the Last Known Good Configuration—the configuration used the last time the computer seemed to be running okay. This means that if installing a new driver prevents your computer from booting as normal, you can use the Last Known Good Configuration to restore the previous driver.

Chapter 14 discusses how to roll back a device driver, and Chapter 12 discusses how to use the Last Known Good Configuration.

NTFS

Where Windows 9x versions used the FAT (File Allocation Table) and VFAT (Virtual File Allocation Table) file systems, XP prefers NTFS, the NT file system. NTFS provides security features (including file-level security) and stability that FAT and VFAT do not.

Chapter 2 discusses how to install (or upgrade to) NTFS.

COMPATIBILITY WITH WINDOWS 9x PROGRAMS

XP aims to be able to run all programs that would run on Windows 9x, Windows NT, and Windows 2000. As you'll know if you've struggled to run a Windows 9x program on NT or Windows 2000, this is quite a challenge. NT-based operating systems (including XP) handle memory and hardware access in a different way than Windows 9x operating systems. These differences mean that programs designed for Windows 9x often won't run satisfactorily on NT and Windows 2000.

Being able to run these legacy programs is a big feature of XP—but because Microsoft has implemented this feature very successfully, it remains hidden most of the time. Usually, you can simply install a legacy program and run it without complications. Behind the scenes, XP may be running the program in its Compatibility mode or applying one of its new AppFixes to the program (to prevent it from detecting the wrong operating system and from causing problems such as referencing memory once it's been freed up), but you often won't know about it. You may need to specifically run some programs in Compatibility mode, and you may see Windows Update automatically downloading new information for AppFixes to keep your copy of Windows up-to-date, but most of the time, your old programs will simply work—which is of course the way it should be.

Chapter 5 discusses how to use Compatibility mode when necessary.

Beware Microsoft's Extravagant Claims

As you've seen in the preceding pages, XP has a lot of strong features—but apparently not enough for Microsoft's marketing folks, who seem to feel bound to stretch the truth enough to trouble even those who like Microsoft's software. For example, XP's installation blurb screens include the claim that "Windows XP not only starts faster than any other version of Windows, but it also runs your programs more quickly and reliably than ever."

Now, there's probably some context behind this claim that they don't give you, but on the face of it, it's completely untrue: XP *doesn't* start faster than every other version of Windows—not by a long way. For example, back in 1993, I had a modest 486DX2/66 with 8MB RAM that would boot DOS and Windows 3.11 in eight seconds flat from pushing the power button. These days, I have a gigahertz-plus computer with 512MB RAM that boots XP Home in about 25 seconds after the time spent fooling around detecting the hardware and inviting me to boot from any bootable CD-ROM in one of the CD drives. XP faster? Not as we currently understand time.

The claim about running programs more quickly seems more likely to be true—but I for one can't detect any difference between the speed of, say, Microsoft Word 2000 running on XP and Word 2000 running on Windows 2000 Professional. Reliability between XP and Windows 2000 Professional seems about the same, too, though XP is unquestionably more stable, and runs programs more reliably, than Windows 9*x*.

Should You Upgrade to Windows XP Home Edition?

Whether you should upgrade to Windows XP Home Edition depends on your needs, how well your current version of Windows is fulfilling them, and whether your hardware is up to the test. The decision is wholly yours (of course), but the following sections offer some suggestions, depending on where you're coming from.

Windows 9*x*

If you're using one of the versions of Windows 9*x*—Windows 95, Windows 98, Windows 98 Second Edition, or Windows Me—the main attractions of XP Home are much greater stability, the enhanced user interface, and the extra features that XP Home includes.

Exactly which extra features XP includes depends—obviously enough—on which version of Windows 9*x* you have. Not surprisingly, later versions of Windows 9*x* offer more features than earlier versions. For example, the Internet Connection Sharing feature debuted in Windows 98 Second

Edition, so ICS might be a reason to upgrade to Windows XP if you have Windows 95 or Windows 98 (first edition), but not if you have Windows 98 Second Edition or Windows Me. (The Internet Connection Firewall feature, however, is new, and is a strong attraction unless you're already using an effective hardware or software firewall.) Likewise, Windows Me includes Windows Media Player 7, a version that greatly improved on the earlier, anemic versions of Windows Media Player but isn't as capable as Windows Media Player 8, the version included in XP. From Windows Me, the new version of Windows Media Player provides only a modest incitement to upgrade, whereas from earlier versions of Windows 9x, it provides much more encouragement—assuming you're interested in multimedia.

Whichever version of Windows 9x you're using, you'll need to make sure that your hardware is up to scratch for XP. Very generally speaking, if your computer is capable of running Windows 98 or Windows Me at a decent clip, it should be able to run XP without much trouble (though you might need to add memory).

You'll find details of XP's hardware requirements in Chapter 2.

Windows 3.1

If you're still using Windows 3.1 and DOS as your main operating system, XP Home represents a considerable upgrade. There are two major considerations in taking this step:

◆ Unless you've installed Windows 3.1 on a modern system (as you might have done for backward compatibility with ancient programs), you'll almost certainly need to get a new PC to run XP. You *could* upgrade an older system, but it'd be a real grandfather's ax of an upgrade: hard drive, processor, RAM, graphics card.... (Don't you remember the anecdote? There's this guy in the bar who says "I have my grandfather's ax. My father replaced the handle, and I gave it a new blade. But it still cuts great!" Your upgraded Windows 3.1 computer would be like that ax, with new components from one end right the way to the other.)

◆ If you will need to continue running DOS programs and 16-bit Windows programs (rather than upgrading to 32-bit programs that provide similar functionality), check to make sure that these programs are compatible with XP before upgrading. As mentioned earlier, XP runs older 32-bit Windows programs quite impressively, but it has problems with some 16-bit programs.

Windows 2000 Professional

If you're currently using Windows 2000 Professional and are happy with it, stick with it for the time being. The "natural" upgrade path from Windows 2000 Professional is to Windows XP Professional Edition, but make this upgrade only after carefully evaluating the benefits that Windows XP Professional will provide.

Should You Upgrade to Windows XP Professional Edition Instead?

So you've decided that XP offers features that you must have—but should you get XP Home or XP Professional? This section discusses the biggest differences between the two. This isn't an exhaustive breakdown of all the differences—just the ones that will probably affect your decision the most.

Intended Usage

As its name suggests (and is designed to suggest), XP Professional is geared toward use in a professional setting—for example, in an office or in a corporate setting. That doesn't mean you can't use it at home if you want, just that it has features designed for use in office and corporate settings. For example, it's designed to connect to Windows 2000 Server servers or Windows .NET Server servers running Active Directory domains, and it has features for being managed remotely by administrators. XP Professional also has features for using a portable computer as a complement to a desktop computer (rather than instead of a desktop computer) and lets you easily synchronize files between two computers.

By contrast, XP Home is designed for home use. It features more relaxed security settings than XP Professional, comes set up for sharing files and folders easily among users of the same computer, and has no interest in being managed remotely by administrators or anyone else.

Connecting to a Windows Domain

XP Home Edition can't connect to a Windows 2000 or Windows .NET domain. So if your computer needs to connect directly to a Windows domain, it needs to run XP Professional rather than XP Home. But an XP Home computer can still connect to resources on a Windows 2000 or Windows .NET network, either directly (for example, across a local area network) or by using a virtual private network (VPN) connection, as discussed in Chapter 34.

Cost

XP Professional is more expensive than XP Home, though if you need the extra features it offers, the price difference probably won't deter you. But you'll certainly want to avoid first buying XP Home and then upgrading to XP Professional.

Hardware Requirements

XP Professional runs adequately on the same hardware as XP Home. While Professional doesn't actually *need* better hardware than Home, it probably *appreciates* better hardware more than Home does, because its extra features (detailed after the next section) can use some extra memory and processing power.

Upgrade Paths to Windows XP

You can upgrade to XP Professional from Windows 98, Windows 98 Second Edition, Windows Me, Windows NT 4 Workstation, and Windows 2000 Professional. You can upgrade to XP Home from only Windows 98, Windows 98 Second Edition, and Windows Me.

Windows XP Professional Features

XP Professional is essentially a superset of XP Home: It has all the features that Home has, plus extra features. You can also look at this the other way around and say that Home is a subset of Professional. In some ways, this might be truer, as Home can be regarded as Professional with a number of features—some very attractive, some less so—taken out.

The following list details the features that Professional has that Home does not have, in descending order of excitement.

Personal Web Server and Internet Information Services   XP Professional includes Personal Web Server and Internet Information Services, which let you run a modest-scale web server on XP.

Fax sharing   As mentioned earlier in the chapter, XP Home has strong fax features for the individual user. XP Professional goes one better by letting you share a fax/modem with other computers: Your computer can provide fax services to other computers to which it is networked, or your computer can send a fax via a fax/modem on another computer. These features can save a great deal of time and effort, not to mention phone lines.

Automated System Recovery (ASR)   XP Professional includes a feature called Automated System Recovery that can be activated from boot-up to restore a damaged system. XP Home doesn't have this feature—though, as mentioned earlier in this chapter, XP Home does have the System Restore feature for rolling back the installation of bad drivers and programs.

Offline files   Offline files let you cache (store) copies of files located on network drives on your local drive so that you can work with them when your computer is no longer connected to the network. XP Professional can encrypt the Offline Files database to help keep the information in the files secure. XP Home offers neither offline files nor encryption.

Multiprocessor support   XP Professional offers multiprocessor support, while Home doesn't. Multiprocessor machines are rare these days, so this limitation will worry few Home users. (If you *do* have a multiprocessor machine, you might consider installing Linux, which will love the extra processor and will cost you less.)

Multiple language support   XP Professional lets you install multiple languages on the same computer. You might need this feature if you need to create documents in foreign languages, or if people with other native languages use your computer. In XP Home, you can use only one language at a time.

Remote Desktop   XP Professional offers Remote Desktop technology, while XP Home doesn't. Remote Desktop is a little confusing because of the terminology. The Remote Desktop component lets you make a computer available for remote control. XP Professional has this capability; XP Home doesn't. The Remote Desktop *Connection* component lets you use a computer to access a remote computer that's running Remote Desktop. Both XP Professional and XP Home have Remote Desktop Connection. So you can use a computer running XP Home to access a computer running XP Professional, but not the other way around. If you need to be able to connect to your computer remotely via Remote Desktop Connection, you need XP Professional rather than XP Home. (Alternatively, you can use NetMeeting's remote features to control a XP Home computer, or one of the many third-party remote-control packages. Web Chapter 3, available from this book's web page at www.sybex.com, discusses NetMeeting.)

Ability to upgrade from more versions of Windows   You can upgrade to XP Professional from Windows 98, Windows 98 Second Edition, Windows NT 4 Workstation, and Windows 2000 Professional.

File encryption   XP Professional includes the Encrypting File System, which lets you use strong encryption to protect your files against intrusion.

File-level access control XP Professional lets you control access at the level of individual files as well as folders, while with XP Home, you can control access only at the folder level. XP Home uses what Microsoft calls Simple File Sharing. (You can use Simple File Sharing with XP Professional as well on a stand-alone computer or one that connects to a workgroup if you want.)

Connection to Windows domains XP Professional computers can log on to Windows 2000 Server and Windows .NET Server domains, whereas XP Home computers cannot. XP Home computers can connect to resources in a domain, either directly or via a virtual private network connection or a remote-access connection, but users have to enter their logon name and password each time they connect to a resource. XP Home computers can only log on to workgroups, which effectively limits them to small or smallish networks.

Connection to NetWare servers Similarly, XP Professional computers can connect to NetWare servers, whereas XP Home computers cannot. (If you've managed to avoid it, Novell's NetWare was the network operating system on which many company networks ran in the 1980s and 1990s. Windows NT Server and Windows 2000 Server have now taken a large part of NetWare's market share.)

Other networking features XP Professional has many networking features that XP Home does not. These include the Simple Network Management Protocol (SNMP), the Client Service for NetWare, Simple TCP/IP Services, and the Multiple Roaming feature.

Management features XP Professional has extensive management features that allow remote administration. XP Home can't log on to an Active Directory domain, so it doesn't have management features associated with domains and remote administration. For example, XP Home doesn't support Group Policy or Microsoft's IntelliMirror feature. Similarly, XP Professional can wake up a laptop via a CardBus LAN card, while XP Home cannot.

64-bit (Itanium) version Microsoft has released a 64-bit version of XP Professional for the Intel Itanium processor. By contrast, XP Home runs only on 32-bit Pentiums and their equivalents. At this writing, there's not much software available for the Itanium, so its breathtaking speed remains largely inaccessible to most users.

As you can see from this list, Microsoft's vision of the differences between users of XP Home and XP Professional is pretty clear: XP Home is intended for home use and perhaps small-office use, while XP Professional is intended for use in companies of any size beyond the very smallest.

If you're still wavering: Broadly speaking, if your computer needs to connect to a domain, or if you need any of the other features discussed in the preceding list, you probably need XP Professional. If not, you'll probably be fine with XP Home.

Up Next

This chapter has discussed what you need to know about XP Home in order to decide whether to upgrade to it, stay with your current version of Windows, or buy XP Professional instead.

The next chapter discusses how to install XP Home, both as an upgrade and as a clean installation from scratch.

Chapter 2

Installing Windows XP Home Edition

THIS CHAPTER DISCUSSES HOW to install Windows XP Home Edition on your computer. Because Microsoft has made the installation process mostly straightforward, and because showing you every step along each of the installation paths would take a lot of pages that are better devoted to more challenging topics, this book doesn't detail each step of installation. Instead, it concentrates, first, on the decisions that you need to make when installing or upgrading to XP and, second, on troubleshooting problems that you may encounter during installation.

NOTE *For step-by-step graphical walkthroughs of an upgrade to XP Home, a new installation of XP Home, and a clean installation of XP Home, visit this book's page on the Sybex website* (**www.sybex.com**).

This chapter covers the following topics:

- ◆ Making sure your computer can run XP Home
- ◆ Choosing a method of installing XP Home
- ◆ Preparing for installation
- ◆ Upgrading Windows 98 or Windows Me to XP
- ◆ Performing a new installation of XP
- ◆ Performing a clean installation of XP
- ◆ Using the Files and Settings Transfer Wizard to transfer files and settings
- ◆ Uninstalling XP and reverting to Windows 98 or Windows Me
- ◆ Removing your old version of Windows
- ◆ Troubleshooting installation
- ◆ Performing an unattended installation

Preparing to Install XP Home

Here's how to go about installing XP Home successfully:

1. First, make sure that your computer will be able to run XP Home. Start by comparing your system specifications with the minimum requirements, and see if you need to upgrade any components.

2. Then—assuming your computer has an operating system loaded already—load the XP Home CD in your computer and run the Windows Upgrade Advisor.

3. If you want to perform a new installation or a clean installation of XP Home rather than an upgrade, but you want your new installation or clean installation to pick up your current settings and some of your files, run the Files and Settings Transfer Wizard to save the settings from your current version of Windows.

4. Then perform the upgrade, new installation, or clean installation.

5. If you ran the Files and Settings Transfer Wizard, run it again to apply your settings to XP Home and to make your files available.

Will Your Computer Be Able to Run Windows XP Home Edition?

First, make sure that your computer will be able to run XP Home. The following sections discuss the main requirements.

Processor

According to Microsoft, XP requires a minimum of a Pentium 233 processor. It'll actually run on a Pentium 166MMX, but the experience is too slow to be truthfully described as enjoyable. Realistically, it's barely worth using XP with a processor slower than a Pentium II 266, a Celeron 300, or a K6 300, because performance is unacceptably slow. A 600MHz or faster processor delivers good performance. A processor faster than 1.5GHz should give snappy performance. Unless you have money to burn or you *must* have the latest and greatest technology to keep ahead of the Joneses (or to play games), it's not worth buying the very fastest processor available, because it'll carry a stiff price premium.

If you don't know what processor your computer has, watch the information that comes up as it boots. This will give you at least the processor speed, though it may give an incorrect classification of the chip. For example, some systems classify Celeron chips as Pentium III chips. (Midrange Celeron chips *are* in fact cut-down Pentium III chips, but your system should really know the difference.)

RAM

XP requires a minimum of 64MB of RAM to install and run. Like the Pentium 233 processor mentioned above, this is an absolute minimum and delivers poor performance unless your processor is extremely fast (in which case the lack of RAM cannibalizes processor performance). 128MB of

RAM gives good performance for one concurrent user session. For multiple concurrent user sessions, get 256MB or more RAM. If you're buying a new computer for heavy-duty use, consider starting with 512MB RAM in a 2×256MB configuration, leaving two memory slots open to take the computer up to 1GB RAM in the future if necessary.

If you don't know how much RAM your computer has, watch the count of RAM when you boot. If the number is in kilobytes, divide by 1024 to get the number in megabytes. Alternatively, right-click the icon for your computer on the Windows Desktop and choose Properties from the context menu. Windows displays the System Properties dialog box with the General page foremost. At the bottom of the page is a readout of the amount of RAM in the computer.

EXPERT KNOWLEDGE: GET PLENTY OF RAM

It's a mistake to try to run XP with minimal RAM. XP will stagger along on 64MB RAM. If the computer has a fast processor, and if you don't use any large programs or large files, performance may be tolerable. But the hard disk will be kept busy as XP continually uses virtual memory to store the information that won't fit in the RAM.

If you're buying a new computer, you'll be much better off saving a little money on the processor and putting it into RAM. Unless you're running the latest 3-D games or performing terrain mapping or other advanced imaging, you'll notice little benefit from having a few hundred extra megahertz on your processor. But another 128MB (better, another 256MB) of RAM will make a huge difference over 64MB on a system with just about any processor.

XP runs adequately on an antiquated processor such as a Pentium II 266 provided the computer has enough RAM—128MB for a single user session running a "normal" number of programs, 192MB for a single user session running a heavy number of programs, and 256MB or more for multiple user sessions running concurrently.

Given this, it's sad to see that many companies that should really know better—including IBM, Dell, and Compaq—are plugging computers with gigahertz-plus processors and a bare minimum of RAM: 128MB in many cases, and 64MB in the more benighted and price-struck areas of the market. They'll happily sell you as much extra memory as you specify, of course—but the implication is that a computer with 64MB RAM is adequately configured to run XP, which it isn't.

If you've been shopping for a new computer recently, you'll know that you can get various types of memory: 100MHz SDRAM, 133MHz SDRAM, 266MHz DDR SDRAM, PC800 RDRAM, and so on. (SDRAM is *synchronous dynamic RAM*. DDR is *double data rate*—in other words, twice as fast. And RDRAM is *Rambus DRAM*, Rambus Inc. being a company that developed a new, faster, and—inevitably—more expensive type of DRAM.) Which types of memory you can use will depend on your motherboard and what type of memory is currently in it. (All the memory needs to be the same type—you can't mix and match different types.)

Generally speaking, having enough RAM is more important than having the fastest RAM around. For example, while 512MB of PC800 RDRAM will significantly outperform 512MB of 100MHz SDRAM, that 512MB of 100MHz SDRAM will greatly outperform 64MB or 128MB of PC800 RDRAM. So if you're stuck with 100MHz SDRAM, don't worry—just make sure you have plenty of it.

NOTE   Why does each successive version of Windows need a faster processor and more RAM to run at a decent speed? Well, it's the Inevitable March of Progress (of course), and the extra features that each version includes (or bundles, depending on your point of view). But more to the point, it's the increase in the number of lines of code that each version of Windows contains in order to provide these features. Whereas Windows NT 3.1 had about 6.5 million lines of code, Windows 95 had about 10 million lines, and Windows 98 had 13 million lines. Windows NT 4 upped the ante to around 17 million lines, Windows 2000 managed nearly 29 million lines, and XP has around 40 million lines of code. This amount of program information needs more storage on disk, more memory space in which to be manipulated, and more processor cycles to manipulate it at a decent speed.

Free Disk Space

XP requires approximately 600MB of free disk space to install, plus space for your paging file (by default, the paging file is set to 1.5 × the amount of RAM in your computer) and for your hibernation file (the same size as the amount of RAM) if your computer supports hibernation. On top of that, you'll need space for any programs you want to install and any files you want to create or transfer to the computer.

In theory, this all adds up to having about 1.5GB of free space on the drive on which you install XP—and that'll work in a pinch. But in practice, it's a good idea to have at least 3GB of free space on that drive, plus space for your programs and files, especially if you're planning to use XP's built-in CD-burning feature, which needs space on the hard drive to create the CD image. (As you'll see in Chapter 28, you can make XP use space on a different drive for this purpose.)

To see how much space is free on a drive, right-click the drive in an Explorer window and choose Properties from the context menu. The General page of the resulting Properties dialog box for the drive shows how much free space it has.

TIP   If you're installing onto a partition other than the system partition after booting from a floppy disk, you still may need a certain amount of space free on the system partition for Setup to be able to store and process its temporary installation files. (A partition is a logical division of a physical disk. A physical disk can contain one or more partitions, each of which appears as a separate drive to operating systems that can read the file system used on the partition.)

The following sections discuss the decisions and considerations involved in getting a new hard drive for your existing computer.

ADD A DRIVE OR REPLACE AN EXISTING DRIVE?

Will you replace your existing hard drive (or one of your existing hard drives) with the new hard drive, or will you add the new hard drive to your existing drive configuration?

If you replace your existing boot drive, you'll need to reinstall all your applications on the new drive and transfer all your files to it. (If you're planning a new installation or clean installation of XP, you'll need to reinstall all your applications anyway, so this is less of a consideration.)

To add a new EIDE/ATA drive to your existing drives, you'll need to have an EIDE cable connector free and a drive bay free. Most motherboards come with two EIDE controllers, each of which supports two devices on one cable, one configured as the master drive and the other as the slave drive.

So with most motherboards, you can attach up to four EIDE drives. These drives can be hard drives, CD-ROM drives, DVD drives, or removable-media drives such as Zip drives or magneto-optical drives. (The floppy drive connects to a separate connector, not to one of the EIDE connectors.)

If you've used up your full complement of EIDE controllers and channels, add more channels by adding a PCI host bus adapter card. At this writing, you can get an Ultra ATA/133 adapter for around $60 that adds two EIDE channels, so you can add four EIDE drives. You'll need an empty PCI slot in your computer, but that's about as difficult as it gets.

Most hard drives these days use the 3.5" form factor, though some still use the 5.25" form factor. If you don't have a 3.5" bay free in your computer, but you do have a 5.25" bay free, you can mount a 3.5" drive in a 5.25" bay by using adapter rails. Some drives come bundled with the rails; for other drives, you'll need to buy them separately.

How Big a Drive Should You Buy?

As with processors, hard disk capacity has now (finally!) managed to draw ahead of the average user's needs, so unless you have huge amounts of data files, you probably don't need to buy the biggest hard disk available. At this writing, commodity hard drives for desktop computers start at 20GB, which is plenty of space to install XP, add a good number of applications, and store a large number of data files. Hard drives of 60GB, 80GB, and 100GB are common, while 120GB and 160GB drives form the upper end of the market. But at the pace at which hard drive capacity is increasing, drives of 300+GB are likely to become widely available in 2003.

For the best value in hard drives, buy a bit behind the curve—don't buy the biggest drive, but perhaps the next size down. If you're buying a new computer, don't pack it with drives right away. Instead, leave yourself space to add another, bigger drive next year, when bigger drives are cheaper—and then maybe a larger drive yet the year after.

How Fast a Drive Should You Buy?

Different desktop hard drives spin at different speeds—typically at 5400RPM (revolutions per minute) or 7200RPM, though some high-performance drives spin at 10,000RPM, and some server drives spin at 15,000RPM. Generally speaking, the faster the drive spins, the more rapidly it should be able to access any given data and the more data it should be able to deliver in a given amount of time. But faster drives also typically make more noise and generate more heat than slower drives and aren't always available in the largest capacities. Faster drives also tend to cost more than slower drives.

If you want snappy performance in a desktop, go for a 7200RPM drive rather than a 5400RPM drive; chances are that you'll find it worth the premium you need to pay. If you want blazing performance, investigate 10,000RPM drives, but be prepared to put up with noise. You may also need to install one or more extra fans to dissipate heat.

For notebook computers, your choices of drive capacity and speed are more limited. Most notebook drives spin at lower speeds than desktop drives to reduce power consumption and the drives' sensitivity to being bumped, and their capacities tend to be lower. But in most cases, replacement drives for notebook computers are so overpriced that they're worth considering only if your existing drive fails (rather than because you're running out of space).

SVGA-Capable Video Adapter and Monitor

Your video adapter and monitor need to be capable of SVGA resolution (800×600 pixels) with 256 or more colors to display XP as it's designed to be displayed. A higher resolution (for example, 1024×768 pixels or 1280×1024 pixels) will give you more Desktop space to work in. More colors (preferably 24-bit color) will make XP look better.

If you're not feeling demanding, just about any PCI or AGP video adapter should work (drivers permitting, of course), as should any CRT or LCD monitor. AGP has greater bandwidth than PCI and so gives a faster display and a better user experience.

As mentioned in the previous chapter, XP supports multiple monitors. In theory, a correctly configured desktop computer can support up to 10 monitors, which would make for a massive amount of Desktop space. In practice, most motherboards have between three and six PCI slots (as well as the one AGP slot), so you'd need video cards capable of multiple displays each in order to get anything like 10 monitors working—even if you didn't need any of those PCI slots for other purposes (such as a modem, network card, or sound card). But also in practice, most multi-monitor users are satisfied with two or three monitors. Five or more monitors and you start needing additional eyes to keep them under surveillance.

CD Drive or DVD Drive

You need a CD drive or DVD drive, or access to one or the other, to install XP. If the drive is on another computer, you can install across a network or copy the files to your local drive and run them from there.

If your computer has a CD drive or DVD drive, but the drive isn't bootable and you're planning a new installation or a clean installation, you'll need to create XP Setup boot disks. To do so, download the appropriate compressed file for your version of XP from the microsoft.com Download Center (www.microsoft.com/downloads/) and run it to create the six boot disks. Number them correctly, or you'll have the wherewithal to get into a horrible mess. Then slot the first of the disks and boot from it. The disks get you to a stage at which you can access the CD-ROM to continue the installation process.

Checking System Compatibility

If your computer's specifications seem to be up to the task, your next step is to make sure that your system's components are compatible with XP.

Running the Windows Upgrade Advisor Program

The easiest way to check whether your computer's hardware is compatible with XP is to run the Windows Upgrade Advisor program. To do so, follow these steps:

1. Insert the XP CD. If your computer doesn't automatically start running the CD, open an Explorer window, navigate to the CD, and double-click the SETUP.EXE program.

2. On the opening screen, click the Check System Compatibility link. Setup offers the choices Check My System Automatically and Visit the Compatibility Web Site.

TIP *You can also run the Windows Upgrade Advisor by issuing the command* cd_drive\i386\winnt32.exe /checkupgradeonly, *where* cd_drive *is the drive letter assigned to your CD drive.*

3. Click the Check My System Automatically link.

4. If an Internet connection is available, Setup runs Dynamic Update to download any new files that may help with the installation. It then runs the Windows Upgrade Advisor program and displays the Upgrade Report page of the Microsoft Windows Upgrade Advisor. Figure 2.1 shows an example of an upgrade report.

FIGURE 2.1

Use the Microsoft Windows Upgrade Advisor to check whether your computer will be able to run XP.

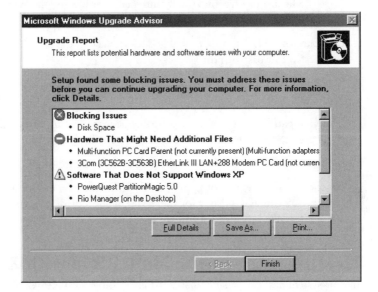

5. If your computer seems to be fit for XP, the report tells you that the check found no incompatibilities or problems. Any problems are listed in the list box in summary form. Click the Full Details button to view the details (broken up into categories such as Blocking Issues, Warnings, and Helpful Information) and advice on what to do about the problems. (Click the resulting Summary button to return to the summary view.) Click the Save As button to save the information to file, or click the Print button to print a copy of it.

6. Click the Finish button. Windows closes the Microsoft Windows Upgrade Advisor.

Follow the Upgrade Advisor's advice to get your computer ready for upgrading to XP. In particular, you need to take care of any blocking issues that the Advisor has identified. An example of a blocking issue is not having enough disk space to install XP. You might need to remove some existing files, or reconfigure your partitions (for example, by using a tool such as PartitionMagic), to resolve such an issue.

Checking Specific Hardware Items Against the HCL

For the latest information on device compatibility with XP (or other versions of Windows), check the Microsoft Hardware Compatibility List (HCL) at the Microsoft Windows Hardware Quality Labs website, www.microsoft.com/hcl/. The site lets you search for products in various hardware categories, such as Storage/Hard Drive, Display (graphics cards), and Modem/Analog. You can enter the manufacturer's name or product name in the Search For text box to narrow the results, or you can search for all the products in a particular category. (Given the wealth of PC hardware available, searching for all products usually produces an awkwardly long list.) The website returns a list of matching devices and their compatibility status.

The HCL has five degrees of compatibility:

Logo   The product has met the requirements for bearing the Windows Logo. In other words, it should be fully compatible.

Compatible   The product probably doesn't meet all the Windows Logo requirements, but it has been tested to work with the OS.

Beta Logo   The product has met the Windows Logo requirements on a beta (prerelease) version of the OS.

Beta Compatible   The product probably doesn't meet all the Windows Logo requirements, but it has been tested to work with a beta version of the OS.

[no icon]   If the device doesn't have an icon, it's not considered compatible for the OS in question.

For the first four degrees of compatibility, a CD icon on the compatibility icon indicates that the CD for the OS contains a driver for the device, while a drive icon with a red arrow indicates that a drive for the device is available for download.

Making Your System Compatible with XP

If your system has components that aren't compatible with XP, you'll need to replace them (or remove them, if they're dispensable) before installing XP. Make sure that any replacement components you buy are on the HCL.

Replacing a component or two—say, a sound card here, a modem there, or perhaps a new hard drive—to make your computer compatible with XP, and perhaps adding 64 or 128MB RAM to bring it up to scratch, makes sense for many computers that aren't thoroughly antiquated. But if your computer is verging on the obsolete and will need many components replaced before it can run XP, think about replacing the computer itself. Unless you have special requirements that give you a strong incentive to reuse as many components of an aging computer as possible, it often makes better financial sense to buy a new computer than to replace many of the components of an old computer.

If you decide to buy a new computer, you shouldn't have any difficulty finding one that's been designed to run XP. If you're in any doubt, consult www.microsoft.com/windowsxp/ready/ for a list of computers that meet Microsoft's Windows XP–Ready and Designed for Windows XP criteria. These criteria include a minimum of 128MB of RAM, a sufficiently powerful processor (a 500MHz Pentium III or local equivalent), peripherals, and (for laptops) Advanced Configuration and Power Interface (ACPI) power management. In 2002, you can meet these criteria at a relatively modest price.

At this writing (August 2002), most PC manufacturers worth mentioning sell computers designed for and preloaded with XP. In fact, it's probably harder to buy a new computer that *isn't* compatible with XP than one that is compatible. So making sure your computer is compatible with XP shouldn't be an issue if you're buying a preconfigured computer from either a major manufacturer or from your local Three Guys and a Goat PC store. For example, manufacturers such as Dell,

Compaq/Hewlett Packard, and IBM offer assorted models of desktop and laptop computers with various configurations, all of which have been thoroughly tested with XP. Small PC builders typically follow a similar path but give you more freedom in your choice of components.

Compatibility is more likely to be an issue if you're building your own PC from an eclectic selection of recycled and new components, or if you're having someone else build a customized PC including some old components. Unless you're an expert, it rarely makes sense to build your own computer from scratch these days, because having a professional build it for you can save you any amount of time and headaches.

Given that the cost of PC hardware continues to fall, it's often better to bite the bullet and buy a new computer, perhaps adding to it a couple of the most valuable (or viable) components of your old computer, rather than flog your old computer into the ground. In particular, it's seldom worth pushing hard drives beyond their usual life span, because eventually they'll either start suffering from bad sectors or simply stop working. Either way, you can easily lose data and waste time.

Choosing Which File System to Use

Once you've decided to install XP, your next decision is which file system to use. As you'll know if you've been working with computers, the *file system* is the way in which the files and folders are organized on hard disks and floppy disks.

XP supports three different file systems: FAT, FAT32, and NTFS. The following sections discuss each file system briefly and tell you why NTFS is the best choice in most cases.

File Allocation Table (FAT)

FAT, at nearly 20 years old the oldest of the three file systems that XP supports, has been used by DOS, Windows 3.1, and Windows 95. FAT is effective for disks with tens of megabytes or a few hundred megabytes, but wasteful for any partition larger than 512MB, because the limited number of clusters it can handle mean that each cluster becomes large and unwieldy. (A *cluster* is the smallest amount of space that a disk uses to store data.) FAT can support partitions up to 2GB, a size fine for its era, but which now seems painfully cramped.

FAT restricts filenames to the 8.3 format that made for short filenames: up to eight characters in the filename itself, and up to three characters in the extension, with a period separating the two. Windows 95 mapped long filenames to the 8.3 entries, which meant that a file with a full name such as `C:\Program Files\Microsoft Office\Winword\Sample Word Document.doc` would actually be named `C:\Progra~1\Micros~1\Winword\Sample~1.doc`. If the filename mapping became corrupted, finding the documents you wanted became difficult.

XP supports FAT solely for backward compatibility with DOS, Windows 95, and NT 4. Unless you're stuck with needing to dual-boot DOS or Windows 95, you should avoid FAT, using FAT32 or NTFS instead. (If you need to dual-boot NT 4 with XP, use NTFS rather than FAT.)

When FAT32 was introduced, FAT was retrospectively termed FAT16 for clarity.

File Allocation Table 32 (FAT32)

FAT32, the later version of the file allocation table file system, is designed to be able to handle larger disks than FAT. FAT32 supports disks up to 2TB (a terabyte is 1024 gigabytes) and can handle

RAID (redundant array of inexpensive disks), a battery of multiple-disk arrangements used to ensure data reliability and integrity. FAT32 also handles clusters more efficiently than FAT, so it's able to use disks more efficiently than FAT.

As you can readily work out from the preceding paragraph, FAT32 is better than FAT. But it's not nearly as good as NTFS, which is discussed in the next section. You should use FAT32 in preference to NTFS only if you need to dual-boot Windows 95 OSR2, Windows 98, or Windows Me with XP, because these versions of Windows can't read NTFS volumes.

NT File System (NTFS)

As its name suggests, NTFS is the file system of preference for NT-based versions of Windows: NT itself, Windows 2000, and XP. But NTFS isn't all plain sailing, because there are two different types of NTFS: NTFS 4, used in NT versions 3.1, 3.5, 3.51, and 4; and NTFS 5, used in Windows 2000 and XP.

Windows 2000 and XP can read NTFS 4 partitions, but NT 4 can't read NTFS 5 partitions unless you upgrade it to Service Pack 5 or later. (NT 3.*x* can't read NTFS 5 partitions, no matter how many service packs you pile on.)

Without getting too technical, NTFS offers a large number of advantages over FAT32 for computers running NT-based OSs. The following list summarizes the major advantages:

Security and encryption   NTFS provides a comprehensive set of permissions for securing files and specifying which users can access them and take other actions with them. In XP Home, you get to work with only a reduced set of the NTFS permissions, whereas XP Professional and Windows 2000 offer all the permissions. NTFS also supports encryption for protecting your files, but Microsoft has removed this feature from XP Home—if you want encryption, you need to fork out the extra money for XP Professional. FAT32 offers neither security nor encryption.

Compression   NTFS lets you compress files and folders easily so that you can fit more on your disks. FAT32 doesn't offer compression unless you add a third-party utility.

Efficiency and partition size   NTFS uses space more efficiently than FAT32 on partitions larger than 8GB—a size increasingly common given the monster hard drives available nowadays. XP can also create larger NTFS partitions than FAT32 partitions. XP can create NTFS partitions of 16TB with the default cluster size, or 256TB if you adjust the cluster size, while its FAT32 partitions are limited to 32GB. (However, you can use Windows 98 or Windows Me to create FAT32 partitions larger than this.)

Use NTFS unless you have a compelling reason to use FAT or FAT32. In most cases, that compelling reason will be the ability to dual boot with Windows 9*x*.

EXPERT KNOWLEDGE: DUAL-BOOTING WITH LINUX, AND SERIOUS MULTI-BOOTING

The XP boot loader handles previous installations of Windows deftly, but it's not designed to work with Linux (or indeed OS/2, Solaris, BeOS, or other non-Microsoft operating systems). If you want to dual-boot XP and Linux, or set up a serious multi-boot arrangement involving more than a handful of operating systems, you need to take a different approach.

Continued on next page

EXPERT KNOWLEDGE: DUAL-BOOTING WITH LINUX, AND SERIOUS MULTI-BOOTING *(continued)*

DUAL-BOOTING WITH LINUX

You can install Linux either before installing XP or after installing XP. In either case, you'll need to keep your partitions straight so that the later installation doesn't overwrite the earlier installation. When installing Linux after XP, make sure that you don't install Lilo (the *Linux Lo*ader) on the master boot record (MBR). Doing so overwrites the XP boot loader, which prevents XP from starting at all.

This means that you shouldn't use an automated installation routine that's designed to take over the whole disk for Linux. For most installations of Linux, you'll need to choose a custom installation. For example, for Red Hat, specify a Custom System on the Install Type screen, and partition the drive manually with Disk Druid (or fdisk if you're feeling bold). On the Lilo Configuration screen, select the First Sector of Boot Partition option button instead of the Master Boot Record option button in the Install Lilo Boot Record On list. Also, make sure the Create Boot Disk check box is selected.

If you don't mind leaving a floppy disk dangling around your floppy drive, you can also boot Lilo off a floppy. XP boots regularly when the floppy drive is empty.

SERIOUS MULTI-BOOTING

If you need to install serious numbers of operating systems on the same computer, it's worth investing in a heavy-duty boot manager such as System Commander from V Communications (www.v-com.com). System Commander lets you install more than 100 operating systems on the same computer. (You'll have a hard time *finding* that many different operating systems, but you can also install multiple copies of the same operating systems to get the numbers up.)

Choosing a Method of Installing XP Home

You can install XP Home in three different ways:

Upgrade   If you have Windows 98 or Windows Me, you can perform an upgrade, essentially overwriting the previous version of Windows with XP Home. (It's not entirely overwritten, because you can restore it if you so choose, provided that you don't convert your file system to NTFS.) Upgrading like this transfers all your files, settings, and programs to XP, so (in theory) you can pick up your work or play straight away in XP where you left off in Windows 9*x*.

New installation   You can install XP alongside your current version of Windows. XP creates a dual-boot setup (or modifies an existing dual-boot setup to create a multiboot setup) so that you can run either operating system. Installing like this lets you compare XP with your previous version of Windows so that you can see whether XP suits you. You can use the Files and Settings Transfer Wizard to copy your files and settings from your previous version of Windows to XP. You'll need to install all the programs you want to use on XP.

Clean installation   You can install XP from scratch on your computer, setting it up as the only operating system but not upgrading from your current operating system. Again, you can use the Files and Settings Transfer Wizard to copy your files and settings from your previous version of Windows to XP. You'll need to install all the programs you want to use on XP.

Which type of installation to perform can be a tricky decision. The longer you've been running Windows on this computer since installing it, the stronger the arguments are for both an upgrade and a clean installation:

◆ By now, you've probably installed all the programs you need and got them working together. By upgrading, you can transition your whole work environment to XP, so that your Desktop, Start menu, and folder structure retain their current settings and your programs all work as before.

◆ Then again, you probably have programs that you no longer use, or programs that no longer work. By performing a clean install, you can strip your system down to only the software you need. It'll take longer, but the result may be better. Similarly, your data folders could probably do with some cleaning out and archiving. It'll be work in the short term, but you'll benefit in the long term.

◆ If you've been suffering either operating-system crashes or program crashes under Windows 98 or Windows Me (and sometimes it's hard to tell the difference between the two types of crash on those operating systems), you have a strong incentive to perform a clean installation to eliminate all possible sources of the crashes.

If you need to install a new hard drive as your main hard drive, you'll need to perform a clean install. (The exception is if you use a hard drive cloning or migration package such as DriveImage or Ghost. These packages are often used for upgrading the hard drives in laptops, where the lack of expansion room forces you to replace the current hard drive rather than add a drive, but some of them work for desktops as well.)

Similarly, if you need to repartition your hard drive to create a new partition on which to install XP, you'll need to perform a clean installation. You can then transfer your files and settings, and install your programs.

EXPERT KNOWLEDGE: PLANNING A PARTITION STRUCTURE FOR YOUR HARD DRIVE

As mentioned earlier, a partition is a logical division of a physical hard disk. Each partition appears as a separate drive to operating systems that can read the file system with which it's formatted.

Each partition can be formatted with a different file system. For example, you could create three partitions on a hard disk and format one with FAT32, the second with NTFS, and the third with the EXT2 file system that Linux uses.

If your computer currently has a single hard disk that's fully occupied by a single partition, and if it contains data you don't want to lose, you'll need to spend some money or effort on partitioning it. These are your choices:

◆ Use a noninvasive third-party partitioning utility such as PartitionMagic to shrink your existing partition to make space in which you can create one or more other partitions.

◆ Back up all your data, then partition the disk by using XP's partitioning tool, install XP (preceded by any other version of Windows with which you want to dual-boot), then restore your data on XP (and on the other version or versions of Windows if necessary).

Continued on next page

EXPERT KNOWLEDGE: PLANNING A PARTITION STRUCTURE FOR YOUR HARD DRIVE *(continued)*

◆ Add another hard disk and partition that as needed. For example, you might add a second hard disk and install XP on it.

If you've decided to upgrade Windows 98 or Windows Me to XP, and you have a single partition fully occupying your hard drive, you don't need to repartition the drive: You can install XP onto your existing partition (which will be formatted with FAT32, or possibly FAT). Setup will offer to convert the partition to NTFS for you. If you're sure about committing to XP, you can accept this offer. But if there's even the slightest chance that you'll need to return to Windows 98 or Windows Me, stay with your current file system for the moment, because once you convert the partition to NTFS, you can't restore Windows 98 or Windows Me without reformatting the partition.

These are the basic parameters for partitioning:

◆ A hard disk can be divided into one, two, three, or four primary partitions.

◆ Any one of the primary partitions can be marked active at any given time. The computer's BIOS looks for a bootable OS on the active partition when you switch the computer on.

◆ Instead of one of the primary partitions, a hard disk can contain one extended partition. The extended partition can't be marked active (so you can't boot from an extended partition) and has to be divided into *logical drives*.

◆ You can have up to 32 drives on a single hard disk—up to three drives on primary partitions and the rest on logical drives on an extended partition. Normally, you won't need anything like this many partitions.

◆ You don't have to fill a hard disk with partitions right away—you can also leave free space on a disk. For example, you might want to create just a couple of partitions to use up half the space on a drive, and leave the rest of the space for partitioning later, when you'd decided how you would use it. And even when you do try to use up all the space on a disk, there are often a few megabytes that go unused.

◆ When you install multiple operating systems on your computer, you need to install each on its own partition to keep it separate from the other operating systems. So dual-booting or multi-booting is a reason for creating multiple partitions. But you may also want to create multiple partitions so that you can keep different files on them. For example, many people prefer to keep their data files (documents, spreadsheets, and so on) on a different partition than their system files. That way, they can back up their data files by backing up everything on that partition.

The clumsiness of the tools that Microsoft provides render partitioning and file system–conversion exciting if not fraught: Choose the wrong partition, and you can destroy all your data with a couple of keystrokes or simply render your current operating system inoperative. So there's a strong argument for buying a partitioning utility such as PartitionMagic (which costs around $70 at this writing) that lets you resize, move, and convert partitions without destroying the data on them.

Preparing for Installation

Once you've established that your computer should be able to run XP Home, prepare for installation by taking those of the following steps that are applicable to the type of installation you're planning (upgrade, new installation, or clean installation).

Read the Latest Release Documentation

Read the latest release documentation for XP Home by loading your XP Home CD and double-clicking the README.HTM file in the root directory of the CD to open the file in your browser. Then browse the Read1st item (which contains information you should read before installing), the Setup item (which contains setup instructions), and the Release Notes item (which contains post-installation information, including late-breaking news of problems with particular hardware items).

Back Up All Your Data Files

If you're installing XP on a computer that already has an operating system installed, back up all your data files shortly before installation using your usual backup medium. For example, from Windows 98 or Windows Me, use the Backup program (Start ➢ Programs ➢ Accessories ➢ System Tools ➢ Backup) to back up your files to removable media.

If you're upgrading from Windows 98 or Windows Me to XP, you shouldn't need to worry about backing up your Windows files, because XP's Setup routine automatically creates a backup of the version of Windows from which you're upgrading, in case you decide you want to revert to it. But it never hurts to have a complete backup of your system, so if your current backup backs up your system files as well as your data files, stick with it.

Write Down Internet Connection Information

If you're planning a new installation or clean installation rather than an upgrade, and you use a dial-up Internet connection, write down the information you need to create the connection: your ISP account username, your password, your ISP's phone number, and your ISP's primary DNS server and secondary DNS server.

Plug In and Switch On All Hardware

Make sure that all the hardware you intend to use with the computer is attached to it and powered on. For example, if you'll use a printer and scanner with the computer, make sure these devices are attached to the computer and powered on, so that Setup can detect them if it's smart enough.

NOTE   *If you're installing XP on a laptop, make sure it's plugged into the mains so that it won't run out of power or put itself to sleep during the installation.*

Use the Files and Settings Transfer Wizard to Transfer Settings

XP includes a wizard for transferring files and settings from one computer or operating system to another. You don't need to use this wizard, which is called the Files and Settings Transfer Wizard, if you're upgrading Windows 98 or Windows Me to XP, because Windows automatically transfers all your settings when you perform an upgrade. But the wizard can save you a great deal of time when you want to transfer files and settings either to a new computer that's running XP or to a new installation of XP on the same computer on which you've kept your previous installation of Windows as a dual-boot. For example, if you choose to test XP on a new partition before committing yourself to it, you can use the Files and Settings Transfer Wizard to transfer your work environment to the new partition so that you can use your regular settings and files.

Before you use the Files and Settings Transfer Wizard, make sure you've connected any network drive you want to use, or that you have a removable disk or recordable CD ready. To transfer files and settings, you'll need plenty of storage. You can save settings files to a floppy drive, but most data files will be too big.

To use the Files and Settings Transfer Wizard, follow these steps:

1. Insert the XP CD. If your computer doesn't automatically start running the CD, open an Explorer window, navigate to the CD, and double-click the SETUP.EXE program. Windows displays the Welcome to Microsoft Windows XP screen.

2. Click the Perform Additional Tasks link.

3. On the next screen, click the Transfer Files and Settings link. Setup starts the Files and Settings Transfer Wizard.

4. Click the Next button. If this computer is running XP, the wizard displays the Which Computer Is This? screen. If it does, select the Old Computer option button and click the Next button. (If this computer isn't running XP, the wizard knows it's the old computer.) The wizard then displays the Select a Transfer Method page (shown in Figure 2.2).

FIGURE 2.2

On the Select a Transfer Method page of the Files and Settings Transfer Wizard, specify how you want to transfer files and settings from the old computer to the new computer.

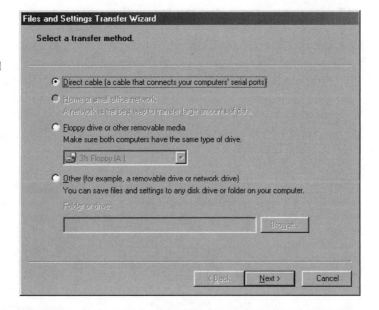

5. Select the Direct Cable option button, the Home or Small Office Network option button (if it's available), the Floppy Drive or Other Removable Media option button (select the drive in the drop-down list), or the Other option button as appropriate. The Other option button lets you use the Browse button and the resulting Browse for Folder dialog box or the Folder or Drive text box to specify a removable drive or a network drive.

6. Click the Next button. The wizard displays the What Do You Want to Transfer? page (shown in Figure 2.3).

FIGURE 2.3

On the What Do You Want to Transfer? page of the Files and Settings Transfer Wizard, specify which settings and files you want to transfer to the new computer (or to XP).

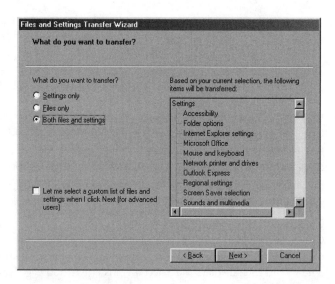

7. In the What Do You Want to Transfer? list, select the Settings Only option button, the Files Only option button, or the Both Files and Settings option button as appropriate. The list box on the right side of the dialog box lists the types of settings and files that will be affected.

8. If you want to customize the list of settings, files, or both, select the Let Me Select a Custom List of Files and Settings when I Click Next check box. Customizing the list of files lets you specify particular folders for transfer. By default, the wizard transfers the \Desktop\ folder, the \Fonts\ folder, the \My Documents\ folder, and the \Shared Desktop\ folder.

9. Click the Next button. If you selected the Customize check box, the wizard displays the Select Custom Files and Settings page (shown in Figure 2.4).

FIGURE 2.4

On the Select Custom Files and Settings page of the Files and Settings Transfer Wizard, choose the files and settings to transfer.

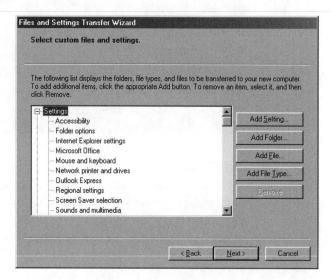

10. Select the files and settings to transfer:

- ◆ To add a setting, click the Add Setting button. The wizard displays the Add a Setting dialog box. Select the setting or settings in the list box and click the OK button. The wizard closes the Add a Setting dialog box and adds the setting or settings to the list.

- ◆ To add a folder, click the Add Folder button. The wizard displays the Browse for Folder dialog box. Select the folder and click the OK button. The wizard closes the Browse for Folder dialog box and adds the folder to the list.

- ◆ To add a file, click the Add File button. The wizard displays the Add a File dialog box (a common Open dialog box in disguise). Select the file and click the Open button. The wizard closes the Add a File dialog box and adds the file to the list.

- ◆ To add a file type, click the Add File Type button. The wizard displays the Add a File Type dialog box (shown in Figure 2.5). Select the file type in the Registered File Types list box; if it's not listed there, enter its extension in the Other text box. Then click the OK button. The wizard closes the Add a File Type dialog box and adds the file type to the list.

- ◆ To remove a setting, folder, file, or file type, select it in the list box and click the Remove button.

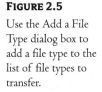

FIGURE 2.5

Use the Add a File Type dialog box to add a file type to the list of file types to transfer.

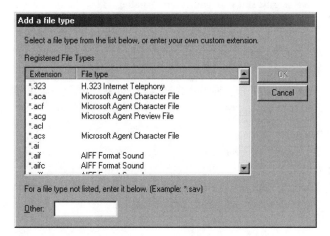

11. Click the Next button. The wizard may display the Install Programs on Your New Computer page, suggesting some programs that you may want to install on your new computer (or new installation of Windows) before transferring settings. If so, note these suggestions.

12. The wizard then displays the Collection in Progress page while it collects your files and settings. It then displays the Completing the Collection Phase page.

13. Click the Finish button. The wizard closes itself.

For details of how to apply your saved files and settings to your new installation of XP, see "Applying Your Files and Settings" later in this chapter.

Stop Any Anti-Virus Software, Disk Utilities, or Boot Managers

Stop any anti-virus software or disk utilities before running the Windows installation, because the installation process needs direct access to your hardware. Disable or uninstall boot-manager software, or make sure that you know how to bypass it during the installation.

A Quick Warning about "Restarting Manually"

At the end of the first phase of Windows Setup, you'll see this message: "Setup will now restart the computer. To restart manually, press the Esc key."

This message is a bit confusing, because in this case, restarting the computer "manually" means aborting the installation, not helping the computer along by giving it a little encouragement. So *don't* press the Esc key when you see this message—just wait for Setup to restart the computer itself.

Upgrading Windows 98 or Windows Me to XP Home

This section discusses the procedure for upgrading your current installation of Windows 9*x* to XP Home. When you upgrade, the installation procedure copies the settings from your current version of Windows 9*x* and applies them to the installation of XP. If the installation doesn't work correctly, or if you find XP doesn't suit you, you can uninstall it and revert to your previous installation of Windows 9*x*.

TIP   When upgrading, keep a boot floppy from Windows 98 or Windows Me so that you can use the tools it provides when necessary. For example, the Windows 98/Me version of FDISK lets you create larger FAT32 partitions than XP can create. (If you don't have a boot floppy, create one before upgrading.)

The list below shows the main steps of the upgrade procedure. For an illustrated step-by-step walkthrough of the upgrade procedure, visit this book's page on the Sybex website (`www.sybex.com`).

1. Insert the XP CD and click the Install Windows XP link on the introductory screen. (If the introductory screen doesn't appear, open an Explorer window, navigate to the drive containing the CD, and double-click the `SETUP.EXE` file.)

2. In the Installation Type drop-down list on the Welcome to Windows Setup page, choose the Upgrade item.

3. Accept the license agreement and enter your product key.

4. Specify the type of upgrade report for your computer (as discussed earlier in this chapter) and deal with any major issues it raises.

5. Wait while Windows Setup upgrades your existing version of Windows to XP (which involves one or more reboots), and then perform the manual parts of configuration as discussed in "The Installation Paths Converge," later in this chapter.

Performing a New Installation of XP and Creating a Dual-Boot Setup

If you decide you want to perform a new installation of XP, thus either creating a dual-boot setup of XP alongside your existing version of Windows or adding XP to an existing dual-boot setup, you need to do some thorough planning and preparation to make sure you get the result you want.

EXPERT KNOWLEDGE: WHEN SHOULD YOU DUAL-BOOT? WHAT'S THE ALTERNATIVE?

XP's Setup routine makes it so easy to set up a dual-boot configuration on a computer that's running an earlier version of Windows that it's tempting to set up a dual-boot configuration when you don't really need to.

Before you go ahead and set up a dual- or multi-boot configuration, you should understand the reasons for doing so and the reasons for *not* doing so. Put most simply, you should dual-boot or multi-boot only if you must run two or more operating systems on the same computer. Otherwise, you shouldn't dual-boot.

WHY DUAL-BOOT?

If you develop software for Windows, you may need to dual-boot or multi-boot so that you can test the software on all the different versions of Windows that you've chosen to support. (You could also use emulation to run the other versions of Windows. More on this in a moment.) Likewise, if you build or maintain websites, you may want to make sure that they appear satisfactorily in browsers not only on all current versions of Windows but also on Linux or perhaps other PC-based operating systems. (You'll probably want to test the websites on Mac OS as well, either using a physical Mac or a Mac emulator such as Executor [www.ardi.com] or SoftMac 2000/XP [www.emulators.com].)

You might also need to dual-boot in order to support older hardware that you still need to use but for which drivers aren't available for your preferred operating system. For example, your old CD recorder, web cam, or video camera might work fine under Windows 9*x*, but their manufacturers might not have bothered to create XP drivers for them, preferring that you buy a new hardware item instead (preferably from the same manufacturer).

Similarly, you might need to run older software that disagrees with your preferred operating system. However, XP's compatibility modes (discussed in Chapter 5) enable XP to run a wide variety of Windows 9*x* programs that wouldn't run on NT or Windows 2000, so older software tends to be less of an issue with XP. But you might need to run a Linux program or BeOS program occasionally to perform a task that you couldn't perform on Windows.

In the shorter term, you might want to dual-boot so that you could evaluate XP (or another OS) without disturbing your current OS.

Beyond these and similar scenarios, the most likely reason that you'll want to dual boot is when you're testing another operating system on your computer. For example, rather than believing the Upgrade Advisor's assurances about compatibility with your hardware and software and upgrading directly to XP, you may prefer to install XP as a dual-boot so that you can try it without affecting your current version of Windows. If everything works fine, you can then upgrade your current Windows installation to XP and remove the test installation, thus ending up with only XP on the computer.

DISADVANTAGES OF DUAL-BOOTING

The first major disadvantage of dual-booting is the amount of space that it takes up. For dual-booting to work well, each OS needs to be installed on its own partition or logical drive. However cannily you calculate the space that each OS and its programs will need (and set up your partition structure accordingly), you'll still be wasting a fair amount of space. Even with today's huge hard drives, that can hurt.

Continued on next page

EXPERT KNOWLEDGE: WHEN SHOULD YOU DUAL-BOOT? WHAT'S THE ALTERNATIVE?
(continued)

Second (and related to the first disadvantage), in most cases, you need to install all your programs that you want to use on any given operating system on that operating system. For example, say you set up a multi-boot arrangement with Windows Me, Windows 2000 Professional, and XP. If you want to use Office on 2000 and XP, you'll need to install it separately on each OS. If you want to use Office on Me as well, you'll need to install it a third time. This eats disk space and chews up time—and you'll need to configure each program on each OS as well. For some programs, you even get into licensing issues: You need a separate copy of the program for each OS on which you'll use it, despite both OSs being installed on the same computer.

If you dual-boot Windows 9*x* with an NT-based version of Windows (NT, 2000, or XP), you'll need to use FAT or FAT32 rather than NTFS for each partition that you want Windows 9*x* to be able to read. This may cause security issues, as may the fact that the Windows 9*x* security model is wide open, allowing each user access to all the files on all drives that Windows 9*x* can read.

THE ALTERNATIVE: EMULATION

If you're testing another operating system to see if you like it (as opposed to seeing if it's compatible with all your hardware and software), you may be able to do so by using an emulation program such as Virtual PC from Connectix (`www.connectix.com`) or VMWare from VMWare (`www.vmware.com`). Emulation uses software to create a *virtual machine*—a PC implemented through software—on which you can install operating systems pretty much to your heart's content.

The virtual machine uses a standardized set of (virtual) hardware devices that the manufacturer has chosen to support and that are unlikely to correspond to the equivalent devices on your computer. For example, Virtual PC includes a virtual CntxCorp (in other words, Connectix Corporation) CD-ROM drive that you won't find in the real world, while as a display adapter it emulates the S3 Trio 32/64 chip, which *is* widely used in the real world but probably isn't the same as the physical display adapter on your computer. So the virtual hardware doesn't tell you anything useful about an OS's compatibility with your physical hardware. By contrast, the software you install on the virtual machine is as "real" as any other software, so you can test it fully for compatibility. (Whether you need to have a separate license for software on the virtual machine depends on subtleties of wording and interpretation of the licensing agreement. The virtual machine is both a separate computer and the same computer. If the software is licensed for a single CPU, you're probably okay.)

Emulation has several advantages and disadvantages. The advantages are that, first, emulation tends to be much less expensive than buying another computer. Second, it's non-destructive: The emulation software installs like just another program, and it creates a virtual disk into which to install each operating system that you want to run under emulation. The virtual disk is essentially a colossal data file, so you can back it up, delete it, and so on. Third, you can install multiple operating systems on the virtual machine. If you have enough system resources, you can run more than one OS on the virtual machine at the same time, which brings us neatly to the disadvantages of emulation.

Continued on next page

EXPERT KNOWLEDGE: WHEN SHOULD YOU DUAL-BOOT? WHAT'S THE ALTERNATIVE?
(continued)

◆ First, an OS running under emulation runs much more slowly than one running on the equivalent real hardware, because the emulation software has to translate all the instructions involved. How much of a problem this is depends on the speed of the hardware, the complexity of the OS running under emulation, and what kind of performance you'll tolerate. If your PC has a fast processor, plenty of RAM, and a fast graphics card, the virtual machine may be able to run a not-too-complex OS at a decent speed. For example, on my current desktop (which has a 1.1GHz Celeron and 512MB RAM), Windows 95 runs at an impressive speed under Virtual PC; Windows 98 is tolerably fast; Windows Me feels a bit sluggish, as does Linux (Mandrake 8.1 with KDE); and XP is uncomfortably slow. This doesn't matter to me, because I'm using emulation for testing XP while I write about it rather than using emulation for more demanding purposes. (Before you ask—the computer is also running XP natively for all the programs I use in the real world.)

◆ Second, emulation doesn't do multimedia well. Sound support tends to be limited, and video performance is intolerably slow. Playing back, say, DVD video would be farcically bad, and you wouldn't want to try playing any action games.

◆ Third, while both Virtual PC and VMWare support an impressive array of standard features, such as networking, modems, serial ports, and parallel ports, they don't support advanced ports. You probably won't be able to plug in your FireWire video camera and use it on the emulated OS.

Given these constraints, emulation isn't an effective solution for actually *running* the operating system in question for most practical purposes. It's more of a niche solution. Emulation is most widely used by developers who need to test the compatibility of their code on different operating systems easily, and by help centers in which the technical support staff needs to be able to run the operating system on which they're assisting the customer without having to reboot their own PC and launch the OS in question.

Emulation is also used by users who need to run one or two programs designed for another operating system so that they can easily work with their colleagues who run that operating system. For example, many companies are PC-based but also have a few Macs for special purposes such as design, layout, or multimedia authoring—but they want to run the same e-mail package on all the computers so that the users can exchange e-mail easily. By installing Virtual PC on the Macs and running Windows under emulation, those companies can have every user use the same Windows e-mail program. (Virtual PC spent many years as a Mac-only program before Connectix released Windows versions as well.)

Though emulation is too slow for running the emulated OS for general use, it's great for assuaging your interest in another operating system without needing to repartition your hard disk or change your file system. So if you want to investigate XP, BeOS, or Linux without disturbing your current version of Windows, you may want to give Virtual PC or VMWare a try. (Each has an evaluation version that you can download from the websites mentioned above.)

If you like, emulation is bit of a dancing bear—it's great that the bear can dance, but you probably won't want to watch it doing so for too long, because it's kinda lumbering and slow. On the other hand, if a dancing bear can help you in your work or play, emulation can be just the thing for you.

Plan Your Partitions

You *can* install two or more OSs on the same partition, but it's almost always a bad idea to do so, because the Windows 9*x* versions share a file structure with each other, while the NT-based versions of Windows share another file structure with each other. For example, Windows 95, Windows 98, Windows Me, and Windows XP all put their system files in a C:\Windows\ folder unless you persuade them otherwise; NT and Windows 2000 use a \winnt\ folder. All these versions of Windows create a \Program Files\ folder for your program files. Windows 2000 and XP create a \Documents and Settings\ folder that contains the folders for documents and settings for each user.

XP's Setup program is smart enough to keep its files out of an earlier installation of Windows, but having multiple \Documents and Settings\ folders and \Program Files\ folders on the same drive can quickly become confusing. By using a separate partition for each operating system, you can avoid such confusion and prevent any operating system from overwriting files belonging to any other operating system.

See the sidebar "Planning a Partition Structure for Your Hard Drive" earlier in the chapter for a discussion of partitioning your hard disk.

Pick Your File Systems

Next, decide which file systems you'll use. As discussed earlier in this chapter, if you're using Windows 9*x* (none of which can read NTFS drives), you'll need to use FAT or FAT32 on your boot partition.

Here's a quick recap on the file systems that the various versions of Windows support:

- ◆ NT 4 supports FAT and NTFS.
- ◆ Windows 95 supports FAT only.
- ◆ Windows 95 OSR2, Windows 98, and Windows Me support FAT and FAT32.
- ◆ Windows 2000 and XP support FAT, FAT32, and NTFS.

NTFS comes in two versions: version 4, which is used by Windows NT 4, and version 5, which is used by 2000 and XP. To upgrade NT 4 to use NTFS 5, install Service Pack 5 or higher. Microsoft recommends not using NT 4 with NTFS 5 as a long-term solution, saying the NTFS update "is provided only to help you evaluate and upgrade to Windows XP."

Back Up Your Files

It's a good idea to back up your files so that you can restore them easily should anything go wrong with creating your dual-boot or multi-boot configuration. Having a recent backup removes all the unnecessary excitement from creating the dual-boot configuration.

Plan Different Computer Names for Domain Use

If your dual-boot or multi-boot operating systems will connect to a Windows 2000 domain, you'll need a distinct computer name for each operating system you use. (You may also need extra licenses for connecting to servers that are licensed on a per-client rather than per-connection basis.)

Install the OSs in the Right Order

Next, depending on which OSs you're installing, you may need to install them in a particular order. If your dual-boot will consist of assorted versions of Windows, the key constraint is that Windows 9x versions have no built-in capability for creating a dual- or multi-boot setup. So you need to install them first; if you install a version of Windows 9x *after* installing NT, 2000, or XP, Windows 9x will happily overwrite the boot sector, leaving you unable to boot NT, 2000, or XP.

The preferred order in which to install the assorted versions of Windows is as follows:

1. Windows 9x (Windows 95, Windows 98, or Windows Me—you can install only one of these on a computer unless you use a special boot utility such as System Commander)
2. Windows NT 4
3. Windows 2000
4. Windows XP

Obviously, you don't have to install all these versions of Windows: Just follow this order for those versions that you do install.

You can install multiple copies of NT 4, Windows 2000, or XP if you want, provided that you follow this installation order. The reason you need to follow it is that the older versions of Windows don't know about the newer versions (understandably enough) and so don't provide the boot facilities they need. For example, if you install Windows 2000 after XP, you'll get an error message when you try to start XP, because Windows 2000's boot loader doesn't know how to start XP. (For a discussion of how to recover from this problem, see the sidebar "Troubleshooting: Problems with a Dual-Boot or Multi-Boot Setup," later in this chapter.)

If you'll be using NT 4 in your dual-boot system, and you haven't yet upgraded NT to Service Pack 5 or a later service pack, upgrade it before installing XP. Otherwise, you won't be able to boot NT after installing XP, because XP uses a later version of NTFS that NT 4 can't read without Service Pack 5 or later.

TROUBLESHOOTING: INSTALLING WINDOWS 2000 OR NT 4 AFTER XP

If you've already installed XP before reading the advice in the previous section, read this sidebar for information on how you can still install other versions of Windows. As you'll see, the result is less than optimal, but it more or less gets you there. Alternatively, invest in a boot manager such as System Commander from V Communications (www.v-com.com), which provides an elegant and effective solution to installing operating systems in the wrong order.

WINDOWS 2000

To install Windows 2000 after XP, start by creating an XP boot floppy as described in "Creating an XP Boot Floppy to Recover from a Faulty Boot Sequence" in Chapter 17. Then start the installation by booting from the CD rather than running WINNT32.EXE from XP. This is because XP recognizes the Windows 2000 CD as containing an older version of Windows (that you presumably *couldn't* be meaning to install intentionally) and disables its setup functionality. Once you've booted, install Windows 2000 as normal into its own partition.

Continued on next page

TROUBLESHOOTING: INSTALLING WINDOWS 2000 OR NT 4 AFTER XP *(continued)*

At this point, all will appear to be well. Windows 2000 will run fine. But when you try to start XP, you either won't get a chance to do so, or you'll find startup fails. If your XP installation was an upgrade from Windows 2000 (either from a previous installation or by using the Windows 2000 CD to prove ownership), you'll get a STOP 0x00000074: BAD_SYSTEM_CONFIG_INFO error on a Blue Screen of Death. If your XP installation wasn't an upgrade, you'll get the message "Windows 2000 could not start because the following file is missing or corrupt: \WINDOWS\SYSTEM32\CONFIG\SYSTEM."

You can fix this problem so that XP boots *but Windows 2000 won't boot* by booting into Windows 2000 and copying the NTLDR file and the NTDETECT.COM file from your boot floppy or the XP CD to the root of the boot partition, thus overwriting the Windows 2000 files of the same names. You'll then need to boot into XP and edit the BOOT.INI file to add an entry for Windows 2000 (and, if necessary, change the default OS and the timeout). Once you've done that, you'll be able to boot both OSs. Alternatively, you can simply use your XP boot floppy to boot XP and have Windows 2000 boot from the hard drive. Messy, sure. But it works fine.

NT 4

Similarly, you can install NT after XP by booting from the NT CD and installing it as usual into a partition of its own—provided that XP isn't installed on your C: drive or that, if it is, that drive is formatted with FAT rather than NTFS.

If XP *is* installed on your C: drive, and that drive *is* formatted with NTFS, NT 4's Setup routine will tell you that "Your C: drive is unformatted, damaged, or formatted with a file system that is not compatible with Windows NT. To continue installing Windows NT, Setup will have to format the drive." You probably won't want to do this.

Once you've installed NT on a separate partition, XP will be less than happy. Typically, XP startup will fail with the message "Windows XP could not start because the following files were missing or corrupted: WINDOWS\SYSTEM32\CONFIG\SYSTEM NTLDR MISSING," which means that NT has replaced the Windows boot files that XP needs. To replace them, boot to the XP Recovery Console (as discussed in "Repairing an XP Installation Using Recovery Console" in Chapter 17), issue the command **fixboot**, and press the Enter key. Reboot and see if XP will start. If not, boot to the Recovery Console again and copy the files NTLDR and NTDETECT.COM from the \i386\ folder on the CD to the root folder on your boot drive. Reboot again.

Performing the Installation

To perform a new installation of XP (without upgrading your current version of Windows), follow the steps below. For an illustrated step-by-step walkthrough of the upgrade procedure, visit this book's page on the Sybex website (www.sybex.com).

1. Insert the XP CD and click the Install Windows XP link on the introductory screen. (If the introductory screen doesn't appear, open an Explorer window, navigate to the drive containing the CD, and double-click the SETUP.EXE file.)

2. In the Installation Type drop-down list on the Welcome to Windows Setup page, choose the New Installation item.

3. Accept the license agreement and enter your product key.

4. On the Setup Options page (see Figure 2.6), choose any applicable language options, installation options, and accessibility options.

FIGURE 2.6

When you perform a new installation, Setup displays the Setup Options page, on which you can choose advanced options and accessibility options.

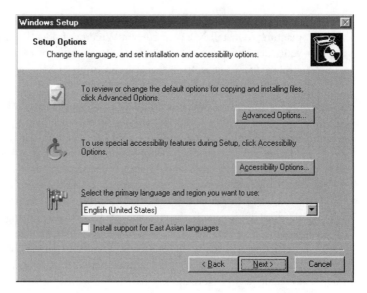

5. To set the advanced options, which let you control the installation folder and specify that you want to select the installation partition, click the Advanced Options button on the Setup Options page. Setup displays the Advanced Options dialog box (shown in Figure 2.7), which offers the following options:

    ◆ The Copy Installation Files from This Folder text box lists the path from which you ran the Setup program (or it ran itself). Usually, you won't need to change this path, but you can if necessary. (You'll notice that the installation folder on the CD is called \i386\. That's an abbreviation for Intel 386, the family of processors that includes the latest Pentium IV chips, and survives as a hangover from the early days of NT, when NT ran on Intel chips, Alpha chips, MIPS chips, and PowerPC chips.)

FIGURE 2.7

In the Advanced Options dialog box, you can specify the installation folder and tell Setup that you want to choose the installation partition.

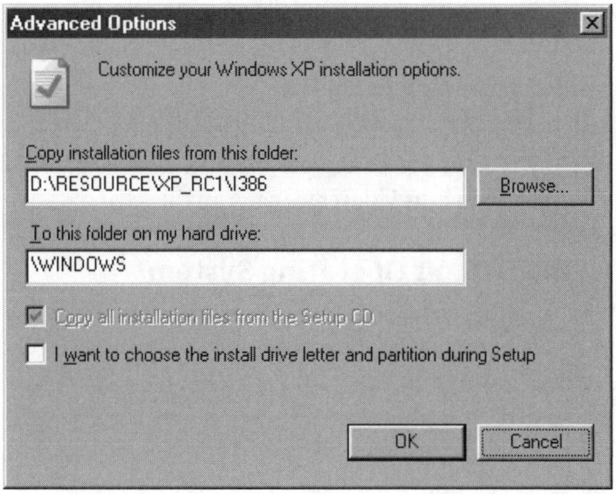

◆ The To This Folder on My Hard Drive text box shows the location to which Setup is planning to install XP: your current Windows folder. If you don't want XP to overwrite your current version of Windows, choose a different folder. For example, you may want to create a dual-boot setup so that you can compare XP to your current version of Windows without removing the latter from your computer yet.

◆ The Copy All Installation Files from the Setup CD check box enables you to force Setup to copy all its files to the hard drive rather than leaving them on the CD. Use this option when installing XP from a CD that will not be available after Setup reboots the computer. For example, when installing XP on a laptop computer using an external CD drive (such as a parallel-port drive, a USB drive, or a PC Card–connected drive), you'll probably need to copy all setup files to the hard drive because the CD drive will not be available from the reboot until Setup is complete. You may also need to use this option if your CD drive will not read the XP CD reliably during the setup routine after the reboot. (This shouldn't happen, but it does. After the reboot, Setup uses a different CD driver that apparently disagrees with some CD drives.) By default, this check box is cleared unless you're installing from a network drive, in which case it's selected but not available (as in Figure 2.7).

◆ The I Want to Choose the Install Drive Letter and Partition during Setup check box lets you tell Setup to display the partitioning screen so that you can specify the partition on which to install XP. If you're performing a new installation of XP, you don't need to select this check box, because Setup automatically displays the partitioning screen so that you can specify where to install XP.

6. Choose whether to use the Magnifier and Narrator accessibility options during Setup. Magnifier is designed for people with limited but viable vision and displays an enlarged version of the selected portion of the screen. Narrator is designed for the blind and those with more limited vision. It reads the contents of the screen aloud. To use these options, click the Accessibility Options button on the Setup Options page. Setup displays the Accessibility Options dialog box. Select the Use Microsoft Magnifier during Setup check box or the Use Microsoft Narrator during Setup check box as appropriate. Then click the OK button. Setup closes the Accessibility Options dialog box and applies your choices.

7. On the Get Updated Setup Files page, choose whether to let Dynamic Update download any updated setup files that are available.

8. Wait while Windows Setup upgrades your existing version of Windows to XP (which involves one or more reboots), and then perform the manual parts of configuration as discussed in "The Installation Paths Converge," later in this chapter.

Specifying the Default Operating System

Once you've set up your dual-boot configuration, specify the default operating system for the XP boot loader to start by following the instructions in step 2 of the section "Setting Start-up and Recovery Options" in Chapter 16.

TROUBLESHOOTING: PROBLEMS WITH A DUAL-BOOT OR MULTI-BOOT SETUP

This sidebar discusses how to troubleshoot common problems with XP in a dual-boot or multi-boot setup.

◆ If you're dual-booting XP with NT 4, when you go to power down the computer from NT, it displays a Shutdown Computer notice telling you that "It is now safe to turn off your computer." You won't be able to turn the PC off by pressing the power button once as you'd expect. Instead, you'll need to hold down the power button for at least five seconds to turn the computer off. This is because the NT boot loader checks to see whether the computer has Advanced Power Management (APM), and the computer's BIOS fails the APM call if the computer uses Advanced Configuration and Power Interface (ACPI) instead.

◆ If you've installed the Lilo (Linux Loader) boot manager on your master boot record (MBR) and need to remove it, boot to Linux, open a terminal window, and issue the `lilo -U` command for the appropriate drive. For example, if you've installed Lilo on the MBR of the master drive on your primary IDE controller, issue the command `lilo -U /dev/hda`.

◆ If you've installed Linux on your computer and then removed it, but you find that XP won't boot because Lilo is still trying to boot Linux, you can restore the master boot record for the disk by booting to DOS (for example, by using a boot disk from a Windows 9x version) and issuing the `fdisk /mbr` command.

◆ If you install XP on a multi-boot system on which you're using the BeOS boot manager, the XP boot manager overwrites the BeOS boot manager. There's not much you can do about this except start BeOS from its startup floppy.

◆ Installing XP may overwrite boot managers such as the PartitionMagic boot manager or the Boot-Magic boot manager. If this happens, you'll need to run the recovery procedure for the boot manager. This should be easy, as most boot managers are designed for easy recovery from being trodden on by operating systems.

◆ XP's Setup program doesn't recognize the file system ID used by PartitionMagic 5 and deems partitions created with PartitionMagic 5 inactive. To get around this problem, update to PartitionMagic 5.01 or a later version.

◆ If the boot menu fails to appear and your computer boots into Windows 9x, it probably means that you've installed that version of Windows 9x after installing XP instead of before installing XP. As a result, Windows 9x has overwritten the XP boot files, causing the computer to boot Windows 9x. To recover from this problem, reinstall or repair XP.

Performing a Clean Installation of XP Home

To perform a clean installation of XP, put the XP CD in your CD-ROM drive or DVD drive and boot from it. (You may have to change the boot settings in your computer's BIOS to boot from the CD.) Setup automatically launches itself.

NOTE For an illustrated step-by-step walkthrough of performing a clean installation of XP Home, visit this book's page on the Sybex website (`www.sybex.com`*).*

First, Setup displays the Welcome to Setup screen. From here, press the Enter key to start the installation. (Press the F3 key if you've reached this stage by mistake and need to quit.) Setup displays the partitioning screen.

Choosing a Hard Disk Partition

The partitioning screen lets you create and delete partitions as well as specify the installation partition. The screen lists the current partitions on the disk, their label, their type (for example, *NTFS* for an NTFS partition, *FAT32* for a FAT partition, and *Raw* for a new, unformatted partition), their size, and the amount of space free on each. Any unpartitioned space is listed as such. Any space you've deliberately left unpartitioned will of course be free, but there will often be a few megabytes of unpartitioned space left over after you've tried to allocate all the space on the disk.

To choose an existing partition for the installation, use ↑ and ↓ to move the highlight to it. Then press the Enter key.

To create a new partition, select some unpartitioned space and press the C key. Setup displays a details screen. Specify the size of the partition in megabytes and press the Enter key.

If you want to install XP and use up the full amount of unpartitioned space, you don't need to explicitly create a partition first. Just select the Unpartitioned Space item and press the Enter key to start the installation.

To delete an existing partition, select it in the list and press the D key. Setup displays a screen confirming the action. Press the L key. If the partition is a system partition, Setup displays a more extensive warning.

Once you've chosen a partition, Setup proceeds. If the partition is a new partition, Setup offers you the choice of formatting it with NTFS or with FAT. For each, there's the option of a quick format. A full format includes a scan of the disk for bad sectors; a quick format skips this scan. Unless you're in a tearing hurry and have checked the disk recently for bad sectors, go with the full format.

NOTE   *If you choose to install XP on a partition that already contains another operating system, Setup displays a page warning you that this may cause problems. Press the C key if you're prepared to continue. Otherwise, press the Esc key to return to the partitioning screen and select another partition.*

Converting the Partition to NTFS

If you're installing XP on an existing partition that uses FAT, Setup offers you the option of converting the installation partition to NTFS. Think seriously about doing so, because NTFS is one of the major improvements in XP Home over Windows Me and other Windows 9*x* versions.

NTFS offers two compelling advantages over FAT. First, NTFS has security features (including auditing) that FAT does not. And second, NTFS keeps a log of activities so that it can restore the disk to order after a hardware or power failure; FAT simply loses your data instead.

WARNING   *Don't convert the partition to NTFS if you're creating a dual-boot configuration with a version of Windows 9x, because Windows 9x cannot read NTFS partitions.*

Next, you see the license agreement. Read it and press the F8 key if you agree and want to proceed. Press the Esc key to cancel installation.

Choosing Regional and Language Options

After this, Setup entertains itself for a few minutes as it performs part of the installation. Next, you see the Regional and Language Options page. From here, you can change the computer's standards and formats setting so that it displays numbers, currencies, and dates in the appropriate formats for the country or user. You can also change the default keyboard layout.

To change the standards and formats setting, click the Customize button. Setup displays the Regional and Language Options dialog box with the Region Options page foremost, as shown in Figure 2.8. In the Standards and Formats group box, select the language and locale you want to use. The text boxes in the Samples area show samples of a number, a currency, a time, a short date, and a long date for that language and locale. (You can change these by clicking the Customize button and working in the Customize Regional Options dialog box.) In the Location drop-down list, select your geographical location so that XP knows which part of the world you're in when its services try to present you with local information. Click the OK button. Setup closes the Regional and Language Options dialog box.

FIGURE 2.8

On the Region Options page of the Regional and Language Options dialog box, specify the standards and formats setting to use and tell XP your location.

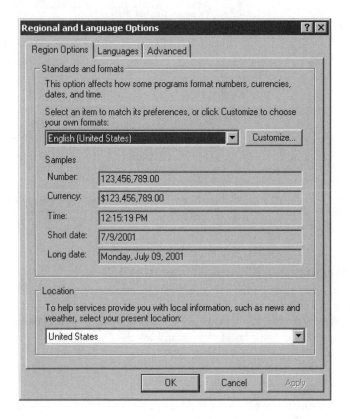

To change the keyboard layout, click the Details button. Setup displays the Text Services and Input Languages dialog box (shown in Figure 2.9). Select the language in the Default Input

Language drop-down list. To add an input language, click the Add button and use the resulting Add Input Language dialog box to specify the input language and keyboard layout. For example, if you use the Dvorak layout for your keyboard, set it as the default keyboard layout. Then click the OK button. Setup closes the Text Services and Input Languages dialog box.

Click the Next button to continue the setup process.

FIGURE 2.9

Use the Text Services and Input Languages dialog box to change your default input language.

Entering Your Name and Organization

Next, Setup displays the Personalize Your Software page, which demands your name and your organization's name. Enter these with due care and consideration, as they get deeply buried within the Registry. (Chapter 12 discusses how to change them if you get them wrong.) You must enter some text in the Name text box, but you can leave the Organization text box empty if you want.

Click the Next button to proceed.

Entering Your Product Key

Next, Setup displays the Your Product Key page. Enter the 25-character product key (it should be on a yellow sticker on the back of the folder or CD box your XP CD came in) and click the Next button to proceed.

TIP   If there's any risk of your misplacing your product key, write it on the XP CD using a felt-tip permanent pen.

Entering the Computer Name

Next, Setup displays the What's Your Computer's Name? page. By default, Setup suggests a complex and unmemorizable name that starts with the first part of the organization name you entered on the Personalize Your Software page. Change this name to something descriptive that you'll be able to remember and associate easily with this computer. The name can be up to 63 characters long, but you'd do well to keep it shorter than this to make it manageable. Names of more than 15 characters will be visible to other computers only via TCP/IP; via other network protocols, they won't be visible.

Click the Next button once again.

Entering the Modem Dialing Information

Next, if the computer has a modem that Setup was able to detect, Setup displays the Modem Dialing Information page. Specify your country or region (for example, United States of America), your area code (which is compulsory), any number you dial to get an outside line, and whether the phone system uses tone dialing or pulse dialing. Then click the Next button to proceed.

Checking the Date and Time

Next, Setup displays the Date and Time Settings page. Check the date, time, and time zone, and select or clear the Automatically Adjust Clock for Daylight Saving Changes check box as appropriate. Then click the Next button.

Specifying Networking Settings

Next, Setup installs some networking components and attempts to detect any network cards installed in your computer. Setup then displays the Networking Settings page, which offers you the choice of Typical Settings or Custom Settings.

The Typical Settings option installs the Client for Microsoft Networks, the QoS Packet Scheduler, File and Print Sharing for Microsoft Networks, and TCP/IP with automatic addressing. Typical Settings are suitable for most computers running XP Home. You can install other services after Setup completes (or remove these services), of course, but if you need other services, usually you'll be better off choosing the Custom Settings option and specifying suitable settings as described in the rest of this section.

If you select the Custom Settings option button and click the Next button, Setup displays the Networking Components page.

You can adjust the default settings by adding other services, uninstalling the default services, or choosing not to apply the selected services to this network adapter. When you remove a service, you make it unavailable to any of the network or dial-up adapters on your computer. So if you need to install a service but not use it for your primary network connection, let Setup install it, but clear its check box on the Networking Components page.

UNINSTALLING A SERVICE

To uninstall one of the services, select it and click the Uninstall button. Setup displays a confirmation message box warning you that uninstalling the component removes it from all network connections. Click the Yes button if you want to remove the service.

ADDING A SERVICE

To add other services to the default services, follow these steps:

1. Click the Install button. Setup displays the Select Network Component Type dialog box.
2. Select the type of component you want to add—Client, Service, or Protocol—and click the Add button. Setup displays the Select Network Client dialog box, the Select Network Service dialog box, or the Select Network Protocol dialog box, as appropriate.
3. Select the client, service, or protocol in the list box. To add an unlisted client, service, or protocol that you have on disk, click the Have Disk button and use the resulting Install from Disk dialog box to identify the file.
4. Click the OK button. Setup installs the client, service, or protocol and closes the Select Network Component Type dialog box.

CONFIGURING TCP/IP

Some of the network components have parameters you can configure. Of these, the key component is TCP/IP, the Internet protocol suite. If you don't run Internet Connection Sharing (ICS) on this computer, connect to the Internet through a computer running ICS, or connect to a DHCP server, you'll probably want to configure TCP/IP manually.

To configure your TCP/IP settings for the primary network card, follow these steps:

1. Select the Internet Protocol (TCP/IP) item in the list box on the Networking Components page.
2. Click the Properties button. Setup displays the Internet Protocol (TCP/IP) Properties dialog box.
3. On the General page, select the Use the Following IP Address option button.
4. Enter the IP address in the IP Address text box (for example, `192.168.0.11`). When you type a three-digit number or a period, XP automatically moves the insertion point to the next box. To move manually, press the spacebar or the → key.
5. Enter the subnet mask in the Subnet Mask text box (for example, `255.255.255.0`). Setup automatically enters a suggested subnet mask appropriate to the IP address you enter, but you may need to change it.
6. Enter the IP address of the default gateway in the Default Gateway text box.
7. Select the Use the Following DNS Server Addresses option button.
8. Enter the IP address of your primary DNS server in the Preferred DNS Server text box.
9. Enter the IP address of your secondary DNS server (if you have one) in the Alternate DNS Server text box.
10. Click the OK button. Setup closes the Internet Protocol (TCP/IP) Properties dialog box and applies your settings.

NOTE   *If necessary, you can also set advanced TCP/IP settings by clicking the Advanced button on the General page of the Internet Protocol (TCP/IP) Properties dialog box and working in the resulting Advanced TCP/IP Settings dialog box.*

Click the Next button to proceed with the installation. You've now chosen all the custom options.

CHANGING DISPLAY SETTINGS

If Setup detects that your screen has a recommended resolution (for example, if it is an LCD panel), or if it detects that you were using the 640×480 screen resolution, Setup displays the Display Settings dialog box, which announces that XP will automatically adjust your screen resolution to improve the appearance of visual elements. Click the OK button. XP adjusts the resolution and displays a Monitor Settings dialog box asking if you want to keep the change. Click the OK button if you do. If not, click the Cancel button or (if the screen isn't legible after the change) wait 30 seconds, after which XP restores the previous screen resolution.

The Installation Paths Converge

The three separate installation paths (upgrade, new installation, and clean installation) converge at the Welcome to Microsoft Windows screen, at which Setup starts playing active elevator music while an animated help logo struts its stuff. Click the Next button to move along.

Setting Up Your Internet Connection

Setup then tries to get your computer connected to the Internet. It tests any detected network adapter to see if it can find an Internet connection. If it detects an Internet connection, Setup displays the Will This Computer Connect to the Internet Directly, or through a Network? screen. Select the Yes, This Computer Will Connect through a Local Area Network or Home Network option button or the No, This Computer Will Connect Directly to the Internet option button as appropriate. (To skip the step of connecting to the Internet, click the Skip button.) Click the Next button. Setup displays the Ready to Activate Windows? screen.

If Setup doesn't detect an Internet connection, it displays the How Will This Computer Connect to the Internet? screen, which offers three options: the Telephone Modem option button, the Digital Subscriber Line (DSL) or Cable Modem option button, or the Local Area Network (LAN) option button.

Select the appropriate option button. If you don't want to configure an Internet connection at the moment—for example, you don't have your ISP or network information—click the Skip button.

The following sections describe what happens when you select each of these options.

TELEPHONE MODEM

If your computer connects with a telephone modem, select the Telephone Modem option button, then click the Next button. Setup displays the Ready to Activate Windows? screen.

After the step of activating XP (or your turning down the invitation to do so), Setup displays the Do You Want to Set Up Internet Access Now? screen, which asks if you want to set up your computer to connect to the Internet. Select the Yes, Help Me Connect to the Internet option button or the No, Not at This Time option button as appropriate.

If you choose the Yes option button, Setup displays the Let's Get on the Internet screen. This offers three choices: The Get Online with MSN option button, the Use My Existing Internet Account with Another Service Provider (ISP) option button, and the Create a New Internet Account after I Finish Setting Up Windows option button. Select the appropriate option button and click the Next button to proceed.

If you choose the Get Online with MSN option button, Setup walks you through the process of signing you up for a new account on MSN (the Microsoft Network) or letting XP know the details of your current MSN account.

If you choose to use your existing Internet account, XP displays the Do You Want Help Finding an Internet Service Provider? screen. If you want assistance setting up your account, select the Yes, I Need Help Finding Information about My Account option button. When you click the Next button, Setup dials a toll-free number to the Microsoft Referral Service to walk you through the steps of identifying your ISP. If you know the details of your account, select the No, I Have My User Name, Password, and My ISP's Name and Phone Number Handy option button. When you click the Next button, XP displays the Set Up Your Internet Account screen.

Enter your username, password, and ISP phone number. By default, XP selects the Obtain IP Automatically (DHCP) check box and the Obtain DNS Automatically (DHCP) check box. If you need to specify a static IP address rather than have the IP address be assigned automatically, clear the Obtain IP Automatically (DHCP) check box and enter the IP address in the Static Internet Protocol (IP) Address text box. Similarly, if your ISP does not supply DNS information automatically, clear the Obtain DNS Automatically check box and enter the IP addresses of the primary and secondary DNS servers in the Preferred DNS text box and the Alternate DNS text box.

When you click the Next button, Setup displays a Congratulations screen telling you that you can connect to the Internet using your phone line. Bear in mind that this isn't necessarily true—you've entered the information, but XP hasn't checked that it works.

If you choose to create a new account, Setup walks you through the process of selecting an ISP from Microsoft's list and entering the connection information for it.

DIGITAL SUBSCRIBER LINE (DSL) OR CABLE MODEM

If your computer connects with a DSL or cable modem, select the Digital Subscriber Line (DSL) or Cable Modem option button, then click the Next button. Setup displays the Do You Use a Username and Password to Connect to the Internet? screen. Select the Yes, I Use a Username and Password to Connect option button or the No, This Computer Is Always Connected to the Internet option button as appropriate. Click the Next button. Setup displays the Ready to Activate Windows? screen.

LOCAL AREA NETWORK (LAN)

If your computer connects through a local area network (LAN), select the Local Area Network (LAN) option button, then click the Next button. Setup displays the Setting Up a High Speed Connection screen.

If your network is set up to automatically supply an IP address and Domain Name System (DNS) information, this screen is easy: Select the Obtain IP Automatically check box and the Obtain DNS Automatically check box, and you're all set. If your network isn't set up to deliver the goods, leave these check boxes cleared and enter your static IP address, your subnet mask, and your default gateway in the left stack of text boxes; your primary DNS server's IP address in the Preferred DNS text box; and your secondary DNS server's IP address (if you have one) in the Alternate DNS text box.

Click the Next button to proceed. Setup displays the Ready to Activate Windows? screen.

Activating XP

Next, Setup displays the Ready to Activate Windows? screen, prompting you to activate Windows. Select the Yes, Activate Windows over the Internet Now option button or the No, Remind Me Every Few Days option button as appropriate.

Activation is a one-time procedure that you need to perform within 30 days of installing XP. If you don't activate XP within that time frame, either over the Internet (the easiest way) or over the phone, it stops working. The activation procedure is intended to reduce software piracy. A side effect is to increase the annoyance to legitimate software users who install XP themselves. (If XP came pre-installed on a computer you bought, chances are that it was activated already by the manufacturer.)

In theory, setup is a convenient time for activating XP, because you get the activation out of the way once and for all. But it's best to wait until you're sure that all your hardware works before activating XP. This needn't take long, and it's much better than needing to get your activation revoked because you need to install XP on another computer instead. If you don't activate XP at setup, it reminds you every few days until you activate it or your grace period ends. (You can also crack the activation by using one of the cracking procedures published on the Internet—but of course such cracking is a violation of your license agreement.)

After your grace period ends, you can boot XP as far as the Welcome screen or the Log On to Windows dialog box, but you can't get any further than that except by pursuing XP's offer to activate it immediately. If you choose not to activate XP, you can reinstall it and get another 30-day period; and you can keep reinstalling XP without activating it as often as you like. Of course, you need to reinstall all your programs, files, and settings each time, and even if you use the Files and Settings Transfer Wizard, this gets old fast.

Activation is a little creepy, even though it doesn't involve supplying any personal information. XP creates what it calls "a unique hardware configuration that represents the configuration of the PC at the time of activation." Briefly, the activation software monitors 10 different hardware components in your computer—everything from the primary display adapter and the processor type to the serial number of the hard drive volume and details of the IDE adapter or SCSI adapter. It uses values derived from this hardware to create a hardware ID (HWID, if you want to be buzzword compliant) that's used with your Product Identification (PID) to create an Installation ID that's transmitted during activation. If you activate XP successfully via the Internet, activation installs a digital certificate containing activation confirmation on your PC.

The Windows Product Activation Privacy Statement reassures you that "Windows can detect and tolerate minor changes to your PC configuration" and that only a complete overhaul will need reactivation. In practice, this means you can change up to four of the 10 monitored hardware components within a 120-day period without triggering an activation alert; any more than four changes within that time, and you'll need to reactivate XP.

TIP It's a good idea to back up the Windows Product Activation file, `WPA.DBL`*, which you'll find in the* `%systemroot%\` `System32\` *folder, in case you have to restore your computer, because restoring the computer may require reactivating it. You're likely to need to reactivate XP only if the computer's hardware configuration for the restoration is substantially different from the configuration on which the backup was made or if the backup was made before XP was activated.*

Registering XP

During activation, you're heavily encouraged to register your copy of Windows XP with Microsoft.

If you've already registered on Microsoft's website, your XP registration information gets merged into your current information. If you haven't registered, Microsoft creates a new profile for you with a personal information number (PIN) and adds the PIN to your hard drive in a cookie file. When you then visit the Microsoft website, it prompts you to create a Registration ID (not usually acronymed to RID). You can keep a profile with personal information—and you can opt out of the communications that Microsoft and the other companies it "occasionally" allows to offer its customers information will bombard you with.

Creating User Accounts

When you've finished with activation and registration, or when you've skipped both, Setup displays the Who Will Use This Computer? screen, which provides an easy way of setting up accounts for one to five users. This screen contains five text boxes. The first is named Your Name; the rest are numbered 2nd User through 5th User.

NOTE   *When you're upgrading from Windows 98 or Windows Me, Setup creates an account for the username under which you upgraded if you yourself forget to do so.*

Enter the names of the users in the text boxes. Each name can be up to 20 characters long, and each must be unique. Names cannot use the characters " * + , / : ; < = > ? [ ] \ or |, and no name can consist of all spaces, all periods, or a combination of the two.

Click the Next button. Setup displays the Thank You! screen telling you you're ready to start using XP.

Click the Finish button. Setup completes a few odds and ends, and then displays the Welcome screen for you to log in. Turn ahead to the next chapter for coverage of this and other basic XP procedures.

Applying Your Files and Settings

To apply the files and settings you saved by using the Files and Settings Transfer Wizard to your new installation of XP, take the following steps:

1. Choose Start ➢ All Programs ➢ Accessories ➢ System Tools ➢ Files and Settings Transfer Wizard. XP starts the Files and Settings Transfer Wizard, which displays the Welcome to the Files and Settings Transfer Wizard page.
2. Click the Next button. The wizard displays the Which Computer Is This? page.
3. Select the New Computer option button.
4. Click the Next button. The wizard displays the Do You Have a Windows XP CD? page, which offers to create a wizard disk that you can use to collect the information from your old computer.
5. Select the I Don't Need the Wizard Disk. I Have Already Collected My Files and Settings from My Old Computer option button.

6. Click the Next button. The wizard displays the Where Are the Files and Settings? page (shown in Figure 2.10).

FIGURE 2.10

On the Where Are the Files and Settings? page of the Files and Settings Transfer Wizard, tell the wizard where you saved the files and settings.

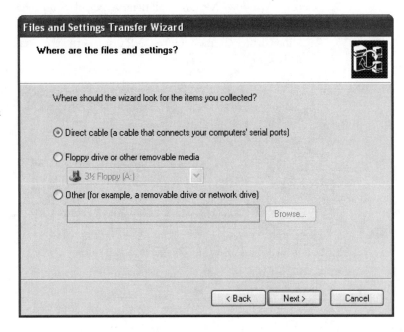

7. Select the Direct Cable option button, the Floppy Drive or Other Removable Media option button, or the Other option button as appropriate.

- ◆ If you select the Floppy Drive or Other Removable Media option button, select the drive in the drop-down list.

- ◆ If you select the Other option button, use the text box and (if necessary) the Browse button and the resulting Browse for Folder dialog box to specify the location of the files and settings.

8. Click the Next button. The wizard displays the Transfer in Progress page as it transfers the files and settings.

9. If the wizard displays a dialog box telling you that you need to log off for the settings to take effect and inviting you to log off now, choose the Yes button. The wizard logs you off and finishes applying the settings.

10. Log back in, and you'll find your settings applied and your files available.

Uninstalling XP Home and Reverting to Windows Me or 98

If you upgraded from Windows Me or Windows 98 to XP Home, you can uninstall XP and revert to your previous version of Windows if necessary. To do so, take the following steps:

1. Choose Start ➢ Control Panel. XP displays Control Panel.

2. Click the Add or Remove Programs link. XP displays the Add or Remove Programs window with the Add or Remove Programs page foremost.

3. Select the Windows XP Uninstall item. XP displays its details, including a Change/Remove button.

4. Click the Change/Remove button. XP displays the Uninstall Windows XP dialog box (shown in Figure 2.11).

FIGURE 2.11

In the Uninstall Windows XP dialog box, choose whether to uninstall XP or to remove the backup of your old version of Windows.

5. Select the Uninstall Windows XP option button.

6. Click the Continue button. XP displays a confirmation dialog box checking that you're absolutely sure.

7. Click the Yes button. XP closes, runs the uninstall procedure, and automatically restarts your computer with your previous version of Windows.

TROUBLESHOOTING: UNINSTALLING FROM SAFE MODE WITH COMMAND PROMPT

If you can't start XP normally or in Safe mode and you want to uninstall XP Home and revert to Windows 9*x*, boot into Safe Mode with Command Prompt (as discussed in Chapter 17), change directory to the %*systemroot*%\System32\ folder, and issue an **osuninst.exe** command.

Removing Your Old Version of Windows

If you decide to stick with XP Home after upgrading to it, you can reclaim the space taken up by the backup of your old version of Windows. To do so, follow the first four steps in the previous section but select the Remove the Backup of My Previous Operating System option button in the Uninstall Windows XP dialog box. Click the Continue button and confirm your choice, and XP deletes the backup of your previous operating system.

Troubleshooting Installation

This section discusses how to troubleshoot common installation problems, starting with general troubleshooting steps that work for a number of problems encountered when upgrading Windows 98 or Windows Me to XP.

Troubleshooting Upgrade Problems

When upgrading from Windows 98 or Windows Me to XP, use these general steps to troubleshoot installation problems that aren't specifically covered in the following sections:

◆ Make sure you've followed the steps discussed earlier in this chapter for preparing your computer for the upgrade.

◆ Ensure that you've got enough disk space to install XP.

◆ If you're running antivirus software, update it with the latest virus definitions, then perform the most detailed scan possible for viruses. When you're satisfied you've eliminated all viruses, disable or (preferably) uninstall the antivirus software you're running, because it is almost guaranteed to interfere with the upgrade. (Reinstall the antivirus software—or install a newer version—once you've upgraded to XP.)

◆ If necessary, perform a clean boot by using the System Configuration Utility. To run the System Configuration Utility, choose Start ➢ Run, entering **msconfig** in the Run dialog box, and click the OK button. Performing a clean boot helps eliminate drivers and terminate-and-stay-resident programs (TSRs) that may conflict with the upgrade.

"WINDOWS COULD NOT START. ...VGAOEM.FON" (WINDOWS 98)

The error message "Windows Could Not Start. The Following File Is Missing or Corrupted: Windows\System\VGAOEM.FON" occurs when you've upgraded an existing Windows 98 installation to XP and the font file VGAOEM.FON is missing or has been damaged. The error occurs when your computer restarts into XP after completing the setup routine.

To recover from this problem, boot into the Recovery Console (as discussed in "Repairing an XP Installation Using Recovery Console" in Chapter 17) and expand the VGAOEM.FO_ file from the \i386\ folder on the XP CD to the \Windows\System\ folder on the drive that contains XP. For example, if your CD drive is drive E: and XP is installed on drive D:, you'd use the following command:

```
expand e:\i386\vgaoem.fo_ d:\windows\system
```

XP displays the message "vgaoem.fon 1 file expanded" if the operation is successful. (If not, use the MAP command to check the drive letters, then try again.)

After expanding the file, issue the **exit** command to exit Recovery Console and to reboot the computer.

CD-Related and CD-ROM-Related Problems

Because XP comes on a CD rather than a shoulder-high stack of floppies, you need a CD drive to install it. Having the CD drive on the computer on which you're installing XP is always easiest, but you can also install using the CD drive on another computer. This section discusses some of the common installation problems involving CDs.

COMPUTER DOESN'T HAVE A CD-ROM DRIVE

If your computer doesn't have a CD-ROM drive, and you have an operating system that's working and can connect to another computer that has a CD-ROM drive, you have two options:

◆ Run the installation across the network, using the second computer's CD-ROM drive as the source. If necessary, select the Copy All Installation Files from the Setup CD check box in the Advanced Options dialog box to make sure that Setup copies all the files so that it can complete the installation after it reboots.

♦ If installing over the network doesn't work (for whatever reason), and you have about 500MB extra space on your hard disk (that's extra space over what you'll need for XP), copy all the files from the root directory of the CD and the entire contents of the \i386\ folder to your CD-less computer's hard drive and run Setup from there. Incidentally, copying the files to the hard drive is called *creating a flat*.

CD-ROM Drive Doesn't Work from DOS

If your CD-ROM doesn't work from DOS, or your CD-ROM drive isn't available for installation for another reason (for example, you're trying to start the installation from DOS, and you don't have a DOS driver for the CD drive), create a "flat" as described in the previous section and run Setup from there.

Computer Won't Boot from CD-ROM Drive

If the computer doesn't offer to boot from the CD-ROM drive, you may need to change the settings in the BIOS on your computer. The settings depend on the type of BIOS your computer has. For example, in an Award Software BIOS, you would change the Boot Sequence setting on the BIOS Features Setup page so that it included your CD-ROM drive before any other bootable drive (for example, the "CDROM, C, A" setting).

"Error Reading CD-ROM in Drive *N*"

You may receive the error message "Error reading CD-ROM in drive *n*" when your computer has two or more CD-capable drives and Setup has decided to look in the wrong drive. Try switching the XP CD to the other drive and pressing the Enter key.

If that doesn't work, try cleaning the CD. If that doesn't work either, create a flat and run Setup from there.

Setup Can't Find CD-ROM Drive

If Setup can't find your CD-ROM drive when you're upgrading from Windows 9*x* to XP, visit the manufacturer's website and see if an updated driver is available. If one is available, download and install it. If not, create a flat and install from it.

CD Won't Read Correctly or "Setup Cannot Copy the File" Error

If the CD won't read correctly or Setup displays the error "Setup cannot copy the file" (followed by a filename), take the following steps:

1. Check the CD for obvious dirt or damage, or for anything unbalancing such as an uncentered heavy label. Clean the CD if necessary. Then check the CD in another CD-ROM or DVD drive to make sure it works there. If it doesn't, contact Microsoft or the supplier for a replacement CD.

2. If the CD seems fine, make sure the CD drive is working by trying a couple of other CDs in it. If nothing will play, you've probably identified the problem. Clean, repair, or replace the drive.

3. If you have multiple drives, make sure that Setup is looking in the right drive. Usually, it's easiest to move the CD to the appropriate drive if Setup is looking in the wrong place, but in extremis you might prefer to disable the CD, either virtually or physically (for example, by disconnecting its power cable).

4. Check your computer for viruses and remove any you find.

More esoteric problems that prevent CD drives from reading CDs correctly include the following:

◆ Overclocking (running the processor at a faster speed than it's rated for) may cause decoding errors when Setup is extracting files from the CD archive.

◆ Mismatched memory modules may also cause decoding errors.

◆ Ultra direct memory access (UDMA) may cause data to move too quickly from the CD-ROM drive. If this happens, turn off UDMA in the BIOS, falling back to Processor Input/Output (PIO) mode (which is slower).

◆ Third-party memory managers may cause errors reading CDs.

Installation Won't Start

If the installation won't start, this usually means that some key device on your computer (for example, your motherboard or your hard drive) isn't compatible with XP. Run the Upgrade Advisor from your XP CD or check the Hardware Compatibility List at www.microsoft.com/hcl. You may need to replace a device before the installation will run. (If the device isn't vital to your computer's operation, you may be able to remove it instead.)

Lack of Disk Space

Lack of disk space is one of the easiest errors to deal with—provided that you can move or delete some of the files or folders on the current partition or make space on other partitions. The easiest way to start freeing up space in Windows 98 or Windows Me is to run Disk Cleanup (Start ➤ Programs ➤ Accessories ➤ System Tools ➤ Disk Cleanup), which lets you empty your Recycle Bin, delete temporary application files and temporary Internet files, remove downloaded program files, and delete other files that you may be able to dispense with.

If you can't make enough space by moving or deleting files, you'll need to either clear an existing partition of 1.5GB or larger or repartition your hard drive to create a new partition of that size or larger. For nondestructive partitioning, use a utility such as PartitionMagic or Partition Commander. For destructive partitioning, you can use the partitioning utility integrated into XP's setup routine.

Setup Errors

This section discusses three specific error messages that you may run into during Setup.

"Setup Can Not Set the Required Windows XP Configuration Information"

The error message "Setup can not set the required Windows XP configuration information," which appears after Setup has copied the installation files to your hard drive, usually indicates that one or more pieces of hardware on your computer are incompatible with XP. If you have an earlier version of Windows installed that you can return to, run the Upgrade Advisor to try to identify the culprits, then remove them.

If you don't have an earlier version of Windows installed, check your hardware manually against the HCL for obvious incompatibilities. Remove any offenders, then run Setup again.

"SETUP HAS DISABLED THE UPGRADE OPTION..."

When upgrading from Windows 98 or Windows Me to XP, you may see the error message "Setup has disabled the upgrade option, could not load the file `D:\i386\Win9xupg\W95upg.dll`. Setup cannot continue, because this version can only install as an upgrade."

If you run into this problem, perform a clean boot in Windows 98 or Windows Me (by using the System Configuration Utility, which you launch by choosing Start ➤ Run, entering `msconfig`, and clicking the OK button) and then try running Setup again.

If that doesn't work, copy all the files from the root directory of the CD and the entire contents of the `\i386\` folder to your hard drive and run Setup from there.

"AN UNEXPECTED ERROR (768) OCCURRED AT LINE 5118..."

The error message "An unexpected error (768) occurred at line 5118..." usually indicates that your computer is using Roxio GoBack (recovery software that lets you return your system to an earlier state). Reboot the computer, press the spacebar to display the GoBack boot menu, and choose the Disable option. (Alternatively, uninstall GoBack and retry installation.)

Computer Hangs During Setup

If your computer seems to hang during Setup, first make sure that it really has hung and that it's not merely in one of the outwardly somnolent phases of Setup during which little or no activity takes place with the hard disk or on the screen. Allow Setup at least 10 minutes of apparent inactivity before taking action.

Next, try rebooting your computer and letting Setup have another go at tackling your hardware. Setup keeps track on how far it has gotten, so it can pick up again from there—it doesn't have to start again from the beginning. It may run into the same problem again, but there's a chance that it'll be able to deal with the problem. Be prepared to try several reboots, allowing each at least 10 minutes' grace before you decide Setup has hung again.

If Setup keeps crashing, it may mean that your hardware is incompatible with XP. If you're upgrading, use the Cancel Windows XP Setup option after your final reboot to return to your previous OS. Then check your hardware against the HCL if you haven't already done so. Remove any incompatible devices and try again. If Setup still hangs, pare down your hardware to essential devices only by removing all devices you can dispense with for the duration of Setup, such as printers, sound cards, network cards, and USB and FireWire devices.

Setup crashing might also indicate that you've left an antivirus program or a boot manager program running. Make sure you haven't. If you have, turn it off and try running Setup again.

TIP   Another trick worth trying if you're still stuck at this stage is to disable Advanced Configuration and Power Interface (ACPI) functionality. To do so, press the F7 key when Setup invites you to press the F6 key to add SCSI drivers. Setup will appear not to respond to the F7 keypress, but it should disable ACPI.

If none of the above prevents Setup from hanging, you may need to upgrade your BIOS. Consult the BIOS manufacturer's website for possible upgrades. In some cases, you may be able to flash your BIOS with an upgrade. In others, you'll need to replace the BIOS.

If even the BIOS upgrade doesn't cure the problem, there's one other thing to try: Specify a Standard PC configuration for the Hardware Abstraction Layer. (Briefly, the Hardware Abstraction Layer, or HAL, provides the logical linkage between NT-based operating systems such as XP and the physical hardware in your computer.) To do so, press the F5 key when Setup displays the message "Press F6 if you need to load a third-party SCSI or RAID driver." You'll see the Windows Setup screen shown in Figure 2.12, which lets you specify the computer type. As you can see in the figure, the list box is badly designed in that it displays only two list items rather than the full list, making you scroll to see the rest of the list.

FIGURE 2.12

As a last resort, you can specify a different Hardware Abstraction Layer for the PC from this screen.

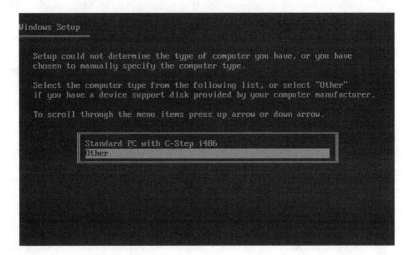

In most cases, you'll want to choose the Standard PC item to bypass any problems that ACPI may be causing. Make your choice and press the Enter key.

Error Messages during First Reboot of Setup

The following error messages may occur during the first reboot of the Setup procedure:

- "Setup has determined that Drive C: is corrupted and cannot be repaired."
- "No operating system"
- "Windows could not start because of the following ARC firmware boot configuration problem. Did not properly generate ARC name for HAL and System path."

These error messages all indicate problems with drive overlay programs, which XP doesn't support. Drive overlay programs are used for assorted purposes such as enabling older BIOSes to support logical block addressing (LBA), making otherwise incompatible hard disks able to work together, and letting a BIOS work with a hard disk that has more cylinders than it was designed to work with. Widely used drive overlay programs include MaxBlast from Maxtor, EZ-BIOS from Western Digital, Disk Manager from Seagate, and Disk Manager 2000 from IBM.

If you're using a drive overlay program, you'll probably know about it, because most of them display a text-based splash screen shortly after you boot your computer, often inviting you to press the spacebar if you want to boot from a floppy disk.

If you're using a drive overlay program, you'll need to repartition your hard disk (and probably update your BIOS) before installing XP. Unless you can discard your data, you'll need to back it up to a safe medium before partitioning the disk.

Troubleshooting Stop Errors (Blue Screen of Death)

If Setup encounters a hardware or software malfunction, you may see a Stop error screen. Stop errors are easy to recognize, as they generally appear as white text (starting with the word STOP) against a deep blue background. In fact, the jocular term for a stop error is the Blue Screen of Death (sometimes abbreviated to BSOD). Sometimes the background is black rather than blue, but the abbreviation still works.

If you run into a Stop error, first note the number displayed for the error. If you have a working Internet connection (for example, from another computer), search for the number displayed for the Stop error in the Microsoft Knowledge Base (`support.microsoft.com`) for the meaning of the error and any specific steps to take to fix it. Otherwise, use the troubleshooting steps outlined in the section "Computer Hangs during Setup," a little earlier in this chapter, to troubleshoot the error.

EXPERT KNOWLEDGE: AUTOMATING THE INSTALLATION OF XP

The installation procedure described in this chapter is effective and relatively straightforward once you know what the options mean. But it still takes between 45 and 90 minutes to complete, depending on the speed of your computer, and requires you to be there at odd moments to answer prompts, so it's a bit of a waste of time.

Still, you need to run the installation procedure only once on any computer. Or do you? Some people find that they need to install XP multiple times on the same computer. Every installation of Windows gradually accumulates unneeded programs, files, and settings. These can cause Windows—even XP—to slow down or even become unstable. Windows 98 was so notorious for this that the joke went that its name specified the number of days you could reasonably run it before expecting enough trouble to set in that a reinstall would be required to fix it.

XP improves your chances of not needing to reinstall by providing tools such as System Restore (discussed in Chapter 17), device driver rollback (discussed in Chapter 14), and Disk Cleanup and Disk Defragmenter (both discussed in Chapter 11) to keep your system in working order. But even these can't fix every problem. If you need a fresh start, or if you maintain a test computer, you may want to blow away all the old files and settings and virtual dust-bunnies by performing a new installation.

To help you do so, XP includes a tool for performing an unattended installation. (You can, of course, use these tools to set up XP the first and only time, but most people don't find it worth their while to do so. About the only reason to do so is that you can customize the unattended installation so that it doesn't include components you don't want. For example, if you consider MSN Explorer useless, you might want to exclude it, because otherwise Setup will install it by default.)

Continued on next page

EXPERT KNOWLEDGE: AUTOMATING THE INSTALLATION OF XP *(continued)*

If you had to guess how the procedure works, you'd probably figure that it'd consist of creating a file ahead of time that gives Windows the information for which it normally prompts you during setup, and then feeding that file to the Setup procedure. That's just how it works. The file is called an *answer file* for obvious reasons. There's a wizard to help you create the answer file, but then you may want to edit it a bit by hand.

To perform an unattended installation, take the following steps:

1. Extract the tools from the \Support\Tools\Deploy.cab folder on the CD to a convenient location. If you already have XP installed on one of your computers, you can extract these files by using Explorer. If you have an earlier version of Windows, use a Zip program (for example, WinZip) from Windows or the EXTRACT command from a command prompt instead. (See the Expert Knowledge sidebar "Extracting a Compressed File from a Cabinet File" in Chapter 17 for information on using the EXTRACT command.)

2. Open an Explorer window to the folder to which you extracted the files.

3. Double-click the SETUPMGR.EXE program. Windows starts the Windows XP Setup Manager Wizard, which displays its first page.

4. Click the Next button. The wizard displays the New or Existing Answer File page.

5. Leave the Create a New Answer File option button selected (as it is by default) unless you already have an answer file that you want to tweak. In that case, select the Modify an Existing Answer File option button and enter the path and filename in the text box, either by typing or by clicking the Browse button and using the resulting Open dialog box.

6. Click the Next button. The wizard displays the Product to Install page.

7. Make sure the Windows Unattended Installation option button is selected.

8. Click the Next button. The wizard displays the Platform page.

9. Select the Windows XP Home Edition option button.

10. Click the Next button. The wizard displays the User Interaction Level page (shown below).

Continued on next page

EXPERT KNOWLEDGE: AUTOMATING THE INSTALLATION OF XP *(continued)*

11. Select the Fully Automated option button.

12. Click the Next button. The wizard displays the Distribution Folder page, which lets you specify that the wizard create a distribution folder on your computer or on a networked drive containing the Windows source files.

◆ Creating a distribution folder lets you not only install without the CD but also add extra files (such as device drivers) to the custom installation. If you like unattended installation so much that you'd like to buy the company that made it—that is, if you want to run unattended installations frequently and you have a convenient drive or folder—you'll probably want to try this option. For the moment, we'll stick with installing from the CD.

13. Select the No, This Answer File Will Be Used to Install from a CD option button.

14. Click the Next button. The wizard displays the License Agreement page.

15. Select the I Accept the Terms of the License Agreement check box and click the Next button. The wizard displays the Windows Setup Manager window (shown below).

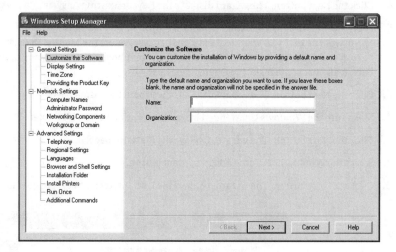

16. Select each page in turn and specify those settings applicable to your installation. Browsing through the pages feels like a sort of Redmond Roulette, because you must fill in any required fields (such as the Name text box on the Customize the Software page) before leaving any given page. If you don't, the wizard halts you in your tracks with a peremptory message box pointing out your omission. So it's best to deal with the pages in order. You can move from page to page by clicking items in the list box or by clicking the Next button.

Customize the Software page   Enter your name in the Name text box (compulsory). If appropriate, enter the organization in the Organization text box.

Display Settings page   You can use the Colors drop-down list, the Screen Area drop-down list, and the Refresh Frequency drop-down list to specify the colors, screen area, and refresh rate to use instead of accepting the XP defaults. For custom settings, click the Custom button and specify them in the Custom Display Settings dialog box.

Continued on next page

Time Zone page Select the time zone in the Time Zone drop-down list.

Providing the Product Key page Enter the product key on this page. (This is compulsory for creating a fully automated answer file.)

Computer Names page Enter the computer name in the Computer Name text box (compulsory).

Administrator Password page Enter the password for the Administrator account in the Password text box and the Confirm Password text box. Select the Encrypt Administrator Password in Answer File check box if you want to do just that. To have XP log the Administrator on automatically, you can select the When the Computer Starts, Automatically Log On As Administrator check box and specify the number of times in the Number of Times to Auto Logon text box. (Auto-logon can be useful for the first boot, but beyond that, it's a severe security threat.)

Networking Components page Select the Typical Settings option button or the Customize Settings option button as appropriate. If you select the latter, customize the settings as discussed in "Specifying Networking Settings" earlier in the chapter.

Workgroup or Domain page Leave the Workgroup option button selected and enter the name of the workgroup in the Workgroup text box.

17. Click the Next button. Windows displays a Windows Setup Manager dialog box telling you that it has created an answer file and inviting you to specify the location for it.

18. Enter the appropriate location and change the filename from its default UNATTEND.TXT to WINNT.SIF. Click the OK button. Windows XP Setup Manager creates the file and saves it under that name.

19. Choose File ➢ Exit. Windows XP Setup Manager closes itself.

Now you've created the basic file. It's ready to go—but before you run it, you probably want to take a look at the contents. (You might also want to add extra parameters. Consult the Setup Manager Help file for possibilities.) Right-click the file in an Explorer window, choose Open With from the context menu, select Notepad in the Open With dialog box, and click the OK button. Windows opens the file in Notepad. Depending on the options you chose, it should look something like this:

```
;SetupMgrTag
[Data]
    AutoPartition=1
    MsDosInitiated="0"
    UnattendedInstall="Yes"

[Unattended]
    UnattendMode=FullUnattended
    OemSkipEula=Yes
    OemPreinstall=No
    TargetPath=\WINDOWS

[GuiUnattended]
    AdminPassword=*
    EncryptedAdminPassword=NO
    OEMSkipRegional=1
```

Continued on next page

EXPERT KNOWLEDGE: AUTOMATING THE INSTALLATION OF XP *(continued)*

```
        TimeZone=85
        OemSkipWelcome=1

[UserData]
        ProductID=NNNNN-NNNNN-NNNNN-NNNNN-NNNNN
        FullName="Andy Rondolophberger"
        OrgName="Rondolophberger Pharmaceuticals"
        ComputerName=Verwirrung

[Display]
        BitsPerPel=32
        Xresolution=800
        YResolution=600
        Vrefresh=85

[Identification]
        JoinWorkgroup=LAUREL

[Networking]
        InstallDefaultComponents=Yes
```

If you've chosen other options—for example, customizing networking or choosing language settings—you'll see further lines covering them. You can also add other lines as necessary to take other actions, such as specifying that the installation repartition the hard drive or convert the file system to NTFS. You'll find details of the possibilities in the Help files contained in DEPLOY.CAB. For example, if you want to prevent MSN Explorer from being installed, add the line **msnexplr=off** to the file. To prevent Windows Messenger from being installed, enter the line **msmsgs=off**.

If you make any changes, save the file. Close it and copy it to a floppy disk. Then boot the computer from the XP CD and put the floppy disk in the floppy drive. XP installs automatically using the settings you specified.

Up Next

This chapter has discussed how to install XP Home, either as a clean installation, as a new installation, or as an upgrade to your current version of Windows 9x. You've also learned how to transfer files and settings from one installation of Windows to XP, how to troubleshoot common installation problems, and how to create an answer file to perform an unattended installation should you need to.

The next chapter discusses how to get started with XP: logging on and off, switching users, finding out who's logged on, and shutting down XP.

Chapter 3

Getting Started with Windows XP Home Edition

THIS CHAPTER DISCUSSES HOW to get started with XP Home Edition. It covers how to log on and log off, how to troubleshoot logon problems, how to switch from one user session to another, how to use the Desktop and the Start menu, and how to exit XP. It also discusses how you can find out who else is logged on to the computer when you're working at it, how you can get an idea of which programs the other users are running, and how you can log off another user (or all other users) to reclaim the resources they're using.

Logging on and off and switching user are straightforward—as they should be, because you'll probably perform each action several times each day you use the computer. But behind these mundane actions lie some important concepts of multiuser computing that you need to understand in order to use XP most effectively. So even at this basic level of coming to grips with XP, we need to lift the hood and glance at what it's hiding beneath it. To do so, we'll use Task Manager, a handy administration tool built into XP.

This chapter covers the following topics:

- Logging on and logging off
- Switching from one user to another
- Seeing who else is logged on to the computer
- Logging another user off
- Sending a message to another user
- Using the Windows key
- Shutting down Windows

NOTE   *Before we start, here's something you need to know. XP Home supports three types of users: Computer Administrator users, Limited users, and the Guest user. By default, all named users are set up as Computer Administrator users, which gives them full authority to configure and customize the computer. Limited users, which you create manually, can perform only minimal configuration and customization. The Guest user, an account that's created automatically by XP, can perform no configuration or customization. This chapter assumes you're logging on as a Computer Administrator user, because that's most likely to be the case. Chapter 9 discusses how to create and manage user accounts and how to set a password on the main Administrator account for your computer.*

TIP   *If you installed XP by upgrading from Windows 98 or Windows Me, or if you've transferred your files and settings from a previous version of Windows by using the Files and Settings Transfer Wizard, XP displays the settings you chose for your previous Desktop rather than its default settings. So items such as your Desktop, Control Panel, and other user-configurable Windows settings may look different from the defaults I describe in this chapter. But if you've used Windows enough to configure the settings in question, I'm sure you'll have no problem dealing with these minor differences.*

Logging On and Logging Off

Logging on and off in XP works differently than in previous versions of Windows. Logging on and off could hardly be easier, but it's important to understand what happens when you log on and off, and how logging on and off differs from simply switching users.

In earlier versions of Windows, only one user at a time could be logged on to a computer running Windows. For a second user to log on, the first user needed to log off. Logging off involved closing all the open programs and files: Either the user could close the programs and files manually before logging off, or Windows would close them automatically when the user issued the Log Off command (and confirmed that they wanted to log off).

Once all the programs and files were closed, and all network and Internet connections were closed as well, Windows displayed the Log On to Windows dialog box or the Enter Network Password dialog box, depending on whether the computer was attached to a network. Another user could then log on to Windows, run programs, open files, establish network and Internet connections, and so on.

In XP, multiple users can be logged on at the same time, though of course only one user can actually be using the computer. Each of those users who is logged on can have programs running and files open. XP lets you switch quickly between users without closing the programs and files.

Only one user can be *active*—actually using the computer—at any time. (Given that most computers have only one keyboard, mouse, and monitor, this may seem too obvious to mention—but things are very different in Unix and Linux, in which multiple users can be actively using the same computer at the same time, some locally and some remotely.) A user who is logged on but not active is said to be *disconnected*.

This means that, for example, Jane and Jack can keep their programs open while Ross is using the computer. When Jane logs back on (in the process disconnecting Ross, who perhaps stepped away for a cup of coffee), XP resumes her session from where she left off, displaying the programs she had running and the files she had open. XP reestablishes any of Jane's persistent network connections, including any Internet connection that's set to connect automatically.

Being able to leave multiple users up and running is great—up to a point. But it has serious implications for performance and file integrity. The following sidebar discusses these considerations briefly.

EXPERT KNOWLEDGE: FAST USER SWITCHING, PERFORMANCE, AND FILE INTEGRITY

Having multiple users logged on to XP at the same time affects performance because each user who's logged on takes up some of the computer's memory. Having a user logged on itself takes up relatively little memory, but each program that the user has running, and each file that they have open, adds to the amount being used.

XP needs a minimum of 64MB of RAM to run at all, and 128MB to run at an acceptable speed. For each light user, reckon another 32MB of RAM; for each moderate user, 64MB; and for each heavy user, 128MB. If you have 256MB of RAM, you should be able to have two or three users logged on and running several programs each without running short of memory.

Another issue is what the programs in a disconnected session are actually *doing*. A program that's running but waiting for user input consumes very few processor cycles, but one that's actively engaged in a task consumes many—sometimes as many as XP can give it. For example, if you leave Microsoft Word open with a document that you're composing displayed, Word will be waiting for user input, and if you disconnect your session, it'll just sit there waiting like the most patient Labrador in the world. But if you start a macro running in Word and then disconnect your session, the macro will keep running like a spaniel pursuing game until it finishes and will consume processor cycles as if there's no tomorrow. Likewise, if you're performing a processor-intensive task such as video rendering in a disconnected session, performance in the active session will be severely degraded. But other programs will essentially suspend themselves when XP disconnects their session and so will not affect the performance of the active session. Experiment with the programs you and the people with whom you share your computer use and establish which programs you can't reasonably leave running in a disconnected session.

Having multiple users logged on at once can also affect file integrity. For example, what happens when two users try to change the same file at the same time? The short answer is, It depends.

Some programs are smart enough to realize that someone else has a copy of the file open. For example, if you try to open in Word 2002 the same document that another user has open, Word displays the File in Use dialog box (shown below) to warn you that the document is locked for editing and to offer you ways to work with the document (open a read-only copy, create a local copy and merge your changes later, or receive notification when the original copy is available).

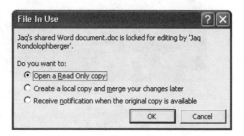

Other programs aren't smart enough to spot the problem. For example, WordPad (XP's built-in word processing program) lets you open a document that another user has open, change it, and save the changes. The other user can then save *their* changes to the same file, which can end up with some of the changes you've made and some that the other user has made. And this is assuming that only two users are editing the document at the same time. For all WordPad knows, half the people in Delaware could be editing the document at the same time and wiping out each other's changes.

Continued on next page

EXPERT KNOWLEDGE: FAST USER SWITCHING, PERFORMANCE, AND FILE INTEGRITY *(continued)*

If your computer has a modest amount of RAM—say, 64MB, 96MB, or 128MB—or if you're having problems with users opening files at the same time, turn off the Fast User Switching feature as discussed in the section "Turning Off Fast User Switching" in Chapter 9. When you turn off Fast User Switching, only one user can be logged on to the computer at any given time, and that user must log off before another user can log on. This reduces the amount of memory needed and avoids most problems with shared files.

Logging On

To start using XP, log on from the Welcome screen. Figure 3.1 shows an example of the Welcome screen, which displays a list of the users who have accounts set up on the computer. (See page 5 of the *Essential Skills* section for a visual guide to logging on.) Any programs a user has running appear listed under the username, together with the number of e-mail messages waiting for them. If a user is logged on but has no programs running, the Welcome screen displays *Logged on* beneath their name.

FIGURE 3.1

The Welcome screen lists the users with accounts on this computer, any tasks the user has running, and any unread e-mail messages they have.

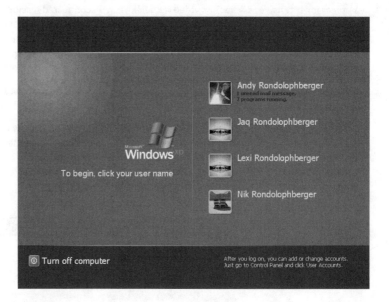

NOTE   *If you set up XP Home with only one user, XP sets that user up to log on automatically, so that when you start XP, it boots straight to their Desktop. You can turn off automatic logon for that user, and you can set up automatic logon for a user on a computer that has multiple user accounts defined. See the section "Implementing and Preventing Automatic Logons" in Chapter 9 for instructions.*

If your computer is set up to use the Log On to Windows dialog box (see Figure 3.2) rather than the Welcome screen, type your username in the User Name text box and your password (if you have one) in the Password text box, then click the OK button to log on. (The User Name text box displays the name of the last user who logged on.)

FIGURE 3.2

If your computer uses the Log On to Windows dialog box, enter your user-name and (if you have one) your password.

By default, user accounts in XP Home are set up without passwords, so you log on by clicking the username under which you want to log on. (If an administrator has set up XP Home to require pass-words, you'll need to enter the password for the account as well.)

When it accepts your logon, XP displays your Desktop with its current settings. (The section "Using the Desktop and Start Menu" a little later in this chapter discusses the basics of the Desktop and Start menu. The next chapter discusses how to customize the Desktop.)

The first time you log on, XP creates your folders and sets up program shortcuts for you—so the logon process takes a minute or two. Subsequent logons are much quicker.

TROUBLESHOOTING LOGON PROBLEMS: YOU CAN'T SATISFY THE PASSWORD PROMPT

In XP Home, logon is intended to be simple, but to provide the level of security set by the Computer Admin-istrator users. By default, no account has a password, so anyone able to access the computer can log on by clicking a username. But if a user has protected their user account with a password, XP provides effective security: Nobody can log on to that account without supplying the correct password.

If you're not able to log on even by using the correct password, make sure that you're entering the password in the correct case, because passwords are case sensitive. To help you avoid problems with the Caps Lock key being on, XP displays a prominent warning when this key is locked down.

Next, if the computer has multiple input languages configured, make sure you're using the right language. When multiple input languages are in use, XP displays a language indicator (for example, EN for English) to the right of the password box on the Welcome screen. To switch to a different input language, press the Alt key and the left Shift key together.

If neither of those simple fixes works, something more complex may be going on.

By default, XP uses the Welcome screen rather than the Log On to Windows dialog box for logon. As you can see in Figure 3.1, the Welcome screen provides a simplified and user-friendly interface for logging on. Unfortunately, this simplicity means that it's not fully equipped to deal with a couple of logon wrinkles that XP Home supports but that Microsoft has chosen to hide from the casual user. So if your computer is using the Welcome screen for logon, XP's only response to a number of different problems is to prompt you for a password—even if you don't have one.

Continued on next page

TROUBLESHOOTING LOGON PROBLEMS: YOU CAN'T SATISFY THE PASSWORD PROMPT *(continued)*

These problems include the user account having been limited to logging on at certain times (and the user trying to log on at a time that's not permitted), the user account having been disabled, and the user account having expired. In each of these cases, the Welcome screen prompts the user for a password, even if they don't have one. If the user has a password and enters it correctly, XP tells them the password was wrong.

If the computer is set up to use the Log On to Windows dialog box instead of the Welcome screen, the user receives a message explaining the problem—for example, that their user account has been disabled.

See the sections "Limiting the Times a User Can Log On," "Disabling and Reenabling a User Account," and "Making a User Account Expire" in Chapter 9 for details on how to impose such restrictions on user accounts.

Logging Off

The counterpart to logging on is (unsurprisingly) logging off. When you log off, XP closes all the programs and files you've been using. If the files contain unsaved changes, XP prompts you to save them.

To log off, display the Start menu by clicking the Start button, and click the Log Off button. If your computer is using the Welcome screen, XP displays the Log Off Windows dialog box shown on the left in Figure 3.3; if not, XP displays the Log Off Windows dialog box shown on the right). Click the Log Off button to log off. See page 6 of the *Essential Skills* section for visual coverage of logging off.

FIGURE 3.3

The Log Off Windows dialog box lets you log off, cancel the command, or switch to another user.

NOTE If you leave your computer unattended for a while, the screen saver usually kicks in—unless you have something open than prevents the screen saver from starting (or you've disabled the screen saver). For example, a dialog box open on-screen usually prevents the screen saver from starting. The default setting is for the screen saver to start after 10 minutes and to display the Welcome screen. The screen saver gives you some protection against prying eyes (particularly if you're using passwords for logging on), but it also makes it harder to see who's doing what on the computer. Chapter 4 discusses how to choose screen saver settings.

Using the Desktop and Start Menu

Once you've logged on successfully, XP displays the Desktop—the background area that XP provides for you to spread your work across. Figure 3.4 shows what the Desktop looks like the first time you start XP and start a couple of programs. Because you can customize the Desktop extensively (as discussed in the next chapter), your Desktop might not look anything like the Desktop shown in the figure: The wallpaper might be different; the Taskbar could be located at a different side of the screen; or various toolbars might be displayed. About the one unchanging thing about the Desktop is the Start menu button—but even this might not be displayed if someone has chosen to hide the Taskbar (of which the Start button is part).

FIGURE 3.4

The components of the XP Desktop

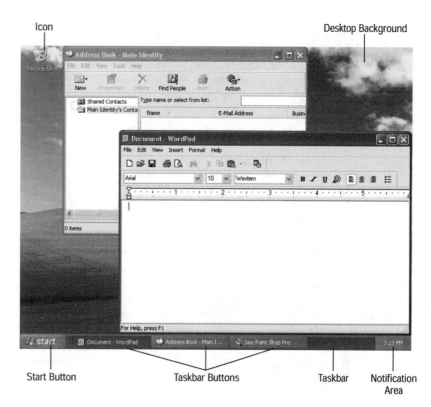

Icon   Desktop Background

Start Button   Taskbar Buttons   Taskbar   Notification Area

We'll examine the Desktop in more detail in the forthcoming chapters, but these are the basic actions for navigating it:

- ◆ The Desktop contains one or more shortcuts to items. Usually, there's an icon for the Recycle Bin, if nothing else. Double-click an icon to run the program associated with it.

- ◆ The Start menu provides access to the full range of programs and features currently installed on XP. To display the Start menu, click the Start button, press the Windows key on the keyboard, or press Ctrl+Esc (for example, if your keyboard doesn't have a Windows key). Choose one of the items that appears on it, or click the All Programs button to display a cascading menu containing further items. See page 9 of the *Essential Skills* section for a visual guide to using the Start menu.

◆ The Taskbar gives you quick access to each program that's currently running. The Taskbar displays a button for each active program window until it runs out of space for reasonable-sized buttons, at which point it groups related windows onto a single button (which expands to show the individual window titles when you click it). To display that window in front of all other windows, click its button. To minimize the program (removing its display from your Desktop, so that only the Taskbar button is left), click its Taskbar button again. See page 14 of the *Essential Skills* section for coverage of how to use the Taskbar to access a window, and pages 12 and 13 for coverage of how to use the Taskbar to arrange windows.

*TIP   If you find that the Taskbar groups program window buttons in a way that isn't helpful, try downloading the Tweak UI PowerToy from the Microsoft Windows XP Downloads site (*www.microsoft.com/windowsxp/home/downloads/ powertoys.asp*) and experimenting with the settings on the Taskbar\Grouping page. These let you group the least-used programs first, group the programs with the most windows first, or group any program with a certain number of windows.*

◆ The notification area contains items that it's useful to have displayed all the time (such as the clock, which is displayed by default), together with information and alerts (which are displayed at appropriate times). Because the notification area tends to get over-stuffed with icons, XP automatically hides those that are inactive.

◆ The Desktop background is a graphic that you can change at will.

Instead of using the Taskbar to switch from one program to another, you can "coolswitch" by pressing the Alt+Tab key combination. Doing so displays a panel of icons for the program windows currently open. Hold down the Alt key and press the Tab key to move the selection to the program window you want, and then release the Alt key to display that program window. Hold down Alt+Shift and press the Tab key to move backward through the list.

*TIP   If you have a lot of program windows open, it can be difficult to establish from the coolswitch panel of icons which window you want. If you find this a problem, download the Alt-Tab Replacement PowerToy from the Microsoft Windows XP Downloads site (*www.microsoft.com/windowsxp/home/downloads/powertoys.asp*) and install it. This PowerToy displays a larger panel that includes a picture of the window represented by the icon you've currently selected, making it much easier to identify the program windows.*

Switching to Another User

As you saw in Figure 3.2, the Log Off Windows dialog box that's displayed when your computer uses the Welcome screen and Fast User Switching also contains a button called Switch User. When you click the Switch User button, XP keeps your programs running (instead of closing them, as it does when you log out) and displays the Welcome screen so that you can log on as another user or (more likely) another user can log on as themselves. See page 7 of the *Essential Skills* section for visual coverage of this procedure.

NOTE   If you upgraded to XP from Windows 98 or Windows Me and your computer has only 64MB of RAM, XP may have disabled Fast User Switching on the grounds that you don't have enough RAM for it to work effectively. To use Fast User Switching, add RAM and then turn Fast User Switching on as discussed in the section "Turning Fast User Switching Off and On" in Chapter 9.

EXPERT KNOWLEDGE: USING THE CONNECT COMMAND TO SWITCH USERS QUICKLY

Switching users as described above is easy but takes a few clicks. There's a quicker way of switching—by using Task Manager as follows:

1. Right-click open space in the Taskbar and choose Task Manager from the context menu. XP opens Task Manager.

2. Click the Users tab. XP displays the Users page (shown in Figure 3.5, later in the chapter).

3. Right-click the user as whom you want to connect and choose Connect from the context menu. If the user's account has a password, XP displays the Connect Password Required dialog box. When you enter the password correctly (or if the account has no password), XP disconnects your session and connects you as the user you selected.

Locking the Computer

To leave your current session running but display the Welcome screen quickly, press Windows key+L. (If you're not using the Welcome screen, XP displays the Log On to Windows dialog box instead.)

Microsoft calls this action *locking* the computer, though the term is neither accurate nor helpful with XP Home's default settings. The computer isn't locked in any useful sense unless all user accounts are protected with effective passwords.

However, if you turn off the Welcome screen and Fast User Switching (as discussed in Chapter 9), XP manages a semblance of locking. When the current user disconnects their session, XP displays a blank background topped by the Unlock Computer dialog box, which tells the user that the computer is in use, that it has been locked, and that only the current user or an administrator can unlock it. If you've applied passwords, this is true; if you haven't, anyone can click the OK button in the Unlock Computer dialog box to unlock the computer and log on as the current user.

Checking Which User Is Currently Active

If you're in any doubt as to which user is currently active, display the Start menu (by clicking the Start button or pressing either the Windows key or Ctrl+Esc) and check the username displayed at the top.

Seeing Who Else Is Logged On to the Computer

As you saw a page or two ago, the Welcome screen displays details of each user logged on to the computer and the number of programs they're running. But if you don't want to display the Welcome screen (and disconnect your session by doing so), you can find out which other users are logged in by using Task Manager as follows:

1. Right-click the Taskbar and choose Task Manager from the context menu. XP displays Task Manager.

2. Click the Users tab. XP displays the Users page (shown in Figure 3.5), which lists the users and their status.

FIGURE 3.5

The Users page of Task Manager shows you which other users are logged on to the computer. You can send them messages, switch to their sessions, or log them off forcibly.

NOTE   Limited users and the Guest user can't see which other users are logged on or which processes they're running. As a result, Limited users and the Guest user can't switch directly to another user's session by using Task Manager, though they can disconnect their own session or log themselves off by using Task Manager.

Seeing Which Programs the Other Users Are Running

It's not easy to see exactly which programs the other users of the computer are running unless you know the names of the executable files for the programs, but you can get an idea by using the Processes page of Task Manager. This page also shows you how much memory each program is using, which helps you establish whether—or why—your computer is running short of memory.

Follow these steps to start Task Manager and display its Processes page:

1. Right-click the Taskbar and choose Task Manager from the context menu. XP displays Task Manager.

2. Click the Processes tab. XP displays the Processes page, which lists the processes you're running.

3. Select the Show Processes from All Users check box. (This check box is cleared by default.) Task Manager adds to the list all the processes that the other users are running as well. Figure 3.6 shows an example of the Processes page. You can sort the list of processes by any column by clicking the column heading. In the figure, the processes are sorted by the User Name column so that it's easy to see which process belongs to which user.

As you can see in the figure, three of the Rondolophbergers are running programs, and between them they're using quite a chunk of memory: The Commit Charge counter in the lower-right corner of the Processes page shows that 172,932K (about 169MB) out of 633,656K (about 619MB) of memory has been used up. In the list, you can see some of the principal offenders: copies of WINWORD.EXE (Word for Windows) that Andy and Jaq are running (24,624K and 18,148K, respectively), several instances of EXPLORER.EXE, and some programs with unpronounceable names such as DEVLDR32.EXE and WPABALN.EXE.

FIGURE 3.6

Use the Processes page of Task Manager to see which programs the other users are running.

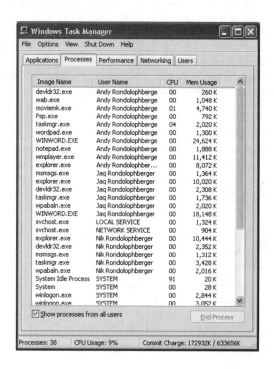

Some of the other names are readily identifiable. For example, WMPLAYER.EXE is the executable for Windows Media Player, as you'd expect, and TASKMGR.EXE is the executable for Task Manager itself. You don't need to memorize the mapping of each executable filename to its program, but if you look at Task Manager now and then, you'll learn to scan the list of processes and see which is running. This will help you decide whether you should go ahead and log another user off XP (as described in the next section) or whether doing so will trash their work and ruin their life.

While you're looking at Task Manager, there are a couple of other things you might as well know.

First, you can also see in the figure that it's not just the Rondolophbergers who are using memory like there were no tomorrow—XP also has a number of processes open on its own account. The LOCAL SERVICE account is running SVCHOST.EXE (service host), as is the NETWORK SERVICE account. The SYSTEM account is running a dozen or more processes, of which you can see only the top few in the figure. Of these, the first, the System Idle Process, is consuming 91 percent of the processor cycles. (This is actually good news. When the System Idle Process is taking up most of the processor cycles like this, the computer is idling along—goofing off until the user does something that presses it into action.)

EXPERT KNOWLEDGE: WHICH NAME CORRESPONDS TO WHICH PROGRAM?

To find out which program corresponds to each executable file, display the Applications page of Task Manager. Right-click a program and choose Go to Process from the context menu. Task Manager displays the Processes page and selects the process for that program.

That's easy enough—but there are many more processes running than programs. Try closing all the programs listed on the Applications page of Task Manager, and you'll see that there's still a goodly list of processes left. Then close as many of the notification area items as you can by right-clicking each icon in turn and choosing any Close command or Quit command that appears on the context menu. Try stopping any obvious services that you can temporarily dispense with, and see if an associated process disappears. For instance, try closing your Internet connection or stopping your PC Cards. Did either of those actions lose you a process? Then you have an idea of what that process does.

 If you're desperate to find out which function or service an executable runs, try searching for the executable. (Chapter 6 describes how to search for a file, and pages 34–36 of the *Essential Skills* section illustrate searching.) The folder that contains the executable may give you a clue as to the program, or there may be a comment on the executable that reveals its purpose. Then again, the executable may prove to be one of the mysterious system files stored in the \Windows\ folder or the \Windows\System32\ folder. If the latter is the case, figure it's something unknowable and leave it alone.

Second, you may have noticed that the numbers in the Mem Usage column don't add up to anything like the 172,932K listed as being committed (even though you can't see the whole column). That's because that committed figure is both physical memory (RAM) used and virtual memory (hard disk space being used to simulate more RAM). If you want to see how much virtual memory each process is taking up, follow these steps:

1. Choose View ➤ Select Columns. Task Manager displays the Select Columns dialog box (shown in Figure 3.7).

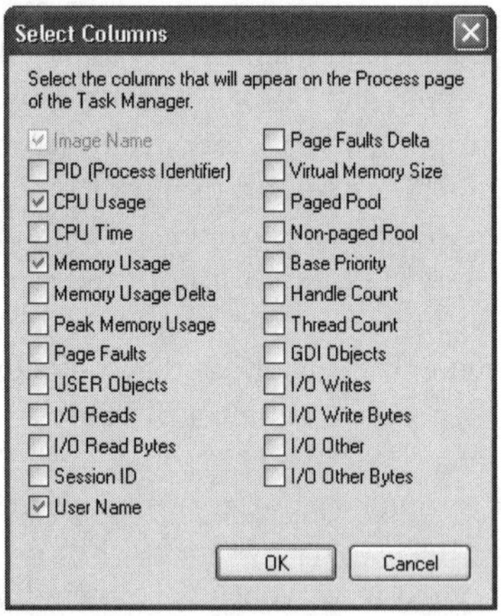

FIGURE 3.7

Use the Select Columns dialog box to add further columns of information to Task Manager's Processes page.

![Select Columns dialog box showing checkboxes: Image Name (checked), PID (Process Identifier), CPU Usage (checked), CPU Time, Memory Usage (checked), Memory Usage Delta, Peak Memory Usage, Page Faults, USER Objects, I/O Reads, I/O Read Bytes, Session ID, User Name (checked); and right column: Page Faults Delta, Virtual Memory Size, Paged Pool, Non-paged Pool, Base Priority, Handle Count, Thread Count, GDI Objects, I/O Writes, I/O Write Bytes, I/O Other, I/O Other Bytes, with OK and Cancel buttons]

2. Select the Virtual Memory Size check box.

   ◆ Also select the check boxes for any other information you want to see in Task Manager. Many of the items here are somewhat arcane, but you might want to look at CPU Time or Peak Memory Usage.

3. Click the OK button. Task Manager closes the Select Columns dialog box and adds the columns you chose to the Processes page.

Figure 3.8 shows the Processes page of Task Manager with the Virtual Memory Size column added and the processes sorted by that column. Notice that the two copies of Word have very heavy memory usage indeed (when you add the Mem Usage column and the VM Size column). SVCHOST.EXE also shows itself as a heavyweight, using a little over 11MB of virtual memory in addition to its 10MB of RAM.

FIGURE 3.8

If you want to see virtual memory usage, add the Virtual Memory Size (VM Size) column to the Processes page in Task Manager.

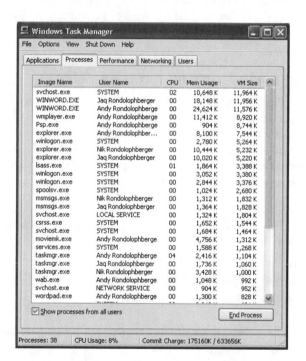

Logging Another User Off

If necessary, any Computer Administrator user can log another user off the computer.

Logging someone else off isn't usually a great idea, because while you can use Task Manager to see which processes they're running (as described in the previous section), you can't see whether they have any unsaved work in them. If you don't use passwords to log on to XP, it's much better to log on as the other user and close the programs and documents manually. Then log off (as the other user) and log back on as yourself. If you do use passwords, you'll need to know the other user's password to log on as them, which defeats the point of having passwords in the first place.

That said, you may need to log another user off if they are running enough programs to affect the computer's performance or if they have open a single-user program or a document that you need to use. If you do so, you may want to send them a message as described in the next section so that they know what's happened.

To log another user off, take the following steps:

1. Right-click the Taskbar and choose Task Manager from the context menu to display Task Manager.

2. Click the Users tab. XP displays the Users page (shown in Figure 3.5, earlier in the chapter).

3. Select the user and click the Logoff button. (Alternatively, right-click the user and choose Log Off from the context menu.) XP displays a confirmation dialog box.

4. Click the Yes button. The other user's session is toast—as is any unsaved work they had open.

Sending a Message to Another User

You can send a message to another user logged in to this computer. Because the other user can't be using the computer at the same time as you, this feature is no use for real-time communication—it's not exactly instant messaging—but it can be useful for making sure a family member or a colleague gets a message the next time they use the computer. (For example, you might ask them not to shut down the computer because you're still using it.) It's also useful for notifying another user that you've had to terminate a program that they were using.

To send a message to another user, take the following steps:

1. Right-click the Taskbar and choose Task Manager from the context menu to display Windows Task Manager.

2. Click the Users tab to display the Users page.

3. Right-click the user and choose Send Message from the context menu. XP displays the Send Message dialog box (shown in Figure 3.9).

FIGURE 3.9

Use the Send Message dialog box (left) to send a message (right) to another user logged on to this computer.

4. Enter the message title in the Message Title text box and the message in the Message text box.

   ◆ To start a new line, press Ctrl+Enter. (Pressing the Enter key on its own registers a click on the OK button, sending the message.)

◆ To type a tab, press Ctrl+Tab. (Pressing the Tab key on its own moves the focus to the next control.)

5. Click the OK button to send the message.

The next time the user logs on to XP, they receive the message as a screen pop.

Using the Windows Key

As mentioned in Chapter 1, XP provides several keyboard combinations for the Windows key, the key (or keys) with the Windows logo on the keyboard. If you're comfortable leaving your hands on the keyboard, these combinations are doubly convenient, because not only can you avoid reaching for the mouse but you can also display with a single keystroke a number of windows and dialog boxes that lie several commands deep in the XP interface.

Table 3.1 lists the Windows key combinations.

TABLE 3.1: WINDOWS KEY COMBINATIONS

WINDOWS KEY COMBINATION	WHAT IT DOES
Windows key	Toggles the display of the Start menu
Windows key+Break	Displays the System Properties dialog box
Windows key+Tab	Moves the focus to the next button in the Taskbar
Windows key+Shift+Tab	Moves the focus to the previous button in the Taskbar
Windows key+B	Moves the focus to the System Tray
Windows key+D	Displays the Desktop
Windows key+E	Opens an Explorer window showing My Computer
Windows key+F	Opens a Search Results window and activates Search Companion
Windows key+Ctrl+F	Opens a Search Results window, activates Search Companion, and starts a Search for Computer
Windows key+F1	Opens a Help and Support Center window
Windows key+M	Issues a Minimize All Windows command
Windows key+Shift+M	Issues an Undo Minimize All command
Windows key+R	Displays the Run dialog box
Windows key+U	Displays Utility Manager
Windows key+L	Locks the computer

TIP   *To add further Windows key combinations—for example, for launching programs—download the free Windows Keyboard Enhancer program from* `www.copernic.com/winkey`.

Shutting Down XP

You can shut down XP in several ways:

- ◆ By clicking the Turn Off Computer button at the bottom of the default Start menu or by choosing Start ➢ Turn Off Computer from the classic Start menu. See page 8 of the *Essential Skills* section for visual coverage of this method.
- ◆ By clicking the Turn Off Computer button on the Welcome screen, then clicking the Turn Off button on the Turn Off Computer screen.
- ◆ By choosing Shut Down ➢ Turn Off from Windows Task Manager.
- ◆ By pressing Alt+F4 with the Desktop active and then clicking the Turn Off button on the Turn Off Computer screen.

From the Turn Off Computer screen, you can also click the Stand By button to make your computer hibernate or the Restart button to restart the computer and XP. If your computer doesn't support hibernation, the Hibernate button doesn't appear on the Turn Off Computer screen. On some APM-compliant or ACPI-compliant systems, you may also be able to press the Shift key to toggle between a Standby option and a Hibernate option.

TROUBLESHOOTING: POWERING DOWN YOUR COMPUTER WHEN XP HAS CRASHED

If XP won't shut down because it has crashed, you'll need to shut it down the hard way. To do so, press the power button on the computer. On ACPI-compliant computers, you may need to hold the power button down for four seconds or more to shut the system down—short presses of the power button may have no effect.

On some computers, a short press of the power button may make XP display the Turn Off Computer screen so that you can specify whether to hibernate, turn off the computer, or restart it. Under normal circumstances, catching the power signal like this is pretty smart, helping to dissuade users from powering down the computer without exiting XP first. But if XP has crashed, you won't be able to do anything from the Turn Off Computer screen.

Up Next

This chapter has discussed how to get started with XP Home Edition. You now know how to log on and log off, navigate the Desktop and Taskbar, switch from one user to another, "lock" the computer, and (if necessary) log another user off by force. More important, you understand the implications of having two or more users logged on to the computer and using programs at the same time, and you know how to see which users are logged on and get a rough idea of which programs each is using.

The next chapter discusses how to customize your Desktop so that you can work comfortably, efficiently, and quickly.

Chapter 4

Customizing Your Desktop

THIS CHAPTER DISCUSSES HOW to get your Desktop into shape so that you can work comfortably, effectively, and enjoyably. Some of these changes are so important to working (or playing) ergonomically in XP that you should perform them right away. These include choosing the best display resolution, configuring the keyboard and mouse, and setting accessibility options (if you need them).

This chapter covers these topics first. After that, it discusses changes that you don't *need* to implement right away, but that you may well want to make before too long. These changes include choosing a screen saver, changing your Desktop background, customizing the Start menu, creating custom toolbars, choosing system sounds, and configuring the Start menu and the Taskbar.

This chapter covers the following topics:

- ◆ Configuring your display and monitor for best viewing
- ◆ Configuring the keyboard and mouse
- ◆ Choosing accessibility options
- ◆ Choosing a screen saver
- ◆ Applying themes and backgrounds
- ◆ Using Desktop web pages
- ◆ Changing the appearance of the Desktop
- ◆ Choosing system sounds
- ◆ Configuring the Start menu and Taskbar
- ◆ Using the Desktop toolbars

NOTE *Some of the topics covered in this chapter are considered "advanced" by some users and many other books. But in order to use XP most effectively, you should know about them immediately—so this book presents them now. If you find you don't need them at the moment, skip over them for the time being.*

Choosing the Best Display Resolution

First, set the best display resolution for you and your computer. If you're squinting at the screen, or if it's flickering at you, or if the display slops over the edges of the monitor, you won't be productive or happy.

Choosing the best display resolution involves three things: your eyesight, your monitor, and your graphics card. The first is up to you and your optometrist. The second and third are discussed below.

Your Monitor

As you'll know from being bombarded with computer ads, there are two widely used types of computer monitors: cathode-ray tube (CRT) monitors, which tend to be bulky and heavy but affordable, and liquid crystal display (LCD) panels, which tend to be thin and light in form but heavy on the wallet.

Most CRTs are capable of multiple resolutions. For example, most modern 15-inch monitors can handle 640×480 resolution, 800×600 resolution, and 1024×768 resolution. Most 17-inch monitors can handle these and 1280×1024 resolution as well. Most 19-inch monitors can also manage 1600×1200 resolution, and larger monitors (such as 20-inch, 21-inch, 22-inch, and 24-inch) can handle resolutions up to 2048×1536—with the right graphics card, of course.

Most LCD panels and some other monitors are designed to deliver optimal quality at only one resolution and only one refresh rate. Some LCD panels will display lesser resolutions as well as their optimum resolution, but the result is jagged and awkward to look at. A few LCD panels—usually on laptops—can display a *higher* resolution than their normal resolution. This can be useful for special effects, but it means that you can't see all of the screen at once, so you usually have to use your keyboard or mouse to scroll down and right to see the southern and eastern regions.

Table 4.1 lists all the resolutions you're likely to see on modern monitors, together with some less usual ones.

TABLE 4.1: STANDARD AND NONSTANDARD SCREEN RESOLUTIONS

RESOLUTION (PIXELS)	NAME	ABBREVIATION	COMMENTS
640×480	Video Graphics Array	VGA	Standard resolution
800×600	Super VGA	SVGA	Standard resolution
1024×480	—	—	Super-wide resolution (laptop LCDs)
1024×768	Extended Graphics Array	XGA	Standard resolution
1152×864	—	—	Standard resolution
1280×1024	—	—	Standard resolution
1400×1050	Ultra XGA	UXGA	Used mostly on laptops
1600×1024	—	—	Super-wide resolution (desktop LCDs)
1600×1200	—	—	Standard resolution
1792×1344	—	—	Standard resolution
1800×1440	—	—	Standard resolution
2048×1536	—	—	Standard resolution

Most CRTs support a variety of refresh rates, while most LCD panels support only one or two. (The *refresh rate* is the frequency with which the graphics card redraws the picture on the monitor. More details in a few pages' time.)

Your Graphics Card

The graphics card in your computer sends information to the monitor. The resolutions and refresh rates that the graphics card supports depend on the amount of video memory it contains. If you want to play games at high resolutions and fast frame rates, you need to make sure that your graphics card is powerful enough (rather than that your processor speed is fast enough).

Choosing Video Settings

To choose video settings, you use the Settings page of the Display Properties dialog box (shown in Figure 4.1): Right-click the Desktop and choose Properties from the context menu. XP displays the Display Properties dialog box. Then click the Settings tab. XP displays the Settings page.

FIGURE 4.1

On the Settings page of the Display Properties dialog box, you can specify the screen resolution and the number of colors XP uses.

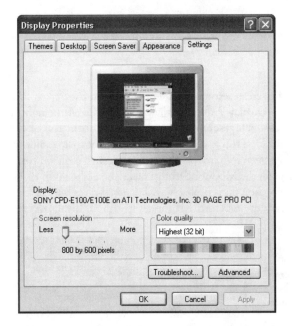

NOTE   *XP supports multiple monitors—you can use up to 10 monitors on a single computer so that you can see a larger amount of information at once. See the section "Setting Up and Using Multiple Monitors" in Chapter 14 for coverage of this feature.*

CHANGING THE SCREEN RESOLUTION

To change the amount of information displayed on the screen, you change the *screen resolution*. The screen resolution affects the number of pixels XP displays on the screen. The more pixels displayed, the more you can see—but the smaller everything on-screen appears. (*Pixel* is short for *picture element* and means one of the elements that make up the display you see on your screen.)

For example, say you're working in a word processing document. At 640×480 resolution, you might see about 500 words of average length in the document window (with some of the screen taken up by the Taskbar, the program's menu bars and toolbars, and so on). At 800×600 resolution, you might see 850 words—not twice as much, but more than one-and-a-half times as much. At 1024×768 resolution, you might see about 1600 words—almost twice as much again. (This example is a little unfair in that the menu bar, toolbars, and the Taskbar take up correspondingly more space at the lower resolution, but it does illustrate roughly what you may see in practice.) Likewise, if you were working with a large spreadsheet, you'd be able to see much more of it on-screen at once by using a higher resolution.

As you can imagine, the higher resolutions let you see more on-screen at the same time, but everything displayed is smaller. In the example with the word processing document, you might need to zoom the display so that you could read the words comfortably at the higher resolution. (You could also use a larger font size, but that changes the document itself rather than just the way it's displayed.)

WARNING   *For some unknown reason, all users of the computer must use the same Desktop resolution. The Welcome screen also uses this resolution. If some of your users see like hawks and others like field mice, try to find a compromise resolution that won't make anyone suffer unduly. Any user can change the resolution, but in doing so, they change it for all other users as well.*

To change the screen resolution, drag the slider in the Screen Resolution group box on the Settings page of the Display Properties dialog box to the left or right. The readout under the slider shows the next available resolution, and the graphic at the top of the dialog box shows an approximation of how your Desktop and a window will look at that resolution.

To apply the screen resolution you chose, click the Apply button. If you haven't used this resolution before, XP displays the Monitor Settings dialog box (shown in Figure 4.2). If you can see the Monitor Settings dialog box, all is probably well. Click the Yes button to apply the screen resolution. (If you have used this resolution before, XP applies it without displaying the Monitor Settings dialog box.)

FIGURE 4.2

If you can see this Monitor Settings dialog box clearly, the screen resolution probably works.

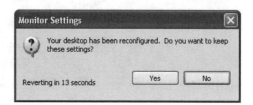

If your display becomes garbled or faded, or if you don't like what you see, either click the No button in the Monitor Settings dialog box or wait the 15 seconds until XP restores your previous video settings.

CHANGING THE NUMBER OF COLORS

You can also change the number of colors that XP uses for the display. Some LCD displays are limited in the number of colors they can display, maxing out at 65,536 colors (High Color), but most CRTs can display the full range of colors—16 million or 4 billion, depending on your graphics card.

As you'd expect, the more colors XP uses, the more lifelike, vibrant, and generally appealing the display looks. But the more colors used, the more video memory is needed on the graphics card, and the slower performance tends to be.

For performance' sake, it's not a good idea to ratchet the colors up as far as they can go if you're spending most of your time working with documents, spreadsheets, and e-mail, which all look more or less as good in 256 colors as they do at True Color. 256 colors tend to be too few for sustained web browsing, as more graphical pages tend to suffer, so you may find you prefer High Color or 24-bit True Color if you spend a lot of time on the Web. Even if you are working with files that need True Color—for example, if you're retouching digital photographs—you'll get better performance at 24-bit True Color than at 32-bit True Color, though in theory 32-bit True Color offers a better representation of every color.

By default, the XP installation routine sets your system to use the highest color quality that your monitor and graphics card support at a reasonable refresh rate. (If you upgrade your installation of Windows, or if you use the Files and Settings Transfer Wizard to transfer your old settings, you should end up with the same color quality as you were using before.) If your graphics performance isn't satisfactory, use the Color Quality drop-down list on the Settings page of the Display Properties dialog box to specify a lower color quality. That should improve graphics performance.

Color settings tend to use confusing terms: either number of colors (from 16 colors up to 16 million or more), number of color bits (16-bit color, 24-bit color), or terms describing the number of colors used (High Color, True Color). Table 4.2 shows you what the terms mean.

TABLE 4.2: NUMBER OF COLORS, COLOR BITS, AND DESCRIPTIVE TERMS

NUMBER OF COLORS	COLOR BITS	DESCRIPTIVE TERM
16	4-bit	—
256	8-bit	—
65,536	16-bit	High Color
16,777,216	24-bit	True Color (24-bit)
4,294,967,296	32-bit	True Color (32-bit)

EXPERT KNOWLEDGE: HOW MUCH VIDEO MEMORY DO YOU NEED?

The number of colors and resolution your graphics card can display depends on the amount of memory it contains. Basically, the more memory the graphics card has, the higher the resolution and the higher the number of colors it should be able to display—up to a point.

This is true only up to a point because there's a limit to the number of colors used in conventional computing (4 billion colors, 32-bit color) and to the resolution that off-the-shelf monitors support (2048×1536 resolution is about the maximum widely used resolution).

In theory, calculating how much video memory you need is straightforward. To get the amount of video memory, you multiply the number of color bits per pixel by the number of pixels on the screen, then divide the result by 8 to get the number of bytes. For example, say you want 24-bit color at 800×600 resolution.

Continued on next page

EXPERT KNOWLEDGE: HOW MUCH VIDEO MEMORY DO YOU NEED? *(continued)*

Okay: 800×600 means 480,000 pixels on the screen. Multiplying 480,000×24 gives 11,520,000 bits. Divide that by 8 and you get 1,440,000 bytes, or a little under 1.4MB of video memory. Given that normal amounts of video memory for current video cards are 8MB, 16MB, 32MB, 64MB, and 128MB, and that older cards have 256KB, 512KB, 1MB, 2MB, and 4MB sizes as well, you'd need a 2MB video card or better to display 24-bit color at 800×600 resolution.

Table 4.3 (which appears after this sidebar) shows the effective amount of memory required to display the color depths at the most widely used resolutions. In this table, the amounts of memory are rounded up to the nearest standard amount of video memory. For example, 1280×1024 resolution at 256 colors requires around 1.25MB of memory—but the nearest larger standard video size is 2MB, so the table lists that.

That calculation seems easy enough, doesn't it? But it's no longer that simple. Here's the problem: In 2002, entry-level video cards come with 16MB or 32MB of video memory. Serious video cards come with 64MB. Gear-head video cards have 128MB—and 256MB cards are lurking around the corner.

Some 8MB cards can manage 1600×1200 resolution, just as the table says they should be able to—but many of them can't. Similarly, to get those really high resolutions—1800×1440 and 2048×1536—you typically need a graphics card with 64MB RAM, not one with the 16MB that the calculation gives you.

What's going on here?

Basically, only some of the RAM on the high-end graphics card is dedicated to creating the bitmap that's shunted off to be displayed on your monitor. The rest of the RAM is trying to display multiple images more quickly (for example, when you're watching a video or playing Quake) and smooth out unevennesses in the transfer of information from one component to another. The results of these endeavors are mostly good, but it means that in order to find out how much memory you need on a graphics card to support a certain resolution and color depth, you need to consult the box (or preferably, the specifications) for each graphics card you're considering rather than just performing the above calculation.

More positively, if you use only a modest resolution (say, 1024×768) on your monitor, or if you have a graphics card with 32MB of RAM or more, you seldom need to worry about video memory, because you've probably got enough already.

TABLE 4.3: VIDEO MEMORY REQUIRED TO DISPLAY COLORS AND RESOLUTIONS

COLORS	BITS	640×480	800×600	1024×768	1152×864	1280×1024	1600×1200	1800×1440	2048×1536
16	4	256KB	256KB	512KB	512KB	1MB	1MB	2MB	2MB
256	8	512KB	512KB	1MB	1MB	2MB	2MB	4MB	4MB
65,536	16	1MB	1MB	2MB	2MB	4MB	4MB	8MB	8MB
16,777,216	24	1MB	2MB	4MB	4MB	4MB	8MB	8MB	16MB
4,294,967,296	32	2MB	2MB	4MB	4MB	8MB	8MB	16MB	16MB

CHANGING THE REFRESH RATE

If your screen flickers noticeably, try adjusting the *refresh rate*—the number of times per second that the video card sends a full screen of information to the monitor. The refresh rate is measured in hertz (Hz)—cycles per second, not the car-rental agency.

NOTE *Technically, this is the* vertical *refresh rate, as opposed to the horizontal refresh rate. Just about the only time you need to worry about the horizontal refresh rate of your monitor is when you're setting an X Windows configuration in Linux. So most of the time people just say "refresh rate" without specifying the dimension involved.*

Flicker is produced by the video card redrawing the image on the monitor slowly enough for you to be able to notice. As a result, your eyes have to work a bit harder to decode what they're seeing, which tends to lead to eye strain and headaches, particularly if you don't take those ergonomically recommended breaks from staring at the screen.

Flicker shows more on large monitors than small monitors. This is not just because there's more of the screen to look at, but also because most people notice flicker more out of the corner of their eye than straight on, and you see more of a larger screen in your peripheral vision.

Some people are much more sensitive to flicker than others. At 60Hz—60 cycles per second—most people find flicker very noticeable on CRT monitors. At 70Hz, many people don't see it. By 75Hz, things look good to most people. At 85Hz, few people can detect flicker. Above that, you're entering the hypochondriac zone—though if your hardware supports a very high refresh rate, there's no reason why you shouldn't use it.

LCD screens flicker far less than CRTs, so they don't need such high refresh rates. Many LCD screens are designed for optimal performance at a refresh rate of 60Hz, and produce a beautifully stable picture at this rate, which would produce very pronounced flicker on a CRT. Other LCDs support refresh rates of 72Hz or 75Hz. Most LCDs don't support refresh rates faster than 75Hz.

Which refresh rates are available to you depends on your graphics card and your monitor. As you'd imagine, both the card and the monitor need to support a refresh rate for you to be able to use it.

To set the refresh rate, take the following steps:

1. Click the Advanced button on the Settings page of the Display Properties dialog box. XP displays the Monitor and Graphics Card dialog box.
2. Click the Monitor tab. XP displays the Monitor page (shown in Figure 4.3).
3. In the Screen Refresh Rate drop-down list, choose one of the settings. If you've configured XP correctly for your hardware, you should be safe choosing the fastest refresh rate listed.
4. Click the Apply button. If you haven't used this refresh rate before, XP displays a Monitor Settings dialog box asking you whether you want to keep the settings. (If you have used this refresh rate, XP simply applies the settings.)
5. If you click the Yes button, XP keeps the settings. If you click the No button, or if you wait 15 seconds, XP reapplies your previous settings.

As you can see in Figure 4.3, the Monitor Settings group box on the Monitor page also contains the Hide Modes That This Monitor Cannot Display check box, which is selected by default. You *can* clear this check box to force XP to list in the Screen Refresh Rate drop-down list refresh rates that XP thinks your monitor doesn't support, and you *can* apply these refresh rates—but doing so is usually a really bad idea, because you can permanently damage a monitor by setting a refresh rate higher than it supports. The only reason to try this is if you are unable (for whatever reason) to get XP to recognize your monitor correctly and you need to trick XP into applying a refresh rate that you know from the monitor's documentation is supported.

FIGURE 4.3

Set the refresh rate on the Monitor page of the Monitor and Graphics Card dialog box.

NOTE *If your screen settings still aren't satisfactory, you may need to take further steps, such as changing hardware acceleration, changing the video driver, or changing XP's misperception of which monitor you're using. Turn to Chapter 14 for details on how to take these (and other) actions.*

Adjusting Your Monitor if Necessary

Once you've settled on a display resolution, color depth, and frequency, adjust your monitor to maximize the image area so that you're seeing the whole image as large as possible. (It's amazing how many people leave an inchwide band of unused space at each edge of the monitor and then complain that they have to peer closely at the image.)

Monitor controls vary, but almost all monitors let you adjust the height, width, and vertical and horizontal positions of the image. Open a program and maximize its window so that you can clearly see where the edges of the screen are. Then use the monitor controls to make your XP Desktop at your chosen resolution fill the display area of your monitor.

Configuring the Keyboard and Mouse

Your next order of business should be to configure the keyboard and mouse (or other pointing device; for simplicity, this section uses the word *mouse*). Both these input devices are vital to getting information into and out of your computer, and each can be a source of great discomfort if you let it.

TIP   If configuring the keyboard and mouse don't give you the control you need, try the accessibility options. The section "Choosing Accessibility Options," later in this chapter, discusses these options.

Configuring the Keyboard

XP offers three keyboard configuration options:

- The *repeat delay* (the length of time that XP waits before repeating a key when you hold it down)
- The *repeat rate* (the speed with which a key repeats its character once the repeat delay is over)
- The rate at which the cursor blinks

To configure your keyboard, follow these steps:

1. Choose Start ➣ Control Panel. XP displays Control Panel.
2. Click the Printers and Other Hardware link. XP displays the Printers and Other Hardware screen.
3. Click the Keyboard link. XP displays the Keyboard Properties dialog box.
4. On the Speed page (shown in Figure 4.4) of the Keyboard Properties dialog box, choose settings by adjusting the Repeat Delay slider, the Repeat Rate slider, and the Cursor Blink Rate slider. Use the Click Here and Hold Down a Key to Test Repeat Rate text box for testing your repeat rate.

FIGURE 4.4

You can adjust the repeat rate, repeat delay, and the cursor blink rate of your keyboard on the Speed page of the Keyboard Properties dialog box.

5. Click the OK button. XP closes the Keyboard Properties dialog box.

NOTE   *The Hardware page of the Keyboard Properties dialog box lets you see which type of keyboard XP thinks you're using. From here, you can access the Properties dialog box for this type of keyboard, so that you can change the driver that it's using.*

Configuring the Mouse

To configure your mouse, follow these steps:

1. Choose Start ➢ Control Panel. XP displays Control Panel.
2. Click the Printers and Other Hardware link. XP displays the Printers and Other Hardware screen.
3. Click the Mouse link. XP displays the Mouse Properties dialog box.

NOTE   *The Mouse Properties dialog box in these figures has the standard controls. If your mouse has custom software, you may see other pages of options in the Mouse Properties dialog box.*

4. The Buttons page (shown in Figure 4.5) offers these options:

    Switch Primary and Secondary Buttons check box   Select this check box if you want to swap the functions of the primary and secondary mouse buttons. This setting is most useful for changing a mouse from right-hand configuration to left-hand configuration.

    Double-Click Speed slider   Drag this slider toward its Fast end or its Slow end to set the double-click speed of your mouse. Double-click in the Test Area box to see if XP is registering your double-clicks properly. When the area registers a double-click, the folder opens; when it registers another, the folder closes.

    Turn on ClickLock check box   Select this check box to turn on the ClickLock feature, which lets you drag without holding down the mouse button all the time. (You click the mouse button again to release the locked item after dragging it.) ClickLock can be useful if you get the hang of it, but it can be an annoyance if you find yourself setting the lock unintentionally when clicking. If you turn ClickLock on, click the Settings button and use the resulting Settings for ClickLock dialog box to tune the lock setting.

5. If you want to use different pointers for your mouse, click the Pointers tab. XP displays the Pointers page (shown on the left in Figure 4.6). This page offers a variety of mouse pointer schemes, some of them fun (for example, the Dinosaur scheme) and others more useful (such as the various large, extra large, and inverted schemes, which can make the mouse pointers much easier to see).

    ◆ In the Scheme drop-down list, select the scheme you want to use.

    ◆ To customize the scheme, select a pointer in the Customize list box. Then click the Browse button, use the resulting Browse dialog box to specify the pointer you want to use instead, and click the Open button. (XP displays the \Windows\Cursors\ folder in the Browse dialog box, but you can navigate to other folders as necessary.) You can also click the Use Default button to use the standard Windows pointer in place of the selected pointer.

FIGURE 4.5

Choose button options on the Buttons page of the Mouse Properties dialog box.

FIGURE 4.6

Choose a pointer scheme—or create a custom pointer scheme—on the Pointers page (left) of the Mouse Properties dialog box. Change the speed and behavior of the mouse on the Pointer Options page (right).

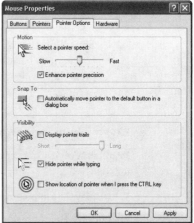

◆ To turn off pointer shadows, clear the Enable Pointer Shadow check box. (It's selected by default.)

◆ To save your customized scheme, click the Save As button, enter the name for the scheme in the Save Scheme dialog box, and click the OK button. Custom pointer schemes are stored in the Registry (in the HKEY_CURRENT_USER key) and are not available to other users.

6. Click the Pointer Options tab to display the Pointer Options page (shown on the right in Figure 4.6). This page offers the following options:

Motion group box   Drag the slider toward its Slow end or its Fast end to adjust the speed at which the pointer moves. By default, the Enhance Pointer Precision check box is selected. This feature makes the mouse pointer decelerate more quickly on-screen as you stop moving the mouse. If you want to try more gradual deceleration, clear this check box.

NOTE   *Unlike in most dialog boxes, XP applies the settings on the Pointer Options page of the Mouse Properties dialog box immediately, so you can see them in action without needing to click the Apply button.*

Automatically Move Pointer to the Default Button in a Dialog Box check box   Select this check box if you want XP to automatically position the mouse pointer over the default button in each dialog box you display. This automatic movement can save you time, but it can also be confusing, because once a dialog box is displayed, the mouse pointer is no longer where you left it.

Display Pointer Trails check box and slider   Select this check box if you want the mouse pointer to display a contrasting trail of phantom pointers when you move it. This option is most useful for dual-scan LCD screens, on which it can be hard to discern the mouse pointer. If you turn this feature on, adjust the slider to give yourself the length of pointer trails that suits you.

Hide Pointer while Typing check box   Select this check box if you want XP to hide the mouse pointer when you're typing. (In some programs, XP hides the pointer when you're typing even if this check box isn't selected.)

Show Location of Pointer When I Press the Ctrl Key check box   Select this check box if you want to be able to make XP identify the mouse key by zooming in a circle on it when you press the Ctrl key. This feature is useful for LCD screens on which the mouse pointer tends to disappear.

EXPERT KNOWLEDGE: CHOOSING ADVANCED SETTINGS FOR YOUR MOUSE

XP offers several advanced settings for configuring your mouse. To access these settings, take the following steps:

1. Display the Mouse Properties dialog box as discussed in the previous section.

2. Click the Hardware tab. XP displays the Hardware page.

3. Click the Properties button. XP displays the *Mouse Type* Mouse Properties dialog box. For example, the illustration below shows the Mouse Properties dialog box for a PS/2 Compatible mouse.

4. Click the Advanced Settings tab. XP displays the Advanced Settings page (shown in the illustration).

Continued on next page

5. Choose advanced settings for the mouse:

> **Sample Rate text box**   The value in this text box specifies how often XP checks the position of the mouse. To increase mouse sensitivity, increase this value; to decrease sensitivity, decrease the value. Like humans, different mouses vary in sensitivity. Setting a higher sample rate than your mouse supports won't net you any improvement.

> **Wheel Detection drop-down list**   This drop-down list controls whether XP checks your mouse for a mouse wheel (or similar rotating button for scrolling). Select the Detection Disabled item if you don't want to use a mouse wheel. Select the Assume Wheel Is Present item if you don't want XP to check whether the mouse has a wheel. Select the Look for Wheel item if you want XP to determine whether the mouse has a wheel. If selecting the Look for Wheel item disables a mouse that has a wheel, Microsoft suggests selecting the Assume Wheel Is Present item instead.

> **Input Buffer Length text box**   The value in this text box specifies the number of packets of information to store in the input buffer for your mouse's location. Increase this number if your mouse is behaving erratically.

> **Fast Initialization check box**   This check box controls whether XP uses fast initialization for the mouse. *Fast initialization* reduces XP's startup time, but it can make the mouse behave erratically—for example, the mouse pointer may move itself, or the mouse may register clicks you haven't generated. If your mouse does this, clear this check box.

6. Click the OK button. XP closes the Mouse Properties dialog box and returns you to the Hardware page of the Mouse Properties dialog box.

Configuring Your Mouse Further with the Tweak UI PowerToy

The settings described in the previous section let you improve your mouse's behavior considerably—but there are several other parameters that you may want to affect that XP doesn't let you get at directly. If you know what you're doing, you can adjust these by editing the Registry (as described in Chapter 12)—but if you download the Tweak UI PowerToy from the Microsoft Windows XP Downloads site (`www.microsoft.com/windowsxp/home/downloads/powertoys.asp`), you can adjust them much more easily.

Tweak UI's Mouse pages let you adjust settings including the following:

◆ How fast XP displays menus after you've summoned them with the mouse—for example, how quickly the Start menu displays a submenu when you move the mouse pointer over the control for the submenu.

◆ The hover sensitivity and hover time of the mouse—how quickly XP decides that you're hovering the mouse over an item that responds to hovering (for example, by displaying a pop-up of information).

◆ Whether the mouse wheel scrolls documents, and if so, by how much at a time.

◆ Whether the mouse behaves like a mouse in X-Windows (the window server for Unix/Linux graphical interfaces) and activates a window by moving over it rather than by clicking in it as you normally would in Windows.

Choosing Accessibility Options

For users with disabilities, XP offers a good selection of accessibility options.

The easiest way to get started with the accessibility options is to run the Accessibility Wizard (Start ➢ All Programs ➢ Accessories ➢ Accessibility ➢ Accessibility Wizard). The Accessibility Wizard walks you through the process of configuring most of these options by asking questions about which accessibility areas you need help with and choosing options accordingly.

To adjust these options, you can run the Accessibility Wizard again. Alternatively, you can use the Accessibility Options dialog box, as discussed in the next section. To display the Accessibility Options dialog box, choose Start ➢ Control Panel, click the Accessibility Options link to access the Accessibility Options screen, and then click the Accessibility Options link (yes, another one).

Keyboard Accessibility Options

This section discusses the options that XP provides to make the keyboard more accessible: keyboard accessibility options, On-Screen Keyboard, and the option of attaching a SerialKey device.

STICKYKEYS, FILTERKEYS, TOGGLEKEYS, AND EXTRA KEYBOARD HELP

XP offers the following keyboard accessibility options on the Keyboard page of the Accessibility Options dialog box (shown in Figure 4.7):

StickyKeys This feature lets you enter keyboard combinations involving the Shift, Ctrl, or Alt keys one key at a time rather than needing to hold down the modifier key while you press subsequent keys.

FilterKeys   This feature lets you tell XP to ignore either repeated keystrokes (such as those caused by holding down a key for longer than a single keypress) or quick keystrokes (such as those caused by accidentally blipping a key while trying to press another key).

ToggleKeys   This feature makes XP sound a tone when you press the Caps Lock key, the Num Lock key, or the Scroll Lock key.

Show Extra Keyboard Help in Programs check box   This feature makes programs show any extra help they contain about using the keyboard.

FIGURE 4.7

The Keyboard page of the Accessibility Options dialog box offers StickyKeys, FilterKeys, Toggle-Keys, and extra keyboard help.

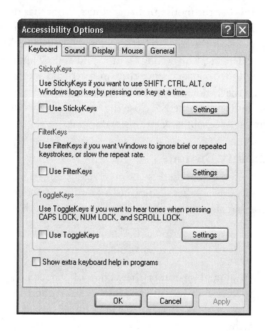

ON-SCREEN KEYBOARD

On-Screen Keyboard displays a keyboard in a window on-screen so that you can enter keyboard commands with a mouse or other pointing device. To start On-Screen Keyboard, choose Start ➢ All Programs ➢ Accessories ➢ Accessibility ➢ On-Screen Keyboard.

Key (no pun intended) options for On-Screen Keyboard include the following:

◆ To make the keyboard click when you press a key, choose Settings ➢ Use Click Sound. (The click sound makes it easier to notice when you've misclicked or clicked twice.)

◆ To make the keyboard enter a key when you hover the pointer over it (so that you don't need to click), choose Settings ➢ Typing Mode. In the resulting Typing Mode dialog box, select the Hover to Select option button and specify the reaction time in the Minimum Time to Hover text box. Click the OK button.

◆ To display a standard keyboard rather than an enhanced keyboard, or to use a block layout rather than the regular offset layout, or to use a 102-key or 106-key keyboard instead of a 101-key keyboard, choose the appropriate command from the Keyboard menu.

ATTACHING A SERIALKEY DEVICE

If you can't (or won't) use a standard keyboard, you can attach a SerialKey device or other augmentative communication device to your computer instead. To use the SerialKey device, select the Use Serial Keys check box on the General page of the Accessibility Options dialog box. Then click the Settings button. XP displays the Settings for SerialKeys dialog box. Specify the serial port and baud rate to use, then click the OK button.

Mouse Accessibility Options

Apart from the control over the mouse that the Mouse Properties dialog box offers, XP provides a feature called MouseKeys that lets you control the mouse pointer by using your keyboard's numeric keys.

To use MouseKeys, select the Use MouseKeys check box on the Mouse page of the Accessibility Options dialog box. Then click the Settings button and choose appropriate settings in the Settings for MouseKeys dialog box. You can change the top speed and acceleration of the mouse pointer, and specify whether to use the Ctrl key to speed up the pointer's movement and the Shift key to slow it down. Click the OK button to make XP close the Settings for MouseKeys dialog box, and then click the Apply button in the Accessibility Options dialog box.

Display Accessibility Options

In addition to the assorted color schemes and font sizes that you can set in the Display Properties dialog box, XP provides a Magnifier feature and a High Contrast display option for improving display accessibility. You can also change the blink rate and the width of the cursor so that it's easier to see.

MAGNIFIER

Magnifier displays a magnified version of the section of the screen around the mouse pointer, the keyboard focus, or the section of text you're editing. This section appears in a panel at the top of the screen. You can resize this panel so that it takes up as much as half of the screen.

Start Magnifier by choosing Start ➤ All Programs ➤ Accessories ➤ Accessibility ➤ Magnifier, then choose settings in the Magnifier Settings window. You can set a magnification level from 1 (normal size) to 9; specify which items to track (the mouse cursor, the keyboard focus, and text editing); choose to invert the colors displayed for the magnified panel; choose to start Magnifier minimized; and choose whether to show Magnifier. Minimize the Magnifier Settings window to get it out of your way.

To stop using Magnifier, click the Exit button in the Magnifier Settings window.

TIP If Magnifier doesn't give you the flexibility you need, check the list of magnification utilities for Windows XP at www.microsoft.com/enable. *If you could just use some help in seeing small items on the Taskbar but can manage the rest of the screen fine, try the Taskbar Magnifier PowerToy, which you can download from the Microsoft Windows XP Downloads site (*www.microsoft.com/windowsxp/home/downloads/powertoys.asp*). Once you've installed this PowerToy, you can toggle it on and off by right-clicking the Taskbar and choosing Toolbars ➤ Taskbar Magnifier from the context menu.*

HIGH CONTRAST

The High Contrast display option makes XP use fonts and colors that are designed to be easy to read (as opposed to, say, looking good). To use this option, select the Use High Contrast check box on the Display page of the Accessibility Options dialog box (shown in Figure 4.8). Then click the Settings button to display the Settings for High Contrast dialog box and select the shortcut to use for toggling high contrast on and off and the color scheme to use.

FIGURE 4.8

On the Display page of the Accessibility Options dialog box, you can apply a high-contrast color scheme to XP and change the blink rate and width of the cursor to make it more visible.

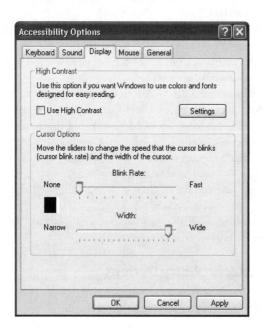

CHANGING THE BLINK RATE AND CURSOR WIDTH

If you find the normal XP cursor hard to see, use the Width slider in the Cursor Options group box on the Display page of the Accessibility Options dialog box to adjust the cursor's width and the Blink Rate slider to change its blink rate.

Sound Accessibility Options

XP offers sound accessibility options that fall into two categories: visual warnings for cues normally indicated by sound, for those with hearing impairments; and reading on-screen text aloud, for those with vision impairments.

VISUAL WARNINGS: SOUNDSENTRY AND SHOWSOUNDS

The SoundSentry option displays visual warnings to indicate when XP makes a sound. To use SoundSentry, select the Use SoundSentry check box on the Sound page of the Accessibility Options dialog box. Click the Settings button to display the Settings for SoundSentry dialog box. Choose the visual warning you want: flashing the active caption bar, flashing the active window, or flashing the Desktop.

The ShowSounds option causes programs to display captions when they make sounds or convey information via spoken words. To use ShowSounds, select the Use ShowSounds check box on the Sound page of the Accessibility Options dialog box.

READING ALOUD: NARRATOR

The Narrator program can read aloud a variety of things from the screen: menu commands, dialog box controls, and characters you type. The voice is synthesized, and its phrasing and cadence make it hard to understand. It's usable in a pinch, but for sustained use you may want to check www.microsoft .com/enable for more powerful alternatives.

Start Narrator by choosing Start ➢ All Programs ➢ Accessories ➢ Accessibility ➢ Narrator. In the Narrator window, select the check boxes for the items you want Narrator to read. Three of the options—Read Typed Characters, Move Mouse Pointer to the Active Item, and Start Narrator Minimized—are self-explanatory. The Announce Events on Screen check box controls whether Narrator announces the program window you're working in and any dialog box on-screen and the controls it contains (or the control you're working with).

To adjust the voice used and the pitch, speed, and volume, click the Voice button and use the options in the Voice Settings dialog box.

To stop using Narrator, select the Exit button in the Narrator window and choose the Yes button in the Exit Narrator dialog box that tries to stop you.

Setting General Accessibility Options

The General page of the Accessibility Options dialog box contains additional controls for specifying accessibility options:

Automatic Reset group box   To turn off accessibility features automatically after a time, select the Use the Turn Off Accessibility Features after Idle for *NN* Minutes check box and specify the period of time in the text box.

Notification group box   Leave the Give Warning Message when Turning a Feature Off check box and the Make a Sound when Turning a Feature On or Off check box selected (as they are by default) if you want XP to warn you when turning a feature off or on.

SerialKey Devices group box   Use these controls (as discussed earlier in this chapter) to set up SerialKey devices.

Administrative Options group box   Select the Apply All Settings to Logon Desktop check box if you want to use the accessibility settings set in the Accessibility Options dialog box each time the current user logs in. Select the Apply All Settings to Defaults for New Users check box if you want to apply these settings to each new user created on this computer. (Normally, it's best to apply the accessibility settings only when a user specifically needs them.)

Using Utility Manager to Start Magnifier, Narrator, and On-Screen Keyboard Automatically

To specify when XP runs Magnifier, Narrator, and On-Screen Keyboard, use Utility Manager (shown in Figure 4.9). Press Windows key+U to start Utility Manager. In the list box, select the entry for Magnifier, Narrator, or On-Screen Keyboard. Then select the Start Automatically when I Log In check box, the Start Automatically when I Lock My Desktop check box (if it's available), and/or the Start Automatically when Utility Manager Starts check box as appropriate. (You can also start and stop the selected utility by using the Start button and Stop button.)

FIGURE 4.9

Use Utility Manager to specify when to run Magnifier, Narrator, and On-Screen Keyboard.

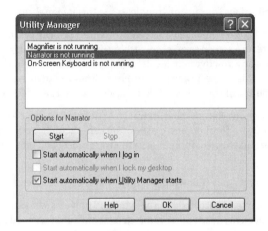

The changes discussed so far in this chapter—display and monitor settings, keyboard and mouse settings, and accessibility settings—are the most vital changes to make. The next changes are less crucial, but can make XP easier to look at and easier to use.

Choosing a Screen Saver

A *screen saver* is a program that blanks out your monitor or displays a moving pattern over it when you haven't used the keyboard or mouse for a specified period of time. XP comes with a variety of screen savers built in. You can also buy commercial screen savers or download them for free from philanthropists, egomaniacs, and advertisers.

Screen savers used to be important in the 1970s and 1980s, because they would save your screen—literally. In those days, text-based displays would burn into the phosphors of the monitor, creating a ghost image that then overlaid whatever else was being displayed. These days, most monitors aren't susceptible to phosphor burn-in, and in any case, graphical displays pose fewer problems with burn-in than text-based displays.

Nowadays, there are only two reasons to use a screen saver:

◆ First, to hide your work (or play) from prying eyes when you've left your computer idle for more than a certain length of time. When you use a screen saver to hide your work, apply a password to the screen saver so that only you can turn off the screen saver.

◆ Second, to have your monitor display something pretty or intriguing to amuse you when you're not actively using the computer. Most screen savers, true to their phosphor-protecting heritage, display moving patterns that can be entertaining to look at, but some display trivia, quizzes, or educational flashcards. XP includes a screen saver called My Pictures Slideshow that displays the pictures in a designated folder one by one. This screen saver seems destined to become a living-room favorite, as it lets you turn the unused computer into a slide show.

TROUBLESHOOTING: AVOID SCREEN SAVERS IF POSSIBLE

Screen savers are notorious for causing trouble, some through malice and some through incompetence.

On the malice front: Free, downloadable screen savers are a favorite tool of the writers of viruses and malware. When they create a screen saver of something diverting (say, a dog relieving itself on the steps of a government office) or an attractive female celebrity (say, Cox Arquette, Kournikova, or Klum), the writer can be almost certain of achieving widespread distribution. They can then use the screen saver as a Trojan horse to get a virus onto the downloader's system, and the virus is free to execute at a time of the writer's choosing.

On the incompetence front: Because they kick in and interrupt normal operations on the computer, screen savers can cause software conflicts and crashes. You can—actually, make that *should be able to*—assume that the screen savers that Microsoft supplies with XP are robust and safe, but *any* screen saver might destabilize your system.

To avoid security threats, never download a third-party screen saver, however attractive it may seem.

If your XP Home computer is part of a home network and provides services such as file sharing, printer sharing, or Internet connectivity to the other computers, there's another good reason not to use a screen saver: Many screen savers give the processor quite a workout in order to produce their intricate patterns. This not only wastes energy but also prevents the computer from responding promptly to requests for services. (You can also configure many screen savers to use less energy by selecting their lowest settings, but doing so tends to make them so much less entertaining that it's better not to use them in the first place.)

One exception worth mentioning is screen savers used to implement distributed-computing projects, such as SETI@home, the Search for Extraterrestrial Intelligence at Home project (setiathome.ssl.berkeley.edu). Such projects actively grab your available processor cycles (so don't run them on a computer providing services) and use them to compute part of a much greater whole.

Even worse, having a vigorous screen saver kick in can ruin a CD or DVD burn if the recorder doesn't have protective features. So if you burn CDs or DVDs and you feel you *must* use a screen saver, configure the screen saver with a long enough delay that any burn you leave running will be long finished before the screen saver starts.

To apply a screen saver, follow these steps:

1. Right-click the Desktop and choose Properties from the context menu. XP displays the Display Properties dialog box.
2. Click the Screen Saver tab. XP displays the Screen Saver page (shown on the left in Figure 4.10).
3. In the Screen Saver drop-down list, select the screen saver to use.
   ◆ To see how a screen saver looks full screen, click the Preview button. XP displays the screen saver in all its glory. Move the mouse or press any key on the keyboard to stop the preview.

FIGURE 4.10

Use the Screen Saver page of the Display Properties dialog box to configure a screen saver. If the screen saver has options, choose them in the resulting Options dialog box, Settings dialog box, or Setup dialog box.

4. To choose settings for the screen saver, click the Settings button and work in the resulting Settings dialog box.

◆ Which settings are available depends on the type of screen saver you chose. Some screen savers have no settings; others have a dozen or more.

◆ The right screen in Figure 4.10 shows the My Pictures Screen Saver Options dialog box, which offers a variety of settings for customizing the slide show, including the following: how frequently the pictures should change, how much of the screen the pictures should occupy, which pictures to use, and whether to use transition effects between pictures. (Tip: Turn off the transition effects unless you're a fan of overdone PowerPoint presentations.)

◆ Use the Preview button again after choosing settings to see if the settings you chose meet your liking.

5. In the Wait text box, enter the number of minutes of inactivity that you want before the screen saver kicks in.

6. If your computer is using the Welcome screen, and you want XP to display the Welcome screen when a user reactivates the computer after the screen saver has been running, select the On Resume, Display Welcome Screen check box. If you're not using the Welcome screen, XP offers a different option: To protect the screen saver with your logon password, select the On Resume, Password Protect check box.

7. Click the Apply button. XP applies your screen saver preferences.

NOTE *From the Screen Saver page of the Display Properties dialog box, you can click the Power button in the Monitor Power group box to display the Power Options Properties dialog box. Power management is an involved topic and is discussed in Chapter 14.*

Applying a Theme

A *theme* is a coordinated look for various different aspects of the XP screen: the Desktop background, colors, font styles and sizes, window sizes, sound events, mouse pointers, icons, and even the screen saver. By applying a different theme, you can change the way XP looks.

To apply a theme, take the following steps:

1. Right-click the Desktop and choose Properties from the context menu. XP displays the Display Properties dialog box with the Themes page (shown on the left in Figure 4.11) foremost.

2. In the Theme drop-down list, select the theme to apply. Watch the Sample box to see how the different themes look.

   ◆ To select a theme that doesn't appear in the Theme drop-down list, select the Browse item. XP displays the Open Theme dialog box. Navigate to and select the file containing the theme, then click the Open button.

3. Click the Apply button. XP applies the theme.

FIGURE 4.11

Use the Themes page of the Display Properties dialog box to apply themes to XP. Use the Desktop page to select a background picture or color for your Desktop.

 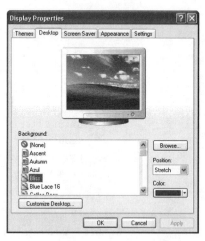

TIP   To create a custom theme, select a theme to start with, and modify it to suit your taste. Then use the Save As button on the Themes page of the Display Properties dialog box, and the resulting Save As dialog box, to save the theme in your My Documents folder. XP then makes the theme available in the Theme drop-down list, from which you can apply it as you would any other theme.

TROUBLESHOOTING: CLASSIC THEMES DON'T DISPLAY CORRECTLY

XP can use either themes specifically designed for XP or themes designed for earlier versions of Windows, such as Windows 98 or Windows Me. Themes designed for XP include a theme file (with the extension .THEME) that's linked to a visual style file (with the extension .MSSTYLE). The visual style file contains visual display elements specific to XP and information that lets XP adapt the theme file to fit the ways in which XP's interface differs from that of earlier versions of Windows.

Continued on next page

TROUBLESHOOTING: CLASSIC THEMES DON'T DISPLAY CORRECTLY *(continued)*

Themes designed for earlier versions of Windows—"classic" themes, as Microsoft calls them—have a theme file (again, with the extension .THEME) but not the visual style file. When you apply a classic theme to XP, the theme doesn't appear correctly, because XP doesn't have the information required to make the theme fit its interface. For example, the large arrow that normally appears on the More Programs button may be replaced by a small arrow, because the classic theme doesn't include a replacement arrow, leaving XP to use a default backup. And in most cases the sounds in older themes won't play.

Changing the Background

You can change the background pattern or image on your Desktop by using the Desktop page of the Display Properties dialog box (shown on the right in Figure 4.11). If you like the default background, there's no obligation to change it—though there is a good reason to do so.

Generally speaking, your computer's graphics performance suffers when you load up a complex picture as a background for your Desktop (though if your graphics card has plenty of memory to spare, you may not notice the hit). The Bliss graphic that's the default background for the XP Home theme is large (about 1.4MB), whereas most of the other pictures are much smaller. For example, the Vortec Space graphic is only about 60K—so if your graphics card seems to be overcome with Bliss as the background, try applying a different background and see if performance improves.

If you do want to change the background pattern or image, select the item in the Background list. To use an image that's not listed, click the Browse button and use the resulting Browse dialog box to navigate to and select the file.

NOTE *By default, XP lists any BMP, JPG, and GIF files in the Windows folder (whatever this folder is called), the* \Web\ *folder in the Windows folder, the* \Wallpaper\ *folder in the* \Web\ *folder, and your* \My Pictures\ *folder and its subfolders.*

If the image you choose is smaller than the screen, you can select one of the choices in the Position drop-down list—Center, Tile, or Stretch—to specify whether to center it, tile it across the screen, or stretch it to fill the screen. If you choose the Center option, or if you choose to have no background image (by selecting the None item), you can change the color by selecting the color you want in the Color drop-down list.

If the image you want to use is a picture from a high-resolution digital camera, it may be *bigger* than the screen. In this case, the Tile option isn't much use. The Center option centers the center of the picture on the screen, so you'll see only part of it. And the Stretch option shrinks the picture to fit the screen.

If the image doesn't have the same proportions as the screen, the Stretch command distorts the image. If you want to have a full-screen picture without distortion, open the image in a graphics program (for example, Paint), crop it to the right proportions, and save the cropped version under a different name for use on your Desktop.

Changing Desktop Items and Desktop Web Pages

As you know, XP displays some items on your Desktop by default, such as the Recycle Bin. You can't get rid of these by conventional means such as deleting them. But you can remove them and, if you wish, add other items by using the Desktop Items dialog box. You can also add live content to your Desktop by using Desktop web pages.

Changing the Items Displayed on Your Desktop

To change the items displayed on the Desktop, click the Customize Desktop button on the Desktop page of the Display Properties dialog box. XP displays the Desktop Items dialog box with the General page (shown on the left in Figure 4.12) foremost.

FIGURE 4.12

Use the Desktop Items dialog box to specify which items appear on your Desktop.

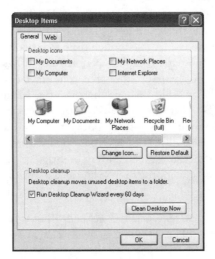

In the Desktop Icons group box, specify which items to display by selecting and clearing the My Documents check box, the My Computer check box, the My Network Places check box, and the Internet Explorer check box.

To change the icon displayed for one of the first three of these items, or for the Recycle Bin in its empty or full state, select the item in the Change Desktop Icon list box and click the Change Icon button. XP displays the Change Icon dialog box. In the Select an Icon from the List Below list box, choose the icon you want to use, and click the OK button to apply it. You can reapply the default icon for an item by selecting the item and clicking the Restore Default button in the Desktop Items dialog box.

TIP   If you don't see an icon you like in the Change Icon dialog box, click the Browse button and use the resulting Change Icon dialog box (a common Open dialog box in disguise) to select a file that contains icons. The file SHELL32.DLL *in the* \Windows\System32\ *folder contains a wide variety of icons, and the file* MORICONS.DLL *(in the same folder) contains a selection of older icons, some of which have amusement value. You can also find a wide variety of icons on the Web, or create your own icons with icon-editor programs.*

Adding Web Content via Desktop Web Pages

If you want, you can add web content to your Desktop. Doing so can make your Desktop more lively and interesting, which can be handy if you spend long periods staring at the Desktop or if you want to keep a stock ticker going. On the other hand, web content tends to be a time-sink, and your computer needs an Internet connection to get it (as you'll see, you can schedule when XP updates content). And if you spend most of your time working in a maximized program window, you'll miss the action on your Desktop.

To use Desktop web pages, take the following steps:

1. Display the Desktop Items dialog box by clicking the Customize Desktop button on the Desktop page of the Display Properties dialog box.

TIP   *Once you've started using Desktop web pages, you can also display the Desktop Items dialog box by clicking the Active Desktop menu button and choosing Customize My Desktop from the menu.*

2. Click the Web tab. XP displays the Web page (shown on the right in Figure 4.12).

3. By default, XP lists your current home page in the Web Pages list box. To use this page, select its check box. (XP doesn't apply the web page to your screen until you close the Desktop Items dialog box *and* click the Apply button in the Display Properties dialog box, so don't worry that nothing happens at this point.)

4. To add a page, click the New button. XP displays the New Desktop Item dialog box.

5. In the Location text box, type in the URL for the web page. Alternatively, if you have the location stored in a favorite, or if you want to add an HTML page that you have stored as a file, click the Browse button. XP displays the Browse dialog box, which is an Open dialog box in disguise, listing your favorites. Navigate to and select the file, and then click the Open button.

6. Click the OK button. XP closes the New Desktop Item dialog box.

NOTE   *At this point, if you have already set this item up as an offline favorite (as discussed in the section "Adding a Page to Your Favorites" in Chapter 19), XP displays the Active Desktop Item dialog box, telling you that you already have a subscription for this Active Desktop item, warning you that the subscription settings for the item will be lost if you continue, and asking if you still want to add this Active Desktop item. As you'll see in a moment, Desktop web pages offer fewer customization settings than offline favorites: You don't get to specify the depth of additional pages to download (because downloading additional pages would be pointless), nor do you get to choose not to download certain items.*

7. XP displays the Add Item to Active Desktop dialog box.

8. If you want to add the web page just as it is to your Active Desktop, click the OK button and skip ahead to step 16. But if you want to create an update schedule for the web page, or if you need to enter a password and username to access it, click the Customize button. XP starts the Offline Favorite Wizard.

9. The first time you run the wizard, you'll see an introductory page. Select the In the Future, Do Not Show This Introduction Screen check box and click the Next button. The wizard displays its synchronization page (shown on the left in Figure 4.13).

FIGURE 4.13

Specify whether you want to use an existing synchronization schedule, create a new schedule (on the page shown on the right), or synchronize the web page manually.

10. Specify how you want to synchronize this favorite. You can choose among the Only When I Choose Synchronize from the Tools Menu option button, the I Would Like to Create a New Schedule option button (which lets you create a custom synchronization schedule for the favorite), and the Using This Existing Schedule option button (which lets you use an existing schedule from the drop-down list). (The Using This Existing Schedule option button becomes available once you've created a schedule.)

11. Click the Next button. If you chose to create a custom synchronization schedule for the favorite, the wizard displays the page shown on the right in Figure 4.13.

12. Specify the schedule:

  ◆ Enter the interval (in days) and the time for the update at the top of the dialog box.

  ◆ Enter a name for the schedule in the Name text box. (The name is displayed when you go to apply an existing schedule to a new offline favorite you create, so make it descriptive, memorable, or both.)

  ◆ If you want your computer to connect to the network or Internet automatically if it is not connected when the time for the synchronization arrives, select the If My Computer Is Not Connected When This Scheduled Synchronization Begins, Automatically Connect for Me check box.

13. Click the Next button. The wizard displays its password page.

14. If the site requires a username and password, select the Yes, My User Name and Password Are: option button and specify your username and password (twice).

15. Click the Finish button to finish scheduling the update. The wizard closes and returns you to the Add Item to Active Desktop dialog box.

16. Click the OK button. XP closes the Add Item to Active Desktop dialog box and displays the Synchronizing dialog box while it synchronizes the web page.

17. Add further items to the Web Pages list if you want.

18. Make sure the check box for each Desktop web page that you want to use is selected.

19. When you're finished specifying Desktop web pages, click the OK button. XP closes the Desktop Items dialog box.

20. Click the OK button in the Display Properties dialog box. XP closes the dialog box and applies your web content to the Desktop.

XP initially displays the first Desktop web page across most of the Desktop (except for the part taken up by icons), with other Desktop web pages appearing as small windows. Move the mouse pointer over the top of a window to display its title bar. You can then click the left control icon (a Maximize button) on the title bar to maximize the web page across your whole Desktop (so that the icons appear on top of it) or click the right icon (a Restore button) to spread the web page across the portion of your Desktop that doesn't have icons on it.

You can also resize a Desktop web page by clicking the down-arrow button at the left end of the title bar and choosing Cover Desktop, Split Desktop with Icons, or Reset to Original Size from the drop-down menu.

NOTE *You can also add a new Desktop item by clicking the Visit Gallery button. XP opens a browser window showing what's available in the Microsoft Desktop Gallery. At this writing, the Desktop Gallery offers an assortment of items including a weather map and a satellite tracker.*

Managing Your Desktop Web Pages

Take the following actions to manage your Desktop web pages:

◆ To switch between Active Desktop web pages, use the Web Pages list box on the Web page of the Desktop Items dialog box.

◆ To remove a Desktop web page from being available, select it in the Web Pages list box and click the Remove button. XP displays a confirmation message box. Click the Yes button.

◆ To hide your Desktop icons, right-click open space on the Desktop and choose Arrange Icons By ➤ Show Desktop Icons from the context menu. XP removes the check mark from the Show Desktop Items item. To display the icons again, repeat the command.

◆ To lock the items on your Desktop so that they cannot be moved or rearranged, right-click open space on the Desktop and choose Arrange Icons By ➤ Lock Web Items on Desktop from the context menu. XP places a check mark next to the Lock Desktop Items item to indicate the locking. To unlock locked items, right-click and choose Active Desktop ➤ Lock Web Items on Desktop again. XP removes the check mark from the Lock Desktop Items item.

Changing the Appearance of XP Items

You can customize the appearance of your Desktop by working on the Appearance page of the Display Properties dialog box (shown on the left in Figure 4.14) and in the Advanced Appearance dialog box (shown on the right in the figure).

NOTE *In previous versions of Windows, the customization features of the Appearance page of the Display Properties dialog box and the Advanced Appearance dialog box all appeared on the Appearance page of the Display Properties dialog box. This was handy for power users but confusing for beginners. XP separates the customization features, making it simpler to see what you're doing. But if you're used to customizing Windows from the Appearance page of the Display Properties dialog box, you may find XP's approach frustrating.*

FIGURE 4.14

Use the options on the Appearance page of the Display Properties dialog box and in the Advanced Appearance dialog box to customize the look of XP.

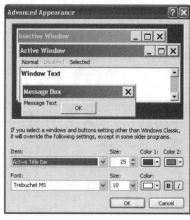

The Appearance page of the Display Properties dialog box offers three adjustments:

Windows and Buttons drop-down list   This drop-down list offers two choices of looks for windows and buttons: Windows XP Style or Windows Classic Style. You can choose advanced customizations only for Windows Classic Style.

Color Scheme drop-down list   This drop-down list provides a selection of color schemes. For the Windows XP style, you can apply only a few color schemes. For the Windows Classic style, you can choose from a wide variety of schemes that range from Windows Classic and Windows Standard through assorted color schemes and some high-contrast schemes.

Font Size drop-down list   This drop-down list gives you three choices of font size for screen fonts: Normal, Large, and Extra Large.

If these three options don't give the effect you want, click the Advanced button. XP displays the Advanced Appearance dialog box, in which you can change the color of just about any part of the screen.

To change the color of an item, select the item in the Item drop-down list, either by selecting it from the list or by clicking its representation in the demo box at the top of the dialog box. Then select attributes in the Size, Color 1, and Color 2 controls as appropriate for the object. If the Font drop-down list is available, you can also specify a font, font size, color, and style for the item.

When you've finished making XP look attractive (or peculiar), click the OK button. XP closes the Advanced Appearance dialog box. Click the Apply button in the Display Properties dialog box to apply your choices.

Choosing Desktop Effects

XP uses a number of visual effects to try to make your Desktop look appealing. Some people find these effects distracting and prefer to turn them off.

To work with effects, click the Effects button on the Appearance page. XP displays the Effects dialog box (shown in Figure 4.15).

FIGURE 4.15

In the Effects dialog box, you can specify the effects that XP uses for your Desktop.

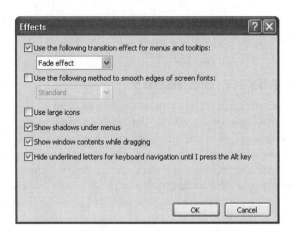

Use the Following Transition Effect for Menus and Tooltips check box and drop-down list
When this check box is selected, XP uses the effect specified in the drop-down list—Fade Effect or Scroll Effect—for the display of menus and tooltips. Clear this check box if you don't like the effect.

Use the Following Method to Smooth Edges of Screen Fonts check box and drop-down list
Select this check box if you want to have XP smooth the edges of screen fonts so that they look less jagged and are easier to read. (Smoothing is usually a good idea.) Then choose one of the options from the drop-down list: Standard or ClearType. ClearType is a Microsoft font-rendering technology that uses subpixel rendering to smooth the edges of fonts, making them easier to read. (Briefly: Instead of turning on a whole pixel, or turning it off, ClearType can turn on *part* of a pixel to achieve a more graduated, less blocky effect.) ClearType is most effective on LCD screens, though it also has some effect on CRT screens as well. If you're used to reading on-screen, ClearType may make you rub your eyes at first, as its effect is to blur the edges of the letters.

Use Large Icons check box   Select this check box if you want XP to display icons at a larger size than usual. This option is useful for high screen resolutions, which can make it hard to distinguish one icon from another.

Show Shadows under Menus check box   Leave this check box selected (as it is by default) to have XP display shadows at the bottom and right-hand edge of menus to give a 3-D effect. Clear this check box if you prefer your menus plain.

Show Window Contents while Dragging check box   Leave this check box selected (as it is by default) to have XP display the contents of a window when you're moving it or resizing it. If your video card struggles to display the window's contents, try clearing this check box. XP then displays only the window's frame when you move or resize it, then displays the contents when you've finished the maneuver.

Hide Underlined Letters for Keyboard Navigation until I Press the Alt Key check box   When this check box is selected (as it is by default), XP doesn't display the underscores under the access keys in menus and dialog boxes until you press the Alt key. (An *access key* is the key you press to access a menu or control. For example, most programs use *F* as the access key for the File menu.)

If you use the keyboard rather than the mouse to select options, clear this check box. You'll then be able to see access keys without needing to press the Alt key.

Choosing System Sounds

If you've got speakers or headphones attached to your computer, you'll have noticed by now that by default XP plays sounds when certain system events occur. For example, when you log on to XP, it plays a sub–Brian Eno tinkle, and when you take an action XP has been programmed to consider unwise, it plays a peremptory little chord at you. (If you don't have speakers or headphones attached to your computer, congratulations—you're saving yourself a good amount of grief.)

Fortunately for your sanity, you can change these sounds. For example, if you decide that you can't abide having a program close without XP declaring "It's just a flesh wound," you could assign a file containing that sound to the Close Program event. You can even create sound schemes so that you can keep multiple sets of system sounds and switch from one set to another as the fancy takes you. To protect other users of the computer from your sonic frenzies, sound schemes are stored in the Registry (in the HKEY_CURRENT_USER subtree, if you're interested; Chapter 12 discusses what the Registry is and how to work with it) and are available only to the user who created them.

To assign system sounds, follow these steps:

1. Choose Start ➤ Control Panel. XP displays Control Panel.
2. Click the Sounds, Speech, and Audio Devices link. XP displays the Sounds, Speech, and Audio Devices page.
3. Click the Change the Sound Scheme link. XP displays the Sounds and Audio Devices Properties dialog box with the Sounds page (shown in Figure 4.16) foremost.

FIGURE 4.16

Use the Sounds and Audio Devices Properties dialog box to configure the sounds assigned to various XP events.

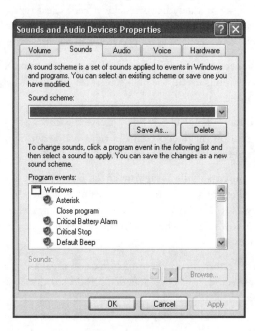

4. To apply an existing sound scheme, select it in the Sound Scheme drop-down list. (To apply peace and quiet, select the No Sounds scheme.)

   ◆ If you were using a custom sound scheme before, but you haven't saved it, XP displays the Save Scheme dialog box prompting you to save it. Choose the Yes button or the No button as appropriate.

5. To customize the current sound scheme, take the following steps:

   ◆ Select an event in the Program Events list box.

   ◆ In the Sounds drop-down list, select the sound you want to assign to the event. To find out how a sound sounds, click the Play button with the sound selected.

   ◆ The Sounds list box lists all the WAV files in the `\Windows\Media\` folder. To make your own WAV files available in the Sounds list box, copy or move them to this folder beforehand. Alternatively, use the Browse button to locate individual files you want to assign to events.

   ◆ To save the customized scheme, click the Save As button. XP displays the Save Scheme As dialog box. Enter the name for the scheme and click the OK button. Once you've saved a scheme, it's available from the Sound Scheme drop-down list. If you tire of it, you can delete it by clicking the Delete button.

6. Click the Apply button to apply your sound settings.

7. Click the OK button. XP closes the Sounds and Audio Devices Properties dialog box.

Arranging Icons on Your Desktop

By default, XP starts you off with just the Recycle Bin on the Desktop. (Your computer's manufacturer may have added other icons to the Desktop.) As you saw earlier in the chapter, you can add icons for My Documents, My Computer, My Network Places, and Internet Explorer by selecting the check boxes on the General page of the Desktop Items dialog box. You can save files to the Desktop and create shortcuts there as you need them (more on this later in the chapter). And many programs place one or more shortcuts on the Desktop when you install them.

One way or another, your Desktop normally gathers icons like an ungroomed dog gathers fleas. To keep things in order, you can arrange the icons on your Desktop by dragging them to wherever you want them to appear or by using one of the commands on the Arrange Icons By submenu of the context menu for the Desktop:

◆ The Name command, Size command, Type command, and Modified command arrange the icons by that attribute. You can choose only one of these commands at a time. XP displays a dot next to the currently selected item on the menu when the Auto Arrange command is active.

◆ The Auto Arrange command controls whether XP automatically arranges the icons into neat columns and rows, starting with a column beginning at the upper-left corner of the screen. You can toggle this command on and off. When it's on, the menu displays a check mark next to it.

◆ The Align to Grid command controls whether XP aligns icons on an invisible grid or lets you place them wherever you want them. You can toggle this command on and off by selecting it; again, it displays a check mark when it's on. This command is notionally independent of the Auto Arrange command, but in practice the Auto Arrange command essentially overrules it: When you let XP arrange your icons, it parks them according to the grid whether the Align to Grid command is on or off.

◆ The Show in Groups command lets you arrange icons in groups. This command is much more useful in Explorer windows than on the average Desktop.

◆ To remove the icons from your Desktop, right-click the Desktop and choose Arrange Icons By ➢ Show Desktop Icons to remove the check mark from the Show Desktop Icons item. To restore the icons, repeat the command.

Desktop Cleanup Wizard

If you leave any of the icons on your Desktop unused for 60 days, the Desktop Cleanup Wizard pops up a prompt in the System Tray urging you to let it help you clean up your Desktop. If you accept this invitation, the wizard displays a list of shortcuts you've never used, or haven't used for a long time, suggesting that you move them to a folder called Unused Desktop Shortcuts, which the wizard creates on your Desktop the first time it runs. Choose which (if any) icons you want to move there, and the wizard will do the rest. You can then access the shortcuts from the folder if you need to—or drag them back to your Desktop so that you can use them directly.

You can run the Desktop Cleanup Wizard manually at any time by clicking the Clean Desktop Now button on the General page of the Desktop Items dialog box. To prevent the Desktop Cleanup Wizard from running, clear the Run Desktop Cleanup Wizard Every 60 Days check box, also on the General page of the Desktop Items dialog box.

Configuring the Taskbar

Both the Taskbar and the Start menu have changed considerably in XP from the way they were in its predecessors, and you may want to restore some of their old behavior. This section discusses how to configure the Taskbar to meet your needs. The section after this discusses how to configure the Start menu.

Resizing and Repositioning the Taskbar

By default, the Taskbar appears at the bottom of the Desktop and is locked so that you cannot expand, shrink, or reposition it. To unlock the Taskbar, right-click open space on it (for example, the partial button at the Taskbar's right end) or in the notification area and select the Lock the Taskbar item from the context menu. XP removes the check mark from the Lock the Taskbar item. (To lock the Taskbar again, repeat this command.)

NOTE   *You can also unlock the Taskbar by clearing the Lock the Taskbar check box on the Taskbar page of the Taskbar and Start Menu Properties dialog box, but this technique is handy only if you have this dialog box displayed already.*

Once you've unlocked the Taskbar, you can resize it or reposition it:

◆ To reposition the Taskbar, click open space in it and drag it toward (or to) one of the edges of the screen so that the Taskbar snaps to it. See page 15 of the *Essential Skills* section for visual coverage of unlocking, resizing, and repositioning the Taskbar.

◆ To resize the Taskbar, drag its inside edge to expand or shrink the Taskbar. The inside edge is the edge nearest to the center of the screen. For example, in the Taskbar's default position at the bottom of the screen, the top edge is the inside edge.

When the Taskbar is positioned at the top or bottom of the screen, it grows and shrinks in increments of its original depth rather than gradually, so you can drag it to one-button depth, two-button depth, and so on. When the Taskbar is positioned at the side of the screen, it grows and shrinks gradually, so you can get exactly the width you want.

TIP   Unless you have a lot of windows open, placing the Taskbar at the side of the screen tends to waste space, because the buttons have a standard depth, leaving the lower half of the Taskbar unused. If you do have a lot of windows open, placing the Taskbar at the side of the screen lets you read the button titles quickly in a column—and you can drag the column width to display more or less of each title as you need.

Using the Taskbar to Navigate between Programs

In XP, the Taskbar looks more decorative than its utilitarian old version in previous versions of Windows, but its function remains the same: to let you see which programs are open; navigate quickly to a program; and maximize, minimize, restore, or close programs easily.

The Taskbar displays a button for each open program window. Note that this said *program window* rather than just *program*: If a program displays multiple separate program windows, the Taskbar shows one button for each window. If the program uses only one program window (including if the program has several document windows open within a program window), the Taskbar shows only one button for it. For example, if you have Excel 2002 or Word 2002 set to display multiple program windows (by selecting the Windows in Taskbar check box on the View page of the Options dialog box in each of the programs), XP displays a Taskbar button for each program window. If you have these programs set to display only one program window, the Taskbar displays only one button for the program.

When the Taskbar has taken up all the available space with buttons, and making the buttons any smaller to display more buttons would make them impractically small, it uses two techniques to present the buttons when you take an action that would add another button to the Taskbar:

◆ First, it groups any related buttons into a single button for the category. For example, if you have five Word documents open, it groups their five buttons into a single group button that contains a menu of the buttons. While the individual buttons bear the names of the document windows, the group button bears the program name and the number of windows the program has open—in this case, 5 Microsoft Word. Similarly, the Taskbar will display an Explorer button named 4 Windows Explorer containing a Control Panel button, a Network Connections button, a My Computer button, and a Recycle Bin button.

♦ Second, if you take actions that require disparate Taskbar buttons that can't be grouped, XP starts a second row of Taskbar buttons and displays scroll buttons at the right end of the Taskbar. Click the scroll buttons to scroll up and down the rows of Taskbar buttons to access the buttons you need.

To display a program, click its button on the Taskbar. (See page 14 of the *Essential Skills* section for visual coverage of using the Taskbar to access a window.) If the button is grouped into a group button, click the group button to display the menu of buttons, then choose the button from the menu. Figure 4.17 shows an example of working with a group button.

FIGURE 4.17

When a program's windows are grouped into a group button, you activate a program window by clicking the group button and choosing the button from the menu displayed.

To resize, move, or close a program window, right-click its Taskbar button and choose Restore, Move, Size, Minimize, Maximize, or Close from the context menu.

To arrange all the program windows, right-click open space in the Taskbar or in the notification area and choose the appropriate command from the context menu. This offers the Cascade Windows command, the Tile Windows Horizontally command, the Tile Windows Vertically command, and the Show the Desktop command. When you've issued a Show the Desktop command, the context menu also contains the Show Open Windows command and the Undo Minimize All command.

TIP *Two quick tips: First, right-click a group button to manipulate all its windows at once. The context menu offers Cascade, Tile Horizontally, Tile Vertically, Minimize Group, and Close Group commands. Second, to work with multiple windows at once, hold down the Ctrl key and select the Taskbar button for each window. Then right-click one of the windows and choose the action from the context menu.*

Configuring the Taskbar's Behavior

To configure the Taskbar, right-click open space in it (in other words, don't click a button) or in the notification area and choose Properties from the context menu. XP displays the Taskbar page of the Taskbar and Start Menu Properties dialog box (shown on the left in Figure 4.18).

The Taskbar Appearance group box offers these five options:

Lock the Taskbar check box   Select this check box (which is selected by default) to prevent the Taskbar from being moved to another edge of the screen or resized. Clear the check box if you want to move or resize it.

FIGURE 4.18

Use the Taskbar page of the Taskbar and Start Menu Properties dialog box and the Customize Notifications dialog box to configure the Taskbar to your liking.

Auto-Hide the Taskbar check box   Select this check box (which is cleared by default) to make the Taskbar hide itself until you move the pointer over its edge of the screen. This option is useful for maximizing the amount of the screen available to you, especially when you've increased the size of the Taskbar to accommodate more programs.

Keep the Taskbar on Top of Other Windows check box   Select this check box (which is selected by default) to have the Taskbar appear on top of any window. Instead of using the Auto Hide feature to hide the Taskbar, you can clear this check box so that the Taskbar remains on-screen. You can then display another window on top of the Taskbar if you want.

Group Similar Taskbar Buttons check box   Select this check box (which is selected by default) to have XP display only one button per program on the Taskbar. (See the previous section for further explanation and an example.) Individual buttons can make it easy to find the window you want, but the buttons take up a lot of space (or each button on the Taskbar gets shrunk to a tiny size to fit them all in).

Show Quick Launch check box   Select this check box to display the Quick Launch toolbar on the Taskbar. See "Using the Desktop Toolbars" later in this chapter for a discussion of the Quick Launch toolbar.

The Notification Area group box offers two options:

Show the Clock check box   Select this check box to have the notification area show the clock (as it does by default). Clear the check box to get rid of the clock and reclaim the space it takes up.

Hide Inactive Icons check box   Select this check box (which is selected by default) to have XP automatically remove from the notification area any items that you haven't used recently. XP hides the items and displays a Show Hidden Icons button that you can use to display them. This option can be useful for keeping your notification area uncluttered. If you find it unsettling to have icons disappear, clear this check box. You can also customize XP's treatment of notification-area icons by clicking the Customize button and working in the Customize Notifications dialog box (shown on the right in Figure 4.18 above). Select the item in the Current Items list or the Past Items list (which doesn't appear in the figure), then choose Hide when Inactive, Always Hide, or Always Show from the context menu. (If you mess up, click the Restore Defaults button to restore XP's default behavior with the notification area.)

Customizing the Start Menu

As you'll notice from your first session with XP, Microsoft has given the Start menu not only a new look but also new behavior. By default, the Start menu appears as a wide panel (shown in Figure 4.19) that automatically adjusts its contents to show your most recently used and most used programs.

FIGURE 4.19

The new-look Start menu appears as a two-column panel with the current user's name at the top.

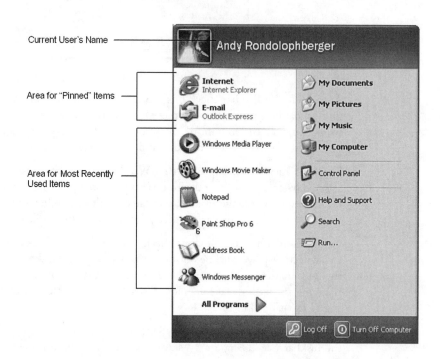

Current User's Name

Area for "Pinned" Items

Area for Most Recently Used Items

TIP If you prefer the "classic" Start menu used in Windows 9x, Windows NT 4, and Windows 2000, you can easily restore it: Select the Classic Start Menu option button on the Start Menu page of the Taskbar and Start Menu Properties dialog box, then click the Apply button. This book assumes that you're using the XP-style Start menu, so if you choose the classic Start menu, you'll need to choose Start menu commands a little differently. The section after next discusses how to customize the classic Start menu, but after that, all coverage uses the XP Start menu.

Whether you use the XP Start menu or the classic Start menu, you can customize it to make your computing a little easier. The following sections discuss how to do so.

Customizing the XP Start Menu

Because the XP Start menu automatically configures itself, it offers fewer customization options than the classic Start menu (which is discussed in the next section).

To customize the XP Start menu, take the following steps:

1. Display the Start menu, then right-click it and choose Properties from the context menu. XP displays the Start Menu page of the Taskbar and Start Menu Properties dialog box.

2. Click the upper Customize button to display the Customize Start Menu dialog box.

3. Choose options on the General page (shown on the left in Figure 4.20).

FIGURE 4.20

On the General page of the Customize Start Menu dialog box, specify how many programs the Start menu should show. On the Advanced page, choose the specific items.

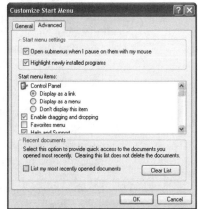

Select an Icon Size for Programs group box Choose the Large Icons option button or the Small Icons option button as suits you.

Programs group box Use the Number of Programs on Start Menu drop-down list to specify the number of programs the Start menu should display. You can set any number from 0 to 30. To wipe the current list of programs, click the Clear List button.

Show on Start Menu group box To display an Internet item on the Start menu, leave the Internet check box selected (as it is by default); to remove this item, clear it. If you leave the check box selected, you can use the drop-down list to select the program used for browsing the Internet. The default is Internet Explorer. Similarly, to display an E-mail item on the Start menu, leave the E-mail check box selected, and specify the program in the drop-down list. The default is Outlook Express.

4. Click the Advanced tab. XP displays the Advanced page (shown on the right in Figure 4.20).

5. Choose options in the Start Menu Settings group box:

Open Submenus When I Pause on Them with My Mouse check box Leave this check box selected (as it is by default) if you want the Start menu to display its submenus when you hover the mouse pointer over them for more than a few milliseconds. Clear this check box if you prefer to have the submenus appear only when you click them.

Highlight Newly Installed Programs check box Leave this check box selected (as it is by default) if you want XP to display a yellow highlight on the Start menu and its submenus to show you the path to newly installed programs. XP removes the highlighting once you've used the program. This highlighting can be useful, but because XP applies it to each new shortcut the freshly installed program has created, the highlighted path persists until you've used each shortcut—which may be awhile for shortcuts to uninstall features, Help files, and documentation. If you don't like the highlighting, clear this check box.

6. The Start Menu Items list box presents a number of items that can appear on the Start menu. Those with an icon and three option buttons (the Display As a Link option button, the Display As a Menu option button, and the Don't Display This Item option button) let you specify whether they appear as a link or as a submenu. For example, you can have Control Panel appear as a link (which opens a Control Panel window), as a menu (which lets you access its categories directly), or never. Those items with a check box let you specify simply whether the item appears (for example, select the Printers and Faxes check box to have the Start menu display a Printers and Faxes entry) or whether a feature is implemented (for example, select the Scroll Programs check box if you want XP to display the All Programs menu as a scrolling item or as multiple pages should it be too long to fit on the screen). Select the check boxes and the option buttons as appropriate.

TIP   If your computer is connected to a network, select the My Network Places check box so that XP displays the My Network Places item on the Start menu.

7. In the Recent Documents group box, select the List My Most Recently Opened Documents check box if you want the Start menu to display a menu for recently used documents. Displaying this item lets you access your recent documents quickly, but it also lets anyone logged on to the computer as you see which documents you've been working with. Click the Clear List button to clear the list of recent documents.

8. Click the OK button. XP closes the Customize Start Menu dialog box.

9. Click the OK button. XP closes the Taskbar and Start Menu Properties dialog box.

TIP   To prevent XP from moving an item on the Start menu, pin it in place. Right-click the item in the Start menu and choose Pin to Start Menu from the context menu. To unpin an item you've pinned, right-click it in the Start menu and choose Unpin from Start Menu from the context menu. To remove an item from the most-used section of the Start menu, right-click the item and choose Remove from This List from the context menu. To prevent an item from finding its way on to the most-used section of the Start menu, use the Taskbar\XP Start Menu page of the Tweak UI PowerToy, which you can download from the Microsoft Windows XP Downloads site (www.microsoft.com/windowsxp/home/downloads/powertoys.asp).

You can also customize the Start menu by dragging items to it and dropping them there:

◆ To pin an item to the Start menu, drag it and drop it on the Start button.

◆ To add an item to the All Programs menu or one of its submenus, drag the item to the Start button, hover the mouse pointer there until XP displays the Start menu, drag the item to the All Programs button and hover there, then drag to the location on the menu where you want the item to appear.

Customizing the Classic Start Menu

You can customize the classic Start menu so that it contains exactly the items you want. To do so, you add items to the menu, remove existing items, and sort the menu if necessary.

Begin by choosing Start ➢ Settings ➢ Taskbar and Start Menu to display the Taskbar and Start Menu Properties dialog box. Select the Classic Start Menu option button if it isn't already selected (if you're using the classic Start menu, it should be selected already). Then click the lower Customize button. XP displays the Customize Classic Start Menu dialog box (shown in Figure 4.21).

FIGURE 4.21

The Customize Classic Start Menu dialog box lets you customize the classic Start menu extensively to put the items you need most right at hand.

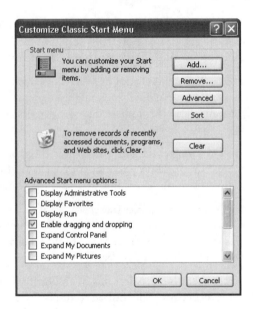

You can add items to the Start menu and remove items from it as follows:

◆ To add an item to the Start menu, click the Add button and follow the steps in the Create Shortcut Wizard that XP displays.

◆ To remove an item from the Start menu, click the Remove button. XP displays the Remove Shortcuts/Folders dialog box. Select the item you want to remove, and then click the Remove button.

◆ To add and remove items freely, click the Advanced button. XP opens an Explorer window showing the Start menu. You can then create and delete shortcuts as you see fit by using standard Explorer techniques.

TIP   *Your Start menu folder is stored in the* `\Documents and Settings\`*Username*`\Start Menu\` *folder. You can navigate to it by using Explorer and manipulate it without bothering the Customize Classic Start Menu dialog box.*

◆   To sort the Start menu alphabetically, click the Sort button.

◆   To clear the details of recently used documents, programs, and websites, click the Clear button.

In the Advanced Start Menu Options list box, choose settings for the following options:

Display Administrative Tools check box   Select this check box to have XP display the Administrative Tools menu on the Programs menu. You can also access these tools through the Administrative Tools page of the Control Panel, but using the menu is quicker for frequent access. This check box is cleared by default.

Display Favorites check box   Select this check box to have XP display the Favorites menu on the Start menu. This menu lets you quickly access your favorites, but it can become unwieldy if you have a large number of favorites. This check box is cleared by default.

Display Run check box   Leave this check box selected (as it is by default) to have the Start menu include the Run item, which you can use for running a program. Clear this check box to remove the Run item. You might want to do this to help discourage users from running programs not on the Start menu.

Enable Dragging and Dropping check box   Leave this check box selected (as it is by default) if you want to be able to use drag-and-drop to move or copy items from one location on the Start menu to another location. Clear this check box to disable drag-and-drop.

Expand Control Panel check box   Select this check box if you want XP to display a menu of Control Panel items instead of opening a Control Panel window when you select Start ➢ Settings ➢ Control Panel. This menu gives you faster access to the Control Panel items than does opening a Control Panel window. This check box is cleared by default.

Expand My Documents check box   Select this check box if you want XP to display a menu listing the items in the My Documents folder instead of displaying a window when you choose Start ➢ Documents. This menu gives you quick access, but it can be hard to navigate if you accumulate many documents and folders in the My Documents folder. This check box is cleared by default.

Expand My Pictures check box   Select this check box if you want XP to display a menu listing the items in the My Pictures folder when you choose Start ➢ My Documents ➢ My Pictures.

Expand Network Connections check box   Select this check box if you want XP to display a menu of network connections instead of displaying a window when you choose Start ➢ Settings ➢ Network Connections. This check box is cleared by default.

Expand Printers check box   Select this check box if you want XP to display a menu of printers instead of displaying a window when you choose Start ➢ Settings ➢ Printers and Faxes. This check box is cleared by default.

Scroll Programs check box   Select this check box if you want XP to display the Programs menu as a scrolling menu when it is too tall to fit on the screen. With this check box cleared, XP displays the Programs menu as two or more columns. This check box is cleared by default.

Show Small Icons in Start Menu check box   Select this check box to have XP display small icons instead of large icons in the Start menu. Small icons let you pack more items on the Start menu but make it harder to read. This check box is cleared by default.

Use Personalized Menus check box   Leave this check box selected (as it is by default) to have XP automatically tailor the Start menu to what it thinks are your needs. For example, if you don't use a program for a long time, XP removes its item from the Start menu on the assumption that you don't need it. When XP has removed items like this, it displays a button at the foot of the menu with a double arrow pointing downward to indicate that more items are available. Click this button to display the items that have been removed.

When you've finished customizing the classic Start menu, click the OK button. XP closes the Customize Classic Start Menu dialog box and applies your choices.

Using the Desktop Toolbars

XP offers four built-in toolbars that you can display on the Desktop. As you'll see in a moment, you can also create custom toolbars of your own to give you quick access to folders and web pages of your choice.

The four toolbars are as follows:

Address toolbar   This toolbar works in the same way as the Address bar in Internet Explorer. Enter a URL and click the Go button (or press the Enter key) to open a web page in Internet Explorer. Enter a drive letter or folder name to open it in an Explorer window. Enter a filename and path to open the file in the program associated with its file type.

Desktop toolbar   This toolbar displays an icon for each item on your Desktop and menus for key folders (for example, the My Computer folder and the My Network Places folder). By displaying this toolbar, you can save yourself having to display the Desktop to access a program, a folder, or a file. Many people find this toolbar most useful reduced to a button. You can then click the toolbar's expansion arrow to get a menu of the items on your Desktop.

Links toolbar   This toolbar is the Links toolbar from Internet Explorer. You can use it to provide quick access to websites you want to be able to access frequently.

Quick Launch toolbar   This toolbar provides quick access to programs and documents you designate. The Quick Launch toolbar initially contains four icons and appears to the right of the Start button (when the Taskbar is at the bottom of the screen): Launch Internet Explorer Browser, Launch Outlook Express, MSN Explorer, and Show Desktop (which brings the Desktop to the foreground, in front of all open windows). You can add other icons to suit your needs, as discussed in the section after next.

Displaying and Hiding the Desktop Toolbars

To display or hide a toolbar, right-click the notification area, choose Toolbars from the context menu, and select the toolbar from the submenu.

Figure 4.22 shows the Quick Launch toolbar, the Desktop toolbar (with its menu displayed), and the Address toolbar. As you can see, cramming several toolbars onto a single-line Taskbar like this makes them impractically small. (The Address toolbar in particular is more or less useless at this size.)

FIGURE 4.22

You can display one or more Desktop toolbars to give you quick access to your programs, your Desktop, and web pages.

Customizing the Quick Launch Toolbar

As you've seen, the new-style Start menu tries to put your most-used programs at your fingertips (or at your mouse pointer) by juggling the Start menu items and letting you pin items to the Start menu. But you may find it even easier to put the programs and documents you use most often on the Quick Launch toolbar and not have to worry about pinning them (or having XP "disappear" them to make room for another program).

There are two easy ways to add a shortcut to the Quick Launch toolbar:

◆ Drag the target file from an Explorer window (or from the Desktop) to the Quick Launch toolbar. XP creates a shortcut to the file (document or program) there. You can also drag Control Panel items to the Quick Launch toolbar by displaying Control Panel in Classic view (choose Start ➢ Control Panel, then click the Switch to Classic View link in the Control Panel task list in Control Panel).

NOTE *Shortcuts on the Quick Launch toolbar don't show the usual shortcut arrow, though if you look at the Quick Launch folder, you'll see that the shortcut arrows are there.*

◆ Right-click open space in the Quick Launch toolbar and choose Open Folder from the context menu. XP displays the Quick Launch folder. (If you want to open this folder the hard way, you'll find it in your \Documents and Settings*Username*\Application Data\Microsoft \Internet Explorer\Quick Launch\ folder.) Create shortcuts by right-dragging any file or folder to this folder and choosing Create Shortcut Here from the context menu.

Once you have the shortcuts you need on the Quick Launch toolbar, drag their icons into the order in which you need them, left to right. This way, if only part of the Quick Launch toolbar is displayed on-screen, you'll be able to access your most-needed icons without needing to display the hidden portion of the toolbar.

EXPERT KNOWLEDGE: ADDING A "LOCK COMPUTER" BUTTON TO YOUR QUICK LAUNCH TOOLBAR

One useful item to add to the Quick Launch toolbar is a button that locks your computer when you click it. To do so, open the Quick Launch folder as described in the second bulleted paragraph above, right-click to display the context menu, and choose New Shortcut. In the Type the Location of the Item text box, enter `rundll32.exe user32.dll,LockWorkStation`. In the Type a Name for This Shortcut text box, enter a name such as Lock Computer and click the Finish button. You can then click the resulting button on the Quick Launch toolbar to lock your computer quickly and easily.

If your keyboard lacks a Windows key, edit the properties for this shortcut and assign to it a keyboard shortcut that you can use to lock XP from the keyboard as well.

Creating and Using Custom Toolbars

In addition to using the four ready-made toolbars, you can create custom toolbars to display the contents of any folder or any website that your computer can access. Using custom toolbars can be a great way of giving yourself access to the documents you use frequently. Custom toolbars aren't much use for web pages—you can't see much of the page on the toolbar. This seems to be a feature that Microsoft implemented because it could rather than because it would benefit users.

To create a custom toolbar, take the following steps:

1. Right-click the Taskbar and choose Toolbars ➤ New Toolbar from the context menu. XP displays the New Toolbar dialog box.
2. Navigate to and select the folder in the list box, or type a URL in the Folder text box (if you want to try creating a useless toolbar of a web page).
3. Click the OK button. XP creates a toolbar for the folder or web page.

Managing Your Desktop Toolbars

If you have the Taskbar locked (as it is by default), you can't resize or move the toolbars you display. But if you unlock the Taskbar, you can resize and move them pretty much to your heart's content by dragging their sizing handles (the dotted area at the left end or upper end of the toolbar). You can drag a toolbar to a large size on the Taskbar, to a free-floating panel on the Desktop, or to a docked position at one of the edges of the screen.

Docking a toolbar like this may seem useless at first, because the toolbar takes up screen real estate that you probably have better uses for. But if you right-click the toolbar once and select the Always on Top attribute, then right-click again and select the Auto Hide attribute, you'll end up with a toolbar that disappears until you move the mouse pointer over its edge of the screen. Using such a toolbar can be a handy way to keep documents quickly accessible.

You can turn off the display of a toolbar's text by right-clicking the toolbar and clicking the Show Text item on the context menu to remove its check mark, or turn off the display of a toolbar's title by right-clicking the toolbar and clicking the Show Title item on the context menu to remove its check mark.

EXPERT KNOWLEDGE: USING MULTIPLE DESKTOPS WITH THE VIRTUAL DESKTOP MANAGER POWERTOY

If you have a huge monitor, or a multiple-monitor configuration, you may have space to display all the programs you need to work with at the same time. If not, you'll have to switch from one program to another, which can get old fast.

To the rescue comes the Virtual Desktop Manager PowerToy, which you can download from the Microsoft Windows XP Downloads site (www.microsoft.com/windowsxp/home/downloads/powertoys.asp). Borrowing a trick from Unix and Linux, which have long had virtual desktops, this PowerToy lets you create four separate virtual desktops. (The term *virtual desktop* is a little confusing, because by definition the XP Desktop is virtual rather than real—but just imagine that the Desktop is real and that you've got four virtual desktops that you can display on it.) On each desktop, you can arrange program windows as you would on your main Desktop. You can switch between the desktops by clicking the controls that the Virtual Desktop Manager puts on the Taskbar.

To enable you to easily identify the desktop that contains the programs with which you want to work next, Virtual Desktop Manager lets you shrink your four virtual desktops down so that they fit on your Desktop temporarily. You then click a virtual desktop to zoom it to your full Desktop size.

Up Next

This chapter has discussed how to configure your Desktop to suit your working needs. By now, you should have chosen display settings, customized the XP Desktop, configured the Start menu and Taskbar, and applied any accessibility options you need in order to use your computer effectively.

The next chapter discusses how to install, remove, and run programs.

Chapter 5

Installing, Removing, and Running Programs

HOWEVER WONDERFUL THE FEATURES built into XP—and some of them *are* pretty wonderful; some less so; see the rest of the book for details—they're not the be-all and end-all of computing. The programs bundled with XP (most of which are discussed in Chapter 7) let you perform a few basic tasks, from creating simple documents to playing music and video to creating simple video movies of your own. But sooner or later, you're going to want to install a third-party program and run it so that you can carry on with your business and your life.

On the assumption that this is probably going to happen sooner rather than later, this chapter discusses how to install, configure, remove, and run programs—and how to shut them down when they fail to respond to conventional stimuli.

The chapter uses various programs as examples, ranging from the latest (and supposedly greatest) programs specially designed for XP to Windows 9x programs to DOS programs that are still only just starting to suspect that graphical environments exist. The odds are overwhelmingly against these programs being the ones you want to use with your copy of XP, but these programs provide examples of many of the issues you'll encounter with installing, running, and removing programs.

This chapter covers the following topics:

◆ Understanding compatibility issues

◆ Understanding multiuser considerations

◆ Who can install and remove programs

◆ Installing and removing programs

◆ Running programs in Compatibility mode

◆ Installing and removing DOS-based programs

◆ Running programs

◆ Making programs run at start-up

◆ Killing a program that's not responding

NOTE *If you performed an in-place upgrade of your previous version of Windows to XP, the installation processes should have configured all your programs for use already, so you shouldn't need to reinstall them. However, if you have old programs that you find don't run properly on XP, you may need to run them in Compatibility mode. If so, turn to the section "Running Programs in Compatibility Mode," later in this chapter.*

Good News on Compatibility

If you've used any of the versions of Windows NT, or if you've used Windows 2000, you'll know that program compatibility has been a major issue for the NT code base. In order to make NT stable and crash-proof, the designers made heavy sacrifices in compatibility. Many Windows 9x programs flat out wouldn't run on NT. Games and other programs that tried to access hardware directly were particularly problematic: Windows 9x lets a program access hardware directly, whereas NT's Hardware Abstraction Layer (HAL) forces all hardware requests to be brokered by the operating system.

In Windows 2000 Professional, Microsoft greatly increased the number of programs that would run on the NT code base—but some Windows 9x programs still wouldn't run, and many DOS-based games wouldn't run either. Direct hardware access was still a problem, because the HAL was still there. Briefly, if the program could run in protected mode, letting the HAL handle the communications with the hardware, it would usually run, though it might run a bit more slowly than on other versions of Windows (or on DOS). If the program insisted on trying to communicate with the hardware directly, HAL gave it grief. (Fill in your own *2001* pun here: "I'm sorry, DOOM, I'm afraid I can't do that," and so on.)

On this front, XP brings very welcome good news: XP is able to run most 32-bit Windows programs without problems. It can also run many 16-bit Windows programs. And it can run a number of DOS programs. Most of this happens transparently: You install the program by running its setup routine or installation routine as usual; you run the program as usual; and that's that. Behind the scenes, XP provides more flexibility in providing the program with the type of environment it needs. On the surface, all is serene.

That's for many programs—perhaps most programs. But some programs don't run properly like this. For some, you need to explicitly use XP's Compatibility mode to fool the program into thinking that it's running on the version of Windows that it expects. XP then mimics the environment of that version of Windows for that program, sustaining the illusion that things are to the program's liking. For example, if a program expects Windows 95 and won't run without it, Compatibility mode tells the program that it's running on Windows 95 and tries to prevent it from finding out the truth. Usually the program then runs fine, though you may notice some loss of performance as XP mollycoddles the program.

NOTE *If you're familiar with the Mac, you might be wondering how XP's Compatibility mode compares with Mac OS X and its Classic technology for running programs that won't run on OS X. Basically, there are similarities between Compatibility mode and Classic, but Compatibility mode is both less gruesome conceptually and far lighter on the memory. Classic essentially loads a hefty chunk of System 9.2 (on top of OS X, which isn't exactly svelte itself) and uses it to run the program, whereas XP essentially dupes the program into a false sense of security by giving it the cues it expects. This duping requires a bit more memory and system resources, but nothing like the overhead that the Mac needs to run a program in Classic mode. But then XP is less of a drastic change from its predecessors than OS X, which is essentially mutated Unix with a new graphical interface—and Classic mode runs almost every program that runs on System 9.2 without requiring you to change any settings or fool around with Compatibility modes.*

EXPERT KNOWLEDGE: 16-BIT PROGRAMS AND 32-BIT PROGRAMS

What *is* a 16-bit program, and what's a 32-bit program? Where does the number of bits come from, and what does it mean?

A layperson's answer to the first question might be that 16-bit programs are programs designed to run on 16-bit versions of Windows (for example, Windows 3.1) and 32-bit programs are programs designed to run on 32-bit versions of Windows (Windows 9*x*, Windows NT, Windows 2000, and XP).

Actually, it's not quite that simple. To get a fraction more technical, 16-bit programs are written to the Win16 application programming interface (API), and 32-bit programs are written to the Win32 API. The APIs are sets of rules that tell programmers how they can access the functionality that an operating system exposes to them and how a program should behave so that it gets along with the operating system and other programs running on it.

Normally, 32-bit programs *are* written for 32-bit operating systems, and 16-bit programs *are* (or, you might hope, *were*) written for 16-bit operating systems (which have largely gone the way of the dodo). But by using the Win32s extensions—a 32-bit operating system extension that sat on top of the 16-bit Windows 3.1 operating environment (which in turn sat on top of the 16-bit DOS operating system)—you could run a 32-bit program on Windows 3.1. So some 32-bit programs were written for a 16-bit operating system. And because 32-bit operating systems can normally run 16-bit programs, many 16-bit programs are used to this day, running more or less happily in virtual machines on 32-bit operating systems. The 32-bit operating system may have to perform a process called *thunking*, essentially gearing down to run a 16-bit program. Thunking typically involves some overhead and a slight loss of performance. But if the 16-bit program ran at an acceptable speed on Windows 3.1 with, say, a 486 processor, it should run at a decent speed on even a modest Celeron or Duron processor, even with any thunking needed.

Just as 32 valves are better than 16 (for making a satisfactory engine growl if not for reaching the speed limit ahead of that pickup in the next lane at the traffic signal), 32 bits are better than 16. The advantage of 32 bits is that you can move more information at once—*much* more information. 32 bits can represent a range of more than 4 billion integer values (4,294,967,296, to be precise), whereas 16 bits can represent only 65,536 integer values. 64 bits can represent correspondingly more than 32 bits, and 64-bit PC operating systems are on their way. In fact, XP Professional has a 64-bit version for Intel's new 64-bit Itanium processor.

That still hasn't answered the second question: Where does the number of bits come from, and what does it mean? The bit-ness of a program essentially comes from the *word size* of the computer it's running on. The word size is the biggest number that the computer can handle in one operation. 286 systems, those fire-breathing speed-demons of the mid-1980s, used a 16-bit word size, enabling them to handle much more data at once than the (exhaust-breathing) 8-bit systems that preceded them. 386 systems upped the ante to a 32-bit word size, at which it has stayed for several generations of chips: Even Pentium IV and Athlon systems use 32-bit words. The Itanium processor has a 64-bit word size, enabling it to handle impressively large chunks of data in a single operation. But until *all* the programs run on the Itanium are 64-bit, a lot of thunking has to go on. That's why the Opteron chip, AMD's 64-bit competitor to the Itanium, offers backward compatibility with the 32-bit Intel x86 processor architecture.

When you're installing programs on XP, you seldom need to worry about how many bits they're going to use, because XP handles any necessary transitions between 32-bit and 16-bit code seamlessly. You *do* sometimes have to worry about *where* you install older programs so that all users of the computer can use them—but more on this a little later in the chapter.

Continued on next page

EXPERT KNOWLEDGE: 16-BIT PROGRAMS AND 32-BIT PROGRAMS *(continued)*

You can easily tell whether a running program is 16-bit or 32-bit as follows:

1. Right-click the notification area and choose Task Manager from the context menu. XP displays Task Manager with the Applications page foremost.

2. Right-click the entry for the program and choose Go to Process from the context menu. XP displays the Processes page of Task Manager and selects the process for the program.

3. If the program is 16-bit, you'll see an entry for WOWEXEC.EXE above the process in the Image name column. If not, the program is 32-bit.

To establish whether a program that's not running is 16-bit or 32-bit, right-click its executable file (you may have to go spelunking in the \Program Files\ folder or your Windows folder) and choose Properties from the context menu. XP displays the Properties dialog box for the program. If the program has a Version tab, it's 32-bit; if not, it's 16-bit.

Once you've set up Compatibility mode for a program, it runs in Compatibility mode each time, so you shouldn't need to tweak it any further unless some of its features misbehave.

Compatibility mode is very impressive, and it's great when it works. But some ancient programs (particularly DOS programs) may never work, even with Compatibility mode. In these cases, your choices of course of action are approximately a) give up on the program, b) dual-boot your system with the version of Windows with which the program was last known to work, or c) use emulation software such as VMWare or Virtual PC to run on top of XP a session of the version of Windows with which the program works.

NOTE *One major category of program that this chapter doesn't talk about is games, which are a subject all to themselves. Games are cordoned off in Chapter 29.*

Programs You Shouldn't Even *Try* to Run on XP

No matter how impressive XP's compatibility with programs designed for earlier versions of Windows (or for DOS), there are some types of programs you should never try to run on XP. These include the following:

Operating systems Obviously, you can't install DOS, an earlier version of Windows, or another operating system or operating environment on top of XP—at least, not without using some kind of PC-emulation software (such as VMWare).

Old anti-virus programs Anti-virus programs designed for previous versions of Windows don't know how to deal with XP. You may be able to update the program so that it'll be able to work with XP. More likely, you'll need to get a whole new version.

Old troubleshooting and cleanup utilities   Most troubleshooting and cleanup utilities designed for earlier versions of Windows will give XP nothing but grief. So will disk utilities (for example, Norton Utilities) designed for earlier versions. As with the anti-virus programs, these utilities don't know how XP works—in fact, most of them assume that Windows works in a completely different way. So despite XP's ability to restore your system after bad software goes on the rampage, it's a mistake to let old troubleshooting and cleanup utilities loose on your system in the first place. Where you still need the added functionality to supplement XP's capabilities, invest in a new utility specifically designed for XP.

Some potential offenders are smart enough to figure out the problem and quit on their own. Figure 5.1 shows the Incorrect Operating System dialog box that an old version of Network Associates' VirusScan displays if you try to install it on XP without using Compatibility mode.

FIGURE 5.1

This old version of VirusScan is smart enough to refuse to be installed on XP.

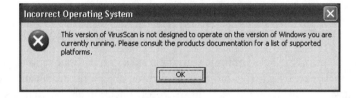

Multiuser Considerations

As you saw earlier in the book, XP offers strong multiuser capabilities. From the start, XP encourages you to set up your computer for multiple different users to use, allowing each their own custom settings. Moreover, multiple users can be logged on to the computer at the same time (though only one user can be active); other users can be running programs in the background (as it were) while the current user is working away unaware of them.

XP's multiuser capabilities raise some issues for programs and files, as discussed in the next section.

Who Can Install Programs?

First, you'll remember that XP Home supports three types of users: Computer Administrator users, Limited users, and the Guest user. Only Computer Administrator users can install and remove programs. Limited users and the Guest user cannot install or remove programs. That said, Limited users (or even the Guest user) may be able to start some Windows 9*x* installation routines that don't understand XP's security system, but these installation routines will usually fail when trying to copy files to folders that XP protects (but that Windows 9*x* versions don't protect).

If a Limited user or the Guest user tries to install a program, XP displays the Install Program As Other User dialog box (shown in Figure 5.2), telling them that they'll probably need administrator rights to do so. The user can specify a valid Computer Administrator username in the User Name text box and the appropriate password in the Password text box in order to proceed with administrative privileges.

FIGURE 5.2

To install or uninstall a program, you need to have Computer Administrator rights. If you don't, XP stops you in your tracks with a warning such as this one.

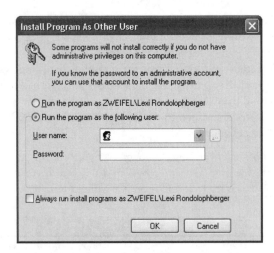

If the user tries to continue with the installation without supplying Computer Administrator credentials, they usually run into an error message and abrupt termination of the setup routine. Figure 5.3 shows a couple of examples from Microsoft Office under different circumstances.

FIGURE 5.3

The Microsoft Office installation grinds to a halt if the user doesn't supply Computer Administrator credentials.

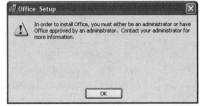

Figure 5.4 shows an example from a program that would prefer to remain nameless.

FIGURE 5.4

Perhaps the ultimate tight-lipped error message. Again, this signified that the installation had crashed because of a lack of permissions.

In most cases, you'll get best results by having a Computer Administrator user install all the programs on XP. By default, XP Home sets up all users you create during setup as Computer Administrator users, so unless you restrict some users manually, everyone will be able to install programs. Alternatively, you could temporarily promote a user to Computer Administrator status to let them install one or more programs, then demote them afterwards. Or you could use the Run

As command (discussed in the sidebar "Running a Program as Another User" later in this chapter) to run the program under the auspices of a Computer Administrator user. But either course of action means entrusting a user you've defined as less trustworthy with administrator-only actions—which you probably don't really want to do.

Who Is the Program Available To?

In some operating systems, you can install a program for some users but not for others. In contrast, XP Home by default makes any program you install available to all users of the computer—provided that the program's setup routine does things in the right way. For example, if you install Office XP, the setup routine automatically creates shortcuts for all users to use the programs, so the next time any user logs on, they'll have a swath of new programs that they can use from the Start menu.

Office XP of course knows all about Windows XP, because they're both Microsoft products and they're roughly the same vintage. Eudora Pro 4.2, on the other hand, is a couple of years old at this writing and hasn't heard of XP. But it installs fine, and is available to all users after installation, because its setup routine was (presumably) constructed along Microsoft's guidelines.

If the program's setup routine is deficient, you may need to install the program again for each user, install it to an explicitly shared location, or simply create shortcuts manually for the program in each user account or in the \Start Menu\Programs\ folder for All Users. For example, if you install Lotus SmartSuite Millennium Edition on XP by using its setup routine, the user who installs Smart-Suite gets the full set of shortcuts for it (plus a slew of shortcuts clogging the notification area, plus the SmartCenter program-launcher and general menace). Other users get none of these—except for shortcuts to Net-It Now! Starter Edition, little-known web-publishing companion software that was included with SmartSuite. This isn't useful, helpful, or even amusing.

TIP   *XP expects all programs to be installed into the* \Program Files\ *folder. Putting them there seems to help make them available for all users, though it's not a guarantee of success. Putting them in another folder is usually not a good idea, though if you need to make small programs easily accessible to all users, you might be tempted to put them in the* \Documents and Settings\All Users\ *folder.*

What Happens when Multiple Users Open the Same File at the Same Time?

As discussed in Chapter 3, problems arise with some programs when different users have the same file open. In Chapter 3, you saw how multiple users can open the same WordPad file at the same time, and each can save their changes into (or through) the other's changes. The result is pretty horrible.

Of course, some files are *designed* to be accessed by multiple users at the same time. For example, most database files are designed so that they can routinely be accessed by dozens, hundreds, or even thousands of users at the same time. The program prevents any *record* from being accessed by more than one user at a time. Some database programs prevent users from accessing records adjacent to any record being accessed by another user, to avoid the problems that can occur when records are added to or deleted from the database, either of which actions changes the numbering of records. But as long as each user is (virtually) cordoned off from all other users in the recordset, all is well. Similarly, Excel lets you explicitly share workbooks with other users.

At the risk of generalizing absurdly, more complex (or perhaps more smartly designed) programs use some form of locking mechanism so that they can tell when another user has a file open. This locking mechanism can consist of flags on the file in question, but often it's implemented as a separate file that's created when the file is opened and is deleted when the file is safely closed. You can see this easily enough with Word, which creates a locking file in the same folder as the document you've opened (or just saved, in the case of a new document) *and* sets a flag on the document. The locking file replaces the first two characters of the file's name with the characters ~$, so that a document named `PENGUINS.DOC` would generate a locking file named `~$NGUINS.DOC`. (Before you ask what happens with two-character filenames—if the file's name is six characters or fewer, Word *adds* the ~$ to the beginning of the filename. Seven characters, it replaces the first character. Eight characters, it replaces the first two.) If you open the locking file in a text editor (such as Notepad), you'll see that it contains the name of the current user (several times over, with variations in the spacing), some extended characters, and a variety of spaces.

NOTE   Word's locking files are hidden, so you won't see them in Explorer or in common dialog boxes unless you've selected the Show Hidden Files and Folders option button in the Advanced Settings list box on the View page of the Folder Options dialog box (Tools ➢ Folder Options) in Explorer.

When you go to open a file, Word takes a quick look through the folder that contains the file to see if there's a locking file for it. If there is, it displays the File in Use dialog box to let you know about the problem and offer you options for proceeding. When you close the file that was open, Word deletes the locking file. But if you delete the locking file while the file is open, Word still knows that the file is open, because the flag is still set on the file.

As you might imagine, any program that doesn't use a locking mechanism so that it can tell when its files are open is going to have problems with multiple users accessing the same file. Very generally speaking, the less complex the program, the less likely it is to check that a file is open, and the more likely you are to have a problem with multiple users opening a file at the same time.

This problem also arises with files that can be opened with two or more different programs that are available on the computer. For example, if you use WordPad to open a Word document, it opens the document without any locking. You can then open the same document in Word while it's still open in WordPad. Word then locks the document, and you won't be able to save changes to the original file from WordPad.

What Happens when Multiple Users Run the Same Program at the Same Time?

By and large, having two or more users open the same document file at the same time (in the same program or in different programs) is more of a problem than having two or more users run the same program at the same time.

The brief answer to this question is as follows:

◆ Some programs are designed to be used by multiple users at once, so they don't cause problems.

◆ Some programs are too dumb to notice that they're being used by multiple users at once, so each session is happy enough. Some of these programs are designed to run multiple instances for any given user anyway, so they're in good shape to run multiple instances for multiple users.

◆ Some programs notice there's a problem with multiple sessions and deal with it gracefully.

◆ Some programs notice there's a problem and sulk conspicuously.

With most programs, the problem comes not with the executable files and libraries (DLLs) but with the settings files. XP handles the executables and libraries, running each in a separate memory space and segregating each user's programs from all other users' programs. But if a program is designed to use a central settings file rather than to implement a separate settings file for each user, the settings file can cause problems. If the program locks the settings file when the first user runs the program, the settings file won't be available when the second user runs the program. The same goes if the settings information is stored in a central location in the Registry.

Perhaps the easiest way around this is to use a separate settings file for each user, or to keep separate Registry entries. As you'd imagine, that's what the Microsoft Office programs do. For example, if you're familiar with Word, you probably know that it stores a lot of information in the global template, which is saved in the file NORMAL.DOT. The global template is always loaded when you're running Word, so Word maintains a separate global template for each user. This way, it avoids problems when users in separate sessions of the same installation of Word change their settings at the same time.

Problems also arise when separate instances of a program try to use the same hardware resources on the computer at the same time—for example, the COM ports, the audio output, or the microphone input—or the same set of data files.

How a program handles a problem gracefully depends on what the program does and what the problem is. In a program that can manage only one instance running on the computer at the same time, when you start a new instance in another user session, you'll typically see a warning dialog box that lets you choose to either cancel running the new instance of the program or forcibly terminate the other user's session of the program.

As you'd expect, some programs are smarter than others. In particular, it shouldn't come as a shattering surprise to learn that current Microsoft programs are much more aware of XP's multiuser functionality than earlier Microsoft programs or programs from other software companies.

For example, Windows Media Player lets you switch user while you're still playing music or video, or copying a CD. The music (or video) continues to run even while the Welcome screen is displayed. If you then log back on as the same user, Windows Media Player simply keeps going without interruption. Only when you log on as another user does Windows Media Player stop playing the music or video (or copying the CD). And—perhaps more important—it exits the instance that was playing or copying for the other user, freeing up the sound and video circuitry together with whatever system resources it was using. (Before you ask—Windows Media Player quits when you switch to another user even if it wasn't playing.)

TIP   If you're experiencing problems with programs that can't run multiple instances successfully at the same time, or with shared documents being opened by multiple users at once, turn off Fast User Switching as discussed in the section "Turning Fast User Switching Off and On" in Chapter 9. All these problems should disappear in a quick puff of logic.

Set a Restore Point before Installing a Program

The installation routines used for many programs, including all the latest Microsoft programs, automatically set a restore point during installation so that you can use XP's System Restore feature (discussed in Chapter 17) to restore XP to its preinstallation state should something go horribly wrong in the installation. But to be sure that a suitable restore point exists, it's a good idea to create one yourself. To do so, follow the procedure described on pages 54 and 55 of the *Essential Skills* section.

Installing a Program

After all that buildup, you're probably raring to install a program. You can do this in a couple of ways. The more formal way is to use the Add/Remove Programs window. The less formal way is to run the setup program manually.

Whichever method you choose, if the program you want to install is on a CD, DVD, or other removable medium, load it into the appropriate drive on your computer. If the program is on a network drive, establish a connection to that drive.

If you have Autoplay enabled, the setup routine may start automatically when you insert the CD or other medium in its drive. Cancel out of the setup routine if you want to use the Add/Remove Programs window for the installation. Alternatively, use the manual installation method described in the section after next.

NOTE *The section "Customizing and Turning Off Autoplay "in Chapter 6 discusses how to customize and turn off Autoplay.*

Installing a Program Using the Add/Remove Programs Window

The Add/Remove Programs window provides the more formal way of installing a program. This way has no particular advantages over the next method except that, because XP explicitly manages the process, it should have no excuse for professing ignorance of the program after you've installed it.

1. Choose Start ➢ Control Panel. XP displays Control Panel.
2. Click the Add or Remove Programs link. XP displays the Add or Remove Programs window.
3. Click the Add New Programs button in the left-hand column of the window. XP displays the Add New Programs page of the window (shown in Figure 5.5).

FIGURE 5.5

The formal way to install a new program is to use the Add New Programs page of the Add or Remove Programs window.

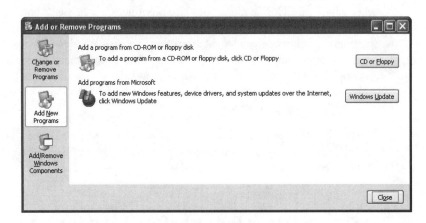

4. Click the CD or Floppy button, even if the program you want to install is on a removable disk, on a network drive, or on your hard drive. XP displays the Install Program from Floppy Disk or CD-ROM page of the Add Programs Wizard.

5. If the program is on a CD or a floppy, and you haven't inserted the disk already, do so now.

6. Click the Next button. XP searches your floppy drives and CD drives for a `SETUP.EXE` file and displays the Run Installation Program dialog box (shown in Figure 5.6). If XP found a `SETUP.EXE` file, it lists it in the Open text box and invites you to make sure it's the correct file; if it didn't (as in the figure), it suggests you browse to find the file manually.

FIGURE 5.6

If XP doesn't find a setup file in your floppy drive or CD drive, the Run Installation Program dialog box lets you choose the file manually.

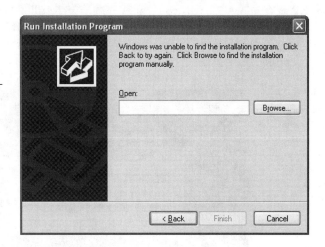

7. If XP didn't find a `SETUP.EXE` file, or if it found the wrong one (which can happen easily enough if you have multiple CD drives and install software frequently), click the Browse button. XP displays the Browse dialog box. Navigate to the folder that contains the setup file, select it, and click the Open button. XP closes the Browse dialog box and enters the program's path and filename in the Open text box.

TIP   If the setup program has a name other than `SETUP.EXE`, `NNSETUP.EXE`, `INSTALL.EXE`, or another widely used name or name variation for setup programs, XP may not list it in the Browse dialog box. Select the Programs entry in the Files of Type drop-down list in the Browse dialog box to make XP list all executable files in the folder. If the setup program isn't an executable file (unlikely but possible), select the All Files entry in the Files of Type drop-down list.

8. Click the Finish button. XP closes the Run Installation Program dialog box and starts the program's setup routine.

What happens next depends on the whims of the setup routine's programmers or (more commonly) on which of the two commonly used Windows installers they used—InstallShield or WISE. Suffice it to say that the usual steps for installing a program include agreeing to its license agreement, choosing which of the program's components to install, selecting a Start menu folder (often still called a Program Group, in an embarrassing hangover from Windows 3.x days), and twiddling your thumbs (or taking a break). For some programs, you'll have to reboot as well.

At the end of the setup routine, you usually get a message box telling you that setup completed successfully. When you dismiss this message box, XP returns you to the Add or Remove Programs window, from which you can add further programs or simply click the Close button.

NOTE *You might be tempted to use the Change or Remove Programs page of the Add or Remove Programs window to see how much space the program you just installed is taking up—but don't bother, because the Change or Remove Programs page doesn't list the new program until you close the Add or Remove Programs window and reopen it.*

You may see some amusing messages when installing old programs. Figure 5.7 shows an example: a Windows 95 Detected dialog box from the setup routine for PhotoWorks 2.01. PhotoWorks identifies XP as Windows 95, tells you that Windows 95 is still in beta, and warns you that PhotoWorks may not work properly because of that. (After this gaffe, PhotoWorks figured out that XP didn't need Win32s, the 32-bit subsystem for Windows 3.1*x*; installed itself correctly; and then ran without problems.)

FIGURE 5.7

The PhotoWorks
2.01 setup routine
identifies XP as
Windows 95—and
warns you that
Windows 95 is
still in beta.

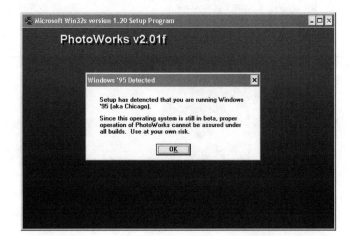

If XP knows about a problem with an application you're installing, it displays a dialog box warning you of the problem. Figure 5.8 shows an example in which XP has detected an issue with Lotus Approach 9.*x*. (If you're using Autoplay, XP performs such a check before even starting the setup routine for the software.) Click the Continue button, the Cancel button, or the Details button as appropriate.

FIGURE 5.8

XP alerts you to any
known issues with
software that you're
about to install.

Installing a Program by Running Its Setup Routine Manually

If you don't like jumping through hoops unnecessarily, you may want to forsake using the Add or Remove Programs window for installing programs, because you can add a program just as easily by running its setup routine manually.

To run a setup routine manually, double-click its file in an Explorer window or on the Desktop. Alternatively, use the Run dialog box as follows:

1. Choose Start ➤ Run or press Windows key+R. XP displays the Run dialog box (shown in Figure 5.9).

FIGURE 5.9

You can also run a setup routine directly from an Explorer window or from the Run dialog box.

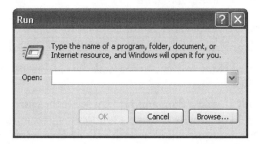

2. In the Open text box, enter the path and filename of the setup program. Either type in the path and filename or browse to it. (Click the Browse button. XP displays the Browse dialog box. Navigate to and select the file, then click the Open button.)

3. Click the OK button. XP closes the Run dialog box and starts running the setup program.

EXPERT KNOWLEDGE: INSTALLING PROGRAMS TO A FOLDER OTHER THAN YOUR \PROGRAM FILES\ FOLDER

Most installation routines for Windows programs are configured to install most of their files in a folder or folder structure in your \Program Files\ folder. If you follow Microsoft's guidelines for installing programs there, and if you have plenty of space on your system partition, this is usually fine. But if you're short of space on your system partition, it's not so convenient.

If the program's installation routine doesn't allow you to select a destination folder, you can make it install its programs in a different folder by editing the Registry. See the section "Changing Your \Program Files\ Folder" in Chapter 12 for details.

Installing the XP PowerToys

As mentioned earlier in the book, Microsoft makes available on the Microsoft Windows XP Downloads site (www.microsoft.com/windowsxp/home/downloads/powertoys.asp) various add-on programs called PowerToys that provide extra functionality for XP.

To install one of these PowerToys, click its link on this site and choose to save it to your disk. When the download is complete, click the Open button in the Download Complete dialog box. (If you've chosen to close the File Download dialog box, open the folder to which you downloaded the file and double-click the file.) XP launches the installation routine for the PowerToy. Most of the PowerToy installation routines offer you a Complete installation or a Custom installation, but because most of the PowerToys have no omissible components, there are no choices worth making in the Custom installation—you're either installing the whole PowerToy, or you're not installing it.

Removing a Program

Removing a program is usually even easier than installing a program, because you don't usually have to have the setup medium (CD, floppy, or whatever) and you have to make even fewer decisions.

Follow these steps to remove a program:

1. Choose Start ➤ Control Panel. XP displays Control Panel.
2. Click the Add or Remove Programs link. XP displays the Add or Remove Programs window.
3. If the Change or Remove Programs page of the window isn't displayed, click its tab. XP displays the page.
4. In the Currently Installed Programs list box, select the entry for the program you want to remove. The Add or Remove Programs window displays information about the program—its size (the approximate amount of space it's taking up on disk), a rough description of how often you've used it over the last 30 days (Frequently, Occasionally, or Rarely), and the date you used it last—together with a Change/Remove button. Figure 5.10 shows these details.

    ◆ If you have a lot of programs installed, use the Sort By drop-down list to sort the programs. You can sort by Name, Size, Frequency of Use, and Date Last Used. Obviously enough, the Name category is useful for finding programs by name. The Size category is good for determining which programs are hogging disk space when you need to free some up in a hurry. And the Frequency of Use category and Date Last Used category are useful for rooting out the programs you installed on a whim and have used hardly at all.

FIGURE 5.10

Use the Change or Remove Programs page of the Add or Remove Programs dialog box to uninstall a 32-bit program.

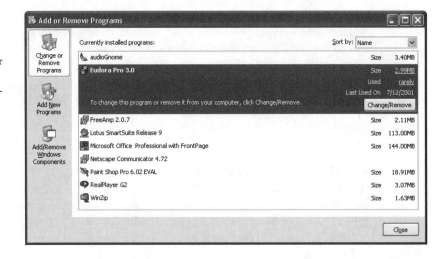

5. Click the Change/Remove button. XP checks to see if other users are using the computer (because they might be using the program that you're about to remove). If any other user is logged on, XP displays the Warning dialog box shown in Figure 5.11.

◆ At this point, you can click the Switch User button to display the Welcome screen, then log on as each user from there and log them off. But usually you'll find it easier to use the Users page of Task Manager to either switch to the other users or simply log them off.

◆ When you're ready, click the Continue button if the Warning dialog box is still displayed. (If it's not, click the Change/Remove button in the Add or Remove Programs dialog box instead.)

FIGURE 5.11

Before letting you uninstall a program, XP warns you if other users are logged on to the computer.

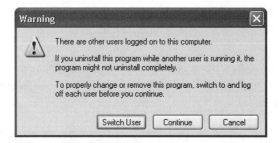

6. Once you've cleared the Warning hurdle, XP invokes the uninstall routine for the program. The next steps vary depending on the program (or on its programmers or the tool they chose), but in most cases, you either specify which parts of the program to uninstall (if the program contains discrete components) or simply confirm that you want to get rid of the program:

◆ Figure 5.12 shows the Confirm File Deletion dialog box that XP displays when you issue the Change/Remove command for Eudora Pro.

FIGURE 5.12

XP invokes the program's uninstall routine. In this case, Eudora Pro offers no partial uninstall and so treats the uninstall as a deletion.

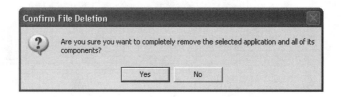

◆ Figure 5.13 shows the Select Lotus SmartSuite Applications dialog box, which lets you specify which SmartSuite programs to uninstall or uninstall the lot.

FIGURE 5.13

XP invokes the program's uninstall routine, which lets you specify which components to uninstall (as in the case with Lotus SmartSuite here) or confirm the uninstallation.

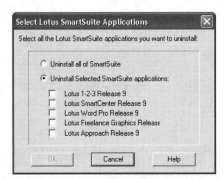

7. Choose uninstall options and click the appropriate button. You'll then typically see something like Figure 5.14, in which unInstallShield (InstallShield's evil twin) is removing Eudora Pro.

FIGURE 5.14

Here's an example of what you see when uninstalling a program. Here, unInstallShield is removing Eudora Pro.

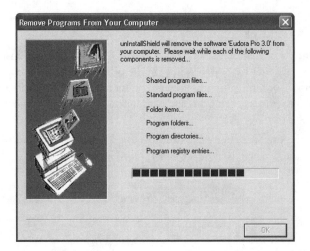

8. If the uninstall routine tells you that it was unable to remove some parts of the program that you've asked to uninstall completely, it usually lets you know which parts are left. For example, unInstallShield provides a Details button that you can click to display a dialog box such as that shown in Figure 5.15. In this case, it's easy enough to delete these folders manually by using Explorer.

FIGURE 5.15

If unInstallShield can't remove all the components of a program, it provides details in the Details dialog box.

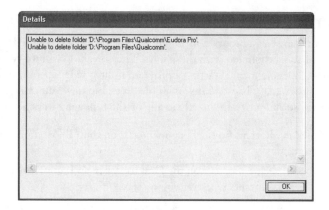

TROUBLESHOOTING: UNINSTALLING 16-BIT WINDOWS PROGRAMS AND DOS PROGRAMS

XP's Add or Remove Programs feature tracks all 32-bit programs installed on the computer, and it's able to track many 16-bit programs as well. But some 16-bit Windows programs and most DOS programs don't show up in the Add or Remove Programs dialog box, so you can't remove them that way.

The preferred way of removing a program that doesn't show up in the Add or Remove Programs window is to run its uninstall routine manually. Some Windows programs add a shortcut to their uninstall routine to the program folder (or, in XP, to the Start menu submenu) that contains their other shortcuts. If there's no shortcut, you'll need to dig through the folder that contains the program to see if it has one. The file might be an EXE file, but it might also be a BAT (batch) file. See if the program includes a README file that contains steps for uninstalling the program.

If the program doesn't have an uninstall routine, you'll need to remove it manually. (If you've only just installed the program, you *could* use the System Restore feature to return your system to its state before you installed the program—but usually you'll have made other changes to your computer since installing the program. Chapter 17 discusses how to use System Restore.) This usually means deleting the folder (or folders) that contains the program and removing any references to it that you can find.

There are two problems with removing a program manually like this. First, you don't necessarily know where the program has put all its files. This is usually more of a problem with Windows programs, which (following Microsoft's own recommendations) often put shared files into the \Windows\ folder or one of its subfolders, than with DOS programs (which probably don't know that the \Windows\ folder exists, and certainly don't care about it even if they do know). So if you simply delete the folder or folders the program created, it may leave detritus in other folders. (This is why uninstall routines exist, of course.) Some utilities, such as the WinDoctor utility included in Norton SystemWorks and Norton Utilities, can take care of "missed links" such as these.

The second problem is that the program may also have added commands to configuration files of their era (such as AUTOEXEC.BAT or WIN.INI) that will cause errors when you've deleted its files. You'll need to discover these additions manually (usually when you get an error message) and delete them or comment them out manually. Because XP uses these configuration files only for compatibility, these errors are likely to cause you annoyance rather than grief—unlike in the old days, when a command for a missing program could make Windows 3.1 refuse to load.

Running Programs

In XP, you can start a program in any of several ways. If you've used a previous version of Windows, you'll probably be familiar with these ways. They break down into two categories: starting a program directly by opening it, and starting a program indirectly by opening a file whose file type is associated with the program. (Chapter 6 discusses file types and how you can associate them with programs.)

You can start a program directly in any of the following ways:

◆ Click its shortcut on the Start menu (or on the All Programs submenu, or on one of its submenus).

◆ Double-click a shortcut on the Desktop or in an Explorer window. (Chapter 6 discusses how to create shortcuts wherever you want.)

◆ Click a shortcut on the Quick Launch toolbar or another Desktop toolbar. (Chapter 4 discusses the Desktop toolbars and how to customize them.)

◆ Choose Start ➤ Run. XP displays the Run dialog box. Enter the name of the program in the Open text box, either by typing or by browsing for it. (Click the Browse button. XP displays the Browse dialog box. Navigate to and select the file, then click the Open button.) Click the OK button.

NOTE *Using the Run dialog box seems a clumsy way of running a program, but it's useful for running utilities for which XP doesn't provide a Start menu entry (for example, the Registry Editor, discussed in Chapter 12) and for running programs for which you don't want to create a shortcut but whose path and filename you can type (or otherwise enter) without undue effort.*

◆ Double-click the icon or listing for the program in an Explorer window (or on the Desktop). You can also use the Search feature (discussed in Chapter 6) to locate the program you want to run.

Almost all setup routines create shortcuts to their programs automatically. Usually, the setup routine puts a shortcut on the Start menu or in a subfolder of the Start menu. Some setup routines place a shortcut directly on the Desktop; some consult you first; others don't. Some setup routines offer to also put a shortcut in the notification area; other setup routines do so without consulting you; while others yet are civilized enough to respect Microsoft's guidelines for notification-area use—that the notification area should be used for warnings and information rather than loaded with shortcuts for every program in sight.

Running Programs in Compatibility Mode

If a program won't run normally on XP, try running it in Compatibility mode. As mentioned earlier in the chapter, Compatibility mode lets you tell XP to emulate Windows 95, Windows 98, Windows NT 4, or Windows 2000 so that a program thinks it's running on the operating system it knows and likes.

TIP *Often, you'll need to run the program's setup routine in Compatibility mode to get the program to install in the first place. Then run the program itself in Compatibility mode as well.*

XP comes with the Microsoft AppCompat database of compatibility problems known about programs. AppCompat is automatically updated by the Windows Update feature, which gives you another incentive to accept Windows Update's offers to download every update available—at least until your computer's hardware and all your software are working as perfectly as you could wish.

NOTE *You can set Compatibility mode only on files on local drives. You can't set Compatibility mode on a program located on a network drive. But you can create a shortcut on a local drive to a program located elsewhere, and then specify Compatibility mode for the shortcut.*

XP provides two ways of setting up a program to run in Compatibility mode. The first way is formal and cumbersome, but it lets you test whether the Compatibility mode you choose works for the program. The second way is much quicker, but you run the risk of getting a program comprehensively hung if Compatibility mode doesn't work.

Let's take it from the top.

The Formal Way of Setting Compatibility Mode

Here's the formal way to run a program in Compatibility mode:

1. Choose Start ➤ All Programs ➤ Accessories ➤ Program Compatibility Wizard. XP displays a Help and Support Center window and starts the Program Compatibility Wizard in it.

2. Read the information and cautions on the Welcome to the Program Compatibility Wizard screen and click the Next button. XP displays the How Do You Want to Locate the Program That You Would Like to Run with Compatibility Settings? screen (shown in Figure 5.16).

FIGURE 5.16

On the How Do You Want to Locate the Program That You Would Like to Run with Compatibility Settings? screen in Help and Support Center, choose how to select the program you want to run in Compatibility mode.

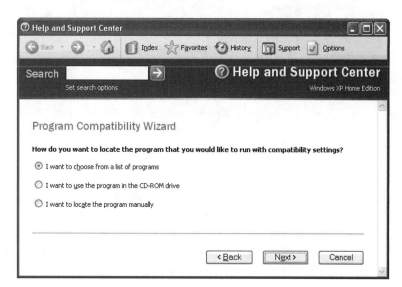

3. Use one of the following three ways to locate the program:

◆ To set Compatibility mode for a program that's already installed, select the I Want to Choose from a List of Programs option button and click the Next button. The wizard scans your hard drive and displays a list of programs. Select the program and click the Next button.

◆ To set Compatibility mode for a program you're installing from CD, insert the CD, select the I Want to Use the Program in the CD-ROM Drive option button, and click the Next button.

◆ To set Compatibility mode for a program that isn't installed and whose installation medium isn't on CD, or if you're just feeling ornery, select the I Want to Locate the Program Manually option button and click the Next button. The wizard displays the Which Program Do You Want to Run with Compatibility Settings? screen. Enter the path in the text box, either by typing or by clicking the Browse button and using the resulting Please Select Application dialog box (a common Open dialog box) to select the program. Click the Next button.

4. The wizard displays the Select a Compatibility Mode for the Program screen (shown in Figure 5.17).

FIGURE 5.17

On the Select a Compatibility Mode for the Program screen of the Program Compatibility Wizard, select the Compatibility mode you want to use.

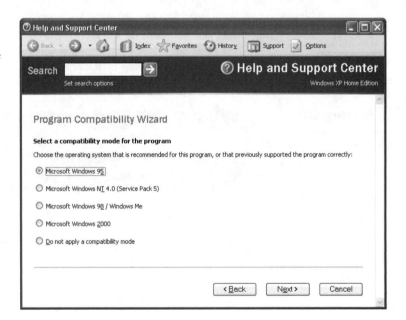

5. Select the option button for the operating system you think the program needs: Windows 95, Windows NT 4.0 (Service Pack 5), Windows 98/Windows Me, or Windows 2000.

6. Click the Next button. The wizard displays the Select Display Settings for the Program screen (shown in Figure 5.18).

FIGURE 5.18

On the Select Display Settings for the Program screen of the Program Compatibility Wizard, you can apply limitations to the display settings used for the program.

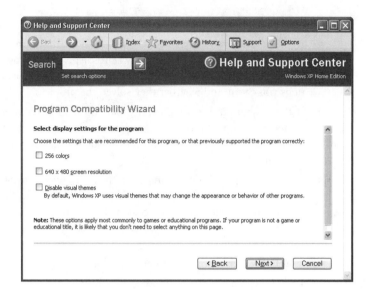

7. If you know the program needs display limitations, select the 256 Colors check box, the 640×480 Screen Resolution check box, or the Disable Visual Themes check box.

   ◆ For most programs, you don't need to select any of these display limitations.

8. Click the Next button. The wizard displays the Test Your Compatibility Settings screen.

9. Check the settings you've chosen, then click the Next button. The wizard launches the program with the compatibility settings you specified and displays the Did the Program Work Correctly? screen (shown in Figure 5.19).

FIGURE 5.19

On the Did the Program Work Correctly? screen, tell the Program Compatibility Wizard whether the program launched correctly with the computer settings.

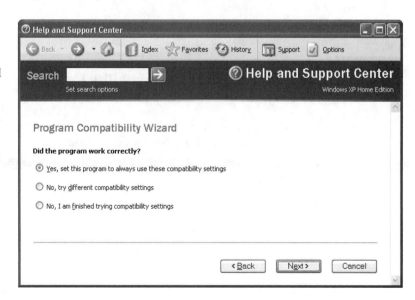

10. Choose the appropriate option button:

   ◆ If the program ran okay, select the Yes, Set This Program to Always Use These Compatibility Settings option button. The wizard displays the Program Compatibility Data screen, on which you can choose whether to send Microsoft information on the program, the settings you chose, and whether they solved the problem.

   ◆ If the program didn't run correctly, but you want to try other settings, select the No, Try Different Compatibility Settings option button. Click the Next button. The wizard returns to the Select a Compatibility Mode for the Program screen. Return to step 5 and try again.

   ◆ When no compatibility settings seem to work, select the No, I Am Finished Trying Compatibility Settings option button. Click the Next button. The wizard displays the Program Compatibility Data screen (discussed above). In this case, you have more incentive for sending Microsoft information, as it may help them fix the problem with this program in the future.

11. Choose the Yes button or the No button as appropriate.

12. Click the Next button. If you chose the Yes button, the wizard sends the compatibility data. Either way, it displays the Completing the Program Compatibility Wizard page.

13. Click the Finish button. The wizard closes itself.

Remember that old version of VirusScan from earlier in the chapter that didn't want to install on XP? It was happy to install in Compatibility mode for Windows 95—but parts of it wouldn't run on XP (see Figure 5.20).

FIGURE 5.20

VirusScan decided it really didn't like XP after all.

The Quick Way of Setting Compatibility Mode

The quick way of setting Compatibility mode is as follows:

1. Right-click the shortcut for the program and select Properties from the context menu. XP displays the Properties dialog box for the shortcut.

2. Click the Compatibility tab. XP displays the Compatibility page. Figure 5.21 shows an example of this page.

FIGURE 5.21

You can also choose Compatibility mode settings on the Compatibility page of the Properties dialog box for the shortcut.

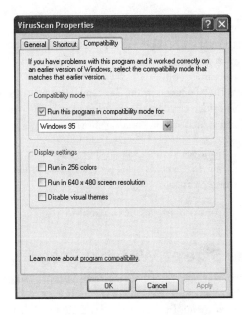

3. Select the Run This Program in Compatibility Mode For check box if it's not already selected.

4. In the drop-down list, select the mode you want to use.

5. In the Display Settings group box, select the Run in 256 Colors check box, the Run in 640×480 Screen Resolution check box, or the Disable Visual Themes check box as necessary. (Again, for most programs, you won't need to set these options.)

6. Click the OK button. XP applies your choice and closes the Properties dialog box.

Even with Compatibility Mode, Some Programs Don't Work

Some programs plain don't work even when you use Compatibility mode. For example, Lotus Smart-Suite 96 won't install on XP, no matter whether you try to run it from the CD or copy its files to a local drive and use Compatibility mode. When you run the SmartSuite 96 installation routine on XP, you get to specify the program folder and the type of installation (typical, minimal, custom). Then the installation crashes with the Output message box shown in Figure 5.22. This message box mentions an overflow (trying to put more information in a memory register than will fit), but beyond that, it tells you next to nothing useful.

FIGURE 5.22

Lotus SmartSuite 96's installation routine crashes with an Output CNTR+318: Over-flow message box.

Making Programs Run at Startup

If you want a program to start every time you log on to XP, place a shortcut to it in your Startup folder. Starting programs automatically like this can save you a few seconds each time you start XP if you always need to use the same programs.

Your Startup folder is the `\Documents and Settings\`*Username*`\Start Menu\Programs\Startup\` folder. Navigating to this folder usually takes nearly as long as placing in it the shortcuts you want. (See the next chapter for instructions on creating shortcuts.)

TIP   *To make a program start automatically each time any user of your computer logs on to XP, place a shortcut to the program in the Startup folder for All Users. As you'd guess, this folder is the* `\Documents and Settings\All Users\Start Menu\Programs\Startup\` *folder.*

To prevent a program from running at startup, remove its shortcut from the Startup folder.

Specifying the Size at Which a Program Runs

By default, most programs start in a "normal" window—one that's not maximized and not minimized. If you'd like the program to start up maximized or minimized, right-click its shortcut and choose Properties from the context menu. In the Properties dialog box that XP displays, choose Maximized or Minimized in the Run drop-down list on the Shortcut page, and click the OK button.

You can do this for any shortcut to a program or to a file—so if you want, you can have shortcuts open different-sized windows for files of the same file type.

EXPERT KNOWLEDGE: RUNNING A PROGRAM AS ANOTHER USER

Sometimes you may need to run a program under a user account other than the user as which you're currently logged on to XP. For example, your current user account might not have permission to access the file or folder you want to manipulate with the program, but you have access to another account that does have permission for that file or folder.

To run a program as another user, create a shortcut to it and set the advanced property called Run with Different Credentials, as described in the section "Setting Advanced Properties for a Shortcut" in the next chapter. When you open that shortcut, XP displays the Run As dialog box, in which you can specify the user account under which you want to run the program.

Killing a Program That's Not Responding

Programs run pretty well on XP—but not all programs run well all the time. Sooner or later, a program will hang or crash on you.

When this happens, first, make sure the program doesn't have an open dialog box that you can't see. When you're working with multiple programs, you can easily get an open dialog box stuck behind another open window. If the dialog box is *application modal*, it prevents you from doing anything else in the program until you dismiss it. (Dialog boxes can also be *system modal,* in which case they prevent you from doing anything else on your computer until you deal with them.)

Minimize all other open windows (right-click the Taskbar and choose Show the Desktop from the context menu), and see if the dialog box appears. If not, you'll probably have the program that's not responding still displayed on your screen, probably with only some parts of the window correctly drawn. For example, typically the areas of the program that were covered by other programs or windows will not be redrawn (or not redrawn correctly).

Next, try using Alt+Tab to switch to the program and bring out from behind it any dialog box that's hiding. Chances are that this won't work either, but it's worth a try. If the dialog box appears, deal with it as usual, and the program should come back to life.

If that didn't work, try using Task Manager to switch to the program:

1. Right-click the Taskbar and choose Task Manager from the context menu. XP displays Task Manager.
2. If the Applications page isn't displayed, click the Applications tab. XP displays the Applications page, which lists each running program and its status. The status can be either Running (all is well with the program, as far as XP is concerned) or Not Responding (XP believes that the program is not responding to conventional stimuli).
3. Select the program that's not responding.
4. Click the Switch To button. Task Manager attempts to switch to the program, and minimizes itself in the process.

If that didn't work either, it's probably time to kill the program. Take the following steps:

1. Restore Task Manager by clicking its button on the Taskbar.
2. Decide whether the program has hung or crashed. (See the nearby sidebar *"Not Responding Status Isn't Always Terminal"* for advice on determining whether the program is still viable.)
3. Select the task in the Task list.
4. Click the End Task button. XP displays the End Program dialog box (shown in Figure 5.23).

FIGURE 5.23

To terminate the program, click the End Now button in the End Program dialog box.

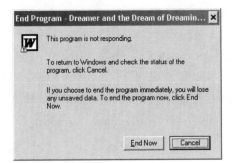

5. Click the End Now button. XP terminates the program and frees up the memory it contained.

If killing the program like this doesn't work, you have several options. Here they are, in descending order of preference:

◆ Close all other programs that are responding. Then log off XP. Doing this should shut down any programs you're running.

◆ If you can't close the program and can't log off XP, but Task Manager is still working (apart from not being able to kill the program), use Task Manager to switch to another user, then log off the user session that contains the crashed program.

◆ At this point, you're pretty much out of options. Reach for the Reset button on your computer.

EXPERT KNOWLEDGE: *NOT RESPONDING* STATUS ISN'T ALWAYS TERMINAL

When you see a program listed as having Not Responding status on the Applications page of Task Manager, you may be tempted to kill it off right away. But you'd do better to stay your hand for a minute or two. Why? Because Not Responding status doesn't necessarily mean that a program has hung or crashed:

◆ First, Not Responding may mean nothing more than that a program is responding more slowly than XP expects; if you give it a few seconds, or perhaps a few minutes, it may start responding normally again. If your computer seems unresponsive overall, back off and give it a few minutes to sort itself out.

◆ Second (and often related to the first point), Not Responding may mean that XP is struggling to allocate enough memory to the program; this often causes the program to run slowly. Task Manager is a little harsh in this respect—it's XP's fault that the program isn't responding, but Task Manager points the finger at the program.

◆ Third, VBA-enabled programs (for example, Microsoft Word and Microsoft PowerPoint) are often listed as Not Responding when they're running a VBA routine or macro. In this case, Not Responding means only that VBA temporarily has control over the program. When VBA releases control of the program— in other words, when the routine ends—Task Manager lists the program as Running again. (If the program shouldn't be running a macro, try pressing Ctrl+Break to stop it.)

Up Next

This chapter has discussed how to install programs, how to run them—using Compatibility mode if necessary—and how to remove them when you tire of them. It's also touched on the types of programs you shouldn't even try to install on XP, and it's shown you how to use Task Manager to kill a program that's crashed.

The next chapter discusses how to manage files in Explorer.

Chapter 6

Managing Your Files and Folders

THIS CHAPTER DISCUSSES HOW to manage files and folders. It starts off by touching briefly on what files and folders *are* (if you've used a computer before, you probably know this already) before getting into what you can do with them and the tools that XP provides.

Tools? It's more like *tool*, actually, because most of your file management takes place in Explorer. As you'll see, you can use Explorer to search for files and folders; to manipulate them; to view them in different ways; and to dispose of them. You can also use Explorer to compress and uncompress files and folders, either to save space or to make archive files that are easy to handle.

At the end of the chapter, after all the other excitement, you'll find a section on how to configure AutoPlay's behavior and how to customize folders in Explorer.

This chapter covers the following topics:

◆ The basics of files and folders

◆ Understanding what Explorer is

◆ Investigating the Windows XP folder structure

◆ Navigating in Explorer

◆ Copying, moving, and deleting files and folders

◆ Finding files and folders

◆ Creating and using shortcuts

◆ Configuring AutoPlay

◆ Customizing Explorer

The Basics of Files and Folders

If you've used computers much in the past, you'll be familiar with the concept of a *file*—a named object containing information that's stored on a disk. The disk in question can be a local hard drive; a networked drive (including a web server); a CD, DVD, or other removable drive; a tape drive; or even a humble floppy drive. Whichever type of drive the file's on, it's stored in a number of clusters on some form of disk. You don't have to worry about the number of clusters a file occupies. In fact, you need worry about the fact that each file occupies various clusters only when your drive needs defragmenting (which you'll find discussed in Chapter 11) or when you need to either wipe out all trace of a file that you've deleted or restore a file that you've deleted (a topic discussed later in this chapter).

Anyway, each file has a name so that you and the computer can distinguish it. In XP, each filename can be up to 255 characters long. Filenames can include letters, numbers, and some punctuation, such as commas (,), periods (.), semicolons (;), single quotation marks ('), or apostrophes ('). Filenames cannot contain forward slashes (/), backslashes (\ ), colons (:), asterisks (*), question marks (?), double quotation marks ("), less-than (<) and greater-than (>) signs, or pipe characters (|), because XP either uses those characters literally or assigns special meanings to them. For example, a colon is used to denote a drive (for instance, C: refers to the C: drive), and an asterisk is a wildcard character that represents one or more characters in searches and commands.

The 255 characters include the path to the file. The *path* (also sometimes called the *directory path*) gives the sequence of drive and folders that describes the location of the file and folders. For example, if a file is in the \My Documents\ folder in the \Nik\ folder of the \Documents and Settings\ folder on the C: drive, the path to that file is C:\Documents and Settings\Nik\My Documents\. That path is 43 characters long, including the backslashes and the spaces, so any file stored in that folder can have a filename of up to 212 characters (255 minus the 43 characters in the path).

A *folder* is a file that can contain other files. (You don't *have* to put any files in a folder, but an empty folder is little use to man or beast.) By using folders, you can organize your files into logical categories (or whimsical categories, if you prefer). Folder names can be up to 255 characters long, but you'll need to keep them shorter than this if you want to use long filenames within the folders. The possible length of a folder name also includes the path to the folder and the length of any filenames that the folder already contains. (If you rename a folder so that the path and filename of a file it contains add up to more than 255 characters, you can no longer access the file.)

When working in a graphical environment such as XP, you don't normally need to type paths to files the way you often had to in DOS and similar text-based operating systems. Instead, you use graphical representations of folders and files to navigate to the folders and files you need, and then manipulate them in graphical windows. Some of this you do with Explorer (discussed in the next section), and some via dialog boxes in the individual programs.

Using Explorer

This section discusses Explorer, starting off with the trickiest thing about it—understanding what it is.

What *Is* Explorer?

If you've used Explorer before, you may think this a dumb question—but Explorer is actually a very complex program. You can use it almost effortlessly in several simple ways. But to understand why it behaves as it does when you take certain actions with it, you need to understand what it is and does. That means wrapping your mind around a few slithery concepts.

Ready?

First, Explorer is the shell for XP. Briefly, in computing terms a *shell* is a logical layer that provides an interface between the user and the computer. In this case, it's a graphical interface—a *very* graphical interface. The Desktop, with its icons and pretty background picture, is run by Explorer, as are the Taskbar, the notification area, and so on. (If you doubt this, see the next sidebar.) Explorer essentially gives you a way to interact with XP without talking code.

Second, Explorer is a utility for managing files and folders—all kinds of files and folders, including the files and folders that make up the Start menu, those that make up Control Panel, and so forth. File management is how most people view Explorer's role, because Explorer windows are the most obvious manifestation of Explorer. We'll investigate Explorer's file-management capabilities in some detail in this chapter.

Third, Explorer is intimately related to Internet Explorer, the web browser that's built into XP. If you look at them together, you see that Explorer (in its second role) and Internet Explorer are basically the same program with somewhat different manifestations and different roles. On the one hand, many of the commands—menu commands, toolbars, keyboard shortcuts—are the same. On the other hand, the Options dialog boxes are substantially different, as are the toolbars. On that first hand, you can use them to do many of the same things (for example, to display the contents of a folder). On that other hand, they're clearly designed to be used in different ways. Most of the time, anyway.

Back to that first hand again, the programs act in much the same way. In fact, Explorer can even switch itself to Internet Explorer when you're using it. This can be freaky until you learn to expect the unexpected. If you enter a URL in the Address bar in Explorer and click the Go button, Explorer opens the website and transmutes itself into Internet Explorer. By contrast, if you enter a local drive letter or path in the Address bar in Internet Explorer, it doesn't entirely change into Explorer. Instead, it just stays as Internet Explorer and displays the contents of the drive or the folder—but with all the Explorer features. For example, if you pull down the Tools menu, you'll see a Folder Options item (the Explorer menu item) rather than an Internet Options item.

But you've got better things to do than worry about how Windows Explorer and Internet Explorer might really be two heads of the same Cerberus-Explorer whose third head is the Desktop shell. If you use Windows Explorer for interacting with files and folders on local and network drives, and Internet Explorer for interacting with anything that might consider itself a website, you'll get on fine.

Besides, Explorer *isn't* Cerberus—at least, in that hewing off one of the heads doesn't affect the body. When you run Internet Explorer, it shows up as a separate process on the Processes page of Task Manager—a process named `IEXPLORE.EXE`. If you point Explorer at a website so that it turns into Internet Explorer, its Taskbar button takes on an Internet Explorer icon, but the process associated with it is `EXPLORER.EXE`, not `IEXPLORE.EXE`. If you terminate Explorer (as described in that next sidebar), Internet Explorer isn't affected. Likewise, if you terminate Internet Explorer, Explorer shouldn't be affected.

To try to keep things clear, the rest of this book uses *Explorer* to refer to Explorer windows (including those for My Computer, Network Connections, Control Panel, and so on), *Internet Explorer* to refer to any Explorer window that calls itself Internet Explorer, and descriptive terms such as *the Desktop, the Taskbar,* and *the notification area* to refer to the named components of the shell.

EXPERT KNOWLEDGE: PROVING THAT EXPLORER RUNS THE DESKTOP AND TASKBAR

If you doubt that Explorer really runs the Desktop, the Taskbar, and so on, you might want to try this little experiment. It's not exactly *recommended*, because it gives XP a vigorous elbow in the solar plexus. But because XP is quite stable and resilient, winding it a little doesn't usually do any damage.

Take these steps:

1. Close all the programs you're running.

2. Right-click open space on the Taskbar and choose Task Manager from the context menu. XP displays Task Manager.

3. Click the Processes tab. XP displays the Processes page.

4. Select the process named EXPLORER.EXE.

5. Click the End Process button. Task Manager displays a Task Manager Warning dialog box warning that terminating the process could lose you data or cause your system to be unstable.

6. Click the Yes button. Task Manager terminates Explorer. The Taskbar and notification area disappear, together with the Start button and all your Desktop icons. Task Manager keeps on chugging along happily enough.

7. Try right-clicking the Desktop. You won't get even a hint of a context menu.

8. Back in Task Manager, click the Applications tab. XP displays the Applications page.

9. Click the New Task button. XP displays the Create New Task dialog box.

10. Enter **explorer** in the Open text box.

11. Click the OK button. XP closes the Create New Task dialog box and runs Explorer. Back come your icons, the Start button, the Taskbar, and the notification area, together with all their functionality.

You don't *have* to try this little experiment at home—but if you just tried it, wasn't it instructive? (Or at least entertaining?) Now, it might be a good idea to restart XP in case it's feeling a little peculiar.

Starting Explorer

You can start Explorer in a variety of ways. The easiest way to start Explorer is to click the Start button so that XP displays the Start menu, and then choose one of the shortcuts associated with Explorer: My Documents, My Pictures, My Music, My Computer, or (if you have it) My Network Places. Each of these opens an Explorer window to the specified folder in Open mode, one of the two modes that Explorer supports.

To open one of these folders in Explore mode (the other mode), click the Start button to display the Start menu, right-click the item for the folder, and choose Explore from the context menu.

You can also run Explorer by choosing Start ➢ All Programs ➢ Accessories ➢ Windows Explorer. Doing so opens a My Computer window in Explore mode.

EXPLORING MY COMPUTER

If you choose Start ➢ My Computer, XP displays an Explorer window showing the contents of the My Computer folder in Open mode, as in the example shown in Figure 6.1.

FIGURE 6.1

The My Computer folder open in an Explorer window

There's a whole bunch of stuff to look at here, even (or especially) if you've used Windows before.

The first thing to notice is how different this looks from Explorer windows in earlier versions of Windows. The window has a title bar as usual, of course, and a menu bar and a toolbar. There's no Address bar, as there was by default in My Computer windows in earlier versions of Windows, but you can display it easily enough by choosing View ➤ Toolbars ➤ Address Bar. (And when you do, you may notice that the toolbar and the Address bar together look suspiciously like those in Internet Explorer....)

The main action is on the left side of the screen, where Explorer is displaying three collapsible panes courtesy of the new WebView and ListView features:

Tasks pane   This pane provides a list of tasks that you might want to perform on the folder or, when you select an object that's displayed, on that object. (More on this in a moment.) For the My Computer folder, the Tasks pane is named System Tasks.

Other Places pane   This pane provides a short list of other folders that you might want to access from the current folder. This list of folders changes to suit the current folder. The list usually includes the parent folder of the current folder (the *parent* of an object is the folder that contains it) and a carefully selected variety of widely used folders such as the Desktop folder, the My Computer folder, the My Documents folder, the Shared Documents folder, and (if your computer is connected to a network) the My Network Places folder. Each of the folders is presented as a link in the list, so you can access the folder by clicking it.

Details pane   This pane displays information about the selected folder or file. For example, when a file is selected, the pane displays the filename, the file type (such as WordPad Document), and the date that the file was modified.

Each pane collapses down to its title bar to save space and make room for its fellow panes. To collapse a pane, or expand it again, click its title bar. If you're feeling the need for precision, you can click the double-arrow button at the right end of the title bar, but the effect is the same as clicking the title bar, so it's not worth making the extra effort.

As you can see in the figure, the main part of the window presents several lists:

Files Stored on This Computer   This list shows the shared folders available to the current user. For a Limited user or the Guest user, this is typically a short list, containing only the \Shared Documents\ folder, which is shared among all users of the computer. Computer Administrator users can see other users' shared folders as well, as in the figure.

Hard Disk Drives   This list shows all the hard drives on the computer.

Devices with Removable Storage   This list shows all the devices with removable storage, such as floppy drives, CD drives, DVD drives, Zip drives, CompactFlash disk reader, and so on.

Network Drives   This list shows all the network drives (if any) to which the computer is attached for the current user.

Below the Network Drives list appears a Scanners and Cameras list if you have one or more scanners or cameras.

The lists of items in the Tasks pane and the Other Places pane are links, so you click them once to take the action on the selected file or folder or to access the other place. The items displayed on the right side of the screen are objects. An *object* is a general descriptor for a distinct entity on a computer—a file, a folder, a computer, and so on. Basically (no pun intended), everything that you see in Explorer is an object. A file is an object; a folder is an object; a computer you can see across the network is an object. Even the links displayed in the Tasks list and the Other Places list are objects.

Each object has *properties*—attributes—that you can view and, in some cases, set. For example, most objects have a name property that contains the name of the object. Many also have a read-only property that can be turned on and off and that determines whether a user can change the object (if the property is off) or not (if the property is on). Most objects also have *methods*—actions associated with the object. For example, many objects have a click method that determines what takes place when you click the object. Link objects execute when you click them, whereas objects such as files and folders become selected when you click them and execute when you double-click them.

WebView and ListView make the display more graphical, and provide quick access to a number of tasks and quick navigation to folders connected to the current folder. In essence, WebView and ListView try to simplify navigating from folder to folder and taking frequently used actions. In particular, they target navigating via the folder tree and taking actions via the context menu. As mentioned earlier in the book, usability tests suggested that 80 percent of Windows users weren't using the context menu effectively.

If you're new to Windows, or if you've never gotten the hang of navigating via the folder tree (*where was that folder again?*) or using the context menus, WebView and ListView may prove welcome. But if you're used to using the folder tree and the context menus, you probably won't find WebView and ListView much of an improvement. You may even find them detrimental, because they make it harder to navigate XP in your time-tested ways. If so, you can turn them off easily enough, as discussed in the section after next. Context menus, which have been enhanced for many folders in XP, almost always contain more commands than the Tasks list, and they're easier to access with the mouse than the Tasks list.

EXPLORE MODE

Okay, so that was My Computer in Open mode. Now open it in Explore mode to see the difference. Click the Start button to display the Start menu, then right-click the My Computer item and choose Explore from the context menu. You get a window like that shown in Figure 6.2.

FIGURE 6.2

Viewed in Explore mode, the My Computer window displays the Folders Explorer bar on the left side for quick navigation.

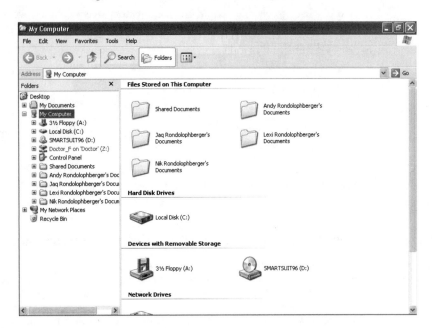

As you can see, in Explore mode, Explorer displays a pane called Folders at the left side of the window pane. The formal name for this pane is the Folders Explorer bar. Clicking the Folders button on the toolbar or choosing View ➢ Explorer Bar ➢ Folders from a My Computer window displayed in Open mode gives you the same effect as opening the window afresh in Explore mode.

Explore mode makes moving up and down the directory tree easy, so Explorer hides the WebView and ListView panes in Explore mode. This also makes more room on the right side of the screen for the files or folders you're presumably interested in. If you find Explore mode useful, you'll probably want to make it the default action for Explorer (as discussed in the next sidebar).

Explore mode is easy to use, but the following details are worth knowing:

◆ Select a drive or folder in the Folders Explorer bar to display its contents in the right pane.

◆ You can select only one drive or folder at a time in the Folders Explorer bar, whereas you can select multiple drives or folders in the right pane.

◆ You can expand or collapse the listing of the folders on a drive or the subfolders in a folder by clicking the plus (+) sign to the left of the drive or folder.

◆ You can move folders by dragging them about in the left pane or the right pane.

◆ To move an item to a folder that's currently collapsed, drag the item to the parent and hover the mouse pointer there until Explorer expands the collapsed folder.

◆ If you accidentally move a folder by dragging it when you intended only to select it, choose Edit ➢ Undo Move to put the folder back where it belongs.

TURNING OFF WEBVIEW AND LISTVIEW

If you're used to blazing up and down a directory tree with a few well-placed clicks of the mouse, you may well find WebView and ListView irritating or worse. You can turn them off easily enough. Follow these steps:

1. From an Explorer window, choose Tools ➢ Folder Options. Explorer displays the Folder Options dialog box with the General page foremost.
2. In the Tasks group box, select the Use Windows Classic Folders option button.
3. Click the OK button. Explorer closes the Folder Options dialog box and applies the change, removing WebView and ListView from all Explorer windows displayed.

To turn WebView and ListView back on, display the Folder Options dialog box again, select the Show Common Tasks in Folders option button in the Tasks group box, and click the OK button. This book assumes you're using WebView and ListView.

EXPERT KNOWLEDGE: SETTING EXPLORER TO USE EXPLORE MODE BY DEFAULT

If you've used a previous version of Windows and you're used to navigating via a tree of folders, you may find Explore mode so much easier and more useful than Open mode that you want to use it all the time. To make Explorer use Explore mode rather than Open mode by default, follow these steps:

1. From an Explorer window (in either Open mode or Explore mode), choose Tools ➢ Folder Options. XP displays the Folder Options dialog box.
2. Click the File Types tab. XP displays the File Types page.
3. Select the (NONE) Folder item. The *(NONE)* bit is in the Extensions list; the *Folder* bit is in the File Types list.
4. Click the Advanced button. XP displays the Edit File Type dialog box for the Folder file type. (You'll find a discussion of file types toward the end of this chapter.)
5. In the Actions list box, make sure the Explore action is selected. (XP usually selects it automatically.)
6. Click the Set Default button. XP applies Explore as the default action for folders.
7. Click the OK button. XP closes the Edit File Type dialog box, returning you to the Folder Options dialog box.
8. Click the Close button. XP closes the Folder Options dialog box.

From now on, XP opens folders using Explore mode. To switch back to Open as the default action, repeat the above steps but choose the Open action in step 5.

Investigating XP's Folder Structure

This section discusses the folder structure that XP creates on your hard drive. You don't *need* to understand the folder structure in order to use XP effectively, because the WebView and ListView features provide an easy way to navigate among the folders that XP wants you to use. But if you want to administer the computer and make the best use of XP's management features, or if you just want to know a bit more about what's going on behind the curtain, it's a great help to understand the folder structure.

XP Home has firm ideas about where it wants you to keep the files you install, create, and use. By and large, you'll get along best if you stick to these guidelines, but they can sure feel restrictive. (If you've used earlier versions of Windows, they'll probably seem familiar.) XP also has firm ideas about what you should look at and what you shouldn't. If you use WebView and ListView, XP attempts to shield you from seeing system folders and program folders. In fact, it tries to discourage you from looking in any folder except those that contain your documents and those that contain settings it expects you to change, such as the Control Panel folder and the Network Connections folder.

NOTE *The folder structure discussed in this section is the one you get when you install a fresh copy of XP on your computer without monkeying around with any settings. If anyone has customized your computer, things might look a bit different.*

XP places all these folders on the same drive XP itself is on.

From the My Computer window (Start ➤ My Computer), double-click the hard disk drive that contains XP. (If you have only one hard disk drive, you shouldn't have a problem. If you have multiple drives, you may need to work out which contains XP.) You'll see something like Figure 6.3, which tells you that "This folder contains files that keep your system working properly. You should not modify its contents."

FIGURE 6.3

By default, XP tries to shield you from the details of the system folders and program folders on your computer.

Click the Show the Contents of This Drive link in the System Tasks task list. XP displays the folders it was hiding. You should see something like Figure 6.4.

FIGURE 6.4

Click the Show the Contents of This Drive link to make XP display the folders.

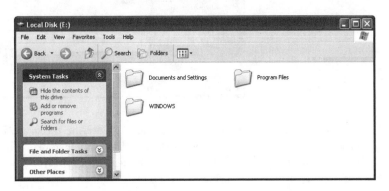

But that's not all the folders. By default, XP hides what it calls *protected operating system files*—translation, any files or folders it would prefer you not to see or mess with. It also hides hidden files and folders—files and folders marked with the hidden attribute. (For example, you'll remember from the previous chapter that Word uses hidden locking files to prevent the same file from being accessed by more than one person at the same time.)

To display hidden files and protected operating system files, follow these steps:

1. Choose Tools ➤ Folder Options. XP displays the Folder Options dialog box.
2. Click the View tab. XP displays the View page.
3. In the Advanced Settings list box, select the Show Hidden Files and Folders option button. (By default, the Do Not Show Hidden Files and Folders option button is selected.)
4. A little further down the Advanced Settings list box, clear the Hide Protected Operating System Files check box. XP displays the Warning dialog box shown in Figure 6.5 when you clear this check box.

FIGURE 6.5

XP displays this Warning dialog box when you choose to display the protected operating system files.

5. Click the Yes button. XP closes the Warning dialog box and returns you to the Folder Options dialog box.
6. Click the OK button. XP closes the Folder Options dialog box and applies the changes. You should now see a list of folders similar to that in Figure 6.6.

FIGURE 6.6

Here's the folder structure that XP creates.

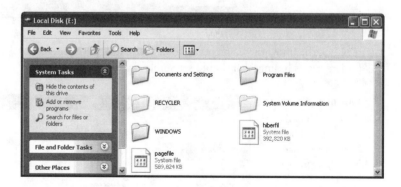

The folder structure contains the \Windows\ folder, the \Program Files\ folder, and the \Documents and Settings\ folder. The following sections discuss these folders. There's also the \Recycler\ folder, which controls the Recycle Bin, and the \System Volume Information\ folder, which XP keeps locked against user intrusion to protect its contents.

THE *\WINDOWS* FOLDER

The \Windows\ folder contains most of the files needed to keep XP running. (As you'll see in a moment, there are a couple of others.) If you open this folder, you'll see a plethora of subfolders and files. (You know how people use the word *plethora* when they really just mean *more than a handful?* Well, this really is a plethora.)

XP is right that it's not a good idea for you to mess with these files: There's very little you can do to them that will benefit you or your PC, and a fair amount you can do to them that will harm your PC. (That said, XP is able to restore many system files after they've accidentally been deleted.)

THE *\PROGRAM FILES* FOLDER

The \Program Files\ folder is designed to hold (almost) all the files for all the programs on the computer. The setup routines for most programs know that they're supposed to install the programs in the \Program Files\ folder, and do so unless you explicitly specify a different location.

Because Microsoft a) created XP and b) is an 800-pound gorilla, however, it can put its program files wherever it wants to. For example, you'll find the program files for Notepad (a limited text-editor program included with XP) in the \Windows\ folder rather than in the \Program Files\ folder.

You'll need to mess with the contents of the \Program Files\ folder only seldom—for example, when something goes wrong with an uninstall routine, or when you're trying to perform a special tweak on a program. But if you have even an averagely curious disposition, you'll probably want to spelunk through this folder to see what it contains.

THE *\DOCUMENTS AND SETTINGS* FOLDER

The \Documents and Settings\ folder contains the documents and settings for each user for whom you create an account on the computer and who has logged on at least once, together with a \My Documents\ folder for the Guest user (also, once they've logged on). This is the place where Microsoft would like you to hang out—though Microsoft would prefer you to access it via the My Documents shortcut, which automatically lands the user in his or her own directory.

If you've been following along, go ahead and double-click the icon for the \Documents and Settings\ folder. You'll see something like the window shown in Figure 6.7.

FIGURE 6.7

The contents of the \Documents and Settings\ folder.

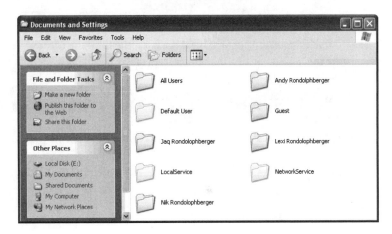

The number of folders you see in your \Documents and Settings\ folder depends on the number of user accounts you set up on the computer. In the figure, the Rondolophbergers have four user accounts, so there's a folder for each of them: the \Andy Rondolophberger\ folder, the \Jaq Rondolophberger\ folder, the \Lexi Rondolophberger\ folder, and the \Nik Rondolophberger\ folder. Then there's an \All Users\ folder, which contains documents and settings that are available to all users. There's the \Default User\ folder, which contains settings that are applied to all new users created (until the user comes along and customizes them). There's the \Guest\ folder, which contains documents and settings for the Guest user. And then there's a \LocalService\ folder and a \NetworkService\ folder. We'll get to these folders in a minute or two.

Each user's folder contains the same folder structure—until the user changes it, anyway. Figure 6.8 shows an example.

FIGURE 6.8

Each user's folder contains this folder structure (until someone changes it).

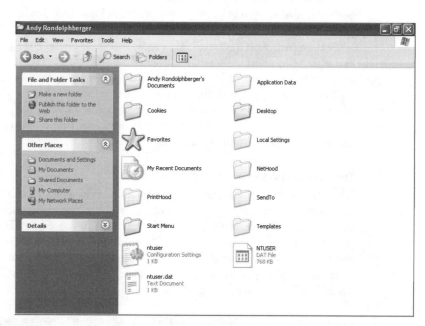

Table 6.1 provides a quick breakdown of the folder structure. We'll examine the \My Documents\ folder in a minute or two. The other folders we'll examine as needed later in the book.

TABLE 6.1: FOLDERS IN EACH USER'S FOLDER STRUCTURE

FOLDER NAME	CONTENTS
\Application Data\	Your settings for programs, including your Address Book data and program templates
\Cookies\	Your cookie files (information used to allow websites to provide user-specific services)

Continued on next page

TABLE 6.1: FOLDERS IN EACH USER'S FOLDER STRUCTURE *(continued)*

FOLDER NAME	CONTENTS
\Desktop\	Your Desktop shortcuts (apart from the standard Desktop shortcuts that XP provides, such as My Computer and the Recycle Bin)
\Favorites\	Your Explorer favorites and Internet Explorer favorites
\Local Settings\	Your Internet Explorer history, temporary files, temporary Internet files, and Desktop settings
\My Documents\	Your documents
\My Recent Documents\	Shortcuts to files and folders you've used recently
\NetHood\	Information about mappings to any network drives that your computer connects to
\PrintHood\	The mappings for any network printers that your computer is set up to use
\SendTo\	The shortcuts, files, and folders that make up your Send To menu
\Start Menu\	Your shortcuts for the Start menu
\Templates\	Templates for programs you install
\Windows\	Your Windows XP settings

THE *MY DOCUMENTS*\ FOLDER

The \My Documents\ folder is where Microsoft would like you to keep all your data files except those that you explicitly want to share with other people. The main advantages to using the \My Documents\ folder (which you can rename to whatever you want) are first that you have a central point of administration that you can protect or back up easily, and second that all the programs know where to look for files.

As you might imagine, which user is active governs which folder is connected to the My Documents link on the Start menu. For example, when Andy Rondolophberger is logged on and active, choosing Start ➢ My Documents causes Explorer to display the \Documents and Settings\Andy Rondolophberger\My Documents\ folder rather than any of the \My Documents\ folders in the other users' folders.

Each user's \My Documents\ folder contains a \My Music\ folder and a \My Pictures\ folder. When you start using videos (for example, the first time you start Windows Movie Maker), XP adds a \My Videos\ folder as well. You get no prizes for guessing what's intended to go in each of these folders. Windows XP–aware programs use these folders by default. For example, WordPad automatically uses the \My Documents\ folder. Windows Media Player has been schooled to save music you copy to folders within the \My Music\ folder, though you can teach it without difficulty to save music elsewhere if you prefer. And Paint uses the \My Pictures\ folder, as does Windows Picture and Fax Viewer.

You can move your \My Documents\ folder from its default location by taking the following steps:

1. Click the Start button. XP displays the Start menu.
2. Right-click the My Computer item and choose Properties from the context menu. XP displays the Properties dialog box with the Target page foremost.

3. Click the Move button. XP displays the Select a Destination dialog box.

4. Select the folder and click the OK button. XP displays the Move Documents dialog box, asking if you want to move all the documents from the old location to the new location.

5. Click the Yes button or the No button as appropriate. Bear in mind that by default your \My Documents\ folder contains your \My Music\ folder and your \My Pictures\ folder (and your \My Videos\ folder, if you have one), so moving the folder may involve moving a large number of files.

XP doesn't provide a simple mechanism for moving your \My Music\ folder and your \My Pictures\ folder out of your \My Documents\ folder—but the Tweak UI PowerToy does. Download this PowerToy from the Microsoft Windows XP Downloads site (`www.microsoft.com/windowsxp/home/downloads/powertoys.asp`), install it, run it by choosing Start ➤ All Programs ➤ PowerToys for Windows XP ➤ Tweak UI for Windows XP, and then use the tool on the My Computer\Special Folders page.

PAGEFILE.SYS AND HIBERFIL.SYS

As mentioned a page or two ago, not *all* the files needed to keep XP running reside in the \Windows\ folder. There are a couple of massive exceptions: the paging file and the hibernation file.

If you look at the root of the drive on which XP is installed, you should see a large file named PAGEFILE or PAGEFILE.SYS. (If you don't see it, turn on the display of protected and hidden files as discussed a couple of pages ago.) This is the *paging file*—a file in which XP stores information temporarily to supplement the RAM (physical memory) in your computer. (Chapter 16 discusses what the paging file does and how you can optimize and move it.) Don't mess with this file via Explorer. It's locked, because it's perpetually in use, so all you can do is stub your toes on it. You probably have better things to do with your time.

You may also see another large file, this one called HIBERFIL or HIBERFIL.SYS. This is the *hibernation file*—the file in which XP stores the contents of RAM when you put the computer into Hibernation mode. It takes up as many megabytes of disk space as you have RAM. Don't mess with this file either. If you don't like sacrificing a chunk of disk space to it, turn off hibernation as discussed in Chapter 14.

You may also see a file called ERRORLOG or ERRORLOG.TXT. As its name suggests, this is a log of critical errors that have occurred on your computer. If you haven't had any critical errors, there won't be an error log file yet.

THE \LOCALSERVICE\ FOLDER AND \NETWORKSERVICE\ FOLDER

The \LocalService\ folder and the \NetworkService\ folder are created and maintained automatically by XP in order to manage local services and network services. These folders are locked so that you cannot access them. You *can* circumvent the locking so that you can open the folders and make changes in them, but there's no point in doing so, because it will make XP seriously unhappy and can do you no conceivable good.

RESTORING THE FOLDER OPTIONS

Now that we've finished our quick tour of the folder structure, you might want to hide the program folders, system folders, and hidden files again so that you see XP as nature—that is, Microsoft—intended. To do so, follow these steps:

1. Choose Tools ➤ Folder Options. XP displays the Folder Options dialog box.

2. Click the View tab. XP displays the View page.

3. In the Advanced Settings list box, select the Do Not Show Hidden Files and Folders option button and the Hide Protected Operating System Files check box.

4. Click the OK button. XP closes the Folder Options dialog box and applies the changes.

Using Views

Explorer supports a number of views to let you browse folders and files comfortably and be able to tell what you're looking at:

Thumbnails view   This view displays a largish icon for each file or folder. Thumbnails view is good for finding the graphics you need, because Explorer displays a miniature version of each graphic. For file types other than graphics, Explorer displays only the icon associated with the program.

Tiles view   This view displays a medium-sized icon for each file or folder. Explorer displays icons rather than miniatures for graphics files. Tiles view is good for sorting through folders that contain relatively few files or folders.

Icons view   This view displays a smallish icon for each file or folder. Again, Explorer displays icons rather than miniatures for graphics files. Icons view is good for sorting through folders that contain a moderate number of files or folders.

List view   This view displays a list of folders and files, showing only the filename or folder name and a small icon for each. List view is good for sorting through folders that contain a large number of files or folders.

Details   This view displays a list of files and folders, showing the filename or folder name, a small icon, the file size, the file type, and the date on which it was modified. (You can customize the details displayed for a folder. See the end of the chapter for, uh, details.) Details view is good for sorting files and folders by different types of information to quickly locate the file or folder you need. You can apply a view in any of these ways:

♦ Pull down the View menu and choose Thumbnails, Tiles, Icons, List, or Details from it.

♦ Click the View button on the toolbar and choose Thumbnails, Tiles, Icons, List, or Details from the menu it displays.

♦ Right-click in an Explorer window, choose View from the context menu, and choose Thumbnails, Tiles, Icons, List, or Details from the submenu that appears.

See pages 18 and 19 of the *Essential Skills* section for a visual guide to using views.

Arranging Icons

Once you've applied a view, you can choose how to arrange the icons displayed in the view. Explorer lets you arrange icons in the following ways:

Name   This arrangement sorts the icons alphabetically by name.

Size   This arrangement sorts the icons by size.

Type This arrangement sorts the icons by their file type. If the folder contains more than a few files, sorting by file type produces groups by file type, so it's a good way of finding all the documents of a particular type (for example, text file) that the folder contains.

Modified This arrangement sorts the icons by the date the file they represent was last modified.

NOTE In some special folders, Explorer offers other arrangements. For example, in the My Computer folder, it offers Total Size, Free Space, and Comments arrangements.

Once you've chosen the arrangement, you can turn on the Show in Groups option to arrange the icons into groups by the attribute on which they're currently sorted. For example, if you're using Details view, and you've sorted by the Modified column, turning on the Show in Groups option divides the icons into groups such as Today and Earlier This Month. If you've sorted Details view by the Type column, turning on the Show in Groups option creates groups based on the types of file— for example, File Folder, Text Document, and so on.

There are two further options that you can toggle on and off as suits you:

Auto Arrange This option tells Explorer to arrange the icons into the specified order automatically. This option is good for keeping the icons in order.

Align to Grid This option tells Explorer to snap the icons back to an invisible grid, thus tidying up the window.

To specify the sorting and arrangement, pull down the View menu, or right-click in open space in the Explorer window to display the context menu. Choose the Arrange Icons By item from the menu, and then select the command from the submenu.

TIP In Details view, you can sort quickly by clicking the heading of the column by which you want to sort. The first click produces an ascending sort (alphabetical order; smallest numbers first). A second click produces a descending sort (reverse alphabetical order; largest numbers first).

Using the Standard Buttons Toolbar

The main Explorer toolbar, which is called the Standard Buttons toolbar, contains six graphical buttons for actions you may well need to take frequently:

Back button Click this button to move back to the previous folder that was displayed. Click the down arrow at the right side of the button to display a drop-down list of the previous folders so that you can move back several steps at once.

Forward button This is the counterpart to the Back button, and becomes available only when you've used the Back button. After you've moved back along the path of folders you've browsed through, you can use the Forward button to move forward through them again. As with the Back button, use the drop-down list to move forward several steps at once.

Up button Click this button to browse to the parent folder of the current folder. (The parent, you'll remember, is the folder that contains the object in question.)

Search button   Click this button to display Search Companion, the tool for searching for files, folders, or computers. (The section "Finding a File or Folder," later in this chapter, discusses how to use Search Companion.)

Folders button   Click this button to toggle the display of the Folders Explorer bar.

Views button   Click this button to display a menu from which you can choose a view for the current window.

USING THE ADDRESS BAR AND THE LINKS BAR

Isn't *Standard Buttons toolbar* quite a mouthful for a plain old toolbar (especially one with only six buttons)? It sure is. But this toolbar needs a distinctive name because Explorer provides two other toolbars: the Address bar and the Links bar. To toggle the display of these toolbars, choose View ➤ Toolbars ➤ Address Bar or View ➤ Toolbars ➤ Links, or right-click the menu bar or a displayed toolbar and choose Address Bar or Links from the context menu.

The Address bar contains a drop-down list box that gives access to folders and files on local and network drives. Figure 6.9 shows an example. Alternatively, you can type in a path or a URL and click the Go button.

FIGURE 6.9

The Address bar provides quick access to the folders on your computer.

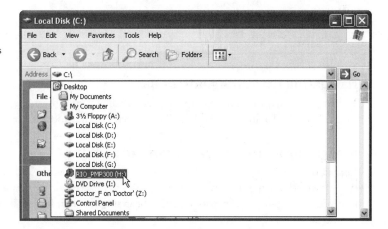

The Links toolbar provides links to websites. We'll discuss this toolbar more when we examine Internet Explorer in Chapter 19.

REARRANGING THE MENU BAR AND TOOLBARS

By default, the toolbars and menu bar are locked so that you can't move them. To unlock toolbars (and the menu bar, which is an honorary toolbar), right-click the menu bar or a displayed toolbar and choose Lock the Toolbars from the context menu, or choose View ➤ Toolbars ➤ Lock the Toolbars.

Once you've unlocked the toolbars, you can drag them and the menu bar to different sizes or arrangements by clicking and dragging the sizing handles (the rows of dots) at their left ends. For example, you can display the Address bar on the same row as the Standard Buttons toolbar to save space.

When the toolbars and menu bar are where you want them, you can lock them again (by repeating the process described two paragraphs above) if you want to prevent yourself from moving them by accident.

Navigating Explorer with the Keyboard

If you prefer the keyboard to the mouse, you can perform some basic navigation with menu commands and keyboard shortcuts. Table 6.2 lists these keyboard shortcuts and menu commands.

TABLE 6.2: KEYBOARD SHORTCUTS AND MENU COMMANDS FOR NAVIGATING EXPLORER

ACTION	KEYBOARD SHORTCUT	MENU COMMAND
Back	Alt+←	View ➤ Go To ➤ Back
Forward	Alt+→	View ➤ Go To ➤ Forward
Up One Level	Backspace	View ➤ Go To ➤ Up One Level
Home Page	Alt+Home	View ➤ Go To ➤ Home Page
My Computer	—	View ➤ Go To ➤ My Computer
Display Address bar drop-down list	F4	—
Refresh	F5	View ➤ Refresh

Navigating Using the Address Bar

You can also navigate from folder to folder by using the Address bar. To display the Address bar, choose View ➤ Toolbars ➤ Address Bar. By default, the Address bar appears below the toolbar.

Navigating by Using Type-Down Addressing

Instead of navigating with the mouse, you can navigate through folders by using the keyboard and type-down addressing. This technique works best for accessing a file or folder whose name and location you know, but you can also use it for browsing through folders or files if you find it fast and comfortable.

Type-down addressing sounds forbidding, but it's easy and intuitive—and a great saver of time and effort. To use type-down addressing, you put the focus in the appropriate area—for example, in an Explorer window or in the Address bar. You can then type down through the contents of the folder. As you type each letter, the program (in this case, Explorer; the technique works for all properly implemented XP programs) selects the files or folders that match what you've typed, progressively narrowing down the possibilities until you reach the file or folder you want. At that point (or before), you can select it as usual.

That sounds a bit vague, doesn't it? Type-down addressing is much easier to do than to describe. Here's an example:

1. Choose Start ➤ My Computer. XP displays an Explorer window showing the contents of the My Computer folder.

2. Click the Address bar to select the current entry (My Computer). Alternatively, press the F4 key and then the Esc key.

   ◆ If the Address bar isn't displayed, choose View ➢ Toolbars ➢ Address Bar to display it.

3. Type the letter of the hard drive on which XP is installed, followed by a colon and a backslash. For example,
   `C:\`

4. Explorer displays a drop-down list of the matching folders and files.

5. Type **m**. XP narrows down the selection to the files and folders that start with the letter *m*—typically, the \My Music\ folder (unless you've created other folders).

6. Press the ↓ key to select the \My Music\ folder.

7. You can then type down through the \My Music\ folder to reach the folder or file you want.

Refreshing the Listing in a Folder

If you take an action in an Explorer window that causes the contents of the folder displayed to change, Explorer automatically refreshes the display. For example, if you create a new folder within the folder, Explorer updates the display to show the new folder along with the previous contents. If you delete a file from the folder, Explorer removes the file from the display.

But if the contents of the folder displayed in an Explorer window change because of an action *not* taken in the window, Explorer doesn't usually notice right away. Periodically, it will reread the contents of the folder and update the display. But if you don't want to wait, you can refresh the display manually. To do so, press the F5 key, or choose View ➢ Refresh, or right-click empty space in the folder and choose Refresh from the context menu.

Choosing Folder Options

The View page of the Folder Options dialog box offers you the following options, some of which you've already met earlier in this chapter:

Automatically Search for Network Folders and Printers check box   Controls whether XP searches the network for shared folders and printers periodically. The items found then appear in your My Network Places folder.

Display File Size Information in Folder Tips check box   Controls whether Explorer displays an information pop-up when you hover the mouse pointer over a folder. As its name implies, this option doesn't apply to files—just to folders. So when you've cleared this check box, XP still displays file information when you hover the mouse pointer over a file in an Explorer window.

Display Simple Folder View in Explorer's Folders List check box   Controls whether Explorer uses XP's new Simple Folder view or the "classic" folder view. Simple Folder view provides more intelligent management of the subfolders displayed in the Folders Explorer bar: Instead of displaying the full list of subfolders, XP displays only those relevant to the subfolder you've chosen to display. When you select a folder in the Folders Explorer bar, Explorer expands the folder to show its subfolders and closes all other currently expanded folders. Explorer also hides the dotted lines used in "classic" folder view to connect the folders and drives.

Display the Contents of System Folders check box   Controls whether Explorer displays the contents of system folders (such as the `\Documents and Settings\` folder, the `\Program Files\` folder, and the `\Windows\` folder. By default, the contents of these folders are hidden.

Display the Full Path in the Address Bar check box   Controls whether Explorer displays the full path in the Address bar (if you've chosen to display the Address bar) instead of just display-ing the folder name. Most people who use the Address bar find this feature useful, but Microsoft has chosen to turn it off by default.

Display the Full Path in the Title Bar check box   Controls whether Explorer displays the full path in the title bar of the Explorer window instead of just displaying the folder name. As with the previous option, many people find this option useful, but Microsoft has chosen to turn it off by default.

Do Not Cache Thumbnails check box   Controls whether XP stores the thumbnail images that it creates for Thumbnail view of a folder. By default, this option is off, so XP stores the thumb-nails. If you turn this option off to save yourself disk space, XP will need to create the thumbnails the next time you display the folder in Thumbnail view, so displaying the folder will take longer than if you'd let XP cache the thumbnails.

Show/Do Not Show Hidden Files and Folders option buttons   Control whether Explorer displays hidden files and folders, such as program files and folders. By default, the Do Not Show Hidden Files and Folders option button is selected.

Hide Extensions for Known File types check box   Controls whether Explorer displays file extensions, the last section of each file's name. (For example, in the filename `MYBOOK.DOC`, the extension is `.DOC`.) By default, this check box is selected, so Explorer hides extensions. But as discussed in "Working with File Associations, File Extensions, and File Types" in Chapter 10, it's usually a good idea to display extensions.

Hide Protected Operating System Files check box   Controls whether Explorer displays or hides operating-system files. Hiding these files is usually a good idea, because it helps you avoid deleting them accidentally. But for some special purposes, you'll need to display these files temporarily.

Launch Folder Windows in a Separate Process check box   Controls whether Explorer displays each separate folder window in a separate area of memory rather than sharing a single area of memory among the folder windows displayed. Using separate folders theoretically increases the stability of XP, because if one instance of Explorer crashes, the others shouldn't be affected. However, using separate folders consumes more memory and processor cycles. This option is turned off by default.

Remember Each Folder's View Settings check box   Controls whether Explorer uses the same view for a folder when you reopen it or whether it reverts to the default view. This option is on by default.

Restore Previous Folder Windows at Logon check box   Controls whether XP reopens Explorer and Internet Explorer windows to the folders and addresses at which they were open when you logged off. This option is off by default but can be useful for helping you pick up work where you left off.

Show Control Panel in My Computer check box   Controls whether Explorer includes a Control Panel item in My Computer. This option is off by default.

Show Encrypted or Compressed NTFS Files in Color check box   Controls whether Explorer displays compressed files on NTFS partitions in green instead of black (in the default color scheme). XP Home doesn't support encryption, but in XP Professional (which does support encryption) encrypted files appear in blue when you select this option. This option is off by default.

Show Pop-up Description for Folder and Desktop Items check box   Controls whether Explorer displays a descriptive pop-up when you hover the mouse pointer over a folder or an item on the Desktop. This option is on by default.

Creating a New Folder

To create a new folder, right-click open space in the folder in which you want to create the new folder and choose New ➤ Folder from the context menu. Alternatively, choose File ➤ New ➤ Folder. XP creates a new folder, assigns it a default name based on `New Folder` (`New Folder`, `New Folder (2)`, and so on), and displays an edit box around the name. Type the name for the folder and press the Enter key or click elsewhere in the window.

NOTE   *You can create a new folder in any folder for which you have permission to make changes. If you're not able to create a folder, the folder you're working in probably belongs to someone else who has chosen not to give you permission to make changes in it.*

See page 21 of the *Essential Skills* section for a visual guide to creating a folder.

Copying a File or Folder

XP supports a variety of ways to copy a file or folder. Because copying is an action you'll need to perform often, this section shows you most of the convenient ways to copy a file or folder. (Comprehensive as these ways may seem, there are a couple of unorthodox ways of copying a file or folder that this section *doesn't* show.) You may end up using only one or two of these ways, but you should try them all out and see which you find easiest in which circumstances.

Some of the ways of copying a file involve opening multiple Explorer windows (or having the Desktop visible). For others, you need have only one Explorer window open (or the Desktop).

This section says "a file or folder," but most of the techniques work just as well for multiple files or folders. As you'll see, one technique doesn't work so well.

See page 23 of the *Essential Skills* section for a visual guide to copying and moving a file or folder.

If the folder to which you're copying or moving a file or folder already contains a file or folder with the same name, XP displays the Confirm File Replace dialog box (see Figure 6.10) asking if you want to replace the existing file with the new file and giving you details on each file. Click the Yes button to replace this file or folder, the Yes to All button to replace all files or folders that share the names of files or folders you're copying or moving in a multi-item operation, the No button to avoid replacing this file or folder but to continue a multi-item operation, or the Cancel button to avoid replacing this file or folder and to cancel the rest of the operation.

FIGURE 6.10

XP lets you decide whether to replace files or folders that have the same names as those you're copying or moving.

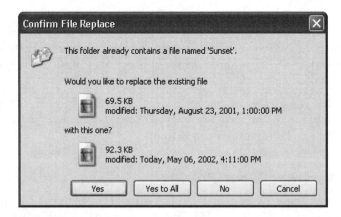

You'll notice there's no "No to All" button that would allow you to specify that you don't want to overwrite any files or folders that have the same names as files or folders you're copying or moving. But you can issue a "No to All" command by holding down the Shift key and clicking the No button.

Copying a File or Folder by Using Drag-and-Drop

To copy a file or folder to another folder on the same drive, take the following steps:

1. Open an Explorer window to the folder that contains the source file or folder.
2. Open another Explorer window to the destination folder.
3. Select the file or folder in the source folder.
4. Hold down the Ctrl key and drag the file or folder to the destination folder. XP displays a plus (+) sign on the mouse pointer to indicate that the file or folder will be copied to the destination.
5. Release the mouse button and the Ctrl key. XP copies the file or folder. While it does so, it displays the Copying dialog box (shown in Figure 6.11), which lists the file or folder being copied and an estimate of how long the whole Copy operation will take.

FIGURE 6.11

The Copying dialog box shows you the progress of the Copy operation.

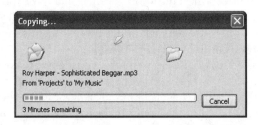

To copy a file or folder to another folder on another drive, use the technique described in the above list, but don't hold down the Ctrl key. When you drag a file to another drive, XP automatically copies the file rather than moving it.

TIP   Because it's easy to get confused about which drive a folder is on, you may prefer to use the right-drag-and-drop technique described in the next section instead of the plain drag-and-drop technique.

Copying a File or Folder by Using Right-Drag-and-Drop

You can also copy a file or folder by using the right-drag-and-drop technique. Follow these steps:

1. Open an Explorer window to the folder that contains the source file or folder.
2. Open another Explorer window to the destination folder.
3. Right-click the file or folder in the source folder and right-drag it to the destination folder. XP displays a context menu of options, as shown below.

4. Select the Copy Here item. XP copies the file or folder.

The advantage of this technique over the plain drag-and-drop technique is that you can always choose whether to copy the file or move it.

Copying a File or Folder by Using the Copy and Paste Commands

You can also copy a file or folder by using the Copy and Paste commands. Follow these steps:

1. Open an Explorer window to the source folder.
2. Select the file or folder.
3. Issue a Copy command by right-clicking and choosing Copy from the context menu or pressing Ctrl+C.
4. Navigate to the destination folder, either in the same Explorer window or in another Explorer window.
5. Select the destination folder.
6. Issue a Paste command by choosing Edit ➢ Paste, right-clicking and choosing Paste from the context menu, or pressing Ctrl+V. XP pastes the copy of the file or folder into the destination folder.

Copying a File or Folder by Using the Copy to Folder Command

Another way of copying a file or folder is by using the Copy to Folder command as follows:

1. Select the file or folder you want to copy.

2. Click the Copy This File link or the Copy This Folder Link in the File and Folder Tasks list, or choose Edit ➤ Copy to Folder. XP displays the Copy Items dialog box (shown in Figure 6.12).

FIGURE 6.12

You can also use the Copy to Folder command to copy a file or folder.

3. Navigate to the folder in which you want to create the copy of the file or folder.

- To create a new folder in the currently selected folder, click the Make New Folder button. XP creates a folder named `New Folder` and displays an edit box around it. Type the name for the folder and press Enter. XP renames the folder and leaves it selected.

4. Click the Copy button. XP copies the file and closes the Copy Items dialog box.

Copying a File or Folder by Using the Send To Command

If you frequently need to copy files or folders to a particular location, using the Send To menu is usually the quickest and most convenient way to do so. For example, you might need to copy files or folders to another folder in order to burn backups of them to CD. You can customize the Send To menu (as described in the nearby sidebar) so that it offers the folder locations you need.

To copy a file or folder via the Send To menu, right-click the file or folder, choose Send To from the context menu, and select the location from the submenu. Figure 6.13 shows an example of using the Send To menu.

FIGURE 6.13

The Send To menu provides a fast and convenient way to copy files or folders into regularly used locations.

EXPERT KNOWLEDGE: CUSTOMIZING THE SEND TO MENU

To make the most of the Send To menu, customize it so that it contains the folders and programs you use most. Take the following steps:

1. Open an Explorer window to My Computer and navigate through the \Documents and Settings\ folder to the \SendTo\ folder. It's under \Documents and Settings*Username*\.

   ◆ To be able to customize the Send To menu, you must have told XP to show hidden files and folders. (From Explorer, choose Tools ➢ Folder Options, display the View page, and select the Show Hidden Files and Folders option button. Click the OK button.)

2. Open another Explorer window and navigate to a folder or program that you want to add to the Send To menu.

3. Arrange the two Explorer windows so that you can see both of them. (For example, if these two windows are the only windows open and not minimized, right-click the Taskbar and choose Tile Windows - Horizontally or Tile Windows Vertically from the context menu.)

4. Right-click the program or folder and right-drag it to the \SendTo\ folder. XP displays a context menu.

5. Select the Create Shortcut(s) Here item from the context menu. XP adds a shortcut to the SendTo folder.

Now, when you display the Send To menu, the folder or program appears on it.

To create a cascading menu off the Send To menu, create a folder in the \SendTo\ folder, then place in that folder shortcuts to programs.

Moving a File or Folder

Windows' drag-and-drop techniques for moving a file depend on whether the source folder (the folder the file is currently in) and the destination folder (the folder to which you want to move the file) are on the same drive or on different drives. You'll notice that the techniques for moving are closely related to the techniques for copying a file.

Moving a File or Folder to a Folder on the Same Drive

To move a file or folder to a folder on the same drive, take the following steps:

1. Arrange one or two Explorer windows so that you can see the source folder and the destination.

2. Drag the file or folder from the source folder to the destination folder, and drop it there. XP moves the file or folder.

Moving a File or Folder to a Folder on a Different Drive

To move a file or folder to a folder on a different drive, take the following steps:

1. Arrange one or two Explorer windows so that you can see the source folder and the destination.

2. Select the file or folder.

3. Hold down the Shift key.

4. Drag the file or folder to the destination folder.

5. Release the Shift key and the mouse button. XP moves the file.

NOTE *This technique doesn't work well for multiple files or folders, because holding down the Shift key and clicking the selected files or folders (in preparation for dragging them) changes the selection.*

Moving a File or Folder by Using Right-Drag-and-Drop

You can also move a file or folder by using the right-drag-and-drop technique. Follow these steps:

1. Open an Explorer window to the folder that contains the source file or folder.

2. Open another Explorer window to the destination folder.

3. Right-click the file or folder in the source folder and right-drag it to the destination folder. XP displays a context menu of options.

4. Select the Move Here item. XP moves the file or folder.

TIP *As with copying a file or folder, the right-drag technique has the advantage of eliminating any ambiguity caused by the result of a drag-and-drop operation depending on whether the destination folder is on the same drive as the source folder.*

Moving a File or Folder by Using the Move to Folder Command

Another way of moving a file or folder is by using the Move to Folder command as follows:

1. Select the file or folder you want to move.

2. Click the Move This File link or the Move This Folder link in the File and Folder Tasks list, or choose Edit ➤ Move to Folder. XP displays the Move Items dialog box.

3. Navigate to the destination folder.
   ◆ To create a new folder in the currently selected folder, click the Make New Folder button. XP creates a folder named New Folder and displays an edit box around it. Type the name for the folder and press Enter. XP renames the folder and leaves it selected.

4. Click the Move button. XP copies the file and closes the Move Items dialog box.

Moving a File or Folder by Using the Cut and Paste Commands

You can also move a file or folder by using Cut and Paste commands. Follow these steps:

1. Open an Explorer window to the source folder.

2. Select the file or folder.

3. Issue a Cut command by choosing Edit ➤ Cut, right-clicking and choosing Cut from the context menu, or pressing Ctrl+X.

4. Navigate to the destination folder, either in the same Explorer window or in another Explorer window.

5. Select the destination folder.

6. Issue a Paste command by choosing Edit ➤ Paste, right-clicking and choosing Paste from the context menu, or pressing Ctrl+V. XP pastes the cut file or folder into the destination folder.

EXPERT KNOWLEDGE: UNABLE TO COPY OR MOVE A FILE OR FOLDER

If you find you can't copy or move a file or folder, especially one on a network drive, you probably don't have the necessary permission. Because moving a file involves deleting its original from the folder it's in, you need permission to change a folder in order to move a file from it. Likewise, you need permission to create a file in the destination folder.

Deleting a File or Folder

Deleting a file or folder is easy once you understand the two-stage process that XP uses to help prevent you from deleting any files or folders unintentionally.

By default, XP maintains a holding area called the Recycle Bin for files or folders that you've deleted. (If you're familiar with Mac OS, you'll find similarities between the Recycle Bin and the Trash.) By default, when you tell XP to delete a file or folder that's stored on a local drive, it confirms that you're sure about the deletion and then moves the file or folder from its current folder to the Recycle Bin. When a file or folder is in the Recycle Bin, it hasn't been deleted yet, and you can retrieve it easily. XP calls this *restoring* a file or folder—restoring it from the Recycle Bin to its previous folder.

Files or folders stay in the Recycle Bin until either you empty it or the Recycle Bin grows to occupy its full allocation of disk space, at which point XP starts discarding the oldest files (or folders) in the Recycle Bin without consultation to make space for further files (or folders) you delete.

WARNING   When you tell XP to delete a file or folder on a network drive, it deletes it immediately without moving the file to the Recycle Bin. Unless you work strictly with files or folders on local drives, it's a bad idea to rely on the Recycle Bin to rescue you from careless Delete operations.

If you want, you can turn off the confirmation of deletion, and you can stop XP from using the Recycle Bin. That way, when you delete a file or folder, it's deleted instantly without confirmation, and there's no easy way of restoring it. (You can sometimes restore deleted files or folders with third-party undelete utilities, but you should rely on doing so no more than you should bank on winning the lottery.)

See page 28 of the *Essential Skills* section for a visual guide to deleting a file or folder.

Moving a File or Folder to the Recycle Bin

All that said, moving a file or folder to the Recycle Bin is easy. Take any of the following actions:

◆ Select the file or folder and press the Delete key.

◆ Right-click the file or folder and choose Delete from the context menu.

◆ Select the file in an Explorer window and click the Delete This File link. For a folder, click the Delete This Folder link.

◆ Select the file or folder and drag it to the Recycle Bin on the Desktop.

Once you've issued a Delete command, XP displays the Confirm File Delete dialog box (shown in Figure 6.14). Click the Yes button if you're sure you want to send the file to the Recycle Bin.

FIGURE 6.14

By default, XP displays the Confirm File Delete dialog box to double-check that you want to move the file to the Recycle Bin when you issue a Delete command.

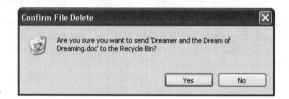

Deleting a folder works in almost exactly the same way as deleting a file, except that you need to worry about the contents of the folder as well as the folder itself. When you delete a folder, XP displays the Confirm Folder Delete dialog box (shown in Figure 6.15) to make sure you've thought about what you're doing. Click the Yes button to proceed.

FIGURE 6.15

When you delete a folder, XP displays the Confirm Folder Delete dialog box to make sure you realize you're deleting the folder's contents as well.

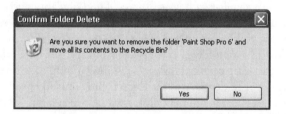

If you accidentally delete a file or folder in an Explorer window, you can recover it by choosing Edit ➤ Undo Delete or by pressing Ctrl+Z before taking any other actions in Explorer.

Deleting a File or Folder without Moving It to the Recycle Bin

To delete a file or folder without moving it to the Recycle Bin, hold down the Shift key as you issue the Delete command:

◆ Select the file or folder, hold down the Shift key, and press the Delete key.

◆ Right-click the file or folder, hold down the Shift key, and press the Delete key.

◆ Select the file or folder in an Explorer window, hold down the Shift key, and click the Delete This File link or the Delete This Folder link.

XP displays the Confirm File Delete dialog box (shown in Figure 6.16) or the Confirm Folder Delete dialog box with different wording. Click the Yes button to delete the file.

FIGURE 6.16

XP also double-checks when you choose to delete a file. Note the different wording in this dialog box from the dialog boxes in the two previous figures.

Confirm File Delete

Are you sure you want to delete 'Illustration of Longevity, Chapter 1.doc'?

Yes   No

EXPERT KNOWLEDGE: FILE DELETION AND RESTORATION

Each file is stored in a number of clusters on your hard disk. The file system—NTFS or FAT—maintains an allocation table of which sectors each file is stored in. When a program goes to open a file, XP gets from the file system the location of the clusters that contain the file and instructs the hard disk to retrieve the information. These clusters may be located pretty much anywhere on the disk partition that contains the drive. If they're located near each other, the hard disk can retrieve them faster, but if your drive is fragmented, they may be scattered all over the place. Either way, the file system puts them together so that XP can present them as a single file in the correct order.

When you delete a file (when you perform a real Delete operation, that is—not when you put a file in the Recycle Bin), XP tells the file system to get rid of the file. The file system does this by deleting the entry that tells it where the clusters containing the file are located. The clusters that the file is actually stored in remain intact but are marked as being available for storing data, so they may be overwritten by another Save operation at any point.

This method of deletion is why some undelete utilities can recover files that have been "deleted" by the operating system. Before the clusters containing the file have been overwritten, the information can be reassembled by synthesizing the entry in the allocation table. This may not work perfectly—often, the result is a bit rough—but it works surprisingly often. After the clusters containing the file have been overwritten, it's much harder to restore the file—though specialists can usually do it. If you followed the Monica Lewinsky affair, you'll probably remember that the NSA was able to restore the contents of Lewinsky's hard drive even though it had been formatted over several times.

If you want to be sure that nobody can easily restore the files you delete, get a shredder utility that overwrites the clusters in which the file's data is stored as soon as you delete the file. (Norton's WipeInfo comes highly recommended.) But if you want to be entirely sure that nobody will ever be able to read the data on your hard disk again, you'll probably need to destroy it. A sledgehammer, an oxy-acetylene lamp, or strong acid might be needed.

Recovering a File or Folder from the Recycle Bin

See page 29 of the *Essential Skills* section for a visual guide to recovering a deleted file or folder from the Recycle Bin.

To recover a file or folder from the Recycle Bin, open the Recycle Bin by double-clicking its icon on the Desktop. Right-click the file or folder in question and choose Restore from the context menu. (Alternatively, select the file or folder and choose File ➤ Restore.) XP restores the file or folder to its previous location.

If you've created another file with the same name in the folder the file to be restored previously occupied, XP displays the Confirm File Replace dialog box to let you decide whether to overwrite the newer file with the one you're restoring.

If you restore a folder from the Recycle Bin after you've created another folder with the same name in the folder into which it'll return, XP displays the Confirm Folder Replace dialog box, which lets you specify whether to overwrite any files in the new folder that have the same names as those that you're restoring. Choose the Yes button, the Yes to All button, the No button, or the Cancel button as appropriate.

Emptying the Recycle Bin

Under normal usage, your Recycle Bin will gradually silt up with files and folders you delete. As mentioned earlier, XP lets the Recycle Bin fill and then automatically deletes the oldest files or folders in it when it needs space for newer files or folders you delete, so you don't *need* to empty the Recycle Bin. But for security, it's a good idea to clear out old files you wouldn't want others to see. So every now and then, visit the Recycle Bin, look through it, recover anything you want to keep, and empty out the rest.

To empty the Recycle Bin, right-click the Recycle Bin icon on your Desktop and choose Empty Recycle Bin from the context menu. (If you've been reviewing the contents of the Recycle Bin and have the Recycle Bin window open, click the Empty the Recycle Bin link in the Recycle Bin Tasks list instead.) XP displays the Confirm Multiple File Delete dialog box asking you to confirm the deletions. Click the Yes button to proceed.

Avoiding Using the Recycle Bin

If you want the files you delete to be removed immediately and stay deleted, you can tell XP not to use the Recycle Bin at all. Right-click the Recycle Bin icon on your Desktop and choose Properties from the context menu. XP displays the Recycle Bin Properties dialog box with the Global page (shown in Figure 6.17) foremost. The Recycle Bin Properties dialog box also contains a page for each hard drive on your computer.

FIGURE 6.17

If you don't want to use the Recycle Bin, you can tell XP to remove files immediately when you delete them.

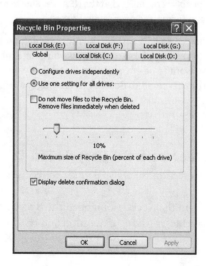

Select the Do Not Move Files to the Recycle Bin. Remove Files Immediately when Deleted check box on the Global page. Click the OK button. XP closes the Recycle Bin Properties dialog box.

Turning Off Confirmation of Deletion

If you're careful or sure in your actions, you may want to prevent XP from double-checking that you know what you're doing each time you delete a file. Right-click the Recycle Bin icon on your Desktop and choose Properties from the context menu. XP displays the Recycle Bin Properties dialog box with the Global page foremost. Clear the Display Delete Confirmation Dialog check box on the Global page. Click the OK button. XP closes the Recycle Bin Properties dialog box. From now on, XP will send files straight to the Recycle Bin without confirming the action.

EXPERT KNOWLEDGE: RESIZING AND MOVING THE RECYCLE BIN

By default, the Recycle Bin is set to take up 10 percent of the space on each hard drive installed in your computer. Depending on the size of your drives and the number and nature of deleted files you want to keep hanging around, this may be far too much space. For example, if you have a couple of 80GB drives in your computer, you probably don't want to devote 16GB of precious space to deleted files.

To configure the maximum amount of space on your drive that the Recycle Bin can take up, right-click the Recycle Bin icon on the Desktop and choose Properties from the context menu. XP displays the Recycle Bin Properties dialog box with the Global page foremost.

On the Global page, you can drag the Maximum Size of Recycle Bin (Percent of Each Drive) slider to change the percentage from 10 percent to a smaller number (or a higher number if you need a larger Recycle Bin). But to give yourself the most control on a computer with multiple drives, select the Configure Drives Independently option button, then use the Maximum Size of Recycle Bin (Percent of Drive) slider on the page for each drive to specify the percentage of that drive you want to set aside for the Recycle Bin.

On each page, you can also select the Do Not Move Files to the Recycle Bin. Remove Files Immediately when Deleted check box if you want to delete files on that drive rather than moving them to the Recycle Bin.

Renaming a File or Folder

To rename a file or folder, right-click it and choose Rename from the context menu. Alternatively, select the file or folder and then click its name. In an Explorer window, you can also select the file and either click the Rename This File link (or the Rename This Folder link) or choose File ➢ Rename.

Whichever of the above actions you take, XP displays an edit box around the filename or folder name, as shown below. Type the new name into the edit box and press the Enter key or click in open space outside the filename.

XP lets you rename multiple files or folders at the same time by selecting the files, pressing the F2 key, and entering the base filename, but the feature is useful only in certain specialized circumstances that seldom occur in real life. Because the renamed files or folders can't have the same name as each other, XP adds ascending numbers in parentheses to all files after the first: (1), (2), and so on. So if you rename the files `Letter to Jane.doc`, `Letter to Fred.doc`, and `Letter to the Bank.doc` with the name **Epic Correspondence**, the files receive the filenames `Epic Correspondence.doc`, `Epic Correspondence (1).doc`, and `Epic Correspondence (2).doc`. Counterintuitively, it's the *last* file in the selection that gets the unadorned name, because this is the file for which XP displays the edit box when you press the F2 key. The first file in the selection gets the (1) name, the second the (2) name, and so on.

If the files you're renaming have different extensions, XP preserves those extensions—even if you have file extensions displayed in Explorer *and* you specify the extension for the file around which the edit box is displayed.

EXPERT KNOWLEDGE: PERFORMING FILE OPERATIONS IN COMMON DIALOG BOXES

You can perform file operations such as Copy, Paste, Rename, and Delete in many common dialog boxes used by Windows programs. Just right-click the listing for a file to display a context menu of the actions you can take, as in the illustration below.

Doing this can save you time because you don't need to open an Explorer window. For example, say you're working in Word and need to save the active document under a name that another document in the same folder already has without overwriting that document. Instead of opening an Explorer window, you can click the listing for the original file twice (with a pause between the clicks) to display an edit box around it, and rename it there.

Before you ask—no, you can't rename multiple files in common dialog boxes. Most common dialog boxes let you select only one item at a time. Enhanced common dialog boxes (such as those in the Microsoft Office programs) let you select multiple files but rename only one at a time.

Viewing and Setting Properties for a File or Folder

As you'll remember from earlier in the chapter, files and folders are objects, and objects have properties.

To view the properties for a file or folder, right-click it and choose Properties from the context menu. (Alternatively, select it and choose File ➤ Properties.) XP displays the Properties dialog box for the file or folder.

Figure 6.18 shows an example of the General page of the Properties dialog box for a file. As you can see, this page contains a lot of information about the file—its name, its file type, its location, its size, and the dates on which it was created, last modified, and last accessed. This page also shows the program that's set to open the target file—in this case, Notepad. (You can change the associated program by clicking the Change button. Chapter 10 discusses the implications of doing so.)

FIGURE 6.18

The General page of the Properties dialog box for a file

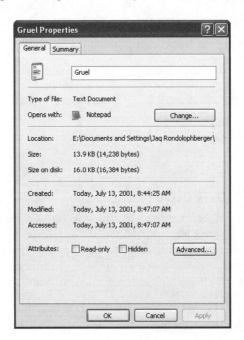

At the bottom of the page, the Attributes line shows the status of the read-only attribute (which governs whether users can modify the file or only view it) and the hidden attribute (which governs whether XP displays the file when Explorer is set to hide hidden files). You can toggle these attributes on and off by selecting or clearing the Read-Only check box and the Hidden check box. You can set advanced attributes for the file or folder by clicking the Advanced button and working in the Advanced Attributes dialog box that XP displays. (Chapter 10 discusses these options.)

The Summary page of the Properties dialog box contains information about the file or folder. This page has two views, Simple view (shown on the left in Figure 6.19) and Advanced view (shown on the right), which you can switch between by clicking the Simple button or the Advanced button. (These buttons replace each other as appropriate.) You can use this page to view existing information, modify it, or add information. Any field whose icon includes a pen in Advanced view is editable; the others are not. For example, in the figure, the Protected field and the Duration field are not editable, but the other fields are.

FIGURE 6.19

The Summary page of the Properties dialog box for a file offers a Simple view (left) and an Advanced view (right).

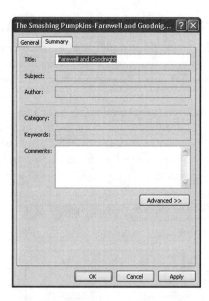

When you've finished examining or changing properties, click the OK button. XP closes the Properties dialog box.

Finding a File or Folder

Unless you're incredibly well organized or have the world's most amazing memory (or you never create any files), you'll probably forget where a particular file or folder is located. XP provides a powerful Search Companion feature that you can use to find files by their name, their size, the date they were created, or even by a word or phrase contained in the body of the file.

See pages 34–36 of the *Essential Skills* section for a visual guide to searching for files.

Displaying Search Companion

First, display Search Companion (see Figure 6.20):

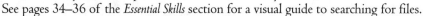

◆ If you have an Explorer window open, click the Search button on the toolbar. (Alternatively, chose View ➤ Explorer Bar ➤ Search or press Ctrl+E.)

◆ Choose Start ➤ Search from the simple Start menu. (From the classic Start menu, choose Start ➤ Search ➤ For Files or Folders.)

TIP *The following sections discuss the different types of search separately, but you can also combine several types of search to really pinpoint the file you need. For example, you can combine searching by filename with searching by a word or phrase in the file, searching for a particular file type, and specifying the time frame in which the file was modified.*

FIGURE 6.20

Use Search Companion to search for files or folders. Search Companion offers custom procedures for searching for pictures, music, or video files, and for searching for documents.

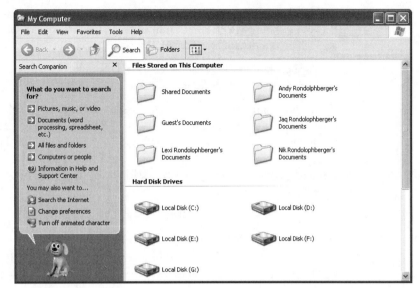

Configuring Searching

By default, XP displays an animated screen character to walk you through your searches. You can turn off this character by clicking the Turn Off Animated Character link that appears at the bottom of the Search Companion pane the first time you display Search Companion (as in Figure 6.20, above). The following examples illustrate searching without the animated screen character.

You can also choose several options for configuring searching at any time by clicking the Change Preferences link. XP displays the How Do You Want to Use Search Companion? box. Click one of the following links to turn that option on or off:

With an Animated Screen Character/Without an Animated Screen Character link   Click this link to toggle between using an animated screen character and not using one. If you use a character, you can click the With a Different Character link to reach a screen on which you can select the character to use.

With Indexing Service (for Faster Local Searches)/Without Indexing Service link   Click this link to toggle Indexing Service on and off. (Turning on Indexing Service lets your computer spend some of its idle moments creating and updating an index of the files stored on it. Having an updated index speeds up searches.) XP displays the Indexing Service screen. Select the Yes, Enable Indexing Service option button and click the OK button. To turn Indexing Service off, click the Without Indexing Service link, then click the No, Do Not Enable Indexing Service link on the Indexing Service screen and click the OK button.

Change Files and Folders Search Behavior link   Click this link to display a screen that lets you choose between the Standard search options (the default) and Advanced search options. Advanced search options provide less hand-holding and give you more freedom of action.

Change Internet Search Behavior link Click this link to display a screen that lets you choose between searching with Search Companion and searching with Classic Internet Search. You can also select your default search engine.

Don't Show Balloon Tips/Show Balloon Tips link Click these links (which replace each other as appropriate) to turn balloon tips off and on.

Turn AutoComplete Off/Turn AutoComplete On link Click these links (which replace each other as appropriate) to turn the AutoComplete feature on and off. AutoComplete suggests the remaining text of items you're typing based on entries you've used before.

Searching for Pictures, Music, Video, or Documents

Search Companion provides custom features for searching for pictures, music, and video files, and for searching for documents (such as Word documents or Explorer workbooks):

◆ To search for pictures, music, or video files, click the Pictures, Music, or Video link in the What Do You Want to Search For? pane and follow the prompts.

◆ To search for document files, click the Documents (Word Processing, Spreadsheet, etc.) link and follow the prompts.

With each of these custom search features, you can also choose advanced options as described in the next sections, which describe the general procedures for searching.

Searching for All Files

To search for a file or folder by name, follow these steps:

1. In the What Do You Want to Search For? pane, click the All File Types link. XP displays the Search Companion screen shown on the left in Figure 6.21.

FIGURE 6.21

Search Companion displays options appropriate to what you're searching for. The left screen shows general search criteria. The center screen shows the What Size Is It? area. The right screen shows the More Advanced Options area.

2. In the All or Part of the File Name text box, enter the entire filename or part of the filename:

   ◆ Enter only as much of the name as you're sure of. Usually, it's better to get multiple results from a search using part of the name than to get no results from using search criteria that are too specific and not quite right.

   ◆ If you know the extension of the file, it's worth entering it. If you're not sure of the extension, omit it.

   ◆ You can use the wildcards * and ? to increase the scope of your search. The wildcard * represents any number of characters, while ? represents just one character. For example, searching for `Letter*` returns a list of all files whose names start with the word *Letter*, while searching for `Letter?` returns a list of all files whose names include *Letter* plus only one other character (for example, *Letters* or *Letter2*).

   ◆ To search for files or folders whose name contains two or more specified words, enter the words separated by spaces. XP searches for any filename that includes both words, irrespective of the order in which they appear.

   ◆ To search for files or folders whose name contains one or more specified words, enter the words separated by semicolons.

NOTE   *If you don't include wildcards in your search, the Search Results pane returns a list of all the files whose filenames include the text you searched for. For example, if you search for* `Letter`, *the Search Results pane lists all files whose names include* Letter, *not just those that start with* Letter.

3. If you can remember a distinctive word or phrase that the file contains, enter that word or phrase in the A Word or Phrase in the File text box.

   ◆ Make the search word or phrase as distinctive as possible to reduce the number of results returned. XP treats the search word or phrase as a literal item; you can't use a semicolon to indicate you want one word or another.

4. In the Look In drop-down list, specify the drives or folders to search.

   ◆ If you opened the Search pane from an Explorer window, the Look In text box suggests the current folder as the starting point for the search. Otherwise, the Look In text box suggests Local Hard Drives.

   ◆ The Look In drop-down list offers further choices, including all local drives (hard drives, CD or DVD drives, floppy drives, or removable drives), mapped network drives, the My Documents folder, and any shared documents folders on this computer.

   ◆ To specify a folder of your choice, click the Browse item on the Look In drop-down list and use the resulting Browse for Folder dialog box to identify the folder.

   ◆ To specify multiple folders, enter them in the Look In text box separated by semicolons. For example, you might search `Local Hard Drives (C:, D:); Z:\Users` to search both your local hard drives and a folder on a networked drive.

NOTE   *If you search My Computer, XP includes any floppy drives, removable drives, CD drives, or DVD drives that contain media.*

5. By default, XP searches all the subfolders of the folder or drive you specify. This is the best way of finding all matching files or folders, but if the locations you specified contain many subfolders and files, the search can take a long time. If you want to restrict the search to only the folder or folders you specified in step 4, expand the More Advanced Options area to display the advanced options. Then clear the Search Subfolders check box.

6. If you remember when the file was modified, expand the When Was It Modified? area by clicking its heading and select the appropriate options. By default, the Don't Remember option button is selected, excluding dates from the search criteria. You can select the Within the Last Week option button, the Past Month option button, the Within the Past Year option button, or the Specify Dates option button. If you choose the Specify Dates option button, use the drop-down list to select Modified Date, Created Date (the date on which the file was first saved), or Last Accessed Date as appropriate, then use the From drop-down list and the To drop-down list to designate the range of dates.

   ◆ To choose dates with the mouse, click the drop-down button and use the resulting panel to specify the date you want. You can change the month and year in the panel by clicking them and using the controls that appear.

   ◆ To specify dates with the keyboard, use the → key and the ← key to move between month, day, and year. Use the ↑ key and the ↓ key to increase or decrease the value for the selected item.

7. To restrict the search to files smaller than or larger than a given size, expand the What Size Is It? area by clicking its heading. The center screen in Figure 6.21 (above) shows this part of the list. By default, the Don't Remember option button is selected, excluding size from the search criteria. Select the Small (Less Than 100KB) option button, Medium (Less Than 1MB) option button, or Large (More Than 1MB) option button as appropriate. Or select the Specify Size option button, choose At Least or At Most in the drop-down list, and specify the size in the text box. For example, to find files over 5MB in size, you might specify At Least 5120KB (or, more realistically, At Least 5000KB).

8. To choose further options, expand the More Advanced Options area by clicking its heading. The right screen in Figure 6.21 (above) shows the options this area contains.

   Search System Folders check box   Select this check box to force XP to include the system folders in the search. Unless you mix your documents in with your system files (which you shouldn't do), you'll need to search your system folders only to find system files, readme files, and the like.

   Search Hidden Files and Folders check box   Select this check box if you want the search to include files and folders marked with the hidden attribute.

   Search Subfolders check box   Select this check box (which is selected by default) if you want the search to include the subfolders of the specified folder. This is usually a good idea.

   Case Sensitive check box   Select this check box (which is cleared by default) to make your searches case sensitive. Case-sensitive searches tend to be most useful when searching for a word or phrase in a file, because you can use distinctive capitalization to search for a word in, say, a title or heading.

Search Tape Backup check box Select this check box (which is cleared by default) to include an attached tape backup drive in your search. Searching a tape backup drive can be nearly as slow as watching grout dry, so don't select this check box until it's necessary.

9. Click the Search button. Search Companion starts the search.

As the search progresses, Search Companion returns a list of matching files and folders in the Search Results window. When the search is finished, Search Companion displays a summary of the results, together with links for finishing searching, starting Indexing Service to make future searches faster (if Indexing Service is not currently running), refining the search, and starting a new search. Figure 6.22 shows an example of the Search Results window. You can sort and arrange these as you would any other files in an Explorer window. For example, to get an overview of the results, you might choose View ➢ Details and then click the Name column heading to sort them by name.

FIGURE 6.22

Search Companion displays the files it has found, together with options for refining the search and starting a new search.

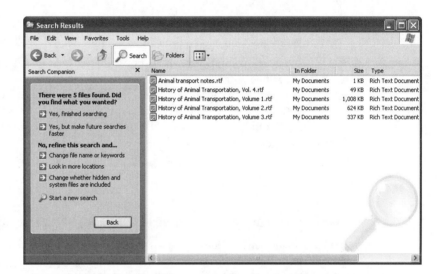

From the Search Results window, you can perform most actions that you can from any Explorer window: Select a file to display its information in the Details pane, double-click a file to open it, press the Delete key to move the selected file to the Recycle Bin, drag a file to another folder, and so on. To open the folder that contains a file you've found, select the file and click the Open Containing Folder link in the Search Results Tasks list. Alternatively, right-click the search result and choose Open Containing Folder from the context menu.

Working with Compressed Files

As you'll know if you've needed to transfer files or store them on limited-capacity media, file-compression programs can save you a lot of time or trouble. There are two widely used forms of compressed files: Zip files and cabinet files. Zip files have the ZIP extension. Cabinet files have the CAB extension and are mainly used by Microsoft for distributing files. XP lets you create Zip folders but not cabinet files.

XP reads compressed files in both formats seamlessly, displaying both Zip files and cabinet files as folders that you can open and browse in Explorer as you would any other folder. A Zip folder appears in Explorer as a closed folder icon with a zipper across it, and a cabinet folder appears as a filing cabinet with an open drawer busy consuming a document. Figure 6.23 shows these icons.

FIGURE 6.23

Zip files appear as folders zipped closed, while cabinet files appear as hungry filing cabinets.

Blueprints 1.cab
77,825 KB

Blueprints1.zip
77,422 KB

You can create compressed folders in the Zip format from one or more files or folders as follows:

◆ To create a compressed folder with the same name as the file or folder it contains, right-click the file or folder and choose Send To ➢ Compressed (Zipped) Folder from the context menu.

◆ To create a new compressed folder, choose File ➢ New ➢ Compressed (Zipped) Folder in an Explorer window, or right-click and choose New ➢ Compressed (Zipped) Folder from the context menu. XP creates a new compressed folder named New Compressed (zipped) Folder (or New Compressed (zipped) Folder.ZIP, if you've displayed extensions) and selects the name so that you can enter a new name. Type the new name and press the Enter key (or click elsewhere in the window) to apply it.

Once you've created a compressed folder, you can add files to it by dragging them to the folder and dropping them in or on it.

EXPERT KNOWLEDGE: DISABLING (AND REENABLING) XP'S ZIP FOLDER SUPPORT

Having Zip compression built into XP is great, because you don't need to get a third-party utility (such as WinZip, PKZip, or TurboZip) to create and use compressed files. But if you prefer to use a third-party Zip utility, you may want to disable XP's support for Zip folders.

To do so, choose Start ➢ Run, enter the command regsvr32 /u %windir%\system32\zipfldr.dll in the Run dialog box, and click the OK button. XP displays a RegSvr32 dialog box like the one shown here.

To reenable Zip folders, enter the command **regsvr32 %windir%\system32\zipfldr.dll** in the Run dialog box and click the OK button. Again, XP displays a RegSvr32 dialog box, but this time it tells you that "DllRegisterServer" succeeded rather than "DllUnregisterServer" succeeded.

Creating and Organizing Shortcuts

This section discusses how to create and organize shortcuts to save time and effort.

What Is a Shortcut?

A *shortcut* is a pointer to a file or folder. (If you're used to the Mac, a shortcut is like an alias.) By placing shortcuts in convenient places, you can give yourself quick access to files and folders stored in remote locations. For example, you could create a shortcut on your Desktop to a WordPerfect document stored in the nethermost subfolder of a network drive. By double-clicking the shortcut from the comfort of your Desktop, you could open the document without browsing through the drives and folders to reach it.

You can create as many shortcuts as you want for any file or folder. You can even create a shortcut to a shortcut if you feel the need. Each shortcut is typically less than 1KB in size, so unless you create a few million of them, you don't need to worry about the amount of disk space they take up.

Shortcuts have been around for many versions of Windows, but Microsoft has been improving them along the way. In the old days, if you renamed or moved the target file or folder to which a shortcut referred, Windows would be unable to find the target file when you double-clicked the shortcut. Nowadays, XP can almost always find the target file unless you move it to somewhere truly inaccessible or delete it. (When you rename or move a file, XP doesn't immediately update any shortcuts that refer to the file to reflect the new name or new location. Instead, it updates a shortcut when you use it to access the file.)

You can tell a shortcut icon on the Desktop or in an Explorer window by the small white box containing an upward-curling black arrow in its lower-left corner. Figure 6.24 shows a text file (on the left) and a renamed shortcut to it. When you let XP name a shortcut, it creates a name consisting of *Shortcut to* and the filename, but you can change the name to anything you want by using standard Windows renaming techniques. (Renaming is discussed earlier in this chapter.)

FIGURE 6.24

A shortcut icon (on the right) bears an upward-curling black arrow in its lower-left corner but can have the same name and icon as the file it leads to.

History of Animal Transportation, Volume 3
Rich Text Document

History of Animal Transportation, Volume 3
Shortcut

NOTE *Shortcuts that appear on the Start menu or on toolbars do not have this arrow. If you prefer none of your shortcuts to have the arrow, or for them to have a lighter arrow or a custom designation (such as a No Entry symbol), download the Tweak UI PowerToy from the Microsoft Windows XP Downloads site (*www.microsoft.com/windowsxp/home/downloads/powertoys.asp*) and investigate the Explorer\Shortcut options.*

It's always safe to delete a shortcut, because deleting a shortcut never deletes the file that it's associated with. And as you saw in Chapter 4, you can customize a shortcut so that it launches the associated program in Compatibility mode or in a window of a specified size.

Creating a Shortcut

You can create a shortcut in several easy ways. The setup routines of most programs install shortcuts automatically for you, so you should already be equipped with shortcuts to your programs. Most of these shortcuts will be on the Start menu. Some programs place shortcuts on the Desktop or in the notification area, despite Microsoft's guidelines to programs designers telling them not to do this. Better-designed programs are courteous enough to consult you before placing shortcuts like this. Other programs go right ahead and please themselves.

See pages 30 and 31 of the *Essential Skills* section for a visual guide to creating a shortcut on the Desktop by using the Create Shortcut Wizard.

CREATING A SHORTCUT THE QUICK WAY

To create a shortcut the quick way, follow these steps:

1. Right-click the file on your Desktop or in an Explorer window and drag it (holding down that right mouse button) to where you want the shortcut to be.

2. Release the mouse button and choose Create Shortcuts Here from the context menu. XP creates a shortcut named *Shortcut to* and the name of the file.

3. If you want to rename the shortcut, right-click it and choose Rename from the context menu. Enter the new name in the resulting edit box and press the Enter key.

CREATING A SHORTCUT ON THE DESKTOP OR IN AN EXPLORER WINDOW

To create a shortcut on the Desktop or in an Explorer window (the more formal way), follow these steps:

1. Right-click open space on the Desktop or in an Explorer window and choose New ➢ Shortcut from the context menu. (Alternatively, choose File ➢ New ➢ Shortcut.) XP displays the Create Shortcut dialog box.

2. Enter the location of the file to which you want to create the shortcut. Either type it in, or click the Browse button, use the resulting Browse for Folder dialog box to navigate to and select the file, and click the OK button.

3. Click the Next button. XP displays the Select a Title for the Program dialog box.

4. Enter the name that you want the shortcut to have. This can be just about anything, so make it descriptive and memorable.

5. Click the Finish button to create the shortcut.

Setting Properties for a Shortcut

To set properties for a shortcut, right-click it and choose Properties from the context menu. XP displays the Properties dialog box. For a shortcut to a document, this dialog box contains two pages: a General page and a Shortcut page. For a shortcut to a program, this dialog box contains a Compatibility page as well.

The General page is just like the one you saw earlier in this chapter, while the Shortcut page (of which Figure 6.25 shows an example) contains a number of items of interest.

Target text box This contains the path and filename of the target file (or folder). To open an Explorer window showing the target in its folder, click the Find Target button.

Start In text box This text box contains the path to the target file. You may need to change this setting occasionally, but not regularly.

Shortcut Key text box To set a shortcut key to run the shortcut, click in this text box and press the letter you want to use. By default, XP creates a shortcut using the Ctrl key and the Alt key, so if you press **P**, it creates the shortcut Ctrl+Alt+P. You can override this default by pressing Ctrl+Shift or Alt+Shift as you enter the letter.

Run drop-down list As discussed in the section "Specifying the Size at Which a Program Runs" in Chapter 5, you can use this drop-down list to make the program run minimized, maximized, or in a "normal" window.

Comment text box In this text box, you can enter a comment associated with the shortcut.

Change Icon button To change the icon displayed for the shortcut, click this button and use the Change Icon dialog box to select an icon you like. As mentioned in Chapter 4, SHELL32.DLL and MORICONS.DLL (both in the \Windows\System32\ folder) contain a selection of icons.

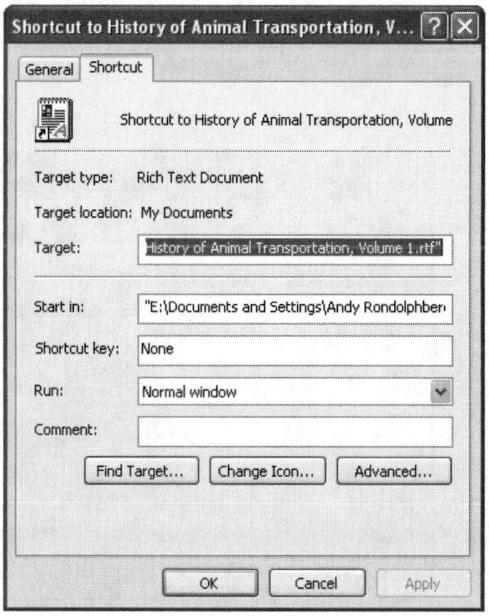

FIGURE 6.25

The Shortcut page of the Properties dialog box for a shortcut

When you've finished tweaking the shortcut, click the OK button. XP closes the Properties dialog box and applies your changes.

Setting Advanced Properties for a Shortcut

You can set two advanced properties for shortcuts that lead to program files. To do so, click the Advanced button on the Shortcut page of the Properties dialog box for the shortcut. XP displays the Advanced Properties dialog box (shown in Figure 6.26).

FIGURE 6.26

The Advanced Properties dialog box for a shortcut to a program lets you specify whether to run the program with different credentials (in other words, as a different user). If the program is 16 bit, you can also choose not to run it in separate memory space.

Run with Different Credentials check box   Select this check box to have XP display the Run As dialog box when you execute the shortcut. This dialog box (shown in Figure 6.27) lets you specify a different user account under which to run the program. This is useful for accessing files of a file type associated with this program in a folder for which the current user account does not have sufficient permission.

FIGURE 6.27

When you've selected the Run with Different Credentials check box in the Advanced Properties dialog box for a program, XP displays the Run As dialog box when you start the program from the shortcut. You can then choose whether to run the program under your current identity or as a different user.

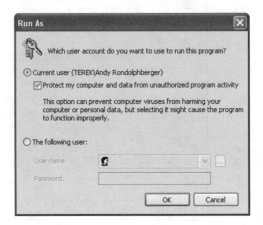

Run in Separate Memory Space check box   You can change this setting only for 16-bit programs, which you can choose *not* to run in a separate memory space. (XP always runs all 32-bit programs in separate memory spaces to prevent them from corrupting each other.) By default, XP runs all 16-bit programs in separate memory spaces, but you may sometimes need to run two or more 16-bit programs in the same memory space so that they can communicate directly with each other (for example, via DDE).

Click the OK button. XP closes the Advanced Properties dialog box and applies the settings you chose.

Customizing Explorer

This section discusses the main ways in which to customize Explorer. It starts off by covering that bane of Windows users, AutoPlay. The bad news is that AutoPlay is still in XP, and it's still enabled by default. The good news is that not only can you disable AutoPlay (as you could before), but you can now customize it so that it takes appropriate actions for different types of files.

After discussing AutoPlay, this section shows you how to customize folders, how to customize the toolbar, and how to specify the columns Explorer displays in Details view.

Customizing and Turning Off AutoPlay

By default, XP is set to use its AutoPlay feature, which tries to automatically run any CD that you insert in your CD drive. What *run* means depends on the contents of the CD and the action that the CD's developer has specified in the CD's AUTORUN.INF initialization file, a hidden file stored at the root of the CD's file system. If the initialization file doesn't contain specific instructions, or if there's no initialization file, XP may pop up a dialog box offering you a choice of possible actions to take with the CD.

These are the usual actions for AutoPlay:

- For a music CD, AutoPlay activates the default player for files of the CD Audio Track type. Usually, this means that Windows Media Player (or whichever program has ousted Windows Media Player as the default player) starts playing the CD.

- For a software installation CD, AutoPlay usually activates the setup routine. There's more good news here: XP is much better than Windows 9x at detecting that you've installed software already, so it doesn't blindly rerun the setup routine when you insert the same CD again. (XP isn't infallible on this score, but it does pretty well.)

- For a game CD, AutoPlay usually starts playing the game.

- For a CD containing video files, AutoPlay may start playing a file.

- For a DVD containing a video, AutoPlay may start playing the video.

AutoPlay also manifests itself in other ways, such as the Removable Disk dialog box, which lets you specify an action to take when you insert a disk that contains a specific type of file.

SUPPRESSING AUTOPLAY TEMPORARILY

To suppress AutoPlay temporarily, hold down the left Shift key as you close the CD drive after inserting a CD. Release the Shift key when XP has loaded the CD (for example, when you see the CD's name and contents appear in an Explorer window). Use the left Shift key because, by default, holding down the right Shift key for eight seconds turns on the FilterKeys accessibility feature. (Alternatively, clear the Use Shortcut check box in the Keyboard Shortcut group box in the Settings for FilterKeys dialog box, which you can access from the Accessibility Options dialog box.)

CUSTOMIZING AUTOPLAY—AND TURNING IT OFF

You can customize AutoPlay for six different types of content: music files, pictures, video files, mixed content, a music CD, and a DVD movie. *Mixed content* is a peculiar description, but in essence it means any CD that isn't exclusively pictures, exclusively music files, or exclusively video, and that isn't an audio CD or a DVD.

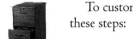

To customize AutoPlay, or turn it off, see pages 52 and 53 of the *Essential Skills* section or follow these steps:

1. Choose Start ➢ My Computer. XP opens an Explorer window showing your drives.

2. Right-click the CD drive or removable drive you want to affect and choose Properties from the context menu to display the Properties dialog box for the drive.

3. Click the AutoPlay tab. XP displays the AutoPlay page. Figure 6.28 shows an example of the AutoPlay page for a DVD drive.

FIGURE 6.28

Customize AutoPlay—or turn it off—on the AutoPlay page of the drive's Properties dialog box.

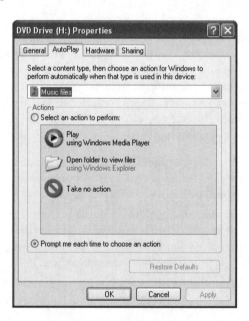

4. In the list box, select the type of files for which you want to specify an action: Music Files, Pictures, Video Files, Mixed Content, Audio CD, or (for a DVD drive) DVD Movie.

5. In the Actions group box, choose the Select an Action to Perform option button or the Prompt Me Each Time to Choose an Action option button. If you choose the Select an Action to Perform option button, choose an action from the list box:

   ◆ For Music Files, you can choose Play, Open Folder to View Files, or Take No Action.

   ◆ For Pictures, you can choose Copy Pictures to a Folder on My Computer, View a Slideshow of the Images, Print the Pictures, Open Folder to View Files, or Take No Action.

   ◆ For Video Files, you can choose Play, Open Folder to View Files, or Take No Action.

◆ For Mixed Content, you can choose Open Folder to View Files or Take No Action.

◆ For Audio CD, you can choose Play Audio CD, Open Folder to View Files, or Take No Action.

◆ For DVD Movie, you can choose Play DVD Video, Open Folder to View Files, or Take No Action.

6. Click the OK button. XP applies your choices and closes the Properties dialog box.

Customizing a Folder

You can customize a folder by designating a particular type of role for it, by applying a picture to it (for Thumbnails view), and by changing the icon displayed for it (for all views other than Thumbnails).

To customize a folder, take the following steps:

1. Right-click the folder and choose Properties from the context menu. XP displays the Properties dialog box for the folder.

2. Click the Customize tab. XP displays the Customize page (shown in Figure 6.29).

FIGURE 6.29

Use the Customize page of a folder's Properties dialog box to customize the folder.

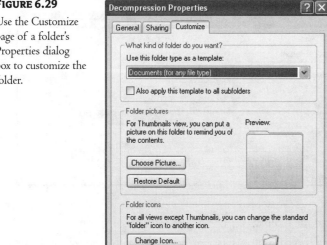

3. In the Use This Folder Type As a Template list box, you can select a template for the folder. XP offers assorted templates for documents, pictures and photos, and music. These templates contain suitable Web View and List View settings for the folder. For example, the music templates offer links for playing music.

◆ If you'll be creating subfolders of this folder and putting the same type of content in them, select the Also Apply This Template to All Subfolders check box.

4. To specify the picture that XP displays on the folder in Thumbnails view, click the Choose Picture button. XP displays the Browse dialog box. Navigate to the picture you want to use, select it, and click the Open button.

   ◆ To reapply the default picture to the folder, click the Restore Default button.

5. To specify the icon that XP displays for the folder in all views other than Thumbnails view, click the Change Icon button. XP displays the Change Icon dialog box. Select an icon and click the OK button.

6. Click the OK button. XP closes the Properties dialog box and applies your choices to the folder.

Customizing the Toolbar

As mentioned earlier, Explorer's Standard Buttons toolbar has a half-dozen buttons by default. But you can customize it by adding and removing buttons so that it contains the actions you need.

To customize the toolbar, take the following steps:

1. Right-click the toolbar and choose Customize from the context menu, or choose View ≻ Toolbars ≻ Customize. XP displays the Customize Toolbar dialog box (shown in Figure 6.30).

FIGURE 6.30

Use the Customize Toolbar dialog box to customize the Explorer toolbar so that it contains the buttons you want.

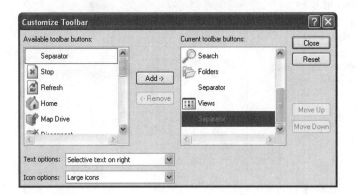

2. To add a button to the toolbar,
   ◆ In the Current Toolbar Buttons list box, select the button above which you want the new button to appear.
   ◆ Select the new button in the Available Toolbar Buttons list box.
   ◆ Click the Add button. Explorer adds the button to the toolbar.

3. To remove a button, select it in the Current Toolbar Buttons list box, then click the Remove button. Explorer removes the button from the Current Toolbar Buttons list box and adds it to the Available Toolbar Buttons list box.

4. To rearrange the order of the buttons in the Current Toolbar Buttons list box, select the button you want to move and use the Move Up button and Move Down button to move it to the position you want.

5. To change the text labels, choose one of the items in the Text Options drop-down list:

   ◆ Show Text Labels makes the text label appear beneath the graphic on each button.

   ◆ Selective Text on Right makes the text labels appear on some buttons (such as Search and Folders) to the right of the graphic. Other buttons display no text label. When a button has no text label, Internet Explorer displays a ScreenTip when you hover the mouse pointer over the button so that you can identify it easily.

   ◆ No Text Labels removes the text labels from the buttons. This option lets you fit more buttons on the toolbar.

6. In the Icon Options drop-down list, select Small Icons or Large Icons to suit your preference. For example, choose small icons and no text labels to really pack the toolbar.

7. Click the Close button to close the Customize Toolbar dialog box.

Choosing the Columns to Display in Details View

You can customize Details view to display the columns you want in any given folder. For example, you might want to add the artist, album, track name, and bitrate to a folder containing MP3 files. Similarly, you might want to display the title and subject for office documents so that you had another means of identifying them apart from their names.

To choose detail settings, follow these steps:

1. Choose View ➤ Choose Details. XP displays the Choose Details dialog box.

2. In the list box, select the check boxes for the columns you want Explorer to display. Clear the check boxes for any currently displayed columns that you want to hide.

   ◆ Which columns are available depends on the template applied to the folder.

3. Use the Move Up button and Move Down button to arrange the columns into the order in which you want them to appear from left to right.

4. To specify the width for a column, enter it in the Width of Selected Column (in Pixels) text box. (Usually it's easier to resize a column manually when you have information displayed and can see how much space it needs.)

5. Click the OK button. XP closes the Choose Details dialog box. Explorer displays the columns you selected.

Up Next

This chapter has discussed what files and folders are, what Explorer is, and how to use Explorer to perform a wide variety of manipulations on files and folders. You've also seen how to apply some simple customizations to Explorer.

This chapter was uncomfortably long. The next chapter is much shorter and discusses how to make the most of the programs that come bundled with XP.

Chapter 7

Making the Most of the Bundled Programs

THIS CHAPTER DISCUSSES THE bundled programs that come with XP: WordPad, Notepad, Character Map, Paint, Calculator, Windows Picture and Fax Viewer, Clipboard Viewer, and Command Prompt.

These programs have relatively limited functionality: They're intended to take care of some basic tasks, but not to discourage you from buying fuller programs from either Microsoft or its competitors. Because they're limited, most of these programs are relatively small and easy to use. So as not to waste time belaboring the obvious, this chapter discusses only the most important features of the programs, leaving you to work out the easy stuff on your own.

This chapter covers the following topics:

- ◆ WordPad
- ◆ Notepad
- ◆ Character Map
- ◆ Paint
- ◆ Calculator
- ◆ Windows Picture and Fax Viewer
- ◆ Command Prompt

WordPad

WordPad is a lightweight word processing program. It provides rudimentary features including font formatting, bulleted lists, paragraph alignment, margin placement, and support for different sizes of paper. It also lets you insert objects such as graphics and parts of other documents, so at a pinch you can create attractive documents with it. WordPad's Print Preview feature (File ➤ Print Preview) lets you make sure your documents look okay before you commit them to paper. But WordPad has no advanced features; for example, it doesn't offer style formatting, tables, or macros. It also lacks a spelling checker or grammar checker, so you'll need to proof and check your documents visually.

Because of these limitations, if you have Microsoft Word, Corel WordPerfect, Star Office, or another full-fledged word processor, you'll probably have little use for WordPad. But if you don't have another word processor, and if you need to create only simple documents, you may find WordPad useful.

WordPad can open documents in Word format, Windows Write format, Rich-Text Format (RTF), and text formats. (Windows Write was WordPad's predecessor for Window 3.*x* versions.) If you have font-formatted documents created in another word processing program, Rich-Text Format may prove the best format for getting them into WordPad.

TIP *Because WordPad can open Word documents but doesn't support macros, you can safely use WordPad to view Word documents that may contain dangerous macros or customizations. WordPad doesn't render all Word's formatting faithfully, but you'll be able to see if the document is valuable or merely a vector for macro viruses. (You can also get a free viewer for Word documents that lets you examine their contents without worrying about macros and viruses. Visit the Microsoft website,* `www.microsoft.com`.)

Each instance of WordPad can have only one document open at once, but you can run multiple instances of WordPad if you need to have two or more documents open at the same time. Each instance of WordPad typically takes up around 4MB of memory (RAM and virtual memory) plus the size of the document, so if you have 128MB RAM or more, you should be able to have several instances of WordPad open without degrading your computer's performance or impairing its ability to run larger programs at a good speed.

Most of WordPad's commands are easily found on its six short menus and two toolbars, but one thing is worth mentioning: As well as using the Tabs dialog box (Format ➤ Tabs) to set and clear tabs, you can set and clear tabs for the currently selected paragraph or paragraphs by working in the ruler. Click in the ruler to place a tab where you click. Drag an existing tab to move it to a different location. Or drag an existing tab downward into the document area to get rid of it.

The most complex part of WordPad is the Options dialog box (View ➤ Options), which has six pages: Options, Text, Rich Text, Word, Write, and Embedded:

- The Options page (of the Options dialog box—WordPad gets a little recursive here) lets you choose measurement units: Inches, Centimeters, Points, or Picas. (Points and picas are type-setting measurements. A *point* is $\frac{1}{72}$ inch, and a *pica* is $\frac{1}{6}$ inch, so there are 12 points to the pica.) It also contains the Automatic Word Selection check box, which controls whether WordPad selects the whole of each second and subsequent word when you click and drag to select from one word to the next. If Automatic Word Selection is turned off, WordPad lets you select character by character. (If you've used Word, you're probably familiar with this behavior.)

- The Text, Rich Text, Word, Write, and Embedded pages contain options for the different document types that WordPad can handle. For each, you can choose word-wrap settings (No Wrap, Wrap to Window, or Wrap to Ruler) and whether you want to display the toolbar, the Format bar, the ruler, and the status bar.

Notepad

Notepad is a *text editor*, a program designed for working with text files. A *text file* is a file that contains only text (characters): It has no formatting and no graphical objects.

NOTE *You may also hear text files described as* ASCII *files.* ASCII *is the acronym for American Standard Code for Information Interchange.*

To make life tolerable in the Spartan environment of text files, Notepad lets you select a font for the display of text on-screen (choose Format ➢ Font). It has a word-wrap option (choose Format ➢ Word Wrap) so that lines of text don't reach past the border of the window to the horizon on your right. And you can insert the time and date in a Notepad file by choosing Edit ➢ Time/Date or pressing the F5 key.

TIP *Notepad automatically adds the TXT extension to files you save. To save a file under a different extension, enter the filename and extension in double quotation marks in the File Name text box in the Save As dialog box.*

Generally speaking, you shouldn't spend any more time using Notepad than you need to, because Notepad is a very limited program. But it's good for several tasks:

◆ Because Notepad is small and simple, you can keep it running without worrying about it slowing your computer down. Because Notepad takes up little memory, you can run multiple instances of Notepad without slowing your computer down appreciably. This can be useful for taking a variety of notes. Notepad lets you open only a single file at a time, but by opening multiple instances of Notepad, you can open as many files as you need.

◆ Notepad is good for editing configuration files for such Windows programs as still use them. But if you're editing any of the standard Windows configuration files that remain in XP (for example, `AUTOEXEC.BAT` or `WIN.INI`), use the System Configuration Editor instead. The System Configuration Editor is essentially Notepad after a couple of doses of steroids and customizations for editing system files. (To run the System Configuration Editor, choose Start ➢ Run or press Windows key+R, enter **sysedit** in the Open text box in the Run dialog box, and click the OK button.)

◆ Apart from working with self-declared text files, Notepad is good for creating and editing other text-only files. For example, it's good for editing playlists for programs such as MP3 players. These are text files, though they use extensions such as M3U and PLS to give them file-type functionality. If you create such a file using Notepad, remember to use double quotation marks around the filename when saving it.

◆ You can use Notepad to open documents other than text files. (Select the All Files item in the Files of Type drop-down list in the Open dialog box.) For example, if Word for Windows crashes, you may end up with a corrupted file that Word itself cannot open. By opening up the file in Notepad, you may be able to rescue part of the text. You'll see a lot of nonalphanumeric characters that represent things like Word formatting (for example, styles), but you'll also find readable text. Figure 7.1 shows an example of this. If the document has been saved using Word's Fast Save feature, you'll even find deleted parts of the document still in the file—which can be intriguing or embarrassing, depending on whether you wrote the document.

FIGURE 7.1

You can use Notepad to recover text from a corrupted Word document—or to view deleted parts of a fast-saved Word document.

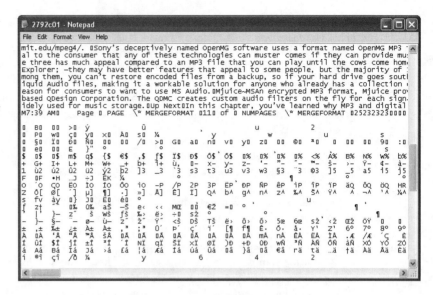

Character Map

Character Map is a small utility that lets you insert in your documents characters and symbols that don't appear on your keyboard. Figure 7.2 shows Character Map in its Standard view with the graphical symbols font Webdings displayed.

FIGURE 7.2

Character Map lets you select any character in any font installed on your computer.

XP hides Character Map on the System Tools menu (Start ➢ All Programs ➢ Accessories ➢ System Tools ➢ Character Map). If you don't find it there but think it's installed on your computer, choose Start ➤ Run (or press Windows key+R) to display the Run dialog box, enter **charmap** in the Open text box, and click the Open button. Failing that, search for **charmap.exe** (it should be in your `\Windows\System32\` folder) and run it from the Search Results window.

Inserting a Character

To insert a character with Character Map, take the following steps:

1. Select the font in the Font drop-down list.

2. Scroll the list box until the character is visible:

   ◆ To display a magnified view of a character, click it. Alternatively, use the arrow keys ($\rightarrow$, $\leftarrow$, $\uparrow$, and $\downarrow$) to select it, and then press the spacebar.

   ◆ Once you've displayed a magnified view, you can use the arrow keys to move the magnifier around the grid of characters.

   ◆ To remove the magnified view, click the magnified character or press the spacebar.

3. Select the character and click the Select button. Character Map copies it into the Characters to Copy text box.

4. Select other characters as necessary, then click the Copy button to copy the character or characters to the Clipboard.

5. Activate the program and paste the characters into it.

NOTE *Some text-based programs cannot accept graphical characters and convert them to the nearest character they support. For example, if you paste a Wingdings telephone character into Notepad, Notepad converts it to a mutated parenthesis. If you paste the same telephone character into WordPad, WordPad displays it correctly. Similarly, many e-mail programs strip incoming messages down to text, so it's a waste of time to send the users of such programs messages that contain unusual characters.*

Inserting a Character in Advanced View

Character Map's Standard view is fine for inserting many weird and wonderful characters in your documents. But if you want to work with a particular character set, you need to use Advanced view. (Character sets are discussed in the nearby sidebar.) Select the Advanced View check box to display Character Map in Advanced view (shown in Figure 7.3).

As you can see in the figure, Character Map in Advanced view has several extra controls:

Character Set drop-down list   Use this drop-down list to select the character set you want to work with. The default selection is Unicode.

Group By drop-down list   When necessary, choose a grouping for the character set. Depending on the character sets installed on your computer, you'll see options such as All, Ideographs by Radicals, Japanese Kanji by Hiragana, Japanese Kanji by Radical, Japanese Shift-JIS Subrange, and Unicode Subrange.

Go to Unicode text box   Use this text box to display the Unicode character associated with a character code. Type the code into this text box. When you type the fourth character of the code, Character Map displays the associated Unicode character.

Search For text box and Search button   Use this text box and button to search for a character by its description. For example, to find the inverted question mark character (¿), enter text such as **question inverted** or **inverted question** and click the Search button. Character Map displays all characters that match the criteria.

FIGURE 7.3

Select the Advanced View check box to work with a particular character set.

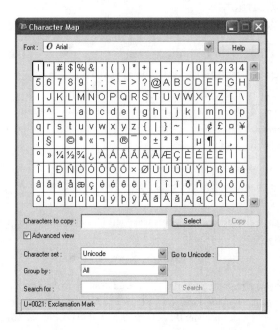

TIP   *If you don't see the character sets you need, they may not be installed on your computer. To install a character set, open Control Panel and click the Date, Time, Language, and Regional Options link. Click the Add Support for Additional Languages link. XP displays the Regional and Language Options dialog box. Click the Advanced tab to display the Advanced page, then specify the languages to add.*

Here's an example of inserting a Japanese kanji using Advanced view:

1. In the Character Set drop-down list, select the Windows: Japanese item.
2. In the Group By drop-down list, select the grouping you want. In the example, this is Japanese Kanji by Hiragana. Character Map opens a window displaying the kanji.
3. In the Japanese Kanji by Hiragana window, select the hiragana (phonetic character) that represents the sound of the kanji character. The main Character Map window (shown in Figure 7.4 with the Japanese Kanji by Hiragana window) displays a scrolling list of kanji that can be pronounced with that sound.
4. Select and copy the character as usual, then paste it into the document.

FIGURE 7.4

Using Character Map's Advanced view to select Japanese kanji.

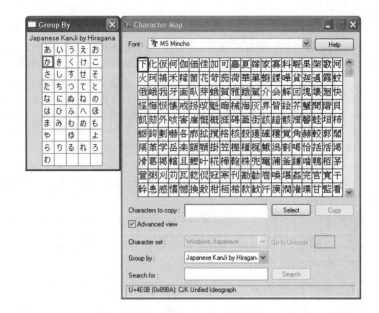

If you need to enter a particular character frequently in your documents and don't want to have to access Character Map each time, select the character in Character Map and memorize the Alt code displayed in the status bar. (Only some characters have these Alt codes.) To enter the character at the insertion point in a document, make sure that Num Lock is on, then hold down the Alt key and type the code for the character.

EXPERT KNOWLEDGE: ASCII, UNICODE, AND CODE PAGES

Okay, time out: What's ASCII? (It sounds kinda familiar....) What's Unicode? And what are code pages?

Briefly, these are all ways of mapping the binary codes that computers use to store characters to a) the characters on whichever keyboard you happen to be using, and b) what you see on-screen.

ASCII (American Standard Code for Information Interchange) and Unicode are both standard character-encoding schemes for text-based data. In other words, if you have information that can be represented in characters (such as this paragraph, for example), you can encode it in ASCII or in Unicode so that a computer can store it.

In ASCII, each character is represented by one byte. There are two forms of ASCII: *Standard ASCII* uses a 7-bit binary number combination to represent each character, which gives enough combinations for 128 characters. *Extended ASCII*, which is also known as *high ASCII*, uses an 8-bit number combination for each character, which gives enough combinations for 256 characters.

Given that the English alphabet uses 26 uppercase letters, 26 lowercase letters, 10 numbers, some punctuation (comma, period, parentheses, and so on), and control characters, standard ASCII's capacity for 128 characters starts to look paltry. Extended ASCII doubles the ante and adds some foreign characters (for example, ¿), graphic symbols, and symbol characters to standard ASCII's set.

Continued on next page

EXPERT KNOWLEDGE: ASCII, UNICODE, AND CODE PAGES *(continued)*

Extended ASCII works pretty well provided you're satisfied with 256 characters. But even 256 characters is a pathetic number if you want anything beyond the main European languages.

Enter Unicode. In Unicode, each character is represented by two bytes (16 bits), which gives 65,536 character combinations (256×256)—enough to cover most of the characters in the world's many languages. As of the year 2000, about 39,000 of those 65,536 combinations had been assigned, with Chinese alone accounting for about 21,000 of them. (Japanese, with its borrowed and mutated kanji, is another of the greedier languages for Unicode combinations.)

When do you have to worry about ASCII and Unicode? XP is pretty savvy about Unicode, so usually you don't have to worry about whether you're using Unicode or ASCII, because XP uses Unicode almost exclusively.

For programs that don't support Unicode, you can use code pages to enable the programs to communicate effectively with the user. Briefly, a *code page* is a table that maps a program's character codes (which are binary) to the keys on the keyboard, the characters on the display, or (preferably) both. Previous versions of Windows used code pages.

If you need to use a program that can't handle Unicode, assign a code page for it as follows:

1. Choose Start ➢ Control Panel. XP displays Control Panel.

2. Click the Date, Time, Language, and Regional Options link. XP displays the Date, Time, language, and Regional Options screen.

3. Click the Regional and Language Options link. XP displays the Regional and Language Options dialog box.

4. Click the Advanced tab. XP displays the Advanced page.

5. In the drop-down list, choose the language in which to display the program.

6. In the Code Page Conversion Tables list box, make sure the check box for the language is selected. If it isn't, select the check box to install the code page conversion table. (You'll need to provide your XP CD or be connected to a network source of XP installation files.)

7. If you want to make the code page settings available to yourself and to all new user accounts that you or other Computer Administrator users set up on this computer, select the Apply All Settings to the Current User Account and to the Default User Profile check box.

8. Click the OK button. If you chose to install a code page conversion table, XP prompts you for your CD or installation source.

EXPERT KNOWLEDGE: USING PRIVATE CHARACTER EDITOR TO CREATE YOUR OWN CHARACTERS

XP includes a hidden applet called Private Character Editor that you can use for creating your own characters and logos. To run Private Character Editor, choose Start ➢ Run or press Windows key+R. XP displays the Run dialog box. Enter **eudcedit** in the Open text box and click the OK button.

Paint

Paint (Start ➤ All Programs ➤ Accessories ➤ Paint) is a basic illustration program that's been included with almost all known desktop versions of Windows. XP's incarnation of Paint lets you create bitmap files (BMP, DIB), GIF files, JPEG files (JPG and JPEG), and TIFF files (TIF)—enough to make it useful for basic illustration needs, and significantly better than the versions of Paint in most versions of Windows 9x, which could work only with bitmaps.

If you're into creating drawings or paintings on the computer, you'll find that Paint's limitations present more challenges than its capabilities do. Paint's Image menu provides tools for flipping and rotating images, stretching and skewing images, changing their attributes (for example, changing a color file to black and white), and inverting colors—but that's about it. If you want to do serious image-editing work, consider a heavy-duty image-editing program such as Paint Shop Pro or Adobe Photoshop. If you want to do serious illustration work, investigate programs such as Adobe Illustrator, Procreate Painter, or CorelDRAW.

If you're *not* into creating drawings or paintings on the computer, you'll probably find Paint quite useful for some basic graphical tasks such as the following:

Creating background images for your Desktop   If you want to use a digital photo or a scan as a background image for your Desktop, you may need to rotate it from a portrait orientation to a landscape orientation or crop it down to size.

Capturing images directly from a web camera   You can capture images directly from a web camera by using the File ➤ From Scanner or Camera command. Chapter 27 discusses how to work with pictures.

Cleaning up scanned images   Images you scan can easily pick up dots from specks of dirt on the scanner or from damage to the picture. You can use Paint to edit pictures and remove small defects such as these.

Capturing screens   If you're preparing documentation on how to use software, you may want to capture the screen, or a window. To capture the whole screen to the Clipboard, press the PrintScreen (PrtScn) key. To capture only the active window to the Clipboard, press Alt+PrintScreen. Then choose Edit ➤ Paste to paste the screen or window into Paint, where you can work with it as you would any other graphic.

Calculator

Calculator (Start ➤ All Programs ➤ Accessories ➤ Calculator) seems such a basic program that it barely deserves mention. But there are several things you should know about it:

◆   Calculator displays itself by default in its Standard view, but it also has a Scientific view that's useful if you need to work in hexadecimal, binary, or octal; calculate degrees or radians; or perform similar tasks. To switch Calculator to Scientific view, choose View ➤ Scientific. (To switch Calculator back to Standard view, choose View ➤ Standard.) Figure 7.5 shows Calculator in Scientific view calculating hex. For hex, octal, and binary, you can choose from four display sizes: Byte (8-bit representation), Word (16-bit representation), Dword (32-bit representation), and Qword (64-bit representation).

◆ When you switch Calculator from Standard view to Scientific view, or switch it back, it wipes the display. To take the current number from one view to the other view, use the MS button to store it, switch view, and then use the MR button to retrieve it. Binary, octal, or hex numbers get converted to decimal when you move them to Standard view by using this technique.

◆ You can operate Calculator entirely from the keyboard if you want to. Choose Help ➢ Help Topics to open the Help file, then investigate the "Using Keyboard Equivalents of Calculator Functions" topic.

FIGURE 7.5

Calculator offers a Scientific view in addition to its Standard view.

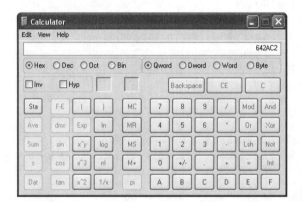

◆ You can use key sequences as functions. For example, the sequence **:p** performs the equivalent of clicking the M+ key. Check the "Using Key Sequences as Functions" topic in the Help file for more information.

◆ If you're working with long numbers, you may want to choose View ➢ Digit Grouping to have Calculator group the digits into threes separated by commas. For example, with digit grouping, 44444444444 appears as 44,444,444,444, making it easier to read.

◆ Press Esc to clear Calculator.

*TIP   If you need more functions than Calculator provides, or you could benefit from features such as being able to view a history of the calculations you've made, try PowerToy Calc, one of the free PowerToys available for download from the Microsoft Windows XP Downloads site (*www.microsoft.com/windowsxp/home/downloads/powertoys.asp*). PowerToy Calc lets you declare and graph functions, convert units of measurement, and enter calculations using Reverse Polish Notation (should you know what that is—yes, "Polish" as in "Poland," not as in "shine"). To launch PowerToy Calc after installation, choose Start ➢ All Programs ➢ PowerToys for Windows XP ➢ PowerToy Calculator.*

Windows Picture and Fax Viewer

Windows Picture and Fax Viewer is a sort of stealth program. It's largely subsumed into Windows Explorer, for which it provides the preview functionality (in views such as Thumbnails view), the Filmstrip view in the My Pictures folder, and slideshow views. There's no shortcut for Windows Picture and Fax Viewer on the Start menu, and there's no convenient way to start it other than by opening one of the file types with which it's associated.

Even when Windows Picture and Fax Viewer is running, XP refuses to acknowledge it as such. The window it runs in is titled Windows Picture and Fax Viewer, but the window is treated as an Explorer window for Taskbar-grouping purposes. This isn't particularly helpful, as it's counterintuitive and means that the Windows Picture and Fax Viewer windows tend to disappear in the welter of Explorer windows that characterizes the busy Desktop. But no doubt it's logical enough. And Task Manager shows you on its Applications page that Windows Picture and Fax Viewer is running, but its Processes page shows only Explorer.

However, when you double-click a picture file in your My Pictures folder (or right-click the file and choose Preview from the context menu), Windows Picture and Fax Viewer springs into action, opening its own window. Figure 7.6 shows an example.

FIGURE 7.6

Windows Picture and Fax Viewer is a stealth program that hides under Explorer's virtual skirts most of the time.

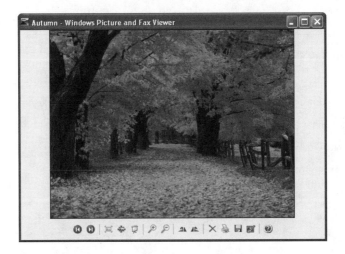

Basic Manipulation of Images

Unlike (almost) all good Windows programs, Windows Picture and Fax Viewer spurns a menu bar in favor of a toolbar. The toolbar icons are marginally intuitive, and Windows Picture and Fax Viewer displays ScreenTips when you hover the mouse pointer over them—but Windows Picture and Fax Viewer displays a different set of buttons depending on which type of image you have opened. Figure 7.7 shows the basic set of buttons on the Windows Picture and Fax Viewer toolbar with labels.

FIGURE 7.7

Windows Picture and Fax Viewer uses a toolbar rather than a menu structure to give you access to its commands.

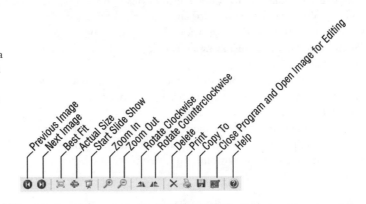

All these buttons are self-explanatory except for the Actual Size button, which displays the image at 100 percent of its actual size (in other words, not zoomed in or zoomed out at all).

To make Windows Picture and Fax Viewer usable from the keyboard despite its lack of menus, most of these buttons have keyboard equivalents. Table 7.1 lists these keyboard equivalents.

TABLE 7.1: KEYBOARD EQUIVALENTS FOR WINDOWS PICTURE AND FAX VIEWER TOOLBAR BUTTONS

BUTTON	KEYBOARD EQUIVALENT
Previous Image	Ctrl+Page Up
Next Image	Ctrl+Page Down
Best Fit	Ctrl+B
Actual Size	Ctrl+A
Start Slide Show	F11
Zoom In	+ on numeric keypad
Zoom Out	– on numeric keypad
Slide Show	—
Rotate Clockwise	Ctrl+K
Rotate Counterclockwise	Ctrl+L
Delete	Delete
Print	Ctrl+P
Copy To	Ctrl+S
Close Program and Open Image for Editing	Ctrl+E
Help	F1

Annotating an Image

Viewing images quickly palls, even if you use the slideshow feature, unless of course the images are unusually stimulating. To counter accusations that it's a featherweight, Windows Picture and Fax Viewer also provides features for annotating TIFF images. You might say that this isn't a task you feel compelled to perform with anything approaching frequency, but these features can be especially useful for annotating incoming faxes before printing them out or shunting them along to your colleagues.

To annotate a TIFF, open it by double-clicking it in an Explorer window. The Windows Picture and Fax Viewer window opens, including the image annotation tools on the toolbar. Figure 7.8 shows the extra buttons with labels.

These annotation tools are mostly self-explanatory and easy to use. The one distinction that you need to know is that a text annotation is plain text with no background, while an attached note annotation is a colored rectangular background to which you can add text. A text annotation works well in open space on the document (for example, in one of the margins), while an attached note annotation is good for slapping over part of the document.

Once you've applied an annotation, you can click the Edit Info button with the annotation selected to display the Annotation Properties dialog box, in which you can change the font or color for the annotation.

Continuing its attempt to build a reputation as a maverick Windows program, Windows Picture and Fax Viewer provides some annotation functionality that's available only through the keyboard (as opposed to being available through both keyboard and mouse, as is the case with most functionality in most Windows programs):

◆ Select an annotation and press ← or → to move it 1 pixel to the left or right.

◆ Select an annotation and press ↑ or ↓ to move it 1 pixel up or down.

◆ Select an annotation and press Ctrl+← or Ctrl+→ to move it 10 pixels to the left or right.

◆ Select an annotation and press Ctrl+↑ or Ctrl+↓ to move it 10 pixels up or down.

When you've finished annotating an image, save it and close the Windows Picture and Fax Viewer window.

FIGURE 7.8

You can use the annotation tools on the Windows Picture and Fax Viewer tool-bar to annotate TIFF files, such as faxes.

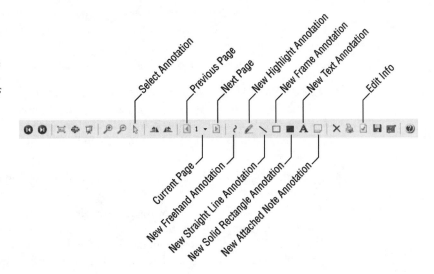

ClipBook Viewer

As you've seen already, XP lets you copy, cut, and paste various kinds of information from one location to another, either within a program or from one program to another. Like other versions of Windows, XP uses an applet called the Clipboard to store the information that you've copied or cut.

You can't view the Clipboard itself directly, but you can use ClipBook Viewer to view the contents of the Clipboard and (if necessary) manipulate them. To run ClipBook Viewer, choose Start ➢ Run to display the Run dialog box, enter **clipbrd**, and click the OK button. XP displays the ClipBook

Viewer (shown in Figure 7.9 with a Clipboard window containing a graphic), which contains the Clipboard window that contains the current contents of the Clipboard.

FIGURE 7.9

The ClipBook Viewer applet lets you examine and manipulate the contents of the Clipboard.

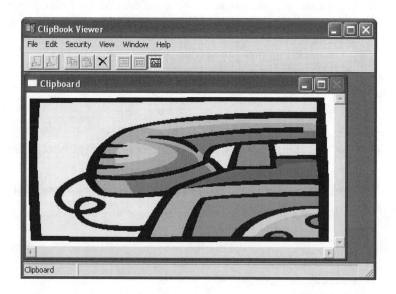

ClipBook Viewer offers several commands, of which these are typically the most useful:

◆ Use the File ➢ Save As command to save the current contents of the Clipboard window as a file, so that you can open it and reuse it later. ClipBook Viewer supports two file formats: NT Clipboard File and Win 3.1 Clipbrd. Both file formats use the CLP extension. Use the NT Clipboard File format unless you need to share files with computers running Windows 3.1*x*.

◆ Use the File ➢ Open command to open a saved file to the Clipboard so that you can paste it into a file.

◆ Use the commands on the View menu to toggle between the available ways of viewing the data that's currently on the Clipboard. Depending on the type of data on the Clipboard, the View menu offers commands such as Text, Unicode Text, Locale, OEM Text, DataObject, HTML Format, Rich Text Format, and OLE Private Data. For example, if you copy some formatted text from a document, you can display it in a variety of text formats.

◆ Choose File ➢ Exit (or click the Close button, or press Alt+F4) to close ClipBook Viewer.

TIP *If you have access to a server running Windows 2000 Server, you may be able to use the command-line utility* clippool.exe *(which is included in the Windows 2000 Server Resource Kit) to share the contents of your Clipboard with other users on your network.*

Command Prompt

Command Prompt (Start ➤ All Programs ➤ Accessories ➤ Command Prompt) gives you a DOS-like command prompt window that you can use to run character-mode programs or to issue commands. Command Prompt is especially useful for command-line utilities such as ping and tracert, which missed the line when the deity of the GUI was doling out interfaces. Figure 7.10 shows ping running in a Command Prompt window.

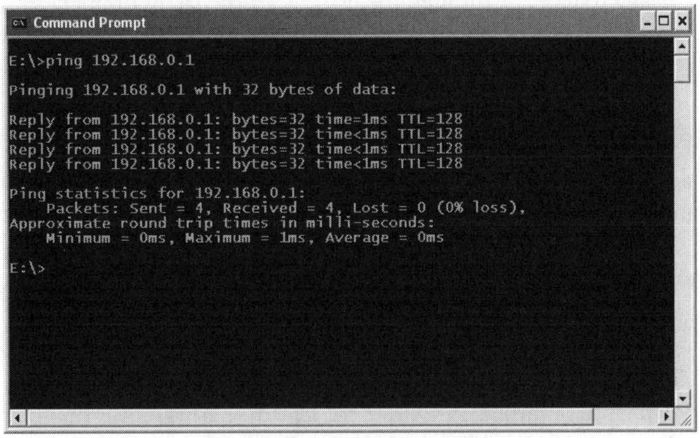

FIGURE 7.10

Running ping in a Command Prompt window.

As you can see in the figure, a Command Prompt window looks like DOS, but in fact it's not DOS. Unlike Windows 9*x* versions, XP doesn't include DOS, which is why you can't boot into DOS from XP. What XP *does* include is called a Virtual DOS Machine (VDM). A VDM runs within XP and synthesizes a computer running DOS so that XP can run programs that require DOS.

For most purposes, there's no advantage in using Command Prompt to issue commands instead of using the Run dialog box (Start ➤ Run, or Windows key+R) except that in Command Prompt you can see the history of the commands you've issued in this session.

Command Prompt may look as simple as an unadorned DOS prompt—and you can use it as simply as that. But if you use Command Prompt extensively, you'd do well to use its editing capabilities and customize its behavior to suit your needs.

If you *really* want Command Prompt to look like a DOS prompt, try running it full screen instead of in a window. To toggle Command Prompt between a window and full screen, press Alt+Enter. There's also an option setting for this, as you'll see in a moment.

TIP   *If you use Command Prompt a lot, download the Open Command Window Here PowerToy from the Microsoft Windows XP Download site (*www.microsoft.com/windowsxp/home/downloads/powertoys.asp*). This PowerToy adds a menu item named Open Command Window Here to the context menu for system folders, so you can quickly open a command-prompt window to a particular folder from an Explorer window.*

Recalling a Command You've Used

Often, you'll need to reuse a command you've used earlier in the current Command Prompt window, or you'll need to issue a similar command. Command Prompt stores the last few commands you've used (as you'll see in a moment, you can customize the number of commands it stores), so that you can recall them quickly.

To recall a command from the current session, press the ↑ key. The first press displays the previous command, the second the command before that, and so on. If you go too far back in the list, press the ↓ key to go back through the list toward the later commands.

Once you've reached the command you want to use, you can edit it or add to it, or simply press the Enter key to run it.

Selecting, Copying, and Pasting in Command Prompt

Selecting, copying, and pasting in Command Prompt windows are much clumsier than in graphical windows, but they work well enough once you know how to do them.

To use the mouse to select text in Command Prompt, you need to turn on QuickEdit mode. You can turn it on either temporarily (choose Edit ➤ Mark from the title-bar context menu or from the control menu) or permanently (select the QuickEdit Mode check box on the Options page of the Console Windows Properties dialog box or the Command Prompt Properties dialog box).

Once you've turned on QuickEdit, click to place an insertion point, or drag to select a block of text.

To copy, right-click after making a selection. (Alternatively, press Enter, or choose Edit ➤ Copy from the title-bar context menu or from the control menu.) Issuing a Copy command in any of these ways collapses the selection, so that it looks as though the Copy operation has failed, but in fact XP has copied the selection to the Clipboard, from which you can paste it into another program or back into the Command Prompt window.

You can also copy information from another program and paste it into Command Prompt by placing the insertion point, then choosing Edit ➤ Paste from either the title-bar context menu or the control menu.

Customizing Command Prompt

By default, Command Prompt uses a white system font on a black background—to look as DOS-like as possible, perhaps—but there's no reason to keep it that way if you don't like that look. You can customize Command Prompt easily enough by using its Properties dialog box.

Actually, it's a little more complicated than that. You can customize the settings for the current Command Prompt window, or you can customize the default settings for the Console Window, which affects all Command Prompt windows you open. You can also choose to apply the settings you specify for the current Command Prompt window to the shortcut from which you started Command Prompt, which means that further Command Prompt windows you start from that shortcut will start with those properties. (This is different from changing the default settings for the Console Window—changing the shortcut affects only the Command Prompt windows you start from the shortcut.)

Let's take it from the top.

CUSTOMIZING THE CURRENT COMMAND PROMPT WINDOW

To customize the current Command Prompt window, right-click its title bar and choose Properties from the context menu. (Alternatively, open the control menu and choose Properties from it.) Command Prompt displays the Properties dialog box.

Options Page

The Options page of the Command Prompt Properties dialog box (shown on the left in Figure 7.11) contains four group boxes of options:

Cursor Size group box   Choose the Small option button, the Medium option button, or the Large option button as appropriate.

Command History group box   In the Buffer Size text box, you can adjust the number of commands that Command Prompt stores in its buffer. (Storing more commands needs a little more memory, but if your computer can run XP at a tolerable speed, it probably has plenty of memory to store a few extra commands.) In the Number of Buffers text box, you can adjust the number of processes allowed to have distinct history buffers. Select the Discard Old Duplicates check box if you want the buffered list to omit repeated commands. Omitting them reduces the list and can make it more manageable.

Display Options group box   If you want your Command Prompt sessions to be displayed full screen, select the Full Screen option button. Otherwise, leave the Window option button selected, as it is by default.

Edit Options group box   Select the QuickEdit Mode check box if you want to be able to use the mouse for cutting and pasting in Command Prompt. Leave the Insert Mode check box selected (as it is by default) if you like the standard way of inserting text at the cursor, moving along any characters to the right of the cursor instead of typing over them. If you prefer typeover, clear this check box.

FIGURE 7.11

On the Options page (left) of the Command Prompt Properties dialog box, specify cursor size, command history, display options, and editing options. On the Layout page (right), specify how you want the Command Prompt window to appear.

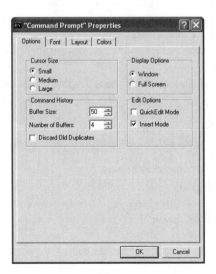
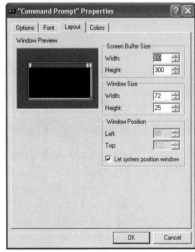

Font Page

On the Font page of the Command Prompt Properties dialog box, select the font and font size you want to use for the Command Prompt window.

Layout Page

On the Layout page of the Command Prompt Properties dialog box (shown on the right in Figure 7.11), specify how the Command Prompt window should look, where it should appear on the screen, and how many commands it should retain:

Screen Buffer Size group box In the Width text box, specify the number of characters that you want each line in the buffer to contain. (Note that this is the buffer, not the window.) In the Height text box, specify the number of lines of data that you want to store.

Window Size group box In the Width text box, specify the number of characters for the width of the window. Usually it's best to set this to the same value as the width of the screen buffer. (You can set it to a smaller value and have the window display scroll bars, but you can't set it to a larger value.) In the Height text box, specify the number of lines for the height of the window.

Window Position group box By default, the Let System Position Window check box is selected, which lets XP position the Command Prompt window as it sees fit. You can clear this check box and use the Left text box and the Top text box to specify the position of the left side and the top of the window.

Colors Page

On the Colors page of the Command Prompt Properties dialog box, you can choose colors for the screen text, the screen background, the pop-up text, and the pop-up background. Use the preview boxes to get an idea of the effect you're creating.

When you click the OK button in the Command Prompt Properties dialog box, XP displays the Apply Properties to Shortcut dialog box asking whether you want to apply the properties you chose to the current window only or to modify the shortcut that you used to open this window. Select the Apply Properties to Current Window Only option button and click the OK button. XP closes the Apply Properties to Shortcut dialog box and applies your choices.

CUSTOMIZING ALL COMMAND PROMPT WINDOWS STARTED FROM A PARTICULAR SHORTCUT

To change how future Command Prompt windows will be displayed, select the Modify Shortcut That Started This Window option button in the Apply Properties to Shortcut dialog box. Then click the OK button.

CUSTOMIZING THE CONSOLE WINDOW SETTINGS

To customize the Console Window settings, right-click the title bar of a Command Prompt window and choose Defaults from the context menu. (Alternatively, choose Defaults from the control menu.) Command Prompt displays the Console Windows Properties dialog box. Choose your customizations and click the OK button to apply them. Note that these customizations don't affect the current Command Prompt window, but they do affect Command Prompt windows that you start by using a shortcut that hasn't been customized or by issuing the **cmd** command.

TROUBLESHOOTING: COMMAND PROMPT ERRORS INVOLVING SPECIAL CHARACTERS

If Command Prompt gives you the error "<name> is not recognized as an internal or external command, operable program or batch file" when you try to run a program, or the error "The system cannot find the path specified" when you try to create, delete, or change directory, chances are that the program or directory name includes a special character such as an ampersand (&), a space, parentheses ((and)), a caret (^), a semicolon (;), a comma (,), or a vertical bar (|). For example, if you have a folder named Bits&Bobs and issue the command cd bits&bobs to change directory to it, Command Prompt will tell you that "The system cannot find the path specified" and that "'bobs' is not recognized as an internal or external command, operable program or batch file"—which is true, but not helpful.

To get around this problem, either put double quotation marks around the name of the item that contains the special character (in the example, cd "bits&bobs") or put a caret immediately before the special character to notify Command Prompt that it's there (for example, cd bits^&bobs). Usually the double quotation marks are easier than the caret, but you may disagree.

Up Next

This chapter has discussed the more challenging features of the programs that come bundled with XP. Between them, these programs provide the bare minimum of features for you to accomplish a number of tasks.

The next chapter discusses how to use XP's help system to find the information you need when things go wrong or just won't work.

Chapter 8

Finding Help to Solve Your XP Problems

THIS CHAPTER DISCUSSES HOW to find the help you need to use XP most effectively. XP includes a greater amount of help than previous versions of Windows and presents that help in a new interface, the Help and Support Center program. This chapter describes how to use Help and Support Center and the various areas it offers, including access to the Knowledge Base on Microsoft Support Services. It also mentions other resources that you may need to turn to when you run into less tractable problems.

This chapter covers the following topics:

- ◆ Finding your way around Help and Support Center
- ◆ Searching for help
- ◆ Searching the Knowledge Base
- ◆ Browsing for help
- ◆ Using the support options
- ◆ Other help resources

Help and Support Center

Help and Support Center is the latest in Microsoft's efforts to provide help resources powerful enough to silence the ringing of the phones on its costly support lines. XP's Help and Support Center builds on the improvements introduced in the Help and Support Center in Windows Me, which introduced a web-style interface to replace the old-style Help-file interface in earlier versions of Windows, by integrating many more external resources. For example, you can now search the Microsoft Knowledge Base, an online database of questions and answers, directly from Help and Support Center instead of having to access it separately by using Internet Explorer. And many hardware manufacturers are now providing product-support information that's accessible through Help and Support Center.

Starting Help and Support Center

Choose Start ➤ Help and Support to open Help and Support Center at the Home page. You should see something like Figure 8.1, except that it will contain some updated information. Your hardware manufacturer may also have customized Help and Support Center by adding content to it or by adapting its interface.

FIGURE 8.1

The Home page in Help and Support Center provides links to the many different areas of Help and Support Center.

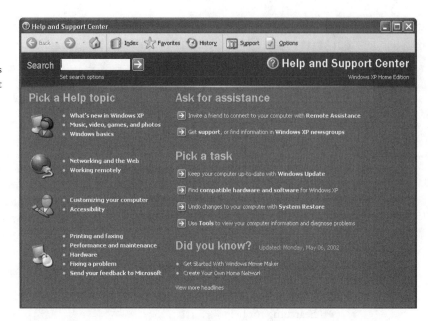

As you can see in Figure 8.1, the Help and Support Center window has a toolbar (at the top, starting with the Back button) for primary navigation rather than a menu bar. This toolbar is called the *navigation bar*. Below the navigation bar appears the Search bar.

TIP   You can open multiple Help and Support Center windows at once, which can be a help when you're searching for different pieces of help information or navigating different routes in search of the same piece of information.

Finding Your Way around Help and Support Center

Help and Support Center has access to a large amount of information in Help files that XP installs on your hard drive, together with troubleshooters for stepping you through the process of finding solutions to common problems and links for running Windows programs (such as Remote Assistance and the System Configuration Utility) that may help you solve or eliminate problems. But Help and Support Center's strongest feature is that it also provides a gateway to information resources on the Web and Internet.

Because of the amount of information and resources that Help and Support Center offers, you may find that it takes you a while to get the hang of navigating around Help and Support Center. This section highlights the main ways of finding the information you need: searching, browsing, using the History feature, and using the Index.

SEARCHING FOR HELP

If you don't see an immediately appropriate link on the Help and Support Center Home page, the easiest way to find information on a particular topic is to search for it.

To search, enter the search term or terms in the Search text box and click the Search button. Help and Support Center displays the Search Results pane on the left side and adds a toolbar containing four buttons (Add to Favorites, Change View, Print, and Locate in Contents) under the right side of the Search bar.

TIP   *When using multiple search terms, you can use the Boolean search terms AND, OR, NOT, and NEAR to specify more exactly what you're searching for. The default search assumption is AND, meaning that you want items that match all your search terms.*

The Search Results list box breaks up the results into three categories:

Suggested Topics   Suggested topics are keyword matches—one or more of your search terms match a keyword in each of these topics. These topics are further broken up into subcategories such as Pick a Task and Overviews, Articles, and Tutorials.

Full-Text Search Matches   Full-text matches are topics that contain one or more of your search terms in the body text of the help topic rather than in the keywords. Because the search term isn't one of the keywords for the help topic, the mention of the search term is likely to be peripheral rather than central to the topic. But you may still dig up nuggets of vital information from full-text matches.

Microsoft Knowledge Base   These results are from the Microsoft Knowledge Base (see the next sidebar). Use them to glean extra or extraneous information beyond that offered by the topics listed in the Suggested Topics and Full-Text Search Matches lists.

To display a category, click its heading. Then click a search result to display it in the right pane, as in the example in Figure 8.2. By default, XP highlights the word or words you searched for, as in the figure. If there are one or two instances, this can be a help, but if there are many instances, this highlighting appears as more of a defacement than an enhancement. But you can get rid of it, as described after the sidebar.

FIGURE 8.2

Click a search result in the Search Results pane to display the page in the right pane.

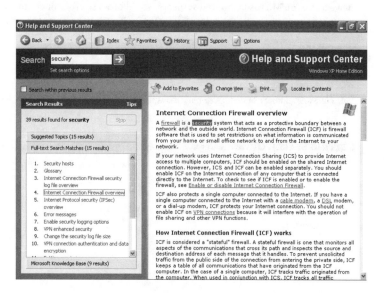

EXPERT KNOWLEDGE: MAKING THE MOST OF THE MICROSOFT KNOWLEDGE BASE

The Microsoft Knowledge Base is an online repository of knowledge and wisdom accumulated by Microsoft about its products. Given that the Knowledge Base is one of the main tools that Microsoft's support engineers use for troubleshooting customer problems with Windows, it's a great resource for searching for solutions to problems that XP's local help resources don't know about.

The disadvantage to the Knowledge Base, and the reason perhaps why it's not more heavily emphasized in Microsoft's battery of help solutions, is the way it's arranged and the necessarily scattershot nature of its coverage. The Knowledge Base consists of a large number of answers that Microsoft's support engineers and other experts have written to questions that frustrated users and developers have submitted. The answers vary greatly in length, depending on the complexity of the problem and user level, ranging from beginner topics to super-advanced (developer-level) topics. Coverage is patchy, because the questions tend to be answered only when they're not covered in the Help files and other more accessible resources. This is why the Help and Support Center Search Results pane presents the Microsoft Knowledge Base list after the Suggested Topics list and the Full-Text Search Matches list: The Knowledge Base's offerings may be helpful, but they may equally well be completely irrelevant to your needs.

Each article is identified by an Article ID number, which consists of the letter Q followed by a six-digit number (for example, Q301950). Each article has a title that describes the problem it covers, information on which products and versions it covers, a summary that you can scan to get an idea of the contents, and the full text of the article. Beyond this, each article is tagged with keywords describing the main areas of its content. By searching for keywords, you can avoid passing references to words you might have included in the search, thus producing a more focused set of results.

For power use, you may get better results by searching the Knowledge Base directly by using Internet Explorer or another browser, because the Knowledge Base's web interface offers extra options that Help and Support Center does not, such as searching for what's new in the last few days on a particular product and being able to display either titles and excerpts from hits found or just titles. To search the Knowledge Base directly, point your browser at search.support.microsoft.com/kb/c.asp.

If you know the number of a particular query, enter it in the Search text box. For example, if you read newsgroups on Microsoft-related subjects, you'll often see references to particular queries (or, more accurately, to the *answers* to particular queries) mentioned as the place to find a fix for a given problem.

NOTE *You can also start searching for help from Search Companion by clicking the Information in Help and Support Center link. There's no advantage to starting searching this way unless you happen to have Search Companion displayed when you want help.*

SETTING SEARCH OPTIONS

Help and Support Center lets you specify how you want it to search. To set search options, take the following steps:

1. Click the Options button on the navigation bar. Help and Support Center displays the Options screen.

2. In the Options list in the left pane, click the Set Search Options link. Help and Support Center displays the Set Search Options screen (shown in Figure 8.3).

FIGURE 8.3

Choose search options on the Set Search Options screen in Help and Support Center.

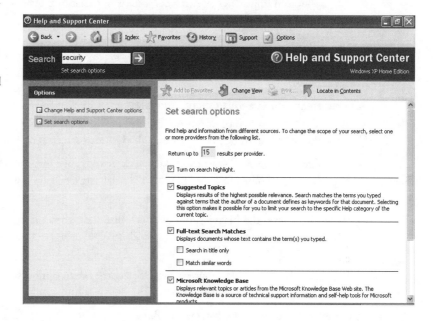

3. In the Return Up to *NN* Results per Provider text box, enter the number of search results you want Help and Support Center to get at once from each source of help. The default setting is 15, but you may want to increase this number if you find 15 doesn't give you the information you need. The disadvantage to returning more search results is that it takes longer to download those that come across your Internet connection.

4. Clear the Turn On Search Highlight check box if you don't want Help and Support Center to highlight your search terms in each result it displays.

5. If you don't want to use the Suggested Topics category, clear the Suggested Topics check box. (Usually, this category is well worth using, but in some circumstances you might want to set up Help and Support Center to search only the Knowledge Base.)

6. If you don't want to use full-text searching, clear the Full-Text Search Matches check box. If you do use full-text searching, you can refine it by selecting the Search in Title Only check box to limit full-text searches to the titles of documents instead of including their body text, or the Match Similar Words check box to have full-text searching include matches with words it thinks are similar to (instead of identical to) your search terms.

7. Clear the Microsoft Knowledge Base check box if you don't want to search the Knowledge Base. You might want to avoid searching the Knowledge Base if you find its suggestions too esoteric or if you're working offline. If you continue to search the Knowledge Base, you can set the following search options to target the results:

♦ In the Select a Product or Topic drop-down list, select the product or topic to search for.

◆ In the Search For drop-down list, choose the search method you want by selecting the All of the Words item, the Any of the Words item, the The Exact Phrase item, or the The Boolean Phrase item. (A *Boolean phrase* is one that uses terms such as AND, OR, or NOT—for example, "Internet NOT Explorer" to search for documents that contain *Internet* but do not contain *Explorer*.)

◆ Select the Search in Title Only check box if you want to limit searches to the titles of documents instead of including their body text.

SETTING HELP AND SUPPORT CENTER OPTIONS

While you're setting search options, your eye will probably be caught by the Change Help and Support Center Options link in the Options pane on the Options screen. These are the options you can set:

Show Favorites on the Navigation Bar check box   Leave this check box selected (as it is by default) to have Help and Support Center display the Favorites button on the toolbar. Clear this check box to remove the Favorites button.

Show History on the Navigation Bar check box   Leave this check box selected (as it is by default) to have Help and Support Center display the History button on the toolbar. Clear this check box to remove the History button.

Font Size Used for Help Content list   Select the Small option button, the Medium option button, or the Large option button to set a font size you find comfortable.

Options for Icons in the Navigation Bar list   Specify whether Help and Support Center should display text on the navigation bar buttons by selecting the Show All Text Labels option button, the Show Only Default Text Labels option button, or the Do Not Show Text Labels option button.

Browsing for Help

As you saw in Figure 8.1, Help and Support Center provides a list of a dozen or so help topics on the left side of its Home page. You can browse any of these help topics by clicking its link.

Click one of the links in the topic area to display the links or information available.

Similarly, Help and Support Center provides a list of key support topics on the right side of its Home page. The Ask for Assistance list provides links to Remote Assistance, Support (from Microsoft), and Windows XP Newsgroups. The Pick a Task list includes links to tools such as Windows Update and System Restore, the Tools area of Help and Support Center for help-specific tools, and Help and Support Center's features for finding XP-compatible hardware and software.

SUPPORT PAGE

The Support page offers a variety of support tools, some of them items that actually provide support (such as Remote Assistance—accessed via the Ask a Friend to Help link—and Microsoft Online Support) and some that are just links to XP utilities (such as My Computer Information and System Configuration Utility).

WINDOWS UPDATE PAGE

The Windows Update page provides an alternative method of accessing Windows Update. (As you'll see in "Keeping XP Updated with Windows Update" in Chapter 17, you can also access Windows Update from the Start menu.)

COMPATIBLE HARDWARE AND SOFTWARE PAGE

The Compatible Hardware and Software page provides a mechanism for searching for information on whether particular products are compatible with XP.

TOOLS PAGE

The Tools page contains the Tools Center, which provides access to a number of tools for configuring and troubleshooting XP. You'll notice that some of these tools have already popped up on other Help and Support Center pages you've seen so far. This illustrates the large number of redundant paths deliberately built into Help and Support Center to make it easier for you to find the information and tools you need to solve a problem.

Creating and Using Favorites in Help

You can create favorites in Help and Support Center so that you can access pages of information quickly whenever you need to.

To add the current page to your favorites, click the Add to Favorites button. Help and Support Center adds the favorite to your Favorites list and displays a message box telling you that it is doing so.

To access a favorite, click the Favorites button on the toolbar. Help and Support Center displays the Favorites pane. Select the favorite you want to display and click the Display button.

To rename a favorite, click it in the Favorites pane, then click the Rename button. Help and Support Center displays an edit box around the favorite's name. Type the new name and press the Enter key.

To delete a favorite, select it in the Favorites pane and click the Remove button.

Using Views

Designed to display a serious amount of information and options at the same time, the Help and Support Center window can threaten visual overload or simply swamp a small screen. To help you retain your sanity and your screen estate, the Help and Support Center window has a reduced view as well.

Click the Change View button to toggle between the full Help and Support Center window (including the left navigation pane, the Search bar, and the toolbar) and the reduced window, which contains only the content page and an abbreviated version of the toolbar.

Navigating with Help History

You can navigate backward and forward in the chain of pages you've browsed by using the Back button and Forward button on the toolbar. If you want to see the history of where you've been, click the History button. Help and Support Center displays the History pane. Click the topic you want to access.

Printing Out Help Information

It goes without saying that you can print out help information if you want to have a hard copy of it handy: To print the current topic, click the Print button, and then click the Print button in the Print dialog box that Help and Support Center displays.

But it's worth pointing out that, instead of printing just an individual screen at a time, you can print a whole section of help by selecting the Print All Linked Documents check box on the Options page of the Print dialog box. You can also select the Print Table of Links check box if you want to print a table of linked pages.

Using the Support Options

This section briefly discusses the three items in the Support pane on the Support page in Help and Support Center. You can access the Support page by clicking the Support button on the navigation bar or the Support link on the Home page in Help and Support Center.

Remote Assistance (Ask a Friend to Help)

The most direct way in which you can get help is by using XP's Remote Assistance feature to let someone else connect to your computer from a remote computer so that they can see what's happening and offer advice via text-based chat or via voice. If you trust your helper well enough, you can even let them take control of your computer so that they can take actions to fix the problem.

Chapter 24 discusses how to configure and use Remote Assistance.

Microsoft Online Support (Get Help from Microsoft)

Microsoft Online Support lets you automatically collect information on a problem you're having and submit it to Microsoft electronically. A Microsoft technician then sends a solution, which appears as a pop-up in your System Tray. You can read the response in the Help and Support Center window and apply the advice it contains to fix the problem.

Microsoft Online Support lets you avoid both long waits on hold and the difficulty of explaining complex problems and system configuration over the phone.

To use Microsoft Online Support, you need to have a Microsoft Passport or a Hotmail account. If you don't have one, Help and Support Center walks you through the process of getting one.

To connect to Microsoft Online Support, click the Get Help from Microsoft link in the Support pane and follow through the steps the Help and Support Center presents. For obvious reasons, your computer needs to have a working Internet connection to use this feature.

Windows Newsgroups (Go to a Windows Web Site Forum)

The Windows Newsgroups are an assortment of Windows-related online newsgroups that you can access through a web-based front end. Though these newsgroups are run under the auspices of Microsoft, they suffer to some extent from the problems of noise and irrelevance that characterize public newsgroups. (See Chapter 21 for a discussion of newsgroups and how to use Outlook Express to access them.)

To access the Windows Newsgroups, take the following steps:

1. Display the Support page of Help and Support Center.
2. In the Support pane, click the Go to a Windows Web Site Forum link. Help and Support Center displays the Windows Newsgroups screen.
3. Click the Go to Windows Newsgroups link. Help and Support Center activates or launches Internet Explorer (or your default browser) and displays the Windows XP Newsgroups home page, which lists the newsgroups.
4. Click one of the newsgroup links. Internet Explorer activates or launches Outlook Express (or your default newsreader) and opens that newsgroup in it.

WARNING   You're probably familiar with the disclaimer "this information comes without guarantee"—in other words, you try whatever is described at your own risk. This goes in spades for the advice you encounter on the Windows Newsgroups. While some of the postings contain high-quality advice from people who know what they're talking about, other postings are wrong or dangerous, and following the advice supplied (with whatever good intent) can threaten or damage your data or your computer. Proceed with caution.

Using the Troubleshooters

XP includes a number of troubleshooters for troubleshooting common problems with hardware and software configuration. Help and Support Center provides a central starting point for running these tools, though XP also offers you the chance to run the appropriate troubleshooter when it detects that you've run into a configuration problem.

To run one of the troubleshooters, follow these steps:

1. From the Help and Support Center Home page, click the Fixing a Problem link. Help and Support Center displays the Fixing a Problem screen.

2. Click the Troubleshooting Problems link in the Fixing a Problem pane. Help and Support Center displays the Troubleshooting Problems screen.

3. Click the List of Troubleshooters link in the Overviews, Articles, and Tutorials list. Help and Support Center displays the List of Troubleshooters page.

4. Click the link for a troubleshooter to run it. Figure 8.4 shows the first screen of the Video Display Troubleshooter.

FIGURE 8.4

XP includes trouble-shooters that attempt to walk you through the steps of solving a problem.

Finding Help on the Internet and Web

If you can't find the information you need through Help and Support Center, try the Internet and the Web.

Help on the Web

With earlier versions of Windows, the first port of call when looking for help on the Web was the Microsoft website, which offered all sorts of resources from the latest patches and drivers to the Knowledge Base. But now that Help and Support Center both seamlessly searches the Microsoft website and provides links to some hardware and software manufacturers' offerings, and Windows Update can automatically download and prompt you to install updates and patches to XP, there's less reason to access the Microsoft website manually unless you need, say, the extra search capabilities that the Knowledge Base website offers.

To find information from hardware and software manufacturers not partnered closely enough with Microsoft to rate inclusion in Help and Support Center's repertoire, to download the latest drivers, or to find other sources of information, the Web can be either valuable or invaluable, depending on your luck and your persistence in searching.

Chapter 19 discusses how to surf the Web with Internet Explorer.

Help in Newsgroups

Another good source of information and help are the many computer-related public newsgroups (such as the `comp.sys` hierarchy) and the Microsoft public newsgroups (in the `microsoft.public` hierarchy).

Chapter 22 discusses how to use Outlook Express to read news.

Up Next

As you've seen in this chapter, Microsoft has done a nice job of integrating internal and external resources into Help and Support Center, bringing many separate sources of information together into a single, searchable front end. But you'll sometimes need to go beyond these offerings to find the solutions to your XP problems. In particular, you may want to go to the newsgroups for unfiltered advice, and to third-party websites for the latest drivers, patches, and tips.

That's the end of the first part of the book. By now, you should be handling XP with aplomb, and you're probably ready to broaden your virtual horizons.

The next part of the book discusses how to administer and troubleshoot XP.

Part II

Administering and Troubleshooting Windows XP Home

In this section:

- ◆ Chapter 9: Managing Users and Accounts
- ◆ Chapter 10: Sharing and File Types
- ◆ Chapter 11: Managing Your Disks and Drives
- ◆ Chapter 12: Working with the Registry
- ◆ Chapter 13: Installing, Configuring, and Managing Printers and Fonts
- ◆ Chapter 14: Managing Hardware, Drivers, and Power
- ◆ Chapter 15: Using XP Home Edition on a Portable Computer
- ◆ Chapter 16: Optimizing Windows XP Home Edition
- ◆ Chapter 17: Backup, Troubleshooting, and Disaster Recovery

Chapter 9

Managing Users and Accounts

As you've read several times already in this book, XP is designed to be a multiuser operating system. To help you keep your users divided if not conquered, XP's setup routine encourages you heavily to create a separate user account for each user. If you do so, each user can keep their own preferences and settings, which helps keep the users from each other's throats. You can also assign users different types of user accounts to reflect the freedom and responsibility you want to give them or (perhaps more likely) the restrictions you want to impose on them in the name of harmony and democracy.

This chapter discusses how to manage users and accounts. First, it muses briefly on what user accounts are and what they're for. Then it details the three different types of user account that XP Home supports, together with their limitations. After that, it tells you how to create, delete, and modify user accounts; how to require passwords for them; how to turn off the Welcome screen; and sundry other associated goodies. Some of the actions described in this chapter are ones that Microsoft apparently doesn't intend you to take in XP Home, because the only ways of performing them are via obscure command-line utilities rather than slick graphical tools. But because some of these hidden capabilities are useful rather than esoteric, I describe the most useful of the command-line actions alongside the graphical tools.

This chapter covers the following topics:

♦ Understanding what user accounts are and what they're for

♦ The three different types of user accounts

♦ Creating and deleting user accounts

♦ Making Windows require passwords

♦ Using password reset disks to recover from lost passwords

♦ Applying a .NET Passport to an account—and removing it

♦ Turning off the Welcome screen

♦ Turning off Fast User Switching

♦ Turning on the Guest account

◆ Implementing and preventing automatic logons

◆ Restricting a user account

◆ Working with the `net user` and `net localgroup` commands

NOTE *If you're the only person who ever uses your computer, you hardly need to worry about user accounts. But if you share your computer with anybody else, you should use user accounts to the full, because they offer great benefits and require minimal setup and administration. Read on.*

What Are User Accounts and What Are They For?

A *user account* is a logical entity that lets you tailor the XP environment to each regular user. By using user accounts, you can let each user set and maintain different preferences on the computer, so they can maintain a custom Desktop that provides the look they like and the shortcuts and information they need. Each user can also keep separate favorites and histories in Internet Explorer. (Chapter 19 discusses Internet Explorer's history and favorites features.) Each user can protect their user account with a password if they choose, and they can choose to share folders with other users via the network. (Chapter 10 discusses how to share folders with other users.)

By using accounts effectively and setting passwords, you can control access to your computer, and you can allow different privileges to different users. For example, you could prevent the less responsible members of the household from accessing critical files by storing them in secure folders. User accounts are particularly useful when your computer is networked (including always-on connections to the Internet).

Each user account is identified by a username that XP uses to manage it. The account has a full-name field that typically contains the full name of the user (which appears on the Welcome screen and at the top of the Start menu) and a comment field that can be used for storing a comment about the user. Each user account has an account type that defines its permissions and a set of folders in which the user's details and preferences are stored.

Three Types of User Accounts

XP Home supports three types of user accounts: Computer Administrator (including the master Administrator account), Limited, and Guest. The following sections discuss what each account can do and which type of account is suitable for which type of user.

Computer Administrator Accounts

Computer Administrator accounts are intended for power users who administer the computer. A Computer Administrator account can perform just about any action on the computer, including installing programs and hardware on the computer and creating, modifying, and deleting user accounts. By default, a Computer Administrator account can access all the files on the computer.

NOTE *A Computer Administrator account in XP is roughly equivalent to the default type of account in Windows 9x.*

By default, during setup XP creates each account as a Computer Administrator account, presumably to spare people from needing to make an awkward decision under (real or imagined) pressure of time. Having everyone be a Computer Administrator suits only groups of people with the most open computing arrangements imaginable. So if you created accounts during setup, you'll probably want to change some of them to Limited accounts.

EXPERT KNOWLEDGE: SECURING THE ADMINISTRATOR ACCOUNT

As well as the Computer Administrator accounts with which Windows Setup generously endows each user you create during installation, Windows Setup also creates a master Computer Administrator account named simply Administrator. This account skulks within the operating system like an airbag in the dashboard—not needed in normal circumstances, hard to get at unless you have advanced knowledge or XP needs to deploy it, but there to prevent you from suffering the consequences of nasty accidents of your own or others' making. (If on your computer the Administrator account *does* appear on the User Accounts page in Control Panel, XP is suffering from a bug. Go to the Microsoft Product Support Services home page, support.microsoft.com, search for Q314412, and follow its advice to fix the problem. Don't use this fix unless you're suffering from the problem.)

The Administrator account is essentially hidden from the user. It doesn't have an entry on the Welcome screen, so you can't access it from there. And even if you turn off the Welcome screen (as discussed later in the chapter), you can't log on using the Administrator account from the Log On to Windows dialog box, because XP Home doesn't allow this. In fact, you can log on to the Administrator account only by starting XP in Safe mode. To do so, take the following steps:

1. Restart XP.

2. When the computer is restarting (after your computer displays any BIOS information), press the F8 key so that XP displays the Windows Advanced Options menu. (If your computer has a multi-boot configuration, press the F8 key from the Please Select the Operating System to Start screen.)

3. Select the Safe Mode item on the menu and press the Enter key. XP boots to a lower-resolution version of the Welcome screen that includes an Administrator entry.

4. Click the Administrator entry to log on using the Administrator account.

Because any potential attacker who can gain access to your computer could log on to the Administrator account in the same way that you've just done, it's important to secure the Administrator account with a strong password instead of the blank password that it receives during setup. You can do so in any of the three ways discussed in the rest of this sidebar. If you've just logged on as Administrator by booting into Safe Mode, follow the first procedure. If you're currently logged on with a Computer Administrator account, use either the second procedure or the third procedure.

CREATING AN ADMINISTRATOR PASSWORD FROM THE ADMINISTRATOR ACCOUNT

Once you're logged on as Administrator, choose Start ➢ Control Panel. XP displays Control Panel. Double-click the User Accounts icon. XP displays the User Accounts screen. Select the Administrator account, and then on the What Do You Want to Change about Your Account? screen, click the Create a Password link.

Log off as Administrator, restart XP if you were using Safe Mode, and log back in as yourself. And be sure not to forget the Administrator password you set.

Continued on next page

EXPERT KNOWLEDGE: SECURING THE ADMINISTRATOR ACCOUNT *(continued)*

CREATING A RANDOM ADMINISTRATOR PASSWORD WITH THE *NET USER* COMMAND

If you don't trust yourself to come up with a suitably random password for the Administrator account, you can have XP create a random password for you. To do so, open a command-prompt window and enter the command **net user administrator /random**. XP generates a random password, assigns it to the Administrator account, and displays it to you. Make a note of it so that you don't forget it.

For various technical reasons involving the predictability of computers and the difficulty of programming spontaneity, passwords generated in this way aren't truly random, but they're close enough to random for anything short of spook work.

CREATING AN ADMINISTRATOR PASSWORD FROM A COMPUTER ADMINISTRATOR ACCOUNT

Alternatively, you can set an Administrator password from a Computer Administrator account by taking the following steps:

1. Choose Start ➢ Run, enter **control userpasswords2** in the Run dialog box, and click the OK button. XP displays the User Accounts dialog box with the Users page foremost. Figure 9.8, later in this chapter, shows the User Accounts dialog box.

2. In the Users for This Computer list box, select the Administrator entry and click the Reset Password button. XP displays the Reset Password dialog box.

3. Enter the new password in the New Password text box and the Confirm New Password text box and click the OK button. XP closes the Reset Password dialog box, returning you to the User Accounts dialog box.

4. Click the OK button. XP closes the User Accounts dialog box.

CHANGING THE NAME OF THE ADMINISTRATOR ACCOUNT

If you're the only person who will administer this computer, you may want to change the name of the Administrator account as an extra security measure. To do so, display the User Accounts dialog box as discussed in the previous section of this sidebar, select the Administrator entry in the Users for This Computer list box, and click the Properties button to display the Properties dialog box for the account. In the User Name text box, type the new name for the account, and then click the OK button.

Limited Accounts

As its name suggests, a Limited account is limited in what it can do—very limited. A Limited account user can change their own picture or password, or remove their password (so that they do not need to use a password to log on to XP).

A Limited user can create, edit, and delete their own files (of course), but they can't read other files that aren't explicitly shared with them. A Limited account user cannot install or remove most programs (they may be able to install *some* programs); cannot install any hardware; cannot create, modify, or delete user accounts; cannot see via Task Manager which other users are logged on to the computer, or log off another user who's locked the computer; and cannot make systemwide changes.

Limited users may also have problems running programs designed for Windows 9*x*—programs that assumed the user had free rein to use the computer and that need to create files in locations that XP doesn't allow them to.

If you want to prevent a household member from rampaging across the computer, making them a Limited user does the job quite nicely.

The Guest Account

The Guest account is a special account for use by guests—either literally guests of your household or company, or figuratively in the sense that the user will need to use the computer only briefly. For longer-term use, create a dedicated account for the user—probably a Limited account.

You can't require a password for the Guest account. That's to prevent one guest from locking out another guest. And you can have only one Guest account on an installation of XP, so the account needs to be shared among guests. You can't create or delete the Guest account, but you can turn it off and on. (For instructions, see the section "Turning the Guest Account On and Off," later in this chapter.) By default, the Guest account is off until you turn it on.

The Guest account cannot access password-protected folders. It can change only supposedly harmless settings. For example, the Guest account can change screen resolution and color schemes, but the only user-account option it can change is the picture displayed for Guest. (Given that the screen resolution applies to all users when you're using Fast User Switching, changing screen resolution can sorely vex other users.)

Creating a User Account

As you've seen, XP encourages you to create user accounts at the end of the setup routine. But you can also create accounts at any time as needed.

The main tool that XP Home provides for working with user accounts is the User Accounts tool that you access by clicking the User Accounts link in Control Panel (Start ➤ Control Panel). This tool is optimized for working with XP Home so that it presents only a limited set of the options that XP Home supports for user accounts. I'll refer to this tool as the "User Accounts tool" when I need to distinguish it from the User Accounts dialog box, which is another graphical tool that XP Home supports and which gives you access to further options for user accounts. Then there are two command-line utilities: `net user` (which you met briefly in the previous sidebar) and `net localgroup`, which you'll meet later in this chapter.

NOTE   If you're used to using Windows in a corporate setting that uses Windows domains, you may be wondering how XP Home behaves when you connect it to a network that uses a domain configuration rather than a workgroup configuration. The answer is that it doesn't: You can't connect XP Home to a domain (though you can connect to resources on a domain by using a dial-up connection or virtual private network connection as discussed in Chapter 34). To connect to a domain, you have to use XP Professional.

To create a user account, log on as a Computer Administrator user and take the following steps:

1. Choose Start ➤ Control Panel. XP displays Control Panel.
2. Click the User Accounts link. XP displays the User Accounts screen (shown in Figure 9.1).

FIGURE 9.1

From the User Accounts screen in Control Panel, you can create, delete, and modify user accounts.

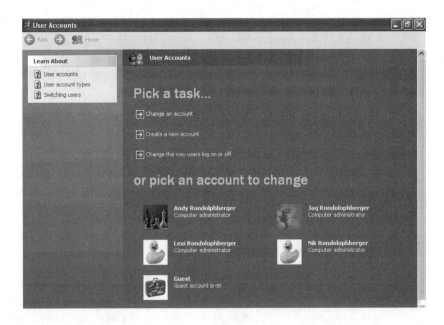

3. In the Pick a Task list, click the Create a New Account link. XP displays the Name the New Account screen (shown in Figure 9.2).

FIGURE 9.2

On the Name the New Account screen, enter the name for the new user account.

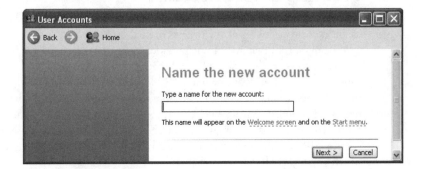

4. Enter a name for the account:

- ◆ Usernames can be up to 20 characters long and are not case sensitive.

- ◆ XP automatically assigns the username you enter in the User Accounts tool as the full name for the user account. You can change this, and add a comment to the user account, by using the User Accounts dialog box or the **net user** command (both discussed later in this chapter).

- ◆ Names can contain letters, numbers, and most symbols. They cannot contain any of these characters: *, ?, +, =, , (comma), : (colon), ; (semicolon), <, >, | (pipe character), " (double quotation marks), [,], /, or \.

- ◆ Names can start with letters, numbers, or symbols. Names can even consist of nothing but underscores.

TIP   It can be amusing to create idiosyncratic names, but consider using a naming convention if you're creating more than a few user accounts and want to keep things formal and organized. If you plan to use command-line utilities to manage users (as discussed later in this chapter), consider creating short usernames that don't include spaces or extended characters, because otherwise you'll need to enter each username in double quotation marks for the utilities to work.

5. Click the Next button. XP displays the Pick an Account Type screen.

6. By default, XP selects the Computer Administrator option button. Select the Limited option button if you want the account to be Limited instead.

7. Click the Create Account button. XP creates the account and displays the User Accounts screen again, with the new user listed.

Understanding User Profiles

Information for each user account is kept in what Microsoft calls the *user profile*, which is stored in the user's folder under the `\Documents and Settings\` folder. This information includes the contents of your Start menu and Desktop, information about your network settings and printers, and so on—all the information listed in Table 6.1 and discussed at some length in Chapter 6.

You *can* copy and delete user profiles by using the controls in the User Profiles dialog box, which you display by clicking the Settings button in the User Profiles group box on the Advanced page of the System Properties dialog box, but doing so doesn't get you far. This is because XP Home provides a much more limited implementation of profiles than XP Professional, which includes roaming user profiles—profiles that let you store your user account information on a server and have it copied automatically to any workstation at which you log on, giving you the same Desktop, Start menu, and other settings no matter which workstation you're using.

NOTE   You can't copy a user profile with which a user is currently logged on—neither the user profile under which you're logged on nor that used for any disconnected user session on a computer that's using Fast User Switching.

To move a user profile from one computer to another, use the Files and Settings Transfer Wizard, discussed in the section "Use the Files and Settings Transfer Wizard to Transfer Settings" in Chapter 2.

Deleting a User Account

If you lose a member of your company or excommunicate a member of your family, you may want to delete their user account from your computer. Deleting the user account is easy, but you need to decide whether to keep the user's Desktop configuration files and their My Documents folder.

To delete a user account, log on as a Computer Administrator user and take the following steps:

1. If the computer is using Fast User Switching, display the Users page of Task Manager (right-click the notification area and choose Task Manager, then click the Users tab) to make sure the user isn't logged on in a disconnected session. If they are, select their entry, click the Logoff button, and click the Yes button in the resulting confirmation dialog box to log them off. Otherwise, you'll get a warning in step 5.

2. Choose Start ➤ Control Panel. XP displays Control Panel.

3. Click the User Accounts link. XP displays the User Accounts screen.

4. Click the user's icon. XP displays the What Do You Want to Change about *Username*'s Account? screen (shown in Figure 9.3).

FIGURE 9.3

Use the What Do You Want to Change about *Username*'s Account? page of User Accounts to make changes to the account.

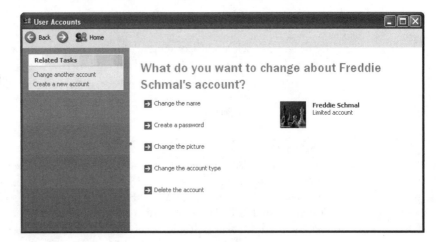

5. Click the Delete the Account link. XP displays the Do You Want to Keep *Username*'s Files? screen (shown in Figure 9.4).

FIGURE 9.4

When you delete a user, you get to choose whether to keep the user's files.

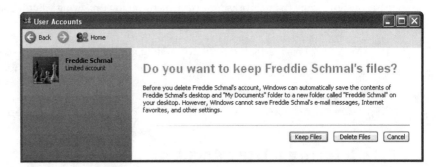

6. Click the Keep Files button or the Delete Files button as appropriate. XP displays the Are You Sure You Want to Delete *Username*'s Account? page to make sure you've thought about what you're doing.

◆ If you chose to keep the files, XP tells you that it will save the user's files to a folder on your Desktop. The folder will bear the soon-to-be-ex-user's name.

7. Click the Delete Account button if you're sure you want to proceed. XP deletes the account and displays the User Accounts screen.

EXPERT KNOWLEDGE: DELETING YOUR OWN ACCOUNT

Sometimes—almost certainly not often—you'll need to delete your own account from a computer. XP makes it hard for you to delete it directly from your own user session, because the account is active and doesn't have a self-destruct button.

So (you've guessed it) you need to delete your account from another Computer Administrator account. If yours is the only Computer Administrator account on the computer, you'll need to create a new Computer Administrator account (either from scratch or by promoting a Limited account to Computer Administrator status) in order to delete your account.

Alternatively, you can use the User Accounts dialog box (Start ➤ Run, enter **control userpasswords2**, and click the OK button) to delete your account while you're logged on to it. This isn't a great idea, as you'll see in the section "Performing Other Management Actions from the User Accounts Dialog Box," later in this chapter, but it does work.

Changing a User Account

If you set up a user account but don't quite get it right, don't worry—you can change it easily. You can change a user account from Limited to Computer Administrator or vice versa; change the account name; change the picture; or add a password to the account.

The actions you can take for a user's account are grouped on the What Do You Want to Change about *Username*'s Account? page (shown in Figure 9.3 above). To display this page, click the user's name on the User Accounts page.

You can then change the account by taking one or more of the actions detailed in the next sections.

Assigning a Picture to a User Account

Assigning a picture to a user account is likely to be one of the most popular account changes made in XP. Even the Guest user can change their picture.

The picture for a user's account can be of the BMP, GIF, JPG, PNG, or TIF file type. XP shrinks the picture down to the appropriate size, but you'll need to take care of any cropping or rotating first. (Windows Picture and Fax Viewer can handle the rotation. Paint can handle both rotation and cropping. See Chapter 7 for a brief discussion of these built-in programs.)

To change the picture for a user, follow these steps from the What Do You Want to Change about *Username*'s Account? page:

1. Click the Change the Picture link. XP displays the Pick a New Picture for *Username*'s Account page (shown in Figure 9.5).

TIP   To change the picture for your user account, click the picture at the top of the Start menu. XP displays the Pick a New Picture for Your Account page.

FIGURE 9.5

Any user can change the picture shown for them on the Welcome screen.

2. To use a built-in picture, select it in the list box. To use a picture of your own, click the Browse for More Pictures link. XP displays an Open dialog box.

3. Navigate to the picture you want to use, select it, and click the Open button. XP adds the picture to the list box.

4. Select the picture and click the Change Picture button.

Now disconnect your session so that you can see how the picture looks on the Welcome screen.

Requiring a Password for an Account

As you've seen, by default XP Home doesn't require a password for any user: Anyone for whom you've created an account can log on by clicking their username on the Welcome screen, and anyone else can log in as Guest once the Guest account is active. (Needless to say, guests can log in under any of the existing user accounts if they're not password protected.)

If you need to tighten your security, start by using passwords. Passwords are more or less mandatory in any serious business setting, and they can be a good idea in many family or dorm situations as well.

You can require passwords from some users but not from others if you want, but in practice this makes little sense, as anyone can log on to any account that doesn't have a password. If you leave a Computer Administrator account unprotected, any user who logs on to that account can make wholesale changes to XP. So if you're going to implement passwords, you should implement them for every user (except the Guest user, who can't have one).

Unfortunately, XP doesn't have an ideal arrangement for implementing passwords. Ideally, there'd be a setting that you (the Computer Administrator user) could set that would make each user apart from the Guest user create a password for their account the next time they used the computer. Each user would then create a password that only they would know, and the computer would be secure against unauthorized users logging on. Each user would be able to change their password whenever they wanted to (or, better, would be made to change the password frequently) and wouldn't be able to remove password protection from the account.

From a security and administration point of view, such an arrangement would be more or less ideal. And in fact this is a crude description of the security you get in XP Professional when you use it in a Windows domain (rather than a workgroup). But in XP Home? Dream on.

Given that XP doesn't have this ideal security arrangement, there are two ways in which you can proceed.

◆ Encourage—no, make that *heavily encourage*—each user to create a password right this moment, change it at least halfway frequently, and never remove it. Stress the benefits of having a strong password that only the user knows.

◆ Create passwords for each user yourself from a Computer Administrator account. This method has two disadvantages. First, you know the passwords. Second, and much worse, *the user loses all the personal certificates they've stored, together with any passwords they've saved for network resources (such as folders and printers) and for websites.* Losing the user this information will make you deservedly unpopular, so the only sensible time to implement passwords in this manner is before the user has used their account.

To make XP require passwords, take these steps from the What Do You Want to Change about *Username*'s Account? page:

1. Click the Create a Password link. XP displays the Create a Password for *Username*'s Account screen (shown in Figure 9.6). If you're creating a password for your own account, you get the same text boxes but not the excitable warnings.

FIGURE 9.6

Use the Create a Password for *Username*'s Account screen to create a password and (if necessary) a password hint for the account.

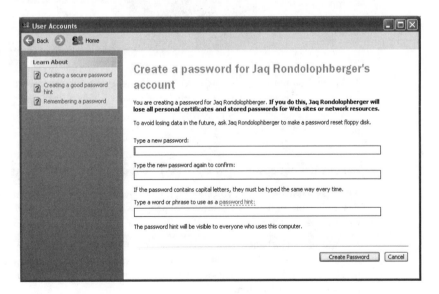

2. Enter the password in the Type a New Password text box and the Type the New Password Again to Confirm text box. For security (is someone looking over your shoulder?), XP displays each character as an asterisk (*). Make sure the two instances of the password match.

3. If you think it appropriate, enter a password hint in the Type a Word or Phrase to Use As a Password Hint text box. Anybody trying to log on to the computer can display the password hint, so you need to tailor it carefully to the person. The password hint must mean something to the user without meaning anything to anyone else. It's much easier to get this wrong than right—and in any case, for security, you shouldn't use password hints. (Every user should memorize their password. Period.)

4. Click the Create Password button. XP applies the password to the account.

5. When you create a password for your own user account, and you're a Computer Administrator user, XP displays the Do You Want to Make Your Files and Folders Private? screen (shown in Figure 9.7), which offers to make your files and folders private so that Limited users won't be able to see them. To accept this offer, click the Yes, Make Private button. To decline it, click the No button. (See Chapter 10 for information on sharing files and folders with other users and implementing security on your computer.)

FIGURE 9.7

XP displays the Do You Want to Make Your Files and Folders Private? screen when you create a password for your own Computer Administrator account.

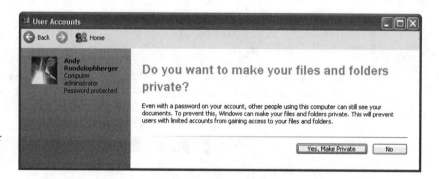

When you require passwords, XP prompts the user for a password when they click their name on the Welcome screen. The user can click the Password Hint link to display the hint for the password.

When a user account is password protected, XP displays *Password protected* under the account type on the User Accounts screens.

EXPERT KNOWLEDGE: HOW—AND WHY—TO CREATE SECURE PASSWORDS

If you use passwords—and you should, if you value your data—it's vital to make sure that they're effective. You wouldn't believe the number of people who don't understand why passwords are important and who see them as an irritant.

Actually, you *might* believe that. But would you believe that between 90 and 95 percent of *all* passwords are the same 100 words? This is what some security experts estimate based on the passwords they see in daily use. Crackers (malevolent hackers) try these popular passwords first when trying to guess a password because they work so often.

To create a secure password, it helps to understand how crackers go about breaking a password. The most common method is to use a *dictionary attack*. The attacker runs a script that tries to match each word in a specified dictionary with your password until it gets a hit. The dictionary can be in any language or a mixture of languages, and will usually contain all popular passwords in all major languages at its beginning.

Continued on next page

EXPERT KNOWLEDGE: HOW—AND WHY—TO CREATE SECURE PASSWORDS *(continued)*

(The dictionary isn't so much a dictionary in the conventional sense as a list of words arranged in some kind of descending order of probability—most likely words first.)

Dictionary attacks are often effective. But if the would-be victim has created a tough password (by using the methods described below), the cracker may resort to *social engineering*—the art of extracting passwords from the unsuspecting by posing as someone in authority (for example, as a system administrator or a troubleshooter for your ISP). Again, security experts tend to be amazed by how freely many users give up their passwords over the phone.

To keep your password secure, *never* write it down (and if you must write it down, don't stick the paper containing it onto your computer or monitor) and *never* tell anyone else what it is. You are the only person who ever needs to know your password. No ISP and no system administrator should need to be given your password, over the phone or in person. ISP personnel and system administrators may need to reset your password or assign you a new password—for example, if you forget your password. In this case, *they'll* give *you* the new password. You then log in with it and create a new, secure password for yourself immediately. (At least, that's the theory.)

Follow these rules to create a secure password:

◆ Create a password of an appropriate length. XP, many ISPs, and most services will let you create passwords of any length between 6 characters and 15 characters. Treat 6 characters as the absolute minimum. Aim for a password of at least 8 characters, and more like 12 if you're feeling insecure. Passwords of 5 characters or fewer are relatively easy to crack by brute force; passwords of 6 characters are much harder; and longer passwords are much harder yet. If you're allowed to create a password of any length, be sensible and limit the password to a length that you can remember and type without undue stumbling.

◆ Never use a real word in any language for a password. Real words can be broken easily by a dictionary attack.

◆ Instead, use symbols (@, $, %, ^, !, &, and so on) as substitute characters in a word or phrase, or reduce a phrase or sentence to its initial letters or key letters. Mix letters and numbers. Use uppercase and lowercase creatively (passwords are case sensitive). Alternatively, open a text editor, close your eyes, and type randomly for a few seconds, making sure to hold down the Shift key at intervals. Then pick a particularly cryptic part of the result to use as a password.

◆ Never use any example password that you see, no matter how compelling it may seem. For example, books on security provide example passwords. These may look wonderfully cryptic, but you should assume that they're all known to crackers and included in cracking dictionaries.

◆ Never use information of personal relevance or importance—your pet's name, a family member's name, your birthday, your driver's license number, your social security number, or (perhaps the ultimate no-no) your credit-card number. Most of these pieces of information can be obtained by trivial searches or the mildest of social engineering, making them near useless as passwords.

◆ Never use any option that offers to save a password for you. For example, XP offers to store your dial-up passwords so that you can access your dial-up accounts more easily. These passwords not only let unauthorized users of your computer access your dial-up accounts effortlessly, but also can be cracked easily by commonly available programs.

Continued on next page

EXPERT KNOWLEDGE: HOW—AND WHY—TO CREATE SECURE PASSWORDS *(continued)*

◆ Use a different password for each account or program that requires one. That way, if one password is compromised, the others will still be secure. (Yes, of course it's difficult. If security were effortless, nobody in the world would have a problem with it.)

◆ Change your passwords frequently, even if you have no reason to suspect that they've been compromised.

◆ As soon as you suspect that a password may have been compromised, change it. Also change any associated passwords.

◆ Never repeat a password you've used in the past. Create an entirely new password each time you change a password.

◆ Memorize your passwords. Never write them down. If you write a password down, you've compromised it. If you must write a password down, keep it in the safest of places. If that place is virtual rather than physical, protect your password stash with another password—a good one.

◆ Never tell anybody any of your passwords—not even the ones you've stopped using. (They might be able to use these passwords to guess at your newer passwords.)

If you can follow the simple advice in this list, you'll be ahead of 99 percent of the computer-using population—and measurably (perhaps immeasurably) more secure than any of them.

That said, be warned that no password is totally secure. Any password can be broken by an attacker who has sufficient time, determination, and computer operations. But most crackers will not be prepared to spend more than a few minutes (or, at the most, hours) on any given password, and will swiftly move on to other pastures that promise to prove greener. So your goal is to keep your passwords secure against random attackers, not against the NSA. If the NSA is on your case, you'll have much worse things to worry about than whether your passwords are strong enough.

TIP *One problem that can occur with passwords is having the Caps Lock feature switched on, either when you're creating the password or when you're subsequently entering it. XP does its best to warn you if the Caps Lock key is on when you're entering a password, but if you miss the warnings, double-check Caps Lock first if XP won't accept your password. On keyboards with an embedded numeric keypad, such as those on most notebooks, you can give yourself a similar problem by having the Num Lock feature on while typing the password. XP won't warn you about this.*

Removing Password Protection from an Account

Just as a Computer Administrator user can apply password protection to another user's account, so they can remove it. But the same problem applies to removal as to application: The user loses all the personal certificates they've stored, together with any passwords they've saved for network resources (such as folders and printers) and for websites. So if you need to remove password protection from an account, it's far better to have the users do it themselves.

To remove password protection from an account, click the Remove the Password link on the What Do You Want to Change about *Username*'s Account? screen. On the Are You Sure You Want to Remove *Username*'s Password? screen, click the Remove Password button.

Creating a New Password for a User

If a user forgets their password, they won't be able to log on to XP. They'll need to get a Computer Administrator user to create a new password—a replacement password, as it were—for them. But again, as with applying and removing passwords, the user loses all the personal certificates they've stored, together with any passwords they've saved for network resources (such as folders and printers) and for websites.

To create a replacement password for another user, log on as a Computer Administrator user and click the Change the Password link on the What Do You Want to Change about *Username*'s Account? screen. XP displays the Change *Username*'s Password screen, which works in the same way as the Create a Password for *Username*'s Account screen shown a page or two earlier: You type a password, confirm it, enter a password hint if appropriate, and click the Change Password button.

You're probably thinking that all this losing of the user's personal certificates and passwords should be avoidable, even if the user is unwise enough to forget their password. And it is avoidable. Read on.

Preventing a User from Changing Their Password

You can prevent a user from changing their password by opening a command-prompt window and issuing a `net user /passwordchg:no` command for the user. For example, the following command prevents the user Kenichi Tanaka IV from changing his password:

```
net user "Kenichi Tanaka IV" /passwordchg:no
```

This locks down *all* password changes for the user: creating a password for their account when it hasn't got a password; replacing their existing password with a new password; and removing password protection from their account.

To allow changes again, reissue the command with the **yes** argument:

```
net user "Kenichi Tanaka IV" /passwordchg:yes
```

NOTE *If you investigate the* `net user` *command, you'll see that its other parameters include a* `/passwordreq` *parameter that you can use to require a user account to use a password. This parameter doesn't work with XP Home. You can specify* `/passwordreq:yes` *until you get bored, and XP Home will blithely ignore you.*

Using Password Reset Disks to Recover from Lost Passwords

If a Limited user forgets their password, they need to get a Computer Administrator user to create a new password for them or remove the password from the account. That's easy enough—but if there's no Computer Administrator user around, it could prove a big waste of time. And the user loses any personal certificates and passwords they have stored.

If any Computer Administrator user forgets their password, they'll need to have another Computer Administrator user create a new password for them (because they won't be able to log on to their own account). That too is easy enough—provided that there's another Computer Administrator user, and that they're handy. Again, though, those personal certificates and passwords go overboard.

But if all available Computer Administrator users forget their passwords, you have a problem bigger than the personal certificates and passwords taking a permanent hike. If you don't prepare for this eventuality, and those Computer Administrator users forget their passwords, you'll need to reinstall XP to get it working again.

To prepare for this eventuality, you need to create a password reset disk. Both Computer Administrator users and Limited users can—and should—do this. You can do this only for your own account.

CREATING YOUR PASSWORD RESET DISK

To create a password reset disk, follow these steps:

1. Click your account on the Pick an Account to Change screen. XP displays the What Do You Want to Change about Your Account? screen.

2. Click the Prevent a Forgotten Password link in the Related Tasks list. XP launches the Forgotten Password Wizard, which displays the Welcome to the Forgotten Password Wizard page.

3. Click the Next button. The wizard displays the Create a Password Reset Disk page, which prompts you to insert a blank, formatted floppy into your A: drive.

4. Insert a blank, formatted floppy disk in the drive.
   - If you have multiple floppy drives, choose the option button for the one you put the floppy in.
   - The floppy doesn't actually have to be blank. The wizard creates only one file, USERKEY.PSW, which is typically only a couple of kilobytes large. So unless the floppy is completely full, the file will usually fit.

5. Click the Next button. The wizard displays the Current User Account Password page.

6. Enter your password in the Current User Account Password text box.

7. Click the Next button. The wizard displays the Creating Password Reset Disk page asking you to wait while it creates the disk. When it has finished, it makes the Next button available.

8. Click the Next button. The wizard displays the Completing the Forgotten Password Wizard screen.

9. Click the Finish button. The wizard closes itself. Remove the disk, label it clearly (or confusingly, if you plan to store it in a shared place), and put it somewhere safe. You can't create another password reset disk without invalidating this disk, so don't try making multiple disks—only the last one will work.

This disk doesn't store your password as such. Instead, it stores encrypted information that enables you to create a new password.

USING YOUR PASSWORD RESET DISK

To use the password reset disk, take the following steps:

1. When you get stuck at the Welcome screen and can't remember your password, insert the disk.

2. Click the green arrow button without entering your password. XP displays the Did You Forget Your Password? pop-up.

3. Click the Use Your Password Reset Disk link in the pop-up. XP starts the Password Reset Wizard, which displays its Welcome screen.

4. Click the Next button. The wizard displays the Insert the Password Reset Disk screen.

5. Insert the disk, specify the drive if necessary, and click the Next button. The wizard displays the Reset the User Account Password page.

6. Enter your new password twice, and enter a hint if you think it wise.

7. Click the Next button. The wizard displays the Completing the Password Reset Wizard page.

8. Click the Finish button. The wizard closes itself and returns you to the Welcome screen.

9. Log on using the new password. Remove the password reset disk and put it away somewhere safe. (You don't need to update it.)

Applying a .NET Passport to an Account

As mentioned earlier in the book, many of XP's communications features (such as Windows Messenger's text, audio, and video messaging capabilities) require you to have and use a Microsoft .NET Passport, a digital persona that's used to identify you online and which raises concerns about Microsoft being able to monitor the actions you take online.

You can apply a Passport to your user account either indirectly—by signing up for a Passport or using a Passport while logged in to the account—or directly by taking the following steps from the What Do You Want to Change about Your Account? page. You'll need to be online at the time. Note that Microsoft tweaks its Hotmail/MSN and Passport sign-up procedures now and then, so you may use a different procedure from that described here.

1. Click the Set Up My Account to Use a .NET Passport link. XP starts the .NET Passport Wizard, which displays its Add a .NET Passport to Your Windows XP User Account page.

2. Click the Next button. The wizard displays the Do You Have an E-mail Account? page.

3. Select the Yes option button or the No. Please Open a Free MSN.com E-mail Address for Me option button as appropriate.

4. Click the Next button.
   ◆ If you chose the Yes button, the wizard displays the What Is Your E-mail Address? page.
   ◆ The wizard displays a series of pages that walk you through the steps of creating an MSN e-mail account that also serves as your passport. You need to give your first name, last name, country or region, state, zip code, time zone, birth date, gender, and occupation. You then get to choose a sign-in name and password and set a secret question and answer for securing the account. By default, the .NET Passport Wizard sets you up to use MSN Explorer to access your e-mail. If you prefer to use another e-mail program, clear the Use MSN Explorer to Access My E-mail check box. You then get to choose whether Microsoft Passport shares your e-mail address, your name, and your other registration information with sites that use Passport. Passport then creates your .NET Passport and applies it to your computer. The wizard ends.

5. Enter the e-mail address in the E-mail Address or Passport text box.

6. Click the Next button. The wizard displays the Type Your .NET Password page.

7. Enter your password.

8. By default, the wizard selects the Save My Passport in My Windows XP User Account check box. Clear this check box if you want to apply your Passport manually to this account or another account.

9. Click the Next button. The wizard checks the password against the Passport and displays the You're Done! screen.

10. Click the Finish button. The wizard closes. You should now be able to access Passport-enabled sites and services from this account.

If necessary, you can change the .NET Passport associated with your user account by clicking the Change My .NET Passport link on the What Do You Want to Change about Your Account? page of User Accounts and clicking the Use a Different Passport button on the resulting What Do You Want to Change about Your .NET Passport? page.

Removing a .NET Passport from an Account

To remove a .NET Passport from a user account, take the following steps:

1. Make sure that Messenger and any other programs that use .NET Passport are closed.

2. Choose Start ➤ Run. XP displays the Run dialog box.

3. Enter **control userpasswords2** in the Open text box and click the OK button. XP displays the User Accounts dialog box with the Users page (shown on the left in Figure 9.8) foremost.

FIGURE 9.8

The two pages of the User Accounts dialog box give you capabilities beyond those available in Control Panel.

4. Click the Advanced tab. XP displays the Advanced page (shown on the right in Figure 9.8).

5. Click the Manage Passwords button in the Passwords and .NET Passports group box. XP displays the Stored User Names and Passwords dialog box (see Figure 9.9).

FIGURE 9.9

In the Stored User Names and Passwords dialog box, you can remove the .NET Passport associated with the current user account.

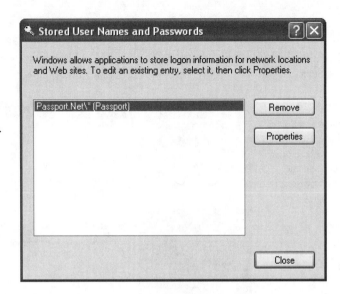

6. In the list box, select the Passport.Net* entry and click the Remove button. XP displays another Stored User Names and Passwords dialog box telling you that "The selected logon information will be deleted."

7. Click the OK button to remove the .NET Passport from the user account.

Removing the "Unread Mail" Readout from the Welcome Screen

By default, XP displays underneath each user's name on the Welcome screen a readout showing how many unread e-mail messages the user has in accounts that XP is aware of—presumably so that a user interested only in e-mail can see at a glance whether they want to bother logging on.

If you find this display intrusive, you can remove it by using the tools on the Logon\Unread Mail page of the Tweak UI PowerToy. You can remove this display for any user or for all users.

Turning Off the Welcome Screen

If you don't like the Welcome screen, or if you don't want users logging on to the computer to be able to see the list of other users, you can make XP display the Log On to Windows dialog box instead of the Welcome screen.

NOTE *Turning off the Welcome screen also turns off Fast User Switching, which means that multiple users won't be able to be logged on to the computer at the same time.*

To turn off the Welcome screen, make sure you're the only user logged on, and then take the following steps:

1. Choose Start ➤ Control Panel. XP displays Control Panel.
2. Click the User Accounts link. XP displays the User Accounts screen.
3. In the Pick a Task list, click the Change the Way Users Log On or Off link. XP displays the Select Logon and Logoff Options screen (shown in Figure 9.10).

FIGURE 9.10

On the Select Logon and Logoff Options screen, you can turn off the Welcome screen and Fast User Switching.

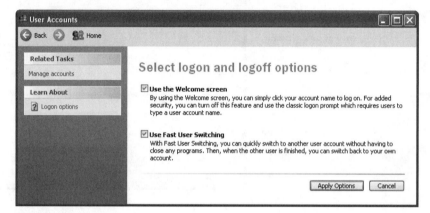

4. Clear the Use the Welcome Screen check box.
5. Click the Apply Options button.

Thereafter, XP displays the Log On to Windows dialog box instead of the Welcome screen. This dialog box neither lists the user accounts on the computer nor offers password hints, so it's more secure than the Welcome screen. However, XP displays the name of the last user in the Log On to Windows dialog box as a convenience in case the same user needs to log back in—so if this account isn't protected by a password, anyone can log on with no trouble at all.

Turning Fast User Switching Off and On

By default, XP's Fast User Switching feature is turned on, allowing you to have multiple user sessions running at the same time (with only one of them active at a time, of course). Fast User Switching is convenient for multiuser situations such as a family computer, but if several users leave a number of programs running, the computer's performance can suffer, especially if the computer has a modest amount of RAM (128MB or less). There's also the risk that one user will try to shut down the computer while another user has unsaved work still open, which will almost always lose the unsaved work. And even if no one terminates anyone else's session, users can have problems trying to open the same files or run the same programs, as discussed in Chapter 5.

To turn off Fast User Switching, make sure you're the only user logged on to the computer. (Log off any other users. If you don't, XP can't turn off Fast User Switching.) Then display the Select

Logon and Logoff Options screen as discussed in the previous section, clear the Use Fast User Switching check box, and click the Apply Options button.

Turning the Guest Account On and Off

Next, ask yourself if you want to have the Guest account enabled on your computer. If you want your computer to be moderately secure, it's a good idea to leave the Guest account turned off until you need it.

In a family setting, the Guest account can be a good idea, particularly if nobody keeps secrets on the computer. In an office, dorm, or just about any other setting, the Guest account is a bad idea because it compromises the security of your computer. The Guest account is more limited in what it can do than Computer Administrator accounts and Limited accounts, but even so, it has the potential to cause trouble, either with local files or via a network or Internet connection.

The Guest account is disabled by default in XP Home. To turn it on, follow these steps:

1. Choose Start ➢ Control Panel. XP displays Control Panel.
2. Click the User Accounts link. XP displays the User Accounts screen.
3. Click the Guest link. XP displays the Do You Want to Turn On the Guest Account? screen.
4. Click the Turn On the Guest Account link. XP turns on the Guest account and displays the User Accounts screen again.

To disable the Guest account, click the Guest link on the User Accounts page. XP displays the What Do You Want to Change about the Guest Account? page. Click the Turn Off the Guest Account link.

Implementing and Preventing Automatic Logons

If you set up XP Home with only one user account, you'll have found that XP sets up that user to log on automatically, so instead of booting to the Welcome screen (and displaying a single user name on it), XP automatically logs the user on and displays their Desktop. Microsoft clearly figured that this habit would be appreciated by people who don't share their computer with anyone else—and it does seem to be. Mind you, its security model is hopeless enough to make computer security consultants throw up their career in despair and opt for a quiet life in air-traffic control instead—but you can change that if necessary.

You can also set up an automatic logon for a user on a computer that has multiple user accounts. Doing so is a massive threat to the security of that user's files and, if the user is a Computer Administrator user, to that of all other users and to the computer itself, so consider security carefully before setting up an automatic logon. However, having a user logged on automatically can be useful when multiple people need to share a user identity that you want to have available all the time. For example, some institutions (such as libraries) use this capability for their public terminals.

TIP *When you've set up a computer to log a user on automatically, you can suppress the automatic logon by holding down the Shift key while the computer is starting up.*

Implementing an Automatic Logon

To implement an automatic logon, take the following steps:

1. Choose Start ➢ Run. XP displays the Run dialog box.
2. Enter **control userpasswords2** in the Open text box and click the OK button. XP displays the User Accounts dialog box, with the Users page (shown on the left in Figure 9.8, earlier in this chapter) foremost.
3. Clear the Users Must Enter a User Name and Password to Use This Computer check box.
4. Click the OK button. XP displays the Automatically Log On dialog box (see Figure 9.11).

FIGURE 9.11

In the Automatically Log On dialog box, enter the user name and password of the user whom you want XP to automatically log on.

5. Enter the username and password (twice) and click the OK button. XP closes the Automatically Log On dialog box and the User Accounts dialog box and sets that user account to automatically log on.

Preventing Automatic Logons

If your computer is set up to automatically log a user on, you can prevent it from doing so by displaying the User Accounts dialog box as described in the previous section, selecting the Users Must Enter a User Name and Password to Use This Computer check box, and clicking the OK button.

NOTE   If you looked at the Advanced User Management group box on the Advanced page of the User Accounts dialog box, you'll have noticed the text "Local Users and Groups can be used to perform advanced user management tasks." That sounds interesting, doesn't it? But if you click the Advanced button, you'll find that the word "can" there should really have been "can't," because Microsoft has chosen to disable the Local Users and Groups snap-in for Microsoft Management Console in XP Home.

Performing Other Management Actions from the User Accounts Dialog Box

From the Users page of the User Accounts dialog box, you can perform other various user account-management actions, such as adding a user account to the computer, removing a user account from the computer, changing a user's password, and resetting a user's password.

For most account management, it makes sense to use XP Home's User Accounts pages in Control Panel, which usher you through each account-management process and steer you toward the choices likely to be most suitable for normal needs. But in certain limited circumstances, you may need the additional flexibility that the tools accessible from the User Accounts dialog box give you.

NOTE   *Note that the User Accounts dialog box is not updated while you're working in it, so any changes you make that should affect the capabilities of the account you're working with won't be reflected immediately. For example, if you log on using a Computer Administrator account and then change the account's permissions to those of a Standard user or a Limited user, you'll still be able to exercise the permissions of a Computer Administrator user until you close the User Accounts dialog box and log off XP. When you then log back on to XP with the same account, XP will have updated the capabilities of the account. The same discrepancy occurs if you, as a Computer Administrator user, change the capabilities of another account that's currently logged on but disconnected on a computer that's using Fast User Switching.*

ADDING A USER

To add a user, click the Add button and use the resulting Add New User Wizard to specify the user's name, description, and password. The good news is that this method lets you specify a wider range of user types (see Figure 9.12) than XP's standard interface for adding user accounts lets you. The bad news is that some of the user types are the same as each other, and one of them doesn't work unless you create the specified group. And only members of the Computer Administrator group, the Limited group, and the Guests group appear on the Welcome screen and in the User Accounts tool.

FIGURE 9.12

By using the Add New User Wizard to add a new user, you can specify different user types.

These are the user types you can create from the Add New User Wizard, together with explanations of what they are and what you have to watch out for:

Standard user   A member of the Power Users group. Unless you create this group first (by using the `net localgroup` command, as discussed in the section "Creating and Deleting Local Groups," later in this chapter), XP returns the error "The group name could not be found" when you try to assign a user to this group. If you create the group, you can then assign the user to it—but the user will not appear on the Welcome screen or in the User Accounts tool.

Restricted user   A Restricted user is the same as a Limited user. Both are members of the Users group.

Administrator user   An Administrator user is the same as a Computer Administrator user, a member of the Administrators group.

Guest user   A Guest user is a member of the Guests group, with the same privileges as the Guest user account that's created by default—in other words, very few privileges.

HelpServicesGroup user   A HelpServicesGroup user is a member of the HelpServicesGroup (naturally enough). This group is used by default for Remote Assistance connections to the computer. You won't normally need to add users to this group.

Power user   A member of the Power Users group. Selecting this group from the Other drop-down list is effectively the same as selecting the Standard User option button. See the "Standard user" item earlier in the list for complications.

DELETING A USER

To remove a user from the computer, select their entry and click the Remove button. XP displays a warning dialog box making sure that you understand you're removing the user's account. Click the Yes button if you want to proceed.

CHANGING A USER'S PROPERTIES

You can change a user's name, full name, description, or group membership by selecting the user, clicking the Properties button, and working on the General page and the Group Membership page of the resulting Properties dialog box. This is the easiest way to change these properties, but you can also change all the properties except the username by using the `net user` and `net localgroup` commands, as discussed later in this chapter.

MAKING USERS PRESS CTRL+ALT+DELETE WHEN LOGGING ON

If you've turned off the Welcome screen (and thus turned off Fast User Switching as well), you can force users to press the Ctrl+Alt+Delete key combination in order to bring up the Log On to Windows dialog box so that they can log on. To do so, select the Require Users to Press Ctrl+Alt+Delete check box in the Secure Logon group box on the Advanced page of the User Accounts dialog box.

The advantage of pressing Ctrl+Alt+Delete (which is also known as the Vulcan Nerve Pinch, the Triple Bucky, and other humorous names) is that it sends an interrupt to XP that causes it to display the Log On to Windows dialog box. This helps to ensure that a malicious hacker can't create a fake Log On to Windows screen that would capture the user's username and password rather than logging them on.

If the computer is using the Welcome screen, selecting Require Users to Press Ctrl+Alt+Delete check box has no effect: The Welcome screen is displayed as usual, and users can log on by clicking their username (and entering their password, if they have one).

Limiting the Times a User Can Log On

By default, any user of an XP Home computer can use it any time they can gain physical access to it, morning, noon, or night. But if you're feeling managerial, you can limit the days and times during which a user can use XP Home. The user then can't log on during days or at times other than those permitted.

Surprisingly, this restriction is a bit toothless if the user is logged on as the active user (in other words, not in a disconnected session) when the end of a permitted time period is reached. You might expect XP to log the user off forcibly, perhaps giving them a five-minute warning so that they could go gracefully rather than wait and be press-ganged, but in fact XP simply allows them to continue working. However, if the user is in a disconnected session, or if they disconnect the active session, XP prevents them from logging back on. Their disconnected session keeps right on rolling, so it might slow down performance for other users.

WARNING *Before we get into the details, a quick warning: XP Home isn't really designed to restrict users in the way described here. If you use the Welcome screen (XP Home's default) rather than the Log On to Windows dialog box for logon, time lockouts are confusing. Instead of receiving a notice that they can't log in at this time because of a time restriction, the user receives a demand for a password—even if they have no password set for their account. If they do have a password set for the account, and enter it correctly, XP rejects it, saying it's wrong.*

To implement time restrictions, issue the **net user** command with the **/times** parameter and the relevant days and times. (For each day, you have to specify the times allowed—you can't just specify certain days, even if that might occasionally be useful.) For days, either spell out the day in full or use the one-letter or two-letter abbreviations M, T, W, Th, F, S, and Su. For times, set them by the whole hour (you can't use minutes) in either 24-hour format or in AM/PM format using either am and pm or **a.m.** and **p.m.** Use hyphens to designate ranges of days or hours, and separate multiple day entries with semicolons. Here are some examples of **/times** arguments:

```
net user "kenichi tanaka iv" /times:M-F,9-17
net user "kenichi tanaka iv" /times:S-Su,12am-12am
net user "kenichi tanaka iv" /times:m-w,9am-1pm,24m-6pm;th-f,8am-6pm
net user "kenichi tanaka iv" /times:Monday,9-13;Wednesday,9-13;Friday,9-13
```

Note that if the username contains one or more spaces, you'll need to put it in double quotation marks, otherwise the **net user** command won't recognize the username. On the plus side, like all good DOS commands, **net user** isn't case sensitive, so you can enter the username, the parameters, and the arguments in lowercase if you find that faster. Each **net user /times** statement sets just the specified times—you can't use it to add times to the existing times. And using a **net user /times** statement without any arguments sets the user account to have no logon times. (However, the account is still technically active. See the next section for instructions on deactivating an account.)

To see the times set for a user account, issue the **net user** command with the username and check the Logon Hours portion of the resulting readout. You might want to do this to double-check that you've set the hours you intended, or to remind yourself of the restrictions previously set on a user account.

As mentioned in the Warning above, XP prompts the user for a password when they try to log on from the Welcome screen. If they have a password, and enter it, XP tells them they've got it wrong.

If the computer is set to use the Log On to Windows dialog box rather than the Welcome screen, the user receives the Logon Message message box shown in Figure 9.13 telling them that their account has time restrictions that prevent them from logging on "at this time" and suggesting they try again later. Unhelpfully, the message box doesn't tell the user what times they *are* allowed to log on—perhaps for security reasons?

To restore the user account to being able to log on at any time under the sun (or moon), issue the **net user** command with the appropriate username and the /Times parameter with the /All argument. For example, the following command restores the ability of the user Kenichi Tanaka IV to log on at any time:

```
net user "Kenichi Tanaka IV" /times:all
```

Disabling and Reenabling a User Account

Instead of deleting a user account to prevent a user from using it, you can disable a user account by deactivating it. The advantage to disabling an account over deleting it is that the account's folders and settings remain intact, so it springs back to life when you reactivate it.

To disable a user account, issue the **net user** command with the appropriate username and the /Active parameter with the No argument. For example, the following command disables the account with the username Kenichi Tanaka IV:

```
net user "kenichi tanaka iv" /active:no
```

When you deactivate an account, XP removes its entry from the Welcome screen, so the user can't log on from there. If the computer is set to use the Log On to Windows dialog box rather than the Welcome screen, the disabled user will need to enter their name manually (and their password, if they have one). They then receive a Logon Message dialog box like that shown in Figure 9.14 telling them that their account has been disabled and suggesting they see their system administrator.

To reactivate an account, issue the **net user** command with the appropriate username and the /Active parameter with the Yes argument. For example, the following command reactivates the user account of our long-suffering Kenichi Tanaka IV:

```
net user "kenichi tanaka iv" /active:yes
```

Making a User Account Expire

Another trick you can perform with the net user command is to make a user account expire at a particular date. To do so, use the /expires parameter with the appropriate date—for example,

```
net user "kenichi tanaka iv" /expire:12/31/02
```

The user account is then locked from the beginning of the day in question. As with the previous two limitations, if the user tries to log on from the Welcome screen, they receive a prompt for a password that they can't satisfy even with the correct password. If the user tries to log on from the Log On to Windows dialog box, they receive a Logon Message message box telling them their account has expired and suggesting they remonstrate with their system administrator.

To get the user account up and running again, set an expiry date in the future. To remove expiration from a user account, use the /expires parameter with the never argument:

```
net user "kenichi tanaka iv" /expires:never
```

Changing Other User Properties with *net user*

net user is a flexible command. Among its other actions are those listed below. In most cases, you can perform these actions more easily by using either the User Accounts tool or (more often) the User Accounts dialog box, but should you prefer to use net user instead, there's nothing to stop you.

Set the full name for the user	net user *username* /fullname:"*name*"
Add a comment to a user	net user *username* /comment:"*comment text*"
Create a user	net user *username* /add
Delete a user	net user *username* /delete
Set the user's password	net user *username* *password*
Set the user's home directory	net user *username* /homedir:*directory*

net user also lets you specify a profile for a user, but this capability doesn't work in XP Home.

WARNING You can delete your own account from the User Accounts dialog box, but it isn't a great idea to do so. The account remains partly alive until you log off, at which point it disappears for good—but the potential for confusing yourself, or confusing XP, is high, because XP doesn't delete the folders that contain the user profile. Likewise, you can delete the user account for a user who's logged on in a disconnected section, but this can easily cause confusion too and so is best avoided.

Creating and Deleting Local Groups

XP Home supports the net localgroup command for displaying the list of groups on the local computer, creating and deleting groups, and adding users to and removing users from groups. That's "supports" in the sense of "it works," but because of the limitations that Microsoft has imposed on XP Home, manipulating user groups in XP Home doesn't really get you anywhere. But if you're interested in creating a "Standard user" using the User Accounts dialog box (as described in the section "Performing Other Management Actions from the User Accounts Dialog Box," earlier in this chapter), you might want to create a Power Users group to which you can assign rights and permissions. You might also want to use groups for identification within a small office (or a big home).

The list below shows the key uses of `net localgroup`, where *groupname* is the group name and *user1* and *user2* are placeholders for usernames. Remember to use double quotation marks around any names that include spaces or other extended characters that would otherwise confuse the `net localgroup` command.

See which groups there are	`net localgroup`
List the members of a group	`net localgroup` *groupname*
Create a new group	`net localgroup` *groupname* `/add`
Delete a group	`net localgroup` *groupname* `/delete`
Add a user to a group	`net localgroup` *groupname* *user1 user2* `/add`
Remove a user from a group	`net localgroup` *groupname* *user1 user2* `/delete`

Up Next

This chapter has discussed what user accounts are, what they're for, and how to work with them to keep users separated from each other and give users scope to take only the actions they need to take. You know why passwords are vital for protecting your data, and you know how to create strong passwords. And you've seen how to turn on and off the Welcome screen, the Fast User Switching feature, and the Guest account.

If this has whetted your taste for administration, turn the page. The next chapter discusses how to share folders with other users, how to use the auditing and security options that XP Home offers, and how to work with file types to make files behave the way you want them to.

Chapter 10

Sharing and File Types

THIS CHAPTER DISCUSSES SHARING and file types—two topics you really need to know about in order to make the most of XP Home.

The chapter starts with a little background about XP Home's approach to security and sharing. After that, it discusses how to share folders with other users of the computer, and how to prevent other users (including Computer Administrator users) from examining folders you want to keep private. It also shows you how to use the Shared Folders snap-in to see at a glance which folders you're sharing and which user has which file open.

Sharing folders is easy. But the topic covered at the end of the chapter—file extensions, file types, and file associations—is tough enough to annoy well-seasoned Windows veterans. If you've gotten confused about why different things happen when you double-click different types of files in Explorer; if you wish you could change the action that results for one file type or another; or if you want to see extensions for all your files—if any of these is the case, read this section.

This chapter might not sound like your idea of fun, but you should probably read it at some point—not necessarily right now, but perhaps when you start having problems with your house-mates accessing your secret files, or with extensions and file types misbehaving.

Part of the problem is that XP Home simply tries to be too friendly, so its security model is wide open by default. Each user created during setup is automatically made a Computer Administrator user, which gives them access to every folder and file on the computer. If you want privacy, you have to tell XP Home so, and tell it explicitly.

This chapter covers the following topics:

◆ The background to sharing
◆ Sharing folders
◆ Making a folder private
◆ Seeing which folders and files you're sharing
◆ Understanding what file types are
◆ Changing the action associated with a file type
◆ Creating a new file type

The Background to Sharing

Windows NT and Windows 2000, as you'll know if you've worked with them, have an impressive range of security and management features, including three different categories of permissions (share permissions, folder permissions, and special permissions) that allow pico-management of what any particular user or group of users can do with a given folder or file. For example, you can allow one user to open files in a particular folder but not change them. Or you can prevent another user from seeing those files in that folder, but allow them to navigate through that folder to a subfolder it contained (and allow them to work with just one of the files in that subfolder).

Because Windows XP has the NT/2000 code base under its hood, it has most of those capabilities too. When you connect a computer running XP Professional to a Windows 2000 Server– or Windows .NET Server–based network, you can implement a set of permissions extensive enough to stun medium-sized mammals. But because XP Home is designed for home use rather than for corporate or military use, and because you don't (or *shouldn't*) need to set permissions such as these in the typical home or home-office setting, XP Home simplifies permissions and security a great deal into an arrangement called Simple File Sharing.

These are the basic parameters of Simple File Sharing:

◆ XP Home differentiates between local sharing and network sharing. Once you read those terms, you probably have a pretty good idea as to what they mean: *Local sharing* is the sharing of files and folders with other users of your computer. *Network sharing* is the sharing of files and folders with users of other computers to which your computer is networked.

◆ By default, most files and folders in XP Home are shared locally. (More on this in a moment.) By default, no files are shared on the network.

◆ XP Home provides a separate area of the file structure for each user: the \My Documents\ folder and its subfolders. Files and folders within the \My Documents\ folder and its subfolders are automatically protected from Limited users and the Guest user. By default, Computer Administrator users can see the contents of any user's \My Documents\ folder and its subfolders, but you can make the contents of your \My Documents\ folder and its subfolders private so that only you can see them.

◆ XP Home provides folders that are automatically shared with all users of your computer (the \Shared Documents\ folder structure). You can't remove this sharing from these folders.

◆ For any folder apart from folders owned and protected by the operating system, you can choose to share the folder on the network. You can even share your \My Documents\ folder if you so choose.

◆ When you share a folder on the network, you can decide whether the users you're sharing it with can only read its contents or can read them and change them. If you let other users change your files, they can delete them as well.

◆ A subfolder inherits privacy from its parent folder (the folder that contains it). For example, say you have a folder named \My Secret Stuff\, located in your \My Documents\ folder, that you make private. If you create a folder named \Top Secret\ within the \My Secret Stuff\ folder, it automatically is made private too. You can't remove privacy from the subfolder of a private folder without removing it from the parent folder.

♦ By contrast, a subfolder *does not* inherit being shared on the network from its parent folder: You need to specify sharing explicitly for the subfolder of a shared parent folder.

♦ You can't set sharing on individual files (but see the next sidebar), so to implement sharing on files, you need to put them in shared folders or private folders as appropriate.

♦ When you create a file or folder, it inherits the permissions of its parent folder (the folder that contains it). When you move a file or folder into another folder, the file or folder takes on the permissions of that new parent folder.

♦ With Simple File Sharing, XP makes each network connection under the permissions of a Guest account.

EXPERT KNOWLEDGE: MANIPULATING PERMISSIONS WITH *CACLS* AND *XCACLS*

If you found that the preceding description of XP Home's Simple File Sharing model sounded a bit restrictive, you'll be glad to know that XP Home *does* include a tool that lets you manipulate permissions on individual files. It's called `cacls`, it's a command-line utility, and it's ugly to use because you need to understand permissions in order to make it do what you want.

`cacls` stands for "change access control lists," and there's a more powerful version of `cacls` called `xcacls` ("extended change access control lists") that you can download for free from the Microsoft website (www.microsoft.com/windows2000/techinfo/reskit/tools/existing/xcacls-o.asp). In XP, an *access control list* or ACL is used to store the permissions for an object such as a file, a folder, a printer, or another resource.

Because `cacls` and `xcacls` are highly esoteric, I'll leave you to explore them on your own if you decide you need them. Use the /? switch from the command line (for example, `cacls /?`) to display the help available.

As mentioned in Chapter 6, XP Home would like you to keep all the documents that you don't want to share in the \My Documents\ folder and its subfolders (such as the \My Pictures\ folder, the \My Music\ folder, and the \My Videos\ folder) and all the documents that you do want to share in the \Shared Documents\ folder and its subfolders (such as the \Shared Music\ folder, the \Shared Pictures\ folder, and the \Shared Videos\ folder). Windows programs are trained to put documents you create using them in the \My Documents\ folder or the appropriate subfolder by default and to look for them there. In theory, this helps you, the user, because you don't lose files, and each program opens automatically in the right folder for the types of files you're likely to want to open in it. Other XP programs and features also use these folders as appropriate. For example, the My Pictures Slideshow screen saver by default looks in the \My Pictures\ folder for pictures.

EXPERT KNOWLEDGE: BENEATH THE HOOD IN XP HOME'S SIMPLE FILE SHARING

Before you start reading this sidebar, a word of warning: Don't read it unless you're curious about how XP's sharing really works. If you're content with using the mechanisms described in this chapter for sharing files (or keeping them private) while not understanding the inner workings of Simple File Sharing, save

Continued on next page

EXPERT KNOWLEDGE: BENEATH THE HOOD IN XP HOME'S SIMPLE FILE SHARING *(continued)*

your time and energy for something more rewarding. But if you're familiar with the permissions structure of NT or Windows 2000, you may find XP Home's nebulous, awkward-details-all-nicely-hidden-for-your-own-good approach to file sharing both irritating and unsettling. Then by all means read this sidebar.

(In case you're curious *and* you're not familiar with permissions, here's a little background: NT-based operating systems use three categories of permissions: share permissions, folder permissions [which apply to files as well], and special permissions. Share permissions are the basic level, providing three permissions: Full Control, Change, and Read. Folder permissions are the next level of permission, providing six permissions: Read, Write, Read & Execute, Modify, List Folder Contents, and Full Control. Special permissions are the finest grade of permission, providing 14 permissions that you can set to define precisely which actions a user can take with a shared folder or file. Each folder permission consists of a set of special permissions. For example, the Write folder permission consists of the Create Files/Write Data, Create Folders/Append Data, Write Attributes, Write Extended Attributes, Read Permissions, and Synchronize special permissions. In the following discussion, the permissions are folder permissions unless specified as share permissions.)

XP Home's Simple File Sharing model uses five levels of access, numbered from Level 1 to Level 5, with Level 1 being the most secure and Level 5 the least secure. The following sections discuss these access levels, how you apply them, and how they relate to permissions.

LEVEL 1: PRIVATE (OWNER ONLY)

Level 1 access is the most secure. You need to apply it manually to a folder. You can apply it only to your \My Documents\ folder or subfolders of your \My Documents\ folder.

XP automatically applies Level 1 access when you take either of the following actions:

◆ You select the Make This Folder Private check box on the Sharing page of the Properties dialog box for the folder.

◆ You apply a password to your account using the User Accounts tool and click the Yes, Make Private button when XP displays the Do You Want to Make Your Files and Folders Private? screen.

You (the owner of the folder) have the Full Control permission for the folder. The System account also has the Full Control permission. Computer Administrator users other than yourself have no access to the folder, and Limited users and the Guest users would have even less access if it were possible. The folder isn't shared on the network.

LEVEL 2: NOT QUITE PRIVATE (OWNER AND COMPUTER ADMINISTRATOR)

Level 2 access is the default access level for each user's \My Documents\ folder and the folders it contains. The owner of the folder, the System account, and all Computer Administrator users for the computer have the Full Control permission for the folder. Other users have no permission for the folder and so cannot access it. The folder isn't shared on the network.

To reapply Level 2 access to a folder in a user's \My Documents\ folder structure, clear both the Make This Folder check box and the Share This Folder on the Network check box on the Sharing page of the Properties dialog box for the folder.

Continued on next page

EXPERT KNOWLEDGE: BENEATH THE HOOD IN XP HOME'S SIMPLE FILE SHARING *(continued)*

LEVEL 3: SHARED WITH OTHER USERS OF THE COMPUTER

Level 3 access is applied to the \Shared Documents\ folder by default. The owner of the folder, the System account, and all Computer Administrator users for the computer have the Full Control permission for the folder, while Limited users and the Guest user have the Read permission for the folder—they can examine its contents, and they can copy them to anywhere they have permission to create files, but they can't change or delete them. The folder isn't shared on the network.

To apply Level 3 access to a folder, move it to the \Shared Documents\ folder.

LEVEL 4: SHARED ON THE NETWORK WITH READ-ONLY ACCESS

Level 4 access is the most secure way of sharing files with remote users—users on other computers. Remote users can see the files (and copy them) but can't change or delete them.

As in Level 3 access, the owner of the folder, the System account, and all Computer Administrator users for the computer have the Full Control permission for the folder, while Limited users and the Guest user have the Read permission for the folder. The folder is shared on the network, with remote users having the Read share permission (so that they can't modify or delete the folder or its contents).

LEVEL 5: SHARED ON THE NETWORK WITH FULL CONTROL

Level 5 access is the least secure and is recommended only for secure networks protected by an effective firewall. In Level 5 access, the owner of the folder, the System account, and all Computer Administrator users for the computer have the Full Control permission for the folder. Remote users have the Full Control share permission. Limited users and the Guest user have the Change permission for the folder (which includes deleting items).

To apply Level 5 access to a folder, select the Share This Folder on the Network check box on the Sharing page of the Properties dialog box for the folder and select the Allow Network Users to Change My Files check box.

From the preceding descriptions, you've probably figured out that these five access levels are mutually exclusive—applying one access level removes the access level that was previously set for the folder, so you can't set two access levels at once. But there's one small quirk that you should be aware of, because it might just possibly bite you if the circumstances were right and you weren't paying attention. If you share a folder with Level 5 access (shared on the network with Full Control) and within it share a subfolder with Level 4 access, local users (those logged on to your computer) will have Level 5 access to the subfolder as well as the folder. Remote users, by contrast, will have Level 4 access to the subfolder, as you intended.

As mentioned in the main text, under Simple File Sharing, a file or folder normally shares the permissions of its parent folder, because the file or folder inherits the permissions of the folder in which it's created or into which it's moved. For a folder, you can then implement different permissions by using the controls on the Sharing page of the Properties dialog box for the folder to set the appropriate level of access. (That's kind of looking at it backward—in practice, you'll specify the type of sharing you want, thereby causing XP to set the appropriate access level and permissions.)

Continued on next page

Expert Knowledge: Beneath the Hood in XP Home's Simple File Sharing *(continued)*

Abnormally, though, a file *can* have different permissions from the folder that contains it. This happens when you do either of the following:

◆ You move a file, using the move command from a command prompt or in a script, from a source folder on the same drive as the destination folder, and the source folder has different permissions from the destination folder.

◆ You use the cacls utility or the xcacls utility (discussed earlier in the chapter) to change the permissions on the file manually.

Sharing a Folder

XP Home provides two easy ways of sharing a folder:

◆ Using the \Shared Documents\ folder to share the folder with all other users of the computer

◆ Using the "share on the network" technique to share the folder with all other users of the same computer and users of computers networked to this computer

The next two sections discuss these ways of sharing a folder.

Sharing a Folder with All Other Users of This Computer

XP provides an easy way to share a folder with all the other users of the computer. To share a new folder, create it in the \Shared Documents\ folder. To share an existing folder, move it to the \Shared Documents\ folder. All other users of the computer can then access the contents of the folder and (by default) change them.

You can share a file by placing it directly in the \Shared Documents\ folder rather than in a subfolder of the \Shared Documents\ folder.

Sharing a Folder "on the Network" with All Other Users

The second way of sharing a folder is called "share on the network." The name is misleading—perhaps intentionally so. A folder shared in this way *is* shared on the network, so that users of other computers networked to this computer can access the folder's contents. But the folder is *also* shared with all other users of this computer.

Before we get into this topic, there are a couple of things you need to know:

◆ First, before you can share a folder on the network, you need to enable remote access to your computer by running the Network Setup Wizard. If you haven't done so, turn to Chapter 31 for coverage of the Network Setup Wizard. Alternatively, you can click the If You Understand the Security Risks but Want to Share Files without Running the Wizard, Click Here link that XP displays in the Network Sharing and Security group box on the Sharing page of the Properties dialog box for a folder until you've run the Network Setup Wizard (or clicked this link). When you click this link, XP displays the Enable File Sharing dialog box. Select the Just

Enable File Sharing option button and click the OK button. XP closes the Enable File Sharing dialog box and makes the Share This Folder on the Network check box available in the Network Sharing and Security group box.

◆ Second, XP prevents you from using the share-on-the-network technique for folders in the `\Program Files\` folder and the `\Windows\` folder structure. These limitations are for your own good, but you need to know about them upfront so that you don't place folders you want to share inside these folders.

To share a folder on the network, follow these steps:

1. Create the folder (if you haven't created it already) in a suitable location for sharing on the network. (That means you shouldn't put it in your `\My Documents\` folder—it's best to keep that to yourself—and you can't put it in the `\Program Files\` folder structure or the `\Windows\` folder structure.) If the folder already exists, and is located in a less-than-prime location, move it to a suitable location.

2. Right-click the folder and choose Sharing and Security from the context menu. (Alternatively, select the folder and choose File ➢ Sharing and Security.) XP displays the Sharing page of the Properties dialog box for the folder. Figure 10.1 shows an example of the Sharing page.

   ◆ If you're sharing a drive, the Sharing page of the Properties dialog box at first contains nothing but a note warning you that sharing the root of a drive isn't recommended (for security reasons) and a link that you can click to acknowledge that you understand the risk but want to share the root of the drive anyway. If you want to share the drive, click this link, and XP displays the controls for the Sharing page.

FIGURE 10.1

Use the Sharing page of the Properties dialog box for a folder or drive to share the folder or drive "on the network."

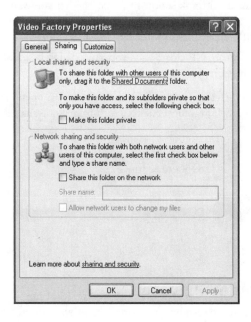

3. Select the Share This Folder on the Network check box. XP enables the Share Name text box and enters the folder's name in it. XP also enables the Allow Network Users to Change My Files check box.

4. Change the name in the Share Name text box if you want. You'll often want to change this to something more descriptive. For example, you might want to change the name to indicate which computer the folder is located on.

   ◆ Remove any commas or semicolons from the share name. XP doesn't allow them, though they're fine in the folder name (and so are entered in the share name automatically). Periods and exclamation points are okay. (If you don't remove these characters, XP hits you with a Sharing dialog box telling you that the share name "contains invalid characters" when you close the Properties dialog box.)

   ◆ You'll need to reduce the share name to 12 characters or fewer if you want to be able to access it from computers running Windows 98, Windows Me, or Windows NT 4. If you don't shorten a long name, Windows hits you with another Sharing dialog box to this effect when you close the Properties dialog box.

TIP *Putting a dollar sign ($) at the end of the share name creates a hidden shared folder—one that doesn't show up when people are browsing the network. Anyone who knows the share name, though, can connect to it easily. You may want to use this trick to make some folders available to users in the know without others running across them.*

5. If you don't want other users to be able to change your files, clear the Allow Network Users to Change My Files check box. "Change" in this sense covers editing the files, renaming them, and deleting them, so think seriously about whether you want to permit changes. (If you don't allow changing, other users can view your files—this is called "reading" them—and can save them under different names in folders of their own.)

6. Click the OK button. XP closes the Properties dialog box and shares the folder with the degree of permissions you specified.

Explorer displays a different icon for a shared folder—an open hand appears underneath the folder—to give you a quick graphical cue to which folders are shared and which aren't. Figure 10.2 shows an example.

FIGURE 10.2

XP displays an icon with an open hand to indicate a shared folder.

Documents and Settings

Video Factory

Making a Folder Private

So far in this chapter, you've seen how to share a folder with all other users of this computer, with them and users of networked computers, and with users you specify.

But what if you want to share a folder with none of the above—in other words, if you flat-out don't want to share a folder? Simply not sharing it (using any of the methods described above) isn't good enough, because Computer Administrator users can see the contents of any folder that isn't specifically protected against them. You need to make it private.

To make a folder private, take the following steps:

1. Right-click the folder and choose Sharing and Security from the context menu. (Alternatively, select the folder and click the Share This Folder link in the File and Folder Tasks list.) XP displays the Sharing page of the Properties dialog box.

2. Select the Make This Folder Private check box.

3. Click the OK button. XP closes the Properties dialog box and applies privacy to the folder.

   ◆ If you don't have a password on your user account when you select the Make This Folder Private check box, XP displays the Sharing dialog box shown in Figure 10.3, warning you that anyone can log in as you, and so access the folder, and inviting you to create a password. If you click the Yes button, XP displays the Create a Password for Your Account screen of User Accounts so that you can create the password immediately.

FIGURE 10.3

When you make a folder private, XP displays this Sharing dialog box to prompt you to password-protect your user account if it's not already protected.

When you make a folder private, other users can still see the folder is there (because they can list the contents of the parent folder), but they can't view its contents. When they try to open it, they get a message such as that shown in Figure 10.4 that the folder is inaccessible and access is denied.

FIGURE 10.4

When you've made a folder private, other users of the computer can't access it.

WARNING   *When you move a folder that you've made private, it loses its private status unless the folder to which you move it is private as well. (By contrast, when you move a folder that isn't private to a folder that is private, XP doesn't make the moved folder private.) So after moving a private folder, explicitly check its sharing status and reapply privacy if necessary.*

Seeing What Files and Folders You're Sharing

However tidy a structure of shared folders you set up, it's easy to lose track of what's being shared and where. You can of course open one or more Explorer windows and go spelunking through your drives looking for shared icons, but this gets old fast, and in any case, Explorer can't show you whether anyone is accessing your shared folders at any given point.

XP's Computer Management tool provides a feature called Shared Folders for seeing which folders and files you're sharing. If necessary, you can close an open file or a user session, but doing so is seldom a good idea.

To access Shared Folders, follow these steps:

1. Choose Start ➢ Control Panel. XP displays Control Panel.

   ◆ Alternatively, click the Start button to display the Start menu, right-click the My Computer item, and choose Manage from the context menu. XP opens the Computer Management window. Go to step 5.

2. Click the Performance and Maintenance link. XP displays the Performance and Maintenance screen.

3. Click the Administrative Tools link. XP displays the Administrative Tools screen.

4. Double-click the Computer Management icon. XP opens the Computer Management window.

5. Expand the System Tools object in the left pane if it's collapsed.

6. Expand the Shared Folders object under the System Tools object.

7. To examine and work with shared folders, select the Shares object. Computer Management displays the list of folders currently being shared and the number of client connections on each. Figure 10.5 shows an example.

FIGURE 10.5

Select the Shares object under the Shared Folders object to see the folders currently shared.

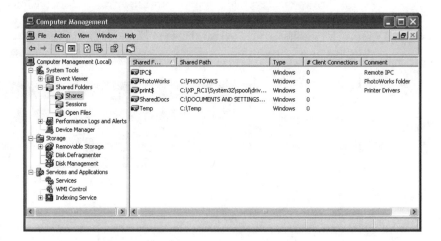

8. To see which users are connected to the computer, select the Sessions object. Computer Management displays a list of the users, the computer from which they're connecting, the number of files they have open, and the length of time for which they've been connected. Figure 10.6

shows an example. To close a session, right-click it and choose Close Session from the context menu (or select the session and choose Action ➢ Close Session), then click the Yes button in the confirmation dialog box.

FIGURE 10.6

Select the Sessions object under the Shared Folders object to see the current sessions connected to the computer.

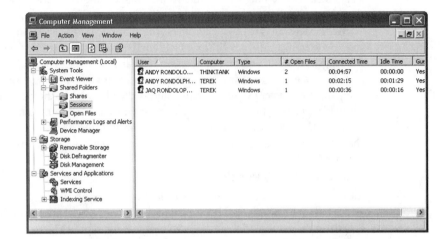

9. To see which files are open, select the Open Files object. Computer Management displays a list of the files and the users accessing them. To close a file, right-click it and choose Close Open File from the context menu (or select the file and choose Action ➢ Close Open File), then click the Yes button in the confirmation dialog box.

10. When you've finished using Computer Management, choose File ➢ Exit. XP closes the program.

Working with File Associations, File Extensions, and File Types

As you know, if you double-click a file with an EXE extension, XP runs the file. If you double-click a file with a TXT extension, XP opens the file in Notepad (or your default text editor). If you double-click a file with an MP3 extension, XP starts it playing in Windows Media Player (or your default audio player for MP3 files).

In each of these examples, the double-click triggers a different action keyed by the file type with which the file extension is associated. This section discusses file extensions, file types, and file associations; how they interact; and how you can customize them to suit your working needs.

What Are File Extensions?

The *extension* is that part of the filename that appears after the last period in the filename. For example, in a file named September 2001 Report.doc, the extension is doc. In a file named September 2001 Report. Edited by Rikki.doc, the extension is still doc, even though there's an earlier period in the filename. A filename doesn't have to have an extension, but almost all files do, because the extension identifies the file type associated with the file, and the file type contains information on the program and action to use for the file. (More on this in a minute.) If a file doesn't have an extension, XP doesn't know what to do with it—unless the file is one of the file types designed to have no extension, such as a folder or a DVD. (By contrast, the Mac splits its files up into a resource fork and a data fork. The resource fork contains information about the file type, while the data fork contains the file's data.)

Most extensions are three characters (for example, EXE, DOC, or AVI), but some are four characters (for example, JPEG, MPEG, or HTML). Extensions can be up to 200 characters long, but this length is impractical and unnecessary for all but the most specialized purposes (though it sure lets you create plenty of different extensions). Despite the proliferation of programs and file types, many three-character extensions remain unused and available, though developers who need to create a new file type may prefer a distinctive four-character extension to an unmemorable three-character extension. Users—particularly those who grew up using DOS—tend to be familiar with three-character extensions, so four-character extensions seem strange or a bit wrong.

What Are File Types?

Ideally, each file extension is linked to a *file type*, a descriptive category with which actions can be associated. For example, the BMP extension is linked by default to the Bitmap Image file type. The default action associated with the Bitmap Image file type is Open. So when you double-click a file with the BMP extension, XP opens the file in the default program (Paint). Other actions associated by default with the Bitmap Image file type are Edit, Print, and PrintTo.

Each extension can be linked to only one file type at a time. If an extension isn't linked to a file type, when you double-click the file, XP displays the Open With dialog box so that you can tell it which program you want to use to open the file. A file that doesn't have a registered file type associated with it is listed as being of the file type "File." (You could argue for or against this really being the file type, just as you could argue about how you can't really call a poem or song "Untitled.")

Multiple extensions can be linked to a given file type. For example, by default the extensions MPA, MPE, MPEG, MPG, and MPV2 are linked to the Movie File (MPEG) file type. So when you double-click a file with any one of those five extensions, XP performs the default action for the Movie File (MPEG) file type: Play.

Registering File Types and Associations

File types and associations are stored in the Registry. You can dig at them there (by using the techniques described in Chapter 12), but it's seldom a good idea unless you know exactly what you're doing. XP provides mostly adequate tools for viewing and changing file types and associations, so you don't need to visit the Registry unless you're trying to create very special effects. (*Mostly* adequate? Yes. More on this in a few pages' time. Hold your horses.)

When you install a program, the setup routine typically handles the registration of any file types associated with the program. The better setup routines check with you before registering the file types, because they may already be registered to other programs. But more aggressive programs monitor the file types associated with them and try to reclaim them each time you run the program. Audio players (particularly MP3 players) and video players tend to be the worst offenders on this front, but they're by no means the only ones. The better programs let you specify whether they should reclaim file types automatically and, if so, which file types.

Specifying the File Type of a File

Typically, you specify the file type of a file by adding the appropriate extension (or one of the appropriate extensions) to it. Most Windows programs use common dialog boxes for Save operations. These common dialog boxes include a Save As Type drop-down list that you use to specify the file type for the file. (By default, the program displays the most likely file type in the Save As dialog box.) If you don't explicitly specify the extension for the file, the program adds it. For example, if you save a workbook file in Excel, Excel suggests the Microsoft Excel Workbook file type in the Save As Type drop-down list. If you don't add an extension to the filename, Excel automatically adds the extension XLS, which is linked to the Microsoft Excel Workbook file type.

Finding Out Which File Type a File Is

Your first clue to which file type a file is should be the icon that XP uses for the file. But if you have a less-than-perfect memory for icons, or if the icon is too small to be identifiable, there are other ways of finding out.

To find out which file type a file is, right-click it in an Explorer window or on the Desktop and choose Properties from the context menu. The General page of the Properties dialog box for the file displays its file type. Figure 10.7 shows an example.

FIGURE 10.7

If you can't identify a file's file type by its icon, display the General page of the Properties dialog box.

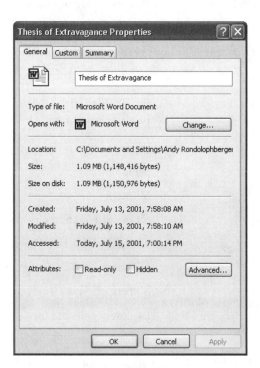

Alternatively, switch the Explorer window to Details view and look at the Type column.

Displaying All File Extensions

Windows has an engrossing love/hate relationship with file extensions. It can't live without them, but it'd sure like to keep them out of sight.

As mentioned a page or two ago, Windows needs file extensions so that it knows the actions it can take with a particular file. But Microsoft seems to feel that extensions look ugly, so it makes XP hide them for as long as possible. This improves the cosmetic look of long filenames and a few other things, but it also has some very undesirable consequences, as you'll see a little later in the chapter.

So by default, XP hides file extensions for registered file types, relying on icons in their various forms (thumbnails, tiles, and icons) to identify the file type and, by (as it were) extension, the extension. In Details view, the Type column in Explorer windows and dialog boxes displays the file type. And because most every file type is registered either by XP itself or by the program you install that creates that type of file, all file extensions remain hidden until you change the settings.

If you're comfortable with and used to icons, this is more or less okay. But if not, you can display most file extensions by choosing Tools ➢ Folder Options from an Explorer window to display the Folder Options dialog box, clearing the Hide File Extensions for Known File Types check box on the View page, and clicking the OK button.

Instead of displaying most file extensions, you can display selected ones by selecting the Always Show Extension check box in the Edit File Type dialog box for the file type. See the next section for details.

Wait a minute—what was that about *most* file extensions? Well, XP kinda figures that there are some file extensions that you really don't need to know about. These extensions include the following:

File Extension	File Type
URL	Internet shortcut or URL
JSE	JScript Encoded file
JS	JScript file
SHS	Scrap object
LNK	Shortcut
SHB	Shortcut to section of a document
JOB	Task Scheduler Task Object file
VBE	VBScript Encoded Script file
VBS	VBScript Script file
SCF	Explorer command file
WSF	Windows Script file

Even when you clear that Hide File Extensions for Known File Types check box and apply the change, XP keeps these extensions hidden. This is partly for the cosmetic reasons mentioned earlier (which sort of stand up under scrutiny) but perhaps more because Microsoft thinks you shouldn't be messing with these files too much, which is (shall we say) misguided. And the overall effect can be disastrous.

As you can see in the list, the LNK file type is used for shortcuts. So if you make XP display the extension for LNK files, you'll see a LNK extension popping up for shortcuts on your Desktop, for shortcuts on your Start menu, and for shortcuts in Explorer windows. The LNK extensions on the Desktop are entirely harmless, but the extensions on the Start menu *are* actually kinda ugly and make it a little more awkward to use. For one thing, the four extra characters—the period and LNK— make each of the cascading menus wider than it would otherwise be. And apart from the visual distraction, it's conceptually a little distracting to realize that many of the items on the Start menu are plain old shortcuts. It's not quite like pulling aside the wizard's curtain, but it gives a feeling that the Start menu is held together by virtual string and sealing wax.

Similarly, the URL file type is for Internet shortcuts and URLs. So if you make XP display the URL extension, it appears on all Internet shortcuts, including those on your Favorites menus. This too looks less than great, and you can see why Microsoft doesn't want these extensions displayed.

The problem with not displaying extensions is that some file types can be used to deliver viruses. All the scripting file types—VBE and VBS files, JSE and JS files, WSF files, even SCF files—can perform a wide variety of actions on your computer without consulting you.

Of course, no savvy user will run a script that arrives unsolicited: It could be just about anything, and the chances of it doing anything pleasant are slimmer than Calista Flockhart. But because XP hides these extensions, a script file can easily masquerade as another file type. For example, say a malefactor creates a script file and names it `Latest Britney Clip.mp3.vbs`. Because the VBS extension is hidden, this file shows up as `Latest Britney Clip.mp3`. If the user double-clicks it, thinking that doing so will start the file playing in their default MP3 player (for example, Windows Media Player), they're in for an unpleasant surprise, because the script will execute instead. The icon will be wrong, but people often miss this, particularly in Details view in Explorer or when opening an attachment from e-mail. (As you know perfectly well, you should never open an attachment without virus-checking it—but people do all the time. Hence the big success of many macro viruses, including the Melissa virus of 1999 and the Anna Kournikova virus of 2001.)

Because of the dangers posed by hidden file extensions, it's best to display *all* file extensions so that you always know exactly what type of file you're double-clicking.

You can display the hidden file extensions by using the manual technique described in the section "Choosing Other Options in the Edit File Type Dialog Box" later in this chapter, but it takes a little while. Another way is to use a program called X-Setup, which you can download for free from the Xteq Systems website, `www.xteq.com/products/xset/`. Expand the Appearance item, then the Files&Folders item, and then the Files item. Then select the Show/Hide File Extensions item and work with the options it displays.

NOTE   *If you're considering getting anti-virus software to protect you from viruses, two of the leading products are Norton Antivirus from Symantec (`www.symantec.com/downloads/`) and McAfee VirusScan from McAfee.com Corporation (`download.mcafee.com/eval/evaluate2.asp`). Each offers an evaluation version from the web address given.*

Changing the File Type Linked to an Extension

As mentioned earlier, some programs grab file types without asking, either during their setup routines or each time you run them. Other programs ask for permission before grabbing. Either way, you'll sometimes need to change file types so that they're associated with the program you want rather than with the grabbiest program around.

To change the file type linked to an extension, follow these steps:

1. Right-click a file with the extension and choose Properties from the context menu. XP displays the Properties dialog box for the file. (See Figure 10.7, earlier in the chapter, for an example of the Properties dialog box.) The General page displays information including the type of file (the Type of File item) and the program associated with it (the Opens With item).

2. Click the Change button. XP displays the Open With dialog box (shown in Figure 10.8).

FIGURE 10.8

Use this Open With dialog box to specify the program with which you want to open the file.

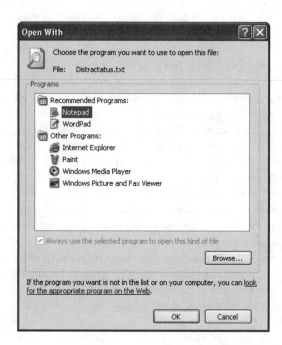

3. In the Programs list box, select the program with which to open the file:
   - XP breaks down the programs it offers into two categories: Recommended Programs and Other Programs.
   - If neither category lists the program you want to use, click the Browse button. XP displays a second Open With dialog box. This dialog box is an Open dialog box in disguise. Navigate to and select the program, then click the Open button. XP closes the second Open With dialog box and returns you to the first Open With dialog box.

4. Click the OK button. XP closes the first Open With dialog box and links the extension to the file type you selected.

5. Click the OK button. XP closes the Properties dialog box for the file.

Restoring the File Type Linked to an Extension

When you customize the file type linked to an extension, XP stores the previous file type for that extension so that you can easily change it back if necessary.

To restore a file association, choose Tools ➢ Folder Options from an Explorer window. XP displays the Folder Options dialog box. Click the File Types tab. XP displays the File Types page. In the Registered File Types list box, select the extension you customized. Click the Restore button (shown in Figure 10.9) to restore the file type previously linked to the extension. Click the Close button to close the Folder Options dialog box.

FIGURE 10.9

When you've customized the file type linked to an extension, the Folder Options dialog box provides a Restore button so that you can restore the previous file type easily if needed.

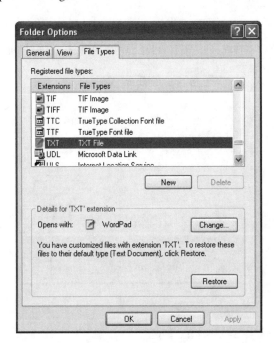

Changing the Program or Action Associated with a File Type

As you saw in the previous couple of sections, you can change the file type linked to an extension easily enough. Chances are, you'll need to do this only occasionally. Much more often, you'll need to change the program associated with a file type, because one program often grabs another program's file types.

NOTE   One way to reassociate a program with all its default file types is to reinstall the program. But if you've customized the program, or if the installation process is complex or lengthy, you'll do better to edit the file associations manually as described in this section.

To change the program or action associated with a file type, open the Edit File Type dialog box as described in the following list:

1. From an Explorer window, choose Tools ➢ Folder Options. XP displays the Folder Options dialog box.

2. Click the File Types tab. XP displays the File Types page.

3. In the Registered File Types list box, select the file type you want to change. By default, this list is sorted alphabetically by extension, but you can sort by file type by clicking the File Types column heading.

NOTE *At this point, you can also change the file type linked to the extension. (Click the Change button. XP displays the Open With dialog box. Select the program as described earlier in this section and click the OK button.) But usually it's easier to change the file type linked to the extension from the Properties dialog box of a file of that type, as described in the previous section.*

4. Click the Advanced button. XP displays the Edit File Type dialog box (shown in Figure 10.10).

Then perform one or more of the changes described in the following sections.

FIGURE 10.10

Use the Edit File Type dialog box to change the behavior or appearance of a file type.

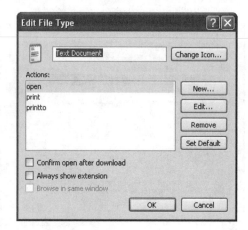

CHANGING THE NAME OF THE FILE TYPE

To change the name of the file type, enter the new name in the text box at the top of the Edit File Type dialog box.

CHANGING THE ICON THAT XP DISPLAYS FOR THE FILE TYPE

To change the icon that XP displays for the file type, follow these steps:

1. Click the Change Icon button. XP displays the Change Icon dialog box, showing the icons associated with the current program for the file type.

2. Either select an alternate icon or click the Browse button and use the resulting Change Icon dialog box (which is a renamed Open dialog box) to identify the icon or the program or library file containing it:

   ◆ Select Icon Files, Programs, Libraries, Icons, or All Files in the Files of Type drop-down list as appropriate.

   ◆ Click the Open button. XP closes the second Change Icon dialog box and returns you to the first Change Icon dialog box.

TIP   As mentioned in Chapter 4, SHELL32.DLL *and* MORICONS.DLL *(both in the* \Windows\System32\ *folder) contain a selection of icons.*

3. Select the icon if necessary.

4. Click the OK button. XP closes the first Change Icon dialog box.

CHANGING THE ACTION ASSOCIATED WITH THE FILE TYPE

Next, you can change the action associated with the file type. For example, instead of having files of the Movie File (MPEG) file type play when you double-click them, you might want to have them open instead.

Some file types have only one action associated with them. Others have anywhere from two up to a half-dozen. You can create new actions, edit existing actions, remove existing actions, and set the default action to be executed when you double-click the file (or select it and press the Enter key).

The default action appears in boldface in the Actions list box.

Creating a New Action

To create a new action for the file type, follow these steps:

1. Click the New button. XP displays the New Action dialog box (shown in Figure 10.11).

FIGURE 10.11

Use the New Action dialog box to specify the name and program for a new action.

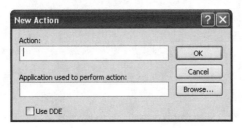

2. In the Action text box, enter the name for the action. Put an ampersand (&) before the letter that you want to use as the access key for the action. Make sure this letter is different from all other access keys on the context menu for this file type.

3. In the Application Used to Perform Action text box, enter the path and name of the program you want to use. Either type in the path and name or use the Browse button and the resulting Open With dialog box to enter them. If you type in the path and name, enclose them in double quotation marks. (If you use the Open With dialog box, it supplies the double quotation marks for you.)

4. After the program's path and name, enter any switches or parameters the program needs to perform the action. (You'll usually need to consult the program's Help files to discover these.)

5. After the switches or parameters (if any), add the parameter "%1" if you need to pass the file-name to the program.

6. If the program uses Dynamic Data Exchange (DDE), select the Use DDE check box and choose further options in the Use DDE group box and extra section of the dialog box that XP displays. Most modern programs don't use DDE, which is an older way of exchanging information, but some older programs still use it.

7. Click the OK button. XP closes the New Action dialog box and adds the new action to the Actions list in the Edit File Type dialog box.

Editing an Existing Action

To edit an existing action, select it in the Actions list box and click the Edit button. XP displays the Editing Action for Type dialog box (shown in Figure 10.12), in which you can edit the action along the lines discussed in steps 2 through 6 in the previous section.

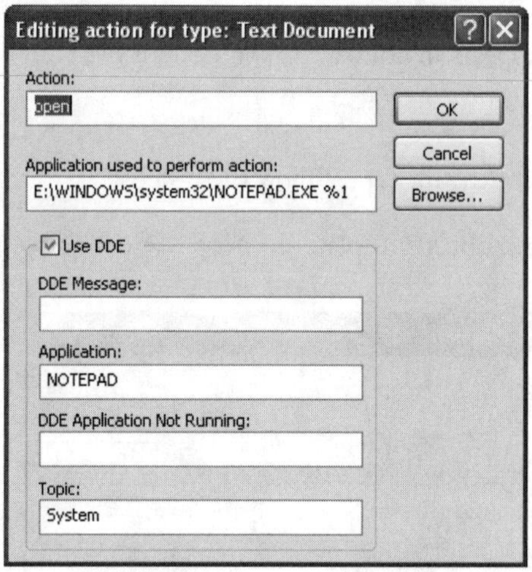

FIGURE 10.12

The Editing Action for Type dialog box is the New Action dialog box in disguise. Use it to edit an existing action for the file type.

Removing an Existing Action

To remove an existing action, select it and click the Remove button. XP displays a File Types message box to confirm the removal. Click the Yes button if you're sure you want to proceed.

It's not a good idea to remove actions built into Windows programs because you may remove functionality that you subsequently need. However, feel free to remove any custom actions you've created.

Changing the Default Action for the File Type

To change the default action (the action that takes place when you double-click the file), select the action you want in the Actions list box and click the Set Default button.

CHOOSING OTHER OPTIONS IN THE EDIT FILE TYPE DIALOG BOX

The Edit File Type dialog box contains three other options that you may want to be aware of:

Confirm Open after Download check box   Select this check box if you want XP to prompt you before opening a downloaded file of this type; clear it if you want XP to open downloaded files without prompting. This check box is selected by default for most file types because of the dangers of opening downloaded files without virus-checking them. The check box is cleared by default for file types such as Windows Media Audio (WMA) files and Video Clip (AVI) files. Clear this check box only for file types that you're sure pose no security risk to your computer.

Always Show Extension check box   Select this check box if you want XP to display extensions for this file type. (If you've set XP to display all extensions already, this check box affects only the extra-hidden file types discussed earlier in the chapter.)

Browse in Same Window check box   Select this check box to make files of this type open in the existing window rather than in a new window. This check box is not available for many file types. Examples of file types for which this check box *is* available include Microsoft Word Document and Microsoft PowerPoint Presentation.

Opening a File with a Program Other than the Associated Program

Once you've got the correct file association in place, double-clicking a file opens it in the associated program. But sometimes you may want to open the file in a different program. For example, you might want to use WordPad instead of Word to open a DOC file or trusty old Notepad instead of your custom 350-BHP multifile text editor to open a TXT file.

To open a file with a program other than the associated program take the following steps:

1. Right-click the file and choose Open With from the context menu. XP displays the Open With dialog box.

   ◆ If XP displays an Open With submenu, select the Choose Program item.

2. In the Choose the Program You Want to Use list box, select the program with which to open the file. Use the Browse button and second Open With dialog box if you need to select a program that doesn't appear in the Recommended Programs list or the Other Programs list.

3. If you want XP to create an Open With submenu for this file type and place an item for this program and the default program for this file type on the submenu, select the Always Use This Program to Open These Files check box.

4. Click the OK button. XP closes the Open With dialog box.

If you selected the Always Use This Program to Open These Files check box in step 3, XP adds an Open With submenu to the context menu for the file type.

EXPERT KNOWLEDGE: CREATING AND REGISTERING A NEW FILE TYPE

If you want, you can create a file of an unregistered file type simply by specifying an extension that hasn't been used. For example, open Notepad, enter a space, and save the new document it automatically creates under the name "Adventures in an Orinda Landscape.888". You'll need to enter the filename and extension within double quotation marks, because otherwise Notepad automatically assigns the TXT extension, which is associated with the TXT File file type. Exit Notepad.

Continued on next page

EXPERT KNOWLEDGE: CREATING AND REGISTERING A NEW FILE TYPE *(continued)*

Now open an Explorer window to that folder, and you'll see the .888 extension displayed. Rather touch-ingly, Explorer decides that the file type for this file is "888 File"; you've created a new file type.

At this point, you can probably still contain your excitement: Creating the file hasn't done you much good. Nor has creating the file type. But now try the following:

1. Double-click the file in Explorer. Wait while XP consults the Registry about the file type and comes up dry. XP then displays the Windows Cannot Open This File dialog box.

2. Choose the Select the Program from a List option button. XP displays a slightly different version of the Open With dialog box.

3. In the Type a Description That You Want to Use for This Kind of File text box, enter the name you want to assign to the file type. Make it as concise and descriptive as possible.

4. In the Programs list box, select the program you want to associate with the file type. If the program isn't listed, click the Browse button and use the resulting Open With dialog box to identify it.

5. Leave the Always Use the Selected Program to Open This Kind of File check box selected, as it is by default.

6. Click the OK button. XP creates the file type, creates Registry entries for it, and opens the file in the specified program.

At the end of this maneuvering, when you double-click a file of your new file type, XP invokes the program you specified, which performs the action you designated.

NOTE   To delete a new file type you've created, use the Remove button on the File Types page of the Folder Options dialog box.

Up Next

This chapter has discussed how to share folders and how to keep folders private, even from Computer Administrator users. It has also covered how to work with file types so that files of a given file type open with the program and the action you want.

The next chapter discusses how to manage your disk and drives.

Chapter 11

Managing Your Disks and Drives

This chapter discusses how to manage your disks and drives, showing you how to understand and undertake the key actions you'll need to perform with them. These actions range from formatting a disk to converting a disk's file system to NTFS; from using compression to free up disk space on an NTFS disk to using quotas to prevent users from grabbing more than their fair share; and from defragmenting your disks to creating and deleting partitions.

This chapter covers the following topics:

◆ Formatting a disk

◆ Changing the computer's name, description, and workgroup

◆ Converting a disk to NTFS

◆ Using compression to free up space

◆ Using quotas to apportion disk space

◆ Defragmenting and cleaning up disks

◆ Scheduling tasks

◆ Creating and deleting partitions

Formatting a Disk

Be it hard, removable, or floppy, a disk needs to be formatted before it's usable. *Formatting* imposes a file system on the disk's physical sectors, arranging them into logical clusters that XP can access and manipulate.

You use the same procedure for formatting hard, removable, and floppy disks. By contrast, recordable (CD-R) and rewritable (CD-RW) discs and writable DVDs need a different kind of formatting because they use different file systems.

NOTE   *XP can format only 1.44MB floppies. It can't format 720KB floppies—neither from the Format dialog box nor from the command-line* **FORMAT** *command—though it can read 720KB floppies formatted using other operating systems.*

To format a disk, follow these steps:

1. Open an Explorer window. (Usually, choosing Start ➤ My Computer gives you the best view for formatting disks.)
2. Right-click the disk and choose Format from the context menu. XP displays the appropriate Format dialog box for the disk:
   - For a local hard disk, XP displays the Format Local Disk dialog box (shown in Figure 11.1).

FIGURE 11.1

In the Format Local Disk dialog box, specify the file system to use for the disk.

   - For a floppy disk, XP displays the Format $3\frac{1}{2}$ Floppy dialog box.
   - For a removable disk, XP displays a dialog box named after the drive's name. For example, for a Zip 100 drive, XP displays a Format ZIP-100 dialog box.
3. When formatting a hard disk, make sure that the Capacity drop-down list is showing approximately the right size for the disk. You shouldn't be able to change this setting, but you should check it in case XP is having trouble reading the disk, which could indicate a physical problem with the disk.

NOTE   *Good news: XP fixes a problem with previous versions of Windows, in which a format operation would grind to a halt if an Explorer window was showing the contents of the disk you tried to format. This problem was especially annoying when you displayed the disk in Explore mode to check that it didn't contain anything worth keeping, and then issued a Format command from the Folders Explorer bar while the contents were still displayed in the right-hand pane.*

4. In the File System drop-down list, choose the file system with which to format the disk: NTFS or FAT32 for a hard disk. You'll recall from Chapter 2 that NTFS offers advantages of security and stability over FAT32 and that the main reason for using FAT32 is if you need an operating system not based on NT—for example, Windows 9x—to be able to read the disk.

5. In the Allocation Unit Size drop-down list, you can specify the cluster size for the disk. By default, XP selects the Default Allocation Size item. Typically the options for NTFS are 512 bytes, 1024 bytes, 2048 bytes, and 4096 bytes. You shouldn't need to specify the cluster size, but see the next sidebar if you're curious as to why not.

6. In the Volume Label text box, you can enter a name for the volume. (A *volume* is an area of storage on a hard disk—typically a partition.) FAT32 volume names can be up to 11 characters long, while NTFS volume names can be up to 32 characters long. There's no obligation to enter a volume label, but doing so makes the volume easier to identify. (This tends to be less important for a floppy disk than for a hard disk volume, especially if you label the outside of the floppy.)

7. In the Format Options group box, select the Quick Format check box if you want to skip scanning the disk for bad sectors. Skipping the scan speeds up the format significantly, because it means that all XP has to do is remove the files from the disk. But it's almost always a good idea to perform the scan by running a standard format. The only exception is if you've very recently scanned the disk for bad sectors and it's come up clean.

8. If the Enable Compression check box is available, you can select it to enable compression on the drive. Compression is available only on NTFS drives. (XP uses the FAT12 file system for floppy disks to make the most of their meager capacity, so you can't use compression on floppies—one of the places where it would be most valuable.) The section "Using Compression to Free Up Space," later in this chapter, discusses the pros and cons of compression.

9. Click the Start button. XP displays a warning dialog box (shown in Figure 11.2) checking that you're sure you want to format the disk.

FIGURE 11.2

Because you're about to wipe the contents of the disk, XP double-checks with this warning dialog box to make sure you know what you're doing.

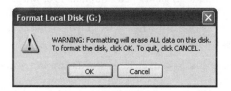

10. If you *are* sure, click the OK button. XP starts the formatting operation.

11. When XP has finished formatting the disk, it displays a Formatting Local Disk dialog box (or a Formatting $3\frac{1}{2}$ Floppy dialog box, or a Formatting ZIP-100 dialog box, or whatever), such as that shown in Figure 11.3, to tell you that the format is complete.

FIGURE 11.3

XP displays a dialog box such as this when it has finished formatting the disk.

12. Click the OK button. XP closes the Formatting Local Disk dialog box and returns you to the Format Local Disk dialog box (or whichever variant of the Format dialog box was previously displayed).

13. Click the Close button. XP closes the Format Local Disk dialog box.

You can now use the formatted disk to store files.

NOTE *The Create an MS-DOS Startup Disk check box lets you create a floppy disk that boots DOS. You can't do much from DOS to an XP computer, so you probably won't need to use this capability.*

EXPERT KNOWLEDGE: WHAT IS THE CLUSTER SIZE, AND SHOULD YOU SPECIFY IT?

The *cluster size* is the smallest amount of disk space that you can allocate for storing a file. As you'll remember from Chapter 6, XP uses clusters as a logical overlay to let it get at the physical sectors on the disk in which the information is actually stored. Most files take up multiple clusters; the smaller the cluster size, obviously enough, the more clusters a file of any given size takes up.

In the days when both disks and files were smaller than they are today, cluster size used to be more of an issue than it is now. Operating systems that used the FAT16 file allocation table, such as DOS and Windows 95, essentially weren't able to create enough clusters to handle large disks efficiently: For a drive of 120MB, FAT16 uses a 2KB cluster size, which is fine; for a 512MB drive, 16KB, which is—let's say—lavish; and for a 3GB drive, 64KB, which is prodigal. Any space not used in the cluster is wasted, so if you stored a 1KB file on that 3GB drive under FAT16, you were wasting 63KB—far worse overheads, so to speak, than in the Mall of the Americas.

Unlike FAT16, FAT32 and NTFS *can* create enough clusters to handle even large disks, so cluster size shouldn't be an issue with XP. As mentioned a moment ago, you can specify cluster sizes of 512 bytes (0.5KB), 1KB, 2KB, and 4KB: all good, small sizes. If you're creating files smaller than 4KB these days, you're doing well—and in any case, hard disks have grown so much that occasionally wasting a few KB seldom causes much pain anymore.

The best cluster size depends on the size of the disk in question. If you're familiar with the cluster size recommended for the size of disk you have, you *can* specify the cluster size you want to use. But because XP is preloaded with information about cluster sizes, it's usually best to let XP allocate the cluster size automatically. To do so, leave the Default Allocation Size entry (the default) selected in the Allocation Unit Size drop-down list.

Normally you set the cluster size, either explicitly or implicitly, when you format a disk. However, some partitioning utilities, such as PartitionMagic, let you change cluster sizes without reformatting, which can save you a huge amount of time and effort.

Changing the Computer's Name, Description, and Workgroup

Each computer has a name and a description, and belongs to a workgroup:

◆ The *name* isn't the name for My Computer (which you can rename to anything you want without affecting anything more than the user interface): It's the name by which the computer appears on the network (if any) to which it's attached. The name is partly for your benefit, partly for the benefit of other users, partly for that of XP, and partly for that of other computers on the network: It enables you, other users, XP, and the other computers to identify your computer.

◆ The *description* is entirely for your and other users' benefit: It's a text field that lets you describe the computer identified by the name. XP doesn't assign a description by default, so the computer doesn't have a description until you enter one.

◆ The *workgroup* is a logical collection of computers intended to work together. By default, the XP Home setup routine adds your computer to a workgroup named MSHOME. As you'll see in Chapter 31, it's a good idea to change the workgroup name, especially if you have a cable modem.

You can change the computer's name, description, and workgroup easily enough. To do so, follow these steps:

1. Press Windows key+Break. (Alternatively, display the Start menu, right-click the My Computer item, and choose Properties from the context menu.) XP displays the System Properties dialog box.

2. Click the Computer Name tab. XP displays the Computer Name page (shown on the left in Figure 11.4), which shows the description, computer name, and workgroup name.

FIGURE 11.4

To change the computer's name, click the Change button on the Computer Name page of the System Properties dialog box (left) and work in the Computer Name Changes dialog box (right).

3. In the Computer Description text box, enter the description for the computer.

4. To change the computer name or workgroup, click the Change button. XP displays the Computer Name Changes dialog box (shown on the right in Figure 11.4).

5. Change the name in the Computer Name text box if necessary.

6. Change the name in the Workgroup text box if necessary.

7. Click the OK button. XP closes the Computer Name Changes dialog box, considers the changes, and (if you changed the name or workgroup) displays another Computer Name Changes dialog box telling you that you need to restart the computer for the changes to take effect.

8. Click the OK button. XP closes the second Computer Name Changes dialog box, returning you to the System Properties dialog box. The Computer Name page now displays a warning telling you that changes will take effect after you restart the computer.

9. Click the OK button. XP closes the System Properties dialog box. If you need to restart your computer, XP displays the System Settings Change dialog box offering to do so immediately.

10. Choose the Yes button if you want XP to restart your computer straight away. Choose the No button if you want to take any other actions and then restart the computer yourself.

Converting a Disk to NTFS

If you need to use XP's security features, compression (discussed next), or quota management (discussed later in this chapter), your volumes need to be NTFS rather than FAT. XP provides a tool for converting a disk from FAT or FAT32 to NTFS, so you can convert your volumes at any time. This is a one-way process, in that you can't convert the disk back to FAT unless you reformat it (which involves removing all the data from the disk), so it's not something to try idly or on a whim.

The best time to convert a disk from FAT to NTFS is when you install XP. The second-best time is when you need to format the disk, because formatting overwrites all the contents of the drive anyway. But if you want to maintain a dual-boot system with Windows 9x until you're sure that XP suits you, you'll need to keep one or more drives formatted with FAT, which means that neither of these options is viable—unless you're prepared to blow away the contents of the FAT disk when you decide to commit to NTFS.

To convert a FAT disk to NTFS without affecting the data on it (other than the file system on which the data is stored), open a command prompt window (Start ➤ All Programs ➤ Accessories ➤ Command Prompt) and issue a convert command. The syntax for the convert command is as follows:

```
convert drive: /FS:NTFS
```

As you'd guess, *drive:* here is the letter of the drive to convert. For example, the following command converts the D: drive:

```
convert d: /FS:NTFS
```

The convert command takes a while to run, depending on how big the drive is and how much it contains. There are a couple of other things that you should know about it:

◆　convert needs a modest amount of space for the conversion, so the disk can't be stuffed to the gills with files when you convert it. (If the disk *is* stuffed—which isn't a great idea anyway—you just need to move some of the files off the drive temporarily while you perform the conversion. You can then move the files back onto the drive, and XP will store the moved files on NTFS.)

- ◆ If you want the files and folders on the converted drive to have no security on them, add the /NoSecurity flag to the command. You won't usually want to do this.

- ◆ Converting the system volume to NTFS requires two reboots. The conversion happens after the reboot, and XP then reboots itself again.

Using Compression to Free Up Space

To save disk space, you can *compress* files, folders, or even an entire drive that uses NTFS. (You can't compress a FAT32 drive using XP.) How much disk space you save depends on the types of file you're compressing. Anything that's already compressed—for example, a Zip file or a compressed multimedia file such as an MP3 music file or an MPEG movie—won't compress much, if at all. Files such as Word documents or Excel spreadsheets compress nicely. Uncompressed graphics— for example, Windows Bitmap (BMP) files—compress a treat.

Compression saves space so that you can pack more information on your drives. To counterbalance this advantage, compression has two main disadvantages: First, your computer will take longer to access a compressed file, folder, or drive; and second, you cannot encrypt a compressed file or folder.

Given that XP Home doesn't offer encryption (unlike XP Professional), the second disadvantage isn't much of a consideration. But the first disadvantage is real enough: If your computer is underpowered, it's probably not wise to compress files that you need to play at full speed. For example, multimedia files may not play back without hiccups if you compress them.

Compressing a File or Folder

To compress a file or a folder, take the following steps:

1. Right-click the file or folder and choose Properties from the context menu. XP displays the Properties dialog box for the file or folder.

2. On the General page, click the Advanced button. XP displays the Advanced Attributes dialog box (shown in Figure 11.5).

FIGURE 11.5

To save space, you can compress a file or folder by selecting the Compress Contents to Save Disk Space check box in the Advanced Attributes dialog box.

3. Select the Compress Contents to Save Disk Space check box.

4. Click the OK button. XP closes the Advanced Attributes dialog box.

5. Click the OK button. XP closes the Properties dialog box.

To uncompress a file or folder, repeat this procedure but clear the Compress Contents to Save Disk Space check box.

Compressing a Drive

Compressing individual folders (let alone individual files) is a slow business, and may not save you a large amount of space. You'll usually get better results from compressing a whole drive.

To compress an NTFS drive, take the following steps:

1. Right-click the drive and choose Properties from the context menu. XP displays the Properties dialog box for the drive.

2. On the General page, select the Compress Drive to Save Disk Space check box.

3. Click the Apply button. XP displays the Confirm Attribute Changes dialog box (shown in Figure 11.6), asking if you want to apply this change only to the root of the drive or to its subfolders and files as well.

FIGURE 11.6

To compress a drive and its contents, select the Apply Changes to *N:*\, Subfolders and Files option button in the Confirm Attribute Changes dialog box.

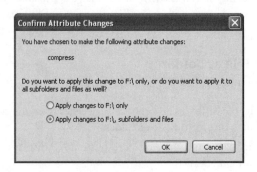

4. Select the Apply Changes to *N:*\, Subfolders and Files option button.

5. Click the OK button. XP closes the Confirm Attribute Changes dialog box, displays the Applying Attributes dialog box, and starts compressing the drive.

   ◆ If XP displays the Error Applying Attributes dialog box telling you that an error occurred applying the attribute to (in other words, compressing) a file because the file is being used by another process, choose the Ignore button, the Ignore All button, the Retry button, or the Cancel button as appropriate.

6. When compression is complete, click the OK button in the Properties dialog box for the drive. XP closes the dialog box.

To uncompress the drive, repeat this procedure, but clear the Compress Drive to Save Disk Space check box.

Setting Archiving and Indexing for a File or Folder

Apart from compression, the Advanced Attributes dialog box (shown in Figure 11.5, earlier in the chapter) for a file or folder offers two other options:

File/Folder Is Ready for Archiving check box   Select this check box (or leave it selected) to specify that the file or folder can be archived. Nothing will happen to the folder until you use a program that checks the archiving status of files.

For Fast Searching, Allow Indexing Service to Index This File/Folder check box   Select this check box (or, again, leave it selected, as the case may be) to include this file or folder in any indexing operations you tell XP to perform. By indexing your files, you can create a database that lets you search more quickly for files matching specified criteria.

When you've finished choosing settings in the Advanced Attributes dialog box, click the OK button. XP closes the Advanced Attributes dialog box. Then click the OK button. XP closes the Properties dialog box for the file or folder.

Using Quotas to Apportion Disk Space

Hard disks have grown in capacity almost as fast as processors have grown in speed, but most users find that they can easily fill even the largest hard disks available. However fast the engineers work out ways to pack more information on a platter and stack more platters in a drive, the number and size of files people want to keep grow even faster.

If you're sharing your computer with other members of your family, or with people in your office, you may want to use XP's quota-management tools to make sure that no one user can hog all the disk space. Quota management may seem a formal and officious thing to implement, but it's easy to do; it can have a salutary effect on users' behavior; and it can help keep your computer running smoothly by preventing it from running out of disk space. Best of all, when you've set quotas on a disk, it appears to the user as if the section of the disk available to them is all the disk space there is. For example, if you have an 80GB drive and set a quota of 20GB per user, each user gets the impression of having a 20GB drive. If you want, you can keep them in ignorance about the rest of the drive....

Quota management is easy—but you need to know three important things to get it right:

- You can use quotas only on NTFS volumes.
- Quotas work on whole volumes, not on individual folders.
- If you implement quotas on your system volume, don't prevent users from using more than their allotted quota of disk space. This is because XP writes information to disk on the system partition when booting. Implementing capped quotas can prevent XP from booting. You'll get entertaining errors as the Network Service and System try desperately to exceed their quotas to do your bidding.

To set quotas, take the following steps:

1. Right-click the volume for which you want to set quotas and choose Properties from the context menu. XP displays the Properties dialog box.

2. Click the Quota tab. XP displays the Quota page (shown in Figure 11.7 with several choices made).

FIGURE 11.7

Use quotas to prevent any user from using up more than their fair share of drive space.

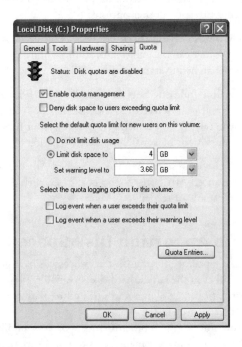

3. Select the Enable Quota Management check box. XP enables the other controls on the Quota page.

4. If you want to prevent a user from using more than their allotted amount of disk space, select the Deny Disk Space to Users Exceeding Quota Limit check box.

WARNING   *Be aware that denying disk space to a user could cause them to lose work or be forced to delete an existing file in order to save a new file. Think carefully before you use this option; and if you use it, make sure that users understand quotas and their implications before they discover the limitations the hard way.*

5. In the Select the Default Quota Limit for New Users on This Volume area, specify whether to limit disk space for new users:

   ◆ If you don't want to limit disk space, select the Do Not Limit Disk Usage option button.

   ◆ To limit disk space for new users, select the Limit Disk Space To option button and enter an appropriate number of megabytes (MB), gigabytes (GB), terabytes (TB), petabytes (PB), or exabytes (EB) in the drop-down list. (You can also enter a number of kilobytes—KB—but any amount of disk space smaller than a megabyte makes no sense.)

NOTE   *By offering terabytes, petabytes, and exabytes, XP is showing it's ready for the future. A terabyte (1TB) is 1024GB, a petabyte (1PB) is 1024TB, and an exabyte (1EB) is 1024PB. At this writing, terabytes are the province of serious servers, petabytes are the province of server farms, and exabytes are provinces of server farms.*

◆ If you limit disk space, use the Set Warning Level To text box and drop-down list to specify the limit at which XP warns the user that they're about to run out of disk space. This limit should be a little less than the amount of disk space they're limited to—enough less that the user will need to create several files of the size they usually work with between triggering the warning and reaching the limit. For this setting, you may want to accept the default that XP offers or manually set a bigger cushion of your own. You can use decimal places with the same unit in the Set Warning Level To text box or select the next smaller item in the drop-down list so that you can work with whole numbers.

6. In the Select the Quota Logging Options for This Volume area, select the Log Event when a User Exceeds Their Quota Limit check box or the Log Event when a User Exceeds Their Warning Level check box if you want XP to log these events.

7. Click the Quota Entries button. XP displays the Quota Entries window (shown in Figure 11.8). The first time you display this window, the only quota it lists is the one for your user identity or the Administrators group.

FIGURE 11.8

Once you've enabled quotas, use the Quota Entries window to set quotas for each user.

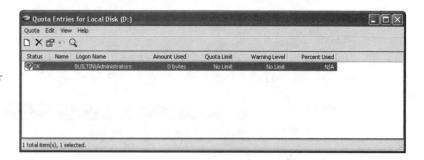

8. Choose Quota ➢ New Quota Entry or click the New Quota Entry button. XP displays the Select Users dialog box.

9. Enter the username in the Enter the Object Names to Select list box and click the OK button. XP displays the Add New Quota Entry dialog box (shown in Figure 11.9).

FIGURE 11.9

Use the Add New Quota Entry dialog box to specify the quota limits for the user.

10. Set a disk space quota and warning level as described in step 5.

11. Click the OK button. XP closes the Add New Quota Entry dialog box and adds the quota entry to the Quota Entries window.

   ◆ To change an existing quota entry, double-click it in the Quota Entries window. XP displays the Quota Settings dialog box for the user. Change the quota settings or warning level and click the OK button.

   ◆ To delete a quota entry, right-click it in the list box and choose Delete from the context menu. Alternatively, select the quota entry and choose Quota ➢ Delete or click the Delete Quota Entry button on the toolbar. XP displays a Disk Quota dialog box confirming the deletion. Click the Yes button.

12. Create further quota entries as appropriate, then choose Quota ➢ Close. XP closes the Quota Entries window and displays the Properties dialog box.

13. Click the Apply button to make XP apply the quotas, or click the OK button to make XP apply the quotas and close the Properties dialog box.

If disk quotas are not currently enabled, when you click the Apply button or the OK button to apply the quotas, XP displays the Disk Quota dialog box (shown in Figure 11.10). This dialog box warns you that when you enable quotas, XP needs to rescan the volume to update disk usage statistics, and that this process can take several minutes. Click the OK button to enable quotas.

FIGURE 11.10

If the quota system isn't enabled for the volume, XP displays the Disk Quota dialog box warning you that it will need to rescan the volume.

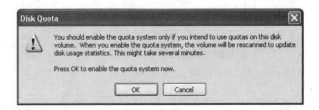

When you've set a quota on a volume, Explorer shows the user the amount of space that remains to them on the volume, not the actual amount of space available on the volume. When a user reaches their warning level, they see a message telling them that they're running out of space.

If you chose to deny disk space to users exceeding their quota limit, they'll see a message such as that shown in Figure 11.11 when they take an action that will exceed their quota limit. Notice that the message isn't that the user is over quota—it's simply that there isn't enough space on disk.

FIGURE 11.11

When a user takes an action that will exceed their quota limit, XP tells them there's not enough space on the disk.

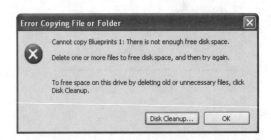

TIP   If you need to apply the same quotas to several volumes, choose Quota ➤ Export to export quotas from one volume to a file. From another volume, choose Quota ➤ Import to import the quota settings file.

Disk Maintenance

Like cars, hard disks can take a fair amount of abuse these days, but the better you treat them, the better performance they give you and the longer they last. Unlike cars, hard disks thrive on running all the time; but like cars, they don't appreciate fragmentation or crashes—and they appreciate a little cleaning-up from time to time.

This section details the steps you can take to keep your disks in good order.

Defragmenting Your Disks

As you know, data is stored on your hard disk in physical areas called sectors that are mapped into logical areas called clusters. Each cluster contains a relatively small amount of information so that XP can use the clusters efficiently. As a result, most files occupy more than one cluster. These clusters can be located just about anywhere on the partition of the drive that contains the volume. Ideally, all the data in a file is stored in contiguous clusters, so that the hard disk's heads can read the data without having to move too far. The further the hard disk's actuator arm has to move to allow the heads to read the clusters that make up the file, the slower the file is to load.

When files are stored in widely spread-out clusters, the volume is said to be *fragmented.* To improve disk performance, you *defragment* (or *defrag*) it using a disk *defragmenter* (or *defragger*). A defragmenter rearranges the data on the disk so that each file occupies contiguous clusters wherever possible.

NOTE   Related to defragmenters but more specialized are tools such as the Microsoft Office optimizer, which defragments a specific set of files and arranges them in a location on the hard drive that the disk heads can quickly access.

Depending on how fragmented a volume is, and how big it is, defragmentation can take anything from a few minutes to a few hours. You *can* work on your computer while defragmentation is going on, but you'll find the computer responding more slowly than usual, and any files that you create, move, or copy may slow down the defragmentation process. Because of this, the best time to defragment a volume is when you're going to leave your computer for a few hours—for example, when you hear the siren song of the mall, an extended lunch hour, or an endless meeting.

To start Disk Defragmenter, choose Start ➤ All Programs ➤ Accessories ➤ System Tools ➤ Disk Defragmenter. Alternatively, right-click the drive icon in an Explorer window, choose Properties from the context menu, display the Tools page in the Properties dialog box, and click the Defragment Now button. Figure 11.12 shows Disk Defragmenter. The list box shows the volumes on your computer, their session status (whether they're being analyzed or defragmented), file system, capacity, amount of free space, and percentage of free space.

FIGURE 11.12

Use Disk Defragmenter to defragment your drives.

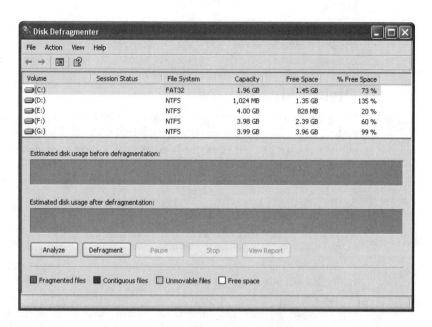

NOTE *You can also run Disk Defragmenter from a Computer Management window. Doing so can be handy if you're working with Computer Management already, but otherwise it conveys no particular benefits. But you need to know about this because, once you access Disk Defragmenter in a Computer Management session, Disk Defragmenter stays active. Now, you can run only one instance of Disk Defragmenter at a time, so if you start Disk Defragmenter while Computer Management is running, XP displays a Disk Defragmenter message box telling you that "This version of Disk Defragmenter does not support running more than one instance." If you've forgotten about the Computer Management session, this message box seems to come out of the blue. (If you're not running Computer Management, this message box may mean that another Computer Administrator user is running Disk Defragmenter.)*

Typically, you'll want to start by analyzing a volume. Select it in the list box and click the Analyze button. Disk Defragmenter examines the volume and displays the Disk Defragmenter dialog box (shown in Figure 11.13) with its recommendations.

FIGURE 11.13

The Disk Defragmenter dialog box tells you the result of the analysis and makes a recommendation.

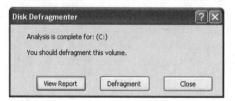

To see the detail of what Disk Defragmenter found on the volume, click the View Report button. Disk Defragmenter displays the Analysis Report dialog box, of which Figure 11.14 shows an example. The Volume Information list box contains everything from the volume size, cluster size, and used space through pagefile fragmentation and Master File Table (MFT) fragmentation. The Most Fragmented

Files list box lists the most fragmented files. You can sort this list by any of the columns—Fragments, File Size, or File Name—by clicking the appropriate column heading.

FIGURE 11.14

The Analysis Report dialog box provides a large amount of information about the volume and the most fragmented files it contains.

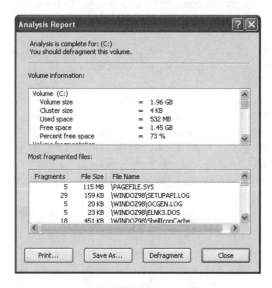

From the Analysis Report dialog box, you can use the Print button to print a copy of the analysis report or the Save As button to save it to a file. More likely, though, you'll want to click the Defragment button to defragment the drive (if Disk Defragmenter recommends doing so) or the Close button to close the dialog box.

If you click the Defragment button in the Analysis Report dialog box or the Disk Defragmenter dialog box, XP closes the dialog box and starts defragmentation. While defragmentation is running, the status bar provides information on the percentage completed and the file currently being moved. (Unfortunately, Disk Defragmenter doesn't offer a full-screen graphical view of the process like Windows 9*x* defragmenters did.) You can use the Pause button and Stop button to pause or stop defragmentation.

When defragmentation is complete, Disk Defragmenter displays another Disk Defragmenter dialog box telling you so. Click the View Report button to display the Defragmentation Report dialog box containing a report (similar to the Analysis Report dialog box's report) on the volume's status, or click the Close button to close the dialog box.

How often you need to run Disk Defragmenter depends on how actively you use your computer and how often you create, modify, or delete files. Under normal usage, running Disk Defragmenter anything from once a week to once every couple of months will keep your files adequately defragmented. Experiment with Disk Defragmenter to establish a schedule that works for you. If Disk Defragmenter says that a volume doesn't need defragmenting, decrease the frequency with which you run Disk Defragmenter.

Cleaning Up Your Disks with Disk Cleanup

Most Windows programs create temporary files that they use to store information temporarily when you're running them. Some programs remember to get rid of these files when you exit them. Others forget. And if your computer loses power or crashes, even the well-behaved programs don't have a chance to get rid of temporary files.

XP's Disk Cleanup feature provides an effective way to remove from local drives not only these temporary files but also temporary Internet files, downloaded program files, offline web pages, and the contents of the Recycle Bin. (Disk Cleanup doesn't work on network drives.)

See page 58 of the *Essential Skills* section for a visual guide to running Disk Cleanup.

Close all programs you're running, then start Disk Cleanup by choosing Start ➤ All Programs ➤ Accessories ➤ System Tools ➤ Disk Cleanup. (Alternatively, right-click a drive and choose Properties so that XP displays the Properties dialog box. Then click the Disk Cleanup button on the General page.) If your computer has multiple hard drive volumes, Disk Cleanup displays the Select Drive dialog box. (If your computer has a single hard drive volume, Disk Cleanup goes ahead and calculates how much space you will be able to free up on the drive.) In the Drives drop-down list, select the drive you want to clean up, then click the OK button. Disk Cleanup examines the disk (which may take a few minutes) and then displays the Disk Cleanup dialog box (shown in Figure 11.15).

FIGURE 11.15

Disk Cleanup presents a list of the items you can remove to clean up your disk.

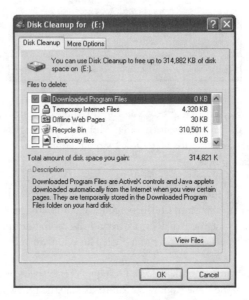

As you can see in the figure, the Disk Cleanup page of the Disk Cleanup dialog box lists the items you can remove and how much space you can recover by doing so. Which of the following items appear in the list depends on the drive's contents:

Downloaded Program Files ActiveX controls and Java applets downloaded by Internet Explorer so that it could display pages that needed them. If you delete these files, Internet Explorer may need to download the controls and applets again when you next access pages that need them, which may slow down your browsing a bit. You can click the View Files button to make XP display an Explorer window containing the files.

Temporary Internet Files   These files are the components of web pages that Internet Explorer has downloaded and has stored on your hard drive so that it can retrieve them quickly when you access the same sites again. Deleting these files means that Internet Explorer will need to download them again the next time you access one of the sites, which will slow down your browsing. Again, you can click the View Files button to have XP display an Explorer window containing these files—but be warned that there are usually thousands of them, and that the format in which they appear is less than informative.

Offline Web Pages   This item appears only if you use offline favorites in Internet Explorer. These files hold the information for the cached copies of your offline favorites. If you use offline favorites extensively, these files may take up a lot of space. If you delete these files, you won't be able to view your offline favorites until you synchronize them again—and synchronizing them will probably reclaim most of the disk space that deleting these files freed up.

Recycle Bin   These files are the contents of the Recycle Bin. As usual, make sure that you want to get rid of these files before you tell Disk Cleanup to delete them. You can click the View Files button to have XP display an Explorer window showing the contents of the Recycle Bin.

Temporary Remote Desktop Files   These files are temporary picture files used to display information more quickly when you're using Remote Desktop Connection.

Temporary Files   These files are temporary storage files that should have been deleted by the program that created them. You can delete with impunity any temporary files that aren't currently being used. (Disk Cleanup leaves alone any temporary files still in use.)

WebClient/Publisher Temporary Files   These files are temporary storage files kept by the WebClient/Publisher service. Deleting these files may affect WebClient/Publisher performance, but it can't lose you any information.

Compress Old Files   To free up some space, you can tell XP to compress files that you haven't used for a while. If you select this check box, select the Compress Old Files item, then click the Options button that appears in the Disk Cleanup dialog box and use the Compress Old Files dialog box (shown in Figure 11.16) that XP displays to specify when to compress files. (The default setting is 50 days.)

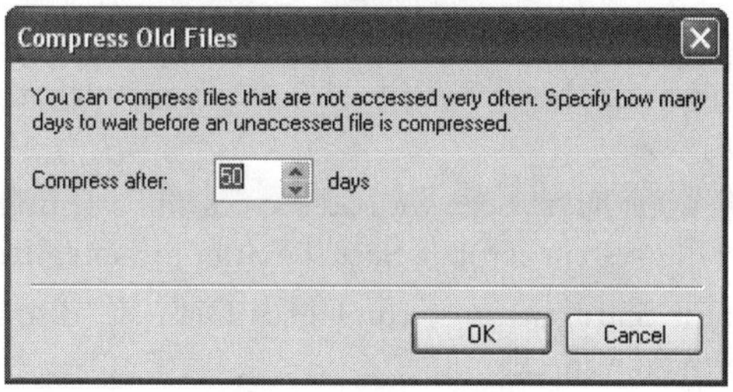

FIGURE 11.16

If you choose to have XP compress old files to free up space on your hard drive, specify in the Compress Old Files dialog box how long the files should remain unaccessed before XP compresses them.

Compress Old Files

You can compress files that are not accessed very often. Specify how many days to wait before an unaccessed file is compressed.

Compress after: 50 days

OK   Cancel

Catalog Files for the Content Indexer These files are leftover catalog files from indexing. There's no downside to deleting them—they don't contain the current index.

Select the check boxes for those items you want to delete and click the OK button. Disk Cleanup displays a Disk Cleanup for *N*: dialog box to confirm that you want to perform the actions (for example, deleting the files). Click the Yes button. Disk Cleanup performs the cleanup.

Checking a Disk for Errors

Once you've cleaned unnecessary files off your hard disk, it's a good idea to check it for errors. Errors typically occur when sectors go bad, which can happen through natural selection (some disks age more quickly in parts) or unnatural intervention (such as physical damage resulting from the disk being bumped or receiving an electrical spike).

To check a disk for errors, follow these steps:

1. Close all programs that are on the disk or that might be accessing the disk. (In practice, it's best to close all programs for the time being.) Close any files open from the disk.

2. In an Explorer window, right-click the drive and choose Properties from the context menu. XP displays the Properties dialog box for the drive.

3. Click the Tools tab. XP displays the Tools page of the Properties dialog box.

4. Click the Check Now button. XP displays the Check Disk dialog box (shown in Figure 11.17).

FIGURE 11.17

In the Check Disk dialog box, specify whether to automatically fix errors in the file system and whether to detect bad sectors and attempt to recover their contents.

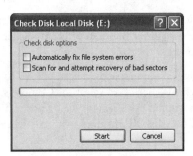

5. If you want XP to repair file-system errors, select the Automatically Fix File System Errors check box.

6. If you want XP to scan for bad sectors and attempt to recover information from them, *and* repair file-system errors, select the Scan for and Attempt Recovery of Bad Sectors check box.

7. Click the Start button to run Check Disk. XP displays the Checking Disk dialog box while it performs the checks.

   ◆ If you see a Checking Disk dialog box such as that shown in Figure 11.18 telling you that "the disk check could not be performed because the disk check utility needs exclusive access to some Windows files on the disk" and asking whether you want to schedule the disk check to take place the next time you restart the computer, select the Yes button. This dialog box typically appears when you're checking a system volume: Because XP is constantly using the volume, Check Disk can't get exclusive access to it.

FIGURE 11.18

The Checking Disk dialog box tells you that it can't get exclusive access to the disk and asks if you want to run the check the next time you restart the computer.

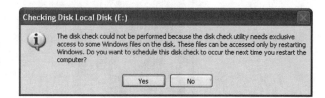

8. When Check Disk has finished, it displays a message box telling you that the disk check is complete.

9. Click the OK button. Check Disk closes and returns you to the Properties dialog box.

10. Click the OK button. XP closes the Properties dialog box.

Scheduling Your Maintenance Tasks with the Scheduled Task Wizard

XP includes a Scheduled Task Wizard that runs you through the process of scheduling the running of just about any program that you want to run at a particular time. This is particularly useful for tedious maintenance tasks—though of course you can also use the Scheduled Task Wizard to schedule regular games of FreeCell or DOOM should you feel the need.

CREATING A SCHEDULED TASK

To create a scheduled task, take the following steps:

1. Choose Start ➤ All Programs ➤ Accessories ➤ System Tools ➤ Scheduled Tasks. (Alternatively, choose Start ➤ Control Panel, click the Performance and Maintenance link, and click the Scheduled Tasks link.) XP displays the Scheduled Tasks folder.

2. Double-click the Add Scheduled Task item. XP launches the Scheduled Task Wizard.

3. Click the Next button on the introductory page. The wizard displays a page with a list box of programs (see Figure 11.19).

4. Select the program in the list. If the program isn't in the list, click the Browse button and use the Select Program to Schedule dialog box to select the program.

5. Click the Next button. The wizard displays a page for naming the task and specifying when it runs (see Figure 11.20).

FIGURE 11.19

On this page of the Scheduled Task Wizard, select the program you want to schedule.

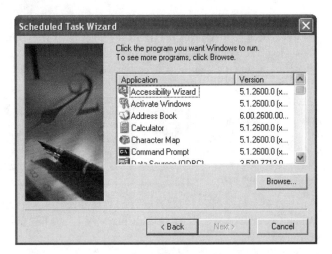

FIGURE 11.20

On this page of the Scheduled Task Wizard, name the task and specify when to run it.

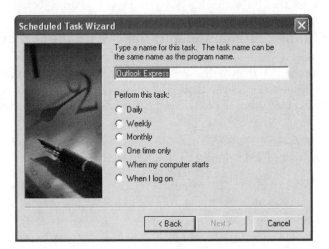

6. The wizard automatically enters the program name as the task name, but you'll usually benefit from entering a descriptive name instead that will enable you to identify the task in the Scheduled Tasks folder.

7. In the Perform This Task list, select the frequency or occasion for the task: Daily, Weekly, Monthly, One Time Only, When My Computer Starts, or When I Log On.

8. Click the Next button. If you chose the Daily option button, the Weekly option button, the Monthly option button, or the One Time Only option button, the wizard displays a page on which you can specify the details. The controls on this page vary depending on your choice. Figure 11.21 shows the Weekly options.

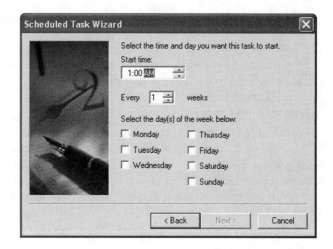

FIGURE 11.21

For a Daily, Weekly, Monthly, or One Time Only task, specify the details. This is the Weekly page.

9. Specify the details as appropriate, and then click the Next button. The wizard displays the name and password page.

10. Specify the username under which to run the task and the password for the user account. Each account that runs scheduled tasks must have a password. You need to enter the password twice to confirm to the wizard that you're typing it correctly, but the wizard doesn't actually check that the password is correct for the account specified. Usually, you'll want the task to be run under your own name, as the wizard suggests. But you might want to use another username only for maintenance tasks. That way, you could let other users know they shouldn't use the computer when that user was logged on, so that the maintenance tasks wouldn't slow down their use of the computer (and vice versa).

11. Click the Next button. The wizard displays its final page, which lists the details for the task.

12. If you want to set further properties for the task (as discussed next), select the Open Advanced Properties for This Task when I Click Finish check box.

13. Click the Finish button. The wizard adds the task to your Scheduled Tasks folder. If you selected the check box in the previous step, the wizard displays the Properties dialog box for the task.

SETTING ADVANCED PROPERTIES FOR A SCHEDULED TASK

The Scheduled Task Wizard gives you access to most of a task's properties, but not to all of them. To set further properties than the wizard offers—for example, to set multiple schedules for the same task—use the task's Properties dialog box.

On the last page of the Scheduled Task Wizard, you can select the Open Advanced Properties for This Task when I Click Finish check box if you want to have the wizard open the task's Properties dialog box automatically. Alternatively, double-click the task in the Scheduled Tasks folder (which resides under Control Panel). XP displays the task's Properties dialog box.

The Properties dialog box for the task has three pages: Task, Schedule, and Settings:

◆ The Task page shows the program assigned to the task, the folder in which the task starts, and the username under which the task runs. There's also a Comments text box in which you can add comments to the task. For example, you might note any changes to the task and why you've made them. Clear the Enabled (Scheduled Task Runs at Specified Time) check box to prevent a task from running.

◆ The Schedule page shows the current schedule or schedules for the task. Select the Show Multiple Schedules check box if you need to set up more than one schedule for a task. (Alternatively, you can set up multiple separate tasks doing the same thing at different times. But using multiple schedules for the same task is neater and usually more efficient.) To specify an end date or a duration for the task, click the Advanced button and work in the Advanced Schedule Options dialog box.

◆ The Settings page contains three group boxes of advanced settings not offered by the Scheduled Task Wizard:

Scheduled Task Completed group box   For a one-time task, select the Delete the Task if It Is Not Scheduled to Run Again check box if you want XP to delete the task automatically once it has run successfully. To prevent a task from running for an inordinately long time, select the Stop the Task if It Runs for *NN* Hours *NN* Minutes check box and specify appropriate values in the two text boxes.

Idle Time group box   This group box contains three self-explanatory options for making sure the task runs when the computer is idle rather than when it is in use: the Only Start the Task if the Computer Has Been Idle for At Least *NN* Minutes check box and text box; the If the Computer Has Not Been Idle That Long, Retry for Up to *NN* Minutes check box and text box; and the Stop the Task if the Computer Ceases to Be Idle check box.

Power Management group box   If you don't want to drain your portable's battery by running the task on battery power, select the Don't Start the Task if the Computer Is Running on Batteries check box and the Stop the Task if Battery Mode Begins check box. If you want XP to wake your computer from its questionably deserved slumber to perform the task, select the Wake the Computer to Run This Task check box.

CHANGING A SCHEDULED TASK

To change the details of a scheduled task, double-click the task in the Scheduled Tasks folder and work in the task's Properties dialog box. (See the previous section for details of the settings you can change.)

PREVENTING A SCHEDULED TASK FROM RUNNING

To prevent a scheduled task from running, clear the Enabled (Scheduled Task Runs at Specified Time) check box on the Task page of the Properties dialog box for the task.

To delete a scheduled task, right-click it in the Scheduled Tasks folder and choose Delete from the context menu. (Alternatively, select the task and click the Delete This Item link in the Folder Tasks list.) Select the Yes button in the confirmation message box.

VIEWING YOUR SCHEDULED TASKS

To view your tasks, display the Scheduled Tasks folder in Details view (the default view for this folder). This view shows columns with the task name, schedule, next run time, last run time, status (blank, Running, Missed, Did Not Start), last result, and creator.

The Last Result column in the Scheduled Tasks folder shows the result of the task as a completion code. The most common codes you'll see are the following:

CODE	MEANING
0x40010004	The task is running.
0x0	The task completed successfully.
0x1	An incorrect function or unknown function was called.
0xa	The environment is incorrect for the task to run.
0xC000013A	The user terminated the task.

RECEIVING NOTIFICATION OF MISSED TASKS

If a task fails to run, XP displays *Missed* in the Status column for the task in the Scheduled Tasks folder. If you want XP to notify you when tasks fail to run, choose Advanced ➢ Notify Me of Missed Tasks from the Scheduled Tasks folder.

VIEWING THE SCHEDULED TASKS LOG

To see which scheduled tasks have been run, display the scheduled tasks log by choosing Advanced ➢ View Log from the Scheduled Tasks folder. This file is named `SchedLgU.txt` and lives in your `%systemroot%` folder.

Contrary to all conventional expectations, Task Scheduler doesn't log events in order, but instead places the note "[***** Most recent entry is above this line *****]" below the latest entry. To find it quickly, choose Edit ➢ Find in Notepad and search for ***** (five asterisks) or [* (opening bracket, space, asterisk).

TROUBLESHOOTING: SCHEDULED TASKS

If tasks you've scheduled don't seem to run as they should, there may be a problem with the scheduling of the task. But you may also have run afoul of some less-than-intuitive aspects of scheduled tasks—so let's start the troubleshooting by discussing those, and then move on to true problems.

"WHEN MY COMPUTER STARTS" TASKS RUN AS NONINTERACTIVE PROCESSES

If you schedule a task to run "when my computer starts," XP runs the task as a noninteractive process the next time anyone boots XP, including a spontaneous reboot after a crash or after a power blip or outage. Because the task is running noninteractively, it will be essentially hidden, and you won't be able to see that it's running without visiting the Scheduled Tasks folder and checking its entry in the Status column. If necessary, you *can* stop a running task by right-clicking its entry and choosing End Task from the context menu, but this crashes the program. If the running task isn't causing you grief, you're usually better off leaving it running until you log off, at which point XP should shut it down gracefully.

Continued on next page

Troubleshooting: Scheduled Tasks *(continued)*

"When I Log On" Tasks Run when *Anyone* Logs On

If you schedule a task to run "when I log on," it actually runs when *anyone* logs on. If you're that anyone, the task runs interactively. For anyone else, the task runs noninteractively. This, um, *quirk* seems guaranteed to trip most users up and makes the "when I log on" scheduling item a bad one to use for most tasks.

And it gets worse. Read on....

"When I Log On" Tasks Run Only When No Other User Is Logged On

If you schedule a task to run "when I log on," XP runs it only when any user logs on (see the previous item) at a time when no other user is logged on. If other users are logged on, the task simply doesn't run. If you've turned off Fast User Switching, this wrinkle won't worry you, but most XP Home users leave Fast User Switching running, so this can often be a problem with scheduled tasks. Note that the logon has to be a "full" logon, not the resumption of a disconnected session.

Task Won't Run with Blank Password

For security reasons, tasks won't run unless you enter the account password for them—even if the account has a blank password. In effect, this means that you need to apply a password to any account under whose auspices you want to run scheduled tasks. Assigning a password to every user account is good security practice, but users in more casual environments may find this restriction a problem.

Task Won't Run Because Password Is Wrong or Has Changed

Because the Scheduled Tasks Wizard doesn't check the password you enter against the user account you specify for a task, if you've entered the wrong password (or entered the password wrongly), the task won't run. If you're solid on your passwords and change them frequently for security, what's more likely to be a problem is that the task was set up with an old password that needs to be updated before the task will run successfully.

Task Won't Run Because Account Name Has Been Changed

If you've changed the name of the user account under which the task was set to run, XP will fail to run the task with the error "Unable to establish existence of the account specified." Edit the properties of the task to make it run under the new user account name.

Make Sure the Task Scheduler Service Hasn't Been Stopped or Paused

If none of your tasks run, chances are that the Task Scheduler service is turned off. You can check and change the status of this service from the Services list in Computer Management, but it's usually easier to work from the Scheduled Tasks folder unless someone has configured the Task Scheduler service for Manual startup. (If this is the case, use Computer Management to configure the service for Automatic startup.)

To turn off the Task Scheduler, choose Advanced ➢ Stop Using Task Scheduler from the Scheduled Tasks folder. To turn it back on, choose Advanced ➢ Start Using Task Scheduler. To pause it, choose Advanced ➢ Pause Task Scheduler. To continue after pausing, choose Advanced ➢ Continue Task Scheduler. If the Start Using Task Scheduler item appears on the Advanced menu, the Task Scheduler service is stopped. If the Continue Task Scheduler item appears, the Task Scheduler service is paused. Take the appropriate action to start or un-pause the service.

TIP If you find yourself needing to schedule many tasks, you may want to investigate the at *command, a command-line tool for scheduling tasks. By default, the* at *command runs under the System account, but you can make it run under a different account by choosing Advanced ➤ AT Service Account from the Scheduled Tasks folder and working in the resulting AT Service Account Configuration dialog box.*

Managing Disks with Disk Management

Formatting disks and converting their file system is all very well—but what if you need to create or delete a partition? For these tasks, XP provides a Computer Management snap-in called Disk Management.

Starting Disk Management

Take the following steps to start Disk Management:

1. Choose Start ➤ Control Panel. XP displays Control Panel.

    ◆ Alternatively, click the Start button to display the Start menu, right-click the My Computer item, and choose Manage from the context menu. XP opens the Computer Management window. Go to step 5.

2. Click the Performance and Maintenance link. XP displays the Performance and Maintenance screen.

3. Click the Administrative Tools link. XP displays the Administrative Tools screen.

4. Double-click the Computer Management shortcut. XP opens a Computer Management window.

5. Expand the Storage item in the console tree if it's not already expanded.

6. Click the Disk Management item. Computer Management starts the Disk Management snap-in, which displays information about your disks. Figure 11.22 shows an example.

FIGURE 11.22

Use Disk Management to manage your disks.

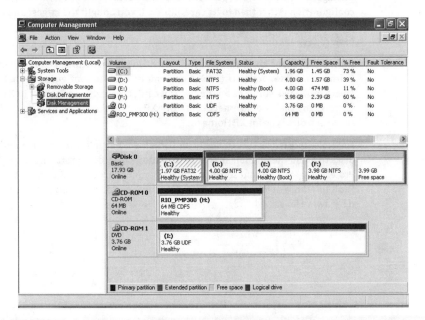

As you can see in the figure, the top section of the right-hand pane lists the volumes currently defined on the system, giving the following information about each volume:

- The letter for the volume (for example, C:).
- The volume's layout—whether it's a full disk or a partition.
- The type (basic or dynamic).
- The file system (FAT32, NTFS, CDFS, UDF, and so on).
- The status—for example, Healthy (Boot) for a boot volume in good condition.
- The capacity in megabytes, gigabytes, or larger units.
- The amount of free space.
- The percentage of the volume free.
- Whether fault tolerance is used on the volume.
- The overhead consumed by fault tolerance (if it's used). You can't see this column in the figure, because it's off the right side of the screen.

Below this list, Disk Management shows a graphical representation of each physical disk attached to the computer and how it's broken down. For example, in the figure, Disk 0 (the first hard disk—computer counting begins at 0) has a FAT32 C: drive, three NTFS drives, and a chunk of free space. Then there's a CD-ROM drive that shows up as CD-ROM 0 and a DVD drive that shows up as CD-ROM 1.

EXPERT KNOWLEDGE: DYNAMIC DISKS AND FAULT TOLERANCE

That bit about basic disks and dynamic disks may have raised your eyebrows a bit—especially since Disk Management shows that your computer has basic disks. But don't worry—the term refers to the disk's configuration rather than to its capabilities. If you bought the largest and fastest hard drive on the block, it'll still be the largest and fastest until the engineers release something better, no matter that it uses the basic disk configuration.

A *basic disk* is one configured to support primary partitions, an extended partition, and logical drives (within that extended partition). A *dynamic disk* is one configured so that you can use fault tolerance or create multidisk volumes on the fly. You can't create dynamic disks in XP Home, but because XP Home borrows the Disk Management tool from XP Professional and Windows .NET Server, Disk Management shows the disk type for XP Home too.

Fault tolerance is a feature typically implemented only in servers or high-end workstations. It uses multiple disks to avoid the possible loss of information when disk problems occur. Windows 2000 Server and XP Professional implement software fault tolerance through redundant array of inexpensive disks (RAID). Fault tolerance involves *overhead*—extra space used to keep extra copies of information so that it isn't lost if hardware fails.

Creating a Partition

If you have free space available, you can create a partition in it. Below is an example of creating a new logical drive using that free space shown back in Figure 11.23. The options available to you will depend on your disk configuration.

1. Right-click the free space and choose New Logical Drive from the context menu. Computer Management starts the New Partition Wizard, which displays an introductory page.

2. Click the Next button. The wizard displays the Select Partition Type page, which offers you such options for creating a new partition as are available: Primary Partition, Extended Partition, or Logical Drive.

3. Select the partition type (if there's a choice) and click the Next button. The wizard displays the Specify Partition Size page (shown on the right in Figure 11.23).

4. In the Partition Size in MB text box, enter the size of partition you want to create. The wizard suggests using all the space available, which you may well not want to do. The readout above the text box shows the minimum and maximum sizes possible.

5. Click the Next button. The wizard displays the Assign Drive Letter or Path page (shown on the right in Figure 11.23).

FIGURE 11.23

On the Specify Partition Size page of the New Partition Wizard, specify the size of the partition. On the Assign Drive Letter or Path page, specify the drive letter to use.

 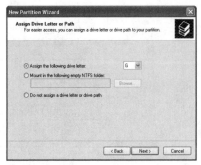

6. Leave the Assign the Following Drive Letter option button selected and specify the letter in the drop-down list.

 ◆ Instead of assigning a drive letter, you can select the Mount in the Following Empty NTFS Folder option button and specify the folder in the text box. See the next sidebar for a discussion of this option.

 ◆ Instead of doing either of the above, you *can* avoid assigning a drive letter or path by selecting the Do Not Assign a Drive Letter or Drive Path option button. The only reason to do this is if you're planning to assign letters (or paths) later after creating other partitions. To access the partition through the XP interface (for example, from Explorer or from an application), you'll need to assign a drive letter or path to it sooner or later—and it may as well be sooner.

7. Click the Next button. The wizard displays the Format Partition page (shown in Figure 11.24).

FIGURE 11.24

On the Format Partition page of the New Partition Wizard, specify the file system and label for the partition.

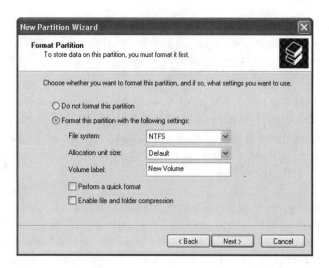

8. Leave the Format This Partition with the Following Settings option button selected and choose settings:

   ◆ Choose the file system (preferably NTFS, but FAT32 or FAT if necessary) in the File System drop-down list.

   ◆ Leave the Allocation Unit Size drop-down list set to Default unless you've got a very good reason to change it.

   ◆ Enter the label for the volume in the Volume Label text box. (The wizard suggests New Volume, but you should be able to come up with something more descriptive. Again, you have 20 characters for the label on an NTFS volume and 11 characters for that on a FAT or FAT32 volume.)

   ◆ Select the Perform a Quick Format check box if you've checked the disk for errors recently and found none. If not, it's better to perform a full format, including the check for errors.

   ◆ Select the Enable File and Folder Compression check box if you want to use compression on the volume.

9. Click the Next button. The wizard displays the Completing the New Partition Wizard page.

10. Click the Finish button. The wizard closes, creates the partition, and formats it. You'll need to wait for the formatting to finish before you can use the volume.

Deleting a Partition

To delete a partition and dispose of all its data, right-click the partition and issue the Delete command from the context menu. For example, if it's a logical drive, choose the Delete Logical Drive item on the context menu. Disk Management displays a Delete Drive dialog box. Click the Yes button to proceed.

Changing the Drive Letter

Disk Management also lets you change the drive letter for a volume other than your system volume or boot volume. This capability comes in handy if you get your drive letters in a tangle. Be aware, though, that changing the drive letter will confuse any program that has learned the path to files on this drive.

To change the drive letter, follow these steps:

1. Right-click the drive whose letter you want to change and choose Change Drive Letter and Paths from the context menu. Disk Management displays the Change Drive Letter and Paths dialog box (shown on the left in Figure 11.25).

2. To change the drive letter, select it (if it's not already selected) and click the Change button. Disk Management displays the Change Drive Letter or Path dialog box (shown on the right in Figure 11.25).

FIGURE 11.25

Use the Change Drive Letter and Paths dialog box (left) and the Change Drive Letter or Path dialog box (right) to change the drive letter for a drive.

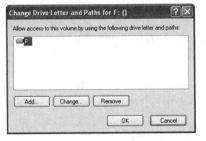

3. Make sure the Assign the Following Drive Letter option button is selected, then select the letter in the drop-down list.

4. Click the OK button. Disk Management displays the Confirm dialog box (shown in Figure 11.26), warning you that changing the drive letter might prevent programs from running.

FIGURE 11.26

Confirm the change in the Confirm dialog box.

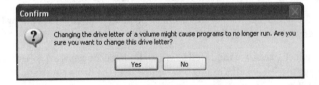

5. Click the Yes button. If files on the drive are open, Disk Management displays the Disk Management dialog box shown in Figure 11.27 telling you that you can continue to use the old drive letter until you reboot and asking if you want to continue.

FIGURE 11.27

Read the small print in the Disk Management dialog box and signal your willingness to proceed.

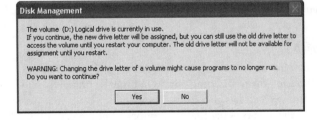

6. Click the Yes button. Disk Management makes the change.

7. Change other drive letters if necessary, then restart your computer so that you can start using the new drive letter assignments.

EXPERT KNOWLEDGE: MOUNTING A PARTITION IN AN EMPTY NTFS FOLDER

Instead of assigning a drive letter to a partition, you can mount the partition in an empty NTFS folder. Doing so has a couple of advantages:

◆ You can connect more drives to your computer than the 26 letters of the alphabet would let you.

◆ You can make files appear to be more readily available or appear to be available in multiple locations. For example, you could keep your videos in a central location but create a subfolder in each user's \My Videos\ folder and assign it to the appropriate drive path.

To do this, take the following steps:

1. Right-click the drive in the list box in Computer Management and choose Change Drive Letter and Paths from the context menu. XP displays the Change Drive Letter and Paths dialog box.

2. Click the Add button. XP displays the Add Drive Letter or Path dialog box, which is the Change Drive Letter or Path dialog box by another name.

3. Make sure the Mount in the Following Empty NTFS Folder option button is selected. (This option button should be selected by default.)

4. Click the Browse button and use the resulting Browse for Drive Path dialog box to specify the folder. Alternatively, type the path in the text box.

5. Click the OK button. XP assigns the path and closes the Add Drive Letter or Path dialog box.

You'll then be able to access the drive through the folder you assigned.

To see if a folder is really a mounted volume, display the Properties dialog box for the folder and see if the Type readout on the General page says *Mounted Volume*.

To check which drives are mounted as which folders, choose View ➢ Drive Paths from Disk Management. XP displays the Drive Paths dialog box, which lists the drive paths and their volume mapping and which includes a Remove button for removing drive mappings.

Exiting Disk Management

When you've finished working in Disk Management, choose File ➢ Exit to close the Computer Management window.

Up Next

This chapter has discussed how to manage your disks and drives, from actions such as formatting and compressing them to setting quotas in order to prevent users from grabbing more than their fair share of disk space. It has also covered how to look after your disks by defragmenting them, checking them for errors, and running Disk Cleanup; and how to use Disk Management to create partitions, delete them, and assign drive letters to them.

The next chapter discusses how to work with the Registry to tweak your computer's configuration in ways that Microsoft failed to provide in the user interface.

Chapter 12

Working with the Registry

THIS CHAPTER COVERS HOW to work with one of the most mentioned but least understood components of Windows—the Registry, the giant repository of Windows' knowledge and wisdom about your computer.

The chapter starts by discussing what the Registry is, what it does, why you might want to mess with it, and what the dangers are of doing so. It then details the step you *must* take before you make any changes to the Registry: backing up the Registry so that you can restore it if something goes wrong. After that, the chapter shows you how to use Registry Editor to examine the contents of the Registry, find what you're looking for, and make changes. It mentions a few Registry changes that you may want to make to change how XP behaves. It concludes by showing you how to goose the Registry so that you can crash your computer with two keystrokes.

This chapter covers the following topics:

- ◆ Understanding what the Registry is and what it does
- ◆ Running Registry Editor
- ◆ Backing up your Registry
- ◆ Restoring the Registry from backup
- ◆ Restoring the Last Known Good Configuration
- ◆ Registry subtrees and data types
- ◆ Finding and changing information in the Registry
- ◆ Examples of working with the Registry
- ◆ Crashing your computer manually

What Is the Registry and What Does It Do?

Put simply, the *Registry* is a hierarchical database of all the settings required by your installation of XP and the programs you've installed. These settings include information on the hardware installed on your computer and how it's configured; all the programs and their file associations; profiles for each user and group; and property settings for folders and files.

The Registry stores the information needed to keep your computer running. XP itself stores a huge amount of information in the Registry, and each program you install stores information there too. You can store information in the Registry yourself if you want to, though unless you're creating programs, there's not much reason to do so.

The number of entries in the Registry depends on the number of users of the computer and the software installed, but between 50,000 and 100,000 entries is normal. This multitude of entries makes browsing through the Registry practical only for those with serious amounts of time weighing on their hands. Even searching through the Registry can be a slow process, because many of the entries contain similar information.

The Registry was introduced in Windows 95, and all 32-bit desktop versions of Windows have used it. In Windows 3.x, information was stored in initialization files—INI files for short. For example, Windows configuration information was stored in files such as WIN.INI and SYSTEM.INI. Most programs typically created configuration files of their own.

Centralizing all the information in the Registry has two main advantages. First, all the information is in a central location. (Actually, it's in a couple of locations. More on this a little later in the chapter.) And second, you can back up the Registry (though most users forget or fail to do so) and restore it.

Not surprisingly, this centralization has the concomitant disadvantage that damage to the Registry can cripple Windows completely.

Why Work with the Registry?

Paradoxically enough, you *don't* work directly with the Registry—most of the time. In theory, you should never need to mess with the Registry.

That's why XP provides no direct way from the user interface to view the Registry and change its contents. If you want to explore and change the Registry, you need to deliberately run the Registry Editor program, which is tucked away in a safe place where no casual user should stumble across it.

Most of the information that's stored in the Registry you'll never need to change. Those relatively few pieces of information that XP is happy for you to change are accessible through the XP user interface, which provides you with an easier—if more restrictive—way of changing them than working in the Registry. For example, the settings in Control Panel applets store most of their information in the Registry, so you *could* edit the Registry and change the information there. But for all conventional purposes, you'll do better to work through those Control Panel applets and let them set the values in the Registry for you. Control Panel is designed to be easy to use, while the Registry isn't. Control Panel shows you your options in (mostly) intelligible ways; the information in the Registry is arcane when not incomprehensible. And Control Panel seldom screws up in translating your choices into hex and binary, whereas the Registry will happily accept input that will instruct XP to disable itself.

That said, sometimes you may need to access the Registry to change a vital piece of information that you cannot change through the user interface. Sometimes you'll need to access the Registry because something has gone wrong, and you need to change an entry manually. But more often, you'll hear about a cool tweak that you can perform by entering a new value in the Registry or by changing an existing value.

TIP *Before you start messing with the Registry to change something you can't reach from the XP interface, check out the Tweak UI PowerToy, which you can download from the Microsoft Windows XP Downloads site (www.microsoft .com/windowsxp/home/downloads/powertoys.asp). Tweak UI lets you change a slew of things that XP itself either doesn't let you change or makes it awkwardly difficult to change.*

You can also use the Registry to store information of your own that you want to have available to XP or to the programs you use. You might want to do this if you write your own programs, or if you use a macro language to create automated procedures in a program—for example, if you use VBA to automate tasks in Word, Excel, or Outlook. (You *could* also use the Registry to store odd information, such as names and addresses—but there are far better ways of spending your life.)

Preparing to Access the Registry

Before you do anything to the Registry, you need to understand this:

If you mess up the Registry, you may disable parts of XP's functionality. You may even disable XP itself so that it cannot boot.

So before you do *anything* to the Registry, back it up by exporting it as discussed in the section after next. In fact, even if you don't make any changes to the Registry, it's a good idea to keep a backup of your Registry in case a program, XP itself, or (more likely) a piece of malware makes a change for the worse.

NOTE *System Restore (discussed in detail in Chapter 17) rolls back Registry entries to their state when the restore point was created, so you can use System Restore to recover from damage to the Registry. Because System Restore also changes other settings, however, it's a clumsy solution that's best avoided unless you've failed to back up your Registry before mangling it. However, you may want to create a new restore point as insurance before monkeying with the Registry.*

Running Registry Editor

To work with the Registry, you use Registry Editor. XP provides no Start menu item for Registry Editor, though you can of course create your own Start menu item or Desktop shortcut if you want.

Unless you create a Start menu item or shortcut, the easiest way to run Registry Editor is to choose Start ➢ Run (or press Windows key+R), enter **regedit** in the Run dialog box, and click the OK button. XP starts Registry Editor (shown in Figure 12.1).

FIGURE 12.1

Launch Registry Editor by choosing Start ➢ Run and entering **regedit** in the Run dialog box.

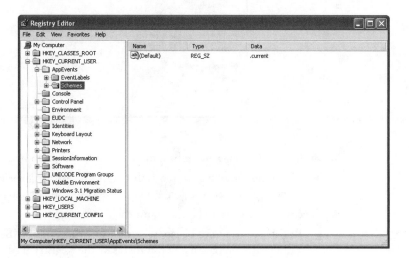

NOTE *If you've worked with the Registry in Windows 2000 or in Windows NT, you'll recall that those OSes included two Registry Editors—*REGEDIT.EXE *and* REGEDT32.EXE. *Both were functional, but* REGEDT32.EXE *offered a few more features than* REGEDIT.EXE. *Good news: XP includes just one Registry Editor,* REGEDIT.EXE, *but there's a stub for* REGEDT32.EXE, *so you can start the same Registry Editor by using either name.*

Backing Up Your Registry

Before you do anything else with Registry Editor—and that includes exploring the subtrees and keys of the Registry, let alone changing any values—back up your Registry.

To back up the Registry, export it by taking the following steps from Registry Editor:

1. Select the My Computer item in Registry Editor.

   ◆ If you want to back up only a subtree of the Registry, select the subtree instead of the My Computer item.

2. Choose File ➢ Export. Registry Editor displays the Export Registry File dialog box (shown in Figure 12.2). As you can see in the figure, this dialog box is a common Save As dialog box with an extra section tacked on at the bottom to house the Export Range group box.

FIGURE 12.2

In the Export Registry File dialog box, specify that you want to export all of the Registry.

3. In the Export Range group box, make sure the All option button is selected.

   ◆ If you chose a subtree in step 1, the Export Registry File dialog box appears with the Selected Branch option button selected and the subtree's name entered in the Selected Branch text box.

4. Specify the filename and location for the file as usual.

   ◆ Registry files tend to be large—on the order of 20–30MB—so don't try to save yours to a floppy. If you have a CD recorder, save the Registry file to disk, then burn it to CD.

5. Click the Save button. XP closes the Export Registry File dialog box and saves the Registry file.

Restoring Your Registry

To restore your Registry (or part of it) from a Registry file you've exported, follow these steps:

1. From Registry Editor, choose File ➢ Import. XP displays the Import Registry File dialog box, which is a renamed Open dialog box.
2. In the Files of Type drop-down list, select the Registration Files item or the Registry Hive Files item as appropriate.
3. Select the Registry file to import.
4. Click the Open button. Registry Editor imports the Registry file and adds it to the Registry.

Restoring the Registry to Its Last Known Good Configuration

If you do to the Registry anything so horrible that XP won't boot anymore, you may need to restore the Registry to its Last Known Good Configuration in order to get XP going again. The *Last Known Good Configuration* is the one with which XP last booted successfully. Restoring the Last Known Good Configuration loses any changes you've made to your XP configuration since the last boot—including whichever change has disabled XP.

To restore the Registry to the Last Known Good Configuration, take the following steps:

1. If XP is still running (and if you need to restore the Registry, XP may well *not* be running), choose Start ➢ Turn Off Computer. From the Turn Off Computer screen, choose the Restart option. If XP isn't running, power up your computer as usual.
2. As XP restarts (or starts), or when (in a multi-boot configuration) it displays the Please Select the Operating System to Start screen, press the F8 key. XP displays the Windows Advanced Options menu.
3. Select the Last Known Good Configuration item and press the Enter key. XP displays the Please Select the Operating System to Start menu but adds the words *Last Known Good Configuration* at the bottom of the screen in blue.
4. Select the operating system to start, and then press the Enter key. XP starts and displays the Welcome screen.

Working in the Registry

Now that your Registry is safely backed up, it's time to examine how the Registry works and how you can change it.

As mentioned earlier in this chapter, the Registry is a hierarchical database. It's hierarchical in that its contents are arranged into a hierarchy of folders organized into five main areas called *subtrees* or *root keys*. You'll also sometimes hear them called *predefined keys*, though the term tends to be confusing because the Registry contains thousands of keys that are predefined—at least, from the user's point of view. As you can see in Figure 12.1 above, the name of each subtree begins with the letters HKEY.

The Five Subtrees of the Registry

These are the five subtrees and the types of information they contain:

HKEY_CLASSES_ROOT   This subtree contains an exhaustive list of the file types that XP recognizes, the programs associated with them, and more.

HKEY_CURRENT_USER   This subtree contains information on the current user and their setup. For example, when you're logged on, all your Desktop preferences are listed in this subtree.

HKEY_LOCAL_MACHINE   This subtree contains information on the hardware and software setup of the computer.

HKEY_USERS   This subtree contains information on the users who are set up to use the computer, together with a DEFAULT profile that's used when no user is logged on to the computer.

HKEY_CURRENT_CONFIG   This subtree contains information on the current configuration of the computer—the hardware with which the computer booted.

Keys, Subkeys, and Value Entries

In Registry Editor, expand the HKEY_CURRENT_USER subtree by clicking the plus (+) sign next to it or by double-clicking its name. Registry Editor displays the items contained within the subtree—an apparently endless list of folderlike objects, many of them containing further objects. Figure 12.3 shows the HKEY_CURRENT_USER subtree with some of its subkeys expanded and the \Control Panel\ Desktop\WindowMetrics key displayed.

FIGURE 12.3

Each subtree contains keys, subkeys, and value entries.

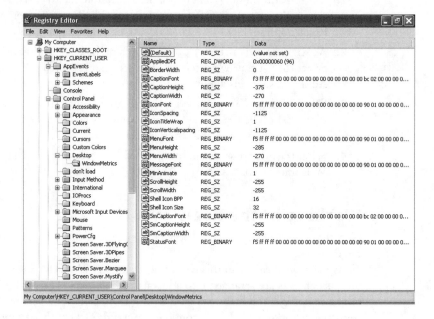

Within each subtree are keys, subkeys, and value entries. A *key* is (as it were) one of the folders within the subtree. Just as a subfolder is a folder within a folder, a *subkey* is a key within a key. Also as with "folder" and "subfolder," many people say "key" rather than "subkey" except when they need to be specific; this chapter does the same.

Each key or subkey can contain subkeys and value entries. The term *value entry* sounds like a management-consultant way of saying "value," but in fact it's not: A value entry is the current definition of a key, and consists of a name, a data type, and the value assigned to the key.

For example, consider the `MinAnimate` key and value entry that you can see in Figure 12.3 in the `HKEY_CURRENT_USER\Control Panel\Desktop\WindowMetrics\` subkey. As you can see in the Data column, the value of `MinAnimate` is 1. This value entry controls whether XP animates windows when you minimize, maximize, or restore them. (The animation zooms the window from its displayed size and position down to its button on the Taskbar, and vice versa, instead of popping it off or back on the screen instantly.) A value of 0 indicates that the animation is off, a value of 1 that the animation is on.

`MinAnimate` is interesting in that it's an example of a key added to the Registry in XP in order to implement functionality already in Windows. In earlier versions of Windows, including Windows NT and Windows 2000, this key wasn't included in the Registry, though its functionality was implemented in Windows. These versions of Windows automatically animated windows that you minimized, maximized, or restored.

This animation was (and remains) pure eye candy—and like much eye candy, this animation didn't appeal to everyone. On a slow computer, or one with an underpowered graphics card, it was particularly irritating, as Windows seemed to be running arthritically. To switch off this animation, you needed to create the `MinAnimate` value entry in the Registry and assign it the value 0, then restart Windows. (You could've also implemented this change by using a utility such as TweakUI, which created and adjusted the `MinAnimate` value entry transparently for you.)

XP lets you control this setting via the Animate Windows when Minimizing and Maximizing check box on the Visual Effects page of the Performance Options dialog box (which you reach by clicking the Settings button in the Performance group box on the Advanced page of the System Properties dialog box). When this check box is selected, `MinAnimate` has the value 1; when the check box is cleared, `MinAnimate` has the value 0.

Registry Data Types

As you can see in Figure 12.3, the `MinAnimate` value entry is of type `REG_SZ`. REG means Registry, as you'd guess; SZ means string, indicating that the value entry contains a string of text (text characters, as opposed to, say, binary data). The `\WindowMetrics\` key also contains value entries of another data type, `REG_BINARY`. You get no prize for guessing that these are binary data.

Strings and binary data are the most widely used of the data types in the Registry. Next comes `REG_DWORD`, a double-word value entry.

The other two most widely used data types are `REG_MULTI_SZ`, multi-string entries, and `REG_EXPAND_SZ`, expandable strings. Table 12.1 provides a roundup of the five most widely used data types.

TABLE 12.1: THE FIVE MOST WIDELY USED REGISTRY DATA TYPES

TYPE	TYPE DISPLAYED	EXPLANATION
String	REG_SZ	Text
Multi-String	REG_MULTI_SZ	Text, but with multiple text values
Expandable String	REG_EXPAND_SZ	Text, but expandable
Binary	REG_BINARY	A binary value, displayed as hexadecimal
DWORD	REG_DWORD	Double-word: A 32-bit binary value displayed as an 8-digit hexadecimal value

You can create and edit value entries with any of these data types. We'll get to that a bit later in the chapter, after discussing where the Registry is stored and how to find information in it.

TIP   *Beyond these five widely used data types, the Registry can contain many different data types, such as* REG_DWORD_BIG_ENDIAN *(a value stored in reverse order of double-word value),* REG_DWORD_LITTLE_ENDIAN *(another type of double-word value),* REG_FULL_RESOURCE_DESCRIPTOR *(a hardware-resource list),* REG_QWORD *(a quadruple-word value), and* REG_FILE_NAME *(three guesses). You shouldn't need to mess with any of these unless you get into programming Windows—in which case you'll need a book more specialized than this one.*

Where the Registry Is Stored

Most of the Registry is stored in several different files on your hard drive. (Part of the Registry is created automatically when XP boots and discovers which devices are attached to your computer.) These files are binary and are called *hives* (think bees, not allergies) or *hive files*.

Perhaps surprisingly, the hives aren't hidden files, so you don't even need to tell XP to display hidden files before you can see them. But you do have to go through XP's veil of secrecy over the files by clicking the Show the Contents of This Folder link.

Hive files containing computer-related information are stored in the *Windows*\system32\config\ folder, where *Windows*\ is your Windows folder. Hive files containing user-specific information are stored in the \Documents and Settings*Username*\ folder for each user.

These are the main hive files:

SYSTEM   This file contains information about the computer's hardware and about XP. This information goes into the HKEY_LOCAL_MACHINE\SYSTEM\ key.

NTUSER.DAT   This file contains information about the user's preferences. XP keeps an NTUSER.DAT file for each user in the \Documents and Settings*Username*\ folder. This information goes into the HKEY_CURRENT_USER subtree.

SAM   This file contains the user database. This information goes into the HKEY_LOCAL_MACHINE\ SAM\ key.

SECURITY   This file contains information on security settings. This information goes into the HKEY_LOCALMACHINE\SECURITY\ key.

SOFTWARE   This file contains information on the software installed on the computer. This information goes into the HKEY_LOCAL_MACHINE\SOFTWARE\ key.

DEFAULT This file contains information about the default user setup. This information goes into the `HKEY_USERS\DEFAULT\` key.

Each of the hive files has a log file named after it: `DEFAULT.LOG`, `SOFTWARE.LOG`, `NTUSER.DAT.LOG`, and so on. These log files note the changes to the hive files so that, if a change is applied that crashes the system, XP can read the log, identify the problem change, and undo it.

Having read this, you're probably longing to lift the lid off a hive so that you can see what's inside it. Perhaps if you use Notepad or another text editor, you can get a peek inside in the same way you did with that Word document in Chapter 7—

Don't.

Taking a text editor to a hive file would be like taking one of those old-fashioned can openers (you know, the ones that leave those nice jagged edges) to your favorite black box of electronic wizardry: clumsy, messy, and ultimately fruitless. In any case, XP keeps the hive files open the whole time it's running so that it can write information to them and retrieve information from them whenever it needs, so they're locked. All you'll get for your pains is a message box telling you something like "The process cannot access the file because it is being used by another process." Translation: XP needs this file. Hands off.

Let's look at what you *can* profitably do with the Registry: find keys and value entries or information in it, change values, and create (and delete) keys and value entries of your own.

Finding Information in the Registry

There are two ways to find information in the Registry: by digging through the Registry looking for it, or by using the Find function.

Digging through the Registry takes minimal explanation, because it's very similar to browsing in Explorer in Explore mode. You can expand and collapse keys as you would drives and folders in Explorer, and you can use type-down addressing to reach the next key or entry matching the letters you type. But because of the number of keys and value entries the Registry contains, you'll usually do better by searching through it rather than browsing.

If you know the name of a key, the name of a value entry, or the data contained in a value entry, you can search for it. For example, if you wanted to find where FTP sites were listed, you might search for **FTP Sites**. If you wanted to find out what the entry for the Microsoft Office AutoCorrect file was called, you might search for **.ACL**, the extension of the AutoCorrect file. Choose Edit ➢ Find (or press Ctrl+F). Registry Editor displays the Find dialog box (shown in Figure 12.4). You can restrict the search by selecting only the check boxes for the items you're looking at—Keys, Values, or Data—in the Look At group box. And you can search for only the entire string by selecting the Match Whole String Only check box. Selecting this check box prevents Find from finding the string you're looking for inside other strings—it makes Find find only whole strings that match the string in the Find What text box.

FIGURE 12.4

Use the Find dialog box in Registry Editor to find the keys, values, or data you want to manipulate.

Because of the volume of information that XP stores in the Registry, the first match you find may not be the key (or value entry, or value) you need. For example, if you use your company's name as the Find item when looking for the `RegisteredOrganization` key for XP, you may find another key, such as the registered organization for Internet Explorer. Close examination of the key will usually tell you whether you've found the key you were looking for. If not, press the F3 key or choose Edit ➤ Find Next to find the next instance.

Editing a Value Entry

To edit a value entry in the Registry, navigate to it and double-click it. (Alternatively, select it and choose Edit ➤ Modify.) XP displays an Edit dialog box appropriate to the type of data the value entry contains.

String values and expandable string values are the easiest values to edit. In the Edit String dialog box (shown in Figure 12.5), enter the text of the string in the Value Data text box, then click the OK button.

FIGURE 12.5

You can edit both string values and expandable string values in the Edit String dialog box.

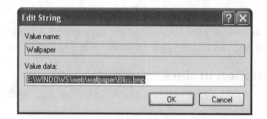

Multi-string values are relatively simple to edit. In the Edit Multi-String dialog box (shown in Figure 12.6), enter all the data for the value entry on separate lines, and then click the OK button.

FIGURE 12.6

Editing a multi-string value in the Edit Multi-String dialog box

Double-word values are the next-easiest values to edit. In the Edit DWORD Value dialog box (shown in Figure 12.7), enter the data in the Value Data text box, then choose the Hexadecimal option button or the Decimal option button as appropriate in the Base group box. (When you're editing a built-in double-word value, you shouldn't need to change the existing Base setting.) Click the OK button.

FIGURE 12.7

Editing a double-word value in the Edit DWORD Value dialog box

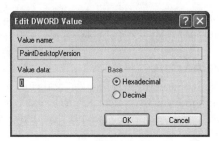

Binary values are brutes to change, and you probably won't want to mess with them for fun. In the Edit Binary Value dialog box (shown in Figure 12.8), edit the data in the Value Data text box with great care, and then click the OK button.

FIGURE 12.8

Editing a binary value in the Edit Binary Value dialog box is hard work.

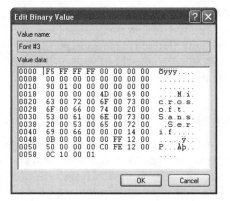

Adding a Key or a Value Entry

You can add a key or a value entry to the Registry either automatically or manually.

To add a key or value entry to the Registry automatically, double-click a REG file that you've received. For example, some programs sold via download use Registry keys to implement a license: You pay for the program and download it. The company then e-mails you a license and a REG file. To add the registration data to your Registry, double-click the REG file. XP adds the necessary keys and value entries to the Registry.

To add a key or a value entry to the Registry manually, follow these steps:

1. Right-click the key in which you want to create the new key or value entry, choose New from the context menu, and choose the appropriate item from the submenu: Key, String Value, Binary Value, DWORD Value, Multi-String Value, or Expandable String Value. Registry Editor creates a new key named New Key #1 or New Value #1 (or the next available number) and displays an edit box around it.

2. Type the name for the key or value entry.

3. Press the Enter key or click elsewhere in the Registry Editor window. Registry Editor assigns the name you specified to the key or value entry.

If you created a value entry, double-click it. Registry Editor displays the Edit dialog box appropriate to its type. Enter the data for the value entry as described in the previous section.

Deleting a Key or a Value Entry

Just as you can create keys and value entries, you can delete them. Generally speaking, it's a bad idea to delete any keys other than those you've created. XP itself and Windows programs protect some keys in the Registry, but you'll find a surprising number that aren't protected and that you can therefore delete freely.

To delete a value entry, right-click it and choose Delete from the context menu. Registry Editor displays the Confirm Value Delete dialog box or the Confirm Key Delete dialog box. Click the Yes button to confirm the deletion.

If the key or value entry is locked against deletion, Registry Editor displays an error message box.

Copying a Key Name

If you're describing to someone how to find particular information in the Registry, you'll need to get the key name right. But you don't need to type it painstakingly—you can copy it instead.

To copy a Registry key name, select it in the left pane in Registry Editor and choose Edit ➢ Copy Key Name. You can then paste it from the Clipboard into a program.

Examples of Working with the Registry

As mentioned at the beginning of the chapter, Microsoft reckons you should seldom (or preferably never) need to make changes to the Registry directly. But you'll probably run into tips and tweaks, online or in magazines, that promise to improve XP's performance, compatibility, or behavior with a judicious change or two. This section presents some examples of working with the Registry to customize your system.

Remember that tinkering with the Registry isn't recommended, because it can have unexpected results. Before you try any of these examples, back up your Registry and make sure that you know how to restore it.

WARNING   Before you try applying any Registry change that you read about online, think carefully about how much you trust the source of the information and whether you're likely to realize the benefits promised by the change. Changes recommended by print magazines and by reputable online magazines are likely to be okay, but changes posted by "friendly" parties in newsgroups or on websites might be malicious rather than helpful. If you have any doubts, spend a few minutes searching for corroboration of the Registry change rather than applying it blindly and suffering the consequences. If you can't find confirmation of what the change does, don't try it.

Changing Your Windows Name and Organization

If you misspelled your name or your organization's name during setup, or if you've bought a computer loaded with XP from someone else, you may need to change the name or organization that appears on the General page of the System Properties dialog box.

There's no way to effect this change through the XP user interface, but by navigating to the HKEY_LOCAL_MACHINE\SOFTWARE\Microsoft\WindowsNT\CurrentVersion\ key and changing the RegisteredOwner and RegisteredOrganization value entries as appropriate, you can fix the problem in a minute or two.

Changing Your *Program Files*\ Folder

If you want to prevent a Windows installation routine from installing a program to your \Program Files\ folder (for example, because you're running out of space on the drive that contains the folder), change the location of your \Program Files\ folder by navigating to the HKEY_LOCAL_ MACHINE\SOFTWARE\Microsoft\Windows\CurrentVersion subkey and changing the ProgramFilesDir value entry to the appropriate drive and folder.

Restart your computer to make the change take effect, then run the installation routine to install the program there. Change the ProgramFilesDir value entry back again to its normal value if you want to install future programs in the \Program Files\ folder.

Clearing the Paging File at Shutdown

If you're concerned about your system's security—well, you ought really to be using XP Professional rather than XP Home. But here's a technique that you can use with both OSes to clear the paging file when you shut down XP. The section "Specifying the Size and Location of the Paging File" in Chapter 16 discusses the paging file in detail; but briefly, it's a huge file on your hard disk that XP uses to store information temporarily so as to spare physical memory (RAM). So the paging file can contain sensitive information that a malicious hacker or a federal agency could recover.

To clear the paging file when you shut down XP, navigate to the HKEY_LOCAL_MACHINE\SYSTEM \CurrentControlSet\Control\Session Manager\Memory Management key and change the value of the value entry ClearPageFileAtShutdown to 1. Then restart your computer.

Preventing Messenger from Running

To prevent Windows Messenger from running automatically, create a new key named Messenger in the key HKEY_LOCAL_MACHINE\Software\Policies\Microsoft. In that key, create a new key named Client. In that key, create a new DWORD value entry with the name PreventRun and the value 1. Then restart your computer.

Changing or Removing the Places Bar

By editing the Registry, you can change the locations shown in the Places bar in common Open and Save dialog boxes—not the Open and Save dialog boxes used in Microsoft Office programs, unfortunately, but in those used by programs such as WordPad and Paint. Or, if you prefer, you can remove the Places bar completely from these dialog boxes.

TIP   Before we get into customizing or offing the Places bar by manipulating the Registry, I should mention that the Tweak UI PowerToy can customize the Places bar more easily for you. Download this PowerToy from the Microsoft Windows XP Downloads site (www.microsoft.com/windowsxp/home/downloads/powertoys.asp), install it, run it from the Start ➢ All Programs ➢ PowerToys for Windows XP submenu, and use the Common Dialogs item.

CUSTOMIZING THE PLACES BAR

By default, the Open and Save common dialog boxes contain buttons for accessing History, My Documents, Desktop, Favorites, and My Network Places. You can change these buttons so that they point to different locations by taking the following steps in Registry Editor:

1. Navigate to the key HKEY_CURRENT_USER\Software\Microsoft\Windows\CurrentVersion\ Policies\comdlg32. (If there's no comdlg32 key in the Policies key, create it.)

2. In the comdlg32 key, create a new subkey named Placesbar.

3. In the Placesbar key, create up to five value entries named Place0, Place1, Place2, Place3, and Place4 and assign values to them. Each value entry should be a String value if you want to assign a path to it or a DWORD entry if you want to assign to it an ID representing a preset location. Table 12.2 lists the IDs for some of the locations you're most likely to want to use.

TABLE 12.2: IDs FOR OFTEN-USED LOCATIONS FOR THE PLACES BAR

ID	LOCATION
0	Desktop
5	\My Documents\ folder (for this user)
6	Favorites (for this user)
8	Recent (for this user)
d	\My Music\ folder (for this user)
e	\My Videos\ folder (for this user)
10	Desktop (for this user)
11	My Computer (for this user)
12	My Network Places (for this user)
22	History (for this user)
24	%systemroot% folder
2e	\Shared Documents\ folder
31	Network Connections folder
35	\Shared Music\ folder
36	\Shared Pictures\ folder
37	\Shared Videos\ folder
3b	\CD burning\ folder (for this user)

Once you've created the value entries in the `PlacesBar` key, open a program that uses the common dialog boxes (for example, Notepad, WordPad, or Paint) and issue an Open command or a Save command. Admire the resulting customized dialog box.

REMOVING THE PLACES BAR

To remove the Places bar, create a new DWORD value entry named **NoPlacesBar** in the key `HKEY_CURRENT_USER\Software\Microsoft\Windows\CurrentVersion\Policies\comdlg32` and assign it the value **1**. (If there's no `comdlg32` key in the `Policies` key, create it.) You don't need to reboot for the change to take effect.

To restore the display of the Places bar, change the value of the `comdlg32` value entry to **0**.

Using the System Attribute for Customized Folders

By default, XP uses the read-only attribute to indicate to itself that a folder is customized. Typically, a customized folder is either a system folder or one that you've customized manually. Either way, the read-only attribute prevents you from changing the folder.

If you actually need to change a customized folder, you can use this trick to make XP use the system attribute rather than the read-only attribute to mark custom folders. In the `HKEY_LOCAL_MACHINE\SOFTWARE\Microsoft\Windows\CurrentVersion\Explorer` subkey, create a new DWORD value entry named **UseSystemForSystemFolders**, assign it the value **1**, and reboot your computer.

Using Registry Favorites to Quickly Access Keys

If you find yourself using the Registry a lot, there's another feature you should know about: Registry favorites. To access the keys you need to work with frequently, you can create favorites in Registry Editor much as you can in Explorer and Internet Explorer.

To create a favorite, follow these steps:

1. Select the key to which you want the favorite to refer.
2. Choose Favorites ➢ Add to Favorites. Registry Editor displays the Add to Favorites dialog box.
3. In the Favorite Name text box, enter the name for the favorite. (By default, Registry Editor suggests the key name, but you may well want to change this to more descriptive text.)
4. Click the OK button. Registry Editor adds the favorite to your Favorites menu.

To access a favorite, display the Favorites menu and choose the favorite from the list.

To remove a favorite from the Favorites menu, choose Favorites ➢ Remove Favorite. XP displays the Remove Favorites dialog box. Choose the favorite in the Select Favorite list box and click the OK button.

EXPERT KNOWLEDGE: CRASHING YOUR COMPUTER ON CUE

Most people want their computer to crash seldom or (preferably) never. But if you want to test what happens when it crashes (for example, to see how memory dumping works), you'll be relieved to know that you don't have to wait for your software to disagree horribly with itself: XP includes a built-in way of crashing itself. You just have to add the right Registry entry, set the appropriate value, and then press a couple of keys.

Here's what to do:

1. Back up your Registry. (Yes, really back it up this time.)

2. Open Registry Editor (for example, choose Start ➢ Run, enter **regedit**, and press the Enter key).

3. Navigate to the `HKEY_LOCAL_MACHINE\SYSTEM\CurrentControlSet\Services\i8042prt\Parameters\` key.

4. Right-click in the right pane and choose New ➢ DWORD Value from the context menu. Registry Editor creates a new value called `New Value #1` and displays an edit box around the new value's name.

5. Enter the name **CrashOnCtrlScroll** and press the Enter key.

6. Double-click the `CrashOnCtrlScroll` value. Registry Editor displays the Edit DWORD Value dialog box.

7. Enter **1** in the Value Data text box. In the Base group box, leave the Hexadecimal option button selected.

8. Click the OK button. Registry Editor closes the Edit DWORD Value dialog box.

9. Close Registry Editor.

10. Restart your computer and log back on.

11. Hold down the Ctrl key on the right side of the keyboard and press the Scroll Lock key twice. XP goes down as if sandbagged, and any memory dumping you've set occurs.

Up Next

This chapter has discussed what the Registry is; what it does; why you *must* back it up before messing with it; how to mess with it; and why you shouldn't mess with it most of the time. It's also shown several examples of how you can edit the Registry to change XP's behavior, including how you can crash your (or someone else's) computer on cue. Use this power only for good.

The next chapter discusses how to install, configure, and manage printers.

Chapter 13

Installing, Configuring, and Managing Printers and Fonts

WITH THE PROMISE OF the paperless office seemingly destined to remain eternally unfulfilled, printing continues to be vital to the average home office, and only marginally less vital to the average home.

This chapter discusses how to install, configure, and manage printers and fonts. Chapter 32 discusses how to share a printer via your network and how to connect to a shared printer.

This chapter covers the following topics:

- The basics of Windows printing
- Installing a local printer
- Configuring a printer
- Removing a printer
- Printing a document
- Managing your print jobs
- Printing offline
- Creating multiple entries for the same printer
- Printing to a file
- Working with fonts

The Basics of Windows Printing

As you'll see in a minute, installing a printer is straightforward enough, with wizards to help you left, right, and center. But before we get into that, let's go over the basics of printing in Windows. First, there's a bit of terminology you ought to understand. Then there are three ways of installing a printer, the first of which this chapter discusses. (Chapter 32 discusses the other two ways.) And there's a little you should know about how an item you print makes its way from the program to the printer.

The Terminology of Windows Printing

Just as the windows in Windows are most likely substantially different from those in your home, Windows terminology for printing is a little different from regular terminology. Here are the terms that you need to know before you consult the Help files or call for tech support:

◆ A *printer* is the hardware device that actually prints the page—in other words, what people normally mean when they say "printer." This doesn't go without saying because Microsoft sometimes refers to a printer as a *print device*. If so, what does Microsoft mean by *printer* at those times? Read on....

◆ When the hardware device is called a *print device*, a *printer* is the software that controls the *print device*. Normally, it's clearer to call this software a printer driver.

◆ A *print job* (or just plain *job*) is an item sent to a printer for printing. For example, if you print the first spreadsheet in an Excel workbook, that's a print job. If you then print three pages of a Word document, that's another print job.

◆ A *network printer*, *shared printer*, or *printer connection* is a printer that's being shared by another computer or by a print server and that you can connect to across the network.

◆ A *print server* is a device (typically a hardware device) that relays print jobs to a printer.

This book uses the terms *printer* for the hardware device and *print driver* for the software that drives it.

Three Ways of Installing a Printer

These are the three ways of installing a printer:

Local printer attached to the computer   The simplest way of installing a printer is to install it *locally*—in other words, attach it directly to the computer. The printer is usually attached directly to the computer with a cable to the parallel port or USB port. There are also more specialized arrangements, such as infrared printer connections for laptop users too impatient to plug into a docking station.

Networked printer attached to a server   The next way of installing a printer is to install it as a *networked*—shared—printer attached to a server. The server in this case doesn't have to be a server in the sense of a computer *dedicated* to providing services to other computers. It can be just another client computer that's sharing a printer directly attached to it and so providing printing services to other computers. Alternatively, it can be a dedicated server running a server operating system. The client computer connects to the networked printer through a network (cabled, wireless, or—rarely—infrared). The network can be the Internet, as XP supports the Internet Printing Protocol (IPP). The section "Printing across the Internet with IPP" in Chapter 32 discusses how to print to a printer across the Internet.

Networked printer attached to a print server   You can also share a printer attached to a print server. A print server is essentially a specialized computer designed for sharing and managing printers. The advantage of using a print server over a networked computer is that you don't need to keep a computer running all the time in order to use the printer. Print servers can be either wired to the network or wireless.

Figure 13.1 illustrates these printer configurations.

FIGURE 13.1

The three basic configurations for printers: a local printer attached directly to the computer, a networked printer shared by another computer, and a networked printer attached to a print server

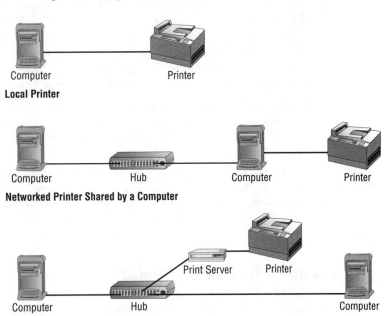

EXPERT KNOWLEDGE: KEEPING DOWN THE COST OF PRINTING

Chances are you're familiar with the axiom about marketing razors and razor blades: The manufacturers sell the razor itself at a low price to get you committed to buying the blades, on which they make plenty of profit.

The economics of printing works in a similar way. Printer manufacturers sell printers at temptingly low prices to get you hooked on buying ink cartridges for them, then they sting you on the cartridges. If you print a lot, the cost of the cartridges for your printer will probably run to between five times and twenty times the printer's cost before the printer gives up the ghost—so it's well worth evaluating the cost per page of each printer you're considering rather than just the printer's price and features.

Because color cartridges tend to be much more expensive than black cartridges, consider getting a printer that uses separate color and black cartridges rather than one that essentially forces you to print using color all the time. (If you print many documents in grayscale, and your color printer uses high-quality and high-cost media, it may even be worth getting a separate printer for your grayscale work.)

Continued on next page

EXPERT KNOWLEDGE: KEEPING DOWN THE COST OF PRINTING *(continued)*

Because printer cartridges are expensive, enterprising companies provide less expensive alternatives. First, some companies provide refilled cartridges that cost less than new cartridges but supposedly deliver similar performance and reliability. Second, other companies sell kits that let you refill ink cartridges, usually with a syringe and needle and a trusty hand. Some people swear by these kits, which have the potential not only to save you money but also to distribute ink where you don't want it, but rather more people swear *at* them. Further adding to the problem is the fact that, because the manufacturers don't design the nozzles in most ink cartridges to be reused, the output quality is likely to degrade if you refill a cartridge.

Another possibility is to print most of your documents in draft mode, which uses lower resolution but is plenty readable enough for everyday use, and save high-quality mode for documents that need the extra resolution (for example, pictures, or text documents that you're going to give to clients rather than use yourself). An extra bonus of this approach is that draft mode is also usually quicker than high-quality mode.

If you print a lot, or if you can afford to take a long-term view, buy a laser printer. Laser printers have much lower per-page running costs than inkjet printers, particularly for standard-quality monochrome printing. The disadvantage is that laser printers tend to be more expensive than inkjets, so you need to make more of an investment up front.

Unfortunately, there's no printer equivalent of an electric razor—except, of course, for viewing documents on screen rather than printing them out on paper. In any case, you should use Print Preview to check that your documents look approximately okay before you print them.

How Does a Print Job Get Printed?

Provided your printer works as it should, you don't need to know how the printing process works. But if anything goes wrong with printing, understanding the basic process can be a great help in troubleshooting the problem.

Here's what typically happens in the print process:

- You issue a Print command for a document you've got open in a program. For example, you're working on a workbook in Excel and you get a worksheet into shape to print. You press Ctrl+P, choose options in the Print dialog box, and click the OK button.

- The program tells Windows that it needs to print the document.

- The printer driver (the print software, or what Microsoft sometimes calls the *printer*) kicks in. The printer driver grabs the information that the program is emitting about what needs to be printed. The printer driver *spools* the printing information, saving it to disk all at once and then feeding it to the printer (the hardware print device) at a speed the printer and its cable can handle. Printer cables transfer data very slowly compared to the wiring inside the computer, and if the printer didn't spool the data, the program would be stuck transferring the information to the printer bit by bit. (This isn't entirely true—some programs are intelligent enough to print in the background while allowing you to continue working in the foreground. But generally speaking, spooling lets you continue your work much more quickly.)

There's one other part to this: Each print job is typically spooled into a *print queue* rather than just fed into the printer. Documents in the print queue are normally printed in the order in which they are submitted, but you can assign different priorities to different users' print jobs if you want. If you have Computer Administrator privileges, you can also manage the print queue, promoting, demoting, pausing, and deleting print jobs.

Printers and Faxes Page

XP's central location for working with printers is the Printers and Faxes page in Control Panel. To display the Printers and Faxes page, choose Start ➤ Control Panel, click the Printers and Other Hardware link, and then click the Printers and Faxes link.

TIP If you find yourself working often on the Printers and Faxes page of Control Panel, put a link to it on your Start menu by selecting the Printers and Faxes check box on the Advanced page of the Customize Start Menu dialog box. (To display this dialog box, right-click the Start button and choose Properties to display the Taskbar and Start Menu Properties dialog box, then click the Customize button on the Start Menu page.)

Installing a Local Printer

If your printer was connected to the computer when you installed XP, Setup should have set it up for you. If you connect it afterward, you'll need to set it up by using the hardware wizards.

In most cases, XP detects the addition of the printer when you connect the printer to the computer's parallel or USB port and switch the printer on. If XP has a driver for the printer, it loads the driver and notifies you that the printer is ready for use. If XP doesn't have a driver for the printer, it starts the Found New Hardware Wizard to walk you through the process of identifying the printer and installing the right driver for it. See the section "Using the Found New Hardware Wizard" in Chapter 14 for information on using the Found New Hardware Wizard.

TIP There are a couple of other reasons why you may need to run the Add Printer Wizard to add a printer. First, you may want to add a new printer configuration for a printer that XP already knows about. Second, you may want to add an entry for a printer to which your computer won't actually connect, so that you can print documents to files formatted for that type of printer (and then print the files later, perhaps from another computer). I'll discuss both these possibilities later in the chapter.

If XP doesn't detect your local printer, use the Add Printer Wizard to install the printer. Take the following steps:

1. Choose Start ➤ Control Panel. XP displays Control Panel.
2. Click the Printers and Other Hardware link. XP displays the Printers and Other Hardware screen.
3. Click the Add a Printer link in the Pick a Task list. (Alternatively, click the Add a Printer link in the Tasks list on the Printers and Faxes screen.) XP starts the Add Printer Wizard, which displays its Welcome page.

4. Click the Next button. The wizard displays the Local or Network Printer page (shown in Figure 13.2).

FIGURE 13.2

On the Local or Network Printer page of the Add Printer Wizard, select the Local Printer Attached to This Computer option button.

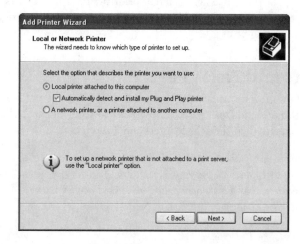

5. Make sure the Local Printer Attached to This Computer option button is selected.

6. If you want to have the wizard search for the printer, select the Automatically Detect and Install My Plug and Play Printer check box. If you prefer to identify your printer yourself, clear this check box.

7. Click the Next button. If you chose to have the wizard search, it does so. If not, the wizard displays the Select a Printer Port page (shown in Figure 13.3).

FIGURE 13.3

On the Select a Printer Port page of the Add Printer Wizard, select the port to which the printer is connected.

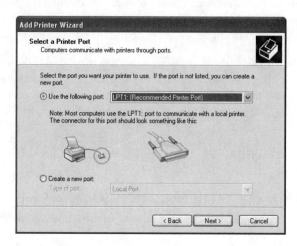

8. Make sure the Use the Following Port option button is selected, then select the port in the drop-down list. The default setting is LPT1, which is typically the port for the parallel port on your computer.

9. Click the Next button. The wizard displays the Install Printer Software page (shown in Figure 13.4).

FIGURE 13.4

On the Install Printer Software page of the Add Printer Wizard, specify the make and model of your printer or provide a driver from another location.

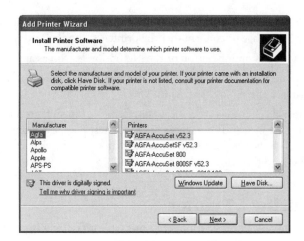

10. To use a driver that XP includes, select the printer's manufacturer in the Manufacturer list box. Then select the printer model in the Printers list box and go to step 12.

11. To provide a driver that you have (for example, on a CD or floppy), follow these steps:
    ◆ Click the Have Disk button. The wizard displays the Install from Disk dialog box.
    ◆ In the Copy Manufacturer's Files From text box, enter the path and filename of the driver file. You can type in this information, but usually it's easier to click the Browse button and use the resulting Locate File dialog box (a common Open dialog box) to select the file, then click the Open button. The wizard closes the Locate File dialog box and enters the path and filename in the text box in the Install from Disk dialog box.
    ◆ Click the OK button. The wizard closes the Install from Disk dialog box and displays the Install Printer Software page, which lists the printer for which the driver is designed.

12. Click the Next button. The wizard displays the Name Your Printer page.

13. In the Printer Name text box, adjust the default name that the wizard suggests for the printer. Keep the name relatively short, because some programs have problems with printer names that are longer than 31 characters including the server's name.

14. If this is the first printer you've installed, XP automatically makes it your default printer. If you've already installed another printer, XP includes the Do You Want to Use This Printer As the Default Printer? list on the Name Your Printer page. Select the Yes option button or the No option button as appropriate.

15. Click the Next button. The wizard displays the Printer Sharing page.

16. If you don't want to share the printer with other users via the network, leave the Do Not Share This Printer option button selected. If you do want to share the printer, select the Share Name option button and adjust the name that the wizard suggests for the printer in the text box.

NOTE *Other users of this computer will be able to use the printer even if you choose not to share the printer on the network.*

17. Click the Next button. The wizard displays the Print Test Page button, which invites you to print a test page to confirm that the printer is installed and working properly.

18. Select the Yes option button or the No option button as appropriate.

19. Click the Next button. The wizard displays the Completing the Add Printer Wizard page, which lists the choices you made.

20. Double-check the list of choices, and click the Finish button if you're satisfied. The wizard installs the printer. If you chose to print a test page, the wizard prints it. If the page prints okay, click the OK button to close the dialog box the wizard displays about the test page. The wizard then closes itself.

Configuring a Printer

This section discusses how to configure a printer—everything from setting a printer as your default to telling it what kind of separator pages to print.

Setting a Printer As Your Default

As you saw, the Add Printer Wizard makes the first printer you install on your computer your default printer and invites you to set each subsequent printer you install as the default printer instead of the incumbent. But you can also change the default printer at any time. To set a printer as your default, right-click it on the Printers and Faxes screen and choose Set As Default Printer from the context menu.

To set properties for a printer, display its Properties dialog box by taking either of the following actions:

♦ Right-click the printer on the Printers and Faxes screen and choose Properties from the context menu.

♦ Select the printer on the Printers and Faxes screen and click the Set Printer Properties link on the Tasks list.

The following sections discuss the standard options in the Properties dialog box for a printer. Depending on the type of printer you're using and the printer driver you installed for it, you may see other pages than these. For example, for a color printer you'll see a Color Management page, on which you can associate color profiles with the printer so that you get approximately the colors you want. For an inkjet printer, you may see a Utilities page or a Maintenance page that offers options such as Nozzle Check and Head Cleaning.

General Page Options

The General page of the Properties dialog box (shown on the left in Figure 13.5) for a printer contains the following options:

Printer Name text box   This text box contains the name you entered for the printer during setup or a default name that XP provided on the basis of the printer driver used. You can change the name by typing in the text box.

Location text box   In this text box, you can enter any location information about the printer. This information is more useful when you're sharing a printer on the network than when the printer is used only by your computer.

Comment text box   In this text box, you can enter further information about the printer. This information too is primarily useful when you're sharing the printer on the network, but you might also use it to note that the printer is loaded with a special type of paper.

Features list box   This list box provides information about the printer's capabilities, such as whether it can print in color, print double-sided, staple, and so on.

Printing Preferences button   Click this button to make XP display the Printing Preferences dialog box, on whose pages you can choose options for layout, paper selection, and print quality. Different settings are available for different printers. The settings are implemented through the printer driver, so updating the driver may make more settings available to you.

Print Test Page button   Click this button to print a test page to the printer to make sure it's handling text and graphics correctly.

FIGURE 13.5

The General page (left) and the Ports page (right) of the Properties dialog box for a printer

 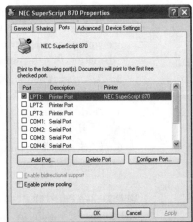

Sharing Page Options

The Sharing page of the Properties dialog box for a printer contains options for sharing the printer on the network. "Sharing a Printer" in Chapter 32 discusses how to use these options.

Ports Page Options

The Ports page of the Properties dialog box for a printer (shown on the right in Figure 13.5) contains options for creating, deleting, and configuring ports.

CREATING A PRINTER PORT

XP automatically provides you with three printer ports (LPT1 through LPT3) and four serial ports (COM1 through COM4), so normally you'll need to add a port only if your printer or other output device requires a specialized port setup or if you need to use a TCP/IP port.

To create a new port, install the device and take the following steps:

1. Click the Add Port button. XP displays the Printer Ports dialog box (shown in Figure 13.6).

FIGURE 13.6

Use the Printer Ports dialog box to create a new local port or TCP/IP port.

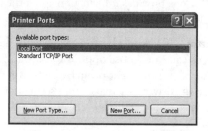

2. To create a new local port, select the Local Port item in the Available Port Types list box, then click the New Port Type button. XP displays the Installing Print Monitor dialog box, which you use to select the printer initialization file containing the port monitor installation information. XP then installs the port.

3. To create a new standard TCP/IP port for a network printer, select the Standard TCP/IP Port item in the Available Port Types list box, then click the New Port button. XP starts the Add Standard TCP/IP Printer Port Wizard, which walks you through the process of adding a TCP/IP port and then returns you to the Printer Ports dialog box.

4. Click the Close button. XP closes the Printer Ports dialog box, returning you to the Ports page of the Properties dialog box for the printer.

DELETING A PRINTER PORT

XP doesn't let you delete any of the system ports that come built in, but you can delete any custom ports that you create.

To delete a port, select it in the Print to the Following Ports list box and click the Delete Port button. XP displays the Delete Port dialog box. Click the Yes button.

CONFIGURING A PRINTER PORT

XP offers only one configuration setting for a parallel port: the number of seconds allowed to elapse before XP decides the printer has taken a hike. To set this timeout, follow these steps:

1. Select the port in the Print to the Following Ports list.

2. Click the Configure Port button. XP displays the Configure LPT Port dialog box (shown in Figure 13.7).

FIGURE 13.7

You can adjust the timeout interval for a parallel port in the Configure LPT Port dialog box.

FIGURE 13.7

You can adjust the timeout interval for a parallel port in the Configure LPT Port dialog box.

3. In the Transmission Retry text box, enter the number of seconds.

4. Click the OK button. XP closes the Configure LPT Port dialog box.

NOTE   *For TCP/IP port monitors, XP offers further configuration options.*

USING BIDIRECTIONAL SUPPORT

If the Enable Bidirectional Support check box is available, you can select it to allow the printer to send status information. For example, the printer can notify you that it's running out of ink or paper.

USING PRINTER POOLING

If you have two or more identical printers, you can *pool* them to create a single logical printer capable of twice the throughput. Set up the printers as usual, then select the Enable Printer Pooling check box for each printer. In the Print to the Following Ports list box, select the appropriate ports. You can then print to the printer pool, and XP will use the first printer that's available.

Advanced Page Options

The Advanced page of the Properties dialog box (shown on the left in Figure 13.8) for a printer contains a slew of options for everything from setting availability times for printers to adding separator pages between print jobs.

FIGURE 13.8

The Advanced page (left) and the Device Settings page (right) of the Properties dialog box for a printer

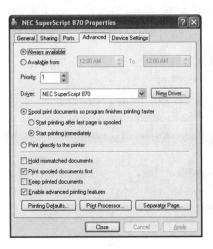

SETTING AVAILABILITY OPTIONS

By default, XP sets the printer to be always available, selecting the Always Available option button. This setting is useful for many home or office situations, but you may want to limit availability in some situations. For example, you might want to prevent people from printing at night if that might disturb the household.

To limit availability, select the Available From option button and use the two time text boxes to specify the range of time the printer should be available.

SETTING THE PRIORITY

To set the priority for the printer, adjust the setting in the Priority text box. You can set priorities from 1 (the lowest priority) to 99 (the highest priority). Each job printed by this printer entry gets the same priority, so there's no point in setting priorities unless you're using multiple printer entries.

CHANGING THE DRIVER

You can change the printer driver to another currently installed printer driver by using the Driver drop-down list. To install a new printer driver, click the New Driver button. XP starts the Add Printer Driver Wizard, which walks you through the process of installing the driver.

CHOOSING SPOOLING OPTIONS

As you'll remember from "How Does a Print Job Get Printed?" earlier in this chapter, the print driver saves information to the hard disk and from there sends it along to the printer. This process, spooling, lets you continue your work without having to wait while the program you're working in forces every byte of the print job down the cable to the printer.

By default, XP selects the Spool Print Documents so Program Finishes Printing Faster option button and its suboption, the Start Printing Immediately option button. If starting printing immediately seems to be causing problems, you can try selecting the Start Printing after Last Page Is Spooled option button to give the printer a chance to get its virtual paws on all the information it needs. If this doesn't help, you can cut out spooling by selecting the Print Directly to the Printer option button—but be warned that printing this way is very slow.

CHOOSING OTHER OPTIONS

The next four options defy easy grouping:

Hold Mismatched Documents check box Select this check box (which is cleared by default) if you want XP to make sure the spooled document matches the printer setup before sending the document to the printer. If the document doesn't match the printer setup, XP holds the document in the print queue.

Print Spooled Documents First check box Select this check box (which is cleared by default) if you want spooled documents to print before partially spooled documents that carry a higher priority. This setting improves printer efficiency but is relevant only if you use printer priorities.

Keep Printed Documents check box Select this check box (which is cleared by default) if you want to keep the spooled files on disk so that you can resend them to the printer from the print queue if necessary. Use this option only if you're having difficulty printing documents correctly—for example, if you're reconfiguring your printer and don't want to waste time and effort by resending the print job from the program. Obviously enough, the spooled files consume disk space.

Enable Advanced Printing Features check box Clear this check box (which is selected by default) if you want to disable advanced printing features (such as booklet printing) in order to troubleshoot printing problems.

SETTING PRINTING DEFAULTS

To set default properties for the printer, click the Printing Defaults button and choose options in the resulting Printing Defaults dialog box.

CHANGING THE PRINT PROCESSOR

To use a different print processor or a different data type, click the Print Processor button and choose settings in the resulting Print Processor dialog box. Don't mess with this setting unless you're sure what you're doing.

USING SEPARATOR PAGES

To make XP print a *separator page* between print jobs, click the Separator Page button. XP displays the Separator Page dialog box (shown in Figure 13.9). Use the Browse button and the resulting Separator Page dialog box (a common Open dialog box) to locate the separator page file, and then click the OK button. XP closes the Separator Page dialog box.

FIGURE 13.9

In the Separator Page dialog box, specify the separator page file to use.

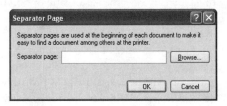

NOTE *XP includes several separator page files, which have the SEP extension. You can also create custom separator files of your own by using a text editor such as Notepad.*

Device Settings Page Options

The Device Settings page of the Properties dialog box (of which the right screen in Figure 13.8 shows an example) contains settings specific to your printer. For example, for many printers you can change the paper assigned to the paper trays or choose options for manual feed.

Color Management Page Options

If your printer supports color printing, its Properties dialog box should include a Color Management page, which offers options for controlling how colors are represented on the printer. Figure 13.10 shows a Color Management page.

FIGURE 13.10

On the Color Management page of the Properties dialog box for a printer, you can add a different color profile to the printer.

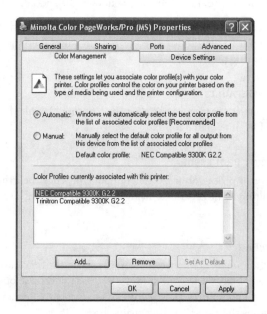

For everyday color printing, you can leave the Automatic option button selected, as it will be by default. But if you need to make sure that the colors you see on-screen match the colors used in output (as you might for professional graphics or art work), you may need to manually associate a color profile with the printer. XP comes with a number of color profiles, but you should also check with your printer manufacturer to see if they provide a custom color profile. If you do get a color profile, you can store it in any folder you want, but the easiest place is probably XP's default folder for color profiles, the %systemroot%\system32\spool\drivers\color\ folder.

To add a color profile, click the Add button on the Color Management page of the Properties dialog box. XP displays the Add Profile Association dialog box, which is a common Open dialog box in disguise. Navigate to and select the profile file, then click the Add button. XP closes the Add Profile Association dialog box and adds the profile to the Color Profiles Currently Associated with This Printer list box.

To apply a profile, select the Manual option button, then select the profile in the Color Profiles Currently Associated with This Printer list box and click the Apply button. (You can only have one active color profile at a time.) Click the Set As Default button if you want to make this profile your default profile.

If you're using a color profile for your printer, you'll probably want to use one for your monitor and scanner as well. To apply a color profile to a monitor, display the Display Properties dialog box by right-clicking the Desktop and choosing Properties from the context menu. Click the Advanced button on the Settings page to display the Properties dialog box for the monitor and graphics, click the Color Management tab to display the Color Management page, and follow the procedures described above for adding and applying a color profile.

Removing a Printer

To remove a printer, select it on the Printers and Faxes screen in Control Panel and click the Delete This Printer link in the Tasks list. XP displays a Printers dialog box asking if you're sure. Click the Yes button. XP closes the Printers dialog box and removes the printer, but it leaves the printer driver on your computer so that you can create the printer again easily if you need to.

Printing a Document

The conventional way of printing a document is by issuing a Print command from the program that created it or from a program designed to handle its file type, choosing any relevant options (which pages to print, or the resolution to use) in the Print dialog box, and then clicking the Print button or OK button. But XP also lets you print directly to the printer from Explorer if you so choose.

You can print a document from Explorer by dragging it and dropping it on the printer in the Printers and Faxes folder (or on a shortcut to the printer). XP prints the document with default settings, so you don't get to choose any of the usual printing options. But usually you won't have the printer (or a shortcut to it) handy enough for this technique to be useful—though of course you can create shortcuts to a printer wherever you need them, such as on the Desktop. For this technique to work, the file must include the extension linked to the appropriate file type and program; otherwise, XP doesn't know which program to use to print the file.

Many programs support printing directly from Explorer and so include a Print command on the context menu for the document. To print a document, right-click it and choose Print from the context menu.

EXPERT KNOWLEDGE: PRINTING FROM DOS PROGRAMS

If you still use DOS programs for anything vital, you'll probably still need to print from them. Printing from a DOS program can be tricky for a couple of reasons.

First, DOS programs mostly come from a simpler time when the printer was almost always connected to the first line printer port, LPT1. As a result, many DOS programs print to LPT1 unless you actively tell them to do otherwise. If your printer is attached to LPT1, of course, this assumption shouldn't cause problems, but if the printer is attached to a different port or is on the network, you won't get a printout.

To work around this problem, open a Command Prompt window and use the net use command to redirect the print output to the appropriate port:

```
net use lpt1: \\servername\printername
```

The second consideration is that DOS programs probably won't be able to tell which printer is set as the default in XP, so you'll usually need to tell them explicitly which printer to use. Telling a printer this usually involves custom settings.

Printing to a Printer on the Internet

XP includes support for printing to printers shared on the Internet. See the section "Printing across the Internet with IPP" in Chapter 32 for a discussion of how to use this feature.

Managing Your Print Jobs

Once you've sent a document to the printer, you can just wait for XP to print it. If you're the only person using this printer, and if there's no problem, it should print more or less right away. But if you're printing many documents, or if you're sharing one or more printers with people who are printing many documents, you may find yourself needing to manage print jobs. This section discusses how to do so.

Pausing and Resuming Printing

To pause printing of all documents on the printer, right-click the printer on the Printers and Faxes screen in Control Panel and choose Pause Printing from the context menu. Alternatively, select the printer and click the Pause Printing link in the Tasks list.

To resume printing, right-click the printer and choose Resume Printing from the context menu. Alternatively, select the printer and click the Resume Printing link in the Tasks list.

NOTE   *On a network printer, you have only the privileges of a Guest user on that computer. This means that you can pause, restart, and delete only your own print jobs: You can't affect other people's print jobs.*

Canceling Printing of All Documents on the Printer

To cancel printing of all documents on the printer, right-click it on the Printers and Faxes screen and choose Cancel All Documents from the context menu. XP displays a confirmation dialog box. Select the Yes button.

WARNING   *It's much easier, neater, and cleaner to cancel a job before it starts printing than after it starts printing—but often you'll only realize that you need to cancel a particular print job when the printer starts spewing out garbage—sheets of paper with only a single column of letters, or with mangled graphics, or page after page of PostScript codes instead of the layout of ink they're supposed to represent. When you cancel a print job that's being printed, the printer may get confused. Give it a minute or two (depending on the printer's speed) to clear its memory of the interrupted job. If that doesn't work, you may need to reset the printer, either by using a hardware reset button, a software reset command supported by the printer's custom software, or by powering the printer off and then back on again.*

Managing Print Jobs by Using the Print Queue

Pausing or canceling all print jobs in the queue is quick and effective. But often you'll want to pause or cancel only some of the print jobs. Other times, you'll want to rearrange the order of the print jobs so that important ones print first.

To manage print jobs, open the print queue by using one of the following methods:

◆ If the notification area is displaying a printer icon, double-click it.

◆ Double-click the printer on the Printers and Faxes screen in Control Panel, or select the printer and click the See What's Printing link in the Tasks list.

Figure 13.11 shows an example of the print queue for a printer.

FIGURE 13.11

Use the print queue to see what's printing, to cancel a print job, or to manage print jobs.

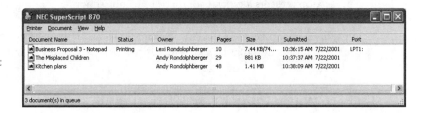

From the print queue, you can take the following actions:

Cancel a print job Right-click the job in the print queue and choose Cancel from the context menu. Alternatively, choose Document ➤ Cancel.

Pause a print job Right-click the job in the print queue and choose Pause from the context menu. Alternatively, choose Document ➤ Pause.

Resume a paused print job Right-click the paused job in the print queue and choose Resume from the context menu. Alternatively, choose Document ➤ Resume.

Restart a paused or failed print job Right-click the paused or failed job in the print queue and choose Restart from the context menu. Alternatively, choose Document ➤ Restart.

Change priorities or time restrictions for a print job Right-click the job and choose Properties from the context menu. XP displays the Document Properties dialog box for the print job. On the General page (shown in Figure 13.12), drag the Priority slider to set the priority for the job, or use the controls in the Schedule text box to set or remove time scheduling. Click the OK button. XP closes the Document Properties dialog box.

FIGURE 13.12

On the General page of the Document Properties dialog box for a print job, you can change the priority and schedule for the print job.

Troubleshooting Printing Problems

This section presents a general approach to troubleshooting printing problems. Given that there are about as many types of printers as there are types of cars, and that the drivers for those printers vary in quality even more widely than the drivers you'll encounter in a trip the length of I-40, the information in this section is just a start—but if you persevere, you should find it can help you solve many problems.

Check Which Printer You're Printing To

(This is almost too obvious to mention—but only almost.)

If your computer is configured to connect to more than one printer, make sure that you're printing to the printer you think you're printing to. Few things are more forehead-slappingly irritating than wasting time troubleshooting an innocent and fully functional printer only to find that you've printed out five copies of the same crucial and secret document on another printer (and that other people have been reading those copies while you've been reading your suspect its rights).

Given that the Print dialog box shows you which printer you're using, this problem is most likely to occur when you issue a Print command that starts the print job without displaying the Print dialog box.

Make Sure the Printer Is Working

Next, make sure the printer is working. Check that it's:

◆ Powered on.

◆ Not set to be offline or paused.

◆ Loaded with ink and paper, and not jammed.

◆ Connected to the computer, print server, or network. If another printer or a print server is involved, check that it's powered on and functional.

Check the Program You're Printing From

If all is well with the printer, make sure you're not doing something wrong in the program from which you're trying to print. In particular, check that you're trying to print the right part of the document. For example, in a spreadsheet, make sure you haven't defined a print area that has the wrong contents. In a multipage document, check that you're trying to print the right pages.

Running the Printing Troubleshooter

If the previous approach doesn't lead you to fix the problem, you can run XP's Printing Troubleshooter and have it walk you through the steps of troubleshooting the problem. From Help and Support Center, click the Printing and Faxing link (which should be on the Help and Support Center home page, unless your OEM has removed it for some inexplicable reason), then click the Fixing a Printing Problem link.

Configuring Your Print Server

Apart from the printer, which you saw how to configure earlier in this chapter, you can also configure your print server—the software that controls the printers attached to your computer. In most cases, the default print server settings work fine, but you can improve your computer's performance and your printing experience of your print server's clients by setting the appropriate options. In particular, you may want to move the print server spool folder to a different location than its default location.

To set print server properties, display the Printers and Faxes folder and choose File ➤ Server Properties. XP displays the Print Server Properties dialog box, which contains four pages: Forms, Ports, Drivers, and Advanced. Figure 13.13 shows the Forms page (on the left) and the Ports page (on the right) of the Print Server Properties dialog box for a relatively typical print server.

FIGURE 13.13

The Forms page and the Ports page of the Print Server Properties dialog box

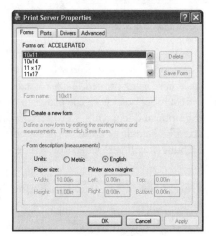 

On the Forms page, you can create a new form based on a current form by selecting the base form in the Forms On list box and selecting the Create a New Form check box, then working with the fields in the Form Description group box and clicking the Save Form button. You can delete forms you've added, but not the preset forms.

On the Ports page, you can add new ports, configure existing ports, and delete ports you've tired of. The port configuration options available depend on the type of port involved—printer port, serial port, COM port, print server port, and so on.

Figure 13.14 shows the Drivers page (on the left) and the Advanced page (on the right) of the Print Server Properties dialog box for the same print server.

On the Drivers page, you can add new drivers, check the properties of existing drivers, replace existing drivers, or delete existing drivers. But as you can see in the figure, the Advanced page is where most of the action is. These are the options you can set on the Advanced page.

FIGURE 13.14

The Drivers page and the Advanced page of the Print Server Properties dialog box

Spool Folder text box The spool folder is a folder on your hard drive in which XP stores the spool files for print jobs as they're being printed. As discussed earlier in this chapter, XP spools the data so that it can return control more quickly to the program that sent the print job. Spool files can be large, particularly for graphical documents, so you may want to move the spool folder to a drive that has plenty of space. The default location for the spool folder is on the partition that contains the XP system files, but XP will perform better if you move the spool folder to a different partition.

Log Spooler Error Events check box Controls whether XP writes printer error events to the System log. Selected by default.

Log Spooler Warning Events check box Controls whether XP writes printer warning events to the System log. Selected by default.

Log Spooler Information Events check box Controls whether XP writes printer information events to the System log. Cleared by default.

Beep on Errors of Remote Documents check box Controls whether XP makes the print server beep when an error occurs when printing a document from another computer. Cleared by default.

Show Informational Notifications for Local Printers check box Controls whether XP displays notification-area information pop-ups when the computer is printing to a local printer or a stand-alone network printer. Cleared by default.

Show Informational Notifications for Network Printers check box Controls whether XP displays notification-area information pop-ups when the computer is printing to a printer attached to another computer. Selected by default.

Notify when Remote Documents Are Printed check box Controls whether XP sends the user a notification when a document has printed. Cleared by default.

Notify Computer, Not User, when Remote Documents Are Printed check box Controls whether XP sends the computer from which the job was sent a notification when a document has printed. This check box is available only when the Notify when Remote Documents Are Printed check box is selected. Cleared by default.

Printing Offline

If you're working offline, or if you want to queue up a number of print jobs and let them all rip at once, put the printer offline. To do so, right-click the printer on the Printers and Faxes screen and choose Use Printer Offline from the context menu. You can then print to the printer as if your computer were connected to it, but instead of sending the data to the printer, XP holds it in the print queue and saves it to disk.

When you've reconnected to the printer (or when you want to print, if you didn't disconnect), right-click the printer on the Printers and Faxes screen and choose Use Printer Online. XP starts sending the print jobs to the printer. The printer must be a local printer—you can't print offline to a network printer.

Creating Multiple Entries for the Same Printer

If you want to use the same printer regularly in different ways, you can create two or more entries for it on the Printers and Faxes screen and set different properties for each. For example, you might set one printer entry to have a higher priority than the other, and then use that printer entry yourself while assigning the lower-priority printer entry to other users.

To create a new entry for the printer, install it again using the technique described earlier in this chapter. When you install the printer again like this, the Add Printer Wizard displays the Use Existing Driver page, which offers you a Keep Existing Driver option button and a Replace Existing Driver option button. Given that the driver is the same, leave the Keep Existing Driver option button selected and click the Next button.

On the Name Your Printer page, assign the printer a name that reflects the role you plan for it. For example, if you create a new entry for a printer so that you can use it to print to a file, include that information in the printer's name (and perhaps add it to the printer's Location and Comment fields as well).

After installing the printer, set properties for it to play the role you intend.

Printing to a File

Sometimes you may want to print a document to a file that you can send to someone else for printing or (less commonly) that you can use in another program. For example, if you need to have a document printed on a high-resolution device in your local print shop, you can print the document to a file, put the file on a portable medium, and take it along to the print shop. That way, the print shop doesn't need to have a copy of the program that created the document, the way it would need one if you just copied the document onto a removable disk or recordable CD and took that along to the print shop instead.

You can print to a file in either of two ways: by selecting the Print to File check box in the Print dialog box from a program, or by configuring the printer to always print to a file. The former technique is useful for printing to a file occasionally. The latter technique is useful for always printing to a file with a particular printer entry.

TIP   *If you often need to print to a file, or if you need to make read-only versions of documents and retain their layout, consider buying Adobe Acrobat. Acrobat produces documents in Portable Document Format (PDF), which you can view on most computer operating systems using the free Acrobat Reader, which is available from the Adobe website (*www.adobe.com*). Acrobat is more expensive than printing to a file, but in many cases it produces better results with service bureaus than simply printing to a file.*

Printing to a File from the Print Dialog Box

To print to a file from the Print dialog box, follow these steps:

1. Issue a regular Print command as usual. (For example, choose File ➤ Print or press Ctrl+P.) XP displays the Print dialog box.
2. Select the Print to File check box.
3. Choose any other appropriate printing options as usual for the program.
4. Click the OK button or the Print button, depending on the program. XP displays the Print to File dialog box (shown in Figure 13.15).

FIGURE 13.15

In the Print to File dialog box, enter the filename (and, if necessary, the path) for the print file.

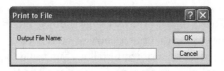

5. Enter the filename for the print file. If you want to specify the folder in which the print file is saved, enter the path to the folder before the filename. Otherwise, XP saves the print file in the program's current folder.
6. Click the OK button. XP closes the Print to File dialog box and the Print dialog box and prints the document to the file. XP gives the file the PRN extension.

Setting a Printer to Always Print to a File

You can also set up a printer so that it prints to a file every time and doesn't let the user print to a physical printer. This capability is useful when you always need to create print files on a particular printer and don't want to risk actually printing a document by forgetting to select the Print to File check box in the Print dialog box, or if the printer in question is never available from your computer.

To make a printer always print to a file, select the FILE port in the Print to the Following Ports list box on the Ports page of the Properties dialog box for the printer. XP clears any other port selected for the printer (unless you've selected the Enable Printer Pooling check box). When you click the OK button and XP closes the Properties dialog box, XP displays a disk on the printer icon to indicate that the printer is set up for printing to a file (shown in Figure 13.16).

FIGURE 13.16

A disk on the printer icon means that
the printer is set up for printing to a file.

NEC SuperScript - FILE
0
Ready

Working with Fonts

XP comes with a number of fonts that you can use to enhance your XP display and your documents.
You can add extra fonts as you need them, either by installing software that includes fonts (such as
Corel WordPerfect Office or Microsoft Office) or by installing fonts directly.

A *font* is the name given to a typeface. A *typeface* is a set of characters. Normally, the characters in a
typeface have similar characteristics, so that they look as though they belong together, but this isn't
an absolute requirement.

Three Categories of Fonts

XP supports three different categories of fonts:

Outline fonts   *Outline fonts* are the newest types of fonts. XP renders outline fonts by using line
and curve commands, which means that it can scale them to any size without distorting them and
can rotate them. XP supports three different types of outline fonts: TrueType fonts (which
Windows has used for many years), OpenType fonts (a more recent extension of TrueType),
and Type 1 fonts (which are created by Adobe Systems for use with PostScript printers and
devices). Outline fonts use the TTF extension.

Vector fonts   *Vector fonts* are an older type of font that are included in XP for backward compatibility. Vector fonts are rendered from a mathematical model and are mostly used with plotters. XP
includes three vector fonts: Modern, Roman, and Script. Vector fonts use the FON extension.

Raster fonts   *Raster fonts* are another older technology that XP includes for backward compatibility. In a raster font, each character consists of a bitmap image that's displayed on the screen or
printed on paper. XP includes five raster fonts: Courier, MS Sans Serif, MS Serif, Small, and
Symbol. Like vector fonts, raster fonts use the FON extension.

Displaying the Fonts Window

To work with fonts, display the Fonts window by taking the following steps:

1. Choose Start ➤ Control Panel. XP displays Control Panel.
2. Click the Appearance and Themes link. XP displays the Appearance and Themes screen.
3. In the See Also list, click the Fonts link. XP displays the Fonts window.

Viewing the List of Fonts

By default, XP displays the Fonts window in Large Icons view. You can switch the window to List
view by choosing View ➤ List or clicking the List button on the toolbar, or to Details view by
choosing View ➤ Details or clicking the Details button on the toolbar.

The Fonts window also offers a List Fonts by Similarity view, which you can invoke by choosing View ➤ List Fonts by Similarity or clicking the Similarity button on the toolbar. Figure 13.17 shows an example of List Fonts by Similarity view. In the List Fonts by Similarity To drop-down list, select the font you're interested in. The Fonts window then lists the other fonts installed on the computer in descending order of similarity to that font, using terms such as Very Similar, Fairly Similar, and Not Similar. (You can click the Similarity To column heading to display the list in ascending order of similarity.)

FIGURE 13.17

Use the Fonts window's List Fonts by Similarity view to see which fonts are similar to a specified font.

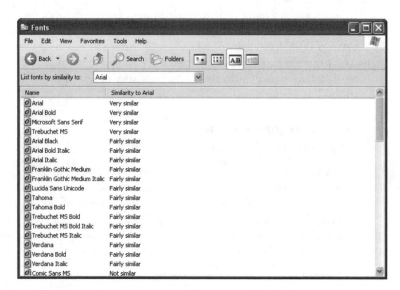

List Fonts by Similarity view is useful for getting an idea of which font is likely to complement another font. To simplify a long list of fonts, you can choose View ➤ Hide Variations. This command tells XP to hide bold and italic variations on a font. So instead of seeing Times New Roman, Times New Roman Bold, Times New Roman Bold Italic, and Times New Roman Italic, you see only Times New Roman. This option makes it easier to get an overview of the different fonts you have available.

To display the full list of fonts once more, choose View ➤ Hide Variations again.

EXPERT KNOWLEDGE: AVOIDING RASTER FONTS AND VECTOR FONTS

If you want to make sure you don't use raster fonts and vector fonts in your documents, you can tell XP to stop showing them to you. Take the following steps:

1. In the Fonts window, choose Tools ➤ Folder Options. XP displays the Folder Options dialog box.

2. Click the TrueType Fonts tab. XP displays the TrueType Fonts page.

3. Select the Show Only TrueType Fonts in the Programs on My Computer check box.

Continued on next page

4. Click the OK button. XP displays the System Settings Change dialog box, telling you that you must restart your computer in order to implement the system change.

5. Click the Yes button if you want XP to restart your computer for you. If not, click the No button to dismiss the System Settings Change dialog box, then restart the computer at your convenience.

Viewing and Printing a Font

To get an idea of what a font looks like, double-click its entry in the Fonts window. XP displays the font in Font Viewer, which shows information on the font type, its file size, and copyright information, together with various sizes of the canonical sentence involving the quick brown fox and the lazy dog and the full set of numbers.

To print the information displayed, click the Print button. XP displays the Print dialog box. Choose the printer and any options, then click the Print button. XP closes the Print dialog box and prints the information.

To close Font Viewer, click the Done button.

Installing a Font

To install a font, take the following steps from the Fonts window:

1. Choose File ➢ Install New Font. XP displays the Add Fonts dialog box (shown in Figure 13.18 with a font selected for installation).

FIGURE 13.18

Use the Add Fonts dialog box to add further fonts to your computer.

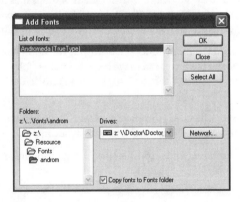

2. Use the Drives drop-down list and the Folders list box to navigate to the drive and folder that contain the font you want to install. (If necessary, click the Network button and use the Map Network Drive dialog box to map a network drive.)

3. In the List of Fonts list box, select the font or fonts you want to install.

◆ Click the Select All button to select all the fonts in the List of Fonts list box.

4. Make sure that the Copy Fonts to Fonts Folder check box at the bottom of the Add Fonts dialog box is selected. This option causes XP to copy the fonts you're installing to the Fonts folder, where you can manage them centrally. This is usually the best way to install fonts, especially when you're installing them from a removable medium (such as a CD). But if the fonts you're installing are already located on your hard drive, and you don't want to make copies of them in the Fonts folder, you can clear this check box. XP then creates a pointer to the folder that contains the font.

5. Click the OK button. XP installs the font or fonts and closes the Add Fonts dialog box, returning you to the Fonts window.

TIP   You can buy commercial font packages from most major software outlets and from many smaller vendors. But first, go to Microsoft's website (www.microsoft.com) and see if Microsoft is offering any fonts for free download. Then check out the free fonts that are available from a number of sites online: You may find a wide enough selection that you don't need to buy any fonts.

Deleting a Font

To delete a font, right-click it in the Fonts window and choose Delete from the context menu. (Alternatively, select the font and press the Delete key or choose File ➢ Delete.) XP displays the Windows Fonts Folder dialog box to confirm the deletion. Click the Yes button. XP closes the Windows Fonts Folder dialog box and deletes the font.

EXPERT KNOWLEDGE: UNLOADING FONTS INSTEAD OF DELETING THEM

If you load your Fonts folder to the gunwales with hundreds or thousands of fonts, don't be surprised if XP handles like a supertanker rather than a speedboat. Loading a huge number of fonts increases the amount of memory XP needs and generally slows down the speed with which it can handle other tasks.

So it's a good idea not to load too many fonts at a time. But you don't have to delete fonts that you temporarily don't want to load. Instead, you can move them to another folder and store them there until you need them again. At that point, move the fonts back to the Fonts folder, and you can use them again in your programs.

If you work with many fonts, consider grouping them into a number of different folders so that you can quickly load the set of fonts you need for a particular type of document.

If you work with a huge number of fonts, consider getting a font-management solution such as Extensis Suitcase (www.extensis.com).

Up Next

This chapter has discussed how to install, configure, and manage printers and fonts.

The next chapter discusses how to manage hardware and power, including how to install, update, and roll back device drivers.

Chapter 14

Managing Hardware, Drivers, and Power

THIS CHAPTER DISCUSSES HOW to install hardware on your computer and how to install, update, and roll back device drivers, the software that makes hardware function. It also covers how to configure power management on your computer and how to install an uninterruptible power supply.

XP greatly simplifies the software end of the process of adding hardware. If the hardware is hot pluggable, XP locates and loads the correct driver automatically. If the hardware is conventional, you use the Found New Hardware Wizard (if XP finds the hardware) or the Add Hardware Wizard (if you have to tell XP that the hardware is there) to install the software for the device. The chapter shows you how to use these wizards and notes special considerations for installing common types of hardware.

NOTE *Chapter 13 discusses how to install, configure, and manage printers. Chapter 27 discusses how to install, configure, and use scanners and digital cameras. Chapter 29 discusses how to install, configure, and use games controllers.*

This chapter covers the following topics:

◆ What hardware can you use with XP?

◆ Using hot-pluggable devices

◆ Using the Found New Hardware Wizard and Add Hardware Wizard

◆ Working with hardware devices

◆ Disabling and uninstalling a device

◆ Adding specific hardware items

◆ Configuring power management and installing a UPS

What Hardware Can You Use with XP?

One of Microsoft's goals in designing XP was to make it capable of picking up the hardware compatibility mantle of Windows 98 and Windows Me, each of which supported an impressive range of hardware both (relatively) ancient and modern. As a result, XP supports a very full range of hardware right out of the box, and it includes compatibility-tested drivers for many products. (A *driver* is a piece of software that enables a hardware device and XP to communicate with each other.)

By using the Windows Update feature to keep your copy of XP up-to-date, and by downloading new drivers from hardware manufacturers' websites as necessary, you can also add the latest hardware to XP. The devices you're more likely to have problems with are legacy devices more than a few years old, particularly those from smaller companies or from companies that have gone out of business.

To check whether a hardware item is compatible with XP, open Help and Support Center (Start ➤ Help and Support), click the Compatible Hardware and Software link on the Home page, and use the search options on the Compatible Hardware and Software page.

Using Hot-Pluggable Devices

Hardware devices that use USB, FireWire, and PC Card (PCMCIA) connections are *hot pluggable*—you can plug in and unplug the device while XP is running without any adverse effects. XP automatically loads and unloads drivers for hot-pluggable devices as needed.

NOTE   *Limited users and Guest users can install hot-pluggable devices. In most cases, only Computer Administrator users can install devices that are not hot pluggable.*

Installing a Hot-Pluggable Device

When you plug in a hot-pluggable device for the first time, XP displays a pop-up from the notification area to let you know that it has noticed the device. Figure 14.1 shows an example.

FIGURE 14.1

XP displays a notification-area pop-up message when it notices you've plugged in a hot-pluggable device.

XP then automatically looks for a driver to let XP and the device communicate with each other. It first checks in its capacious driver cache, which contains a wide variety of preinstalled drivers. If it draws a blank there, and if your computer is connected to the Internet, it checks the Windows Update site for a driver for the device; if it finds a driver, it downloads it and installs it. If XP is able to find a suitable driver in either the driver cache or Windows Update, it unpacks and installs the driver, displaying a pop-up identifying the device as it does so. Figure 14.2 shows an example of such a pop-up.

FIGURE 14.2

If XP can find a driver for the hot-pluggable device, it loads it.

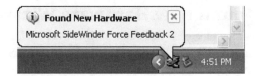

When the driver is installed and working, XP displays a pop-up telling you that the hardware is ready to use. Figure 14.3 shows an example of such a pop-up.

FIGURE 14.3

XP lets you know when the device is ready to use.

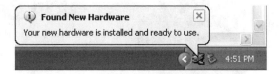

If XP can't find a driver for the device, it starts the Found New Hardware Wizard, so that you can supply the driver for the device manually. See "Using the Found New Hardware Wizard" later in this chapter for a walkthrough of using the Found New Hardware Wizard.

Removing a Hot-Pluggable Device

How you remove a hot-pluggable device depends on the type of device it is. If XP is displaying the Safely Remove Hardware icon (a gray PC Card with a green arrow above it) in the notification area, click this icon (you may have to right-click) and see if the resulting context menu displays an item for the device you're about to remove. PC Card devices always use the Safely Remove Hardware feature. Devices such as FireWire drives and USB memory-card readers typically have entries on the Safely Remove Hardware menu because Windows mounts them as drives, while items such as web cams and USB modems typically don't have entries. But check for an entry before removing a device.

If there *is* an item for the device on the Safely Remove Hardware menu, it'll read `Safely remove device`, where `device` is the name by which XP knows the device (for example, `Safely remove USB Mass Storage Device - Drive(E:)`). Click this item and wait until XP displays a pop-up telling you that it's safe to remove the device.

If there's no entry for the device on the Safely Remove Hardware menu, or if the Safely Remove Hardware icon isn't displayed in the notification area (make sure that it's really not there and that it's not just temporarily hidden), you don't need to use the Safely Remove Hardware feature to remove the device. Simply unplug it. XP notices that you've removed the device and unloads its driver.

Plugging a Hot-Pluggable Device In Again

When you plug a hot-pluggable device in again, XP notices it and loads the driver without displaying any pop-up—in theory, anyway. In practice, XP doesn't remember some hot-pluggable devices and decides to install them again. For example, I have an Intel Pocket Concert audio player that XP discovered and reinstalled each of the first five times I connected it to its USB cable.

Using the Found New Hardware Wizard

For devices that aren't hot pluggable, or for hot-pluggable devices for which XP can't find a suitable driver, you use XP's two hardware wizards, the Found New Hardware Wizard and the Add Hardware Wizard.

When XP discovers some hardware new to it (or that XP thinks it doesn't know about), it starts the Found New Hardware Wizard. Figure 14.4 shows the first page of the Found New Hardware Wizard.

As you can see in the figure, the wizard lists the type of hardware it has found—in this case, Multimedia Controller. If the wizard can't identify the type of hardware, it displays *Unknown device*.

FIGURE 14.4

XP displays the first page of the Found New Hardware Wizard when it discovers new hardware. Choose whether to install the software for the hardware automatically or specify the details of the software you want to install.

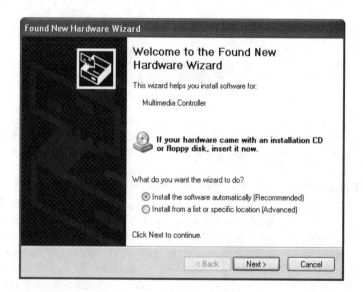

The What Do You Want the Wizard to Do? list gives you two options:

Install the Software Automatically option button   Select this option button (which is usually selected by default) if you want the wizard to try to install the software needed for the hardware. This is usually a good option: The wizard often manages to set up the hardware, and if it doesn't, you can easily return to this stage and try the second option. Click the Next button. The wizard searches for the software and installs it automatically.

Install from a List or Specific Location option button   Select this option button if you want to specify a particular driver for the hardware. Then follow the procedure described in the next section.

If the Found New Hardware Wizard *doesn't* find the software it needs, it displays the Cannot Install This Hardware page. At this point, you have three choices:

◆   If you want to give up on installing the software for this hardware completely (or at least for the foreseeable future), make sure the Don't Prompt Me Again to Install This Software check box is selected. Then click the Finish button. The wizard closes itself and makes a note not to find this piece of hardware again. Doing so makes it harder to install the device afterward—but you *can* do so, as discussed later in this chapter.

◆ If you want to give up on installing the software for the time being, clear the Don't Prompt Me Again to Install This Software check box. Then click the Finish button. Each time you restart XP (or run the Add Hardware Wizard), the Found New Hardware Wizard will offer to install the hardware. These offers get old fast, but you may sometimes want to leave the installation of hardware for a day or two while you dig out the driver disk, download a new driver manually, or run Windows Update to see if it can find a driver.

◆ To try to identify the necessary software yourself, click the Back button to return to the start of the wizard. Then follow the steps below.

Installing a Driver from a Specific Location

To install a driver from a specific location, take the following steps:

1. On the first page of the Found New Hardware Wizard, select the Install from a List or Specific Location option button.

2. Click the Next button. The Found New Hardware Wizard displays the Please Choose Your Search and Installation Options page (shown in Figure 14.5).

FIGURE 14.5

On the Please Choose Your Search and Installation Options page of the Found New Hardware Wizard, choose whether to search for a driver or specify a particular one.

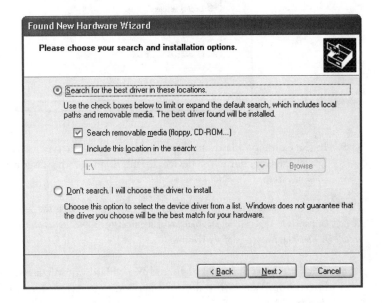

3. Choose whether to let the wizard search for a driver or to specify a specific driver:

◆ To let the wizard search, leave the Search for the Best Driver in These Locations option button selected. Then select the Search Removable Media (Floppy, CD-ROM) check box if you want the wizard to search your floppy and CD-ROM drives. (Insert a floppy or CD at this point if appropriate.) Alternatively, or additionally, select the Include This Location in the Search check box and use the text box, drop-down list, or Browse button to specify the location to search.

◆ To specify a driver yourself, select the Don't Search. I Will Choose the Driver to Install option button.

4. Click the Next button.

   ◆ If you chose to search for a driver, the wizard searches for one, installs it (if it finds one), and displays the Completing the Found New Hardware Wizard page.

   ◆ If you chose to specify a driver, the wizard displays the Hardware Type page (shown in Figure 14.6).

FIGURE 14.6

On the Hardware Type page of the Found New Hardware Wizard, choose the type of hardware you're installing.

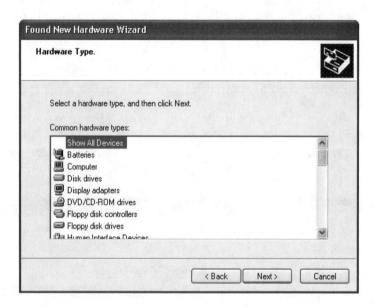

5. In the Common Hardware Types list box, select the type of hardware you're installing. The list is extensive, but if the device doesn't fit any of the descriptions, select the Show All Devices item.

TIP *If you're installing a driver from a floppy or a CD, it's not crucial that you get the hardware type right. The function of this page is to display the appropriate list of manufacturers and devices on the Select the Device Driver You Want to Install for This Hardware page of the Wizard.*

6. Click the Next button. The Found New Hardware Wizard displays the Select the Device Driver You Want to Install for This Hardware page. Figure 14.7 shows this page with all devices shown.

7. If XP has a driver for the device, you can select it by selecting the manufacturer in the Manufacturer list box and the device in the Model list box. But usually the Found New Hardware Wizard will have identified the driver if XP has it already, so you'll be visiting this page of the wizard only if you need to install a driver that XP *doesn't* have. Click the Have Disk button. XP displays the Install from Disk dialog box.

8. If you have the driver on a floppy or a CD, insert it in the appropriate drive and select the drive in the Copy Manufacturer's Files From drop-down list. If you have the driver on a

local drive or network drive, click the Browse button, use the resulting Locate File dialog box (a common Open dialog box) to locate the driver file, and click the Open button to enter its name and path in the Copy Manufacturer's Files From text box.

FIGURE 14.7

On the Select the Device Driver You Want to Install for This Hardware page, select the manufacturer and device, or use the Have Disk button to identify the driver by its file.

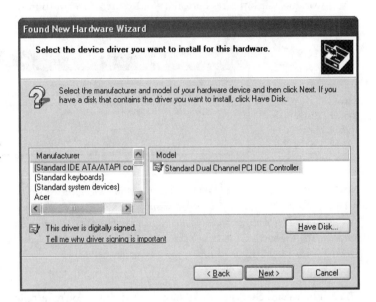

9. Click the OK button. The wizard displays the Select the Device Driver You Want to Install for This Hardware page (shown in Figure 14.8) with the name of the hardware model or models identified by the driver.

FIGURE 14.8

When you specify the driver to use, the wizard displays the Select the Device Driver You Want to Install for This Hardware page.

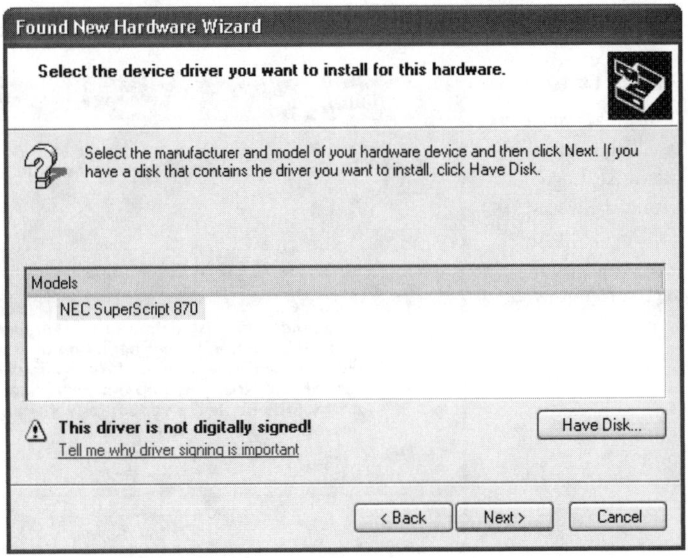

10. Select the driver and click the Next button. If XP doesn't think the driver is correct for the device, it displays the Update Driver Warning dialog box (shown in Figure 14.9), warning you that the hardware may not work and that your computer might become unstable or stop working. Click the Yes button if you're sure you want to install this driver. Otherwise, click the No button and select another driver.

FIGURE 14.9

The Update Driver Warning dialog box warns you if you've chosen a driver that appears not to match your device.

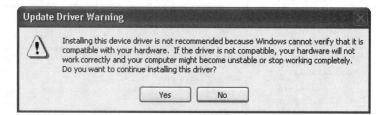

NOTE *If the wizard can't find hardware information in the location you specified, it displays the Select Device message box telling you that the location you specified doesn't contain information about your hardware. The wizard then displays the Install from Disk dialog box again so that you can specify a different location for the file. If you get to this stage, you're probably stuck. You can click the Cancel button to close the Install from Disk dialog box and return to the Select the Device Driver You Want to Install for This Hardware page so that you can select a built-in driver, but that's about it. Click the Cancel button to cancel the wizard.*

11. The wizard checks to make sure that the driver you're installing has passed the Windows Logo testing to verify its compatibility with XP. (See the next Note for an explanation of Windows Logo testing.) If the driver has passed Windows Logo testing, all is well; if it hasn't passed, the wizard displays the Hardware Installation dialog box (shown in Figure 14.10) warning you of the problem and strongly discouraging you from installing the driver. If you're sure the driver is okay, click the Continue Anyway button. If you have any doubts about the driver, click the STOP Installation button.

FIGURE 14.10

If the driver you're installing hasn't passed XP Logo testing, the wizard displays the Hardware Installation dialog box to warn you.

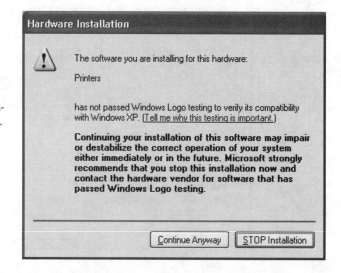

NOTE *Windows Logo testing isn't testing a logo, as its name implies, but rather a Windows compatibility test. When a product passes the test, the manufacturer is allowed to display the Designed for Microsoft Windows logos on the product. Drivers that pass Windows Logo testing are digitally signed by Microsoft to verify their compatibility. The wizard checks for the digital signature and raises Cain if it's not there. Some hardware companies don't bother with Windows Logo testing, so there's a fair chance that you may need to install a driver that isn't certified as compatible with XP. Before you do so, closely read the documentation (for example, the README file) supplied with the hardware so that you can judge whether you want to proceed. (This boils down to the question of whether you trust the hardware company involved.)*

12. If XP finds no problem with the driver, it installs it and displays the Completing the Found New Hardware Wizard page.

13. Click the Finish button. The wizard closes itself, and the hardware is ready for use.

If the Found New Hardware Wizard is unable to install the device, it displays the Cannot Install This Hardware page telling you what the problem was. Figure 14.11 shows an example in which the driver file ("the third-party INF"—*inf* is short for *initialization file*) didn't contain digital signature information.

FIGURE 14.11

The Found New Hardware Wizard displays the Cannot Install This Hardware page if it runs into a problem installing the device.

NOTE *Help and Support Center contains a system for referring searches for drivers that don't come with XP or with the hardware device. When you plug in a new hardware device, and XP finds that it doesn't have a driver for it and you can't supply a driver, XP invites you to send information about the hardware to Microsoft. Once you've sent the information, you can take a variety of actions depending on what information is available. For example, you might be able to view a list of compatible devices (if any), search for information on compatible devices or Knowledge Base articles about the hardware, or find a link to the vendor's website.*

Running the Add Hardware Wizard

If XP doesn't find the new hardware you install, run the Add Hardware Wizard so that you can add the hardware manually. As you'll see, there's considerable overlap between the Add Hardware Wizard and the Found New Hardware Wizard, so don't be surprised if some of the steps in this list duplicate those in the previous section.

To run the Add Hardware Wizard, take the following steps:

1. Choose Start ➢ Control Panel. XP displays Control Panel.
2. Click the Printers and Other Hardware link. XP displays the Printers and Other Hardware screen.
3. Click the Add Hardware link in the See Also pane. XP starts the Add Hardware Wizard, which displays the Welcome to the Add Hardware Wizard page.
4. Click the Next button. The wizard searches for new hardware and displays the The Following Hardware Is Already Installed on Your Computer page (shown in Figure 14.12).

FIGURE 14.12

On the The Following Hardware Is Already Installed on Your Computer page of the Add Hardware Wizard, select the Add a New Hardware Device item.

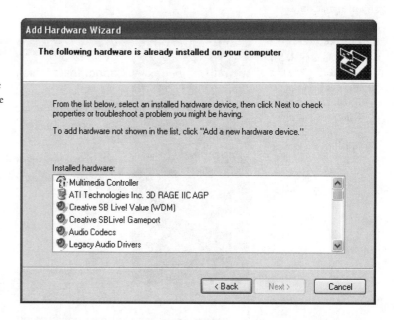

NOTE   *If the Add Hardware Wizard doesn't find any hardware it didn't already know about, it displays the Is the Hardware Connected? page, which asks whether you've already connected the hardware to the computer. Select the Yes, I Have Already Connected the Hardware option button or the No, I Have Not Added the Hardware Yet option button as appropriate. If you select the Yes, I Have Already Connected the Hardware option button, the wizard displays the The Following Hardware Is Already Installed on Your Computer screen. If you select the No, I Have Not Added the Hardware Yet option button, the wizard displays the Cannot Continue the Add Hardware Wizard screen, which offers to turn off the computer for you so that you can connect the hardware and try the Add Hardware Wizard again.*

5. If the device you want to install is listed in the Installed Hardware list box, select it. If it's not, select the Add a New Hardware Device item in the list box—the last item in the list.

6. Click the Next button. The wizard displays the The Wizard Can Help You Install Other Hardware page (shown in Figure 14.13), offering to search for the hardware.

FIGURE 14.13

The Add Hardware Wizard offers to search for the hardware, but usually you'll do better to select it manually.

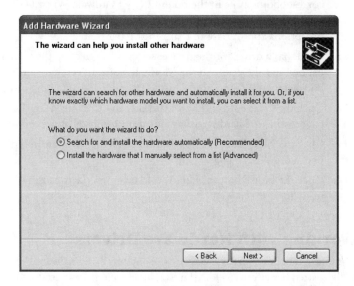

7. Select the Install the Hardware That I Manually Select from a List option button.

8. Click the Next button. The wizard displays the From the List Below, Select the Type of Hardware You Are Installing page (shown in Figure 14.14).

FIGURE 14.14

On the From the List Below, Select the Type of Hardware You Are Installing page, select the category of hardware that you're installing.

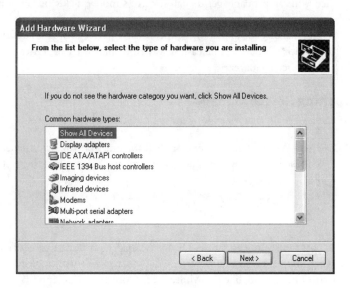

9. In the Common Hardware Types list box, select the type of hardware you're installing. Again, if the device doesn't fit any of the descriptions, leave the Show All Devices item selected (as it is by default).

10. Click the Next button. If you chose the Show All Devices item, the wizard displays the Select the Device Driver You Want to Install for This Hardware page, which is similar to the corresponding page in the Found New Hardware Wizard (shown in Figure 14.8, earlier in this chapter). If you chose a specific type of hardware, the wizard leads you off on a byway of options appropriate to that type of hardware.

11. If XP has a driver for the device, select it by selecting the manufacturer in the Manufacturer list box and the device in the Model list box. If you have a new driver, click the Have Disk button and use the resulting Install from Disk dialog box to specify the location of the driver.

12. Click the Next button. The wizard displays the The Wizard Is Ready to Install Your Hardware page, listing the hardware that's lined up for installation.

13. Click the Next button. The wizard installs the hardware and displays the Completing the Add Hardware Wizard page.

14. Click the Finish button. The Add Hardware Wizard closes itself. The hardware should be ready for use.

Working with Hardware Drivers

Without a functional driver, XP can't use any piece of hardware. And using the wrong driver or a badly written driver can make XP unstable or even make it crash.

Hardware manufacturers frequently release new versions of drivers for their hardware to improve performance, to banish bugs, or both. If you want to keep your hardware running to the best of its capacity, check the manufacturers' sites and the Windows Update site for updated drivers. In theory, Windows Update should be able to supply you with the latest drivers for most of your hardware. In practice, you can probably get the latest drivers more quickly by haunting the hardware manufacturers' websites and newsgroups.

To view, change, or uninstall the driver for a device, display the Driver page of the Properties dialog box for the device. The easiest way to display the Properties dialog box for the device is to go through Device Manager.

Opening Device Manager

To display the Device Manager window, take the following steps:

1. Press Windows key+Break or click the Start button, right-click the My Computer item, and choose Properties from the context menu. XP displays the System Properties dialog box.

2. Click the Hardware tab. XP displays the Hardware page.

3. Click the Device Manager button. XP displays the Device Manager window (shown in Figure 14.15).

As you can see in the figure, Device Manager presents a categorized tree of the devices on the computer in its default view. Any device that isn't working or has a problem is marked with a question-mark icon, like the Multimedia Controller that appears in the figure. When all is well with a category of device, Device Manager presents the category collapsed. In the figure, the Display Adapters category and the IDE ATA/ATAPI Controllers category are expanded to show their entries.

FIGURE 14.15

Use Device Manager to access hardware devices you want to configure.

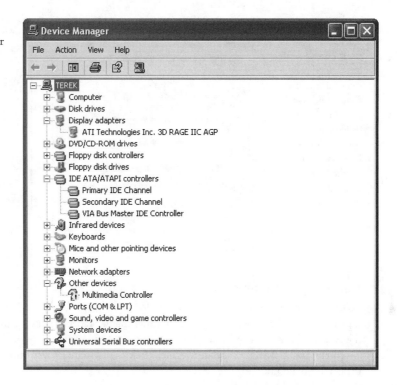

You can change the view by displaying the View menu and choosing Devices by Type (the default view), Devices by Connection, Resources by Type, or Resources by Connection from the menu. You can display hidden devices by choosing View ➤ Show Hidden Devices.

If you leave Device Manager open while you plug in a hot-pluggable device, you may need to refresh the listing in Device Manager to make it list the device. To do so, choose Action ➤ Scan for Hardware Changes.

To check or set properties for a device, double-click its entry in Device Manager (or right-click the entry and choose Properties from the context menu). XP displays the Properties dialog box for the device.

Checking the Details of a Driver

The Driver page of the Properties dialog box for a device shows some details of the driver: the provider of the driver (the company that supplied the driver to your computer), the date, the version, and the *digital signer*—the owner of the digital certificate applied to the driver. The left screen in Figure 14.16 shows an example of the Driver page of the Properties dialog box for a graphics card driver.

To display further information, click the Driver Details button. XP displays the Driver File Details dialog box, which displays further information: the filenames and paths of the driver files, the provider (the company that originally provided the driver), the file version, the copyright information, and the digital signer (again). The right screen in Figure 14.16 shows an example of the Driver File Details dialog box.

FIGURE 14.16

The Driver page of the Properties dialog box (left) shows some information about the driver. The Driver File Details dialog box (right) contains further information, including the filenames and paths of the driver files.

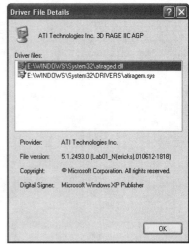

Updating a Driver

To update a driver, you use the Hardware Update Wizard. You'll have no problems with the Hardware Update Wizard, because it's essentially another manifestation of the Found New Hardware Wizard and the Add Hardware Wizard that you met earlier in the chapter.

To run the Hardware Update Wizard, click the Update Driver button on the Driver page of the Properties dialog box for the device.

Rolling Back a Driver

If a new driver you've installed doesn't work, or doesn't improve things, revert to the previous driver by using the driver rollback feature. To use the rollback feature, click the Roll Back Driver button on the Driver page of the Properties dialog box for the device.

Disabling a Device

If you want to stop using a device temporarily, you can disable it. For example, you might want to disable a device that you think is making XP unstable.

To disable a device, right-click it in Device Manager and choose Disable from the context menu. XP displays a confirmation message box such as that shown in Figure 14.17. Click the Yes button. XP closes the message box and disables the device.

FIGURE 14.17

XP displays a confirmation message box when you instruct it to disable a device.

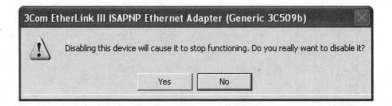

Uninstalling a Device

If you want to stop using a device permanently and remove it from your computer, uninstall it first. To do so, right-click the device in Device Manager and choose Uninstall from the context menu. XP displays the Confirm Device Removal dialog box, of which Figure 14.18 shows an example. Click the OK button. XP closes the dialog box and uninstalls the device.

FIGURE 14.18

XP displays the Confirm Device Removal dialog box for confirmation when you uninstall a device.

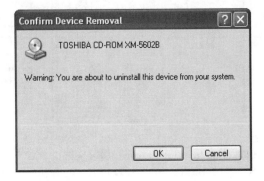

NOTE *You can also uninstall a device by clicking the Uninstall button on the Driver page of the Properties dialog box for the device.*

Adding Specific Hardware Items

The following sections discuss considerations for adding particular hardware items that need configuration beyond the driver. Many hardware items do not.

The easiest place to start configuring most hardware items is Device Manager.

Adding a CD Drive or DVD Drive

The Properties dialog box for a CD-ROM or DVD drive has two settings on its Properties page (shown on the left in Figure 14.19):

CD Player Volume slider Drag the slider to set the volume you want the CD player to deliver when playing audio CDs. This setting controls the output of the CD drive. You can control the output volume from your sound card by using Volume Control (discussed in Chapter 26).

Enable Digital CD Audio for This CD-ROM Device check box Select this check box if you want to use digital output rather than analog output from the CD drive for audio CDs. Digital output typically gives you higher audio quality, especially when you're copying audio CDs to your hard drive. (Chapter 26 discusses how to copy audio CDs to your hard drive.) Most newer CD-ROM drives and just about all DVD drives support digital output, but some older CD-ROM drives don't. If digital output doesn't work for you, clear this check box to return to analog output.

NOTE *Depending on the audio software you use, you may not be able to rip (extract) and encode music tracks from an audio CD if you disable digital output. Some audio software can handle analog ripping, but the results are lower in quality than pure digital copies. Other audio software can't handle analog ripping.*

FIGURE 14.19

The Properties page (left) of the Properties dialog box for a CD-ROM drive or DVD drive contains controls for setting the CD's volume and specifying whether to use digital CD audio. The DVD Region page displays the current encoding region for a DVD drive.

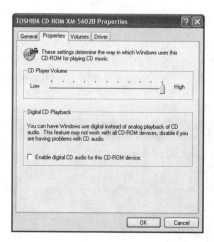
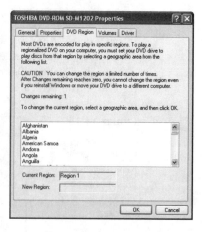

The Properties dialog box for a DVD drive also contains a DVD Region page (shown on the right in Figure 14.19), which displays the DVD encoding region currently set for the DVD player. To change the region, select the country you want in the list box and click the OK button.

Adding a Removable Drive

The first time you plug in a removable drive or local drive and XP finds pictures or audio files on it, XP displays the Removable Disk dialog box or Local Disk dialog box to let you specify whether you want to set a default action to take with files of this type. Figure 14.20 shows an example of the Removable Disk dialog box for a CompactFlash card in a PC Card adapter. The CompactFlash card contains picture files, so the Removable Disk dialog box contains actions that XP can take with picture files: Print the Pictures, View a Slideshow of the Images, Copy Pictures to a Folder on My Computer, Open Folder to View Files, or Take No Action.

FIGURE 14.20

In the Local Disk dialog box or Removable Disk dialog box (shown here), you can specify which action you want XP to take for a particular content type when you add a local disk or removable disk.

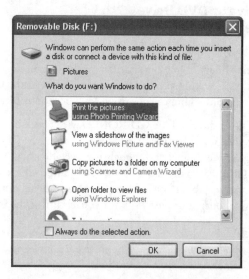

Select the action you want to take. If you want XP to take this action for every disk you add that contains this type of file, select the Always Do the Selected Action check box. Then click the OK button. XP closes the Local Disk dialog box or Removable Disk dialog box and takes the action you specified.

> **EXPERT KNOWLEDGE: DVD ENCODING REGIONS**
>
> In case you've managed to avoid the question of DVD encoding regions: As far as DVDs are concerned, the world is divided into eight regions or *locales*. Region 1 is the U.S., Canada, and U.S. Territories. Region 2 is Europe, Japan, South Africa, and the Middle East. Region 3 is Southeast Asia, East Asia, and Hong Kong. Region 4 is Australia, New Zealand, the Pacific Islands, South America, Central America, Mexico, and the Caribbean. Region 5 is Eastern Europe, Mongolia, North Korea, the Indian subcontinent, and Africa. Region 6 is China. Region 7 is "reserved" (for off-world use, perhaps). And Region 8 is for international vessels such as airplanes and cruise ships.
>
> DVD players are encoded to play only DVDs for their region. Almost all DVDs are encoded for the region in which they're intended to be sold. (There are also *all-region* DVDs that'll play in any region.) So to play a DVD, you need a player with a matching region code.
>
> Most consumer-electronics DVD players are coded for one region only. Some players—typically more expensive ones—can play discs for two, more, or all regions. Other players can be *chipped* (modified, either by adding hardware, modifying the built-in hardware physically, or by entering an engineer's code to reprogram the device) to play DVDs with different regional encoding or even to play any regional encoding. Chipping is legal in most countries (though some manufacturers pretend to disagree) but typically costs a proportion of the cost of a cheap DVD player.
>
> PC DVD drives are a little more flexible than most consumer-electronics DVD players. With most drives, you can switch region a certain number of times on a DVD drive before it goes into a locked state in which you can no longer change the region. The DVD Region page of the Properties dialog box for the DVD drive displays the number of times you can change the region again. Use them sparingly.
>
> Why do DVDs have regional encoding anyway? In theory, it's to let the movie studios control the release of the movie in different countries. For example, U.S.-made movies are usually released in the U.S. several months before they're released in Europe, and DVDs and videos of the movie are often released in the U.S. while the movie is still running in Europe. Regional encoding prevents most of the Europeans from viewing the movie on DVD until it's released with Region 2 encoding.
>
> In practice, regional encoding also enables the distributors to charge different prices for DVDs in different countries without being undercut by imported DVDs from the least expensive regions. For example, at this writing, DVDs in Region 2 are substantially more expensive than those in Region 1, and the European Union has been investigating whether this constitutes price-fixing.

Adding a Modem

XP automatically loads the driver for a USB modem, a PCI modem, or a PC Card modem if it can find the driver. It sometimes loads the driver for a serial modem too, but other times, it fails to notice that you've added a serial modem. If this happens, run the Add Hardware Wizard manually and specify the details of the modem.

SPECIFYING YOUR LOCATION

The first time you go to use a modem, XP displays the Location Information dialog box (shown in Figure 14.21) demanding your location information unless you've given it already.

Specify the details: your country and region; your area code or city code; any carrier code you need to enter; any number you dial to access an outside line; and whether the phone system uses tone dialing (the norm for most modern exchanges) or pulse dialing. Then click the OK button. XP closes the Location Information dialog box.

FIGURE 14.21

Sooner or later, XP prompts you for information about your location. Supply it once, and you should be free from all future demands.

SPECIFYING PHONE AND MODEM OPTIONS

After you close the Location Information dialog box, XP displays the Phone and Modem Options dialog box with the Dialing Rules page foremost. Figure 14.22 shows this page of the dialog box.

FIGURE 14.22

Edit your locations on the Dialing Rules page of the Phone and Modem Options dialog box.

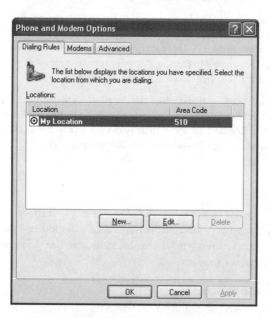

XP provides you with a default location named My Location with the area code you specified in the Location Information dialog box. Rename this location to something descriptive (for example, *Home* or the name of the city or town): Click the Edit button and enter the new name in the Location Name text box on the General page of the Edit Location dialog box that XP displays. Click the OK button. XP closes the Edit Location dialog box. Click the OK button. XP closes the Phone and Modem Options dialog box.

NOTE *For a laptop or other computer you take traveling, you'll probably want to create other locations as well. Chapter 15 discusses how to do this.*

Adding a Video Card

When you install a new video card, XP may detect it on boot-up and display the Found New Hardware Wizard so that you can install the correct driver for it. Other times, you may have to change the video driver manually by using the Hardware Update Wizard.

After installing the driver for the new video card, you usually need to restart XP. When you log back in, XP displays the Display Properties dialog box so that you can test and apply the screen resolution and color quality you want. See the section "Choosing Video Settings" in Chapter 4 for a discussion of how to choose a suitable screen resolution and color depth.

Adding a Monitor

Adding a monitor tends to be simplicity itself, involving only a couple of cables. But XP identifies many monitors simply as Plug and Play Monitor, assigning them a generic driver. This driver works well enough for undemanding programs, but to get the best performance, use the Hardware Update Wizard to install the latest driver for your specific type of monitor.

If you're seeing corrupt images on your monitor, or if the mouse pointer doesn't respond properly to conventional stimuli, or if DirectX isn't working, you may need to change the graphics hardware acceleration on your computer or disable write combining. (*Write combining* is a method of shunting more information from the video card to the monitor at once. It can cause screen corruption by providing the monitor with more information than it can handle.) To do so, take the following steps:

1. Right-click open space on the Desktop and choose Properties from the context menu. XP displays the Display Properties dialog box.
2. Click the Settings tab. XP displays the Settings page.
3. Click the Advanced button. XP displays the Monitor and Graphics Card Properties dialog box.
4. Click the Troubleshoot tab. XP displays the Troubleshoot page (shown in Figure 14.23).
5. Move the Hardware Acceleration slider one notch at a time from Full (or wherever you find it) toward None until the problems disappear. At each setting, click the Apply button, and check your computer to see what effect the change has had.
6. Alternatively, or additionally, try clearing the Enable Write Combining check box to prevent screen corruption. Click the Apply button and see what effect the change has had.

FIGURE 14.23

If you see corrupt images on the screen, try reducing hardware acceleration or disabling write combining on the Troubleshoot page of the Monitor and Graphics Card Properties dialog box.

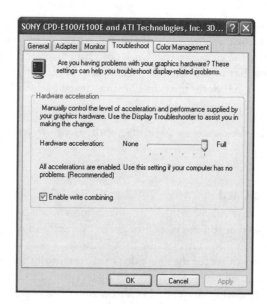

7. When the screen seems to be behaving as it should, click the OK button. XP closes the Monitor and Graphics Card Properties dialog box, returning you to the Display Properties dialog box.

8. Click the OK button. XP closes the Display Properties dialog box.

Setting Up and Using Multiple Monitors

Like Windows 98 Second Edition, Windows Me, and Windows 2000 Professional, XP lets you attach multiple monitors to your computer to increase the amount of Desktop space available to you. This feature can make both work and play much easier—but it can also lead you to loading your desk with more monitors than it can comfortably provide a footing for.

This discussion of using multiple monitors concerns only desktop computers to which you can add one or more extra graphics cards. But XP includes a feature called DualView that lets you use multiple monitors with portable computers and graphics cards with multiple outputs. The section "Using DualView" in Chapter 15 discusses DualView.

WARNING   Setting up multiple monitors can be a tricky and frustrating business. With some combinations of motherboards and graphics cards, you need to install the graphics cards in the right sequence in order to get them to work. Others work fine immediately. Others never work. Before you try to implement multiple monitors, check the Hardware Compatibility List (HCL) at the Microsoft website, `www.microsoft.com`, *for details of the graphics cards that are known to work in multiple-monitor configurations with XP.*

To use multiple monitors, you need to make sure that your graphics cards work together (some graphics cards don't) and that your computer's motherboard supports multiple monitors (some motherboards don't). In most cases, you'll want to use an AGP graphics card and one or more PCI graphics cards, but two or more PCI graphics cards without an AGP card can provide a satisfactory solution as well if you don't need ultimate performance on your primary monitor. You can also find motherboards that can use both an onboard video chipset and an AGP card together, and advanced graphics cards that can handle two (or in some cases four) monitors apiece.

The monitors, by contrast, don't need to know about each other—each gets its own input, so each can believe it's the only monitor in town if it wants to. So any monitors should do. You can mix CRTs and LCDs provided that each graphics card you use can handle the monitor to which it's connected.

NOTE *In the 1990s, large monitors were so expensive that it was much cheaper to buy two, three, or even four small monitors than one large one. That's now changed, at least with cathode-ray tube monitors (large LCD monitors are still prohibitively expensive). 19-inch monitors are reasonably affordable, and even 21-inch and 22-inch monitors are worth thinking about if you need a serious amount of Desktop space. But there's no reason why you shouldn't have a monster monitor and a couple of satellite monitors if you want—or even two or more monsters. . . .*

To set up multiple monitors, first get everything working to your satisfaction with one monitor and graphics card. Then power down your computer and insert the new graphics card. (You *can* install multiple graphics cards and monitors at a time, but unless you're very lucky and everything works, you'll be looking at some doubly confusing troubleshooting.) Connect the second monitor, then power everything on. Don't be surprised if the boot-up display appears on the second monitor rather than your primary one. After you log on to XP, it should discover the new hardware, which will trigger a Found New Hardware notification-area pop-up followed by the Found New Hardware Wizard. If XP affects not to have noticed the new hardware, run the Add Hardware Wizard manually to add the graphics card and monitor.

Next, display the Settings page of the Display Properties dialog box. (Figure 14.24 shows an example.) For each monitor you want to use (hint: all of them), select the monitor and then select Extend My Windows Desktop onto This Monitor. Once you've done that, let XP know where the monitors are positioned in relation to each other by dragging the monitor icons into their relative positions. If you get confused as to which monitor is which, click the Identify button to have XP flash up the number of each monitor on the monitor.

FIGURE 14.24

Configuring two monitors in a multiple-monitor setup

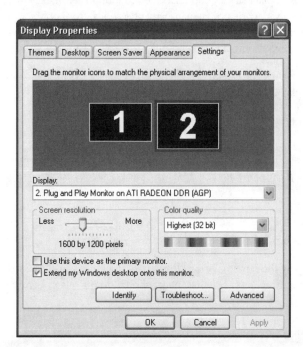

Your primary monitor is the monitor on which Windows displays the Welcome screen. You can change the primary monitor by clicking the icon for the monitor you want to make primary and selecting the Use This Device As the Primary Monitor check box. Because only the primary monitor can perform full DirectX acceleration and run DirectX programs full-screen, it's almost always best to make your primary monitor the one that's connected to your fastest graphics card. In most cases, the fastest graphics card will be the AGP card.

Set the screen resolution, color depth, and refresh rate for each monitor as usual (see the section "Choosing Video Settings" in Chapter 4 for details).

Once you close the Display Properties dialog box, you should have a substantially enlarged Desktop. By default, the Taskbar appears on your primary monitor (the one that shows the boot sequence), but you can drag it to any of the other monitors as you see fit.

Maximizing a window maximizes it for the monitor it's currently (or mostly) on. You can extend a "normal" window across two or more monitors by dragging its window border to the appropriate size. Doing so can occasionally be useful when you need to see a lot of information at the same time.

Configuring Power Management

If you have a laptop computer and use it on the road, power management tends to be an exciting part of your computing life. You've probably developed strategies to maximize your battery life while traveling, such as dimming the screen or slowing down the processor when you can accept poorer performance in the interests of longevity. (Chapter 15 discusses the features that XP offers for portable computers.)

If you have a desktop computer, power management tends to be a much less stimulating topic, because leaving your computer running usually isn't a problem. But to keep your computer healthy, to keep your (or your employer's) electrical bill to a minimum, and perhaps to contribute to keeping the polar icecaps in place, it's a good idea to configure power management on your computer.

XP offers a variety of power-management settings, from power schemes and hibernation to attaching an uninterruptible power supply (UPS) to your computer. The following sections discuss these options.

To configure power management, open the Power Options Properties dialog box as follows:

1. Right-click the Desktop and choose Properties from the context menu. XP displays the Display Properties dialog box.

2. Click the Screen Saver tab. XP displays the Screen Saver page.

3. Click the Power button. XP displays the Power Options Properties dialog box.

NOTE   *Because the Power Options Properties dialog box displays different pages depending on how your computer is configured, the following sections show the Power Options Properties dialog box from different computers.*

Choosing a Power Scheme

First, choose a power scheme and adjust it as necessary:

1. Display the Power Options Properties dialog box as discussed in the previous section. By default, the Power Schemes page (shown on the left in Figure 14.25) is displayed.

FIGURE 14.25

Choose basic power-management options on the Power Schemes page (left) of the Power Options Properties dialog box and, if necessary, further power-management options on the Advanced page (right).

2. In the Power Schemes drop-down list, select the power scheme that seems best to describe your computer's role: Home/Office Desk, Portable/Laptop, Presentation, Always On, Minimal Power Management, or Max Battery. The Presentation scheme never turns off the monitor and is intended for computers left to run kiosk-style presentations (for example, at a trade show). The Always On scheme is useful for a computer that's acting as a server. The Minimal Power Management scheme aims to get the maximum performance out of a computer without worrying about conserving power.

3. The Settings for Power Scheme group box contains adjustable settings for the power scheme. Which settings there are depends on which of your computer's components are designed for power management. For most computers, XP offers the Turn Off Monitor drop-down list and the Turn Off Hard Disks drop-down list. If your computer offers power features for standby and hibernation, the Settings for Power Scheme group box displays a System Standby drop-down list and a System Hibernates drop-down list as well.

NOTE *If you adjust the settings for a power scheme, you can save your custom power scheme by clicking the Save As button and specifying the name for the scheme in the Save Scheme dialog box that XP displays.*

4. Click the Apply button to apply the power scheme to your computer.

Choosing Advanced Power Options

The Advanced page of the Power Options Properties dialog box (shown on the right in Figure 14.25, above) offers various advanced power-management options. Which of these options you see depends on the hardware configuration of your computer.

Always Show Icon on the Taskbar check box Select this check box to make XP display a power icon in the System Tray. This option is most useful for laptop computers, as you can see at a glance whether the computer is plugged in (XP displays a plug icon) or running on battery power (a battery icon).

Prompt for Password when Computer Resumes from Standby check box   Select this check box if you want XP to make you enter your password when you wake the computer from a standby state. This is a good idea when security is important.

When I Press the Power Button on My Computer drop-down list   In this drop-down list, select the action you want XP to take when you press the Power button on your computer when XP is running. The options are Do Nothing, Ask Me What to Do, Sleep, Hibernate, and Shut Down.

When I Press the Sleep Button on My Computer drop-down list   In this drop-down list, select the action you want XP to take when you press the Sleep button on your computer. As for the Power button, the options are Do Nothing, Ask Me What to Do, Sleep, Hibernate, and Shut Down.

Enabling and Disabling Hibernation

Hibernation suspends your computer in its current state with programs and documents open. When you tell your computer to hibernate, it writes all the data held in RAM to a hibernation file on the hard disk. This way, even if the computer's battery runs out, all your information is safe. (If the battery *does* run out, hibernation saves you no time over shutting the computer down.)

The more RAM you have, the longer it takes for your computer to enter hibernation and to emerge from it again. But using hibernation is usually substantially faster than shutting down the computer and restarting it, especially as hibernation allows you to keep your programs and documents open, so that you can restart your work where you left off.

To enable hibernation, select the Enable Hibernation check box on the Hibernate page of the Power Options Properties dialog box.

Enabling and Disabling Advanced Power Management

If your computer supports Advanced Power Management (APM), XP displays an APM page in the Power Options Properties dialog box. On this page, you can toggle APM on and off by selecting and clearing the Enable Advanced Power Management Support check box.

NOTE   *For portable computers, XP includes an Alarms page in the Power Options Properties dialog box. These options are discussed in the next chapter.*

Configuring XP to Use an Uninterruptible Power Supply

One of the great benefits of a laptop computer is that its battery protects it from data loss when a power outage occurs. To get similar protection in a desktop computer, you need to attach a separate device—an uninterruptible power supply (UPS). A UPS is about the most important hardware add-on purchase you're likely to make for your computer, so this section discusses in some depth which features you should look for in a UPS.

Like backup media, a UPS is seldom if ever included in a PC bundle.

WHAT IS A UPS?

A *UPS* is essentially a large battery of above-average intelligence that sits between your computer and the electricity supply and ensures a steady power stream to your computer to protect it from blackouts, brownouts, and surges. Different UPSes do this in two different ways.

The simpler way is for the device to monitor power fluctuations and kick in when the power supply falls outside acceptable thresholds. Technically, this type of device is called a *standby power supply (SPS)* rather than a UPS, but you'll often hear SPSes described as UPSes, because consumers will pay more money for them that way.

The more complicated—and better—way is for the device to feed power to the computer continuously, charging itself when the power supply is running within acceptable parameters. This device is technically a UPS. This way of supplying power is better because the UPS delivers conditioned power to the computer all the time, protecting it better from fluctuations and avoiding the critical moment of changeover from mains power to battery power that can be a drawback with an SPS.

CHOOSING A UPS

If you're looking for a UPS, keep these features in mind:

Operating system support   Make sure the UPS is designed for use with XP. With operating system support and an appropriate system management port (discussed next), the UPS can warn XP when the electricity supply has failed. XP can then shut itself down automatically if the computer is unattended. (More on this in a moment.)

System management port   Make sure the UPS has an appropriate system management port for your computer. Many UPSes use a serial port connection. Others use a USB connection.

Indicators for line voltage and battery power   The UPS should have an indicator to indicate when the incoming power to the UPS is okay, and another indicator to indicate when the devices attached to the UPS are running on battery power. (Many UPSes also sound an alarm when battery power is being used.)

Multiple power outlets   Make sure the UPS has enough outlets for all the devices you want to plug into it directly.

Enough power and battery life   Before buying the UPS, work out how much power and battery life you need it to have. Make a list of the computers and devices you'll need to have plugged into the UPS, then use a power-supply template such as that on the American Power Conversion Corp. website (`www.apc.com`) to calculate the number of volt-amps (VA) you'll need to keep the equipment running. (You can simply add up the voltages listed on the equipment, but be aware that the power-supply rating on your computer equipment shows the maximum power rather than typical power usage.) Then decide the amount of time you'll need to shut down the computers once the power alarm goes off. Generally speaking, the more power and battery life you need, the more the UPS will cost and the bigger and heavier it will be. If you just want a few minutes to allow you to shut down XP under control (or to have XP shut itself down), a modest and inexpensive UPS may fit the bill.

TIP   *Unless you're convinced that you'll need to print during a power outage, don't plan to plug your printer into your UPS. Printers are power hogs. Laser printers are such power hogs that they can kill a UPS.*

INSTALLING A UPS

Once you've bought a UPS and lugged it home, power down your computer and install the UPS. Bring up the computer again, log on to XP, and display the UPS page of the Power Options Properties dialog box (shown in Figure 14.26 before and after installing a UPS).

FIGURE 14.26

The UPS page
of the Power
Options Properties
dialog box before
(left) and after
(right) installing a
UPS

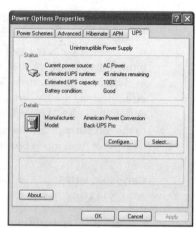

To let XP know about your UPS, take these steps:

1. Click the Select button. XP displays the UPS Selection dialog box (shown in Figure 14.27
   with American Power Conversion chosen in the Select Manufacturer drop-down list).

FIGURE 14.27

Use the UPS Selec-
tion dialog box to
specify which UPS
you're using and
the port it's
connected to.

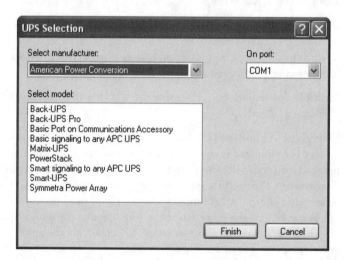

2. In the Select Manufacturer drop-down list, choose the manufacturer of your UPS. If the
   manufacturer isn't listed, choose the Generic item.

3. If the manufacturer was listed, specify the model of UPS in the Select Model list box, and
   select the port in the On Port drop-down list. Click the Finish button. XP closes the UPS
   Selection dialog box, returning you to the Power Options Properties dialog box.

4. If the manufacturer wasn't listed, select the Custom item in the Select Model list box. Then
   click the Next button. XP displays the UPS Interface Configuration dialog box (shown in
   Figure 14.28). Consult your documentation, then choose settings for Power Fail/On Battery,

Low Battery, and UPS Shutdown as appropriate. Then click the Finish button. XP closes the UPS Interface Configuration dialog box.

FIGURE 14.28

If XP doesn't list the manufacturer of your UPS, use the UPS Interface Configuration dialog box to configure signal polarities for the UPS.

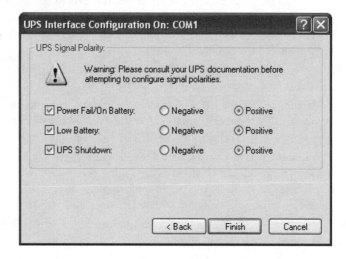

5. In the Power Options Properties dialog box, click the Configure button. XP displays the UPS Configuration dialog box (shown in Figure 14.29).

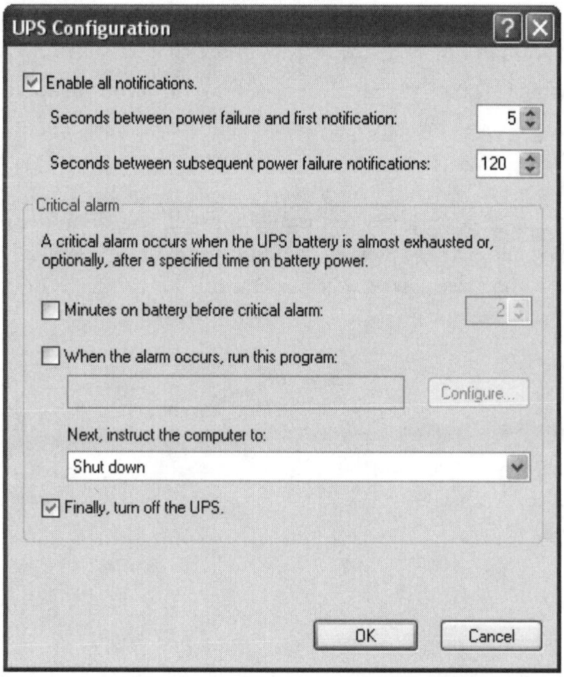

FIGURE 14.29

Use the UPS Configuration dialog box to choose settings for the UPS.

6. Select or clear the Enable All Notifications check box as appropriate. Adjust the value in the Seconds between Power Failure and First Notification text box and the Seconds between Subsequent Power Failure Notifications text box to suit your needs. For example, if your electricity supply suffers from mini-outages of a few seconds each, you might increase the Seconds between Power Failure and First Notification setting to a value such as 20 or 30 seconds so that the UPS raises the alarm only for a more serious outage than usual.

7. In the Critical Alarm group box, specify what actions XP should take when the UPS sends XP a critical alarm, warning XP that the UPS is almost out of battery power.

    Minutes on Battery before Critical Alarm check box and text box   Select this check box if you want XP to sound an alarm after the specified number of minutes running on battery power.

    When the Alarm Occurs, Run This Program check box and text box   If you want XP to run a program when an alarm occurs, select this check box and specify the program in the text box. For example, you might want to run a custom shutdown utility or use a program to send a warning to users of connected computers.

    Next, Instruct the Computer To drop-down list   In this drop-down list, choose Shut Down or Hibernate as appropriate.

    Finally, Turn Off the UPS check box   Leave this check box selected (as it is by default) to have XP turn off the UPS (and stop the alarm).

8. Click the OK button. XP closes the UPS Configuration dialog box.

9. Click the Apply button. XP applies your UPS settings. The Status group box shows status information on your UPS, and the Details group box shows the UPS's type. The right-hand illustration in Figure 14.26, earlier in the chapter shows an example.

10. Click the OK button. XP closes the Power Options Properties dialog box.

Up Next

This chapter has discussed how to install, uninstall, and disable hardware; update, roll back, and remove drivers; and manage power, including configuring a UPS.

The next chapter discusses the considerations for using XP on a portable computer.

Chapter 15

Using XP Home Edition on a Portable Computer

THIS CHAPTER DISCUSSES HOW to use XP Home Edition on a portable computer. It starts by discussing how to use the power-management features specific to portables to prolong your battery life and warn you when it's running out. It continues by showing you how to use the Safely Remove Hardware feature for PC Cards (PCMCIA cards) and how to use hardware profiles to manage different hardware configurations. It mentions how to use ClearType for better readability on some LCD screens, and DualView for connecting an extra display to some portables. Last, it shows you how to use locations in dial-up networking and points you to information on connecting your portable to your desktop computer so that you can transfer files between them and keep files synchronized between them.

This chapter covers the following topics:

◆ Using the power-management features for portable computers
◆ Safely removing PC Cards
◆ Using ClearType
◆ Using DualView
◆ Using hardware profiles for different hardware configurations
◆ Using locations for dial-up networking
◆ Transferring files between a desktop computer and a portable
◆ Synchronizing files between a desktop and a portable

Before We Begin...

Before we get started with this chapter, a word or two of explanation on why this chapter is relatively short. Portable computers are growing more capable and more popular by the year if not by the month, and if you have a portable, you may well feel portables deserve more coverage.

Here's why this chapter is relatively short:

◆ First, many of the features that apply to portable computers also apply to desktop computers and have been covered in other chapters. The chapter mentions these features and refers to the chapters in which they're covered. For example, the last chapter discussed power management, which applies to both desktop computers and portable computers. This chapter discusses some additional power-management options that apply only to laptops. Some of the topics that *are* discussed in this chapter aren't entirely specific to portable computers, but because they mostly apply to portable computers, they're discussed here.

◆ Second, XP Home doesn't have one of the killer features for portable computers that XP Professional has: offline folders. Offline folders let you create copies of folders that are located on another PC and work with them when you're not connected to that PC. For example, you can make copies of your desktop computer's data folders on your portable computer, then work with them on your portable computer wherever you happen to be. When you return to your desktop computer, you synchronize the offline copies (on the portable) with the folders on the desktop computer, so that the folders on the desktop computer contain all the changes you've made.

You'll have no problem using XP Home on a portable computer that's your main computer. But you'll find it difficult—at least, more difficult than it should be—to use a portable computer running XP Home as a satellite to your main computer. You may even get the impression that Microsoft would like you to use XP Professional instead for a portable with this type of role.

Using the Power-Management Features for Portables

In addition to the power-management features discussed in the previous chapter, XP provides six power-management features for portable computers. Three of these features are configurable from the Power Options Properties dialog box; the other three are implemented behind the user interface. As you'll remember from the previous chapter, the easiest way to display the Power Options Properties dialog box is to click the Power button on the Screen Saver page of the Display Properties dialog box—and the easiest way to display *that* dialog box is to right-click the Desktop and choose Properties from the context menu.

Choosing Power Settings for Running on Batteries

On the Power Schemes page of the Power Options Properties dialog box for a portable computer, you can choose different power settings for when the computer is plugged in and when it is running on batteries. The left screen in Figure 15.1 shows an example of the Power Schemes page for a portable computer.

You shouldn't need much advice on how to choose settings for when the computer is running on battery power: The sooner you let the computer turn off one of the power-draining components, such as the monitor or the hard disk, the longer your battery will last. That said, don't set a minimal timeout (1 or 2 minutes, say) for the monitor if you tend to work on the computer on documents that require pauses for thought—having the monitor black out when you're constructing a formula or a sentence can be very distracting.

FIGURE 15.1

On the Power Schemes page (left) of the Power Options Properties dialog box, specify power settings for running on batteries. On the Alarms page (right), you can set a low battery alarm and a critical battery alarm.

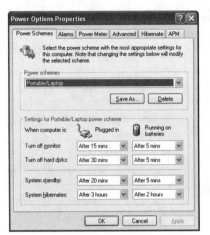
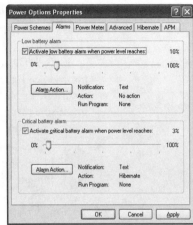

Setting Battery Alarms

If XP recognizes your computer as a portable that can run off a battery, it includes the Alarms page (shown on the right in Figure 15.1) in the Power Options Properties dialog box.

To set battery alarms, take the following steps:

1. Use the controls in the Low Battery Alarm group box to specify the battery level and the action for a low battery alarm. To use the alarm, select the Activate Low Battery Alarm when Power Level Reaches check box and drag the slider to a suitable level.

   ◆ By default, the alarm displays a message box warning you of the low battery level. To change what the alarm does, click the Alarm Action button. XP displays the Low Battery Alarm Actions dialog box (shown on the left in Figure 15.2).

FIGURE 15.2

Use the Low Battery Alarm Actions dialog box to specify the action that you want XP to take when the battery reaches the low battery threshold. Use the Low Battery Alarm Program dialog box to configure a program to run automatically.

◆ In the Notification group box, select the Sound Alarm check box or the Display Message check box as appropriate.

◆ In the Alarm Action group box, select the When the Alarm Goes Off, the Computer Will check box if you want the computer to take an action when the alarm is triggered. In the drop-down list, choose Stand By, Hibernate, or Shut Down as appropriate. Select the Force Stand By or Shutdown Even if a Program Stops Responding check box if you want to make sure that a hung program or driver doesn't prevent XP from shutting the computer down or putting it into Sleep mode.

◆ In the Run a Program group box, select the When the Alarm Occurs, Run This Program check box if you want to run a program automatically when the alarm is triggered. Click the Configure Program button. XP displays the Low Battery Alarm Program dialog box (shown on the right in Figure 15.2), in which you can create a task as described in the section "Creating a Scheduled Task" in Chapter 11.

◆ Click the OK button. XP closes the Low Battery Alarm Actions dialog box.

2. In the Critical Battery Alarm group box, specify the criteria for a critical battery alarm—the alarm that XP raises when your battery is very close to running out of power. The options for the critical battery alarm are the same as those for the low battery alarm.

3. Click the Apply button. XP applies your alarm settings.

WARNING *Because the battery alarms use the Task Scheduler, the account under which you run a program when an alarm occurs must have a password. If it doesn't have a password, XP gives you the error message "The scheduled task did not run because no user account password was entered" and fails to run the program. The alarm task also won't run if you've paused or stopped the Task Scheduler.*

Power Meter

For portable computers that it recognizes, XP also includes the Power Meter page in the Power Options Properties dialog box. This page shows the current power source and the percentage of battery power remaining.

Processor Power Control

XP supports processor power control. If the computer has a processor that supports running at multiple speeds, such as an Intel SpeedStep processor, XP can use the computer's power-management features to run at full speed when on AC power and at a lesser speed when running on battery power (to deliver longer battery life at somewhat lesser performance).

Dimming and Turning Off the Display

Slowing down the processor saves some battery power, but in most portables, the display consumes far more power than the processor. To save power, XP automatically turns off the display when the user closes the lid of the computer.

Similarly, XP automatically decreases the brightness of LCD screens when they're running on battery power. This reduces the amount of power needed, and so prolongs battery life, but it can make it hard to work on screens that aren't too bright in the first place. To restore the screen to its full brightness, use a hardware command (these vary depending on the laptop and its manufacturer).

Hibernation when Battery Runs Low

If the portable computer's battery runs low, and the user doesn't respond to warnings, XP puts the laptop into hibernation rather than letting it run out of power and crash.

TROUBLESHOOTING: RECOVERING A HUNG LAPTOP

If your laptop gets so thoroughly hung that it no longer responds to the power button, even when you hold the power button down for four or five seconds, you may need to disconnect the laptop from the AC wall socket and remove the battery in order to reset it. But before you do, make sure that you're not missing a hardware reset button on the laptop. Many laptops have these, but to prevent you from pressing them accidentally, they're usually located in a really awkward position. For example, on some computers, you need to poke the end of a paper clip or a similar thin, blunt instrument through a small hole in the bottom of the machine to press the reset button. If in doubt, consult the manual for your laptop before poking it with a paper clip.

Safely Removing PC Cards

You can install PC Card devices by inserting them like any other hot-pluggable devices. (See the section "Using Hot-Pluggable Devices" in Chapter 14 for brief details—but basically, you just plug in hot-pluggable devices.) As with some USB and FireWire devices, before removing a PC Card device, you're supposed to stop it by using the Safely Remove Hardware feature. *Supposed*? Yes—you can often get away without using this feature, though it's never a good idea to do so. Usually, XP handles the unannounced removal of hot-pluggable hardware gracefully. Sometimes, though, removing hardware without using Safely Remove Hardware causes the computer to lock up or become unstable. Your attitude may be different from mine, but your mileage is likely to be more or less the same.

You can use the Safely Remove Hardware feature in two ways: the quick way and the slow way. Guess which we'll start with? Right.

The Quick Way of Using Safely Remove Hardware

To use Safely Remove Hardware the quick way, follow these steps:

1. Click the Safely Remove Hardware icon in the notification area. XP displays a pop-up menu of devices (shown in Figure 15.3).

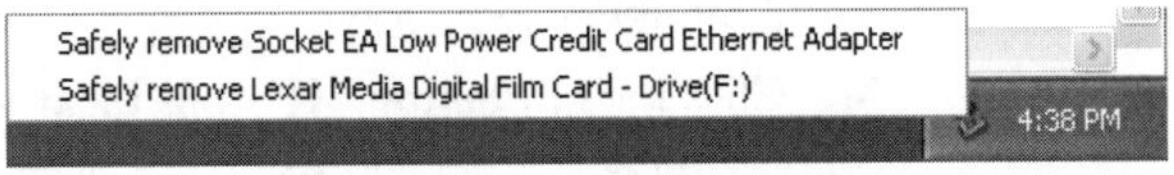

FIGURE 15.3

Click the Safely Remove Hardware icon in the notification area and select the device to stop in the pop-up menu.

Safely remove Socket EA Low Power Credit Card Ethernet Adapter
Safely remove Lexar Media Digital Film Card - Drive(F:)

4:38 PM

2. Select the device you want to remove. XP stops the device and displays a Safe to Remove Hardware pop-up (shown in Figure 15.4).

FIGURE 15.4

XP displays a Safe to Remove Hardware pop-up when it's safe to remove the device.

3. Remove the device.

The Slow Way of Using Safely Remove Hardware

To use Safely Remove Hardware the slow way, follow these steps:

1. Right-click the Safely Remove Hardware icon in the notification area. XP displays the Safely Remove Hardware dialog box (shown on the right in Figure 15.5).

FIGURE 15.5

You can also use the Safely Remove Hardware dialog box (left) to stop the device. In the Stop a Hardware Device dialog box (right), confirm that you want to stop the PC Card device.

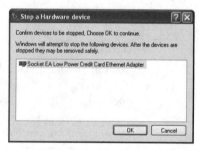

2. Select the device you want to remove.

  ◆ If you want to display more information about the device's components, select the Display Device Components check box. (This check box is selected in the figure.) Confusion about the components of a device is the main reason for using the slow way.

3. Click the Stop button. XP displays the Stop a Hardware Device dialog box (shown on the right in Figure 15.5).

4. Click the OK button. XP stops the device and displays a Safe to Remove Hardware pop-up (as in Figure 15.4 above).

5. Remove the device.

6. Click the Close button. XP closes the Safely Remove Hardware dialog box.

Using ClearType

Unless your portable is one of the very few portables that doesn't have an LCD screen, it's worth trying the ClearType resolution-enhancement technology to see if it makes fonts look better. Some people find ClearType a help; others find it produces an irritatingly smeary effect unless they peer closely at it. Your mileage will vary depending on your screen and your eyesight.

To enable ClearType, display the Display Properties dialog box and click the Effects button on the Appearance page. XP displays the Effects dialog box. Select the Use the Following Method to Smooth Edges of Screen Fonts check box and select ClearType in the drop-down list. (See "Choosing Desktop Effects" in Chapter 4 for more details.)

Using DualView

DualView is a great new feature in XP that enables you to extend your Desktop onto an external display connected to your portable's external graphics port. DualView exploits the capability of the graphics cards in almost all portables to send two signals at once: a digital signal to the portable's LCD screen, and an analog signal to the external graphics port. Normally, the portable sends the same signal both internally and externally, which is useful for giving presentations but not much else. By contrast, DualView uses the external port and monitor as an extension of your Desktop, much as in a multi-monitor setup.

DualView works with only some graphics cards, but if you have an external monitor, it shouldn't cost you more than a few seconds' effort to connect it to the external graphics port and see what happens. On some portables, the external graphics port is switched off to conserve battery power, so you'll need to turn it on, typically by using custom configuration software supplied by the manufacturer or poking in the BIOS. You'll then need to set your computer to send signals to both ports; most portables have a built-in key combination to do this.

If you find that DualView works for your portable, configure it as you would a desktop multi-monitor setup (as described in the previous chapter). The main difference is that with DualView, you can't specify the primary monitor, because the portable's built-in display must always be the primary monitor.

Using Hardware Profiles

XP'S *hardware profiles* let you create different hardware configurations for the same computer. Hardware profiles are useful for computers that you regularly use with two or more different hardware configurations. You can set up different hardware configurations with a desktop computer by dint of diligent plugging and unplugging of a set of hardware, but it's much easier to achieve the same effect with a laptop that you use both docked and undocked or that has swappable components—and that's what hardware profiles are usually used for.

NOTE *Hardware profiles can seem forbidding until you start using them, at which point most people find them surprisingly easy. Even if you don't have a docking station and need a profile only for something as simple as using your portable with an external monitor (with perhaps a higher resolution than your portable's screen) or an external mouse, profiles can save you a lot of time and effort.*

Creating a Hardware Profile

To create a hardware profile, take the following steps:

1. Press Windows key+Break or click the Start button, right-click the My Computer item, and choose Properties from the context menu. XP displays the System Properties dialog box.

2. Click the Hardware tab. XP displays the Hardware page.

3. Click the Hardware Profiles button. XP displays the Hardware Profiles dialog box (shown in Figure 15.6). By default, XP starts you off with a profile named `Profile 1`, which it lists in the Available Hardware Profiles list box. It displays `(Current)` next to the current profile, so you should see `Profile 1 (Current)` before you create a new profile.

FIGURE 15.6

In the Hardware Profiles dialog box, create profiles for the different configurations your computer uses.

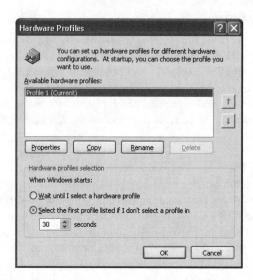

4. In the Available Hardware Profiles list box, select the profile you want to copy.

5. Click the Copy button. XP displays the Copy Profile dialog box (shown in Figure 15.7).

FIGURE 15.7

In the Copy Profile dialog box, specify the name for the copy you're making of the profile.

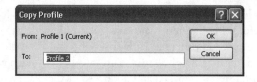

6. Enter the name for the copy of the profile in the To text box. XP suggests a default name of `Profile N`, where N is the next unused number, but you'd be wise to opt for something more descriptive.

7. Click the OK button. XP closes the Copy Profile dialog box and creates the profile.

8. Set properties for the profile:

   ◆ Select the profile in the Available Hardware Profiles list box.

   ◆ Click the Properties button. XP displays the Properties dialog box for the profile. Figure 15.8 shows an example of the Properties dialog box.

FIGURE 15.8

Use the Properties dialog box for a profile to set options.

   ◆ If this is a portable computer, select the This Is a Portable Computer check box. XP enables the options in the group box. Select the appropriate option button: The Docking State Is Unknown, The Computer Is Docked, or The Computer Is Undocked.

   ◆ In the Hardware Profiles Selection group box, select the Always Include This Profile As an Option when Windows Starts check box if you want XP always to present this profile in the start-up menu of profiles. If you don't select this check box, XP includes the profile in the start-up menu of profiles only if it determines that the profile is relevant to the hardware configuration it has detected.

   ◆ Click the OK button. XP closes the Properties dialog box for the profile and applies your changes to it.

9. Create further profiles as necessary. (Or delete one or more profiles by using the Delete button.)

10. To rename a profile (for example, the `Profile 1` profile), select it in the Available Hardware Profiles list box and click the Rename button. XP displays the Rename Profile dialog box. Enter the new name for the profile in the To text box and click the OK button. XP closes the Rename Profile dialog box and renames the profile.

11. Use the up-arrow button and down-arrow button to sort the profiles in the Available Hardware Profiles list box into the order in which you want XP to present them. If you want to use a profile as the default, put it at the top of the list.

12. In the Hardware Profiles Selection group box in the Hardware Profiles dialog box, choose the Wait until I Select a Hardware Profile option button or the Select the First Profile Listed if I Don't Select a Profile in *NN* Seconds option button as appropriate. If you choose the latter, enter the number of seconds in the text box. (The default is 30 seconds, which makes for slow booting.)

13. Click the OK button. XP closes the Hardware Profiles dialog box, returning you to the System Properties dialog box, and applies your changes.

14. Click the OK button. XP closes the System Properties dialog box.

Choosing a Hardware Profile

Once you've set up hardware profiles as described in the previous section, XP displays the Hardware Profile/Configuration Recovery Menu screen when the computer reboots. (If you're using a multi-boot configuration, the Hardware Profile/Configuration Recovery Menu screen appears after you choose the Windows XP entry from the Please Select the Operating System to Start menu—as you'd expect if you think about it.)

Use the ↑ key and ↓ key to select the profile from the menu, and then press the Enter key. XP starts the computer with that profile.

Setting Up the Hardware in the Profile

Once you've started XP with the profile you want, make the hardware changes and install drivers to suit the profile. These changes apply only to the current profile.

Using Dial-up Networking from Multiple Locations

If you travel with your portable computer, you'll probably want to create multiple locations for dial-up networking. To do so, display the Phone and Modem Options dialog box by taking the following steps:

1. Choose Start ➢ Control Panel. XP displays Control Panel.

2. Click the Network and Internet Connections link. XP displays the Network and Internet Connections screen.

3. Click the Phone and Modem Options link in the See Also pane. XP displays the Phone and Modem Options dialog box.

Creating a New Location

To create a new location, take the following steps:

1. Click the New button on the Dialing Rules page of the Phone and Modem Options dialog box. XP displays the New Location dialog box with the General page foremost (shown on the left in Figure 15.9).

FIGURE 15.9

Create the new location on the General page of the New Location dialog box. If necessary, use the New Area Code Rule dialog box to create area code rules.

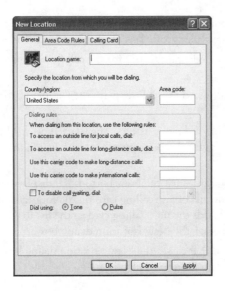
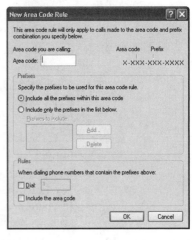

2. Enter the name for the location in the Location Name text box.

3. In the Country/Region drop-down list, specify the country or region in which you'll use this location.

4. Enter the area code for the location in the Area Code text box.

5. In the Dialing Rules group box, specify access numbers for outside lines and carrier codes for long-distance calls and international calls as appropriate.

6. If you need to disable call waiting, select the To Disable Call Waiting, Dial check box and enter the appropriate code in the text box, either by typing or by selecting one of the standard codes from the drop-down list.

7. If the location uses pulse dialing, select the Pulse option button. (The Tone option button is selected by default.)

8. If necessary, create area code rules for dialing from the new location:

   ◆ Click the Area Code Rules tab. XP displays the Area Code Rules page.

   ◆ Click the New button. XP displays the New Area Code Rule dialog box (shown on the right in Figure 15.9).

   ◆ Enter the area code in the Area Code text box.

   ◆ In the Prefixes group box, select the Include All the Prefixes within This Area Code option button or the Include Only the Prefixes in the List Below option button as appropriate. If you choose the latter, click the Add button and use the resulting Add Prefix dialog box to specify the prefixes (separated by spaces or commas).

   ◆ In the Rules group box, select the Dial check box if these numbers require an extra number; if so, enter it in the text box. Select the Include the Area Code check box if necessary.

◆ Click the OK button. XP closes the New Area Code Rule dialog box and enters the rule in the Area Code Rules group box on the Area Code Rules page.

9. If you need to use a credit card to pay for the call from the location, specify it by following the steps below.

   ◆ Click the Calling Card tab. XP displays the Calling Card page of the New Location dialog box.

   ◆ To use one of the card types listed in the Card Types list box, select its option button and enter the details in the Account Number text box and the Personal ID Number (PIN) text box.

   ◆ To add a calling card, click the New button. XP displays the New Calling Card dialog box. Enter the details of the calling card on the four tabs of this dialog box, then click the OK button. XP adds the new calling card to the list in the Card Types list box on the Calling Card page of the New Location dialog box.

10. Click the OK button. XP closes the New Location dialog box and adds the new location to the Phone and Modem Options dialog box.

Editing a Location

To edit a location, select it in the Locations list box on the Dialing Rules page of the Phone and Modem Options dialog box and click the Edit button. XP displays the Edit Location dialog box, which is a renamed version of the New Location dialog box. Make the necessary changes and then click the OK button. XP closes the Edit Location dialog box and applies your changes to the location.

Using a Location

To use a location, select it in the Phone and Modem Options dialog box and click the OK button. XP closes the Phone and Modem Options dialog box and uses the location you chose for calls you dial.

Transferring Files between a Desktop Computer and a Portable

If you have both a desktop computer and a portable computer, chances are that you'll want to transfer files between them, be it occasionally or often, more simply than by using floppy disks or removable disks. You can easily do so by using a variety of methods that I'll mention here but discuss later in the book:

◆ If both the computers involved have FireWire ports, you can connect them directly to each other using a six-pin-to-six-pin FireWire cable. See the section "Creating a FireWire Network" in Chapter 31 for details.

NOTE   *If you don't have FireWire ports on your portable and desktop, but you do have USB ports, look for a USB network connection cable instead. You'll need to get software to go with it. If possible, choose USB 2.0 rather than USB 1.x, because USB 2.0 is far faster than USB 1.x.*

- ◆ If a FireWire connection isn't an option, you can put a network card in each of them and connect them either via a network (wired or wireless) or directly via a crossover cable. See the section "Cabling an Ethernet Network" in Chapter 31 for information on how to network your computers.

- ◆ If you don't want to buy network cards and can tolerate low transfer speeds, connect the computers by using a serial cable, a parallel cable, or an infrared connection. See the section "Setting Up a Direct Connection" in Chapter 31 for details of how to do this.

Once you've got the computers connected, you can transfer files between them by sharing folders and drives (see the sections "Browsing the Network" and "Mapping and Disconnecting Network Drives" in Chapter 31 for details). But you may also want to use XP's Briefcase feature, discussed in the next section, to keep files synchronized between the computers.

Using Briefcase to Synchronize Files between Two Computers

The Windows Briefcase is a utility for creating Briefcases, a special type of folder that lets you keep its contents synchronized with copies that you make on another computer. The classic scenario for using Briefcase—and the scenario from which Briefcase takes its name—is that you need to take files with you on a trip. You copy them from your desktop computer (or server) to the Briefcase on your laptop so that you can work on the files when you don't have access to the desktop computer or server. When you return home (or to the office), you synchronize the files contained in the Briefcase so that your desktop computer or the server contains the latest versions.

That's the classic scenario, and it can work pretty well. But if the original file on the desktop computer or the server has changed as well as the copy on your laptop having changed, overwriting either file with the other file is going to lose some changes. When this happens, Briefcase asks you what you want to do. Choosing the newer version of the file won't necessarily help—and even when standardizing on the newer version of the file is your solution, it can be complicated by the file on the laptop having been changed in a different time zone than the original file. When you run into a situation like this, you'll probably need to review both files and incorporate changes from both manually.

Alternative Approaches to Synchronization

As mentioned earlier in this chapter, XP Professional's Offline Folders feature provides seamless synchronization with files stored on a server. You designate which folders you want to be able to access when you're offline, and XP handles the rest, copying the folders to your computer, making the programs use the files in those folders when the server isn't available, and synchronizing the changed files and folders when you go back online with the server. By comparison with Offline Folders, Briefcase is a very poor cousin.

But if you don't have XP Professional, Briefcase is all you've got. But if your computing setup is that of the desktop computer and laptop computer outlined above, and you plan to use Briefcase to keep files on the laptop synchronized with their originals on the desktop computer when you travel, consider an easier solution: Keep the files on the laptop computer and share them with the desktop computer from there. This way, when you hit the road with the laptop, you'll know that you have the full set of files with you, and they'll all be up-to-date.

Using Briefcase

This section describes how to use Briefcase. It assumes that you've read the preceding sections about how Briefcase works and the perils of synchronization.

Briefcase is a little peculiar, because you don't run the program and then create a new Briefcase. Instead, you create a Briefcase and then open the Briefcase to open an Explorer window that gives you access to the Briefcase commands.

CREATING A NEW BRIEFCASE

You can create a Briefcase on the Desktop or in any folder—for example, on a removable disk or floppy that you'll then transfer to the other computer. If you can connect the two computers so that you can transfer files or folders between them, the best place to create the Briefcase is on the hard drive of the laptop computer.

To do so, right-click the Desktop or open space in the folder and choose New ➤ Briefcase from the context menu. (From an Explorer window, you can also choose File ➤ New ➤ Briefcase.) XP creates a new briefcase and names it New Briefcase (or New Briefcase (2) if there's already a new Briefcase in the folder).

RENAMING THE NEW BRIEFCASE

You can leave the new Briefcase with the name New Briefcase if you want, but usually it's a much better idea to assign it a descriptive name immediately. Rename the Briefcase by using standard Windows techniques. For example, select the Briefcase, press the F2 key to display an edit box around the name, type the new name, and press the Enter key.

You can then double-click a Briefcase to open it in an Explorer window that includes Briefcase commands. The first time you open a Briefcase, XP displays the Welcome to the Windows Briefcase dialog box, which provides a quick introduction to Briefcase basics.

ADDING FILES TO THE BRIEFCASE

To add files to the Briefcase, copy them there by using any form of the Copy command. For example, you can use the Copy to Folder dialog box or drag-and-drop to copy files to the Briefcase. When you copy an item to the Briefcase, XP displays an Updating Briefcase dialog box rather than a Copying dialog box, so you shouldn't be in any doubt as to what's happening.

TIP   If you use a Briefcase a lot, create a shortcut to the Briefcase in the \SendTo\ folder. See the "Expert Knowledge: Customizing the Send To Menu" sidebar in Chapter 6 for instructions on creating shortcuts in the \SendTo\ folder.

WORKING WITH FILES IN THE BRIEFCASE

Once you've got the files in the Briefcase, and the Briefcase on your laptop, you're ready to work with the files. Open them as you would any other files, edit them, save them, and close them.

You can also create new files in the Briefcase. A new file is called an *orphan*, because it doesn't have a parent file and isn't copied to the desktop computer or server during an update, so you'll need to copy it manually to wherever you want it to belong.

You can delete a file from the Briefcase as you would any other file. The file disappears into the Recycle Bin as usual, from where you can restore it if necessary. When you update the files, the original of that file will be deleted.

VIEWING THE STATUS OF BRIEFCASE FILES

To view the status of files in the Briefcase, open the Briefcase in an Explorer window in Details view and examine the Status column, which lists the status—Up-to-Date, Needs Updating, or Orphan—of each file. (Details is the default view in which Briefcases open.) Figure 15.10 shows a small Briefcase open in an Explorer window.

FIGURE 15.10

You can view the status of Briefcase files by opening the Briefcase in an Explorer window.

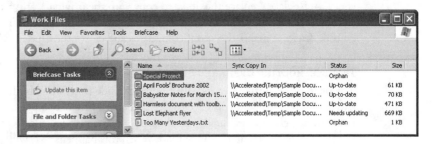

For more specifics on the update status of a file or folder, right-click it and choose Properties to display its Properties dialog box, then click the Update Status tab to display the Update Status page. This page includes a Find Original button that you can click to open an Explorer window showing the folder that contains the original of the file or folder.

SPLITTING A BRIEFCASE FILE FROM ITS ORIGINAL

Sooner or later, you'll probably work on a file stored in Briefcase and create a file that you don't want to synchronize with the original of the file on the desktop computer or server. When this happens, you can *split* the file stored in Briefcase from its counterpart selecting it in a Briefcase window and choosing Briefcase ➢ Split from Original. You can also issue this command by clicking the Split from Original button on the Update Status page of the Properties dialog box for the file.

UPDATING THE FILES IN THE BRIEFCASE

When you bring the laptop back to the mothership, you need to update the files in the Briefcase so that the originals of the files contain any edits you made while on the road. Connect the laptop to the desktop computer or server, or put the floppy or removable disk containing the Briefcase in the desktop computer. Then issue an Update command in either of the two following ways:

- ◆ Right-click the icon for the Briefcase and choose Update All from the context menu.
- ◆ Open the Briefcase in an Explorer window and then click the Update All Items link in the Briefcase Tasks list or choose Briefcase ➢ Update All.

NOTE *To update just some of the items in the Briefcase, open an Explorer window to display the contents of the Briefcase, select the item or items you want to update, and click the Update This Item link or the Update the Selected Items link in the Briefcase Tasks list or choose Briefcase ➤ Update Selection. (You can also right-click the item or selection and choose Update from the context menu.)*

Briefcase checks the status of each file that you've requested (directly or indirectly) to update and displays the Update dialog box for you to confirm the actions to be taken.

To change an action, right-click the file and choose the appropriate option from the context menu. For a file that's marked to be deleted, the options are Delete, Create, and Don't Delete. For a file that's marked to be replaced, the options are → Replace (replace the original with the updated copy), ← Replace (replace the updated copy with the original), and Skip.

When you've finished reviewing the updates and changing them if necessary, click the Update button. Briefcase makes the specified updates and closes the Update dialog box.

TROUBLESHOOTING ORPHANED FILES

The main problem that occurs with Briefcase (aside from when both the original file and the copy have been changed, and you have to decide between their competing claims to your affections or integrate the changes manually) is when one of the original files gets renamed or moved while its counterpart is being edited on the road. When this happens, XP will either tell you that the file has been deleted or that "Filename Is an Orphan. It Was Not Updated."

If this happens, take the following steps:

1. Rename the modified copy of the file.
2. Copy the original file back to its previous location in Briefcase.
3. Open the modified copy of the file and save it under the name of the original file you just copied in step 2.
4. Delete the orphan file (the renamed modified copy whose contents you've just saved under the original filename).
5. Issue an Update command to synchronize the files.

Up Next

This chapter has discussed considerations for using XP on a portable computer: using the power-management features for portables; using the Safely Remove Hardware feature for PC Cards; using ClearType if it suits you; using DualView if you can; using hardware profiles for different hardware configurations; and using dial-up networking locations. It has also discussed how to use Briefcase to keep files synchronized between two computers, and alternatives to using Briefcase.

The next chapter discusses how to troubleshoot, optimize, and dual-boot XP.

Chapter 16

Optimizing Windows XP Home Edition

YOU'VE READ SEVERAL TIMES already in this book that XP is much more reliable than Windows 9x—and it's quite true. But things still sometimes go wrong with XP: a program hangs; you start getting bizarre error messages about some strangely named component not having done something it should; or XP starts to slow down, behave oddly, or become unstable.

This chapter discusses how to use the tools that XP provides for dealing with untoward occurrences such as these. It also discusses some steps you may want to take to optimize XP in the hope of keeping it running smoothly and as swiftly as your hardware permits. And it shows you how to set up a dual-boot arrangement so that you can use both XP and another operating system on your computer.

This chapter covers the following topics:

- Dealing with program hangs
- Using Event Viewer to identify problems
- Keeping XP updated with Windows Update
- Optimizing performance
- Setting environment variables
- Enabling error reporting
- Setting startup and recovery options
- Monitoring performance with the Performance tool

Dealing with Program Hangs

When a program hangs, it'll usually be very obvious. The program stops responding to direct stimuli (keystrokes and mouse commands issued in its window) and indirect stimuli (for example, commands issued via the Taskbar or via another program). If you move another program window in front of the hung program's window and then move it away, the hung program's window fails to redraw correctly, leaving either parts of the window that you've moved or a blank, undrawn area on the screen.

Ending a Program

Sometimes XP notices when a program has hung and displays the End Program dialog box automatically so that you can choose whether to end the program. Other times, you'll need to use Task Manager to tell XP to end the program. To do so, take the following steps:

1. If you have Task Manager running already, switch to it. If not, press Ctrl+Alt+Delete. XP displays Task Manager with the Applications page foremost.

2. Select the task you want to end.

3. Click the End Task button. If XP can end the task easily, it does so. Otherwise, XP displays the End Program dialog box, of which Figure 16.1 shows an example.

FIGURE 16.1

If XP can't close the program easily, it displays the End Program dialog box to let you end it forcibly.

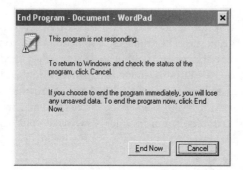

4. Click the End Now button. XP ends the program. You lose any unsaved data in the program.

5. After shutting the program down and containing any virtual shrapnel that results, XP displays a message box such as that shown in Figure 16.2, inviting you to tell Microsoft about the problem. If you pass this information on to Microsoft, you can be sure that they're aware of the problem you've experienced; and if enough people report the same problem, chances are that Microsoft will respond sometime in the future with a fix that Windows Update can download for you. But understand that this error reporting isn't a personal service—Microsoft won't be contacting you directly with apologies for the problem you've suffered and a quick fix for it.

FIGURE 16.2

XP displays a dialog box such as this one when you've used the End Program dialog box to end a program. Choose whether to send Microsoft information on the problem.

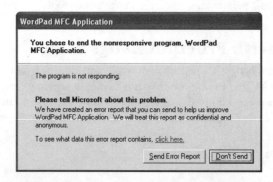

6. Click the Send Error Report button or the Don't Send button as appropriate. (To see details on what information you'll be sending to Microsoft, click the Click Here link before dismissing the dialog box.)

You can turn off or tweak this error reporting if you want. See the section "Enabling and Disabling Error Reporting" later in this chapter.

NOTE   By default, Task Manager appears with its Always on Top attribute on, so that it always appears as the topmost window on the Desktop, no matter which program window is active. Always having Task Manager on top makes it easy to keep track of Task Manager, but it means that Task Manager often blocks dialog boxes or error messages in the programs you're using, particularly at low screen resolutions such as 800×600. If you find Task Manager useful and often keep it open to see what's happening with your programs, choose Options ➢ Always on Top to remove the check mark from the Always on Top menu item and make the Task Manager window behave like a normal program window. (To turn Always on Top back on, repeat the command.) Also on the Options menu are two other items that are both on by default: Minimize on Use, and Hide When Minimized.

Ending a Process or a Process Tree

Instead of ending a program, you can end a process. A *process* is the executing environment in which program components called *threads* operate. Many programs run as a single process much of the time, but others involve multiple processes.

There are two problems with ending a process. First, doing so may make your computer unstable, so it's a last resort. Second, you need to know which process does what. Now, as you saw in Chapter 3, you can use the Go to Process command from a program on the Applications page of Task Manager to identify the process on the Processes page. This command can be useful for learning the name under which the main process for a program is executing, but it's not much use for ending a process, because usually you'll do much better to end the program itself from the Applications page. Ending the program takes out all the processes associated with the program. So the only reason to end a process directly is if it doesn't have its associated program listed on the Applications page. This is the case for a system process, but it's not a good idea to end a system process unless you're certain what it's doing. But if you overload XP, it can sometimes get confused about which programs are running and lose a program's listing from the Applications page while keeping its process or processes going.

If this happens, you can end a process by selecting it on the Processes page and clicking the End Process button. XP displays the Task Manager Warning dialog box shown on the left in Figure 16.3 warning you that ending the process may make your system unstable or lose you data. If you're prepared to risk such consequences, click the Yes button. XP terminates the process.

FIGURE 16.3

XP displays the Task Manager Warning dialog box on the left when you tell it to end a process, and the dialog box on the right when you tell it to end a process tree.

To end all the processes associated with a process, right-click the process and choose End Process Tree from the context menu. XP displays the Task Manager Warning dialog box shown on the right in Figure 16.3 with a variation of its message about the possible undesirable results of stopping processes. Click the Yes button if you want to continue. XP stops the processes.

Using Event Viewer to Identify Problems

If your computer seems to be behaving strangely, you can use Event Viewer to try to pinpoint the source of the problem.

To open Event Viewer, take the following steps:

1. Choose Start ➢ Control Panel. XP displays Control Panel.
2. Click the Performance and Maintenance link. XP displays the Performance and Maintenance screen.
3. Click the Administrative Tools link. XP displays the Administrative Tools screen.
4. Double-click the Event Viewer shortcut. XP starts Event Viewer (shown in Figure 16.4).

FIGURE 16.4

Use Event Viewer to identify problems and to learn what's happening behind the scenes in your computer.

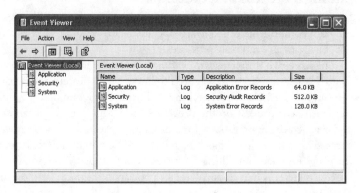

As you can see in the figure, Event Viewer contains three logs: the Application Log, the Security Log, and the System Log.

NOTE   *Event Viewer automatically opens the current logs. You can also open old logs by choosing Action ➢ Open Log File. Event Viewer displays a common Open dialog box with two peculiarities: a Log Type drop-down list and a Display Name text box. Navigate to the log and select it. Then select the appropriate type of log—Application, Security, or System—in the Log Type drop-down list. The Display Name text box automatically displays Saved Type Log, where Type is the log type selected (for example, Saved Application Log for an Application Log). You can change this description as necessary. Click the Open button. Event Viewer opens the log file and adds it to the left pane. (You can also rename it here by using standard Windows editing techniques, such as selecting the name and pressing the F2 key.)*

The System Log

The System Log contains information about Windows processes. The System Log uses the following three types of events:

Error events   A notification that an error has occurred. Errors can be anything from mildly serious (for example, "The device U.S. Robotics 56K FAX EXT disappeared from the system without first being prepared for removal") to seriously serious (for example, a system error described only by forbidding error codes).

Warning events   A notification that something has gone wrong, but not disastrously so. For example, you might see a warning that "The browser was unable to retrieve a list of servers from the browser master on the network." This isn't bad—it just means that the browser (a service that finds out which resources are available on the network) has to find another browser master (a computer that's coordinating information on available resources).

Information events   Events worth noting in the System Log but that are not considered errors and do not merit warnings. For example, when you start XP, it starts the event log service and logs this as an Information event. Other examples include XP's starting to use a network adapter that it has detected is connected to the network, or that the browser has forced an election on the network because a master browser was stopped.

The System Log is stored in the SYSEVENT.EVT file in the \Windows\System32\Config\ folder.

The Application Log

The Application Log contains information about programs running on the computer. Like the System Log, the Application Log supports three types of events: Error events, Warning events, and Information events. Program developers specify the events that their programs raise and which event type each event has.

The Application Log is stored in the APPEVENT.EVT file in the \Windows\System32\Config\ folder.

The Security Log

The Security Log contains information on security-related events. In XP Home, these events are limited to Account Logon actions, Logon/Logoff actions, Policy Change actions (initiated by the System object), and System Events (such as the loading of authentication packages). XP Home audits these events automatically. (In XP Professional, you can enable auditing on files and folders, which lets you track which users take which actions on those files and in those folders.)

The Security Log is stored in the SECEVENT.EVT file in the \Windows\System32\Config\ folder.

Viewing an Event Log

To view one of the three event logs, select it in the left pane of the Event Viewer window. Event Viewer displays the events in the log in the right pane. Figure 16.5 shows an example of viewing the System Log.

To view the details of an event, double-click it (or right-click it and choose Properties from the context menu). XP displays the Event Properties dialog box (shown in Figure 16.6). The dialog box shows the date, time, type, user (if appropriate), computer, source, category, and ID number of the event. The Description text box displays the description of the event, and the Data text box displays any data for it. You can toggle the display of the data between bytes and words by clicking the Bytes option button or the Words option button. With the dialog box open, you can use the Previous Event button (the up-arrow button) and the Next Event button (the down-arrow button) to display the details for the previous event or next event, or the Copy Event Details to Clipboard button (the button below the Next Event button) to copy the details of the event to the Clipboard.

FIGURE 16.5

Use Event Viewer to find out which events have occurred on your system.

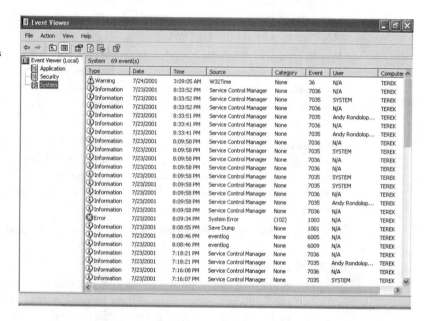

FIGURE 16.6

Use the Event Properties dialog box to view the properties for an event.

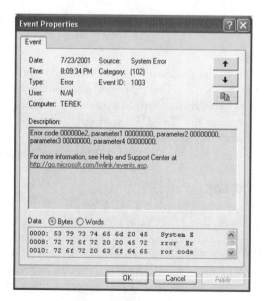

Managing the Event Logs

As you can imagine, event logs grow in size, particularly when many events occur that need logging. XP offers features to keep the size of your event logs under control.

To manage the event logs, take the following steps:

1. Right-click the event log in question and choose Properties from the context menu. XP displays the Properties dialog box for the log. The left screen in Figure 16.7 shows the General page of the Properties dialog box for the Application Log.

FIGURE 16.7

Use the General page (left) of the Properties dialog box for an event log to specify a maximum size for the log file and which events to overwrite. Use the Filter page (right) to filter the types of events displayed.

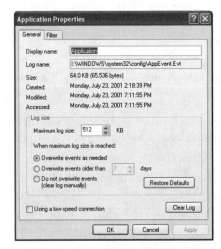

2. In the Maximum Log Size text box, you can specify the maximum size to which the file can grow. The default size is 512KB, but you can set any size from 64KB upward. Having the log file grow to a couple of megabytes shouldn't be a problem unless you're backing it up from another machine, but there's no particular reason to keep a large amount of log-file data.

3. In the When Maximum Log Size Is Reached area, select one of the option buttons to specify what XP should do when the log file reaches its maximum size:

   Overwrite Events As Needed option button   Select this option button to have XP delete the oldest event to make room for the newest event, thus keeping the log file around its maximum size.

   Overwrite Events Older Than *NN* Days option button   Select this option button (the default setting) to make XP overwrite events older than a particular number of days in order to make room for new events. If you archive your log files, set the number of days in the text box to match your frequency of archiving. The default setting is 7 days. Be aware that if the log file reaches its maximum size within the allotted number of days and contains no events older than that number of days, XP stops writing events to the log file. (This isn't usually a good idea.)

Do Not Overwrite Events option button   Select this option button if you want to prevent XP from overwriting any events. This means that you'll need to clear the event log manually. Until you clear the log, XP writes no more events to the log once it has reached its maximum size.

4. If your computer is connected to the network via a modem and is receiving event information from other computers (or is transmitting event information to other computers), select the Using a Low-Speed Connection check box. This option reduces the amount of information transmitted.

5. Click the OK button. XP applies your changes and closes the Properties dialog box for the event log.

FILTERING THE EVENT LOG

Your event logs can fill up quickly, especially when there's something wrong with your system or with a program. To find particular events, you can use the Filter page of the Properties dialog box to apply filters. Take the following steps:

1. Right-click the event log in question and choose Properties from the context menu. XP displays the Properties dialog box for the log.

2. Click the Filter tab. XP displays the Filter page (shown on the right in Figure 16.7 above).

3. In the Event Types group box, select the check boxes for the types of events you want to see. Clear the other check boxes.

4. Use the controls on the lower two-thirds of the page to specify the details of the events you want to see.

5. Click the OK button. XP applies your choices and closes the Properties dialog box.

CLEARING THE EVENT LOG

To clear a log, right-click it in Event Viewer and choose Clear Log from the context menu. Alternatively, display its Properties dialog box and click the Clear Log button on the General page.

Event Viewer displays an Event Viewer dialog box asking if you want to save the log before clearing it. Click the Yes button or the No button as appropriate.

Keeping XP Updated with Windows Update

XP's Windows Update feature helps you keep XP up-to-date by automatically checking for Windows updates, service packs, and fixes for security holes, and notifying you that they're available for installation. This section discusses how to use Windows Update in its default configuration and how to configure it to suit your needs.

When Windows Update Runs

By default, Windows Update runs automatically when an Administrator user is logged in. (Microsoft assumes that you don't want Limited users—let alone guests—to install or refuse updates.) If multiple Administrator users are logged on to the computer at the same time, Windows Update runs for only one of them. Windows Update "runs" in the sense that if it's set to check automatically for updates, it does so; and if it's set to download those updates automatically before notifying you that they're available, it does that too.

What actually runs is the Automatic Updates service, which you'll find running whenever any user is logged in. This service implements your choice of settings for Windows Update, which we'll discuss next.

EXPERT KNOWLEDGE: SWITCHING OFF THE AUTOMATIC UPDATING SERVICE

The Automatic Updates service runs even if you turn off automatic updating so that you can run Windows Update manually when you need it. Running this service probably doesn't slow down XP much, if at all, but if you turn off automatic updating, you may want to turn this service off too in the hope of improving performance.

To do so, log on as a Computer Administrator user and take the following steps:

1. Right-click the My Computer item on the Start menu and choose Manage from the context menu. XP displays the Computer Management window.

2. Expand the Services and Applications item.

3. Expand the Services item.

4. In the Services list, right-click the Automatic Updates item and choose Properties from the context menu. XP displays the Properties dialog box for the service.

5. On the General page, click the Stop button. XP stops the service.

6. In the Startup Type drop-down list, choose Manual.

7. Click the OK button. XP closes the Properties dialog box.

8. Choose File ➢ Exit to close the Computer Management window—or go spelunking in other services while you've got the window open.

Controlling What Windows Update Does

As mentioned earlier, Automatic Updates is automatically configured to search for and download updates. The first time a Computer Administrator user logs on to a new installation of XP Home, XP displays a nag icon for the Automatic Updates Setup Wizard in the notification area. When curiosity gets the better of the user and they click the icon, the Automatic Updates Setup Wizard launches and displays its Notification Settings page to let the user confirm how Automatic Updates should behave.

Under normal circumstances, that's the only time you get to see the Automatic Updates Setup Wizard, but you can also change your Automatic Updates settings at any time on the Automatic Updates page of the System Properties dialog box (see Figure 16.8). To display the System Properties dialog box, press Windows key+Break or right-click the My Computer item on the Start menu and choose Properties from the context menu.

FIGURE 16.8

You can configure Windows Update on the Automatic Updates page of the System Properties dialog box.

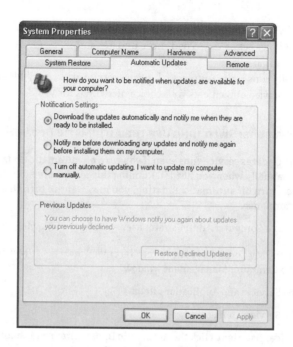

The Notification Settings group box offers the following three option buttons:

Download the Updates Automatically and Notify Me when They Are Ready to Be Installed option button   The default, this setting is convenient if you want to use automatic updating and you have a fast Internet connection. Periodically, when your computer is connected to the Internet, Automatic Updates checks the Windows Update site for new updates (ones that haven't been applied to this installation of XP Home and that you haven't been offered and declined). When it finds new updates, Automatic Updates downloads them in the background, using bandwidth-throttling technology to make sure it doesn't prevent you from using your Internet connection by grabbing all bandwidth when you need it. (*Bandwidth-throttling* means that Automatic Updates throttles back the amount of bandwidth the download is taking up, not that it throttles your bandwidth—though on a slow connection, it may feel like the latter even though Automatic Updates is trying to leave you enough bandwidth to operate.) If you're not using your Internet connection, Automatic Updates downloads the update files as fast as possible. Once the update files are downloaded, Windows Update notifies you (assuming you're an Administrator) that they're available and invites you to install them.

Notify Me before Downloading Any Updates and Notify Me Again before Installing Them on My Computer option button   Use this setting if you want to use automatic updating but want to be aware of when Windows Update is downloading updates. You might want to know this because your Internet connection isn't fast enough to support your surfing (or downloading MP3s) at the same time as Windows Update is trying to squeeze a large update through it, or because you don't like unexplained activity across your Internet connection.

Turn Off Automatic Updating. I Want to Update My Computer Manually option button
Select this option button if you prefer to control not only when Windows Update downloads and installs updates but when it checks for them—or if you don't want to use Windows Update at all.

As you can see in Figure 16.8, the Automatic Updates page of the System Properties dialog box also contains a Previous Updates group box, which offers you a Restore Declined Updates button. This button becomes available when you decline an update that Windows Update has offered you. By clicking this button, you can restore all updates you've declined, so that Windows Update will offer them to you again (so that you can install them this time).

Once you've chosen the appropriate setting, click the OK button. XP closes the System Properties dialog box.

Windows Update in Action

If you choose to have Automatic Updates download updates automatically, it checks automatically for updates and, when it finds them, automatically starts downloading them when it thinks your Internet connection is either idle or being consistently lightly used over a period of time (for example, if your e-mail program is checking for mail every few minutes and finding nothing, but no other activity is taking place).

When Automatic Updates is downloading updates, it displays an icon in the notification area. You can make XP display the status of the download (what percentage is complete) by hovering the mouse pointer over the icon. You can pause the download manually by clicking the icon and choosing Pause from the resulting menu, and resume a paused download by clicking the icon and choosing Resume from the menu.

When you click this icon or its message, it displays the Automatic Updates: Ready to Install dialog box shown on the left in Figure 16.9, which offers you three command buttons:

◆ Clicking the Details button displays another Automatic Updates: Ready to Install dialog box like the one shown on the right in Figure 16.9. This dialog box lets you read details for each update and specify which updates to install (by leaving their check boxes selected). This dialog box contains a Settings button that you can click to display an Automatic Updates dialog box that's essentially the Automatic Updates page of the System Properties dialog box in disguise, a Remind Me Later button (see the next paragraph), and an Install button (see the paragraph after next).

◆ Clicking the Remind Me Later button displays an Automatic Updates dialog box in which you can specify the timeframe for a reminder—anything from 30 minutes to three days. When you click the OK button to close this dialog box, XP closes the Automatic Updates: Ready to Install dialog box too.

◆ Clicking the Install button starts XP installing the updates.

FIGURE 16.9

The Automatic Updates: Ready to Install dialog boxes let you review the updates that XP has downloaded and is ready to install and choose whether to apply them immediately or later.

If you choose to have Windows Update notify you when new updates are available, Windows Update checks periodically for new updates. When it finds some, it displays a Windows Update icon in the notification area with a pop-up message telling you that new updates are available. When you click the icon or the message, XP displays the Automatic Updates: Updates for Your Computer dialog box, of which Figure 16.10 shows an example.

FIGURE 16.10

The Automatic Updates: Updates for Your Computer dialog box lets you choose which updates to download for installation.

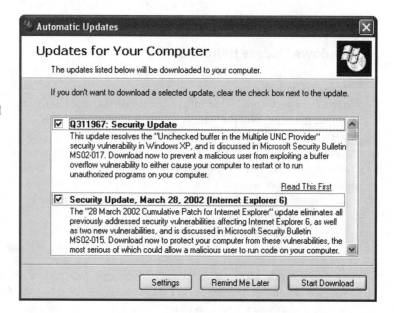

The Automatic Updates: Updates for Your Computer dialog box offers you the following options:

- Clicking the Settings button displays an Automatic Updates dialog box that is essentially the Automatic Updates page of the System Properties dialog box in disguise.

- Clicking the Remind Me Later button displays an Automatic Updates dialog box in which you can specify the timeframe for a reminder, as described above.

- Clicking the Start Download button starts Windows Update downloading the updates you left selected. (By default, Automatic Updates selects the check boxes for all the available updates. You clear the check boxes for the updates you don't want to download.) Again, Windows Update uses bandwidth throttling during the download so that it doesn't hog all your bandwidth when you're trying to use it.

If you turned off Automatic Updates, or if you want to check for updates right now, you can run Windows Update manually by choosing Start ➢ All Programs ➢ Windows Update or by following the Windows Update link in Help and Support Center.

Removing Updates

You can remove some updates applied by Windows Update by using the Add or Remove Programs window, as discussed in Chapter 5. Select the entry for the update on the Change or Remove Programs page and click the Change/Remove button that it displays. XP displays a Windows XP Uninstall dialog box such as that shown in Figure 16.11 to confirm the removal. Click the Yes button if you're sure. Other updates applied by Windows Update are permanent: You can never remove them once you've installed them.

FIGURE 16.11

XP double-checks
that you want to
remove an update.

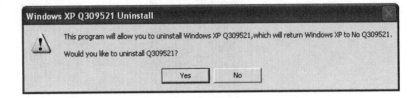

As you can see in the figure, each update, hotfix, or service pack is linked to a Q number—the number of the article in the Microsoft Knowledge Base (support.microsoft.com) that discusses the problem that the update, hotfix, or service pack solves.

Downloading Updates Manually from the Windows Update Website

If you prefer not to use the Automatic Updates feature, you can use the Windows Update website instead. Choose Start ➢ All Programs ➢ Windows Update. XP opens the Windows Update site in Internet Explorer. (Alternatively, you can run Internet Explorer yourself and enter the URL manually: www.windowsupdate.com.) Once there, click the Scan for Updates link to see which updates are available.

If the site finds updates, follow the Review and Install Updates link to examine the updates. In most cases, you'll want to click the Install Now button to install all the updates. But if you want to pick and choose, use the Remove buttons to remove from the list any updates that you don't want to download and install. Then click the Install Now button.

When you access the Windows Update website, you may see one or more Security Warning dialog boxes like that shown in Figure 16.12 asking if you want to install and run assorted Windows Update Controls. (If you're running antivirus software, it may block these controls or display an additional warning.) To use Windows Update, you'll need to click the Yes button and install each control. Before you do, read briefly through the description in the Security Warning dialog box and make sure that the control has to do with Windows Update, that it comes from the appropriate entity (at this writing, the designation is "Microsoft Windows XP Publisher"), and that the publisher's authenticity has been verified. (If you're feeling trusting, you *can* select the Always Trust Content from *Publisher* check box, but most people prefer to be aware of each control that's being installed on their computer.)

FIGURE 16.12

You may see Security Warning dialog boxes such as this one when accessing the Windows Update website.

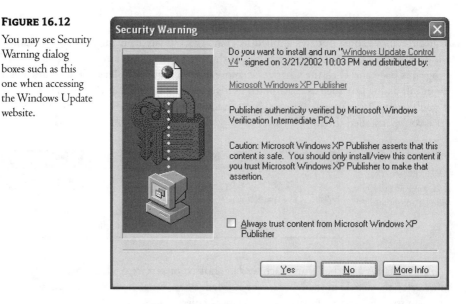

Downloading Updates Manually for Multiple Computers

As you've seen, Windows Update is essentially configured for use on a single computer: It works out which updates are necessary, downloads them automatically (if you let it), and walks you through applying them. If you have a single computer, that's great. But if you have multiple computers that need updating, you may not want to waste time downloading the same files for each computer—particularly if you have a single Internet connection.

You can get around downloading the same files multiple times, but it's a bit of work, because you need to download the files manually from the Windows Update website and then apply them manually to each computer. Here's how to do so:

1. Browse to the Windows Update website (`www.windowsupdate.com`).
2. Click the Windows Update Catalog link in the See Also list in the left column. The Windows Update site displays the Welcome to Windows Update Catalog page.
   - ◆ If you don't see the Windows Update Catalog link, click the Personalize Windows Update link to display the Personalize Your Windows Update Experience page. Select the Display the Link to the Windows Update Catalog check box and click the Save Settings button. The Windows Update site adds the Windows Update Catalog link to the See Also list.
3. Click the Find Updates for Microsoft Windows Operating Systems link. The site displays a page with a list of operating systems and a list of languages.
4. Select the Windows XP Home Edition item in the Operating System drop-down list.
5. If necessary, select the appropriate language in the Language drop-down list. (Internet Explorer selects your local language by default.)

6. If you want to restrict the search, click the Advanced Search Options link and use the resulting controls to specify what to search for. You can choose a specific timeframe (for example, the last month), specify search words, or choose to search for particular categories of updates: critical updates and service packs, recommended updates, or multi-language features.

7. Click the Search button to search, and then follow the links that the site returns.

8. Click the appropriate Add buttons on the results page to add the updates you want to download to your Download Basket.

9. Click the Go to Download Basket link. The site displays your Download Basket.

10. In the Type or Browse to the Download Location of Your Choice text box, enter the location of the folder to which you want to download the updates. (For example, if you want to apply the updates to multiple computers, you might want to download the updates to a shared folder or network drive.) The easiest way to specify the location is to click the Browse button and use the resulting Browse for Folder dialog box.

11. Click the Download Now button. Internet Explorer downloads the update files.

12. Apply the files to the relevant computers by navigating to the folder and double-clicking each file in turn.

If you get confused as to which updates you've downloaded and which you haven't, click the View Download History link on the Windows Update Catalog page of the Windows Update website.

Optimizing Performance

This section discusses steps you can take to optimize the performance of your computer and of XP. These steps range from getting more RAM (if you need it), through setting suitable performance options for your computer, to specifying the size and location of the paging file. You should also defragment your disk or disks as discussed in "Defragmenting Your Disks" in Chapter 11.

RAM: Do You Have Enough?

If your computer's performance seems disappointing, make sure that your computer has plenty of RAM to run XP itself plus all the programs that may be running in the background. As mentioned earlier in the book, 128MB is usually enough for running a single user session at reasonable speed, and 256MB is usually enough for several user sessions running conventional programs. If you want multiple users to be able to open large programs or large files at the same time, you might need 384MB or 512MB.

If your computer is light on RAM, consider adding more. At this writing, RAM prices have reached an all-time low, and you can get 256MB of SDRAM for less than $100.

There are various ways of finding out how much RAM you have on your computer. Normally, when the computer starts, you'll see the boot routine take a quick count of the RAM. (Some computers hide this part of the boot process behind a custom splash screen.)

Once XP is running, the easiest way to find out the amount of RAM is to display the System Properties dialog box (press Windows key+Break, or right-click the My Computer item on the Start menu and choose the Properties item from the context menu) and look at the Computer section of the General page.

Choosing Performance Options

Next, make sure that XP is configured to give the best performance possible for your needs.

As mentioned in Chapter 1, getting the best performance out of XP on a computer that isn't screamingly fast is partly a question of choosing the right balance between visual delight and speed: the more graphics and visual effects that XP is using, the slower their display will be, and the heavier the demands placed on the processor as well as the graphics subsystem. The more visual effects you can sacrifice, the better performance you'll get.

You also need to give the foreground program as much of a boost as possible, make sure that memory usage is optimized for programs rather than system cache, and set an appropriate size for your paging file.

To set performance options, follow these steps:

1. Press Windows key+Break. Alternatively, choose Start ➤ Control Panel, click the Performance and Maintenance link, and then click the System link. XP displays the System Properties dialog box.

2. Click the Advanced tab. XP displays the Advanced page (shown in Figure 16.13).

FIGURE 16.13

The Advanced page of the System Properties dialog box is the starting place for setting performance options.

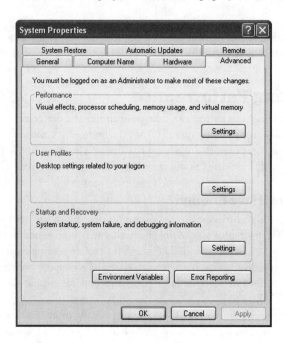

3. Click the Settings button in the Performance group box. XP displays the Performance Options dialog box.

4. On the Visual Effects page of the Performance Options dialog box (shown on the left in Figure 16.14), select one of the option buttons:

   ◆ Select the Let Windows Choose What's Best for My Computer option button to have XP apply the mixture of settings it deems most appropriate to your computer's speed and your graphics card's capabilities.

- ◆ Select the Adjust for Best Appearance option button to turn on all the effects.
- ◆ Select the Adjust for Best Performance option button to turn off all the effects.
- ◆ Select the Custom option button if you want to apply a custom set of effects. Then select the check boxes for the effects you want to use. Most of the effects are self-explanatory— for example, the Animate Windows when Minimizing and Maximizing check box controls whether XP animates windows when minimizing and maximizing them. (In fact, this item isn't precisely named, as the effect is applied to windows that are being restored as well as minimized or maximized—but no matter.) The fewer visual effects you use, the better the performance you'll enjoy, but the plainer and less subtle the XP interface will seem.

5. Click the Advanced tab. XP displays the Advanced page of the Performance Options dialog box (shown on the right in Figure 16.14).

FIGURE 16.14

To improve performance, turn off unnecessary visual effects on the Visual Effects page (left) of the Performance Options dialog box. On the Advanced page (right), make sure that processor scheduling and memory usage are optimized for applications.

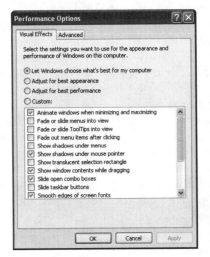 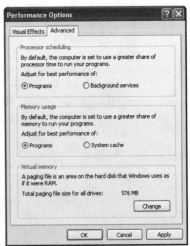

6. In the Processor Scheduling group box, make sure that the Programs option button is selected. The Programs option button causes XP to give priority to the foreground program—the active program—giving you faster response time in it. (Select the Background Services option button only if you're using this computer as a sort of server and are not running programs on it or if you want a background task, such as Backup Utility, to get more attention so that it'll run faster.) In case you're wondering what the difference is: For the Programs option, XP allocates short, variable-length *quanta* (time slices) to programs, whereas for the Background Services option, XP allocates longer, fixed-length quanta.

7. In the Memory Usage group box, make sure the Programs option button is selected so that XP manages memory to give the maximum performance boost to the foreground program. Select the System Cache option button only if you want to optimize the system cache performance at the expense of program performance or if you're running programs that you know need a large cache.

8. If necessary, change the size of the paging file by following the instructions in the next section.

9. Click the OK button. XP applies your changes and closes the Performance Options dialog box.

10. Click the OK button. XP closes the System Properties dialog box.

Specifying the Size and Location of the Paging File

The *paging file* is space reserved on the hard disk for XP to use as virtual memory. *Virtual memory* involves storing memory information on the hard disk so that more information can be loaded into memory (both real and virtual) at the same time. XP juggles virtual memory automatically, swapping information between the RAM and the paging file, so its use should be imperceptible to you. (You'll hear the hard drive working, of course; but then the hard drive works so much when XP is running that you'll hear it even when no virtual memory swapping is taking place.)

Being able to load more information into memory at a time is good, but because the hard drive is much slower to access than RAM, storing memory information in virtual memory makes your computer run more slowly than it would if it were to store all memory information in RAM. In XP—unlike NT 4 and Windows 2000—you *can* turn off the paging file to force the OS to use RAM all the time. But given the demands that XP can make on memory, Microsoft doesn't recommend it—even if you have a huge amount of RAM (say, 512MB or 768MB).

XP automatically creates the paging file on the drive that XP itself is installed on, not because this is the best place to have it—it isn't—but because it'd be antisocial to put it anywhere else. (If you're familiar with Linux, you'll know that it requires a separate partition for its swap file, which is roughly analogous to the paging file in Windows.) You may well want to move the paging file to a different partition to improve performance by separating the disk read and write requests for the system folder from those for the paging file.

You might also want to move your paging file to a faster drive than the drive it's currently on. For example, if you had a small but screamingly fast SCSI drive in your computer as well as a slower but much larger EIDE drive, you might want to move the paging file to the SCSI drive to improve performance. (This would work for a large and fast SCSI drive as well—but you'd probably have installed XP on that drive in the first place, so the paging file would already be there.) Similarly, you may be able to improve performance by moving the paging file to an otherwise unused EIDE drive, should you have one hanging around.

Before you move the paging file, though, there's a gotcha you need to know about. For XP to be able to create a memory dump file for debugging STOP errors, you need to have a paging file on the boot partition. (See the section "Setting Startup and Recovery Options" later in this chapter for a discussion of memory dumps.) So in most cases it's best to split the paging file between the boot partition and one or more other partitions. When you do this, XP uses an internal algorithm to determine which paging file to use, allowing it to use the paging file on the less frequently accessed partition (or partitions) in preference to that on the boot partition (which will be heavily accessed).

The paging file takes up anything from about 100MB to a gigabyte or more. By default, the paging file is initially set to 1.5 times the amount of RAM in the computer: a 96MB paging file for a computer with 64MB RAM, 192MB for 128MB RAM, 384MB for 256MB RAM, and so on. So if you have a small drive or partition, you may want to move the paging file off it when you start running low on disk space. You can also split the paging file between different partitions if you're running low on space on all the partitions or if you want to optimize performance. (More on this in a moment.)

The paging file is called `PAGEFILE.SYS`. It's a hidden and protected operating system file, so if you feel the urge to look at its entry in an Explorer window, you'll need to select the Show Hidden Files and Folders option button and clear the Hide Protected Operating System Files check box on the View page of the Folder Options dialog box to see it. (To display the Folder Options dialog box, choose Tools ➢ Folder Options in an Explorer window.)

NOTE *If you look for the paging file, you may also see the hibernation file,* HIBERFIL.SYS. *(Your computer will have a hibernation file only if your computer supports hibernation.) By default, the hibernation file is stored on the same drive as the paging file, and is approximately the same size as the amount of RAM your computer contains. For example, if the computer has 256MB RAM, the hibernation file will be about 256MB as well. That's because XP writes the contents of RAM to the hibernation file before entering hibernation—RAM doesn't store information when it's powered down.*

As you've undoubtedly guessed, you shouldn't delete the paging file (even if you can see it). In fact, XP won't let you delete it—if you try to do so, it prevents you with an Error Deleting File or Folder message box telling you that the file "is being used by another person or program" and suggesting that you close any programs that might be using the file (but not any people!) and try again. You *can* delete the paging file by booting another operating system and attacking it from there, but there's little point in doing so—you can manage the paging file easily enough by following the procedure described next.

EXPERT KNOWLEDGE: USE A FIXED-SIZE PAGING FILE ON EACH PHYSICAL DRIVE

As you can see in the following list, XP lets you specify the size and location of your paging file. You can choose to place a paging file of just about any size on each fixed drive. (You can also place paging files on writable removable volumes, but this is seldom a good idea.) Or you can choose not to use a paging file at all.

For optimum performance, create one paging file on each physical drive in your computer, and make each paging file a fixed size by choosing the Custom Size option button and entering the same value in the Initial Size text box and the Maximum Size text box. Using a fixed-size paging file means not only that XP doesn't need to waste time resizing the paging file on-the-fly but also, more important, that the paging file can be written to disk in one contiguous area of the hard disk in question rather than fragmented over various parts of the disk. If the paging file isn't fragmented, access to virtual memory will be faster. Also—less of a bonus but important when things go wrong—memory dumps are less likely to contain errors if the paging file isn't fragmented than if it is.

Instead of creating a fixed-size paging file, you can create one on its own partition and allow XP to manage its size. Having no other files on the partition will prevent fragmentation from occurring.

To ensure that there's plenty of space in your fixed-size paging files, make their total size (on all drives together) equal to twice the amount of RAM in your computer.

When creating your paging files, make sure that you're clear about which volume resides in which partition of which physical drive so that you can avoid putting two or more paging files in different partitions on the same physical drive. (Doing so will rob you of the performance benefits of spreading out your paging files.) Also, make sure you don't put your paging files on removable drives—particularly on SmartMedia, CompactFlash, or Memory Stick cards that appear in the drives list. (Because XP constantly writes data to and reads data from the paging file, these types of removable storage will quickly reach the end of their life cycle and start developing errors if you put paging files on them.)

To specify the size and location of the paging file, follow these steps:

1. Click the Change button in the Virtual Memory group box on the Advanced page of the Performance Options dialog box. XP displays the Virtual Memory dialog box (shown in Figure 16.15).

FIGURE 16.15

In the Virtual Memory dialog box, you can specify the size of the paging file and the drive on which to locate it.

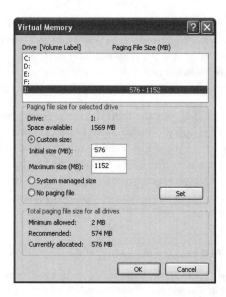

2. In the Drive list box, select the drive (or one of the drives) that contains the paging file.

3. In the Paging File Size for Selected Drive list box, specify the size of the file:

- If you want XP to manage the paging file's size, select the System Managed Size option button.

- If you want to manage the paging file's size yourself, select the Custom Size option button. Enter appropriate values in the Initial Size text box and the Maximum Size text box, based on the Recommended readout and the Currently Allocated readout in the Total Paging File Size for All Drives group box. Click the Set button.

- To remove the paging file from this drive, select the No Paging File option button. Click the Set button.

TIP   If you want, you can use the No Paging File option on each drive that currently contains a paging file to remove that paging file, leaving you with no paging file at all. Unless you have a huge amount of RAM—between 512MB and 1GB, depending on how many user sessions you typically have running at once and on how many programs and files each typically uses—this isn't usually a good idea. In theory, turning off the paging file should speed up XP (again, given plenty of RAM) because XP won't waste time writing memory data to disk and retrieving it from there. But in my experience turning off the paging file doesn't seem to deliver much of a performance boost, and it increases the likelihood of XP's running out of memory and crashing.

4. Specify paging file sizes for the other drives as appropriate by repeating steps 2 and 3.

5. Click the OK button. XP closes the Virtual Memory dialog box and returns you to the Advanced page of the Performance Options dialog box.

6. Click the OK button. XP closes the Performance Options dialog box and returns you to the Advanced page of the System Properties dialog box.

You'll need to restart XP before your changes to the paging file take effect.

TIP   Because your paging file can contain sensitive information, you may want to clear its contents when XP shuts down. To do so, see "Clearing the Paging File at Shutdown" in Chapter 12.

EXPERT KNOWLEDGE: WHAT HAPPENS WHEN YOU RUN OUT OF VIRTUAL MEMORY?

The main point of having virtual memory, of course, is to prevent you from running out of physical memory—as far as possible. But what happens if you run out of virtual memory as well?

Between the memory used by XP itself, the memory any running program occupies, and the memory taken up by whatever data files you've got open, RAM itself goes quickly enough. It's easy to chew up 128MB of RAM on a single-user session. And if a couple of other users have sessions running in the background, perhaps with a few large graphics files open for editing between them, 256MB can disappear faster than a sixteen-inch pepperoni pizza waylaid by teenagers.

Of course, XP doesn't allocate the RAM just like that to itself, the programs, and the files. Instead, it monitors your memory usage the whole time, doling out RAM and virtual memory as it judges best to keep itself running (the first priority) and the programs you're using in the foreground responding smoothly. As you work, XP is constantly shunting pages of memory from RAM to the paging file on the hard disk and vice versa, trying to keep ahead of the game.

If you want to get a rough picture of what's happening in memory and the page file, open Task Manager (right-click the notification area or open space in the Taskbar and choose Task Manager from the context menu). Look at the PF Usage readout and the Page File Usage History graph on the Performance page to see how much memory is being used. That reading is in megabytes or gigabytes. Then look at the Physical Memory (K) group box, which lists the total memory, available memory, and system cache. These figures are in kilobytes, so you'll need to divide by 1024 to get exact megabytes, but dividing by 1000 will give you figures close enough for government work.

The left illustration below shows the computer struggling. You can see that the CPU usage has been high but has dropped a bit. Memory usage is massive and has been steadily increasing. And there's only a pathetic amount of physical memory unused and available: less than 1 percent of the total.

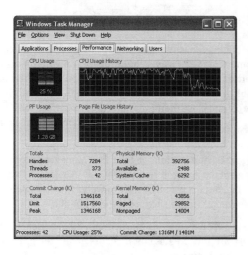

Continued on next page

EXPERT KNOWLEDGE: WHAT HAPPENS WHEN YOU RUN OUT OF VIRTUAL MEMORY? *(continued)*

Then display the Processes page and look at what's going on there. Select the Show Processes from All Users check box so that you see all the processes that are going on. Then choose View ➢ Select Columns to display the Select Columns dialog box. Select the Virtual Memory Size check box and click the OK button. Task Manager adds the VM Size column to the columns displayed. You can then sort the running processes by the Mem Usage column or by the VM Size column to see how much memory and virtual memory each is taking up. The right illustration above (which doesn't show processes from all users) explains why the computer in the left illustration was struggling: Two processes have absurdly large virtual machines. Also, check out the Commit Charge readout at the bottom of the Taskbar window. There's a runt's helping of memory left, and that's all.

For more precise monitoring of performance, use the Performance tool, as discussed in "Monitoring Performance with the Performance Tool" later in this chapter.

If you watch the readouts in Task Manager, you'll see that XP tries to keep some RAM available for as long as possible. When most of the RAM is gone, the amount of virtual memory consumed grows faster to accommodate your memory demands. But if you keep using up more memory (for example, by opening large files), and you've set a maximum size for your paging file, you'll eventually run out of virtual memory as well as RAM.

When you run out of virtual memory, XP displays the Windows – Virtual Memory Minimum Too Low pop-up in the notification area (shown below), telling you that it is increasing the size of your virtual memory paging file and that, while this is happening, requests for memory may be denied. XP is serious about denying requests for memory—it starts responding glacially slowly, and you'll probably be less frustrated if you leave it alone until it has finished increasing the size of the paging file. Click the pop-up to dismiss it, then sit back for a minute or two. Again, if you have Task Manager open, you can see XP increasing the size of the paging file—the size of the second Commit Charge figure on the Processes page will increase to show the new amount of memory available.

Once XP has grabbed more memory for the paging file, and has written as much data to disk as it must in order to get things moving again, it'll become more responsive—but probably only a *bit* more responsive. You can try to start using XP normally again at this point, but in most cases you'll be better off reducing the amount of memory you're using. This could mean closing some programs; closing some big files; using the Users page of Task Manager to log someone off and close their programs (losing any unsaved data if necessary); or shutting down XP and restarting it. (Restarting XP will also terminate any other user sessions and lose any unsaved data they contain.)

When XP is struggling for memory, you'll see the Applications page of Task Manager list programs as *Not Responding* when in fact they *are* responding but are doing so very slowly. You can use the End Task button to kill any program that really isn't responding, but it's usually better to wait a few seconds (or a few minutes) to see if the program comes back to life when XP is able to feed it more memory.

If you start any memory-hungry program when XP is struggling for memory, XP may clobber the program without notifying you. Again, it's better to wait until XP has stabilized itself and the programs that are currently running before you try to run any more programs.

Setting Environment Variables

From the Advanced page of the System Properties dialog box, you can click the Environment Variables button to display the Environment Variables dialog box (shown in Figure 16.16).

FIGURE 16.16

You can examine user variables and system variables in the Environment Variables dialog box.

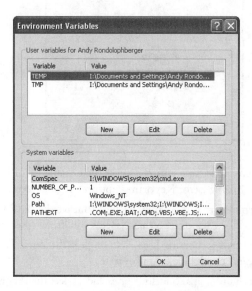

Environment variables have largely been superseded by Registry values, so you probably won't need to do much in this dialog box. You *can* use the New buttons, the Edit buttons, and the Delete buttons to create, edit, and delete user variables and system variables, but you shouldn't need to do so. And you *can* find out some information about XP and your system from the System Variables list box—but most of this information is more easily found elsewhere. For example, you'll find processor information in the System Info applet, which you can access from the Help and Support Center window.

Click the OK button or the Cancel button to close the Environment Variables dialog box when you've finished gazing at the wonders it offers.

Enabling and Disabling Error Reporting

If you've ever complained about software crashing on Windows, or about Windows itself crashing, you should like XP's error-reporting features, which by default are set up to enable error reporting on XP itself and programs running on it. You can turn off error reporting if it doesn't suit you, or you can choose to include or exclude specific programs from error reporting. For example, if you're developing a program, and it keeps crashing because you haven't programmed it right, you'd probably want to exclude it from error reporting on the grounds that Microsoft hadn't even heard of it yet (and they might not want to hear of it until you improve it).

To configure error reporting, follow these steps:

1. Click the Error Reporting button on the Advanced page of the System Properties dialog box. XP displays the Error Reporting dialog box (shown in Figure 16.17).

FIGURE 16.17

Use the Error Reporting dialog box and the linked dialog boxes to configure error reporting to your taste.

2. To turn off error reporting entirely, select the Disable Error Reporting option button. Otherwise, leave the Enable Error Reporting option button selected (as it is by default).

   ◆ If you turn off error reporting, it's best to leave the But Notify Me When Critical Errors Occur check box selected so that XP lets you know when something goes badly wrong.

3. In the Enable Error Reporting list, select or clear the Windows Operating System check box and the Programs check box as appropriate.

4. To specify which programs to include or exclude, select the Programs check box. Then click the Choose Programs button. XP displays the Choose Programs dialog box.

5. In the Report Errors for These Programs area, select the All Programs option button (the default setting) or the All Programs in This List option button as appropriate.

6. If you selected the All Programs in This List option button, select or clear the check boxes in the list box to indicate the programs you're interested in. Use the upper Add button and the resulting Add Program dialog box to add programs to this list.

7. To exclude specific programs from error reporting, use the lower Add button and its Add Program dialog box to build a list of programs for exclusion in the Do Not Report Errors for These Programs list box. Select and clear the check boxes for the programs you add to the list as appropriate.

8. Click the OK button. XP closes the Choose Programs dialog box.

9. Click the OK button. XP closes the Error Reporting dialog box.

Setting Startup and Recovery Options

XP includes several startup options that you should know about if you're running a dual-boot setup. (If you're not, just ignore these options: They don't apply to you at the moment.) And it lets you specify what it should do when it encounters a system failure—an error bad enough to crash the system.

To set startup and recovery options, follow these steps:

1. Click the Settings button in the Startup and Recovery group box on the Advanced page of the System Properties dialog box. XP displays the Startup and Recovery dialog box (shown in Figure 16.18).

FIGURE 16.18

Use the System Startup options in the Startup and Recovery dialog box to specify the default operating system to boot and for how long XP should display the boot list of operating systems. Use the System Failure options to specify what XP should do if it suffers a system failure.

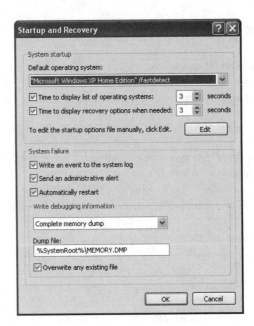

2. If you have a dual- or multiple-boot system, choose options in the System Startup group box:

   ◆ In the Default Operating System drop-down list, select the operating system that you want to boot by default.

   ◆ If you want XP to display the boot list of operating systems for a number of seconds before booting one, so that you can boot an operating system other than the default one, select the Time to Display List of Operating Systems check box and enter a suitable value in the text box. You can enter any value from 0 seconds to 999 seconds. The default value is 30 seconds, but most people find a shorter value more useful—long enough to give you time to select the operating system (or just tap a key) without needing pro-sports reflexes, but short enough to pass quickly if you just want to boot the default operating system.

TIP *You can edit the boot options file,* **BOOT.INI**, *manually by clicking the Edit button in the System Startup group box. The section "Creating a Dual-Boot Setup" at the end of this chapter discusses how to edit the boot options file.*

3. Whether you're using a single-boot system or a multiple-boot system, leave the Time to Display Recovery Options when Needed check box selected, and enter an appropriate number of seconds in its text box. When XP is rebooting after a failed boot, it displays the Recovery Options menu so that you can restart it in Safe mode if you want.

4. Choose options in the System Failure group box:

   Write an Event to the System Log check box   Select this check box (which is selected by default) if you want XP to write an event to the System Log. ("The System Log" earlier in this chapter shows you how to view and interpret the System Log.)

   Send an Administrative Alert check box   Select this check box (which is selected by default) if you want XP to display an Alert dialog box when a system failure occurs. Having a visual indication of narrowly averted or impending disaster can concentrate the mind wonderfully.

Automatically Restart check box Select this check box (which is selected by default) if you want XP to automatically reboot if there's a system failure. (XP reboots after writing that event to the System Log and sending an administrative alert, if you left those check boxes selected.)

TIP *It should go without saying that these recovery options aren't a panacea. Any crash serious enough to be called a system failure will almost invariably result in the loss of any unsaved data sitting around in the programs affected. Besides, despite sitting stably on the New Technology bedrock of Windows NT and 2000, XP still suffers occasional lockups, particularly with misbehaving hardware drivers. If your system hangs (freezes), you'll probably need to reboot it manually, because the auto-reboot functionality will be frozen as well. After rebooting, you'll find that no event was written to the System Log and no administrative alert was sent, because XP was just as blindsided by the hang as you were.*

Write Debugging Information group box In the drop-down list, select the type of debugging information that you want XP to write in the event of a crash. Your choices are None, Small Memory Dump, Kernel Memory Dump, and Complete Memory Dump. The None choice turns off the writing of debugging information. A Small Memory Dump creates a file with a name built of the prefix MINI, the date in MMDDYY format, a hyphen, the number of the dump, and the DMP extension. For example, the first dump on Christmas Day 2002 is named MINI122502-01.DMP. The dump file is stored in the directory specified in the Small Dump Directory text box and contains the smallest possible amount of memory information to be useful for debugging. With each crash, XP creates a new file. To create a Small Memory Dump, XP needs a paging file of at least 2MB on the boot volume of your computer. A Kernel Memory Dump dumps only the kernel memory into a file called MEMORY.DMP by default and needs between 50 and 800MB of space for the paging file on the boot volume (not on another volume). A Complete Memory Dump, as its name suggests, dumps all the information contained in system memory when the crash occurred. Again, this goes into a file named MEMORY.DMP by default. To create a complete memory dump, you need to have a paging file on the boot volume (again, not on another volume) of at least the size of your computer's RAM plus 1MB (for example, a paging file of at least 97MB if your computer has 96MB RAM). Choose the location and name for the dump file in the text box in the Write Debugging Information group box, and select the Overwrite Any Existing File check box if appropriate. (This check box isn't available for Small Memory Dump, because this option creates a sequence of files automatically.)

NOTE *A small memory dump happens instantaneously. A kernel dump takes a bit longer. A complete memory dump takes anything from a few seconds to a minute or two. For a kernel dump or a complete dump, XP displays a Blue Screen of Death with a percentage counter as it writes the contents of memory to disk. When this is done, the computer reboots (if you've left the Automatically Restart check box selected).*

5. Click the OK button. XP closes the Startup and Recovery dialog box.

TIP *To check how the memory dump works, or to experience a crash in action, try using the CrashOnCtrlScroll Registry key as discussed in the "Expert Knowledge: Crashing Your Computer on Cue" sidebar in Chapter 12. On some computers, this produces a dump followed by a reboot. On other computers, it produces a custom Blue Screen of Death and nothing beyond it.*

Monitoring Performance with the Performance Tool

As you saw earlier in the chapter, you can monitor performance to some extent by using Task Manager—and if any program gets out of hand, you can shut it down without much difficulty from there. But if you want to see more precisely what's happening on your computer, use the Performance tool instead.

To run Performance, take the following steps:

1. Choose Start ➢ Control Panel. XP displays Control Panel.

2. Click the Performance and Maintenance link. XP displays the Performance and Maintenance screen.

3. Click the Administrative Tools link. XP displays the Administrative Tools screen.

4. Double-click the Performance shortcut. XP starts Performance (shown in Figure 16.19).

FIGURE 16.19

If Task Manager doesn't give you the detail you need on your computer's performance, use the Performance tool to monitor performance.

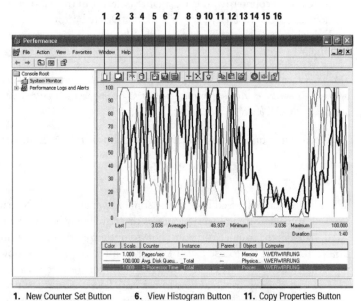

1. New Counter Set Button
2. Clear Display Button
3. View Current Activity Button
4. View Log Data Button
5. View Graph Button
6. View Histogram Button
7. View Report Button
8. Add Button
9. Delete Button
10. Highlight Button
11. Copy Properties Button
12. Paste Counter List Button
13. Properties Button
14. Freeze Display Button
15. Update Data Button
16. Help Button

In grayscale, this looks like a spider taking a polygraph test, but in color, it's easy enough to read. As you can more or less see in the figure, Performance starts you off in Graph view tracking three counters: Pages/Sec, Avg. Disk Queue Length, and % Processor Time (listed in the list box at the bottom of the window).

You can add further counters by taking the following steps:

1. Click the Add button. XP displays the Add Counters dialog box.

2. Either select the Use Local Computer Counters option button or select the Select Counters from Computer option button and choose your computer in the drop-down list. It doesn't

matter which. Performance is designed to allow administrators to monitor computers remotely, but you can't use this capability with XP Home.

3. In the Performance Object drop-down list, select the category of item you want to monitor. For example, you might select Memory. XP displays a list of the counters available for that performance object in the left list box.

4. With the Select Counters from List option button selected (as it is by default), select the first counter in the left list box and click the Add button to add it to the Performance window.

   ◆ Click the Explain button to display a window explaining the meaning of the current counter.

5. Add further counters by repeating steps 3 and 4.

6. Click the Close button. XP closes the Add Counters dialog box.

To remove a counter from Performance, select it in the list box at the bottom of the Performance window and press the Delete key or click the Delete button.

To highlight a counter with a thick black line, select the counter in the list box and click the Highlight button.

TIP   Once you've set up a view in Performance that shows the items you want to track, you can add it to your favorites by choosing Favorites ➢ Add to Favorites, specifying the name for the favorite in the resulting Add to Favorites dialog box, and clicking the OK button.

When you've finished using Performance, choose File ➢ Exit. XP closes Performance.

Up Next

This chapter has discussed how to use some key tools to keep XP running as smoothly as possible. You've learned how to deal with programs that have hung; how to configure Windows Update to keep XP updated in the manner you want; how to optimize performance, and how to monitor performance. You've also seen how to use Event Viewer to identify problems, how to enable and disable error reporting, and how to set environment variables for the rare occasions when you may need them.

The next chapter discusses how to use XP's Backup Utility to protect your valuable data, how to troubleshoot common but vexing problems, and how to recover from disaster when it strikes.

Chapter 17

Backup, Troubleshooting, and Disaster Recovery

THIS CHAPTER IS LIKE an extended visit to the dentist, so I'll forgive you if you approach it with a spectacular lack of enthusiasm and if you find it hard going. But if you skip it, I doubt you'll ever forgive yourself should things go wrong.

There are various reasons to visit the dentist, but for most people, the reasons break down to fear, guilt, pain, and disaster, not necessarily in that order and not necessarily separated from each other. (If you disagree, you're either very lucky or you're a dentist. Either way, don't change.)

First, I'm going to tell you—wait, make that *remind* you—why you must floss regularly so that you don't lose your data. Then I'm going to discuss XP's built-in gum-shield, Windows File Protection, and how it can spare you grief. Then I'll show you how to protect your teeth from ill-judged actions and how to use the toothpick that XP provides for digging out detritus that gets stuck. Last, I'll show you how to recover from boot problems—no, no, that has nothing to do with teeth, I hope…

Before we start, one general point: After restoring any system files from the XP CD, it's a good idea to run Windows Update (as discussed in the previous chapter) to make sure that you have the latest versions of all system files.

This chapter covers the following topics:

- ◆ Backing up your data—and restoring it
- ◆ Understanding how the Windows File Protection feature works
- ◆ Using System Restore to protect and restore your system
- ◆ Repairing an XP installation using Recovery Console
- ◆ Troubleshooting boot problems

Backing Up Your Data—and Restoring It

This section discusses how to install and use XP's Backup Utility to back up your data for protection against problems and restore it when problems arise. It starts by talking about *why* you must back up your data, and the equipment and media you'll need to do so, before discussing the actual procedures for using Backup Utility.

Why You Must Back Up Your Data

If you've used most any computer for any length of time, you likely don't need to be told why you *must* back up your data: Because if you don't, you may lose it irretrievably. XP is arguably more stable than any other version of Windows yet released, but XP itself can still crash, as can any program running on it. If XP or a program crashes, you're likely to lose unsaved data.

Even if all your software is stable, your data is at risk from several other threats, of which the following are the most frequent repeat offenders:

Hardware problems If your hard drive develops bad sectors or gets corrupted, you can lose anything from a file to all your files. Or your computer may get physically damaged: Laptops can get dropped, spilled upon, or baked (or frozen) when left in cars. Desktop computers usually avoid such trials of gravity, precipitation, and thermodynamics but are threatened by the attention of children, pets, and worse.

Electrical problems Even if you use an uninterruptible power supply (UPS) to protect against power outages (as discussed in the section "Configuring XP to Use an Uninterruptible Power Supply" in Chapter 14), severe electrical storms or disruptions can still damage your computer. For example, a man I used to work with suffered a complete data loss when a truck backed into a transformer at the electric utility just down the street from him, shorting some circuits and sending an estimated 7000 volts through the wires that toasted all his electrical equipment from doorbell to refrigerator. This is once-in-a-lifetime bad luck, but you should be prepared for something this bad, just as you should carry insurance against unpleasant if unlikely things happening to you and yours.

Viruses and worms Even if you always use anti-virus software and firewalls to protect your computer from as many threats as possible (and you should), you may run into a virus or worm that damages your data.

User error You or another user may overwrite or delete files, deliberately or by accident.

Theft and vandalism Whether at work, at home, on the road, or in the air, your computer could be stolen. Even if you use a third-party encryption solution to secure your data against prying eyes, you'll still need a backup so that *you* can get at it.

The only reason for *not* backing up your data is if you're prepared to lose everything on your computer at a moment's notice. For example, say you keep a computer set aside for testing viruses, and you never put any valuable data on it. You might then be prepared to reinstall Windows and all applications from scratch at any point. But even then, you might do better to back the computer up so that you can restore it quickly to a pristine state by using a partition-cloning utility such as PartitionMagic (discussed in the section "Creating Drive Images" later in this chapter).

NOTE   If you're using XP Home in your home business, backing up your files is even more vital for a couple of reasons. First, you may be obliged to keep records of your business for a certain number of years. Second, however humble they may seem to you—a customer database in Address Book, spreadsheets in Works or Excel workbooks containing income and expenses, pending orders in Access, proposals in Word or WordPad—those files are probably even more vital to your business than you imagine. A survey conducted by McGladrey and Pullen, LLP, a firm of UK accountants, found that any company that's unable to get at its data for 10 days will never recover fully (yes, never), and 43 percent of them will go out of business sooner or later. In short, data loss is benign only if you're Enron or Andersen—and if you are one of those entities, you've got plenty of other problems.

What to Back Up

There's a temptation to back up *everything* on your computer, so that, if needed, you could restore it to the state it was in before the problem occurred with your computer or your data. But there's not much sense in doing this, because some of the files on your computer are essentially useless and others are easily replaceable. For example, there's no sense in backing up your paging file or your hibernation file, because they don't contain any data that you can actually use. And if you still have your XP installation CD (or network installation source), you can reinstall your operating system files easily. Generally speaking, you'll want to back up your data files—the information you've created with the sweat of your virtual brow—and your configuration files, but not the system files and program files that you can easily reinstall from CD or DVD.

Backup Utility *does* let you back up just about all the data on your computer, but you won't want to do this frequently, because it takes a long time and requires capacious backup media. In most cases, you'll do better to craft a strategy of regular complete backups with frequent incremental backups that will provide near-total cover of the files you've sweated over. That means backing up your data files and configuration files.

Backup Utility makes this process fairly easy, but you can help make it even easier by arranging your folders suitably for backup. In particular, keep your documents in a separate folder structure than your program files, as XP encourages you to do (and as most Windows guidelines–compliant programs also suggest).

Tech moment: Windows files have an *archive bit* that can be set on or off to indicate the backup status of the file. When the archive bit is on, the file needs backing up; when the bit is off, the file doesn't need backing up. Most backup operations set the archive bit to the Off position once they've backed up the file (but see the description of differential backups in the next section for an exception). The next time a program changes a file, it sets the archive bit to the On position again, so the backup program knows that the file needs to be backed up once more.

When to Back Up Your Data

Back up your data regularly and frequently enough that you never expose yourself to the chance of losing more data than you can recreate comfortably and easily. If you use your computer mostly for e-mail and entertainment, you might be comfortable backing it up only once a week or once every couple of weeks. If you use your computer for business, you might want to back it up every day, or even every few hours.

Instead of performing ultra-frequent backups, you may prefer to manually copy your current working documents to a removable medium (such as a Zip disk or a CD recorder running packet-writing software) every few hours. Doing so can be quicker and easier than running backup software.

TIP   If you back up your computer infrequently, also back it up after making major hardware changes to it. Otherwise, if you end up needing to restore from a backup that was made on substantially different hardware than the computer now has, you may fall afoul of the hardware-snooping checks in Windows Product Activation and need to reactivate your copy of XP. (For a discussion of Windows Product Activation, see the section "Activating XP" in Chapter 2.)

Backup Types

Backup Utility supports these five backup types: normal, copy, differential, incremental, and daily. You can save a great deal of time and effort by choosing the backup type appropriate to your needs.

Normal backup   A normal backup backs up every file and folder specified and clears the archive bit. The files and folders then aren't backed up again until they've been changed.

Copy backup   A copy backup copies every file and folder specified to the backup media.

Differential backup   A differential backup backs up all the files that have been changed since the last full backup. Differential backups *don't* clear the archive bit and thus grow in size. Say you perform a full backup on a Friday, then a differential backup on each other weekday. Monday's differential backup contains files that have changed on Saturday, Sunday, and Monday; Tuesday's contains changes from Saturday through Tuesday; and so on. To restore a computer using a full backup and a differential backup, you need only the latest differential backup and the full backup. But you'll need more capacious backup media (discussed in the next section) than for incremental backups (discussed next).

Incremental backup   An incremental backup backs up all the files that have been changed since the last full backup or incremental backup. An incremental backup clears the archive bit for the files it backs up, so that they don't need backing up until they change again. Incremental backups after the first have the advantage of being smaller than differential backups (again, after the first), but they have the corresponding disadvantage that you need to reapply each incremental backup in turn on top of the last full backup to fully restore the file set. If your backup media are capacious enough to store differential backups, differential is a better option than incremental.

NOTE   *Incremental backups and differential backups also have the disadvantage that if you need to perform a partial restore, you need to find the files involved: With an incremental backup, you may need to check all the incremental backups as well as the full backup. With a differential backup, you'll need to check the latest differential backup and the full backup. Further, incremental backups increase your exposure to backup media problems, because you have fewer backup copies of the files.*

Daily backup   As its name suggests, a daily backup backs up only the files modified on the day you run the backup. To get full coverage with daily backups, you need to run them literally every day: Skip a day, and you might miss backing up an important file. But if you're conscientious about backing up daily, and you know the date on which you last changed the file you're looking for, you should be able to find it easily.

Choosing Backup Media

Ideally, you want to back up your data to a medium that's capacious enough to hold it all but portable enough to keep in a safe place. The medium would also be inexpensive enough for you to be able to create backups as frequently as needed—say, every day, or several times a week.

Given the amount of data most people back up, such a medium is hard to find. These are the main contenders:

◆   Backup tapes have the capacity but are too slow for easy use. DAT drives largely haven't crossed into the consumer realm, being still perceived as tools for system administrators and professional users. QIC-Travan drives *are* in the consumer realm but still are not very widely used.

- Recordable DVDs offer impressive capacity—9.4GB on a single DVD-RAM disc, 4.7GB on a DVD-RW , DVD+RW , or DVD-R disc—but are still too expensive for most people for regular use.

- Recordable CDs are inexpensive and easy to use, but their limited capacity means that most people will need to split backups across several CDs. Backup Utility can't back up directly to a CD, but you can back up to a file and then copy it to a CD.

- Removable media such as Zip disks are relatively inexpensive and very easy to use. Zip disks have a capacity far more limited than that of recordable CDs, but alternatives such as the Orb (5.7GB; `www.castlewood.com`) offer far greater capacity.

- A network drive can provide plenty of space, good space, and extreme simplicity for a backup, but ideally you need to have offsite backup as well. (If your network is extensive enough that your network drive *is* effectively offsite, you're on to a winner here.)

- A second (or subsequent) hard disk offers the capacity and speed for a complete backup. External USB 2.0 or FireWire hard drives offer portability as well. But few people can afford one or more extra external hard drives for backup.

TIP   With backup, you don't need to put all of your virtual eggs in one basket. Whatever form of backup you choose for most of your files, consider backing up key files in a safe location online. This can be particularly valuable if you travel for work and need immediate access to backups of your data if a crisis strikes—for example, if your laptop fritzes out when a flight attendant accidentally christens it with coffee.

- Online backup offers easy access from any computer that can connect to the Internet—but compared to other backup media, it's slow and expensive. If you have enough money and a fast enough Internet connection, you can back up *all* your data online. But for most people, online is an option only for small amounts of data.

Installing Backup Utility

Windows Setup doesn't install Backup Utility on Windows XP Home by default, so you'll need to install it manually from your XP installation CD. Double-click the file `NTBACKUP.MSI` in the `\VALUEADD\MSFT\NTBACKUP\` folder on your XP Home installation CD. XP runs the Windows Backup Utility Installation Wizard, which installs Backup for you. There are no options to choose— all you need to do is click the Finish button to close the wizard when it has finished installing Backup.

Creating a Backup

Once you've installed Backup Utility, you can create a backup by taking the following steps:

1. Choose Start ➢ All Programs ➢ Accessories ➢ System Tools ➢ Backup. XP launches Backup Utility.

2. Click the Next button. The wizard displays the Backup or Restore page.

3. Make sure the Back Up Files and Settings option button is selected, and then click the Next button. The wizard displays the What to Back Up page (see Figure 17.1).

FIGURE 17.1

On the What to Back Up page of the Backup or Restore Wizard, select the appropriate option button. *Don't* select the All Information on This Computer option button, because it won't work with XP Home.

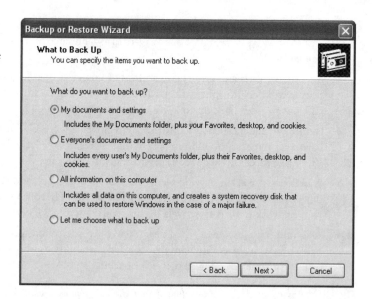

4. Select the appropriate option button:

My Documents and Settings option button   Selecting this option button backs up your user profile—all the configuration information for your user account—including your Desktop and all the documents stored in your \My Documents\ folder and its subfolders.

WARNING   The My Documents and Settings backup option works only if your \My Documents\ folder is in its default location. If you've moved it to a different location, select the Let Me Choose What to Back Up option button instead and specify the location of your \My Documents\ folder manually.

Everyone's Documents and Settings option button   Selecting this option button backs up user profiles for all the user accounts on the computer. (Essentially, this option backs up all the files in the \Documents and Settings\ folder.)

All Information on This Computer option button   This option button is used for an XP Professional feature called Automated System Recovery (ASR), which lets you make a backup of your entire system, together with a floppy disk that contains a couple of key files telling ASR what goes where on your hard disk (the partition structure, and so on). XP Home *doesn't* include support for ASR, but Backup Utility isn't fully aware of this. Don't try to use this option with XP Home, because it doesn't work.

Let Me Choose What to Back Up option button   This option button lets you specify exactly which files and folders you want to back up. This option gives you much greater flexibility than the first two options, but it raises the risk that you'll forget to back up something important.

5. Click the Next button. If you selected the Let Me Choose What to Back Up option button, the wizard displays the Items to Back Up page (see Figure 17.2). If you selected one of the other items, go to step 7.

FIGURE 17.2

On the Items to Back Up page of the Backup or Restore Wizard, specify exactly which files and folders you want to back up.

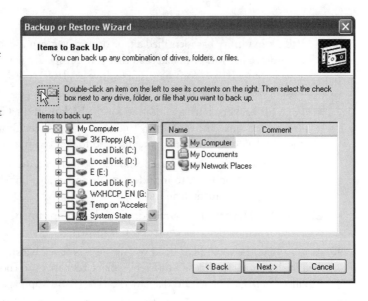

6. Select the folders and files you want to back up, and then click the Next button. The wizard displays the Backup Type, Destination, and Name page (see Figure 17.3).

   ◆ Click a plus (+) sign to expand one of the entries so that you can see the items it contains.

   ◆ You may want to back up the System State data, which consists of the Registry, the boot files, and the COM+ Class Registration Database.

FIGURE 17.3

On the Backup Type, Destination, and Name dialog box, specify what type of backup to create and where to place it.

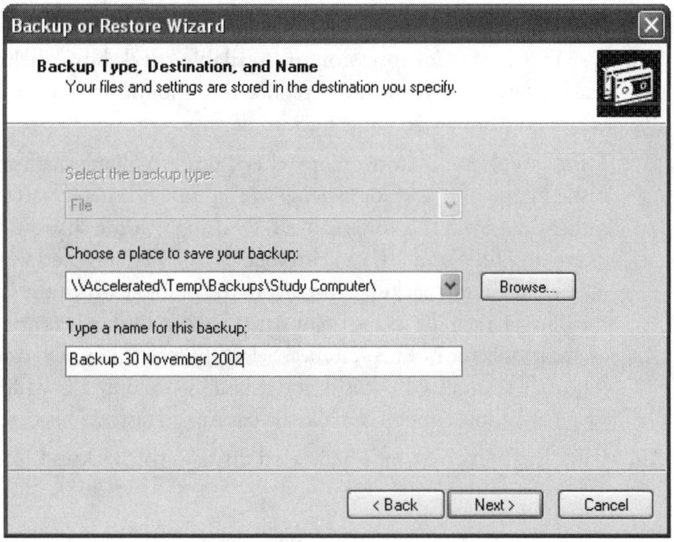

Backup or Restore Wizard

Backup Type, Destination, and Name
Your files and settings are stored in the destination you specify.

Select the backup type:

| File | ▾ |

Choose a place to save your backup:

| \\Accelerated\Temp\Backups\Study Computer\ | ▾ | Browse...

Type a name for this backup:

| Backup 30 November 2002 |

< Back   Next >   Cancel

7. Choose options as appropriate:

   ◆ If Backup Utility has identified a tape drive that it can use, the Select the Backup Type drop-down list will be available so that you can specify whether to make a tape backup or a file backup. If you don't have a tape drive available, this drop-down list will be unavailable, because you can make only a file backup.

   ◆ For a file backup, enter the location for the backup in the Choose a Place to Save Your Backup text box. The easiest way to do this is to use the Browse button and the resulting Save As dialog box to specify the disk and folder, but you can type the path if you prefer.

   ◆ In the Type a Name for This Backup text box, enter a descriptive name for the backup. Usually it's a good idea to include the date and details on what type of backup it is—full, differential, incremental, and so on.

8. Click the Next button. The wizard displays the Completing the Backup or Restore Wizard page, which summarizes the choices you've made.

9. At this point, the wizard has lined you up for a Normal backup. To go ahead with this, click the Finish button. To choose a different type of backup, or to choose further options, click the Advanced button. The wizard displays the Type of Backup page.

10. In the Select the Type of Backup drop-down list, select Normal, Copy, Incremental, Differential, or Daily as appropriate. (See the section "Backup Types," earlier in the chapter, for an explanation of the different backup types.) Click the Next button. The wizard displays the How to Back Up page.

11. Choose the appropriate options:

    Verify Data after Backup check box   Always verify your data after backup. If the backup isn't okay, you haven't just wasted time (and perhaps media), but you've also compromised the security of your data.

    Use Hardware Compression, if Available check box   Select this check box if you want to use hardware compression to reduce the amount of space the backup consumes. This option is available only with some backup devices.

    Disable Volume Shadow Copy check box   Volume shadow copy is a technology that makes an instant copy of the volume being backed up and then creates the backup from the shadow copy rather than from the volume itself. By using volume shadow copy, you can continue to use programs and files (and XP can continue to run services) even while the backup is being created, and all the data in the backup comes from the point at which the backup was started rather than from the state of each file at the point when Backup Utility gets around to it. Volume shadow copy is available only for NTFS volumes. Select this check box if you want to disable volume shadow copy. The only reason to do so is if you're backing up only a few files or folders, in which case *not* using volume shadow copy may make the backup go faster. This check box is available only sometimes.

12. Click the Next button. The wizard displays the Backup Options page (see Figure 17.4).

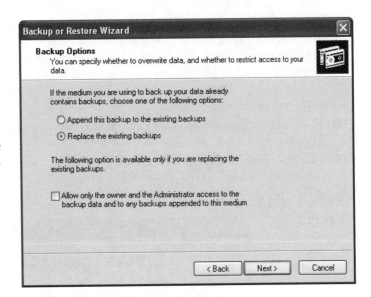

FIGURE 17.4

On the Backup Options page of the Backup or Restore Wizard, you can choose whether to append this backup to your existing backups or overwrite the existing backups.

13. If the location to which you're backing up already contains a backup, select the Append This Backup to the Existing Backups option button or the Replace the Existing Backups option button as appropriate. If you select the Replace the Existing Backups option button, XP makes available the Allow Only the Owner and the Administrator Access to the Backup Data and to Any Backups Appended to This Medium check box. Select this check box if you want to restrict access to the backups.

14. Click the Next button. The wizard displays the When to Back Up page (see Figure 17.5).

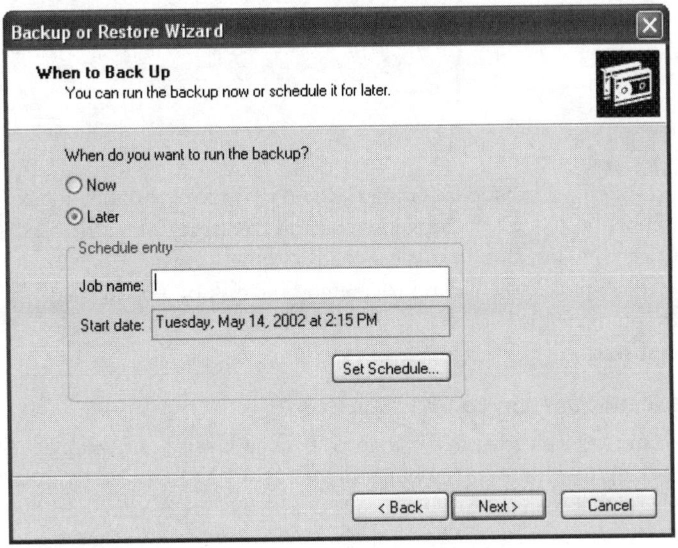

FIGURE 17.5

On the When to Back Up page of the Backup or Restore Wizard, you can create a schedule for running the backup job later.

15. To have the backup job run immediately, leave the Now option button selected, as it should be by default. To run the job later, select the Later option button and use the controls in the Schedule Entry group box to specify when to run the job. Click the Set Schedule button to display the Schedule Job dialog box, in which you can set specifics for the schedule. (See the section "Setting Advanced Properties for a Scheduled Task" in Chapter 11 for a discussion of these options.)

16. Click the Next button. The wizard again displays the Completing the Backup or Restore Wizard page, but this time there's no Advanced button to click.

17. Click the Finish button. The wizard closes. If you chose to run the backup immediately, XP displays the Backup Progress dialog box (see Figure 17.6), which shows you what's happening as the backup runs.

FIGURE 17.6

XP displays the Backup Progress dialog box while the backup is running.

When the backup is complete, the Backup Progress dialog box offers a Close button and a Report button. Click the Report button to display a text file containing the details of the backup. Click the Close button to close the Backup Progress dialog box.

If you made the backup to a removable disk or a backup tape, label it and store it in a safe place. If you made the backup to a file with the intention of transferring it to a recordable CD, read the next section.

BACKING UP FILES TO A WRITABLE CD

As mentioned earlier in the chapter, Backup Utility can't back up directly to a CD drive, but you can back up to a file and then burn that file to a CD. Provided that you can keep the size of the backup file smaller than the maximum size of the CD you're using (650MB or 800MB, depending on the type of CD), the procedure is as simple as right-clicking the backup file, choosing Send To ➢ CD Drive, and then running the CD Burning Wizard (as discussed in Chapter 28).

If you want to cut one step out of the process, back up to a file in the \CD Burning\ folder and then burn it to CD from there. The \CD Burning\ folder is located at *%userprofile%*\Local Settings\ Application Data\Microsoft\CD Burning—for example, C:\Documents and Settings\Philippa User\Local Settings\Application Data\Microsoft\CD Burning. (You can move this folder by using the tool on the My Computer\Special Folders page of the Tweak UI PowerToy.)

Restoring Files from Backup

To restore files from backup, take the following steps:

1. Choose Start ➢ All Programs ➢ Accessories ➢ System Tools ➢ Backup. XP launches Backup Utility.

2. Click the Next button. The wizard displays the Backup or Restore page.

3. Select the Restore Files and Settings option button and click the Next button. The wizard displays the What to Restore page (see Figure 17.7), which contains a list of the items that you can restore.

FIGURE 17.7

On the What to Restore page of the Backup or Restore Wizard, select the files or folders that you want to restore.

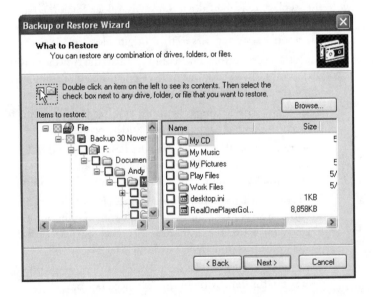

4. If the Items to Restore list box contains the backup file or backup source you want to use, select the items in the list boxes. If not, use the Browse button and the resulting Open Backup File dialog box to identify the backup file you want to use.

5. Click the Next button. The wizard displays the Completing the Backup or Restore Wizard page. As with the backup process, you can click the Finish button to proceed with the restoration with default options, or you can click the Advanced button to choose further options.

6. If you click the Advanced button, the wizard displays the Where to Restore page, which lets you specify the location to which to restore the files:

Original Location   Selecting this option makes Backup Utility restore the files and folders to the drive and folder they were originally in. Select this option when restoring a full backup to a drive you've reformatted. If the drive contains data, you may overwrite existing files.

Alternate Location   To restore the files to a different location from where they were before, select this option and enter the path in the Alternate Location text box that the wizard displays. (You can browse to the location.) Using this option lets you restore files without risking overwriting existing files. You can then examine the restored files and the existing files and perform any necessary overwriting manually.

Single Folder   To restore all the files you're restoring to a single folder of your choosing, select this option and enter the path in the Folder Name text box that the wizard displays. (Again, you can browse to the location.) This option is most useful when you're restoring a small number of files from separate folders.

7. Click the Next button. The wizard displays the How to Restore page, which offers three option buttons for you to specify whether Backup Utility should overwrite existing files that have the same names as files you're restoring. Choose the Leave Existing Files option button, the Replace Existing Files if They Are Older Than the Backup Files option button, or the Replace Existing Files option button as appropriate. (This option is usually relevant only when you're restoring files to their original location.)

8. Click the Next button. The wizard displays the Advanced Restore Options page, which offers the options discussed in the following list. These options are available only if they are applicable to the restore operation you're performing.

Restore Security Settings check box   Select this check box to make Backup Utility reapply the security settings to the files and folders being restored.

Restore Junction Points, but Not the Folders and File Data They Reference check box
Select this check box to make Backup Utility restore any junction points you've created (you'll know if you have) and you need to restore both the junction points and the data they point to.

Preserve Existing Volume Mount Points check box   Select this check box if you're restoring an entire drive but you don't want the existing mount points on the volume to be overwritten. If you've formatted the drive, clear this check box so that Backup Utility restores the mount points in the backup together with the data.

9. Click the Next button. The wizard displays the Completing the Backup or Restore Wizard page again, this time without the Advanced button.

10. Review the choices you've made, and click the Finish button if you're ready to commit the restore operation.

XP displays the Restore Progress dialog box as it performs the restore operation. When the backup is complete, the Restore Progress dialog box offers a Close button and a Report button. Click the Report button to display a text file containing the details of the restore operation. Click the Close button to close the Restore Progress dialog box.

Using Backup Utility in Advanced Mode

By default, Backup Utility runs in Wizard mode as the Backup or Restore Wizard and displays the Welcome to the Backup or Restore Wizard screen. And as you've seen in the preceding sections, the Backup or Restore Wizard simplifies the process of backing up and restoring data.

If you're an experienced user, you may want to give yourself more control of Backup Utility and access advanced settings. To do so, clear the Always Start in Wizard Mode check box on the Welcome page of the Backup or Restore Wizard and click the Advanced Mode link. The wizard displays Backup Utility in Advanced mode as a program window with menu bar and four tabbed pages.

Welcome page This page contains a Backup Wizard button, a Restore Wizard button, and an Automated System Recovery Wizard button. The Automated System Recovery feature is not included in XP Home, so don't try to use the third button.

Backup page This page (shown in Figure 17.8) lets you select the items you want to back up, the destination for the backup, and the filename to use. Click the Start Backup button to start running the backup.

FIGURE 17.8

You can also use Backup Utility in Advanced mode, which lets you use more options.

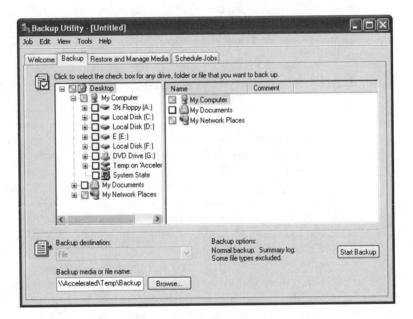

Restore and Manage Media page This page lets you select the items you want to restore and specify a restore location. Click the Start Restore button to start the restore operation.

Schedule Jobs page This page contains a month-by-month calendar and an Add Job button that you can click to start creating a scheduled backup.

You can access most of Backup Utility's configuration options through the five pages of the Options dialog box (Tools ➢ Options). In particular, you may want to explore the Exclude Files page, which lets you specify which files to exclude from the backups you make. Backup Utility automatically excludes a number of files that you're very unlikely to need to back up, including the paging file and the hibernation file.

Creating Drive Images

Backing up your data files so that you can restore them gives you a good amount of protection against disaster. But what if you want to back up your computer's whole configuration—operating system files, program files, and data—so that you can restore everything at once?

As mentioned earlier in this book, XP Professional has a feature called Automated System Recovery (ASR) that lets you create a more-or-less complete backup set that you can use to restore your computer to the state it was in when you made the ASR backup. To use ASR, you boot from your XP CD, then provide XP with the floppy disk (which tells XP where the partitions go and which files to load) and the backup file.

ASR is a little clunky and best reserved for emergencies. In any case, ASR isn't included in XP Home, so if you want the kind of backup ASR provides, you need to look elsewhere.

At this writing, the most satisfactory solution is software that creates a *drive image*—a file containing all the information from the specified drive or partition. Leading drive-imaging programs include Drive Image from PowerQuest Corporation (`www.driveimage.com`) and Norton Ghost (`www.ghost.com`). Drive Image and Ghost let you create drive images on local hard disks, on networked drives, and on recordable CDs (splitting the image file into multiple parts small enough to fit on CDs).

You also create boot disks ("rescue disks" for Drive Image) that enable you to boot from a floppy drive and access your drive-image files so that you can restore from them.

Understanding Windows File Protection

As mentioned in Chapter 1, XP includes a feature called Windows File Protection that limits the damage that you can do by ill-advisedly pruning the contents of your system folders or that programs, installation routines, or malware can cause by overwriting system files such as dynamic-link libraries (DLLs) and executable files with unauthorized versions of files with the same name.

Windows File Protection uses digital signatures and catalog files produced by code signing to check that the files are authorized versions. You may remember from Chapter 14 that XP is very reluctant to let you install a driver that doesn't have the appropriate digital signature. (Figure 14.9 showed an example of the type of protest you'll get if you try.) Windows File Protection extends this protection to all key system files, including all SYS, DLL, EXE, TTF (TrueType font), FON (font), and OCX (ActiveX component) files.

If you delete a protected file, or if a program overwrites or replaces a protected file, Windows File Protection restores the file from its own cache (stored in the *%systemroot%*\system32\dllcache\ folder) or from the distribution media for the software as soon as it notices the file is missing. XP then displays an alert message box to an administrator notifying them that the file has been replaced.

There are no interface settings for Windows File Protection: It's on all the time, and you shouldn't want to turn it off. You shouldn't need to change settings for Windows File Protection—but if you're terminally curious, you *can* make the changes discussed in the following sections. To do so, you need to be logged on as a Computer Administrator user—but you'd guessed that already.

Change the Size of the Dllcache Folder

You can adjust the amount of space that the Dllcache folder has available for caching copies of the protected files by changing the value of the SFCQuota value entry in the HKEY_LOCAL_MACHINE\Software\ Microsoft\Windows NT\CurrentVersion\Winlogon key in the Registry. The default setting is 0xffffffff, which tells XP to cache all protected system files on the local hard disk. If you change this setting, be sure to allow plenty of space for the cached files.

Change the Location of the Dllcache Folder

You can move the Dllcache folder to a different location by creating an expandable string value entry named `SFCDllCacheDir` in the `HKEY_LOCAL_MACHINE\Software\Microsoft\Windows NT\CurrentVersion\Winlogon` key in the Registry. As mentioned above, the default location of the folder is *%systemroot%*`\System32`. (You need to create the value entry because XP doesn't really want you to move this folder.) The folder needs to be on a local drive rather than a network drive.

Disable Windows File Protection

You can disable Windows File Protection—but only if you've hooked up a kernel debugger to the computer to debug a process. If you've done that, you can set the value entry `SFCDisable` in the `HKEY_LOCAL_MACHINE\Software\Microsoft\Windows NT\CurrentVersion\Winlogon` key in the Registry to 1 or 2 instead of its normal setting of 0 (enabled). A setting of 1 disables Windows File Protection permanently, but XP prompts you to reenable it at each boot. A setting of 2 disables Windows File Protection only for the next boot.

Of more interest is the setting of 4, which leaves Windows File Protection enabled but disables any pop-up messages it generates.

Checking Files with System File Checker

If you suspect that there may be a problem with your files, you can set the System File Checker tool to scan your protected system files and verify their versions. System File Checker is a command-line tool that runs after you reboot the computer. If it finds a protected file has been damaged or over-written, it replaces it with the correct file from the *%systemroot%*`\system32\dllcache\` folder, which is a storage area for copies of protected files. You may need to provide your XP CD if System File Checker needs files that aren't held in the cache.

You need to be logged on as a Computer Administrator user to run System File Checker.

To set System File Checker to run, open a command-prompt window and enter the `sfc` command with the appropriate options using the following syntax:

```
sfc [/scannow] [/scanonce] [/scanboot] [/revert] [/purgecache] [/cachesize=x]
```

These are the parameters:

Parameter	Explanation
/scannow	Makes System File Checker scan all protected system files immediately.
/scanonce	Makes System File Checker scan all protected system files once.
/scanboot	Makes System File Checker scan all protected system files each time the computer boots XP.
/revert	Makes System File Checker revert to its default scanning.
/purgecache	Makes System File Checker delete all files in the Windows File Protection file cache and scan all protected system files immediately.
/cachesize=n	Sets the size of the Windows File Protection file cache to *n*MB.

System File Checker can also repair damage to the `%systemroot%\system32\dllcache\` folder if you use the `/scannow`, `/scanonce`, or `/scanboot` parameter.

Checking System Files and Drivers with File Signature Verification

XP includes a tool called File Signature Verification for checking that critical files on your computer include the appropriate digital signatures. You can run File Signature Verification by choosing Start ➤ Run, typing **sigverif** in the Open text box, and clicking the OK button.

File Signature Verification features a point-and-click interface that has a Start button for starting the verification process, a Close button for closing the program when you've finished, and an Advanced button for displaying the Advanced File Signature Verification Settings dialog box, which lets you specify exactly what to search for, where to search, and how and where to log the results.

Using the System Restore Feature

XP's System Restore feature provides a way of recovering from the consequences of installing the wrong hardware driver (or a buggy driver) or a dysfunctional piece of software.

How System Restore Works

System Restore uses a system of *restore points* that include information about the state of the computer's software configuration when the restore point was created. XP creates some restore points automatically (one after the first boot, then one every 24 hours) and before you install an unsigned driver or a program that uses the Windows Installer or the InstallShield installer. To supplement these automatic restore points, you can create restore points manually whenever you want to. For example, you might choose to create a restore point manually before you install a new driver (signed or not) or program, just in case XP doesn't create a restore point and things turn out for the worse.

If your computer starts misbehaving, you can return your computer to one of the restore points before whatever change precipitated the trouble. You run System Restore and specify the restore point you want to return to. XP then restores the computer's software configuration using the information stored in the restore point.

System Restore is very impressive technology, but it can't fix every problem. It affects only your system files (as opposed to your data files or backup files), so rolling back the computer to an earlier state doesn't delete any data files that you've created or downloaded in the meantime. Likewise, returning to a restore point doesn't reinstate any data files that you've deleted since that point in time.

Adjusting the Amount of Space System Restore Takes Up

System Restore stores the restore-point information in files on your hard disk. The more restore points XP creates automatically and you create manually, the more space they take up. XP automatically reserves space on each hard drive volume for System Restore files. It fills this space gradually with restore-point information as it creates restore points, so you don't lose all the reserved space at once—it disappears only as System Restore actually uses it.

By default, System Restore reserves 400MB on any drive smaller than 4GB and 12 percent of any drive of 4GB or more. That's a serious investment of space, and you don't really need to use System Restore on any drive but the one that contains your XP files and your program files. Once you've gotten your computer fixed up with the hardware and software you need, and everything seems to be working to your satisfaction, you may want to reduce the amount of space devoted to System Restore. To do so, take the following steps:

1. Press Windows key+Break; or click the Start button, right-click the My Computer item on the Start menu, and choose Properties from the context menu. XP displays the System Properties dialog box.

2. Click the System Restore tab. XP displays the System Restore page. Figure 17.9 shows two examples of the System Restore page, because the page shows different controls depending on whether your computer has one hard drive (as in the left example) or multiple hard drives (as in the right example). XP displays *Monitoring* for a drive you're monitoring and *Turned Off* for a drive on which you've turned off System Restore.

FIGURE 17.9

On the System Restore page of the System Properties dialog box, you can turn off System Restore or adjust the amount of space it takes up.

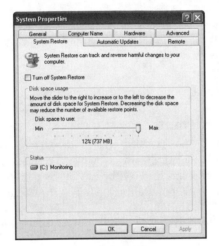

3. If you have only one hard drive, drag the Disk Space to Use slider to specify the amount of space to use for System Restore.

4. If you have multiple hard drives, follow these steps for each drive:

   ◆ Select the drive in the Available Drives list box and click the Settings button. XP displays the Settings dialog box for the drive. Figure 17.10 shows an example of the Settings dialog box for a system drive (on the left) and an example for a nonsystem drive (on the right).

   ◆ For a nonsystem drive, you can turn off System Restore by selecting the Turn Off System Restore on This Drive check box.

   ◆ Drag the Disk Space to Use slider to specify the amount of space to use for System Restore.

   ◆ Click the OK button. If you chose to turn off System Restore, XP displays a confirmation dialog box warning you that you won't be able to undo harmful changes on the drive. Click the Yes button. XP closes the Settings dialog box.

FIGURE 17.10

If you have multiple drives, use the Settings dialog box to choose settings for each drive. The Settings dialog box on the left is for a system drive. The Settings dialog box on the right is for a nonsystem drive.

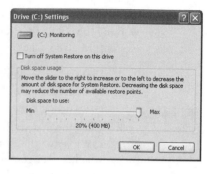

NOTE *If you're desperate enough to trade recoverability for space, you can turn off System Restore by selecting the Turn Off System Restore check box or the Turn Off System Restore on All Drives check box. But usually it's a much better idea to keep using System Restore but devote less space to it.*

5. Click the OK button. XP closes the System Properties dialog box.

Setting System Restore Points

XP automatically creates restore points called *system checkpoints* periodically—usually one or two a day. It also creates restore points automatically when you install certain types of software.

You can create system checkpoints manually by running System Restore (Start ➢ All Programs ➢ Accessories ➢ System Tools ➢ System Restore), selecting the Create a Restore Point option button, and following the prompts.

See pages 54 and 55 of the *Essential Skills* section for a visual walkthrough of setting system restore points.

Restoring Your System to a Restore Point

To restore your computer to a restore point, close all programs, run System Restore (Start ➢ All Programs ➢ Accessories ➢ System Tools ➢ System Restore), select the Restore My Computer to an Earlier Time option button, and follow the prompts. Note that the Select a Restore Point screen shows boldface dates (which represent days with restore points available) only for the current month. To view restore points for the previous month, you need to move the calendar back to that month before System Restore displays its dates in boldface.

See pages 56 and 57 of the *Essential Skills* section for a visual guide to restoring your system to a system restore point.

After restoring your system to the restore point, check your system to make sure that it's running properly. If the restoration didn't produce the effect you wanted, run System Restore again. You can either choose a restore point further in the past or undo your last restoration.

NOTE   *For System Restore, NTFS offers various advantages over FAT32: First, the restore-point files are compressed, so they take up less space on NTFS than on FAT32. (Remember how much of your hard drive System Restore likes to take up, and you'll be grateful for the compression.) Second, NTFS uses permissions intelligently to protect the restore-point files, preventing anyone except the System account from accessing or deleting them. By contrast, FAT32 doesn't have permissions and so can't protect the restore-point files—which means any user can delete them either deliberately or accidentally.*

Keeping and Deleting Old Restore Points

System Restore keeps restore points for 90 days (provided that it has enough space to do so) and then deletes them automatically. You can change this time period by running Registry Editor and changing the RPLifeInterval value in the HKEY_LOCAL_MACHINE\Software\Microsoft\WindowsNT\ CurrentVersion\SystemRestore key from its default setting of 7,776,000 seconds (90 days).

If during that 90-day period (or whatever period you've changed it to) the System Restore files grow to take up more than 90 percent of the storage space it has reserved, System Restore starts deleting restore points, beginning with the oldest, until it has 25 percent of the reserved space available in which to create new restore points.

You can cause System Restore to delete restore points in any of the following ways:

◆   Reduce the RPLifeInterval value as discussed above. Doing so isn't guaranteed to delete restore points, but it's likely to.

◆   Select the System Restore option in Disk Cleanup (discussed in the section "Cleaning Up Your Disks with Disk Cleanup" in Chapter 11). Disk Cleanup deletes all the restore points except the latest one.

◆   Turn off System Restore on the System drive as discussed in the section "Adjusting the Amount of Space System Restore Takes Up" a little earlier in this chapter. Unless you're desperate to reclaim every last byte of disk space that System Restore has been using, this isn't usually a good idea.

TROUBLESHOOTING: SYSTEM RESTORE FREEZES

XP suspends System Restore when a drive that System Restore is tracking runs very low on space. For a system drive, the threshold is 200MB of free space. For a non-system drive, the threshold is 50MB. (With any luck, you'll never get this low on free space.) For either type of drive, the trigger for the suspension is the copying, modifying, or deletion of a file that System Restore is tracking.

What's confusing about the suspension of System Restore is that it applies to *all* the drives on the computer, not just the drive that caused the problem. To activate System Restore again, you need to free up enough space—200MB on a system drive, 50MB on a non-system drive; preferably much more—and choose Start ➢ All Programs ➢ Accessories ➢ System Tools ➢ System Restore. (Alternatively, wait 15 minutes for System Restore to notice that it has enough space again and start itself automatically.)

Restoring the Last Known Good Configuration

System Restore can work wonders—provided that your system can boot XP. But if your system can't boot XP, you need to take other measures. Your first step should be to try restoring the Last Known Good Configuration, as discussed in "Restoring the Registry to Its Last Known Good Configuration" in Chapter 12. Failing that, try using Recovery Console as described in the next section.

Repairing an XP Installation Using Recovery Console

If using the Last Known Good Configuration does you no good, or if you want to go nuclear without taking conventional recovery steps, try Recovery Console. Recovery Console gives you a command-prompt skeleton of XP that you can use to perform basic file maintenance (for example, replacing a corrupted system file) or to issue repair commands for getting XP running again.

WARNING   *Some OEM versions of XP don't include Recovery Console. If yours doesn't, you might need to borrow an XP CD from a friend in order to be able to use Recovery Console. (Don't install from that CD—just use Recovery Console to repair your installation of XP.)*

To start Recovery Console, take the following steps:

1. Boot from your XP CD as if you were installing XP from scratch. Wait while Setup loads all the files required for setup.

2. On the Welcome to Setup screen, press **R**. Setup displays the Recovery Console, which gives you a momentary prompt to press Enter if you want to select a non-standard keyboard layout (for example, Dvorak) and then presents you with a numbered list of the operating systems that it has identified on the computer. The operating systems are identified by the drive and folder that contains them rather than by type, so make sure you select the right one if the computer has multiple operating systems installed.

3. Type the number of the operating system you want to recover and press the Enter key. (To cancel out of Recovery Console, press the Enter key without typing a number.) Setup prompts you for the Administrator password for the account.

4. Type the password for a Computer Administrator account and press the Enter key. (If your account doesn't use a password, just press the Enter key.) Setup displays a command prompt to the system root folder for the operating system.

The command prompt doesn't look very exciting, but it gives you the entrée to the operating system that you need to fix XP. Recovery Console supports regular DOS commands. For example, you can use the COPY command to copy files from a floppy or from a CD (for example, the XP CD) to replace files. Recovery Console also supports commands for taking the following actions:

Partitioning the disk   Invoke the DISKPART command to display a partitioning screen that you can use to create and delete partitions.

Creating a new boot sector   Use the FIXBOOT command to create a new boot sector on a partition you specify and make that partition active.

Repairing the master boot record   Use the FIXMBR command to repair the master boot record on the drive. (If you don't know what the master boot record is, you probably shouldn't be using this command.)

WARNING *The* FIXMBR *command in XP (and in Windows 2000, incidentally) has a bug in it that causes it to display the following error message even when there's no problem: "This computer appears to have a non-standard or invalid master boot record. FIXMBR may damage your partition tables if you proceed. This could cause all the partitions on the current hard disk to become inaccessible. If you are not having problems accessing your drive, do not continue. Are you sure you want to write a new MBR?" Type* y *to continue. If the* FIXMBR *command is able to write a new MBR, it displays a message telling you so.*

Listing the devices and services on your computer   Use the LISTSVC command to list the devices and services on your computer.

Checking the drive mapping on your computer   Use the MAP command to display a table of the devices and partitions on your computer and the drive letters assigned to them.

Enabling and disabling devices   Use the ENABLE command and the DISABLE command to enable or disable a specific device or service. (Use the LISTSVC command to list the devices or commands that you can enable or disable.)

Logging on to a different operating system   Use the LOGON command to log on to another operating system so that you can repair it.

Returning to the system root folder   Use the SYSTEMROOT command to return to the system root folder.

You can also use the BOOTCFG command from the Recovery Console to repair your boot configuration, as discussed in the next section.

Using the *BOOTCFG* Command to Repair Your Boot Configuration

If your boot configuration has gone haywire, you may be able to repair it by using the BOOTCFG command from the Recovery Console. This section details its use.

Command and Switches	Explanation
bootcfg /list	Lists the entries in the boot menu.
bootcfg /default	Lists the entries in the boot menu and lets you specify which to use as the default.
bootcfg /add	Scans the computer for NT, Windows 2000, and XP installations that you might want to add to the boot menu.
bootcfg /rebuild	Scans the computer for NT, Windows 2000, and XP installations that you might want to use to create a boot menu.
bootcfg /scan	Scans the computer for NT, Windows 2000, and XP installations and displays a list of them with their operating system load options and their OS path.
bootcfg /redirect	Enables redirection in the boot loader, allowing you to perform what's called Headless Administration via a COM port. Example: bootcfg /redirect com2 115200.
bootcfg /disableredirect	Disables redirection in the boot loader. Use this command to turn off Headless Administration.

TIP   *System Configuration Utility (discussed in the section "Using System Configuration Utility to Disable Startup Items or to Clean Boot," later in this chapter) also provides options for repairing your boot configuration.*

Exiting Recovery Console

To exit Recovery Console and restart your computer, issue the EXIT command and press the Enter key.

Troubleshooting Boot Problems

Boot problems can be the most frustrating problems to encounter with XP, because if XP won't boot, your computer is essentially crippled. If you have another computer, you can access online resources for advice, but if you don't, you're completely stuck.

With any luck, you won't need all the information in this section to get your computer booting again, so this section is arranged in order of seriousness of problem, starting with creating a boot floppy to recover from a trashed boot sector.

Because of the difficulty of dealing with boot problems, this section covers them at some length. If you never experience any boot problems, you may never need the contents of this section—in which case, feel free to skip all but the first section with my blessing. But do a) read the first section and b) create the boot floppy as described in it, because a boot floppy can save you a large amount of grief should things go awry.

EXPERT KNOWLEDGE: WHAT HAPPENS WHEN YOUR COMPUTER BOOTS?

To be able to troubleshoot boot problems effectively, you need to have at least a modest understanding of what actually happens in hardware and software when your computer boots. This sidebar discusses the major steps involved without getting into more details than will help you in your troubleshooting.

POWER-ON SELF TEST (POST)

The power-on self test, often shortened to the acronym POST, is the test performed by the computer's BIOS after you start the computer. The POST typically includes checking the amount of memory, checking that there's a hard disk and other vital devices, and retrieving system configuration settings from complementary metal-oxide semiconductor (CMOS) memory on the motherboard.

SEARCH FOR BOOT MEDIA

After the POST, the computer searches the devices specified in the BIOS for boot media. In most BIOSes, you can specify different boot sequences. For example, the widely used Award BIOS includes the boot sequences CDROM, C, A; C, CDROM, A; C, A, SCSI; A, C, SCSI; LS/ZIP, C; C Only; SCSI, C, A; SCSI, A, C; and others depending on the hard drives installed on the computer. (LS is the LS-120 super-floppy drive that failed to take over the world in the late 1990s.) If the computer has a bootable disk in a floppy drive, LS-120 drive, or Zip drive that's searched, the computer boots from it automatically. If the computer has a bootable CD or a bootable DVD in a CD drive or DVD drive, the computer offers to boot from it (but by default doesn't). If the computer finds no bootable media in any drives it has been instructed to search, it boots from the hard drive.

Continued on next page

NTLDR BOOT LOADER LOADS

Next, the computer loads NTLDR, the NT boot loader. NTLDR does a couple of things you really don't want to know about (okay, okay: It sets the processor to run in 32-bit flat memory mode instead of in real mode—I *told* you you didn't want to know—and it starts the file system). Then it reads the BOOT.INI file to find out where the boot partition is and whether the computer has a multi-boot configuration that requires NTLDR to display the boot menu for the user to choose the operating system to boot.

If the BOOT.INI file contains only a single entry, NTLDR starts NTDETECT.COM (see the next subsection). If the BOOT.INI file contains multiple entries, NTLDR displays the boot menu. If the user chooses the entry for XP (or for another NT-based operating system, but let's assume we're booting XP here), NTLDR starts NTDETECT.COM; if the user chooses an entry for a non-NT OS, NTLDR passes control to the boot sector for that OS, which then boots that OS (or fails to, as the case may be).

NTDETECT.COM DETECTS THE HARDWARE

Once NTLDR starts it, NTDETECT.COM detects the hardware on the computer (bus type, video cards, keyboards, mouses, ISA devices, and so on) and checks for ACPI information. NTDETECT.COM also retrieves hardware profile information and, for a portable computer, selects the docked or undocked configuration if it can determine from the attached hardware which to use.

NTLDR LOADS THE NT KERNEL AND THE HARDWARE ABSTRACTION LAYER

NTDETECT.COM passes the hardware information collected back to NTLDR, which then loads the NT kernel (NTOSKRNL.EXE) and the hardware abstraction layer (HAL), which provides the logical linkage between the OS and the physical hardware in your computer. XP comes with various HALs for different types of computers, and in extremis you may need to specify a different HAL manually (see the section "Computer Hangs during Setup" in Chapter 2 for instructions on how to do so). The HAL for a Standard PC is named HAL.DLL, but if XP uses one of the other HALs (which have different names), it renames it to HAL.DLL after loading it—so whichever HAL is in use on your computer is currently called HAL.DLL.

HAL AND THE KERNEL INITIALIZE THE WINDOWS EXECUTIVE, WHICH STARTS DRIVERS AND SERVICES

Once loaded, HAL and the NT Kernel initialize the Windows Executive, a group of software components that then work their way through the configuration information stored in the Registry and start running the services and drivers that XP is configured to run. A *driver*, as you probably know, is a software component required to make a particular hardware device (for example, a hard disk or a video card) work. Drivers work in *kernel mode* (at the highest priority; the lower priority is *user mode*), which gives them access to the kernel of the OS; this is why badly written drivers can cause such havoc with the operating system. A *service* is a component that supports an operating-system function or application—for example, the Network Location Awareness (NLA) service gathers and stores network configuration and location information and makes it available to programs that need to know what's on the network and where.

As you'll see later in this chapter, the starting of drivers and services is where many boot problems start (and end). Boot drivers and file-system drivers have to be loaded in order for XP to start (for example, the computer won't be able to start if it can't access its hard disk), but you can eliminate many services in order to locate the source of a boot problem.

Continued on next page

EXPERT KNOWLEDGE: WHAT HAPPENS WHEN YOUR COMPUTER BOOTS? *(continued)*

SESSION MANAGER SWITCHES FROM TEXT MODE TO GRAPHICS MODE

After starting the required drivers and services, the kernel launches Session Manager (SMSS.EXE). Session Manager does the following:

◆ Creates environment variables (look back to the section "Setting Environment Variables" in Chapter 16 if what these are escapes you).

◆ Starts the kernel-mode part of the Windows subsystem (WIN32K.SYS). You'll know this has happened because XP switches from text mode to graphics mode.

◆ Starts the user-mode part of the Windows subsystem (CSRSS.EXE), which allows processes to run in user mode.

◆ Starts Logon Manager (WINLOGON.EXE; see the next section).

◆ Checks the Registry for services that should now be started.

LOGON AND PLUG-AND-PLAY DEVICE DETECTION

The Logon Manager starts the Service Control Manager (SCM; SERVICES.EXE), the Local Security Authority process (LSASS.EXE), and displays the Welcome screen or the Log On to Windows dialog box (depending on which XP is set to use). When a user logs on, the Local Security Authority process receives the username and password (if any) from the Graphical Identification and Authentication component (GINA—a nice acronym, if forced) and authenticates the user (or denies them logon). If the logon is successful, XP updates the Last Known Good Configuration control set with the Clone entry, which is a copy, created at boot time, of the CurrentControlSet key in the Registry. Local security policies are applied. Logon scripts are processed. And programs set to run on startup are launched.

At the same time as logon is taking place (or the computer is waiting for a user to log on), XP organizes resources for the plug-and-play devices it knows about and checks for any new devices.

WHERE THINGS CAN GO WRONG

So that's the XP boot process in some detail. Where can things go wrong?

As you'll see in the next sections, the answer is, Pretty much anywhere. Booting may fail at the POST. No boot medium or bootable drive may be present. Your boot sector or master boot record may have become corrupted. The boot loader can be mangled, missing, or simply not found. There can be problems with the BOOT.INI file. NTDETECT.COM may not work for any of various reasons. XP may be trying to use the wrong HAL for your computer. Drivers and services may cause XP to crash. Or the logon process might fail to start.

The following sections discuss how to troubleshoot common boot problems.

Creating an XP Boot Floppy to Recover from a Faulty Boot Sequence

If your boot sector or master boot record (MBR) has become corrupted, XP has been infected with a boot-sector virus, or your NTLDR or NTDETECT.COM files are missing in action, you may need to create a boot floppy in order to restore your system to booting normally. This section discusses how to do so.

TIP   Instead of creating a boot floppy, you can create a boot CD if you have CD-burning software that'll create a bootable CD. There's no particular advantage to doing so unless you have a floppy drive–free PC—for example, a laptop or a legacy-free (or legacy-lite) PC. Bootable CDs use the El Torito recording format.

CREATING THE BOOT FLOPPY BEFORE TROUBLE STRIKES

If you're creating this boot floppy before trouble strikes, congratulations—it's easy to do. Format a floppy disk as usual using the procedure described in "Formatting a Disk" in Chapter 11, then open an Explorer window to the root directory on your boot drive; select the files NTLDR, NTDETECT.COM, and BOOT.INI; right-click the selection; and choose Send To ➢ $3\frac{1}{2}$ Floppy from the context menu. If you're using a SCSI disk, copy the NTBOOTDD.SYS file as well. If you have a multi-boot configuration that includes DOS or OS/2, copy the file BOOTSECT.DOS as well.

NOTE   If you can't see the files in the root folder of your boot drive, choose View ➢ Folder Options to display the Folder Options dialog box. Select the Show Hidden Files and Folders option button to display hidden files and folders. Then clear the Hide Protected Operating System Files check box on the View page of the Folder Options dialog box and click the Yes button in the Warning dialog box that XP displays. Click the OK button to close the Folder Options dialog box.

CREATING THE BOOT FLOPPY AFTER TROUBLE HAS STRUCK

Creating the boot floppy after trouble has struck is a little more work. First, you need a computer running some version of Windows (most likely a different computer than the one that's giving you grief). Format a floppy disk as usual for the OS and copy the files NTLDR and NTDETECT.COM from the XP CD to the floppy disk. (For example, select the files and choose File ➢ Send To ➢ $3\frac{1}{2}$ Floppy.)

So far, so easy. But next comes the hard bit: You need to create on the floppy a BOOT.INI file that matches the disk configuration of the computer you're trying to rescue. (This would be a convenient point at which to discover a backup of the BOOT.INI file on a friendly floppy.)

Here's an example of a BOOT.INI file for a computer that has XP Home installed in the \WINDOWS\ folder on the first partition of the first EIDE drive and Windows 2000 Professional installed in the \WINNT\ folder on the second partition of that drive. XP Home is set as the default operating system.

```
[boot loader]
timeout=30
default=multi(0)disk(0)rdisk(0)partition(1)\WINDOWS
[operating systems]
multi(0)disk(0)rdisk(0)partition(1)\WINDOWS="Microsoft Windows XP Home Edition"
➥/fastdetect
multi(0)disk(0)rdisk(0)partition(2)\WINNT="Microsoft Windows 2000 Professional"
➥/fastdetect
```

Here's a breakdown of the components of a BOOT.INI file:

timeout   Specifies the wait period before starting the OS. Use the value 0 (zero) to omit the timeout. This argument applies only when the computer is configured for dual- or multi-boot. Otherwise the computer boots the default (a.k.a. the only) OS without consulting the user.

default   Specifies the default OS.

multi()   Specifies the hard disk controller of the disk on which the operating system in question is installed. Numbering starts at 0 (zero), because it's computer counting.

disk() Specifies the hard disk on which the operating system is installed. disk() is used only when scsi() is used; otherwise, it's included in the boot menu item but has no function. Again, numbering begins at zero.

rdisk() Specifies the hard disk on which the operating system is installed. Once again, numbering begins at zero.

partition() Specifies the partition on which the operating system is installed. Just to be confusing, numbering starts at 1.

If XP or Windows 2000 is installed on a FAT32 partition, there's also a signature() component to the boot menu item. This specifies the disk controller.

If the operating system is installed on a SCSI disk without an active BIOS, the boot menu item has a scsi() component that specifies the hard disk controller. For example,

```
scsi(0)disk(0)rdisk(1)partition(1)\WinXP="Windows XP Home Edition"
```

When using a SCSI disk, there's an additional complication: You need to copy the device driver for the SCSI controller to the boot floppy as well. Once you've copied it, rename it to NTBOOTDD.SYS.

The /fastdetect switch turns off the detection of serial mouses. You can also use this switch with a specific COM port to turn off detection on that port—for example, /fastdetect=COM1.

NOTE You can add several other switches to the boot file for troubleshooting. I'll discuss these in the section "Using a Modified BOOT.INI File," later in this chapter, along with System Configuration Utility, a tool that helps you troubleshoot your boot configuration.

Once you've created the boot floppy, restart your computer so that it boots from the floppy. (You may need to adjust your BIOS settings to make it do so.) Copy the NTLDR and NTDETECT.COM files from the CD to your boot drive. Check (and if necessary) recreate your BOOT.INI file.

TROUBLESHOOTING BOOT ERROR MESSAGES

If you don't get the BOOT.INI file exactly right, XP may not be able to boot. Table 17.1 lists the boot error messages you're most likely to see, explains the problems they typically indicate, and tells you how to fix the problems.

TABLE 17.1: BOOT ERROR MESSAGES AND THEIR MEANINGS

"WINDOWS COULD NOT START BECAUSE...	MEANING	REMEDY
...of a computer disk hardware configuration problem. Could not read from the selected boot disk. Check boot path and disk hardware."	Wrong controller or disk.	Specify the right controller or disk.
...of the following ARC firmware boot configuration problem: did not properly generate ARC name for HAL and system paths."	Wrong path to system files, or path includes drive letter. On first boot of Setup: Incompatible drive overlay program (see "Troubleshooting Installation" in Chapter 2).	Correct the path or remove the drive letter.

Continued on next page

TABLE 17.1: Boot Error Messages and Their Meanings *(continued)*

"Windows Could Not Start Because...	Meaning	Remedy
...the following file is missing or corrupt: <Windows root>\system32\hal.dll. Please reinstall a copy of the above file."	Wrong partition.	Specify the right partition.
...the following file is missing or corrupt: <Winnt_root>\System32\Ntoskrnl.exe. Please reinstall a copy of the above file."	Default value in BOOT.INI is missing or invalid, or XP isn't installed in the location specified.	Supply or correct the Default value in BOOT.INI or use BOOTCFG /REBUILD command in Recovery Console to add the Windows installation to BOOT.INI.

Recovering from Failed Boot with "NTLDR Is Missing" Message

If your computer fails to boot and gives you the message "NTLDR is missing. Press Ctrl+Alt+Del to restart," it means either that someone has deleted, moved, or renamed the NTLDR file (which contains the boot loader) or that you've marked as active a partition that's not bootable. (You can do this by using the Disk Management tool, as discussed in the section "Managing Disks with Disk Management" in Chapter 11.)

There are three ways of recovering from this problem. Here they are, in descending order of preference.

1. The easiest way to recover from this problem is to use the XP boot floppy that you created in the previous section to boot your computer. You can then restore the NTLDR file from the XP CD (or from your boot floppy) or use Disk Management to set the correct partition active.

2. The next best way to recover from this problem is to insert your XP CD and boot into the Recovery Console (as discussed in "Repairing an XP Installation Using Recovery Console" earlier in this chapter). Copy the NTLDR file from the \i386\ folder on the CD to the active partition. (If necessary, copy NTDETECT.COM as well.) Issue the **exit** command to exit Recovery Console, and reboot your computer.

3. The third and least preferable way to recover from this problem is as follows: If you didn't create an XP boot floppy and don't want to guess your way through creating a BOOT.INI file that'll work; and if you have a Windows 9*x* boot floppy to hand; and you're sure the problem was caused by your setting the wrong partition active; and the partition you need to set active uses the FAT32 file system—if all those things *and* the sun is shining in Tibet, boot from that Windows 9*x* boot floppy to a command prompt. Run the FDISK utility by typing **fdisk** and pressing the Enter key. When FDISK prompts you to enable large disk support, choose Yes. Then select the Set Active Partition item, type the number of the partition you want to make active, and press the Enter key. Press the Esc key to quit FDISK, eject the boot floppy, and

press Ctrl+Alt+Delete to restart your computer. If you got the partition right and NTLDR is present and functional, XP will boot. This way of recovering from the problem is more work and more risky than using an XP boot floppy, so don't use it unless you must.

Recovering from Black Screen Hang after POST

If booting fails with a black screen after the computer finishes its power-on self test (see the beginning of the "Expert Knowledge: What Happens When Your Computer Boots?" sidebar earlier in this chapter if you don't know what the power-on self test is) and before the Windows logo appears, the MBR, the boot sector, or the partition tables may have been corrupted, or the NTLDR file may be corrupted or missing.

To recover from this problem, locate your XP boot floppy (or create it, if you've been shirking doing so) and boot from it. If you're able to do so, the partition table on your computer is okay, which is good news. That means that the MBR, the boot sector, or the NTLDR file is the problem.

When XP is running, run Disk Management (as discussed in the section "Managing Disks with Disk Management" in Chapter 11) and double-check that your partition structure is okay. Then run a virus scan on your computer to identify and remove any virus.

After that, back up all your data so that you can approach the remaining problem with a clear conscience. Then replace the copy of the NTLDR file on your boot drive with a fresh copy from your XP CD and try rebooting your computer from the hard disk. (Remove the boot floppy before doing so.)

If that solves the problem, well and good. If not, insert your XP CD and boot from that to the Recovery Console. Then run the FIXMBR command to repair the MBR. If your primary boot partition is a FAT partition (and it shouldn't be), run the FIXBOOT command to create a new boot sector, and then run the FIXMBR command. Issue an **exit** command to exit Recovery Console, ensure that your computer boots normally, and check your computer for viruses again.

Recovering from Black Screen Hang after POST and "NTDETECT Failed" Message

If booting fails after the POST, the message "NTDETECT failed" appears briefly (you'll have to watch closely to see it) and the computer reboots and repeats the problem, your NTDETECT.COM file is absent without leave. To recover from this problem, boot from your boot floppy, then replace the copy of NTDETECT.COM on your boot drive with a fresh copy from your XP CD and try rebooting your computer from the hard disk. (Remove the boot floppy before doing so.)

Recovering from "Invalid Partition Table" Message

This section's heading is a bit optimistic, because you can't really recover from this error. If your partition table has been damaged, you'll need to recreate it. The easiest way to do so is to reinstall XP from scratch. As you'd imagine, doing so deletes your existing partitions and all the data they contain, with all the unwelcome consequences the loss of partitions (and data) entails.

Recovering from Hang at Welcome Screen after Restart

If XP starts fine as far as the Welcome screen and then stops responding to the mouse and keyboard, your computer may have accessed a corrupted memory snapshot from Hibernate mode. When you restart the computer (by resetting it or by cycling the power), it gives you the message "System restart has been paused" and a menu consisting of two items, a Continue with System Restart item and a Delete Restoration Data and Proceed to System Boot Menu item. Select the Delete Restoration Data and Proceed to System Boot Menu item to discard the data from the corrupted memory snapshot so that XP can restart as normal.

Booting into Safe Mode

As you saw earlier in the book, you can boot into Safe mode to set a password on the Administrator account. Normally, if you boot into Safe mode, it's to troubleshoot XP. This section discusses how to do so.

WARNING *Between the devil and the USB... One of the modernizing features that XP supports is legacy-free PCs that don't have serial ports or PS/2 ports—the venerable old ports traditionally used for connecting devices such as mouses and keyboards. Such computers typically connect the keyboard and mouse to USB ports. Being legacy-free is all well and good until the computer stops working and you need to use Safe mode, which disables the USB ports. To work around this problem, you need to either attach a non-USB keyboard and mouse (which you won't be able to do if your computer doesn't have serial or PS/2 ports), or a) have a BIOS that supports USB devices in USB legacy mode and b) have enabled USB legacy mode in that BIOS.*

To boot into Safe mode, restart XP (or start it if it's not currently running). When the computer is restarting, press the F8 key so that XP displays the Windows Advanced Options menu (see Figure 17.11). (If your computer has a multi-boot configuration, press the F8 key from the Please Select the Operating System to Start screen.) Then select the Safe Mode option (or another, more appropriate option) from the menu and press the Enter key to boot with it.

FIGURE 17.11

Use the Windows Advanced Options menu to boot into Safe mode.

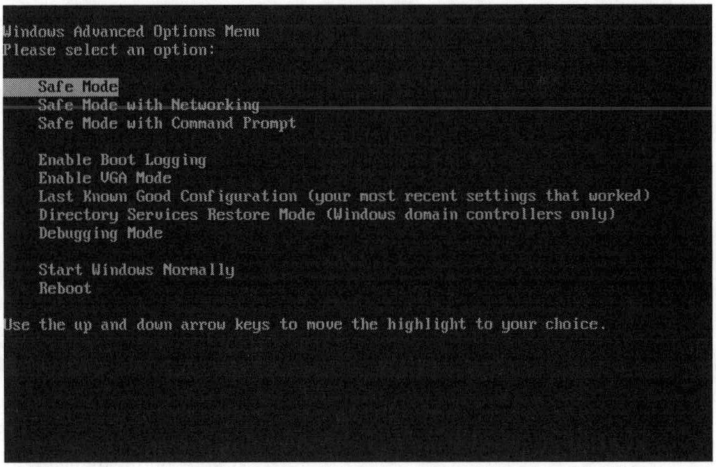

```
Windows Advanced Options Menu
Please select an option:

    Safe Mode
    Safe Mode with Networking
    Safe Mode with Command Prompt

    Enable Boot Logging
    Enable VGA Mode
    Last Known Good Configuration (your most recent settings that worked)
    Directory Services Restore Mode (Windows domain controllers only)
    Debugging Mode

    Start Windows Normally
    Reboot

Use the up and down arrow keys to move the highlight to your choice.
```

The Windows Advanced Options menu offers the options listed in Table 17.2.

TABLE 17.2: OPTIONS ON THE WINDOWS ADVANCED OPTIONS MENU

OPTION	EXPLANATION
Safe Mode	Starts XP with as few services and drivers as is possible, and uses the VGA.SYS alternative VGA video driver (at 640×480 resolution, and in 16-color mode) to force video compatibility. Use Safe mode for troubleshooting drivers and services, including video driver problems.
Safe Mode with Networking	Starts XP in Safe mode but adds the network drivers and services. Use this option for troubleshooting drivers and services when you need to connect to a network (for example, to get replacement files) or for troubleshooting networking.
Safe Mode with Command Prompt	Starts XP in Safe mode but with a command prompt instead of the Explorer shell. Use this option for troubleshooting using command-line tools or when your mouse seems to be causing the problem. To shut down XP, press Ctrl+Alt+Delete and select the Shut button. Alternatively, issue the **explorer** command and choose the Yes button in the Desktop dialog box that XP displays, then use the Start button to shut down XP as usual.
Enable Boot Logging	Turns on logging of the boot process for any Safe mode option except Last Known Good Configuration. XP logs the boot information in the NTBTLOG.TXT file in the %systemroot% folder.
Enable VGA Mode	Starts XP using VGA (640×480) resolution but with the current video driver rather than the backup video driver (VGA.SYS). Use this option for troubleshooting display resolutions when the driver itself isn't the problem—for example, if the refresh rate or display size is set higher than the monitor can handle.
Last Known Good Configuration	Starts XP using the Last Known Good Configuration. See the section "Restoring the Registry to Its Last Known Good Configuration" in Chapter 12 for a discussion of this option.
Directory Services Restore Mode	Applies only to Windows-based domain controllers, not to computers running XP Home.
Debugging Mode	Enables debugging mode using the COM2 serial port. To use this option, use the COM2 serial port to connect this computer to another computer that's running a debugging program. Expert stuff.
Start Windows Normally	Starts the computer normally, as it says. Use this option when XP automatically displays the Windows Advanced Options menu after rebooting following an incomplete start caused by problems that you've eliminated (for example, power problems) or when you've displayed the Windows Advanced Options menu by mistake.

Continued on next page

TABLE 17.2: OPTIONS ON THE WINDOWS ADVANCED OPTIONS MENU *(continued)*

OPTION	EXPLANATION
Reboot	Reboots the computer. Use this option if you're not sure whether you have (or someone else has) displayed the Windows Advanced Options menu by mistake.

Using System Configuration Utility to Disable Startup Items or to Clean Boot

System Configuration Utility is a graphical tool for troubleshooting your system (as opposed to a tool for *configuring* your system) by disabling startup programs and services that you suspect of causing problems at bootup.

RUNNING SYSTEM CONFIGURATION UTILITY

System Configuration Utility doesn't get a Start menu entry under normal circumstances (you can of course always create one), but you can run it either from Help and Support Center or by running the MSCONFIG.EXE file in the *%systemroot%*PCHEALTH\HELPCTR\Binaries folder. This folder should be in your path, so you can run System Configuration Utility by choosing Start ➢ Run, entering **msconfig** in the Run dialog box, and clicking the OK button. (If for some reason the folder isn't in your path, either enter the full path in the Run dialog box or navigate to the file in an Explorer window and double-click it.)

TIP   To display a particular page of System Configuration Utility, you can use the –n switch when launching it from the Run dialog box, where n is a number between 1 and 6 representing the page you want to display. The pages are numbered from left to right: 1 gives you the General page (which is displayed by default), 2 the SYSTEM.INI page, 3 the WIN.INI page, 4 the BOOT.INI page, 5 the Services page, and 6 the Startup page.

Only Computer Administrator users can actually *use* System Configuration Utility—but in most XP Home configurations, Limited users can *run* System Configuration Utility but not save changes to it. The System Configuration Utility interface registers changes that a Limited user makes, and lets them click the Apply button, but System Configuration Utility is then unable to write the changes to disk. Once this has happened, the user can't close System Configuration Utility by using its Close button (the command button in the window), the Close button at the upper-right corner of its window, or the Control command on the command menu. Instead, they'll need to use the End Task command from Task Manager to close System Configuration Utility. Note that Task Manager may list System Configuration Utility as "Running" rather than as "Not Responding," because System Configuration Utility is still responding to some of the user's commands.

Once System Configuration Utility is running, you can work with the options on its six pages. Most of the action takes place on the General page (shown foremost in Figure 17.12), which provides overarching options that turn on or off the sets of options presented on the other five pages of System Configuration Utility.

FIGURE 17.12

System Configuration Utility is a troubleshooting tool that lets you turn off boot elements— drivers, services, initialization files— in order to pin down problems.

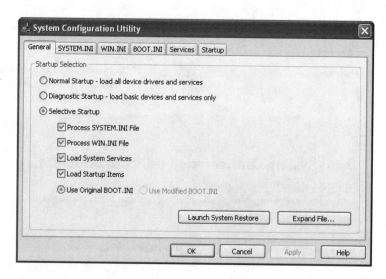

The General page offers three main option buttons:

Normal Startup – Load All Device Drivers and Services option button   This option button, which is selected by default, causes XP to load all drivers and services. Leave this setting alone if the computer is operating normally. (But if it is, you probably won't be using System Configuration Utility. ...)

Diagnostic Startup – Load Basic Devices and Services Only option button   Select this option button when you want to strip down the device driver's XP loads and the services it starts to a bare minimum. The services that XP disables when you select this option prevent you from using some of the tools in Control Panel. This option is primarily useful for determining whether you have a problem with a basic driver or service or whether the problem lies later on in the boot process.

Selective Startup option button   Selecting this option button lets you selectively turn off items by using the four or more check boxes and two option buttons below the Selective Startup option button. These check boxes and option buttons relate to the sets of controls presented on the other five pages of System Configuration Utility and are discussed in the following sections.

The General page also includes a Launch System Restore button for launching System Restore from System Configuration Utility (a minor convenience over having to wade to the System tools submenu on the Start menu) and an Expand File button that displays the Expand One File from Installation Source dialog box (see Figure 17.13) that you can use to expand a file from a source folder to a particular folder. This feature is designed for easily replacing corrupted files with clean versions.

FIGURE 17.13

The Expand One File from Installation Source dialog box lets you extract a replacement file for a corrupted file.

> **Expand One File from Installation Source** ☒
>
> Specify the file you would like to restore, the source location containing the installation files, and the destination location for the file.
>
> File to restore: | [ ] [Browse File...]
>
> Restore from: [⌄] [Browse From...]
>
> Save file in: [⌄] [Browse To...]
>
> [Expand] [Cancel]

HOW TO PROCEED WITH SYSTEM CONFIGURATION UTILITY

The basic methodology for troubleshooting boot problems using System Configuration Utility is to perform a clean boot to eliminate all possible causes of the problem, then gradually load drivers, start services, and launch startup programs until the problem reoccurs and you can isolate it. Take the following steps:

1. Close any other programs and run System Configuration Utility.
2. On the General page, select the Selective Startup option button.
3. Clear the Process SYSTEM.INI File check box, the Process WIN.INI File check box, the Load System Services check box, and the Load Startup Items check box. If you have an OEM version of XP that includes further check boxes (for custom features), clear those check boxes too.
4. Make sure the Use Original BOOT.INI File option button is selected.
5. Click the OK button. System Configuration Utility applies your changes and displays the System Configuration dialog box shown here, telling you that you need to restart the computer and offering to do so for you.

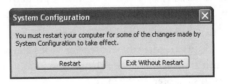

6. Click the Restart button. System Configuration Utility causes XP to reboot. When XP comes back up and you log on, XP displays the System Configuration Utility dialog box shown here. You'll notice that XP has turned off most of its window-beautifying effects, so this dialog box has square corners.

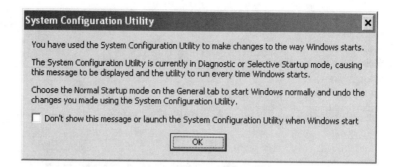

7. If appropriate, select the Don't Show This Message or Launch the System Configuration Utility when Windows Starts check box. (Usually, having this dialog box displayed and System Configuration Utility launched automatically is a helpful reminder.)

8. Click the OK button. XP launches System Configuration Utility (unless you told it not to).

9. If XP seems to be working all right (try running a few programs), select the Process SYSTEM .INI File check box on the General page of System Configuration Utility, click the OK button, and click the Restart button in the System Configuration dialog box.

   ◆ If XP *isn't* working okay, work with the items on the SYSTEM.INI page of System Configuration Utility to identify the culprit and remove it. See the section "Controlling the Processing of the `SYSTEM.INI` File" (next) for details.

10. When XP restarts, see if it seems to be running okay. If it is, select the Process WIN.INI File check box and let System Configuration Utility restart the computer again.

    ◆ If XP *isn't* working okay at this point, work with the items on the WIN.INI page of System Configuration Utility to identify the offender. Clear its check box to prevent it from running. See the section "Controlling the Processing of the `WIN.INI` File," a little later in this chapter, for details.

11. When XP restarts, again see if it's running properly. If it is, select the Load System Services check box and let System Configuration Utility restart the computer.

    ◆ If XP *isn't* running properly, work with the items on the Services page of System Configuration Utility to identify the service that's causing the trouble. Disable that service to prevent it from running. See the section "Controlling the Loading of System Services," later in this chapter, for details.

12. When XP restarts, see if it's running okay. If it is, select the Load Startup Items check box and let System Configuration Utility restart the computer yet again.

    ◆ If XP *isn't* running properly, work with the controls on the Startup page of System Configuration Utility to identify the program that seems to be causing the instability. Prevent that program from running. See the section "Controlling Which Programs Are Started at Startup," later in this chapter, for details.

If the problem seems to be with your `BOOT.INI` file rather than with the initialization files, drivers, services, or startup programs, use the controls on the BOOT.INI page of System Configuration Utility to adjust your boot configuration. See the section "Using a Modified `BOOT.INI` File," later in this chapter, for details.

Once you've identified the problem and removed it, select the Normal Startup – Load All Device Drivers and Services check option button on the General page of System Configuration Utility and click the OK button. Let System Configuration Utility reboot your computer, and verify that it's running normally after it comes back up.

CONTROLLING THE PROCESSING OF THE *SYSTEM.INI* FILE

The SYSTEM.INI file is a configuration file used for backward compatibility to initialize older versions of software that aren't young and smart enough to save their configuration information in the Registry. If you suspect that one of the instructions in the SYSTEM.INI is causing problems, you can safely switch off the processing of the SYSTEM.INI file (by clearing the Process SYSTEM.INI File check box) without affecting the way XP itself runs. Alternatively, you can leave this check box selected and use the options on the SYSTEM.INI page of System Configuration Utility (see Figure 17.14) to disable individual components of the SYSTEM.INI file or to rearrange the order in which they're processed.

FIGURE 17.14

On the SYSTEM .INI page of System Configuration Utility, you can turn off the processing of individual entries in the SYSTEM.INI file.

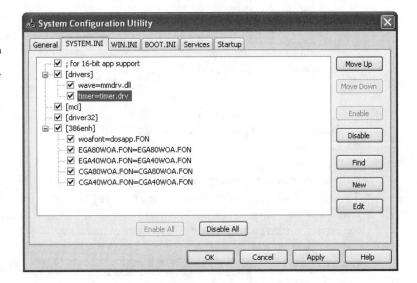

CONTROLLING THE PROCESSING OF THE *WIN.INI* FILE

Like the SYSTEM.INI file, the WIN.INI file is used for backward compatibility with older versions of programs that don't use the Registry, so if you suspect it of fomenting trouble, you can take it out of the equation (by clearing the Process WIN.INI File check box) without affecting how XP itself runs. Or you can leave this check box selected and use the options on the WIN.INI page of System Configuration Utility to disable individual components of the WIN.INI file or to rearrange the order in which they're processed.

CONTROLLING THE LOADING OF SYSTEM SERVICES

The Services page of System Configuration Utility (see Figure 17.15) lets you disable individual services from running. The list shows the service name, whether it's essential to the running of XP

(Yes appears in the Essential column if it is), the manufacturer of the service, and its status (Running or Stopped). You can sort the entries by any column by clicking the column heading. Select the Hide All Microsoft Services check box to hide the entries for all Microsoft services and make it easier to spot third-party services that might be causing problems.

FIGURE 17.15

On the Services page of System Configuration Utility, you can disable individual services that you suspect of causing problems.

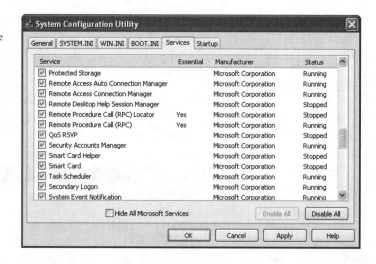

You can turn off all services by clicking the Disable All button on the Services page or by clearing the Load System Services check box on the General page.

CONTROLLING WHICH PROGRAMS ARE STARTED AT STARTUP

To control which programs XP starts at startup, use the check boxes on the Startup page of System Configuration Utility (see Figure 17.16). To disable all startup programs, click the Disable All button on the Startup page or clear the Load Startup Items check box on the General page.

FIGURE 17.16

On the Startup page of System Configuration Utility, you can prevent individual programs from starting up automatically.

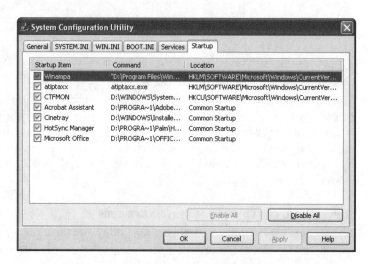

USING A MODIFIED *BOOT.INI* FILE

Last but emphatically not least, you can modify your BOOT.INI file by using the controls on the BOOT.INI page of System Configuration Utility (see Figure 17.17).

FIGURE 17.17

The BOOT.INI page of System Configuration Utility (left) and the BOOT.INI Advanced Options dialog box (right) provide tools for tweaking your BOOT.INI file to overcome boot problems.

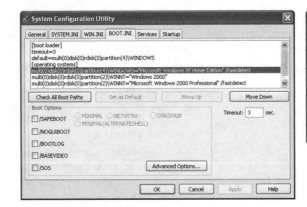

To tweak the BOOT.INI file, select the entry you want to affect in the list box and click the appropriate control:

Check All Boot Paths button   Click this button to make System Configuration Utility check all the boot paths for validity and display a message box showing its findings.

Set As Default button   Click this button to set the selected item as the default operating system to load.

Move Up button and Move Down button   Use these buttons to move the selected item up or down the boot menu. (Such rearranging is cosmetic: It doesn't affect the default operating system but can make it easier for the user to select the appropriate operating system.)

Timeout text box   Change the value in this text box to change the time for which the boot menu is displayed. System Configuration Utility edits the value in the timeout= line.

Boot Options group box   Select the check boxes for the options you want to use (see Table 17.3 for the meaning of the options). For the /SAFEBOOT check box, select the appropriate option button as well.

In extreme situations, you may need to limit the memory that XP uses or prevent XP from dynamically assigning resources to PCI devices. To do so, click the Advanced Options button and choose options in the BOOT.INI Advanced Options dialog box (shown on the right in Figure 17.17). Again, the options add switches to the selected entry in the boot menu, and Table 17.3 shows their meaning.

TABLE 17.3: BOOT OPTIONS SWITCHES

SWITCH	EXPLANATION
SAFEBOOT:Minimal	Boots Safe mode (with the minimal set of drivers and services).
SAFEBOOT:Network	Boots Safe mode with network support.
SAFEBOOT:Minimal(AlternateShell)	Boots Safe mode with a command prompt instead of the Explorer shell.
SAFEBOOT:DSREPAIR	Boots Safe mode for restoring Active Directory from a backup. Not applicable to XP Home.
/NOGUIBOOT	Disables the VGA video driver used to display graphics during the boot process (and to display Blue Screen crashes, should you get any).
/BOOTLOG	Makes XP create a log of the boot process in a file named NTBTLOG .TXT in the %systemroot% folder. View the log to see which drivers load successfully and which don't.
/BASEVIDEO	Makes XP use the standard VGA display driver when moving to graphical mode.
/SOS	Forces XP to display driver names while they're being loaded and, after that, information on the file-system check. This switch is useful for determining at what point the boot process is failing.
/MAXMEM	Limits XP to using the specified number of megabytes of memory.
/NUMPROC	Limits XP to using the specified number of processors. XP Home can't use multiple processors, so you won't need this option.
/PCILOCK	Prevents XP from dynamically assigning input-output addresses and interrupt requests (IRQs) to PCI devices, leaving the devices as configured by the BIOS.
/DEBUG	Enables kernel-mode debugging. If you choose this option, you can select the /DEBUGPORT check box and specify the port in the drop-down list. For a COM port, select the /BAUDRATE check box and specify the baud rate to use. For an IEEE1394 (FireWire) port, select the /CHANNEL check box and specify the channel to use.

NOTE *The Use Original BOOT.INI option button and the Use Modified BOOT.INI option button on the General page of System Configuration Utility let you switch between your original* BOOT.INI *file and the modified version that you've created by using the controls on the BOOT.INI page. As soon as you make changes on the BOOT.INI page, System Configuration Utility automatically selects the Use Modified BOOT.INI option button, so you'll need to select the Use Original BOOT.INI option button if you've changed your mind about the modifications you've made.*

EXPERT KNOWLEDGE: EXTRACTING A COMPRESSED FILE FROM A CABINET FILE

If XP won't boot because it has corrupted a vital system file (or you've somehow managed to delete a vital system file), you'll need to replace the system file in order to get XP working again.

The best place to get a replacement system file is your XP CD. If you don't have a second PC handy on which to extract the file from the compressed cabinet file that contains it, you can use the DOS-based EXTRACT command from Windows 9x to extract the file.

The basic syntax for the EXTRACT command is as follows, where *cabinet* is the name of the cabinet file and *filename* is the name of the file to extract:

```
EXTRACT cabinet filename
```

To display a directory listing of the contents of the CAB file, use the following syntax, where *cabinet* is the name of the cabinet file:

```
EXTRACT /D cabinet
```

"System Has Recovered from a Serious Error" Message after Each Restart

If XP suffers a serious error that causes it to crash, when it restarts, the Windows Error Reporting tool appears, prompting you to report the problem to Microsoft. As usual, you can choose to send the problem or not send it.

But if XP continues to display the Windows Error Reporting tool after each restart with the same message (without any other serious error having occurred in the meantime), it means that XP has a flag set about the error that it's unable to clear. To solve this problem, you need to download an update from the Microsoft Download Center. See Q317277 in the Microsoft Support Knowledge Base (`support.microsoft.com`) for a link to the file to download.

Choosing System Startup Options for Booting XP

When you've created a dual-boot setup as described in Chapter 2, you can specify which of the operating systems the boot loader boots by default. You can also edit the boot menu (which is stored in the `BOOT.INI` file) to change the order in which the operating systems are listed and the way in which they are listed. You may also need to remove boot menu items that have become superfluous or confusing.

To choose system startup options, take the following steps:

1. Press Windows key+Break. Alternatively, choose Start ➤ Control Panel, click the Performance and Maintenance link, click the Other Control Panel Options link, and click the System link. XP displays the System Properties dialog box.

2. Click the Advanced tab. XP displays the Advanced page.

3. Click the Settings button in the Startup and Recovery group box. XP displays the Startup and Recovery dialog box (shown in Figure 16.19, in the previous chapter).

4. In the Default Operating System drop-down list, select the operating system that you want to boot by default.

5. If you want XP to display the boot list of operating systems for a number of seconds before booting one, so that you can boot an operating system other than the default one, select the Time to Display List of Operating Systems check box and enter a suitable value in the text box. You can enter any value from 0 seconds to 999 seconds. The default value is 30 seconds.

6. If you want to change the names and descriptions of the items on the boot menu, click the Edit button. XP opens the BOOT.INI file in a Notepad window. Figure 17.18 shows an example of a BOOT.INI file open in Notepad.

FIGURE 17.18

You can edit the BOOT.INI file to change the list of entries displayed and the order in which they're listed.

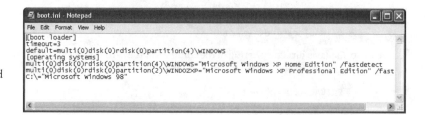

♦ Edit the descriptions of the operating systems as necessary within the double quotation marks. For example, you might add to the name of an operating system a note about when it should be used:

```
multi(0)disk(0)rdisk(0)partition(1)\WINDOWS="Windows XP Home - test
    configuration" /fastdetect
```

WARNING *Don't change any of the disk, volume, or partition information. Doing so may prevent XP from booting.*

♦ To change the number of seconds the boot menu is displayed, change the timeout= value. (It's usually easier to do this in the Startup and Recovery dialog box.)

♦ Similarly, you *can* change the default= line to change the default operating system, but it's usually much easier to use the Default Operating System drop-down list in the Startup and Recovery group box.

♦ Press Ctrl+S or choose File ➢ Save to save the BOOT.INI file, then press Alt+F4 or choose File ➢ Exit to close it.

7. Click the OK button. XP closes the Startup and Recovery dialog box.

8. Click the OK button. XP closes the System Properties dialog box.

Up Next

This chapter has discussed how to use XP's tools to identify problems on your computer and troubleshoot them. It has concentrated on troubleshooting boot problems, because by their nature these tend to be the most difficult problems to troubleshoot—especially as they often prevent you from accessing your data (for example, to work with it on another computer) until you get the problem fixed.

That's the end of Part II of the book. Part III discusses communications, the Internet, and the Web.

Part **III**

Communications, the Internet, and the Web

Chapter 18

Connecting to the Internet

THESE DAYS, AN INTERNET connection is almost a must-have for anyone with a computer—and indeed XP's setup routine heavily encourages you to connect your computer to the Internet by any viable means that it can find.

This chapter discusses how to connect to the Internet with XP and how to secure your Internet connection. Along the way, it discusses the different types of Internet connection and the benefits they offer; what dial-up networking is, how it works, and how to configure and troubleshoot it; and how to work with digital certificates so that you can establish the authenticity of a document or transaction.

This chapter covers the following topics:

◆ Choosing an Internet connection type and ISP

◆ Creating an Internet connection

◆ Establishing an Internet connection

◆ Using multiple modems on a dial-up connection

◆ Securing your Internet connection

◆ Troubleshooting dial-up Internet connections

◆ Getting and using digital certificates

NOTE *One topic that isn't covered in this chapter is how to share your Internet connection with other computers in your household or office. Chapter 32 discusses the Internet Connection Sharing feature. (This chapter does cover how to share your Internet connection with other users of this computer.)*

Choosing an Internet Connection Type and ISP

This section provides a brief summary of the options you should be considering if you don't have an Internet connection or you need to improve on your existing connection.

Unless you're very unusual, you'll want an Internet connection as fast as you can a) get and b) afford. You'll also want your ISP to provide the features you need.

In the old days of the late 1990s, shopping around for an ISP used to involve minute comparisons of the details of the services that competing dial-up ISPs offered: This ISP offered you three more mailboxes than that ISP, but that ISP had more points of presence nationwide. These days, such comparisons hold if you're looking for a dial-up connection (a connection that uses a modem and a phone line), but you're more likely to want a high-speed connection—if one is available. If one is, selecting an ISP is more likely to involve choosing among as few as two or three providers of high-speed access. In some cases, your only choice may be between your incumbent high-speed provider and poky old dial-up.

Trying to move with the times, this section starts by discussing the connection types in descending order of speed, starting with the type that's by far the fastest but also the one you're least likely to be able to get.

Fiber

The fastest affordable Internet connection available in the U.S. is optical fiber, which can deliver speeds of around 100Mbps—the same speed as the Fast Ethernet networks used in many companies and on many campuses. This bandwidth is typically shared, so you usually won't be able to download at the full 10+MB per second it offers, but you'll find it plenty fast enough.

If you can get fiber, go for it. Unfortunately, the chances of your being able to get it are minimal at this writing. Some new housing communities in high-tech areas (such as Silicon Valley, Silicon Island, Silicon Prairie—hmm, there's a theme here) are being built with fiber to the home, and some apartment buildings in major cities are being refitted with fiber. But if you live anywhere else, you're apt to be straight out of luck.

As you'd expect, fiber tends to be more expensive than other technologies, but when it's run to the home (rather than to a business), it's usually more or less affordable—especially if you need the speed it delivers.

Cable Modem

If cable modem access is available where you live, go for it. After fiber, cable provides the fastest affordable residential access—up to several megabits (millions of bits) per second.

Cable has three main drawbacks:

◆ First, the bandwidth is shared with your neighbors, so if everyone gets online at the same time, the speed drops. Ask the cable company what the network's capacity is, how many people share that capacity, and what the minimum bandwidth they guarantee you is. (They may not guarantee *any* minimum bandwidth.) If you find the speed dropping to unacceptable levels, lobby the cable company vociferously to add bandwidth to your loop. Get your neighbors to lobby too—if you can pry them away from their computers.

◆ Second, many cable companies implement an *upload speed cap*, which limits the amount of data you can upload per second, typically to prevent you from running a web server or FTP server. (Their user agreements usually forbid you to run such servers anyway.) If you're neither going to be running a server nor sharing many files via P2P technologies, this shouldn't be a problem, but make sure that you know what the company's policy is before you sign up.

◆ Third, because the wire is shared, your computer is essentially networked with your neighborhood, so it's vital that you use a firewall to secure it. Also, be sure to turn off file-sharing on any computer that's connected to the Internet via a cable modem.

Digital Subscriber Line

If digital subscriber line (DSL) connectivity is available and affordable where you live, get it. DSL typically offers between 384Kbps and 1.5Mbps downstream (to the consumer) and slower upstream (to the ISP) speeds. At this writing, the Baby Bells are vying with the cable companies for high-speed customers, so the cost of DSL is reasonable—from $20 to $50 per month for good service, including an account with their ISP.

Because DSL is always on, your computer is continuously connected to the Internet, so there's a threat of your computer being attacked across the wire. With DSL, the threat is significantly lower than with cable (because the wire isn't shared in most U.S. implementations), but you'll still need a firewall.

EXPERT KNOWLEDGE: DIFFERENT TYPES OF DSL

There are many different types of DSL, but you're most likely to encounter the following:

Asymmetric DSL (ADSL) ADSL delivers faster speed downstream (downloading data to your computer) than upstream (uploading data). ADSL is currently the most widely used form of DSL for residential connections. ADSL can manage up to 6.1Mbps downstream and 640Kbps upstream, but most reasonable-priced offerings give 384Kbps to 1.544Mbps downstream and 128Kbps to 384Kbps upstream. The disadvantage to ADSL is that it requires a device called a *splitter* to be installed at the consumer end of the line to split the line between data use and voice use. Installing the splitter is a professional job and so requires a (technical term) *truck roll*—in theory, only one per installation, but enough to greatly increase the cost and time needed for deployment.

Consumer DSL (CDSL) CDSL is a new implementation of DSL by Rockwell that's designed (as its name suggests) for the consumer market and to be easier to install than ADSL: It doesn't need a splitter at the consumer end of the line. It delivers 1Mbps downstream and slower speeds upstream.

DSL Lite (G.Lite) DSL Lite wins the competition for the most names, as it's also known as *splitterless ADSL* and *Universal ADSL*. As you'd guess from the first of those alternative names, DSL Lite doesn't require a splitter to be installed at the consumer end of the line. It delivers from 1.544Mbps to 6Mbps downstream and from 128Kbps to 384Kbps upstream.

Rate-adaptive DSL (RADSL) RADSL adjusts its speed to the capabilities of the phone line. It requires a splitter and can deliver from 640Kbps to 2.2Mbps downstream and from 272Kbps to 1.088Mbps upstream.

Symmetrical DSL (SDSL) SDSL delivers the same data rate (1.544Mbps) upstream and downstream, making it suitable for businesses (or individuals) who need to transmit a lot of data—for example, running a web server. SDSL requires a splitter and is usually considerably more expensive than ADSL.

That's probably more DSLs than you really want details on—and we haven't even mentioned x2/DSL, HDSL, IDSL, or UDSL.

It's likely that your provider will offer only one flavor of DSL for residential service. That flavor is likely to be ADSL.

Unlike with cable, you're not on the same local network as your neighbors, so the bandwidth isn't shared, and you should be able to get the minimum guaranteed rate (sometimes referred to as the *committed information rate* or *CIR*) any time of the day or night.

The main disadvantage of DSL is that it works only within a relatively short distance from the telephone company's central office, which means in effect that it's confined to urban locations. Some non-telco DSL providers are more aggressive with the distance than the telcos, but you'll typically have to pay more, and you'll get a lower-speed connection. If you live out in the sticks, you're almost certainly beyond the range of DSL.

Integrated Services Digital Network

If you can't get cable or a DSL, your next choice should be ISDN (Integrated Services Digital Network). An ISDN is a digital line that's not as fast as a DSL but is more widely available, especially for people outside major metropolitan areas. ISDN's *basic rate interface (BRI)* provides two *bearer channels* that deliver 64Kbps each, plus a 16Kbps signaling channel, so it delivers decent speeds when both bearer channels are open. The signaling channel is more formally called a *data channel*, and you'll sometimes hear BRI referred to as *2B+D*—two bearer channels plus one data channel.

Check the prices before you order ISDN: It's traditionally been a business service, and it can be expensive, with most companies levying per-minute charges for each channel. It requires professional installation, for which you'll probably have to pay, and extra hardware (likewise). Also, because you can establish an ISDN connection only to another ISDN number, your ISP has to support ISDN as well. They also may charge you extra for the privilege.

The good news about ISDN (apart from its wide availability) is that most implementations are symmetrical, so you get the same speed upstream as downstream.

Satellite Solutions

If you're too rural to get ISDN, or if ISDN is too slow for you, consider one of the satellite solutions available, such as DirecPC (`www.direcpc.com`) or StarBand (`www.starband.com`). These solutions typically offer speeds of around 400Kbps downstream, so they can be good if you need to download large chunks of data (such as audio or video files).

Satellite solutions used to have one major drawback: The satellite provided only downlink capabilities, so you had to use your phone line to send data to your ISP to tell them which information to deliver by satellite. Less-expensive satellite solutions still use this method, but if you pay more, you can send your outgoing data via satellite as well, which makes satellite much more attractive.

But there are several caveats:

◆ First, the satellite dish and installation can be pricey. (Watch for special offers.)

◆ Second, check the plan or pricing scheme carefully. Make sure it provides enough hours each month so that you don't start incurring expensive extra hours every month on your normal level of usage.

◆ Third, some satellite services have a *fair access policy (FAP)* by which they reserve the right to throttle back your download speed if you continuously run it full bore—in other words, you can have your 400Kbps (or whatever speed the provider offers), but you can't have it all the time. This can put a serious crimp into your ability to download a massive amount every day via a satellite hookup. So read your sign-up agreement carefully for details of the fair access policy, and be especially wary of clauses that allow the service provider to modify the terms of the contract without your explicit consent.

◆ Fourth, you typically can't share one-way satellite connections via Internet Connection Sharing. You also can't use ICS to share some satellite connections that connect to your computer via USB.

Wireless Services

If you need mobility with your Internet connection, check out the wireless services available. At this writing, you *can* hook up a laptop to a mobile phone, but the resulting data rates are too slow for anything but checking e-mail—and you're paying your usual call rates for the mobile phone. Several more promising wireless solutions (such as Ricochet from Metricom) were deployed in the late 1990s, but most of them either went bankrupt or were heavily cut back during the dotcom collapse of 2000 and 2001—leaving the field wide open for new entrants that may have emerged by the time you read this.

Criteria for Choosing an ISP

If the connection type you chose isn't the only game in town, you may have a choice of ISPs as well. If you're using dial-up, you'll probably have plenty of choice. This section suggests the main criteria to use when evaluating the offerings of competing ISPs.

How many e-mail accounts do you get?   These days, a single e-mail account gets you about as far as a single tire on a car. Many ISPs offer five or so e-mail accounts for residential accounts—one for each member of the nuclear family, including the dog. You may want more than this, particularly if you use your computer for business. The better ISPs give you as many e-mail accounts as you need. Other ISPs charge you for additional mailboxes.

How much connect time are you allowed?   (Dial-up connections only.) Some ISPs and some plans allow unlimited connection time. Others allow you a certain number of hours per month and charge extra for each hour or part of an hour beyond that.

Does your ISP provide a full suite of newsgroups?   Almost all ISPs provide newsgroups, but some filter out newsgroups they consider offensive or that have exceptionally high volumes of traffic.

How much web space and traffic are you allowed?   Make sure that your ISP provides enough space for your website: Some ISPs offer 10MB, some 20MB, some 50MB. If you plan to get a lot of visitors to your website, check the amount of traffic that the ISP permits before charging you extra. Some ISPs permit unlimited traffic, but others charge beyond a certain limit (usually measured in gigabytes per month).

How many dial-up points of presence does it have?   First, make sure that the local point of presence (POP) is within your unrestricted calling area. Second, if you're traveling, you'll want to be able to connect at local rates. Make sure that your ISP has POPs in enough geographical areas or the right geographical areas. Your ISP might also have an 800 number that you can use when traveling; it'll probably have a per-minute charge, but it should cost less than calling long-distance with hotel surcharges.

Can you use multilink? (Dial-up connections only) Multilink lets you connect with two or more modems at the same time to get faster throughput. You'll need a second phone line to use multilink, and many ISPs who support multilink charge extra for it.

How good is the service? This question is best asked of people who are already using the service. If they report slow browsing and e-mail outages, look elsewhere.

Does the ISP support XP? Sooner or later, just about every ISP will support XP, but many have been slow to add XP support. Some require you to use their proprietary software, which typically offers a customized front end to the Web but in many cases proves less flexible than using Internet Explorer or another browser.

Can you access your e-mail via the Web? This feature can be useful when you're traveling without your PC. Many ISPs don't support it.

TIP *If you're prepared to have advertising displayed at you the whole time you're connected to the Internet, you may be able to connect to the Internet for free. Check out the list of Cheap and Free ISPs at Freedomlist.com (`www.freedomlist.com`) for more information.*

Creating an Internet Connection

This section discusses how to create an Internet connection manually.

NOTE *If you have an always-on DSL connection or always-on cable connection, your computer should already be connected to the Internet, and you shouldn't need to follow this procedure. (For other types of broadband, such as cable modems that don't sustain a permanent connection, follow this procedure unless XP tells you that you don't need to.) If you have a CD from your ISP that promises to set up your Internet connection for you, use that instead of following this procedure.*

To create an Internet connection, take the following steps:

1. Choose Start ➤ Connect To ➤ Show All Connections. XP displays the Network Connections folder.

   ◆ If you haven't created a network connection, the Connect To item doesn't appear on the Start menu. Choose Start ➤ Control Panel. XP displays Control Panel. Click the Network and Internet Connections link. XP displays the Network and Internet Connections screen. Click the Network Connections link. XP displays the Network Connections folder.

2. Click the Create a New Connection link in the Network Tasks list. XP starts the New Connection Wizard, which displays its Welcome to the New Connection Wizard page.

   ◆ If you haven't identified the country (or region) and area code that you're in, or your phone and modem options, XP prompts you for them. See the sections "Specifying Your Location" and "Specifying Phone and Modem Options" in Chapter 14 for details.

3. Click the Next button. The wizard displays the Network Connection Type page (shown in Figure 18.1).

FIGURE 18.1

On the Network Connection Type page of the New Connection Wizard, select the Connect to the Internet option button.

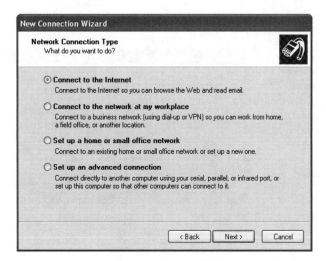

4. Select the Connect to the Internet option button (if it's not selected by default).

5. Click the Next button. The wizard displays the Getting Ready page (shown in Figure 18.2).

FIGURE 18.2

On the Getting Ready page of the New Connection Wizard, tell the wizard how you want to connect to the Internet.

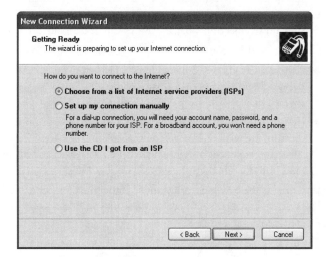

6. Select the Set Up My Connection Manually option button.

◆ If you select the Choose from a List of Internet Service Providers (ISPs) option button, the wizard displays the Completing the New Connection Wizard page when you click the Next button. On that page, you have the choice to set up Internet access using MSN Explorer (for the U.S. only) or to select from a list of other ISPs listed on the Microsoft Internet Referral Service.

◆ If you select the Use the CD I Got from an ISP option button, the wizard displays the Completing the New Connection Wizard page when you click the Next button. It then essentially tells you to run the ISP's CD to set up your connection.

7. Click the Next button. The wizard displays the Internet Connection page (shown in Figure 18.3).

FIGURE 18.3

On the Internet Connection page of the New Connection Wizard, specify whether you'll be connecting via a dial-up modem or via broadband.

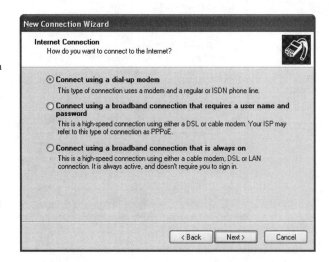

8. Select the Connect Using a Dial-up Modem option button, the Connect Using a Broadband Connection That Requires a User Name and Password option button, or the Connect Using a Broadband Connection That Is Always On option button as appropriate.

9. Click the Next button.

- ◆ If you selected the Connect Using a Dial-up Modem option button or the Connect Using a Broadband Connection That Requires a User Name and Password option button, the wizard displays the Connection Name page.

- ◆ If you selected the Connect Using a Broadband Connection That Is Always On option button, the wizard displays the Completing the New Connection Wizard page, telling you that your connection should already be configured and ready to use. Click the Finish button and find out whether the wizard is right.

10. Enter the name by which you want to know the connection. The wizard suggests using your ISP's name, but there's no need to do so if you find another name more suitable.

11. Click the Next button.

- ◆ If you selected the Connect Using a Dial-up Modem option button, the wizard displays the Phone Number to Dial page. Take the next two steps.

- ◆ If you selected the Connect Using a Broadband Connection That Requires a User Name and Password option button, the wizard displays the Internet Account Information page. Go to step 14.

12. Enter the phone number for your ISP, including any area code or long-distance number.

13. Click the Next button. The wizard displays the Internet Account Information page (shown in Figure 18.4).

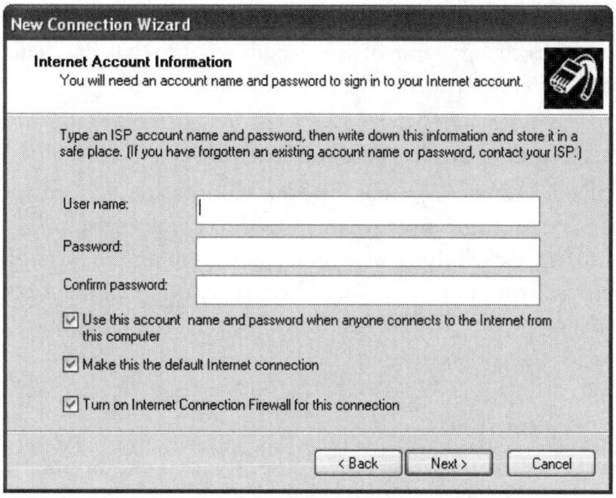

FIGURE 18.4

On the Internet Account Information page of the New Connection Wizard, enter your username and password and choose options for the connection.

New Connection Wizard

Internet Account Information
You will need an account name and password to sign in to your Internet account.

Type an ISP account name and password, then write down this information and store it in a safe place. (If you have forgotten an existing account name or password, contact your ISP.)

User name:

Password:

Confirm password:

☑ Use this account name and password when anyone connects to the Internet from this computer

☑ Make this the default Internet connection

☑ Turn on Internet Connection Firewall for this connection

< Back   Next >   Cancel

14. Enter your username in the User Name text box, and your password in the Password text box and the Confirm Password text box.

15. If you want other users of this computer to be able to connect to this Internet connection by using this username and password, leave the Use This Account Name and Password when Anyone Connects to the Internet from This Computer check box selected (as it is by default). If you want users to have to enter a username and password to establish an Internet connection, clear this check box.

16. If you want this connection to be the default Internet connection for this computer, leave the Make This the Default Internet Connection check box selected (as it is by default). Otherwise, clear this check box.

NOTE   *XP displays a white check mark in a black circle on the icon for the default Internet connection in the Network Connections window. To stop this connection from being the default connection, right-click its icon and choose Unset As Default Connection from the context menu. (To set it as the default connection again, right-click again and choose Set As Default Connection.)*

17. If you want to use XP's Internet Connection Firewall (ICF) to protect your computer and others that connect to the Internet via your computer from attack via this Internet connection, leave the Turn On Internet Connection Firewall for This Connection check box selected (as it is by default). If you don't want to use ICF, clear this check box. See "Securing Your Internet Connection" later in this chapter for more information about firewalls in general and ICF in particular.

18. Click the Next button. The New Connection Wizard displays the Completing the New Connection Wizard page, which summarizes the choices you've made.

19. Select the Add a Shortcut to This Connection to My Desktop check box if you want the wizard to create a shortcut on the Desktop for each user.

20. Click the Finish button. The New Connection Wizard finishes creating the connection and closes itself.

You can then connect as described in the section after next, "Establishing a Connection." But first you may want to change some of the default settings that the New Connection Wizard applied to the connection, as described in the next section.

Configuring the Connection Manually

Most of the default settings that the New Connection Wizard applies to Internet connections are appropriate, but in some cases you may need to tweak the settings in order to get better performance.

To do so, right-click the icon for the connection on the Network Connections page and choose Properties from the context menu. (Alternatively, if the New Connection Wizard displayed the Connect dialog box for the connection, click the Properties button.) XP displays the Properties dialog box for the connection.

GENERAL PAGE OPTIONS

The General page of the Properties dialog box for a dial-up Internet connection (shown on the left in Figure 18.5) contains the following controls:

Connect Using list box　Select the modem or other device to use for the connection. If you have only one dial-up device, you won't have a choice. If you have multiple dial-up devices, select the check box for each that you want to use. (The section "Using Multiple Modems on a Dial-up Connection," later in this chapter, discusses how to use multiple dial-up devices.)

FIGURE 18.5

The General page (left) and the Options page (right) of the Properties dialog box for a dial-up Internet connection.

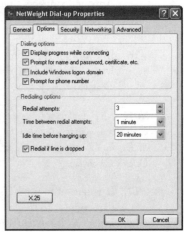

Configure button　Click this button to display the Configuration dialog box for the selected dial-up device.

Phone Number group box　Specify the phone number for the dial-up device to dial and choose whether to use dialing rules.

◆ When you select the Use Dialing Rules check box, XP enables the Dialing Rules button, the Area Code drop-down list, and the Country/Region Code drop-down list. Click the Dialing Rules button to display the Dialing Rules page of the Phone and Modem Options dialog box, in which you can create dialing rules as discussed in the section "Using Dial-up Networking from Multiple Locations" in Chapter 15.

◆ If your ISP provides more than one dial-up number for this location, click the Alternates button. XP displays the Alternate Phone Numbers dialog box (shown on the left in Figure 18.6). To add a number, click the Add button and work in the resulting Add Alternate Phone Number dialog box (shown on the right in Figure 18.6). To edit an existing number, select it, click the Edit button, and work in the Edit Alternate Phone Number dialog box. To delete an existing number, select it and click the Delete button. Once you've added the phone numbers, use the up and down buttons to shuffle them into the order in which you want XP to dial them. XP automatically selects the If Number Fails, Try Next Number check box, and usually you'll want to leave it selected. If you have no preference among the numbers, you may want to select the Move Successful Number to Top of List check box to allow XP to migrate successful numbers to the top of the list on the basis that they'll be the best ones to try next.

FIGURE 18.6

If your ISP provides multiple dial-up numbers, add them to the list in the Alternate Phone Numbers dialog box (left) by using the Add Alternate Phone Number dialog box (right).

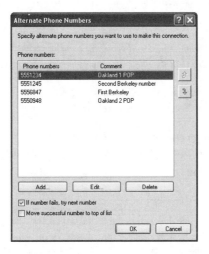

Show Icon in Notification Area when Connected check box   This check box, which is selected by default for a dial-up connection, controls whether XP displays an icon for the connection in the notification area. This icon lets you monitor the status of the connection easily and disconnect it quickly, so most people find it useful.

OPTIONS PAGE OPTIONS

The Options page of the Properties dialog box for a dial-up connection (shown on the right in Figure 18.5) contains the following controls:

Dialing Options group box   This group box lets you specify whether XP should display message boxes showing its progress as it establishes dial-up connections (the Display Progress while Connecting check box), prompt you for your name and verification (the Prompt for Name and Password, Certificate, Etc. check box), include the Windows logon domain in the logon information it sends (the Include Windows Logon Domain check box), and prompt you for the phone number for the connection (the Prompt for Phone Number check box). Make sure the Include Windows Logon Domain check box is cleared for a dial-up Internet connection. (You need to use this setting only when connecting to a corporate network via dial-in or a VPN connection. We'll discuss these actions later in this book.) The other three check boxes are cleared by default, but you may want to experiment with turning some off. If you turn all these check boxes off, when you double-click the connection, XP dials it without displaying the Connect dialog box.

Redialing Options group box   This group box lets you control how XP redials the connection if it can't connect at the first attempt or if the line or connection is dropped. Use the Redial Attempts text box to specify the number of times XP should attempt to establish the connection and the Time between Redial Attempts drop-down list to specify the pause between attempts. (You can set values between 1 second and 10 minutes.) In the Idle Time before Hanging Up drop-down list, specify what length of inactivity XP should allow before dropping the connection automatically. (You can set values from 1 minute to 24 hours, or you can choose Never to maintain the connection as long as possible.) Select the Redial if Line Is Dropped check box if you want XP to automatically redial the connection if it's dropped at the other end.

TIP   *To maintain as permanent a connection as your phone line and ISP permit, select the Redial if Line Is Dropped check box on the Options page and select Never in the Idle Time before Hanging Up drop-down list.*

Clicking the X.25 button displays the X.25 Logon Settings dialog box for configuring networking settings for X.25 networks. You're very unlikely to be using X.25 at home or in a home office.

NOTE   *If your computer has multiple dial-up devices available for connections, the Options page also contains a Multiple Devices group box. The section "Using Multiple Modems on a Dial-up Connection," later in this chapter, discusses how to use this group box.*

SECURITY PAGE OPTIONS

The Security page of the Properties dialog box for a dial-up connection (shown on the left in Figure 18.7) contains controls for specifying how to authenticate and secure the connections you made. Because these controls work in combination, I'll discuss them by function rather than individually.

FIGURE 18.7

The Security page (left) and the Networking page (right) of the Properties dialog box for a dial-up Internet connection.

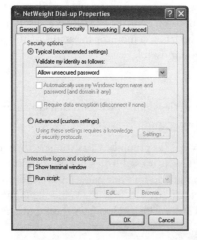

In the Security Options group box, you have a choice of two option buttons for specifying a category of security settings: the Typical (Recommended Settings) option button and the Advanced (Custom Settings) option button.

By default, XP selects the Typical option button for a dial-up Internet connection and selects the Allow Unsecured Password item in the Validate My Identity As Follows drop-down list. This setting allows XP to validate your identity by using an unsecured password if it's not able to validate it by using a secured password. (XP tries the secured password first, then drops back to the unsecured password if necessary.)

For increased security, select the Require Secured Password item in the Validate My Identity As Follows drop-down list to prevent XP from using the unsecured password. For this to work, your ISP must support secured passwords for your connection—if your ISP doesn't, XP won't be able to establish the connection. Once you select the Require Secured Password item, XP makes available the Automatically Use My Windows Logon Name and Password (and Domain if Any) check box and the Require Data Encryption (Disconnect if None) check box. Select the former check box only if your dial-up account uses the same username and password as your XP user account. This is very unlikely to be the case for an Internet connection, but it may be the case for a dial-up network connection to a corporate network. (I'll discuss connecting to a corporate network in the section "Creating a Dial-up Connection to a Remote Network" in Chapter 34.) Select the Require Data Encryption (Disconnect if None) check box if your ISP supports encryption and you feel compelled to use it. (This setting too is one you're much more likely to need for connecting to a corporate network than to an ISP.)

If you have a smart card for the connection, select the Use Smart Card item in the Validate My Identity As Follows drop-down list—but very few ISPs support smart cards at this writing. (That said, you may need a smart card for some company connections.) When you select the Use Smart Card item, XP makes available the Require Data Encryption (Disconnect if None) check box. Select it if necessary.

If you know which security protocols you can (or must) use for your Internet connection, select the Advanced (Custom Settings) option button, click the Settings button, and work in the Advanced Security Settings dialog box. Because you're far more likely to need these options for a remote connection to a corporate network than for an Internet connection, I'll discuss these options in Chapter 34 rather than here.

NETWORKING PAGE OPTIONS

Compared with the Security page, the Networking page of the Properties dialog box for a dial-up connection (shown on the right in Figure 18.7 above) is refreshingly straightforward.

Type of Dial-up Server I Am Calling drop-down list   In this drop-down list, you'll almost always want the PPP: Windows 95/98/NT 4/2000, Internet item, which XP will have selected by default. The only other option is the SLIP: Unix Connection item, which you'll need if you have a SLIP connection to the Internet. (Briefly, PPP is a newer technology than SLIP and offers more flexibility.)

This Connection Uses the Following Items check box   In this list box, the Internet Protocol (TCP/IP) item and the QoS Packet Scheduler item should be selected already. You shouldn't need to select any further items. In particular, make sure that the File and Printer Sharing for Microsoft Networks item is *not* selected, because you don't want to be sharing your files and printers automatically with everyone on the Internet.

ADVANCED PAGE OPTIONS

The Advanced page of the Properties dialog box for a dial-up connection lets you configure the settings for Internet Connection Firewall (ICF) and Internet Connection Sharing (ICS). I'll discuss the Internet Connection Firewall options in the section "Enabling and Disabling Internet Connection Firewall," later in this chapter, and the Internet Connection Sharing options in the section "Configuring ICS Manually" in Chapter 32.

Establishing a Connection

To establish a connection, take the following steps:

1. If you created a shortcut for the connection on your Desktop, double-click it. If not, choose Start ➢ Connect To and choose the connection from the submenu. XP displays the Connect dialog box for the connection (shown in Figure 18.8).

FIGURE 18.8

The Connect dialog box

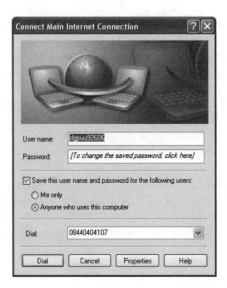

2. If necessary, enter your username in the User Name text box and your password in the Password text box. You won't need to enter these if whoever set up the connection chose to store the username and password in the connection.

   ◆ If you want XP to store the username and password, make sure the Save This User Name and Password for the Following Users check box is selected. Then select the Me Only option button or the Anyone Who Uses This Computer option button as appropriate.

3. Click the Dial button (for a dial-up connection) or the Connect button (for a broadband connection). XP dials the connection or attempts to connect and displays the Connecting dialog

box to keep you informed of its progress. If it receives an answer, it checks your username and password and, all being well, logs you in.

4. When the connection is established, XP displays a notification-area pop-up giving the connection name and the connection speed.

If you chose to have the connection display an icon in the notification area, XP places the icon there.

Viewing the Status of a Connection

The two monitor screens on the icon in the System Tray show light blue as data is transferred. When no data is being transferred, they appear dark. When a short burst of information is transferred, they flicker blue briefly; when sustained data transfer is taking place, both stay blue.

To view brief statistics for the connection, hover the mouse pointer over the icon. XP displays a pop-up showing the connection name, the speed, and the number of packets sent and received, as shown on the left side of Figure 18.9.

To get a closer reading of what's happening on the connection, double-click the icon in the System Tray. XP displays the Status dialog box for the connection. The General page of the Status dialog box (of which the right side of Figure 18.9 shows an example) gives the connection status, duration, speed, and details including the number of bytes of information sent and received and the number of errors.

FIGURE 18.9

Two ways of checking what's happening on a connection: Hover the mouse pointer over the System Tray icon to get a quick readout (left), or double-click the System Tray icon to display the Status dialog box with more details.

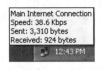

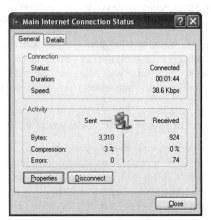

As you can see in the figure, the General page of the Status dialog box contains three buttons. Click the Properties button to display the Properties dialog box for the connection. Click the Disconnect button to disconnect the connection and close the Status dialog box. Click the Close button to close the Status dialog box without disconnecting the connection.

The Details page of the Status dialog box for a connection displays information about the server type, transport protocol, authentication, compression, PPP multilink framing, and IP addresses for the server and the client.

EXPERT KNOWLEDGE: WHEN DOES UNEXPECTED DATA TRANSFER INDICATE A PROBLEM?

As mentioned a page or so ago, the monitor screens on the System Tray icon for a dial-up connection appear light blue as data is transferred and black when no data is being transferred. By watching this icon, you can see at a glance whether the connection is transferring data. By displaying the Status dialog box for the connection, you can see details of the flow of bytes in and out.

When you're browsing the Web, or when you're downloading files, data is being transferred—obviously enough. When you're uploading files, you'll usually know about it. When you're in a conference with Net-Meeting, packets will be zipping back and forth. If you make phone calls over your Internet connection, it'll be busy in both directions. (And if you stream video, you'll be giving your connection a fair workout.)

At other times, when you're not obviously doing things on the Internet or Web, you'd expect the connection not to be transferring data. But often it will be—sometimes for a long period at a stretch. What's going on? Has someone cracked your security screen? And are they busily downloading your Quicken or Money files?

They may have, and they may be. But before you yank the modem or network connection out of the computer, make sure you know why your computer might be uploading or downloading data without your knowledge. Here are some of the reasons for apparently unexplained activity:

◆ TCP/IP sends acknowledgment packets while receiving data so that the computer sending the information knows that it has been received. So when you're downloading information, there will always be some outbound packets. The normal ratio is about one outbound packet for every eight inbound packets. If your connection to the computer that's sending the packets is unreliable, and some inbound packets are being lost, you may see a higher ratio of outbound to inbound packets.

◆ If you set your e-mail program to check your mail server regularly, it will do so until you tell it to stop. Checking e-mail shows up as a brief flicker on the screens when you don't have mail to send or retrieve. Sustained downloading can indicate that someone has attached a huge PowerPoint presentation or a dozen uncompressed 4.3 megapixel digital pictures of their dog.

◆ If you run Windows Messenger, it keeps sending packets to tell the service that you're still online (or that you're Away, when it decides you're so). Other IM programs do much the same thing.

◆ If you run a P2P file-sharing program, you'll see a bunch of activity taking place on your connection even when you're not downloading or uploading a file, searching, or chatting. Gnutella is the worst offender in this regard, because its searches are not coordinated through a central network of servers but through the peer computers with which each Gnutella client is connected. So your computer ends up relaying a lot of packets of information for search requests—plus the packets for the responses to those requests, of course.

◆ Windows Update automatically downloads update files in the background when it discovers that they're available and your computer needs them. As mentioned earlier in the book, Windows Update uses bandwidth-throttling techniques that try to prevent the download from interfering with your activity across the connection. These techniques increase the time it takes to download a file, and work better on fast connections than on slow ones. So apparently suspicious activity that goes on for a long time may be nothing worse than Windows Update downloading an update.

As you can see, there are a lot of activities that could legitimately be using your Internet connection without your direct involvement. At the same time, you could have been hacked. Read the section "Securing Your Internet Connection" later in this chapter to learn how you can prevent that from happening.

Disconnecting a Connection

There are three easy ways to disconnect a network connection. Which you find most convenient depends on whether you have the connection configured to display an icon in the notification area and whether you have its Status dialog box open:

- ◆ If you have the Status dialog box for the connection open, click the Disconnect button.
- ◆ If the connection has a status icon in the notification area, right-click that icon and choose Disconnect from the context menu.
- ◆ If neither of the above is the case, choose Start ➢ Connect To ➢ Show All Connections. XP displays the Network Connections window. Then right-click the icon for the connection and choose Disconnect from the context menu.

Whichever method you choose, XP closes the connection. If the Status dialog box or a status icon was displayed, XP removes it from the screen.

If the connection fails, or if XP disconnects it when the screen saver or Welcome screen kicks in after a period of inactivity, XP displays the Reconnect dialog box, which is a renamed version of the Connect dialog box shown earlier in Figure 18.8. Connect as described earlier in this chapter.

NOTE   *If your Internet connection is running when you log out, XP displays a dialog box asking if you want to close the connection.*

Connecting Automatically to the Internet

If you set any of your Internet-enabled programs to connect to the Internet automatically (or they set themselves to do so), XP displays the Dial-up Connection dialog box shown in Figure 18.10 when a program tries to connect via a connection that's not open. Click the Connect button to let the program connect. If you want the program to be able to use the connection without your intervention, select the Connect Automatically check box first.

FIGURE 18.10

XP displays the Dial-up Connection dialog box when a program tries to connect to the Internet via a connection that's not open.

Preventing Internet Explorer from Connecting Automatically

To prevent Internet Explorer, Outlook Express, or another Internet-related program from automatically launching your Internet connection when you start it, take the following steps:

1. Choose Start ➢ Control Panel. XP displays Control Panel.
2. Click the Network and Internet Connections link. XP displays the Network and Internet Connections page.
3. Click the Internet Options link. XP displays the Internet Properties dialog box.
4. Click the Connections tab. XP displays the Connections page.
5. Select the Never Dial a Connection option button.
6. Click the OK button. XP closes the Internet Properties dialog box.

Switching Easily between Different Dial-up Numbers for the Same ISP

If your ISP provides you with multiple numbers that you'll need to use frequently (for example, if the ISP has multiple different local numbers in your area code, or if you need to call different numbers when you travel), create an entry for the ISP as described earlier in this chapter, then copy it by right-clicking it and choosing Create Copy from the context menu. (Alternatively, choose File ➢ Create Copy.) Rename the connection by using the Rename This Connection link in the Network Tasks list, then edit its properties and change the phone number.

Using Multiple Modems on a Dial-up Connection

If your ISP supports multilink and you have two phone lines and two modems, you can use multilink to improve your aggregate connection speed and increase the amount of data you can transmit. Connecting with two multilinked modems of the same speed doesn't quite double the speed you get, because there's some overhead in coordinating them, but it can still net you a considerable increase in speed.

To use multilink, take the following steps:

1. Install and configure both modems as described in Chapter 14.
2. Set up a dial-up connection as described earlier in this chapter using the first modem.
3. In the Network Connections window, right-click the icon for the dial-up connection and choose Properties from the context menu. XP displays the Properties dialog box for the connection with the General page foremost (shown on the left in Figure 18.11).
4. In the Connect Using list box, select the check boxes for the modems you want to use for the connection. Use the up-arrow button and down-arrow button to arrange the modems into the order in which you want them to connect.
5. By default, XP selects the All Devices Call the Same Numbers check box. To change this, clear this check box, select the modem that needs to dial a different number in the Connect Using list box, and enter the other number in the Phone Number list box.
6. Click the Options tab. XP displays the Options page of the Properties dialog box (shown on the right in Figure 18.11).

FIGURE 18.11

On the General page (left) of the Properties dialog box for the connection, select the modems you want to use for the connection and specify the phone numbers to use. On the Options page (right), specify which devices to dial.

7. In the Multiple Devices drop-down list, select the Dial All Devices item (the default) if you want to have both (or all) lines open all the time. Select the Dial Devices Only As Needed item if you want XP to dial the second and subsequent lines only when the first is at or near capacity.

8. If you choose the Dial Devices Only As Needed item, you can specify settings for when XP dials another line and when it drops the connection by clicking the Configure button and working in the resulting Automatic Dialing and Hanging Up dialog box (shown in Figure 18.12) that XP displays.

FIGURE 18.12

In the Automatic Dialing and Hanging Up dialog box, specify criteria for when to dial additional lines and when to drop them.

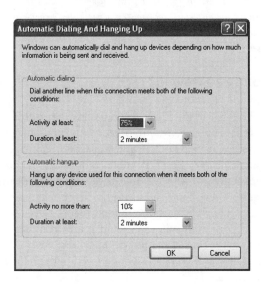

9. Click the OK button. XP closes the Properties dialog box and applies your choices.

Securing Your Internet Connection

As you read earlier in the chapter, XP includes a personal firewall that you can use as a first line of defense for your computer or your network. (That's the first line of defense seen from an inside perspective.) You may also want to consider adding a third-party firewall, either software or hardware—or even both.

But we're getting ahead of ourselves. What *is* a firewall, and what does it do?

What Is a Firewall?

A *firewall* is a device used to secure the connection between one computer or network and another computer or network. For example, a home user would typically use a firewall to secure the connection between their computer (or their home network) and the Internet. An IT department might use various firewalls to secure the connections between a corporate network and the Internet, or between two corporate networks that are linked together.

A firewall can be implemented in hardware, in software, or in a combination of the two. Loosely speaking, hardware firewalls are more expensive than software firewalls, but because the hardware is dedicated to its job (as opposed to having to run an operating system, manipulate spreadsheets, and play Quake on command), it tends to be more reliable and effective than a software firewall.

A firewall monitors the packets of information being sent and received from the computers inside the network. Depending on the configuration of the firewall, it may pass all the packets it receives (both ingoing and outgoing) to a proxy server that checks whether the packets are allowed to pass the firewall. If the packets are allowed, it passes them on. If they're not allowed, it stops them in their tracks.

NOTE *In case you're wondering—the term* firewall *comes not from buildings but from automobiles, in which the firewall is the fireproof shielding between the engine compartment and the passenger compartment designed to protect you from having foot flambé when the engine decides to combust externally for a change. (The analogy with networking is a bit strange, but the term sounds cool, and so it has stuck.) You may also hear a firewall called a* security-edge gateway, *though the term isn't used nearly as often as* firewall. (Security-edge gateway *just isn't snappy enough.)*

Do You Need to Use a Firewall?

The brief and simple answer to the question in the heading is, Yes, you should use a firewall. Every computer connected directly to the Internet should use a firewall. That goes in spades for any computer that provides Internet connectivity to other computers—for example, a networked computer that shares an Internet connection via XP's Internet Connection Sharing feature.

As usual, though, life tends to be a little more complicated than that. In some circumstances, you may decide not to use a firewall—for example, because you consider the threats to your computer to be minimal, or because a firewall interferes with the functionality of a program, or because you need to use virtual private networking and find that a firewall prevents it from working properly. But before you decide not to use a firewall, you should at least consider the threats to your security and balance them against such problems as a firewall may cause you.

Generally speaking, if you have a persistent connection to the Internet (for example, a connection through a cable modem or a DSL), a firewall is vital. Because your computer is connected to the Internet all the time, and because it most likely has a static IP address, a malicious hacker (often referred to as a *cracker*) can poke and prod at it at will to see if your computer is easy to break into. Often crackers will run what's called a *port scan* on a number of computers they're eyeing. The port scan explores the TCP/IP ports open for communication on the computer and sees if there are any obvious vulnerabilities. A port scan is an automated routine that can be run quickly with minimal effort.

If you have a dial-up connection to the Internet, and your ISP assigns your computer an IP address dynamically each time you connect, you're unlikely to have the same IP address from one session to the next. (It's possible, but it probably won't happen before you win that lottery for which you've been buying tickets for half your life.) The changing IP address, and the fact that the computer will be offline at least some of the time, make it a little less vulnerable to attack, especially if somebody is targeting your computer in particular (as opposed to any other computer they might be able to break into). Your computer is still vulnerable all the time that it's online, but if you're working at it while it's online, you're in a reasonable position to detect signs of suspicious activity (though you may be too late to do anything about them).

EXPERT KNOWLEDGE: RUNNING A PORT SCAN ON YOURSELF

If you want to see how your computer checks out on a basic port scan and unauthorized incoming requests for information, point your browser at the Gibson Research Corporation website (www.grc.com). This offers several free checks, including ShieldsUP!, PortProbe, and NanoProbe, designed to help you identify weaknesses in your security arrangements.

Enabling and Disabling Internet Connection Firewall

Internet Connection Firewall (ICF) is a software firewall rather than a hardware firewall. Technically, ICF is a *stateful* firewall: It monitors all the communications that pass it, checking the source, the destination, and the content of each packet that passes it.

How does ICF know which incoming packets are legitimate and which aren't? Basically, ICF watches the outgoing packets and builds a table from the information. It then compares incoming packets against the entries in the table, letting pass the packets for which there's a matching outbound entry and jettisoning all other packets.

As you saw earlier in this chapter, XP encourages you to enable ICF when you set up your Internet connection. You can also enable and disable ICF manually at any time by taking the following steps:

1. Choose Start ➢ Connect To ➢ Show All Connections. XP displays the Network Connections window.
2. Right-click the Internet connection and choose Properties from the context menu. XP displays the Properties dialog box for the connection.
3. Click the Advanced tab. XP displays the Advanced page (shown in Figure 18.13).
4. Select or clear the Protect My Computer and Network by Limiting or Preventing Access to This Computer from the Internet check box.
5. Click the OK button. XP starts or stops ICF and closes the Properties dialog box.

FIGURE 18.13

Enable the Internet Connection Firewall (ICF) on the Advanced page of the Properties dialog box for the Internet connection.

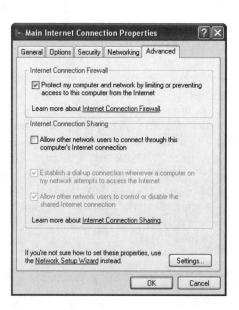

NOTE   The steps shown above enable Internet Connection Firewall with its default settings, which are suitable for connecting a single computer or a simple home network to the Internet. You can also specify advanced settings for Internet Connection Firewall manually to let data pass on specific ports so as to reach specific computers within the firewall—for example, if you run a web server on a computer that connects to the Internet through a shared connection protected by ICF. The section "Configuring ICF to Pass Data for Specific Programs and Services" in Chapter 32 discusses how to choose these settings and those for Internet Connection Sharing.

Troubleshooting Your Internet Connection

This section discusses how to troubleshoot a direct connection to the Internet—in other words, a connection attached to your computer. If your computer connects to the Internet through another computer, see the sidebar "Troubleshooting: You Can't Access or Use the Shared Internet Connection" in Chapter 32 for troubleshooting advice.

The Modem Doesn't Dial

If your connection uses a modem, and the modem doesn't dial, start your troubleshooting by checking the usual suspects:

1. Check that the phone line is working. The easiest way is to plug in a phone and see if you get a dial tone.

2. Check that the phone line is plugged into the modem. If the modem has a pass-through for your phone, check that the phone line (to the telephone network) and the cable to your telephone are plugged into the correct sockets.

3. If the modem is external and needs a power source (as most serial modems do), check that it has a power supply and that it's powered on.

4. Check the connection between the modem and the computer. Make sure that no cable is loose (or missing) and that each end is connected to the appropriate type of connector.

Those four steps are almost too obvious to detail, but they take care of the majority of modem problems. But if they don't solve your modem problem, check that the modem is working by taking the following steps:

1. Choose Start ➤ Control Panel. XP displays Control Panel.
2. Click the Network and Internet Connections link. XP displays the Network and Internet Connections page.
3. Click the Phone and Modem Options link in the See Also list. XP displays the Phone and Modem Options dialog box.
4. Click the Modems tab. XP displays the Modems Page.
5. Select the modem and click the Properties button. XP displays the Properties dialog box for the modem.
6. Click the Diagnostics tab. XP displays the Diagnostics page.
7. Click the Query Modem button. If all is well, you'll see details of the modem's response to the query in the Command | Response list. If you see an error message, you'll know that you need to troubleshoot the modem. Choose Start ➤ Help and Support to display a Help and Support Center window, search for **modem troubleshooter**, and follow its prompts.

The Modem Makes Mating Noises but Can't Connect

If your modem receives an answer and makes squealing noises but can't establish a connection with the ISP, check that the modem is compatible with the ISP's equipment. In some cases, you may be able to upgrade a modem by "flashing" an updated BIOS onto it. (You'd get the modem firmware update from the manufacturer's website.) Failing that, you'll probably need a different modem.

"The Protocol Is Not Configured" Error Message

If you receive the error message "The protocol is not configured" when trying to connect to your ISP, it means that XP is trying to use the wrong networking protocol for the connection. Phone the ISP, ask which protocol you need to use and which settings to apply to it, and then use the controls on the Networking page of the Properties dialog box for the connection to install the protocol (if necessary) and configure it.

TIP You may also need to remove the IPX/SPX protocol from a connection to prevent XP from trying to connect by using it.

The Connection Fails after Dialing

If the connection fails immediately after dialing, one of several things may be wrong.

◆ Your account name or password may be wrong.
◆ Your ISP might have frozen your account (for example, for nonpayment—real or imagined) or terminated it (for example, for spamming).
◆ Your ISP may be temporarily down.

To help you find out which, make sure XP is displaying progress messages while connecting. (To display messages, display the Options page of the Properties dialog box for the connection, then select the Display Progress while Connecting check box in the Dialing Options group box.)

THE CONNECTION FAILS AT VERIFYING USERNAME AND PASSWORD SCREEN

If the connection fails when you're viewing the progress message "Verifying username and password," you've probably mistyped the account name or password.

ERROR 691 ("ACCESS WAS DENIED")

If you get Error 691 ("Access was denied because the username and/or password was invalid on the domain") when trying to connect, it's most likely that you've mistyped your username or password. Another possibility is that you've got the Include Windows Logon Domain check box selected on the Options page of the Properties dialog box for the connection and that you've entered some text in the resulting Domain text box that appears in the Connect dialog box. (If you leave the Domain text box blank, having the Include Windows Logon Domain check box selected usually doesn't cause problems. But it's still better to make sure you're not using this option when you don't need it.)

ERROR 734 ("THE PPP LINK CONTROL PROTOCOL WAS TERMINATED")

If you get Error 734 when trying to connect, it may mean that you've required a secured password (by selecting the Require Secured Password item in the Validate My Identity As Follows drop-down list on the Security page of the Properties dialog box for the connection) but that the ISP doesn't support secured passwords. Select the Allow Unsecured Passwords item instead.

This error may also indicate that the ISP doesn't support Link Control Protocol (LCP) extensions. On the Networking page of the Properties dialog box for the connection, click the Settings button and clear the Enable LCP Extension check box in the PPP Settings dialog box.

ERROR 678 ("THE REMOTE COMPUTER DID NOT RESPOND")

Error 678 ("The remote computer did not respond") usually indicates that the computer you're trying to contact is down or too overloaded to respond to the request for connection.

The Modem Connection Closes Unexpectedly

If your modem connection sometimes closes unexpectedly, and you have call waiting on that line, check that you've selected the To Disable Call Waiting, Dial check box and chosen the appropriate command code in the drop-down list on the General page of the Edit Location dialog box for the connection.

The Modem Connection Closes after a While

If your modem connection always closes after a similar length of time, adjust the Idle Time before Hanging Up drop-down list setting in the Redialing Options group box on the Options page of the Properties dialog box for the connection.

Some programs' Internet activities don't seem to register with the idle timer, so you may find that XP closes the connection even when you've got a program open that you know is using the connection.

The other possibility is that your ISP aggressively cuts off users after a short period of inactivity in order to keep enough of their dial-up lines free.

To keep the connection up as much of the time as possible, select the Redial if Line Is Dropped check box in the Redialing Options group box on the Options page of the Properties dialog box for the connection.

You Can't Access Websites or Mail Servers by Name

If you connect to your ISP without problem, but then can't connect to any websites by their URL and can't connect to your ISP's mail servers, chances are that your ISP's DNS server is down. To find out, try sending a ping packet to the site by its IP address rather than by its URL, as described in the next section. If ping fails, try using tracert, as described in the section after next.

USING PING TO TEST NETWORK CONNECTIONS

Ping (Packet InterNet Groper) is a simple tool for checking connectivity between two computers on a network. If you can't access a website or a mail server by its name, you can use ping to establish whether the server is active and answering or not. The *not* in this case isn't definitive, because it may indicate either that the site or server is not active or that it's simply not providing answers to ping packets. (As you'll see later in this book, XP's ICF feature lets you specify whether to answer ping packets that other people send your way. For security, it's usually best *not* to answer ping packets.)

The most basic usage of ping is with an IP address (for example, `ping 66.218.71.113`) or a host name (for example, `ping yahoo.com`). By default, ping sends four data packets and displays the replies it receives. Here's an example of a successful ping:

```
C:\>ping yahoo.com

Pinging yahoo.com [66.218.71.113] with 32 bytes of data:

Reply from 66.218.71.113: bytes=32 time=212ms TTL=51
Reply from 66.218.71.113: bytes=32 time=210ms TTL=51
Reply from 66.218.71.113: bytes=32 time=205ms TTL=51
Reply from 66.218.71.113: bytes=32 time=205ms TTL=51

Ping statistics for 66.218.71.113:
    Packets: Sent = 4, Received = 4, Lost = 0 (0% loss),
Approximate round trip times in milli-seconds:
    Minimum = 205ms, Maximum = 212ms, Average = 208ms
```

If ping can't get a reply from the specified address, it displays the message "Request timed out." If ping can't resolve a host name to an IP address, it displays the message "Ping request could not find *host name*."

If you can't connect to a website or a server by its URL or host name, you can use ping with the IP address instead of the URL or host name to see if the site is alive. For example, as you can see in the ping output above, Yahoo is using the IP address `66.218.71.112` at this writing, so you can `ping` Yahoo there by using that address. Obviously, to do so, you'll need to know the IP address for the site ahead of time—so it's a good idea to write down ahead of time the IP addresses for a couple of sites you may want to ping to establish whether an apparent connectivity problem is with the site rather than with your Internet connection.

You can also use ping for testing connectivity on your local network. For example, you can use ping to make sure that one computer is connecting properly to another computer (for example, ping 192.168.0.44). Or you can use ping to make sure that the network adapter attached to your computer is working by using what's called the *loopback address*, 127.0.0.1. If you receive four "reply from" packets, you'll know that TCP/IP is correctly bound to the adapter.

Usually, you can find out what you need to know by using ping without switches, but ping does have 11 switches that you can add for more sophisticated use. To see these switches, type **ping /?** at a command prompt.

USING TRACERT TO TRACE THE PATH TO A HOST

Tracert ("trace route") is like ping on steroids. It lets you trace the path to the specified host or IP address by sending Internet Control Message Protocol (ICMP) echo packets to it. Use tracert when you can't ping a host and you want to find out where the problem lies.

To return the list of routers along the path to the host or IP address, tracert uses a neat trick with IP packets. Briefly, each properly formed IP packet includes a value called *time to live* (TTL), which specifies how many routers it's allowed to pass through before it expires. (If IP packets didn't have TTL values, they could go ricocheting around the Internet more or less forever, clogging up the wires big-time.) As a router passes along a packet, it decreases its TTL by 1 (or sometimes more) so that the value remains valid. When a packet's TTL reaches zero, the router it's at sends the source computer a "Time exceeded" message.

So tracert sends out a number of echo packets with different TTL values, starting at 1 and going up to the specified maximum (the default is 30). Back come the "Time exceeded" messages as the TTL values reach zero at each router along the path. Tracert displays a list of the routers in the path, from first to last, with the times the packets took to reach them. Here's an abbreviated example:

```
C:> tracert www.sybex.com

Tracing route to www.sybex.com [63.99.198.12]
over a maximum of 30 hops:

1   135 ms   137 ms   143 ms   so-2-0-0.pr1.lga4.us.mfnx.net [64.124.232.6]
2   148 ms   167 ms   137 ms   ibr02-g2-1.nycm01.exodus.net [216.32.132.5]
3   139 ms   143 ms   137 ms   64.15.224.225
...
Trace complete.
```

You may see "Request timed out" messages. These come from routers configured to silently drop packets with a TTL of zero.

Usually, you can get the results you need by using tracert in its basic form, supplying just the host name or IP address, as in the above example (tracert www.sybex.com). Tracert does support four switches, of which the most useful is –h, which lets you specify the maximum number of hops that tracert should use (for example, tracert –h 5 www.sybex.com). To see information on the other three switches, type **tracert /?** at a command prompt.

Using Digital Certificates

In the physical world, we're used to proving our identity in various ways, such as brandishing a driver's license when the cops pull us over for speeding, producing a credit card and corresponding signature to pay for goods, or presenting a passport at Immigration Control at the airport.

In the virtual world, we need to prove our identity without a piece of paper or plastic. Up until around the turn of the millennium, this was largely done at the personal level by using the mechanisms adapted from the real world for the telephone over the previous couple of decades. Online merchants accepted your credit card (linked to your physical address) as proof of identity. Credit card companies already knew about your credit card and demanded your social security number, mother's maiden name, and perhaps a code phrase of your choosing. But these methods, while still workable, are growing increasingly clumsy as more of the world gets wired and its less-honest elements latch on to the possibilities on offer. (For example, identity theft is growing apace.)

Digital certificates are starting to be accepted as a way of authenticating the provenance of an item, be it a piece of code that Internet Explorer needs to install in order to perform an especially clever piece of 3D animation, or simply establishing that an e-mail is from the person or company it claims to be from.

If you trust the source of, say, an ActiveX control to produce a control that's safe and beneficial to use, you may want to install it. If you know nothing about the source of the control or suspect it to be malignant, you'll want to avoid it at all costs. Similarly, you may need to prove your identity to others—for example, in order to execute a transaction.

This section discusses what digital certificates are, what they mean in the real world, how to get hold of them, and how to import them, export them, and examine them. If this seems a bit theoretical and useless, hold your horses: In the next chapter, you'll see how you can use digital certificates in Internet Explorer to control the content you accept or reject, and in Chapter 21 you'll learn how to use digital certificates to apply digital signatures to messages you send.

What Is a Digital Certificate?

A *digital certificate* is essentially a piece of code that uniquely identifies its holder. You use your digital certificate to prove your identity.

Getting a Digital Certificate

There are several types of digital certificates: those you create yourself, those you get from your company or organization, and those you get from a commercial certification authority. As you might imagine, a digital certificate you create yourself is of little use to people beyond you and those who trust you, whereas a certificate from a commercial certification authority should be good enough for anyone short of the Homeland Security Department. A certificate issued by your company falls in the middle, depending on how much faith you—or, more to the point, other people—put in your company verifying the identity of those to whom it issues certificates.

The following sections briefly examine these different ways of getting a digital certificate. After that, we'll look at how you install the certificates.

CREATING A DIGITAL CERTIFICATE OF YOUR OWN

The quickest and easiest way of getting a digital certificate is to create one yourself. There are various utilities for creating digital certificates, including one, SELFCERT.EXE, that ships with most versions of Microsoft Office. Creating a digital certificate yourself won't make anybody else trust you, but it will help you work with digital certificates.

GETTING A DIGITAL CERTIFICATE FROM YOUR COMPANY

Your second option is to get a digital certificate from a digital certificate server that your company has. The details of this procedure will vary from company to company. The key point is that the certificates the company provides via its digital certificate server are generated in the same fashion as the digital certificates distributed by the commercial certification authorities discussed in the next section. The difference is that the company decides who to allocate the certificates to.

GETTING A DIGITAL CERTIFICATE FROM A COMMERCIAL CERTIFICATION AUTHORITY

Your third choice is to get a digital certificate from a commercial certification authority, such as VeriSign (www.verisign.com); Thawte, Inc. (www.thawte.com); or GlobalSign NV-SA (www.globalsign.net). Thawte is now owned by VeriSign, a deal that made Thawte's founder, Mark Shuttleworth, rich enough to buy a ticket to ride to the International Space Station in April 2002. Most commercial certification authorities work together in an arrangement called a public-key infrastructure (PKI), which means that customers of one certification authority should be able to trust digital certificates issued by another certification authority, because the root certification authorities trust each other.

If you're planning to use the digital certificate with Microsoft products (as seems likely if you're reading this), run Outlook Express and click the Get Digital ID button on the Security page of the Options dialog box. Alternatively, look for the list that Microsoft usually provides on its website (www.microsoft.com) of certificate authorities that provide certificates for use with Microsoft products. (Try searching for **certificate authorities** and see what you find.)

Several different types of certificate are available, depending on what you want to do—prove your personal identity, distribute software, prove your corporate identity, and so on. Each involves an online enrollment form, a pledge of good conduct, and a check with a suitable agency—a credit service such as Equifax or TRW for an individual certificate, Dun & Bradstreet Financial Services (if the company has a Dun & Bradstreet number) for a company, and so on. Almost all involve payment.

If all goes well, you typically receive an e-mail containing an URL and a PIN. You access the URL, enter the PIN, and get the digital ID, which you install to your computer. This installation means that you have the digital certificate: It's been assigned to you by the certification authority, you've downloaded it, and you've got it as a file on your computer. (You should also create a backup of your digital certificate on a floppy disk or—preferably—a CD and store it away somewhere secure, such as a bank deposit box.)

EXPERT KNOWLEDGE: HOW TRUSTWORTHY ARE DIGITAL CERTIFICATES?

If you believe the certification authorities, digital certificates are eminently trustworthy. But in reality, there are many problems with them. This section examines the problems briefly—just enough to get you worried, I hope. For a thorough dissection of the strengths and weaknesses of digital certificates, see *Secrets and Lies* by Bruce Schneier (Wiley, 2000).

The first problem with digital certificates is that you need to trust the root certification authority to be trustworthy. Now, if the certification authority were run by a major government, perhaps you could necessarily trust it. (Then again, maybe not.) But at this writing, the root certification authorities are private companies. And each root certification authority issues its own root certificate. Basically, the root certification authority says, "Trust us—we're trustworthy. Because we say we are." The root certification authorities certify intermediate certification authorities, so if you trust the root certification authorities, you should be able to trust the intermediate certification authorities. But that's a big *if*.

The second problem is that you need to trust the certification authorities to verify the identity of the people or organizations to whom they issue digital certificates. But for some certificates, the checks are rudimentary. For example, at this writing, you can buy a personal digital certificate from VeriSign by providing little more than an e-mail address and valid credit-card payment information. Credit cards can be stolen, and e-mail addresses can be forged, so such personal digital certificates inspire minimal trust. Other types of certificates require stronger proof of identity, but in most cases, the certification authority uses an existing mechanism to verify the identity of the applicant. If that mechanism is weak, so is the level of trust inspired (if that's the word).

The third problem is that digital certificates can be stolen, borrowed (with or without the permission of the certificate holder), applied by other people, applied inadvertently, or applied automatically against the intentions of the certificate holder. For example, as you'll see in Chapter 21, you can use a digital certificate to apply a digital signature to an e-mail message in Outlook Express. Because Outlook Express can be automated, a virus or a script can send a message in your name, using your digital certificate to create a digital signature.

The fourth problem is that it's hard to tell whether a certificate has been revoked. XP and Internet Explorer include no features for automatically downloading a certificate revocation list (CRL) from the root certification authorities to check for certificates that have been revoked. For example, in Spring 2002, VeriSign was conned into issuing a couple of digital certificates in Microsoft's name to persons unknown. Unless you have access to an up-to-date CRL, these digital certificates are undistinguishable from certificates belonging to Microsoft—which creates a huge problem.

The fifth problem is that, even if the root certification authority is trustworthy, the certification authority has verified the identity of the certificate holder with the utmost diligence (and success), the digital certificate hasn't been stolen and has been applied intentionally by the holder, and the digital certificate hasn't been revoked, it still may not be very helpful. The digital certificate may prove that the message was signed by Bob Smith, but that doesn't help you establish that this Bob Smith is the Robertson W. Smith IV of 44 Main Street, Anytown (MI), whom you know to be a fine, upstanding citizen and a developer of rock-solid code, rather than Bobo Smith, the notorious malicious hacker.

Given these problems, I suggest you approach digital certificates with caution. They can be very useful, but you shouldn't trust them blindly.

Installing a Digital Certificate

Getting the digital certificate is the first step. You then need to install it so that Internet Explorer knows where it is.

NOTE   You may find that the digital certificate is automatically stored where it needs to be on the computer on which you created or downloaded it. For example, the SELFCERT.EXE *certificate-generator program automatically registers the certificates it creates on the computer on which it creates them. So if you created a digital certificate for yourself, you shouldn't need to install it on the same computer.*

Here's how to install a digital certificate:

1. Start or activate Internet Explorer.
2. Choose Tools ➢ Internet Options. XP displays the Internet Options dialog box.
3. Click the Content tab. XP displays the Content page.
4. In the Certificates group box, click the Certificates button. XP displays the Certificates dialog box, shown in Figure 18.14.

FIGURE 18.14

Internet Explorer provides the Certificates dialog box for managing digital certificates.

5. Click the Import button. XP starts the Certificate Import Wizard.
6. Click the Next button. XP displays the File to Import stage of the Certificate Import Wizard dialog box.
7. In the File Name text box, enter the name of the certificate file you want to import. Either type the name of the certificate by hand, or click the Browse button. XP displays the Open dialog box. Locate the certificate as usual. (Make sure the Files of Type drop-down list in the Open dialog box is set to the appropriate type of certificate, so that the certificate's file shows up in the dialog box.) Click the Open button. XP closes the Open dialog box and enters the certificate name and path in the File Name text box.

8. Click the Next button. XP displays the Certificate Store page of the Certificate Import Wizard dialog box, shown in Figure 18.15.

FIGURE 18.15

On the Certificate Store page of the Certificate Import Wizard, choose the certificate store in which to store the certificate you're importing.

9. Specify whether to store the certificate in the default certificate store for that type of certificate or in a certificate store of your own choosing. By default, Internet Explorer suggests a certificate store it deems appropriate. You may need to change this store.

◆ To do so, select the Place All Certificates in the Following Store option button. Then click the Browse button. XP displays the Select Certificate Store dialog box, shown on the left in Figure 18.16. Choose the certificate store (for example, Personal) and click the OK button.

FIGURE 18.16

Use the Select Certificate Store dialog box to specify the certificate store in which you want to store the certificate. The screen on the left shows the categories of stores; the screen on the right shows the physical stores displayed.

◆ To specify a particular location within a certificate store, select the Show Physical Stores check box and then click the plus (+) sign next to the store in question. XP displays its subfolders, as shown in the screen on the right in Figure 18.16. Select the folder you want, and then click the OK button. Internet Explorer closes the Select Certificate Store dialog box and displays your selection in the Certificate Store text box in the Certificate Import Wizard.

10. Click the Next button to finish setting up the import procedure. The wizard displays the Completing the Certificate Import Wizard dialog box to confirm the choices you've made.

The list box shows the certificate store that you or the wizard chose, the type of content you're putting in it (a certificate, a certificate trust list, a certificate revocation list, and so on), and the name of the file from which the content is being drawn.

11. If you (or the wizard) decide to import the certificate into the root certificate store, Internet Explorer displays the Root Certificate Store dialog box, asking you to confirm that you want to add the certificate to the root store. If placing this certificate in the root certificate store is correct, click the Yes button. Otherwise, click the No button.

12. If you're ready to go, click the Finish button. The Certificate Import Wizard imports the certificate (or whatever) and displays a message box confirming that the operation was successful.

Now that you've imported the certificate, it shows up in the Certificates dialog box on the appropriate page.

Exporting a Certificate

You may need to export a certificate for backup or so that you can install it on another computer. To export a certificate, select it in the Certificates dialog box and click the Export button. XP starts the Certificate Export Wizard, which walks you through the process of exporting the certificate. If you choose to export the private key with the certificate, be sure to protect it with a password.

Removing a Certificate

Sometimes you'll need to remove a digital certificate from the store—perhaps because a once-trusted associate has turned rogue, or an esteemed competitor has gone belly-up, or another event has occurred that obviates your need for that digital certificate's services.

To remove a digital certificate from the digital certificate store in Internet Explorer, take the following steps:

1. Display the Certificates dialog box by clicking the Certificates button on the Content page of the Internet Options dialog box.

2. Display the page that contains the digital certificate in question, and then select the certificate you want to remove.

3. Click the Remove button. XP displays a Certificates dialog box warning you of the consequences of deleting the digital certificate and asking you to confirm the deletion:

   ◆ Figure 18.17 shows the warning you get when removing a certification authority.

FIGURE 18.17

XP displays this Certificates dialog box to warn you of the consequences of removing a certificate authority's certificate.

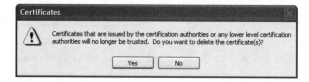

   ◆ Figure 18.18 shows the warning you get when removing one of your personal certificates.

4. Click the Yes button to delete the certificate. Click the No button if the warning has persuaded you to relent.

FIGURE 18.18

XP displays this Certificates dialog box to warn you of the consequences of removing one of your personal certificates.

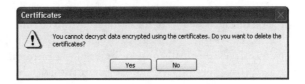

Examining a Certificate

So far, we've discussed how to go about getting, installing, and exporting digital certificates. This section discusses how to examine a certificate that identifies someone else.

Often, you'll want to examine a certificate because Internet Explorer asks you whether you want to trust the person, company, or organization that the certificate is supposed to identify. The next couple of pages show an example of this. But if you want to follow along on your PC, and you haven't got a handy website that will raise a certificate question, open the Certificates dialog box, select a certificate, and click the View button. (Alternatively, just double-click the certificate.) To open the Certificates dialog box: From Internet Explorer, choose Tools ➤ Internet Options, and then click the Certificates button on the Content page of the Internet Options dialog box.

When there's a problem with a certificate for a site you're visiting, Internet Explorer brings it to your attention, typically by displaying a Security Alert dialog box. Internet Explorer recommends that you view the certificate to determine whether you want to trust the certifying authority. Clicking the View Certificate button displays the certificate in the Certificate dialog box.

The General page of the Certificate dialog box explains any problem that XP has identified with the certificate. Figure 18.19 shows an example of the Certificate dialog box for a certificate with a problem (on the left) and an example of the Certificate dialog box for a certificate that seems to be okay (on the right). When there's a problem, you'll see explanations such as "This certificate cannot be verified up to a trusted certification authority" or "Windows does not have enough information to verify this certificate." This page also displays some basic information about the certificate: to whom the certificate is issued, by whom it was issued, and the period for which it's valid.

FIGURE 18.19

Use the Certificate dialog box to examine the properties of a certificate and learn of any problems that XP has identified with it.

When there isn't a problem with the certificate, this page displays a list of the purposes for which the certificate is intended: for example, "Protect e-mail messages," "Ensure the identity of a remote computer," "Protect software from tampering after publication," or "Ensure software came from software publisher." When you're examining a certificate, make sure that the stated purposes cover the bases you're expecting. If Internet Explorer thinks the certificate is valid, the Issuer Statement button will be enabled. Clicking this button is supposed to make XP displays a statement by the issuer. (At this writing, it doesn't always work.)

The Details page of the Certificate dialog box, shown on the left in Figure 18.20, contains about a score of specifics on the certificate. If the information in a field overflows the list box, click the field. XP displays its value in the text box below. To restrict the view to a subset of the fields available, select one of the following choices in the Show drop-down list: Version 1 Fields Only (which displays the X.509 basic certificate fields); Extensions Only (the X.509 extension fields); Critical Extensions Only (fields that ensure safe operation when security is needed, such as the Key Usage Restriction field and the SpcSpAgencyInfo field); or Properties Only (the Thumbprint Algorithm field, the Thumbprint field, the Friendly Name field, and the Description field).

FIGURE 18.20

The Details page (left) of the Certificate dialog box contains a host of details about the certificate. The Certification Path page displays the path by which the certificate has been issued from the issuing authority to the holder.

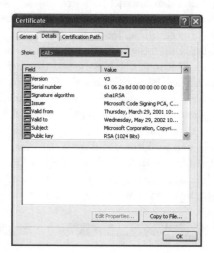 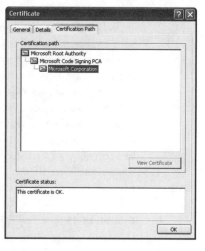

From the Details page, you can edit some of the properties of a certificate by clicking the Edit Properties button. The next section, "Editing the Properties of a Certificate," discusses this.

On the Certification Path page (shown on the right in Figure 18.20), you can follow the chain of certificates up from the current holder to the issuing authority to find one that's trustworthy. To check one of the links in the chain, select it in the Certification Path list box and click the View Certificate button (if it's available). XP displays the Certificate dialog box for the certificate in question. You can then pursue the certification path for that certificate if you choose, or click the OK button to dismiss the second (or subsequent) Certificate dialog box and return to the previous one.

If on examination and reflection you decide the certificate is okay, you can install it on your computer by clicking the Install Certificate button on the General page of the Certificate dialog box and letting the Certificate Import Wizard shepherd you through the process as discussed earlier in this section. Alternatively, you can click the Yes button in the Security Alert dialog box to proceed without installing the certificate; or you can click the No button in the Security Alert dialog box if you choose not to proceed.

When you finish exploring the certificate, click the OK button. Internet Explorer closes the Certificate dialog box.

EDITING THE PROPERTIES OF A CERTIFICATE

On the Details page of the Certificate dialog box, clicking the Edit Properties button displays the Certificate Properties dialog box, shown in Figure 18.21. In this dialog box, you can change the friendly name and description for the certificate, and specify the purposes for which the certificate can be used. The *friendly name* is a name that humans can read easily; it shows up in the Certificates dialog box in the Friendly Name column and also appears as a property on the Details page of the Certificate dialog box. The description is a text description to accompany the friendly name; it appears on the Details page of the Certificate dialog box.

FIGURE 18.21

You can edit the properties of a certificate in the Certificate Properties dialog box.

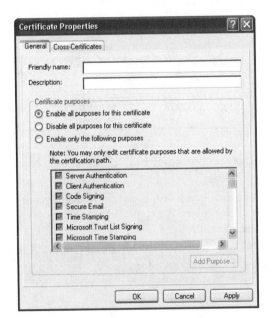

In the Certificate Purposes group box, choose the purposes for which you want to use the certificate by selecting one of the three option buttons:

◆ The Enable All Purposes for This Certificate option button enables all the purposes for which the certificate is valid.

◆ The Disable All Purposes for This Certificate option button prevents use of the certificate.

◆ The Enable Only the Following Purposes option button lets you select the check boxes for the purposes you want. Note that the list box displays only the purposes you can edit, not necessarily the full set of purposes for the certificate.

Click the OK button. XP closes the Certificate Properties dialog box and applies your choices.

SPECIFYING ADVANCED PURPOSES

You can designate the purposes that you want XP to list as advanced for certificates. To do so, take the following steps:

1. Click the Advanced button in the Certificates dialog box. XP displays the Advanced Options dialog box (shown in Figure 18.22).

FIGURE 18.22

In the Advanced Options dialog box, specify the purposes that you want XP to list as advanced.

2. In the Certificate Purposes group box, select the check boxes that you want to designate as advanced.

3. In the Export Format group box, you can select the default format for XP to use when you drag a certificate to a folder. For some formats, you can choose whether to include all certificates in the certification path.

4. Click the OK button. XP closes the Advanced Options dialog box, applies your choices, and returns you to the Certificates dialog box.

Up Next

This chapter has discussed how to choose an Internet connection type and ISP (if you have the choice); how to create an Internet connection; how to start and stop it; and how to secure it by implementing XP's built-in firewall. It has also covered what digital certificates are, where to get them, and how to import them, export them, and examine them.

The next chapter discusses how to use Internet Explorer to surf the Web.

Chapter 19

Surfing the Web with Internet Explorer

THIS CHAPTER DISCUSSES HOW to browse the Web with Internet Explorer, the web browser built into XP, and how to configure Internet Explorer's most important settings, including the security settings. At the end of the chapter is a short introduction to MSN Explorer, Microsoft's Internet service. The chapter assumes that you have already configured an Internet connection as discussed in the previous chapter.

The chapter also assumes that you *have* Internet Explorer on your computer. At this writing, Internet Explorer ships with XP Home—and indeed Internet Explorer is an integral part of XP Home. But thanks to the recent antitrust action against Microsoft, Microsoft may soon be supplying versions of XP with which OEMs can install browsers other than Internet Explorer—for example, the Netscape browser, the Opera browser, or the Mozilla browser.

If your version of XP doesn't have Internet Explorer, and you want to get it, you can download it from the Microsoft website (www.microsoft.com). Similarly, you can download Netscape (www.netscape.com), Opera (www.operasoft.com), Mozilla (www.mozilla.org), or NeoPlanet (www.neoplanet.com) if you want to try them instead of your current browser.

This chapter covers the following topics:

◆ Starting Internet Explorer

◆ Using the Internet Explorer interface

◆ Opening and saving documents

◆ Creating and using favorites

◆ Changing your home page and Quick Links

◆ Managing your temporary Internet files

◆ Controlling your history

◆ Choosing security options

◆ Using Content Advisor to screen out objectionable content

◆ Managing your AutoComplete information

◆ Choosing advanced options

◆ Browsing offline

◆ A quick introduction to MSN Explorer

Starting Internet Explorer

These are the easiest ways of starting Internet Explorer:

◆ Choose Start ➢ Internet.

◆ Click the Launch Internet Explorer Browser shortcut on your Quick Launch toolbar (if you have the Quick Launch toolbar displayed).

◆ Double-click a URL or another file type associated with Internet Explorer.

EXPERT KNOWLEDGE: HOW TO STOP INTERNET EXPLORER, NETSCAPE, AND OPERA FROM DUELING FOR DOMINANCE

If you have two or more web browsers installed on your computer, they'll bicker for your attentions like puppies or MP3 players. Each time you run a different browser, it'll prompt you to make it your default browser. The default browser gets pole position, including possession of the coveted Internet shortcut at the top of the Start menu and the associations for the many Internet file types (for example, HTM, HTML, URL, and so on). The illustrations below show Opera (on the left) and Internet Explorer (on the right) competing for attention.

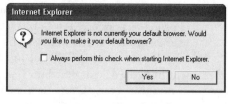

To prevent Internet Explorer from asking to be your default browser, clear the Always Perform This Check when Starting Internet Explorer check box before dismissing the Internet Explorer dialog box. Alternatively, choose Tools ➢ Internet Options. Internet Explorer displays the Internet Options dialog box. Click the Programs tab. Internet Explorer displays the Programs page. Clear the Internet Explorer Should Check to See whether It Is the Default Browser check box. Click the OK button. Internet Explorer closes the Internet Options dialog box and applies the settings.

To prevent Opera from bugging you about making it the default browser, select the Do Not Show This Dialog Again check box before dismissing the Opera dialog box shown above. Alternatively, choose File ➢ Preferences. Opera displays the Preferences dialog box. Select the Default Browser category. Clear the Check if Opera Is Default Browser on Startup check box. In the File Types group box, select the file types that you want to associate with Opera. In the Protocols group box, select the protocols that you want to associate with Opera. Click the OK button. Opera closes the Preferences dialog box and applies the settings.

Continued on next page

EXPERT KNOWLEDGE: HOW TO STOP INTERNET EXPLORER, NETSCAPE, AND OPERA FROM DUELING FOR DOMINANCE *(continued)*

To suppress Netscape's ambitions to be your default browser and commandeer file types, choose Edit ➢ Preferences. Netscape displays the Preferences dialog box. Expand the Advanced category and select the Desktop Integration item. In the File Types group box, select the file types you want to associate with Netscape. In the Internet Shortcuts group box, select the Internet shortcuts you want to associate with Netscape. Clear the Check that Windows Is Set Up to Match These Preferences Each Time Netscape Starts Up check box. Click the OK button. Netscape closes the Preferences dialog box and applies the settings.

TROUBLESHOOTING: "IEXPLORE CAUSED AN INVALID PAGE FAULT IN MODULE KERNEL32.DLL" ERROR

The error message "iexplore Caused an Invalid Page Fault in Module kernel32.dll" occurs when you've installed multiple operating systems on the same partition. The only solution is to reinstall the operating systems, each on its own partition.

Using the Internet Explorer Interface

Figure 19.1 shows the main features of the Internet Explorer window.

FIGURE 19.1

The main features of the Internet Explorer window

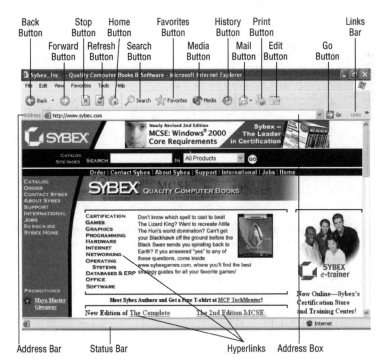

The status bar shows information on the current operation (for example, *Connecting to site www.sybex.com*) or information on any hyperlink the mouse pointer is currently pointing to.

As you can see in the figure, Internet Explorer provides three toolbars for navigating the Web and Internet. When you start Internet Explorer, the Address bar is displayed as the lower layer of the toolbar, with the Links bar reduced to just a button at the right end of the Address bar.

Unlocking the Toolbars and Menu Bar

By default, the Internet Explorer toolbars are locked, so to move them, you need to unlock them. To do so, right-click the menu bar or any displayed toolbar and choose Lock the Toolbars from the context menu. Internet Explorer removes the check mark from the Lock the Toolbars item on the context menu, unlocks the toolbars and menu bar, and displays handles at their left ends so that you can move and resize them.

You can then customize the size and position of the three toolbars by dragging the handles. For example, you can drag the toolbar handles of the Links bar to the left from their default position to display more of the Links bar and less of the Address bar. Alternatively, you could drag the Links bar down to display it below the Address bar.

TIP *To dispose of the toolbars, menu bar, and status bar quickly so that you can see more of the current web page, use Full Screen view. To enter Full Screen view, choose View ➤ Full Screen or press the F11 key. To turn Full Screen off again, press the F11 key.*

Using the Toolbar Buttons

Here's how to use the buttons on the toolbar in Internet Explorer:

◆ Click the Back button to move to the previous page you were on. To move back more than one page in a single jump, click the downward-arrow button on the Back button to display a list of pages that you can go back to.

◆ Click the Forward button to move forward to a page you were on before you clicked the Back button. To move forward more than one page, click the downward-arrow button on the Forward button to display a list of pages that you can go forward to.

NOTE *Until there is a page to go forward or back to, the Back button and the Forward button are dimmed and unavailable.*

◆ Click the Stop button to stop Internet Explorer from pursuing a jump that's in progress. (For example, if the jump has stalled or if the page is loading very slowly, you might want to stop it.)

◆ Click the Refresh button to have Internet Explorer reload the current page. You might want to do this if part of the page fails to transfer properly, or if you think the page may have changed since you loaded this instance of it.

◆ Click the Home button to jump to your home page (the page that Internet Explorer displays by default).

◆ Click the Search button to display Search Companion, which offers natural-language searching of the Web.

◆ Click the Favorites button to display the Favorites Explorer bar. ("Creating and Using Favorites" later in this chapter discusses favorites.)

◆ Click the Media button to display the Media bar, which gives you quick access to Windows-Media.com.

◆ Click the History button to display the History Explorer bar, which you can use to navigate to a site you've visited recently.

◆ Click the Mail button to display a menu of mail and news commands. For example, choosing the Read Mail item from this menu launches or activates your default e-mail client.

◆ Click the Print button to print the current page. (Internet Explorer doesn't display the Print dialog box—it goes right ahead and prints the page.)

◆ Click the Edit button to open the current page for editing in your default HTML editor. (You can change your default HTML editor on the Programs page of the Internet Options dialog box.)

Using Keyboard Shortcuts

Internet Explorer supports many of the same keyboard shortcuts as Explorer. For example, you can press the F4 key to display the Address drop-down list and select the current entry in the Address bar. Refer back to Table 6.2 in Chapter 6 for a list of keyboard shortcuts for Explorer.

Opening a Web Page or a Document

Each website or web page is identified by an address called a *Uniform Resource Locator*, or *URL* for short. (URL is usually spelled out as "U-R-L," but it's sometimes pronounced "earl.") For example, the URL for the Microsoft website is `http://www.microsoft.com`. By pointing your browser at this URL, you can access the Microsoft website.

See pages 37–39 of the *Essential Skills* section for a visual guide to browsing the Web with Internet Explorer.

Opening a Web Page or a Document the Easy Way

The easiest way to open a URL is to click in the Address box on the Address bar, type in the address of the document, and press Enter to accept it. You don't need to include the `http://` prefix: Internet Explorer adds that automatically if you enter a valid URL. Similarly, to access an FTP site, you don't need to enter the `ftp://` prefix: Just enter the address, and Internet Explorer adds the prefix. (Occasionally this prefix-adding doesn't work. In that case, enter the prefix manually.)

If the URL starts with `www.` (after the `http://` prefix) and ends with `.com`, you can enter those parts of the address automatically by pressing Ctrl+Enter. For example, to access the Sybex website, **www.sybex.com**, you could type **sybex** and press Ctrl+Enter to have Internet Explorer enter `http://www.sybex.com`.

WARNING *Internet Explorer's AutoComplete feature does its best to make a complete URL out of whatever you enter. If you enter part of a URL, AutoComplete adds `http://www` to it and then tries the `.com`, `.edu`, and `.org` domain suffixes (in that order). Be warned that if you give Internet Explorer this much latitude in constructing URLs, you may get some sites you didn't bargain for. The canonical example of this is `www.whitehouse.com`, a pornographic site, which people access accidentally when trying to reach the White House (government) site (`www.whitehouse.gov`).*

If the address you're typing matches an address you've visited within Internet Explorer's memory, Internet Explorer displays a drop-down list of URLs. If one of them is right, use the ↓ key to select it, and then press the Enter key. If not, finish typing the new URL and then press the Enter key or click the Go button.

You can also open a document stored on a local drive or network drive in the same way by using type-down addressing in Internet Explorer, just as you can in Explorer. Type the drive letter (for example, D:), and Internet Explorer displays a drop-down list of the folders on the drive. Type down to select one of them (or use the ↓ key and the ↑ key) to select one, and Internet Explorer displays a drop-down list of the contents of that folder. This can be a quick way of accessing a document provided you know its name and location. For general digging through directories, browse as usual using an Explorer window or an Internet Explorer window.

TIP   If you don't like the AutoComplete feature, turn it off. Choose Tools ➢ Internet Options and clear the Use Inline AutoComplete check box on the Advanced page of the Internet Options dialog box.

Opening a Web Page or a Document the Formal Way

There's also a more formal (and almost invariably slower) way of opening a web page or a document on a local drive, a network drive, or an intranet. This way is useful for opening documents because it lets you browse through folders, so you don't need to know the exact name and location of the document. A more dubious benefit is that opening a URL or a document this way doesn't add the URL or filename to the Address drop-down list, so it's a little more private. (However, the Address drop-down list does suggest it in AutoComplete items.)

Here's the formal way of opening a web page or document:

1. Choose File ➢ Open. Internet Explorer displays the Open dialog box (shown in Figure 19.2).

FIGURE 19.2

To open a document on the Web, choose File ➢ Open, enter the address in the Open text box, and click the OK button.

2. In the Open text box, enter the address for the document or file you want to open, using any of the following three methods:

◆ Type the name of the document or file into the Open text box.

◆ To open a document or file you've accessed recently, click the down-arrow button at the right end of the Open text box and select the file from the drop-down list.

◆ Click the Browse button. Internet Explorer displays the Microsoft Internet Explorer dialog box (a common Open dialog box in disguise). Select the file and click the Open button. Internet Explorer enters the file's name and path in the Open text box in the Open dialog box. To open a file of a file type not explicitly associated with Internet Explorer, select All Files in the Files of Type drop-down list.

3. Click the OK button in the Open dialog box. Internet Explorer closes the Open dialog box and opens the file.

Internet Explorer includes built-in support for a large number of file formats, including HTML pages, text files, and several types of graphics files (such as GIF, JPEG, and PNG). When you encounter a file type that needs an add-on program or a plug-in, Internet Explorer warns you and seeks permission to download and install the add-on or plug-in.

TROUBLESHOOTING: SOLVING PROBLEMS ACCESSING WEB PAGES

This sidebar discusses some of the most common reasons for not being able to access web pages.

"SERVER TOO BUSY" ERROR

The "Server Too Busy" message typically means that the web server the browser contacted was too busy right then handling other requests to deal with your request for information. Click the Refresh button on the toolbar to try the link again. Often, you'll get straight through on the second attempt; but if the server is truly busy, you may need to retry a number of times, or wait until later.

HTTP ERROR 404: "PAGE NOT AVAILABLE"

When you receive HTTP Error 404: "Page Not Available," the page may in fact not be available, but try refreshing it by clicking the Refresh button on the toolbar, choosing View ➢ Refresh, or pressing the F5 key in case the request simply timed out.

HTTP ERROR 403: "YOU ARE NOT AUTHORIZED TO VIEW THIS PAGE"

The error message HTTP Error 403: "You Are Not Authorized to View This Page" typically means either that you've requested a page that you're really not allowed to access or that you haven't authenticated yourself enough for the website to recognize that you are in fact authorized to view the page. If you think you *have* authenticated yourself, check that the page isn't on a subscription website to which you don't have access because you haven't paid (or because the website has started charging for content, as many have done following the dotcom bust).

"THE PAGE CANNOT BE DISPLAYED... CANNOT FIND SERVER OR DNS ERROR"

The error message "The Page Cannot Be Displayed... Cannot Find Server or DNS Error" typically means that the page isn't at that URL anymore. It may also mean that the website has gone to the great bit-bucket in the sky, either temporarily or permanently. Try reducing the URL to the domain name (for example, reduce `http://www.sybex.com/sybexbooks.nsf/d31811de243c22668825693b00793e3c/d51dd94518472837` `882569e70037096c!OpenDocument` to `http://www.sybex.com`) and see if the website is still there. If it is, try to navigate to the page you want by using whatever search or navigation mechanisms the site provides.

If you know that the address exists, try it later, when the server may be back online. If not, and if you typed in the URL, double-check each character to make sure you didn't miss or add anything. Then try it again.

Failing the previous suggestions, this error may indicate simply that your Internet connection isn't working. Check the connection manually if you're not certain it's functional.

Continued on next page

TROUBLESHOOTING: SOLVING PROBLEMS ACCESSING WEB PAGES *(continued)*

CHECK YOUR SECURITY SETTINGS

If the website you're trying to reach is secure, make sure that your security settings match its requirements:

◆ In the Security section of the Advanced page of the Internet Options dialog box, choose settings for SSL 2.0, SSL 3.0, or TLS 1.0 as necessary. (See the "Security Category" section near the end of this chapter for a discussion of SSL and TLS.)

◆ If the site requires 128-bit security, make sure that your version of Internet Explorer has it. Choose Help ➢ About Internet Explorer and check the Cipher Strength readout in the About Internet Explorer dialog box. (Some export versions of Internet Explorer use 56-bit security because of government restrictions.)

Jumping to a Hyperlink

Many web documents contain *hyperlinks*, which are jumps to other locations. Hyperlinks are typically displayed as underlined text, graphical objects, or pictures. (For example, Figure 19.1 contains a large number of hyperlinks, several of which are labeled.)

When you move the mouse pointer over a hyperlink, the mouse pointer takes on the shape of a hand with a finger pointing upward. To jump to the hyperlinked location, click the hyperlink. If the hyperlink involves another program, XP activates that program. For example, a hyperlink in an e-mail message may launch Internet Explorer (or your default browser), or a hyperlink on a web page to a PDF file may launch Adobe Acrobat.

TIP By default, Internet Explorer makes a clicking sound when you click a link, to give you audio feedback that you've clicked it. To turn this clicking off, or to change the sound played, work with the Start Navigation event in the Program Events list box on the Sounds page of the Sounds and Audio Devices Properties dialog box. See the section "Choosing System Sounds" in Chapter 4 for step-by-step instructions. (There's also a Complete Navigation event that you can configure if you like having sound cues.)

Returning to a Previous Document

Because you'll often access dead ends or pages that don't offer the information you need, you'll often want to return to the previous document you accessed. There are several ways to move back to a document you've visited before:

◆ Click the Back button on the toolbar, or use its drop-down list, as described earlier in the chapter. Alternatively, press Alt+← to move back one page. (To move forward, use the Forward button or press Alt+→.) This technique works well when you're browsing in a single window. If you're using multiple windows (as discussed in the next section), each will have a different sequence of sites visited, so it may be more difficult to find the one you want.

◆ Click the down arrow at the right end of the Address box and choose the document from the drop-down list. This drop-down list gives you quick access to a good number of the sites you've visited.

◆ Choose one of the items listed in the View ➢ Go To menu (for example, View ➢ Go To ➢ Back, View ➢ Go To ➢ Home Page, or View ➢ Go To ➢ *one of the listed sites*).

◆ Click the History button (or choose View ➢ Explorer Bar ➢ History) to display the History Explorer bar (shown in Figure 19.3). This pane contains a complete list of the pages you've visited and the documents you've opened recently, organized into folders by day and site. Use the View context menu to sort the history sites by date, site, or most visited, or by order visited today; or use the Search feature to search the history sites by keyword. Then click the shortcut for the item you want to return to. You can also copy the shortcut to another folder, create a favorite from it, or delete it.

FIGURE 19.3

Use the History Explorer bar to return to a previous document.

TIP   *By default, Internet Explorer stores history for 20 days. You can change the number of days to anything from 0 to 999 by adjusting the number in the Days to Keep Pages in History text box on the General page of the Internet Options dialog box (Tools ➢ Internet Options). When you set this number to 0, Internet Explorer doesn't keep pages from one day to the next, but you can still access pages on the same day. See the upcoming section "Keeping Control of Your History" for information on how to prune and clear your history.*

Opening Multiple Internet Explorer Windows

Given the amount of information on the Web, you'll often want to have several Internet Explorer windows open at once so that you can see multiple web pages at the same time without having to move back and forth from one to the other. All Internet Explorer windows share your connection (whether modem, cable, DSL, or network) and slow each other down.

You can open multiple windows in several ways:

◆ To open another copy of the page displayed in the current window, press Ctrl+N or choose File ➢ New ➢ Window.

◆ To open a hyperlinked location in a new browser window, so that the current window still displays the current page, right-click the hyperlink and choose Open in New Window from the context menu.

◆ To start a new instance of Internet Explorer, click its shortcut on the Quick Launch toolbar or choose Start ➤ Internet.

◆ Some websites will open a new browser window for you. This tends to happen when you've chosen to display a page that doesn't involve their site. Keep an eye on the number of browser windows you have open, because there may be more than you have opened yourself—and some of them may be showing items that you haven't specifically chosen to see.

To close a window, click its Close button (the × button), choose File ➤ Close, or press either Alt+F4 or Ctrl+W.

TIP   *If you want to open each link you follow in a new window instead of in the same window, clear the Reuse Windows for Launching Shortcuts check box on the Advanced page of the Internet Options dialog box (Tools ➤ Internet Options).*

Making a Page Easier to Read

One of the problems with viewing web pages is that they tend to look different when displayed in different browsers. Because Internet Explorer is so widely used, commanding between half and three-quarters of the total browser market for Windows and the Mac, this is less of a problem with Internet Explorer than with Netscape or Opera. A bigger problem for Internet Explorer users is that web designers design pages for optimal viewing at a certain screen resolution (for example, 800×600). When you view them at a different resolution, they can be hard to read.

Depending on how the web designer has created the page, you can do a couple of things to make it easier to read. The first thing to try is adjusting the text size displayed. Choose View ➤ Text Size and choose one of the items from the Text Size submenu: Largest, Larger, Medium, Smaller, or Smallest. (The size currently used appears with a dot next to it on the menu.) If your mouse has a wheel, you can change text size by holding down the Ctrl key and turning the wheel forward (to move to a smaller size) or backward (to move to a larger size).

NOTE   *When you change the text size by using the View ➤ Text Size submenu, your choice carries through to subsequent pages you visit in this browser window or other browser windows you launch from it. Other browser windows already displayed when you issue the command are not affected.*

If all goes well, Internet Explorer increases or decreases the text size when you issue this command. But if the text size doesn't change—perhaps because the website designer has used Cascading Style Sheets (CSS) to specify exact sizing and placement of the text and other elements on the page—you need to take the following steps:

1. Choose Tools ➤ Internet Options. Internet Explorer displays the Internet Options dialog box.
2. Click the Accessibility button on the General page. Internet Explorer displays the Accessibility dialog box (shown in Figure 19.4).

3. Choose options in the Formatting group box:

- Select the Ignore Colors Specified on Web Pages check box to ignore colors.
- Select the Ignore Font Styles Specified on Web Pages check box to override font styles.
- Select the Ignore Font Sizes Specified on Web Pages check box to override font sizes.

FIGURE 19.4

If choosing a different text size doesn't change the page, use the Accessibility dialog box to override the web designer's settings.

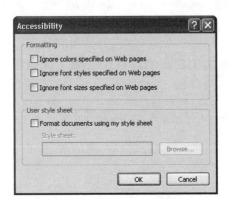

4. Click the OK button. Internet Explorer closes the Accessibility dialog box and applies your choices.

TIP   If you have persistent difficulty in reading other people's web pages, try creating a style sheet of your own that uses font sizes you find comfortable to read. (Consult a web design book for advice on creating a style sheet.) In the Accessibility dialog box, select the Format Documents Using My Style Sheet check box, then specify the style sheet in the Style Sheet text box by clicking the Browse button and navigating to the file that contains it.

If you're generally dissatisfied with how web pages look in Internet Explorer, change the default font size and font color to see if that improves things. Choose Tools ➢ Internet Options. Internet Explorer displays the Internet Options dialog box. To change the font size and color, click the Fonts button and use the resulting Fonts dialog box to select a typeface and size that please you. To change the color, click the Colors button to display the Colors dialog box:

- To change the text and background colors, clear the Use Windows Colors check box and use the Text button and Background button to select colors.
- To change the colors of links, use the Visited button and the Unvisited button.
- To make Internet Explorer display a link over which you're hovering the mouse pointer in a different color, select the Use Hover Color check box and use the Hover button to pick the color. The hover color is especially useful for identifying which link you're about to select on a busy page that presents several links close to each other.

Saving a Document

Although you cannot create new documents in Internet Explorer, you can use Internet Explorer to save documents to your computer. For example, you might want to save a copy of a web page or intranet page to your hard disk so that you can examine it in detail when your computer is offline.

To save the current page, choose File ➤ Save As. Internet Explorer displays the Save Web Page dialog box. Choose a location for the file as usual, specify a filename, and click the Save button. Internet Explorer closes the Save As dialog box and saves the file.

NOTE   *Instead of saving a page like this, you can have Internet Explorer create an offline favorite for it—a copy of the page that you can access when your computer isn't connected to the Internet. See the upcoming section "Creating and Using Favorites" for details.*

Saving, Printing, or E-mailing a Picture

When you hover the mouse pointer over a picture on a web page, Internet Explorer displays the Image toolbar (see Figure 19.5), which offers buttons for saving the image, printing it, sending it in an e-mail message, and opening the My Pictures folder.

FIGURE 19.5

The Image toolbar, which appears when you hover the mouse pointer over a picture, contains buttons for manipulating pictures.

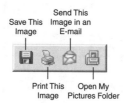

If you don't use the Image toolbar, you can turn it off by clearing the Enable Image Toolbar in the Multimedia section of the Advanced page of the Internet Options dialog box. You need to restart Internet Explorer before this change takes effect.

Printing a Document

To print the web page you're viewing, click the Print button on the toolbar. Internet Explorer prints the page without displaying the Print dialog box.

To display the Print dialog box so that you can choose printing options, choose File ➤ Print. Internet Explorer displays the Print dialog box. Choose options as usual. For example, the Options page of the Print dialog box offers options for printing frames (layout areas of web pages), printing all linked documents, and printing a table of links.

Downloading Files

Apart from surfing the Internet, you'll probably find yourself using Internet Explorer for downloading a lot of files: drivers, patches, updates, programs, games, screen savers, audio, video, or whatever. Internet Explorer lets you download files seamlessly via both HTTP and FTP. Most of the time, you don't need to worry about whether the download is happening via HTTP or FTP. (The exception is when you're accessing a password-protected FTP server. More on this in a minute.)

Here's what usually happens when you download a file: You click a link to download a file. If the extension on the file indicates that the file is of a file type registered on your computer, Internet

Explorer displays a File Download dialog box (of which Figure 19.6 shows an example) offering you the choice between opening the file from its current location, saving it to disk, canceling the download, or getting more information. (If the file appears to be of a file type that isn't registered on your computer, Internet Explorer doesn't offer to open it from its current location.) Click the Open button to open the file, the Save button to save it to a file on your computer, or the Cancel button to cancel the download. Clicking the More Info button opens an Internet Explorer Help window to a topic explaining about downloading files and the risk of viruses.

FIGURE 19.6

In the File Download dialog box, choose whether to open the file from its current location or save it to disk.

The File Download dialog box also contains the Always Ask before Opening This Type of File check box, which is selected by default. If you *always* want to perform the same operation with this type of file—always open this type of file from its current location, or always save this type of file to disk—clear this check box, and Internet Explorer will not prompt you for files of this file type that you download in the future. This check box isn't available for executable files (such as EXE files or COM files).

TIP *To avoid having Internet Explorer prompt you about opening a file you're downloading and that you want to save, right-click its link (instead of clicking it) and choose Save Target As from the context menu.*

Sometimes you'll want to open the file from its current location. For example, the setup routines for some programs involve opening them from the Web so that they can examine your computer and download only the components they need rather than a huge file that contains all the components. But usually, if Internet Explorer offers you this choice, you'll want to download the file and save it locally.

If the file you're downloading is of a file type registered to play, Internet Explorer starts it playing rather than giving you the opportunity to save it to disk. For example, if you click a link for an audio stream, Internet Explorer starts it playing. For copyright reasons, most companies and individuals that stream audio and video try to prevent the listener or viewer from saving the file. This is because streaming a file is legally analogous to broadcasting, whereas distributing savable files is legally analogous to copying them.

If you choose to save the file, Internet Explorer displays the Save As dialog box so that you can choose a drive, folder, and filename for it. Once you've specified these, the download continues as usual. The Download window (of which Figure 19.7 shows an example) displays the progress of the download, with a percentage-complete readout in its title bar that shows on the Taskbar button for the window as well.

FIGURE 19.7

Internet Explorer displays the progress of the download in the Download window.

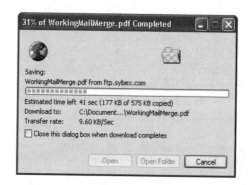

When the download finishes, Internet Explorer changes the Download window title to Download Complete and provides three command buttons. Click the Open button to open the downloaded file in the associated program, if there is one. (Bear in mind that you may well want to virus-check the downloaded file before opening it.) Click the Open Folder button to open an Explorer window showing the folder containing the downloaded file. Or click the Close button to close the Download Complete window. If you regularly find yourself clicking the Close button, select the Close This Dialog Box when Download Completes check box if you want Internet Explorer to close the Download window automatically when it has received the whole file.

You can download multiple files at the same time by setting multiple downloads in motion. All downloads share your Internet connection, so running multiple downloads will make each take longer than it would if it were the only download running—unless you have a fast Internet connection that is being held back by slow (or busy) servers at the other end *and* each of your downloads is coming from a different server. On the other hand, you may want to run multiple downloads concurrently if you're planning to take a break from your computer.

TIP   *If you download many files over an unreliable dial-up connection, consider getting a download manager that can resume downloads from the point at which they get broken off. Download managers include RealDownload (www.real.com) and Go!Zilla (www.gozilla.com).*

EXPERT KNOWLEDGE: SUPPLYING AN FTP USERNAME AND PASSWORD IN INTERNET EXPLORER

Internet Explorer handles accessing FTP servers via anonymous logon transparently. But if the FTP server requires you to supply a username and password, you need to enter it in the Address bar as follows:

   ftp://*username*:*password*@*ftpserver*/*url*

As you can see, this makes for tricky typing. If you access password-protected FTP servers frequently, consider getting a dedicated graphical FTP client such as WS_FTP Pro (www.ipswitch.com) or CuteFTP (www.globalscape.com).

Creating and Using Favorites

Internet Explorer lets you designate URLs as *favorites*, which allows you to access them quickly using the Favorites menu or the Favorites Explorer bar. (Other web browsers such as Netscape call favorites *bookmarks*.) Regular favorites are simply shortcuts to sites, but Internet Explorer can also create *offline favorites*, cached copies of pages that you can access when your computer isn't connected to the Internet.

NOTE   *Because they're stored on your hard drive (or another local drive or network drive) and don't need to be downloaded, offline favorites load very quickly. But to counteract this advantage, they have several disadvantages: They may not be up to date (because a web page may have changed since you last synchronized its offline favorite), they take up disk space, and (if the website tries to prevent web-crawling) they may not synchronize properly.*

To use favorites, you create them as described in the next section, then access them from the Favorites menu or the Favorites Explorer bar (shown in Figure 19.8).

FIGURE 19.8

Internet Explorer provides the Favorites Explorer bar for accessing your favorites quickly.

NOTE   *By default, Internet Explorer customizes your Favorites menu, hiding items that you haven't accessed recently so that other items are easier to find. To prevent Internet Explorer from customizing the menu, clear the Enable Personalized Favorites Menu item on the Advanced page of the Internet Options dialog box (Tools ➤ Internet Options).*

Adding a Page to Your Favorites

To add the current URL (the page that Internet Explorer is currently displaying) to your list of favorites, follow these steps:

1. Choose Favorites ➤ Add to Favorites. Internet Explorer displays the Add Favorite dialog box (shown in Figure 19.9).

FIGURE 19.9

To add a URL to your list of favorites, choose Favorites ➢ Add to Favorites. Internet Explorer displays the Add Favorite dialog box.

2. In the Name text box, enter the name by which to identify the favorite. You will often need to change the default name, which will be the title of the page, to something shorter, more descriptive, or more memorable.

3. If you want to have the favorite available offline (when your computer is not attached to the network or the Internet), select the Make Available Offline check box. Then choose a schedule and details by using the Offline Favorite Wizard as follows:

   ◆ Click the Customize button. Internet Explorer starts the Offline Favorite Wizard. The first time you run the wizard, you'll see an introductory page. Select the In the Future, Do Not Show This Introduction Screen check box and click the Next button.

   ◆ On the page shown on the left in Figure 19.10, choose whether you want to download just this page or pages linked to it. To download just this page, leave the No option button selected (this is the default). To download linked pages, select the Yes option button (as shown in the figure) and specify the depth of links you want to download by entering a number in the Download Pages *NN* Links Deep from This Page text box. Then click the Next button.

FIGURE 19.10

In the Offline Favorite Wizard, decide whether to download just this page or the pages linked to it as well (left) and how you want to synchronize the favorite (right).

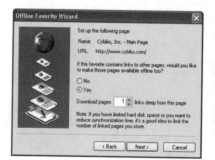

WARNING *Don't set too deep a level of links to download. Setting more than one level can quickly fill up your hard drive and monopolize your Internet connection with synchronization. If you want to try this feature, experiment cautiously, setting a minimal level of links at first for any given favorite. (Bear in mind that each favorite is likely to need a different level of links.)*

   ◆ On the next page of the Offline Favorite Wizard, shown on the right in Figure 19.10, decide how you want to synchronize this favorite. You can choose among the Only when I Choose Synchronize from the Tools Menu option button, the I Would Like to Create a New Schedule option button (which lets you create a custom synchronization schedule for the favorite), and the Using This Existing Schedule option button (which lets you use an existing schedule from the drop-down list). The Using This Existing Schedule option button (which doesn't appear in the figure) isn't available until you create a schedule. Click the Next button to proceed.

◆ If you chose to create a custom synchronization schedule for the favorite, Internet Explorer displays the Offline Favorite Wizard page shown on the left in Figure 19.11. Specify the interval (in days) and the time for the update at the top of the dialog box. Enter a name in the Name text box. If you want your computer to connect to the network or Internet automatically if it is not connected when the time for the synchronization arrives, select the If My Computer Is Not Connected when This Scheduled Synchronization Begins, Automatically Connect for Me check box. Click the Next button.

FIGURE 19.11

If you chose to create a custom synchro-nization schedule for the favorite, specify the details (left). If the site requires you to log on, enter your username and password (right).

◆ On the final page of the Offline Favorite Wizard (shown on the right in Figure 19.11), choose the Yes, My User Name and Password Are option button and specify your user-name and password (twice) if the site requires you to enter a password when accessing it. Click the Finish button to finish scheduling the update.

4. Choose where you want to create the favorite. You can create the favorite either at the top level, so that it appears directly on the Favorites menu (and in the Favorites Explorer bar), or in a folder.

◆ To create the favorite in a different folder, click the Create In button in the Add Favorite dialog box. Internet Explorer displays an additional part of the dialog box (shown in Figure 19.12).

FIGURE 19.12

Use the additional part of the Add Favorite dialog box to specify where to create the favorite.

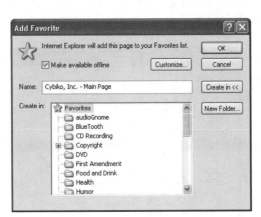

◆ Select an existing folder or create a new folder. To create a new folder beneath the cur-rently selected folder, click the New Folder button, enter the name in the Folder Name text box in the resulting Create New Folder dialog box, and click the OK button.

5. Click the OK button. Internet Explorer closes the Add Favorite dialog box and creates the favorite. If you chose to make this favorite an offline favorite, you'll see the Synchronizing dialog box as Internet Explorer performs the initial synchronization.

Thereafter, Internet Explorer will synchronize the favorite automatically if you set up a schedule. If not, or to force an immediate synchronization, choose Tools ➤ Synchronize. Internet Explorer displays the Items to Synchronize dialog box, which offers both a compact view and an expanded view (shown in Figure 19.13) that you can access by clicking the Details button. Select the items you want to synchronize, and then click the Synchronize button.

FIGURE 19.13

Use the Items to Synchronize dialog box to force a synchronization.

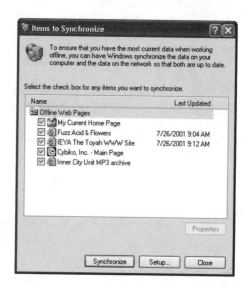

You'll see the Synchronizing dialog box (shown in Figure 19.14) as Internet Explorer synchronizes the pages. The dialog box closes automatically when synchronization is complete.

FIGURE 19.14

Internet Explorer displays the Synchronizing dialog box while it synchronizes your pages.

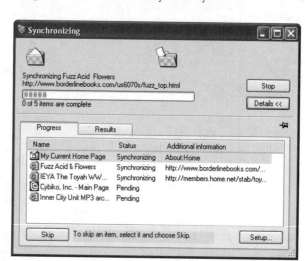

NOTE   *Internet Explorer keeps the list of offline favorites in the* `\Windows\Offline Web Pages\` *folder. You can examine them here if you want—but usually you'll find it easier to work with them via the Favorites menu, the Favorites Explorer bar, or the Organize Favorites dialog box (Favorites ➤ Organize Favorites). All users can see this folder, but each user sees only the offline favorites that belong to them.*

Choosing Further Options for Offline Favorites

The Offline Favorite Wizard offers you a good range of options for your offline favorites—but it doesn't offer you several key options. For the extra options, you need to edit the properties of the offline favorite after creating it.

TIP   *You can turn a regular favorite into an offline favorite by editing its properties as described here.*

Right-click the favorite in the Favorites Explorer bar, on the Favorites menu, or in the Organize Favorites dialog box and choose Properties from the context menu. Internet Explorer displays the Properties dialog box for the favorite. The left screen in Figure 19.15 shows an example of this Properties dialog box for an offline favorite.

NOTE   *The Properties dialog box for a regular favorite displays only two pages—the General page and the Web Document page. When you select the Make This Page Available Offline check box to turn the favorite into an offline favorite, the dialog box displays the Schedule page and Download page as well.*

Click the Download tab. Internet Explorer displays the Download page (shown on the right in Figure 19.15). Then select options as follows:

◆ In the Download Pages *NN* Links Deep from This Page text box, enter the number of links to pursue from this page. (This option is available in the Offline Favorite Wizard.) Valid numbers are 0, 1, 2, and 3. 0 downloads no pages linked to this one; 1 downloads the pages directly linked; 2 downloads all the pages linked to those; and 3 downloads all the pages linked to *those*. As in the movie-buff game Six Degrees of Kevin Bacon, each increment of the number increases the area covered almost exponentially. (A setting of 6 here—were Internet Explorer to offer it—might net you enough of the Web to fill the average hard disk.)

FIGURE 19.15

Use the Properties dialog box for an offline favorite to adjust its synchronization schedule or the amount of information to download (left) and to specify whether to follow outside links and whether to limit the amount of hard disk space the favorite can consume.

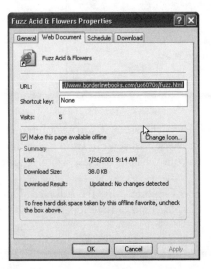

◆ If you set 1, 2, or 3 in the previous step, the Follow Links outside of This Page's Web Site check box is available. (If you set 0, this check box is unavailable because it doesn't apply.) Select this check box if you want Internet Explorer to follow links to other sites. Leave this check box cleared (as it is by default) if you don't. Use this option with great caution—for example, monitor the first synchronization session to get an idea of whether it's reasonable to go outside the favorite's website.

WARNING   *Be aware that the Follow Links outside of This Page's Web Site option can cause Internet Explorer to try to download large amounts of information. For example, if you set a value of 3 in the Download Pages NN Links Deep from This Page text box and select the Follow Links outside of This Page's Web Site check box for an offline favorite of a book on Sybex's website, Internet Explorer will end up trying to download substantial chunks of the Amazon.com website, the Barnes & Noble.com Professional, Technical & Business Bookstore website, and so on.*

◆ To cap the amount of space this offline favorite and its associated pages can consume, select the Limit Hard-Disk Usage for This Page To check box and enter a value in the Kilobytes text box. Internet Explorer suggests 500KB by default, but you'll often want to increase this. If you want to download a large amount of a particular website but make sure that you don't end up downloading half the Web (so to speak), set a value of between 5MB (5120KB) and 20MB (20,480KB). The maximum value you can set is 32,767KB, or a hair under 32MB.

Then click the Advanced button. Internet Explorer displays the Advanced Download Options dialog box (shown in Figure 19.16). Specify which items to download by selecting or clearing the Images check box, the Sound and Video check box, and the ActiveX Controls and Java Applets check box. Not downloading sound and video saves you the most bandwidth (if the pages contain them), but if you really want to pare down the content, clear the Images check box as well.

FIGURE 19.16

Use the Advanced Download Options dialog box to specify which items Internet Explorer should download for offline favorites.

Select the Only to HTML Pages check box if you want Internet Explorer to follow only links to HTML pages. By selecting this check box, you can avoid having Internet Explorer waste time downloading items such as Zip files—but the links to these will of course be nonfunctional when you're browsing offline.

Click the OK button. Internet Explorer closes the Advanced Download Options dialog box. Then click the OK button. Internet Explorer closes the Properties dialog box for the offline favorite.

EXPERT KNOWLEDGE: GETTING NOTIFIED BY E-MAIL WHEN A WEBSITE CHANGES

If you need to keep close track of a site, you can get Internet Explorer to automatically send you an e-mail when the site changes. To do this, you need to set the site up as an offline favorite as described in the previous section.

Right-click the favorite and choose Properties from the context menu. Internet Explorer displays the Properties dialog box for the favorite. On the Download page, select the When This Page Changes, Send E-mail To check box. Then enter your e-mail address in the E-mail Address text box and the address of your *outgoing* mail server (the SMTP server) in the Mail Server (SMTP) text box. (Internet Explorer needs this information in order to send the message.) Then click the OK button. When the site changes, you'll receive a message titled *Internet Explorer Notice* and the name of the favorite.

Chances are, you won't want to do this for more than a few key offline favorites, because many sites change frequently, and you've probably got better things to do than constantly deleting website–change messages from your Inbox.

Organizing Your Favorites into Folders

Internet Explorer automatically sorts your favorites alphabetically on the Favorites menu, which works well enough for a short list of favorites. But if you use the Web vigorously, you'll soon build a collection of favorites that will overrun the Favorites menu. You'll need to organize these favorites into folders.

To organize your favorites, take the following steps:

1. Choose Favorites ➤ Organize Favorites. Internet Explorer displays the Organize Favorites dialog box (shown in Figure 19.17). Alternatively, if you have the Favorites Explorer bar displayed, click the Organize button at the top of it.

FIGURE 19.17

Use the Organize Favorites dialog box to organize your favorites into folders.

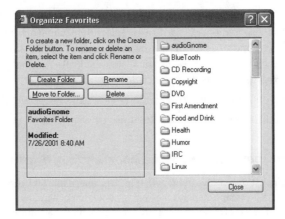

2. Organize your favorites into folders by using the following techniques:

   ◆ To move a favorite to a folder, either drag it to the folder in the list box (this is difficult if your Favorites menu is long) or select the favorite and click the Move to Folder button. Internet Explorer displays the Browse for Folder dialog box. Select the folder, and click the OK button. Internet Explorer closes the Browse for Folder dialog box and moves the favorite.

- ◆ To change the order of the list, drag a favorite or a folder up or down the list box.
- ◆ To rename a favorite or a folder, select it and click the Rename button. Type the new name over the existing name and press the Enter key.
- ◆ To delete a favorite or a folder, select it and click the Delete button. Internet Explorer displays the Confirm Folder Delete dialog box. Click the Yes button. Internet Explorer closes the dialog box and deletes the favorite or folder.
- ◆ To create a new folder, click the Create Folder button. Internet Explorer creates a new folder called New Folder at the bottom of the list box and selects its name. Type in the new name for the folder and press the Enter key.

3. Click the Close button. Internet Explorer closes the Organize Favorites dialog box.

Changing a Favorite So That It's Available Offline

To make one of your designated favorites available even when you're not online, take the following steps.

1. Choose Favorites ➢ Organize Favorites. Internet Explorer displays the Organize Favorites dialog box.
2. Select the favorite in the panel on the right side of the dialog box so that its details appear in the pane on the lower left of the dialog box.
3. Select the Make Available Offline check box. (This check box appears when you select a favorite in the list box.) When you select the check box, Internet Explorer displays a Properties button below the check box.
4. Click the Properties button. Internet Explorer displays the Properties dialog box for the favorite.
5. Click the Schedule tab. Internet Explorer displays the Schedule page of the Properties dialog box.
6. In the Synchronize This Favorite area, select the Only when I Choose Synchronize from the Tools Menu option button if you want to control synchronization manually. If you want to schedule synchronization, select the Using the Following Schedule(s) option button and the check boxes for the schedule or schedules you want to use.
7. Click the OK button. Internet Explorer closes the Properties dialog box.
8. Click the Close button. Internet Explorer closes the Organize Favorites dialog box.

EXPERT KNOWLEDGE: USING NETSCAPE BOOKMARKS IN INTERNET EXPLORER

To use a bookmark list that you've put together in Netscape, export it from Netscape: Choose Bookmarks ➢ Manage Bookmarks. Netscape displays the Manage Bookmarks window. Choose File ➢ Export Bookmarks. Netscape displays the Export Bookmark File dialog box, which is a common Save As dialog box. Specify the location and filename for the file and click the Save button. Netscape closes the Export Bookmark File dialog box and saves the file.

Then, in Internet Explorer, choose File ➢ Import and Export. Internet Explorer starts the Import and Export Wizard. Follow the wizard's prompts to import the file.

Using the Explorer Bars

Internet Explorer provides a handful of Explorer bars that provide some additional functionality and an alternate way of accessing certain features. The drawback to using these Explorer bars is that they take up a chunk of your browsing area. Some people find these bars useful; others find them a waste of screen space. But you should know about them so that you can use them if you'll benefit from doing so. You've already met a couple of them in this chapter.

To display an Explorer bar, choose View ➤ Explorer Bar and choose the bar's name from the submenu, or (where appropriate) press the key combination listed below. To hide the bar again, repeat the command or click the Close button (the × button) on the bar. Most of the Explorer bars appear at the left side of the Internet Explorer window; you can display only one of these Explorer bars at once. The Tip of the Day Explorer bar and the Discussion Explorer bar (which grafts itself onto Internet Explorer when you install Microsoft Office XP or Microsoft Office 2000) appear across the bottom of the window.

These are the main Explorer bars:

Search Explorer bar (Ctrl+E)   This bar provides tools for searching for a web page, a person's address, a business, or a map. The contents of the Search Explorer bar change depending on which item you're searching for. You can customize your search settings by clicking the Customize button and working in the Customize Search Settings dialog box.

Favorites Explorer bar (Ctrl+I)   This bar lists your favorites, essentially duplicating the Favorites menu in a more visible way.

History Explorer bar (Ctrl+H)   This bar displays a list of the websites you've visited and the documents you've opened recently.

Folders Explorer bar   This bar displays a tree showing your Desktop and the folders accessible from it: My Documents, My Computer, My Network Places, and Recycle Bin. This bar can be useful for opening documents in Internet Explorer. For general file-management tasks, you'll normally be better off using an Explorer window.

Media Explorer bar   This bar provides quick access to WindowsMedia.com's music, radio, movies, and entertainment, together with play controls.

Tip of the Day Explorer bar   This bar displays tips. Use it to quickly view all tips by clicking the Next Tip link; implement or memorize the good ones; and then turn this bar off to reclaim the space it wastes.

Customizing Your Home Page and Quick Links

Apart from favorites, Internet Explorer provides several features for quickly accessing particular sites. These features include your home page, your search page, and Quick Links buttons.

Your *home page* is the page that Internet Explorer automatically opens when you start Internet Explorer and when you click the Home button on the toolbar. You'll usually want to change your home page from the default setting (MSN) to the site you want to see first in every Internet Explorer session.

EXPERT KNOWLEDGE: CREATING A CUSTOM HOME PAGE LOCALLY

One of the problems with most home pages is that, even with the fastest of connections, they take a few seconds to load. If you want to see what's new on the home page, that may be well and good. But if you just want to use the home page as a jumping-off point for sites further afield, the delay may be annoying.

To avoid this delay, create a custom home page and store it on your hard drive. It needs to contain no more than a little HTML—though you can make it as complex as you like. Alternatively, start with a blank page, which will not only load like lightning but won't automatically connect to the Internet (useful if you don't have a permanent Internet connection).

The Links bar provides Quick Links to regularly updated Microsoft sites, such as Free Hotmail and the Windows site. (The names of these Quick Links vary a little in different versions of Internet Explorer. Your hardware provider may also have customized the Quick Links.) You can access any of these sites by clicking its button on the Links bar.

To customize the Quick Links bar, navigate to a site that you like, then drag the page icon from the beginning of the Address box to the Quick Links bar. Drop the icon in an open space on the bar. Internet Explorer creates a link for it.

See page 40 of the *Essential Skills* section for a visual guide to changing your home page, or take the following steps:

1. Navigate to your target page.
2. Choose Tools ➤ Internet Options. Internet Explorer displays the Internet Options dialog box with the General page foremost.
3. Click the Use Current button in the Home Page group box on the General page.
   ◆ You can also type the address into the Address text box, but it's usually easier to display the site first.
   ◆ Alternatively, click the Use Blank button to make Internet Explorer start with a blank page. (A blank page displays immediately but doesn't get you far.)
4. Click the OK button. Internet Explorer closes the Internet Options dialog box.

WARNING *Installing or updating Microsoft programs may reset your home page to its default setting without warning you. In case this happens, create a favorite for your start page so that you will be able to access it quickly in order to restore it as your home page.*

To make more space on the Quick Links bar, rename the existing buttons on it with shorter names.

Customizing the Toolbar

You can customize the Internet Explorer toolbar by adding, removing, or rearranging buttons, and changing the presentation of the labels on the buttons you display. You customize the Internet Explorer toolbar in the same way as you customize the Explorer toolbar. See the section "Customizing the Toolbar" in Chapter 6 for details.

You can rearrange the toolbars and menu bar by dragging them by their handles (the raised line at the left end of the toolbar). For example, you might drag the bars so that they occupy two rows across the screen rather than their default three. You can also toggle off the display of the toolbars by right-clicking the menu bar or any displayed toolbar and choosing Standard Buttons, Address Bar, or Links as appropriate. You can toggle off the display of the status bar by choosing View ➤ Status Bar.

TIP   *To get the maximum display area in the Internet Explorer window, press the F11 key or choose View ➤ Full Screen, then right-click the toolbar and choose Auto Hide from the context menu. Press the F11 key again to toggle Full Screen view off.*

To restore your toolbar buttons to their default state, removing any customizations, click the Reset button in the Customize Toolbar dialog box.

Configuring Internet Explorer

This section discusses the most important options that Internet Explorer offers for controlling how it runs. You can configure most aspects of its behavior—everything from the font size Internet Explorer uses to display text, to security, to improving performance over a slow Internet connection.

Internet Explorer has a plethora of options, so this section doesn't discuss all of them. Instead, it concentrates on the options that will make the most difference in your daily surfing.

All these options live in the Internet Options dialog box. Start by choosing Tools ➤ Internet Options. Internet Explorer displays this dialog box.

Cleaning Up Temporary Internet Files

Every time you view a page on the Internet or on an internal network, the information on the page is transferred to your computer. That's no surprise—that's why download times matter so much to the surfing experience. But it's not so obvious that this information is written into temporary files on your hard drive. This enables you to view the information more quickly the next time you access the page, as Internet Explorer has to download only new items if the page has changed. Over a high-speed network, that may not make a big difference, but over the average Internet connection, it can save anything from a few seconds to a minute or two.

The disadvantages to having the files on your hard drive are, first, that they take up space, and second, that you can have embarrassing or dangerous information stored on your computer without your knowledge. So it's a good idea to clear out your temporary files periodically.

To clean up temporary Internet files, click the Settings button in the Temporary Internet Files group box on the General page of the Internet Options dialog box. Internet Explorer displays the Settings dialog box (shown in Figure 19.18).

In the Check for Newer Versions of Stored Pages list, select an option button to determine how frequently Internet Explorer should check for newer versions of stored pages: Every Visit to the Page, Every Time You Start Internet Explorer, Automatically, or Never. The first, second, and fourth of these options are self-explanatory. The default setting, Automatically, causes Internet Explorer to build its own schedule for updating each stored page. If you return to a page the same day and during the same Internet Explorer session as your previous visit, Internet Explorer doesn't check for a new version of the page (unless you issue a Refresh command). If your last visit was in an earlier session or on an earlier day, Internet Explorer updates the page. Subsequently Internet Explorer monitors the page and tries to establish a schedule that approximately reflects the page's frequency of change. Internet Explorer isn't psychic and can't intuit the frequency of changes, so the schedule it establishes may result in you seeing an out-of-date version of the page.

In the Temporary Internet Files Folder group box, check the amount of disk space Internet Explorer is using for temporary files. If you have space to burn and you're not concerned about having potentially embarrassing information stored, devote anything up to several gigabytes to temporary files, because storing more of them may speed up your browsing.

From the Settings dialog box, you can take three other actions:

◆ Move the folder to another folder or drive if necessary by clicking the Move Folder button and using the resulting Browse for Folder dialog box to designate the folder. If you do this, you need to restart Internet Explorer.

◆ Display an Explorer window showing your temporary files by clicking the View Files button. You probably won't need to do this unless you want to delete an objectionable item (for example, a graphics file) that you know Internet Explorer has downloaded.

◆ Display an Explorer window listing the objects installed—for example, ActiveX controls—by clicking the View Objects button. From this window, you can check an object's properties by right-clicking it and choosing Properties from the context menu; remove it by right-clicking it and choosing Remove from the context menu; or update it by right-clicking it and choosing Update from the context menu.

When you've chosen suitable settings, click the OK button. Internet Explorer closes the Settings dialog box.

To clear out your current temporary files, click the Delete Files button in the Temporary Internet Files group box. Internet Explorer displays the Delete Files dialog box (shown in Figure 19.19). To delete all your offline content, select the Delete All Offline Content check box. Usually, you'll want to keep the offline content but get rid of everything else. Click the OK button. Internet Explorer closes the Delete Files dialog box and deletes your temporary files.

FIGURE 19.19

Use the Delete Files dialog box to delete your temporary Internet files.

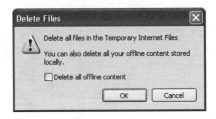

NOTE *Another way to delete temporary files is to use the Disk Cleanup Wizard (as discussed in the section "Cleaning Up Your Disks with Disk Cleanup" in Chapter 11) or a commercial program such as Norton CleanSweep.*

To delete your cookies, click the Delete Cookies button in the Temporary Internet Files group box on the General page of the Internet Options dialog box. Internet Explorer displays the Delete Cookies dialog box to confirm that you want to delete all your cookies. Click the OK button. Internet Explorer closes the Delete Cookies dialog box and deletes your cookies.

Keeping Control of Your History

As you saw earlier in the chapter, Internet Explorer's History feature tracks where you've been. History is a great feature for retracing your steps to find a site you forgot to bookmark, but it's also a threat: Those who study your history can repeat your movements step by step—which, depending on what you've been doing, could be a threat to your business' security, to your family's good name, or to the recipient's blissful ignorance of that perfect Christmas present you bought well ahead of time.

If you perceive a security threat, reduce the Days to Keep Pages in History text box entry in the History group box on the General page of the Internet Options dialog box to a minimum—perhaps 0 days. Then click the Clear History button to clear your current history. Click the OK button in the confirmation message box that appears.

If clearing your history would raise suspicions, you can delete a particular shortcut or a web location by right-clicking it and choosing Delete from the context menu.

Choosing Security Options

The History feature touches on security, but Internet Explorer has a bunch of explicit security features as well. Click the Security tab in the Internet Options dialog box. Internet Explorer displays the Security page (shown on the left in Figure 19.20).

FIGURE 19.20

Choose canned
security options
on the Security page
of the Internet
Options dialog box
(left) or use the
Security Settings
dialog box to
implement custom
security settings.

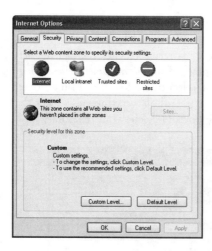

The Select a Web Content Zone to Specify Its Security Settings box at the top of the page contains four categories of sites. The easiest way to explain them is in reverse order:

◆ Restricted Sites (sites you've specifically designated as potentially dangerous)

◆ Trusted Sites (sites you've specifically designated as trusted not to damage your computer or your data)

◆ Local Intranet (local sites not specifically designated as restricted or trusted)

◆ Internet (everything else)

You can set a different level of security for each category by selecting the category, clicking the Default Level button so that Internet Explorer displays the Security Level for This Zone slider, and then dragging the slider up or down. If you understand the specifics of security, you can also specify a custom level for a zone by selecting the category and clicking the Custom Level button. Internet Explorer displays the Security Settings dialog box (shown on the right in Figure 19.20). Select settings for the different categories, then click the OK button. Internet Explorer closes the Security Settings dialog box and implements your settings.

By default, the Internet category has a Medium security level designed to let you browse effectively while protecting you from harmful content. Local Intranet has a Medium-Low level; Trusted Sites has a Low level; and Restricted Sites has a High level.

To change your list of Local Intranet sites, Trusted Sites, or Restricted Sites, select the category and click the Sites button. Internet Explorer displays the Local Intranet dialog box, the Trusted Sites dialog box, or the Restricted Sites dialog box (shown in Figure 19.21). To add a site to the list, enter its URL in the Add This Web Site to The Zone text box and click the Add button; to remove a site from the list, select it in the Web Sites list box and click the Remove button. Click the OK button to close the dialog box.

NOTE *The security zone for the current site appears in the status bar.*

FIGURE 19.21

Use the Restricted
Sites dialog box
(shown here), the
Trusted Sites dialog
box (not shown), or
the Local Intranet
dialog box (not
shown) to adjust
your list of restricted
sites, trusted sites, or
local intranet sites.

Choosing a Level of Privacy

For the Internet zone, you can choose the level of privacy to use. Click the Privacy tab. Internet
Explorer displays the Privacy page of the Internet Options dialog box (shown in Figure 19.22).

FIGURE 19.22

Use the Privacy page
of the Internet
Options dialog box
to specify your
privacy preferences
for the Internet zone.

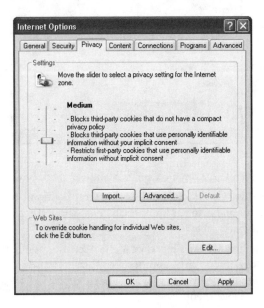

Drag the slider in the Settings group box to specify the level of security to use. Beside the slider,
Internet Explorer displays specifics for that level of privacy.

If you prefer to have the boundaries of your privacy designed by other people, you can download privacy settings files from privacy organizations. Then click the Import button and use the
resulting Privacy Import dialog box to import the file, which applies the preferences it contains.

Handling Cookies

A key aspect of privacy is handling *cookies*, the text files that websites place on your computer in order to track your dealings with their site. For example, if you visit an e-commerce site and fill out a form to buy a product, the information you enter in the form is typically stored in a cookie so that the website can maintain the information in the fields if you need to go back to a previous page. Only the website that creates a cookie can read it; other websites cannot. Most cookies are *persistent*, lasting from one session to another so that their information can be used when you revisit a site in a later session, but there are also *temporary cookies* or *session cookies* that last only until the end of the current Internet Explorer session.

To specify custom cookie handling, take the following steps:

1. Click the Advanced button on the Privacy page of the Internet Options dialog box. Internet Explorer displays the Advanced Privacy Settings dialog box (shown in Figure 19.23 with some settings chosen).

FIGURE 19.23

Use the Advanced Privacy Settings dialog box to specify custom handling of cookies.

2. Select the Override Automatic Cookie Handling check box.

3. In the First-Party Cookies list, choose the Accept option button, the Block option button, or the Prompt option button as appropriate. *First-party cookies* are those that come from the website you're viewing.

4. In the Third-Party Cookies list, choose the Accept option button, the Block option button, or the Prompt option button as appropriate. *Third-party cookies* are those that come from websites associated with the one you're viewing. They're often used for advertising or marketing, so you might want to block them.

5. If you want to use session cookies no matter what your settings in the First-Party Cookies list and the Third-Party Cookies list, select the Always Allow Session Cookies check box. Session cookies are temporary cookies maintained during a session to facilitate communication with websites. Internet Explorer deletes session cookies when you close it.

6. Click the OK button. Internet Explorer closes the Advanced Privacy Settings dialog box and applies your choices.

That custom cookie handling you just set applies to all websites. If you want to be more specific about which sites can and cannot place cookies on your computer, click the Edit button in the Web Sites group box. Internet Explorer displays the Per Site Privacy Actions dialog box (shown in Figure 19.24).

FIGURE 19.24

You can use the Per Site Privacy Actions dialog box to specify which websites may use cookies and which websites are blocked.

To allow or block cookies from a website, enter the domain name in the Address of Web Site text box and then click the Allow button or the Block button as appropriate. Use the Remove button to remove a blocked or allowed site from the Managed Web Sites list box, or use the Remove All button to clear the list.

Click the OK button. Internet Explorer closes the Per Site Privacy Actions dialog box and applies your choices.

Internet Explorer monitors cookies and displays messages such as that shown in Figure 19.25 when there's a problem that you might want to know about. You'll probably want to accept Internet Explorer's offer to turn off this warning, but watch for the privacy icon in the status bar.

FIGURE 19.25

Internet Explorer displays this Privacy dialog box to alert you to restricted cookies.

When Internet Explorer displays the privacy icon in the status bar, you can double-click it to display a Privacy Report dialog box (shown in Figure 19.26). Use the Show drop-down list to toggle between Restricted Web Sites and All Web Sites. Click the Settings button if you want to move to the Privacy page of the Internet Options dialog box (for example, to block a new offender). Or click the Close button to close the Privacy Report dialog box.

FIGURE 19.26

In the Privacy Report dialog box, you can see which sites are being blocked from sending you cookies.

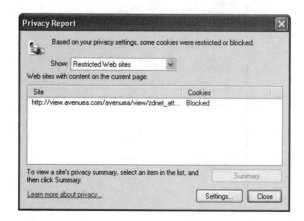

NOTE *To delete all your cookies, click the Delete Cookies button in the Temporary Internet Files group box on the General page of the Internet Options dialog box and then click the OK button in the Delete Cookies dialog box that Internet Explorer displays. Bear in mind that deleting all cookies denies you any benefit those cookies offered.*

Screening Out Objectionable Content

The Content Advisor feature enables you to set up content screening based on the ratings of the Recreational Software Advisory Council rating service for the Internet (RSACi). Content Advisor is very useful if children or easily offended friends or relatives may be using your computer.

To set up Content Adviser, take the following steps:

1. Click the Content tab of the Internet Options dialog box. Internet Explorer displays the Content page.

2. Click the Enable button in the Content Advisor group box. Internet Explorer displays the Content Advisor dialog box.

3. On the Ratings page, select the item in the Category list box and drag the Rating slider to a suitable level (shown on the left in Figure 19.27). Each of the items has five levels, ranging from 0 (none of the offensive item) to 4 (lots of it). For example, the Violence levels are No Violence (0), Fighting (1), Killing (2), Killing with Blood and Gore (3), and Wanton and Gratuitous Violence (4). The Language levels are Inoffensive Slang (0), Mild Expletives (1), Moderate Expletives (2), Obscene Gestures (3), and Explicit or Crude Language (4).

4. Click the Approved Sites tab. Internet Explorer displays the Approved Sites page (shown on the right in Figure 19.27).

FIGURE 19.27

Choose rating levels on the Ratings page of the Content Advisor dialog box (left). Use the Approved Sites page (right) to specify sites that should be always viewable or never viewable regardless of their rating.

5. Set up your list of approved and disapproved sites by taking the following steps:

◆ In the Allow This Web Site text box, enter the URL of the website you want to make always viewable or never viewable.

◆ Click the Always button or the Never button as appropriate. Internet Explorer adds the site to the List of Approved and Disapproved Web Sites list box and marks it with the corresponding icon.

◆ To remove a website from the List of Approved and Disapproved Web Sites list box, select it and click the Remove button.

6. Click the General tab. Internet Explorer displays the General page (shown in Figure 19.28).

FIGURE 19.28

Choose general options on the General page of the Content Advisor dialog box.

7. Choose options as appropriate:

   ♦ Select the Users Can See Sites That Have No Rating check box if you want users to be able to view websites that don't use ratings. This check box is cleared by default, because unrated websites may well have offensive content.

   ♦ Leave the Supervisor Can Type a Password to Allow Users to View Restricted Content check box selected (as it is by default) if you want to be able to let other users view restricted sites by your entering a password. If not, clear this check box.

   ♦ To change the supervisor password, click the Change Password button and specify the new password in the resulting Change Supervisor Password dialog box.

TIP   If you don't find RSACi adequate, you can add other rating systems to Internet Explorer by using the controls in the Rating Systems group box on the General page of the Content Advisor dialog box. The Advanced page contains controls for adding a ratings bureau and PICSRules to Content Advisor. You're unlikely to need to use these options for home or home-office computing.

8. Click the OK button. Internet Explorer closes Content Advisor. The first time you close Content Adviser, Internet Explorer displays the Create Supervisor Password dialog box (shown in Figure 19.29).

FIGURE 19.29

Create a supervisor password in the Create Supervisor Password dialog box.

9. Enter the password in the Password and Confirm Password text boxes, then click the OK button. Internet Explorer displays a Content Advisor message box telling you that Content Advisor has been installed and to close Internet Explorer.

10. Click the OK button. Internet Explorer closes the Content Advisor dialog box and returns you to the Internet Options dialog box, where the Enable Ratings button has changed to the Disable Ratings button.

11. Click the OK button. Internet Explorer closes the Internet Options dialog box.

12. Exit all Internet Explorer windows, then reopen one.

To adjust the settings for Content Advisor, click the Settings button in the Content Advisor group box on the Content page of the Internet Options dialog box. Internet Explorer displays the Supervisor Password Required dialog box. Enter your password and click the OK button to display the Content Advisor dialog box, then change the settings and click the OK button.

To disable ratings again, click the Disable button in the Content Advisor group box on the Content page of the Internet Options dialog box. Internet Explorer displays the Supervisor Password Required dialog box. Enter your password and click the OK button. Internet Explorer displays a Content Advisor message box telling you that Content Advisor has been turned off.

When users hit a site that contains unapproved content, they see a Content Advisor dialog box such as the one shown in Figure 19.30. If you're the user, you can enter the supervisor password and choose the Always Allow This Web Site to Be Viewed option button (to make a lasting exception for the site), the Always Allow This Web Page to Be Viewed option button (to make a lasting exception for the page but not the site), or the Allow Viewing Only This Time option button (to make a temporary exception). Then click the OK button. Internet Explorer closes the Content Advisor dialog box and displays the site. (A user without the supervisor password will need to click the Cancel button and will not be able to reach the site.)

FIGURE 19.30

Content Advisor in action

Managing Your AutoComplete Information

AutoComplete is a great feature that can save you a lot of fuss with passwords and often-repeated information. But it can also severely compromise your digital persona and your finances, so you need to understand what it does and how it works so that you can use it appropriately.

Briefly put, AutoComplete automatically fills in URLs and entries on forms for you. To do so, it needs to watch as you enter URLs and information on forms, and store that information. Then, when you start typing a URL or access a form it recognizes, it can fill in the information for you. For example, the first time you access your Hotmail account via Internet Explorer, AutoComplete can learn your username and password, and offer to fill them in for you in the future.

You can see the downside to this: Internet Explorer is storing sensitive or secret information, which means that other people who use your computer can more easily masquerade as you. There's also a risk that your computer could be hacked to give up this information, though this risk is less severe than the direct risk from people who can physically access your computer.

To configure AutoComplete, follow these steps:

1. Click the AutoComplete button in the Personal Information group box on the Content page of the Internet Options dialog box to display the AutoComplete Settings dialog box (shown in Figure 19.31).

FIGURE 19.31

Choose Auto-
Complete options in
the AutoComplete
Settings dialog box.

2. In the Use AutoComplete For group box, specify the items for which you want to use AutoComplete:

◆ The Web Addresses check box controls whether AutoComplete tracks the URLs you access and suggests matching URLs in the Open dialog box and the Address box.

◆ The Forms check box controls whether AutoComplete tracks your entries in forms other than usernames and passwords.

◆ The User Names and Passwords on Forms check box controls whether AutoComplete tracks the usernames and passwords you enter in forms. This is the most sensitive information, so you may want to clear this check box. If you leave it enabled (as it is by default), leave the Prompt Me to Save Passwords check box selected so that Internet Explorer gets your consent each time it's about to store a password of yours. (This way, you can use AutoComplete for less sensitive passwords but not for high-security passwords.)

3. If you want to clear your form information or passwords stored to date, click the Clear Forms button or the Clear Passwords button in the Clear AutoComplete History group box and click the OK button in the Internet Options confirmation dialog box that Internet Explorer displays.

4. Click the OK button. Internet Explorer closes the AutoComplete Settings dialog box.

Specifying Programs for Internet Services

The Programs page of the Internet Options dialog box (shown on the left in Figure 19.32) lets you specify which program XP should use for Internet-related tasks such as editing HTML and reading newsgroups. Use the six drop-down lists to specify the programs to use. By default, Internet Explorer chooses Outlook Express for E-mail and Newsgroups, NetMeeting for Internet Call, and Address Book for Contact List.

FIGURE 19.32

On the Programs page (left) of the Internet Options dialog box, you can manually configure the programs that you want XP to use for Internet services. On the Advanced page (right), you can choose advanced settings.

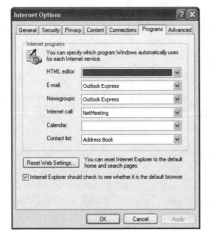

Advanced Options

The Advanced page of the Internet Options dialog box (shown on the right in Figure 19.32) contains a formidable number of options organized in a number of categories. The following sections discuss the key options.

WARNING   Because many of the options on the Advanced page control important behavior on the part of Internet Explorer, don't change them unless you understand exactly what they do and what the results can be. If you think you've chosen some unwise settings, you can click the Restore Defaults button to restore the default settings.

BROWSING CATEGORY

These are the key options in the Browsing category:

Automatically Check for Internet Explorer Updates check box   This check box controls whether Internet Explorer checks for any available updates. It's a good idea to select this check box even if you use Windows Update regularly: Because Internet Explorer handles a wide range of duties and has extensive contact with the Internet, any vulnerabilities can prove painful.

Enable Offline Items to Be Synchronized on a Schedule check box   Make sure this check box is selected if you want to create offline favorites.

Notify when Downloads Complete check box   Leave this check box selected (as it is by default) if you want Internet Explorer to prompt you when it finishes downloading a file. Clear this check box if you find the notification annoying.

Reuse Windows for Launching Shortcuts check box   When selected (as it is by default), this check box causes Internet Explorer to display the page for a hyperlink you click in the current window. Clear this check box if you want Internet Explorer to display the linked page in a new window by default.

Underline Links option buttons   Select the Always option button (the default), the Hover option button, or the Never option button to specify whether and when Internet Explorer should underline links. (*Hover* means that you position the mouse pointer over the link.)

Use Inline AutoComplete check box   This check box controls whether Internet Explorer offers AutoComplete suggestions when you're typing an address or URL in the Address box or in Explorer. Most people find AutoComplete helpful, but its suggestions can be embarrassing if you've been visiting URLs or viewing documents you shouldn't have.

Use Passive FTP check box   Select this check box if you want to use passive FTP—FTP in which your computer does not need to supply its IP address. Because of this, passive FTP is normally more secure than regular FTP. Depending on your network settings, you may need to use passive FTP—for example, if you have a vigilant firewall. Generally speaking, stick with regular FTP unless you find it doesn't work, in which case, try passive FTP.

Use Smooth Scrolling check box   This check box (which is selected by default) controls whether Internet Explorer scrolls the contents of its window in a smooth and gentle fashion or in jerks (as most Windows programs do). If you're used to regular Windows behavior, or if you find the smooth scrolling sick-making, try clearing this check box.

MULTIMEDIA CATEGORY

These are the key options in the Multimedia category:

Play Animations in Web Pages check box   This check box controls whether Internet Explorer plays animations. If your computer or connection is slow, you may want to turn animations off.

Play Sounds in Web Pages check box   This check box controls whether Internet Explorer plays sounds. Because sound files can be big, consider clearing this check box to speed up your downloads.

Play Videos in Web Pages check box   This check box controls whether Internet Explorer plays videos. Video files can be huge, so if you have a slow connection, consider turning videos off to speed up your browsing.

Show Pictures check box   This check box controls whether Internet Explorer displays pictures. If your Internet connection is really slow (for example, if you're surfing via a cell-phone hookup), you may want to turn pictures off—but the Web is so graphical nowadays that some pages may be tough going without their pictures.

SECURITY CATEGORY

You should understand most of the items in the Security category:

Check for Publisher's Certificate Revocation check box   Select this check box to have Internet Explorer check that a software publisher's digital certificate is still valid before accepting it. Checking a certificate slows down the installation of add-on software but offers you a little extra protection against bad software.

WARNING   *Surprisingly, even some major software publishers have been known to let their certificates lapse. If you select the Check for Publisher's Certificate Revocation check box, you may occasionally have to override warnings that a certificate is out of date in order to install add-ons you need.*

Check for Server Certificate Revocation check box   This check box (which is cleared by default) controls whether Internet Explorer checks an Internet site's certificate to make sure it hasn't been revoked.

Do Not Save Encrypted Pages to Disk check box   Select this check box (which is cleared by default) to prevent Internet Explorer from saving encrypted web pages to disk.

Empty Temporary Internet Files Folder when Browser Is Closed check box   This check box (which is cleared by default) controls whether Internet Explorer deletes all temporary files each time you close Internet Explorer. If you're concerned about security, select this check box.

Enable Integrated Windows Authentication check box   Leave this check box selected if you want to use Integrated Windows Authentication.

Enable Profile Assistant check box   Leave this check box selected (as it is by default) if you want to use Internet Explorer's Profile Assistant for providing information requested by websites. The Profile Assistant manages the requests for information and lets you specify which information to share with each website and whether to respond automatically to future requests from that site. Clear this check box to turn off the Profile Assistant. (See "Editing Your Profile for Address Book" in Chapter 20 for coverage of Profile Assistant.)

Use SSL 2.0 check box and Use SSL 3.0 check box   Leave these check boxes selected (as they are by default) if you want to use the Secure Sockets Layer Level 2 (SSL 2) and Secure Sockets Layer Level 3 (SSL 3) protocols for securing the transmission of information. As you'd guess from the number, SSL 3 is supposed to be more secure than SSL 2. At this writing, SSL 2 is almost universally used, but SSL 3 is starting to supplant it.

Use TLS 1.0 check box   Select this check box (which is cleared by default) if you want to use Transport Layer Security (TLS) to secure the transmission of information. TLS is not widely used.

Warn about Invalid Site Certificates check box   This check box (which is selected by default) controls whether Internet Explorer warns you if a digital certificate is invalid. Keep this check box selected.

Warn if Changing Between Secure and Not Secure Mode check box   This check box (which is selected by default) controls whether Internet Explorer warns you when you are switched from a secure (encrypted) connection to a server to an insecure connection. Keep this check box selected until you've got the hang of secure connections. When the warnings become an irritant, clear this check box.

Warn if Forms Submittal Is Being Redirected check box   This check box (which is selected by default) controls whether Internet Explorer warns you when a form you've submitted is being redirected to a different destination than its apparent destination. Many forms contain sensitive information, so keep this check box selected.

Browsing Offline

Once you've set up offline favorites as described earlier in the chapter, you're ready to browse them offline.

If your computer isn't currently connected to the network or Internet, you'll automatically be offline. If your computer is connected to the network or Internet, choose File ➤ Work Offline to start working offline. Internet Explorer displays an indicator on the status bar—a network cable with a red cross on it and a gray cloud above it—to show that you're currently offline. (Choose File ➤ Work Offline again to switch back to online mode.)

As long as you stay within the material you have available offline, you'll be able to surf as usual. Because the pages are stored on your hard drive, the surfing will probably be quicker than when you have to download them. When you hit a link that leads to a page that's not available, or you enter an address that's not available, Internet Explorer displays the Web Page Unavailable while Offline dialog box (shown in Figure 19.33). Click the Connect button to connect to the Internet or the Stay Offline button to cancel the connection request.

FIGURE 19.33

If you try to go to a URL that's not available, Internet Explorer offers you the choice of connecting to the network or staying offline.

A Quick Introduction to MSN Explorer

This short section discusses MSN Explorer, Microsoft's latest effort to take a bite out of AOL's pie and make a larger chunk of the Web its own.

MSN Explorer provides a highly graphical interface that integrates e-mail (via MSN and Hotmail), instant messaging (via Windows Messenger), discussion groups (the MSN Communities), online shopping (from big names including Amazon.com, RadioShack, and Nordstrom), and music and entertainment (via WindowsMedia.com). MSN Explorer also delivers personalized news and information; provides an online calendar facility; gives you a location to store your own web pages, including photos; and offers MoneyCentral, an area for managing your finances (if you care to do so online).

Figure 19.34 shows the e-mail component of the MSN Explorer interface. As you can see in the figure, the toolbar provides quick access to the main areas of MSN with large and colorful buttons, while the panel on the left gives access to the calendar, stock tracking, websites you're a member of, your photo albums, and a search facility.

FIGURE 19.34

MSN Explorer provides a colorful and graphical interface to MSN and Microsoft's services.

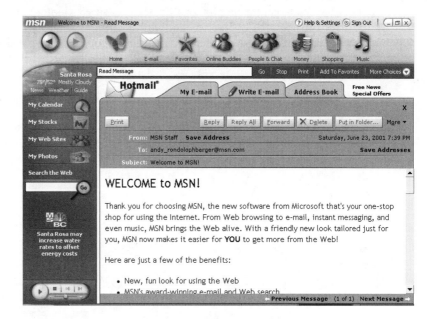

To get started with MSN Explorer, choose Start ➤ All Programs ➤ MSN Explorer. MSN Explorer walks you through a setup routine that involves the following steps:

- Specifying how MSN Explorer should connect to the Internet—via modem, via DSL or your LAN, or having you establish the connection manually

- Identifying a Hotmail or MSN e-mail address that you already have or getting a new e-mail address

- For a new account, providing a good bit of personal information, including your name (or an approximation of it), country, state and Zip code, your occupation, and your date of birth. (The date of birth controls whether MSN gives you an adult's account or a child's account. MSN Internet Access members must be 18 or older.)

- Choosing a secret question in case you lose your password and need to request it

- Reading and accepting the MSN Internet Access Member Agreement

- Choosing an e-mail name (if you didn't already have one) and specifying whether to list yourself in Internet directories and whether to receive notifications of "new services and opportunities"

TIP *If you never use MSN Explorer, you might want to remove it from your computer to free up a few megabytes of disk space. To do so, choose Start ➤ Control Panel, click the Add or Remove Programs link, click the Add/Remove Windows Components button, and use the Windows Components Wizard to remove the MSN Explorer item.*

Up Next

In this chapter, you've learned the key skills to surfing the Web with Internet Explorer; to using favorites; and to configuring Internet Explorer for speed, comfort, and security. You've also read a word or two about MSN Explorer and what it offers.

The next chapter discusses how to use Address Book to store contact information.

Chapter 20

Using Address Book

XP COMES WITH AN address book program, unimaginatively named Address Book, for storing contact information: names of people, companies, and organizations; their phone numbers, addresses, and e-mail addresses; their birthdays and anniversaries; and even the details of their digital IDs.

Address Book doesn't advertise itself aggressively, and as a result even many experienced Windows users don't make the most of its capabilities. While Address Book isn't as powerful as Microsoft's desktop information management program, Outlook—let alone professional contact management programs such as ACT! and GoldMine—it provides more than enough features for efficient contact management for many home or home-business users. (In other words, try it before you reject it. It's free.)

Each person with a user account on the PC can maintain a separate list of contacts. Address Book also offers a Shared Contacts folder so that each user can share contact information with other users. You can group contacts to manage them efficiently, and you can use group addresses for easy multiple (or mass) mailings.

Address Book is integrated with Outlook Express, so you can quickly create e-mail messages to contacts in Address Book. Conversely, you can create new contacts from the information contained in e-mail addresses.

This chapter covers the following topics:

◆ Starting Address Book
◆ Adding and deleting contacts
◆ Sharing contacts with other users
◆ Editing your profile
◆ Importing and exporting information
◆ Using folders and groups to organize your contacts
◆ Sending mail to a contact

◆ Finding a contact in Address Book or in Internet directories

◆ Printing out your Address Book

◆ Copying or moving your Address Book

Starting Address Book

You can start Address Book from the Start menu (Start ➤ All Programs ➤ Accessories ➤ Address Book) or in various ways from Outlook Express: Click the Addresses button, choose Tools ➤ Address Book, or press Ctrl+Shift+B. You can also access Address Book via the Select Recipients dialog box that Outlook Express displays when you click the To button or the Cc button from the New Message window.

To make Address Book more quickly accessible from the Desktop, copy or move its shortcut from the Accessories submenu. Alternatively, create a new shortcut to the Address Book executable file, WAB.EXE.

When you start Address Book, it displays the contacts for the identity you're currently using in Outlook Express. By default, this will be your main identity. (For a discussion of identities, see the section "Using Identities to Keep Multiple E-mail Accounts Separate" in Chapter 21.) When you first open Address Book, you probably won't have any entries in it. Figure 20.1 shows Address Book with a number of entries already entered in it.

FIGURE 20.1

Address Book with a number of contacts entered.

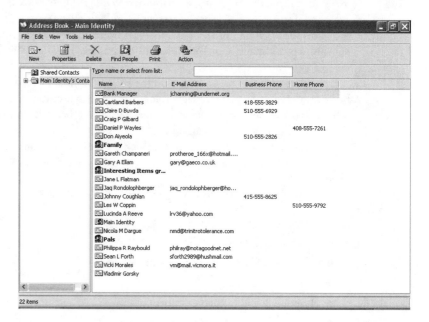

TIP *If you use multiple identities in Outlook Express, you can make Address Book display the contacts for all your identities by launching it with the command* **wab /a** *from the Run dialog box (Start ➤ Run). Otherwise, when run conventionally, Address Book displays just the contacts for your current identity.*

EXPERT KNOWLEDGE: USING ADDRESS BOOK WITH OUTLOOK

Provided that you don't use identities in Outlook Express, you can use Address Book with Outlook as well as with Outlook Express. Doing so can be very handy, because it allows you to keep a single address book for contacts you create from both Outlook Express and Outlook.

To use Address Book in this way, run Registry Editor (as described in Chapter 12), navigate to the HKEY_ CURRENT_USER\Software\Microsoft\Wab\WAB4\ key, and set the value of the UseOutlook DWORD value entry to 1. (If UseOutlook doesn't exist, create it. If UseOutlook's value is already set to 1, leave it be.)

The problem with using identities is that Outlook takes over the Folders and Groups pane to display its Contacts folder, so you can't use this pane to navigate between your identity's contacts and the shared contacts.

Adding a Contact to Your Address Book

The most conventional way to add a contact to your Address Book is as follows.

1. In the Folders and Groups pane, make sure you have selected your identity's contacts or the Shared Contacts folder as appropriate.

2. Click the New button on the toolbar and choose New Contact from the drop-down menu. (Alternatively, choose File ➤ New Contact or press Ctrl+N.) Address Book displays the Properties dialog box for a new contact, with the Name page foremost (see Figure 20.2).

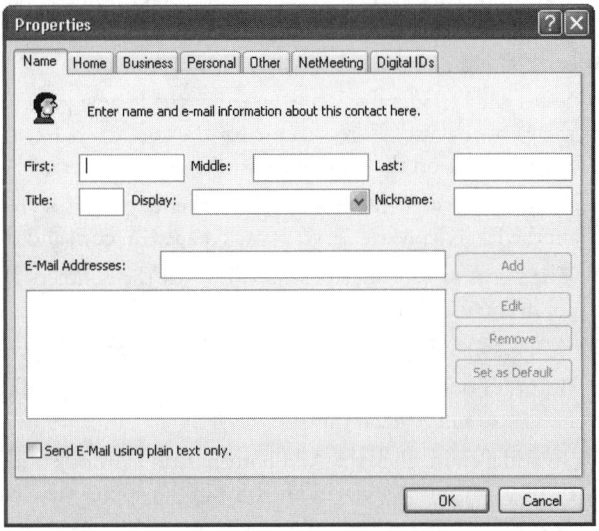

FIGURE 20.2

Use the Properties dialog box to create a new contact.

3. On the Name page, enter the contact's name, title, nickname, and e-mail addresses:

   ◆ Once you've entered the contact's first, middle, and last names, Address Book automatically builds entries for the Display drop-down list. Its default format is First Middle

Last—for example, Randall A Chaucer—but you can choose a different format (Chaucer Randall A or Chaucer, Randall A) in the Display drop-down list. You can also type something completely different—for example, a description such as Bank Manager.

◆ You can use the Nickname field in two ways. First, you can use it to hold a nickname associated with the contact but that you don't want to use instead of their actual first name. But even if the contact doesn't have a nickname, you can use this field as a unique identifier within Address Book and Outlook Express. You can type a nickname in the To field or Cc field in a new message in Outlook Express and issue a Check Names command. Outlook Express fills in the corresponding e-mail address. For example, if you entered **Law** as the nickname for your attorney in Address Book, you could enter **Law** as the address in Outlook Express. (If two or more contacts have the same nickname, Outlook Express displays the Check Names dialog box so that you can pick the one you want.)

◆ You can enter multiple e-mail addresses for a contact. By default, the first e-mail address you enter is set as the default address. If you add multiple e-mail addresses and want to use one other than the first as the default, select the address to use as the default and click the Set As Default button. Address Book adds an envelope icon to the left of the listing and the text *(Default E-mail)* to its left.

◆ If you need to send plain-text e-mail rather than formatted or HTML e-mail to the contact, select the Send E-mail Using Plain Text Only check box. If you're not sure whether a contact can receive formatted e-mail, select this check box. That way, the contact will be able to read your message.

4. On the Home page and the Business page, enter home-related information and business-related information for the contact. Almost all the fields and controls on these pages are self-explanatory, but these three deserve comment:

◆ Select the Default check box on either the Home page or the Business page to specify that this is the default address to use for the contact. Selecting the Default check box on one page clears it on the other page if it is selected there.

◆ Clicking the View Map button on either page causes your browser to look up the address on the Expedia Maps service (`maps.expedia.com`) and display a map of the area to you.

◆ The Business page includes a text box for the contact's IP telephone address, which is useful if you use IP telephony.

5. On the Personal page, enter any personal information known for the contact:

◆ Address Book creates all contacts as being of "Unspecified" gender. With luck, you should be able to improve on this.

◆ To add a child, click the Add button. Address Book adds an entry named New Child and displays an edit box around it. Type in the appropriate name and press the Enter key. (If you need to change the child's name afterward, select the child and click the Edit button.)

6. If you have other information about the contact, enter it in the Notes text box on the Other page. This page also contains the Group Membership text box, which lists any of your Address Book groups the contact belongs to.

7. If you have conferencing information for the contact, enter it on the NetMeeting page. This page also contains a Call Now button that you can click to place a NetMeeting call to the contact.

8. To import a digital ID for the contact, display the Digital IDs page, click the Import button, and follow through the import procedure. You can also export a digital certificate from here, view its properties, and choose which digital certificate to use as the default for a contact. (Chapter 18 discusses digital IDs.)

9. Click the OK button to close the Properties dialog box. Your contact appears in Address Book.

Deleting a Contact

To delete a contact, right-click it and choose Delete from the context menu. Address Book displays a dialog box asking you to confirm the deletion. Click the Yes button.

Moving a Contact from One Identity to Another

You can move a contact from one identity to another by dragging it from the list box to the appropriate folder in the Folders and Groups pane. For example, to move a contact from your main identity to the Shared Contacts folder, drag the contact to the Shared Contacts folder and drop it there.

EXPERT KNOWLEDGE: CREATING A CONTACT RECORD FROM AN E-MAIL MESSAGE

When you're reading e-mail in Outlook Express, you can add a sender to your Address Book by right-clicking the message in the Inbox and choosing Add Sender to Address Book from the context menu. (Alternatively, select the message and choose Tools ➤ Add Sender to Address Book.) Outlook Express adds the name and e-mail address directly to Address Book. So when you do this, it's usually a good idea to display Address Book and immediately add all the information you know about the contact—before you forget.

From a message window, you can create contacts from the sender, a Cc addressee, or everyone on the addressee list of the message (except any Bcc addressees). Choose Tools ➤ Add to Address Book ➤ Sender; Tools ➤ Add to Address Book ➤ Everyone on To List; or one of the e-mail addresses listed on the Add to Address Book submenu. Alternatively, double-click the From listing, one of the To listings other than yourself, or one of the Cc listings.

Outlook Express displays the Properties dialog box for the contact with a Summary page added and displayed. At this point, the information is minimal. Click the Name page of the dialog box and start improving the information while it's fresh, or just click the Add to Address Book button if you're in a hurry.

Editing Your Profile for Address Book

Address Book creates a profile called Main Identity for each user with a user account on the PC. When you start Address Book, it displays the Main Identity profile for the user account under which you logged on to XP.

Address Book is integrated with the Profile Assistant tool in Internet Explorer. To enable Address Book to provide Internet Explorer with the information it needs for websites that request data such as your e-mail address or a digital certificate, you need to create a profile for yourself and associate it with the Main Identity. To do so, follow these steps:

1. Choose Edit ➤ Profile. Address Book displays the Address Book – Choose Profile dialog box (shown in Figure 20.3).

FIGURE 20.3

In the Address Book – Choose Profile dialog box, choose whether to create a new entry for your profile or to use an existing entry.

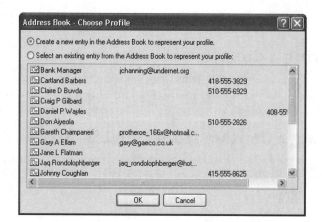

2. Choose whether to use an existing entry for your profile or to create a new entry. If you choose the Select an Existing Entry from the Address Book to Represent Your Profile option button, choose the profile from the list box.
3. Click the OK button. Address Book closes the Address Book – Choose Profile dialog box. If you chose to create a new entry, Address Book displays the Properties dialog box for an identity named Main Identity. Fill in the information as you would for any other contact (though perhaps with more care), and change the name from Main Identity to your name.

When Profile Assistant receives a request for information from a website, Profile Assistant tells you the URL or IP address of the site requesting the information, the types of information requested, how the site claims it will use the information (invariably for good—*your* good—of course), and whether the connection to the site is secured with SSL. You can choose which information to give the site. If the connection is secure, you can view the certificate for the site to help you decide.

Importing Information into Your Address Book

If you already have information in a data source (for example, in an organizer or in a database), you can import it into Address Book. Address Book can handle formats that include Windows address books, the vCard business-card format, Address Books in Works, Exchange, Microsoft Internet Mail for Windows 3.1, Eudora (Pro and Light), Netscape and Netscape Communicator, and the LDAP Data Interchange Format. If your data is in a different format (for example, a spreadsheet or an organizer), the best way of exporting and importing the information is to use a *comma-separated values* file (CSV file for short)—a file in which the fields are separated by commas.

WARNING *With some data sources, Address Book may fail to preserve divisions between address books—for example, it may lump entries from multiple separate address books into the same category in Address Book. Make sure you keep your data source until you've checked your imported data carefully in case Address Book messes things up and you need to import it all again.*

Importing a Windows Address Book

Importing a file in Windows address book (WAB) format is a straightforward process: Choose File ➢ Import ➢ Address Book (WAB), use the Select Address Book to Import From dialog box to identify the file, and click the Open button. Then dismiss the message box telling you that the address book has been imported.

Importing a vCard

Importing a record stored in a vCard business card is equally straightforward. Choose File ➢ Import ➢ Business Card (vCard), use the Import Business Card (vCard) dialog box to select the file, and click the Open button. Address Book displays the Properties dialog box for the contact so that you can check that the information is in the right slots and add any other data you want. Then click the OK button. Address Book closes the Properties dialog box and files away the information.

NOTE *You should also be able to add a contact to Address Book quickly by double-clicking a vCard (VCF) file. If double-clicking a vCard doesn't add a contact to Address Book, you need to change the file type linked to the VCF extension. See the section "Changing the File Type Linked to an Extension" in Chapter 10 for instructions.*

Importing Information Stored in Another Format

Importing address information stored in another format tends to be a more involved process, because you usually need to map the fields in the data source to the fields in Address Book.

> **EXPERT KNOWLEDGE: EXPORTING YOUR ADDRESS INFORMATION FIELDS IN THE BEST ORDER**
>
> If the program from which you're exporting the address information lets you name the fields and specify their order, use this order and these names: First Name, Last Name, Middle Name, Name, Nickname, E-mail Address, Home Street, Home City, Home Postal Code, Home State, Home Country, Home Phone, Home Fax, Mobile Phone, Personal Web Page, Business Street, Business City, Business Postal Code, Business State, Business Country, Business Web Page, Business Phone, Business Fax, Pager, Company, Job Title, Department, Office Location, and Notes. Using this sequence makes the information snap into the fields in Address Book without any remapping.

Here's an example using a comma-separated values (CSV) file:

1. Choose File ➢ Import ➢ Other Address Book. Address Book displays the Address Book Import Tool dialog box (see Figure 20.4).

FIGURE 20.4

In the Address Book
Import Tool dialog
box, select the type
of information you
want to import and
then click the
Import button.

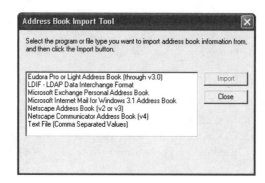

2. In the list box, choose the appropriate format. The example uses Text File (Comma Separated Values).

3. Click the Import button. Address Book displays the first CSV Import dialog box, which lets you select the file to import.

4. Either type in the name and path or click the Browse button to display the Open dialog box, specify the location and name as usual, and click the Open button.

5. Click the Next button. Address Book displays the second CSV Import dialog box (shown on the left in Figure 20.5).

FIGURE 20.5

In the second CSV
Import dialog box
(left), check and
change the field
mapping using the
Change Mapping
dialog box (right),
and then click the
Finish button.

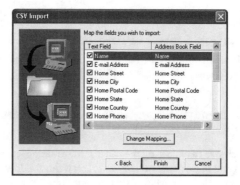
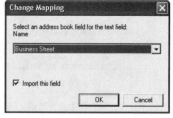

6. Check that each field in the data source (the first column) is *mapped* (matched) to an appropriate field in Address Book (the second column) and that each text field that you want to import has its check box selected:

   ◆ To change the mapping of a field, select it and click the Change Mapping button. Address Book displays the Change Mapping dialog box (shown on the right in Figure 20.5). In the drop-down list, select the target Address Book field, select the Import This Field check box, and click the OK button.

   ◆ If your data source doesn't have column headings, you'll have to look at it to see which field contains which information. If possible, open it in a spreadsheet program such as Excel, because doing so separates the information into separate columns, making it easier to read. If you don't have a spreadsheet program, open the data source in Notepad and count the commas. (If you have Word, open the data source in Word and convert it to a table.)

7. Click the Finish button to perform the import:

   ◆ If any of the information you're importing does not match the expected field, Address Book displays the Error Importing Contact dialog box, of which Figure 20.6 shows an example. Click the OK button to proceed or the Cancel button to cancel the whole import procedure. Select the Don't Show Me Error Messages Anymore check box if you want to suppress further error messages when proceeding.

FIGURE 20.6

By default, Address Book displays the Error Importing Contact dialog box to warn you when it encounters data it thinks is unsuitable for a field.

8. When Address Book has finished importing the data, it displays a message box telling you so. Close this dialog box and then click the Close button to close the Address Book Import Tool dialog box.

Double-check the resulting Address Book entries for duplicates and errors before you use them.

Exporting Information from Your Address Book

As you'd expect, you can also export information from Address Book so that you can import it into an organizer, database, or spreadsheet.

If the recipient program can read the WAB format, use that. Choose File ➤ Export ➤ Address Book (WAB), specify the filename and location in the Select Address Book File to Export To dialog box, and click the Save button. Address Book exports the information and displays a message box telling you that it has done so. Click the OK button to dismiss the message box, and you're done.

To export a single record, save it as a vCard. Choose File ➤ Export ➤ Business Card (vCard), specify the filename and location in the Export As Business Card (vCard) dialog box, and click the Save button.

To export your address book in a format other than WAB, use a CSV file as follows:

1. Choose File ➤ Export ➤ Other Address Book. Address Book displays the Address Book Export Tool dialog box.

2. In the list box, select the Text File (Comma Separated Values) entry.

3. Click the Export button. Address Book displays the first CSV Export dialog box.

4. In the Save Exported File As text box, enter the name under which to save the exported file. Either type in the name and path or click the Browse button, use the resulting Save As dialog box to specify the location and filename, and click the Save button.

5. Click the Next button. Address Book displays the second CSV Export dialog box (shown in Figure 20.7).

FIGURE 20.7

In the second CSV Export dialog box, select the fields you want to export and then click the Finish button.

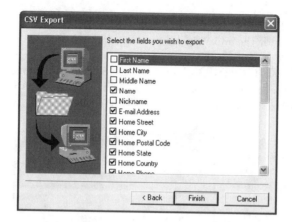

6. Select the fields you want to export. By default, the CSV Export dialog box does not select the check boxes for the First Name, Last Name, and Middle Name fields, because it lumps the names together into a single field (called Name), which it selects. If you need to have the individual fields as well, select their check boxes too.

7. Click the Finish button. Address Book exports the address book and displays a message box telling you that it has completed the export procedure. Click the OK button to dismiss the message box, then click the Close button to close the Address Book Export Tool dialog box.

You can now import the CSV file into your organizer, database, or spreadsheet.

Organizing Your Contacts into Folders and Groups

To prevent your contact list from growing to the length of the San Andreas fault, you can divide your contacts up among a number of folders. For example, in a home situation, you might create a folder to contain family members, one for friends, one for local businesses, another for emergency contacts, and so on. You can also create groups to help administer your contacts.

Normally, a folder actually contains a contact, while a group contains only a pointer to a contact. You *can* create contacts that reside only within groups, but usually you'll want to use groups mostly to organize contacts rather than contain them.

Creating a Folder

As you saw earlier in this chapter, Address Book starts you off with a Shared Contacts folder (shared with all the other users of the computer) and a Main Identity's Contacts folder (of which each user has one to her- or himself). Under each of these, you can add as many folders as you need to sort your contacts into logical containers.

To create a new folder, follow these steps:

1. Right-click the folder that will contain it (Shared Contacts or Main Identity's Contacts) in the Folders and Groups pane and choose New ➢ New Folder from the context menu. (Alternatively, select the folder and choose File ➢ New Folder, or press Ctrl+R.) Address Book displays a Properties dialog box.

2. Enter the name for the folder in the Folder Name text box.

   ◆ Address Book displays the folders in alphabetical order. To implement a specific order of your own, add numbering to the beginning of the folder names. To force a single folder to float to the top of the list without numbering, put a space at the beginning of its name.

3. Click the OK button. Address Book creates the folder.

You can then move contacts to the folder by dragging them from their current location and dropping them on the folder.

Deleting a Folder

To delete a folder, right-click it in the Folders and Groups pane and choose Delete from the context menu, then select the Yes button in the confirmation message box.

Deleting a folder deletes all the contacts it contains and is not undoable. Consider backing up Address Book before deleting a folder.

Creating a Group

To create a group, follow these steps:

1. Click the New button on the toolbar and choose New Group from the drop-down list (or choose File ➢ New Group or press Ctrl+G). Address Book displays the Properties dialog box for the group with the Group page displayed. Figure 20.8 shows an example.

FIGURE 20.8

Use the Properties dialog box for a group to define the group and add contacts to it.

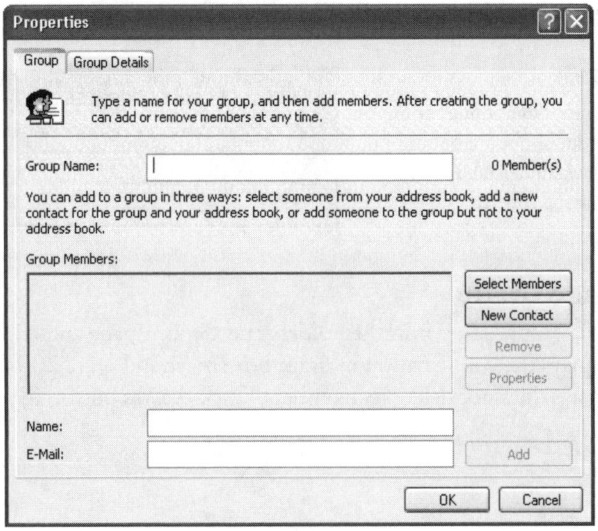

2. Enter the name for the group in the Group Name text box. This is the name that appears in the Folders and Groups pane.

3. Click the Select Members button to display the Select Group Members dialog box.

4. In the left-hand list box, select the contacts to add to the group and then click the Select button to transfer them to the group:

   ◆ Double-click a contact to add it to the Members list box.

   ◆ Use Shift+click and Ctrl+click to select multiple contacts at once.

   ◆ To remove a contact from the right-hand list box, right-click the contact and choose Remove from the context menu.

5. Click the OK button. Address Book closes the Select Group Members dialog box. The Group Members list box in the Properties dialog shows the members you added.

TIP *To add a contact to the group but not to Address Book, enter the contact's name and e-mail address in the Name text box and E-mail text box in the Properties dialog box and click the Add button. To add a contact to both the group and Address Book, click the New Contact button and create the contact as usual in the Properties dialog box for the contact.*

6. If you have details to add for the group (such as an address, phone number, or notes), click the Group Details tab to display the Group Details page, then enter the information there.

7. Click the OK button. Address Book closes the Properties dialog box for the group.

NOTE *You can check which groups a contact belongs to on the Other page of the contact's Properties dialog box.*

Removing a Contact from a Group

To remove a contact from a group, select the group in the Folders and Groups pane, then right-click the contact in the list box and choose Delete from the context menu. Address Book displays the confirmation dialog box shown in Figure 20.9 to let you know that you're removing the contact from the group rather than deleting them. Click the Yes button.

FIGURE 20.9

When you remove a contact from a group, Address Book checks to make sure you understand you're not deleting the contact.

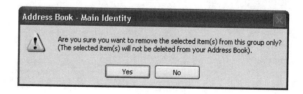

Deleting a Group

To delete a group, select it in the Folders and Groups pane and click the Delete button. Address Book displays the confirmation message box shown in Figure 20.10, reminding you that getting rid of the group does not delete its members. Click the Yes button if you want to proceed.

FIGURE 20.10

Address Book double-checks to make sure you want to delete a group.

Changing the Fields Displayed

By default, Address Book displays the Name, E-mail Address, Business Phone, and Home Phone columns. You can change any of these fields except the Name field or E-mail Address field by right-clicking its column heading and choosing a different field from the context menu of fields that appears.

Using Views

Address Book offers four views for scrutinizing your contacts: Details view (the default view), Large Icon view, Small Icon view, and List view. You'll recognize these views from the views in Windows Explorer—they're essentially the same. (Unfortunately—or perhaps otherwise—there's no Thumbnails view, so you can't assign a different picture to each contact.) Details view tends to be the most useful, because it puts the most information on-screen at the same time, but you may want to use Small Icon view or List view occasionally so that you can see a larger number of contacts at once.

To change view, choose View ➤ Large Icon, View ➤ Small Icon, View ➤ List, or View ➤ Details as appropriate.

Sorting Your Contacts

By default, Address Book sorts your contacts alphabetically by first name. If you're on a first-name basis with them, or have relatively few contacts, this works fine. If not, you'll probably need to sort your contacts into a different order sooner or later.

To sort the contacts by one of the columns displayed, click the column heading once for an ascending sort (alphabetical order) or twice for a descending sort (reverse alphabetical order).

To sort by last name, choose View ➤ Sort By ➤ Last Name. To restore the default first-name sorting, choose View ➤ Sort By ➤ First Name.

Sending Mail to a Contact

To send e-mail to a contact, right-click the contact's name and choose Action ➤ Send Mail from the context menu. Address Book activates Outlook Express and starts a new message to the contact you chose.

If the contact has no e-mail address, Address Book displays an exclamation message box alerting you to the problem and doesn't activate Outlook Express.

Finding a Forgotten Contact in Address Book

To access a contact whose name you remember in Address Book, you can type down through the list box until you reach the entry you want. If you can't remember the contact's name but can remember other information about the contact, use the Find feature to locate the contact as follows:

1. Click the Find People button on the toolbar, or choose Edit ➢ Find People, or press Ctrl+F, to display the Find People dialog box (shown in Figure 20.11 after a successful search).

FIGURE 20.11

Use the Find People dialog box to find a contact whose full name you can't remember. If it finds matches, you can work directly from the results.

2. In the Look In drop-down list, make sure Address Book is selected if you want to search Address Book. (The alternatives are to search information repositories such as Active Directory and online directory services.)

3. In the Name, E-mail, Address, Phone, and Other text boxes, enter such information as you can remember about the person:

   ◆ The Name, E-mail, Address, and Phone text boxes cause Address Book to search *all* name fields, all e-mail addresses, all address fields, and all phone fields for the contact.

   ◆ Each piece of information doesn't have to be complete: For example, you might enter only part of the last name in the Name text box and only an area code in the Phone text box.

   ◆ The more specific the information you enter, the fewer matches you'll get. If you enter information the contact record doesn't contain, you won't find the contact.

4. Click the Find Now button to perform the search. If it finds matches, the Find People dialog box displays a lower section containing them. If not, it displays a message box saying that it found no matches.

5. Click the Properties button to open the Properties dialog box for the contact. Click the Delete button to delete the contact. Or click the Close button to close the Find People dialog box.

Searching Internet Directories for People

If Address Book doesn't have the contact you need, you can search Active Directory or an Internet directory as follows:

1. Click the Find People button on the toolbar, or choose Edit ➤ Find People. Address Book displays the Find People dialog box.

2. In the Look In drop-down list in the Find People dialog box, select one of the directories: Active Directory, Bigfoot Internet Directory Service, VeriSign Internet Directory Service, WhoWhere Internet Directory Service, or one of the other directory services listed. The Find People dialog box reduces the number of fields on its People page to just the Name text box and the E-mail text box but displays an Advanced page as well (shown in Figure 20.12).

FIGURE 20.12

Use the Advanced page of the Find People dialog box to define criteria when searching for people on directory services.

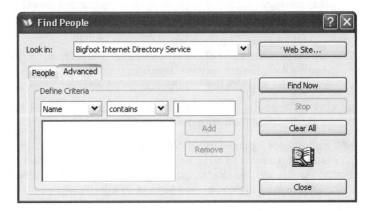

3. Use the Define Criteria group box on the Advanced page to define criteria for your search:

   ◆ In the first drop-down list, choose Name, E-mail, First Name, Last Name, or Organization as appropriate.

   ◆ In the second drop-down list, choose the appropriate condition: Contains, Is, Starts With, Ends With, or Sounds Like. (The Sounds Like item can give you some peculiar results, but it's worth trying when all else fails.)

   ◆ In the text box, enter the text for the criterion. For example, you might specify **Last Name Starts With Rob** to find people with last names such as Robson, Roberts, or Robertson.

   ◆ Click the Add button to add the criterion to the list box. Then define other criteria as necessary by repeating these steps.

4. Click the Find Now button to execute the search.

NOTE   *If the Web Site button is available, you can click it to open an Internet Explorer window showing the directory's website, which may offer further search options.*

EXPERT KNOWLEDGE: ADDING AND CONFIGURING DIRECTORY SERVICES

If you often need to search for people on directory services, you can add to Address Book's preconfigured list of directory services to increase your chances of finding who you're looking for. You can also remove directory services that you don't find useful. And if you use more than one directory service to check names when sending e-mail, you can change the order in which Address Book and Outlook Express check the directory services.

To add a directory service,

1. Choose Tools ➤ Accounts. Address Book displays the Directory Service page of the Internet Accounts dialog box.

2. Click the Add button. Address Book starts the Internet Directory Server Name feature of the Internet Connection Wizard.

3. Enter the address of the directory server (for example, `ldap.yahoo.com` for the Yahoo directory server) in the Internet Directory (LDAP) Server text box.

4. If you have to log on to your LDAP server before you can use it, select the My LDAP Server Requires Me to Log On check box. When you click the Next button, the Internet Connection Wizard displays the Internet Directory Server Logon panel. Enter your account name and password, and select the Log On Using Secure Password Authentication check box if necessary.

5. Click the Next button. The Internet Connection Wizard displays the Check E-mail Addresses panel. Select the Yes option button if you want to use this directory service to check e-mail addresses. (The No option button is selected by default. This isn't a good idea for conventional e-mail use.)

6. Click the Next button to proceed to the Congratulations panel of the Internet Connection Wizard. Click the Finish button. The wizard closes itself.

Address Book adds the directory service to the list on the Directory Service page of the Internet Accounts dialog box under a name based on its address. To give the directory service a descriptive name, select the directory service and click the Properties button to display its Properties dialog box (shown below). Enter the descriptive name in the upper text box and click the OK button.

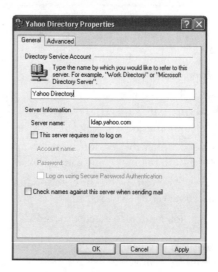

Continued on next page

> **EXPERT KNOWLEDGE: ADDING AND CONFIGURING DIRECTORY SERVICES** *(continued)*
>
> On the General page of the Properties dialog box, you can also change whether you log on to the LDAP server, your account name and password, whether you use Secure Password Authentication, and whether Outlook Express checks names against the server when sending e-mail. The Advanced page offers further options, including the maximum number of matches to return from the directory service and whether to use a search base (a grouping) in the directory service.
>
> To change the order in which Outlook Express uses the directory servers when checking names against them, click the Set Order button in the Internet Accounts dialog box. In the resulting Directory Services Order dialog box, use the Move Up button and Move Down button to arrange the accounts into the appropriate order, and then click the OK button.

Printing Out Your Address Book

As you'd expect, you can print out your Address Book entries by issuing a Print command—for example, File ➢ Print.

To print only some contact records, select them before issuing the Print command. Then make sure that Address Book has selected the Selection option button rather than the All option button in the Print Range group box in the Print dialog box.

The Print dialog box also contains a Print Style group box that contains three option buttons for printing different amounts of information for those contact records:

Memo   Prints all the information in the contact records. Because a contact record can contain a bunch of information, this option is best used for selected records only.

Business Card   Prints a business-card format that contains the contact's full name, job title, company name, business address, telephone numbers (all except IP Phone), and e-mail addresses (all).

Phone List   Prints the full name of the contact and all their phone numbers (except IP Phone) in an alphabetically separated list.

Copying or Moving Your Address Book

By default, your Address Book is stored in the file *username*.wab in the folder \Application Data\ Microsoft\Address Book\ in your user profile. If you're not sure where your Address Book is stored, choose Help ➢ About Address Book from Address Book and check the entry in the File text box in the About Address Book dialog box.

You can copy your Address Book by copying this WAB file, but for many purposes it's easier to export your Address Book to a WAB file by following the procedure described in the section "Exporting Information from Your Address Book," earlier in this chapter.

To move your Address Book to a different folder (for example, to keep it on another computer), move the WAB file by using standard Explorer techniques, then run Registry Editor and change the value of the (Default) value entry in the HKEY_CURRENT_USER\Software\Microsoft\Wab\WAB4\Wab File Name\ folder. You need to change this value entry because if you don't, Address Book checks the default location, finds that you don't have an Address Book, and creates a new one for you.

EXPERT KNOWLEDGE: RECOVERING FROM A CORRUPT ADDRESS BOOK

If you back up your data as described in Chapter 17 (and you should), your Address Book is one of the key files to include in the backup. But sometimes you may need to recover from a corrupt or damaged Address Book file. To do so, check your \Application Data\Microsoft\Address Book\ folder for a file with the WA~ extension. This is a backup of the WAB file.

If you find the WA~ file, rename the WAB file to another extension (for example, WA1). Then rename the WA~ file to the WAB extension and run Address Book to see if the backup file contained usable data.

Up Next

This chapter has discussed how to use Address Book for storing and managing contact information. As you've seen, Address Book is limited compared to professional contact management packages, but it provides enough capabilities for most home and home-office use. And the price is right.

You'll hardly have been able to miss that many of Address Book's features are designed for use with the e-mail capabilities of Outlook Express, which form the topic of the next chapter.

Chapter 21

E-mail with Outlook Express

THIS CHAPTER DISCUSSES HOW to use the e-mail features of Outlook Express, the powerful e-mail and newsreader program built into XP. (The next chapter discusses how to use the newsreader features.)

This chapter covers the following topics:

◆ Setting up e-mail with Outlook Express
◆ Configuring Outlook Express
◆ Creating and sending e-mail messages
◆ Reading e-mail messages
◆ Replying to an e-mail message
◆ Managing your e-mail messages
◆ Filtering your messages
◆ Using multiple e-mail accounts
◆ Creating and using identities

Before you can do anything with Outlook Express, you need to configure it to work with your ISP, so that's the first order of business. After that, the chapter shows you how to create and send e-mail messages; read e-mail messages; send and receive attachments; and use the multiple identities (personalities or roles) that Outlook Express supports to maintain multiple e-mail accounts—for example, one for business use and one for personal use. Along the way, you'll learn how to filter your e-mail, how to block e-mail from certain people, and how to implement e-mail security.

Information You Need to Get Started

To work through this chapter, you'll need to have a modem or network connection to the Internet and an account with an ISP or e-mail provider. You'll need to know the following information: your logon name and password, your e-mail address, your incoming mail server and its type (POP, IMAP, or HTTP), your outgoing mail server, and whether to use Secure Password Authentication (SPA).

For the next chapter, you'll also need to know the name for your ISP's news server, whether you need to log on to it, and (if you do log on) whether you need to use Secure Password Authentication. So if you're asking your ISP for information, include those questions.

EXPERT KNOWLEDGE: CHANGING YOUR DEFAULT E-MAIL PROGRAM

Outlook Express is included with XP (at this writing) and has been included with most other versions of Windows for the last few years, so it's widely used—but it's far from the only game in town. Other popular e-mail programs include Eudora (from Qualcomm, Inc.; www.eudora.com); Netscape Mail (from Netscape Communications; www.netscape.com); and Microsoft's heavier-duty e-mail program, Outlook (which also comes bundled with Microsoft Office).

If you've installed another e-mail program, you may need to instruct XP which one to use as the default e-mail program. To do so, right-click the Start button and choose Properties from the context menu to display the Taskbar and Start Menu Properties dialog box, then click the Customize button. In the E-mail drop-down list on the General page of the Customize Start Menu dialog box, select the program, then click the OK buttons to close first the Customize Start Menu dialog box and then the Taskbar and Start Menu Properties dialog box.

Starting Outlook Express

In XP's default configuration, the easiest way to start Outlook Express is to choose Start ➤ E-mail.

Alternatively, create a shortcut to Outlook Express on your Quick Launch toolbar, on your Desktop, or in another handy location. If you want to run Outlook Express automatically each time you start XP—not a bad idea, given how vital e-mail is these days—put a shortcut to Outlook Express in your Startup group.

TROUBLESHOOTING: OUTLOOK EXPRESS WON'T START AFTER UPGRADE TO XP

If Outlook Express crashes with the error "Outlook Express has encountered a problem and needs to close" when you first try to launch it after upgrading from Windows 98 or Windows Me to XP, the Identities key in the Registry may have become corrupted. To repair this, you need to perform a detailed series of steps. For instructions, see Q314422 in the Microsoft Knowledge Base (support.microsoft.com).

Setting Up E-mail with Outlook Express

The first time you start Outlook Express, you'll need to set it up to work with your Internet connection and ISP. Follow these steps:

1. Choose Start ➤ E-mail. XP starts the Internet Connection Wizard, which displays the Your Name page.

2. In the Display Name text box, enter your name the way you want it to appear in outgoing messages. (For example, you might choose to use your full name with middle initial, or you might prefer to use your diminutive and your last name. Or you might choose an alias.)

3. Click the Next button. The wizard displays the Internet E-mail Address page.

4. Enter your e-mail address in the E-mail Address text box.

5. Click the Next button. The wizard displays the E-mail Server Names page (shown in Figure 21.1):

- ◆ In the My Incoming Mail Server Is a *XXX* Server drop-down list, choose POP3, IMAP, or HTTP, as appropriate for your ISP. (If you're curious about these acronyms and their implications, see the next sidebar.)

- ◆ In the Incoming Mail (POP3, IMAP or HTTP) Server text box, enter the name of your ISP's incoming mail server.

- ◆ In the Outgoing Mail (SMTP) Server text box, enter the name of your ISP's outgoing mail server.

FIGURE 21.1

On the E-mail Server Names page of the Internet Connection Wizard, specify the e-mail servers you'll use.

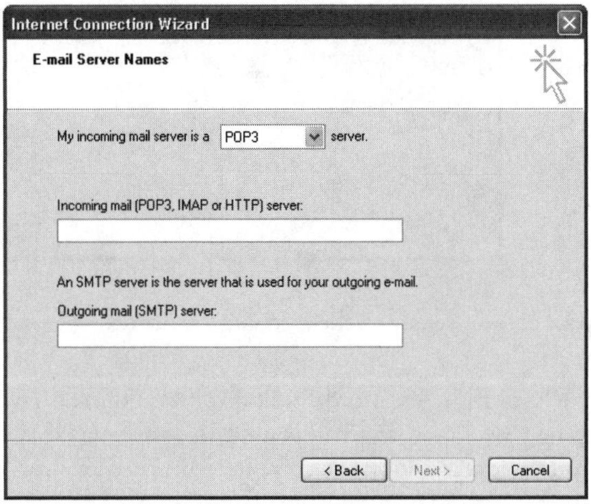

- ◆ If you entered a Hotmail address on the Internet E-mail Address page, the wizard pre-fills the E-mail Server Names page with Hotmail information, as shown in Figure 21.2. You shouldn't need to change these settings.

FIGURE 21.2

The Internet Connection Wizard automatically enters server information if you specified a Hotmail address.

6. Click the Next button. The wizard displays the Internet Mail Logon page (shown in Figure 21.3).

FIGURE 21.3

On the Internet
Mail Logon page of
the Internet Connec-
tion Wizard dialog
box, specify your
account name and
password.

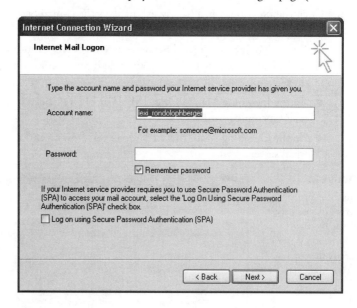

7. Enter your account name in the Account Name text box and your password in the Password text box.

8. Select the Remember Password check box if you think it's wise. (Using this option saves you time typing your password when you retrieve your mail, but it means that anyone who can access your user account on the computer can check your mail, too.)

9. Select the Log On Using Secure Password Authentication (SPA) check box if you need to use SPA.

10. Click the Next button. The wizard displays its Congratulations page, telling you that you've successfully entered all the information needed to set up your e-mail account.

11. Click the Finish button. The wizard closes itself and launches Outlook Express. If you just set up a Hotmail account, Outlook Express offers to display a list of available folders for the account. Click the Yes button.

EXPERT KNOWLEDGE: POP3, IMAP, HTTP, AND SMTP

POP3, IMAP, HTTP, SMTP—that's a pretty dish of acronyms to set before a king. What do they mean, and how much should you worry about them?

To answer the second question first, you shouldn't worry about them too much beyond giving Outlook Express the correct information. Usually you won't have a choice of server types—your ISP will support either POP3 or IMAP for incoming mail and will use SMTP for outgoing mail. If you use Hotmail, or a similar web-based e-mail service that can work with Outlook Express, both your incoming mail server and your outgoing mail server will be HTTP.

Continued on next page

But you're waiting for an answer to the first question: What do these terms mean?

HTTP   Hypertext Transfer Protocol, the protocol on which much of the Web is based.

SMTP   Simple Mail Transfer Protocol, the protocol used for sending e-mail. SMTP is part of the TCP/IP protocol suite (which is largely responsible for the running of the Internet).

POP3   Post Office Protocol, the common-or-garden variety Internet mail-server protocol for storing and passing on mail. POP3 works well and is very widely used, but it doesn't have advanced features that IMAP has. POP3's major limitation is that when you check your mail, you have to download all the messages waiting for you. You can leave copies of all your messages on the server, but each time you download them, you download everything waiting for you. (Tech moment: POP3 actually uses SMTP to move the messages from the one server to another, and from the server to the client.)

IMAP   Internet Mail Access Protocol, a newer protocol than POP3 and one that has more features. IMAP offers strong authentication and supports Kerberos security, but from the average user's point of view, IMAP's big advantage is that it's smart enough to allow you to manage your mail on the server. You can download just the headers of the messages so that you can decide which you want to download, delete messages off the server without reading them, and shuttle them between different folders on the server. These capabilities make IMAP especially useful for checking mail from multiple computers—for example, when traveling.

From the user's point of view, IMAP offers many advantages over POP3. (The only disadvantage is that you may have to do more configuration with IMAP than with POP3, depending on how smart your mail client is.) Unfortunately, many ISPs aren't enthusiastic about implementing IMAP because doing so would probably result in a huge amount more mail lying around on their servers than is currently on them (which is already more than enough). Given that spam still seems to be increasing, and that legitimate (nonspam) advertising e-mail messages seem to be getting not only more frequent but also larger, *and* that more people are using e-mail and sending more messages, you can understand their concern.

Getting a Hotmail or MSN Account

If you don't have an e-mail account (but you do have an Internet connection), web-based e-mail such as Hotmail and MSN (Microsoft Network) can be attractive. As their name suggests, web-based e-mail services let you access your e-mail from any web browser, so you can easily check your e-mail from just about any computer—from a friend's computer, from an Internet café, or (perhaps most popular) from a computer at work.

Hotmail, owned by Microsoft and more or less integrated with MSN (or is it that MSN is integrated with Hotmail? It's kinda hard to tell) is one of the biggest free e-mail services, but it's far from being the only game in town. Other free e-mail services you might want to consider include those offered by Netscape (`www.netscape.com`), Nettaxi.com (`www.nettaxi.com`), SoftHome.net (`www.softhome.net`), and HotPOP (`www.hotpop.com`). HushMail (`www.hushmail.com`) is noted for its security features for inter-HushMail messages (messages to non-HushMail users don't have the security), but it's also widely used for conventional e-mail. (Yahoo! Mail, one of the most popular free e-mail services, started charging for its service in April 2002.)

Because they're owned and operated by Microsoft, Hotmail and MSN offer strong interoperability with Outlook Express. Accessing your e-mail through a web browser is great for using assorted computers, but it's much more convenient to use Outlook Express's features for downloading Hotmail and MSN messages to your Inbox on your regular computer. Some other web-based e-mail services offer similar functionality; others are browser-only.

If you don't have an e-mail account and decide Hotmail or MSN would be a good place to have one, point your web browser at the Hotmail website (`www.hotmail.com`) or the MSN website and follow the sign-up procedure. These procedures are straightforward and almost identical, but the following points are worth noting:

- Because many million Hotmail and MSN accounts have been created (though many have been abandoned by their users, and many others have been closed by Hotmail and MSN), snappy usernames are in short supply. Be prepared to get creative with underscores to get something resembling the name you want.

- Hotmail passwords can include only letters and numbers—they can't include symbols—so you'll have to work harder to create a secure password. Make the effort, because you don't want anyone breaking into your Hotmail account. (Hotmail may be free, but it shouldn't be easy.) MSN passwords can include "standard" symbols (but not spaces or international characters), which gives you more flexibility.

- Hotmail encourages you to list yourself in the Hotmail Member Directory and register yourself in the Internet White Pages. MSN encourages you to list yourself in the Hotmail Member Directory. These aren't quite the Internet equivalent of being listed or unlisted in the phone book, but they come close enough for a conventional comparison. Some people want to be listed; others don't. It's up to you.

- Worse, Hotmail encourages you to flood your Inbox by signing up for receiving Special Offers and newsletters. You don't have to be all that cynical to see these Special Offers as junk mail. Some of the newsletters can be worthwhile—if you really want to read them. Worst of all, Hotmail even sends you unsolicited e-mail messages of its own.

- The user agreements are vigorous enough to be worth reading carefully. For example, Hotmail users agree not to send spam from their accounts—and to pay Microsoft $5 for each piece of spam they send if actual damages for spamming can't be reasonably calculated.

- The Inbox Protector feature lets you specify filtering for messages so that you can keep some unwanted messages out of your Inbox. This feature is only partly effective, but it's better than nothing, and is well worth using.

- Both Hotmail and MSN sign-up procedures suggest you share your e-mail address, your first and last names, and your other registration information with .NET Passport–enabled sites. Before choosing to do so, weigh carefully the benefits of sharing this information automatically with sites against the cost of needlessly advertising your presence. In many cases, it makes more sense to sign in manually to sites that demand to know your e-mail address, name, or other details.

To help remind people to keep up their accounts, Hotmail and MSN mark as "inactive" any user accounts that are left unused for more than 30 days. When an account is marked as inactive, all its messages, folders, and addresses are deleted.

NOTE   *At this writing, both Hotmail and MSN offer free accounts. But each tries to "up-sell" you to a paid account that costs $19.95 per year, doesn't expire if you neglect it, offers you more space for e-mail and MSN Communities (discussed briefly in Chapter 25), and automatically scans all e-mail attachments. Beyond the obvious disadvantage of your having to pay for the account, these paid accounts have the further disadvantage that Hotmail or MSN gets to associate your .NET Passport with your verifiable credit-card information, making your .NET Passport an identifier that points to you personally.*

The Outlook Express Screen

Once you've configured Outlook Express, and thereafter when you start it, it displays your Start page, as shown in Figure 21.4.

FIGURE 21.4

The Start page provides links to the main features of Outlook Express.

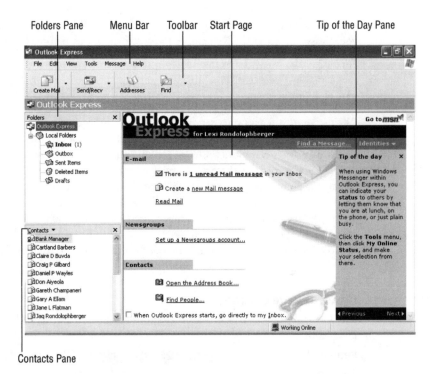

TIP   *If you have a small monitor, get rid of the Tip of the Day pane by clicking the close button in its upper-right corner to give yourself more room on the Start page.*

If you prefer to start your Outlook Express session in the Inbox rather than on the Start page, select the When Outlook Express Starts, Go Directly to My Inbox check box at the bottom of the Start page. Thereafter, when you start Outlook Express, it displays the Inbox first.

If the Internet Connection Wizard didn't persuade you to enter your password and have Outlook Express remember it, you'll need to log on when you launch Outlook Express. Figure 21.5 shows an example of the Logon dialog box you'll see. This Logon dialog box is for Hotmail.

FIGURE 21.5

If you didn't save
your password, you'll
need to enter it in
the Logon dialog
box in order to log
on to the mail
servers.

If the tediousness of having to log on each time lulls your fears about the inadvisability of saving your password, select the Remember Password check box before clicking the OK button in the Logon dialog box.

Choosing Options for Outlook Express

At this point, you *could* start sending e-mail straight away, but it's a good idea to configure Outlook Express first. This section discusses the configuration options that Outlook Express offers.

Because of its complexity, Outlook Express has a host of options, many of which it's a good idea to know about. Because there are so many options, you may prefer not to read through this section in full at this point—it's uncomfortably long unless you're sitting very easy and in no hurry. That's fine; go ahead and start using e-mail, and see how the default settings suit you. Just know that if you want to change an aspect of Outlook Express's behavior, you probably can. Return to this section, find the appropriate option, and set it.

To configure Outlook Express, choose Tools ➤ Options. Outlook Express displays the Options dialog box. Then choose settings as appropriate.

General Page Options

The General page of the Options dialog box (shown on the left in Figure 21.6) contains three sets of options.

FIGURE 21.6

The General page
(left) and Read page
(right) of the
Options dialog box

GENERAL AREA

The General area of the General page contains four options:

When Starting, Go Directly to My "Inbox" Folder check box   This check box performs the same function as the When Outlook Express Starts, Go Directly to My Inbox check box on the Start page. Select it if you want Outlook Express to start in your Inbox; clear it to make Outlook Express start with the Start page.

Notify Me if There Are Any New Newsgroups check box   Leave this check box selected (as it is by default) if you want Outlook Express to notify you of new newsgroups on the news server you're using. This option is a double-edged sword: It may be good to learn about new newsgroups that might interest you, but new newsgroups are created so often that leaving this option selected means that Outlook Express will offer you new newsgroups every time you fire up the newsreader. This gets old fast.

Automatically Display Folders with Unread Messages check box   Leave this check box selected (as it is by default) if you want Outlook Express to automatically display e-mail folders and newsgroup folders that contain messages you haven't read. Most people find this option helpful. If you don't, clear this check box.

Automatically Log On to Windows Messenger check box   Leave this check box selected (as it is by default) if you want to start Windows Messenger automatically when you start Outlook Express. If Messenger is already running, this option does nothing.

SEND/RECEIVE MESSAGES AREA

The Send/Receive Messages area of the General page contains four options:

Play Sound when New Messages Arrive check box   Leave this check box selected (as it is by default) to have Outlook Express automatically play a sound when it receives a new message. Clear this check box if you prefer to be uninterrupted; the Outlook Express status bar will still indicate any new messages that come in.

Send and Receive Messages at Startup check box   Leave this check box selected (as it is by default) if you want Outlook Express to send any pending mail and receive any incoming mail when you start it. Clear this check box if you want to choose when to send and receive mail.

Check for New Messages Every *NN* Minutes check box and text box   Leave this check box selected (as it is by default) if you want Outlook Express to check for messages at regular intervals. Specify the interval in the text box (the default is 30 minutes). Clear this check box if you prefer to check for messages manually.

TIP   *If you run Windows Messenger, it alerts you to incoming messages on your Hotmail account or MSN account.*

If My Computer Is Not Connected at This Time drop-down list   If you leave the Check for New Messages check box selected, use this drop-down list to specify what you want Outlook Express to do if your computer isn't connected to the Internet when Outlook Express needs to send and receive mail. Your options are Do Not Connect, Connect Only when Not Working Offline, and Connect Even when Working Offline. Use the second option when your computer is disconnected from its Internet connection (for example, if it's a laptop and you're on the move). Use the third option for dial-up Internet connections.

DEFAULT MESSAGING PROGRAMS AREA

The Default Messaging Programs area of the General page notes whether Outlook Express is your default mail handler and news handler. In the figure, Outlook Express is both; but if it's not, you can click the Make Default button to make it the default.

Read Page Options

The Read page of the Options dialog box (shown on the right in Figure 21.6) contains three areas.

READING MESSAGES AREA

The Reading Messages area of the Read page contains the following options:

Mark Message Read after Displaying for *NN* Seconds check box and text box   Leave this check box selected (as it is by default) if you want Outlook Express to mark a message as having been read when you've displayed it for the specified number of seconds in the Preview pane. Adjust the number of seconds if you want to be able to browse quickly through messages in the Preview pane without Outlook Express marking them as read. Clear this check box if you prefer to mark messages as read manually.

Automatically Expand Grouped Messages check box   Select this check box (which is cleared by default) if you want Outlook Express to automatically expand threads of messages in newsgroups. Clear this check box to have Outlook Express display just the original message.

Automatically Download Message when Viewing in the Preview Pane check box   Leave this check box selected (as it is by default) if you want Outlook Express to download the body of a message when you select its header in the message list. Most people find this option useful—but be warned that you'll also get any attachments the message has, which can slow things down greatly if you have a dial-up Internet connection. If you don't, clear this check box and press the spacebar to display the body for the selected header.

Show ToolTips in the Message List for Clipped Items check box   Leave this check box selected (as it is by default) to have Outlook Express display a tooltip over a message header when the header is too long to fit in its column. To display the tooltip, hover the mouse pointer over the header.

Highlight Watched Messages drop-down list   Select the color you want to use for watched conversations. (More on this later in the chapter.)

NEWS AREA

The News area of the Read page contains two options:

Get *NN* Headers at a Time check box and text box   These controls let you choose between downloading the specified number of headers from the newsgroup (if there are that many; otherwise you get however many there are) and downloading all the messages. If you frequent very busy newsgroups, keep this check box selected (as it is by default), and reduce the number in the text box if necessary.

Mark All Messages As Read when Exiting a Newsgroup check box   Select this check box (which is cleared by default) if you want Outlook Express to mark all messages in a newsgroup as read when you exit the newsgroup. Clear this check box to have Outlook Express mark the messages as read only when you've read them. This check box is useful if you tend to browse newsgroups that have a high volume of traffic with many posts that you don't want to read or manually mark as read but that you want Outlook Express to know that you've dealt with.

FONTS AREA

This area contains two buttons:

◆   The Fonts button displays the Fonts dialog box, in which you can choose font settings for reading messages. For example, you might increase the font size or choose a different font.

◆   The International Settings button displays the International Read Settings dialog box, in which you can specify whether to use default encoding for all incoming messages. You shouln't need to do this unless you find yourself coming up against apparently garbled messages that use different language encoding.

Receipts Page Options

The Receipts page of the Options dialog box (shown on the left in Figure 21.7) contains three areas.

REQUESTING READ RECEIPTS AREA

The Requesting Read Receipts area of the Receipts page contains only one option, but it's an important one: the Request a Read Receipt for All Sent Messages check box.

FIGURE 21.7

On the Receipts page of the Options dialog box (left), choose options for requesting and returning read receipts. For secure receipts, click the Secure Receipts button and work in the Secure Receipt Options dialog box (right).

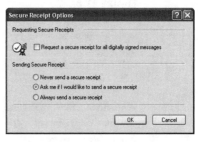

Select this check box (which is cleared by default) if you want to try to get a notification of when the recipient opens ("reads") the message. Whether you receive a receipt depends on whether the recipient has chosen to send receipts. It may also depend on their ISP's server software, though these days it's more likely to work than it did a few years ago.

If you want to request receipts only on certain messages you send, leave this check box cleared and choose Tools ➤ Request Read Receipt from the New Message window when composing a message for which you want a receipt. Similarly, if you want to request receipts on all but a few messages you send, select this check box and choose Tools ➤ Request Read Receipt from the New Message window to turn off the request on any given message.

A read receipt appears as a regular message in your Inbox, with the subject *Read:* and the original subject (for example, *Read: Dinner at 8?* for a message with the subject "Dinner at 8?") and details of when the message was sent and when it was read.

RETURNING READ RECEIPTS AREA

The Returning Read Receipts area of the Receipts page contains three option buttons and a check box for specifying how Outlook Express deals with requests you receive for read receipts.

Select the Never Send a Read Receipt option button, the Notify Me for Each Read Receipt Request option button (the default setting), or the Always Send a Read Receipt option button as appropriate to your needs. If you select the Always Send a Read Receipt option button, you can select the Unless It Is Sent to a Mailing List and My Name Is Not on the To or Cc Lines of the Message check box to prevent you from sending read receipts to mailing lists. Sending these receipts will annoy everyone on the group if they're not filtered out by software or by humans, so this check box is selected by default (and comes highly recommended).

If you select the Notify Me for Each Read Receipt Request option button, you get to choose whether to send the receipt. When you open a message with a request for a read receipt, Outlook Express displays the Outlook Express dialog box shown in Figure 21.8. Click the Yes button or the No button as appropriate to the message and your temper.

FIGURE 21.8

This Outlook Express dialog box appears when you read a message that has a request for a read receipt.

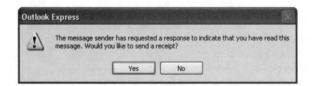

WARNING *Read receipts aren't the only way that someone can track that you've read a message. Instead (or in tandem), they can include in an HTML-formatted message a hyperlink to a graphic or other content on a website. When Outlook Express goes to retrieve that graphic or content in order to display it to you, the sender of the message will know that you've read the message. (If you display the message multiple times, causing multiple downloads of the data, they'll know that too.)*

SECURE RECEIPTS AREA

The Secure Receipts area of the Receipts page contains only the Secure Receipts button. If you want to receive secure receipts for digitally signed messages you send, click the Secure Receipts button. Outlook Express displays the Secure Receipt Options dialog box (shown on the right in Figure 21.7), which contains similar options to the Returning Read Receipts area, except for secure receipts. Choose the options you want and click the OK button.

Send Page Options

The Send page of the Options dialog box (shown in Figure 21.9) contains three areas, as discussed in the following sections.

FIGURE 21.9

The Send page of the Options dialog box

SENDING AREA

The Sending area of the Send page contains the following options:

Save Copy of Sent Messages in the "Sent Items" Folder check box Leave this check box selected (as it is by default) to have Outlook Express save a copy of each message you send in the Sent Items folder. Clear this check box if you don't want to keep copies of messages you send.

Send Messages Immediately check box Leave this check box selected (as it is by default) if you want Outlook Express to send messages immediately rather than put them in your Outbox until you issue a Send and Receive command.

Automatically Put People I Reply To in My Address Book check box Leave this check box selected (as it is by default) if you want Outlook Express to create Address Book entries for any person whose message you reply to who doesn't already have an entry. This option can be a labor saver, but it can also pack your Address Book with useless entries consisting of just an e-mail address. If you prefer to add Address Book entries manually (for example, if you send replies to people you don't want in your Address Book), clear this check box.

WARNING *Two quick warnings about the Automatically Put People I Reply To in My Address Book option. First, if you make the mistake of replying to spam (either to buy or to request your removal from the spammer's list), this option will add the spammer's address to Address Book too. Second, if someone who already has a contact entry in your Address Book writes to you using an e-mail address other than their usual one, you'll get a duplicate entry for them that you'll later need to weed out of your Address Book to keep it current and accurate. This gets old fast.*

Automatically Complete E-mail Addresses when Composing check box   Leave this check box selected (as it is by default) if you want Outlook Express to attempt to help you out by suggesting e-mail addresses from your Address Book to match addresses you type in the To, Cc, and Bcc fields in message windows. This option can be helpful, but it doesn't suit everyone. If it annoys you, turn it off so that you can type the addresses in peace.

Include Message in Reply check box   Leave this check box selected (as it is by default) to include the message in the reply. Clear this check box to create blank replies.

Reply to Messages Using the Format in Which They Were Sent check box   Leave this check box selected (as it is by default) to have Outlook Express create replies in the same format—plain text or HTML—as the message. This option is intended to help prevent you from sending HTML messages to people who prefer text, and vice versa, and is usually a good idea. Clear this check box to send all messages in the format you specify in the Mail Sending Format area.

MAIL SENDING FORMAT AREA

In this area, select the HTML option button or the Plain Text option button to specify which format to use for mail you send. This setting is overridden by the Reply to Messages Using the Format in Which They Were Sent option if you selected its check box.

If you want to tweak the settings for the format you choose, click the HTML Settings button or the Plain Text Settings button. The HTML Settings dialog box (shown on the left in Figure 21.10) contains the following settings:

Encode Text Using drop-down list   If necessary, change this setting from Quoted Printable (the default setting) to None or Base 64. (You shouldn't need to change this setting.)

Allow 8-Bit Characters in Headers check box   Select this check box (which is cleared by default) if you want Outlook Express to display foreign character sets, double-byte character sets, and extended ASCII characters in the header without encoding. If you don't know what these character sets are, leave this check box cleared, and Outlook Express encodes these characters in the header.

EXPERT KNOWLEDGE: SHOULD YOU USE PLAIN TEXT OR HTML? AND WHAT ABOUT STATIONERY?

When the Internet was young, all e-mail was plain text, because that was all that e-mail programs were designed to send. Plain-text messages were as plain as the term suggests, but they were small, and they traveled quickly through Internet servers and the wires. Then HTML mail was developed.

The advantages of HTML formatting (also called rich-text formatting) are clear: You can add to your messages not only formatting (such as colors, bulleted lists, and paragraph styles) but also hyperlinks, graphics, and background colors. By using HTML formatting, you can create messages that pack far greater punch than plain-text messages. From the recipient's point of view, the mail can look more or less like a web page, full of color, light, and impact.

Continued on next page

Provided, of course, that the recipient can receive HTML mail. If they can receive only plain-text e-mail, they'll receive a plain-text version of your message plus a text version containing all the HTML codes. If the message contained pictures, they'll come through as attachments, and the recipient will need to view them separately. The resulting message will look pretty sorry, and all your effort in formatting it will be wasted. So it's not a great idea to send HTML mail to someone who can receive only plain-text messages.

These days, many (perhaps most) e-mail programs can receive HTML mail and display it accurately; but quite a few cannot. If you receive HTML mail from someone, you can be sure that their e-mail client can handle HTML, so you're safe sending them an HTML reply. And if you know the recipient is using Outlook Express, you can feel free to send HTML mail. But if you know that someone is using plain-text e-mail, don't send them HTML mail if you can avoid it. Simple enough—but if you're used to sending HTML mail, it's easy to forget that some people won't be able to read it, especially when you're sending messages to multiple recipients.

So—much of the time, you're probably safe in sending HTML mail. But think before you add gratuitous formatting to your messages. Just because you can add, say, a picture or a background color to your messages doesn't mean that you should. Use these features only if they will enhance the recipient's reading or understanding of your message. This applies in spades to colorful stationery, which tends to be more appropriate to personal settings than business settings. For example, if you wrote to your bank, you'd probably use regular paper (or letterhead) rather than a colorful greeting card. Likewise, if you send your bank e-mail, use no stationery or simple stationery rather than inappropriately colorful stationery.

Last, remember that HTML messages are larger than plain-text messages, particularly if you stuff them with finery. Anyone who has a slow Internet connection probably won't welcome an HTML message bloated with stationery and pictures where a humbler text message would have sufficed.

Send Pictures with Messages check box   Leave this check box selected (as it is by default) if you want Outlook Express to send pictures or background images included in the message with the message. Clear this check box if you don't want to send pictures (Outlook Express includes a reference to the picture instead) or if the recipients will already have access to the pictures.

Indent Message on Reply check box   Leave this check box selected (as it is by default) if you want Outlook Express to indent the text of a message to which you're replying. Usually, indenting the original message is a good idea, because it enables the recipient to distinguish it from your reply. If you clear this check box, Outlook Express left-aligns the original message.

Automatically Wrap Text at *NN* Characters, when Sending text box   This option is available only if you choose the None setting in the Encode Text Using drop-down list. Set the number of characters at which to wrap the lines of text in outgoing messages. This is so that they don't wrap when displayed in text-only e-mail clients or when indented in replies. As a standard line length for text-only e-mail clients is 80 characters, the default setting of 76 characters allows for an indent of three or four characters on a reply before wrapping occurs. To allow two indentations without wrapping, choose a setting of 72 characters.

FIGURE 21.10

Use the HTML Settings dialog box (left) or the Plain Text Settings dialog box (right) to specify formatting for your messages.

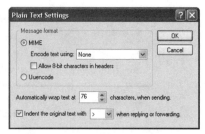

The Plain Text Settings dialog box (shown on the right in Figure 21.10) lets you choose between sending messages in MIME format and Uuencode format. (See the next sidebar for a quick explanation of MIME and Uuencode.) If you choose MIME, you can specify text encoding and whether to allow 8-bit characters in headers, just as you could in the HTML Settings dialog box. For either MIME or Uuencode, you can specify the number of characters for text wrapping. The Plain Text Settings dialog box offers a different indentation option:

Indent the Original Text with *Character* when Replying or Forwarding check box   Leave this check box selected (as it is by default) if you want to indent original text in replies and forwarded messages. Select a character—>, |, or :—in the drop-down list. Clear this check box if you want original text to appear flush left.

NEWS SENDING FORMAT AREA

The News Sending Format area of the Send page essentially duplicates the Mail Sending Format area, except that its controls apply to news rather than mail. Select the HTML option button or the Plain Text option button as appropriate, and use the HTML Settings button or the Plain Text Settings button to set options for that format.

EXPERT KNOWLEDGE: MIME AND UUENCODE

MIME is the acronym for Multipurpose Internet Mail Extension, an Internet specification for sending multimedia and multipart messages. MIME is widely used, and you should use it unless you have a good reason not to. S/MIME is the abbreviation for Secure MIME, a MIME extension that adds RSA security to MIME. S/MIME is a good choice for secure e-mail.

Uuencoding is a method of converting a binary file (for example, a graphic or an audio file) into a text file so that it can be sent in a text-only message. Uuencode is the utility for uuencoding, and there's a corresponding utility called Uudecode for decoding the resulting text (usually after transfer) back to the binary file. Uuencode and Uudecode essentially enabled the transfer of binary files via e-mail and newsgroups, but they've largely been superseded by MIME. You'll still find uuencoded files in Usenet newsgroups and on systems that need to maintain backward compatibility with old standards.

Compose Page Options

The Compose page of the Options dialog box (shown on the left in Figure 21.11) contains three sets of options for composing mail and news.

FIGURE 21.11

The Compose page (left) of the Options dialog box lets you choose fonts, stationery, and business cards for your mail and news messages. The Signatures page lets you create signatures to add to your outgoing messages.

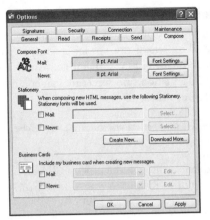

COMPOSE FONT AREA

The Compose Font area contains four controls:

Mail text box and Font Settings button   This text box displays the font and font size currently selected for mail. Click the Font Settings button to display the Font dialog box, in which you can change the font, font size, style, and effects (for example, underline, strikeout, and color).

News text box and Font Settings button   This text box displays the font and font size currently selected for news. Again, you can click the Font Settings button to display the Font dialog box to change the settings.

STATIONERY AREA

The Stationery area contains controls for specifying the stationery to use for HTML messages for mail and news. To use stationery, select the Mail check box or the News check box, then click the Select button. Outlook Express displays the Select Stationery dialog box. Select the stationery item to use, and click the OK button.

Click the Create New button to start the Stationery Setup Wizard, which walks you through the process of creating custom stationery.

Click the Download More button to open a browser window showing the Outlook Express area on the Microsoft website, which offers more stationery files.

BUSINESS CARDS AREA

The Business Cards area contains controls for specifying a business card to include as a vCard with mail and news messages you send. To include a business card, select the Mail check box or the News check box as appropriate, then choose the business card from the drop-down list, which contains the contacts in your Address Book. To edit the business card, click the Edit button. Outlook Express displays the Properties dialog box with the details for the contact.

Signatures Page Options

The Signatures page of the Options dialog box (shown on the right in Figure 21.11 with a couple of signatures added) contains three sets of options for creating signatures and adding them to your messages. A *signature* is text that usually gives your name (or assumed name), e-mail address or other immediately relevant contact information, and sometimes an epigram or quote. Use a signature only if it will benefit recipients of your messages.

TIP   Signatures are best kept short. Try not to be one of those people who become so delighted by the possibilities of signatures that they include far too much text.

These options are best explained through the process of creating and using signatures. To create signatures and add them to your messages, follow these steps:

1. Click the New button. Outlook Express adds to the Signatures list box a signature named Signature #1 (or the next available number), selects it, and positions the insertion point in the Edit Signature Text text box.
    ♦   Outlook Express makes the first signature you create the default signature.
2. Type the text for the signature.
    ♦   If you have multiple accounts and want to use the signature for only one of them, click the Advanced button. Outlook Express displays the Advanced Signature Settings dialog box. Select the check box for the account, and click the OK button. Outlook Express closes the Advanced Signature Settings dialog box and applies the signature to that account.
    ♦   Instead of creating a signature in Outlook Express, you can create one in a text file (for example, by using Notepad) and then tell Outlook Express to use it. To use a file, select the File option button, click the Browse button, use the resulting Open dialog box to select the file, and click the Open button. Outlook Express enters the path and filename in the File text box.
    ♦   To make the signature your default signature, click the Set As Default button. (Outlook Express automatically makes the first signature you create the default, so you need take this action only with subsequent signatures.)
3. Click the Rename button. XP displays an edit box around the signature's name in the Signatures list box. Type the name for the signature and press the Enter key.
4. To delete a signature, select it in the Signatures list box and click the Remove button.
5. Select the Add Signatures to All Outgoing Messages check box if you want to do just that.
    ♦   If you select this check box, select or clear the Don't Add Signatures to Replies and Forwards check box. By default, this check box is selected, preventing Outlook Express from adding signatures to replies and forwarded messages.
    ♦   If you choose not to add signatures to all your outgoing messages, you can apply a signature to an individual message from the New Message window.

Security Page Options

The Security page of the Options dialog box (shown on the left in Figure 21.12) contains options for securing Outlook Express. These options work closely with those you set for Internet Explorer (discussed in Chapter 19).

VIRUS PROTECTION AREA

The Virus Protection area of the Security page contains the following options:

Select the Internet Explorer Security Zone to Use list   Select the Internet Zone option button or the Restricted Sites Zone option button.

FIGURE 21.12

Choose security settings on the Security page of the Options dialog box (left) and in the Advanced Security Settings dialog box (right).

Warn Me when Other Applications Try to Send Mail As Me check box   Select this check box (which is cleared by default) if you want Outlook Express to warn you when other programs try to send mail under your identity. This setting offers some protection against viruses that send mail in your name, but it may also cause you to thwart some legitimate operations. For example, sending Remote Assistance requests via e-mail triggers this warning.

Do Not Allow Attachments to Be Saved or Opened That Could Potentially Be a Virus check box   Select this check box (which is cleared by default) if you want Outlook Express to refuse documents of file types that might contain viruses. This setting offers you some protection against viruses, but it may cause Outlook Express to discard some harmless documents because their file type is suspect. In many cases, you'll be better off using good, up-to-date anti-virus software than using this setting. See the sidebar "Expert Knowledge: Protecting Yourself Against Malicious Attachments," later in this chapter, for advice on how to handle attachments.

SECURE MAIL AREA

The Secure Mail area of the Security page contains three command buttons and two check boxes for specifying how to handle secure mail—messages that are either encrypted to protect their contents or signed with a digital certificate to verify the sender.

To send an encrypted message, you need to have added the recipient's certificate to your Address Book. Likewise, anyone who wants to send you an encrypted message needs to have your public key.

Tell Me More button   Click this button to display the Sending Secure Messages topic in the Outlook Express Help file.

Digital IDs button   Click this button to display the Certificates dialog box (discussed in the section "Using Digital Certificates" in Chapter 18).

Get Digital ID button Click this button to open a browser window containing information from the Microsoft website on where to obtain a digital certificate.

Encrypt Contents and Attachments for All Outgoing Messages check box Select this check box if you want to try to encrypt all the messages and attachments you send. As mentioned a moment ago, you need to have the recipient's certificate in your Address Book in order to send an encrypted message or attachment. If you select this option and send messages or attachments to people whose digital certificates you don't have, Outlook Express warns you of the problem and offers you the choice of sending the item without encryption or canceling sending it.

Digitally Sign All Outgoing Messages check box Select this check box if you want to digitally sign all the messages you send.

To choose advanced security settings, click the Advanced button. Outlook Express displays the Advanced Security Settings dialog box (shown on the right in Figure 21.12).

The Advanced Security Settings dialog box offers the following options:

Warn on Encrypting Messages with Less Than This Strength drop-down list Select the minimum acceptable level of encryption for messages: 40 bits, 56 bits, 64 bits, 128 bits, or 168 bits. (See the next sidebar for an explanation of the bit-ness of encryption—but basically, the higher the number, the more secure.) Outlook Express then warns you if you're about to send a message with a lower level of encryption.

Always Encrypt to Myself when Sending Encrypted Mail check box Leave this check box selected (as it is by default) if you want Outlook Express to encrypt with your digital certificate the copy of the message that it puts in your Sent Mail folder. (If you don't encrypt this copy, you won't be able to read it.)

Include My Digital ID when Sending Signed Messages check box Leave this check box selected (as it is by default) to send your digital certificate with a digitally signed message so that the recipient can use the public key to read it. (If the recipient already has your public key, you don't need to send the digital certificate again.)

Encode Message before Signing (Opaque Signing) check box Select this check box (which is cleared by default) if you want to encode your digitally signed messages in order to keep the signature secure. If you use this option, the recipient's e-mail program must support S/MIME. Otherwise, they won't be able to read the message.

Add Senders' Certificates to My Address Book check box Leave this check box selected (as it is by default) to have Outlook Express automatically add certificates from messages you receive to Address Book. This option is usually a good way to build your collection of certificates so that you can gradually send secure messages to more people (assuming you want to do so).

Check for Revoked Digital IDs list Select the Only when Online option button or the Never option button to specify when to check that digital IDs you receive are current and haven't been revoked.

Click the OK button. Outlook Express closes the Advanced Security Settings dialog box and returns you to the Options dialog box.

EXPERT KNOWLEDGE: SHOULD YOU USE ENCRYPTION? AND IF SO, HOW MUCH?

Internet e-mail is inherently insecure, because it passes through a shared medium (the Internet). The standard analogy used to illustrate the insecurity of Internet e-mail is that of a postcard sent through the mail: At any point, anyone who can get hold of it can read its contents. Conversely, anyone looking for that particular postcard would have a hard time finding it among all the other mail being sent unless they were able to intercept it close to its source or its destination.

So the standard advice goes that you shouldn't write anything in an unencrypted e-mail that you wouldn't mind the whole world reading, because anyone who reads the e-mail could publish it worldwide almost instantly by posting it on a website or to a newsgroup. (The recipient could also do this, but presumably you trust them enough to read the content of the message.)

There's much truth in this, but (at this writing, at least) most people send unencrypted e-mail all day long without suffering any adverse consequences. But if you want to make sure that nobody who intercepts a message can read it, you need to secure the message by using encryption.

As you saw a page or so ago, Outlook Express offers various strengths of encryption: 40 bit, 56 bit, 64 bit, 128 bit, and 168 bit. Which should you use?

Very generally speaking, the more bits, the more secure the encryption, and the more processing power it takes to encode and decode. The weakest encryption strengths, 40 bit and 56 bit, are those the U.S. government allows software firms to export. (Unlike with beer, export-strength encryption is weaker than the normal article.) 64-bit encryption is a little more exciting than 40-bit and 56-bit, but probably not enough so to be worth using if you're concerned about security. 128-bit encryption is considered strong encryption and should be enough for most civil purposes, but if you're trying to make the NSA and Echelon think that you have material worth cracking, you might want to step up to the 168-bit level—which Outlook Express suggests you use in the first place.

Of course, if you want to be truly secure, you need to make sure that nobody else can access your computer to attempt to hack it. Unplug the modem and seal the computer in a lead-lined room in an underground bunker....

If you want greater security without severing all links with the outside world, consider using external encryption software such as Pretty Good Privacy (PGP), which you can get from Network Associates (www.pgp.com).

Connection Page Options

The Connection page of the Options dialog box (shown on the left in Figure 21.13) contains refreshingly few options:

Ask before Switching Dial-up Connections check box   Leave this check box selected (as it is by default) if you want Outlook Express to check with you before switching from a connection that isn't working to another connection. If you have only one dial-up connection, you don't need to worry about this setting.

Hang Up after Sending and Receiving check box Select this check box (which is cleared by default) if you want Outlook Express to hang up your dial-up connection once it has finished sending and receiving mail when you issue a Send and Receive command. This setting is most useful with pay-as-you-go Internet connections.

Change button Click this button to display the Connections page of the Internet Properties dialog box (discussed in the section "Preventing Internet Explorer from Connecting Automatically" in Chapter 18).

FIGURE 21.13

The Connection page (left) and Maintenance page (right) of the Options dialog box

 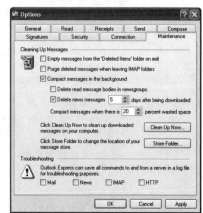

Maintenance Page Options

The Maintenance page of the Options dialog box (shown on the right in Figure 21.13) contains a double-handful of options for keeping Outlook Express running smoothly without silting up your hard disk.

These are the options on the Maintenance page:

Empty Messages from the "Deleted Items" Folder on Exit check box Select this check box (which is cleared by default) to have Outlook Express empty all the deleted messages in your Deleted Items folder when you exit Outlook Express. By default, Outlook Express keeps the deleted messages until you empty the Deleted Items folder manually.

Purge Deleted Messages when Leaving IMAP Folders check box Select this check box (which is cleared by default) to have Outlook Express dispose of all messages you've marked as deleted when you close an IMAP folder. If your server doesn't use IMAP, you don't need to worry about this option.

Compact Messages in the Background check box Leave this check box selected (as it is by default) to have Outlook Express squeeze extra space out of messages in the background as you're working. If you clear this check box, you can compact messages by clicking the Clean Up Now button. The next three controls are available only when this check box is selected.

Delete Read Message Bodies in Newsgroups check box   Select this check box (which is cleared by default) if you want Outlook Express to delete all the message bodies of messages you've read when you quit Outlook Express. This option saves a lot of space, but it means that you'll need to download a message again if you want to reread it.

Delete News Messages *NN* Days after Being Downloaded check box and text box   Leave this check box selected (as it is by default) and specify the number of days in the text box if you want Outlook Express to automatically delete messages after a set time. Clear this check box if you want to keep old messages for reference.

Compact Messages when There Is *NN* Percent Wasted Space text box   In this text box, specify the percentage of wasted space at which Outlook Express should compact messages.

Clean Up Now button   Click this button to display the Local File Clean Up dialog box, which provides actions for compacting and deleting messages. The section "Compacting and Cleaning Up Messages" later in this chapter discusses these actions.

Store Folder button   Click this button to display the Store Location dialog box, which you can use for changing the folder in which your message store is located. The section "Moving Your Message Store" later in this chapter discusses this process.

Troubleshooting area   If you're having problems communicating with a mail or news server, you can select the Mail check box, the News check box, the IMAP check box, or the HTTP check box to make Outlook Express log the commands used for that server. (All these check boxes are cleared by default.) The log file may help cast light on the problem. The log files have the extension LOG and are named after the account they log. For example, the HTTP mail log is called `HTTPMail.log`, and the news log for the account `news.demon.com` would be called `news.demon.com.log`. You'll find these files in the message store folder.

Reading E-mail Messages

To read e-mail, click the Read Mail link on the Start page. Outlook Express displays your Inbox. Figure 21.14 shows a sparsely populated Inbox.

As you can see in the figure, Outlook Express displays icons to indicate information about the message headers:

◆   The Attachment icon means that the message has one or more files attached to it. (You'll learn how to work with attachments later in this chapter.)

FIGURE 21.14

The Inbox

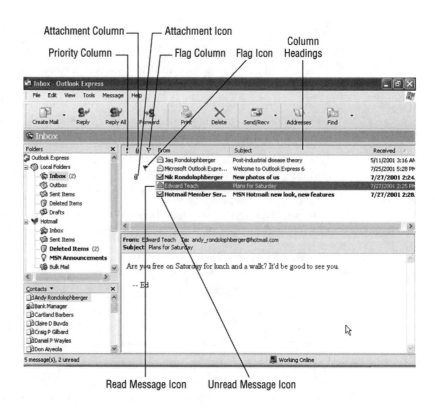

◆ The Unread Message icon indicates that a message has not been read.

TIP *You can mark a message as unread or read by right-clicking its header and choosing Mark As Unread or Mark As Read, as appropriate, from the context menu.*

◆ The Read Message icon indicates that a message has been read.

◆ A flag is a mark you can set on a message to indicate that you need to deal with it. To set or remove a flag, click in the Flag column beside the message's header.

◆ If a message is marked as high priority, it displays a red exclamation point in the Priority column.

To read a message in the Preview pane, click it in the message headers listing. Outlook Express displays it in the Preview pane.

To read a message in a separate window, double-click its message header listing. Outlook Express displays the message in a separate window, as shown in Figure 21.15.

To sort your messages by one of the column headings, click the heading once for an ascending sort (alphabetical order) or twice for a descending sort (reverse-alphabetical order).

FIGURE 21.15

Instead of reading a message in the Preview pane, you can display it in a separate window if you prefer.

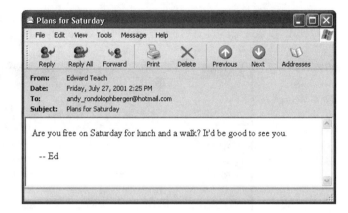

To view a subset of your messages, choose View ➢ Current View ➢ Hide Read Messages or View ➢ Current View ➢ Hide Read or Ignored Messages. To restore the view to all messages, choose View ➢ Current View ➢ Show All Messages.

If you have multiple messages from the same conversation (on the same topic, with the same subject), choose View ➢ Current View ➢ Group Messages by Conversation to group the messages. Issue the command again to ungroup the messages.

To ignore a conversation that's going on, select one of the messages and choose Message ➢ Ignore Conversation.

TROUBLESHOOTING: "SERVER NOT FOUND" ERROR

A "Server not found" error from Outlook Express may mean that your Internet connection isn't working when Outlook Express expects it to be. If you want Outlook Express to dial the connection automatically when necessary, select the Dial Whenever a Network Connection Is Not Present check box on the Connection page of the Options dialog box.

Sending E-mail

You can generate e-mail in Outlook Express by creating new messages, replying to messages you've received, or forwarding either messages you've received or messages you've created and sent before.

Composing a New Message

To create a new message, take the following steps:

1. Click the Create Mail button on the toolbar to create a new message. Outlook Express opens a message window containing a new message. Figure 21.16 shows an example.

   ◆ To create a message using Outlook Express's stationery, click the Create Mail button's drop-down list button and choose the type of stationery from the drop-down menu.

◆ To create a message to a contact, double-click the contact in the Contacts pane, or right-click the contact in the Contacts pane and choose Send E-mail from the context menu.

FIGURE 21.16

Create your message in the New Message window.

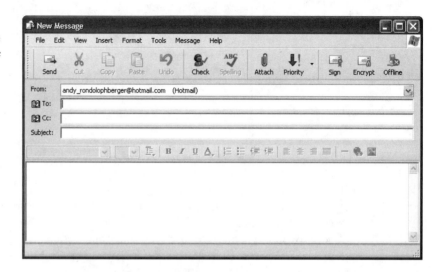

2. If you have multiple e-mail accounts, choose the account from which you want to send the account by using the drop-down list at the right end of the From text box.

3. Enter the e-mail address of the recipient or recipients in the To text box and the names of cc: recipients in the Cc: text box. Separate multiple addresses with semicolons. You can either type each address in or choose it from Address Book as follows:

◆ Click the To button. Outlook Express displays the Select Recipients dialog box (shown in Figure 21.17).

FIGURE 21.17

Use the Select Recipients dialog box to designate the recipients for the message.

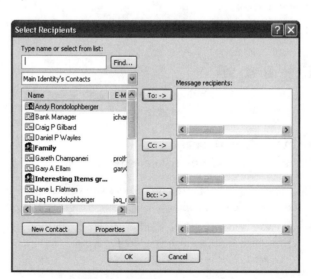

◆ In the Type Name or Select from List list box, select the name and click the To: button, the Cc: button, or the Bcc: button to add the selected name to the appropriate box of message recipients.

◆ Add further names to the To:, Cc:, and Bcc: lists as applicable, and then click the OK button. Outlook Express closes the Select Recipients dialog box and adds the recipients to the appropriate boxes in the New Message window.

4. Click in the Subject text box and enter the Subject line for the message. The more descriptive, informative, and concise the Subject line is, the more useful it will be to the recipients of the message—and the more likely they will be to read the message.

5. In the message box, enter the text of the message:

◆ You can enter and edit the text using the standard Windows commands (such as cut-and-paste, and drag-and-drop) and format the text (if you're sending a formatted message) by using the buttons on the Formatting toolbar, shown in Figure 21.18.

◆ To switch the message from plain text to rich text (HTML) or vice versa, choose Format ➤ Rich Text (HTML) or Format ➤ Plain Text.

FIGURE 21.18

Use the Formatting toolbar to format your messages if necessary.

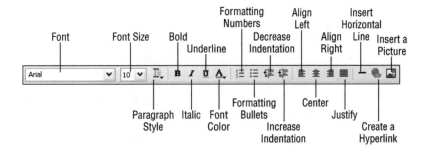

◆ To insert a horizontal line, click the Insert Horizontal Line button on the toolbar.

◆ If you type a recognizable hyperlink, Outlook Express automatically converts it to a hyperlink. To insert a hyperlink manually, select the text to include in the hyperlink and click the Create a Hyperlink button on the toolbar. Outlook Express displays the Hyperlink dialog box (shown in Figure 21.19). Choose the type of hyperlink from the Type drop-down list (for example, http for a regular connection, https for a secure connection), enter the URL in the URL text box, and click the OK button. Outlook Express closes the Hyperlink dialog box and inserts the hyperlink in the message.

FIGURE 21.19

You can use the Hyperlink dialog box to insert a hyperlink manually.

◆   To insert a picture, click the Insert a Picture button. Outlook Express displays the Picture dialog box (shown in Figure 21.20). Enter the path and filename for the picture in the Picture Source text box (use the Browse button and the resulting Picture dialog box if necessary to select the picture). In the Alternate Text text box, enter text to be displayed in case the recipient cannot view the picture. Choose alignment and border thickness options in the Layout group box and horizontal and vertical spacing options in the Spacing group box, then click the OK button. Outlook Express closes the Picture dialog box and inserts the picture in the message.

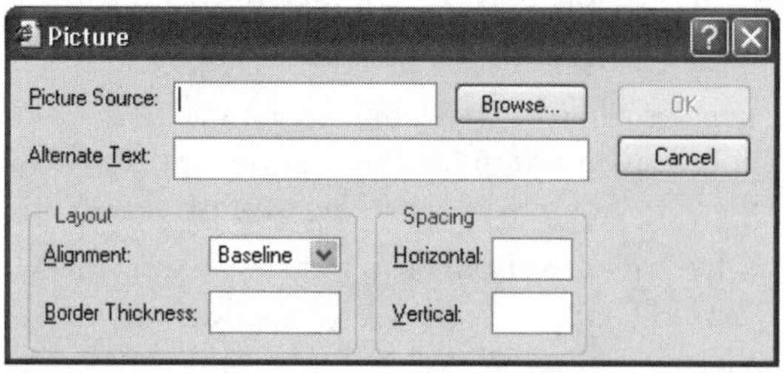

FIGURE 21.20

Use the Picture dialog box to insert a picture. Always specify alternate text in case the recipient cannot view the picture.

TIP   *As you can see from the preceding paragraphs, Outlook Express offers some basic formatting options for HTML messages. But if you want to create a complex layout for a message, you'll do better to use a custom web-design program (for example, FrontPage) to create it as a web page. Then paste the contents of the page into the message in Outlook Express. Before sending the message to others, send a copy to yourself to make sure everything works.*

6.   To override for this message your default setting for requesting read receipts, choose Tools ➤ Request Read Receipt.

7.   To override for this message your default setting for encrypting messages, choose Tools ➤ Encrypt.

8.   To override for this message your default setting for digitally signing messages, choose Tools ➤ Digitally Sign.

◆   If you turn on digital signing and want to request a secure receipt, choose Tools ➤ Request Secure Receipt.

9.   You're now ready to send the message. Read through the message quickly to make sure it conveys what you want it to and that you haven't written anything rash or ambiguous. Spell-check the message if necessary. Then click the Send button or choose File ➤ Send to send the message on its way.

If you try to send an encrypted message without having a digital certificate with which to encrypt it for yourself, Outlook Express displays the Security Warning dialog box shown in Figure 21.21. Choose the Yes button to send the message, or choose the No button to cancel sending the message so that you can change the encryption setting or find your digital certificate.

FIGURE 21.21

Outlook Express displays this Security Warning dialog box if you try to send an encrypted message when you don't have a digital certificate.

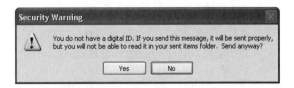

If you try to send an encrypted message to someone whose digital certificate you don't have, Outlook Express displays the Outlook Express Mail dialog box shown in Figure 21.22. Click the Don't Encrypt button to send the message without encryption. Click the Cancel button to cancel sending the message.

FIGURE 21.22

You'll see this Outlook Express Mail dialog box if you try to send an encrypted message to someone whose digital certificate you don't have.

Replying to an E-mail Message

To reply to a message from the Inbox, click the Reply button on the toolbar, or right-click the message header and choose Reply to Sender from the context menu. Alternatively, press Ctrl+R.

To reply to a message from a message window, click the Reply button on the toolbar in the message window.

If you weren't the only recipient of a message, you can use the Reply to All feature to reply quickly to all the recipients of that message (and to cc: everyone on the Cc: list, if the message has one). From the Inbox, click the Reply All button on the toolbar, or right-click and choose Reply to All from the context menu. Alternatively, press Ctrl+Shift+R. From a message window, click the Reply All button on the message window's toolbar.

Outlook Express opens a message window for the reply. Compose your reply, add any extra recipients, and send the message as usual.

When you reply to a message, Outlook Express adds RE: to the Subject line so that the recipient can easily see that the message is a reply.

Adding a vCard to Your Outgoing Messages

You can include a *vCard*—a virtual business card—with your outgoing messages either automatically or manually. Usually it's better to include vCards manually when necessary so that you don't barrage your friends and colleagues with useless vCards. vCards are small, but they travel as attachments to messages, so they can make attachments folders silt up.

To send a vCard with every message, select the Mail check box in the Business Cards area of the Compose page of the Options dialog box (Tools ➢ Options), then choose the appropriate contact entry from the context menu.

To send a vCard manually, specify the vCard as described in the previous paragraph, but then clear the Mail check box in the Business Cards area. You can then choose Insert ➢ My Business Card from a message window to add the vCard to a message.

Adding vCards You Receive to Address Book

When you receive a vCard as an attachment, you can quickly add it to Address Book by taking the following steps:

1. Click the icon for the vCard in the message window and choose Open from the pop-up menu. Outlook Express displays the Open Attachment Warning dialog box (shown in Figure 21.23).

   ◆ Alternatively, select the message in your Inbox and click the icon for the vCard in the Preview pane header.

FIGURE 21.23

In the Open Attachment Warning dialog box, select the Open It option button to add a vCard you receive as an attachment to Address Book.

2. Select the Open It option button.
3. Click the OK button. Outlook Express displays the Properties dialog box for the vCard.
4. Click the Add to Address Book button to make the contact information editable, and then edit it as usual.

Forwarding a Message

You can easily forward a message to someone else. To forward a message from the Inbox, click the Forward button on the toolbar or right-click the message header and choose Forward from the context menu. Alternatively, press Ctrl+F.

To forward a message from a message window, click the Forward button on the toolbar in the message window.

Outlook Express opens a message window for the forwarded message. Choose recipients, enter your contribution to the message, and send it as usual.

When you forward a message, Outlook Express adds FW: to the Subject line so that the recipient can easily see that the message was forwarded.

Sending and Receiving Attachments

In addition to sending and receiving e-mail messages, you can send and receive files as attachments to messages. Attachments are a great way of sharing files and getting information from point A to point B.

Sending Attachments

To send a file as an attachment, start a message as usual (or reply to a message, or forward a message), then click the Attach button on the toolbar. Outlook Express displays the Insert Attachment dialog box. Select the file or files to attach, and click the Attach button. Outlook Express closes the Insert Attachment dialog box and displays the Attach box on the message (shown in Figure 21.24) with details of the attachment. You can then complete and send the message as usual.

FIGURE 21.24

When you've attached one or more files to a message, the message displays the Attach box.

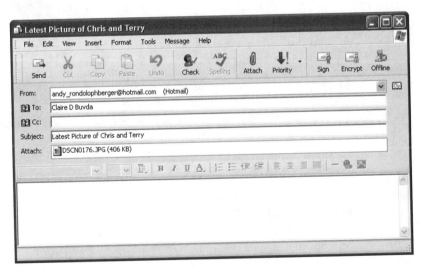

TIP *If the attachment you're sending is much larger than 1MB, it may be rejected by a mail server on the way. If this happens (or to prevent this from happening), select the Break Apart Messages Larger than NN KB check box on the Advanced page of the Properties dialog box for the mail account and specify a value of 1MB (1024KB) or smaller in the text box. Outlook Express then breaks up the message into parts, and the recipient can recombine the parts, by using either an e-mail program with recombining capability (for example, Outlook Express or Outlook) or a separate recombining utility. See the "Configuring an Individual Account" section later in the chapter for details.*

EXPERT KNOWLEDGE: RESIZING PICTURES YOU SEND VIA E-MAIL

Large graphics files can be slow to transmit. XP lets you resize (or, more accurately, down-resolve) a graphics file to produce a smaller file size that will transmit more quickly.

To use this feature, take the following steps:

1. Open an Explorer window to the folder containing the file.

2. Select the file, then click the E-mail This File link in the File and Folder Tasks list. (Alternatively, right-click the file and choose Send To ➤ Mail Recipient from the context menu.) XP displays the Send Pictures via E-mail dialog box (shown on the left below).

 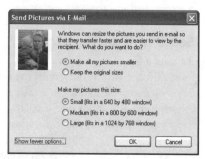

3. Click the Show More Options link. XP displays a hidden part of the Send Pictures via E-mail dialog box, as shown on the right above.

4. In the Make My Pictures This Size list, select the Small option button, the Medium option button, or the Large option button as appropriate. (Each size lists the resolution used.)

5. Click the OK button. XP creates a new version of the file using the specified resolution, starts a new message, and attaches the file.

6. Finish the message and send it as usual.

Receiving Attachments

When someone sends you a file with an attachment, the message header in your Inbox displays an Attachment icon, as you saw earlier in this chapter. If you open the message in a message window, it displays an Attach box.

WARNING   *Before you open an attachment, make sure it's harmless. See the next sidebar for details.*

To save an attachment, take the following steps:

1. Select the message header.

2. Choose File ➤ Save Attachments. Outlook Express displays the Save Attachments dialog box (shown in Figure 21.25).

FIGURE 21.25

Use the Save Attachments dialog box to save the attachments from an e-mail message to a folder of your choosing.

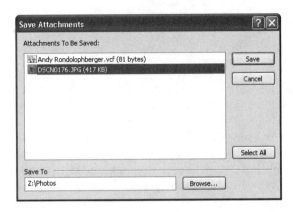

3. For each attachment, specify a destination location in the Save To text box (use the Browse button and the resulting Browse for Folder dialog box if necessary), then click the Save button.

4. Check the detached file with virus-checking software before you open it.

If you receive an attachment that has been broken into multiple parts, select all the messages in the Inbox, right-click one of them, and select the Combine and Decode command.

EXPERT KNOWLEDGE: PROTECTING YOURSELF AGAINST MALICIOUS ATTACHMENTS

Attachments are one of the easiest ways for a malicious hacker to attack your computer, so have your wits about you each time you open an attachment. This sidebar discusses the ways in which attachments can pose a threat to your computer and the best way to protect yourself.

AN EXECUTABLE FILE OR SCRIPT FILE CAN DO DAMAGE

The most straightforward threat is an attachment containing an undisguised executable file or script file that you can be persuaded to run. By the beginning of the twenty-first century, most computer users know that it's a really bad idea to execute an executable file or script file that they receive as an e-mail attachment— even if it comes from someone they know, trust, or even love—so most malefactors have taken to disguising the executables or scripts they send.

AN APPARENTLY HARMLESS FILE MAY BE A DISGUISED EXECUTABLE OR SCRIPT

Unless you've chosen to display *all* file extensions (as discussed in the section "Displaying All File Extensions" in Chapter 10), the true extension of the file can be hidden behind a part of the filename masquerading as the extension.

For example, if XP is hiding extensions (as it does by default), and someone sent you the executable file New Shakira pic.jpg.exe, it would appear to be named New Shakira pic.jpg. Since JPG is a graphics file format, you might think it safe to open the file—but opening it directly would cause the executable file to run. (Trying to open the file from a graphics program would cause an error, as the graphics program wouldn't be able to open the executable file.)

Continued on next page

EXPERT KNOWLEDGE: PROTECTING YOURSELF AGAINST MALICIOUS ATTACHMENTS *(continued)*

Even if you'd cleared the Hide File Extensions for Known File Types check box on the View page of the Folder Options dialog box (from Explorer) so that XP displays most extensions, a file with one of the super-hidden extensions (URL, JSE, JS, SHS, LNK, SHB, JOB, VBE, VBS, SCF, or WSF) would still appear to be a different type of file. For example, New Shakira Hit.mp3.js would appear to be named New Shakira Hit.mp3 unless you'd specifically told XP to display the super-hidden extensions as well.

AN DOCUMENT FILE MAY CONTAIN VBA OR OTHER EXECUTABLE CODE

Even if the file is of the file type its extension suggests, it can still be dangerous. For example, a file created by a program that acts as a Visual Basic for Applications (VBA) host—such as a Word or WordPerfect document, an Excel workbook, a PowerPoint presentation, or an AutoCAD drawing—can contain executable code in macros or user forms that can attack your computer. VBA and other scripting languages can take extensive actions on a computer—anything from formatting a disk to installing a back-door administration program or silently e-mailing your most private files to persons unknown.

ALWAYS VIRUS-CHECK ALL ATTACHMENTS YOU RECEIVE

Because of these dangers, it's best *never* to open *any* attachment *from anyone* without virus-checking it first. Even if you know the sender and you've checked their e-mail address to make sure the message and attachment are really from that person, bear in mind that their computer could be infected with a virus that's using the e-mail client automatically to spread itself. Alternatively, your apparent correspondent's e-mail account could have been hijacked, either at the computer or at the server, and used to distribute malware. Or the person could have sent you, intentionally and in good faith, a document that they didn't know had been infected with a virus.

This exhortation—to always virus-check every attachment—may seem impractical if you regularly send documents back and forth, and I'll admit to not always following it myself. But having to disinfect a computer that's caught a virus wastes far more time than virus-checking attachments. Restoring data from backup takes even longer. And having to recreate data files you've lost because of an attack that struck when you didn't have a backup takes longest of all. So it's well worth investing in an anti-virus program that automatically checks all incoming e-mail and attachments.

TURN OFF THE PREVIEW PANE IN OUTLOOK EXPRESS

For extra security, you may want to avoid using the Preview pane in Outlook Express, because the act of displaying the message in the Preview pane can run a script that can trigger a virus such as the Klez virus. (To stop using the Preview pane, choose View ➢ Layout. Outlook Express displays the Window Layout Properties dialog box. Clear the Show Preview Pane check box in the Preview Pane area, and click the OK button.) However, because the Preview pane helps you process your e-mail quickly, and because most viruses travel as attachments, most people choose to continue using the Preview pane. Some anti-virus programs can also guard against this type of script.

Continued on next page

EXPERT KNOWLEDGE: PROTECTING YOURSELF AGAINST MALICIOUS ATTACHMENTS *(continued)*

USE THE "DO NOT ALLOW ATTACHMENTS TO BE SAVED…" OPTION

As discussed in the section "Security Page Options," earlier in this chapter, the Security page of the Options dialog box for Outlook Express includes a check box called Do Not Allow Attachments to Be Saved or Opened That Could Potentially Be a Virus. If you select this check box, Outlook Express won't let you save or open attachments whose file types *could* contain a virus or code. These file types include executable files and scripts, of course, but also include documents that could contain VBA code or code in another scripting language.

The problem with this option is that when you use it, Outlook Express typically ends up "protecting" you from a large number of harmless files that you want to work with, such as Word documents that contain customized toolbars. So if you use this option, you'll need to toggle it on and off frequently: Keep it on until Outlook Express notifies you that it has suppressed an attachment because it might be dangerous; turn it off so that you can sic your anti-virus program on the file and decide if it's a friend or a foe; and then turn it back on again so that Outlook Express is protecting you once more. Because of all this maneuvering, many people find that anti-virus software, run constantly and updated whenever possible, provides a more satisfactory solution to the problem of dangerous attachments. This is especially true because malefactors can produce new types of viruses that inhabit supposedly harmless files. For example, JPEG images used to be safe, but now they can be loaded with code that can be run automatically by an extractor program that has been surreptitiously installed on your computer. (If the extractor program hasn't been installed on your computer, the code in the doctored JPEG images does nothing.)

Managing Your E-mail Messages

To keep your Inbox in order, you'll need to manage your messages carefully, by deleting messages, moving them to folders, and being able to locate messages for reference. You may also need to move your message store, and you should certainly back it up to safeguard against data loss.

Deleting a Message

To delete a message from the Inbox, select it and click the Delete button on the toolbar or press the Delete key. Doing so moves the message to the Deleted Items folder. To delete everything in the Deleted Items folder, right-click the folder, choose Empty "Deleted Items" Folder from the context menu, and click the Yes button in the confirmation message box that appears.

Compacting and Cleaning Up Messages

If you send and receive many messages, and subscribe to a number of newsgroups, the messages and posts can take up a lot of space on your hard disk. To reduce the amount of space taken up, or the amount of information stored, follow these steps:

1. Choose Tools ➢ Options. Outlook Express displays the Options dialog box.
2. Click the Maintenance tab. Outlook Express displays the Maintenance page.
3. Click the Clean Up Now button. Outlook Express displays the Local File Clean Up dialog box (shown in Figure 21.26).

FIGURE 21.26

In the Local File Clean Up dialog box, select the action you want to take to free up more disk space.

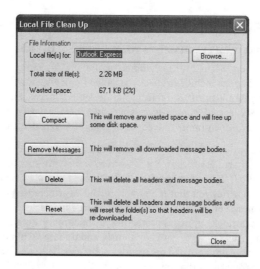

4. In the Local File(s) For text box, make sure the right account is selected. If it's not, click the Browse button, select the account in the resulting Outlook Express dialog box, and click the OK button.

5. Click the button for the action you want to take:

◆ The Compact button compresses the files, removing any wasted space, but keeps all the messages. This action saves you the least disk space—the amount shown in the Wasted Space readout in the File Information group box—but is worth performing if you have a huge number of messages.

◆ The Remove Messages button deletes the bodies of downloaded messages but keeps the headers. Because the bodies tend to be bulkier than the headers (especially for messages that have attachments), this action can recover a good amount of space.

◆ The Delete button deletes all the messages (both headers and bodies). This action reclaims even more space, but it doesn't leave much behind.

◆ The Reset button deletes all the messages (again, both headers and bodies) *and* resets the folder so that it will download the message headers again. This action is best saved for when an account has become corrupted.

6. Click the Close button. Outlook Express closes the Local File Clean Up dialog box and returns you to the Options dialog box.

7. Click the OK button. Outlook Express closes the Options dialog box.

Moving a Message to a Folder

You can move a message to a folder in several ways:

◆ From the Inbox, click the message header and drag it to the appropriate folder in the Folders pane.

◆ From the Inbox, right-click the message and choose Move to Folder from the context menu, or choose Edit ➤ Move to Folder. Outlook Express displays the Move dialog box. Select the folder and click the OK button.

◆ From a message window, choose File ➤ Move to Folder. Outlook Express displays the Move dialog box. Proceed as described in the previous paragraph.

TIP   You can also copy a message to a folder (instead of moving it) by using the Copy to Folder command instead of the Move to Folder command.

Moving Your Message Store

By default, Outlook Express puts your *message store* (the folder in which the messages are kept) in a folder deeply buried under the folder for your account on the computer. The folder for your account is named with your username, a period, and the computer name. For example, if your username is Jaq Rondolophberger and the computer's name is ZWEIFEL, the folder for your account is named `Jaq Rondolophberger.ZWEIFEL`. The folder for your account lives in the `\Documents and Settings\` folder.

If you need to, you can move your Outlook Express message store to a different folder. For example, you might want to move the message store to a different drive if the current drive were getting full.

To move the message store, follow these steps:

1. Choose Tools ➤ Options. Outlook Express displays the Options dialog box.
2. Click the Maintenance tab. Outlook Express displays the Maintenance page.
3. Click the Store Folder button. Outlook Express displays the Store Location dialog box (shown in Figure 21.27).

FIGURE 21.27

Use the Store Location dialog box to move your message store to a different folder or drive.

4. Click the Change button. Outlook Express displays the Browse for Folder dialog box.
5. Select the folder for the new location and click the OK button. Outlook Express moves the folder and returns you to the Store Location dialog box.
6. Click the OK button. Outlook Express displays a dialog box telling you that the store location will not be changed until you exit and restart Outlook Express.
7. Click the OK button. Outlook Express closes the Store Location dialog box and returns you to the Options dialog box.
8. Click the OK button. Outlook Express closes the Options dialog box.
9. If you want to move your message store immediately, exit Outlook and restart it.

Finding a Message

To find a particular message, take the following steps:

1. Click the Find a Message link on the Start page, or choose Edit ➢ Find ➢ Message. Outlook Express displays the Find Message window (shown in Figure 21.28 with a search performed and a message found).

FIGURE 21.28

Use the Find Message window to find a particular message by specifying information it contains.

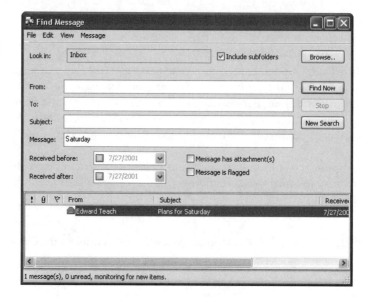

2. Enter such information as you can muster about the message in the From, To, Subject, and Message text boxes; specify dates in the Received Before and Received After boxes if possible; and select the Message Has Attachment(s) check box or the Message Is Flagged check box if applicable to narrow the field further.

3. Click the Find Now button. The Find Message window displays the messages it finds in a list box at the bottom of the window, as shown in the figure.

4. Double-click a message to open it.

If you're sure that the message you're looking for is in the current folder, choose Edit ➢ Find ➢ Message in This Folder. Outlook Express displays the Find dialog box (shown in Figure 21.29), which offers simpler searching capabilities.

FIGURE 21.29

Use the Find dialog box to perform simple searches.

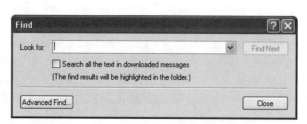

Filtering Your E-mail

Business queries, love letters, spam, messages from your family, and solicitations for mass-mailing software and pornography—these days, you never know exactly what to expect in your Inbox, though most people can count on an increasing number of messages arriving.

To help you manage the mayhem, Outlook Express lets you create rules for filtering e-mail and news. By creating a rule that defines certain conditions, you can take action when a matching message arrives. That action can be anything from moving or copying the message to a particular folder, to forwarding the message automatically to people, to deleting it unread. For example, you could create a rule that deleted any message that contained the word *marketing*.

Better yet, with Outlook Express you can block specific senders, no matter what kind of message they try to send you. Read on.

Creating Rules for Filtering E-mail

Your first priority in filtering should be to filter the e-mail you receive. By filtering e-mail, you can move messages to different folders or even delete them without your ever seeing them.

To create a rule for filtering e-mail, take the following steps:

1. Choose Tools ➤ Message Rules ➤ Mail. Outlook Express displays the New Mail Rule dialog box. Figure 21.30 shows the New Mail Rule dialog box with a rule underway.

FIGURE 21.30

Use the New Mail Rule dialog box to create rules for filtering e-mail.

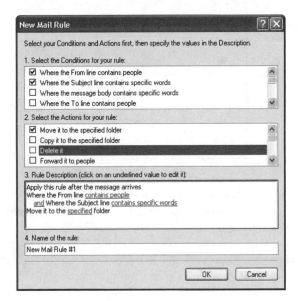

2. In the Select the Conditions for Your Rule list box, select the condition or conditions under which you want the rule to operate. For example, you might choose the Where the From Line Contains People condition in order to take action on messages from a particular e-mail account. (You get to specify which people in a moment.) You might also choose the Where the Subject Line Contains Specific Words condition to filter the subject line for particular words.

3. In the Select the Actions for Your Rule list box, select the action that you want Outlook Express to take when the condition is met. For example, you might choose the Move It to the Specified Folder action to move the message to a particular folder. (Again, you get to specify which folder in a moment.)

4. In the Rule Description list box, Outlook Express has built the general rule. Now click one of the underlined values to edit it.

♦ Continuing the example, you'd click the Contains People link. Outlook Express displays the Select People dialog box (shown in Figure 21.31). Enter a name in the text box and click the Add button to add it to the list box. Or click the Address Book button to display the Rule Addresses dialog box, select the names, move them to the Rule Addresses list box, and click the OK button. Outlook Express closes the Rule Addresses dialog box and updates the Contains condition in the Rule Description list box to reflect the names you chose.

FIGURE 21.31

Use the Select People dialog box to specify which people the rule should work on.

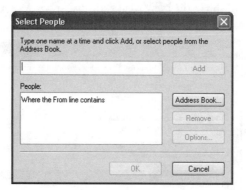

♦ You'd then click the And link in the Rule Description list box. (This link appears when you've created two or more criteria that can be complementary.) Outlook Express displays the And/Or dialog box (shown in Figure 21.32). Select the Messages Match All of the Criteria option button if you want messages to meet each condition for the rule to kick in, or select the Messages Match Any One of the Criteria option button to have one condition suffice. (The example uses the Messages Match All of the Criteria option button.) Click the OK button. Outlook Express closes the And/Or dialog box and updates the Rule Description list box.

FIGURE 21.32

In the And/Or dialog box, choose whether messages must match all the criteria (an And condition) or any one of the criteria (an Or condition).

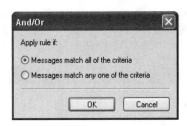

◆ You'd then click the Contains Specific Words link. Outlook Express displays the Type Specific Words dialog box (shown in Figure 21.33 with several words added). Type one word at a time into the text box, then click the Add button to add them. Click the OK button. Outlook Express closes the Type Specific Words dialog box and updates the Where the Subject Line Contains condition to contain the words.

FIGURE 21.33

In the Type Specific Words dialog box, enter the words for which you want to filter.

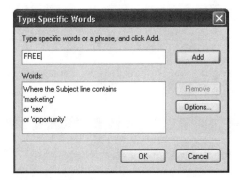

◆ You'd then click the Specified link. Outlook Express displays the Move dialog box. Select the folder in the folder structure as usual (create a new folder if necessary) and click the OK button. Outlook Express closes the Move dialog box and returns you to the New Mail Rule dialog box.

TIP   You can also create a rule that applies if a message does not contain the specified information—for example, if a message does not come from a specified sender. Click the Options button in the selection dialog box (the Select People dialog box, the Type Specific Words dialog box, or another selection dialog box). Outlook Express displays the Rule Condition Options dialog box. Choose options as appropriate, and then click the OK button to return to the selection dialog box.

5. In the Name of the Rule text box, enter a memorable name for the rule.

6. Click the OK button. Outlook Express closes the New Mail Rule dialog box, creates the rule, and displays the Message Rules dialog box (shown in Figure 21.34).

FIGURE 21.34

Manage your mail rules on the Mail Rules page of the Message Rules dialog box.

7. Click the Apply Now button. Outlook Express displays the Apply Mail Rules Now dialog box (shown in Figure 21.35).

FIGURE 21.35

In the Apply Mail Rules Now dialog box, choose which rules to apply to which folder.

8. In the Select Rules to Apply list box, select the rules you want to apply.

9. By default, the rule is applied to the folder you were working in when you created it. If necessary, use the Browse button and the resulting Apply to Folder dialog box to designate a different folder, and click the OK button. If the folder has subfolders to which you want to apply the rules, select the Include Subfolders check box.

10. Click the Apply Now button to apply the rules you chose. Outlook Express displays a message box telling you that it has applied the rules to the folder.

11. Click the OK button. Outlook Express closes the message box.

12. Click the Close button. Outlook Express closes the Apply Mail Rules Now dialog box and returns you to the Message Rules dialog box.

13. If you're using multiple mail rules, use the Move Up and Move Down buttons to arrange the rules in the best order.

14. Click the OK button. Outlook Express closes the Message Rules dialog box.

Next, if possible, send yourself a message that meets the condition. (For example, if you created the rule described, you could send yourself a message with *FREE Sex* in the Subject line.) Make sure the filter catches the message. If not, adjust the filter until it works.

Blocking a Sender

To quickly block a sender from the Inbox, choose Message ➤ Block Sender to add the sender of the current message to your blocking list. Outlook Express displays the Outlook Express dialog box shown in Figure 21.36, offering to remove from the current folder all messages from that sender. Click the Yes or No button as appropriate.

FIGURE 21.36

When you block a sender, Outlook Express offers to remove from the current folder all messages sent by that sender.

To unblock a sender that you've blocked:

1. Choose Tools ➤ Message Rules ➤ Blocked Senders List. Outlook Express displays the Blocked Senders page of the Message Rules dialog box (shown in Figure 21.37).

FIGURE 21.37

To unblock a sender, use the Blocked Senders page of the Message Rules dialog box.

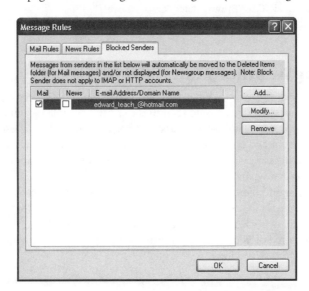

2. Select the sender and click the Remove button. Outlook Express displays a confirmation message box.

3. Click the Yes button. Outlook Express closes the message box and unblocks the sender.

4. Click the OK button. Outlook Express closes the Message Rules dialog box.

EXPERT KNOWLEDGE: MINIMIZING SPAM

If you've used e-mail for more than a few days, you probably know what spam is—unsolicited commercial e-mail offering you a variety of supposedly can't-miss opportunities for medicines, pyramid and multi-level marketing schemes, mail-order spouses, pornography, or spam-them-yourself software.

No matter how inventive you get with e-mail filters, and no matter how determinedly you block any sender or domain that offends you, spam will still get through to you. When it does, there's only one thing to do: Delete it.

It's never—repeat, *never*—worth responding to spam (unless you want to buy whatever the spammer is selling). *Never* reply to spam that thoughtfully provides an address for removing yourself from the spammer's list, because sending mail to this address proves that your e-mail address is a live one: The spammer will put you on the list of live addresses that they share with other spammers, so you'll get more spam. And never respond to spam with flames, either—however much vitriol you muster, it's unlikely to be read, and again you prove that the address from which you sent it is live.

When posting to newsgroups, use a variation of your e-mail address that'll trip up robotic harvesting of e-mail addresses but will let sentient beings read your e-mail address easily. (More on this in the next chapter.)

Think twice before you make your e-mail address available in online directories (or indeed offline directories). Balance your privacy against the need of other people to find your e-mail address for positive reasons. Alternatively, get a secondary e-mail account (perhaps a free account), make that account's address available, and be prepared for a high noise-to-signal ratio on that account. By doing so, you can keep your primary e-mail account mainly on signal but still publicize an e-mail address at which people with whom you haven't shared your primary address can contact you.

If you're interested in actively fighting spam, check out the website of the Coalition Against Unsolicited Commercial Email (CAUCE; www.cauce.org).

Adding Another Mail Account

If you have multiple mail accounts, you can check them all from a single identity or by using multiple identities (as described in "Using Identities to Keep Multiple E-mail Accounts Separate" later in the chapter). If you check multiple accounts from a single identity, messages to all accounts except your Hotmail account end up in the same Inbox, where you can deal with them as if they had all been addressed to the same account. Outlook Express maintains a separate set of folders for Hotmail, so you can keep that separate from your main Inbox.

Which you find more convenient will probably depend on whether you're using the accounts for different purposes (for example, business and personal use) and need to be able to keep the messages for each separate or whether you have (as it were) legacy mailboxes that you can't afford to get rid of because too many of your contacts are still using them (and can't be persuaded to change the e-mail address they have stored for you).

To add another mail account to Outlook Express, take the following steps:

1. Choose Tools ➤ Accounts. Outlook Express displays the Internet Accounts dialog box with the Mail page foremost (shown in Figure 21.38).

FIGURE 21.38

Use the Internet Accounts dialog box to create new accounts and set properties for existing accounts.

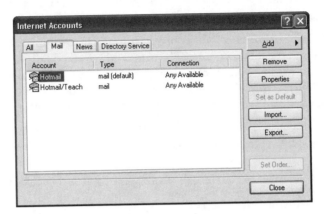

2. Click the Add button and choose Mail from the resulting pop-up menu. Outlook Express starts the Internet Connection Wizard.

3. Enter the details for the account just as you did with your first account in "Setting Up E-mail with Outlook Express" at the beginning of this chapter.

Removing a Mail Account

To remove a mail account, select the account in the Internet Accounts dialog box and click the Remove button. Outlook Express displays an Internet Accounts dialog box to confirm that you want to delete the account. Click the Yes button.

Configuring an Individual Account

You may have thought there were plenty of configuration options earlier in the chapter when you configured Outlook Express—but Outlook Express also lets you configure individual accounts. For example, you might need to change the server used for incoming or outgoing mail; you might want to change the name for the account so that it's easier to recognize when Outlook Express is checking it; or you might want to use a particular digital certificate for one account but not for others.

To change the properties of an account, choose Tools ➤ Accounts. Outlook Express displays the Internet Accounts dialog box with the Mail page foremost. Select the account and click the Properties button. Outlook Express displays the Properties dialog box for the account.

The next sections discuss the options on the pages of the Properties dialog box. The number of pages in the Properties dialog box varies depending on the type of account: It has four pages for an HTTP account, five for a POP3 account, and six for an IMAP account.

General Page Properties

The General page of the Properties dialog box (shown on the left in Figure 21.39) for a mail account contains the following settings:

Mail Account area   Enter the descriptive name for the mail account in the text box. This is the name that you see when Outlook Express is accessing the account or otherwise dealing with it.

User Information area   Enter or adjust your name, organization, e-mail address, and reply address in the four text boxes. The name and e-mail address will be filled in already with the information you entered while setting up the account. Specify the organization if you want to use one. Enter a reply address only if you want replies to your e-mail to be automatically sent to a different e-mail address than the address entered in the E-mail Address text box.

Select the Include This Account when Receiving Mail or Synchronizing check box if you want Outlook Express to check this account for new messages each time you check for new messages.

FIGURE 21.39

The General page (left) and Servers page (right) of the Properties dialog box for a mail account

Servers Page Properties

The Servers page of the Properties dialog box (shown on the right in Figure 21.39) for a mail account contains the following settings:

Server Information area   Enter or adjust the information for the incoming mail server and the outgoing mail server. If you entered this information correctly when setting up the account, you should need to change it only if your ISP changes server type or server name.

Incoming Mail Server area   Enter or adjust your account name and password. Select the Remember Password check box if you want Outlook Express to store your password; clear it if you don't. If this server requires you to use Secure Password Authentication, select the Log On Using Secure Password Authentication check box.

Outgoing Mail Server area   If you need to log on to your outgoing mail server, select the My Server Requires Authentication check box. If you need to use different settings than those for your incoming mail server, click the Settings button. Outlook Express displays the Outgoing Mail Server dialog box (shown in Figure 21.40). Select the Log On Using option button. Enter your account name and (if you wish) your password. Select or clear the Remember Password check box and the Log On Using Secure Password Authentication check box as appropriate. Then click the OK button. Outlook Express closes the Outgoing Mail Server dialog box and returns you to the Properties dialog box.

FIGURE 21.40

If you need to log on to your outgoing mail server, you can use the Outgoing Mail Server dialog box to set the account name and password to use.

Connection Page Properties

The Connection page of the Properties dialog box for a mail account lets you instruct Outlook Express to use a specific dial-up connection or LAN connection for connecting to the account.

To use a specific connection, select the Always Connect to This Account Using check box and select the connection in the drop-down list. Clicking the Settings button displays the Properties dialog box for the connection. Clicking the Add button starts the New Connection Wizard so that you can create a new connection.

Security Page Properties

The Security page of the Properties dialog box (shown on the left in Figure 21.41) for a mail account contains the following settings:

Signing Certificate area   To specify a digital certificate to use for signing messages from this account, click the Select button. Outlook Express displays the Select Default Account Digital ID dialog box. Select the certificate and click the OK button. Outlook Express closes the Select Default Account Digital ID dialog box and enters the name of the certificate in the text box in the Signing Certificate area.

Encrypting Preferences area   To specify an encryption certificate and algorithm, use the Select button and the resulting Select Default Account Digital ID dialog box to enter the name of the certificate in the text box. If necessary (and it shouldn't be), change the algorithm in the Algorithm drop-down list.

FIGURE 21.41

The Security page (left) and Advanced page (right) of the Properties dialog box for a mail account

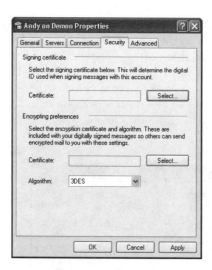

Advanced Page Properties

The Advanced page of the Properties dialog box (shown on the right in Figure 21.41) for a mail account contains a full house of advanced options. This page is not available for HTTP connections such as Hotmail.

Server Port Numbers area   If necessary, change the port number in the Outgoing Mail (SMTP) text box from the default setting (25) to another port specified by your ISP. Likewise, change the port number in the Incoming Mail (POP3) text box if your ISP uses a different port. Also if necessary, select the This Server Requires a Secure Connection (SSL) check box. Again, your ISP will let you know if you need to apply this setting.

Server Timeouts area   If Outlook Express is timing out when you feel it shouldn't be, drag the slider to increase the length of the server timeout interval.

Sending area   Select the Break Apart Messages Larger than *NN* KB check box and enter an appropriate value in the text box if you want Outlook Express to automatically divide large files you attach to a message into a number of smaller parts. This option is useful for making sure that large files don't get rejected by mail servers.

Delivery area   This area of the dialog box is displayed only for POP3 servers. Select the Leave a Copy of Messages on Server check box (which is cleared by default) if you want to leave a copy of messages on the server while downloading the full set of messages. This option is useful when you need to check your mail from a computer other than your usual one but later download the same messages to your usual computer, so as to have the full set of messages on your usual computer. Don't use this option on your usual computer, because the number of messages on the server will build up as you receive more mail, and Outlook Express will download all of them each time you check mail. To reduce this problem, if you leave a copy of messages on the server, you can select the Remove from Server after *NN* Days check box and use the text box to specify the number of days after which Outlook Express should instruct the server to delete the messages you've downloaded.

You can also select the Remove from Server when Deleted from "Deleted Items" check box to make Outlook Express tell the server to delete the messages you've downloaded after you've deleted them *and* removed them from your Deleted Items folder (for example, by emptying the Deleted Items folder).

IMAP Page Properties

The IMAP page of the Properties dialog box (shown in Figure 21.42) for a mail account appears only for accounts that use an IMAP server. It contains the following options:

Folders area In the Root Folder Path text box, enter the name of the root folder—the folder that contains all your folders. For a Unix server, this is usually the `Mail` folder in the folder named with your username. For example, if your username is `ppiper`, your root folder path would usually be `~ppiper/Mail`. (Don't add a forward slash (`/`) to the path, because this invalidates the name.) For a Cyrus IMAP server, the root folder is the Inbox.

Leave the Check for New Messages in All Folders check box selected if you want Outlook Express to check all folders (including hidden folders) for new messages.

Special Folders area If you want to store Outlook Express's Sent Items folder and Drafts folder on the IMAP server, leave the Store Special Folders on IMAP Server check box selected (as it is by default) and enter the appropriate paths in the Sent Items Path text box and the Drafts Path text box.

FIGURE 21.42

The IMAP page of the Properties dialog box for an IMAP mail account

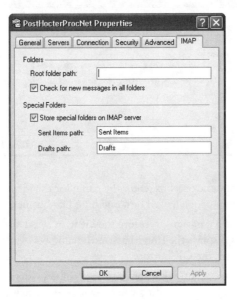

When you've finished adjusting properties in the Properties dialog box, click the OK button. Outlook Express closes the Properties dialog box and returns you to the Internet Accounts dialog box. Click the Close button to return to Outlook Express.

Using Identities to Keep Multiple E-mail Accounts Separate

To enable you to check multiple e-mail accounts, Outlook Express provides support for *identities*— different personalities, either for the same person or for different people. By using identities, you can maintain separate online personae for your business and personal selves, or for different activities that you undertake online. Your Outlook Express identities work for Address Book as well.

NOTE   *In Windows 9x installations that didn't use user profiles, identities were useful for implementing a separate account for each member of the family or household. In XP, it's much better to have each user log on using a separate username, which gives them access to (as it were) their own copy of Outlook Express.*

Outlook Express starts you off with an identity called Main Identity that you get to use by default. After that, it's up to you to create and use identities as you need them.

Creating an Identity

To create an identity, follow these steps:

1. Choose File ➢ Identities ➢ Add New Identity. Outlook Express displays the New Identity dialog box (shown in Figure 21.43).

FIGURE 21.43

Use the New Identity dialog box to create a new identity.

2. In the Type Your Name text box, enter the name for the identity. (This won't necessarily be your name—it might equally well be something like Business or Personal.)

3. If you want to use a password to secure the identity, select the Require a Password check box. Outlook Express displays the Enter Password dialog box. Enter the password in both text boxes and then click the OK button.

4. Click the OK button. Outlook Express closes the New Identity dialog box and displays the Identity Added dialog box, inviting you to switch to the new identity.

5. Click the Yes button or the No button as appropriate. If you select Yes, Outlook Express starts the Internet Connection Wizard so that you can set up the e-mail account for the identity. Do so as usual.

When you've created the account, Outlook Express switches you to the new identity. You'll see that everything looks as normal, except that the title bar and the Outlook Express bar bear the name you gave the identity to remind you who you currently are. Similarly, when you're using your main identity, Outlook Express displays *Main Identity*.

TIP   *You can also use the Identities drop-down list on the Start page to work with identities. This drop-down list contains a Switch Identities item, an Add New Identity item, a Manage Identities item, and a Log Off Current Identity item and provides an alternative way to issue these commands.*

Managing Identities

To manage your identities, follow these steps:

1. Choose File ➢ Identities ➢ Manage Identities. Outlook Express displays the Manage Identities dialog box (shown in Figure 21.44).

FIGURE 21.44

Use the Manage Identities dialog box to manage your identities.

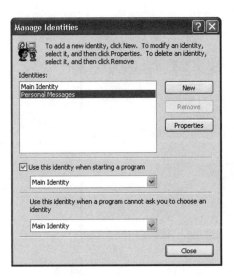

2. To specify which identity Outlook Express should use when you start it, select the Use This Identity when Starting a Program check box and choose the identity in the drop-down list.

3. In the Use This Identity when a Program Cannot Ask You to Choose an Identity drop-down list, select the identity that you want Outlook Express to use for automatic processes.

4. To delete an identity you've created, make sure you're currently using another identity. Then select the victim in the Identities list box and click the Remove button. Outlook Express displays a Warning dialog box (shown in Figure 21.45). Click the Delete button. You can't delete your main identity.

FIGURE 21.45

Outlook Express displays this Warning dialog box when you ask it to delete an identity.

5. Click the Close button. Outlook Express closes the Manage Identities dialog box.

Switching Identities

To switch from one identity to another, follow these steps:

1. Close any message windows that you've been working in.
2. Choose File ➤ Switch Identity. Outlook Express displays the Switch Identities dialog box (shown in Figure 21.46).

FIGURE 21.46

Use the Switch Identities dialog box to switch between your different identities.

3. In the list box, select the identity you want to switch to.
4. If the identity requires a password, enter it in the Password text box.
5. Click the OK button. Outlook Express closes the Switch Identities dialog box and switches you to the identity you chose.

Logging an Identity Off

By default, Outlook Express starts as the identity you chose in the Manage Identities dialog box. But if you like, you can force it to ask you at startup which identity to use. To do so, log off your current identity.

To log off your current identity, close any messages you have open and then take the following steps:

1. Choose File ➤ Switch Identity. Outlook Express displays the Switch Identities dialog box.
2. Click the Log Off Identity button. Outlook Express displays the Log Off Current Identity dialog box.

3. Click the Yes button. Outlook Express logs you off and closes itself.

The next time you start Outlook Express, it displays the Identity Login dialog box (shown in Figure 21.47). Select the identity, enter the password if necessary, and click the OK button.

FIGURE 21.47

When you log an identity off from Outlook Express, Outlook Express displays the Identity Login dialog box the next time you start it.

Importing Messages before Deleting an Identity

As you saw a couple of pages ago, you can delete an identity from the Manage Identities dialog box—but before you delete it, you may want to import the identity's messages into an identity you're keeping. You can do this by taking the following steps:

1. Choose File ➢ Import ➢ Messages. Outlook Express starts the Outlook Express Import Wizard.

2. Select the Microsoft Outlook Express 6 item and click the Next button. The wizard displays the Import from OE6 page (see Figure 21.48).

FIGURE 21.48

Before deleting an identity, you can use the Import from OE6 dialog box to import that identity's messages to another account.

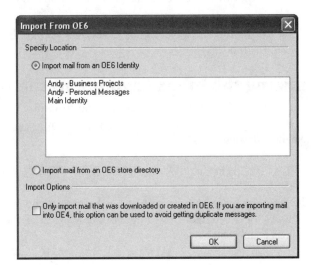

3. Select the identity from which to import the messages and click the Next button. The wizard displays the Location of Messages page, which shows you the current location of the mail folder for the identity you chose.

4. Check the location, correct it if necessary by using the Browse button or by typing the right path, and click the Next button. The wizard displays the Select Folders page.

5. Specify which folders to import by selecting the All Folders option button (the default setting) or by selecting the Selected Folders button and selecting the folders. Click the Next button. The wizard performs the import and displays the Import Complete page.

6. Click the Finish button. The wizard closes itself.

Customizing the Columns Displayed in the Inbox

By default, the Inbox displays six columns: Priority, Attachment, Flag, From, Subject, and Received. For most purposes, these are the most widely useful columns. Outlook Express offers five more columns—Account, Size, Sent, To, and Watch/Ignore—that you can add if you want. You can also remove the default columns, specify widths for all the columns you display, and change the order in which they appear.

NOTE *You can also customize the Hotmail Inbox. This Inbox displays a different set of columns: Attachment, Mark for Offline, From, Subject, and Received. You can add a Size column and a Watch/Ignore column.*

To customize the columns displayed in the Inbox, take the following steps:

1. Right-click a column heading and choose Columns from the context menu, or choose View ➤ Columns. Outlook Express displays the Columns dialog box.

2. In the list box, clear the check box for any column that you don't want to have appear. Select the check box for any column you want to add. For any column you display, you can specify a suitable width in the The Selected Column Should Be *NN* Pixels Wide text box.

3. To rearrange the order of the columns, select a column and use the Move Up or Move Down button.

4. Click the OK button. Outlook Express closes the Columns dialog box and implements your changes to the Inbox.

Customizing the Inbox Layout and the Toolbar

In addition to changing the columns displayed, you can customize the layout of your Inbox, displaying only the elements you want, arranging the Preview pane where you need it, and customizing the toolbar. Take the following steps:

1. Choose View ➤ Layout. Outlook Express displays the Layout page of the Window Layout Properties dialog box.

2. In the Basic area, select the check boxes for the components you want to see, and clear the check boxes for the components you want to hide. Most of the items you've seen already, but there are a couple you haven't:

   ◆ The Outlook bar is a vertical bar that you can display at the left side of the Inbox to provide navigation between the main Outlook Express folders (the Inbox, the Outbox, the

Sent Items folder, the Deleted Items folder, and the Drafts folder). In Outlook itself, which has many more features, the Outlook bar is a useful navigational tool, but in Outlook Express, it's seldom necessary.

◆ The Views bar is a horizontal bar that appears below the toolbar and provides a drop-down list of different views: Show All Messages, Hide Read Messages, or Hide Read or Ignored Messages.

3. To customize the toolbar, click the Customize Toolbar button. Outlook Express displays the Customize Toolbar dialog box. This dialog box works the same as the Customize Toolbar dialog box for Explorer and Internet Explorer. Use the methods discussed in "Customizing the Toolbar" in Chapter 6 to customize it to your liking.

4. In the Preview Pane area, choose options for the Preview pane:

◆ Clear the Show Preview Pane check box if you don't want to use the Preview pane.

◆ If you do use the Preview pane, choose the Below Messages option button or the Beside Messages option button to determine its placement.

◆ Select the Show Preview Pane Header check box if you want to have the Preview pane header displayed. (The Preview pane header is the gray strip at the top of the Preview pane that shows information about the current message.)

5. Click the OK button. Outlook Express closes the Window Layout Properties dialog box and applies your choices.

Backing Up and Restoring Your Outlook Express Folders

If you use Outlook Express extensively, and you use most of the features discussed in this chapter, you'll soon have not only a large quantity of data stored in Outlook Express but also a considerable amount of effort invested—writing and responding to messages, building your list of contacts, configuring your accounts, and constructing rules to highlight important mail and trash as much spam as you can. It only makes sense to back up your Outlook Express folders and configuration so that you can restore your data and your configuration should disaster strike.

The easiest way to back up your Outlook Express data is to use Backup Utility as discussed in Chapter 17. If you store your Outlook Express data in the default location (within your user profile folders), you can back it up by backing up your profile, and restore it by restoring your profile. This data includes your folders, Internet accounts (mail, news, and directory services), mail rules, news rules, and blocked senders.

Alternatively, you can back up individual components by using the following commands:

◆ You can export and import individual mail, news, or directory service accounts by using the Export button and the Import button on the All page or the Category page (Mail, News, or Directory Service) of the Internet Accounts dialog box (Tools ➤ Accounts).

◆ You can back up the message store for an identity by backing up the `\Outlook Express\` folder in the appropriate `\`*`username`*`\Local Settings\Application Data\Identities\` folder. The easiest way of getting to the message store is to display the Store Location dialog box by clicking the Store Folder button on the Maintenance page of the Options dialog box (Tools ➤ Options), copy the path to the folder, choose Start ➤ Run, paste the path into the Run dialog box, and click the OK button. XP opens an Explorer window to the folder.

◆ Similarly, you can back up an individual mail folder within the message store. Open the message store as described in the previous paragraph and back up the appropriate DBX file.

TIP *Two quick tips. First, compact the mail folders before backing them up (unless you've recently compacted them). Second, if you need to back up your mail folder frequently (which is a good idea), you may want to invest in a custom solution for doing so. Products that let you do this include Express Assist from AJSystems.com, Inc. (*`www.ajsystems`*
`.com/oexhome.html`; $29.95 at this writing, with a 15-day evaluation period).*

◆ You can export your Address Book to a file by using the File ➢ Export ➢ Address Book command, as discussed in Chapter 20.

◆ Data for your Outlook Express identities is stored in the `\HKEY_CURRENT_USER\Identities\` key in the Registry. Each identity appears as a globally unique identifier (GUID), such as `{105ABA80-F7BD-44D1-BDA84ACF3919D179}`. Within each identity, you can find data such as your Block Senders list (`\HKEY_CURRENT_USER\Identities\`*GUID*`\Software\Microsoft\Outlook Express\5.0\Block Senders\`) and details of your mail and news rules (`\HKEY_CURRENT_USER\ Identities\`*GUID*`\Software\Microsoft\Outlook Express\5.0\Rules\`). You can back up this data by selecting the appropriate key, choosing File ➢ Export, and exporting the data to a Registry file. You can then restore it, or apply it to another computer, by using the File ➢ Import command from Registry Editor.

Up Next

This chapter has discussed how to set up Outlook Express and how to use its mail features to send and receive e-mail, with and without attachments; manage your e-mail effectively; filter your e-mail by creating custom rules; check multiple accounts; use multiple identities to keep them separate if you need to; customize the Inbox; and back up your Outlook Express data.

The next chapter discusses how to use Outlook Express' newsreader features to read and participate in newsgroups.

Chapter 22

Reading News with Outlook Express

THIS CHAPTER DISCUSSES HOW to use the newsreader features of Outlook Express to read messages posted to Internet newsgroups and to post messages yourself. It assumes that you've already read (and perhaps taken to heart) the previous chapter, setting up Outlook Express and creating as many identities as you need. In this chapter, you'll need to do a little more setup, configuring Outlook Express to access the right news server.

This chapter covers the following topics:

◆ What is news?
◆ The dangers of newsgroups
◆ Setting up Outlook Express to read news
◆ Reading messages in newsgroups
◆ Posting to a newsgroup
◆ Filtering news
◆ Working offline

What Is News?

News in this context refers to Internet newsgroups, a very loose collection of discussion areas based on the Network News Transport Protocol (NNTP). A *newsgroup* consists of the messages (and sometimes attachments) that people post to the list. These messages, often referred to as *posts*, are available to anyone who chooses to take part in the group (or, in a moderated newsgroup, anyone the moderators allow to take part).

Internet newsgroups encompass most every topic under the sun, the moon, and the earth. In the olden days of the early 1990s, newsgroups were divided up into a relatively formalized infor-mal structure based around a dozen or so hierarchies of newsgroups with names such as alt (alternative topics), biz (business topics), comp (computer topics), and assorted others, with many groups in subgroups under each hierarchy. Nowadays, in concert with the near-anarchy into which the Web has grown, newsgroups are often named capriciously, so the best way to find a newsgroup covering topics you're interested in is to search for keywords (or get a recommendation from a friend).

The Dangers of Newsgroups

Before you dive into Internet newsgroups, there are several things that you should keep in mind—even if you're fully up to speed on the dangers of the Internet and the Web in general.

First, Internet newsgroups are public. In most cases, anyone who can get online can post to them. If you dip into the right newsgroups (or maybe the *wrong* newsgroups), you'll sooner or later run into the full range of online humanity—the good, the bad, the ambivalent, the mediocre, and of course the resoundingly ugly.

Some of these people post things that most people would much rather they didn't. Sooner or later (probably sooner), you're likely to run into such posts.

TIP   In addition to public, free-for-all newsgroups, there are also members-only newsgroups that you may be lucky enough to be invited to join. If so, behave yourself.

Second, much of the information you find in newsgroups is incomplete, inaccurate, wrong, misinformation, disinformation, lies, or even advertising. Chances are, you don't believe even a quarter of what you read on the Web; you'd be wise to apply an even greater standard of disbelief to newsgroups.

Third, newsgroups tend to get archived. (For an example of an archive, point your web browser at Google's Deja.com, `groups.google.com/`, where you can search through a truly frightening number of postings recent and ancient.) This archiving means that every throwaway posting has a good chance of remaining available more or less forever—or at least long enough to severely embarrass the poster. Before you dash off an inflammatory post, remember that it may stick around to haunt you for years. Likewise, don't post any personal information that you don't want to share with the whole wired world.

Fourth, spammers use *bots* (robot programs) to harvest e-mail addresses from newsgroups, both for direct use and for selling to other people. (Perhaps you've already received spam offering you *2 million valid e-mail addresses for only $29.99*? Right—many of those e-mail addresses have been harvested from newsgroups.) This harvesting means that if you expose your real e-mail address, you're likely to get spam almost immediately from the current crop of spammers.

Many people who post to newsgroups change their e-mail addresses in a way that will defeat bots but enable humans to establish the real e-mail address with a minimal application of sentience. For example, if your e-mail address is `peterpiper@pacbell.net`, you might post with an address of `peterpiper@removethis.pacbell.net` and add a note saying "remove `removethis` from the address when replying." This type of custom addition to an address is enough to defeat most bots while remaining manageable for anyone with even minimal command of English. Other people consider it unwise to include any form of their e-mail address in public newsgroups. Others yet are happy to expose their real addresses.

Fifth, many of the more specialized newsgroups tend to attract an expert audience that doesn't tolerate off-topic or ill-considered questions well. Before posting, be sure to read the Frequently

Asked Questions list (the FAQ) for the newsgroup, and check through its archives to make sure that the topic of your posting a) is on topic for the newsgroup, and b) hasn't been answered five times already in the last three months.

Still raring to get to those newsgroups? Okay, read on.

Setting Up Outlook Express to Read Newsgroups

To get Outlook Express set up to read newsgroups, take the following steps:

1. Open Outlook Express and display your Start page.
2. Click the Set Up a Newsgroups Account link. Outlook Express starts the Internet Connection Wizard, which displays the Your Name page and enters on it the name for your current identity.

NOTE *If Outlook Express detects an existing news account, it displays a dialog box asking whether you want to create a new Internet news account or use an existing account. The steps shown here apply to creating a new account.*

3. Enter the name you want to use for your news messages. Depending on whether you'll be posting personally or professionally, you may want to use a pseudonym or a variation of your name, at least for some of your identities.
4. Click the Next button. The wizard displays the Internet News E-mail Address page.
5. The wizard suggests this identity's current e-mail address in the E-mail Address text box. You may well want to use a different address to throw off spammers, as discussed in the previous section. If so, enter it now.
6. Click the Next button. The wizard displays the Internet News Server Name page.
7. Enter the name of your news server in the News (NNTP) Server text box.
8. If you need to log on to the news server, select the My News Server Requires Me to Log On check box.
9. Click the Next button. If you didn't select the check box in the previous step, the wizard displays its Congratulations page. Go to step 11.
10. If you did select the My News Server Requires Me to Log On check box, the wizard displays the Internet News Server Logon page (shown in Figure 22.1). Enter your account name and password. Select the Remember Password check box if you think it's wise. Select the Log On Using Secure Password Authentication (SPA) check box if you need to use SPA. Then click the Next button. The wizard displays the Congratulations page.
11. Click the Finish button. The wizard closes. Outlook Express displays a message box prompting you to download the current list of newsgroups from the news account.
12. Click the Yes button or the No button as appropriate. You'll need to download the list of newsgroups at some point—so if this is a convenient time, go ahead. Depending on the speed of your Internet connection, downloading the list will take a few minutes. Skip ahead to the section "Downloading the List of Newsgroups."

FIGURE 22.1

On the Internet
News Server Logon
page of the Internet
Connection Wizard,
enter the logon
information for
your news server.

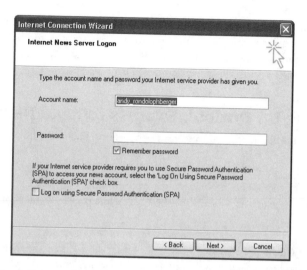

Configuring Outlook Express for newsgroup access like this adds newsgroup items to your Start page. Your Start page now contains links for Create a New News Message, Read News, and Subscribe to Newsgroups. An item for the news server you added appears in the Folders pane. Figure 22.2 shows an example of the changes to the Start page.

FIGURE 22.2

Your Start page now
has links for news,
and the Folders
pane contains an
entry for the news
server you added.

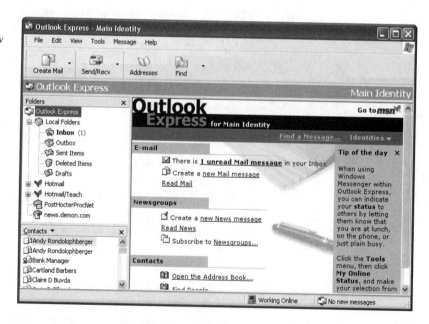

Adding Another News Account

You can add another news account at any time by running the Internet Connection Wizard again. To do so, follow these steps:

1. Choose Tools ➢ Accounts. Outlook Express displays the Internet Accounts dialog box.

2. Click the Add button and choose News from the pop-up menu. Outlook Express starts the Internet Connection Wizard for news.

Changing the Properties for a News Account

You can change the properties for a news account you've set up by working in its Properties dialog box. For example, you might want to change the name that Outlook Express displays for the news account to something snappier, or you might need to change your password or connection information.

To display the Properties dialog box for the account, take either of the following actions:

◆ Right-click the news account in the Folders pane and choose Properties from the context menu.

◆ Choose Tools ➤ Accounts. Outlook Express displays the Internet Accounts dialog box. On the News page, select the account and click the Properties button.

General Page Properties

The General page of the Properties dialog box (shown on the left in Figure 22.3) for a news account contains the following options:

News Account area   In the text box, enter the name that you want displayed for the news account. Changing the name doesn't affect the server.

User Information area   Enter or adjust your name, organization, e-mail address, and reply address in the four text boxes. Select the Include This Account when Checking for New Messages check box if you want Outlook Express to check this account's newsgroups for new messages each time you check for new messages. (Doing so tends to slow down checking for mail.)

FIGURE 22.3

The General page (left) and Server page (right) of the Properties dialog box for a news account.

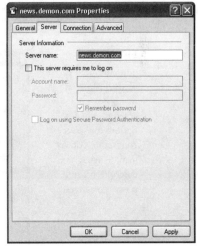

Server Page Properties

The Server page of the Properties dialog box (shown on the right in Figure 22.3) for a news account contains the connection information for the server that you entered during setup. Change this information if necessary to connect to the server. (For example, your ISP might start requiring you to log on or to use Secure Password Authentication.)

Connection Page Properties

The Connection page of the Properties dialog box for a news account lets you specify which connection to use for connecting to the account. In many cases, you won't need to change the settings on this page.

Advanced Page Properties

The Advanced page of the Properties dialog box (shown in Figure 22.4) contains the following options:

Server Port Number area   If necessary, change the port number in the News (NNTP) text box from the default setting (119) to another port specified by your ISP. Also if necessary, select the This Server Requires a Secure Connection (SSL) check box. Again, your ISP will let you know if you need to apply this setting.

Server Timeouts area   If Outlook Express is timing out when you feel it shouldn't be, drag the slider to increase the length of the server timeout interval.

Descriptions area   Select the Use Newsgroup Descriptions check box if you want Outlook Express to download newsgroup descriptions. Doing so can be informative but slows down the downloading of the list of newsgroups.

Posting area   Select the Break Apart Messages Larger than *NN* KB check box and enter an appropriate value in the text box if you want Outlook Express to automatically divide large files you post into a number of smaller parts. (This setting is primarily useful if you're posting large attachments, but it will also help protect the denizens of the newsgroups if you start posting million-word theses on a regular basis.) Select the Ignore News Sending Format and Post Using check box and select the HTML option button or the Plain Text option button if you want Outlook Express to override the format in which you compose your messages.

FIGURE 22.4

The Advanced page of the Properties dialog box for a news account provides options for server connections, downloading newsgroup descriptions, and posting messages.

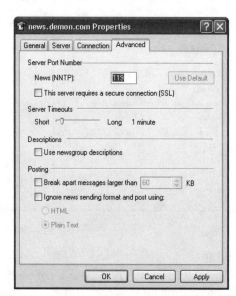

When you've finished choosing options in the Properties dialog box, click the OK button. Outlook Express closes the Properties dialog box and applies your choices.

Downloading the List of Newsgroups

As mentioned in the previous section, Outlook Express encourages you to download the list of newsgroups from the news server you've just added. If you prefer not to do so right away, you can download the list the first time you issue the Tools ➢ Newsgroups command.

Outlook Express displays the Downloading Newsgroups dialog box while downloading the list of newsgroups. The number of newsgroups available depends on the ISP. Some ISPs offer as many newsgroups as they can get (usually a figure upward of 50,000), whereas others provide only the newsgroups that they think their customers want (or should want).

When Outlook Express has finished downloading the list of newsgroups, it displays the list in the Newsgroup Subscriptions box. The next section covers how to subscribe to newsgroups.

Subscribing to Newsgroups

At this point, you're ready to start reading news. You can do this either by subscribing to newsgroups that interest you or simply by opening newsgroups that might interest you and browsing through them.

To subscribe to a newsgroup, follow these steps:

1. Click the Subscribe to Newsgroups link on your Start page, or choose Tools ➢ Newsgroups, or press Ctrl+W. Outlook Express displays the Newsgroup Subscriptions dialog box (shown in Figure 22.5 with two groups subscribed).

FIGURE 22.5

Subscribe to newsgroups in the Newsgroup Subscriptions dialog box.

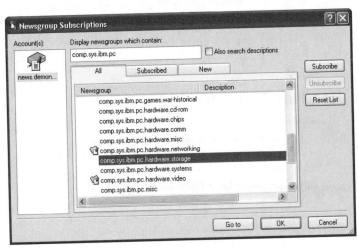

2. In the list box, select a newsgroup that you want to subscribe to, and click the Subscribe button to subscribe:

    ◆ The Newsgroup Subscriptions dialog box has three pages: All, Subscribed, and New. Typically, you'll want to start on the All page, so that you can access all the newsgroups.

Once you've subscribed to the newsgroups you're interested in, use the Subscribed page to access them quickly, and use the New page to check out new newsgroups from time to time.

♦ To filter the thousands of newsgroups down to a manageable number, enter search text in the Display Newsgroups Which Contain text box. For example, if you're interested in PC-compatible computer systems, you could enter `comp.sys.ibm.pc` to display the set of newsgroups that contain that string of text, as shown in the figure.

♦ Select the Also Search Descriptions check box if you want to search the newsgroup descriptions for the terms in the Display Newsgroups Which Contain text box. (Many of the newsgroups lack descriptions, however, so this step may not get you far.)

♦ Outlook Express places an icon to the left of newsgroups you're subscribed to, as you can see with the `comp.sys.ibm.pc.hardware.networking` and `comp.sys.ibm.pc.hardware.video` newsgroups in the figure.

♦ To unsubscribe from a newsgroup you're subscribed to, select the newsgroup and click the Unsubscribe button.

♦ To download the latest newsgroups, click the Reset List button. You'll see the Downloading Newsgroups dialog box again.

NOTE *If a newsgroup you want to read isn't available even after you've reset your list of newsgroups, your ISP probably doesn't carry it. Try requesting the ISP to carry it—if it's a new newsgroup, it may not have appeared on their radar yet. If they won't carry it (for example, because other people might find its content offensive), you might need to buy a subscription to a dedicated news server that carries it.*

3. When you've assembled your list of newsgroups, click the OK button. Outlook Express closes the Newsgroup Subscriptions dialog box and returns you to your Start page, where the Folders pane lists the newsgroups you subscribed to under the news server.

To read a newsgroup without subscribing to it, select its name in the Newsgroup Subscriptions dialog box and click the Go To button. Outlook Express displays the newsgroup.

Reading Newsgroup Messages

To read the messages in a newsgroup you've subscribed to, double-click the newsgroup in the Folders pane to display it. Outlook Express downloads the first batch of headers for the newsgroup—up to 300, at the default setting, if there are that many—and displays them in the Header pane.

Click a message to display it in the Preview pane, as shown in Figure 22.6. Alternatively, double-click a message to display it in a separate window. If a message has an attachment, you can open it by using the same techniques as for e-mail messages with attachments.

TIP *When a large file has been posted in multiple parts, you can reconstitute it by downloading the messages for each part, selecting the messages, right-clicking one of them, and issuing the Combine and Decode command.*

FIGURE 22.6

As with e-mail, you can read newsgroups in the Preview pane or in a separate window.

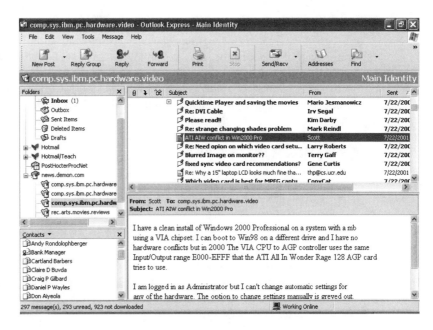

Where posters have replied to a message using the same Subject line, the messages are *threaded*—linked together in a sequence—as you see in Figure 22.7. You can expand a collapsed thread by clicking the + sign next to it, and collapse an expanded sign by clicking its – sign. Each generation of a threaded message is indented more than the previous generations.

FIGURE 22.7

Threaded messages

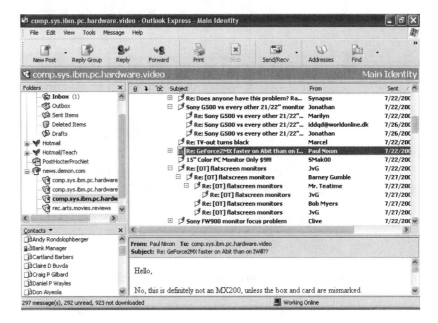

The status bar shows you the current status of your subscription to the newsgroup: how many messages there are in the newsgroup, how many you've read, and how many more you haven't downloaded yet. For example, the status bar in Figure 22.7 displays *297 message(s), 292 unread, 923 not downloaded*.

To download message headers you haven't downloaded yet, choose Tools ➤ Get Next 300 Headers. To display another newsgroup, double-click it in the Folders pane.

Posting to a Newsgroup

You can post to a newsgroup either by creating a new post or by replying to a post:

◆ Click the New Post button on the toolbar to start a new post. Don't use stationery for a post to an Internet newsgroup, because chances are that many people won't be able to see it— they'll probably have to download it as an attached graphic, which improves nobody's temper. Outlook Express starts a new post to the newsgroup.

◆ To reply to the newsgroup, click the Reply Group button on the toolbar. Outlook Express creates a reply message to the group, quoting the text of the original post (shown in Figure 22.8). Reduce this text to the minimum needed for context, because surplus quoted text is a killer in highly trafficked newsgroups.

FIGURE 22.8

Creating a reply to a posting in the `alt.beer` newsgroup

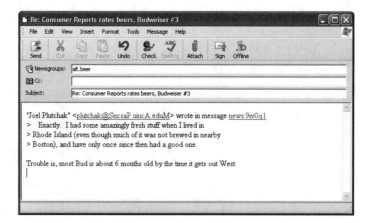

Once you've written your post, set it aside for 10 minutes. Then read it carefully to make sure its meaning is clear, that there's nothing offensive in it, and that you're not about to annoy people by writing in all capitals (doing so is considered to be shouting). Make changes as necessary, and spell-check it if appropriate. Then click the Send button to send the post.

You may also want to reply only to the author of the post (particularly if you don't want to broadcast your response to the post) or to forward the post to someone else:

◆ To reply only to the author of the post, click the Reply button on the toolbar. Outlook Express creates a regular reply for you, as if you were replying to an e-mail message.

◆ To forward a post, click the Forward button on the toolbar. Outlook Express creates a regular forwarded message.

Posting an Attachment

To attach a file to a post, follow the same procedure as for an e-mail message:

1. Click the Attach button or choose Insert ➢ File Attachment. Outlook Express displays the Insert Attachment dialog box.

2. Select the file.

3. Click the Attach button. Outlook Express attaches it to the post.

If you're posting large attachments, make sure that you've selected the Break Apart Messages Larger than *NN* KB check box on the Advanced page of the Properties dialog box for the news account and entered an appropriate value in the text box. What's appropriate will depend on the size of the files you're posting and the sensitivity (or lack of sensitivity) of the news server. For example, if you're posting your latest compositions in MP3 format, consider breaking the files down into segments of 100KB or so by using this option.

NOTE   *Don't post any copyrighted material that you don't have specific permission to distribute. See the section "Understanding Copyright Issues" in Chapter 25 for a brief discussion of copyright.*

Creating Rules for Filtering News

In Chapter 21, you learned how you can filter e-mail to perform preordained maneuvers on messages that match certain criteria. As you'd guess, you can filter news messages as well. For example, you might want to create a rule that captured every message with particular keywords in the header.

Here's the brief version of what to do (for more specifics, look at the section titled "Creating Rules for Filtering E-mail" in Chapter 21):

1. Choose Tools ➢ Message Rules ➢ News. Outlook Express displays the New News Rule dialog box (shown in Figure 22.9).

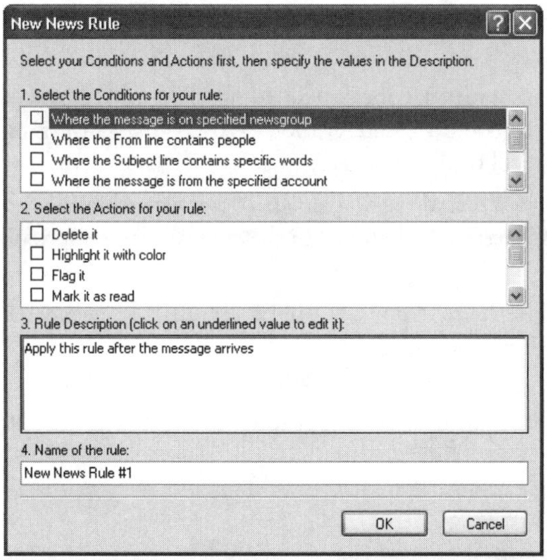

FIGURE 22.9

Use the New News Rule dialog box to create rules for handling news.

2. In the Select the Conditions for Your Rule list box, select the conditions to apply to the messages.

3. In the Select the Actions for Your Rule list box, select the actions to take when the conditions are met.

4. In the Rule Description list box, click the links to edit them as appropriate.

5. In the Name of the Rule text box, enter a memorable name for the rule.

6. Click the OK button to close the New News Rule dialog box. Outlook Express displays the Message Rules dialog box.

7. Click the Apply Now button to display the Apply News Rules Now dialog box.

8. Select the rule in the Select Rules to Apply list box.

9. Use the Browse button and the resulting Apply to Folder dialog box to apply the rule to a different newsgroup if necessary.

10. Click the Apply Now button to apply the rule. Outlook Express displays a message box telling you when the rule has been applied.

11. Click the OK button to close the message box.

12. Click the Close button to close the Apply News Rules Now dialog box.

13. Click the OK button to close the Message Rules dialog box.

Working Offline

If you don't have a permanent Internet connection, you can work offline with newsgroups. Briefly, you download the headers for the newsgroups, mark those you want to download, and then download them when you go back online.

To work offline, follow these steps:

1. When you're ready to go offline, choose File ➢ Work Offline. Outlook Express stops working online and switches to offline mode. The status bar displays *Working Offline*.

2. Browse the headers for the newsgroups you subscribe to. Mark any messages you want to download:

   ◆ To mark a message for downloading, right-click it and choose Download Message Later from the context menu. Outlook Express marks the message with an arrow to indicate that it will be downloaded.

   ◆ To mark a thread for downloading, right-click one of the messages in it and choose Download Conversation Later from the context menu. Outlook Express marks the messages with arrows.

3. When you're ready to go back online, choose File ➢ Work Online or double-click the *Working Online* indicator on the status bar.

4. With the newsgroup selected, choose Tools ➢ Synchronize Newsgroup. Outlook Express displays the Synchronize Newsgroup dialog box (shown in Figure 22.10).

FIGURE 22.10

In the Synchronize Newsgroup dialog box, specify which items to download.

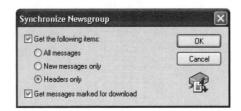

5. Leave selected the Get Messages Marked for Download check box. To download further headers, select the Get the Following Items check box and the Headers Only option button.

6. Click the OK button. Outlook Express downloads the items you specified.

7. Choose File ➤ Work Offline to go offline again to read the items.

Up Next

In this chapter, you've seen how to use Outlook Express' newsreader features to read Internet newsgroups and to post to newsgroups. Along the way, you've learned what newsgroups are, and you've been lectured a bit about the unpleasant things that may happen to you in newsgroups if you don't pay attention.

The next chapter discusses how to use Windows Messenger for instant messaging.

Chapter 23

Instant Messaging with Windows Messenger

THIS CHAPTER DISCUSSES HOW to use Windows Messenger, the instant-messaging software built into XP. Actually, that should probably be "kinda built into XP," because Windows Messenger is one of the "middleware" items that Microsoft may be legally obliged to remove from XP for competitive reasons. So if you can't find Messenger on your computer, that's probably why. In that case, you may want to download Messenger from Microsoft's MSN website (`messenger.msn .com`)—or you may prefer to use other instant messaging software, some of which whoever provided your version of XP may have supplied.

Windows Messenger (hereafter plain *Messenger* except where we need to be formal) provides solid instant-messaging capabilities: You can keep a list of online buddies; see at a glance which of them are online; and communicate instantly with them via text-based chat, voice, and even video (if you have the hardware). You can also transfer files to them and receive files from them.

Sad to say, Messenger also has a major downside, in that you need to have a Microsoft .NET Passport in order to use Messenger. (In case you haven't run into it yet, Microsoft .NET Passport is a sort of electronic identity.) If you have a Hotmail account or MSN account, you can use that as your .NET Passport, but there's no other way around the requirement. (This is one of the reasons why you may want to use other instant messaging software.)

This chapter covers the following topics:

- ◆ Configuring Windows Messenger
- ◆ Adding and removing contacts
- ◆ Chatting with one or more people
- ◆ Using emoticons in your messages
- ◆ Adding voice and video to a conversation
- ◆ Blocking and unblocking users
- ◆ Transferring files via Messenger
- ◆ Collaborating and program sharing

NOTE *In addition to Messenger, XP includes NetMeeting, a chat, communication, and collaboration program that Microsoft has supplied with the last several generations of Windows. NetMeeting can do many of the things that Messenger does, but it doesn't tie into a central server system and it doesn't require you to have a .NET Passport. NetMeeting outdoes Messenger in several ways, such as letting you share programs with multiple people at a time, whereas Messenger is limited to sharing with one other person. Web Chapter 3, available from the Sybex website (`www.sybex.com`), discusses NetMeeting in some depth.*

Why Instant Messaging Is Hot

Instant messaging (IM) is hot because it's a great way to keep in touch with people. The big advantage to IM is that the communication—the conversation, if you will—takes place in real time. If someone is online at the same time you are, you can communicate with them. Like other IM software, Messenger notifies you when your contacts come online (and notifies your contacts when *you* go online), so you know who's available to chat. The disadvantage to IM, of course, is that the person or people with whom you're communicating need to be online at the same time as you. If they're not online (or are pretending not to be online), you can't communicate with them.

NOTE *At this writing, Microsoft and AOL are continuing their face-off over instant messaging, with AOL refusing to give users of IM software other than its own AOL Instant Messenger (AIM) software access to AIM users. This means that if you use Windows Messenger and your buddy uses AIM, you can't send them instant messages—you'll need to install AIM instead. On the plus side, AIM is free, doesn't require that you have an AOL account, and works well. On the minus side—well, nobody wants to be compelled to run a particular software package or sign up for a particular network identity, do they?*

Starting Messenger

To start Messenger, choose Start ➢ All Programs ➢ Windows Messenger. Alternatively, if Messenger is displaying an icon in the notification area, double-click it.

If you haven't added a .NET Passport to your XP user account, Messenger displays a Click Here to Sign In link in its window. Clicking this link starts the .NET Passport Wizard, which shepherds you through the process of adding an existing .NET Passport to XP or getting a new .NET Passport and adding that to XP. Once you've done that, Messenger signs you in.

Once you've started Messenger, it displays an icon in your notification area. Click this icon to display a menu of actions you can take with Messenger.

When Messenger appears on your screen, chances are that it tells you that you don't have anyone in your contacts list and suggests you click the Add button to start adding contacts. (If you've just set Messenger up, your lack of contacts should be no surprise.) Figure 23.1 shows Messenger with a modest number of contacts added. As you can see in the figure, Messenger tells you the number of new messages you have in your Hotmail or MSN account (if you have one).

You're probably itching to add some contacts and get on with messaging. But before you do that, configure Messenger by choosing options as described in the next section.

FIGURE 23.1

Messenger with
some contacts added

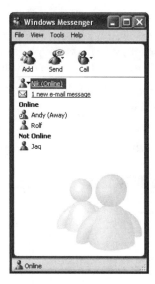

Configuring Messenger

Messenger comes with a raft of configuration options. You don't need to set all of them at once (but this section covers them all in case you want to), but you should know about them before using Messenger. At the very least, you should edit your public profile so that you know what information other people can access about you.

Choose Tools ➢ Options to display the Options dialog box, then configure your choice of the options described in the following sections.

NOTE *The following sections discuss the options available in Windows Messenger 4.6, the version current at this writing. XP Home ships with Windows Messenger version 4, but Messenger actively encourages you to update it to the latest version available—and you'll probably want to do so. But the later versions of Messenger offer some different features from the earlier versions, and they put some controls on different pages of the Options dialog box—so if you're using a version other than 4.6, you may need to do a little sleuth work to find the information you need.*

Personal Page Options

The Personal page of the Options dialog box (shown on the left in Figure 23.2) contains a couple of important settings and a couple of trivial ones.

My .NET Messenger Service Display Name text box   Enter the name you want Messenger to display for you.

Edit Profile button   If you have a Hotmail account or an MSN account, click the Edit Profile button to edit the profile of information that .NET Messenger Service maintains on you for display to other users. Depending on which version of Messenger you have, the first time you click this button, you may see a message box telling you that you need to go to the Add-in website and install an add-in. Click the Yes button, download the add-in, agree to the license agreement, and install it, then click the Edit Profile button again. Messenger opens an Internet Explorer window to the MSN Member Directory website. On this, you can provide information including your real name and whether to share it with other people; your location, age, gender, marital status, occupation, interests; and whether to allow people to contact you at an e-mail address of your choosing.

Change Font button   Use this button and the resulting Set My Message Font dialog box to specify the font you want to use in IM windows.

Show Graphics (Emoticons) in Instant Messages check box   Clear this check box (which is selected by default) if you want to prevent Messenger from displaying emoticons (for example, ☺).

FIGURE 23.2

On the Personal page of the Options dialog box, set your display name and edit your Passport public profile. On the Phone page, specify your country or region code and enter the phone numbers you want Messenger to know.

 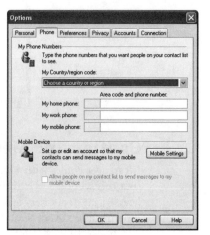

TROUBLESHOOTING: "THE DISPLAY NAME YOU CHOSE WAS INVALID" ERROR MESSAGE

The error message "The display name you chose was invalid. Please choose another display name and try again" means that you've included in your display name a trademarked name or another word that Microsoft has decided not to let you use. For example, if you try to set "Messenger" as your display name, you'll provoke this message. The same goes for any of the major obscenities. But you can call yourself "Bill Gates" without Messenger objecting.

Phone Page Options

The Phone page of the Options dialog box (shown on the right in Figure 23.2) lets you specify your country or region code and your home, work, and mobile phone numbers.

If you want your contacts to be able to send messages to your mobile phone or other mobile device, click the Mobile Settings button. Messenger opens an Internet Explorer window to the MSN Mobile website, which walks you through the signup process. You'll need your phone to be powered on and receiving for the signup process to work.

Once you've signed up, you can select or clear the Allow People on My Contact List to Send Messages to My Mobile Device check box to control whether your contacts can send messages to your mobile.

Preferences Page Options

The Preferences page of the Options dialog box (shown on the left in Figure 23.3) contains a slew of options that affect Messenger's behavior:

Run This Program when Windows Starts check box   Leave this check box selected (as it is by default) if you want XP to launch Messenger every time you log on to XP. Clear this check box if you prefer to run Messenger manually when you need it.

Allow This Program to Run in the Background check box   Leave this check box selected (as it is by default) if you want Messenger to be able to run in the background and lurk in your notification area when you're not actively using it. Keeping Messenger running in the background lets you know instantly when one of your contacts comes online or sends you a message, but it also means that you need to keep your Internet connection open all the time. If you don't want Messenger to run in the background, clear this check box, and Messenger will exit when you close its window.

Show Me as "Away" when I'm Inactive for *NN* Minutes check box and text box   Leave this check box selected (as it is by default) if you want Messenger to change your status to Away after the specified period of inactivity. (Adjust the number of minutes in the text box as necessary. The default setting is 10 minutes, which is too short for many busy people.) Clear this check box if you don't want Messenger to monitor you in this way. If you clear this check box, Messenger changes your status to Away when your screen saver kicks in. (If you're not using a screen saver, your status will remain Online until you change it.)

Display Alerts when Contacts Come Online check box   Leave this check box selected (as it is by default) if you want Messenger to pop up an alert above the notification area when one of your contacts comes online.

Display Alerts when an Instant Message Is Received check box   Leave this check box selected (as it is by default) if you want Messenger to pop up an alert above the notification area when you receive an instant message.

Display Alerts when E-mail Is Received check box   Leave this check box selected (as it is by default) if you want Messenger to pop up an alert above the notification area when you receive an e-mail message. This option works only for Hotmail accounts and MSN accounts.

Play Sound when Contacts Sign In or Send a Message check box   Leave this check box selected (as it is by default) if you want Messenger to play a sound when contacts of yours sign in or send you a message. This audio alert is especially useful if you turn off the two visual alerts. If you use this option, you can click the Sounds button to customize the sounds displayed. XP displays the Sound and Audio Devices Properties dialog box. In the Program Events list box on the Sounds page, scroll down to the Windows Messenger category, and assign sounds that you like to the Contact Online event (when a contact signs in), the New Alert event (when Messenger displays an alert), the New Mail event, and the New Message event. Then click the OK button. XP closes the Sound and Audio Devices Properties dialog box.

Files Received from Other Users Will Be Put in This Folder text box   Specify the folder in which you want Messenger to put files that you receive from your contacts. The default setting is your \My Documents\My Received Files\ folder.

FIGURE 23.3

On the Preferences page (left) of the Options dialog box, customize Messenger's behavior. On the Privacy page (right), maintain your Allow List and your Block List.

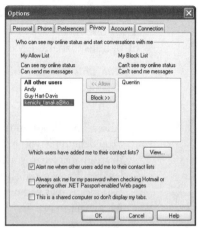

Privacy Page Options

The Privacy page of the Options dialog box (shown on the right in Figure 23.3) is where you maintain your Allow List (people who can see your online status and can send you messages) and your Block List (people who can do neither).

To move a contact from one list to another, select them in the appropriate list box and click the Allow button or the Block button.

TIP By default, Messenger allows all other users to contact you and view your status until you block them. If you want to use Messenger privately, consider blocking all other users until you decide to allow them. To do so, select the All Other Users item in the My Allow List and click the Block button to move it to the My Block List.

To see which users have added you to their contacts lists, click the View button. Messenger displays the Which Users Have Added You? dialog box, which provides an unadorned list of names. You can right-click a name and choose Add to Contacts from the context menu to add the person to your list of contacts, or choose Properties from the context menu to display a Properties dialog box giving information about the person.

Alert Me when Other Users Add Me to Their Contact Lists check box   Leave this check box selected (as it is by default) to have Messenger notify you when another user adds you to their contact list. Clear this check box if you prefer peace.

Always Ask Me for My Password when Checking Hotmail or Opening Other .NET Passport-Enabled Web Pages check box   Select this check box (which is cleared by default) if you want to enter your Passport password manually each time it's required by a website. Entering the password manually improves your security, but you may find yourself needing to enter the password too often for speedy or comfortable browsing.

This Is a Shared Computer So Don't Display My Tabs check box   Select this check box (which is cleared by default) if you share your user account with other people and want to prevent them from seeing the tabs you have added to Messenger. See the section "Working with Tabs," toward the end of this chapter, for a discussion of what tabs are and what you're supposed to do with them.

Accounts Page Options

The Accounts page of the Options dialog box (see Figure 23.4) provides controls for controlling whether Messenger signs into .NET Messenger Service or another communications service first. Briefly, a communications service in this context is an instant-messaging service implemented within a corporate network or another network, either using the Microsoft Exchange Server software or a Session Initiation Protocol (SIP) server package. (SIP is a signaling protocol for messaging, conferencing, and telephony over TCP/IP networks.) Because XP Home is designed not to connect to such networks, you're less likely to use a communications service with XP Home than with XP Professional, which is designed to be connected to such networks.

FIGURE 23.4

On the Accounts page of the Options dialog box, you can specify which account Messenger should log on to first.

In the Sign In with This Account First area, select the .NET Passport option button (which should be selected by default) to make Messenger sign into .NET Messenger Service first. Select the Communications Service option button to sign into your designated communications service first.

If you select the .NET Passport option button, Messenger makes available the My Contacts Include Users of a Communications Service check box. If you do use a communications service alongside .NET Messenger Service, select this check box, and then configure your communications service account as described below.

If you select the Communications Service option button, Messenger makes available the My Contacts Include Users of .NET Messenger Service check box. If you use .NET Messenger Service as well as your communications service, select this check box. You don't need to enter further information, because you've already signed in using your .NET Passport, so .NET Messenger Service knows all it needs to know about you.

If you're using a communications service account, you need to set it up. Depending on how the service is configured on your network, you may need to do no more than enter your username in the

Sign-In Name text box: Messenger's automatic-configuration option will take care of the rest. But in many cases you'll also need to click the Advanced button to display the Communications Service Connection Configuration dialog box (see Figure 23.5). Select the Configure Settings option button, enter the server's name or IP address in the Server Name or IP Address text box, and select the TCP option button, the TLS option button, or the UDP option button as appropriate. (You will probably need to ask your communications service administrator for these settings.) Then click the OK button to close the Communications Service Connection Configuration dialog box.

FIGURE 23.5

If you use a communications service (other than .NET Messenger Service) with Messenger, you may need to set options in the Communications Service Connection Configuration dialog box.

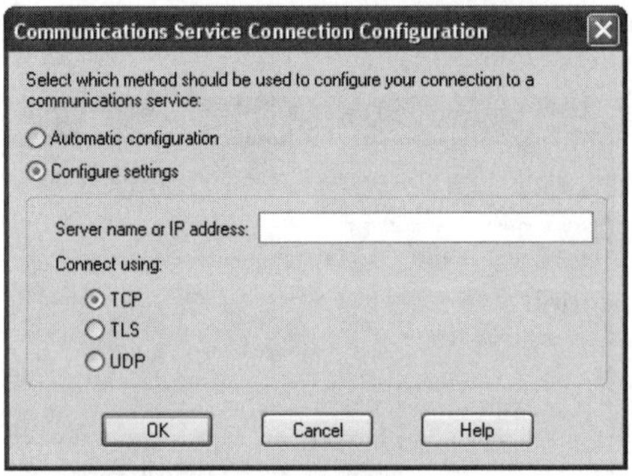

Connection Page Options

On the Connection page of the Options dialog box, you can specify proxy server settings if you connect to the Internet through a proxy server (for example, through a company network). If not, leave these settings alone.

Running the Audio and Video Tuning Wizard

If you have speakers (or headphones) and a microphone, you can use them to make voice calls via Messenger. If you have a web cam or another live video camera, you can make video calls as well. To set Messenger up for making voice and video calls, make sure your sound and video hardware is plugged in and working, and then run the Audio and Video Tuning Wizard by choosing Tools ➢ Audio and Video Tuning Wizard. The wizard walks you through the process of identifying the microphone and camera to use and choosing appropriate microphone-sensitivity and speaker-volume settings.

Signing Out and Signing Back In

Messenger automatically signs you in when you start it. But you can sign out manually, leaving Messenger running, by choosing File ➢ Sign Out.

The first time you sign out, if you have things going on, Messenger displays a dialog box explaining that signing out will close all your conversations and stop any file transfers. Click the OK button to proceed. After that, Messenger doesn't give you any warning when you sign out.

To sign back in as the same user, click the Click Here to Sign In As *Username* link in the Windows Messenger window. Messenger signs you in. To sign in using a different Passport, click the Or, Click Here to Sign In As Someone Else link, choose File ➤ Sign In, or click the Messenger icon in the notification area and choose Sign In from the menu it displays. Messenger displays the .NET Messenger Service dialog box (shown in Figure 23.6). Enter your sign-in name and password, then click the OK button.

FIGURE 23.6

Signing back in to Messenger Service

TROUBLESHOOTING: MESSENGER SIGN-IN AND CONNECTION ERRORS

This sidebar discusses the two most common errors you may suffer when trying to sign in with Messenger.

YOU CAN'T LOG ON TO .NET MESSENGER SERVICE

The most likely causes of not being able to log on to Messenger are that .NET Messenger Service is down or that you've got your .NET Passport name or password wrong. Take the following steps:

1. Use Internet Explorer to check the status of .NET Messenger Service at messenger.microsoft.com/ support/status.asp. If there's a problem listed, you'll probably need to wait for a while before logging on.

2. Make sure that you don't have Caps Lock on, making you mistype your password.

3. Go to a .NET Passport–enabled website for which you have an account (for example, the Hotmail website or the MSN website) and try to sign in. If you can, your .NET Passport is still valid.

MESSENGER IS BLOCKED BY A FIREWALL, NAT DEVICE, OR ROUTER

Messenger usually gets along well with XP's Internet Connection Firewall (ICF), because both are Microsoft products and were taught from the cradle to work together, but other firewalls may cause Messenger grief, and you may need to open ports manually on the firewall so that Messenger can communicate through it. You may also need to reconfigure any other NAT device or router you use for your Internet connection to get it to pass Messenger traffic.

Messenger uses TCP port 6901 and UDP port 6901 for incoming voice calls; UDP ports 6801, 6901, and 2001–2120 for computer-to-phone voice calls; and TCP ports 6891–6900 for file transfer. If you need to open these ports on ICF, see the section "Configuring ICF to Pass Data for Specific Programs and Services" in Chapter 32 for instructions. For other firewalls, you're on your own.

Adding a Contact

You can add a contact to your list of contacts in several ways: by using their e-mail address or Passport sign-in name; by searching for them in a directory; by adding them when they contact you; or by reciprocating when they add you as a contact.

Adding a Contact by E-mail Address or Passport Sign-In

If you know a contact's e-mail address or Passport sign-in name, you can add them to your contacts list as follows:

1. Click the Add button in the Messenger window (or choose File ➤ Add a Contact). Messenger displays the How Do You Want to Add a Contact? page of the Add a Contact Wizard.
2. Leave the By E-mail Address or Sign-In Name option button selected, as it is by default.
3. Click the Next button. Messenger displays the Please Type Your Contact's Complete E-mail Address page.
4. Enter the e-mail address and click the Next button. Messenger searches for a matching user. If it finds one, it displays a Success screen telling you that it has added the contact to your list. If Messenger doesn't find a match, it offers to send a message to the user inviting them to try Messenger. Take up this request if you like.

Adding a Contact by Searching for Them

You can also add a contact to your contacts list by searching for them:

1. Click the Add button in the Messenger window (or choose File ➤ Add a Contact). Messenger displays the How Do You Want to Add a Contact? page of the Add a Contact Wizard.
2. Select the Search for a Contact option button.
3. Click the Next button. Messenger displays the Type Your Contact's First and Last Name page.
4. Enter the person's first name and last name. If you're sure of their country or region, specify that in the Country/Region drop-down list. By default, Messenger searches in the Hotmail Member Directory. You may be able to choose another search location, such as your Address Book, in the Search for This Person At drop-down list.
5. Click the Next button. Messenger displays a Search Results page showing possible matches.
6. Select the right person and click the Next button. Messenger then walks you through the process of having the .NET service send an e-mail to the person and tell them how to install Messenger and contact you. You can add your own message to this e-mail, but Messenger won't give you the person's e-mail address so that you can contact them directly.

Adding a Contact when Someone Adds You to Their Contacts List

You can also add a contact quickly by adding a person who adds you to *their* contacts list (unless you've configured Messenger not to notify you when this happens).

When someone adds you to their contacts list, Messenger displays the Windows Messenger dialog box shown in Figure 23.7 asking whether you want to allow this person or block them. Select the

Allow This Person to See when You Are Online and Contact You option button or the Block This Person from Seeing when You Are Online and Contacting You option button as appropriate. If you want to add the person to your contacts list, leave the Add This Person to My Contact List check box selected. If not, clear it. Then click the OK button. Messenger closes the dialog box and takes the actions you specified.

FIGURE 23.7

Messenger displays this Windows Messenger dialog box when someone adds you to their contacts list. Specify whether to allow the contact or block them.

Removing a Contact from Your Contacts List

To remove a contact from your contacts list, select their entry and press the Delete key (or choose File ➤ Delete Contact). Alternatively, right-click the contact and choose Delete Contact from the context menu. Messenger deletes the contact without confirmation.

Chatting

To chat with a Messenger user, double-click the user's entry in the Online list, or right-click the user's entry in the Online list and choose Send an Instant Message from the context menu.

Messenger opens a Conversation window of chat with the user. Figure 23.8 shows an example. Type a message into the text box and press the Enter key (or click the Send button) to send it.

FIGURE 23.8

Starting a conversation in Messenger

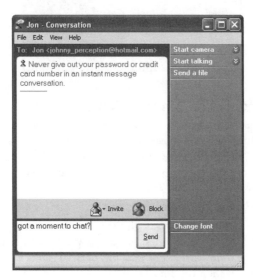

The other user receives a screen pop (of which Figure 23.9 shows an example) telling them that you've sent them a message and a minimized Conversation window. The user can display the Conversation window by clicking the screen pop (if they're quick enough to catch it before it disappears) or by clicking the Conversation window's button on the Taskbar.

FIGURE 23.9

Messenger displays a screen pop like this when someone sends you a message.

Figure 23.10 shows chat getting started in a Conversation window. Note the readout at the bottom that tells you that the other protagonist in the chat is typing a message. This alert helps you avoid sending overlapping messages and having the conversations spiral off into multiple threads.

FIGURE 23.10

Chatting in a Conversation window. The readout at the bottom warns the user that the other participant is typing a message.

Adding More People to a Conversation

To add a third or fourth person to your current conversation, choose File ➢ Invite ➢ To Join This Conversation. From the submenu, select one of your contacts from the context menu. Alternatively, select the Other item, specify the user's e-mail address in the Invite to This Conversation dialog box, and click the OK button. Messenger adds the user to the conversation if they're online.

Including Emoticons in Your Messages

To include *emoticons* (also called *smileys* or *glyphs*) in your messages, type in the appropriate text sequence. Table 23.1 lists the possibilities. Note that where the main protagonist is a letter, you can type it either uppercase or lowercase. For example, both **(d)** and **(D)** produce a martini-glass icon—so use whichever capitalization you find easier to type.

TABLE 23.1: TEXT SEQUENCES FOR PRODUCING EMOTICONS

EMOTICON	TYPE	ALTERNATIVE	EMOTICON	TYPE
	:)	:-)		(X)
	:d	:-D or :-> or :>		(Z)
	:o	:-O		(P)
	:P	:-P		(B)
	;)	;-)		(D)
	:(	:-(or :-< or :<		(T)
	:-S	:S		(@)
	:|	:-|		(C)
	(Y)			(I)
	(N)			(H)
	(L)			(S)
	(U)			(*)
	(K)			(8)
	(G)			(E)
	(F)			(M)

When you send a sequence that contains the text sequence for an emoticon, Messenger converts the text sequence and displays the emoticon on both your screen and that of the person (or people) you're chatting with.

To prevent Messenger from displaying emoticons, choose Edit ➤ Show Emoticons so that Messenger removes the check mark from the Show Emoticons item on the menu. You'll then see the characters intended to make up the emoticon still as text. To allow Messenger to display emoticons again, issue the command again.

Setting Font, Style, and Color for Text You Send

If you want to be distinctive, you can change the font, style, and color for text you send to others and that you see on your screen. For the text you see in the Messenger windows, you can change the size as well. (You can't change the size of the text others see, and they can't change the size you see.)

To set the font, style, color, and size, choose Edit ➤ Change Font. Messenger displays the Change My Message Font dialog box. Choose settings you like and click the OK button to apply them.

Adding Voice to a Conversation

If both participants have functioning audio hardware, you can add voice to a Messenger conversation between two people. (You can't use voice in a conversation that has three or four people.)

As usual for Internet telephony, the audio that's transmitted is converted from its (spoken) analog form to a digitized version, transmitted digitally, and then converted back to analog output at the sound card, headphones, or speakers on the other end. As a result, the quality tends to suffer compared to a regular phone call, in which the audio stays analog the whole way. That said, you can get intelligible audio quality over a connection as slow as 21.6Kbps, acceptable quality in the 40–53Kbps range, and good quality over faster connections.

NOTE *If you haven't run the Audio and Video Tuning Wizard, Messenger runs it the first time you click the Start Talking heading.*

To add voice to your current conversation, click the Start Talking heading in the right pane in the Conversation window. Messenger displays a Speakers volume control and a Microphone Mute check box (shown in Figure 23.11) and notifies the person you're chatting with that you want to have a voice conversation. They get to accept this or decline it. If they accept, Messenger establishes the connection.

FIGURE 23.11

When you add voice to a Messenger conversation, the Conversation window displays a Speakers volume control and a Microphone Mute control.

To hang up the voice portion of the call, click the Stop Talking heading.

TROUBLESHOOTING: SOLVING AUDIO PROBLEMS IN MESSENGER

Audio in Messenger is usually pretty straightforward: If you can get audio, it works okay. And if you have plenty of bandwidth, audio sounds pretty good. If you don't have enough bandwidth (for example, a slow modem connection), audio may be low quality or choppy. But there are a few wrinkles to Messenger audio that you may run into. Read on....

WINDOWS MESSENGER CAN'T SEND AUDIO OR VIDEO TO MSN MESSENGER

At this writing, Windows Messenger can send audio and video only to other computers running Windows Messenger (in other words, computers running XP), not to MSN Messenger (computers running earlier versions of Windows).

Continued on next page

TROUBLESHOOTING: SOLVING AUDIO PROBLEMS IN MESSENGER *(continued)*

YOU GET FEEDBACK OR ECHO

If audio in Messenger suffers from feedback or echoing, and you use a USB camera that uses Microsoft USB audio, download the Messenger update that includes Acoustic Echo Cancellation (AEC) from the Microsoft Support website (`support.microsoft.com`). The easiest way to do so is to search for Q310507 and follow the link that the resulting article provides.

Once you've installed the AEC update, you can turn AEC off by running the Audio Tuning Wizard and selecting the I Am Using Headphones check box on the Select the Microphone and Speakers You Want to Use page. (To turn AEC back on, clear this check box.)

If you don't use a USB camera that uses Microsoft USB audio, try using headphones instead of speakers.

MICROPHONE SLIDER IN CONVERSATION WINDOW DOESN'T WORK

If the microphone slider in a Conversation window doesn't seem to work, the problem is most likely that Messenger is using XP's microphone setting for playback rather than for recording. To fix this problem, take the following steps:

1. Choose Start ➢ Control Panel. XP displays Control Panel.

2. Click the Sounds, Speech, and Audio Devices link. XP displays the Sounds, Speech, and Audio Devices page.

3. Click the Advanced Volume Controls link in the See Also list. XP displays the volume control window for playback. This window uses different names depending on your hardware and software configuration, but is often called Play Control or Master Volume.

4. Choose Options ➢ Properties. XP displays the Properties dialog box.

5. In the Adjust Volume For group box, select the Recording option button.

6. Click the OK button. XP closes the Properties dialog box and displays the volume control window for recording. As with the playback window, this window uses different names depending on your configuration, but it's often called Record Control or Recording Control.

7. Choose Options ➢ Exit to close the volume control window for recording.

Now, you may feel that this procedure was missing a step between steps 6 and 7—that you should have *done* something in the volume control window for recording. But this little four-step and shuffle should have changed the association of the Messenger microphone setting from the playback control to the recording control.

MOVING THE SPEAKER SLIDER MOVES THE MICROPHONE SLIDER

Because of Messenger's automatic gain control, moving the Speaker slider *does* move the Microphone slider as well—by design. Don't worry about it. Messenger doesn't provide an option for turning off automatic gain control, so there's not much you can do about this.

CAN'T TRANSFER VOICE OR VIDEO ACROSS NON-SIP ROUTERS

Messenger uses Session Initiation Protocol (the acronym is SIP) for transferring voice and video. For SIP to work, your Internet connection–sharing device needs to be SIP-aware. ICS is SIP-aware, as are most newer hardware routers, but older routers tend not to be. You may be able to upgrade some older routers by flashing their BIOS.

Adding Video to a Conversation

If one or both participants have video hardware installed, you can add video to a Messenger conversation between two people. (As with voice, you can't use video in a conversation that has three or four people.)

To add video to a conversation, click the Start Camera heading. Messenger displays a camera panel on your computer with a picture-in-picture picture of the video you're sending, and invites your victim to take part in the video conversation. If they accept, they receive a larger version of the picture.

To toggle your picture-in-picture picture on and off, click the Options button and choose Show My Video As Picture-in-Picture from the menu.

To stop transmitting or receiving video, click the Stop Camera heading.

TROUBLESHOOTING: SOLVING VIDEO PROBLEMS IN MESSENGER

Compared to NetMeeting (which is discussed in Web Chapter 3, available on the Sybex website, www.sybex.com), Messenger has relatively few video problems. These are the problems you're most likely to run into.

WINDOWS MESSENGER CAN'T SEND VIDEO TO MSN MESSENGER

As mentioned in the previous sidebar, at this writing, Windows Messenger can send audio and video only to other computers running Windows Messenger (in other words, computers running XP), not to MSN Messenger (computers running earlier versions of Windows).

MESSENGER DOESN'T RECOGNIZE YOUR VIDEO CAMERA

If Messenger appears not to recognize your video camera, take the following steps:

1. Check that the camera is plugged into the correct jack on your computer.

2. Check that Windows Image Acquisition has identified the camera: Choose Start ➢ My Computer to open a My Computer window, and see if the camera appears in the Scanners and Cameras area at the bottom of the window. (The Scanners and Cameras area doesn't appear at all if XP hasn't recognized any scanner or camera.) If Windows Image Acquisition hasn't recognized the video camera, use Device Manager to uninstall the camera, then run the Add Hardware Wizard to install it.

3. Check that the video camera is working with Windows Image Acquisition. The easiest way to do this is to open Paint (Start ➢ All Programs ➢ Accessories ➢ Paint), choose File ➢ From Scanner or Camera, and see that the Capture Pictures from Video dialog box shows an image feed from the camera.

4. Run the Audio Tuning Wizard from Messenger (Tools ➢ Audio Tuning Wizard) and make sure that Messenger is trying to use the right video camera.

YOU NEED TO USE AN UNSUPPORTED ANALOG TV TUNER ADAPTER OR DV CAMCORDER

If you need to use an analog TV tuner adapter or a digital-video camcorder that Messenger doesn't support out of the (XP) box, download the Messenger update that includes Acoustic Echo Cancellation, as described in the sidebar "Troubleshooting: Solving Audio Problems in Messenger," earlier in this chapter. This fix includes support for analog TV tuners and digital-video camcorders as well as AEC.

Blocking and Unblocking Users

To block somebody from chatting with you, take one of the following actions:

◆ In a Conversation window with the person you want to block, click the Block button or choose File ➤ Block.

◆ In a Conversation window with multiple people, click the Block button and choose the person from the pop-up menu, or choose File ➤ Block and choose the person from the submenu.

◆ From the Windows Messenger window, right-click the person and choose Block from the context menu.

When you block a user from a Conversation window, Messenger displays the Windows Messenger dialog box shown in Figure 23.12 telling you that the blocked user will not be able to contact you or see your online status. When you unblock a user, Messenger displays a similar dialog box telling you that the other user *will* be able to do these things. In either case, you get an OK button to proceed with the blocking or unblocking, a Cancel button to cancel it, and a Don't Show Me This Message Again check box that you can select to prevent Messenger from telling you what you already know.

FIGURE 23.12

When you block a user, Messenger displays a dialog box to make sure you understand the consequences of your action. Select the Don't Show Me This Message Again check box to prevent Messenger from displaying this dialog box again.

To unblock a user, take one of the following actions:

◆ In a Conversation window, choose File ➤ Unblock.

◆ In a Conversation window with multiple participants, choose File ➤ Block and select the blocked user from the submenu.

◆ In the Windows Messenger window, right-click the blocked user and choose Unblock from the context menu.

Changing Your Status

To let people know what you're up to, you can change the status that Messenger displays for you. To do so, click your icon in the Windows Messenger window and choose Online, Busy, Be Right Back, Away, On the Phone, Out to Lunch, or Appear Offline from the pop-up menu. You can also set your status by choosing File ➤ My Status and selecting the status from the submenu.

When you change your status to Appear Offline, Messenger displays the Windows Messenger dialog box shown in Figure 23.13 warning you that your instant message windows and Conversation windows will be closed and your file transfers will be canceled. Click the OK button if this is okay, or click the Cancel button to cancel the status change.

FIGURE 23.13

You can change your status to Appear Offline, but doing so closes your instant message and conversation windows and cancels your file transfers.

Transferring Files

Messenger provides an easy way to transfer files quickly to other Messenger users who are currently online. You can transfer only one file at a time to any given user, but you can have up to 10 separate file-transfer operations going at the same time with other users. These 10 file-transfer operations include both inbound and outbound file transfers.

Sending a File

To send a file to someone via Messenger, take the following steps:

1. Choose File ➢ Send a File To and select either an existing user or the Other item from the submenu. Messenger displays the Send a File To dialog box, which is an Open dialog box in disguise.

    ◆ If you select the Other item, Messenger displays the Send a File dialog box (shown in Figure 23.14). Enter the person's e-mail address, select the service in the Service drop-down list (if applicable), and click the OK button.

FIGURE 23.14

Use the Send a File dialog box to send a file to a Messenger user who isn't one of your contacts.

    ◆ To send a file to a user you're chatting with in a Conversation window, click the Send a File heading or choose File ➢ Send a File. You don't need to identify the user because Messenger knows it already. (If you're chatting with multiple people, Messenger displays the Send a File submenu listing the people in the conversation.)

2. Navigate to the file, select it, and click the Open button. Messenger contacts the user, asking them if they want to accept or decline the file. You can cancel the transfer by pressing Alt+Q or clicking the Cancel link.

3. If the user accepts the file, Messenger displays a progress readout in the Conversation window. When the file transfer is complete, Messenger lets you know that too.

If the user doesn't accept the transfer, or if it fails, Messenger tells you that the user declined the file or the file could not be sent.

Receiving a File

Receiving a file via Messenger is even easier than sending one. Here's what happens:

1. If you're using pop-ups, Messenger displays a pop-up telling you that someone is trying to send you a file. (Messenger identifies the user and the file by name.)

2. Click the pop-up to display the Conversation window. (If you're already in a messaging session with this user, you'll go directly to this step.)

3. To accept the file, click the Accept link (or press Alt+T). To decline the file, click the Decline link (or press Alt+D).

4. If you choose to accept the file, Messenger displays a Windows Messenger dialog box warning you that files may contain harmful viruses or scripts and advising you to make sure that the file you're receiving is from a trustworthy source. Click the OK button to dismiss this dialog box. You can select the Don't Show Me This Message Again check box before dismissing the dialog box if you're fully aware of malware tricks and you carefully check every file you receive before running it.

5. Messenger transfers the file, stores it in the folder specified on the Preferences page of the Options dialog box, and displays a link that you can click to open the file.

To access your received files folder, choose File ➢ Open Received Files.

TROUBLESHOOTING: PROBLEMS WITH FILE TRANSFER

This sidebar discusses the two most prevalent problems with file transfer using Messenger—that it doesn't work at all, or that you can transfer only one file at a time.

FILE TRANSFER DOESN'T WORK AT ALL

If you can't get file transfer to work at all, you've probably run into one of the following problems:

Your Computer Connects through a NAT Device That Doesn't Support UPnP If your computer connects to the Internet through a NAT device that doesn't support Universal Plug & Play (UPnP), you won't be able to perform file transfers. Check to see if there's an update available for the NAT device to add UPnP capabilities to it.

Your Firewall Is Configured to Prevent File Transfer via Messenger For you to perform file transfers via Messenger, TCP ports 6891–6900 need to be open on your firewall (be it ICF or another firewall). If you have access to the firewall, open those ports.

Your ISP Has Configured Its Routers to Prevent File Transfer via Messenger Another possibility is that your ISP has blocked TCP ports 6891–6900 to prevent users from transferring files, either because of the amount of bandwidth file transfer can take up or for copyright concerns. Ask the ISP if they're blocking file transfer. If they are, ask them to desist.

Continued on next page

> **TROUBLESHOOTING: PROBLEMS WITH FILE TRANSFER** *(continued)*
>
> **FILE TRANSFER IS LIMITED TO ONE TRANSFER AT A TIME**
>
> As mentioned earlier, Messenger lets you transfer only one file at a time to, or receive only one file at a time from, any other user. But you can send files to, and receive files from, multiple users at the same time—provided that the right ports (TCP ports 6891–6900) are open on the firewall and on your ISP's routers.
>
> If you can achieve only one file transfer at a time, your firewall or your ISP's routers have only one of these ports open. If the firewall is the culprit, reconfigure it. If your ISP is the culprit, try yelling at it politely.

Making PC-to-Phone Calls

By signing up for a voice service provider (VSP), you can make PC-to-phone calls with Messenger. Whether you'll want to do so will probably depend on whether you benefit from doing so, either by saving money or by gaining in convenience. At this writing, most VSPs charge about the same fees for long-distance and international calls as do the lower-cost carrier plans, so you may not be able to save money. And in most cases, the only convenience you'll gain is in being able to have the PC dial the call for you. Against this, you have to set off the disadvantage of only being able to make calls when at your PC. And while it's great to be able to call any regular phone in the world from your PC, you can do that just as well by making a normal call from a regular phone.

Messenger lets you use only one VSP at a time, so research your options before making a commitment. To sign up with a VSP, take the following steps:

1. Click the Make a Phone Call link in the Action pane of the Messenger window. (Alternatively, choose Actions ➤ Make a Phone Call.) XP checks that your computer has a direct connection to the Internet (see the next sidebar). If it does, Messenger displays a Get Started Here button. If not, Messenger displays a message of regret telling you that you can't make PC-to-phone calls from this PC.

2. Click the Get Started Here button. Messenger displays the Select a Voice Service Provider window, which contains links to VSPs.

3. Sign up with a VSP and pay for some minutes or hours.

After you complete the sign-up procedure with a VSP, Messenger displays the VSP's name in the Phone window, as in Figure 23.15. You can then make a phone call by entering the phone number and clicking the Dial button. To hang up the call, click the Hang Up button that replaces the Dial button.

To change your VSP, cancel your current VSP account by choosing Tools ➤ Change Voice Service from the Phone window. Messenger connects to your current VSP, where you can cancel that account. Then click the Get Started Here button in the Phone window to go through the sign-up procedure for another VSP account.

FIGURE 23.15

Messenger also lets you make PC-to-phone calls by signing up with a voice service provider (in this case, Callserve).

TROUBLESHOOTING: CAN'T MAKE PC-TO-PHONE CALLS VIA ICS OR NAT

At this writing, Messenger's PC-to-phone calls don't work through network address translation (NAT) devices such as Internet Connection Sharing (ICS), wireless network access-sharing devices, and other Internet-sharing devices. So to use Messenger's PC-to-phone capabilities, your PC needs to have a direct connection to the Internet.

Preventing Messenger from Running

Not everyone finds Messenger useful or wants to have it lurking in the background the whole time ready to run at the slightest provocation. If you're one of these people, you can prevent Messenger from running by editing the Registry using the technique described in the section "Preventing Messenger from Running" in Chapter 12.

Whiteboarding and Sharing Programs

As well as letting you chat with another person by text or by voice, Messenger provides a shared Whiteboard tool for brainstorming and a program-sharing feature that lets you work together in a program on one computer or the other.

If you've used NetMeeting (discussed in Web Chapter 3), you'll recognize these features, which Messenger borrows from NetMeeting. However, whereas NetMeeting lets you whiteboard or share programs with multiple other users, Messenger limits you to one other user, which greatly cuts down the amount of collaboration you can achieve in a session.

Using Whiteboard

Whiteboard is a basic graphical tool for brainstorming and discussions. It's essentially a cut-down version of Paint with a few multiuser features grafted onto it, so if you can use Paint, you'll have no trouble with Whiteboard. It's neither powerful nor pretty, but it can be useful for showing people how to do things from a distance.

You can start Whiteboard either from an existing Conversation window or from the main Messenger window by clicking the Start Whiteboard link in the I Want To list or choosing Actions ➤ Start Whiteboard. If you're in a conversation with one other person, Messenger starts the Whiteboard session with that person. Otherwise, Messenger displays the Start Whiteboard dialog box with the My Contacts page foremost so that you can choose the contact with whom you want to whiteboard. Do so and click the OK button.

Messenger then displays an invitation for that person. If they accept it, Messenger displays the Sharing Session window (shown here), establishes the Whiteboard session, and displays the Whiteboard window.

Figure 23.16 shows an example of using Whiteboard to brainstorm.

FIGURE 23.16

You can use Whiteboard for brainstorming.

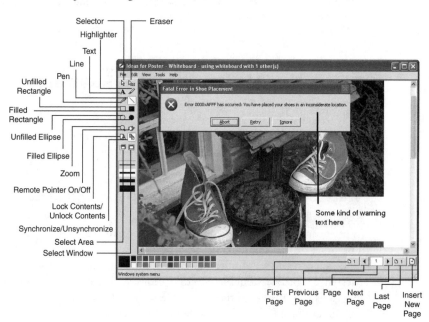

Web Chapter 3 (which covers NetMeeting) details the actions you can take using Whiteboard. Here's the brief version. You can

◆ Add text and graphics by using the controls shown in Figure 23.16.

◆ Add graphical items (for example, images) by pasting them in using the Edit ➤ Paste command.

◆ Use multiple pages for different items (or different versions of items). To insert a new page, click the Insert New Page button or choose Edit ➤ Insert Page. To navigate between pages, use the buttons in the lower-right corner of the Whiteboard window.

◆ Lock the contents of Whiteboard so that you can work on it without interference.

◆ Unsynchronize the contents of Whiteboard so that you can work on them without your collaborator seeing the changes, then synchronize Whiteboard to share the changes.

◆ Use the remote pointer (click the Remote Pointer button) to point out items on-screen.

◆ Save the contents of Whiteboard by choosing File ➢ Save.

TROUBLESHOOTING: PROBLEMS AND LIMITATIONS OF WHITEBOARD AND PROGRAM SHARING

As I mentioned earlier, Messenger borrows Whiteboard and program sharing from NetMeeting—and at this writing, not all that effectively. Here are problems and limitations you should know about before you commit time to Whiteboard and program sharing from Messenger.

WHITEBOARD AND PROGRAM SHARING IN MESSENGER ARE LIMITED TO TWO USERS

In Messenger, you can use Whiteboard or share programs with only one other user. In NetMeeting, you can use Whiteboard or share programs with multiple users.

WINDOWS MESSENGER CAN'T WHITEBOARD WITH MSN MESSENGER

Windows Messenger can't share Whiteboard or programs with MSN Messenger—Messenger running on versions of Windows other than XP. NetMeeting can share Whiteboard or programs with versions of Windows back to Windows 95.

WHITEBOARD IN MESSENGER CRASHES TOO OFTEN FOR COMFORT

Whiteboard run from Messenger seems far less stable than Whiteboard run from NetMeeting.

The only workaround for these two limitations and one problem is to run Whiteboard from NetMeeting rather than from Messenger. See Web Chapter 3 for instructions on running and using NetMeeting.

Sharing a Program—or Your Desktop

Messenger also lets you share one or more programs—or your whole Desktop—with one of your contacts. Such sharing can be useful for collaborating on a document, demonstrating a program, or troubleshooting problems, but Remote Assistance (described in Chapter 24) is a better and safer tool for troubleshooting in most cases.

You can even allow another Messenger user to control a program or your entire Desktop. Unless you have a lot to gain by doing so, or you trust the other person absolutely *and are completely certain that it's them at the other computer*, there's seldom any reason for using this capability, because it's a huge security risk. If you give someone control of your Desktop, they have free rein to do whatever they want to your system—start programs, rummage through your files, delete anything they want, or install programs or viruses. You can in theory stop them at any point, but you might be too late, and in any case you might not notice something subtle they did.

To share your Desktop or a program, click the Start Application Sharing in the I Want To list or choose Actions ➢ Start Application Sharing in either a Conversation window or the main Messenger window. If you're in a conversation with one other person, Messenger starts the sharing session with that person. Otherwise, Messenger displays the Start Application Sharing dialog box with the My Contacts page foremost so that you can choose the contact with whom you want to share a program. Do so and click the OK button.

Messenger then displays an invitation for that person. If they accept it, Messenger displays the Sharing Session window and the Sharing window (see Figure 23.17).

FIGURE 23.17

Use the Sharing window to share your Desktop or a program.

In the list box, select the program you want to share and click the Share button. You can then unshare the program by selecting it and clicking the Unshare button or by clicking the Unshare All button.

If the program you share is part of a group, NetMeeting shares the whole group. For example, if you share one of three Explorer windows you have open, NetMeeting shares all three.

The other user sees a window titled with your NetMeeting name and *Programs*. (Yes—the name you've set for yourself in NetMeeting, not your Messenger display name.) The windows appear on a featureless gray Desktop in the positions in which you currently have them. If you place an unshared window over one of the shared windows, it blocks the other user's view of the shared window, but its contents aren't transmitted. When you're setting up sharing, the Sharing Session window and the Sharing window often block the view of the other windows, so you need to remember to move them out of the way or minimize them once you've arranged the sharing.

Usually, it's better to minimize the Sharing window than to close it. But if you do close it, you can reopen it by clicking the App Sharing button in the Sharing Session window.

To let the other user (or users) control your shared programs, display the Sharing window (if it's not already displayed) and click the Allow Control button. Clicking this button makes available the Automatically Accept Requests for Control check box and the Do Not Disturb with Requests for Control Right Now check box, which you can use to automatically accept and to disable requests for control. Once you've clicked the Allow Control button, it changes into a Prevent Control button that you can click to prevent control of the shared programs.

Usually, you'll want to retain manual control over allowing other users control of your programs. When you click the Allow Control button but leave the Automatically Accept Requests for Control check box cleared, Messenger displays the Request Control dialog box to alert you to incoming requests for control.

If you accept the request for control, the user is able to control the program much as if it were on their own Desktop. You see every action they take, including movements of the mouse pointer. You can regain control temporarily by clicking your mouse in one of the shared windows or regain control permanently by clicking the Prevent Control button in the Sharing window or by unsharing the program.

If you reject the request for control, or do not respond to it within the timeout period, the user requesting control sees a Request Control Failed dialog box.

To share your Desktop and all open programs, select the Desktop item at the top of the Share Programs list box. If you allow control of your Desktop, the other user can take more or less any action that XP supports—bar anything that closes Messenger, of course. Again, you see the actions they take.

NOTE *In a multi-monitor configuration, XP shares programs on the primary monitor only.*

To close your sharing session, click the Close button in the Sharing Session window.

Working with Tabs

Because Messenger has a stylized interface, it's not immediately obvious to everyone that the blue column that normally appears down the left side of the Messenger window is a display area for tabs that display different pages that give access to other .NET services that tie into Messenger.

By default, Messenger displays the Messenger page foremost. It also displays the .NET Alerts tab on the tab panel, with other tabs hidden until you choose to display them.

To display a tab, either click the Tabs button at the foot of the blue column and choose the tab from the resulting context menu or choose Tools ➢ Show Tabs and choose the tab from the Show Tabs submenu. To hide a displayed tab, repeat the process.

To access one of these pages, click its tab, just as you would click the tab in a multipage dialog box to display the page attached to the tab. When you click a tab, Messenger automatically logs you into the website for the service using your .NET Passport.

Messenger 4.6 comes configured with tabs for Messenger itself, Microsoft .NET Alerts (time-sensitive notification messages—for example, bidding notifications from eBay and uBid Online Auctions or travel offers from Expedia.com—delivered to Messenger, to your mobile, or to your e-mail inbox), CNBC on MSN Money (your stock list), Expedia (travel information and deals), FYE (entertainment), McAfee.com (security alerts and virus news), and MSN Carpoint (live traffic updates, personalized traffic forecasts, and local gas prices). Microsoft promises further tabs and services in the future.

As mentioned earlier in this chapter, you can configure Messenger to hide your tabs on a shared computer so that other people can't use them by selecting the This Is a Shared Computer So Don't Display My Tabs check box on the Privacy page of the Options dialog box (Tools ➢ Options). Other users then can't see your tabs (and can't turn on the display of the tabs either).

TIP   You can navigate from one displayed tab to the next by pressing Ctrl+Tab (to move to the next tab downward) or Shift+Ctrl+Tab (upward).

Up Next

This chapter has discussed how to use Messenger for everything from instant text messaging to making audio and video calls to sending and receiving files.

You can also use Messenger to send—and respond to—requests for Remote Assistance. The next chapter discusses these capabilities.

Chapter 24

Giving and Getting Remote Assistance

REMOTE ASSISTANCE IS A powerful new XP feature that lets you permit a designated helper to connect to your computer, see what's going on, and help you out of trouble. The helper—a friend, an administrator, or a Microsoft support professional; whomever you choose—can control the computer directly if you give them permission, or you can simply chat with them and apply yourself such of their advice as you deem fit. Or you can use Remote Assistance to help another person who requests your assistance.

This chapter covers the following topics:

- ◆ Understanding the basics of Remote Assistance
- ◆ Security considerations for Remote Assistance
- ◆ Setting limits for Remote Assistance
- ◆ Enabling and disabling Remote Assistance
- ◆ Receiving help via Remote Assistance
- ◆ Giving help via Remote Assistance

Understanding the Basics of Remote Assistance

Remote Assistance lets a user who needs help share the display of their screen and, if they wish, control of their computer, with another user across a network or Internet connection. For ease of reference, the user requesting assistance is termed the *novice*, though of course they may be an experienced user. The user providing assistance is termed the *expert*; again, the usual connotations needn't apply.

Like Remote Desktop Connection (discussed in Chapter 34), Remote Assistance uses XP's Terminal Services feature to achieve its effects. Terminal Services (discussed in more detail in the sidebar "Expert Knowledge: Remote Desktop Connection Is Terminal Services by Another Name" in Chapter 34) is a technology that passes keystrokes, mouse movements and clicks, and video display information across a network or Internet connection, allowing remote control of a computer running XP Professional.

At the risk of stating the obvious, Remote Assistance is substantially different from Remote Desktop Connection. Remote Desktop Connection is designed to let you remotely control a computer on which you have a user account. While you're remotely controlling the computer, the monitor attached to the computer displays the Welcome screen (or the Log On to Windows screen, depending on how it's configured), so nobody physically at the computer can see what you're doing or take actions on the computer till you disconnect. By contrast, you can't connect to a computer using Remote Assistance unless there's somebody (the novice) at the computer who can respond to the request for the Remote Assistance session. Both the novice and the expert see the screen of the novice's computer. And the novice has control of their computer until and unless they specifically decide to grant the expert control of it.

To use Remote Assistance, both the novice's computer and the expert's computer must be running XP. The novice sends an invitation via e-mail or via Windows Messenger, or saves it as a file (for example, to a network location designated for Remote Assistance request files, or on a floppy or CD that they then pop in the snail mail). When the expert responds, the novice decides whether to accept their help.

Each of the three methods of requesting Remote Assistance has its advantages and disadvantages. An e-mail invitation lets the novice include details of the problem with which they need help—but the novice doesn't know when the expert will check their e-mail, or if the novice will be online when the expert tries to respond. A Messenger invitation will be received immediately (because you can't send an invitation to someone who isn't online), but the novice can't include details of the problem. A file invitation, like an e-mail invitation, lets the novice include details of the problem, but they have no idea of when they'll receive a response to it (if ever).

On the other end of the wire, you can offer help via Remote Assistance. All you need is for someone to send you an invitation by any of the three methods discussed above.

Security Considerations for Remote Assistance

Like all remote-control technologies, Remote Assistance has serious security implications that you need to consider before using it.

If you give another person control of your computer, they can take actions almost as freely as if they were seated in front of the computer. You can watch these actions, and you can take back control of the computer at any time, but you may already be too late: It takes less than a second to delete a key file, and only a little longer to plant a virus or other form of malware.

Even if you *don't* give the expert control, and simply chat, keep your wits about you when deciding which of their suggestions to implement. Malicious or ill-informed suggestions can do plenty of damage if you apply them without thinking. Never take any actions that could compromise your security or destroy your data. Above all, treat any incoming files with the greatest of suspicion and virus-check them using an up-to-date anti-virus program before using them.

One particular problem is that you can't tell that the person at the other computer is who they claim to be. For this reason alone, always protect the Remote Assistance invitations that you send via e-mail or save to a file with a strong password known only to the person from whom you're requesting help. That way, if someone else is at their computer or has identity-jacked them, they won't be able to respond to the Remote Assistance invitation you send.

Enabling and Disabling Remote Assistance

Remote Assistance is enabled by default. To find out if Remote Assistance is enabled on your computer, take the following steps:

1. Display the System Properties dialog box (for example, by pressing Windows key+Break or clicking the System link on the Performance and Maintenance screen of Control Panel).

2. Click the Remote tab. XP displays the Remote page.

3. Check the status of the Allow Remote Assistance Invitations to Be Sent from This Computer check box. If this check box isn't selected, select it to enable Remote Assistance.

4. Click the OK button. XP closes the System Properties dialog box.

Setting Limits for Remote Assistance

To set limits for Remote Assistance, take the following steps:

1. Click the Advanced button in the Remote Assistance group box on the Remote page of the System Properties dialog box. XP displays the Remote Assistance Settings dialog box (shown in Figure 24.1).

FIGURE 24.1

Set limits for Remote Assistance in the Remote Assistance Settings dialog box.

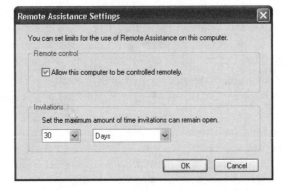

2. In the Remote Control group box, clear the Allow This Computer to Be Controlled Remotely check box if you don't want your helpers to be able to control the computer. (This check box is selected by default.) Even when this check box is selected, you need to approve each request for control of the PC manually, so you're not signing your virtual life away by leaving it selected.

3. In the Invitations group box, use the two drop-down lists to specify an expiration limit for Remote Assistance invitations that your computer sends out. The default setting is 30 days; you might want to shorten this period considerably for security.

4. Click the OK button. XP closes the Remote Assistance Settings dialog box, returning you to the System Properties dialog box.

5. Click the OK button. XP closes the System Properties dialog box. You're now ready to start sending out invitations for Remote Assistance.

Sending a Remote Assistance Invitation via E-mail

To send a Remote Assistance invitation as an e-mail message via your existing e-mail account, follow these steps:

1. Choose Start ➤ All Programs ➤ Remote Assistance. XP opens a Help and Support Center window to the Remote Assistance topic.

2. Click the Invite Someone to Help You link. Help and Support Center displays the Remote Assistance—Pick How You Want to Contact Your Assistant screen.

3. In the Or Use E-mail area, enter the expert's e-mail address in the Type an E-mail Address text box. Either type in the address (get it right, because Remote Assistance doesn't validate e-mail addresses) or click the Address Book button and use Address Book to specify the address.

4. Click the Invite This Person link. Help and Support Center displays the Provide Contact Information screen.

5. Change the name in the From text box if you want.

6. In the Message text box, enter a description of the problem and any blandishments necessary to get the help you want.

7. Click the Continue button. Help and Support Center displays the Set the Invitation to Expire screen.

8. In the Set the Invitation to Expire area, specify the time limit for the recipient to accept the invitation. Choose a number in the first drop-down list and a time period—Minutes, Hours, or Days—in the second drop-down list. This is the maximum length of time the invitation stays open. You can manually "expire" the invitation at any time after creating it.

9. To set a password, make sure the Require the Recipient to Use a Password check box is selected, then enter the password in the Type Password text box and the Confirm Password text box.

10. Click the Send Invitation button. Help and Support Center creates a file named `rcBuddy` `.MsRcIncident` containing the invitation and sends it via your default e-mail client with a message explaining how to use it. Help and Support Center then displays a screen telling you that the invitation has been sent successfully.

    ◆ If Help and Support Center can't send the file—for example, if your ISP's mail server is down—it invites you to save the file and send it manually.

    ◆ Depending on its sentience and settings, your e-mail program may warn you if other programs attempt to send mail in your name. Outlook Express displays an Outlook Express dialog box such as that shown on the left in Figure 24.2, warning you that a program (Help and Support Center) is trying to send a message. Click the Send button. Eudora Pro displays a Warning dialog box like that shown on the right in Figure 24.2, recommending that you view the message before letting Eudora send it. Click the Yes button if you want to read the Help and Support Center message.

FIGURE 24.2

Your e-mail program may warn you that Help and Support Center is trying to send a message on your behalf. The example on the left is from Outlook Express. The example on the right is from Eudora Pro.

NOTE *To change the default program for e-mail, choose Tools ➤ Internet Options from Internet Explorer to display the Internet Options dialog box, display the Programs page, and change the entry in the E-mail drop-down list, then click the OK button.*

TROUBLESHOOTING: CAN'T SEND REMOTE ASSISTANCE INVITATION VIA NON-MAPI E-MAIL PROGRAM

If you use an e-mail program that isn't MAPI compliant, you won't be able to send a Remote Assistance invitation from it. (MAPI is the Messaging Application Programming Interface, a layer of code that enables the automation of messaging features—for example, sending an e-mail message automatically the way Remote Assistance does.) Non–MAPI compliant e-mail programs include MSN Explorer, Hotmail, and AOL.

To get around this problem, either use Messenger to send your Remote Assistance invitation or save it to a file, attach it to a message in your MAPI-free e-mail program, and send it. For security, you might consider encrypting the Remote Assistance invitation file—for example, using Pretty Good Privacy (PGP).

Sending an Invitation via Windows Messenger

To send an invitation via your existing Messenger account, follow these steps:

1. Start Messenger as usual, or activate it from the notification area.

2. Choose Actions ➤ Ask for Remote Assistance (or click the Ask for Remote Assistance item in the I Want To drop-down list) and use the Ask for Remote Assistance dialog box to specify the contact you want to ask.

   ◆ You can also send an invitation to an existing contact by right-clicking them in the Online list and choosing Ask for Remote Assistance from the context menu.

   ◆ You can also issue an Ask for Remote Assistance command from the Actions menu or the I Want To list in a Conversation window that you've already opened. If multiple people are in the conversation, XP displays the Ask for Remote Assistance dialog box.

3. Messenger opens an Instant Message window on the specified user's computer and displays a note saying that you've invited the user to start Remote Assistance. To cancel the invitation, click the Cancel link in the Instant Message window, or press Alt+Q.

4. Wait for a response, then proceed as described in "Receiving Remote Assistance," later in this chapter.

TIP   Because you can't use password protection on Remote Assistance connections that you establish via Messenger, it's a good idea to chat with your contact to make sure that it's actually them at their computer rather than someone logged on to .NET Messenger Service under their account. It's easiest to check by chatting via Messenger before issuing the Remote Assistance request, but you can also check after establishing the Remote Assistance connection—preferably before you take any advice from the person.

Saving an Invitation As a File

Saving an invitation as a file works in essentially the same way as sending an invitation as an e-mail message, except that instead of specifying an e-mail address, you click the Save Invitation As a File link, create the invitation, and then specify a filename and location in the Save File dialog box.

There are three main scenarios for saving a Remote Assistance invitation as a file:

Your e-mail program isn't MAPI-compliant   By saving an invitation as a file, you can send it as an attachment in a non–MAPI compliant e-mail program, such as Hotmail, MSN Explorer, or AOL.

Your company uses a drop-box for Remote Assistance invitations   Your company might designate a network folder as a drop-box for Remote Assistance invitations. Administrators would then examine the contents of the folder and respond to the invitations accordingly.

You need to mail the invitation on a disk   Sometimes—rarely—you may need to use snail mail to get the invitation to the expert. Save the file to a floppy disk or other removable medium and mail it. You'll be lucky to receive Remote Assistance before the next ice age, but this option may be useful sometimes.

NOTE   Remote Assistance invitation files are tiny—around 1KB—so there's no need to use a medium more capacious than a floppy. But if you're sending the medium through the mail, consider using a recordable CD instead, because the mail-scanning systems instituted since 9/11 may damage floppies.

Viewing the Status of Your Invitations

To view the status of the Remote Assistance invitations you've sent (or saved), display the Remote Assistance screen in Help and Support Center.

Click the View Invitation Status link. XP displays the Remote Assistance—View or Change Your Invitation screen. Figure 24.3 shows an example.

From here, you can view the details of an invitation by clicking the Details button, kill off an open invitation by clicking the Expire button, resend an invitation by clicking the Resend button, or delete an invitation by clicking the Delete button. If you need to resend an invitation because your computer's IP address has changed, XP displays "Resend required" in the Status column for the invitation.

FIGURE 24.3

On the View or Change Your Invitation screen, you can view the Remote Assistance invitations you've sent, "expire" them, resend them, or delete them.

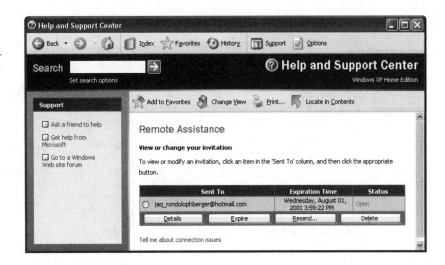

Receiving Remote Assistance

The following sections describe what happens when you receive a response to your Remote Assistance request. The details depend on what type of Remote Assistance request you sent out.

E-mail Invitation

When an expert responds to an e-mail invitation, XP displays a Remote Assistance dialog box such as that shown in Figure 24.4, telling you that the person has accepted the invitation and asking if you want to let them view your screen and chat with you. Click the Yes button to start the Remote Assistance session.

FIGURE 24.4

You'll see this Remote Assistance dialog box when the expert has accepted your e-mail invitation and is ready to get down to business.

NOTE   *Two quick notes: First, if you don't take any action for a few minutes, XP assumes you're not in the market for Remote Assistance and times out the connection. Second, Remote Assistance automatically configures its settings based on the speed of the connection established with the expert, so that it sends only an appropriate amount of information. But if the connection between you and the expert is slow (for example, a modem connection), it will take 30 seconds to a minute for the expert to see changes that appear on your screen in milliseconds—so you need to be patient. (Exactly how long it takes depends on the nature of the changes and the screen resolution you're using as well as on the speed of the connection.)*

Windows Messenger Invitation

When the expert responds to a Messenger request for Remote Assistance, XP displays a Remote Assistance window such as that shown in Figure 24.5.

FIGURE 24.5

You'll see a Remote Assistance window such as this when the expert responds to a Messenger request for Remote Assistance.

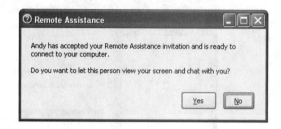

File Invitation

When the expert responds to a Remote Assistance request saved in a file, XP displays a Remote Assistance window telling you that the person has accepted the invitation and asking if you want to let them view your screen and chat with you. Click the Yes button to start the Remote Assistance session.

Receiving Assistance

Once the Remote Assistance session is established, Remote Assistance displays on the novice's screen the Remote Assistance window shown in Figure 24.6, which provides a chat pane and control buttons.

FIGURE 24.6

During a Remote Assistance session, this Remote Assistance window provides a chat pane and control buttons.

CHATTING WITH THE EXPERT

You can chat with the expert both via text and by using voice (if both computers are set up for audio):

◆ Type a message in the Message Entry text box and press the Enter key or click the Send button to send it.

◆ To start voice transmission, click the Start Talking button. The expert then sees a dialog box asking if they want to use a voice connection. If they click the Yes button, Remote Assistance establishes the voice connection. Talk as usual, and then click the Stop Talking button when you want to stop using the voice connection.

NOTE   The first time you use the talk feature, Remote Assistance runs the Audio and Video Tuning Wizard if you haven't run it before.

◆ To choose voice settings, click the Settings button. XP displays a Remote Assistance Settings dialog box. Choose the Standard Quality option button or the High Quality option button as appropriate. Alternatively, click the Audio Tuning Wizard button (if it's available) to run the Audio and Video Tuning Wizard to optimize your speaker and microphone settings. Close the Remote Assistance Settings dialog box when you've finished.

GIVING THE EXPERT CONTROL OF YOUR COMPUTER

If the expert requests control of your computer, XP displays the Remote Assistance dialog box shown in Figure 24.7. Click the Yes button or the No button as appropriate.

FIGURE 24.7

When the expert requests control of the computer, decide whether you trust them.

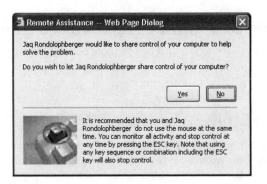

You can regain control by pressing the Esc key, by pressing Alt+C, or by clicking the Stop Control button.

If the expert leaves the Remote Assistance connection untouched for around an hour when they have control of your computer, Remote Assistance times out the connection and closes it. You'll need to establish a new connection in order to enjoy (if that's the word) further assistance.

DISCONNECTING THE EXPERT

To disconnect the expert, click the Disconnect button. Remote Assistance closes the connection and restores your Desktop to its full complement of colors (if you chose to optimize performance for the expert).

When the expert disconnects themselves, XP displays a Remote Assistance dialog box telling you so. Click the OK button to close this dialog box, then close the Help and Support Center window.

TROUBLESHOOTING: WHEN REMOTE ASSISTANCE CAN'T CONNECT THROUGH A FIREWALL

If Remote Assistance can't connect through your firewall or Internet connection–sharing device, make sure that TCP port 3389 is open. You shouldn't need to open this port manually on Internet Connection Firewall (ICF), because ICF opens it automatically when Remote Assistance comes knocking. But you may need to open it (or have a network administrator open it for you) on other firewalls or Internet connection–sharing devices.

If you're not able to establish a Remote Assistance connection from an invitation sent via e-mail (or via a file drop), try establishing a connection via Messenger instead. The advantage of this method is that because Messenger already has a connection between the novice's computer and the expert's computer, Remote Assistance is better positioned to deal with firewall problems. If the expert's computer doesn't receive a Remote Assistance connection attempt from the novice's computer within five seconds of the expert's acceptance of the Messenger invitation, the expert's computer sends what's called a *forward connect* to the location specified in the invitation. Usually, this backup attempt at communication is enough to solve communications problems caused by firewalls and Internet connection–sharing devices.

Responding to a Remote Assistance Invitation

This section discusses how to respond to a Remote Assistance invitation that someone sends you. As you'd expect, the specifics vary depending on whether it's an e-mail invitation, a Messenger invitation, or a file invitation.

EXPERT KNOWLEDGE: *OFFERING* **REMOTE ASSISTANCE**

If you're the helpful sort, you might have noticed a distinct hole in Remote Assistance's capabilities. Having the novice request Remote Assistance is all very well, but what if the novice doesn't know they need help, or is reluctant to imply ignorance by asking for help, or can't figure out how to request Remote Assistance? Shouldn't the expert be able to offer their services unsolicited?

There's good news and bad news on this front. The good news is that Microsoft has anticipated this request and catered for it. The bad news is that Microsoft has provided the capability to offer Remote Assistance only in XP Professional, and then only when the computer's administrator (or the domain administrator) has actively chosen to enable it—it's not enabled by default.

XP Home doesn't offer this feature, presumably to protect people who don't really want help from those who want to foist it on them. And because the computers involved need to be either members of the same domain or members of domains that trust each other, both need to be XP Professional PCs—you can't use an XP Professional computer to offer help to an XP Home user.

E-mail Invitation

When someone sends you a Remote Assistance invitation via e-mail, you receive an e-mail message with the Subject line "YOU HAVE RECEIVED A REMOTE ASSISTANCE INVITATION FROM *USERNAME*." The message comes with explanatory text augmenting whatever message text the requester entered, and an attached file with the name rcBuddy.MsRcIncident. (If the file is called rcBuddy.MsRcIncident1, see the next sidebar.)

Open the file by double-clicking it. Alternatively, in Outlook Express, click the Attachment icon, select the file from the drop-down menu, select the Open It button in the Open Attachment Warning dialog box, and click the OK button. XP displays a Help and Support Center window such as that shown in Figure 24.8, giving the details of the Remote Assistance invitation: who it's from, and when it expires.

FIGURE 24.8

Double-click the file you receive to open the Remote Assistance invitation.

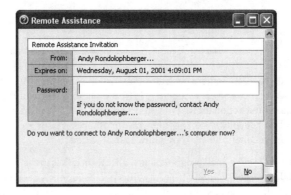

Enter the password (if the window includes a Password text box) and click the Yes button to start the help session. XP tries to contact the novice's computer.

TROUBLESHOOTING: SOLVING PROBLEMS RESPONDING TO REMOTE ASSISTANCE INVITATIONS SENT BY E-MAIL

This sidebar discusses how to deal with the two most common problems with Remote Assistance invitations sent via e-mail.

"WINDOWS CANNOT OPEN THIS FILE: RCBUDDY.MSRCINCIDENT1" ERROR

If when you try to open the Remote Assistance invitation file, you see the Windows dialog box and error message shown here, rest assured that nothing is really wrong: You've merely run into a piece of wretched design and programming on Microsoft's part.

Continued on next page

TROUBLESHOOTING: SOLVING PROBLEMS RESPONDING TO REMOTE ASSISTANCE INVITATIONS SENT BY E-MAIL (continued)

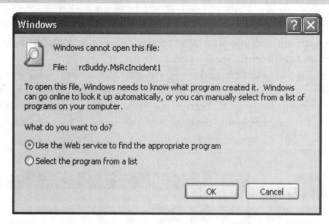

As mentioned above, each Remote Assistance invitation comes in a file named rcBuddy.MsRcIncident. The extension MsRcIncident is associated with the Microsoft Remote Assistance Incident file type by default, and the default action for that file type is to open the file using Help and Support Center—so when you double-click an rcBuddy.MsRcIncident file (or otherwise issue an Open command for it), XP opens it in Help and Support Center, which knows how to deal with it.

So far, so good. But if your e-mail program places all attached files in the same directory, it'll be able to store only one rcBuddy.MsRcIncident file. Any files it subsequently receives with that name it'll need to rename so that it doesn't overwrite the first file. Now, to preserve the file association, XP should keep the MsRcIncident extension on the file, renaming the second file, say, rcBuddy1.MsRcIncident, the third file rcBuddy2.MsRcIncident, and so on. But instead, it renames the second file rcBuddy.MsRcIncident1, the third file rcBuddy.MsRcIncident2, and so on. And because the extensions MsRcIncident1, MsRc-Incident2, and so on have no associated file type in XP, XP doesn't know how to handle them. So when you tell XP to open a file with such an extension, it displays the Windows dialog box shown above.

To deal with this problem, click the Cancel button in the Windows dialog box. If you haven't saved the Remote Assistance incident file to disk (for example, if you've tried to open the file as an attachment from Outlook Express), save it to disk in a folder that doesn't already contain an rcBuddy.MsRcIncident file. Then rename the file with the MsRcIncident extension and double-click it to open it in Help and Support Center.

After responding to a Remote Assistance invitation, delete the rcBuddy.MsRcIncident file from your computer so that it can't get in the way of invitations you subsequently receive.

If you anticipate misnamed MsRcIncident files being a major problem, you can create file types with the extensions MsRcIncident1, MsRcIncident2, and so on, by taking the following steps:

1. Choose Start ➢ My Computer. XP displays a My Computer window.

2. Choose Tools ➢ Folder Options. XP displays the Folder Options dialog box.

Continued on next page

TROUBLESHOOTING: SOLVING PROBLEMS RESPONDING TO REMOTE ASSISTANCE INVITATIONS SENT BY E-MAIL *(continued)*

3. Click the File Types tab. XP displays the File Types page.

4. Click the New button. XP displays the Create New Extension dialog box (shown below with its Advanced section displayed).

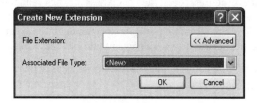

5. In the File Extension text box, enter MsRcIncident1.

6. Click the Advanced button. XP displays the Advanced section of the dialog box, thus making the Associated File Type drop-down list available.

7. In the Associated File Type drop-down list, select the Microsoft Remote Assistance Incident item.

8. Click the OK button. XP closes the Create New Extension dialog box.

9. To create further new extensions (MsRcIncident2, and so on), repeat steps 4 through 8.

10. Click the Close button. XP closes the Folder Options dialog box.

Once you've done this, you'll be able to open MsRcIncident1 files by double-clicking them.

"A REMOTE ASSISTANCE CONNECTION COULD NOT BE ESTABLISHED" ERROR

The error message "A Remote Assistance connection could not be established" (see the dialog box shown below), which occurs when the expert opens the invitation and tries to establish a connection with the novice, can mean any of the following:

◆ The novice's Internet connection is down.

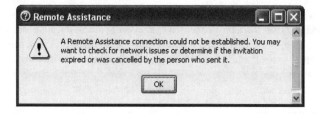

Continued on next page

TROUBLESHOOTING: SOLVING PROBLEMS RESPONDING TO REMOTE ASSISTANCE INVITATIONS SENT BY E-MAIL *(continued)*

◆ The novice's IP address has changed, and Remote Assistance has no way of identifying the computer's new IP address. (If both computers are on the name network, Remote Assistance can look the computer up from the name information contained in the Remote Assistance invitation, but it can't do this across the Internet.) If the expert can communicate with the novice via e-mail or chat, the expert can learn the novice's new IP address, open the rcBuddy.MsRcIncident file in a text editor such as Notepad, and enter the new IP address to make the connection work. But in most cases it's easier to have the novice resend the invitation from Help and Support Center. If the expert can communicate with the novice via Messenger, the novice can issue a new invitation in Messenger.

◆ The novice has manually expired the Remote Assistance invitation.

Windows Messenger Invitation

When someone sends you a Remote Assistance invitation via Messenger, you see a Conversation window telling you that the person "is inviting you to start using Remote Assistance." Click the Accept link (or press Alt+T) to accept the invitation or click the Decline link (or press Alt+D) to decline it.

TROUBLESHOOTING: SOLVING PROBLEMS RESPONDING TO REMOTE ASSISTANCE INVITATIONS ISSUED FROM MESSENGER

This sidebar discusses how to deal with the two most common problems with Remote Assistance invitations issued from Messenger.

THE EXPERT RECEIVES AN "UNABLE TO ACCEPT INVITATION" MESSAGE

If the novice sends a Remote Assistance invitation to someone running a version of Windows other than XP, that person is likely to see the message "Unable to accept invitation." This happens because Remote Assistance works only with XP, not with earlier versions of Windows.

THE NOVICE DOESN'T RESPOND TO THE EXPERT'S REPLY

If the novice doesn't respond to the expert's reply to an invitation issued via Messenger, the novice may have used Fast User Switching to switch to another account. Because Messenger keeps running in a disconnected session, the expert will see that the novice is still online with Messenger, but because the novice won't be able to see that the expert is trying to take up their invitation, they won't respond.

File Invitation

If you find a file invitation waiting for you, or receive one on a physical medium, double-click the file to open it. The rest of the procedure is the same as for an e-mail invitation, discussed in the section before last.

Providing Remote Assistance

If XP is able to contact the novice's computer, and if the novice accepts the Remote Assistance connection, XP displays the Remote Assistance window (shown in Figure 24.9). As you can see, this features a chat pane, a view pane that shows the novice's Desktop, and assorted command buttons. If the novice's Desktop uses multiple monitors, the Remote Assistance window displays all of them in one window.

FIGURE 24.9

When you're supply-ing the assistance in a Remote Assistance session, you can view the screen and chat with the novice.

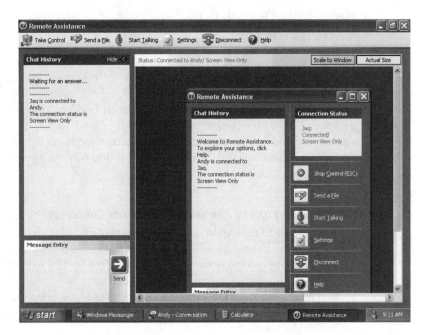

CHATTING WITH THE NOVICE

To chat with the novice via text, click the Show Chat button to display the chat pane if it's not cur-rently displayed. Type a message in the Message Entry text box and press the Enter key or click the Send button to send it.

To hide the chat pane so that you can see more of the remote screen, click the Hide button.

To chat via voice, click the Start Talking button. Remote Assistance displays a dialog box asking the novice whether they want to use voice. If they click the Yes button, Remote Assistance activates the audio hardware. Click the Stop Talking button to stop using voice to chat.

SCALING THE DISPLAY

You can scale the remote display to shrink it down to fit in the area available on your screen by clicking the Scale to Window button, and restore it to its actual size by clicking the Actual Size button. (You can't scale the remote display to larger than its actual size, no matter how much screen real estate you have.) Depending on the resolution you and the novice have set, scaling the display may make the fonts illegible, but viewing the whole screen at once may make it easier for you to see what's happen-ing on the computer than being able to see only a partial screen and having to scroll to see its outer reaches.

TAKING CONTROL OF THE REMOTE COMPUTER

To request control of the remote computer, click the Take Control button. XP displays a Remote Assistance dialog box on the remote screen asking the novice if they want to give you control. If they click the Yes button, you get a Remote Assistance dialog box telling you so. When you dismiss this dialog box, you have control of the computer and can take any action with it as if you were working directly on it. To release control, click the Release Control button or press the Esc key.

WARNING   *Avoid pressing the Esc key when taking keyboard actions on the remote computer. Even combinations that use the Esc key will release control.*

When you have control of the remote computer, you're working in the novice's security context: If they're a Computer Administrator user, you can take most any action on the computer; if they're a Limited user, you're limited in your actions; and if they're the Guest user (or a member of the Guests group), you're wearing a virtual straitjacket buckled down tight. If you're just trying to show the novice how to do something they ought to be able to do, you shouldn't have any problem working within a Limited or Guest account, but if you're trying to fix a problem, the security context may give you grief. You can't use the RunAs command to run a program in a different security context from Remote Assistance.

TRANSFERRING FILES TO AND FROM THE REMOTE COMPUTER

To transfer a file to the remote computer, click the Send a File button. XP displays a Remote Assistance dialog box. Use the Browse button to locate the file, and then click the Send File button to send it. The novice then gets to decide whether to keep the file and in which folder to save it. (If you have control of the computer, you can make these decisions.)

To transfer a file from the remote computer to your computer, have the novice click the Send a File button in their Remote Assistance window. Alternatively, if you have control of the computer, you can do this yourself.

DISCONNECTING FROM THE REMOTE COMPUTER

To disconnect from the remote computer, click the Disconnect button. Then close the Remote Assistance window manually. Unless you expect you'll need to reconnect to the remote computer to help the novice further during the time remaining before the Remote Assistance invitation expires, delete the invitation file before you forget.

If the novice disconnects the connection, XP displays a Remote Assistance dialog box telling you so.

Up Next

This chapter has discussed how to use XP's Remote Assistance feature to request, receive, and provide assistance from a distance.

The next chapter discusses how to publish information to the Web.

Chapter 25

Publishing Information to the Web

THIS CHAPTER DISCUSSES HOW to publish information to the Web. The material isn't difficult (or even long), but there are three questions you need to consider: First, what will you publish? Second, where will you publish it? And third, how will you get it there?

This chapter covers the following topics:

◆ Understanding copyright issues involved in publishing to the Web

◆ Performing quality control

◆ Deciding where to publish your material

◆ Publishing material to the Web

What Will You Publish?

The first question is what you're going to publish. You'll have your own answer to this question, of course—anything from your family photos to your political opinions, from your recipes to your music and videos.

But before you publish anything, there's one issue you *must* consider: copyright. And there's another issue you really ought to consider: quality control. This section discusses those issues.

Understanding Copyright Issues

Before you publish any material to the Web, make sure you can legally do so. This means either understanding the basics of copyright law or consulting a lawyer. Three guesses as to which is less expensive.

Right. So here's an executive summary:

◆ If you created an original work yourself, you hold the copyright to it. For example, if you take an original digital photo, write an original story, or compose an original song, you hold the copyright to it. (If the work isn't original, you've probably infringed copyright. For example, taking a digital photo of someone else's work is unlikely to create an original work.) You can post that work to the Web if you want. (And you can try to defend your copyright against anyone who infringes it.)

◆ As the copyright holder, you have five main rights to the work: the Reproduction Right (making copies of the work), the Distribution Right (distributing it), the Modification Right or Derivative Works Right (creating other works based on the work), the Public Performance Right (performing or transmitting the work), and the Public Display Right (displaying the work in a public place). You can exercise these rights yourself or grant them to other people. For example, the author of a book often grants to a publisher the Reproduction Right and the Distribution Right, so that the publisher can print copies of the book and distribute them.

◆ If someone else created the work, you probably need to get explicit permission to publish or distribute it. The fact that someone has posted a work on a website or a newsgroup doesn't make it public domain (discussed in the next paragraph), and you should be wary of airy claims by such posters that works are in the public domain.

◆ Some works are in the *public domain*, a notional area that contains all works that are not protected by copyright and which you can therefore publish and distribute freely. Some works are never protected by copyright, because they're not copyrightable due to their nature (for example, facts, URLs, and names are not copyrightable), because they're not copyrighted (for example, U.S. Government publications under the authorship of the Federal Government are not copyrighted), or because the creator of the work has chosen to put it in the public domain. Other works go out of copyright because the copyright has expired or has been lost.

WARNING   *Some website hosting services use their Terms and Conditions to claim copyright of any original material you post. Read the small print before you post anything on these services.*

Those are the bare bones of what you need to know about copyright to avoid committing copyright violations left, right, and center. Here are some resources for understanding copyright:

◆ Brad Templeton's *10 Big Myths about Copyright Explained* site (`www.templetons.com/brad/copymyths.html`) debunks the biggest myths about copyright.

◆ The U.S. Copyright Office (`www.loc.gov/copyright/`) offers several resources on copyright, including the Copyright FAQ (`www.loc.gov/copyright/faq.html`) and a Copyright Basics section (`www.loc.gov/copyright/circs/circ1.html`).

◆ The Copyright Clearance Center (`www.copyright.com`) provides a central location for getting permission to reproduce many copyrighted works. (For others, you may need to contact the creator of the work directly.)

◆ Chapter 2 of *Internet Piracy Exposed* (Sybex, 2001; shameless plug: also by me) discusses copyright law in the context of what you can and cannot legally do with material on the Internet.

Performing Quality Control

As you'll have noticed if you've spent more than a few hours surfing, the Web already suffers from a severe lack of quality control. You'll improve your karma if you don't add to this problem.

Historically, the high cost of publishing a work has acted as a strong incentive for the publisher to ensure that the work is of a high enough quality that it will appeal to its intended audience. For example, if a publisher publishes a book that's so bad (or on so unappealing a topic) that nobody buys it, they lose money. If a record company issues an unlistenable CD, they're unlikely to achieve significant sales (and they may even have to pay the "artist" huge sums of money to make her go away). And if an artist paints wretched pictures, the chances of their finding a market are slim.

By contrast, the Web is more or less a free-for-all. The cost of publishing to the Web can be extremely low (or nothing): You need do little more than create files and post them on a website, and anyone with an Internet connection and web browser can access them. If they don't like what they find at your site, they probably won't return, but the cost to you remains minimal.

But if you want people to look at what you post, make sure that its quality is at least acceptable:

- Don't post just anything (or *everything*) you have. Select the best items and post them. If they draw acclaim (or rapture), consider posting more.

- Spell-check any text you post. If your grammar isn't the greatest, get someone competent to check it for you. Involve an editor or proofreader if you're looking to be professional and persuasive. (For editors and proofreaders, the unedited and unproofed content on the Web can be painful to experience but at the same time gratifying in that it illustrates the need for their often unseen and unsung services.)

- Use graphics in moderation—and make sure they contribute to your site. Gratuitous graphics grate on the visitor nearly as badly as artless alliteration.

- Produce any audio material to a reasonable standard. Your band's live tapes might not make the cut unmixed; mixed, they might.

- Produce any video material to a higher standard. Because downloading video is a serious investment of time and bandwidth over any but the very fastest connections, you'll need to give people a good reason to download your video—and try not to disappoint them.

Above all, beware technologies that make it too easy to post material to the Web. Just because you *can* publish material directly to the Web doesn't mean you should; in fact, it often means just about the opposite. For example, as you'll see in Chapter 27, XP's Scanner and Camera Wizard offers to copy pictures you download from a digital camera or images you acquire via a scanner directly to the Web. In most cases, this is a very bad idea:

- Even if you've edited the photos on the digital camera ruthlessly so that you're sure you're not downloading any duds, you may need to crop the pictures, change their size or resolution, or otherwise manipulate them before posting them to the Web.

- Unless you hold the copyright to the documents you are scanning, or the documents are in the public domain or otherwise not copyrighted, you will need to get permission before publishing them to the Web.

Similarly, Windows Movie Maker (covered in Web Chapter 2) offers a feature for publishing a movie to a web server. This feature is more reasonable, in that Windows Movie Maker lets you preview the movie before you publish it. All the same, think twice before uploading huge amounts of scantily reviewed material to the Web.

Where Will You Publish Your Content?

Once you've established that you've got content you think is worth posting, you need somewhere to publish it. In most cases, your choice will be between your ISP and a free web hosting service such as MSN.

As discussed in Chapter 18, one of the factors you should evaluate when choosing an ISP is how much web space they give you and how much traffic they allow your site as part of your monthly fee (or free, as the case may be). Make sure that the ISP allows you plenty of space for as much material as you'll need to post at once (you can always delete some of the fatter files to make room for new material) and that they'll sell you more space and bandwidth for a modest fee should the need arise.

How Will You Publish Your Content?

XP offers two ways of getting material onto your website: creating it offline and using FTP to transfer a copy of it, and using Web Sharing (WebDAV) to create the files directly online.

FTP

The standard way of getting material onto your website is to create and assemble the material offline and then upload it to the website via FTP. If you're uploading a new version of a page, the upload overwrites the existing page. You can spend as long as you need to creating and saving the content, and because the files you're working with are stored on a local drive, you can access them at full speed.

There are three main methods of transferring material to and from an FTP site:

◆ Create a network place for the site and access it via the My Network Places folder.

◆ Access the site from Internet Explorer and create a favorite for it.

◆ Use an FTP client to access the site.

We'll discuss these methods in a moment or two. But first: WebDAV.

Web Sharing (WebDAV)

If your ISP supports Web Sharing (or, more formally, Web Digital Authoring and Versioning—WebDAV for short), you can use the new and snappier method of getting material onto your website, which is to create it or edit it in situ by using any program that can save directly to a web folder or to an FTP site. Web Sharing is based on the Hypertext Transfer Protocol (HTTP) on which the Web runs.

This method can simplify the process of making minor edits to a page and seeing the effects of the changes. But there are two problems:

◆ First, because even the fastest residential Internet connection is hundreds of times slower than the data-transfer speeds inside even a modest PC, this method makes for painfully slow opening and saving of documents. If there's a problem with the Internet connection, the document you're working on can become corrupted. If this is the only copy you have of the document, you may lose everything in it. Figure 25.1 shows the Windows – Delayed Write Failed dialog box, which gives an example of such unwelcome news.

FIGURE 25.1

Saving files directly to your website doesn't always work—and when it fails, you can lose the document involved.

Windows - Delayed Write Failed

Windows was unable to save all the data for the file \andy_rondolophberger@hotmail.com/files/Andy's Folder on MSN/Theory of Industrialization.rcv. The data has been lost. This error may be caused by a failure of your computer hardware or network connection. Please try to save this file elsewhere.

OK

♦ Second, most ISPs cache web pages so that they can deliver them more frequently. This means that changes you make to your site may not be propagated through the network until the cache is refreshed. This refresh may take anything from a few minutes to (in extreme cases) a day or two.

These two problems mean that the second way of adding content to a website is best left for intranet situations, where you can access the site at full network speeds and perhaps manipulate the refresh process yourself.

Because XP implements WebDAV, XP-aware programs can save directly to FTP sites and web folders. For example, the ability (mentioned earlier in the chapter) of the Scanner and Camera Wizard and Windows Movie Maker to save material directly to the Web comes courtesy of WebDAV. Similarly, Microsoft Office programs such as Word and Excel can save directly to web folders—all you need do (in theory) is use the My Network Places list in the Save As dialog box to select the network place, and you're away.

Using Network Places to Access an FTP Site or Web Folder

Network places provide the easiest built-in way to access an FTP site or web folder for transferring files. A network place essentially puts a pretty face on copying to an FTP site or a web folder by disguising it to look like a folder on your hard drive. You'll notice the difference, because when you save or copy a file to a network folder, the operation takes place at the speed of your Internet connection rather than at normal blazing computer speeds. But otherwise, the operation is seamless and almost effortless.

CREATING A NEW NETWORK PLACE

XP provides the Add Network Place Wizard for creating a new network place and adding it to your My Network Places list. Take the following steps:

1. Choose Start ➢ My Network Places. XP displays the My Network Places window. If your Start menu doesn't include a My Network Places link, choose Start ➢ My Computer, then click the My Network Places link in the Other Places list in the My Computer window.

2. Click the Add a Network Place link in the Network Tasks list. XP starts the Add Network Place Wizard, which displays its Welcome page.

NOTE *You can also start the Add Network Place Wizard by clicking the Network Place or Site link in the Map Network Drive dialog box (Tools ➢ Map Network Drive).*

3. Click the Next button. The wizard displays the Where Do You Want to Create This Network Place? page (shown in Figure 25.2).

FIGURE 25.2

On the Where Do You Want to Create This Network Place? page of the Add Network Place Wizard, choose the service you want to use.

4. In the list box, select the web host or local network location you want to use. In the figure, your choices are limited to MSN Communities or Choose Another Network Location. The next sections discuss these choices.

Creating a Network Place on MSN

To create a network place on MSN, select the MSN Communities item on the Where Do You Want to Create This Network Place? page of the Add Network Place Wizard. Click the Next button. The wizard walks you through the process of creating a place called My Communities on MSN. This place is linked to your Passport identity.

MSN Communities have their strengths and weaknesses. The strengths are that a Community provides an easy way of implementing a basic site with a canned set of features that include a Pictures area for sharing photos and other graphics, a Documents folder for documents that aren't graphics, a Calendar of Events for the Community, and a Chat area in which members of the Community can chat. You can rate your Community (General, Mature, or Adult); choose whether the Community is public, public with approval of membership, or private; decide whether to moderate the Community or let anyone post whatever they want; and decide how to list it in the MSN Community directory.

The weaknesses are that you have to possess a .NET Passport in order to create a Community; that your Community receives only a tiny amount of space unless you pay for more, and that it expires if it doesn't receive attention for a while; and that you can't roll your own set of features for it.

Creating a Network Place in Another Network Location

To create a network place in another network location, take the following steps:

1. On the Where Do You Want to Create This Network Place? page of the Add Network Place Wizard, select the Choose Another Network Location item.

2. Click the Next button. The wizard displays the What Is the Address of This Network Place? page (shown in Figure 25.3).

FIGURE 25.3

On the What Is the Address of This Network Place? page of the Add Network Place Wizard, specify the folder or FTP site containing the network place.

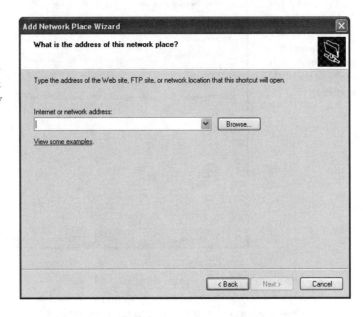

3. In the Type the Address of the Web Site, FTP Site, or Network Location That This Shortcut Will Open text box, enter the location of the network folder, web folder, or FTP site. For most purposes, you'll want to use one of these three formats:

Network Place	Format
Shared folder on network	\\server\folder
Web folder	http://server/folder
FTP site	ftp://ftp.domainname.domain

4. Click the Next button. The wizard checks the type of authentication required and displays the appropriate dialog box:

◆ For an FTP site, the wizard displays the User Name and Password page (shown in Figure 25.4 with the Log On Anonymously check box cleared). If you log on anonymously to this network place, leave the Log On Anonymously check box selected, as it is by default. If you need to supply a username and password (as is more likely), clear the Log On Anonymously check box and enter your username in the User Name text box. Click the Next button.

FIGURE 25.4

On the User Name and Password page of the Add Network Place Wizard, choose whether to log on anonymously or specify your username.

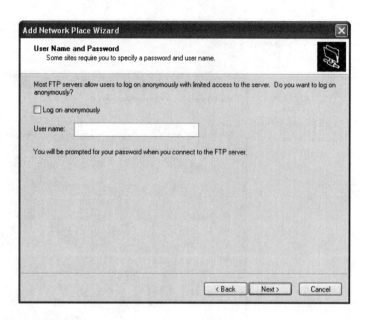

◆ For a web folder, the wizard displays the Enter Network Password dialog box (shown in Figure 25.5). Enter your username and password. Select the Save This Password in Your Password List check box if you think it advisable. Then click the OK button.

FIGURE 25.5

In the Enter Network Password dialog box, enter your username and password for the web folder.

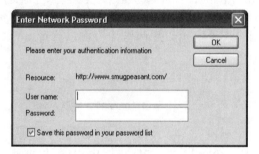

5. The wizard displays the What Do You Want to Name This Place? page (shown in Figure 25.6).

6. Enter the name for the network place. This name is for your benefit, so make it descriptive. By default, XP suggests a variation on the address for the network place, so you'll often want to change it.

7. Click the Next button. The wizard displays the Completing the Add Network Place Wizard page.

8. If you want to open the network place immediately, leave the Open This Network Place when I Click Finish check box selected. Otherwise, clear this check box.

9. Click the Finish button. The Add Network Place Wizard closes itself and creates the network place.

FIGURE 25.6

On the What Do You Want to Name This Place? page of the Add Network Place Wizard, specify the name you want to use for the network place.

ACCESSING A NETWORK PLACE

Once you've created a network place, you can access it from Explorer by using the My Network Places window (Start ➢ My Network Places).

To open a network place, double-click it. If you saved your password for the network place, XP opens the network place at the full speed of your Internet connection. If the network place is on MSN, XP automatically logs you in to the network place using your .NET Passport.

If the network place is an FTP site, XP displays the Log On As dialog box (shown in Figure 25.7). Enter the password. Select the Save Password check box if you want XP to store your password so that you can access this network place without interruption next time. (Remember that storing a password compromises your security.) Then click the Log On button.

FIGURE 25.7

For an FTP site, you need to enter your password in the Log On As dialog box.

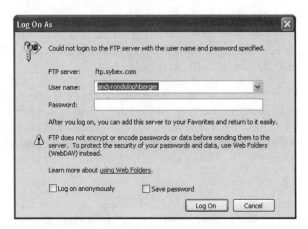

You can add files to the network place by using regular Explorer techniques. For example, you can drag files from another folder and drop them on the icon for a network place to copy them to that network place.

Opening Web Folders

To open a web folder, run Internet Explorer and choose File ➢ Open. Internet Explorer displays the Open dialog box. Select the Open As Web Folder check box, enter the address in the Open text box, and click the OK button. Enter your login name and password if the site requires them.

Once you've accessed the site, the Internet Explorer window changes to an Explorer window and displays the contents of the web folder. Internet Explorer adds the web folder's URL to your My Network Places list so that you can access it more easily from My Network Places in the future.

If a web folder appears to be empty when you're sure it isn't, chances are that the Directory Listing property for the folder needs to be enabled. You'll need to get whoever manages the web folder to set this property. (It's also possible that the web folder actually *is* empty. You never know.)

FTP via Internet Explorer

As you saw in Chapter 18, you can use Internet Explorer for FTP. There's no particular advantage to using Internet Explorer when you can use a network place instead, but Internet Explorer works well enough to be worth considering as an alternative.

To transfer files via FTP using Internet Explorer, take the following steps:

1. Choose Start ➢ Internet. XP launches Internet Explorer.

2. In the Address bar, enter the FTP address, username, and password (if you choose) using the following format:

   ```
   ftp://username[:password]@ftpserver/url
   ```

3. Click the Go button or press the Enter key. If you specified your password (and got it right), XP connects to the FTP server and displays the folder. If you chose not to specify your password, XP displays the Login As dialog box, in which you can enter your password and choose whether to save it.

TIP　*Once you've connected to the FTP site, create a favorite for it so that you can access it quickly in the future.*

FTP via an FTP Client

Network places provide smooth access to web folders and FTP sites, but for more powerful FTP capabilities, you may want to invest in a graphical FTP client such as WS_FTP Pro (`www.ipswitch.com`) or CuteFTP (`www.globalscape.com`).

NOTE　*XP includes an FTP client built in—but unfortunately it's a command-line client, which means that to use it, you need to use Unix-style commands. If you know these commands, launch the FTP client by choosing Start ➢ Run, entering* ftp *in the Open text box in the resulting Run dialog box, and clicking the OK button. If you don't know these commands and don't want to learn them, stick with Internet Explorer or a graphical FTP client.*

Up Next

This short chapter has discussed the main considerations in publishing material to the Web: what you can legally publish and the importance of performing quality control; where to publish your material; and how to get the material from your computer to the web host.

This is the end of Part III of the book. Part IV, which begins overleaf, discusses how to enjoy audio, video, and games on XP.

Part IV

Audio, Video, and Games

Chapter 26

Windows Media Player

THIS CHAPTER DISCUSSES HOW to use Windows Media Player, the powerful multimedia player included with XP. A vast improvement on its predecessors of the same name, Windows Media Player not only provides features for enjoying audio and video—including DVDs, if you add software—but also supports copying compact discs (CDs) to your hard disk in WMA format (or MP3 format, if you add further software). The main problems that Windows Media Player face are those of being *bloatware* (software that consumes a large amount of memory and processing power) and of being buggy, but if it's included with the version of XP that you have, try it and see how you get along with it before spending money on an alternative.

NOTE *Windows Media Player is one of the "middleware" components that Microsoft has been legally obliged to make removable. So your copy of XP may include an alternative program instead of Windows Media Player.*

This chapter starts by discussing how to configure Windows Media Player, because you'll almost certainly want to change some of its default settings. It then shows you how to play music with Windows Media Player, how to "copy" music from CDs to your hard drive, and how to tune into Internet radio. In between, it discusses digital rights management and how to back up and restore digital licenses for audio and video files. The chapter ends by showing you how to use the Volume Control applet to control input and output and how to record and convert sounds using the Sound Recorder applet. Volume Control and Sound Recorder are relatively straightforward, but each has a couple of subtleties that you'll want to be aware of.

This chapter covers the following topics:

- Configuring Windows Media Player
- Playing music with Windows Media Player
- Understanding digital rights management
- Copying a CD to your hard disk
- Tuning into Internet radio

◆   Backing up and restoring digital licenses

◆   Using Volume Control to control output and input

◆   Recording and converting sounds with Sound Recorder

Getting Started with Windows Media Player

Start Windows Media Player by choosing Start ➢ All Programs ➢ Windows Media Player. By default, Windows Media Player starts on its Media Guide page, which is essentially a browser window that displays the latest news from the WindowsMedia.com website.

Figure 26.1 shows Windows Media Player in its Full mode, with a track playing. By default, the menu bar and window frame hide themselves automatically when Windows Media Player appears in a normal (not maximized) window, giving Windows Media Player the irregular effect you see here. You can display the menu bar by moving the mouse pointer over the area it occupies or by clicking the Show Menu Bar button at the left end of the gray bar across the top of the window.

FIGURE 26.1

Windows Media Player 8, shown here in its Full mode, provides full-ish capabilities for audio and video and is a huge improvement over the versions of Windows Media Player included in Windows 95, 98, NT, and 2000.

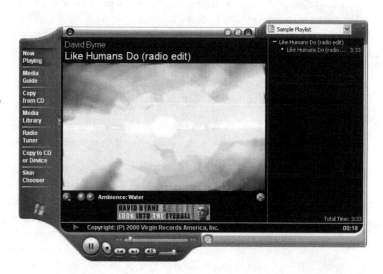

As you can see in Figure 26.1, Full mode takes up a serious chunk of a small screen, even when Windows Media Player isn't maximized and the menu bar and window frame are hidden. For sustained use, you'll be better off using Skin mode, shown in Figure 26.2.

FIGURE 26.2

In Skin mode, Windows Media Player occupies a more reasonable amount of your screen.

EXPERT KNOWLEDGE: DIGITAL RIGHTS MANAGEMENT, LICENSES, AND COPY-PROTECTION TECHNOLOGIES

Being able to store audio and video in digital format on a PC, play them back easily, and even transfer them via the Internet or removable media, is great for consumers of audio and video content. But it can be way less than great for creators of audio and video content: These computer capabilities pose a severe threat to their livelihoods by compromising their copyrighted works and robbing them of sales.

COMPUTERS HAVE MADE DIGITAL PIRACY EFFORTLESS, FAST, AND CHEAP

In the past, audio and video works have largely been distributed on physical media, such as CDs, audio cassettes, LPs, video cassettes, and DVDs. The tangible nature and physical presence of such media generally make it clear when a theft has occurred: Physical media can't walk out of stores by themselves. Making unauthorized copies of a work distributed on a physical medium such as a videotape involves cost (for the media for the copies and for any duplicating equipment needed), time (typically real-time copying), and effort. Distributing those copies involves further cost, time, and effort. And the illegality of such pirated works is widely known (and recognized, if not exactly appreciated): Most consumers are aware that it's illegal to distribute (let alone sell) copies of copyrighted works. Besides, copies of works on analog media (such as videotape or audiotape) are lower fidelity than the originals, so the inauthenticity of late-generation copies is clear.

By contrast, any work stored in a digital medium accessible by a PC can be copied in seconds at almost zero cost, and the copies are perfect every time. These perfect copies can be distributed via the Internet, again at negligible cost. And they can be distributed in quantities and over distances unthinkable for physical media. For example, if someone buys a CD in Sioux Falls, makes MP3 files of its tracks, and makes them available on a file-sharing service such as GnutellaNet or Freenet, anyone with Internet connectivity anywhere in the world—from Vladivostok to Tierra del Fuego, from Juneau to Java—can download them and then distribute them further.

PROTECTING THE RIGHTS OF CONTENT CREATORS

At this writing, several technologies exist to protect the rights of content creators (and their authorized distributors) while allowing consumers to use the content. For example, most DVDs use an encryption system called Content Scrambling System (CSS), which requires an encryption key in order to be decoded. CSS keys were licensed and tightly controlled by the DVD-Copy Control Association (DVD-CCA)—tightly controlled, that is, until Norwegian hackers in the LiVid (Linux Video group) created a utility called DeCSS by reverse engineering some unencrypted code they discovered in a sloppily constructed software DVD player. Now that DeCSS is widely available, CSS-encrypted content can be deciphered by anyone who has the code.

Perhaps the most promising of the technologies designed to protect content is the digital license. A *digital license* is encrypted information that links a particular copy of a downloaded work to a particular computer or individual. For example, in the current model of digital licenses for audio, if you download a track that uses a digital license, you buy or are otherwise granted a license to play the track on the computer on which you downloaded it. If you transfer the track to another computer, it won't play, because the computer lacks the necessary license information.

Continued on next page

EXPERT KNOWLEDGE: DIGITAL RIGHTS MANAGEMENT, LICENSES, AND COPY-PROTECTION TECHNOLOGIES *(continued)*

So far, so good. But in order to be viable enough to become widely accepted, digital licenses need to be not only easy and intuitive to use but also compatible with both generally used technology and with the prevailing laws. For example, the First Sale Doctrine laid out in the Copyright Act allows consumers to sell or give a copy they've legitimately acquired of a copyrighted work to another person. Any copyright-protection technology that prevents consumers from doing this effectively (for example, because any subsequent recipient would not be able to view or listen to the work because it was locked by encryption and a non-transferable license to the first purchaser's computer) would be open to heavy-duty legal challenges.

Leaving aside such details for the moment... digital licenses are now being used to secure some copyrighted content. Windows Media Player adopts a two-pronged approach to digital licenses for audio content, supporting digital licenses for both tracks you buy and download and tracks you copy from CD. Windows Media Player automatically issues a license for each track you copy from a CD (unless you set it to copy tracks without licensing them).

At this writing, Windows Media Player lets you choose whether to use digital licenses or to be free, easy, and possibly illegal. As long as you use those tracks on the PC with which you created them, there's no problem with using licenses. But if you want to be able to play the tracks from another computer, you've got a problem, because the license ties the associated digital media file to the PC for which the license is issued: You'll need to acquire a new license or transfer a license from the original computer. Similarly, you may not be able to download a copy of a licensed track to a portable player without licensing gymnastics.

Now, simply *playing* a track from another computer should be fine, legally, because it's the same file that you created from the CD. So should be moving the track to another computer that belongs to you and using it on that computer. Only if you create an illegal copy of the track—and particularly if you distribute it—should there be a problem. More on this later in the chapter; but you can see that the implementation of digital licenses tends to be problematic, partly because of the nature of the beast and partly because of the assumption of those who implemented the technology that anything unlicensed will tend to be licentious. There's no good reason for using digital licenses for the tracks you copy from CD unless you can't trust yourself (or other users of your computer) not to take illegal actions with them.

If you choose to use digital licenses for the tracks you copy from CD and the tracks you purchase and download (or download for free), you need to back up your licenses in case you lose them and need to restore them. If your computer crashes, if you reinstall XP, or if you install another operating system, you'll need to restore your licenses in order to be able to use the tracks.

License files are small, so you can store a good number of them on a floppy disk. If you're not good at keeping your floppy disks in order, or if you want to protect them against local or natural disasters, back them up to an Internet drive instead.

BEWARE OF NON-CD AUDIO DISCS

In 2001 and 2002, some of the major record companies began releasing audio discs that used copyright-protection technologies intended to prevent users from ripping and encoding their contents on computers and (by extension) sharing the resulting files with other people in authorized ways.

Continued on next page

Expert Knowledge: Digital Rights Management, Licenses, and Copy-Protection Technologies *(continued)*

Typically, copy-protected discs include some form of deliberate corruption designed to confuse computer CD and DVD drives, which are more sensitive than audio-only CD drives because they need to be able to read data CDs as well as audio CDs. Some of the copy-protection mechanisms mess with the error-correction capabilities built into CD players, raising concerns that these discs will degenerate faster than genuine CDs because they're less resistant to scratches.

Some of the more prominent discs involved include Michael Jackson's *Invincible*, Shakira's *Laundry Service*, and some pressings of Natalie Imbruglia's *White Lilies Island*. Identifying these offending audio discs is difficult because record companies release different versions in different markets—and they've been known to issue protection-free versions of discs if enough consumers in a particular market complain about protected versions.

These protected discs play fine on most audio CD players, though some cause problems on older CD players and specialized CD players, such as car CD players. But they won't play on many (perhaps most) computer CD drives. Other CD drives—particularly DVD drives and CD-RW drives—can play these discs (and rip and encode them) without problems. If you have such a drive, and you rip and encode a copy-protected audio disc, you will have committed a crime under Title I of the Digital Millennium Copyright Act (DMCA), which makes it illegal to "circumvent a technological measure that effectively controls access to a work protected under this title." If you do this "willfully and for purposes of commercial advantage or private financial gain" (which can include providing another person with a track you've ripped and encoded and receiving just about anything—even a single audio track—from them in return), you can be savaged with fines of up to a half-million dollars and a sentence of five years in jail.

Some protected discs have caused extreme problems with Apple iMacs, because some models of iMac lack a manual eject mechanism that can eject a CD when the operating system has disagreed with it (or vice versa). In some cases, owners have had to take iMacs to dealerships for physical repairs to remove copy-protected audio discs from the CD drives. There have been isolated reports of non-CD audio discs causing CD drives on PCs to function incorrectly, but in general, the problems appear to be less severe. Typically, a copy-protected disc won't play, but it will eject normally. If it won't eject normally, the user can almost always use the drive's manual-eject mechanism (for example, poking a straightened paper-clip into the tiny hole in the drive's front panel) to get the disc out the hard way.

Technically and legally, these copy-protected audio discs are *not* compact discs, because they don't conform to the Red Book compact disc specification. This means that, legally, such discs can't be sold as CDs and must not bear the CD logo that certifies that the disc is a CD.

Some users report being able to crack the copy protection by using lo-tech techniques such as coloring the outer track of the CD with a dark marker or carefully sticking a strip of tape over it. Your mileage on doing so will vary depending on the type of copy protection on the disc and the type of drive you have. If you can't play the disc on your CD drive, and you have an audio CD player that can play the disc, you can always feed the signal from the CD player's output into the audio input on your sound card (or into a USB input) and record it from that input. If your CD player's output is digital (for example, an SPDIF), you can make a pure digital copy. If your CD player's output is analog, the audio will need to be converted from digital to analog and back again, so the resulting files will be lower in quality than the original, but for most purposes they'll be plenty listenable if your CD player, sound card, and cable are up to scratch. (Again, you'll have committed a crime under the DMCA.)

Configuring Windows Media Player

Windows Media Player has a raft of configuration options on the eight or nine pages of its Options dialog box (the DVD page appears only if your computer has a DVD drive and a DVD player installed). The following sections discuss the most important options. If you want some music while you read, go ahead and load a CD. Windows Media Player should start playing it automatically unless you've disabled Autoplay for music. Then choose Tools ➤ Options. Windows Media Player displays the Options dialog box.

Player Page Options

Almost all of the options on the Player page (shown on the left in Figure 26.3) are worth knowing about:

Automatic Updates group box   Select the Once a Month option button (unless you want Windows Media Player to prompt you to upgrade more frequently). Leave the Download Codecs Automatically check box selected (as it is by default) if you want Windows Media Player to download and install any new codecs (coder/decoder software) it needs to play back audio streams or files. Clear this check box if you prefer to have Windows Media Player prompt you before it installs new codecs.

TIP   *You can force Windows Media Player to check for updates by choosing Help ➤ Check for Player Updates, then following the Windows Media Component Setup process that ensues.*

Internet Settings group box   The Allow Internet Sites to Uniquely Identify Your Player check box sounds like it's threatening to broadcast your personal information all over the Web. In fact, this check box controls whether Windows Media Player passes an identifier to streaming media servers to enable the servers to monitor the connection and adjust the stream to improve playback quality. For best quality of streaming audio, leave this check box selected, as it is by default. The Acquire Licenses Automatically check box controls whether Windows Media Player tries to automatically get a license when a file requires one. (See the sidebar earlier in this chapter on digital rights management and licenses for a discussion of licenses.)

Player Settings group box   Choose whether to start the player on the Media Guide page, whether to display the player always on top in Skin mode, whether to display the anchor window (a small reference window) when the player is in Skin mode, and whether to let the XP screen saver kick in while music or video is playing back. The anchor window is more or less useless, but having the player always on top makes it easy to access. The screen saver seldom improves playback, even of music: Visualizations provide better entertainment. Select the Add Items to Media Library when Played check box if you want Windows Media Player to add new tracks to the Media Library when you play them. If you select this check box, you get the choice of selecting the Include Items from Removable Media check box, which controls whether Windows adds tracks from removable media such as CDs or removable disks to the Media Library. (This isn't usually a good idea.)

FIGURE 26.3

The Player page
(left) and Copy
Music page (right)
of the Options
dialog box

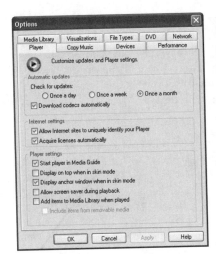
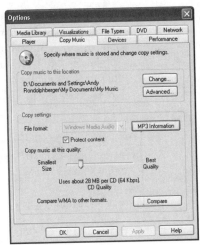

Copy Music Page Options

The Copy Music page of the Options dialog box (shown on the right in Figure 26.3) contains four options that control the "copying" of music from CDs to your hard drive. These options are largely set-and-forget, though you may want to use different music quality settings for different CDs that you copy.

These are the options:

Copy Music to This Location group box   This group box contains a label that shows the folder to which Windows Media Player copies music. The default location is your \My Music\ folder, in which Windows Media Player creates folders by artist and, within these, folders by album name. To change the location, click the Change button, use the resulting Browse for Folder dialog box to navigate to and select the location, and then click the OK button.

By default, Windows Media Player names the files by track number and track name (or *song title*, as Windows Media Player refers to it)—for example, 01 Clock without Hands.WMA. To change the naming, click the Advanced button and work in the resulting File Name Options dialog box. Select the check boxes for the items you want to include in the filename (track number, song title, artist, album, and so on). Use the Move Up button and Move Down button to shuffle the selected items into order. And use the Separator drop-down list to specify which separator character to use: none, a space, a dash, a dot, or an underline. Then click the OK button. Windows Media Player closes the File Name Options dialog box and applies your choices.

NOTE   *Windows Media Player shares the Media Library among all users, so you don't need to use the* \Shared Documents\ *folder to share music with other users of the computer.*

Copy Settings group box   In the File Format drop-down list, select the file format you want to use for the files: Windows Media or MP3. (See the next sidebar for details on how Windows Media and MP3 stack up to each other.) In practice, you'll need to use the Windows Media format unless you buy an MP3 Creation Pack from a third-party developer such as Cyberlink Corp., InterVideo Inc., or Ravisent. (Click the MP3 Information button in the Copy Settings group box to open a browser window to a page with details of the MP3 Creation Packs available for Windows Media Player.)

> *TIP*   *If you don't feel like paying for the privilege of creating MP3 files, there's no need to do so, because you can get various high-quality MP3 rippers and encoders for free. One of the best is MusicMatch Jukebox (*www.musicmatch .com*), which comes in a free Basic version and a paid Plus version. For details of other MP3 rippers and encoders, visit the MP3.com website (*www.mp3.com*). You may also want to get a dedicated MP3 player, such as Winamp (*www.winamp.com*), rather than using Windows Media Player all the time.*

Leave the Protect Content check box selected (as it is by default) if you want to use Windows Media Player's features for personal licensing of CD tracks you copy. See the previous sidebar for a discussion of the advantage (*sic*) and disadvantages of using this feature. Clear this check box if you want more flexibility in what you can do with WMA files.

Use the Copy Music at This Quality slider to specify the quality at which to encode the files you copy. Windows Media Player offers six bitrates (48Kbps, 64Kbps, 96Kbps, 128Kbps, 160Kbps, and 192Kbps) graded from Smallest Size (48Kbps) to Best Quality (192Kbps). Higher bitrates take up more space but sound better. Experiment with this setting on a variety of music and find the bitrate that suits you best:

- If you have plenty of hard disk space for the music you want to copy, choose the 192Kbps bitrate as a hedge against getting a better sound card or speakers in the future.
- If you want to use the files with a portable player with limited memory, use the lowest bitrate that sounds good on the player.
- Microsoft describes the 64Kbps bitrate as "CD Quality." This is optimistic enough to qualify as deluded in most people's terms.

EXPERT KNOWLEDGE: HOW DO MP3 AND WMA STACK UP TO EACH OTHER?

Audiophiles, gearheads, and Microsoft-haters have had a long-running argument about whether MP3 or WMA is better. Impressive amounts of research have been done by interested parties, but the resulting articles and papers have drawn such diametrically opposed conclusions that you'd be forgiven for dismissing them all as propaganda. The argument tends to get polarized into a holy war, and neither the crusaders nor the infidels (or heretics, depending on your point of view) have a monopoly on fact, reason, or logic. In fact, each side often seems to have at best a tenuous grasp on all three. If you want to see Microsoft's side of the story, click the Compare button on the Copy Music page of the Options dialog box.

To really appreciate the nuances of the different sides of the argument, you need to understand a bit about how audio compression works. If you could bear to know some more, try my book *MP3 Complete* (Sybex, 2001).

Continued on next page

EXPERT KNOWLEDGE: HOW DO MP3 AND WMA STACK UP TO EACH OTHER? *(continued)*

In the meantime, though, you no doubt want some sensible advice. That's easy enough, because from a lay point of view, the situation is very simple. Here's what you need to know:

◆ Even at the highest quality settings they offer, and on the best equipment, neither MP3 nor WMA sound quite as good as CD-quality audio, which is uncompressed and uses a comprehensive range of samples across the whole area of audio frequencies audible to the human ear. This is because each format uses lossy compression to reduce the size of the audio files. As you'd guess from its name, *lossy compression* involves discarding data from the original in order to compress it. (The opposite of lossy compression is *lossless compression*, which essentially involves squeezing files in such a way that they can be reexpanded to a copy that contains the same information as the original. Zip files use lossless compression, so the files you extract from a Zip file are functionally identical to their originals, though not actually the same file.)

◆ Unless you've got amazing ears, very good hi-fi, or perhaps both, the advantages of compression outweigh the disadvantages. Compressed files are small enough to store in large numbers on computers, to carry in small numbers on ultraportable players, and to transfer easily via removable media, networks, or the Internet.

◆ MP3 and WMA use different encoding methods, but the results are roughly comparable in quality.

◆ MP3 is a more widely used file format than WMA. A wide variety of software MP3 players are available for every conceivable computing platform, and you can get hardware MP3 players in an impressive variety of shapes and sizes. Many software MP3 players and some hardware MP3 players can handle WMA files as well as MP3 files.

◆ In June 2001, Thomson Multimedia (www.thomson-multimedia.com) released a demo version of mp3PRO, a new version of MP3 that delivers better sound quality than MP3 at lower bitrates. mp3PRO is more expensive to license than other MP3 encoders, so it's hard to say how quickly or widely it will be integrated into MP3 solutions.

Whether you choose MP3, WMA, or another format will probably boil down to what you want to do with digital audio, how high your standards are, and how much time, effort, and money you're prepared to invest.

If all you want to do is rip your CDs, encode them, and store the results on your hard disk so that you can play them back from your computer, Windows Media Player and WMA provide an effective solution. Choose a bitrate that delivers satisfactory audio quality through your sound card and speakers, load the first CD, and you're away. In this case, it may be a good idea to use Windows Media Player's licensing features, because they ensure that you can't inadvertently break the law by using the files on another computer. (You can transfer them to another computer, but because it doesn't have the right license information, it won't be able to play them.)

If you want to use digital audio on a portable player, WMA may not be such a suitable choice. While an increasing number of portable digital-audio players do support WMA as well as MP3, many do not. Even for those players that do support WMA, you may find that MP3 provides more options or easier administration. For example, to use WMA files on a portable player that doesn't support the SDMI specification, you'll need to turn off Windows Media Player's licensing features; by contrast, with MP3 files, you don't need to worry about digital licenses.

Devices Page Options

The Devices page of the Options dialog box (shown on the left in Figure 26.4) lets you configure your CD and DVD drives for playing back and copying CDs and any portable devices for downloading tracks from Windows Media Player.

FIGURE 26.4

The Devices page of the Options dialog box (left) lists your CD drives, DVD drives, and portable devices. To choose analog or digital audio, display the Properties dialog box (right) for the drive.

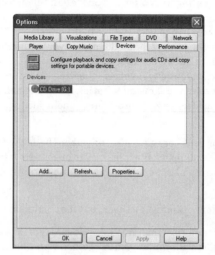
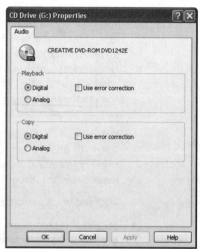

SETTING PROPERTIES FOR A CD DRIVE OR DVD DRIVE

To set properties for a CD drive or DVD drive, select it in the Devices list box and click the Properties button. Windows Media Player displays the Properties dialog box for the drive. The screen on the right in Figure 26.4 shows an example of the Properties dialog box for a DVD drive.

In the Playback group box and the Copy group box, choose between the Digital option button and the Analog option button. Digital audio extraction is preferable to analog audio extraction because it maintains a higher-fidelity signal. The main reason not to use digital audio extraction is if your CD drive does not support it or cannot deliver it successfully. If you choose digital audio extraction, you can select the Use Error Correction check box if you want Windows Media Player to use its error-correction features to try to remove errors that occur during playback or copying. Error correction uses a bit more CPU power than regular playback or copying; it slows down copying considerably; and its effect is often undetectable. You may want to try playing your CDs without error correction and turn it on only if you hear odd noises in the playback. Unless you have a savage degree of impatience encoded in your chromosomes, it's a good idea to use error correction for copying music, because any defects in the copied tracks tend to be much more annoying than spending a few extra minutes copying each CD.

NOTE *If Windows Media Player finds, when you insert a CD, that your CD drive doesn't support digital playback, it displays a message telling you so and warning you that visualizations, the graphic equalizer, and SRS WOW will not work. Windows Media Player then switches to analog mode.*

Click the OK button. Windows Media Player closes the Properties dialog box for the CD drive.

ADDING A PORTABLE DEVICE

To add a portable device, click the Add button. Windows Media Player opens an Internet Explorer window to the WindowsMedia.com site, which maintains a list of compatible devices and links to the software that you can download to make the devices agree with Windows Media Player. This list is becoming extensive, but older portable devices (such as the original Rio 300PMP) need not apply.

TIP   Most portable devices come with effective software for loading tracks and playlists onto them. Because this software is specifically designed for the portable device, it may offer enhancements that Windows Media Player does not. However, some portable device software packages cannot rip, encode, and load to the portable device in one move, as Windows Media Player can with some of the players it supports.

Performance Page Options

The Performance page (shown on the left in Figure 26.5) of the Options dialog box offers these options:

Connection Speed group box   By default, the Detect Connection Speed (Recommended) check box is selected. This setting usually works well. If you find the results disappointing, try selecting the Choose Connection Speed option button and specifying the speed in the drop-down list.

Network Buffering group box   By default, the Use Default Buffering (Recommended) option button is selected, so Windows Media Player buffers the default number of seconds of audio before starting to play it. (The *buffer* is the quantity of audio that Windows Media Player downloads before starting to play an audio stream and holds in reserve so that it can even out any minor interruptions in the audio stream when it's playing.) If you hear interruptions in the audio with the default buffering, note the buffering time the next time you access streaming audio, then try selecting the Buffer For option button and specifying a larger number in the Seconds text box. The disadvantage to buffering more audio is that you have to wait longer for the audio to start playing.

Video Acceleration group box   If your video playback in Windows Media Player is unsatisfactory, you can try adjusting the Video Acceleration slider to improve the speed or smoothness.

FIGURE 26.5

If necessary, specify a connection speed on the Performance page of the Options dialog box (left). To choose further video settings, work in the Video Acceleration Settings dialog box (right).

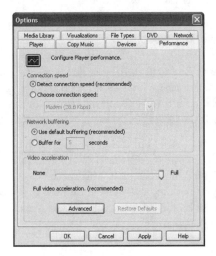

For further video acceleration settings, click the Advanced button. Windows Media Player displays the Video Acceleration Settings dialog box (shown on the right in Figure 26.5). The key settings here are the Digital Video slider, which adjusts the size of the picture, and the Display Full-Screen Controls check boxes in the Video Acceleration group box and the DVD Video group box. The Enable Full-Screen Mode Switch check box in the Video Acceleration group box, which is cleared by default, attempts to expand the video image for viewing at full-screen size in full-screen mode. This capability typically doesn't work with digital video. The Digital Video slider (which, as its name suggests, works only for digital video, not for analog video) kicks in when you expand the Windows Media Player window to a larger size than the original video and Windows Media Player needs to stretch the video to fit. The Large setting allows Windows Media Player to interpolate (add) pixels that are not in the original video in order to stretch the picture. The Small setting keeps the video more faithful to the original but requires more CPU power. For best results, experiment with this setting.

If you have both hardware and software DVD decoders installed, you'll be able to choose the Hardware option button or the Software option button in the Preferred Decoder area. Click the OK button. Windows Media Player closes the Video Acceleration Settings dialog box.

Media Library Page Options

The Media Library page (shown on the left in Figure 26.6) of the Options dialog box contains three crucial settings for keeping control of your Media Library. You may want to stay with the default settings, which are suitable for many people, but you should understand these options.

Access Rights of Other Applications group box   The three option buttons in this group box control whether other programs installed on your computer can access your Media Library. The default setting is the Read-Only Access option button. This setting is useful if you want other programs to be able to read your Media Library (for example, if you use a jukebox other than Windows Media Player to play music sometimes) but not change it. If you want other programs to be able to change your Media Library, select the Full Access option button. If you're sure none of your other programs will need to access your Media Library, select the No Access option button.

Access Rights of Internet Sites group box   The three option buttons in this group box control whether Internet sites can access your Media Library. The default setting is the No Access option button. *Change this setting to the Read-Only Access option button only if you want Internet sites to be able to access your Media Library to collect information about the audio and video you have.* At this writing, there seems no good reason to select the Full Access option button—but no doubt someone will invent a program that requires this.

Media Files group box   Leave the Automatically Add Purchased Music to My Library check box selected if you want Windows Media Player to automatically add to your Media Library all the music you purchase online and download. This check box is selected by default, and leaving it selected is the easiest way of building your Media Library. If you don't want to add all the music you purchase to your Media Library, clear this check box. You can then add music to your Media Library manually after you purchase it.

FIGURE 26.6

On the Media Library page (left) of the Options dialog box, you can specify access rights to your Media Library. On the Visualizations page (right), choose the visualization collection to use for visual accompaniment.

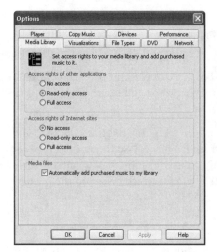

Visualizations Page Options

On the Visualizations page (shown on the right in Figure 26.6) of the Options dialog box, you can choose the visualization collection to use for enhancing your listening pleasure.

Some visualizations have properties that you can set by selecting the entry in the list box and clicking the Properties button to display a Properties dialog box.

You can add other visualizations that you've downloaded by clicking the Add button, using the resulting Open dialog box to identify the visualizations file, and clicking the Open button.

You can remove some visualizations by selecting them and clicking the Remove button. Other visualizations are built in and wish to remain so.

File Types Page Options

On the File Types page (shown on the left in Figure 26.7) of the Options dialog box, you can select and clear check boxes to specify which file types Windows Media Player is associated with. For example, if Windows Media Player has associated itself with the MP3 file type, but you want to use another player for MP3 files, clear the MP3 Format Sound check box.

FIGURE 26.7

Use the File Types page (left) of the Options dialog box to specify the file types to associate with Windows Media Player. If you have a DVD drive, you can choose parental control settings and language settings on the DVD page (right).

DVD Page Options

If your computer has a DVD drive and a DVD player installed, the Options dialog box includes the DVD page (shown on the right in Figure 26.7). This page offers these options:

Parental Control group box To implement parental control on DVDs played on the computer, select the Parental Control check box and use the Select a Rating drop-down list to specify the rating to apply.

Language Settings group box Use the Subtitles drop-down list to specify whether you want subtitles and, if so, in which language. Use the Audio drop-down list and the Menu drop-down list to specify the language to use for movie audio and on-screen menus. The default setting for these two controls is Title Default, which gives you the primary language with which the DVD was encoded.

Network Page Options

On the Network page, you can choose which protocols to use for receiving audio and video streams over a network. Unless you know your protocols well enough not to need advice on configuring them, you probably shouldn't mess with the default selections.

Letting Windows Media Player Know about the Media Files on Your Computer

You've configured Windows Media Player, but you still need to let it know about all the audio and video files on your computer. (If you display the Media Library page before you've searched your computer for media files, Windows Media Player prompts you to search for files.)

To let Windows Media Player know about the media files on your computer, choose Tools ➤ Search for Media Files or press the F3 key. In the Search for Media Files dialog box that Windows Media Player displays, specify which drives (and if necessary, which folders) to search, and choose any advanced search options needed. Then click the Search button to set the search going. If you have a hard drive of any size, the search takes a few minutes. Windows Media Player lists the files it found on the Media Library page.

WARNING *The Media Library is shared with all other users of the computer, including the Guest user. Don't put anything in your Media Library that you don't want other users to see or hear.*

Playing Audio Files from Disk

Once you've let Windows Media Player discover the tracks that you have on your computer and list them in the Media Library, you can play any track by navigating to it and double-clicking it (or by selecting it and clicking the Play button).

You can also open a file by choosing File ➤ Open (or pressing Ctrl+O) to display the Open dialog box, navigating to and selecting the file, and clicking the Open button.

Playing Music from the *My Music*\ Folder

If you prefer to locate your music by browsing through your \My Music\ folder or the \Shared Music\ folder rather than by using Windows Media Player, you can launch Windows Media Player and start music playing by selecting a folder of music (or a track) and clicking the Play Selection link in the Music Tasks pane or by clicking the Play All link with no track selected in a folder of music.

To make these links available to other folders, customize each folder and apply one of the music templates: the Music (Best for Audio Files and Playlists) template, the Music Artist (Best for Works by One Artist) template, or the Music Album (Best for Tracks from One Album) template.

Creating Playlists

Playing audio files from disk is easy enough, but you can make it even easier by creating playlists of the audio files you like to play together.

To create a new playlist, take the following steps:

1. Click the New Playlist button on the Media Library page. Windows Media Player displays the New Playlist dialog box.
2. Enter the name for the playlist in the New Playlist dialog box.
3. Click the OK button. Windows Media Player closes the New Playlist dialog box and creates a new playlist in the My Playlists list.
4. Populate the playlist by dragging tracks to it.

To start a playlist playing, double-click it on the Media Library page. To switch from one playlist to another, use the drop-down list in the upper-right corner of Windows Media Player.

Playing a CD

Unless you turn off Autoplay (as discussed in the section "Customizing and Turning Off Autoplay" in Chapter 6), Windows Media Player automatically starts playing an audio CD you insert in your CD drive. If your computer is connected to the Internet, Windows Media Player attempts to retrieve the CD information by submitting the CD's ID number to the WindowsMedia.com database of information. (According to Microsoft, Windows Media Player doesn't submit any information about you other than the Globally Unique Identifier [GUID] and your IP address, which is required to get the information about the CD back to your computer.)

If Windows Media Player doesn't automatically display the track names, or if it shows them as Unknown Artist – Unknown Album, you'll need to retrieve them manually. Click the Get Names button, and Windows Media Player leads you through a search for the artist and album. The process is clumsy, but it works well enough if WindowsMedia.com has the artist and album listed.

Unfortunately, the WindowsMedia.com database isn't very complete at this writing. It's nothing like as complete as CDDB, the online database of CD information (www.cddb.org) that is widely used by MP3 rippers and that contains impressively accurate information for a very wide range of CDs. CDDB works in the same way as WindowsMedia.com: It uses the unique identifying code that each commercially released audio CD contains. By submitting this code, a program can download the CD information: artist name, CD name, and track titles. Most rippers handle this process automatically when you insert a CD.

NOTE *Part of CDDB's wide coverage of CDs is due to its receiving many entries from its users. If a CD you try to look up in CDDB doesn't have an entry, you can submit one. Many MP3 rippers have a built-in mechanism for submitting entries to CDDB.*

If the artist isn't listed, click the Not Found button. Windows Media Player displays a screen that lets you add the CD's information to your local database.

Using the Graphic Equalizer and Sound Effects

Windows Media Player includes a minimalist graphic equalizer for improving the sound that emerges from your speakers or headphones. It's minimalist in that, although it comes with several preset equalizations and allows you to adjust 10 bands of frequency to your taste, it does not let you save your custom equalizations or load equalizations automatically with tracks.

The Graphic Equalizer appears on the Now Playing page of Windows Media Player when the Equalizer and Settings panel is displayed. If the Equalizer and Settings panel is not displayed, choose View ➢ Now Playing Tools ➢ Show Equalizer and Settings. Then choose View ➢ Now Playing Tools ➢ Graphic Equalizer to display the Graphic Equalizer if one of the other Now Playing tools is displayed. Figure 26.8 shows the Graphic Equalizer.

FIGURE 26.8

Use the Graphic Equalizer to improve the sound of audio.

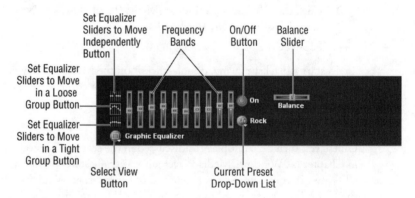

The Graphic Equalizer is straightforward to use:

◆ To turn the Graphic Equalizer on and off, click the On/Off button.

◆ To apply a preset equalization, choose it from the Current Preset drop-down list.

◆ To apply custom equalization, drag each frequency-band slider to an appropriate position. The frequency bands start with the lowest frequencies at the left side and progress to the highest frequencies at the right side.

◆ To specify whether the frequency-band sliders move independently or together, click one of the three buttons on the control to the left of the frequency bands. Click the top button to make the sliders move independently. Click the middle button to make the sliders move together in a loose group. Click the bottom button to make the sliders move together in a tight group.

To apply sound effects, click the Select View button and choose SRS WOW Effects from the context menu. Windows Media Player displays the SRS WOW Effects panel (shown in Figure 26.9). From here, you can use the On/Off button to turn the effects on and off, set bass boosting with the TruBass slider, set the wow effect with the WOW Effect slider, or choose a different speaker setting.

FIGURE 26.9

Use the SRS WOW Effects panel to apply sound effects to audio.

Copying (Ripping) a CD

Windows Media Player provides features for what it calls "copying" an audio CD to your hard drive. This doesn't mean copying each file on the CD bit for bit, but rather extracting the audio data from the CD (a process normally called *ripping*) and encoding it to a compressed format called Windows Media Audio (WMA).

As you probably know, CD-quality audio files are huge, taking up about 9MB per minute. (This is why about 74 minutes of audio fits on a 650MB CD.) WMA files can be encoded at various bitrates, including the six bitrates that Windows Media Player offers: 48Kbps, 64Kbps, 96Kbps, 128Kbps, 160Kbps, and 192Kpbs. Windows Media Player's default bitrate is 64Kbps. This bitrate sounds borderline okay to many people and is good if you're trying to pack as much music as possible onto a portable device. But to make the files you copy sound good when you play them back on your PC, increase the bitrate to 128Kbps, 160Kbps, or 192Kbps—the higher the better, especially if you're likely to upgrade your sound card or your speakers before you change your taste in music.

See pages 45 and 46 of the *Essential Skills* section for a visual guide to copying a CD.

Windows Media Player can encode to MP3 if you add a third-party codec. Click the MP3 Information button on the Copy Music page of the Options dialog box to display an Internet Explorer window containing information on the MP3 Creation Pack for Windows XP and how to get it.

The first time you go to rip a CD with Windows Media Player, it displays a Windows Media Player dialog box that tells you that Windows Media Player is configured to protect your content from "unauthorized use," and that you won't be able to play content that's protected like this on any computer other than this one.

This restriction makes a lot of sense for Microsoft, because it prevents you from using illegal copies of these tracks and thus violating copyright law. (See the nearby Expert Knowledge sidebar for an explanation of what you can and cannot legally do with digital audio.) But it doesn't protect you from violating copyright law in one important way: by borrowing a CD from someone else and copying it, or by lending someone one of your CDs so they can copy it.

If you're fine with this restriction, click the OK button. If you're not, select the Do Not Protect Content check box to disable the protection, then click the OK button. This means that you'll be able to use the files you copy on other PCs. It also means that you can commit extra copyright violations either intentionally or unintentionally.

EXPERT KNOWLEDGE: WHAT CAN YOU LEGALLY DO WITH DIGITAL AUDIO?

If you're going to enjoy digital audio, you need to know what you can and cannot do with it. Here's what you can legally do:

◆ Listen to streaming audio from a website or an Internet radio station, even if the site or person streaming the audio is doing so illegally.

◆ Record audio from a medium you own (for example, a CD) to a different medium (for example, a cassette) so that you can listen to it at a different time or in a different place.

◆ Download a digital file that contains copyrighted material from a website or FTP site *provided that the copyright holder has granted the distributor permission to distribute it.*

◆ Download a digital file from a computer via P2P technology (for example, Morpheus, Freenet, or Gnutella) *provided that the copyright holder has granted the distributor permission to distribute it.*

◆ Create digital-audio files (for example, WMA files or MP3 files) of tracks on CDs you own for your personal use.

◆ Distribute a digital-audio file to which you hold the copyright or for whose distribution the copyright holder has granted you permission.

◆ Download (or copy) legal MP3 files or digital-audio files in other supported formats to portable audio devices or PDAs.

◆ Broadcast licensed audio across the Internet.

Here are some of the key things that you cannot legally do with audio:

◆ Download a digital-audio file that contains copyrighted material if the copyright holder has not granted the distributor permission to distribute it.

◆ Distribute a digital-audio file that contains copyrighted material if the copyright holder has not granted you permission to distribute it.

◆ Lend a friend a CD so that she can create digital-audio files from it.

◆ Borrow a CD from a friend and create digital-audio files from it.

◆ Upload digital-audio files from a portable audio player that supports music uploading (which most portable players don't) to another computer. (In this scenario, you're essentially using the portable player to copy the files from one computer to another.)

To copy a CD, follow these general steps:

1. Load the CD in your CD drive.
2. If Windows Media Player starts playing the CD, stop it.
3. Click the Copy from CD tab. XP displays the Copy from CD page.
4. If Windows Media Player doesn't automatically retrieve the CD information, use the Get Names feature to retrieve the information manually. (If necessary, type in the information.)

5. If necessary, edit the information retrieved. You can edit any of the changeable fields (such as the track names, the artist's name, or the genre) by clicking the field twice (with a pause in between—*not* double-clicking). Windows Media Player displays an edit box around the field. Type the correction and press the Enter key.

6. If necessary, change (or check) the Copy Music at This Quality slider setting on the Copy Music page of the Options dialog box.

7. Select the check boxes for the tracks you want to copy. Use the check box in the column header to change the status of all the individual check boxes at once.

8. Click the Copy Music button. Windows Media Player starts ripping and encoding the music, adding the tracks to the Media Library when they're finished.

If you notice a problem, click the Stop Copy button to stop copying the tracks.

TROUBLESHOOTING: TRACKS "COPIED" USING WINDOWS MEDIA PLAYER CONTAIN ONLY SILENCE

If you find that the tracks you've copied (in other words, ripped and encoded) using Windows Media Player contain nothing but the sound of silence, the cause may be that the CD drive is set to use digital mode but Windows Media Player is set to use analog mode. To solve this problem, set both the drive and Windows Media Player to analog or both to digital.

To set Windows Media Player to use digital mode, follow these steps from Windows Media Player:

1. Choose Tools ➢ Options to display the Options dialog box.

2. On the Devices page, select the device and click the Properties button. Windows Media Player displays the Properties dialog box for the drive.

3. Select the Digital option button in the Copy group box on the Audio page.

4. Click the OK button. Windows Media Player closes the Properties dialog box.

To set the CD drive to use analog mode, follow these steps:

1. Start Device Manager. For example, click the Start button, right-click the My Computer item and choose Properties from the context menu to display the System Properties dialog box, click the Hardware tab to display the Hardware page, and click the Device Manager button.

2. Expand the DVD/CD-ROM Drives item.

3. Right-click the drive and choose Properties from the context menu to display the Properties dialog box.

4. Click the Properties tab to display the Properties page.

5. In the Digital CD Playback group box, clear the Enable Digital CD Audio for This CD-ROM Device check box.

6. Click the OK button to close the Properties dialog box.

7. Close Device Manager and the System Properties dialog box.

Playing a DVD

Once you've installed a DVD drive and a DVD player, you can play a DVD by putting it in the drive and choosing Play ➤ DVD or CD Audio. Windows Media Player uses the standard Play controls for DVDs and displays a list of the DVD chapters in the playlist area.

NOTE *If you have a DVD drive but no player for it, consult the DVD Troubleshooter for details of compatible players.*

To make the most of your DVDs, you'll probably want to view them full-screen. To do so, choose View ➤ Full Screen or press Alt+Enter. Windows Media Player switches to full-screen view. You can display pop-up controls on-screen by moving the mouse. These disappear after a few seconds when you stop moving the mouse.

To display DVD controls (such as a Variable Play Speed control and a Next Frame control), choose View ➤ Now Playing Tools ➤ DVD Controls.

When you play a DVD with Windows Media Player, Windows Media Player contacts a Microsoft-controlled server via the Internet to retrieve information about the DVD so that it can list the DVD's title and chapter names for you. Windows Media Player also passes the server a unique ID number for your player—so Microsoft effectively knows which DVDs you're watching. While Microsoft probably isn't associating this information with your e-mail address to build a database of your movie preferences, you might want to avoid the risk of their doing so by using a stand-alone DVD player.

TROUBLESHOOTING: WINDOWS MEDIA PLAYER WON'T PLAY A DVD

If Windows Media Player won't play a DVD, first make sure that you've installed a DVD software plug-in for Windows Media Player, because Windows Media Player doesn't include DVD playback software.

Next, open Device Manager: Press the Windows key+Break to display the System Properties dialog box, click the Hardware tab to display the Hardware page, and click the Device Manager button. Check that Device Manager has identified the drive as a DVD drive and shows it to be functioning correctly. If not, install the drive or update the driver for it.

While you have Device Manager open, check that Device Manager has identified any hardware decoder that you have installed, and shows it to be functioning correctly too. If the hardware decoder isn't working, you'll need to install a driver for it.

Next, choose Start ➤ My Computer to open a My Computer window, right-click the DVD, and choose Explore from the context menu. (Don't double-click the DVD, because chances are that its default action is Play rather than Open or Explore.) Make sure that Explorer displays a list of contents for the DVD. It should include at least the folders \Video_TS\ and \Audio_Ts\. (There may be other folders or files as well.) This check ensures that XP can read the DVD.

If all the previous suspects turn out not guilty, check your software decoder, and reinstall it if necessary.

Tuning Into Internet Radio

Windows Media Player provides good features for tuning into Internet radio—radio broadcast across the Web via streaming audio servers such as SHOUTcast, icecast, or RealAudio. To listen to Internet radio, click the Radio Tuner tab to display the Radio Tuner page. Figure 26.10 shows the Radio Tuner page with a station playing.

FIGURE 26.10

Use Windows Media Player's Radio Tuner page to listen to radio stations broadcasting across the Internet.

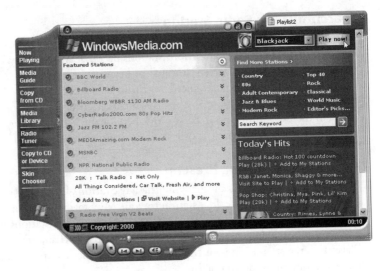

Connecting to an Internet Radio Station

The easiest way to connect to a radio station is to use a preset. Windows Media Player comes with several presets built in. You can edit these and create your own presets as you want.

To listen to a preset station, select the category of presets in the Featured Stations list. Then click the preset you want to listen to. Windows Media Player displays information about the station. Click the Play link.

Windows Media Player displays the message *Connecting to media* while it is connecting to the radio station. Next, it displays the word *Buffering* and a percentage-completed readout as it fills the buffer for the signal. When buffering is complete, Windows Media Player starts playing the station.

NOTE *Windows Media Player sometimes needs to download a codec (a coder/decoder) in order to play back a station. Some codecs may take a minute or two to download—so if you're planning to listen to a broadcast on a station you haven't accessed before, allow time for a codec download. Depending on the settings you've chosen for Windows Media Player, installing a codec may well raise a Security Warning dialog box. Check the publisher's digital certificate if you're in any doubt about the authenticity of the codec.*

Windows Media Player displays a browser window containing information about the radio station. Use this window to learn more about the station and its programming. But if you're listening to radio over a dial-up connection, you may find that this window is taking up bandwidth, especially if it's slow to load or if it runs tickers or animations. If this is happening, close the window so that it doesn't take bandwidth from the signal.

TIP *If you're using a dial-up connection and the signal keeps stopping and rebuffering, increase the size of the buffer on the Performance page of the Options dialog box.*

Searching for a Radio Station

You can browse for a radio station by following the category links (Country, 80s, Adult Contemporary, and so on) under the Find More Stations heading. Alternatively, click the Find More Stations link and use the resulting screen to search by keyword or zip code.

You can also perform an advanced search. To do so, click the Use Advanced Search button to display the Advanced Search panel. Specify whichever criteria you want—Genre, Language, Country, State (in the U.S. only), Speed, Band (AM, FM, or the Net); or Keyword, Call Sign, or Frequency—and click the Search button to locate stations that match.

Creating and Editing Presets

You can edit your presets by changing the My Stations list as you need. You cannot change the Featured Stations list. To add a station to your My Stations list, expand its heading and click its Add to My Stations link. To remove a station from your My Stations list, expand its heading in the My Stations list and choose Remove from My Stations. To change the order in which Windows Media Player lists the stations in your My Stations list, use the red up-arrow and down-arrow buttons to move a station up or down the list.

Applying Skins

You can apply *skins* (custom graphical looks) to Windows Media Player to change its appearance in Skin mode. Windows Media Player comes with a selection of skins built in. To apply a skin, display the Skin Chooser page of Windows Media Player. Select a skin in the list box to see how it looks. When you find one you like, click the Apply Skin button to apply it.

TIP   You can also apply a skin quickly by double-clicking its file in an Explorer window or on your Desktop.

To download extra skins, click the More Skins button on the Skin Chooser page. Windows Media Player opens a browser window of the appropriate page of the WindowsMedia.com website, which maintains a gallery of skins, some created by Microsoft and others by users. (You'll also find skins in online software archives such as CNET's Download.com, but WindowsMedia.com is a good place to start.)

When you download a skin package, XP displays the Windows Media Download dialog box. From this, you can click the View Now button to display the skin or the Close button to dismiss the dialog box.

NOTE   Windows Media Player skins can have the file type Windows Media Player Skin File and the WMS extension, but you'll usually find them compressed into files of the Windows Media Player Skin Package file type. These have the WMZ extension.

To delete a skin from Windows Media Player, select it in the list box and click the Delete button, then click the Yes button in the Confirm Skin Delete dialog box that Windows Media Player displays.

You can create your own custom skins for Windows Media Player. To do so, download the Windows Media Player Software Development Kit from the Microsoft website and follow the tutorials on the Microsoft Developer Network (MSDN; `msdn.microsoft.com/workshop/imedia/windowsmedia/wmpskins.asp`). When you've created a skin, store it in the `\Program Files\Windows Media Player\Skins\` folder, and Windows Media Player will automatically list it on the Skin Chooser page.

Choosing Visualizations

When it's playing audio, Windows Media Player shows visualizations (graphical displays) on the Now Playing page. To toggle a visualization to full screen, press Alt+Enter or choose View ➤ Full Screen. Press the Esc key (or Alt+Enter again) to toggle off full screen. To change the visualization, choose View ➤ Visualizations and make a choice from one of the submenus.

Editing MP3 and WMA Tags

WMA files and MP3 files include a *tag*, a virtual container with slots for several pieces of information, such as the artist's name, the track name, the album name, the genre, and so on. By using these tags, you can not only keep your music clearly identified, but you can also sort the tracks by any of the pieces of information. For example, you could sort tracks by artist or by album.

To edit the tag on an MP3 file or a WMA file, take the following steps:

1. In an Explorer window, right-click the file and choose Properties from the context menu. XP displays the Properties dialog box for the file.

2. Click the Summary tab. XP displays the Summary page. Figure 26.11 shows an example. If the Summary page is displaying an Advanced button, click it to display the Summary page in Advanced view. XP replaces the Advanced button with a Simple button that you can click to return to Simple view.

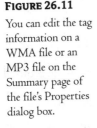

FIGURE 26.11

You can edit the tag information on a WMA file or an MP3 file on the Summary page of the file's Properties dialog box.

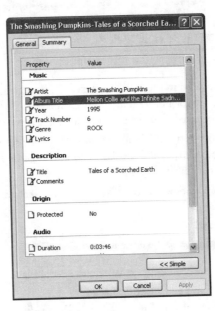

3. Edit the tag information as appropriate. You can change any field that has a pen on its icon. You can't change fields such as Duration, Bitrate, and License.

4. Click the OK button. XP applies the changes to the track's tag and closes the Properties dialog box for the file.

Backing Up and Restoring Licenses

If you download tracks secured with digital licenses, or if you use digital licenses on tracks you copy to disk, back up your licenses in case you have disk trouble. Should you lose the licenses, you won't be able to play the tracks.

Backing Up Your Licenses

To back up your licenses, follow these steps:

1. Choose Tools ➤ License Management. Windows Media Player displays the License Management dialog box (shown in Figure 26.12).

FIGURE 26.12

Back up your digital licenses so that you can restore them if you have computer trouble.

2. Check the folder indicated in the Location text box. If necessary, click the Browse button and use the resulting Browse for Folder dialog box to specify a different folder. For safety, keep the backup on a removable medium, or make a copy of it on an online drive.
3. Click the Backup Now button. Windows Media Player closes the first License Management dialog box, copies the licenses, and displays a second License Management dialog box when the licenses have been safely backed up.
4. Click the OK button. Windows Media Player closes the second License Management dialog box.

Restoring Your Licenses

To restore your licenses from backup, take the following steps:

1. Choose Tools ➤ License Management. Windows Media Player displays the License Management dialog box shown in Figure 26.12 (above).
2. Click the Restore Now button. Windows Media Player displays a License Management dialog box warning you that the restoration needs Internet access and that Windows Media Player will send your GUID to a Microsoft service.

3. Click the OK button. Windows Media Player contacts the Microsoft site for authorization. If it receives authorization, Windows Media Player copies the licenses and displays another License Management dialog box to let you know the operation has succeeded.

4. Click the OK button. Windows Media Player closes the License Management dialog box.

Playing Videos

Playing a video file could hardly be easier:

◆ To play a video file listed in your Media Library, double-click it.

◆ To play a video file that's not listed in your Media Library, choose File ➤ Open and use the resulting Open dialog box to select the video to open.

◆ To play a streaming video from a website, click its link.

◆ To change the brightness, contrast, hue, saturation, and size of the image, choose View ➤ Now Playing Tools ➤ Video Settings and work with the resulting Video Settings tools.

TROUBLESHOOTING: WINDOWS MEDIA PLAYER PLAYS ONLY PART OF A DOWNLOADED VIDEO CLIP

If you watch a video file while it's downloading, so that the video stops playing before the download is complete, you may find you can't watch the whole of the video file even when the download is complete. This happens because Windows Media Player's cache file has stored information on the section of the file that you watched and thinks this section represents the whole of the file.

To get around this problem, you need to clear the Windows Media Player cache. To do so, open an Explorer window to the folder \%`allusersprofile`%\Application Data\Microsoft\Media Index\ and delete the file named `wmplibrary_v_0_12.db`. Windows Media Player creates a new cache file the next time you start it.

Deleting this cache file also prevents other users from trawling through the cache to find out what videos or DVDs you've been watching and what audio you've been listening to. This data isn't easy to decipher, but you may prefer not to have these incriminating details hanging around.

Setting Output Volume and Recording Volume

As you saw earlier in the chapter, you can adjust the output volume by moving the Volume slider in Windows Media Player. If you prefer, you can put a Volume control in the notification area (the System Tray) so that it's always at your mouse-tips even when Windows Media Player or your other favorite noise-maker is minimized or hidden behind other windows.

This section starts by showing you how to do that. It then covers the Volume Control program that XP provides for controlling output volume and recording volume, adjusting the sound balance, choosing input and output, and so on.

Displaying the Volume Control in the Notification Area

For immediate access to a Volume control, you can put one in the notification area. Take the following steps:

1. Choose Start ➤ Control Panel. XP displays Control Panel.

2. Click the Sounds, Speech, and Audio Devices link. Control Panel displays the Sounds, Speech, and Audio Devices screen.

3. In the Pick a Task list, click the Adjust the System Volume link. Control Panel displays the Volume page of the Sounds and Audio Devices Properties dialog box (shown in Figure 26.13).

FIGURE 26.13

To make XP display the Volume control in the System Tray, select the Place Volume Icon in the Taskbar check box on the Volume page of the Sounds and Audio Devices Properties dialog box.

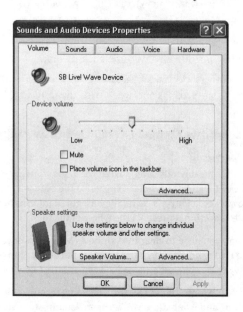

4. Select the Place Volume Icon in the Taskbar check box.

5. Click the OK button. XP closes the Sounds and Audio Devices Properties dialog box and displays the Volume control in the notification area.

TIP *By default, XP applies its default notification-area behavior to the Volume control: Hide When Inactive. You'll probably want to change the Volume control's behavior to Always Show so that it's always available.*

To set the volume, click the Volume control. XP displays a pop-up panel bearing a Volume slider and a Mute check box (shown in Figure 26.14). Drag the slider up and down to set the volume. XP emits a Ding chord when you release the slider so that you can hear the approximate loudness of that volume. Click anywhere other than the pop-up panel to make the panel disappear.

When you mute the sound by selecting the Mute check box on the pop-up panel, XP displays a red circle and bar beside the Volume control as a visual reminder.

FIGURE 26.14

Setting volume with
the notification-area
Volume control

You can double-click the Volume control, or right-click it and choose Open Volume Control from the context menu, to display the Play Control window. And you can right-click the Volume control and choose Adjust Audio Properties from the context menu to display the Volume page of the Sounds and Audio Devices Properties dialog box.

Setting Volume from the Sounds and Audio Devices Properties Dialog Box

If you seldom need to change the volume being output by your computer (for example, if you have a physical volume control strapped to your keyboard or elsewhere within reach), you probably won't want to waste notification-area space on the Volume control. Instead, you can use the Device Volume slider on the Volume page of the Sounds and Audio Devices Properties dialog box to set the volume and the Mute check box to mute the sound.

Setting Speaker Balance

To set speaker balance on the signal output by your sound card (as opposed to setting it via your amplifier), click the Speaker Volume button in the Speaker Settings group box on the Volume page of the Sounds and Audio Devices Properties dialog box. XP displays the Speaker Volume dialog box (shown in Figure 26.15). Drag the sliders to suitable positions; select the Move All Slide Indicators at the Same Time check box if you want synchronized sliding. Then click the OK button. XP closes the Speaker Volume dialog box.

FIGURE 26.15

To set speaker bal-
ance on your sound
card's output, use
the Speaker Volume
dialog box.

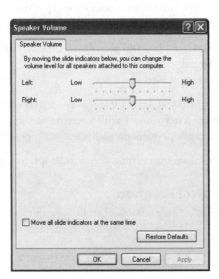

Setting Advanced Audio Properties

Beyond the speaker balance settings, XP also offers advanced audio settings. You can specify your speaker layout, the degree of hardware acceleration to use on audio playback, and the sample rate conversion quality to use.

To choose advanced audio settings, click the Advanced button in the Speaker Settings group box on the Volume page of the Sounds and Audio Devices Properties dialog box. XP displays the Advanced Audio Properties dialog box.

The Speakers page of the Advanced Audio Properties dialog box (shown on the left in Figure 26.16) contains only one setting: the Speaker Setup drop-down list. Choose the appropriate option for your speakers or headphones. Your choices range from Desktop Stereo Speakers through to 7.1 Surround Sound Speakers (seven satellites and a subwoofer).

FIGURE 26.16

Specify your speaker setup on the Speakers page (left) of the Advanced Audio Properties dialog box, and choose audio performance settings on the Performance page (right).

The Performance page of the Advanced Audio Properties dialog box (shown on the right in Figure 26.16) contains two settings:

Hardware Acceleration slider Drag this slider to set the amount of hardware acceleration you want to use. On most computers, it's best to start with full acceleration and decrease it only if your computer exhibits audio problems.

Sample Rate Conversion Quality slider Drag this slider to choose a balance between audio quality and CPU usage. XP usually starts you off with a setting of Good. Try improving this, and reduce it again only if your computer's performance suffers.

Click the OK button. XP closes the Advanced Audio Properties dialog box.

Using the Volume Control Program

XP's Volume Control program provides close control over audio output and input.

Volume Control can initially be confusing for several reasons:

◆ First, the window in which it appears isn't even called Volume Control. (See the next objection.)

◆ Second, Volume Control has separate manifestations for output and input. Depending on the sound card installed on your computer, you'll see different names for each. For example, with most Sound Blaster cards, the output manifestation of Volume Control appears as a window named Play Control, and the input manifestation appears as a window named Record Control. With other sound cards, you'll see other names, such as Master Out and Recording Control.

◆ Third, Volume Control hides advanced options until you force it to display them.

◆ Fourth, the set of controls that Volume Control displays changes depending on the capabilities of your sound card.

◆ Fifth, you can choose which of the available controls are displayed.

USING PLAY CONTROL

To use Play Control (or whatever your sound card calls it), display its window by taking one of the following actions:

◆ Choose Start ➤ All Programs ➤ Accessories ➤ Entertainment ➤ Volume Control.

◆ If XP is displaying the Volume control in the notification area, double-click it.

◆ Click the Advanced button in the Device Volume group box on the Volume page of the Sounds and Audio Devices Properties dialog box.

Figure 26.17 shows a typical Play Control window.

FIGURE 26.17

Play Control lets you control the output source and volume for the sound card.

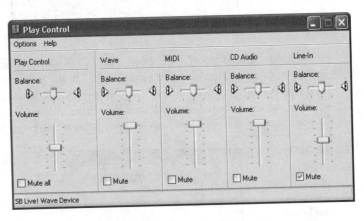

The controls in the Play Control window are intuitive enough to use:

◆ The leftmost set of controls (which appears in Figure 26.17 as Play Control, but which with other sound cards appears with other names such as Master Out) is the master control. Move the Volume slider to control the master volume (doing so manipulates the Volume control in the notification area directly); move the Balance control to change the master left-right balance; and select the Mute All check box to silence all output from the sound card.

◆ Set the volume, balance, and muting for the other controls as appropriate. Which controls appear depends on your sound card, but typically you'll see entries such as Wave, MIDI, Digital, CD Audio, Line In, and Auxiliary.

◆ Select the Mute check box to mute any given output. Select the Mute All check box to mute all the outputs.

◆ To display any advanced options your sound card supports, choose Options ➤ Advanced Controls. The window displays an Advanced button beneath the master Volume controls. Click this button, and XP displays the Advanced Controls dialog box, which offers bass and treble controls together with any other controls your sound card offers. Figure 26.18 shows an example of the Advanced Controls dialog box.

FIGURE 26.18

Use the Advanced Controls dialog box to set any advanced options your sound card offers.

◆ To change the set of controls displayed, choose Options ➤ Properties. Volume Control displays the Properties dialog box (shown in Figure 26.19). In the Show the Following Volume Controls list box, select the check boxes for the controls you want in the window and clear the check boxes for those you don't want. Then click the OK button. Volume Control closes the Properties dialog box and adjusts the window to show the controls whose check boxes you selected.

FIGURE 26.19

In the Properties dialog box, choose the controls you want the Volume Control window to display.

TIP   *If your computer has multiple sound cards, you can switch between them by using the Mixer Device drop-down list in the Properties dialog box for Volume Control.*

USING RECORD CONTROL

To display the Record Control window (or whatever your sound card calls it), take the following steps:

1. Display Play Control as described in the previous section.
2. Choose Options ➤ Properties. Volume Control displays the Properties dialog box.
3. Select the Recording option button and click the OK button. Volume Control closes the Properties dialog box and displays the Record Control window (shown in Figure 26.20).

FIGURE 26.20

The Record Control window lets you control the input devices, volume, and balance.

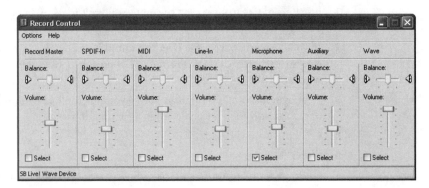

As with Play Control, Record Control has a Balance slider and a Volume slider for each input device. Where Play Control has a Mute check box for each device, Record Control has a Select check box. Select the Select check box for the input device you want to use, and choose appropriate volume and balance settings. (With most sound cards, the Select check boxes actually work like a set of option buttons—selecting one Select check box automatically deselects all the other Select check boxes.)

Recording Audio Files with Sound Recorder

If you need to create some simple WAV files, use Sound Recorder, which comes with XP. Sound Recorder is a simple program with some severe limitations. The worst limitation is that its maximum file length is a mere 60 seconds, so while it's fine for recording sound effects, short memos, and so on, it's no good for, say, recording a song of even modest length.

You can also use Sound Recorder for converting WAV files to some other formats, including MP3. But Sound Recorder is limited in this, too, offering bitrates of only 56Kbps and lower for MP3 files.

Starting Sound Recorder

To start Sound Recorder, choose Start ➤ All Programs ➤ Accessories ➤ Entertainment ➤ Sound Recorder. Figure 26.21 shows Sound Recorder.

FIGURE 26.21

Sound Recorder is useful for recording WAV files.

Recording a Sound File with Sound Recorder

To record a sound file with Sound Recorder, take the following steps:

1. Use Record Control to select the input you want to use. Choose appropriate volume and balance settings.

2. If you currently have a file open in Sound Recorder, choose File ➤ New. Sound Recorder closes the current file, prompting you to save it if it contains unsaved changes, and opens a new file.

3. Get the input ready. For example, bring your microphone within kissing distance of your mouth or throat, or feed in a signal through the Line In jack.

4. Click the Record button.

5. Start the input.

6. Click the Stop button to stop recording. (Sound Recorder automatically stops recording after 60 seconds.)

7. Save the file by choosing File ➤ Save and specifying the name and path in the Save As dialog box.

Once you've recorded a sound, you can take assorted self-explanatory actions with it:

◆ Click the Play button to play back the file.

◆ Drag the slider to move to a specific position in the file.

◆ To add to the end of a sound file you've created, or to record over part of it and add to the end of it, position the slider at the end or at the position at which you want to start recording over its current contents. Then click the Record button.

◆ To truncate the file, place the slider in the appropriate position and choose Edit ➤ Delete before Current Position or Edit ➤ Delete after Current Position as appropriate.

◆ Apply one of the effects by using the Effects menu: Increase Volume (by 25%), Decrease Volume, Increase Speed (by 100%), Decrease Speed, Add Echo, and Reverse.

TIP *Because Sound Recorder doesn't offer an Undo feature, it's a good idea to save the sound file before adding to a file or applying an effect. If you don't like the result, you can then close the file without saving changes.*

Converting a File to Another Format

To convert a WAV file to another format, follow these steps:

1. Open the WAV file.

2. Choose File ➤ Save As. Sound Recorder displays the Save As dialog box.

3. Click the Change button at the bottom of the Save As dialog box. Sound Recorder displays the Sound Selection dialog box (shown in Figure 26.22).

FIGURE 26.22

Use the Sound Selection dialog box to specify the format of the sound file when converting a WAV file to another format.

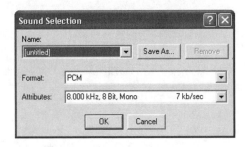

4. Choose the format in the Format drop-down list.

5. Choose any applicable attributes (for example, the bitrate) in the Attributes drop-down list.

6. Click the OK button. Sound Recorder closes the Sound Selection dialog box and returns you to the Save As dialog box.

7. Specify the filename as usual in the Save As dialog box.

8. Click the Save button. Sound Recorder closes the Save As dialog box, converts the file to the specified format, and saves it under the name you chose.

Up Next

This chapter has concentrated on audio, discussing how to make the most of Windows Media Player for listening to CDs, copying CDs to your hard disk, and tuning into Internet radio. You've also seen the assorted ways of controlling the volume that XP outputs, and how to record sounds with the distressingly limited tool that XP provides for the purpose.

It's time to get graphical. The next chapter discusses how to work with pictures and videos.

Chapter 27

Working with Pictures and Videos

XP PROVIDES STRONG FEATURES for working with pictures and videos—everything from easily viewing and rotating a picture to making a video of your own. The chapter starts by discussing the tools that XP provides for manipulating pictures via Explorer. It then discusses how to install scanners and digital cameras, how to scan documents, and how to retrieve images from a digital camera. After that, it covers how to capture still pictures from a video camera and how to copy your pictures to the Web.

XP uses a bundle of features called Windows Image Acquisition (abbreviated to WIA) to communicate with imaging devices ranging from digital cameras and web cams to scanners and digital camcorders. WIA attempts to cover more ground than earlier imaging connectivity technologies such as TWAIN (as in "never the twain shall meet," but popularly supposed to be an acronym for Technology Without An Interesting Name) and ISIS (Image and Scanner Interface Specification). In most cases, you'll do best to use WIA if it supports your hardware, because WIA is more powerful and flexible than TWAIN. For example, XP activates WIA as soon as you attach and turn on a supported imaging device, whereas TWAIN requires you to start image transfers manually. Second, TWAIN supports only scanning and still images, but WIA supports video as well. But if WIA doesn't support your hardware, fall back to TWAIN or ISIS.

This chapter covers the following topics:

◆ Using the Photo Album template image-manipulation features

◆ Installing a scanner or digital camera

◆ Scanning an image

◆ Working with a digital camera

◆ Capturing still pictures from a video camera

◆ Copying your pictures to the Web

Using the Photo Album Template Tools

The most convenient place to work with pictures just so happens to be the \My Pictures\ folder—the folder in which XP would like you to save all pictures you're not sharing. The next most convenient place is the \Shared Pictures\ folder, which shares the features of the \My Pictures\ folder but is a little slower to access. This folder is where XP would like you to save all the pictures you're sharing with other users. However, you can store your pictures in any folder you choose and still use the image-manipulation features that XP provides.

When XP detects that all the files in a folder you're opening for the first time are graphics, it applies to it the Photo Album template. This template displays the Picture Tasks list and makes Filmstrip view available. Figure 27.1 shows a folder of pictures in Filmstrip view with the Picture Tasks list displayed.

FIGURE 27.1

The Photo Album template provides the Picture Tasks list and Filmstrip view for manipulating graphics.

The Picture Tasks list provides the following links:

Get Pictures from Camera or Scanner link   Clicking this link starts the Scanner and Camera Wizard, discussed in the section after next. This link appears only if XP detects a scanner or camera attached to your computer.

View As a Slide Show link   Clicking this link makes XP display a full-screen slideshow of the pictures in the folder. To have a slideshow of just some pictures, select them first. To control the slideshow, use the buttons on the toolbar that XP displays when you move the mouse, or use the following keys:

Key	Effect
Spacebar	Pause the slide show or restart it.
→, ↓, or Enter	Next picture.
← or ↑	Previous picture.
Ctrl+L	Rotate picture 90 degrees counterclockwise.
Ctrl+K	Rotate picture 90 degrees clockwise.
Tab	Toggle display of the toolbar.
Esc	End slide show.

Order Prints Online link   Clicking this link makes XP start the Internet Print Ordering Wizard, which walks you through the steps of ordering prints (or T-shirts, sweatshirts, ceramic mugs, and so on) from your choice of a number of online photo services. These services can be convenient, but you may find that your local photo-processing joint or drugstore offers a similar service in a shorter time.

Print This Picture link   Clicking this link makes XP start the Photo Printing Wizard. See the section "Printing Pictures with the Photo Printing Wizard" later in this chapter for more information.

Set As Desktop Background link   Clicking this link makes XP apply the picture as your Desktop background. XP stretches the picture to fit your Desktop. This produces strange effects with portrait-orientation pictures. If that's a problem for you, crop the picture first.

The Filmstrip toolbar contains four buttons for manipulating pictures. Figure 27.2 shows the Filmstrip toolbar with labels. The buttons are self-explanatory to use.

FIGURE 27.2

You can use the buttons on the Filmstrip toolbar to manipulate pictures.

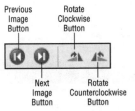

You can also move from picture to picture by pressing the ← key and the → key. You can issue the rotation commands from the context menu from the picture or from the File menu.

The rotation commands issued from Filmstrip view affect only the picture displayed. To rotate multiple pictures in a single operation, switch to Thumbnails view, select the pictures, right-click in the selection, and issue the appropriate rotation command from the context menu.

TIP If when you create a new folder within an existing folder that has the Photo Album template applied to it, and you paste pictures into the new folder, XP doesn't automatically apply the Photo template to that folder, you can force XP to automatically apply the Photo Album template to the folder by clicking the Up button to move to the next folder up, then double-clicking the folder to open it again.

EXPERT KNOWLEDGE: THREE POWERTOYS FOR WORKING WITH IMAGES

If you work with pictures, you may want to use the following three PowerToys. You can download them from the Microsoft Windows XP Downloads site (www.microsoft.com/windowsxp/home/downloads/powertoys.asp).

◆ The Image Resize PowerToy adds to the context menu for a graphics file a Resize Pictures item that you can click to display the Resize Pictures dialog box, which lets you resize the selected picture or pictures to assorted widely used resolutions or to a custom resolution.

◆ The CD Slide Show Generator PowerToy lets you view a slide show of images stored on a CD.

◆ The HTML Slide Show Wizard PowerToy walks you through creating a slide show of your images that you can then post on the Web so that other people can view them. The slide show is silent, but the process is easy. Once you've installed this PowerToy, launch it by choosing Start ➤ All Programs ➤ PowerToys for Windows XP ➤ Slide Show Wizard.

Installing a Scanner or Digital Camera

To install a scanner or digital camera, connect it to your computer. If XP notices the scanner or camera, it displays a notification-area pop-up such as that shown in Figure 27.3 and attempts to locate the software for the device. If XP doesn't have drivers for the scanner, install them manually from the manufacturer's installation media or website.

FIGURE 27.3

If you're in luck, XP automatically detects your scanner or camera when you plug it in.

NOTE You may prefer to use the manufacturer's latest drivers rather than those included with XP, as they may include extra features. To change the driver, follow the procedure described in the section "Working with Hardware Drivers" in Chapter 14.

If XP doesn't automatically detect your scanner or camera, use the Scanner and Camera Installation Wizard to identify it. Start the wizard by taking the following steps:

1. Choose Start ➤ Control Panel. XP displays Control Panel.

2. Click the Printers and Other Hardware link. XP displays the Printers and Other Hardware page.

3. Click the Scanners and Cameras Link. XP displays the Scanners and Cameras page.

4. Double-click the Add an Imaging Device icon. XP starts the Scanner and Camera Installation Wizard, which displays the Welcome to the Scanner and Camera Installation Wizard page.

To install your scanner or camera, follow the wizard. This example shows the pages involved in installing a camera:

1. Click the Next button. The Scanner and Camera Installation Wizard displays the Which Scanner or Camera Do You Want to Install? page (shown in Figure 27.4), which should look familiar from Chapter 14.

FIGURE 27.4

On the Which Scanner or Camera Do You Want to Install? page of the Scanner and Camera Installation Wizard, select the driver or provide one of your own.

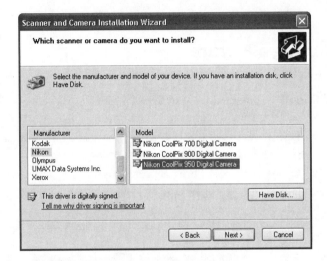

2. Use the Manufacturer list and the Model list to specify your camera, or use the Have Disk button and its resulting dialog boxes to give XP a new driver.

3. Click the Next button. The Scanner and Camera Installation Wizard displays the Connect Your Device to Your Computer page.

4. Connect the device, and choose the appropriate port in the Available Ports list. Alternatively, leave the Automatic Port Detection item selected.

TIP   If you have a choice, connect your digital camera to a USB port or a FireWire port rather than a serial port. The USB port or FireWire port will transfer pictures many times faster than the serial port.

5. Click the Next button. The Scanner and Camera Installation Wizard displays the What Is the Name of Your Device? page, which lets you adjust XP's name for the device or enter a new name. This is the name under which the device appears in Explorer, so make sure it's descriptive and clear.

6. Click the Next button. The Scanner and Camera Installation Wizard displays the Completing the Scanner and Camera Installation Wizard page.

7. Click the Finish button. The wizard copies the files, adds the device to the Scanners and Cameras page of Control Panel and to the Scanners and Cameras list in Explorer, and closes itself.

Once you've installed a scanner or a camera, it appears as an entry in the Scanners and Cameras list in My Computer. Double-clicking a scanner or a camera launches the Scanner and Camera Wizard.

TIP   To change the program associated with the scanner or camera, right-click its icon in the My Computer window and choose Properties from the context menu. XP displays the Properties dialog box for the device. On the Events page, use the Select an Event drop-down list to specify the event you want to affect (for example, Scan Button for a scanner), and then select the program in the Start This Program drop-down list. Alternatively, choose one of the other actions available for the event.

Scanning a Picture

To scan a picture, load it in your scanner and take the following steps:

1. Start the Scanner and Camera Wizard in either of the following ways. The Scanner and Camera Wizard starts and displays its Welcome page.

    ◆   Display your \My Pictures\ folder (for example, by choosing Start ➢ My Pictures) and click the Get Pictures from Camera or Scanner link in the Picture Tasks list.

    ◆   Choose Start ➢ All Programs ➢ Accessories ➢ Scanner and Camera Wizard.

    If you have two or more scanners or cameras, the wizard displays the Select Device dialog box (shown in Figure 27.5). Select the scanner you want to use and click the OK button. The Scanner and Camera Wizard displays its Welcome page.

FIGURE 27.5

In the Select Device dialog box, choose the scanner you want to use.

2. Click the Next button. The Scanner and Camera Wizard displays the Choose Scanning Preferences page (shown on the left in Figure 27.6 after clicking the Preview button).

FIGURE 27.6

Select your preferences for scanning on the Choose Scanning Preferences page (left) of the Scanner and Camera Wizard. Use the Properties dialog box (right) to set custom scanning options.

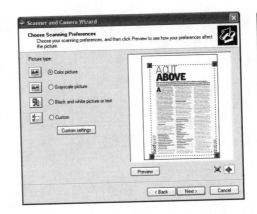
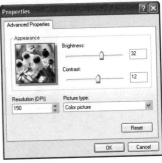

3. In the Picture Type list, select the Color Picture option button, the Grayscale Picture option button, the Black and White Picture or Text option button, or the Custom option button as appropriate. Click the Preview button to scan the image with that picture type and display it in the preview box. (Scanning the image takes a few seconds, so be patient.)

- If you select the Custom option button, click the Custom Settings button. The wizard displays the Properties dialog box. The properties in this dialog box vary depending on your scanner and its features. The right screen in Figure 27.6 above shows an example.

- In the Appearance group box, drag the Brightness and Contrast sliders until the sample image looks good to you.

- In the Resolution (DPI) text box, specify the resolution you want to use. The wizard offers values supported by your scanner.

- In the Picture Type drop-down list, choose the Color Picture item, the Grayscale Picture item, or the Black and White Picture or Text item as appropriate.

- Click the OK button. The wizard closes the Properties dialog box.

4. Adjust the size of the preview image if necessary. Drag the four sizing handles to select the area of the picture you want to scan. Click the Enlarge button (the left button above the Cancel button) to enlarge the selected area to fill the whole page. Click the Show the Entire Image button (the right button) to display the full picture and the sizing handles again.

5. Click the Next button. The Scanner and Camera Wizard displays the Picture Name and Destination page (shown in Figure 27.7).

6. In the Type a Name for This Group of Pictures drop-down list, enter the base name that you want to use for all the images you scan. XP adds automatically incremented numbers to this name to form a unique name for each image. The default base name is *Picture*.

7. In the Select a File Format drop-down list, select the file format to use for the images. Your choices are BMP, JPG, TIF, or PNG:

- BMP (bitmap image) uses no compression, so it produces large files. But this format can be read by a wide variety of old software, so it may be useful for backward compatibility. Because a bitmap retains the full amount of information about the image, it's a good format for archiving images to recordable CDs so that you can work with them later.

FIGURE 27.7

On the Picture
Name and Destina-
tion page of the
Scanner and Camera
Wizard, specify the
location, format,
and naming for the
picture files.

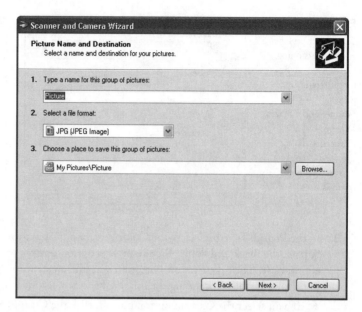

- ◆ JPG (JPEG image; Joint Pictures Experts Group) is the default format. JPG uses lossy
  compression, so you lose image quality when you use this format, but the results are good
  for general use. JPG files have a relatively small file size, which is good for saving and
  transferring the images.

- ◆ TIF (TIFF image; Tagged Image File Format) uses lossless compression, so it produces
  medium-large files. TIFFs are widely used, but not as widely as BMPs. Use this format if
  you want to use Windows Picture and Fax Viewer's image-annotation features or if you
  want to use the files on the Mac as well. (Not all TIFFs are compressed, but the ones that
  the Scanner and Camera Wizard produces are compressed.)

- ◆ PNG (PNG image; Portable Network Graphics) is a lossless compression format designed
  for handling computer-generated images on the Web. PNG is generally considered less
  suitable than JPG for scanned images or photographs.

8. In the Choose a Place to Save This Group of Pictures drop-down list, specify the folder in
which to save images. The default location is a folder named with the text in the Type a Name
for This Group of Pictures text box and created in your \My Pictures\ folder, but the drop-
down list offers other locations (such as your computer's \Shared Pictures\ folder) and naming
methods. Alternatively, click the Browse button and use the resulting Browse for Folder dialog
box to specify the folder.

9. Click the Next button. The wizard displays the Scanning Picture page and starts scanning the
picture with the settings you specified.

10. When the wizard has finished scanning the picture, it displays the Other Options page.

11. Choose any other action you want to take with the pictures:

   ◆ If you want to copy the pictures to a website immediately, select the Publish These Pictures to a Web Site option button. (See "Copying Your Pictures to the Web" later in the chapter for details of this process.)

   ◆ If you want to order prints of the pictures, select the Order Prints of These Pictures from a Photo Printing Web Site option button. When you click the Next button, the wizard walks you through the process of selecting a printing company and placing the order.

   ◆ Otherwise, leave the Nothing. I'm Finished Working with These Pictures option button selected. Click the Next button. The wizard displays the Completing the Scanner and Camera Wizard page.

12. To display the picture in an Explorer window, click the link on the page. Otherwise, click the Finish button. The Scanner and Camera Wizard closes itself.

Working with a Digital Camera

This section discusses the three main actions you're likely to want to take with a digital camera: finding out how many pictures it contains, downloading them onto your computer, and deleting the pictures from the camera. It also touches on another action you may want to take: burning the pictures directly to a writable CD.

To work with your digital camera, display its folder by taking the following steps:

1. Choose Start ➤ My Computer. XP opens an Explorer window to My Computer.

2. In the Scanners and Cameras list, double-click the item for the camera. XP opens the folder for the camera and establishes communication with it. Figure 27.8 shows an example of a camera's folder with thumbnails downloaded from the camera.

FIGURE 27.8

The folder for a digital camera includes a Camera Tasks list.

As you can see, the camera's folder includes a Camera Tasks list that contains camera-related actions.

Downloading Pictures from a Still Camera

To download pictures from a still camera, you use the Scanner and Camera Wizard. Take the following steps from the camera's folder:

1. Click the Get Pictures from Camera link. XP starts the Scanner and Camera Wizard, which displays the Welcome to the Scanner and Camera Wizard page.

2. Click the Next button. The Scanner and Camera Wizard displays the Choose Pictures to Copy page (shown in Figure 27.9). This page displays Downloading Preview placeholders until it has downloaded previews of the pictures from the camera.

3. Select the check boxes for the pictures you want to download. (By default, the Scanner and Camera Wizard selects all the check boxes.) Use the Select All button and Clear All button to toggle selection of all the pictures on and off. Use the Rotate Clockwise button and Rotate Counterclockwise button to rotate an image for better viewing. To find out the size of a picture, click the Properties button (to the right of the Rotate Counterclockwise button). The wizard displays the Properties dialog box for the picture, which contains the picture's size, name, and image format, and the time and date it was taken.

4. Click the Next button. The wizard displays the Picture Name and Destination page.

5. In the Type a Name for This Group of Pictures drop-down list, enter the base name for all the pictures you download. Again, the default base name is *Picture*.

FIGURE 27.9

On the Choose Pictures to Copy page of the Scanner and Camera Wizard, select the pictures you want to download.

6. In the Choose a Place to Save This Group of Pictures drop-down list, specify the folder in which to save pictures. The default location is a folder named with the text in the Type a Name for This Group of Pictures text box and created in your `\My Pictures\Picture\` folder.

7. Select the Delete Pictures from My Device after Copying Them check box if you want to do just that. This check box is cleared by default.

8. Click the Next button. The wizard displays the Copying Pictures page while it downloads the pictures.

9. When the wizard has finished copying the pictures, it displays the Other Options page.

10. Choose any other action you want to take with the pictures:

    ◆ If you want to copy the pictures to a website immediately, select the Publish These Pictures to a Web Site option button. (See "Copying Your Pictures to the Web" later in the chapter for details of this process.)

    ◆ If you want to order prints of the pictures, select the Order Prints of These Pictures from a Photo Printing Web Site option button. When you click the Next button, the wizard walks you through the process of selecting a printing company and placing the order.

    ◆ Otherwise, leave the Nothing. I'm Finished Working with These Pictures option button selected. Click the Next button. The wizard displays the Completing the Scanner and Camera Wizard page.

11. Click the Finish button. The Scanner and Camera Wizard closes itself.

Burning Pictures to CD from the Camera

If you want to burn pictures directly to CD, drag the folder from your digital camera to the CD-R icon and drop it there. XP copies the files to the queue for the CD, from where you can burn them to CD as usual.

Finding Out How Many Pictures Are on the Camera

To find out how many pictures the camera contains, click the Show Camera Properties link in the Camera Tasks list in the camera's folder. XP contacts the camera for information and displays the Properties dialog box for the camera, which includes a Pictures Taken readout.

Deleting Pictures from the Camera

As you saw, you can delete pictures from the camera after downloading them—but in many cases you won't want to, especially if your camera has enough storage for a good number of pictures.

To delete pictures, click the Delete All Pictures on Camera link in the Camera Tasks list. XP displays the Confirm Multiple File Delete dialog box. Click the Yes button. XP deletes the pictures from the camera.

Capturing Still Pictures from a Video Camera

To capture still pictures from a video camera, connect it to your computer and take the following steps:

1. Choose Start ➤ All Programs ➤ Accessories ➤ Paint. XP launches Paint.

2. Choose File ➢ From Scanner or Camera. If you have multiple devices, Paint displays the Select Device dialog box (shown in Figure 27.5, earlier in the chapter). If you have only one device configured, Paint doesn't need to ask you which device to use.

3. Select the device and click the OK button. Paint displays the Capture Pictures from Video dialog box (shown in Figure 27.10) with a feed running from the camera into the left pane.

FIGURE 27.10

Use the Capture Pictures from Video dialog box to capture still pictures from a video camera.

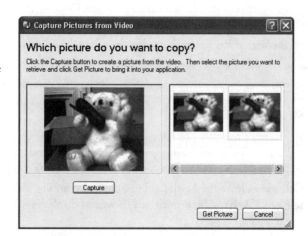

4. Click the Capture button to capture the current frame. Paint displays a thumbnail of the resulting picture in the right pane.

5. Capture further frames if you want.

6. Choose the thumbnail of the picture you want in the right pane, then click the Get Picture button. Paint closes the Capture Pictures from Video dialog box and displays the captured frame as a new picture in Paint, where you can work with it and save it as usual.

TIP   *If you have a web cam, there's a PowerToy that may interest you: TimerShot. This PowerToy lets you take pictures at intervals with your web cam and save them to a folder of your choosing. As with the other PowerToys, you can download it from the Microsoft Windows XP Downloads site (***www.microsoft.com/windowsxp/home/downloads/powertoys.asp***). To run TimerShot, choose Start ➢ All Programs ➢ PowerToys for Windows XP ➢ TimerShot.*

Printing Pictures with the Photo Printing Wizard

The Photo Printing Wizard tries to simplify the process of printing pictures by walking you through the process of selecting the pictures and choosing the appropriate paper size and layout.

To print one or more pictures with the help of the Photo Printing Wizard, warm up your color printer (for example, run a nozzle-cleaning routine if necessary) and take the following steps:

1. Click the Print Pictures link in the Picture Tasks list in the \My Pictures\ folder. XP launches the Photo Printing Wizard, which displays the Welcome to the Photo Printing Wizard page. If you prefer, you can select the pictures you want to print and then click the Print the Selected Pictures link. Alternatively, choose File ➢ Print or right-click a picture and choose Print from the context menu.

2. Click the Next button. The wizard displays the Picture Selection page.

3. Select the check box for each picture you want to print. Use the Select All button and Clear All button if appropriate.

4. Click the Next button. The wizard displays the Printing Options page.

5. In the What Printer Do You Want to Use? drop-down list, select the printer.

6. If the What Type of Paper Do You Want to Use? drop-down list is available, use it to select the paper to use. If necessary, specify further settings by clicking the Printing Preferences button and working in the resulting dialog box.

7. Click the Next button. The wizard displays the Layout Selection page (shown in Figure 27.11).

FIGURE 27.11

On the Layout Selection page of the Photo Printing Wizard, specify the layout for the paper.

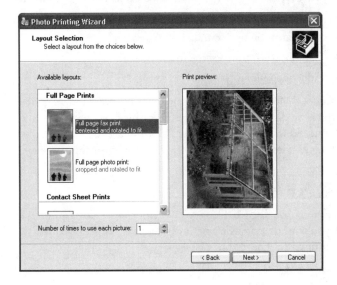

8. In the Available Layouts list box, select the layout to use. The Print Preview box displays an approximation of how it will look.

9. Click the Next button. The wizard starts sending the pictures to the printer. While it does so, it displays the Please Wait page. When it finishes, it displays the Completing the Photo Printing Wizard page.

10. Click the Finish button. The wizard closes itself.

Copying Your Pictures to the Web

If you want, you can copy pictures directly from your camera or scanner onto the Web. This is impressive technology, but in most cases it's not a good idea, because usually it's a good idea to check the quality of your pictures or scans (and perhaps manipulate them) before posting them to the Web.

But if you want to use this feature, select the Publish These Pictures to a Web Site option button on the Other Options page of the Scanner and Camera Wizard. Click the Next button. The wizard displays the Change Your File Selection page, on which you can select the pictures you want to copy to the Web. Click the Next button. The wizard displays the Where Do You Want to Publish These Files? page, which offers you choices similar to those discussed in Chapter 25 for creating a network place on MSN or on another web provider's site.

Select the provider and click the Next button. The wizard walks you through the procedure for copying the pictures to the site. (This procedure varies from site to site.)

Making Movies with Windows Movie Maker

Windows Movie Maker is a basic video-editing program that lets you do the following:

◆ Transfer home movies from a video camera to your computer and edit them there

◆ Break a movie down into clips (shorter segments) to make it more manageable

◆ Add narration or a soundtrack to a movie

◆ Capture stills from a scene in the movie

◆ Add video files to your movies

Windows Movie Maker is relatively straightforward to use, but it benefits from a graphical treatment for which we didn't have enough space in this book without omitting some of the more advanced XP topics. So we've put the Windows Movie Maker coverage on the Web. To download Web Chapter 2, "Making Movies with Windows Movie Maker," visit the Sybex website (www.sybex.com).

Up Next

This chapter has discussed how to use XP's features for capturing and manipulating still pictures.

If you want to share your pictures or videos via mail, you may want to burn them to CD. The next chapter discusses how to burn CDs.

Chapter 28

Burning CDs on XP

FROM BEING AN EXOTIC, expensive, and erratically performing technological marvel in the mid 1990s, the recordable CD has progressed to being the most convenient and most cost-effective backup and file-transfer medium for the early 2000s. Standard recordable CDs now hold up to 700MB of data and can be burned in as little as four minutes. So it should perhaps come as no surprise that XP improves on previous versions of Windows by offering CD-writing capability built into the operating system. This chapter discusses how to use those features, how to choose a CD recorder drive if you don't have one, and how to choose recordable CD media.

This chapter covers the following topics:

◆ Understanding the basics of recording CDs

◆ Choosing a CD recorder

◆ Choosing recordable CDs

◆ Configuring a recordable CD drive

◆ Burning CDs from Explorer

◆ Burning CDs from Windows Media Player

◆ Features to look for in other CD-recording packages

CD-Recording Basics

To record CDs, you need to have a CD or DVD recorder. If you have one, you're all set to record CDs. If you don't have one, see the next sidebar for advice on choosing a CD recorder.

You also need media—blank recordable CDs or rewritable CDs. The next section discusses those.

EXPERT KNOWLEDGE: CHOOSING A CD RECORDER

Because of its value for backup and file transfer, a CD recorder is almost indispensable nowadays. Most new PCs—including some high-end laptops—have built-in CD recorders. If your PC doesn't have a CD recorder and you want to get one, this sidebar explains what you need to know.

This chapter uses the term "CD recorder" to refer to any drive designed to record data to CD. Whereas older CD recorders could record only once on a CD, modern CD recorders can write either once or multiple times to the same disc, depending on the disc's format. CD-R discs are *Write Once, Read Multiple* media—*WORM* for short—while CD-RW discs are *Write And Read Multiple* or *WARM* media.

The following sections discuss the main considerations for choosing a CD recorder.

SPEED

CD recorder speed is measured by the same rating system as regular old read-only CD drives: 1X, 2X, 4X, and so on. Each X represents 150Kbps (the nominal read rate of the first CD drives), so a 4X drive chugs through 600Kbps, an 8X drive handles 1200Kbps (1.2Mbps), a 12X drive manages 1800Kbps (1.8Mbps), a 16X drive cranks out 2400Kbps (2.4Mbps), a 20X drive burns 3000Kbps (3Mbps), a 24X drive blazes through 3600Kbps (3.6Mbps), a 32X drive toasts 4800Kbps (4.8Mbps), and a 40X drive incinerates 6000Kbps (6Mbps).

CD recorder speed keeps on improving. At this writing, 40X drives are just beginning to appear. These can burn a full CD in less than 4 minutes (other constraints, such as the speed of your system, permitting). 40X drives and 32X drives are still on the expensive side. 24X drives, 20X drives, and 16X drives are more reasonably priced, and can burn a full CD in around 5 minutes. 12X drives are starting to look like old technology, taking more like 6 minutes. 8X drives take about 9 minutes, 6X drives take about 12 minutes, and 4X drives take about 18 minutes.

Those speeds are for the initial writing to the CD. On high-speed drives, the rewriting speeds are typically considerably slower than the writing speeds. For example, a drive might write at 24X but rewrite at 12X, and a 12X drive might rewrite at only 4X. By contrast, slower drives (for example, 4X) may rewrite at the same speed as they write.

CD recorder speeds are given with the write speed first, the rewrite speed second, and the read speed third. For example, a 40×12×48 drive is one that writes at 40X, rewrites at 12X, and reads at 48X.

As you can see, the higher speed ratings don't translate as directly into a speed gain as the lower speeds do. There are two reasons for this. First, the faster speeds are reached only some of the time (for technical reasons we won't get into here). Second, no matter how fast the drive is able to burn the bulk of the data to the CD, there's some overhead in creating the file system on the CD and wrapping up the writing process. So until prices on the fastest drives come down, there's little advantage in buying them over buying slightly slower drives at a much more reasonable price.

CD recorders almost invariably read data at a faster rate than they write it. Some CD recorders now read up to 48X, making them almost as fast as a dedicated CD drive. Even so, unless you're out of drive bays or connectors, look to add a CD recorder to your computer rather than replace your existing CD drive with a CD recorder. That way, you'll be able to duplicate a CD (assuming that you have the right to do so) or install Return to Castle Wolfenstein at the same time as listening to music.

DVD recorders can also burn all recordable CD formats. XP doesn't have built-in support for burning DVDs—you need third-party software for that.

Continued on next page

Expert Knowledge: Choosing a CD Recorder *(continued)*

Buffering and BurnProof

The faster a drive tries to write (or rewrite) a CD, the more susceptible it is to buffer underrun problems. A *buffer underrun* sounds like something a train might suffer on a bad day, but in CD-recording terms it's what happens when the computer's hard drive subsystem can't deliver data to the CD drive quickly enough for the writing to run smoothly. The data stream from the computer is likely to be irregular because the computer is tending to system tasks and user input at the same time as burning a CD, so CD recorders include a buffer to store a certain amount of data to let the recorder smooth out any inconsistencies in the data stream. The bigger the buffer, the bigger the disruptions in the data stream that the recorder can smooth out.

But if the computer is really thrashing away at other tasks, even a big buffer may not be enough to prevent a buffer underrun, which wrecks the CD being recorded. Enter BurnProof, a technology developed by Sanyo, which lets the CD-burning laser pause when a buffer underrun is about to occur and then pick up from the point it let off, all without turning the disc into a coaster.

At this writing, most CD drives don't have BurnProof. But if you're looking for a new CD recorder, and you need the performance, make sure that the drive includes BurnProof.

Internal or external?

Generally speaking, an internal drive will cost you less than an external drive, but you'll need to have a drive bay free in your computer for an internal drive, and you'll need to do a little work with cables (or have someone else do it for you). An external drive will usually cost more, will occupy space on your desk, and will need its own power supply. In addition, most external drives are much noisier than internal drives because they contain their own fans. But if your main computer is a notebook, or if you want to be able to move the drive from computer to computer without undue effort, or if you're looking for an easy connection, you'll need an external drive.

EIDE drives are all internal. SCSI drives can be internal or external. Because the parallel port, the USB ports, and any FireWire ports are external connections, almost all of these drives are external only. (You can find internal FireWire CD recorder drives if you look hard enough.)

EIDE, SCSI, Parallel Port, USB, or FireWire?

If you have a SCSI card in your computer, you'll probably want to get a SCSI CD recorder, because it will typically perform better *and* put much less burden on the processor than an EIDE CD recorder will. SCSI drives are usually more expensive than EIDE drives of the same speed, but if your computer's already got SCSI, the extra cost is probably worth it. If you need to copy CDs, bear in mind that most SCSI CD recorders will copy CDs directly only from other SCSI drives, not from EIDE drives. If you have a SCSI CD recorder and an EIDE CD drive, you'll need to copy the CD to the hard disk and then burn it to CD from there.

If you don't have SCSI and want an internal drive, or if your CD player is EIDE and you want to do a lot of CD-to-CD duplicating, choose EIDE. Before you buy, make sure that you have an EIDE connector available on your computer. If it's already chock-full of drives (most modern machines can take four EIDE devices), you won't be able to add another without sacrificing an existing one.

If you're looking at an external non-SCSI drive, your current choices are a parallel-port drive, a USB drive, or a FireWire drive. Parallel-port drives perform so slowly—2X at best—that they're barely worth using. USB drives using the USB 1.0 standard are only a bit better—they're limited to 4X speeds by the limitations of USB. USB 2.0 drives, which are just starting to arrive at this writing, go right up to the fastest speeds. FireWire drives offer full speed and great convenience, but if your computer doesn't have a FireWire card, you'll need to add one. (You can get FireWire PCI cards for $50 or so and FireWire PC Cards for a few dollars more.)

Recordable CDs and Rewritable CDs

CDs on which you can record data come in two basic types:

CD-R discs CD-R discs, usually referred to as *recordable CDs*, are CDs that you can record data to only once. Once you finish recording data, you can't change the information on the disc. Regular CD-R discs hold 650MB, the same amount as a standard audio CD. (650MB holds 74 minutes of uncompressed audio.) Extended-capacity CD-R discs hold 700MB, a small increase that's worth having if you don't have to pay extra for it. 700MB holds 80 minutes of uncompressed audio at 128Kbps.

CD-RW discs CD-RW discs, usually referred to as *rewritable CDs*, are CDs that you can record data to multiple times. You can record data to the CD in multiple recording sessions until it is full. You can then erase all the data from the CD (a process that some recording programs call formatting) and use it again. CD-RW discs specify a theoretical safe maximum number of times that you can reuse them, but if you like your data, you'd be wise not to push them that far. CD-RW discs hold 650MB. CD-RW discs are more expensive than CD-R discs.

To simplify (or perhaps complicate) the terminology, XP uses the term *writable CD* to refer to recordable and rewritable discs. This isn't a standard term, but it now seems destined to become one.

EXPERT KNOWLEDGE: CHOOSING CD-R AND CD-RW MEDIA

When buying CD-R and CD-RW discs, you need to balance economy with quality. Beware of cheapo discs, because they may give you skips and errors—or even lose your precious music or data. If you can, buy a few discs for testing before you buy a quantity that you'll regret if they're not up to snuff.

One way to save some money is to buy CD-R and CD-RW discs without jewel cases. This makes for a good discount, as the jewel cases are relatively expensive to manufacture and bulky to package (and easy to break, as you no doubt know from personal experience). The discs are typically sold on a spindle, which makes for handy storage until you use them—after which you'll have to find safe storage for them on your own. (One possibility is a CD wallet, which can be especially handy if you need to take your CDs with you when you travel. If you buy one, make sure it has soft pockets that won't scratch the CDs as you insert them, and sweep out travel grit frequently. You can also buy CD binders that can safely hold up to 256 discs. These binders fit on a bookshelf and allow you to quickly and easily find the disc you're looking for.)

For the faster drives, you may need to buy CD-R or CD-RW media designed for use in faster drives. For example, at this writing most fast drives request discs rated at their maximum speed, suggesting that regular (and less expensive) discs will have too many errors to use. Your mileage will vary depending on your discs and your drive, but it's worth testing less expensive discs to see how they perform in a fast drive. If the drive ends up burning at, say, 32X instead of 40X, you lose around 30 seconds. Unless you're holding your breath for the duration of the burn, you're unlikely to notice the difference.

Audio CDs and Data CDs

As of this writing, CDs come in enough different formats to stun your average donkey. Full-bore CD-burning software packages typically offer a full range of formats, which means you'll probably need to learn a bit about the formats in order to make the right choices for the CDs you burn. The section "If XP's CD-Writing Capabilities Aren't Enough," later in this chapter, discusses CD formats beyond those that XP supports.

In this respect, XP's limited capabilities for burning CDs are both a boon and a bane—a boon in that XP shields you from potentially difficult decisions (and from getting them wrong) and makes it easy to create the two types of CDs you're most likely to want to create, and a bane in that you can't create any of the more exciting forms of CDs even if you know all about them.

XP can create audio CDs and data CDs:

Audio CDs Audio CDs contain uncompressed audio in pulse code modulation (PCM) format. (PCM files are essentially WAV files with different header information at the beginning of the file.) They can be read by both audio CD players and CD-ROM drives. Audio CDs don't have names, though pressed audio CDs are identified by an ID number linked to the artist and the work. Technically, the audio CDs that XP burns use the Red Book format. XP can't burn CD Extra discs. (For more on Red Book and the other colors of CD books, see the section "If XP's CD-Writing Capabilities Aren't Enough," later in this chapter.)

Data CDs Data CDs can contain any file type. They can be read by CD-ROM drives but not by audio CD players. Data CDs can have names up to 16 characters long. Technically, these data CDs use the Orange Book format. XP can't burn specialized data CDs such as video CDs or CDs containing slideshows.

WARNING *Because CD-RW discs use a different technology than regular CD-ROMs, they're not as compatible with all CD-ROM drives. If you want to share a CD with someone else, a CD-R disc is a better bet than a CD-RW disc. Likewise, only the most recent audio players can play CD-RW discs, whereas most audio players can play only pressed audio CDs and audio CD-R discs. Another problem you may run into is that older versions of Windows, older versions of Mac OS, and older versions of Linux and Unix can't read the Joliet file system that Windows XP uses for recording CDs.*

Configuring a Recordable CD Drive

Before you try to burn a CD, it's a good idea to check the settings that XP has chosen for your CD recorder. You may want to tweak the configuration or change the drive used for holding temporary files when burning a CD on the Desktop.

To configure a recordable CD drive, follow these steps:

1. Choose Start ➢ My Computer. XP opens an Explorer window showing My Computer.
2. Right-click the CD drive and choose Properties from the context menu. XP displays the Properties dialog box for the drive.
3. Click the Recording tab. XP displays the Recording page (shown in Figure 28.1).
4. Choose settings that meet your needs:

   Enable CD Recording on This Drive check box Select this check box to use this drive for recording. XP lets you use only one drive at a time for recording. This check box is selected by default on the first recordable CD drive on your system and cleared by default on subsequent recordable CD drives.

FIGURE 28.1

Check the configuration of your drive on the Recording page of its Properties dialog box.

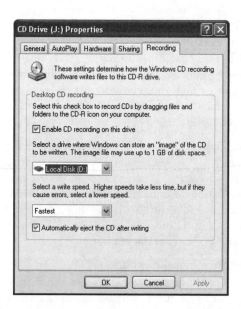

Select a Drive drop-down list   In this drop-down list, select the drive on which XP should store an *image* of the CD (temporary files containing the data to be written to the CD) when creating the CD. XP commandeers up to 1GB of space on the drive for a high-capacity CD, so make sure the disc you choose has more than that amount available. (For a standard CD, XP needs around 700MB of space.)

Select a Write Speed drop-down list   In this drop-down list, you can specify the speed that XP should use when recording a CD. The default setting is Fastest—the highest speed your drive supports. If Fastest doesn't give good results, try the next lower rate. XP automatically adjusts this speed to match the speed of the current disc, so you may not need to change it manually.

Automatically Eject the CD after Writing check box   Leave this check box selected (as it is by default) to have XP eject the CD when it has finished writing to it. When you're burning CD-R discs, this ejection can be a useful visual signal that the disc is done, but you may want to disable this option when burning CD-RW discs or when using a laptop in a tight space.

5.   Click the OK button. XP closes the Properties dialog box and applies your choices.

EXPERT KNOWLEDGE: HOW ARE RECORDABLE CDS DIFFERENT FROM REGULAR CDS?

If you've looked at CD-R or CD-RW discs, you'll know that most of them look very different from pre-recorded audio or data CDs (*pressed* CDs). Depending on their make and type, CD-R and CD-RW discs may have a gold, green, or bluish coating on their data side. Typically, this is a polycarbonate substrate over a reflective layer of 24-carat gold or a silver-colored alloy like aluminum.

Information is transferred to CD-R and CD-RW discs by a different process than for pressed CDs. While pressed CDs are pressed in a mold from a master CD, CD recorders use a laser to burn the information onto

Continued on next page

the CD-R or CD-RW media. Pressed CDs use physically raised areas called *lands* and lowered areas called *pits* to store the encoded data. Recordable CDs have a dye layer in which the laser burns marks that have the same reflective properties as the lands and pits. To be pedantic, the laser doesn't actually *burn* anything, but it heats the dye layer (which discolors or melts the dye) to produce the marks. But because the term is not only evocative but also distinguishes from the CD-recording that music artists do, it has stuck: CD recorders are widely referred to as *CD burners*, and people speak of *burning a CD*.

Not only do CD-R and CD-RW discs look different from pressed CDs, but they're also less robust. You can damage them more easily with extreme heat and moderate cold, by scratching or gouging them, or by leaving them in direct sunlight. The data is actually stored closer to the label side of the CD than to the business side, so if you're compelled to scratch one side of the CD, go for the business side over the label side.

Burning CDs from Explorer

Burning CDs from Explorer is an easy three-step process:

1. Copy the files to the storage area.
2. Check the files in the storage area to make sure that they're the right files and that there aren't too many of them.
3. Write the files to CD.

 The following sections discuss these steps. See pages 26 and 27 of the *Essential Skills* section for a visual guide to copying files to a CD.

If you can't burn CDs on your CD drive, the problem may be that XP doesn't know that the drive is a CD recorder. To check, choose Start ➢ My Computer to open a My Computer window, then right-click the icon for the CD drive and choose Properties from the context menu to display the Properties dialog box for the drive. If the Properties dialog box includes a Recording page, XP recognizes the drive as a CD recorder. If not, it doesn't. Leave the Properties dialog box for the drive open for the moment, because you'll need to use it.

If XP seems to think your CD-R drive or CD-RW drive is nothing more than a plain CD-ROM drive, and your drive is on the Hardware Compatibility List (HCL), try the three steps detailed in the next subsections. Stop when a step works.

UPDATE THE DRIVER IF POSSIBLE

First, try updating the driver. On the Hardware page of the Properties dialog box you displayed a moment ago, select the CD-RW in the All Disk Drives list box and click the Properties button to display the Properties dialog box for the device. Click the Driver tab to display the Driver page, then click the Update Driver button and let the Hardware Update Wizard walk you through the process of updating the driver. If no new driver is available, the wizard will tell you so.

Continued on next page

REMOVE AND REINSTALL THE CD RECORDER

If updating the driver didn't help, or the Hardware Update Wizard found no updated driver available, try removing the CD recorder from your system and then reinstalling it. To do so, take the following steps:

1. Press the Windows key+Break (or click the Start button, right-click the My Computer item, and choose Properties from the context menu). XP displays the System Properties dialog box.

2. Click the Hardware tab. XP displays the Hardware page.

3. Click the Device Manager button. XP launches Device Manager.

4. Expand the DVD/CD-ROM Drives category so that you can see the listings for the DVD and CD drives on your system.

5. Right-click the offending drive and choose Uninstall from the context menu. Device Manager displays the Confirm Device Removal dialog box.

6. Click the OK button. Device Manager removes the CD recorder from your system.

7. Choose File ➢ Exit. Device Manager closes, returning you to the Hardware page of the System Properties dialog box.

8. Click the Add Hardware Wizard button and let it walk you through discovering and installing your CD recorder.

EDIT THE REGISTRY

If using Device Manager to remove and then reinstall your CD-R or CD-RW drive doesn't make XP recognize the device for what it is, you may be able to force XP to recognize the drive by editing the Registry. Be warned that this procedure doesn't always work: Even if XP recognizes the drive as a CD-R or CD-RW drive, it may refuse to write on it at any speed above 1X, or CD writing may not work at all. (If your drive isn't on the XP HCL, CD writing may well not work.) But if you're stuck, this procedure is worth trying.

Run Registry Editor, open the HKEY_CURRENT_USER\Software\Microsoft\Windows\Current-Version\Explorer\CD Burning\Drives key, and open the key named Volume{*GUID*}, where *GUID* is the globally unique identifier for the CD drive. (If you have multiple CD drives, you may have to guess at which GUID represents which CD.) Edit the Drive Type value entry, changing its value to 2 for a CD-RW drive and 1 for a CD-R drive. (The value will probably be 3, which denotes a common-or-garden CD drive.)

Display the Properties dialog box for the drive, and the Recording page should appear on it. See if it now works.

Copying the Files to the Storage Area

The first step in burning files (or folders) to CD is to copy them to the storage area. You can do so in several ways, of which these three are usually the easiest:

◆ Select the files in an Explorer window or in a common dialog box. Then right-click in the selection and choose Send To ➢ CD Drive from the context menu. (Alternatively, choose File ➢ Send To ➢ CD Drive.) This technique is the most convenient when you're working in Explorer or in a common dialog box.

◆ Drag the files and drop them on the CD drive in an Explorer window or on a shortcut to the CD drive. For example, you could keep a shortcut to the CD drive on your Desktop so that you could quickly drag files and folders to it. This technique is good for copying to CD files or folders that you keep on your Desktop.

◆ Open an Explorer window to the storage area, then drag files to it and drop them there. This technique is mostly useful for adding files when you're checking the contents of the storage area. When you insert a blank CD in your CD drive, XP displays a CD Drive dialog box offering to open a folder to the writable CD folder.

WARNING *Two quick warnings here. First, it can take several minutes to copy the files to the storage area. Don't click the Write These Files to CD link before the copying is complete, because the files won't all be present and correct, and problems will result with the burn. Second, and related, XP doesn't lock the storage area even when you start the CD Burning Wizard, but after you start the wizard, you can't add any more files to the storage area for inclusion on the CD. You can paste more files to the storage area, but they won't be written to the CD you're burning, and they'll be deleted when the CD-burning operation ends. Again, don't do this.*

When you take one of these actions, XP copies the files to the storage area and displays a notification-area pop-up telling you that you have files waiting to be written to the CD. If you already have an Explorer window open to the CD drive, XP doesn't display the pop-up.

Either click the pop-up or (if it has disappeared) open a My Computer window and double-click the icon for the CD drive. XP opens an Explorer window showing the storage area, which appears as a list called Files Ready to Be Written to the CD. (For a CD-RW that already contains files, the storage area also contains a list of Files Currently on the CD.) Figure 28.2 shows an example of the storage area. As you can see in the figure, XP displays a downward-pointing arrow on the icon for each file or folder to indicate that it's a temporary file destined to be burned to CD and then disposed of.

FIGURE 28.2

The storage area holds the copies of files to be burned to the CD. The downward-pointing arrow on each file icon and folder icon indicates that the item is temporary and will be deleted after being burned to CD.

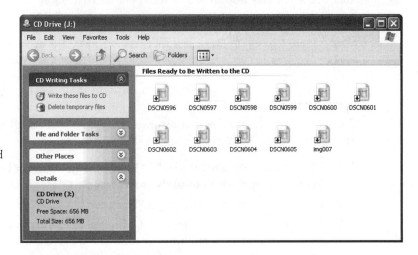

While XP copies the files, the CD drive will appear to be busy, but it won't actually be writing any information to CD yet.

> **NOTE** *If you have Roxio's DirectCD packet-writing software installed on your computer (which will be the case if you've installed Roxio's Easy CD Creator package or bought a computer that has an OEM version of Easy CD Creator prein-stalled), things will be substantially different from how they're described in this section, because DirectCD lets you write files directly to the CD without placing them in the storage area first. Abandon this book and consult your DirectCD documentation if confused.*

Checking the Files in the Storage Area

Once you've copied to the storage area all the files that you want to burn to the CD, activate the window that Explorer opened to the storage area and check that the files are all there, that you don't want to remove any of them, and that there aren't too many to fit on the CD. (If you closed the window showing the storage area, you can display the storage area again by opening an Explorer window to My Computer and double-clicking the icon for the CD drive.)

> **NOTE** *By default, the storage area is located in the* \Local Settings\Application Data\Microsoft\CD Burning\ *folder under the folder for your account in the* \Documents and Settings\ *folder. The easiest way to move this folder to a location of your choosing is to use the tool on the My Computer\Special Folders page of the Tweak UI PowerToy, but you can also move it manually if you want. To do so, you'll need to display hidden files and folders (by selecting the Show Hidden Files and Folders option button on the View page of the Folder Options dialog box from Explorer) in order to access the* \CD Burning\ *folder.*

To check the size of files in the storage area, select them all (for example, by choosing Edit ➤ Select All), then right-click and choose Properties from the context menu. XP displays the Properties dialog box for the files. Check the Size readout on the General page.

XP doesn't let you view the contents of a compressed folder (a Zip file or a CAB file) that's in the storage area. The only workaround is to examine the contents of the compressed folder before copying it to the storage area.

> **NOTE** *If you copied the files from a drive that uses NTFS, the copies in the storage area retain their attributes. If you copied the files from a FAT or FAT32 drive, XP doesn't preserve the attributes of the original files on the copies.*

Writing the Files to CD

Once you've looked at the files in the storage area and are satisfied all is well, start the process of writing the files to CD. Take the following steps:

1. Click the Write These Files to CD link in the CD Writing Tasks list. XP starts the CD Writing Wizard, which displays its first page.

2. Enter the name for the CD in the CD Name text box. CD names can be up to 16 characters long.

3. If you want the wizard to close itself when the CD is finished, select the Close the Wizard after the Files Have Been Written check box. If you select this check box, you won't have the option of creating another CD containing the same files, because the wizard automatically clears the storage area.

4. Click the Next button. The CD Writing Wizard displays a *Please wait* message as it burns the CD. The burning goes through three stages: Adding Data to the CD Image, Writing the Data Files to the CD, and Performing Final Steps to Make the CD Ready to Use.

5. When the wizard has finished burning the CD, it displays the Completing the CD Writing Wizard page and ejects the CD.

6. If you want to create another CD containing the same files, select the Yes, Write These Files to Another CD check box.

7. Click the Finish button. The wizard closes itself and deletes the files from the storage area unless you selected the Yes, Write These Files to Another CD check box.

TROUBLESHOOTING: AVOIDING AVOIDABLE PROBLEMS WHILE BURNING

Even with today's overmuscled computers powered by multigigahertz processors and loaded with enough RAM to stun a charging hippopotamus, burning a CD can be a demanding task that requires a fair amount of the computer's concentration. You can help your computer by not disturbing its concentration while it's burning. And you can copper your bet by using a BurnProof drive.

Most of the things you shouldn't do are almost too obvious to mention, but not quite. These are the usual suspects:

◆ Don't run processor-intensive programs or operations. That means no terrain-mapping and no video-rendering, of course, not to mention the more demanding games. But you should also watch for other programs that tend to hog processor cycles. A perennial culprit is Visual Basic for Applications (VBA) macros in programs such as those in Microsoft Office: VBA seems to think that 100-percent processor usage is efficient, which is like the person in front of you clearing the smorgasbord so that the staff can refill it more easily for you. Many macros execute quickly, but you should avoid running those that take longer while you're burning.

◆ Don't try to suspend your computer or put it into hibernation while burning a CD. Under most circumstances, this is likely only to happen if the computer is running on batteries or a UPS and the battery state or UPS state triggers suspension or hibernation. Avoid burning a CD on battery power if possible (you'll know if it's not) and be prepared to lose a CD you're burning if a power outage knocks you back to UPS power.

◆ Don't let your screen saver kick in while you're burning a CD. The screen saver might do the burn no harm, but it sure can't do it any good. Either don't use a screen saver (better by far) or configure your screen saver to start after a period of inactivity long enough to cover even a burn that's been slowed down to, say, a 2X crawl by media problems.

When Things Go Wrong Writing the CD...

If you try to write more files to a CD than will fit on it, the CD Writing Wizard displays the Cannot Complete the CD Writing Wizard page. You can remove some files from the storage area, then select the Retry Writing the Files to CD Now option button, and click the Finish button if you want to try to fix the problem while the CD is open, but in most cases you'll do best to leave the Close the

Wizard without Writing the Files option button selected and click the Finish button, then return to the storage area, fix the problem, and restart the writing process.

The CD Writing Wizard may also warn you that there was an error in the recording process, and the disc may no longer be usable. This is the other reason why people like the term *burning* for recording CDs—when things go wrong, you get burned and the disc is toast. In this case, you'll probably want to try writing the files to another CD.

When you've finished creating the CD, test it immediately by opening an Explorer window to its contents and opening some of them. Make sure all is well with the CD before archiving it or sending it on its way.

NOTE *If the CD you create won't read or play properly, it may have suffered recording errors. Try reducing the burning speed by using the Select a Write Speed drop-down list on the Recording page of the Properties dialog box for the drive.*

Clearing the Storage Area

If you end up deciding not to create the CD after all, clear the storage area by deleting the files in it. To do so, click the Delete Temporary Files link in the CD Writing Tasks list. XP displays the Confirm Delete dialog box (shown in Figure 28.3) to make sure you know the files haven't yet been written to CD. Click the Yes button. XP deletes the files and removes the Files Ready to Be Written to the CD heading from the Explorer window.

FIGURE 28.3

XP displays the Confirm Delete dialog box to make sure you want to delete all the files from the storage area.

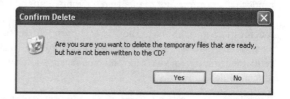

Working with Rewritable CDs

You record the first set of information to rewritable CDs (CD-RW discs) by using the same procedure as for recordable CDs (CD-R discs). But you can then add further files to them and erase all files from them. The following sections discuss how to take these actions.

NOTE *Because XP doesn't support packet writing (otherwise known as UDF, or Universal Disc Format), you can't delete individual files from a rewritable CD—you have to erase the whole thing.*

ADDING FURTHER FILES TO A REWRITABLE CD

You can add further files to a rewritable CD by following the same procedure as for initially burning files to it. As mentioned earlier in the chapter, the storage area for a rewritable CD displays a Files Currently on the CD list for a CD-RW that already contains files or folders. Figure 28.4 shows an example of the storage area for a rewritable CD with a file queued for adding to the CD.

FIGURE 28.4

The storage area for a rewritable CD displays a Files Currently on the CD list.

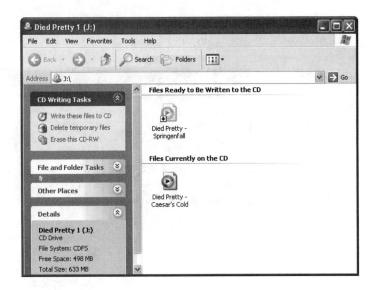

ERASING ALL FILES FROM A REWRITABLE CD

You can erase all the files off a rewritable CD so that all its space is free again. To do so, take the following steps:

1. Open an Explorer window to the CD drive.
2. Click the Erase This CD-RW link in the CD Writing Tasks list. XP starts the CD Writing Wizard, which displays another Welcome to the CD Writing Wizard page.
3. If you want the wizard to close itself after erasing the files, select the Close the Wizard when Erase Completes check box.
4. Click the Next button. The wizard displays the Erasing the CD page while it erases the files.
5. When the wizard has finished erasing the files on the CD-RW, it displays another Completing the CD Writing Wizard page.
6. Click the Finish button. The wizard closes itself.

TIP   If you're not able to erase files from a CD-RW disc that's completely full, it probably means that your CD-RW drive has outdated firmware. If the manufacturer is still around, see if you can get an update to the firmware.

Creating an Audio CD from Explorer

To create an audio CD, you use Windows Media Player, which includes features for creating PCM files from other audio file formats. But you can start the process from Explorer by copying only audio files to the storage area. When you then start the CD Writing Wizard, it displays the Welcome to the CD

Writing Wizard page as usual for you to name the CD, but after that it displays the Do You Want to Make an Audio CD? page (shown in Figure 28.5).

FIGURE 28.5

When the CD Writing Wizard notices that all the files for the CD are audio files, it displays the Do You Want to Make an Audio CD? page.

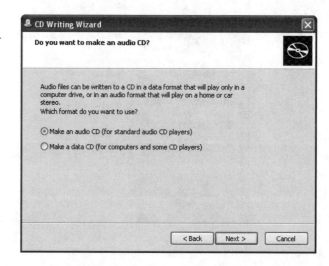

To create an audio CD, select the Make an Audio CD option button and click the Next button. The CD Writing Wizard launches or activates Windows Media Player, passes the information across to it, and then closes itself. Create the CD as described in the next section.

To create a data CD, select the Make a Data CD option button and click the Next button. The CD Writing Wizard then continues its usual course.

NOTE *If XP decides that the contents of the current folder displayed in an Explorer window are predominantly music, it displays the Music Tasks list. You can then select a file or folder and click the Copy to Audio CD link. Doing so opens Windows Media Player with the tracks loaded ready for copying to an audio CD.*

Burning CDs from Windows Media Player

Windows Media Player includes a feature for burning audio CDs directly from playlists. You can use MP3, WAV, and WMA files to create CDs up to 74 minutes long. (Windows Media Player can't create 80-minute audio CDs.)

TIP *If you want to include tracks in other formats on CDs you burn, convert them to WAV format first. Many sound programs can convert audio files. Sound Recorder (discussed in Chapter 26) can convert a wide range of formats.*

Burning a CD from Windows Media Player is even easier than burning a CD from Explorer. That's because the only choice you have to make is which tracks you want to include on the CD: You don't have to name the CD (because it's an audio CD), and you don't have to specify whether it's a data CD or an audio CD (for the same reason). You also don't have to choose whether to leave the CD open (so that you can write another session) or to close it, because Windows Media Player closes the CD automatically so that it will work properly on audio CD players. (This means that you can't create a CD, then add more tracks to it.)

The only other thing you have to worry about is this: if the tracks have digital licenses, whether the licenses allow the tracks to be copied to CD. If they don't, Windows Media Player will warn you of the problem. (If you're not clear on what you can and cannot legally do with digital-audio files, look back to Chapter 26 for a summary.)

To burn a CD from Windows Media Player, take the following steps:

1. Open the playlist you want to burn to CD, or create a new playlist containing the tracks.

2. Check the number of minutes shown: It must be 74 or fewer, otherwise the burning will grind to a halt when the disc is full. Remove tracks if necessary. (Or add more if you have space left.)

3. Choose File ➢ Copy ➢ Copy to Audio CD. Windows Media Player displays the Copy to CD or Device page and inspects the tracks to make sure that there aren't any license problems. Figure 28.6 shows the Copy to CD or Device page with a playlist queued for writing to CD.

FIGURE 28.6

Windows Media Player ready to write a playlist to CD

4. Click the Copy Music button. Windows Media Player begins the copying process, which consists of these three steps:

   Converting   Writing out the audio files to uncompressed WAV files. While Windows Media Player converts the tracks, it displays *Converting* and a percentage readout next to the track it's working on.

   Copying to CD   Copying the WAV files to the CD. Windows Media Player displays *Copying to CD* and a percentage readout next to each track in turn as it copies the track to the CD.

   Closing the disc   When all of the WAV files have been written to the CD, Windows Media Player closes the disc.

5. When Windows Media Player has closed the disc, it ejects the CD. Check the CD manually to make sure that it works (for example, put it back in the drive and try playing it), then label it.

NOTE   *You can also launch Windows Media Player and get it ready to burn CDs by selecting music files, right-clicking, and choosing Copy to Audio CD from the context menu. (Alternatively, choose File ➤ Copy to Audio CD.)*

TROUBLESHOOTING: WINDOWS MEDIA PLAYER WON'T RECORD USING YOUR CD RECORDER

If Windows Media Player seems to think your CD recorder is just a CD drive, make sure that XP knows the drive is a recorder by using the procedure described in the sidebar "Troubleshooting: XP Doesn't Recognize Your CD Recorder," earlier in this chapter.

If XP *has* recognized your CD recorder but it doesn't work with Windows Media Player, make sure that the Enable CD Recording on This Drive check box on the Recording page of the Properties dialog box for the drive is selected. Remember that only one CD recorder drive can be enabled for recording at a time, so if you have two or more recorder drives, enabling one drive disables whichever drive was previously enabled.

Copying a CD

You can make a copy of a CD by using the same techniques as for copying any other files: Copy the files to the storage area, and then write them to CD. Remember that copying CDs of copyrighted works involves copyright issues.

If you have a CD drive (or DVD drive) other than your CD-R or CD-RW drive, you can simply open an Explorer window to My Computer, then drag the icon for the CD and drop it on the icon for the CD-RW drive. XP copies the files to the storage area. Click the Write to CD link to start the CD Writing Wizard.

If XP's CD-Writing Capabilities Aren't Enough

XP offers strong but basic features for burning CDs, letting you burn data CDs easily from Explorer and audio CDs even more easily from Windows Media Player. But if you need more advanced CD-burning features (or more bells and whistles), you'll need to buy third-party CD-burning software. The following subsections discuss some bells and whistles you'll probably want to look for in CD-burning software you buy.

Packet-Writing Capability

XP's CD-R–burning capabilities force you to record a CD all at once. By contrast, packet-writing/UDF software such as Roxio's DirectCD lets you write data to a CD-R more or less as if it were a removable disk: a few files here now, a few files there later, and a huge set of files when the cows deign to come home. You can also delete files from the CD, though doing so doesn't reclaim the space they occupied. When you've finished writing to the CD-R, you close the writing session, either temporarily (so that you can write further files to the disc later) or permanently (so that the disc's contents can't be changed). If you use a CD-RW disc with DirectCD, you can erase it completely and reuse it when necessary.

Ability to Create Discs in Other Formats

Whereas XP can create data-only CDs or audio-only CDs, other programs can also create CDs in other formats such as the following:

CD Extra   CD Extra format lets you add a data track to a CD after writing audio tracks to it. CD Extra discs are typically used to create "enhanced" audio CDs that include added-value items such as video tracks, lyric sheets or tablatures, pictures, or links to the artist's website. But you can also use them to create a mostly data CD that also has a couple of audio tracks. To audio CD players, CD Extra discs appear to be regular audio CDs, with the extra content appearing only when the disc is in a computer's CD drive or another data-capable CD drive. (A standard mixed-mode disc, on the other hand, has data stored within the first tracks and can't be played in a typical audio CD player.)

CD-ROM XA (multisession)   The CD-ROM XA format lets you create *multisession* CDs—CDs that contain multiple, separate tracks of data, of which you can access only one at a time. Multisession CDs have largely been overtaken by packet-writing software, which offers most of the advantages of multisession without any of multisession's substantial cons, but they're still available for specialized use. (Technically, such a disc is a *multivolume* multisession disc. You can also create *incremental* multisession discs that present one session that you can update with data from additional sessions—but you're unlikely to need to create such discs.)

ISO 9660   The ISO 9660 format lets you create discs that can be read by just about every computer operating system around. The trade-off for ISO 9660's wide compatibility is that the number of directories you can make is limited, as is the length of filenames.

Video CD   The Video CD format lets you create video discs that play in CD drives and most DVD drives, including menus for table of contents and scene selection. Most DVD players designed for use with televisions can also read Video CDs.

Creating a Bootable CD

You may want to be able to create bootable CDs—for example, so that you can easily resuscitate a computer that's gone down for the count. Bootable discs use the strangely named El Torito format.

Testing before Writing

Many CD-writing programs let you test the capabilities of your CD recorder (and your computer's subsystem) before actually writing to disc. Testing lets you find out whether a buffer underrun could toast a coaster for you and make adjustments (for example, slowing down the recording speed) so that it doesn't happen when you burn.

The Obvious Contender: Easy CD Creator

Many software packages for recording CDs are available, but one package you might consider is Easy CD Creator from Roxio, Inc. (You might also consider Easy CD Creator Deluxe, which comes with not only bells and whistles such as those discussed above but also gongs such as features for designing CD labels.) Why consider Easy CD Creator in particular? Well, for one thing, you're using Roxio technology already—the CD-burning functionality in XP is licensed from Roxio. For another, Roxio is a company spun off in 2001 from Adaptec, Inc., a company that has long been one of the major names in CD burning. Finally, Easy CD Creator is the most complete CD recording package on the market, and it can handle all of the exotic formats mentioned above.

Up Next

This chapter has discussed how to burn CDs from Explorer and from Windows Media Player. It has also provided advice on choosing recordable CD media and CD recorders.

The next chapter discusses how to play games on XP.

Chapter 29

Playing Games on XP Home Edition

GAMES AND BACKWARD COMPATIBILITY have long frustrated users of Windows NT and Windows 2000 Professional. Many people wanted to use NT or Windows 2000 for the extra stability they delivered for general use and business programs—but they also wanted to kick some alien butt in Duke Nukem, frag each other in Quake, or tranquilly explore a puzzle or two. To their dismay, they found that (forgive the puns) id Software games were doomed to incompatibility, Mystscapes were riven by graphics problems, and playing Rebel Assault sucked big asteroids just when they were supposed to be steering a rockless road through them.

Good news: XP changes almost all that.

This chapter starts by discussing briefly the games that come with XP—a handful of single-player games (including old favorites such as Solitaire and FreeCell) and about the same number of multiplayer games for the Internet. It then goes on to discuss the hardware you'll need for "serious" games, how to install and configure game controllers, how to deal with compatibility problems, and how to get the best performance from your computer when running games.

This chapter covers the following topics:

◆ Playing XP's bundled games

◆ The hardware you need for serious gaming

◆ Adding and configuring game controllers

◆ Getting the best performance on games

Playing the Bundled Games

XP comes with more games than previous versions of Windows. This isn't saying all that much (most distributions of Linux come with more games than XP), but it does mean that you have some games to keep you entertained the next time you get stuck waiting for a connection in O'Hare—even if you're thoroughly sick of plain old Solitaire.

All the games are on the Games submenu of the Start menu (Start ➤ All Programs ➤ Games).

Playing Single-Player Games

XP includes six single-player games:

FreeCell FreeCell is a solitaire variation that involves building descending columns of cards of opposite colors until you can transfer each suit in ascending order onto the four home cells. To enable you to do so, there are four free cells (from which the game gets its name), each of which can hold one card at a time. All 1 million FreeCell games are theoretically winnable, though some are much harder than others. You can start a new random game by choosing Game ➤ New Game (or pressing the F2 key) or a new game of a specified number by choosing Game ➤ Select Game (or pressing the F3 key), entering the game number in the resulting Game Number dialog box, and clicking the OK button.

Hearts Hearts is a computerized implementation of the classic four-person card game. In this implementation, the computer plays the other three players. The Hearts Options dialog box (Game ➤ Options, or press the F7 key) offers a choice of animation speed (Slow, Normal, or Fast) for the movement of the cards, and you can set the names of your cybernetic opponents if you wish.

Minesweeper Minesweeper is a classic Windows logic game in which you attempt to clear a minefield. Click a square to detonate it. Right-click a square to mark it as a mine (one click) or a possible mine (another click). Click both left and right buttons on a square whose mines you've marked to clear the surrounding area as far as any unmarked mines. Minesweeper has three sizes of field—Beginner, Intermediate, and Expert—that you can choose from the Game menu. You can also create custom minefields up to 30 rows wide by 24 rows high by using the Custom Field dialog box (Game ➤ Custom).

Pinball Pinball is a virtual implementation of the classic arcade and bar favorite. You can play either in a window or full screen (Options ➤ Full Screen, or press the F4 key). You can play single player (the default) or two, three, or four players (Options ➤ Select Players, then choose the number of players from the submenu). The default controls are the spacebar to launch the ball (hold the spacebar down for a moment to build up the spring), the Z key to flip the left flipper, the / (forward slash) key to flip the right flipper, the X key to bump the table left, the . (period) key to bump the table right, and the ↑ key to bump the table up. You can change the controls in the Player Controls dialog box (Options ➤ Player Controls, or press the F8 key).

Solitaire The classic solitaire card game, Solitaire should need no introduction. The only thing worth mentioning is the Options dialog box (Game ➤ Options), in which you can choose whether to draw one card or three; whether to use standard scoring, Vegas scoring (with or without cumulative scoring), or no scoring; and whether to time the game, display the status bar, and use outline dragging (which improves display speed on older graphics cards).

Spider Solitaire Spider Solitaire is a challenging solitaire game. You can play at three levels of difficulty (Easy, Medium, or Difficult) by choosing Game ➤ Difficulty (or pressing the F3 key). If you're new to Spider Solitaire, press the M key or choose Game ➤ Show an Available Move to see an available move. You can save one game by choosing Game ➤ Save This Game or pressing Ctrl+S, and you can open the saved game by choosing Game ➤ Open Last Saved Game or pressing Ctrl+O.

Playing Multiplayer Games

XP's multiplayer games are Internet Backgammon, Internet Checkers, Internet Hearts, Internet Reversi, and Internet Spades. (More's the pity, Microsoft has chosen not to provide a chess game with XP.) These games are implemented through Zone.com.

To play these games, you need to be connected to the Internet. When you start the game from the Games submenu (Start ➤ All Programs ➤ Games) on the Start menu, XP displays an explanatory screen, of which Figure 29.1 shows an example for Hearts. If you don't want to see this screen again, clear the Show This Every Time check box.

FIGURE 29.1

XP displays an explanatory screen when you start an Internet game.

XP then connects to the Internet game server and searches for the appropriate number of other players. Once it has found them, it starts the game.

The Game menu offers game-appropriate options, such as Find New Opponent(s) and Skill Level. You can switch chat on or off by selecting the On option button or the Off option button in the Chat area. To use chat, select one of the canned messages from the list.

Choosing Hardware for Serious Gaming

Any computer that can run XP at a decent pace should be able to run most games well enough for you to see what they're like. But to get the most out of more demanding games, you need heavier-duty hardware than XP itself needs. At the risk of preaching to the converted, this section discusses the hardware needed for serious gaming.

Sound Card and Speakers or Headphones

Basic sound systems such as those you find in run-of-the-mill bargain PCs are fine for standard audio tasks such as Windows system sounds and listening to Internet radio, and may be good enough for a little light CD, WMA, or MP3 audio if your ears aren't too picky. But to enjoy the sonic excesses of serious gaming, you need a sound system built for it.

For most people, that means getting a sound card that delivers 3-D audio and environmental audio and a subwoofer system with surround sound or home-theater capabilities (for example, a Dolby 5.1 setup—five satellites and a subwoofer—or 7.1 setup). Subwoofer systems are more expensive than subless systems, but because the subwoofer does the heavy lifting, it tends to be the most important part of a speaker upgrade.

When buying speakers, choose ones designed for the use or uses you'll give them: Some speakers are designed for classical music, some for rock, and some for rockets and explosions. Speakers that overlap the latter two categories may be your best bet unless you have no interest in music.

Headphones come in enough styles—circumaural (over the ear), supra-aural (on the ear), and assorted buds (in the ear)—designs, and sizes that they're almost entirely a personal choice. While cheap headphones are almost guaranteed to sound bad, you don't need to spend a huge amount to get acceptable sound quality and comfort.

Generally speaking, sound quality and comfort are what you should look for in headphones. Style and looks should be secondary considerations (if you consider them at all). If headphones promise special features, evaluate them carefully rather than taking them at face value, because many aren't really worth having. For example, Evergreen Technologies (`www.evertech.com`) makes the RumbleFX Force Feedback Headphones, which claim to deliver force feedback through your ears but actually do little more than put subwoofers rather closer to your brain than any reputable doctor would recommend. Apparently some people love these headphones.

Video Card

Games are one area where an investment in a capable 3-D AGP video card with plenty of video memory pays dividends. At this writing, the amount of video memory on video cards appears to be doubling year by year: 16MB cards and 32MB cards are now entry level, 64MB cards are almost unexciting, and the latest 128MB cards are checking their rear-view mirrors for 256MB cards and 512MB cards closing in on them. PCI cards have less exciting amounts of memory, but they can perform well enough if your computer doesn't support AGP.

Video-card technologies change at least as fast as fashion. To find out the latest and greatest video-card technologies when you read this, consult serious gamers or visit games websites such as GameSpot (`www.gamespot.com`).

Joystick, Game Pad, Steering Wheel, or Other Human Interface Device

Keyboards and mice are great for regular input to Windows computers, but to enjoy most games to the max, you'll probably want to add a game controller such as a joystick, game pad, or steering wheel with rudder pedals. These devices are commonly referred to as *game controllers* or *human interface devices*.

Which type of device you choose depends of course on the types of games that you want to play. *Force-feedback devices* (such as joysticks) provide better tactile sensation for some games (for example, flying simulations). As you'd expect, they cost more than regular devices.

Adding and Configuring Game Controllers

This section discusses how to add and configure game controllers such as those discussed in the previous section.

Adding a Game Controller

How you add a game controller usually depends on how it connects to your PC. If the controller uses a USB connection, you should be able to plug in the controller and have the Found New Hardware Wizard detect it automatically. If XP has an appropriate driver for the controller, it loads it automatically; if not, it prompts you to supply a driver. Do so.

If the controller uses a connection that XP is unable to detect automatically, you can install the controller either by running the Add Hardware Wizard (as described in Chapter 14) or by using the Game Controllers dialog box.

To display the Game Controllers dialog box, take the following steps:

1. Choose Start ➤ Control Panel. XP displays Control Panel.

2. Click the Printers and Other Hardware link. XP displays the Printers and Hardware screen.

3. Click the Game Controllers link. XP displays the Game Controllers dialog box (shown on the left in Figure 29.2).

To add a game controller, click the Add button in the Game Controllers dialog box. XP displays the Add Game Controller dialog box (shown on the right in Figure 29.2). Then add a listed type of game controller by using the technique described in the next section, or add an unlisted type of game controller by using the technique described in the section after that.

FIGURE 29.2

Use the Game Controllers dialog box to add game controllers that XP doesn't detect and install automatically. Use the Add Game Controller dialog box to add a game controller.

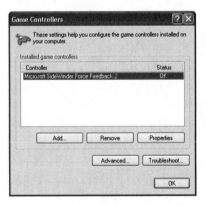

ADDING A GAME CONTROLLER OF A LISTED TYPE

To add a game controller of a type that XP lists in the Add Game Controller dialog box, take the following steps:

1. Select the controller in the Game Controllers list box.

2. If the controller has rudder controls or pedals (for example, for driving games), select the Enable Rudders and Pedals check box.

3. Click the OK button. XP closes the Add Game Controller dialog box and triggers the Found New Hardware Wizard, which searches for drivers for the new game controller. Again, if XP has an appropriate driver for the controller, it loads it automatically; if not, it prompts you to supply a driver.

ADDING A GAME CONTROLLER THAT'S NOT LISTED

To add a game controller that's not listed, take the following steps:

1. Click the Custom button in the Add Game Controller dialog box. XP displays the Custom Game Controller dialog box (shown in Figure 29.3).

FIGURE 29.3

If your game controller isn't listed, use the Custom Game Controller dialog box to define a custom entry for it.

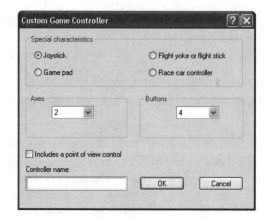

2. In the Special Characteristics group box, select the option button that most closely describes the controller. Your choices are the Joystick option button, the Game Pad option button, the Flight Yoke or Flight Stick option button, and the Race Car Controller option button.

3. In the Axes drop-down list, specify the number of axes (plural of *axis*, not of *ax*) the controller has: 2, 3, or 4.

4. In the Buttons drop-down list, specify the number of buttons the controller has.

5. If the controller has a point-of-view (POV) hat, select the Includes a Point of View Control check box.

6. In the Controller Name text box, enter the name you want to use for the controller.

7. Click the OK button. XP closes the Custom Game Controller dialog box, creates an entry for the controller you defined, and adds it to the Game Controllers list box in the Add Game Controller dialog box.

8. Click the OK button. XP closes the Add Game Controller dialog box and triggers the Found New Hardware Wizard, which searches for drivers for the new game controller. XP prompts you to supply a driver for the device.

Removing a Game Controller

To remove a game controller from your system, select its entry in the Installed Game Controllers list box in the Game Controllers dialog box and click the Remove button. XP displays a Remove Controller dialog box. Click the Yes button to remove the controller.

Choosing the Game Controller to Use for Legacy Programs

If you have the money and the ports, nothing's stopping you from installing multiple game controllers on the same PC. To tell XP which game controller to use for legacy programs that may get confused by a surfeit of game controllers, take the following steps:

1. Click the Advanced button in the Game Controllers dialog box. XP displays the Advanced Settings dialog box (shown in Figure 29.4).

FIGURE 29.4

Use the Advanced Settings dialog box to tell XP which game controller you want to use.

2. In the Preferred Device drop-down list, select the game controller you want to use.
3. Click the OK button. XP closes the Advanced Settings dialog box and applies your choice.

Testing and Calibrating a Game Controller

To test and calibrate a game controller, take the following steps:

1. Select the game controller in the Installed Game Controllers list box in the Game Controllers dialog box.
2. Click the Properties button. XP displays the Properties dialog box for the game controller with the Test page foremost. The left screen in Figure 29.5 shows the Test page of the Properties dialog box for a SideWinder Force Feedback 2 Joystick.

FIGURE 29.5

The Test page (left) of the Properties dialog box for a game controller lets you test and calibrate the controller. The Settings page (right) includes the Calibrate button for starting the Device Calibration Wizard.

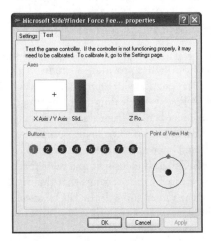

3. Use the controls on the Test page to make sure that your game controller is working as it should. For example, in the Properties dialog box shown, you can check the range of movement on the axes and make sure that the buttons and the point-of-view hat control are working correctly.
4. If you decide you need to calibrate your controller, click the Settings tab. XP displays the Settings page, of which the right screen in Figure 29.5 shows an example (again for the SideWinder Force Feedback 2 Joystick).

5. Click the Calibrate button. XP starts the Device Calibration Wizard.

6. Follow the prompts as the Device Calibration Wizard walks you through calibrating your game controller. When the wizard finishes, it returns you to the Properties dialog box for the controller.

7. Click the OK button. XP closes the Properties dialog box, applies the settings you chose, and returns you to the Game Controllers dialog box.

Troubleshooting a Game Controller

To troubleshoot a problem with a game controller, take the following steps:

1. Click the Troubleshoot button in the Game Controllers dialog box. XP launches or activates Help and Support Center and starts the Games and Multimedia Troubleshooter.

2. Select the I Am Having a Problem with a Joystick or Another Game Device option button.

3. Click the Next button. The Games and Multimedia Troubleshooter walks you through the steps for troubleshooting the game controller—for example, establishing whether the device is USB and whether the game you're trying to play is configured to use the controller.

Getting the Best Performance on Games

To get the best performance on games, follow the recommendations in this list.

Get plenty of RAM   You've heard this before many times in the book—but many computers don't have enough RAM to run demanding programs effectively without frequent swapping to disk. And games are some of the most demanding programs around. For example, Unreal Tournament typically devours around 60MB of RAM and virtual memory—*each*. And if you have an AGP video card (and you should), there's another reason to have plenty of RAM. Read the next item.

Assign a big AGP aperture size   One of the reasons why AGP video cards can blow the socks off PCI video cards (apart from AGP's providing a bandwidth of 533MBps to PCI's 132MBps) is that they can offload the less exciting video-processing tasks onto system RAM so that they can devote their video RAM (VRAM) to dealing with the most exciting and demanding video-processing tasks. To get the most benefit from this, assign a big AGP aperture size. Restart your computer and display the BIOS screen. (On many computers, you can do this by pressing the Delete key or the F2 key during boot-up.) Find the setting called AGP Aperture Size (or something similar, depending on your BIOS), and increase it to a value that's around half the amount of system RAM you have. (You'll be limited to the settings that the BIOS provides, but choose a setting around this amount.) Save the values and exit the BIOS screen. AGP will then be able to take as much RAM as it needs for video-processing tasks.

Assign plenty of swap-file space   Give XP plenty of space for the paging file so that it can write to disk as much information as it needs. (See the section "Specifying the Size and Location of the Paging File" in Chapter 16 for details.)

Get the latest stable drivers   Get the latest stable versions of drivers for your hardware. If your hardware is from big-name manufacturers or enthusiastic manufacturers, you'll probably be able to download new drivers via Windows Update. But for the latest drivers the moment they're released, visit the hardware manufacturers' websites directly. Resist any temptation to test beta drivers, because they can destabilize your computer. Though System Restore (discussed in Chapter 17) can work wonders, you probably won't want to use it any more frequently than you have to.

Keep your disks defragmented   Keep your disks defragmented, as discussed in Chapter 11. This speeds up the retrieval of game data from the hard drive and optimizes the performance of virtual memory.

Choose appropriate display settings   Choose a screen resolution, color depth, and refresh rate appropriate to the game you're playing. For example, for action games, you may want to reduce the resolution, color depth, and refresh rate to increase the frame rate of the game and produce a smoother flow of play. For a nonaction game that uses high-quality graphics, you'll probably want a higher resolution, color depth, and refresh rate. (If your hardware is supremely rugged, handsome, and windswept, you may be able to manage an impressive frame rate with high resolution and true color.)

Disable high-end graphics features you can't afford   If your computer is struggling to run a game fast enough for you, you may be able to turn off some of the flashier features to buy yourself more speed. For example, some games let you turn off high-quality textures and shadows. You might also be able to lower the sound quality used.

Stop unnecessary software   Before running a game, exit as many open programs as possible to free up memory. Check your startup group for background services that may be running when you don't need them to. (The Microsoft Office Find Fast utility is a perennial offender.) If you're using a screen saver, disable it so that it won't try to kick in while you're playing a game.

Up Next

This chapter has discussed the games that XP provides, how to install and configure game controllers, and how to get good games performance on XP.

That's the end of Part IV of the book. The last part, Part V, discusses how to network your XP PCs and how to share resources.

Part V

Networking Windows XP Home Edition

Chapter 30

Understanding Windows Networking

THIS CHAPTER DISCUSSES WHAT a network is, why you might want to implement one in your home or home office, and what hardware you'll need to get in order to implement a network. Along the way, it tells you what you need to know about network architectures, network topologies, and network equipment. The chapter's quite short—more of an overview than seriously detailed information—so don't feel that you need to skip it. As you'll see, XP includes all the software you need to create a fully functional network. You might not even need to buy any extra hardware, but if you do need to buy hardware, it shouldn't be too expensive, and it'll be fairly easy to set up the network.

If you're already sold on the benefits of a network and you know the basics of networking, skip this chapter and go straight to the next chapter, which discusses how to start implementing a network.

This chapter covers the following topics:

◆ Why network your home?
◆ Network architectures
◆ Network topologies
◆ Network protocols
◆ Planning your network
◆ Choosing between wired and wireless
◆ Choosing hardware for a wired network
◆ Choosing hardware for a wireless network

Why Network Your Home or Home Office?

A *network* is simply computers connected to each other so that they can share resources or exchange information. A network can consist of as few as two computers or as many as are connected to the Internet. In a home or a home office, you'll probably have anything from a couple computers to a half-dozen computers networked together.

By networking your computers, you can share files and resources, so that you can perform the following actions and more:

◆ Transfer files from one computer to another. (For one-time use, such as when you're upgrading from an old computer to a new one, you might choose to use a direct connection via a FireWire, parallel, or serial port instead of establishing a connection via network cards.)

◆ Share files. For example, if several users need to collaborate on a project from different computers, you can give them all access to a networked drive to use as a central location.

◆ Back files up easily from each of the networked computers. By centralizing backup to one computer or standard media, you can protect your files against loss and corruption.

◆ Share Internet connections, thus making better use of broadband connections (such as DSLs, cable, and satellite links) or simply reducing hardware and telephony costs.

◆ Share printers, CD-ROM and CD recorder drives, scanners, and other hardware.

◆ Play multiplayer games with either other users of your network or people on the Internet (or both).

Network Architectures

There are two basic network architectures: client/server networks and peer-to-peer networks. The following sections discuss the key points of each, so that you're clear on the differences. Both are worth considering for your home or home-office network, though at this writing peer-to-peer networks are far more popular for such small networks. (As you'll see, client/server networks deserve more of a look-in than they get.)

Client/Server Networks

Client/server networks are the type of networks used by most companies that have more than a dozen or so users. In a *client/server network* (also sometimes called a *server-based network*), there are two different types of computers: *server computers* that provide services such as file storage and printing, and *client computers* that use those services. The point of using servers is to centralize files, coordinate the sharing of resources, and improve security while decreasing the number of points of failure. In most client/server networks, the client computers are managed by software running on the servers, but looser arrangements, in which the client computers enjoy some autonomy while tasting the benefits that servers can deliver, are possible too.

A client/server network can have just one server, but most corporate networks of any size have multiple servers of different types, each type having a specialized purpose. *File servers* provide networked storage for the users' files. *Print servers* manage printers, queuing the print jobs that the users send and coordinating the printers. *Applications servers* run programs so that users' desktop PCs can be 98-pound weaklings or the modern equivalent of dumb terminals. *Internet-access servers* such as proxy servers handle users' Internet requests, routing demands for URLs outward and the corresponding data inward. (Most proxy servers are set to check incoming and outgoing information for sins such as sports sites and sex sites on the way.) *E-mail servers* handle e-mail and groupware. *Fax servers*... okay, you get the idea.

The servers make it easier to manage, back up, and troubleshoot the network. Instead of having files scattered all around the building (or the campus, or offices spread right across North America) on the hard drives of individual users' computers, the administrators can have files saved on network drives that they can easily back up (and restore if necessary) from a central location. Instead of having an inexpensive and flaky printer crowding each user's cubicle, the administrators can funnel printing through centralized printers the size of refrigerators, making troubleshooting and management easy. Instead of installing programs locally (on the users' hard drives), they can install them on the applications server, where they can maintain and upgrade them with minimal effort. Security and permissions are handled centrally through the servers, so an administrator can easily prevent users from taking actions they shouldn't.

Needless to say, there's a downside to this centralization as well. If everyone in the office has been well behaved and stored all their files on the file server (as they're usually told to do), nobody will be able to do any work on those files if the file server flatlines. If the Internet-access server takes an extended coffee break, all users' contact with the Internet and the Web is cut off. And if one of the cubicle-sized printers decides to eat paper rather than spit it out at 40 sheets a minute, even the network administrators won't be able to print out their resume.

That said, when client/server networks work well, they work *very* well. With proper planning, client/server networks can *scale* (grow) to have thousands of workstations on them, whereas (even with good planning) peer-to-peer networks seldom work well with more than a couple dozen workstations.

Figure 30.1 shows part of a client/server network, omitting most of the clients so that the figure fits on the page.

FIGURE 30.1

In a client/server network, servers centralize tasks such as file storage, faxing, e-mail, and Internet access.

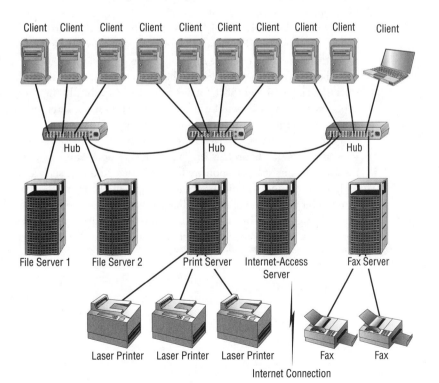

Normally, the server or servers in a client/server network run a server operating system such as Windows 2000 Server, Windows .NET Server, NT Server, Novell NetWare, Mac OS X Server, Linux, or Unix. But this isn't an absolute requirement. If you want, you can set up a small client/server network in which the server runs XP (or even a version of Windows 9x). More on this in a moment.

Peer-to-Peer Networks

In a *peer-to-peer network*, the computers are all equals—*peers*—from the administration and security points of view. Instead of connecting to one or more servers, the peer computers connect to each other. Instead of getting services from servers, the peer computers get services from each other and provide each other with services. Instead of being managed centrally by administrators, each peer computer is managed by its user, making security and backup more difficult without deliberate coordination by the users.

Typically, each computer on a peer-to-peer network is both a client and a server: It's a client when it accesses a resource on another computer, and it's a server when it supplies a resource to another computer. (The word *typically* is there because quite often one or more computers in a peer network will act only as clients, in that they share no resources with their peers.) For example, when you share a folder with other users, your computer is acting as a server. And when you access the printer connected to another computer, your computer is acting as a client. But most of the time, you don't need to worry about whether your computer is acting as a client or as a server, because it all happens seamlessly behind the scenes. You set up the sharing, and after that, the resources are available, and you can use them. It's as simple as that.

Figure 30.2 shows a simple peer-to-peer network that's sharing folders, two printers, and a dial-up Internet connection. This also illustrates the main weakness of peer-to-peer networks: Each computer that's sharing a resource must be powered on and have its operating system functioning all the time that the resource is needed. If the computer that's sharing folders is switched off (or has hung or crashed), the files in those folders won't be accessible. If the computer that's sharing the printers is powered off, nobody will be able to print. And for the Internet connection to be accessible all the time, that computer must keep humming along.

Peer-to-peer networks have another disadvantage worth mentioning here—a disadvantage that you can't see in the figure. Sharing a resource occupies some of the computer's processing power and memory, making it less responsive for user-oriented duties such as running programs.

If in your mind you move around a couple of the resources shared in Figure 30.2 (and perhaps squint a bit), you can see that the line between a client/server network and a peer-to-peer network can be quite fine. If one of the computers were sharing all the resources, it'd be a server; and if the network were administered centrally, it would be a client/server network rather than a peer-to-peer network.

FIGURE 30.2

In a peer-to-peer network, the computers share resources with each other.

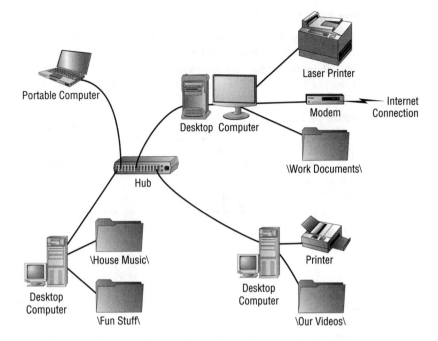

Network Topologies

This section discusses the two main network topologies you're likely to want to use for networking your home or home office. It also mentions two network topologies that are less used nowadays.

These topologies are physical. There are also logical topologies that describe how the data travels along the wires. We'll get to these in a few minutes' time.

Star Topology

The *star topology* is the most used topology for networks nowadays, because it's easy to implement and fault tolerant. In a star topology, all the computers connect to a central hub or switch (or several hubs or switches connected to each other). Both the client/server network shown in Figure 30.1 and the peer-to-peer network shown in Figure 30.2 use star topologies.

A star topology uses more cable than a bus topology (discussed in the next section), because each computer is wired to the hub or switch. Extra cable costs more money, of course, but for a small network, the difference in cabling cost between a star topology and a bus topology isn't usually a significant amount. And because each computer is connected to the hub or switch, a cable failure affects only one computer.

The hub or switch in a star topology does represent a single point of failure. But because hubs and switches are typically very reliable, this isn't usually a problem.

Bus Topology

In a *bus topology*, all the computers and devices are attached to a single run of cable. As you can see in Figure 30.3, which illustrates a bus topology, the bus is a simple network design, and one that's economical on cable. The terminators at each end of the bus essentially tell the signal that it's reached the end of the cable and that it should stop rather than bouncing back along the cable.

FIGURE 30.3

In a physical bus topology, the computers and devices are attached to a single run of cable.

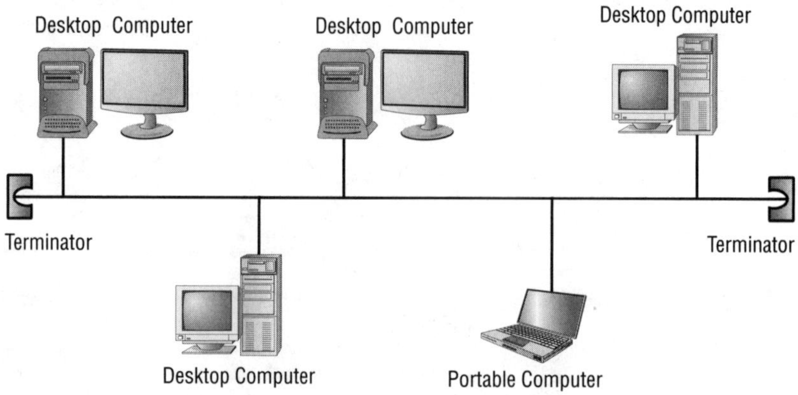

The main drawback to a bus topology is that any break in the cable takes down the entire network. Bus topologies are seldom used for Ethernet and Fast Ethernet nowadays, but they're used in other networking technologies, such as HomePNA phone-line networks.

Other Topologies: Ring and Mesh

Star and bus aren't the only topologies for networks—there are also ring topologies and mesh topologies.

In a *ring topology*, the computers are laid out in a topological ring, with each connected to its two neighbors. Ring topologies aren't fault tolerant, and because each computer on the network needs two cables, they tend to be more expensive than star or bus topologies.

Mesh topologies are fault tolerant and are used where uptime is vital. In a true mesh, each computer is directly connected to each other computer, giving a network diagram that looks like a mesh or a cat's cradle. As you can imagine, a true mesh involves a huge number of connections, and is rarely implemented for more than a handful of computers. More frequently, a partial mesh topology is implemented, with the most critical computers having multiple connections to each other so that they can maintain connectivity even if they lose a connection or two.

Logical Topologies

As mentioned a few minutes ago, the topologies discussed so far are physical topologies. A network also has a *logical topology* that describes how the data travels along the wires. A network can have the same logical topology as physical topology, or the two can be different.

There are three widely used logical topologies:

◆ In a *logical bus topology*, the signal travels to all the computers on the network, but only the computer identified by the address picks the packets of data off the wires. Ethernet uses a logical bus topology.

◆ In a *logical ring topology*, the signal travels around the network from one attached computer to the next. Each computer checks to see if the signal is intended for it; if it isn't, the computer passes the signal along to the next computer. When the signal reaches the computer identified by the address, that computer picks the packets off the wire, and they travel no further. A token ring network is an example of a logical ring topology.

◆ In a *logical mesh topology*, the signal can take any of a number of paths from its source to its destination. The Internet is an example of a logical mesh topology.

Network Protocols

A network protocol is a set of rules that lay out how data is transmitted between computers (or other devices) on a network. For two devices to communicate effectively, they need to use the same protocol.

For general networking purposes, XP's preferred protocol is TCP/IP, the suite of protocols on which the Internet is based. XP can also run Internetwork Packet Exchange/Sequenced Packet Exchange (IPX/SPX), a set of protocols developed by Novell, Inc. and used in Novell's NetWare network operating system. If you use XP Home, you're unlikely to need to run IPX/SPX unless you have a networking program or device that requires IPX/SPX in order to operate. (For example, some LinkSys print servers require the computer administering them to have IPX/SPX installed.) By contrast, if you use XP Professional, you might well need IPX/SPX to connect to a server running NetWare.

Also included in XP, but not supported by Microsoft, is NetBIOS Enhanced User Interface (NetBEUI, pronounced "net-booey"), a local area network protocol that many previous versions of Windows supported. You might need to run NetBEUI to enable older programs to communicate. Otherwise, you're unlikely to need to bother with it.

NOTE *XP doesn't support AppleTalk, a networking protocol used by Macs, or LocalTalk, a printing protocol used by Macs. (Some earlier versions of Windows, such as Windows 2000 Professional, supported LocalTalk.) However, more recent versions of Mac OS have TCP/IP built in, so unless you're using an older version of Mac OS, you shouldn't need AppleTalk or LocalTalk.*

XP uses various other network protocols for particular purposes that include the following:

Dial-Up Network Connections XP uses Point-to-Point Protocol (PPP) for dial-up connections such as Internet connections via modems or ISDN.

Broadband Internet Connections XP uses Point-to-Point Protocol over Ethernet (PPPoE) for broadband Internet connections such as cable connections and DSL connections.

Virtual Private Network Connections XP uses Point-to-Point Tunneling Protocol (PPTP) and Layer 2 Tunneling Protocol (L2TP) for virtual private network (VPN) connections. (Chapter 34 discusses how to create and use VPN connections.)

Automatic Network Configuration and Device Discovery XP uses Universal Plug and Play (UPnP) to enable networked devices to communicate their presence to each other and configure themselves to work with each other. For example, if you enable Internet Connection Sharing (ICS) on an Internet connection, it uses UPnP to advertise its presence to other computers so that they can connect to the Internet through the shared connection.

In most cases, XP handles the protocols shown in the above list seamlessly, so you don't need to worry about them. For example, if you set up a dial-up networking connection by using the New Connection Wizard, it'll configure the connection to use PPP by default; if you set up a broadband connection, XP will automatically use PPPoE. If you enable ICS, XP automatically uses UPnP. But sometimes you may need to install an additional protocol (such as IPX/SPX or NetBEUI) or configure a protocol manually.

EXPERT KNOWLEDGE: IP ADDRESSES AND HOW THEY WORK

You don't need to know this information in order to implement a Windows network, but understanding what Internet Protocol (IP) addresses are and how they work can be a great help when troubleshooting network problems.

TCP/IP uses an IP address to identify each computer or device on a network. An IP address takes the form $x.x.x.x$, where each x is a number between 0 and 255—for example, 216.43.28.244. Different ranges of IP addresses give different network sizes, or *classes*, but we don't need to get into the details of those here.

IP addresses are either public or private. *Public IP addresses* are centrally assigned by the Internet's registration authorities, which keep detailed records of which organization or individual has which IP address. *Private IP addresses* are IP addresses that you can assign yourself for internal use within your network. Private IP addresses are nonroutable, which means that packets sent to private IP addresses can't be passed across routers and so can't escape from your network to the Internet.

There are three private address ranges. The range 10.0.0.0 to 10.255.255.255 is used for large organizations. The range 172.16.0.0 to 172.31.255.255 is used for medium-sized organizations. The range 192.168.0.0 to 192.168.255.255 is used for small networks and home networks. XP's Internet Connection Sharing (ICS) uses the last-mentioned range for home and small-office networks.

As you might imagine, there are basically two ways for a computer to get an IP address appropriate to its needs: Either you can set a fixed address manually, or the computer can contact a computer that doles out IP addresses on request and reclaims them when they're released. On Microsoft networks, the doling-out of IP addresses is handled by a protocol named Dynamic Host Configuration Protocol (DHCP).

In a Windows domain, a server running Windows NT Server, Windows 2000 Server, or Windows .NET Server runs a DHCP service that allocates IP addresses to computers as necessary. In mixed networking, the DHCP service often runs on another operating system, such as Linux or Unix (for example, Solaris or BSD).

Many devices designed for sharing Internet access in the home or small office, such as residential gateways, implement a basic DHCP service as well. ICS includes a DHCP allocator, which is a stripped-down DHCP server.

Continued on next page

ICS uses the third of the address ranges shown above and automatically configures a network using these addresses. The computer running ICS gets the IP address 192.168.0.1 and allocates IP addresses to other computers on request when they boot up and look to join the network.

In most cases, using DHCP is more efficient than allocating fixed IP addresses manually, because DHCP prevents a computer that's switched off (or disconnected) from hogging an IP address when another computer might need it. But in some cases it's useful to keep a fixed IP address for one or more given computers so that you always know which address they're using. Besides, if you're using only half-a-dozen or so computers and other devices on your network, you have IP addresses to burn.

XP Home assumes that you'll be using DHCP (probably in the form of ICS) to allocate IP addresses, but it also provides a feature called Automatic Private IP Addressing (the acronym is APIPA) in case you're not using DHCP (or fixed IP addresses) or your DHCP allocator isn't available. If XP Home doesn't get a response to its request for an IP address, it automatically chooses an IP address in the range 169.254.0.1 to 169.254.0.254 and checks to see if any other computer already on the network is already using this address. If the IP address is free, XP Home assigns itself that address; if not, it chooses another, checks that, and so on.

Even after assigning itself an address via APIPA, XP keeps checking the network for the presence of a DHCP server every three minutes. If XP finds a server, it applies for an IP address and switches to it. If not, it waits another three minutes and then checks again. This constant checking severely impinges on network performance, and you'll probably want to avoid it if possible. If you don't have a computer running ICS or another DHCP service, simply assign an IP address manually to each computer on the network.

You'll notice that the 169.254.0.1 to 169.254.0.254 range isn't one of the private ranges mentioned earlier in this sidebar. But this range is private in a way, because Microsoft reserved it for APIPA—so if you're using XP, you can use this address range freely (or XP can use it automatically for you).

Planning Your Network

This section discusses how to go about planning your network. You need to make the following decisions:

- Should the network be client/server or peer-to-peer?
- Should the network be wired or wireless?
- If the network will be wired, which wired networking technology will you use?
- Where will you keep your files?
- Which resources will you share on the network?

Client/Server or Peer-to-Peer?

The first question you should answer is whether you want to create a client/server network or a peer-to-peer network.

At first sight, you may be surprised by this question. Didn't the book just say that most home networks and many home-office networks are peer-to-peer? That's right—but just because most of these networks are peer-to-peer doesn't necessarily mean that they're better off so.

Even if your network needs are relatively modest, it's worth considering having a server, especially if you have a spare computer, or a pensioned-off old laptop or desktop, that you'd like to get a bit more use out of. A server doesn't have to have a fast processor or a ton of RAM. Nor does it need to be running the latest and greatest operating system (read: XP). That Pentium-166 with 64MB RAM that you reluctantly decided couldn't handle XP could still play a valuable role in your computing life. Put an old copy of Windows NT Workstation or Windows 2000 Professional on it—or Linux, if you can handle Linux—and it can provide services to the network. The server doesn't have to manage the computers on the network—it just has to provide resources and services to authenticated users.

TIP   Another alternative is to add to the network dedicated devices for sharing resources so that you don't need to keep as many computers running. For example, you could add a DSL modem and router or cable modem and router to share your Internet connection, or a print server to share one or more of your printers. You can also get stand-alone, dedicated file servers designed for home-office or small-office use, although these tend to be far more expensive than a humble PC providing equivalent capabilities. Each of these is an independent device that connects to your network hub. Once it's connected, it can be accessed by any computer that's running.

Wired or Wireless?

After you decide between a client/server network and a peer-to-peer network, your second decision should be whether you want a wired network, a wireless network, or a combination of the two.

As with most things in life, both wired and wireless networks offer advantages and disadvantages. Wired networks have three main advantages over wireless networks: speed, cost, and reliability. Wireless networks offer two main advantages over wired networks: flexibility and lack of cables. The following sections examine these advantages.

One point on which wired networks and wireless networks are about tied is simplicity. In theory, a wireless network should be easier to implement than a wired network, because less hardware is involved—for example, there are no cables. But it doesn't always work out that way in practice, as anyone will attest who's spent time struggling to configure a wireless access point to talk to the wireless network adapter located a full six inches from it.

Wired networks are relatively simple to configure. You add a network card to each computer, attach a cable to the network card and the hub or switch, and you're in business.

Another point on which wired networks often score over wireless networks is security: Because the range of a wireless access device often extends beyond the physical boundaries of the location it's covering, someone can tap into the network from outside the location. But as you'll see in the section "Securing a Wireless Network" in Chapter 33, if you take some basic measures to secure it, a wireless network can be just about as secure as a wired network—secure enough, anyway, for most conventional use.

ADVANTAGES OF WIRED NETWORKS OVER WIRELESS NETWORKS

This section discusses the advantages of wired networks over wireless networks: speed, cost, and reliability.

Speed

Wired networks offer higher speed than wireless networks. Fast Ethernet—as you'll see, the best choice for a wired network—provides 100Mbps. Most wireless network adapters conform to the IEEE 802.11b standard, which is also known as WiFi and offers a theoretical 11Mbps. (Some OEMs sell double-rate 802.11b equipment that produces theoretical data rates up to 22Mbps.) Almost all of these adapters drop down to lower speeds—5.5Mbps, 2.4Mbps, 1.1Mbps—if conditions don't allow 11Mbps, as is often the case. The more distance and the more walls or floors that you put between your wireless adapter and the nearest access point, the lower the transmission speed will drop.

At this writing, 802.11a equipment is gradually spreading onto the market. In a reversal of normal alphabetical order, 802.11a offers greater power, speed, and distance than 802.11b: 802.11a offers data rates of up to 54Mbps to 802.11b's 11Mbps. 802.11a also offers greater distance than 802.11b as well, with some products claiming full-speed ranges of 100 feet in an "open environment" and 60 feet in a "closed environment" and maximum ranges of up to 1200 feet (at 6Mbps) in an open environment and 300 feet (again at 6Mbps) in a closed environment. The bad news is that 802.11a isn't directly compatible with 802.11b, so you can't migrate to 802.11a without upgrading (read: junking) all your 802.11b equipment. Some manufacturers are building access points that provide both 802.11a and 802.11b service, but buying one of these access points tends to be at least as expensive as buying an 802.11a access point and a separate 802.11b access point. (Besides, you've most likely already got an 802.11b access point—otherwise you'd probably go straight to 802.11a.)

NOTE *All the distances and data rates mentioned here are for 802.11 equipment in off-the-shelf condition. You can greatly boost range on many wireless products by attaching an external antenna to supplement the on-board antenna, which tends to be relatively feeble and, in the case of wireless network adapters, hard to orient for maximum effect. (You might get better wireless range by standing your laptop on edge, but your work, play, or neck would suffer.) Omnidirectional antennae provide the widest coverage. (Coverage is actually pancake-shaped rather than spherical, because moles and airplanes tend not to need boosted signals.) Yagi antennae provide extended range in a general direction. Parabolic grid antennae provide the greatest range in a more specific direction. Wireless maniacs—I'm sorry, wireless enthusiasts—can get ranges of 15 to 20 miles with boosted WiFi gear, given a suitably open landscape.*

Next, currently on the horizon, is 802.11g, which restores normal alphabetical order with a vigorous skip, offers the same speed as 802.11a (54Mbps), and is essentially an upgrade to 802.11b. 802.11g is expected to become a standard toward the end of 2002, and equipment based on that standard should follow shortly after that. 802.11g equipment is expected to work with 802.11b equipment.

Having several competing standards makes it difficult to choose wireless networking equipment at this writing. 802.11b equipment is least expensive, and many higher-end notebook PCs come with built-in 802.11b cards, so if you've bought one of these notebooks, you've essentially made the choice already. 802.11b is being deployed for community wireless networks, coffee-shop networks, and the like. Microsoft's "home-companion" portable PC code-named Mira is also scheduled to use 802.11b. 802.11a delivers far better performance but is essentially incompatible with 802.11b. The HomeRF Working Group has backed 802.11a as the standard for "high-bandwidth entertainment applications"—presumably they mean voice and video over the airwaves rather than virtual reality or DVD karaoke, but we'll have to wait and see. And 802.11g, when it arrives, will offer similar performance to 802.11a and an upgrade path from 802.11b.

Cost

Wired network adapters cost much less than wireless network adapters. You can get a bargain-basement wired network adapter for $10, though you'll usually be better advised to spend more like $20 to $50. Then you'll need a hub or a switch. A hub costs less than $10 per port; a switch costs $10 to $20 a port.

Most wireless network adapters cost between $100 and $200. You can create a peer-to-peer network with two or more adapters, but to improve performance, you may want to get a wireless access point instead. Most hardware wireless access points cost between $200 and $800. Some manufacturers offer software wireless access points that are less expensive ($100 to $200). A software wireless access point usually involves putting a second, wireless network interface card in a computer that's already wired to the network. This computer then acts as a bridge between the wired portion and the wireless portion of the network. The disadvantage to software wireless access points is that you need to keep that computer running all the time you want to use the wireless portion of the network. However, if you decide to have a server on the network, adding a wireless software access point to it can be relatively painless.

Reliability

Wired networks tend to be more reliable than wireless networks. Unless there's a problem with one of the network cards, the cables, or the hub (or switch), a wired network should deliver its full performance all the time.

By contrast, throughput on a wireless network can be affected not only by the distance and obvious obstacles such as walls and floors but also by its immediate surroundings. For example, a PC Card wireless network adapter can be blocked by the user's hand on a laptop that has its PC Card slots toward the front, by the user's legs when the computer is being used on the user's lap, or by books or other objects placed near the adapter. It shouldn't happen, but it does.

ADVANTAGES OF WIRELESS NETWORKS OVER WIRED NETWORKS

This section discusses the advantages of wireless networks over wired networks: flexibility, and the lack of cables.

Flexibility

Because the computers in a wireless network aren't constrained by cables, a wireless network offers greater flexibility than a wired network. You can move the computers from room to room without trailing cables. Even if you're not interested in roaming with your laptop, being able to move it about freely can be a boon.

For desktop computers, the mobility offered by a wireless network connection is less of a draw, though it can come in useful in shared computers. For example, if you put a desktop computer on a wheeled workstation, you can move it easily from room to room (or from schoolroom to schoolroom).

You can also get multifunction wireless devices that act as a network access point, a print server, and an Internet sharing device. If you can find one of these devices that suits your needs and is within your budget, you should be able to connect your key devices with a minimal number of wires.

Lack of Cables

Wireless networks are great for locations where, for whatever reason, you don't want to (or cannot) install cables. For example, in a temporary office location, you can set up a wireless network without having unsightly cables strung like trip wires from room to room. Likewise, if you're renting an apartment whose landlord wouldn't appreciate your drilling holes from room to room (or floor to floor) or stapling cables or raceways along the baseboards, a wireless network will probably seem more attractive than a wired network.

NOTE   *In the near future, you may be able to add Voice over IP (VOIP) phones to wireless networks, so that you could make phone calls via your Internet connection from a cordless phone that connected to your wireless network. When this capability is widely available, it'll be a strong argument in favor of wireless networks in many homes.*

COMBINING WIRED AND WIRELESS IN YOUR NETWORK

You can get the best of both worlds by combining wired and wireless in your network. For example, you may want to implement a wired network with a wireless access point that allows your laptops to connect via wireless network interface cards from wherever in the building they happen to be. The wired portion of your network will be fast, and the wireless portion of your network will be flexible. The cost will be considerably more than that of a wired-only network, but it should be significantly less than that of a wireless-only network.

If you decide to combine wired and wireless networks, create the wired network as described in "Installing Your Network Hardware" in Chapter 31, and then add wireless to it as described in "Installing a Wireless Network" (also in Chapter 31).

Where Will You Keep Your Files?

Your next decision is where to keep the files on the network. It's vital to make this decision when implementing the network, because it can save you a great deal of time and effort later on.

In a peer-to-peer network, each user typically saves the files they create (or download) on the hard drive of their computer. To share files, they either use the `\Shared Documents\` folder on their computer, designate another folder on their computer for sharing, or use a folder someone else is sharing on another computer.

There's nothing to stop you from keeping your files scattered about on the hard drives (or removable drives) of all the computers attached to the network. But the files will be very difficult to back up effectively from their various locations, and unless each user of the network has a good memory, it'll probably become hard to remember which file is stored in which folder on which computer.

To keep your shared files in order, designate a minimum number of shared locations. This is one of the strongest arguments for creating a client/server network rather than a peer-to-peer network. By concentrating all your shared files on the server, you'll be able to back them up easily. All the users of the network should be able to find the shared files without wasting time and effort. And because the server will be running all the time, you'll avoid the problem that arises when a user wants to access a file in a shared folder whose host computer is currently powered down or whose operating system has temporarily given up the ghost.

How Much Space Do You Need for Your Files?

If you decide to keep all your shared files in a central location, estimate how much space you'll need for the files. This is much easier said than done, because it's always difficult to know how much space you need until you find out that you have far too little. But you need to start by making an educated guess at the amount of space required so that you can provide it to start with.

How much space you need will vary wildly depending on the types of files you want to share. If you're networking your home office, you'll probably want to share documents, spreadsheets, presentations, address books, and so on. If you're networking your computers to make their entertainment resources available to each computer in the household, you may need much more space. For example, if you're planning to implement a network so that you can play your vast collection of MP3 files from any connected computer, you'll need a huge amount of storage space. If you want to share video files, the demand for storage space will be even more intense. You might even want to look into creating a RAID array on a network file server for maximum space and speed. (RAID is the acronym for Redundant Array of Inexpensive Disks.)

Which Resources Will You Share?

Next, make a list of the resources that you want to share via the network. The most obvious resources are files and folders, your Internet connection, and your printers, though not necessarily in that order.

Right out of the box, XP lets you share files and folders, an Internet connection, and printers directly (as it were) from one computer to another. For example, if Computer A is sharing a printer, Computers B and C can print to it via the network. If Computer B is sharing its Internet connection, Computers A and C can use the Internet connection to access the Internet. With custom software, you can also share other resources. For example, you can network your TV or your DVD, or implement a video-communication or baby-monitoring program across the network.

You may also want to share other resources that you can't share directly like this. For example, you can't share a digital camera or scanner directly unless you unplug it and carry it from computer to computer. So the best way to share a digital camera or scanner is to set it up on a computer that any member of the household can use. If the server is in a central location, it might be the best computer for this role. (Alternatively, you could invest in enough USB or FireWire extension cords to plug the scanner or camera into each computer without moving the device itself....)

Choosing Network Hardware for a Wired Network

Once you've decided to implement a wired network, you have a further choice to make: Fast Ethernet, FireWire, phone line (HomePNA), or power line. The following sections discuss how to choose hardware for each of these types of wired network.

WARNING   *Network hardware is unglamorous compared to graphics cards, fast processors, and thundering subwoofer systems, but don't make the mistake of buying the cheapest hardware you can find for your network just because the network is boring. In particular, don't skimp on the hub (or switch) and the cables. Sure, you can shave a few bucks off the price, but you need your network to be reliable because it will be carrying your valuable data. False economies you make here can cost you far more in troubleshooting and downtime in the future.*

Choosing Hardware for a Fast Ethernet Network

For a Fast Ethernet network, you need network interface cards, cables, and a hub or switch.

NOTE The only reason to consider a regular Ethernet network over a Fast Ethernet network is if you already have a full set of regular Ethernet equipment ready to use. If you don't, you'll do much better to go directly to Fast Ethernet. Fast Ethernet cards, cables, and hubs used to be much more expensive than standard Ethernet ones, but now the differences are just about negligible. Even if you have regular Ethernet cards and hubs, buy Fast Ethernet cables, because you can use them for higher data rates if you upgrade your network interface cards and switches. The cables should last for many years unless you allow dogs, rodents, or small children near them.

At this writing, Gigabit Ethernet prices are heading in the right direction—down—but have a long way to go before they're affordable for most people. Unless you have more money than ideas about how to dispose of it, or you absolutely must have the fastest network available, stay with Fast Ethernet rather than going to Gigabit Ethernet.

NETWORK INTERFACE CARDS

The main consideration when buying Fast Ethernet network interface cards is which types of slots your computers have free. In general, PCI cards are better than ISA cards, because you'll have fewer IRQ conflicts. But if your computer is stuffed to the gills with PCI cards and has only an ISA slot free, ISA will work fine.

For a portable computer that doesn't have a built-in Fast Ethernet port, your only viable choice will be a PC Card or CardBus network interface card, depending on whether your computer supports CardBus. USB 1.*x*–connected Ethernet network interface cards can't deliver anything like Fast Ethernet speeds, so you should use them only as a last resort for either portable computers or desktop computers. USB 2.0–connected Ethernet cards, when they arrive, should be more promising.

Whichever types of network card you choose, make sure they're listed on the Windows Hardware Compatibility List (HCL) at the Microsoft Windows Hardware Quality Labs website, www.microsoft .com/hcl/.

CABLE

When choosing Fast Ethernet cable, keep these points in mind:

◆ For general-purpose use, go with unshielded twisted-pair (UTP) Category 5 (*Cat 5* for short) cable or Category 5 Enhanced (Cat 5E) cable. This delivers excellent performance at reasonable cost.

◆ If you need to run cable in suspended ceilings, inside walls, or between the floors of a building, get plenum cable. Plenum cable has a Teflon coating designed to resist catching fire and to give off nontoxic smoke if it does catch fire. (A *plenum* is essentially an enclosed space that's full of matter.)

◆ For fast and easy connection, buy ready-made cables. Most networking suppliers stock cables anything from 18 inches to 100 feet in length and in a wide variety of colors. Colored cables can help you identify different cables more easily in a crowded environment, but if you want your cables to be inconspicuous, you'll probably want to settle for the color that best matches your décor.

◆ If you need a lot of cables, or if you feel compelled to have cables of exactly the right length rather than any of the ready-made lengths, you can make your own cables easily enough. You'll need a reel of cable, some RJ-45 connectors, and a crimping tool with a die for crimping RJ-45 connectors. You'll probably also want to get a cable-stripper tool for stripping the outer plastic sheath off the cable neatly, but you can strip it with a knife if you have the steady hand and patience required.

NOTE   *Buying a crimping tool, a reel of cable, and connectors can save you money over buying a large number of ready-made cables.*

HUB OR SWITCH

In the star network topology used for Fast Ethernet, the hub or switch forms the central point of the network, with the network cables from all the computers and other network-aware devices plugging into its ports.

When a computer sends data, the hub receives it on one port and broadcasts it on all the other connected ports so that the computer or device to which the data is addressed can receive it.

This arrangement works well enough, but it means that there's a lot of data bouncing around the network unnecessarily. Say you have eight computers, imaginatively named A through H, connected to your hub. When A is sending data to B, it sends it to the hub, and the hub broadcasts the data to all the ports but the port the data is coming in on—in other words, the ports to which computers B through H are connected. B picks the data off the wire. The data to ports C through H is unnecessary and decreases the performance of the network.

This is why you should seriously consider buying a switch rather than a hub. A *switch* (or *switching hub*) is essentially a more intelligent version of a hub. A switch builds a table of the hardware addresses of the computers and devices connected to its ports. Then, instead of taking the data passed to it on one port and blindly blasting it out on all other connected ports, it examines the address on the data and passes the data along only to the appropriate port (and thus to the appropriate computer). By doing this, a switch provides more available bandwidth on the network and improves performance.

There is, of course, a downside: A switch costs a little more than a hub. But if you're planning to use your network extensively—especially if you'll be using your network for audio and video files—you'll find the investment worthwhile.

NOTE   *The switches discussed in this book are* unmanaged *switches—switches that essentially look after themselves once you've connected them to your network. High-performance networks often use* managed *switches, on which the administrator can configure the performance of each port—for example, allowing a computer connected to one port large amounts of bandwidth and a high quality of service while making a computer connected to another port scratch along with minimal bandwidth and a miserable quality of service. Managed switches are far more expensive than unmanaged switches.*

Buy a hub or switch with enough ports for both your current needs and your future needs. If you have four computers in your home or office now, but might add either more computers or more network-aware devices in the near-ish future, it makes little sense to buy a four-port hub. Instead, buy an eight-port or twelve-port hub or switch.

Alternatively, make sure that your four-port hub or switch includes an uplink port, so that you can attach another hub or switch to it.

If you have both standard Ethernet (10BaseT) equipment and Fast Ethernet (100BaseT) equipment, make sure that your hub or switch is dual-speed, so that you can connect all the equipment to it, and that it lets each port communicate at the full speed of the device attached to it rather than knocking the whole network back to standard Ethernet speed as soon as you attach a single standard Ethernet device.

Choosing Hardware for a FireWire Network

You can also connect FireWire-enabled computers using a six-pin to six-pin (6–6) FireWire cable. (If a computer doesn't have a FireWire port, you can add one or more by using a PCI card or a PC Card, provided that you have a PCI slot or a PC Card slot free.) These cables are far more expensive than network cables, but given the performance they can deliver, you may well think them worth the cost.

Because FireWire can transfer data very fast (up to 400Mbps), and because it's plug and play, it can be a great networking solution for a home or home office. The main problem with FireWire networking is that the maximum cable length is 15 feet (4.5 meters), so each of the computers on the FireWire network needs to be within 15 feet of another computer. That 15 feet needs to be "as the cable flies," of course—around or over any obstacles that the cable can't go through, and preferably not strung like a thigh-high tripwire between desks.

TIP   You can also bridge a FireWire network with an Ethernet network. So if you have a cluster of computers in the den, you can network them to each other with FireWire, and then network one of them to an Ethernet network with a cable run to the distant reaches of your dwelling.

Choosing Hardware for a Phone-Line Network

Phone lines can be one of the easiest ways to network your home quickly, provided that you have wires and jacks where you need them. (If you don't, you *could* run extension leads—but these offer little advantage over network cable.)

Here's what you need to know about phone-line networks:

◆ Phone-line networks are limited in speed. The industry body, the Home Phoneline Networking Alliance (HomePNA; `www.homepna.org`), has so far set two standards: HomePNA 1.0 offers speeds of 1Mbps. HomePNA 2.0 offers speeds of 10Mbps—the same speed as a regular Ethernet network, a tenth of the speed of Fast Ethernet. HomePNA 3.0, a new specification, is in the works and is intended to deliver 100Mbps performance.

◆ Logically enough, the phone jacks you use for the network need to be on the same phone line.

◆ Most phone-line network adapters include a splitter, so that you can use the network and the phone at the same time.

◆ Most phone-line network adapters plug into a parallel port or USB port.

◆ Phone-line networks use a physical bus topology and a logical bus topology. This means that you don't need a hub. It also means that if you cut the phone line, the whole network stops working—but you'd figured that out already. Phone lines are terminated automatically, so you don't need to add termination devices to the ends of the bus.

This is about as much as you need to know. If the speed is adequate for your needs, and you have the jacks, you can buy a phone-line networking kit, plug in the adapters, and install the software, and you should be away.

EXPERT KNOWLEDGE: ETHERNET OVER PHONE WIRES

There are actually *two* ways in which you can network your home by using the existing phone lines.

One way is to use special network adapters designed for phone-line networks, as described in this section. The other is to use the spare pair of wires present in most existing phone cabling that's used for only one line to run regular Ethernet.

Regular phone cable has two pairs of wires—the telephone companies like to be able to sell you a second line without having to install more cable. Each phone line uses one pair of wires. So if you have only one telephone line, you may be able to use the second pair of wires to carry data.

Be warned that this approach to networking requires much more patience and technical skill than the other means of creating a network. Also, because phone cable has minimal shielding and isn't designed for data use, you may experience interference and slowdowns on the network... but if you have the wires free and they surface where you need the computers to be, this can be a handy solution to wiring a network.

Choosing Hardware for a Power-Line Network

Plug the network adapter into your parallel port, then plug it into the electrical socket... given the damage that a little snap of static can do to a computer's sensitive parts, this instruction seems dangerously wrong, doesn't it? But a power-line network can be one of the easiest ways to network your home, drawing ahead of phone-line networks in the simplicity stakes because most dwellings have many more electrical outlets than they do phone jacks. You shouldn't need to buy any cables for a power-line network beyond the cables for connecting the computer's parallel port or USB port to the electrical socket.

Utility companies have also been experimenting with delivering Internet connectivity via power lines, with some promising to deliver, uh, *electrifying* speeds. (Yes, at least one company has actually used that word.)

At this writing, power-line networks aren't as fast as other network types. Most offer rates of between 2Mbps and 4Mbps—enough for sharing documents among a handful of computers, but not enough for heavy-duty audio or video use—but newer models offer rates of up to 12Mbps, making them competitive with plain Ethernet. And most power-line network adapters require a power conditioner to make sure that the computer receives no untoward signal from variations in the power supply that normal electrical equipment can shrug off.

Various manufacturers make power-line network equipment. One of the leaders is Inari (formerly Intelogis; www.inari.com), which licenses power-line networking equipment to OEMs.

Given that there are various manufacturers, you'd expect there to be various types of power-line network adapters—and indeed there are. Most types plug into a parallel port or a USB port, making them easy to attach to most computers.

Power-line networks have a couple of limitations worth mentioning. One is that some power-line networks don't work well with bidirectional printer cables: You need to disable the features that let the printer give feedback to the computer, such as telling the computer that it's out of ink or that it's managed to jam again on your expensive letterhead.

A second limitation is that, because multiple apartments or even houses can be on the same ring main, power-line networking can inadvertently network you with your neighbors. So it's vital that you implement security on a power-line network to protect your data and your devices.

Choosing Hardware for a Wireless Network

Choosing hardware for a wireless network is both easier and harder than choosing hardware for a wired network. It's easier in that you need less equipment—you can skip the cables for a start—but harder in that you should evaluate that equipment even more carefully than you would wired networking equipment.

For a simple wireless network involving two computers, you need nothing more than a pair of wireless network interface cards. For desktop computers, PCI card network interface cards are usually the best choice. For portable computers, PC Card or CardBus network interface cards are usually the only viable choice.

NOTE *You can get wireless 802.11b network interface cards with USB connections, but even wireless's unexciting speeds can overtax USB 1.0's bandwidth. USB 1.0 can manage a maximum of 12Mbps for all the devices on the bus; 802.11 wireless devices can manage a maximum of 11Mbps, so if anything else is taking up bandwidth on the bus, you won't get the maximum wireless rate. At this writing, USB 2.0 devices are becoming available, which will make wireless USB NICs much more viable. Having a wireless NIC dangling off the back of your computer doesn't improve its aesthetics, but it gives you more flexibility in pointing the NIC's built-in antenna at its access point than PCI mounting does.*

For a more complex or more capable wireless network, get a wireless access point for the wireless network interface cards to connect to. The access point typically plugs into your Ethernet hub, forming a wireless bridge to the network and letting the wireless computers access the wired portions of the network.

Usually it's best to get all your wireless equipment from the same manufacturer or from manufacturers known to be friendly to each other. In theory, standards-based 802.11b devices are able to interoperate with each other, and standards-based 802.11a devices can interoperate with each other (but not with 802.11b devices). In practice, many of them sulk or resort to data rates low enough to make you regret the experiment.

When evaluating wireless networking equipment, keep the following considerations in mind:

Price With wireless networking equipment, you'll have a hard time forgetting this consideration, but don't buy anything cheap and dysfunctional.

Range If you've used cordless phones, it'll come as no surprise that the maximum range listed for most wireless network cards turns out to be wildly optimistic or achievable only under atmospheric conditions and surroundings that can be recreated in laboratories but not real life. As mentioned earlier, some 802.11a devices available at this writing claim to deliver 6Mbps at 1200 feet—plenty far enough to work wirelessly on your laptop at your local coffee shop or bar, perhaps, while maintaining a connection to your home network. Typically, the ranges you'll experience in the real world are far less. Try to get a demo of a device's range before buying if at all possible.

External Antenna Attachment   If you need to extend the range of wireless networking equipment, make sure the cards and access point you buy have a socket for attaching an external antenna.

Roaming   Usually more of a consideration in offices than in home buildings, roaming is worth thinking about if you need wireless access from an area greater than a single access point can cover. First, make sure that the network interface cards and access points you buy can handle roaming, so that you'll be able to move from one access point's coverage to the next's without dropping your network connection. (If you just need to be able to establish a connection from the garden or the garage, you won't necessarily need roaming—you can disconnect from the network, go to the garden or garage, and establish a new connection with the nearest access point.) And second, work out how many access points you need.

Number of access points   From the range and the need for roaming, establish the number of access points you need to provide effective coverage for your building or area.

Placement of access points   Whether you get one access point, two, or ten, you need to place them optimally in order to balance the widest possible coverage with the fastest possible connections. The nearer you are to an access point, the better your chances of getting the full data rate the hardware supports.

Up Next

This chapter has discussed why you might implement a network in your home or home office; the different network architectures, physical topologies, and logical topologies available to you; and the different types of networking equipment. It has suggested how to approach choosing the type of network you want and the types of network equipment you'll need for it.

The next chapter discusses how to set up the network.

Chapter 31

Building a Home or Home-Office Network

THIS CHAPTER DISCUSSES HOW to build an effective network for your home or your home office. It assumes that you've read the previous chapter, decided on the network type you want to use, and purchased the necessary hardware for it.

This chapter starts with arguably the simplest type of network that you can create: a direct connection from one computer to another using a parallel cable, a serial cable, or infrared rays. Direct connections are useful for infrequent networking—for example, for transferring files from one computer to another. The chapter then moves on to setting up a regular network (wired or wireless) by using the Network Setup Wizard.

This chapter covers the following topics:

◆ The different ways of setting up a network with XP

◆ Setting up a direct connection via cables or infrared

◆ Installing your network hardware

◆ Setting up a network using the Network Setup Wizard

◆ Browsing the network

◆ Mapping and disconnecting network drives

◆ Changing your computer's workgroup

◆ Connecting Macs and Linux boxes to the network

The Different Ways of Setting Up a Network with XP Home

You can set up a network with XP Home in several different ways:

◆ You can connect two computers with a serial cable, a parallel cable, or infrared ports and use the New Connection Wizard to create a direct connection between them.

- You can install network hardware and then run the Network Setup Wizard and perform most of your network configuration in one fell swoop. Provided that you're satisfied with a Windows-only network and a basic if effective network design, the Network Setup Wizard can get you networking very easily and efficiently.

- If you add additional computers to the network, you can run the Network Setup Wizard to configure their pieces of the network.

- If you install your network hardware piecemeal, or if you want a heterogeneous network (for example, including a Linux server), you'll need to perform some configuration manually.

The Network Setup Wizard does a creditable job of creating a peer-to-peer network with these basic parameters:

- It uses the nonroutable 192.168.0.*x* TCP/IP subnet and implements a Dynamic Host Configuration Protocol (DHCP) allocator on the computer that's sharing its Internet connection. The DHCP allocator gets the IP address 192.168.0.1 and assigns IP addresses on-the-fly to each computer that joins the network.

- It creates a workgroup called MSHOME (or another name of your choosing). (As you'll see, it's a good idea to change the name of the workgroup, especially if you're using a cable modem.)

- It shares the Internet connection you designate with every computer on the network so that each computer can start the connection and disconnect it as necessary.

- It automatically implements Internet Connection Firewall (ICF) to protect your network from probes and attacks across your Internet connection. Because XP Home shares folders by default, using ICF is vital.

- It automatically shares the \Shared Documents\ folder on each computer with every computer on the network.

- It automatically shares any printers that it can find with every computer on the network.

You can change any of these default settings after using the Network Setup Wizard to set up your network, as described in this chapter. Alternatively, you can avoid the Network Setup Wizard almost entirely and set up your network manually, as described in the next chapter.

Setting Up a Direct Connection

If you just need to transfer files from one computer to another once or occasionally, create a direct connection using a serial port, parallel port, or infrared port. You then configure one computer as the host computer and the other computer as the guest computer, connect the two with the cables or infrared rays, and establish the connection. The guest computer can then access files on the host computer. The host computer can't access files on the guest computer, but the guest computer can upload files to the host computer, so you can transfer files back and forth easily enough.

TIP   *If you'll need to connect the two computers frequently, you'll be better off using a network connection than a direct connection. If both computers have FireWire ports, you can connect them to each other with a six-pin to six-pin (6–6) FireWire cable. If both have network interface cards, you can connect them to each other with a crossover cable—a cable that reverses the wires that send and receive signals so that connection doesn't need to pass through a hub or switch.*

Infrared, Parallel, or Serial?

Which port you use depends on which ports your computer has and which of them are available. But your order of preference should be as follows:

1. Infrared port   Of these three types of port, infrared ports offer the fastest connection—up to 4Mbps for an IrDA 2.0 connection, or between a third and a half of 10BaseT speeds. This speed is fast enough for most networking purposes, including playing streaming video. (IrDA 1.0, on the other hand, offers a miserly 115Kbps—about the speed of a serial port.) Most laptop computers have IrDA ports built in; pre-1998 laptops tend to have IrDA 1.0 ports, post-1998 laptops mostly have IrDA 2.0. However, most of these ports get so little use that the manufacturers might as well not have bothered. That's because IrDA has remained firmly the province of laptop computers, and few multiple-computer people have two or more laptops—most have one laptop and one desktop. You *can* add IrDA ports to desktops, typically via USB or a serial port (USB is preferable, because a serial port isn't fast enough), but most people prefer to use parallel or serial cables or network cards for networking instead.

2. Parallel cable   Parallel cables offer as easy a way to connect two computers as serial cables, and they can be much faster. A common-or-garden parallel cable offers speeds of around 400Kbps, but you can also get enhanced parallel cables specifically designed for file transfer that offer speeds of up to 4Mbps—nothing like as fast as Fast Ethernet, but more than satisfactory for performing backups, transferring files, installing programs, and sharing anything but the fastest Internet connections.

The main disadvantage to using parallel ports is that they tend to be in use by printers, multimedia card readers, or MP3 players.

TIP   *If you choose to use a parallel-cable connection, check the BIOS settings on your computers to make sure that the parallel port you're using is running in the fastest mode possible. Most modern parallel ports offer a standard setting, an Enhanced Parallel Port (EPP) setting, and an Enhanced Capabilities Port (ECP) setting. ECP mode is usually used for printers, while EPP mode is often used for scanners, digital cameras, and the like. If your BIOSes support EPP or ECP, try these, as they should give you much faster data transfer than the standard setting.*

3. Serial cable   Serial cables are much slower than parallel cables, managing only 115Kbps, but they're good enough to transfer files in a pinch. If you're planning to back up a large number of files, or to install a large program over a serial connection, plan plenty of time for doing it. For example, you might want to set it running and leave it going overnight.

As with parallel ports, your serial ports (or port—many computers offer only one nowadays) may be occupied for other purposes. While you can add a couple of serial ports or parallel ports to a desktop easily enough by using an add-in card, you'd probably be better off spending the same time, money, and effort getting and installing a network card instead.

To establish a connection via IrDA, keep the limitations of infrared firmly in mind and position the computers accordingly:

Distance   Keep the distance between the computers as short as possible. In theory, IrDA works over distances of up to three feet. In practice, you'll find it much more reliable over distances of an inch to a foot.

Horizontal alignment   Keep the angle of alignment between the IrDA ports as close to 90 degrees as possible. An IrDA port throws out a 15–30-degree arc of infrared light, but the signal is strongest in the middle of the arc.

Vertical alignment   Position the two IrDA ports on the same level as each other. IrDA ports don't spread the beam out much vertically, so if the ports are at different levels, you may not be able to establish a satisfactory connection.

Clear path   Make sure the path between the IrDA ports is clear. Even a sheet of paper can block infrared transmission quite effectively.

Avoid direct sunlight   Direct sunlight can interfere with an infrared signal because sunlight contains infrared rays. (Besides, your laptop won't thank you for being placed in direct sunlight.)

Make sure the infrared ports are enabled   Last but far from least, make sure the infrared ports are enabled. Many laptops ship with the infrared ports disabled (partly to conserve battery power, partly as a security measure), so you have to turn them by changing a BIOS setting or using a manufacturer-supplied configuration utility.

Reading this list may make you think that the IrDA ports should be just about kissing each other for maximum effect—and that's not far off true. Get the ports as close to each other as is practical, and you'll experience many fewer problems.

Direct Connection via Cable or Infrared

This section discusses how to create a direct connection via cable or infrared.

CONNECTING THE CABLE

If you're using a cable for the connection, connect it to the appropriate port on each computer.

TIP   If you're buying a parallel or serial cable for the purpose, be sure to get the right type—a serial-port null-modem cable (or asynchronous modem eliminator cable) or parallel-port data-transfer cable with male connections at each end. Many serial cables have male connections at one end and female connections at the other. If you have nine-pin serial ports, get a cable with male DB9 connectors at each end. Most parallel cables are for connecting printers and have a male DB25 connection at one end and a Centronics connector at the other. You need a cable with male DB25 connectors at each end so that you can connect the two parallel ports. Make sure that the cable is specifically designed for PC-to-PC connections. You can get cables with two male DB25s that aren't designed for this purpose; they won't work, and XP won't be able to tell you that the cable is the problem.

SETTING UP THE HOST FOR THE DIRECT CONNECTION

Next, set up the host computer for the direct connection. Before you start, be warned that because of the security features that XP includes, this process is more complicated than setting up the guest computer. It's not exactly difficult, but be prepared to spend a few minutes on it. You need to be logged on as a Computer Administrator user to set up this connection.

To set up the host computer, take the following steps:

1. Choose Start ➤ Connect To ➤ Show All Connections. XP displays the Network Connections folder. If you haven't created a network connection, the Connect To item doesn't appear on the Start menu. Choose Start ➤ Control Panel. XP displays Control Panel. Click the Network and Internet Connections link. XP displays the Network and Internet Connections screen. Click the Network Connections link. XP displays the Network Connections folder. (You can also choose Start ➤ All Programs ➤ Accessories ➤ Communications ➤ Network Connections.)

2. Click the Create a New Connection link in the Network Tasks list. XP starts the New Connection Wizard, which displays its Welcome to the New Connection Wizard page.

3. Click the Next button. The New Connection Wizard displays the Network Connection Type page.

4. Select the Set Up an Advanced Connection option button.

5. Click the Next button. The wizard displays the Advanced Connection Options page.

6. Select the Accept Incoming Connections option button.

7. Click the Next button. The wizard displays the Devices for Incoming Connections page, which lists the modems and direct connections currently available on your computer. When you first set up your computer to accept incoming connections, the Devices for Incoming Connections page doesn't include serial ports (COM ports) in the list. To set up a direct connection via a serial port, leave the check boxes for the parallel port and any modems clear and complete the wizard as described in the rest of this list. Then follow the instructions in the section "Adding a Serial Connection to Your Incoming Connections," immediately after this section.

8. Select the check box for the port or the modem that you want to use for the connection.

9. Click the Next button. The wizard displays the Incoming Virtual Private Network (VPN) Connection page.

10. Select the Do Not Allow Virtual Private Connections option button.

11. Click the Next button. The wizard displays the User Permissions page (shown on the left in Figure 31.1), which lists the users set up on this computer, together with a HelpAssistant user (for Remote Assistance) and a Support user (for getting help from Microsoft).

12. Specify which users may connect via this connection:

    ◆ To enable one of the listed users to use the connection, select their check box.

    ◆ To add a user, click the Add button. The wizard displays the New User dialog box (shown on the right in Figure 31.1). Enter the user's details—username, full name, password, and confirmation of password—and click the OK button. The wizard adds the user to the Users Allowed to Connect list and selects their check box.

FIGURE 31.1

On the User Permissions page of the New Connection Wizard, specify which users may connect to the host computer. To add a user, click the Add button and work in the New User dialog box (right).

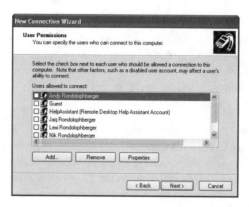

◆ To remove one of the listed users *from your system* (not just from the list of users allowed to use this connection), select their entry in the Users Allowed to Connect list and click the Remove button. The wizard displays the Incoming Connections Warning dialog box (shown in Figure 31.2). If you're sure you want to remove the user, click the Yes button.

FIGURE 31.2

When you go to delete a user from the Users Allowed to Connect list, XP displays this Incoming Connections Warning dialog box to warn you that you're about to remove the user permanently from your system.

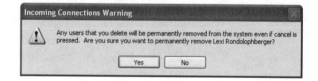

◆ To change a user's password, select the user in the Users Allowed to Connect list and click the Properties button. The wizard displays the Properties dialog box for the user. On the General page, change the password in the Password text box and the Confirm Password text box. Click the OK button. XP closes the Properties dialog box.

WARNING   *Changing a user's password in the Properties dialog box changes it for logging on to XP as well.*

◆ If you want a user to be able to use callback for a modem connection, select the user in the Users Allowed to Connect list and click the Properties button. The wizard displays the Properties dialog box for the user. Click the Callback tab. XP displays the Callback page. Then select the Do Not Allow Callback option button (the default setting), the Allow the Caller to Set the Callback Number option button, or the Always Use the Following Callback Number option button. Not allowing callback is the most secure option, followed by the option for specifying the number that must always be used. Allowing the caller to set the callback number is not secure but may be necessary when the caller will be calling in from the road. Click the OK button. XP closes the Properties dialog box.

13. Click the Next button. The wizard displays the Networking Software page (shown in Figure 31.3). If you think this dialog box looks familiar from when you set up XP, you're right.

FIGURE 31.3

On the Networking Software page of the New Connection Wizard, specify which networking components the host computer should use for the connection.

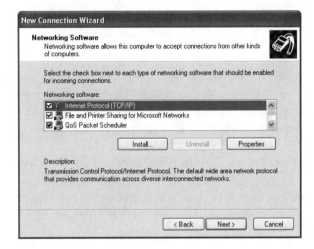

14. Select (or leave selected) the check boxes for the networking components that you want XP to use for the cable connection:

◆ If a component's check box is shaded, it's vital to the connection, and you can't disable the component for the connection.

◆ If you try to clear the check box for File and Printer Sharing for Microsoft Networks, XP displays the Incoming Connections Warning dialog box shown in Figure 31.4. This dialog box warns you that in order to disable this networking component, you need to stop the Server service, and that doing so stops sharing on any currently shared folders or printers. Choose the No button in this dialog box if you don't want to take this (relatively drastic) step. If you do want to turn off sharing, click the Yes button. XP displays the Computer Management window. Expand the Services and Applications branch of the tree, then select the Services item. In the right list box, select the Server item, then click the Stop the Service link. XP displays the Stop Other Services dialog box, warning you that stopping Server will also stop Computer Browser (and perhaps other services, depending on your setup). Click the Yes button. XP displays the Service Control dialog box while it stops the Server service. When the service is stopped, the Server entry in the Status column no longer displays *Started*. When you've finished using the cable connection, restart the Server service by selecting it in the Services list and clicking the Start the Service link.

FIGURE 31.4

It's best not to try to disable File and Printer Sharing for Microsoft Networks for the cable connection, because doing so also disables any shared folders or printers on your computer.

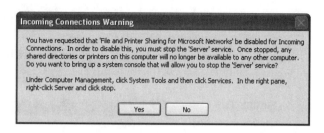

15. Click the Next button. The wizard displays the Completing the New Connection Wizard page, which tells you that the connection is named *Incoming Connections*.

16. Click the Finish button. The New Connection Wizard closes, naming the connection *Incoming Connections* and adding it to the Incoming category in your Network Connections folder.

ADDING A SERIAL CONNECTION TO YOUR INCOMING CONNECTIONS

If you want to use a serial connection for the incoming connection, you need to retrace your steps a bit, because XP hides the serial ports to encourage you to favor the parallel port (because the parallel port is usually a better choice). Take the following steps:

1. Follow steps 1 to 5 in the previous list to reach the Advanced Connection Options page of the New Connection Wizard.

2. Select the Connection Directly to Another Computer option button.

3. Click the Next button. The wizard displays the Host or Guest? page.

4. Select the Host option button.

5. Click the Next button. The wizard displays the Connection Device page.

6. In the Device for This Connection drop-down list, select the appropriate Communications Port entry.

7. Click the Next button. The wizard displays the User Permissions page.

8. Change user permissions if necessary (see step 12 of the previous list) and then use the Next button and the following Finish button to finish the New Connection Wizard.

SETTING UP THE GUEST COMPUTER FOR THE CABLE CONNECTION

Next, follow these steps to set up the guest computer for the connection:

1. Follow steps 1 to 5 in the previous list to reach the Advanced Connection Options page of the New Connection Wizard.

2. Select the Connect Directly to Another Computer option button.

3. Click the Next button. The wizard displays the Host or Guest? page.

4. Select the Guest option button.

5. Click the Next button. The wizard displays the Connection Name page.

6. In the Computer Name text box, enter the name you want to use for the connection. You don't need to enter the name of the other computer; this name is for your benefit.

7. Click the Next button. The wizard displays the Select a Device page.

8. In the Select a Device drop-down list, select the port to use. For example, select Direct Parallel (LPT1) to use your printer port.

9. Click the Next button. The wizard displays the Completing the New Connection Wizard page, which summarizes the choices you've made.

10. If you want the wizard to create a shortcut on your Desktop for this connection, select the Add a Shortcut to This Connection to My Desktop check box.

11. Click the Finish button. The New Connection Wizard closes itself, creates the connection, adds it to the Network Connections window, adds a shortcut to the Desktop if appropriate, and displays the connection's Connect dialog box. Go directly to step 3 in the next section if you want to establish a connection right now.

TIP *You can copy a direct connection by right-clicking it and choosing the Create Copy item from the context menu. You can then adjust the properties of the copy to connect differently from the original—for example, using a different port.*

ESTABLISHING A CABLE CONNECTION

Once you've set up the host and the guest, and connected the two via the cable (or configured infrared), you should be ready to connect.

To connect, take the following steps on the guest computer. (This example uses a parallel connection.)

1. Choose Start ➤ Connect To ➤ Show All Connections. XP displays the Network Connections window.

2. Double-click the icon for the connection. XP displays the Connect dialog box. Figure 31.5 shows an example.

FIGURE 31.5

Connecting to another computer via a parallel connection

3. Enter your username *for the other computer* in the User Name text box and your password in the Password text box. If you want XP to save your password (a convenience, but a security threat), select the Save This User Name and Password for the Following Users check box for the connection and choose the Me Only option button or the Anyone Who Uses This Computer option button as appropriate.

4. Click the Connect button. XP attempts to connect via the specified connection.

As with an Internet connection, XP displays in the notification area on both the guest computer and the host computer an icon showing two computers to represent the direct connection. To see the status of the connection, hover the mouse pointer over this icon until XP displays a pop-up, or click the icon to display the Status dialog box for the connection.

Once you're connected, you can work with the shared folders on the host computer by choosing Start ➤ My Computer and then clicking the My Network Places link.

HANGING UP THE DIRECT CONNECTION

To hang up the connection, right-click the icon and choose Disconnect from the context menu. You can disconnect the connection from either computer.

TIP   You can connect a computer running Windows 9x to a computer running XP by using the Direct Cable Connection feature on the Windows 9x computer. (To run Direct Cable Connection, choose Start ➤ Programs ➤ Accessories ➤ Communications ➤ Direct Cable Connection. If there's no Direct Cable Connection item on the Communications submenu, you'll need to install from the Communications item on the Windows Setup page of the Add/Remove Programs Properties dialog box.) In many cases, it's easier to set up the Windows 9x computer as the host for the direct connection and the XP computer as the guest rather than the other way around. This is because Windows 9x's security and authentication model is much more open than XP's.

EXPERT KNOWLEDGE: TROUBLESHOOTING DIRECT CONNECTIONS

Direct connections can be a bit twitchy, for reasons that usually remain unexplained. If you're having trouble establishing a direct connection, here are a couple of things to try:

◆ First, check the cable (if you're using a cable): Make sure it's correctly attached at both ends, and that it's the right kind of cable. You need to do this because XP isn't as smart with cable connections as it might be. In particular, XP sometimes displays the Connecting *Connection Name* message box containing the *Verifying Username and Password* message when it hasn't actually contacted the other computer. If you suspect this is happening, try disconnecting the cable and seeing if XP produces the same error when the computers are definitely not connected.

◆ Second, try switching the host and guest roles. Sometimes trying to establish a connection from Computer A to Computer B produces nothing but error messages and denials that usernames and passwords are valid when you know they're fine, but connecting from Computer B to Computer A is a snap.

Installing Your Network Hardware

To put your Ethernet network together, install your network hardware by following these basic steps:

1. Install a network interface card in each computer.

2. If your network uses a hub or switch (for example, if you're creating a Fast Ethernet network using a star configuration), position the hub or switch in a convenient central location. If you're using multiple hubs or switches, position them so that each is located conveniently for the computers that will connect to it, and then connect the hubs or switches via the uplink port on one and a regular port on the other.

3. For a regular (wired) network interface card, connect a network cable from the card to one of the ports on the hub or switch.

4. Power on the hub or switch.

5. Power on each computer in turn. Use the Found New Hardware Wizard or Add Hardware Wizard as described in Chapter 14 to install the driver for each network card.

When the Found New Hardware Wizard or the Add Hardware Wizard has finished setting up the network card, it displays a notification-area pop-up suggesting that you run the Network Setup Wizard to configure your network settings. You can start the Network Setup Wizard by clicking this pop-up. Alternatively, you can start the Network Setup Wizard manually as described in the section "Setting Up a Network Using the Network Setup Wizard," a little later in this chapter.

Reduced to their essentials, those steps for installing the network look straightforward enough—even friendly. But as with many things in meat-space, the devil is in the details. The next sections discuss how to install network cards, how to cable an Ethernet network, and how to create a FireWire network.

Installing Network Cards

Installing a network card is typically straightforward in XP as long as XP supports the network card. If in doubt, check the HCL before buying a new card.

◆ For a PCI card or an ISA card, shut down XP, switch off the computer (if shutting down XP didn't do so), and unplug the power. Open the case and ground yourself to dissipate any static electricity by touching a metal part of the case. Locate an empty slot of the right type, install the card, and close the case again. Plug the power back in and power up your computer again.

◆ For a PC Card or CardBus card, insert it while the computer is running.

◆ For a USB Ethernet connection, plug it in while the computer is running.

XP should detect the card automatically and display the Found New Hardware Wizard to walk you through the process of selecting and installing the appropriate driver for the card.

If XP seems not to detect the card, run the Add Hardware Wizard. If the wizard doesn't think there's any new hardware, check Device Manager to see if the device has been added without notification or without your noticing.

INSTALLING TWO OR MORE NETWORK CARDS IN A COMPUTER

If you need to share a broadband connection from a computer without using a hardware router, or if you need to connect to two or more discrete networks, you'll need to install two or more network cards in the same computer. You may also need to install multiple network cards in the same computer if you need to bridge two networks (as discussed in the section "Connecting Two Networks via a Bridge" in Chapter 32).

Provided that both your network cards are compatible with XP and that you have enough slots of the appropriate type available in your computer, installing two network cards should be little more difficult than installing just one. The most important thing is to avoid any confusion as to which card is which—in particular, to avoid creating two network connections named "Local Area Connection" and then having to figure out which is actually your broadband connection.

If the computer already has one of the network cards installed and configured, check the card's configuration and make sure that it's working as it should. If the connection is named Local Area Connection and the other connection will receive the same name, rename the connection to something more informative before installing the second network card and configuring its connection. Label the card so that you'll be able to tell easily which it is when you've installed the second card. Then go ahead and install the second card.

If you're installing both network cards from scratch, install them one at a time. Again, once you've got the first card and connection working, rename it to avoid any confusion with the second card. Then install the second card and configure it. Rename the resulting connection if necessary, and label the card.

Cabling an Ethernet Network

On a scale of difficulty from breaking an egg to building a house, cabling an Ethernet network falls well at the lower end of the scale—say, roughly the same difficulty as installing internal telephone cables. And like installing telephone cables, you can cable an Ethernet network quickly and dirtily or you can do the job properly.

SHOULD YOU DIY OR PAY A PROFESSIONAL?

If all your computers inhabit the same room, or if you're content to have the Ethernet cables trail across the floor from room to room, cabling can be as easy and swift as uncoiling the cables, plugging each into the appropriate sockets on the hub or switch and the computers and other network-enabled devices, and supplying power to the hub or switch. In other words, you can have your network in place in a matter of minutes.

At the other extreme, if you want your network cables to run almost invisibly from room to room and emerge tidily at wall plates into which you can plug patch cables when you need to connect, you'll need to invest some time and effort. You'll need to buy some tools (unless you already have all you need). Unless you're happy spelunking in drywall, ceilings, and basements, you might want to think about calling in a professional cabling contractor instead. A professional's rates are likely to seem steep, but using a professional should get you a neat and effective cabling system that will add value to your property rather than detract from it. As usual when hiring someone for a task, see if your friends or colleagues can recommend anybody; ask for references; check how quickly they'll fix any problem that crops up; and make sure that the deal includes full documentation on the specifications, location, configuration, and upkeep of the cabling system.

NOTE *If you're a DIY person, you may not like the idea of paying a cabling contractor to do work that you can do yourself. But at the very least, invest in a book on cabling such as* Cabling: The Complete Guide to Network Wiring, Second Edition *(by David Groth, Jim McBee, and David Barnett; Sybex, 2001) that will help you analyze your requirements and learn the most efficient and cost-effective ways of fulfilling them.*

If your property is cabling-friendly—say, you're doing a major refit, or you're having a new house built—consider having it wired to the Residential Telecommunications Cabling Standard, or ANSI/TIA/EIA-507-A for short. (That's one of the less usual values of "short.") This standard calls for one outlet in each bedroom, family room, and study, one outlet in the kitchen, and one outlet in any wall that has an unbroken space of 12 feet or more or in which a device would have to be 25 feet or more from an outlet (in other words, two or more outlets in big rooms). Under Grade 1 of this standard, each outlet is connected to one cable. Under Grade 2, each outlet is connected to two cables.

If that brief précis of ANSI/TIA/EIA-507-A raised your eyebrows, rest assured that you're not alone. For most homes in 2002, Grade 1 is way surplus to requirements, and Grade 2 seems like serious overkill. But as home-entertainment electronics and computers continue to grow into each other's roles, many people will need to be able to transfer data easily from one part of their home to another. For example, having two cables running to each room will let you share video from one room to another without swamping your computer network. Or you can integrate your telephone system with the network, so that you can make voice calls from any room. (Or you could Internet-enable your fridge.) Besides, when you're installing cable, the hardware costs—the cable itself, the wall plates, the patch panel—tend to be far less than the labor costs, so it makes sense to go the whole hog if you can afford it.

DOING IT YOURSELF

When installing network cables yourself, approach the job in as focused and rational a way as possible. Assess your needs. Work out the best placement for the hub or switch (or hubs or switches). Measure the distances involved. Round up the equipment. And then install the network.

TIP *It's tempting to go hog-wild and try to set up your whole network in a grand slam—pull all the cables, punch them down into wall plates or a patch panel, attach the computers and other devices, and then power on the whole lot at once. If everything works, you'll feel a wonderful surge of techno-potency (and you may even deserve it). But if everything doesn't work, you'll have the mother of all troubleshooting jobs on your plate. So it's much better to start small: Connect two computers, make sure everything's working, and then build from there, adding one computer at a time. Doing so will let you identify any problems far more easily and quickly than the grand-slam approach.*

Choose Home-Run Cabling if Possible

If possible, use a star topology with *home-run cabling*—cabling in which each wall outlet is connected back to the same patch panel or switch—rather than having outlets *daisy-chained* (connected in series). A home-run arrangement gives better performance with less degradation than a daisy-chained arrangement. It also makes troubleshooting easier.

Choosing the Location for the Hub or Switch

If your computers are spread out through your home (or another building), choosing a location for the hub or switch becomes a key decision. Ideally, in a small area, you'll use a single hub or switch to keep your network simple. But you can use multiple hubs or switches if necessary to avoid running a large number of wires running along the same course. Figure 31.6 shows an example of a network layout using two switches.

FIGURE 31.6

To avoid running long cables, you can use multiple hubs or switches connected by the uplink port or cascade port to the central hub or switch.

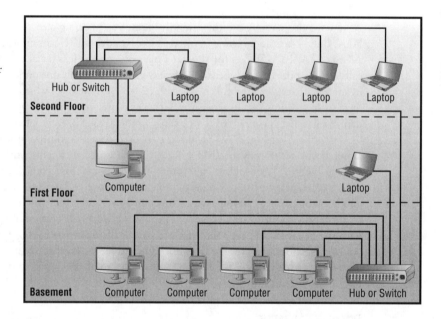

Each hub or switch needs to be powered, so the location will need to be within striking distance of a power outlet. Alternatively, look for a hub or switch that can use Power over Ethernet (PoE), drawing power via the Ethernet cable from another device.

Most hubs and switches have an *uplink port* or *cascade port* to which you can connect a regular Ethernet cable from a standard port on another hub or switch. (On some hubs and switches, there's a switch to toggle one of the ports between being a standard port and an uplink port.) If the hub or switch doesn't have an uplink port, you can connect it by using a crossover cable to a standard port.

Measuring the Distances

Measure the distance that the cables will need to run from each computer to the hub. Make sure that you include any vertical rises and drops that the cable run will need to include. Then, if you're cutting custom lengths of cable, allow a few feet extra on each cable to make sure they're long enough. (As with anything cut to length, you can always cut it shorter if necessary, but it's hard to make it longer.) If you're buying ready-made cable, buy the next longer length. You can always coil up any surplus length and stow it away discreetly.

Rounding Up the Equipment

Next, round up the equipment you need. At the minimum, you'll need a hub or switch and either ready-made patch cables of the appropriate lengths or a reel of cable, a cutting tool, and a cable stripper. If you're going to create your own patch cables, you'll need a crimping tool and an RJ-45 die for it. If you're going to bring the wires to a patch panel or wall plates, you'll need the panel or the plates and a matching punch-down tool for attaching the wires.

If you need to run cables through walls or between floors of a building, you'll need conventional builder's tools such as a drill and a Sheetrock saw.

For attaching cables to surfaces such as baseboards or floors, you'll need either a cable tacker (also known as a *cable stapler*) designed for the job and loaded with the right caliber of cable staples or a hammer and rigid cable clips (which you can get from a computer-supply store). For straight runs of cable, you may want to use *raceways* (wiring channels) and cable guards to hide the cables and give them some degree of protection. *Don't* use ordinary staples to secure cables, because it's very easy to drive them in too far and so damage the cable. (If you *must* use ordinary staples, do so with great care.)

For making sure the cables are working properly, a remote cable tester can save you a great deal of time and grief. A *remote cable tester* is a device into which you plug both ends of the cable you want to test and then send a signal through it to see if the wires are connected correctly. The most useful models have a detachable transmitter unit that you either use attached to the unit (for testing a patch cable) or attach to the far end of the cable run you're testing and then use the main unit on the near end of the cable.

Running the Cable

Once you've rounded up the equipment, you should be ready to get down and dirty. Here are basic tips for running cable:

- When securing the cable to baseboards, desks, floors, or other surfaces, do so carefully.

- Cat 5 UTP is reasonably resilient, but don't stress it any more than you must. When routing cable around baseboards, try not to bend it too sharply. If you end up pulling lengths of cable through wall or floor cavities yourself, be careful not to overstretch it, because that can degrade the quality of the signal or prevent the cable from working at all. You *can* get cable lubricant for greasing the cable's way around tight corners, but the lubricant means that not only does the cable tend to pick up any dirt it passes but it also sets into a facsimile of ancient crud in remarkably short order. You'll often do better to pull the cable in shorter stages (around one corner, then around a second) rather than longer stages (around both corners at once) to reduce the strain on the cable.

- When routing your cables, avoid electric wiring and any electrically noisy devices (such as air conditioning or refrigerators).

Connecting the Hub or Switch

Most hubs and switches have one or more lights for each port. At a minimum, most have a light to show whether the port is active. When you plug a cable into the hub or switch and into a functioning network card at the other end, the light should go on, showing that the cable is connected correctly.

Many dual-speed hubs and switches also have lights to show whether each port is running at 10Mbps or 100Mbps. Some hubs and switches also have lights to show whether the port is using full duplex or half duplex transmission. (Full duplex uses two pairs of wires to transmit data, while half duplex uses one pair.)

TROUBLESHOOTING: NO LIGHT ON HUB OR NETWORK CARD

If you don't get a light on the hub (or switch) or on the network card when you connect a computer or other device with a cable, the connection isn't working. Check the three candidates—the hub, the network card on the device, and the cabling—by taking the following steps:

1. Check that the hub is powered on. Chances are that it has a power light that'll be on if it's getting power. If you've connected cables to other ports, those lights should be on.

2. Check that you're not using a crossover cable by mistake. Crossover cables can look exactly the same as regular patch cables, but they won't transmit data to a standard port. (Crossover cables can transmit data to an uplink port just fine. See the next section for a description of uplink ports.)

3. Check you haven't plugged a standard patch cable into an uplink port.

4. Check the patch cable by using it to replace a patch cable that's you know is good—for example, one that's connecting another computer to one of the ports on the hub. Replace the patch cable if it's bad.

5. If the patch cable works for the second computer, try connecting the first computer to a different port on the hub. If that works, you've got a bad port. If it doesn't work, you've got a bad network card. Try replacing the network card and trying again.

6. If the hub, patch cable, and network card all check out okay, check your cabling, wall plates, and patch panel (if you have one). To test these most effectively, get a remote cable tester.

TIP *If you need to connect just two computers via Ethernet, you don't need a hub or switch. Instead, get a crossover cable—a cable that reverses the wires that send and receive signals so that connection doesn't need to pass through a hub or switch—and plug it into each network card, and you'll be done. If the crossover cable isn't clearly marked as such, mark it before you forget, because otherwise crossover cables can be easy to confuse with regular Ethernet cables.*

Creating a FireWire Network

By comparison with cabling an Ethernet network, cabling a FireWire network is simplicity itself: You don't need a hub or switch, and the length limit of FireWire cables (15 feet) reduces the number of decisions you need to make.

If any of the computers you want to join to the network doesn't have a FireWire port, install a FireWire PCI card, PC Card, or CardBus card in it.

Then, with the computers running, connect each computer on the network to the next computer with one cable. Make sure that you don't connect any of the computers to any other computer with two cables.

Installing a Wireless Network

What you need to do when installing a wireless network depends on the type of wireless network.

For a wireless-only network—one in which all the computers communicate with each other via wireless—you won't need to install any cables. You'll need to install a wireless network card in each computer that will participate in the network and install a driver for each wireless network card. Depending on the type of wireless network card, you may need to install wireless client-management software or an additional networking service. Your wireless network cards should come with full details of all hoops you need to jump through to get the hardware working.

If you're adding a wireless section to your network by using a wireless access point that includes bridging capabilities, connect the wireless access point to the network hub with a cable. You'll then need to run some configuration software on the access point in order to set its IP address, wireless ID, and network group.

CONNECTING TO A WIRELESS NETWORK

If your wireless access point is configured to broadcast its service set identifier (SSID), as most access points do by default, you should be able to connect to it almost effortlessly. When you log on to XP on your wireless-enabled PC, or when you insert your wireless network adapter (for example, a PC Card adapter) in your computer, XP automatically loads the drivers and searches for an available wireless network and connects to it. XP then displays a notification-area pop-up like that shown in Figure 31.7 telling you that the connection has been established and giving you the connection strength (Excellent, Very Good, Good, Low, or Very Low).

FIGURE 31.7

XP displays a notification-area pop-up telling you the strength of the wireless connection.

If your wireless network isn't broadcasting its SSID, you'll need to configure your wireless network connection as described below. (Disabling SSID broadcasts on a wireless access point is a good idea for security, as you'll see in the section "Securing a Wireless Network" in Chapter 33.)

To configure your wireless network connection and connect to a wireless network, take the following steps:

1. Choose Start ➢ Connect To ➢ Show All Connections. XP displays the Network Connections screen.

2. Right-click the Wireless Network Connection icon (it may have been renamed) and choose View Available Wireless Networks from the context menu. XP displays the Connect to Wireless Network dialog box (shown in Figure 31.8).

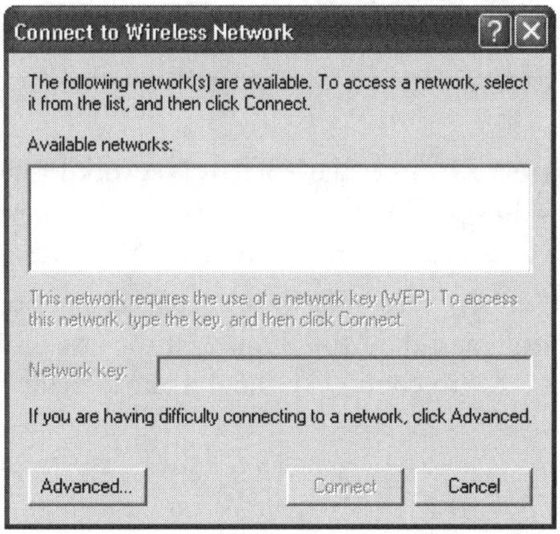

FIGURE 31.8

If the Connect to Wireless Network dialog box lists no available wireless networks, click the Advanced button to configure a connection.

3. Click the Advanced button. XP displays the Wireless Network Connection Properties dialog box with the Wireless Networks page foremost (shown on the left in Figure 31.9).

FIGURE 31.9

From the Wireless Networks page of the Wireless Network Connection Properties dialog box (left), display the Wireless Network Properties dialog box to add a new wireless connection.

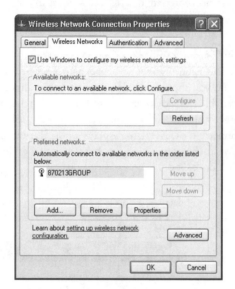

4. The list box in the Available Networks group box lists the networks that are available. If necessary, click the Refresh button to search for networks that have just become available (for example, if you've moved within range of an access point since displaying the Wireless Network Connection Properties dialog box).

5. To add a new connection, click the Add button. XP displays the Wireless Network Properties dialog box (shown on the right in Figure 31.9).

6. In the Network Name (SSID) text box, enter the SSID of the network.

7. In the Wireless Network Key (WEP) group box, choose settings for data encryption and network authentication as necessary. See the section "Securing a Wireless Network" in Chapter 33 for a discussion of these settings.

8. If the wireless network is a peer-to-peer network rather than one that uses an access point, select the This Is a Computer-to-Computer Network; Wireless Access Points Are Not Used check box.

9. Click the OK button. XP closes the Wireless Network Properties dialog box, returns you to the Wireless Networks page of the Wireless Network Connection Properties dialog box, and adds the network to the list box in the Preferred Networks group box.

10. If the list box in the Preferred Networks group box contains more than one entry, use the Move Up button and the Move Down buttons to shuffle the entries into the order in which you want XP to connect to them if more than one network is available at the same time.

11. If necessary, you can choose further settings by clicking the Advanced button and working in the resulting Advanced dialog box (shown in Figure 31.10). The Advanced dialog box offers the following settings:

Networks to Access group box Select the Any Available Network (Access Point Preferred) option button, the Access Point (Infrastructure) Networks Only option button, or the Computer-to-Computer (Ad Hoc) Networks Only option button as appropriate. The Any Available Network (Access Point Preferred) option button is the default.

Automatically Connect to Non-Preferred Networks check box Select this check box (which is cleared by default) if you want XP to automatically connect to wireless networks that you haven't added to the Preferred Networks list on the Wireless Networks page of the Wireless Network Connection Properties dialog box. This option can be useful if you often use public wireless networks (for example, in airports), but you may prefer to connect to such networks manually when you need to.

FIGURE 31.10

You can choose further wireless networking settings in the Advanced dialog box.

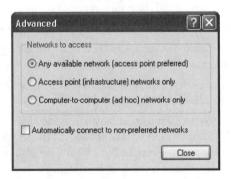

12. When you've finished choosing settings, click the OK button in the Wireless Network Connection Properties dialog box.

NOTE You can edit an existing wireless network connection by either selecting it in the list box in the Available Networks group box and clicking the Configure button or by selecting it in the list box in the Preferred Networks group box and clicking the Properties button. Either action displays the connection in the Wireless Network Properties dialog box, where you can edit it using the techniques described above.

ADDING A PRINTER TO A WIRELESS NETWORK

You can add a printer to a wireless network in any of the following ways:

◆ Connect the printer to one of the computers participating in the network and share it from there.

◆ Connect the printer to a wireless print server and position it wherever best suits the needs of the users who will use it. (As mentioned earlier, you may be able to get a wireless device that combines Internet access with a print server and other features.)

◆ Get a network-aware printer and connect it using a wireless network card or (for a network that's not fully wireless) an Ethernet cable.

Setting Up a Network Using the Network Setup Wizard

This section discusses how to use the Network Setup Wizard to set up a network. The procedure is a little different for the computer that's sharing the Internet connection than for the other computers, so we'll deal with that first.

Setting Up the Computer That's Sharing the Internet Connection

Start with the computer that will share the Internet connection. Before running the Network Setup Wizard, set up your Internet connection as discussed in Chapter 18. Then use the Network Setup Wizard to configure the computer by taking the following steps:

1. Establish your Internet connection.

2. Choose Start ➢ All Programs ➢ Accessories ➢ Communications ➢ Network Setup Wizard. The wizard displays the Welcome to the Network Setup Wizard screen.

3. Click the Next button. The wizard displays the Before You Continue page, which tells you to plug in your devices, turn on all the computers and devices, and connect to the Internet.

4. Click the Next button. The wizard displays the Select a Connection Method page.

5. Make sure the This Computer Connects Directly to the Internet. The Other Computers on My Network Connect to the Internet through This Computer option button is selected.

6. Click the Next button. The wizard displays the Select Your Internet Connection page, which lists the Internet connections available.

7. In the Select Your Internet Connection from the Following List list box, select your Internet connection. In this example, there's no confusion, as the wizard is listing a dial-up connection and the local area network connection. But if you have configured multiple dial-up connections or broadband connections, you may have to pay a little more attention to this choice. XP establishes the connection you chose.

8. Click the Next button. The wizard displays the Give This Computer a Description and Name page.

9. Enter the description for your computer in the Computer Description text box. This description is for your benefit and that of other users of the network, so make it concise and descriptive.

10. In the Computer Name text box, enter the name for your computer. Typically, for dial-up connections and DSL connections, you can choose more or less any name that suits you (within Windows' naming conventions). For cable-modem connections, you may have to use a name designated by your ISP.

11. Click the Next button. The wizard displays the Name Your Network page.

12. In the Workgroup Name text box, enter a name for the network. It's best to use a unique name rather than the default name, MSHOME, in case your network or Internet connection puts you on the same network loop as your neighbors. (For more details, see "Changing Your Computer's Workgroup" later in the chapter.)

13. Click the Next button. The wizard displays the Ready to Apply Network Settings page.

14. Click the Next button. The wizard starts configuring the home network. While it works, it displays the Please Wait page.

15. When the wizard has finished configuring the computer, it displays the You're Almost Done page, which offers to create a network setup disk for use on non-XP computers connecting to the same computer.

16. If you want to create a network setup disk, select the Create a Network Setup Disk option button. Otherwise, select the Just Finish the Wizard; I Don't Need to Run the Wizard on Other Computers option button. (Selecting the Use the Network Setup Disk I Already Have option button or the Use My Windows XP CD option button brings up a page of instructions for using the network setup disk or the CD.)

17. Click the Next button.

   ◆ If you chose the Create a Network Setup Disk option button, the wizard displays the Insert the Disk You Want to Use page.

   ◆ Insert a floppy disk in the floppy drive.

   ◆ If you need to format the floppy disk, click the Format Disk button and use the resulting Format $3\frac{1}{2}$ Floppy dialog box to format the disk as usual. Then click the Close button. XP closes the dialog box.

   ◆ Click the Next button. XP copies files to the floppy and then displays the To Run the Wizard with the Network Setup Disk page, which contains instructions for using the disk.

   ◆ Click the Next button.

18. The wizard displays the Completing the Network Setup Wizard page, which provides links to Help and Support topics on sharing files and folders.

19. Click the Finish button. The Network Setup Wizard closes itself.

Setting Up a Client Computer

Next, set up the first of your client computers. Make sure the Internet connection is still open on the computer you set up to share it, and then take the following steps:

1. Start the Network Setup Wizard:

   ◆ On an XP computer, choose Start ➤ All Programs ➤ Accessories ➤ Communications ➤ Network Setup Wizard. The wizard displays the Welcome to the Network Setup Wizard page.

   ◆ On a computer running an earlier version of 32-bit Windows, put the network setup disk you made earlier in the floppy drive. Open an Explorer window to the floppy drive and double-click the file named NETSETUP (or NETSETUP.EXE, if you've set Windows to show file extensions). The wizard displays three Network Setup Wizard dialog boxes in sequence. The first dialog box tells you that the wizard needs to install network support files on your computer. Click the Yes button. The second dialog box tells you to remove the floppy and warns you that it will prompt you to restart your computer. Remove the floppy and click the OK button. The third dialog box prompts you to restart your computer. Click the Yes button. After the restart, the wizard displays the Welcome to the Network Setup Wizard page.

2. Click the Next button. The wizard displays the Before You Continue page.

3. Click the Next button. The wizard displays the Do You Want to Use the Shared Connection? page (shown in Figure 31.11).

FIGURE 31.11

On the Do You Want to Use the Shared Connection? page of the Network Setup Wizard, consent to using the shared connection.

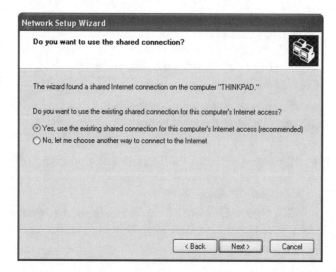

4. If the wizard has identified the right connection, leave the Yes, Use the Existing Shared Connection for This Computer's Internet Access option button selected. If not, select the No, Let Me Choose Another Way to Connect to the Internet option button.

5. Click the Next button.

   ◆ If you chose the No, Let Me Choose Another Way to Connect to the Internet option button, XP displays the Select a Connection Method page.

   ◆ Make sure the This Computer Connects to the Internet through Another Computer on My Network or through a Residential Gateway option button is selected.

   ◆ Click the Next button. If your computer has more than one Internet connection, the wizard displays the Your Computer Has Multiple Connections page. Otherwise, it displays the Give This Computer a Description and Name page.

   ◆ By default, the wizard selects the Determine the Appropriate Connections for Me option button. If you leave this option button selected, the wizard guesses which Internet connection you want to use. If you prefer to choose the connection yourself, select the Let Me Choose the Connections to My Network option button.

   ◆ Click the Next button. The wizard displays the Select the Connections to Bridge page (shown in Figure 31.12), which lists the connections available for bridging.

   ◆ Select the check boxes for the connections you want to bridge. Clear the check box for any direct Internet connection. Then click the Next button. The wizard displays the Give This Computer a Description and Name page.

FIGURE 31.12

On the Select the Connections to Bridge page of the Network Setup Wizard, you can specify which connections to bridge.

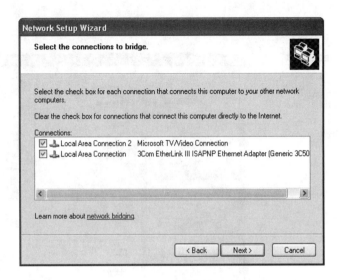

6. Enter the description and name for the computer. (See steps 9 and 10 in the previous list.) Because this computer isn't connecting to the Internet directly, you should be free to use any name you want for it even if your ISP requires that you use a specific name for the computer that's directly connected.

7. Click the Next button. The wizard displays the Name Your Network page.

8. In the Workgroup Name text box, enter the name you chose earlier for the network.

9. Click the Next button. The wizard displays the Ready to Apply Network Settings page.

10. Click the Next button. The wizard displays the Please Wait page while it configures the computer. It then displays the You're Almost Done page.

11. Select the Just Finish the Wizard; I Don't Need to Run the Wizard on Other Computers option button.

12. Click the Next button. The wizard displays the Completing the Network Setup Wizard page.

13. Click the Finish button. The wizard closes itself and displays the System Settings Change dialog box telling you that you need to restart your computer before the new settings will take effect.

14. Click the Yes button if you want to restart your computer immediately. Click the No button if you want to close some programs and then restart your computer manually.

Browsing the Network

To browse the network that the Network Setup Wizard has created, choose Start ➤ My Network Places. XP displays the My Network Places window (shown in Figure 31.13). This window displays the resources that are directly shared. In the figure, the four SharedDocs folders represent the \Shared Documents\ folders on the four XP computers connected to the network, and the drives on Doctor are drives on a server in the workgroup.

To access one of the shared folders, double-click its icon.

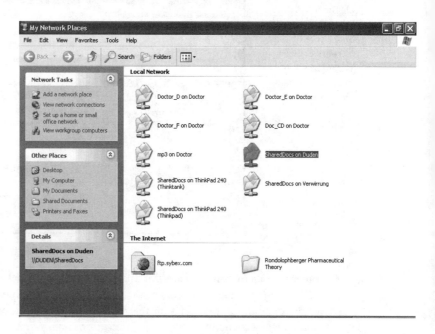

TIP   If running the Network Setup Wizard hasn't added the My Network Places to your Start menu, customize the Start menu (as discussed in "Customizing the Start Menu" in Chapter 4) and add the My Network Places item to it. You can also display the My Network Places page by choosing Start ➢ My Computer and then clicking the My Network Places link in the Other Places list in the My Computer window.

To browse the computers on your network, click the View Workgroup Computers link in the Network Tasks list. You can then browse any shared resources on a computer by double-clicking its icon and drilling down to the resources.

By default, XP automatically finds network folders and network printers so that it can show you the list of what's available. Automatically discovering these items is a good idea on small peer-to-peer networks, but if you have a large number of computers on your network sharing many items, automatic discovery may consume network bandwidth that you'd prefer to use for other purposes. To turn off automatic discovery, clear the Automatically Search for Network Folders and Printers check box in the Files and Folders section of the Advanced Settings list on the View page of the Folder Options dialog box (choose Tools ➢ Folder Options from an Explorer window).

For a small network, it's usually easiest to browse network resources from the My Network Places window. But if you turn off automatic discovery (as discussed in the previous paragraph), you may need to find items manually. To do so, open an Explorer window, click the Folders button to display the Folders bar, and then expand the Entire Network item, the Microsoft Windows Network item under it, and the workgroup item that appears under that. (The workgroup item will have the name of your workgroup.) Inside the workgroup you'll find the computers that belong to the workgroup, and you can browse through the resources they're sharing (if any). You can also use Search Companion to search from the My Network Places window as you would from any other window—just click the Search button to display Search Companion.

You can add shortcuts to the My Network Places window by using the Add Network Place Wizard or by dragging folders or URLs to the My Network Places window.

In addition to the SharedDocs folder on each computer, such folders as the users have shared manually, and any shared printers, you'll see other shared items, such as the Scheduled Tasks folder and the Printers and Faxes folder. These are used for remote administration. Also, several shared items are normally hidden, because they're used by XP itself rather than by users. These (since you ask) include a hidden share for each hard drive (named C$, D$, E$, and so on), a print$ folder for sharing printer drivers with computers on the network, an ADMIN$ folder for remote administration, and an IPC$ share for remote procedure calls. You'll notice that each name ends in a dollar sign ($), which is the designation for a hidden item.

TROUBLESHOOTING: UNABLE TO BROWSE THE NETWORK

If you're unable to browse the network or access resources on it, take the following steps to troubleshoot it. This procedure assumes that your network is using TCP/IP, XP's standard networking protocol.

1. Check that your hub or switch is powered on, that the necessary cables are connected, and that the lights for the relevant ports are lit. (If the lights aren't on, see the sidebar "Troubleshooting: No Light on Hub or Network Card," earlier in this chapter.)

2. Open a command-prompt window (Start ➢ All Programs ➢ Accessories ➢ Command Prompt) and ping the loopback address for your network adapter to see if it's working: Type **ping 127.0.0.1** and press the Enter key. You should get four Reply from 127.0.0.1 packets in response. If not, your network adapter isn't working. Open Device Manager from the Hardware page of the System Properties dialog box and see if Device Manager thinks the network adapter is working. If not, you may need to change the driver for the adapter, uninstall and reinstall the adapter, or (if XP doesn't support the adapter) get a new adapter.

3. In the command-prompt window, issue an **ipconfig** command (and press the Enter key) to check the IP addresses assigned to the network adapters on your computer.

4. Next, ping the IP address for your computer—for example, **ping 192.168.0.99** (and press the Enter key). Again, you should get four replies in the format Reply from 192.168.0.99. If not, the problem is with the network card on your computer.

5. If pinging your computer works, run the **ipconfig** command on another computer on the network to find out its IP address. Ping that IP address from the first computer. If that works, ping the first computer from the second. If you can ping each computer from the other by IP address, but you can't connect by browsing from Explorer, open the System Properties dialog box and check on the Computer Name page that the computers belong to the same workgroup. If not, make the workgroups match. If you can't ping one computer from another, the problem lies in the physical network connection. Double-check the network connections, the cables, and the hub.

6. Ping the other computer by its host name to test host name resolution. Again, you should get four replies in the format Reply from. If you get the message "Ping request could not find host *hostname*" or "Unable to resolve target name system," the problem lies with your DNS server (for example, the DNS service supplied by Internet Connection Sharing).

Mapping and Disconnecting Network Drives

You can access a shared folder as described in the previous section. But if you need to access the folder frequently or quickly, and especially if the folder is buried deep within the folder structure, you can save time and effort by mapping a network drive to the folder. By mapping the network drive, you essentially tell XP that you want to refer to the folder as (say) Z: instead of (say) \\VERWIRRUNG\Andy's Documents\Reading\Recommended\Plain Text\. Mapping the drive makes it not only easier to connect but also faster, because XP keeps a connection open to the shared folder (as long as it's available).

The two backslash characters at the beginning of that share name are part of the Universal Naming Convention (UNC for short). The two backslashes indicate the name of the server (the computer providing the shared service).

You can map as many network drives as you have free letters of the alphabet on your computer. Previous versions of Windows used to start network drive mapping with the letter F, but these days, many computers need A through G (or further) for local drives—floppy, CD, CD-RW , DVD, Zip, or other removable drives, and of course one or more hard disk volumes. (B is often unused these days, because very few computers have two floppy drives.) So XP automatically starts mapping drives with the letter Z, then walks backward through the alphabet with each subsequent drive. But you can override XP's choice of drive letter with one of your own if you prefer.

Mapping a Network Drive

To map a network drive, take the following steps:

1. From an Explorer window, choose Tools ➤ Map Network Drive. XP displays the Map Network Drive dialog box (shown on the left in Figure 31.14).

FIGURE 31.14

Use the Map Network Drive dialog box (left) and the Browse for Folder dialog box (right) to map a drive letter to a shared network folder so that you can access the folder quickly.

2. In the Drive drop-down list, select the drive letter you want to use. The list shows all currently unused letters. By default, XP selects the last available letter.

TIP   You don't have to select a drive letter here. If you don't want to assign a drive letter, select the (None) item at the bottom of the Drive drop-down list. When you do this, XP maintains a connection to the shared folder but doesn't add it to the My Computer window.

3. Enter the path and folder name in the Folder text box. You can type in the path or (when you've mapped drives before) choose it from the drop-down list, but usually it's easier to click the Browse button and use the resulting Browse for Folder dialog box to select the folder, then click the OK button. As you can see in the screen on the right in Figure 31.14, the Browse for Folder dialog box displays the My Network Places tree. You can drill down through this tree to the local network, the computers on it, and the folders they contain, or you can select one of the \SharedDocs\ folders, which appear conveniently at the first level of the My Network Places list. (You can't see them in the figure because they're too far down the list.)

TIP *Instead of using the procedure described in the above steps, you can browse through the network by using the Folders pane until you find the network drive or folder to which you want to connect. Then right-click the drive or folder and choose Map Network Drive from the context menu. XP displays the Map Network Drive dialog box with the computer's name and the folder's path entered already.*

NOTE *You can map a drive either to the root of a shared drive or to a subfolder. Mapping a drive to a subfolder can give you quicker access to that subfolder.*

4. If you want XP to try to reconnect the network drive each time you log on, make sure the Reconnect at Logon check box is selected.

5. By default, XP tries to log on to the network drive using the username and password (if any) under which you're currently logged on. To log on to the network drive under a different username, take the following steps:

◆ Click the Connect Using a Different User Name link. XP displays the Connect As dialog box (shown in Figure 31.15).

FIGURE 31.15

Use the Connect As dialog box to specify a different username for connecting to the network drive.

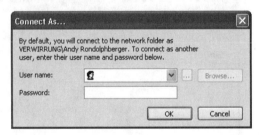

◆ Enter the username in the User Name text box. If the network drive is in a different workgroup than the workgroup your computer is currently in, specify the network drive's workgroup and the appropriate username in it. For example, to use the username Rikki in the workgroup Group2, use \\Group2\Rikki.

◆ Enter the password for the username in the Password text box.

◆ Click the OK button. XP closes the Connect As dialog box, returning you to the Map Network Drive dialog box.

6. Click the Finish button. XP connects the network drive to the specified folder and closes the Map Network Drive dialog box.

◆ If XP can't find the folder you specified by typing in the Folder text box, it displays a Windows message box. Click the OK button. XP closes the message box and returns you to the Map Network Drive dialog box so that you can try again.

◆ If XP can't connect the drive because the username is invalid or the password is wrong, it displays a Connect To dialog box telling you the problem. Correct the username or password and click the OK button to try again.

Reconnecting a Network Drive at Logon

If you selected the Reconnect at Logon check box in the Map Network Drive dialog box when mapping the drive, XP tries to reestablish the network mapping each time you log on.

If XP isn't able to connect a network drive, it displays a pop-up in the notification area telling you so. Click the pop-up to display a My Computer window showing all the drives. Check which drives XP wasn't able to reconnect, and reconnect them manually if they're available. (The usual reason for not being able to reconnect a network drive is that the computer it's on is currently not sharing it.)

Disconnecting a Network Drive

To disconnect a network drive you've mapped, take the following steps from an Explorer window:

1. Choose Tools ➢ Disconnect Network Drive. XP displays the Disconnect Network Drives dialog box (shown in Figure 31.16), which lists the network drives to which your computer is currently connected.

FIGURE 31.16

Use the Disconnect Network Drives dialog box to disconnect one or more network drives.

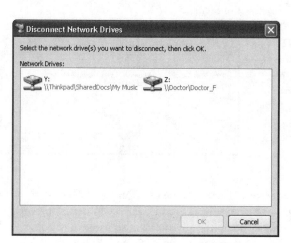

2. Select the drive or drives you want to disconnect.

3. Click the OK button. XP closes the Disconnect Network Drives dialog box and disconnects the drive or drives. If you have any files or folders open on the drive or drives, XP displays the

Disconnect Network Drive dialog box (shown in Figure 31.17) to warn you that you may lose data if you disconnect the drive while files are open. Click the Yes button if you want to proceed. Click the No button if you want to close the files before you disconnect the drive.

FIGURE 31.17

XP warns you if you have files open on the drive you're disconnecting.

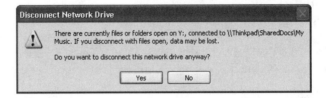

You can also disconnect a single network drive by right-clicking the network drive in an Explorer window and choosing Disconnect from the context menu.

Changing Your Computer's Workgroup

As mentioned earlier, it's not a good idea to accept the default workgroup name, MSHOME, for a couple of reasons. First, MSHOME isn't the greatest name for a workgroup. It's not snappy. It's not intuitive. It's barely even pronounceable. You can come up with a much better name based on your family name, your dog's name, your knowledge of cult movies or Norse mythology, or a combination of the three.

Second, if your network is connected to the Internet via a cable modem, using a workgroup named MSHOME may be dangerous, because it can share your network with any of your neighbors who are also using a workgroup named MSHOME. You can protect your own computers and resources by using strong passwords, but even so, chances are that if you browse the network, you'll see many folders being shared without protection.

This problem is now widely recognized and, as a result, somewhat mitigated. But in the late 1990s, people in areas that had recently gotten cable Internet access reported seeing literally thousands of shared folders and printers, most of which weren't protected by a password. Apart from the security risks of having unknown people able to access drives, the amount of information about shared folders and devices bombing around the network could cause network slowdowns.

WARNING   Should you be cruising a large MSHOME network with apparently unprotected drives and be tempted to take a peek at them, remember that this lack of security can cut both ways: An unprotected shared drive containing juicy items such as MP3 files, MPEG files, JPEGs, or (uh) sensitive information can be a great way to distribute viruses, Trojan horses, and other malware. Having people steal malware like this might also provide an interesting defense for its author, who could claim to have never intended to let it out of the lab environment in which they were testing it for security purposes. . . .

To change your computer's workgroup, change the name in the Workgroup text box in the Computer Name Changes dialog box. For details, see the procedure described in "Changing the Computer's Name, Description, and Workgroup" in Chapter 11.

After changing the workgroup, you have to reboot your computer before the change takes effect. Do so as soon as possible.

Connecting Macs and Linux Boxes to the Network

This section gives brief details on connecting Mac and Linux clients to your Windows network.

Mac Clients

XP doesn't come with any software to provide connectivity with Macs. Unless you upgrade to Windows 2000 Server (or Windows .NET Server) or you run Mac OS X exclusively, your best bet is probably to buy third-party software such as DAVE (Thursby Software Systems Inc.; `www.thursby.com`) or DoubleTalk (Connectix; `www.connectix.com`) that provides TCP/IP connectivity between Macs and PCs.

Mac OS X can connect directly to servers running the Server Message Block (SMB) protocol. (SMB is the native sharing protocol for Windows OSes. Linux can provide SMB sharing as well if you use its Samba utility.) Mac OS X doesn't automatically display the names of SMB servers in the Connect to Server dialog box, but you can add them manually as follows:

1. Open the Finder.
2. Choose Go ➢ Connect to Server to display the Connect to Server dialog box.
3. In the Address text box, enter the server name and the share name in the form `SMB://servername/sharename/` and click the Connect button. The Finder adds the drive if it's available, prompting you for the workgroup, username, and password as necessary.

You can then connect to the drive by using the Finder as you would for any other networked drive.

WARNING *It's best—indeed, advisable—to connect to only one SMB server at a time. This is because Mac OS X may suffer a kernel panic (yes, that's the technical term) if you connect to two SMB servers at the same time. So before you connect to a second SMB server, drag the volume for the first SMB server to the Trash to eject it. (Mac OS X 10.2 is due to fix this problem.)*

TIP *If your SMB connection doesn't seem to be working, use the Mac OS X Network Utility to ping the IP address of the Windows (or Linux) computer to make sure it's working.*

To give a Mac access to the Internet through Internet Connection Sharing (ICS), configure its TCP/IP Control Panel to use DHCP. Alternatively, manually assign the Mac an IP address in the `192.168.0.x` subnet (`192.168.0.0` to `192.168.0.255`). Don't use the `192.168.0.1` address, because the computer running ICS claims that for itself.

Linux Clients

Linux clients are better equipped than the Mac for sharing files with computers running XP, but this is thanks to Linux's capabilities rather than any largesse on Microsoft's part.

To enable the Linux box to access shared folders on a XP computer, you have several options:

◆ Use a `mount -t smbfs` command to mount a shared folder on the XP computer to a mount point on the Linux box.

- Use a `smbmount` command to mount a shared folder on the XP computer to a mount point on the Linux box. (Using `smbmount` is very similar to using `mount -t smbfs`, but `smbmount` sometimes works when `mount -t smbfs` won't work, so it's worth keeping in mind as an alternative.)

- Use `smbclient` to attach to a shared folder. `smbclient` has the advantage of being much less ticklish than the previous two options, so it almost always works, even when they don't. The disadvantage is that when you make a connection via `smbclient`, you're stuck with using FTP-like commands to manage files. For example, you can use `get` and `mget` to copy files from the XP computer and `put` and `mput` to copy files to it. You want a graphical interface? Then get one of the previous two options to work....

So far, so good—but that's only one-way traffic. If you need the Windows computers to be able to access files on the Linux box, set up Samba on the Linux box. Get it right (Samba's configuration options are good material for a GUI-lover's nightmare), and your Windows computers will be able to access the shared folders on the Linux box as if it were running Windows. (Which, incidentally, is what the Windows computers will think it's running.)

You can give a Linux box access to the Internet through ICS in the same way as you can a Mac. Either configure it to use DHCP or manually assign it an IP address in the `192.168.0.x` subnet (`192.168.0.0` to `192.168.0.255`). Again, don't use the `192.168.0.1` address, because the computer running ICS will be using it.

Up Next

This chapter has discussed how to create a network in the two ways you're most likely to want to network your XP computers: by using a direct connection for slow-and-dirty file transfer between two computers, and by using the Network Setup Wizard to configure a straightforward network sharing folders, printers, and an Internet connection. It has also discussed how to browse the network; how to map and disconnect network drives; how to change your computer's workgroup to something more appealing or obscure than MSHOME; and how to connect non-XP computers to the network.

So much for the easy way to share resources. You can also roll most of your network the hard way, as described in the next chapter. Grip those sharp-edged dice and turn the page.

Chapter 32

Sharing Resources on Your Network

IN THE PREVIOUS CHAPTER, you saw how to use the Network Setup Wizard to create a basic network configuration for sharing resources including folders, printers, and an Internet connection. This chapter discusses how to share (and unshare) resources manually. So if you set up your network with the Network Setup Wizard in the previous chapter and everything is fine, you can probably ignore this chapter for now.

But if you need (or want) to perform some manual configuration, here's what this chapter contains: First, it shows you how to share your Internet connection and how to use an Internet connection that another computer is sharing. It then moves on to sharing printers connected to your computer and using printers shared by other computers, mapping a drive by using the **net use** command, and configuring network components manually. It ends by discussing how to connect two networks using a network bridge.

This chapter covers the following topics:

- ◆ Connecting your network to the Internet
- ◆ Sharing your Internet connection with networked computers
- ◆ Using a shared Internet connection
- ◆ Sharing a printer
- ◆ Using a shared printer
- ◆ Repairing a network connection
- ◆ Mapping a drive by using the **net use** command
- ◆ Configuring network components manually
- ◆ Configuring TCP/IP manually
- ◆ Connecting two networks via a bridge

Connecting Your Network to the Internet

If you have a home network, you'll probably want to connect it to the Internet through a shared Internet connection so that each of the computers can send e-mail, browse the Web, and enjoy instant messaging and the other delights of the wired. (Or you may prefer not to let any of the other people on the network access the Internet.)

This section discusses the pros and cons of connecting your network to the Internet, ways of doing so, and considerations to keep in mind. As you'll see, you need to answer several questions, and the answers to the questions are related. The next section discusses how to implement XP's Internet Connection Sharing (ICS) feature, should you choose that as your way of connecting your network to the Internet.

Should You Connect Your Network to the Internet?

Instead of connecting the whole network through a single Internet connection, you can let individual computers connect through their own Internet connections. Doing so has the following advantages:

♦ If you can access the Internet only via dial-up, and you have multiple phone lines, you may prefer to have each computer connect separately so that each computer can enjoy as fast a connection speed as possible. Sharing, say, a 33.6Kbps connection among three or four computers will be no fun for anyone. (An alternative is to establish a multilink connection and share that—if your ISP supports multilink.)

♦ Each computer that connects directly to the Internet will be able to use the full range of features in programs that can't operate fully via a shared connection protected with a firewall— for example, Messenger or NetMeeting.

♦ You can restrict use of the Internet to those computers that have a direct connection.

Having computers connect to the Internet individually has the following disadvantages:

♦ If the computers are trying to connect to the Internet by using the same phone line, only one will be able to connect at a time. If the computers are using separate phone lines, you'll need to pay for those phone lines. You'll probably also have to pay for multiple ISP accounts rather than just one account.

♦ Having more computers connect to the Internet increases the number of points at which your network can be attacked. (Chapter 33 discusses how to secure your network.)

Should You Use Multiple IP Addresses or NAT?

If you do decide to connect your network to the Internet, your next decision is whether to use multiple public IP addresses—one for each computer on your network that connects to the Internet—or a single IP address with Network Address Translation (NAT).

NOTE   See the sidebar "Expert Knowledge: IP Addresses and How They Work" in Chapter 30 for a discussion of the differences between public and private IP addresses.

MULTIPLE IP ADDRESSES

Whether you *can* use multiple IP addresses depends on your connection. Typically, in order to use multiple IP addresses, you'll need an always-on connection such as a DSL or a cable connection that can be assigned a fixed IP address. You'll need to request *routed Internet service* from your ISP, who will assign you the appropriate number of fixed IP addresses. Some ISPs will provide a handful of IP addresses for the same price as your regular connection, whereas others consider supplying multiple IP addresses to be "business" service rather than "residential service" (a single IP address), and charge accordingly.

Routed Internet service has a couple of advantages over NAT. First, because with routed Internet service each computer has a public IP address, all features in all Internet programs should work on each computer, because the computer is directly accessible from the Internet. Second, you can publish the IP address or the name of any given computer so that people can connect directly to it. If you get your ISP to implement what's called *inverse DNS* for your domain name, you can also allow people on the Internet to look up the name of your computer.

The disadvantages to routed Internet service are that it'll almost invariably cost you more than sharing an Internet connection using NAT and that it increases your exposure to security threats, because you'll need to protect each of the computers on the network against direct attack. If you use inverse DNS, any website you access will be able to tell the name of the computer that accessed it, whereas when you access a website via NAT, the website can tell only the IP address of the computer or device running NAT.

Over software NAT devices (as opposed to hardware NAT devices), routed Internet service has another advantage: Because the service is implemented via a hardware device, you don't need to leave a host computer running the whole time you want any computer on the network to be able to access the Internet.

NETWORK ADDRESS TRANSLATION

In most cases, you'll do better to use Network Address Translation (NAT) for a network based on computers running XP Home. Network Address Translation, which is also known as *IP masquerading* (particularly in the Linux world), lets multiple computers connect through a single Internet connection using a single public IP address. So if you have an Internet connection on one of your PCs, you can easily share it with the other computers on the network. This sharing is more appealing for a high-speed connection than for a modest dial-up connection, but it works just as well for either. But there are a couple of catches, as you'll see later in this section.

The NAT host acts as an intermediary between the client (the PC connected to the network) and the server (the Internet server that is supplying information). Basically, NAT receives any packets sent by the client to destinations not on the local network, changes the source IP address on the packets so that they appear to come from the NAT host rather than from the client, assigns a source port to them that lets itself track reply packets, and sends the packets on to the destination. When the replies come back, NAT matches them to the original packets and forwards them to the client.

In NAT, the identity of the client submitting a request is hidden: Instead, the request appears to come from the host. This can be good and bad. NAT gives you more freedom in the IP addresses you assign within the network. Typically, you'll want to use nonroutable internal IP addresses within the network so that incoming packets can reach a computer only through the router, which gives you some protection against attacks. On the bad side, if someone on your network takes some illegal or offensive action (for example, posting libelous comments or downloading unsuitable material), the culprit will appear to be the host rather than the individual concerned. (If you had multiple IP addresses, only the specific IP address involved would appear to be guilty.)

As mentioned earlier, you need only one ISP account and one IP address (either static or dynamic) to connect your network to the Internet via NAT. This usually makes NAT the most economical option for connecting a network to the Internet. If you regularly have a half-dozen users thrashing your broadband connection, your ISP will probably suspect that you have multiple users connected, but all the traffic *will* be coming from the single IP address they've assigned to you. Unless you're actually violating any terms of service you've subscribed to, the chances that they'll pull the plug on your connection are low.

The main disadvantage of NAT is that not every program works across NAT, depending on the NAT device used and on the needs of the program. Problems are most likely to arise when a computer connected to the Internet through your NAT device is trying to connect to a computer that itself connects to the Internet through another NAT device.

What usually happens with NAT is one of the computers inside the network originates the conversation with a computer on the Internet. For example, consider Figure 32.1. This shows two simple home networks, unimaginatively named West Network (in the blue trunks) and East Network (in the red). Each network contains a computer that's connected to the Internet (West 1 and East 1) and running NAT so that it can provide Internet connectivity to the two other computers in its network (West 2, West 3, East 2, and East 3). In the middle of the figure is the Internet, represented by its traditional cloud of uncertainty. And right below the cloud (quite coincidentally) is the Sybex web server, represented by a computer the size of a walk-in freezer.

FIGURE 32.1

Two networks using NAT to connect internal computers to the Internet

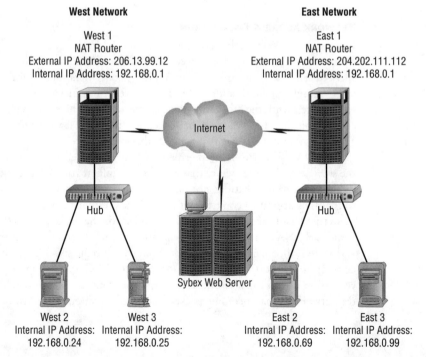

West Network

West 1
NAT Router
External IP Address: 206.13.99.12
Internal IP Address: 192.168.0.1

East Network

East 1
NAT Router
External IP Address: 204.202.111.112
Internal IP Address: 192.168.0.1

Hub

Internet

Sybex Web Server

Hub

West 2
Internal IP Address:
192.168.0.24

West 3
Internal IP Address:
192.168.0.25

East 2
Internal IP Address:
192.168.0.69

East 3
Internal IP Address:
192.168.0.99

So far, so good. Now, here's the problem that used to occur with NAT. The computers that connect through the NAT devices have only internal IP addresses. That means they can originate a conversation with a computer on the Internet, but they can't take part in a conversation originated from beyond their NAT devices. For example, West 2 can access the Sybex web server with no problem. It sends its request to the NAT router on West 1, which says the binary equivalent of "ah, an address on the Internet" and shunts the request out through its external connection. The Sybex web server responds to the request and sends back a response to West 1. The NAT router intercepts this response, matches it to the outgoing request, says "ah, it's for West 2" (again in binary), and passes the data on to West 2. And so it continues: West 2 (and the other internal computers) can access Internet sites provided that it starts the conversation.

But if West 3 wants to start a conversation with East 2, it can't, because it can't see East 2 through the NAT router on East 1. It can get as far as East 1, because that computer has an external IP address. But the computers beyond the NAT router are hidden from view. So you can't access them for a quick DeathMatch, for videoconferencing, for chat—well, for anything. And with NAT routers becoming widely implemented thanks to the rapid spread of broadband availability, that quickly becomes a problem. At one end of the connection, the activity has to take place on the computer running the NAT router rather than on the "inside" machine you want to use.

XP offers good news and bad news on this front. The good news is that XP's implementation of ICS fixes this problem, letting you communicate across two NAT routers, from one inside machine to another inside machine. This is quite clever, because both the server (the NAT router) and the client (the inside machine) need to understand what's going on and work together. Some of the software has to be reworked to make the connection work, but you'll find that many things work. The bad news is that you need to use ICS in order to enjoy this benefit. If you use another NAT device, your computers may well not be able to connect to computers behind another NAT device.

Because NAT shields the internal computers on your network from direct access from the Internet, NAT makes it a little harder for you to provide Internet services from a computer on the network. For example, if you want to run a web server on a computer that connects to the Internet via NAT, you need to do a little more setup than if the computer has a public IP address. However, both ICS and many NAT devices let you forward all packets directed to a specified port to a particular internal IP address on the LAN, so it's not too difficult.

Should the Connection Connect Automatically to the Internet?

If you do decide to connect your network to the Internet, and your means of connection is a dial-up connection rather than an always-on connection, your next decision is whether to have the connection be established automatically whenever one of the computers on the network tries to access the Internet or whether to require the connection to be established manually.

Because having the connection established automatically is by far the most convenient arrangement for most networks, you'll probably want to connect automatically unless you have a good reason not to. Such reasons include the following:

◆ You want to restrict Internet usage to certain times of day for whatever reason (for example, to avoid per-minute charges in the daytime, or to make sure that your children do their homework and don't spend the night online).

◆ Your dial-up connection shares your voice line, and you want to prevent the Internet connection from gate-crashing your voice calls.

◆ You want to make sure that no program is able to "call home" by establishing an Internet connection of its own accord. Many Trojan-horse programs and viruses do this, but many other programs may be configured to automatically establish a connection. For example, Windows Messenger and other instant-messaging programs are often set by default to sign you in as soon as you log on to Windows. If your network isn't connected to the Internet at the time, these programs will establish the connection.

A dial-up modem connection tends to be the least satisfactory way of connecting a network to the Internet, because the time needed to establish a connection makes for a poor user experience on one of the networked computers. Because the user probably won't be able to hear the modem dialing as the computer sharing the modem tries to set up the connection at their demand, the connection will seem not to be working. So if you have a flat-rate dial-up connection, you may want to set it to redial automatically when the connection is dropped so as to keep the connection open as much of the time as possible. To do so, display the Options page of the Properties dialog box for the connection, select the Redial if Line Is Dropped check box, choose Never in the Idle Time before Hanging Up drop-down list, and reduce the time specified in the Time between Redial Attempts drop-down list to a sensibly small value.

Should You Use ICS or Another NAT?

If you've decided that NAT is the way to go, your final decision in this chain of consequence is whether you want to use XP's Internet Connection Sharing (ICS) or another NAT device (either hardware or software).

ICS has several strong points:

◆ ICS is included with XP, so the price is right. By contrast, a hardware NAT device will typically set you back $100 to $200. (This price often includes additional functionality as part of an Internet router device, such as a built-in hub, so it's not as bad as it looks.)

◆ ICS includes the various networking components that you need to share a network connection: NAT, a proxy server, a router, and a DHCP allocator (a minimalist DHCP server). ICS even gets around some of the problems of computers not being able to communicate with each other when each is behind a different NAT device.

◆ ICS is integrated with Internet Connection Firewall (ICF). This integration lets you set up a shared and fairly well firewalled Internet connection with minimal effort. You can poke holes through ICF easily to enable programs that have specific connectivity needs.

◆ ICS and ICF are fully aware of XP's features and middleware and are designed to work with them. For example, Windows Messenger knows how to automatically ask ICS and ICF to open the ports that it needs to communicate. Likewise, ICS and ICF open ports for remote-connection technologies such as Remote Assistance (discussed in Chapter 24) and Remote Desktop Connection (discussed in Chapter 34).

ICS has two significant limitations:

1. You need to keep the ICS host computer running all the time so that it can handle the Internet connection and the sharing.

2. Because of the way ICS is set up, you can share only one Internet connection at the same time on the same network by using ICS. To share two Internet connections, you'll need to set one up manually for sharing via another technology. (Alternatively, you can create two separate networks with an ICS connection in each, but doing so is usually much more work than setting up a second shared connection manually, because those two networks won't be able to talk to each other directly without ICS conflicts.) You can also use unshared Internet connections alongside your shared connections without any problems.

You can get around the limitation of needing to keep the host computer running by using a hardware NAT device—for example, a cable router, DSL router, or ISDN router—instead of ICS.

Almost all these routers have NAT built in, and most can run DHCP as well, so they provide an effective means of sharing an Internet connection. Some routers have firewalls built in as well, which you can use instead of or in addition to XP's Internet Connection Firewall (ICF).

Some models are designed to connect to a network switch or hub and have two ports: An internal port for connecting to the switch or hub and an external port for connecting to the cable modem or DSL splitter. Others have hubs or switches built in, so if you haven't yet bought the hub or switch for your network, you can solve all your connectivity needs with a single box.

If you do decide to get a hardware NAT device, install it according to the instructions supplied. If you decide to stick with ICS, and you haven't set it up using the Network Setup Wizard, set it up and configure it as described in the following sections.

Configuring ICS Manually

If you haven't had the Network Setup Wizard set up Internet Connection Sharing (ICS) for you, configure it manually by taking the following steps:

1. Choose Start ➢ Connect To ➢ Show All Connections. XP displays the Network Connections screen.

2. Right-click the dial-up connection for which you want to implement ICS and choose Properties from the context menu. XP displays the Properties dialog box for the connection.

3. Click the Advanced tab. XP displays the Advanced page (shown in Figure 32.2).

4. Select the Allow Other Network Users to Connect through This Computer's Internet Connection check box.

5. If you want other computers to be able to cause ICS to start up the network connection when it's not running, make sure the Establish a Dial-up Connection whenever a Computer on My Network Attempts to Access the Internet check box is selected. Clear this check box if you want only the computer with the connection to be able to start the connection.

6. If you want users of the other computers on the network to be able to control the Internet connection, make sure the Allow Other Network Users to Control or Disable the Shared Internet Connection check box is selected. Clear this check box if you don't want them to be able to manipulate the Internet connection directly.

FIGURE 32.2

Setting up ICS on the Advanced page of the Properties dialog box for an Internet connection

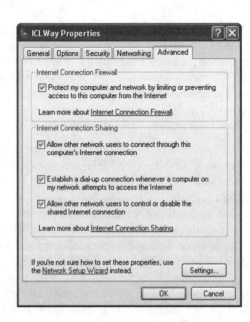

7. If you want to use Internet Connection Firewall on this connection, select the Protect My Computer and Network by Limiting or Preventing Access to This Computer from the Internet check box in the Internet Connection Firewall group box. Unless you're using a separate firewall or you've established that ICF interferes with an Internet program that you must run, it's a good idea to use ICF on your Internet connection. A computer connected to the Internet but not protected by a firewall is a prime target for malicious hackers.

8. Click the OK button. XP closes the Properties dialog box for the connection, changes the IP address of your network adapter to the static IP address `192.168.0.1`, and starts telling the other computers to get their IP addresses from it (if there's no other DHCP server on the network).

NOTE *If you have another computer on the network using the* `192.168.0.1` *IP address, XP gives you an angry message telling you to change that IP address on the other computer before it will let you implement ICS on this computer. You're likely to be using this IP address only if you've previously set up ICS on another computer, you have another NAT device currently managing the network, or the stars have decided you're due for a bad-horoscope day. If you have another NAT device, remove it. If you have another computer running ICS, display the Properties dialog box for its shared connection and clear the Allow Other Network Users to Connect through This Computer's Internet Connection check box, then click the OK button. If the other computer isn't running ICS but has the* `192.168.0.1` *IP address set manually, either set a different address manually or switch to automatic addressing.*

At this point, ICS should be up and running. The shared connection appears with a palm-upward hand on its icon to indicate that it's shared. If it's your default connection, the icon has a white check mark in a black circle. And if you're using ICF, the connection has a lock icon in its upper-right quadrant. Figure 32.3 shows one of these busy icons.

FIGURE 32.3

The icon for your Internet connection shows that it's shared (the hand), that it's the default (the check mark on the circle), and that it uses ICF (the lock icon).

ICLWay
Connected, Shared, Firewalled
U.S. Robotics 56K FAX EXT

At this point, most Internet-enabled programs on computers that connect to the Internet through the ICS host should be working. In theory, ICS shares the details of the connection via UPnP, so the client computers learn of the ICS host automatically, but in some cases you may need to run the Network Setup Wizard on the client computer to formally identify the network connection it's supposed to use. If the client computer still can't access the Internet after you've run the Network Setup Wizard, see the sidebar "Troubleshooting: You Can't Access or Use the Shared Internet Connection," later in this chapter, for advice on how to proceed.

Other programs and services have special requirements for Internet connectivity and so run afoul of the protection provided by Internet Connection Firewall (ICF). For example, if you've chosen to host a website on a computer that connects to the Internet through an ICS host, you'll need to configure ICF to pass on the requests to the web server, because otherwise ICF will treat the incoming requests as hostile and discard them automatically. For such programs and services, follow the instructions in the section "Configuring ICF Manually," a little later in this chapter.

SETTING THE IP ADDRESSES OF CONNECTED COMPUTERS

If your Windows computers are set to get IP addresses via DHCP, they should automatically get IP addresses from ICS within a few minutes of your implementing ICS. If you're configuring IP addresses manually, you'll need to set each computer an IP address in the 192.168.0.2 to 192.168.0.255 range.

TURNING OFF ICS

To turn off ICS, clear the Allow Other Network Users to Connect through This Computer's Internet Connection check box on the Advanced page of the Properties dialog box for the connection, then click the OK button. XP closes the Properties dialog box, and changes your computer's IP address from using 192.168.0.1 to obtaining an IP address automatically.

If you have a DHCP server on your network, XP grabs an IP address from it on the next go-around of network polling. If XP doesn't find a DHCP server (which will be the case if ICS was handling DHCP for you before you turned it off), XP falls back on its alternate TCP/IP configuration, which uses Automatic Private IP Addressing (APIPA) to automatically assign an IP address in the range 169.254.0.1 to 169.254.255.254.

Configuring ICF Manually

By default, ICF is configured to block any incoming traffic that it can't match to an outgoing request, not to log dropped packets or successful connections, and not to respond to Internet Control Message Protocol (ICMP) messages. You can change these settings as described in the following subsections.

To configure ICF, you work in the Advanced Settings dialog box for the connection. To display this dialog box, take the following steps:

1. Right-click the shared connection and choose Properties from the context menu. XP displays the Properties dialog box.
2. Click the Advanced tab. XP displays the Advanced page.
3. Click the Settings button. XP displays the Advanced Settings dialog box with the Services page foremost.

CONFIGURING ICF TO PASS DATA FOR SPECIFIC PROGRAMS AND SERVICES

To configure ICF to pass data for specific programs and services, you work on the Services page of the Advanced Settings dialog box (shown on the left in Figure 32.4). The list box on this page contains the services that come preconfigured with XP, together with any services that XP has added automatically on your behalf (for example, services related to Windows Messenger, Remote Desktop Connection, or Remote Assistance) and any services you've defined manually.

In the Services list, select the services running on your network that you want Internet users to be able to access. By default, none of these services are accessible from outside the network—you need to turn them on explicitly. Don't turn on a service unless you actually need it, because packets being redirected to a destination that's not ready to receive them opens a security hole into your network.

To add a service, click the Add button and work in the Service Settings dialog box (shown on the right in Figure 32.4). Enter the description of the service, the name or IP address of the computer hosting the service, and the port number and port type (TCP or UDP) of the service, and click the OK button. XP closes the Service Settings dialog box and adds the service to the Services list box.

FIGURE 32.4

On the Services page of the Advanced Settings dialog box for a shared Internet connection, specify which network services you want Internet users to be able to access. Use the Service Settings dialog box (right) to add a service.

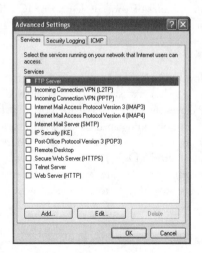

You can change one of the listed services by selecting it, clicking the Edit button, and working in the resulting Service Settings dialog box. For example, to pass packets sent to TCP port 80 to a web server running on an ICS client, select the Web Server (HTTP) item in the Services list box and click the Edit button. In the resulting Service Settings dialog box, enter the name or IP address of the web server and then click the OK button. (For the predefined services, you can edit only the computer running the service, not the description of the service or the port used.)

To delete a service you've created, select it and click the Delete button. XP deletes the service from the list without confirmation.

NOTE *If you've selected the Allow Other Network Users to Control or Disable the Shared Internet Connection check box on the Advanced page of the Properties dialog box for the Internet connection, other computers on the network will be able to configure ICF to pass data for programs and services: if you've cleared this check box, only your computer will be able to configure ICF. Even if you've selected this check box, other computers can't configure security logging or ICMP.*

CONFIGURING SECURITY LOGGING

To find out which packets ICF is discarding, or to log the successful connections that ICS makes, you need to configure security logging. To do so, you work on the Security Logging page of the Advanced Settings dialog box (shown on the left in Figure 32.5).

FIGURE 32.5

On the Security Logging page (left) of the Advanced Settings dialog box, choose which connection attempts to log and where to store the log file. On the ICMP page (right), specify how the computers on the network respond to incoming requests for information.

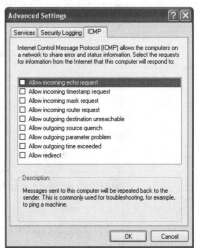

Select the Log Dropped Packets check box if you want to log dropped data packets. These are the packets that ICF discards because it can't match them to an outgoing request. They may reveal attempts to scan your system for a security hole. They may also help you identify legitimate programs that are having problems communicating across the firewall.

Select the Log Successful Connections check box if you want to log successful inbound and outbound connections (for example, to see which Internet sites the computers on your network are connecting to and which computers are connecting to your network from the Internet). If you use your Internet connection actively, logging successful connections will rapidly fill up your firewall log.

In the Log File Options group box, use the Name text box (and if necessary the Browse button and its resulting Browse dialog box) to specify where to store the log file. If you want, use the Size Limit text box to change the size limit for the security log file. The default setting is 4096KB—in other words, 4MB—but you may want to increase it if you choose to log successful connections.

The log is a text file, so you can view it in any text editor (for example, Notepad). The easiest way to open the firewall log file in your default text editor is to display the Run dialog box by choosing Start ➤ Run, enter **pfirewall.log**, and click the OK button. You can also open it from an Explorer window or directly from a text editor or word processor.

ENABLING AND DISABLING ICMP SERVICES

On the ICMP page of the Advanced Settings dialog box (shown on the right in Figure 32.5, above), you can choose whether XP should respond to certain types of Internet Control Message Protocol packets. ICMP packets are used for sharing data on transmission status and errors. By default, XP is configured not to respond to any packets, because not responding is usually safer than responding.

For example, the Allow Incoming Echo Request check box controls whether the computers respond to ping packets sent to them. Usually, it's best not to respond to ping packets, because it tells other people—including malicious hackers—that there's a computer at that IP address. But if you're trying to establish that your network is alive when you're stuck in a remote location, echoing ping requests becomes very valuable.

Select the check boxes for the ICMP (Internet Control Message Protocol) packets you want to use. When you select an item in the list box, XP displays information about it in the Description text box.

APPLYING YOUR CHOICES

Once you've made your choices for services, security logging, and ICMP packets, click the OK button. XP closes the Advanced Settings dialog box, returning you to the Properties dialog box for the connection. Click the OK button. XP closes the Properties dialog box.

If the connection is open when you close the Properties dialog box, XP displays the Network Connections dialog box warning you that some changes may not take effect until the next time you start the connection. Click the OK button.

Using a Shared Internet Connection

Depending on how a shared Internet connection is configured, you can use it in much the same way as you can use a regular Internet connection on your computer.

The shared connection appears under the Internet Gateway heading in the Network Connections window with a flashy icon. Figure 32.6 shows an example.

FIGURE 32.6

A shared connection appears in the Internet Gateway list in the Network Connections window.

Internet Gateway

ICLWay on THINKTANK
Disconnected
ICLWay on THINKTANK

To tell XP to display an icon in the notification area when the connection is connected, take the following steps:

1. Right-click the connection and choose Properties from the context menu. XP displays the Properties dialog box for the connection.

2. Select the Show Icon in Notification Area when Connected check box.

3. Click the OK button. XP closes the Properties dialog box and applies the setting.

If the connection is configured to start automatically on demand, you can start the connection by starting a program that attempts to access the Internet. For example, if you start Internet Explorer or Outlook Express, ICS automatically starts the connection.

If the connection is configured to let you control it, you can start it manually by double-clicking its entry on the Network Connections screen, and you can disconnect the connection by right-clicking its notification-area icon and choosing Disconnect from the context menu.

TROUBLESHOOTING: YOU CAN'T ACCESS OR USE THE SHARED INTERNET CONNECTION

This sidebar discusses the best way of approaching the troubleshooting of problems with an Internet connection shared using ICS.

If you have immediate access to the ICS host, go to it and check that it's running, check that the modem is powered on and connected to a live phone line, and perform all the other checks detailed in the section "Troubleshooting Your Internet Connection" in Chapter 18. If someone else is using the ICS host, interrogate them closely but within the restrictions imposed by the Geneva Convention. In particular, you'll probably want to know whether they've stopped sharing the Internet connection or prevented you (and other client computers) from activating it.

If you don't have immediate access to the ICS host, start by using ping to check that the network connection to the ICS host is working. Open a command-prompt window (Start ➢ All Programs ➢ Accessories ➢ Command Prompt) and enter a ping command for the ICS host's address:

```
ping 192.168.0.1
```

If the connection is working, you'll see four "Reply from" lines giving statistics on the connection. If it's not working, you'll get "Request timed out" messages. You'll then need to troubleshoot the network connection, as discussed earlier in this book. Check that the network hardware is in place, in order, and powered on, that XP knows about your network card, and that TCP/IP is working. See the sidebar "Troubleshooting: Unable to Browse the Network," near the end of Chapter 31, and the section "Using Ping to Test Network Connections" in Chapter 18 for advice.

If the connection *is* working, the problem lies with the ICS host. Again, your most immediate course of action is to walk over to the host and examine it (and perhaps anyone using it) closely. But if the host (and its user) is inaccessible to you, you're essentially stuck—unless you can manipulate that user remotely.

Sharing a Folder or Drive

To share a folder or a drive, use the technique described in the section "Sharing a Folder 'on the Network' with All Other Users" in Chapter 10. To recap briefly: Right-click the folder and choose Sharing and Security from the context menu. On the Sharing page of the Properties dialog box for the folder, select the Share This Folder on the Network check box, and specify in the Share Name text box the name under which to share the folder. If you haven't run the Network Setup Wizard, you'll need to either run it first or click the If You Understand the Security Risks but Want to Share Files without Running the Wizard, Click Here link.

As discussed in the section "Mapping and Disconnecting Network Drives" in Chapter 31, folders are shared under Universal Naming Convention (UNC) names, which start with two backslashes (\\) before the name of the computer sharing them. For example, if the computer named `WinBox01` is sharing a folder under the share name `MP3s`, the UNC name for the share is `\\WinBox01\MP3s\`.

Sharing a Printer

Over the past few years, printer prices have dropped nearly as dramatically as printers' capabilities have risen—but even so, a printer worth having costs the best part of a year's supply of Krispy Kremes (okay, a *month's* supply if you're a heavy user), so you don't want to buy any more printers than you absolutely need for your home or office. Still, for many households and most offices, that means a minimum of two or more printers to handle different printing tasks. For example, you might have a laser printer for handling home-office and school chores such as printing documents and spread-sheets, and a color printer for photographs and fun items.

In any case, the printer itself works out to be the smallest cost in the long run of printing. Ink cartridges are expensive—that's where the printer manufacturers make money, just like razor makers take losses on the razors but rake in the profits on the replacement blades. Fancy paper for high-quality color printers and photo printers runs expensive. And printers tend to break if abused or if given the evil eye more than once a week.

Bulging preamble, hidden point: To get the most out of your printers, you can share them across your network with your other networked computers. XP makes it easy to share printers and to connect to shared printers.

To share a printer that you've already set up on your computer, take the following steps:

1. Display the Printers and Faxes screen of Control Panel. (For example, choose Start ➢ Control Panel, click the Printers and Other Hardware link in Control Panel, and click the Printers and Faxes link on the Printers and Other Hardware screen.)

2. Right-click the printer and choose Sharing from the context menu. Alternatively, select the printer and click the Share This Printer link in the Tasks list. XP displays the Sharing page of the Properties dialog box for the printer.

3. Select the Share This Printer option button. XP activates the Share Name text box and enters a suggested name for the shared printer. This shared name is derived from the first eight char-acters of the printer's existing name—an improvement on the stunningly unoriginal `Printern` name that the Network Setup Wizard uses for the printers it networks, but nonetheless improvable.

4. Change the name in the Share Name text box if you want. Keep the name down to eight or fewer characters if you need the printer to be accessible to computers running Windows 3.*x* or DOS. If all your computers use 32-bit versions of Windows, you can make the name longer and more descriptive. For example, you might want to include the computer's name or description so that when users print to the printer, they're clear as to where they'll find their printouts.

5. If the computers with which you'll be sharing the printer use versions of Windows other than XP, click the Additional Drivers button. XP displays the Additional Drivers dialog box (shown in Figure 32.7).

FIGURE 32.7

If you'll be sharing this printer with computers running other versions of Windows, use the Additional Drivers dialog box to install drivers for them.

6. Select the appropriate check boxes in the Environment column. The Alpha environment is computers using the DEC Alpha processor (for which Microsoft provided versions of Windows NT). The IA64 is Intel's 64-bit chip code-named Itanium. The other environments you should recognize.

7. Click the OK button. If XP needs you to provide drivers for any of the operating systems you chose, it displays the Printer Drivers dialog box. Use the Browse button and the resulting Locate File dialog box to identify the drivers, and then click the OK button. XP installs the drivers and closes the Additional Drivers dialog box, returning you to the Properties dialog box for the printer.

8. Click the OK button. XP closes the Properties dialog box and displays a shared icon for the printer (a printer with an open hand in front of it).

Other computers can now connect to the shared printer as described in the next section.

TIP   If you want remote users to receive a notification when their print jobs are printed, select the Notify when Remote Documents Are Printed check box on the Advanced page of the Print Server Properties dialog box. See the section "Configuring Your Print Server" in Chapter 13 for details.

Connecting to a Shared Printer

To connect to a shared printer, take the following steps:

1. Choose Start ➤ Control Panel. XP displays Control Panel.

2. Click the Printers and Other Hardware link. XP displays the Printers and Other Hardware screen.

3. Click the Add a Printer link in the Pick a Task list. (Alternatively, click the Add a Printer link in the Tasks list on the Printers and Faxes screen.) XP starts the Add Printer Wizard, which displays its Welcome page.

4. Click the Next button. The wizard displays the Local or Network Printer page.

5. Select the A Network Printer, or a Printer Attached to Another Computer option button.

6. Click the Next button. The wizard displays the Specify a Printer page.

7. Choose one of the following three ways of specifying the printer:

   ◆ Usually, it's best to leave the Browse for a Printer option button selected and use the browse procedure to locate the printer as described in the next steps.

   ◆ If you know the printer's name and location, select the Connect to This Printer option button and enter the path and printer name in the Name text box. For example, if the computer Requiem is sharing a printer named Laser1, you would enter \\Requiem\Laser1.

   ◆ Similarly, if you know the URL for the printer, select the Connect to a Printer on the Internet or on a Home or Office Network option button and enter the URL in the URL text box.

8. Click the Next button. If you chose to browse for a printer, the wizard displays the Browse for Printer page (shown in Figure 32.8 with the network tree expanded).

FIGURE 32.8

Use the Browse for Printer page of the Add Printer Wizard to identify the shared printer you want to use.

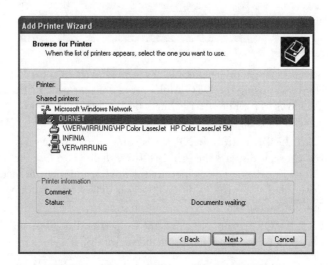

9. In the Shared Printers list box, expand the network tree until you reach the printer you want, then select the printer. The wizard enters the printer's full name in the Printer text box.

10. Click the Next button. The wizard displays the Default Printer page, which asks whether you want to use the printer as your default printer.

11. Select the Yes option button or the No option button as appropriate.

12. Click the Next button. The wizard displays the Completing the Add Printer Wizard page, which details the printer you've chosen.

13. Click the Finish button. The wizard closes and adds the printer to your Printers and Faxes list. The icon for the printer has a network cable underneath it, indicating that the printer is connected via the network.

You can then use the printer as you would a local printer, except that you can't set Sharing options or Advanced options for the printer.

NOTE   *If the computer sharing the printer doesn't have a printer driver for XP, XP alerts you to the problem and invites you to install the printer driver on your computer. Click the OK button and use the Add Printer Wizard to identify the type of printer.*

Using a Print Server

As discussed in Chapter 13, one of the most appealing ways of making one or more printers available on your network is to add a print server to the network. Having a print server means that you don't need to keep the computer sharing the printer running in order for any of the computers connected to the network to be able to print. It also means that you can locate the print server and its printers anywhere on your network that has access to an Ethernet cable (or a wireless connection) and a power socket (or Power over Ethernet, if you have an adapter for it)—the print hardware doesn't have to be within a bidirectional parallel cable's distance of your computer.

Once you've bought and unpacked your print server, connect the printer or printers to it, and then connect it to the network and to its power supply (if it needs one). For some print servers, you may need to install TCP/IP redirection software that captures the print jobs and directs them to the print server.

So far, so easy. You then have to decide how to use the print server. If part of your motivation for getting the print server was to free up the computer that previously managed the printer or printers from its print-management duties, install the print software on all the computers that will need to print to the printers. That way, each can print independently, and each will be able to manage all print jobs on the printer. Alternatively, you can install the printer on one computer and share it from there, so that this computer will be able to manage all print jobs on the printer while other computers will be able to manage only their own print jobs—but the computer sharing the printer will need to be running all the time for the other computers to be able to print.

Connecting to an LPR Printer

Some printers are designed to be connected directly to a network (rather than to a computer or to a print server) and print using LPR/LPD, a protocol originally developed for Unix. XP can print to LPR printers as long as you install LPR support, which isn't installed by default.

INSTALLING LPR SUPPORT

To install LPR support, take the following steps:

1. Open the Network Connections window.
2. Choose Advanced ➢ Optional Networking Components. XP displays the Windows Optional Networking Components Wizard, which is essentially a subcomponent of the Windows Components Wizard.
3. Select the Other Network File and Print Services check box and click the Next button. The wizard prompts you for your XP Home CD or installation source and, when you supply it, installs Print Services for Unix, which is the only item in the Other Network File and Print Services category.
4. Click the Finish button. The wizard closes itself.

ADDING AN LPR PRINTER

Once you've installed LPR support, you can add an LPR printer by running the Add Printer Wizard and making the following choices:

1. On the Local or Network Printer page of the wizard, select the Local Printer Attached to This Computer option button (yes, this is counter-intuitive, but do it anyway) and clear the Automatically Detect and Install My Plug and Play Printer check box.

2. On the Select a Printer Port page of the wizard, select the Create a New Port option button and then select the LPR Port item in the Type of Port drop-down list.

3. When you click the Next button, XP displays the Add LPR Compatible Printer dialog box (see Figure 32.9).

FIGURE 32.9

Enter the details of the LPR printer in the Add LPR Compatible Printer dialog box.

Add LPR compatible printer	
Name or address of server providing lpd:	OK
Name of printer or print queue on that server:	Cancel
	Help

4. In the Name or Address of Server Providing LPD text box, enter the host name or IP address of the server.

5. In the Name of Printer or Print Queue on That Server text box, enter the name of the printer or the print queue.

6. Click the OK button. XP checks that it can access the printer. If it can, XP then lets you specify the type of printer and choose other options. If XP can't access the printer, it displays the LPR Port Configuration Warning dialog box (see Figure 32.10), which lists possible causes of the problem. Click the OK button to continue with the installation (for example, if you know the print settings are right but the printer is offline) or the Cancel button to return to the Add LPR Compatible Printer dialog box and change the settings.

FIGURE 32.10

XP displays the LPR Port Configuration Warning dialog box if it can't connect to the printer you specified.

LPR Port Configuration Warning

The LPD Server did not respond as expected to a test command. Any of the following can cause this error:

The entry for IP Address or Queue name is incorrect.

The TCP/IP print device (LPD server) does not support the test command.

The specified TCP/IP print device is not available.

If the information typed in the previous screen is correct, you can ignore this message. Click OK to continue, or click Cancel to return to the previous screen and verify settings.

OK   Cancel

Printing across the Internet with IPP

IPP is the Internet Printing Protocol, an HTTP-based protocol that lets you print to a shared printer across the Internet. IPP is appealing to business travelers and others who often need to print to a remote printer via an Internet connection. You might also want to use IPP to deliver a printed copy of, say, a proposal to a client rather than send them a (possibly editable) file to print out themselves. Or you might need to print certain jobs to a high-quality printer at a service bureau. (In both of the last two cases, an alternative is to send a print file or PDF to the recipient so that they can print it themselves. See the section "Printing to a File" in Chapter 13 for a discussion of how to create print files.)

If you need to print across the Internet with IPP, set up the printer by following steps 1–6 of the list in the section "Connecting to a Shared Printer," earlier in this chapter. On the Specify a Printer page of the Add Printer Wizard, select the Connect to a Printer on the Internet or on a Home or Office Network option button and enter the URL for the printer in the URL text box. Provide your username and password for the printer, and install a driver for it on your computer if XP prompts you to do so. You'll then be set up to use that printer.

To see the IPP printers available at a particular location, use Internet Explorer to view the URL `http://server/Printers`, where *server* is the name or IP address of the server. The Printers page displays a list of the printers. To install a printer on your computer, click the link for the printer to display its page, and then click the Connect link in the Printer Actions list.

Once you've installed an IPP printer on one of your computers that's running XP, you can share it with other computers on your network. Doing so tends to be easier than installing the printer on each of them.

NOTE   *To share a printer yourself for use with IPP, you need to be running Internet Information Services, which come built into XP Professional but are not part of XP Home.*

Repairing a Network Connection

If a network connection seems not to be working or seems to be malfunctioning, you may need to repair it. To do so, choose Start ➤ Connect To ➤ Show All Connections. XP displays the Network Connections screen. Either select the connection and click the Repair This Connection link in the Network Tasks list, or right-click the connection and choose Repair from the context menu.

EXPERT KNOWLEDGE: MAPPING DRIVES FROM THE COMMAND LINE VIA THE *NET USE* COMMAND

You can map a drive quickly from the command line by using the net use command. Choose Start ➤ All Programs ➤ Accessories ➤ Command Prompt to open a Command Prompt window, and then follow the instructions in this sidebar.

The basic syntax for the net use command is as follows:

```
net use drive path
```

Here, *drive* is the drive letter that you want to use to access the shared folder, and *path* is the path to the folder. For example, the following command connects the shared folder \\TBC\users as drive F:

```
net use f: \\TBC\users
```

If XP is able to assign the share, it reports "The command completed successfully." If XP isn't able to assign the share because it can't find the network drive, it returns a system error 53 and tells you "The network path was not found."

Continued on next page

EXPERT KNOWLEDGE: MAPPING DRIVES FROM THE COMMAND LINE VIA THE *NET USE* COMMAND (*continued*)

To make the mapping persistent, use the /persistent parameter with the argument yes. For example, the following command connects the shared folder \\TBC\users as drive F and will reconnect at each subsequent logon:

```
net use f: \\TBC\users /persistent:yes
```

If you want net use to use the next available drive letter for the share, enter an asterisk in the command instead of specifying the drive letter. For example,

```
net use * \\TBC\users
```

If you need to supply an account name and a password for the drive you're connecting to, specify them in this format:

```
net use drive path password /user:domain\username
```

Here, *password* is the password, and *domain\username* is the domain or workgroup name, a backslash, and the username. For example, the following command connects drive Z to the shared folder \\TBC\users using the password 1llumin8! and the username Jaq in the workgroup MSHome:

```
net use z: \\TBC\users 1llumin8! /user:MSHome\Jaq
```

You can also use the server's IP address instead of its name. This can be especially useful if you're connecting to the server across the Internet.

If you see the message *The credentials supplied conflict with an existing set of credentials*, usually accompanied by a system error 1219, it can mean either of two things. First, that you already have a connection to this share using a different username and (valid) password, and that net use doesn't approve of your trying to connect with another username or password. Or second, that the computer to which you're trying to connect has decided, on the basis of a failed connection attempt you've made, that you're persona non grata as far as it's concerned.

In either case, use the net use *drive:* /d command to disconnect from the server, then try to connect again:

```
net use Z: /d
```

If you're in doubt as to which folders are connected to which drive, type **net use** at the command prompt without any arguments and press the Enter key. XP displays a list of the local drives, the remote folders, and their status.

To see the status of a network drive, type **net use *drive:*,** where *drive* is the drive letter. You'll see a printout something like the following, giving the name of the remote folder, the resource type, the status, the number of files open, and the number of connections.

```
C:\>net use q:
Local name        Q:
Remote name       \\Donner\SharedDocs\Fun
Resource type     Disk
Status            OK
# Opens           3
# Connections     1
The command completed successfully.
```

Configuring Networking Components Manually

XP automatically installs and configures the most widely used network components—network clients, network services, and network protocols—when you install the OS. The Network Setup Wizard installs and configures further network components as necessary when you run it, depending on the type of network configuration it finds. And the Found New Hardware Wizard and the Add Hardware Wizard also add networking components when they discover new networking hardware that's not covered by your existing networking components. But you can also install, configure, and remove networking components manually as described in this section if you so choose.

The following subsections describe the networking components that XP provides, starting with the standard configuration for a LAN connection and for a dial-up connection, and then examining the less usual components and discussing when and how to add them.

Standard Configuration for a LAN Connection

XP's standard configuration for a LAN connection consists of the components shown in the following list. You'll find these components listed in the This Connection Uses the Following Items list box on the General page of the Local Area Connection Properties dialog box. To display this dialog box, choose Start ➤ Control Panel, click the Network and Internet Connections link, and then click the Network Connections link. Then right-click the Local Area Network Connection icon and choose Properties from the context menu.

CLIENT FOR MICROSOFT NETWORKS

The Client for Microsoft Networks enables your computer to access files and printers that other computers on the network are sharing. Normally, you won't need to configure Client for Microsoft Networks unless you're using Distributed Computing Environment (DCE) server or client kits, which is very unlikely. (If you *are* using DCE, select the Client for Microsoft Networks item in the This Connection Uses the Following Items list and click the Properties button. XP displays the Client for Microsoft Networks Properties dialog box, which contains only one page, the RPC Service page. In the Name Service Provider drop-down list, change from the default item, Windows Locator, to DCE Cell Directory Service. Specify the network address in the Network Address text box. Then click the OK button to close the dialog box.)

FILE AND PRINTER SHARING FOR MICROSOFT NETWORKS

File and Printer Sharing for Microsoft Networks enables your computer to share files and printers with other computers on the network. The Network Setup Wizard enables File and Printer Sharing by default, but if this computer doesn't have any resources that you want to share with other computers on the network, clear the check box for this item to prevent the connection from using it.

QoS PACKET SCHEDULER

The QoS Packet Scheduler organizes the sending and receiving of packets (chunks of data packaged for transmission) so as to maintain quality of service (QoS).

That may sound esoteric (and the details are), but the principle is straightforward enough. Some data transmissions suffer more than others from a delay in the stream of packets. For example, when you transfer a data file from one computer to another, it doesn't much matter if there's a hiatus while the data is being delivered: After all the packets of data have arrived, the network card and network client software kick the packets back into the correct order and reassemble them into a file that you can work with. By contrast, if you're listening to streaming audio or watching streaming video across a network connection, a hiatus in the stream of packets will produce a break in the audio or video, spoiling the experience. So the QoS Packet Scheduler gives priority to data that would suffer from being interrupted over data that's less sensitive to time lags.

INTERNET PROTOCOL (TCP/IP)

TCP/IP is the protocol suite on which the Internet is based and is XP's default network protocol. TCP/IP has a number of properties that you can set in the Internet Protocol (TCP/IP) Properties dialog box. The section "Configuring TCP/IP Manually," later in this chapter, discusses how to set these properties.

Standard Configuration for a Dial-up Internet Connection

A standard dial-up Internet connection uses the Internet Protocol (TCP/IP) and QoS Packet Scheduler items.

Make sure that your dial-up Internet connection isn't using the File and Printer Sharing for Microsoft Networks item, because this exposes your shared files and printers to everyone on the Internet.

Other Components and When You May Need to Use Them

This section discusses the other networking components that XP provides and when you may need to use them.

CLIENT SERVICE FOR NETWARE

Client Service for NetWare is a network client that lets you connect to a network server running Novell, Inc.'s NetWare (or IntraNetware). Unless you have a NetWare server in your home or home office, you shouldn't need this network client.

NWLINK IPX/SPX/NETBIOS COMPATIBLE TRANSPORT PROTOCOL

IPX/SPX is the protocol traditionally used by Novell, Inc.'s NetWare network operating system and by client computers connecting to it. You can use IPX/SPX on a home network or home-office network that has nothing to do with NetWare, but in most cases, TCP/IP is a better bet.

NETWORK MONITOR DRIVER

Network Monitor Driver is a tool that lets a network administrator monitor your computer's network transmissions (for example, to diagnose a problem). Very rarely will you need to install Network Monitor Driver in a home or home-office network.

SERVICE ADVERTISING PROTOCOL

Service Advertising Protocol (SAP) is a protocol that advertises the presence of servers, services, and addresses on a network. SAP is primarily used on large networks. You shouldn't need it on a small network.

Installing and Removing Networking Components

To install the networking components discussed in the previous section, follow the procedure in the next subsection. To remove an installed networking component from all connections, follow the procedure in the subsection after next. To disable an installed networking component for a particular connection (rather than remove it from all connections), follow the procedure in the third subsection.

INSTALLING A NETWORKING COMPONENT

To install a networking component from the Properties dialog box for a connection, take the following steps:

1. Click the Install button on the General page of the Properties dialog box for the connection. XP displays the Select Network Component Type dialog box (see Figure 32.11).

FIGURE 32.11

In the Select Network Component Type dialog box, choose Client, Service, or Protocol as appropriate.

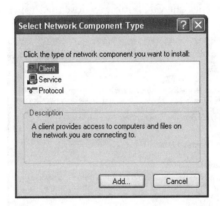

2. In the list box, select the Client item, the Service item, or the Protocol item as appropriate.

3. Click the Add button. XP displays the Select Network Client dialog box, the Select Network Service dialog box, or the Select Network Protocol dialog box as appropriate. Figure 32.12 shows the Select Network Protocol dialog box.

FIGURE 32.12

In the Select Network Protocol dialog box (shown here), the Select Network Client dialog box, or the Select Network Service dialog box, select the protocol, client, or service to install.

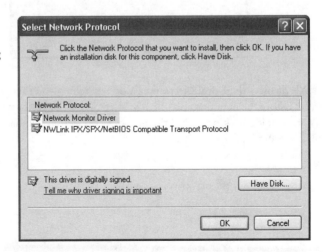

4. In the list box, select the component to add. If you have on disk a component that XP doesn't provide, click the Have Disk button and use the resulting Install from Disk dialog box to specify the location of the file containing the component, then select the component itself.

5. Click the OK button. XP installs the component and returns you to the Properties dialog box for the connection.

6. If the component has configurable properties that you want to configure, select it in the This Connection Uses the Following Items list box and click the Properties button. (If the component has no configurable properties, this button will be dimmed and unavailable.) XP displays the Properties dialog box for the component. Figure 32.13 shows an example: the NWLink IPX/SPX/NetBIOS Compatible Transport Protocol Properties dialog box. (Not surprisingly, the title bar of the dialog box abbreviates this long-winded name.) Choose properties as appropriate and then click the OK button to close the Properties dialog box.

FIGURE 32.13

Depending on the networking component you install, you may need to set properties for it.

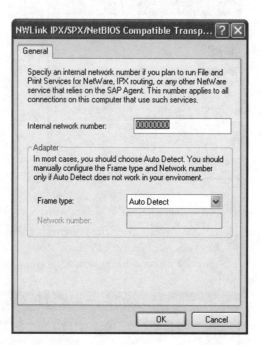

7. If XP displays the Local Network dialog box telling you that you need to restart your computer before the new settings will take effect, click the Yes button. XP restarts your computer. When you log back on to XP, the network connection will have the client, service, or protocol installed and available for use.

EXPERT KNOWLEDGE: INSTALLING NetBEUI

As mentioned in Chapter 30, XP includes NetBEUI, an older networking protocol used by DOS and early versions of Windows. Microsoft doesn't support NetBEUI on XP, and XP doesn't install NetBEUI automatically, but it still works, and in rare circumstances you may need to install it—for example, for running older software that can't handle TCP/IP. Some classic multiplayer games, such as the original DOOM and Heretic, require NetBEUI.

To install NetBEUI, close all running programs and take the following steps:

1. Dig out your XP CD and insert it in a CD drive. Alternatively, make sure that you're connected to a flat of XP (a copy of the installation files).

2. Open an Explorer window to the \VALUEADD\MSFT\NET\NETBEUI\ folder on the CD or the flat.

3. Copy NBF.SYS to your *%systemroot%*\System32\Drivers\ folder.

4. Copy NETNBF.INF to your *%systemroot%*\INF\ folder.

Once you've copied the files, you can install NetBEUI by following the procedure described in this section. You'll need to reboot your computer to complete the installation.

NetBEUI has no configurable properties. You can turn it off for the connection by clearing its check box on the General page of the connection's Properties dialog box.

REMOVING A NETWORKING COMPONENT

To remove a networking component, select it on the General page of the Properties dialog box for a Local Area Connection and click the Uninstall button. XP displays a confirmation dialog box warning you that uninstalling the component removes it from all network connections (not from just the connection from which you're uninstalling it). Click the Yes button to proceed.

Depending on the component, you may need to shut down and restart your computer after removing the component.

DISABLING A NETWORKING COMPONENT

If you don't want to uninstall a networking component for all network connections, disable it for the connection in question by displaying the connection's Properties dialog box and clearing the check box for the component.

Installing and Removing Network Components via Windows Setup

Beyond the networking components discussed so far that you can install (or remove) from the Properties dialog box for a network connection, XP offers several other networking components that you can install or remove by using the Windows Components Wizard. (To run the Windows Components Wizard, choose Start ➢ Control Panel, click the Add or Remove Programs link, and then click the Add/Remove Windows Components button in the Add or Remove Programs window.)

In the Windows Component Wizard, the extra components are listed under the categories Networking Services, Other Network File and Print Services, and (less intuitively) Management and Monitoring Tools. Select one of these items and click the Details button to drill down to the individual components.

NETWORKING SERVICES

The Networking Services category includes the following components:

RIP Listener   A tool that enables XP to listen to Router Information Protocol (RIP) broadcast packets giving information about router availability and reconfigure its TCP/IP routing tables accordingly. You won't normally need RIP Listener on a small network.

Simple TCP/IP Services   A group of TCP/IP services (including a Quote of the Day service and an Echo generator) that you're unlikely to need. Don't install them unless you're sure you need them, because they can be used in denial-of-service (DoS) attacks by malware that gets onto your computer. Worse yet, some personal firewall software packages don't monitor these services.

Universal Plug & Play   Universal Plug & Play (UPnP) lets networked devices advertise their presence, discover each other, and configure themselves to work with each other. If you install UPnP (as you will want to if you have a device that requires it), install the patch that Microsoft provides for it, because the version originally shipped with XP is vulnerable to a buffer-overflow attack. (A *buffer overflow* occurs when a program tries to put too much data into a memory buffer. The data that won't fit in the buffer overflows and can be used to execute programs.) You can get the patch either through Windows Update or from the link on article Q315000 on the Microsoft Knowledge Base (`support.microsoft.com`).

OTHER NETWORK FILE AND PRINT SERVICES

The Other Network File and Print Services category includes only one item: Print Services for Unix, which enables Unix or Linux computers to print to printers that your computer is sharing.

MANAGEMENT AND MONITORING TOOLS

The Management and Monitoring Tools category includes the following tools:

Simple Network Management Protocol   This protocol, SNMP, is used to manage larger networks (for example, remotely administering routers and switches). You shouldn't need to install it on a home network or a home-office network.

WMI SNMP Provider   This component lets Windows Management Interface (WMI) programs access SNMP information. You shouldn't need this component on a home network or home-office network.

Configuring TCP/IP Manually

For most home network or home-office network configurations, it's easiest to use a DHCP server of some sort to assign IP addresses automatically when they're needed. For example, if you use Internet Connection Sharing (ICS) to share your Internet connection, XP Home automatically configures the ICS host to use ICS' built-in DHCP allocator to supply IP addresses to the computers on your network. Similarly, many residential gateways and other shared Internet access devices offer built-in DHCP servers that automatically allocate IP addresses for computers connected to the same network.

That said, sometimes you'll need to configure TCP/IP manually to specify a fixed IP address and DNS server details. To do so, take the following steps:

1. Choose Start ➤ Connect To ➤ Show All Connections. XP displays the Network Connections screen.

2. Right-click the Local Area Connection icon in question and choose Properties from the context menu. XP displays the Local Area Connection Properties dialog box with the General page foremost.

3. In the This Connection Uses the Following Items list box, select the Internet Protocol (TCP/IP) item.

4. Click the Properties button. (Alternatively, double-click the Internet Protocol (TCP/IP) item.) XP displays the Internet Protocol (TCP/IP) dialog box. If your computer is configured to obtain an IP address automatically, this dialog box contains a General page and an Alternate Configuration page, as shown on the left in Figure 32.14. If it's configured to use a specific IP address, the dialog box contains only the General page, as shown on the right in Figure 32.14.

FIGURE 32.14

If necessary, you can configure TCP/IP manually in the Internet Protocol (TCP/IP) dialog box. When the computer is using DHCP to obtain an address, this dialog box contains a General page and an Alternate Configuration page (left). When the computer is using a fixed IP address, this dialog box contains only the General page (right).

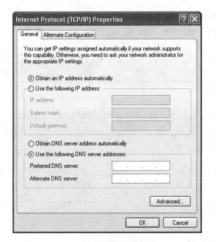

5. Select the Use the Following IP Address option button. XP hides the Alternate Configuration tab, because it's not relevant when you use a fixed IP address.

6. In the Use the Following IP Address group box, enter the details of the IP address: the IP address itself (for example, **192.168.0.44**), the subnet mask (for example, **255.255.255.0**), and the default gateway (for example, **192.168.0.1**).

7. In the Use the Following DNS Server Addresses group box, enter the IP addresses of your preferred (or *primary*) DNS server and alternate (or *secondary*) DNS server.

8. If you need to add further DNS servers, click the Advanced button. XP displays the Advanced TCP/IP Settings dialog box.

9. Click the DNS tab. XP displays the DNS page (see Figure 32.15).

FIGURE 32.15

You can adjust your DNS configuration on the DNS page of the Advanced TCP/IP Properties dialog box.

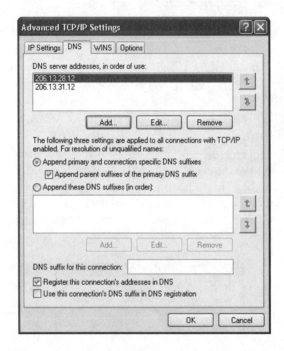

10. In the DNS Server Addresses, in Order of Use list box, arrange the list of DNS servers into the order in which you want the servers queried:

- ◆ Use the Up button and the Down button to shuffle the listed servers into order.
- ◆ Use the Add button and the resulting TCP/IP DNS Server dialog box to add a server to the list.
- ◆ Use the Edit button and the resulting TCP/IP DNS Server dialog box to edit an existing server entry.
- ◆ Use the Remove button to remove a server.

11. Click the OK button. XP closes the Advanced TCP/IP Settings dialog box.

12. Click the OK button. XP closes the Internet Protocol (TCP/IP) dialog box.

NOTE *Before you ask: You'll rarely need to change the settings on the IP Settings page and the WINS page of the Advanced TCP/IP Settings dialog box. (WINS is the acronym for Windows Internet Name Service, a service that TCP/IP uses to resolve NetBIOS names.) The Options page of the Advanced TCP/IP Settings dialog box lets you implement TCP/IP filtering on your computer. TCP/IP filtering lets you specify that only data packets that match certain criteria will be accepted, thus making it more difficult for an attacker to reach your network. See "Filtering TCP/IP to Keep Out Unauthorized Data Packets" in Chapter 33 for coverage of implementing TCP/IP filtering.*

Connecting Two Networks via a Bridge

As mentioned earlier, XP lets you *bridge* (connect) two separate networks so that they essentially function as a single network. For example, you might need to connect a wireless network to a wired network or a FireWire network to a wired Ethernet network. Or you might need to connect a FireWire network to a wireless network—that works too.

The networks can be of different types (as in those examples) or of the same type. For example, you can bridge two local area networks running TCP/IP if you need to. Or you could bridge a local area network running TCP/IP with a local area network running IPX/SPX.

As discussed earlier in this chapter, the Network Setup Wizard can automatically set up bridging for your network if all your network connections are present and correct when you run the wizard. But you may also need to set up bridging manually as described in this section so that you have more control over the connections established.

The computer on which you implement the bridging needs to be connected to both networks, so it will have at least two network interfaces, one connected to each network.

To bridge the network connections, select them on the Network Connections screen of Control Panel, then right-click the selection and choose Bridge Connections from the context menu. XP creates the bridge, applies it to the network connections, and displays an icon named Network Bridge. If you're likely to forget which connections are bridged, rename the Network Bridge icon to something more descriptive (for example, add the names of the connections that the bridge connects).

Once you've created a bridge, the bridged network adapters have the same IP address, and XP forwards all data packets from each segment to the other network segment. To configure properties for the bridged network adapters, work with the bridge rather than with the individual network adapters: Right-click the bridge and choose Properties from the context menu to display its Properties dialog box, then make the changes there.

Apart from configuring the bridge's properties, you can manipulate it from the context menu as follows:

- To add a connection to the bridge, right-click it and choose Add to Bridge from the context menu.
- To remove a connection from the bridge, right-click it and choose Remove from Bridge from the context menu.
- To disable the bridge, right-click it and choose Disable from the context menu.
- To delete the bridge, right-click it and choose Delete from the context menu. Confirm the deletion.

Up Next

This chapter has discussed how to configure your networked devices and how to share your Internet connection, your printers, and your folders.

The next chapter discusses how to secure your network.

Chapter 33

Securing Your Network

THIS CHAPTER COVERS HOW to secure your network against both external and internal threats. It discusses how to identify the points of weakness on a typical network and the best ways of securing them, and it provides in-depth coverage of how to secure wireless networks, which have additional security considerations.

This chapter covers the following topics:

◆ Understanding the points of weakness on your network

◆ Normal methods of securing a home network

◆ Securing your Internet connection with a firewall

◆ Using antivirus software

◆ Securing your browsers and programs

◆ Limiting user access to computers and files

◆ Maintaining your hardware and software

◆ Filtering TCP/IP to keep out unauthorized data packets

◆ Backing up data on your network

◆ Securing a wireless network

WARNING   For many home network and home-office network administrators, the main problem with network security is getting people—including perhaps yourself—to take it seriously. It's tempting to believe that your computer or your network is unlikely to be attacked and that therefore you don't really need to bother securing it. After all, if several hundred million computers are on the Internet, why should anyone pick on yours? Similarly, you might choose not to pay for home insurance on the assumption that your home is very unlikely to be broken into. But unlike your home, which is vulnerable only to thieves in the neighborhood, a computer or network connected to the Internet is vulnerable to everyone else who's online—and unlike thieves, hackers have automated tools with which they can scan Internet addresses for unprotected computers and attack them automatically. People who have secured their networks often find in their firewall logs frequent attempts to access their networks from IP addresses all over the world. And if an attacker is subtle rather than savage, they can access your unprotected computer, read your files, and steal your secrets without your being any the wiser.

Understanding the Points of Weakness on Your Network

As everyone knows, a house has certain obvious points of weakness for an attacker: the doors; the windows; the chimney (possibly); and any hole in the roof, walls, floors, or ceiling. An attacker could brazenly try to open a door or window. They could try to slip into the house undetected by weaseling through a rat hole in the baseboard. They could simply smash their way in by using a bulldozer. Or they could try to persuade you (or your house) to open the door for them.

Similarly, an individual stand-alone computer has obvious points of weakness, the usual suspects being the floppy drive, the CD or DVD drives, and any other removable drives, any of which can be used to load infected files or malware onto the computer. The computer may also be open to physical attacks, such as cutting off the power supply (either at the computer, at the wall socket or breaker box, or outside the building) or trying to open it with a sledgehammer.

As soon as you connect your computer to the Internet, you open another channel for attack or infection. In many cases, the Internet connection poses a far greater threat to the security of the computer than do the floppy, CD, and removable drives.

When two or more computers are connected in a network, each point of weakness on an individual computer becomes a threat to the other computers on the network. And when you connect the network to the Internet, each computer connected to the network becomes vulnerable to attack and infection through the Internet connection. Unless the Internet connection is tightly protected, an attacker can take control of a computer on the network and use it to attack or infect the other computers on the network.

To keep your network safe, you essentially want to make it the equivalent of a tightly controlled gated community surrounded by a high-risk area: Each computer attached to the network must be a known quantity, just as each house in a community must be (houses outside the community can't suddenly become part of the community). Users of networked computers have levels of access appropriate to their trustworthiness, just as community members do. For example, most community members will be allowed to access their own house but not other people's houses. Most users on the network will be allowed to use their own computer (or a computer they share with other people) but not other computers. Just as the road into the community from the outside needs to be guarded so that community members can come and go freely but unauthorized traffic is kept out, so the Internet connection needs to be firewalled and policed to prevent unauthorized data from entering the network. And the community leaders (read: the Computer Administrator users) supervise what's happening in the community, check periodically that the gatekeeper is doing its job (read: examine the firewall logs), and generally keep an eye on things.

Your home network is likely to have three main points of weakness:

◆ The network's Internet connection (or connections) can give an attacker access to your network; can bring in viruses, malware, or inappropriate material; and can send out your private data.

◆ The removable-media drives on the computers can be used to introduce dangerous material to your network or to copy your private data.

◆ The users of the computers on the network can delete files, steal files, install dangerous software, or introduce malware or inappropriate material to the network.

If your network is a home or home-office network, as this chapter is assuming, your users probably pose less of a threat than do the users of a corporate, governmental, or military network. But don't discount them as a threat, because even well-intentioned actions can damage your valuable data. For example, if someone decides to, say, install Linux on the same partition as your data files, you'll find yourself giving your backup and disaster-recovery strategy an impromptu workout—together with your central nervous system, most likely.

Normal Methods of Securing a Home Network

The normal methods of securing a home or home-office network are as follows:

- Secure the Internet connection with a firewall and configure the connection to prevent file sharing across it.
- Scan all incoming files for viruses. Monitor each computer for unusual activity.
- Choose browser settings to minimize the dangers of hostile web pages, scripts, and infected files. Choose high-security settings for programs that allow the execution of macros, scripts, and user forms.
- Use user accounts actively to control which computers users can use and which actions they can take on them.
- Use permissions to prevent users from accessing files you don't want them to access.
- Educate users about security risks and how to minimize them.
- Prevent untrustworthy users from physically accessing computers that contain sensitive or otherwise important data, or that are mission-critical. For example, in a home setting, lock your office so that young children or pets can't turn your financial files from Quicken to dead.
- For each computer that contains important data files or delivers services to other computers, keep the hardware and software maintained so that no computer stops working unexpectedly. (You should maintain *all* your computers, of course, but if time is short, concentrate your efforts on those that contain important data.)
- To make sure that no unauthorized traffic can enter certain parts of your network, implement TCP/IP filtering on key computers.

Besides securing the network using these techniques, you need to have a disaster-recovery plan for when the network's security is compromised. As with a stand-alone PC, that means backing up all the data files that you can't easily recreate and knowing how to restore the files.

The rest of this chapter discusses these steps in more detail, referring you to features covered in other chapters where appropriate.

EXPERT KNOWLEDGE: HOW ARE HIGH-SECURITY NETWORKS SECURED?

These security measures discussed so far in this section are adequate for most home and home-office networks. But what about networks that need really high security—corporate networks, governmental networks, and military networks? What do they use? This sidebar discusses some of the common techniques for securing networks. You could apply some of these measures to your home or home-office network if you felt the need—actually, you *could* just conceivably apply all of them. But as you'll see, that'd be extreme.

As mentioned earlier in this book, there's a foolproof way of making your computer truly secure from being hacked: Disconnect it from any network, unplug the modem, and seal the computer in a lead-lined room in a bunker deep underground. There you can compute in near-total security.

Continued on next page

EXPERT KNOWLEDGE: HOW ARE HIGH-SECURITY NETWORKS SECURED? *(continued)*

Most people don't find this approach practical, because it prevents them from working or playing as they need to or want to. But many high-security installations do follow this approach to a certain extent: Vital networks and workstations are kept physically isolated and protected. This isolation may involve anything from a secure room or secure area of a building up to a secure site protected by a patrolled and mined boundary fence.

For security, many networks aren't connected to the Internet at all. They may be completely isolated, or they may have secure connections to other high-security networks via private communication lines.

If the network has any Internet access, it'll be through at least one hardware firewall. Only users with a valid reason are allowed to access the Internet, and this access is likely to be through a proxy server, a computer that filters requests for web pages and retrieves those that are for permitted sites. A proxy server also stores the most frequently accessed web pages so that it can deliver them quickly when a user requests them.

Any publicly accessible servers and services are kept outside the firewall in what's called a demilitarized zone (DMZ) in a tribute to Korea or Berlin, depending on your historical preference. The DMZ is created by placing the computers that need to be in it between the firewall and the Internet connection. Computers placed in the DMZ contain no sensitive data and are locked down tightly so that people who access them can manipulate them only in approved ways and cannot use them to attack computers located inside the firewall. The computers in the DMZ are checked frequently to make sure they haven't been cracked and taken over.

E-mail—again, only if it's used, and usually it'll be used only for some users—goes through an e-mail gateway that filters both ingoing and outgoing messages to prevent messages from being sent to or arriving from forbidden addresses and to prevent inappropriate material from entering or leaving the network. For example, an e-mail gateway might check the content of incoming and outgoing messages, blocking or referring to an administrator any messages that fell afoul of its rules. Almost certainly, it would also scan all attachments for viruses and for content.

All files coming into the network—whether via an Internet connection, a network connection, or on physical media—are scanned for viruses and to make sure that their content is appropriate to its destination. Any executable files, and all new code, are tested in simulated environments to make sure they perform as they should before they're introduced to the working environment.

All personnel are closely evaluated for security before being employed. Access to the secure site or area requires an identity check. And personnel's actions at work are likely to be monitored or recorded.

As you can see, you *could* apply some of these measures to your home or home-office network. But in most cases you'll do best to stick with the simpler and less stringent measures outlined in the previous section.

Securing Your Internet Connection with a Firewall

If your network is connected to the Internet, securing your Internet connection is a vital step in securing your network. To secure the Internet connection, you need to implement a firewall on it. (If your network has multiple Internet connections, you need to implement a firewall on each connection.)

If you use Internet Connection Sharing (ICS) to share the connection, you have an easy solution available: Internet Connection Firewall (ICF) is included with XP, and the Network Setup Wizard enables it by default. You should also use ICF on any other Internet connections that computers on your network have—for example, if your network connects via a shared broadband connection, but one or two computers have additional dial-up connections, you need to implement ICF on those dial-up connections as well as on the shared broadband connection.

If you're not sure whether Internet Connection Firewall is enabled, open the Network Connections screen of Control Panel and see whether the icon for the connection has a lock symbol on it. If it doesn't, display the Advanced page of the Properties dialog box for the connection and select the Protect My Computer and Network by Limiting or Preventing Access to This Computer from the Internet check box. (See the section "Enabling and Disabling Internet Connection Firewall" in Chapter 18 for more information on ICF.)

If you need tight security, or you don't entirely trust ICF, or both, add a hardware firewall to the network. You can either implement a hardware firewall on its own, or you can use it to harden a network protected by a software firewall such as ICF. See a book about firewalls (such as *Firewalls 24seven* by Matthew Strebe and Charles Perkins, Sybex, 2002) for advice on choosing a hardware firewall. Check that the hardware firewall supports Universal Plug & Play (UPnP) if you want to be able to use programs such as Messenger across it.

Make sure you haven't bound File and Printer Sharing to the network adapter for your Internet connection. Display the Networking page of the Properties dialog box for the connection and verify that the File and Printer Sharing for Microsoft Networks check box in the This Connection Uses the Following Items list box is cleared. If not, clear it, then close the Properties dialog box and restart your Internet connection if it's currently connected.

Once your firewall is in place, check that it's working. One easy method is to run the free probe tools at the Gibson Research Corporation website (`www.grc.com`). This offers several free checks, including ShieldsUP!, PortProbe, and NanoProbe, designed to help you identify weaknesses in your security arrangements.

Using Antivirus Software

Next, use antivirus software to scan all incoming files for viruses and to monitor each computer for unusual activity, such as programs being run remotely or Trojan horses coming to life.

As mentioned earlier in the book, two of the leading antivirus products are Norton Antivirus from Symantec (`www.symantec.com/downloads/`) and McAfee VirusScan from McAfee.com Corporation (`download.mcafee.com/eval/evaluate2.asp`). Each offers an evaluation version from the web address given. Some companies offer free antivirus software, but as you'd expect, it doesn't provide as many features as the leading products.

Because each computer that gets infected can then infect other computers on the same network, it's vital to use antivirus software on all computers on your network. There's no sense in implementing Baked-Alaska security, in which your network is hard to attack on the outside but easy to attack on the inside. By the same token, educate the users about viruses and other threats to the network so that they can pull their weight in keeping the network secure rather than blithely compromising security by downloading Trojan-loaded screensavers and pirated software.

Securing Your Browsers and Programs

In theory, any program can compromise the security of your computer (or network), but in practice, the three leading contenders are web browsers, e-mail clients, and programs that include programming or scripting languages. By choosing as high security as you can for these programs, you can limit the amount of damage they can cause.

Securing Your Web Browsers

Because they're designed to access a wide variety of different types of content on the Internet, web browsers are a prime source of danger and contagion across the Internet connection. To help keep your network secure, you'll want to limit the amount of harm that browsers can do while enabling your Internet users to surf as widely as they wish (or you wish them to).

If you're using Internet Explorer, see the sections "Choosing Security Options," "Choosing a Level of Privacy," "Handling Cookies," "Screening Out Objectionable Content," and the "Security Category" subsection in the "Advanced Options" section in Chapter 19 for a discussion of the security options that Internet Explorer offers. If you're using another browser, consult its documentation for details of its security options.

Securing E-mail Clients

Your e-mail client can also pose a considerable threat to the security of your computer or network, because it brings in messages and attachments from anyone who chooses to send them to you (or whose computer has caught an e-mail virus that automatically sends messages to people in the address book).

If your e-mail client includes a programming language or scripting language (as both Outlook Express and Outlook do), it poses an even greater threat, as an incoming e-mail message can include a script that runs when you display the message (or when the program automatically displays it to you in the preview pane).

If you're using Outlook Express, see the section "Security Page Options" and the sidebar "Expert Knowledge: Protecting Yourself Against Malicious Attachments" in Chapter 21 for a discussion of how to secure Outlook Express. If you're using a different e-mail client, investigate its security options.

Securing Programmable Programs

In much the same way that e-mail clients that include programming or scripting languages can host an attack on your computer, so can any program that includes a programming or scripting language. To counter this threat, choose high-security settings for programs that allow the execution of macros, scripts, and user forms.

Visual Basic for Applications (VBA) is a favorite tool of malicious hackers, because it's used in a huge range of widely used programs—Microsoft Word, Excel, PowerPoint, Access, Visio, Corel WordPerfect, AutoCAD, and many others—it's easy to learn, and it's very powerful. Other programming languages (such as LotusScript, which is used by programs such as Lotus Notes) are equally powerful but tend to be seen as less juicy targets.

If you're using a VBA-enabled program, take the following steps to secure it:

1. Choose Tools ➢ Macro ➢ Security. The program displays the Security dialog box.
2. On the Security Level page, select the High option button if you don't use macros yourself or the Medium option button if you do.
3. On the Trusted Sources page, reduce the number of trusted sources to a minimum. (A trusted source is someone you trust to develop safe macros or code.)

4. If you have any doubts about the quality of macros or code in templates already installed on your computer, clear the Trust All Installed Add-ins and Templates check box.

5. Click the OK button. The program closes the Security dialog box and applies your changes.

NOTE *If you don't know whether a program is VBA-enabled, see if there's a Tools* ➢ *Macro* ➢ *Visual Basic Editor command. If there is, the program hosts VBA. Secure it.*

Limiting User Access to Computers and Files

Next, you need to limit users' access to the computers and files on your network. Restrict each user as far as you reasonably can without preventing them from taking the actions they need to. For example,

◆ Create only those user accounts you need to. Don't create a user account for each member of the household on each computer unless each user will need to use each computer. (Alternatively, create the accounts but disable extra accounts until they're needed.)

◆ Create user accounts as Limited accounts rather than as Computer Administrator accounts. That way, the users can do less damage if they're attacked by bad intentions or bad ideas.

TIP *If you can stomach the minor inconveniences involved, it's a good idea not to use Computer Administrator accounts for daily work. Instead, create a Limited account for each user for daily work and keep your Computer Administrator account or accounts for when you need to make a configuration change that a limited user isn't permitted to make.*

◆ Use strong passwords on all user accounts. Discourage users from sharing their passwords with each other.

◆ Apply Level 1 access (private—owner only access) to each user's \My Documents\ folder. Level 2 access (the default for the \My Documents\ folder) isn't secure enough for any but the most trusting environments.

◆ Share on the network only as many files as you absolutely need to. Use Level 4 access (shared with read-only access) unless you must use Level 5 access (shared with full control).

NOTE *See Chapter 10 for a full discussion of file sharing and permissions.*

◆ Lock away any computer that you can't afford to have other people in the house mess with. (Alternatively, get a removable hard drive and take it with you to prevent others from accessing your data.)

Maintaining Your Hardware and Software

Maintain your hardware and software so that your computers don't quit unexpectedly on you. This advice is so dangerously close to being a truism (or platitude—take your pick) that far too many people ignore it. It goes almost without saying that you should maintain your hardware and software to keep your computers running. But the point is that in a network, the failure of even one of the less interesting computers can deny the other computers data or services that they need.

If you know you'll need to repair or upgrade a computer, plan the process ahead of time so that you can transfer your data files to another computer for the duration of the upgrade or repair.

Filtering TCP/IP to Keep Out Unauthorized Data Packets

To take control of the IP packets flowing across your network adapters and trying to worm their way through your firewall, you can add TCP/IP filtering to your network adapters. TCP/IP filtering lets you specify that only packets destined for specific TCP ports or UDP ports, or specific IP protocol numbers, can pass the adapter. TCP/IP filtering can be a great way of keeping unauthorized traffic out of your network, but you need to apply it with care, because if you don't configure the filters to pass the packets needed for *your* TCP/IP communications, you won't be able to communicate with the other computers on your network.

TCP/IP filtering applies to all network connections, so if you apply it, you need to get the filters right so that you don't disable your network. Getting the filters right means knowing which port is used for which purpose. The best place to get a list of TCP/IP port assignments is www.iana.org/assignments/port-numbers.

To implement TCP/IP filtering, take the following steps:

1. Choose Start ➤ Connect To ➤ Show All Connections. XP displays the Network Connections folder.

2. Right-click the Local Area Network Connection icon and choose Properties from the context menu. XP displays the Properties dialog box for the connection with the General page foremost. (You can actually use the Properties dialog box for any network connection, but the Local Area Network Connection is usually the easiest.)

3. Double-click the Internet Protocol (TCP/IP) item in the list box. XP displays the Internet Protocol (TCP/IP) Properties dialog box.

4. Click the Advanced button. XP displays the Advanced TCP/IP Settings dialog box.

5. Click the Options tab. XP displays the Options page.

6. In the Optional Settings list box, double-click the TCP/IP Filtering item. XP displays the TCP/IP Filtering dialog box (shown in Figure 33.1 with some filters set).

FIGURE 33.1

In the TCP/IP Filtering dialog box, you can specify exactly which TCP and UDP ports can receive packets and which IP protocols can pass across your network adapters.

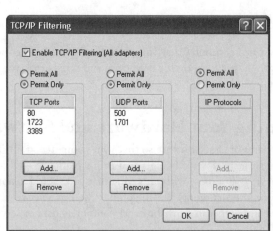

7. Select the Enable TCP/IP Filtering (All Adapters) check box.

8. To apply TCP filters, take the following steps:

   ◆ Select the Permit Only option button in the left column.

   ◆ Click the Add button. XP displays the Add Filter dialog box (shown in Figure 33.2).

FIGURE 33.2

In the Add Filter dialog box, enter the port or protocol to permit.

   ◆ Enter the port number in the TCP Port text box.

   ◆ Click the OK button. XP closes the Add Filter dialog box and adds the filter to the TCP Ports list box.

9. To apply UDP filters, take the following steps:

   ◆ Select the Permit Only option button in the center column.

   ◆ Click the Add button. XP displays the Add Filter dialog box.

   ◆ Enter the port number in the UDP Port text box.

   ◆ Click the OK button. XP closes the Add Filter dialog box and adds the filter to the UDP Ports list box.

10. To filter IP traffic by protocol, take the following steps:

    ◆ Select the Permit Only option button in the right column.

    ◆ Click the Add button. XP displays the Add Filter dialog box.

    ◆ Enter the IP protocol number in the IP Protocol text box.

    ◆ Click the OK button. XP closes the Add Filter dialog box and adds the filter to the IP Protocols list box.

11. Click the OK button. XP closes the TCP/IP Filtering dialog box.

12. Click the OK button. XP closes the Advanced TCP/IP Settings dialog box.

13. Click the OK button. XP closes the Internet Protocol (TCP/IP) Properties dialog box.

14. Click the OK button. XP closes the Properties dialog box for the Local Area Network Connection (or whichever network connection you used).

Now that you've applied filtering, XP checks all the packets that pass your network connections and compares them to the filters you've set. Any packets not specifically allowed to pass are discarded.

Before you forget, quickly check your network and Internet connectivity. Be sure to use the full range of programs that you need to be able to use in your work or play. If any of the programs doesn't work, the problem is most likely that you need to apply a filter to enable it to work. Check the list of port assignments, create the necessary filter to allow the packets to pass, and try again.

Backing Up Data on Your Network

Having a network lets you back up all the important data from each computer on the network to a central location, whether you have a peer-to-peer network or a server-based network. And back the data up you must, because (as discussed earlier in this chapter), having a network also increases the number of threats to your data.

As with a stand-alone PC, you can back your network's data up to a CD-R, CD-RW, recordable DVD, or removable disk if that gives you enough capacity. Removable media have the advantage that you can implement an off-site backup by sending the media elsewhere. If your network contains too much data for such media, back up your data either to an internal hard drive or an external hard drive. External hard drives (for example, FireWire drives) have the advantage that you can easily move them to another computer, making them an attractive solution for speed and capacity. However, it's hard to implement off-site backups unless you can afford a large number of external hard drives.

Another possibility is to back data up to an Internet backup site. Unless you've got both the money to pay for plenty of storage and a broadband Internet connection that's fast upstream as well as downstream, you'll probably want to back up only a small amount of critical data online—and because online backups raise security concerns, you'll probably want to encrypt the data before backing it up.

Backup procedures are essentially the same as described in Chapter 17. Connect the backup unit to (or install it on) a computer that will always be running when the other computers on the network need to back up data. This is particularly important if you schedule the backups to take place when no one is using the computers (but they're not powered down or in hibernation), as you'll probably want to do.

Securing a Wireless Network

Wireless networks require more security measures than wired networks, because they're often easily accessible from outside the property they cover and because most wireless access points automatically broadcast the network name so that clients can easily connect to it. Some neighborhoods have used these capabilities positively, to implement WiFi area networks for sharing a high-speed Internet connection with people in the same group of houses or street. Less positively, in the same way, if you don't secure your wireless network, your neighbors will be able to access your network, use any Internet connection you've shared, and perhaps even dip into your files.

This section discusses the steps you can take to secure your wireless network. It presents the steps separately because you may want to implement only some of them. It discusses the significance, benefits, and drawbacks of each security step.

NOTE   Corporations are enthusiastic implementers of wireless networks, because it allows their employees to lug their laptops to meetings and squeeze in a little more work. But many corporations are amazingly lax in securing their wireless networks. Hackers report performing "war drives" in San Francisco and being able to access different corporate networks from anywhere on the downtown section of Market Street.

Use Wired Equivalent Privacy

The first step in securing your wireless network is to turn on Wired Equivalent Privacy. As its name suggests, Wired Equivalent Privacy (WEP) is supposed to provide wireless networks with security equivalent to that of a physical (wired) network cable. Turning on WEP is essential to securing your wireless network and has no disadvantages.

Unfortunately, the WEP algorithm is flawed, with problems that include weaknesses in the method (hold on, the virtual water gets deep fast) of using a stream cipher to encrypt the packets of data sent over the wireless network. You don't need to know the details, but it means that WEP traffic can be hacked into by performing a series of computations. Worse, because many 802.11b networking cards use the same encryption key, they're also vulnerable to hacking. So if you need your wireless network traffic to be really secure, you can't rely on WEP. The best solution is to use virtual private networking, which is discussed in detail in Chapter 34.

To turn on WEP, take the following steps:

1. Connect to the wireless network from a wireless network client.

2. Choose Start ➢ Connect To ➢ Show All Connections. XP displays the Network Connections folder.

3. Right-click the wireless network connection icon (it'll be named Wireless Network Connection by default unless someone has renamed it) and choose Properties from the context menu. XP displays the Properties dialog box for the connection with the General page foremost.

4. Click the Wireless Networks tab. XP displays the Wireless Networks page (shown in Figure 33.3).

FIGURE 33.3

The Wireless Networks page of the Properties dialog box for a wireless network connection lists the wireless network available to you and lets you set the order in which to attempt to access preferred networks.

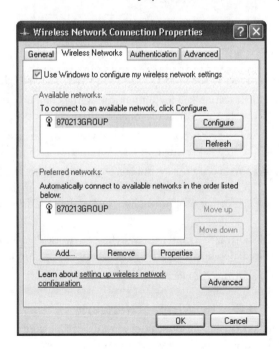

5. In the Available Networks group box, select the entry in the list box for the network you want to configure. (If you have only one wireless access point, it'll be the only entry.)

6. Click the Configure button. XP displays the Wireless Network Properties dialog box (shown in Figure 33.4).

FIGURE 33.4

In the Wireless Network Properties dialog box, you can turn Wired Equivalent Privacy (WEP) on and off, and you can change the service set identifier (SSID) for the wireless network.

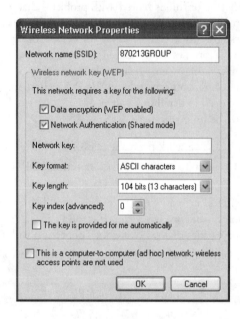

7. To enable WEP, select the Data Encryption (WEP Enabled) check box.

8. To use an authentication key for authenticating the computer to the wireless access point, select the Network Authentication (Shared Mode) check box.

   ◆ If your wireless access point automatically provides the authentication key for you, make sure the The Key Is Provided for Me Automatically check box is selected.

   ◆ If you need to specify the key manually, make sure the The Key Is Provided for Me Automatically check box is cleared. Then enter the details of the key in the Network Key text box, the Key Format drop-down list, the Key Length drop-down list, and the Key Index text box.

9. Click the OK button. XP closes the Wireless Network Properties dialog box, returning you to the Properties dialog box for the wireless network connection.

10. Click the OK button. XP closes the Properties dialog box.

Change the SSID for the Wireless Network

Once you've turned on WEP, your next move toward securing your wireless network is to change the service set identifier (SSID) for the wireless network. The reason for changing the SSID is that many SSIDs are easy to guess, which makes it easier for an attacker to contact the access point. Changing the SSID is not essential but a good step to securing your network. It has no disadvantage beyond requiring a small amount of effort on your part.

To change your wireless network's SSID, take the following steps:

1. Follow steps 1 to 6 of the list in the previous section to display the Wireless Network Properties dialog box.

2. In the Network Name (SSID) text box, enter the new SSID for the network. Make it something hard to guess but that you'll easily remember. As with passwords, don't use any real word in any language.

3. Click the OK button. XP closes the Wireless Network Properties dialog box.

4. Click the OK button. XP closes the Properties dialog box for the wireless network connection.

Configure Your Access Point Not to Broadcast Its SSID

The next step in securing your wireless network is to configure your access point not to broadcast its SSID. Most access points let you make this change, but the details depend on the access point's configuration mechanism, so I won't show you an example here. This change isn't essential, but it does greatly increase your wireless network's security, and it goes hand-in-hand with the previous step, so you'll probably want to perform it.

TIP *While you're configuring your access point not to broadcast its SSID, change the access point's password as well if you haven't done so already. Many manufacturers use feeble passwords on their access points, and you should assume that hackers know these standard passwords by heart. Use a password that you've never used before—don't reuse one of your existing passwords or previous passwords.*

If you followed the advice in the previous section to change the SSID of your wireless network, you'll see why you should turn off SSID broadcasting: By doing so, you make it much more difficult for an attacker to access your wireless network. Otherwise, they can just tune in on the WiFi frequency, and the access point will obligingly tell them the SSID so that they can attack it.

The disadvantage to turning off SSID broadcasts is that you won't be able to browse the network for wireless connections either. Instead, you'll need to connect to the network manually. To do so, take the following steps:

1. Follow steps 2 to 4 in the section "Use Wired Equivalent Privacy," earlier in this chapter, to display the Wireless Networks page of the Properties dialog box for the wireless network connection.

2. Click the Add button. XP displays the Wireless Network Properties dialog box (shown in Figure 33.4, earlier in the chapter).

3. In the Network Name (SSID) text box, enter the SSID of the network.

4. In the Wireless Network Key (WEP) group box, enter the details of the WEP key.

5. Click the OK button. XP closes the Wireless Network Properties dialog box.

6. Click the OK button. XP closes the Properties dialog box for the wireless network connection.

Use Password Protection on Your Files

To protect your files from anyone unauthorized who succeeds in accessing your network, implement password protection on all your data files.

Use Virtual Private Networking to Secure the Data You're Transmitting

As mentioned earlier, because the WEP algorithm is flawed, data transmitted across wireless networks secured with WEP can be decrypted relatively easily by determined hackers. For any data that you absolutely need to keep private, use virtual private networking to secure the data transmitted across the wireless network.

See the section "Creating and Using VPN Connections" in Chapter 34 for a discussion of what virtual private networking is and how to implement it.

Reposition Your Access Point for Security

Another step you can take is to position your access point so that it provides as little coverage outside your property as possible.

In theory, this is a good move, because if you could confine the access point's coverage to the boundaries of your property, you could more easily prevent most unauthorized people from accessing your wireless network. Unfortunately, you won't be able to do this short of investing in lead-lined walls, floors, and roofs—even if your property covers a large area. By using booster antennae or parabolic dishes, hackers can pick up wireless network signals from distances of up to about 15–20 miles (even from over the horizon, with determination), so if they're really out to get you, you have good reason to be paranoid.

Still, they're probably *not* out to get you specifically, so you may want to take your wireless-enabled laptop or Pocket PC for a walk around your property and its immediate surroundings to see where your access point is accessible from. Relocate it if necessary, being careful not to lose access from the places you need it.

Try to Hack into Your Own Network

Once you've taken the measures discussed above to secure your wireless network, try to hack into it yourself. Download a tool such as NetStumbler for Windows or Mini Stumbler for Pocket PC (both from `www.netstumbler.com`) and take a quick stumble around your property to see what you can pick up. Change your security configuration as necessary depending on what you find—or warn your neighbors that you're picking up their wireless networks' SSIDs loud and clear.

Up Next

This chapter has discussed the points of weakness of most networks and the basic principles for securing them. Coverage has included ways of securing wireless networks, which by their nature are less secure than wired networks.

The next chapter discusses the technologies that XP Home provides for connecting to a remote computer or network: Remote Desktop Connection, dial-up networking connections to a remote access server, and virtual private network (VPN) connections.

Chapter 34

Connecting to a Remote Computer or Network

So FAR IN THIS book, we've been assuming that you're working locally at your computer—computing the normal way, as it were. But XP also provides technologies for working remotely, both for remotely controlling a computer running XP and for connecting remotely to a network.

- Remote Desktop Connection lets you connect to a remote computer running XP Professional from a computer that's running XP Home or XP Professional or another version of Windows with Remote Desktop Connection installed. For example, if your computer at work runs XP Professional and your computer at home runs XP Home, you could connect from your home computer to your work computer. Once connected, you can work on the remote computer as if you were sitting at it (provided your Internet or network connection is fast enough—otherwise everything happens much more slowly).

- Dial-up networking lets you establish a dial-up connection to a server. For example, you might use dial-up networking to connect your home computer to a remote-access server on your company's network so that you can access files and resources from home.

- Virtual Private Network (VPN) connections let you connect to a network via a secure connection across an insecure medium. Usually the insecure medium is the Internet. You establish your Internet connection via your ISP as usual, then create an encrypted "tunnel" to a VPN host on the destination network. Once you've connected to the VPN host, you can work as if your computer were directly attached to the network. For example, you might use a VPN connection to connect to your company's network so that you could upload or download files, or work with e-mail, from your home computer.

This chapter covers the following topics:

- Using Remote Desktop Connection
- Creating a dial-up connection to a corporate network
- Creating and using VPN connections
- Troubleshooting VPN connections

Using Remote Desktop Connection

This section discusses what Remote Desktop Connection is, what it does, and how to use it.

What Is Remote Desktop Connection For?

Remote Desktop Connection lets you connect via a dial-up connection, via a local area network connection, or across the Internet and take control of somebody's computer (or your own).

Remote Desktop Connection is designed to let you access and control one computer (say, your work computer) from another computer (say, your home computer or your laptop). It's great for catching up with the office when you're at home, or for grabbing the files that you forgot to load on your laptop before you dived into the taxi for the airport.

TIP Remote Desktop Connection is also great for sharing a program from other computers without needing to buy extra copies to install on them. For example, say you need to manipulate digital photos using Adobe Photoshop. By installing Photoshop on a computer that's running XP Professional, you can connect with Remote Desktop Connection from other computers on your home or home-office network (one at a time) so that you can use the same copy of Photoshop to manip-ulate photos as needed. That saves a lot of money over needing to buy a copy of Photoshop for each computer you have.

You can also use Remote Desktop Connection for other purposes, such as helping a friend or family member find their way out of a computing problem from a distance. It's not really designed for this, though, and you'd do better to use XP's Remote Assistance feature, which is designed for precisely that. Similarly, Remote Desktop Connection is not good for collaboration, because only one user can be working with the computer at a time. For collaboration, turn back to Chapter 23 (which discusses Windows Messenger and its collaboration features) or Web Chapter 3, which discusses NetMeeting (which includes more powerful collaboration features than Messenger has).

NOTE XP Professional also supports Remote Desktop Web Connection, a version of Remote Desktop Connection that lets you connect to a computer running XP Professional from a remote computer using just Internet Explorer. XP Home doesn't support Remote Desktop Web Connection.

TIP If you need to connect to a computer that's not running XP Professional, you can't use Remote Desktop Connection, but you may be able to use another remote-connection technology that XP provides, Remote Desktop Sharing. Remote Desk-top Sharing is a feature of NetMeeting, a program that comes built into XP but is hidden until you seek it out. Remote Desktop Sharing lets you control your Desktop remotely by connecting via NetMeeting. Remote Desktop Sharing is less powerful than Remote Desktop Connection and has some defects, but you may find it useful when you can't use Remote Desktop Connec-tion. Web Chapter 3 discusses how to set up NetMeeting and use its features, including Remote Desktop Sharing.

Remote Desktop Connection Terminology and Basics

Remote Desktop Connection terminology is a little confusing. Here are the terms:

◆ The *home computer* is the computer on which you're working. The home computer needs to have Remote Desktop Connection installed. Remote Desktop Connection is installed by default in XP Home.

◆ The *remote computer* is the computer that you're accessing from the home computer. The remote computer needs to have Remote Desktop installed. Remote Desktop is separate from Remote Desktop Connection and is included in XP Professional and Windows .NET Server. Remote Desktop is not included in XP Home.

So the typical scenario is for the home computer to be running XP Home and the remote computer to be running XP Professional. You can also access one XP Professional computer from another XP Professional computer.

NOTE *You can access more than one remote computer at a time from the same home computer. Unless you have impressive bandwidth, though, this results in slow sessions.*

For you to be able to connect to another computer via Remote Desktop Connection, any active session (whether local or connected via another Remote Desktop Connection) on that computer needs to be disconnected. Both you and the other user receive warnings about this. If you choose to proceed, the remote computer displays the Welcome screen while your Remote Desktop Connection session is going on. There's no easy way for anyone looking at that computer to tell that you're remotely connected to it.

If a user comes back and starts using the remote computer while your Remote Desktop Connection session is going on, your session will be terminated.

In lay terms, Remote Desktop Connection works as follows:

◆ Keystrokes and mouse clicks are transmitted from the home computer to the remote computer via the display protocol. The remote computer registers these keystrokes and clicks as if they came from the keyboard attached to it.

◆ Programs run on the remote computer as usual. (Programs aren't run across the wire—that would be desperately slow.) Documents you create and save during a Remote Desktop Connection session are saved on the remote computer, just as if you were working at it, unless you specifically save them elsewhere (for example, on drives local to the home computer, as discussed below).

◆ Screen display information is passed to the home computer, again via the display protocol. This information appears on the display as if it came from the video adapter (only rather more slowly, and usually in a window).

Sound can be passed to the home computer as well, so that you can hear what's happening at the remote computer. Transferring sound like this enhances the impression of controlling the remote computer, but sound takes so much bandwidth that transferring it isn't a good idea on slow connections. The default Remote Desktop Connection setting is to transfer sound, but you may well want to switch it off.

EXPERT KNOWLEDGE: REMOTE DESKTOP CONNECTION IS TERMINAL SERVICES BY ANOTHER NAME

Remote Desktop Connection is the snappy new name for the Terminal Services Client, a feature from the black lagoon days of Windows NT 4. A couple of years after releasing NT Server 4, Microsoft loosed NT Server 4 Terminal Server Edition, a version of NT Server with a multiuser technology called Terminal Server added to it. In Windows 2000 Server, Terminal Server was integrated into the server and renamed Terminal Services, but the underlying technology remained the same.

Here's what happens with Terminal Services. The user has a local computer as usual, but they don't run programs on it. Instead, they run a smallish program called Terminal Services Client that lets them run programs on a server but have the output displayed on the local computer. The server does all the heavy lifting, so as long as the server is big and fast, the local computer can be small, underpowered, or outdated. All it needs to do is send keystrokes and mouse clicks to the server and display the output it receives back across the wire. Given a fast server and a fast network, performance can be quite snappy, so there's no problem from the users' end.

With Terminal Services, corporations can save big money by continuing to use ancient hardware (we're talking 486s and early Pentiums here) several years past their sell-by date for running modern programs. For example, some early Pentium computers had 250MB hard drives. Office 2000 needs about 340MB to get comfortably settled, even before you create any data files. Sure, you can put a bigger hard drive in an old PC like this, but why bother if you don't have to? Turn it into a Terminal Services client and you can flog it until it collapses. Better yet, make the user save their files and settings on the server, and not only will they be able to use any client with their own preferences, but both files and preferences will be safe when the client finally expires, so you can just swap in another client with minimal fuss.

Terminal Services also greatly reduces administration: Instead of needing to install—and maintain—programs on each client, administrators can install them on the servers instead. And they can lock down the lame old clients so that users can't waste good company time trying to configure their Desktops ... but that's another story.

So much for the history of Terminal Services. With XP, Terminal Services has been renamed Remote Desktop and integrated into the Professional version as well as the Server version. (You could look at this another way and say that XP Home and XP Professional, with their capabilities to support multiple concurrent user sessions, are in fact a cut-down version of Windows .NET Server running both the server and the client sessions on the same computer.) Terminal Services Client has been renamed Remote Desktop Connection.

As you'll see in this chapter, Remote Desktop Connection is installed automatically in XP. But on the XP CD, you also get a copy of Remote Desktop Connection that works on previous versions of Windows as well. To install Remote Desktop Connection on an earlier version of Windows, run the SETUP.EXE program on the CD and follow the Perform Additional Tasks link, then click the Set Up Remote Desktop Connection link.

Setting the Remote Computer to Accept Incoming Connections

The first step in getting Remote Desktop Connection to work is to set the remote computer to accept incoming connections. Remember that this is the computer that's remote from you and that's running XP Professional (or Windows .NET Server).

To set your remote computer to accept incoming connections, take these steps:

1. Display the System Properties dialog box in whichever way you find easiest. For example, press Windows key+Break. Or click the Start button to display the Start menu, right-click the My Computer link, and choose Properties from the context menu.

2. Click the Remote tab. XP displays the Remote page (shown on the left in Figure 34.1).

3. To allow users to connect to your computer, select the Allow Users to Connect Remotely to This Computer check box.

4. To specify which users may connect via Remote Desktop Connection, click the Select Remote Users button. XP displays the Remote Desktop Users dialog box (shown on the right in Figure 34.1). The list box shows any users currently allowed to connect to the computer. Below the list box is a note indicating that you (identified by your username) already have access—as you should have.

FIGURE 34.1

To allow incoming connections, select the Allow Users to Connect Remotely to This Computer check box on the Remote page of the System Properties dialog box. Then use the Remote Desktop Users dialog box to specify which users may connect.

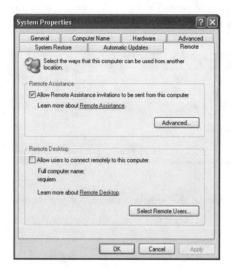
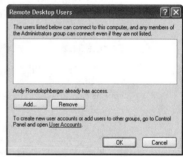

5. Click the Add button. XP displays the Select Users dialog box.

6. Select a user or group, and then click the OK button. XP adds them to the list in the Remote Desktop Users dialog box.

7. Add further users or groups as necessary.

8. To remove a user or a group, select them in the list box and click the Remove button.

9. Click the OK button. XP closes the Remote Desktop Users dialog box.

10. Click the OK button in the System Properties dialog box. XP closes the dialog box and applies your changes.

The remote computer is all set. Leave it up and running and return to the home computer.

NOTE *There's one other thing that you might need to do on the remote computer—but it's something that you'll almost certainly have done already: Apply a password to any user account that will be used to access the computer via Remote Desktop Connection. (See the section "Requiring a Password for an Account" in Chapter 9 for details of how to apply a password to an account.)*

Choosing Settings for Remote Desktop Connection

Next, choose settings for Remote Desktop Connection on the home computer. Remote Desktop Connection has a modestly large number of settings, but many of them are set-and-forget. Even better, you can save sets of settings so that you can quickly apply them for accessing different remote computers (or the same remote computer under different circumstances, such as when the cable modem is working and when it's flaked out on you).

To choose settings for Remote Desktop Connection, follow these steps:

1. Choose Start ➤ All Programs ➤ Accessories ➤ Communications ➤ Remote Desktop Connection. XP starts Remote Desktop Connection and displays the Remote Desktop Connection window in its reduced state (shown in Figure 34.2).

FIGURE 34.2

The Remote Desktop Connection window appears first in its reduced state.

2. Click the Options button. XP displays the rest of the Remote Desktop Connection window.

3. The General page of the Remote Desktop Connection window (shown in Figure 34.3) offers these options:

Computer drop-down list   Enter the name or the IP address of the computer to which you want to connect; or select it from the drop-down list; or click the Browse for More item from the drop-down list to display the Browse for Computers dialog box, then select the computer in that.

User Name text box   Enter the username under which you want to connect to the remote computer. XP enters your username by default.

Password text box   If you want to store your password (for the remote computer) for the connection, enter it in this text box and select the Save My Password check box. If you don't enter your password here, you get to enter it when logging on to the remote computer, which takes longer but is more secure.

Domain text box   If the remote computer is part of a domain, enter the domain name here. If the computer is part of a workgroup, you can leave this text box blank.

Save My Password check box   Select this check box if you want to save your password with the rest of the Remote Desktop Connection information. This can save you time and effort, but it compromises your security a bit.

Connection Settings group box   Once you've chosen settings for a connection, you can save the connection information by clicking the Save As button and specifying a name for the connection in the Save As dialog box that XP displays. Remote Desktop Connection connections are saved as files of the file type Remote Desktop File, which by default is linked to the RDP extension, in the `\My Documents\Remote Desktops\` folder. You can open saved connections by clicking the Open button and using the resulting Open dialog box.

NOTE *You'll see a file named* `DEFAULT.RDP` *in the* `\My Documents\Remote Desktops\` *folder. XP automatically saves your latest Remote Desktop Connection configuration under this name when you click the Connect button. But by explicitly saving your settings under a name of your choice, you can easily maintain different configurations for different Remote Desktop Connection settings.*

FIGURE 34.3

The General page of the expanded Remote Desktop Connection window

4. The Display page of the Remote Desktop Connection window (shown on the left in Figure 34.4) offers three display options:

   Remote Desktop Size group box Drag the slider to specify the screen size you want to use for the remote Desktop. The default setting is Full Screen, but you may want to use a smaller size so that you can more easily access your home computer's Desktop. When you display the remote Desktop full screen, it takes over the whole of the local Desktop, so that you can't see your local Desktop. (To get to your local Desktop, you use the connection bar, discussed in a moment or two.)

   Colors group box In the drop-down list, select the color depth to use for the connection. Choose a low color depth (for example, 256 colors) if you're connecting over a low-speed connection, because reducing the number of colors decreases the amount of data that XP needs to transfer to draw the screen on your computer. This choice will be overridden by the display setting on the remote computer if you ask for more colors than the remote computer is using.

Display the Connection Bar when in Full Screen Mode check box   Leave this check box selected (as it is by default) if you want XP to display the connection bar when the remote Desktop is displayed full screen. The connection bar provides Minimize, Restore/Maximize, and Close buttons for the remote Desktop. (When the remote Desktop is displayed in a window, that window has the control buttons, so the connection bar isn't necessary.)

FIGURE 34.4

Choose display settings on the Display page (left) of the Remote Desktop Connection window. Specify how to handle sound, keystrokes, and local devices on the Local Resources page.

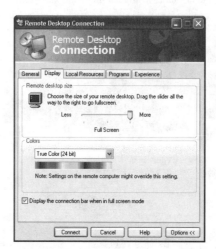
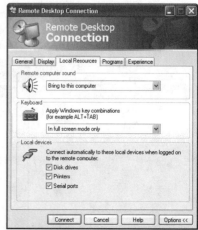

5. The Local Resources page of the Remote Desktop Connection window (shown on the right in Figure 34.4) offers the following options:

   Remote Computer Sound group box   In the drop-down list, specify what you want XP to do with sounds that would normally be generated at the remote Desktop. The default setting is Bring to This Computer, which transfers the sounds to the home computer and plays them there. This setting helps sustain the illusion that you're working directly on the remote Desktop, but it's heavy on bandwidth, so don't use it over low-speed connections. Instead, choose the Do Not Play setting or the Leave at Remote Computer setting. The Leave at Remote Computer setting plays the sounds at the remote computer and is best reserved for occasions when you need to frighten somebody remotely or pretend to be in your office.

   Keyboard group box   In the drop-down list, specify how you want XP to handle Windows key combinations that you press (for example, Alt+Tab or Ctrl+Alt+Delete). Select the On the Local Computer item, the On the Remote Computer item, or the In Full Screen Mode Only item (the default) as suits your needs. In Full Screen Mode Only tends to be the most convenient option, because it's the closest to working normally in Windows—whichever Desktop you're viewing full-screen receives the key combinations.

   Local Devices group box   Select the Disk Drives check box, the Printers check box, and the Serial Ports check box if you want these devices on your home computer to be available from the remote computer. This means that you can save documents from the remote computer to local drives, print them on your local printer, or transfer them via devices attached to serial ports (for example, a PDA). Local disk drives appear in the Other category in Explorer windows, named *Driveletter on COMPUTERNAME*. Local printers appear with *from COMPUTERNAME* in parentheses after them.

6. The Programs page of the Remote Desktop Connection window (shown on the left in Figure 34.5) lets you specify that XP run a designated program when you connect via Remote Desktop Connection. Select the Start the Following Program on Connection check box, then enter the program path and name in the Program Path and File Name text box. If you need to specify the folder in which the program should start, enter that in the Start in the Following Folder text box.

FIGURE 34.5

On the Programs page (left) of the Remote Desktop Connection window, specify any program to run automatically when you connect. On the Experience page (right), choose which graphical information Remote Desktop Connection should transmit.

 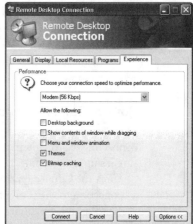

7. The Experience page of the Remote Desktop Connection window (shown on the right in Figure 34.5) contains the following options:

   Choose Your Connection Speed to Optimize Performance drop-down list In this drop-down list, select one of the four listed speeds to apply a preselected set of settings to the five check boxes on this page. The choices in the drop-down list are Modem (28.8Kbps), Modem (56Kbps), Broadband (128Kbps–1.5Mbps), LAN (10Mbps or Higher), and Custom. If you change a setting applied by one of the preset sets, XP selects the Custom item for you.

   Desktop Background check box This check box controls whether Remote Desktop Connection transmits the Desktop background. Because Desktop backgrounds are graphical, transmitting them is sensible only at LAN speeds. (If you clear this check box, Remote Desktop Connection uses a blank Desktop background.)

   Show Contents of Window while Dragging check box This check box controls whether Remote Desktop Connection transmits the contents of a window while you're dragging it, or only the window frame. Don't use this option over a modem connection, because the performance penalty outweighs any benefit you may derive from it.

Menu and Window Animation check box This check box controls whether Remote Desktop Connection transmits menu and window animations (for example, zooming a window you're maximizing or minimizing). Don't use this option over a modem connection—it's a waste of bandwidth.

Themes check box This check box controls whether Remote Desktop Connection transmits theme information or uses "classic" Windows–style windows and controls. Transmitting theme information takes a little bandwidth, so you can improve performance over a very slow connection by clearing the Themes check box. But bear in mind that XP will look different enough to unsettle some inexperienced users.

Bitmap Caching check box This check box controls whether Remote Desktop Connection uses bitmap caching to improve performance by reducing the amount of data that needs to be sent across the network to display the screen remotely. Caching could prove a security threat, so you *might* want to turn it off for security reasons. But in most cases, you're better off using it.

8. If you want to save the settings you've chosen under a particular name so that you can reload them at will, click the Save As button on the General page of the Remote Desktop Connection window.

Connecting via Remote Desktop Connection

Once you've chosen settings as outlined in the previous section, you're ready to connect. If you're connecting via the Internet (rather than a local network) and you have a dial-up connection, make sure it's up and running.

Click the Connect button in the Remote Desktop Connection window. XP attempts to establish a connection to the computer you specified.

If XP is able to connect to the computer, and you didn't specify your username or password in the Remote Desktop Connection window, it displays the Log On to Windows dialog box. Enter your username and password and click the OK button to log in. XP then displays the remote Desktop. (If you chose to provide your password on the General page of the Remote Desktop Connection window, you shouldn't need to enter it again.)

If you left a user session active on the computer, Remote Desktop Connection drops you straight into it—likewise if you left a user session disconnected and no other user session is active. But if another user *is* active on the remote computer when you submit a successful logon and password, XP displays the Logon Message dialog box shown in Figure 34.6 to warn you that logging on will disconnect the user's session. Click the Yes button if you want to proceed. Click the No button to withdraw stealthily.

FIGURE 34.6

XP displays the Logon Message dialog box when you're about to bump a user off the remote computer by logging on.

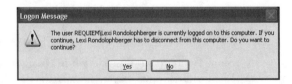

If you click the Yes button, the active user gets a Request for Connection dialog box such as that shown in Figure 34.7, which tells them that you (it specifies your name) are trying to connect to the computer, warns them that they'll be disconnected if you do connect, and asks if they want to allow the connection.

FIGURE 34.7

XP displays the Request for Connection dialog box to tell the active user of your incoming session.

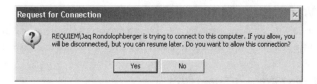

The active user then gets to click the Yes button or the No button as appropriate to their needs and inclinations. If XP doesn't get an answer within 30 seconds or so, it figures they're not there, disconnects their session, and lets you in.

If the active user clicks the Yes button in the Request for Connection dialog box, XP logs them off immediately and logs you on. But if the active user clicks the No button, you get a Logon Message dialog box such as that shown in Figure 34.8 telling you that they didn't allow you to connect. XP displays this Logon Message dialog box for a few seconds, and then closes it automatically, returning you to the Remote Desktop Connection window.

FIGURE 34.8

XP displays this Logon Message dialog box when the active user decides not to let you interrupt their session on the computer.

If XP is unable to establish the connection with the remote computer, it displays one of its Remote Desktop Disconnected dialog boxes to make you aware of the problem. Figure 34.9 shows two examples of the Remote Desktop Disconnected dialog box.

FIGURE 34.9

If XP is unable to connect, you'll see a Remote Desktop Disconnected dialog box.

The first example of the Remote Desktop Disconnected dialog box tells you that the client couldn't connect to the remote computer and suggests that you try again later. The second example tells you that the remote computer couldn't be found and suggests checking that the computer name or IP address are correct. This should indeed be your first move—but if that doesn't work, that's about all you can do. If the remote computer has been shut down (or has crashed); or if its network or Internet connection has gone south; or if someone has reconfigured the computer not to accept Remote Desktop Connection connections, or has revoked your permission to connect—if any of these has happened, you're straight out of luck, and no amount of retyping the computer name or IP address will make an iota of difference.

Working via Remote Desktop Connection

Once you've reached the remote Desktop, you can work more or less as if you were sitting at the computer. The few differences worth mentioning are discussed briefly in this section.

USING KEYBOARD SHORTCUTS

Most mouse actions are straightforward with Remote Desktop Connection: If the mouse pointer is working in the Remote Desktop Connection window (or full screen), mouse clicks and movements are interpreted there. Much the same happens with keystrokes, with the exception of the Windows keyboard shortcuts listed in Table 34.1.

TABLE 34.1: SPECIAL KEYBOARD SHORTCUTS FOR REMOTE DESKTOP CONNECTION

REMOTE DESKTOP CONNECTION SHORTCUT	ACTION
Alt+Page Up	Coolswitches between programs (as Alt+Tab does locally).
Alt+Page Down	Coolswitches in reverse order (as Alt+Shift+Tab does locally).
Alt+Insert	Switches among programs in the order in which you started them (as opposed to the order in which they appear).
Alt+Home	Displays the Start menu (as Ctrl+Esc does locally).
Alt+Delete	Displays the control menu for the active window.
Ctrl+Alt+– (minus on numeric keypad)	Copies the active window to the Clipboard (as Alt+PrintScreen does locally).
Ctrl+Alt++ (plus on numeric keypad)	Copies the remote Desktop to the Clipboard (as PrintScreen does locally).
Ctrl+Alt+End	Displays Task Manager (as Ctrl+Alt+Delete does locally).

USING CUT, COPY, AND PASTE BETWEEN THE LOCAL AND REMOTE COMPUTERS

You can use Cut, Copy, and Paste commands to transfer information between the local computer and the remote computer. For example, you could copy some text from a program on the local computer and paste it into a program on the remote computer. Or you could use the Ctrl+Alt+– (the minus key on the numeric keypad) keystroke to copy the active window to the Clipboard and then paste it into a window on the local computer.

COPYING FROM REMOTE DRIVES TO LOCAL DRIVES

You can copy from remote drives to local drives by working in Explorer. The drives on your local computer appear in Explorer windows on the remote computer marked as *Driveletter on*

COMPUTERNAME. The drives on the remote computer appear as regular drives. You can copy and move files from one drive to another as you would with local drives. Depending on the speed of your connection to the remote computer, copying large files from one computer to another may take a while.

PRINTING TO A LOCAL PRINTER

You can print to a local printer from the remote Desktop by selecting the local printer in the Print dialog box just as you would any other printer.

Printer settings are communicated to the remote Desktop when you access it. If you add a local printer during the remote session, the remote Desktop won't be able to see it. To make the printer show up on the remote Desktop, log off the remote session and log back on.

EXPERT KNOWLEDGE: REMOTE DESKTOP CONNECTION WRINKLES

This sidebar discusses some wrinkles of Remote Desktop Connection that you probably would like to know about before you run into them firsthand.

ACCOMMODATING DIFFERENT DISPLAY SETTINGS

The most pressing of these wrinkles concern the logistics of translating what's on the display or displays of the remote computer to the display on the local computer.

If the local computer is using a lower resolution than the remote computer, XP reduces the size of program windows as necessary to make them fit on the screen.

If the remote computer has multiple monitors configured, XP shows just the primary display, as you'd expect—it doesn't try to show both (or all) the displays, even if the local computer has the same number of monitors as the remote computer. If the Taskbar is displayed on a monitor other than the primary monitor, XP moves it to the primary monitor so that you can see it. (This happens even if the Taskbar is locked.) Similarly, XP shunts all the open windows onto the primary monitor, packing them on like the Tokyo subway people-pushers.

It'd be nice if XP restored the remote Desktop to its previous condition when you disconnect a Remote Desktop Connection session—but it doesn't. So if you use Remote Desktop Connection a lot, it's a good idea to designate the monitor on which your Taskbar appears as the primary monitor. Otherwise, when you return to the remote computer, you'll find your Taskbar rearranged, and you'll need to unlock it (if you keep it locked) and move it back to where it belongs. Your program windows will be rearranged anyway, but there's not much you can do about this—XP doesn't restore them to their previous size when you disconnect the Remote Desktop Connection session.

USING DIFFERENT KEYBOARD LAYOUTS

The keyboard setting on the remote computer decides how your keystrokes are interpreted—the keyboard setting on the local computer isn't used when you're working on the remote computer. For example, if you want to use a Dvorak keyboard layout on the remote computer, you need to apply that layout to the remote computer. You can't apply the layout to the local computer instead and send (as it were) translated keystrokes.

Continued on next page

EXPERT KNOWLEDGE: REMOTE DESKTOP CONNECTION WRINKLES *(continued)*

DAISY-CHAINING REMOTE DESKTOP CONNECTION CONNECTIONS

Last, while you *can* connect via Remote Desktop Connection to a computer (let's call it remote computer A) that in turn is connected to another computer (remote computer B) via Remote Desktop Connection, things tend to get confused when you try to control remote computer B from your local computer. You probably won't want to create such daisy-chains. Instead, connect directly from the home computer to each remote computer that you want to control.

Returning to Your Local Desktop

If you have the remote Desktop displayed in a window rather than full screen, you can return to your local Desktop by clicking anywhere outside the Remote Desktop Connection window. But if the remote Desktop is displayed full screen, you need to use the connection bar to return to your local Desktop.

If you chose to display the connection bar, it hovers briefly at the top of the screen, then slides upward to vanish like a docked toolbar with its Auto-Hide property enabled. To pin the connection bar in position, click the pin icon at its left end. (To unpin it, click the pin icon again.) To display the connection bar when it has hidden itself, move the mouse pointer to the top edge of the screen, just as you would do to display a docked toolbar hidden there.

The connection bar provides a Minimize button, a Restore/Maximize button, and a Close button. Use the Minimize button and the Restore button to reduce the remote Desktop from full screen to an icon or a partial screen so that you can access your local Desktop. Maximize the remote Desktop window to return to full-screen mode when you want to work with it again. Use the Close button as discussed in the next section to disconnect your remote session.

Disconnecting the Remote Session

You can disconnect the remote session in either of the two following ways:

- On the remote Desktop, choose Start ➢ Disconnect. XP displays the Disconnect Windows dialog box (shown in Figure 34.10). Click the Disconnect button.

FIGURE 34.10

You can disconnect the remote session by issuing a Start ➢ Disconnect command and clicking the Disconnect button in the Disconnect Windows dialog box.

- Click the Close button on the connection bar (if the remote Desktop is displayed full screen) or on the Remote Desktop window (if the remote Desktop is not displayed full screen). XP displays the Disconnect Windows Session dialog box (shown in Figure 34.11). Click the OK button.

FIGURE 34.11

The Disconnect Windows Session dialog box appears when you click the Close button on the connection bar. Click the OK button to end your remote session while leaving the programs running.

XP disconnects the remote session but leaves the programs running for the time being. You can then log on again and pick up where you left off.

Logging Off the Remote Session

To log off and end your user session, click the Start button on the remote Desktop and choose Log Off from the Start menu. XP displays the Log Off Windows dialog box (shown in Figure 34.12). Click the Log Off button.

FIGURE 34.12

To log off from the remote computer, choose Start ➤ Log Off and click the Log Off button in the Log Off Windows dialog box.

When someone else bumps you off the remote Desktop (by logging on locally or remotely), XP displays a Remote Desktop Disconnected dialog box telling you that the remote session "was ended by means of an administration tool."

If the network connection between the home computer and the remote computer is broken, the home computer displays another Remote Desktop Disconnected dialog box.

Shutting Down or Restarting the Remote Computer

You can also shut down the remote computer from Remote Desktop Connection. XP doesn't offer access to the Turn Off Computer command from the Start menu on the remote computer, presumably either on the assumption that you won't often want to do this or that having this command available would make it too easy for you to turn off the remote computer when you actually meant to turn off the local computer. So the Start menu on the remote computer offers only the Disconnect button and the Log Off button.

But sometimes you *will* need to shut down the remote computer—for example, say you've left it running so that you can retrieve files via Remote Desktop Connection, you've now retrieved them, and you don't need to access it any more. Other times you'll need to restart the computer—for example, if it seems to be unstable, or if it has suffered memory leaks that have crippled its performance—so that you can connect to it again using Remote Desktop Connection.

To shut down or restart the remote computer, display Task Manager (right-click the Taskbar or notification area and choose Task Manager from the context menu) and choose Shut Down ➤ Turn Off Computer or Shut Down ➤ Restart Computer from there. XP displays the confirmation dialog box shown in Figure 34.13. Click the Yes button.

FIGURE 34.13

XP double-checks that you know what you're doing when you issue a Turn Off Computer command for the remote computer via Remote Desktop Connection.

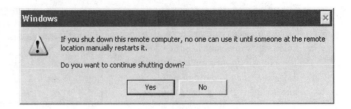

> **NOTE** *If other users have disconnected sessions on the computer you're proposing to shut down (or restart), XP warns you that you'll terminate these sessions.*

Troubleshooting Remote Desktop Connection Connections

This section discusses an error message and a problem that you may run into when using Remote Desktop Connection, what causes them, and how to solve them.

"THE LOCAL POLICY OF THIS SYSTEM DOES NOT PERMIT YOU TO LOGON INTERACTIVELY" ERROR

If Remote Desktop Connection fails to connect with the error message "The local policy of this system does not permit you to logon interactively," it means you need to add your account to the Remote Desktop Users group. Log on as a Computer Administrator user locally and then add your account to the group by following the steps in the section "Setting the Remote Computer to Accept Incoming Connections," earlier in this chapter. (You can also effect this change by using the net localgroup command, but it's easier to work from the System Properties dialog box.)

REMOTE DESKTOP CONNECTION PROMPTS FOR YOUR PASSWORD EVEN WHEN YOU'VE SAVED IT

If Remote Desktop Connection prompts you for your password even when you've saved your password in the connection, it means that the computer running Remote Desktop is set to always prompt for the password at connection time.

If you administer the computer running Remote Desktop, disable the Always Prompt Client for Password upon Connection policy in the Local Computer Policy\Computer Configuration\Administrative Templates\Windows Components\Terminal Services\Encryption and Security\item in Microsoft Management Console. If someone else administers the computer, ask them to do this.

Creating a Dial-up Connection to a Remote Network

The most direct way to connect directly to a remote network is via dial-up connection. The remote network needs to have a remote access server, which in most cases means that it'll be a corporate network rather than a home network—but you can install a remote access server on your home network so that you can access it remotely if you so choose.

> **NOTE** *Another way of connecting to a remote network is to use a virtual private network (VPN) connection as discussed in the next section.*

Creating a dial-up connection to a remote network is like creating an Internet connection, only with a few wrinkles. Start by assembling the following information:

- Your username and password for the remote access server.
- The telephone number and area code of the remote access server.
- The modem type required (for example, V.92 or V.90), to make sure your modem is compatible.
- Whether the remote access server uses Dynamic Host Configuration Protocol (DHCP) to assign IP addresses or whether you need to specify a particular IP address. (If the latter, you need to know the IP address.)
- The protocol or protocols used on the remote network. In most cases, it'll be TCP/IP, but you may need to use IPX/SPX for some remote access servers.
- The names or IP addresses of any mail servers that you'll need to connect to.

To create the dial-up connection, take the following steps:

1. Choose Start ➤ Connect To ➤ Show All Connections. XP displays the Network Connections page of Control Panel. If you haven't created a network connection before, choose Start ➤ Control Panel, click the Network and Internet Connections link, and then click the Network Connections link.

2. Click the Create a New Connection link. XP starts the New Connection Wizard, which displays its Welcome page.

3. Click the Next button. The wizard displays the Network Connection Type page.

4. Select the Connect to the Network at My Workplace option button and click the Next button. The wizard displays the Network Connection page.

5. Make sure the Dial-up Connection option button is selected and click the Next button. If you have multiple dial-up devices available, the wizard displays the Select a Device page. If you have only one dial-up device available, the wizard displays the Connection Name page; skip step 6.

6. Select the appropriate dial-up device and click the Next button. The wizard displays the Connection Name page.

7. In the Company Name text box, enter a descriptive name for the connection and click the Next button. (This name is for your benefit and doesn't have to have anything to do with the name of any company involved.) The wizard displays the Phone Number to Dial page.

8. Enter the phone number, including any long-distance code and area code necessary, and click the Next button. The wizard displays the Completing the New Connection Wizard page.

9. If you want to have a shortcut for this connection on the Desktop, select the Add a Shortcut to This Connection to My Desktop check box.

10. Click the Finish button. The wizard closes itself and opens the Connect dialog box for the connection.

If necessary, you can tweak the connection by displaying its Properties dialog box (for example, by clicking the Properties button in the Connect dialog box or by right-clicking the connection's icon and choosing Properties from the context menu) and working on its five pages. These properties are the same as those for a dial-up Internet connection, discussed in the section "Configuring the Connection Manually" in Chapter 18.

One difference is that you'll often want to have the Client for Microsoft Networks bound to a dial-up connection for a remote network (whereas you'll seldom need this client for an Internet connection). Another is that you're likely to need different security settings for a connection to a remote network—particularly a connection to a corporate network—than to your ISP. Ask the network's administrator for specifics if they don't actively press them upon you.

Creating and Using VPN Connections

This section discusses what virtual private network (VPN) connections are, what you use them for, how you create them, and how you use them.

What Is Virtual Private Networking?

Virtual private networking is a method of connecting two computers securely across an insecure network. In practice, the insecure network is usually the Internet, though in theory it can be any network, public or private, on which the prevailing level of security isn't adequate for the needs of the connection. VPN connections are typically used for connecting a remote PC securely to a computer on a corporate network so that the remote PC can use network resources (files, printers, and so on) as though it were connected directly to the network. But VPN connections can also be used for connecting a remote computer to a stand-alone computer or to a home network or small-business network.

The computer that makes the connection is the *VPN client*, while the computer that accepts the connection is the *VPN server* or *VPN host*. If you're using XP to call in to a network (which is probably the most likely scenario), you'll need to configure a VPN client connection on your computer. But XP also includes a stripped-down version of the Windows 2000 remote access server, which allows your computer to host a single incoming VPN connection at a time. For example, you might provide a VPN connection to friends so that you could let them browse a folder of files that you wanted to make available to them. Or you might leave your home computer accepting incoming VPN connections so that you could connect to it with your laptop when on the road, pick up any files you'd forgotten, and make backups of new documents you'd created.

How Virtual Private Networking Works

Here's the straightforward version of how virtual private networking works:

◆ The company or individual hosting the VPN server connects the server to the Internet (either directly to an ISP or indirectly through a shared Internet connection) and configures the server to accept incoming connections from specified users.

◆ The user—the VPN client—establishes a connection to the insecure network as it usually would. In practical terms, this usually means that the remote user establishes an Internet connection through their ISP just as they normally would when accessing the Internet. When using a VPN over a LAN, the user would establish a LAN connection as usual. (Typically, the user's computer would already be directly connected to the LAN.)

◆ The user then connects to the VPN server across the insecure network, providing such authentication as necessary—for example, a username and a password, a certificate, or a smart card. Once the user has authenticated, they can connect to the resources on the server—and, if the server is configured to permit them to do so, on the network—as if they were connected locally to it.

◆ The VPN client and server use the protocols of the insecure network to transfer data as usual—for example, if they're connecting across the Internet, they'll use TCP/IP much as for any other Internet connection. But the client and server tunnel under those protocols to create a direct, secure connection between the two endpoints. The connection is secured by encrypting each packet (or frame, depending on the network protocol used) of data to be transmitted and encapsulating it in another packet (or frame) for transmission. The resulting packet (or frame) receives a new header for transmission. At the destination, the other computer removes the header, extracts and decrypts the packet (or frame), and reassembles the data in its unencrypted form.

XP supports the Point-to-Point Tunneling Protocol (PPTP) and the Layer 2 Tunneling Protocol (L2TP) for VPN connections. We won't get into the details of the protocols here, but I should at least tell you that L2TP is much more secure than PPTP (which is sometimes referred to disparagingly by cryptographers as *kiddy crypto* because its encryption is reckoned easy to break). When connecting to a VPN server, XP can use either PPTP or L2TP. As a VPN server, however, XP can use only PPTP. Once again, Microsoft has deliberately limited XP's capabilities—but if you need to accept incoming VPN connections with more security than PPTP can offer, you should probably be using either a different software solution or a different operating system in the first place.

We'll look at the details of VPN connections in a moment. First, though, let's consider the advantages and disadvantages of VPN connections.

Advantages of VPN Connections

For remote access to a network, VPN connections have compelling advantages over direct dial-up connections for both users and network administrators.

VPN connections let the user connect at the full speed of their broadband Internet connection (assuming they have broadband) rather than at dial-up speeds. As you can no doubt imagine if you've tried transferring files over a dial-up connection, using broadband for such tasks can make a huge difference to the user's experience of remote networking. If the user doesn't have broadband, the dial-up connection to the ISP won't be any faster than a dial-up connection to a remote access server, but it should normally be a flat-rate local call rather than a metered call.

Meanwhile, the network administrator doesn't need to worry about buying (or building) and maintaining a monster remote access server with dozens of modems connected to a corresponding number of phone lines—nor paying for those phone lines or the metered (or long-distance) calls charged back to the company. All they need do is configure the VPN server carefully, connect it to the Internet, keep it running, and perhaps monitor who's logging on and what actions they're performing remotely.

Creating a VPN Client Connection

To connect to a remote VPN server, create a VPN client connection by following these steps:

1. Choose Start ➤ All Programs ➤ Accessories ➤ Communications ➤ New Connection Wizard. XP starts the New Connection Wizard. (Alternatively, display the Network Connections folder and click the Create a New Connection link in the Network Tasks list.)

2. On the Network Connection Type page of the wizard, select the Connect to the Network at My Workplace option button and click the Next button.

3. On the Network Connection page of the wizard, select the Virtual Private Network Connection option button and click the Next button.

4. On the Connection Name page of the wizard, enter a name for the connection in the Company Name text box. As before, this name is for your benefit and doesn't need to have anything to do with any company.

5. If the wizard displays its Public Network page, which offers to dial an initial connection to the Internet (or another public network) before establishing the VPN connection, specify whether to dial a connection. To dial a connection, select the Automatically Dial This Initial Connection option button and choose the connection in the drop-down list. To avoid dialing, select the Do Not Dial the Initial Connection option button. Click the Next button.

6. On the VPN Server Selection page of the wizard, enter the host name or IP address of the VPN server and click the Next button.

7. On the Completing the New Connection Wizard page, select the Add a Shortcut to This Connection to My Desktop check box if appropriate, and then click the Finish button. The wizard creates the connection, creates the shortcut if appropriate, and quits.

Configuring the VPN Client Connection

As far as the wizard is concerned, your VPN connection is now set up and ready for use—but you may well need to configure it further by using its Properties dialog box as discussed in this section. To display the Properties dialog box for the connection, choose Start, display the Connect To menu, right-click the VPN connection, and choose Properties from the context menu.

The General page (shown on the left in Figure 34.14) contains the following options:

Host Name or IP Address of Destination text box   Enter the host name (for example, vpnserver.mycompany.com) or the IP address (for example, 206.13.48.12) of the VPN host to which you're connecting. If you entered the name or address while setting up the connection with the wizard, you shouldn't need to change it unless the company changes the host or the host uses a dynamic IP address.

First Connect group box   If you need XP to dial an Internet connection before trying to establish the VPN connection, select the Dial Another Connection First check box and choose the connection in the drop-down list. Again, you should have chosen these settings in the wizard.

Show Icon in Notification Area when Connected check box   As usual, select this check box to have XP display a notification-area icon for this connection when it's connected.

The Options page (shown on the right in Figure 34.14) contains the same options as for a dial-up connection, except that it doesn't offer the options directly related to dialing a connection: the Prompt for Phone Number check box, the Multiple Devices group box controls, and the X.25 button.

FIGURE 34.14

The General page (left) and Options page (right) of the Properties dialog box for a VPN connection

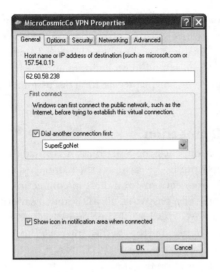

The Security page (shown on the left in Figure 34.15) contains the same items in the Security Options group box as a dial-up connection, but instead of the Interactive Logon and Scripting group box it offers an IPSec Settings button that you can use to configure IPSec settings. (More on security and IPSec later in this chapter.)

The Networking page (shown on the right in Figure 34.15) contains the same This Connection Uses the Following Items list box as other network connections, but at the top of the page is a Type of VPN drop-down list that you can use to select the type of VPN connection you want to establish: L2TP IPSec VPN (the more secure option), PPTP VPN (less secure), or Automatic (the default). When you choose the Automatic item, the connection tries L2TP first, then falls back to PPTP if it can't connect via L2TP.

FIGURE 34.15

The Security page (left) and Networking page (right) of the Properties dialog box for a VPN connection

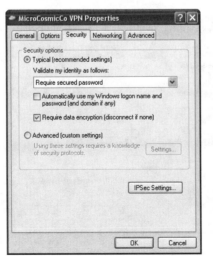

The Advanced page (not shown) contains the same controls—the Internet Connection Firewall group box, the Internet Connection Sharing group box, and the Settings button—as for a dial-up connection. See the section "Enabling and Disabling Internet Connection Firewall" in Chapter 18 for a discussion of the Internet Connection Firewall options and the section "Configuring ICS Manually Sharing Your Internet Connection" in Chapter 32 for a discussion of the Internet Connection Sharing options.

Establishing a VPN Connection

To establish a VPN connection, click the Start button, display the Connect To submenu, and select the VPN connection from it. XP displays the Connect dialog box for the connection, which looks much like the Connect box for a dial-up connection but doesn't include a phone number. Enter your username and password. If you want to save them so you don't need to enter them again, select the Save This User Name and Password for the Following Users check box and select the Me Only option button or the Anyone Who Uses This Computer option button as appropriate.

If you've configured the connection to connect to an Internet connection before establishing the VPN connection, it'll display the Initial Connection dialog box to prompt you to connect to the Internet. Select the Yes button or the No button as appropriate. If you want XP to go ahead and dial without prompting you, or to refrain from prompting you, select the Don't Display This Reminder Again check box before dismissing the Initial Connection dialog box.

If you're connecting to a VPN server that has a dynamic IP address rather than a fixed address or host name, click the Properties button in the Connect dialog box and enter the host's current IP address in the Host Name or IP Address of Destination text box on the General page of the Properties dialog box.

Click the Connect button to establish the connection. If your username or password isn't recognized, or if you need to provide domain information, XP displays the Connect dialog box shown in Figure 34.16 for you to enter correct information or further information.

FIGURE 34.16

If necessary, correct your username or password or enter your domain name in this Connect dialog box.

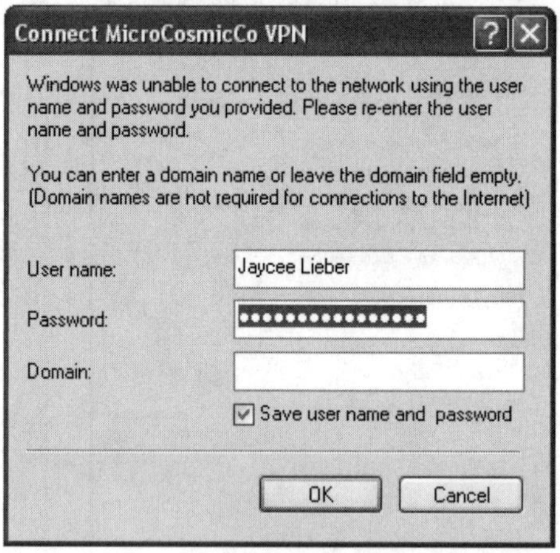

This sidebar discusses two reasons why you may not be able to connect to the network via your VPN connection.

A FIREWALL BLOCKS YOUR CONNECTION TO THE VPN

If the firewall is Internet Connection Firewall, check that the Services page of the Advanced Settings dialog box for the connection shows an Incoming Connection VPN (L2TP) check box and an Incoming Connection VPN (PPTP) check box, and that both check boxes are selected.

At the server end, TCP port 1723 on the firewall needs to be open for PPTP VPN connections. Port 1701 needs to be open for L2TP VPN connections. And IP protocol 47 needs to be enabled.

On the client end, TCP ports 1024–65535 on the firewall need to be open, and IP protocol 47 needs to be enabled.

If both the client and the server are correctly configured, the problem may lie in between. Ask your ISP if they're blocking the ports you need for VPN connections.

ERROR 619 OR ERROR 645

If you get Error 619 ("The port was disconnected") or Error 645 ("Dial-Up Networking could not complete the connection to the server") when trying to connect to a Windows 2000 Routing and Remote Access Services (RRAS) server via a VPN connection, the RRAS server needs to be registered in Active Directory. Until it is, you can't make client connections to Active Directory objects. Ask the network administrator to make this change.

Working via the VPN Connection

When you've connected, you'll be able to access your usual network drives, printers, and other resources, but the connection takes place at the speed of your Internet connection, which typically means that performance will be far slower than that of a LAN connection.

If you chose to display a notification-area icon for the connection, you can close the connection by right-clicking the icon and choosing Disconnect from the context menu. Otherwise, select the icon for the connection in the Network Connections folder and click the Disconnect This Connection link in the Network Tasks list (or right-click the icon and choose Disconnect from the context menu).

If you can establish a VPN connection to the VPN host but you then can't browse the network, the most likely explanation is that your TCP/IP configuration is incorrect. Display the Properties dialog box for the connection, double-click the Internet Protocol (TCP/IP) item in the This Connection Uses the Following Items list box on the Networking page, and specify either the IP address and DNS server information supplied by the network's administrator or tell XP to obtain the IP address and DNS server address manually.

A less likely explanation is that the VPN host is configured to prevent you from accessing any computers beyond the host itself. If this is the case, you're stuck with the host's offerings unless you can persuade the network's administrator to upgrade your access.

> **TROUBLESHOOTING: USING YOUR VPN DISABLES YOUR OTHER INTERNET PROGRAMS**
>
> If using a VPN connection appears to disable your other Internet programs, make sure that XP isn't trying to access the Internet via the VPN connection. Display the Networking tab of the Properties dialog box for the VPN connection and double-click the Internet Protocol (TCP/IP) entry to display the Internet Protocol (TCP/IP) Properties dialog box. Click the Advanced button to display the Advanced TCP/IP Settings dialog box and clear the Use Default Gateway on Remote Network check box on the General tab. Click the OK button in all three dialog boxes to close them.
>
> You may also need to flush the DNS cache. To do so, open a command-prompt window and issue a `ipconfig /flushdns` command.

Configuring XP to Accept Incoming VPN Connections

To accept incoming connections—or, more precisely, to configure XP's VPN server to accept one incoming connection at a time—take the steps shown in the following list. As for most configuration tasks, you need to be logged on as a Computer Administrator user.

1. Start the New Connection Wizard by choosing Start ➢ All Programs ➢ Accessories ➢ Communications ➢ New Connection Wizard or by clicking the Create a New Connection link in the Network Tasks list on the Network Connections page in Control Panel.

2. Click the Next button. The wizard displays the Network Connection Type page.

3. Select the Set Up an Advanced Connection option button and click the Next button. The wizard displays the Advanced Connection Options page.

4. Leave the Accept Incoming Connections option button selected and click the Next button. The wizard displays either the Devices for Incoming Connections page or the Incoming Virtual Private Network (VPN) Connection page.

5. If the wizard displays the Devices for Incoming Connections page, click the Next button. This page lets you specify which devices (modems, parallel ports, serial ports, and so on) you want to use for incoming connections, but for VPNs, this choice isn't relevant—you don't need to select *any* of the check boxes. When you click the Next button, the wizard displays the Incoming Virtual Private Network (VPN) Connection page.

6. Select the Allow Virtual Private Connections option button and click the Next button. The wizard displays the User Permissions page.

7. Specify which users may connect via this connection, as discussed in steps 11 and 12 of the list in "Setting Up the Host for the Direct Connection" in Chapter 32. Then click the Next button. The wizard displays the Networking Software page.

8. In most cases, the Networking Software list on the Networking Software page will list the item Internet Protocol (TCP/IP), File and Printer Sharing for Microsoft Networks, and QoS Packet Scheduler. Select the Internet Protocol (TCP/IP) item and click the Properties button. The wizard displays the Incoming TCP/IP Properties dialog box (see Figure 34.17).

FIGURE 34.17

In the Incoming
TCP/IP Properties
dialog box, choose
whether to let
incoming callers
access your network
and specify how to
assign IP addresses
to them.

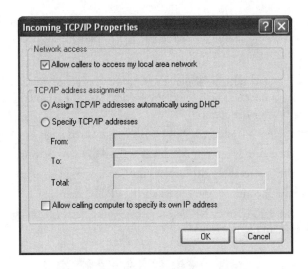

9. To allow callers to access computers and resources (such as printers) on your network, select the Allow Callers to Access My Local Area Network check box. To restrict callers to just the VPN server, clear this check box.

10. In the TCP/IP Address Assignment group box, choose how to assign IP addresses to callers.

   ◆ The easiest solution is to leave the Assign TCP/IP Addresses Automatically Using DHCP option button selected, as it is by default, which lets ICS's DHCP allocator assign an IP address to the caller.

   ◆ If you want, you can select the Specify TCP/IP Addresses option button and enter a starting value in the From text box and an ending value in the To text box. The Total text box displays the number of IP addresses in the range you've allocated. Because XP can accept only one incoming VPN connection at a time, you can enter a range of only two addresses if you want—for example, from 192.168.0.99 to 129.168.0.100. (XP won't let you enter a range of only one IP address.)

   ◆ For special effects, you may need to select the Allow Calling Computer to Specify Its Own IP Address check box so that the caller can designate the address. The problem with doing so is that the IP address the caller chooses may already be in use on the network, which produces an IP address conflict.

11. Click the OK button to close the Incoming TCP/IP Properties dialog box and return to the Networking software page of the New Connection Wizard. Then click the Next button. The wizard displays the Completing the New Connection Wizard page.

12. Click the Finish button. The wizard sets up the incoming connection, names it Incoming Connections, and exits.

If the computer you configured to accept VPN connections has an Internet connection, either one that it shares with other computers on your network or one it keeps all to itself, your connection is all set to go. But if your computer connects to the Internet through ICS running on another computer, you need to configure that computer to pass PPTP packets to the VPN server. Take the following steps on the ICS host:

1. Click the Start button, display the Connect To menu, right-click the entry for the shared Internet connection, and select Properties from the context menu. XP displays the Properties dialog box for the connection.

2. Click the Advanced tab. XP displays the Advanced page.

3. Click the Settings button. XP displays the Advanced Settings dialog box.

4. Click the Services tab. XP displays the Services page.

5. Select the Incoming Connection VPN (PPTP) item.

6. Click the Edit button. XP displays the Service Settings dialog box, which should show details like those in Figure 34.18.

FIGURE 34.18

Use the Service Settings dialog box to configure the Incoming Connection VPN (PPTP) service to pass PPTP packets along to the VPN server.

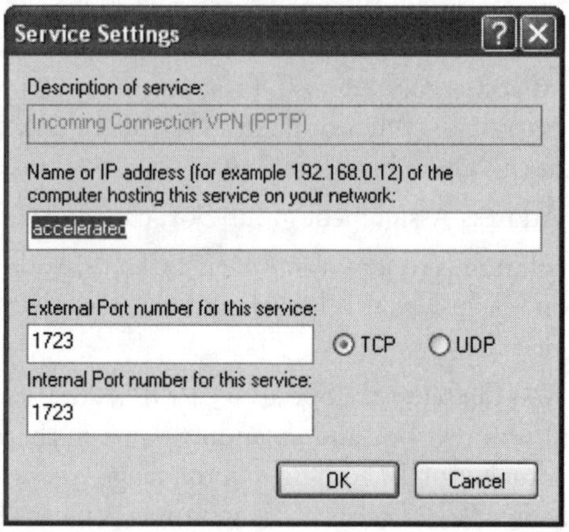

7. In the Name or IP Address of the Computer Hosting This Service on the Network text box, enter the IP address (for example, `192.168.0.5`) or qualified name (for example, `MyVPNBox.MSHOME.NET`) of the VPN server.

8. Click the OK button. XP closes the Service Settings dialog box.

9. Click the OK button. XP closes the Advanced Settings dialog box.

10. Click the OK button. XP closes the Properties dialog box for the connection.

TIP   *You can't directly rename the Incoming Connection VPN (PPTP) item. To rename it, delete the Incoming Connection VPN (PPTP) item and create another item by clicking the Add button and using the resulting Service Settings dialog box. Enter **1723** in both the External Port Number for This Service text box and the Internal Port Number for This Service text box.*

Turning Off the VPN Connection

To turn the VPN connection off temporarily without deleting its details, follow these steps:

1. Right-click the Incoming Connections icon on the Network Connections page of Control Panel and choose Properties from the context menu. XP displays the Incoming Connections Properties dialog box with the General page foremost.

2. Clear the Allow Others to Make Private Connections to My Computer by Tunneling through the Internet or Other Network check box in the Virtual Private Network group box.

3. Click the OK button. XP closes the Incoming Connections Properties dialog box.

To turn the VPN connection back on, repeat the steps but select the check box.

Choosing Security Settings and Configuring IPSec

This section discusses the settings that XP provides for making your VPN connections as secure as possible. The settings are different for outgoing VPN connections and incoming VPN connections.

SECURITY FOR OUTGOING VPN CONNECTIONS

Here are some suggestions for implementing security on your outgoing VPN connections from a computer running XP. Which of them you use depends on the capabilities and security configuration of the VPN server to which you're connecting.

Security Options for Connecting to an XP VPN Server

If you're connecting to a VPN server that's running XP, implement these two security settings:

◆ On the Networking page of the Properties dialog box for the VPN connection, select PPTP VPN in the Type of VPN drop-down list. Do this only if you're sure that the VPN server is running XP. Otherwise, select Automatic, which makes XP try L2TP first, then fall back to PPTP if it can't establish an L2TP connection.

◆ Select the Require Data Encryption (Disconnect if None) check box on the Security page of the Properties dialog box for the VPN connection.

Security Options for Connecting to a Windows 2000 Server VPN Server

If you're connecting to a Windows 2000 Server VPN host, take the following steps:

◆ On the Networking page of the Properties dialog box for the VPN connection, select Automatic in the Type of VPN drop-down list, so that XP will try to establish a VPN connection using L2TP first. If you want to make sure the connection uses L2TP, select L2TP IPSec VPN instead, but be aware that this will prevent you from establishing the VPN connection if L2TP isn't available for whatever reason.

◆ To choose IPSec settings for a VPN connection using L2TP, click the IPSec Settings button on the Security page. XP displays the IPSec Settings dialog box (see Figure 34.19). Select the Use Pre-Shared Key for Authentication check box and enter the key in the Key text box. Then click the OK button to close the dialog box.

FIGURE 34.19

In the IPSec Settings dialog box, specify the pre-shared key to use for authentication.

◆ Select the Require Data Encryption (Disconnect if None) check box on the Security page of the Properties dialog box for the VPN connection.

Even better than simply requiring data encryption is to use strong authentication such as Extensible Authentication Protocol (EAP) or Microsoft Challenge Handshake Authentication Protocol version 2 (MS-CHAP v2). However, these settings need to mesh with those on the VPN host to which you're connecting, so whether you get to use them will normally be a question for the administrator of the VPN host (for example, your company's network administrator) rather than for you. If you do need to use EAP or MS-CHAP v2, you apply it by selecting the Advanced (Custom Settings) option button on the Security page of the Properties dialog box for the VPN connection, clicking the Settings button, and working in the resulting Advanced Security Settings dialog box (see Figure 34.20).

FIGURE 34.20

If your VPN host requires strong authentication (such as EAP or MS-CHAP v2), apply it to the VPN connection by using the Advanced Security Settings dialog box.

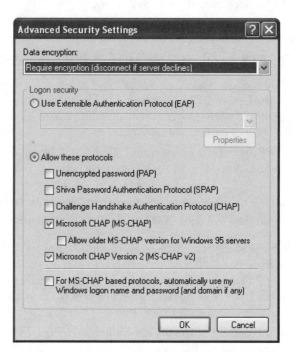

SECURITY FOR INCOMING VPN CONNECTIONS

Because XP offers only PPTP on its incoming VPN connections, and PPTP is less secure than L2TP, it's a good idea to implement the following security measures on your incoming VPN connections:

◆ Select the Require All Users to Secure Their Passwords and Data check box on the Users page of the Incoming Connections Properties dialog box. This forces the users to select the Require Data Encryption (Disconnect If None) check box before they can connect.

◆ Use DHCP to allocate IP addresses rather than letting callers specify IP addresses for themselves.

Up Next

This chapter has discussed how to use Remote Desktop Connection to take control of and work remotely at a computer running XP Professional, how to create a direct dial-up connection to a remote network, and how to use virtual private networking to establish secure connections over an insecure network.

The next chapter—well, there isn't one. This is the end of the book, except for Appendix A, "Windows Basics," which you've probably read already if it's relevant to you, and Appendix B, "Faxing and Telephony." Go well, go in peace, and go with XP until a better operating system comes along.

Appendix A

Windows Basics

THIS APPENDIX PRESENTS THE basic things you need to know about the Windows XP graphical user interface (GUI) in order to get started with the main text of the book. If you've used Windows before and are comfortable with the GUI, you probably don't need to read this appendix, though you might want to skim through the sections about Windows controls to make sure you're clear on the terms involved.

This appendix covers the following topics:

- ◆ Mouse basics and terminology
- ◆ Selection basics
- ◆ Drag-and-drop
- ◆ Working with windows and dialog boxes

Mouse Basics and Terminology

For navigating the XP GUI, a pointing device is almost essential. You can get a bewildering variety of pointing devices that work with XP—everything from a conventional mouse or trackball with two, three, or more buttons to a set of foot pedals that provide mouse functionality to a head-mounted infrared reflector that reflects a beam sent from a device mounted on your monitor to track your head movements and so move the mouse pointer. But the basic principle of all these devices is the same: You move the pointer around the screen to indicate one or more objects on which you want to take an action. You then click in one of the following ways to take the action:

Click   Press the primary mouse button once (and release the button). The primary mouse button on a conventional mouse is the left button, on which your right forefinger rests.

Double-click   Press the primary mouse button twice in quick succession.

Right-click   Press the secondary mouse button once.

Drag   Press the primary mouse button to select the object, keep holding the mouse button down, and move the mouse to drag the object to where you want it to appear. Release the mouse button.

Right-drag   Drag (as described in the previous paragraph) except using the secondary mouse button.

Selection Basics

These are the basic moves for selecting objects in XP:

◆ To select one object, click it with the primary mouse button. Alternatively, use the arrow keys to move the focus (the current selection) to the object, and then press the spacebar.

◆ To deselect a selected object, click in open space elsewhere in its window. With the keyboard, use the arrow keys to move the focus off the object.

◆ To select multiple objects that appear next to each other (for example, in a dialog box or in an Explorer window), click the first object to select it as usual. Then hold down the Shift key and click the last object in the range. Release the Shift key.

◆ To select multiple objects that don't appear next to each other, click the first object to select it as usual. Then hold down the Ctrl key while you click each of the other objects in turn. Release the Ctrl key.

◆ To deselect some of multiple objects you've selected, hold down the Ctrl key and click each selected object that you want to deselect in turn. Release the Ctrl key.

◆ To select multiple objects that appear near each other on your Desktop or in a folder in Tiles view, Icons view, or Thumbnails view, click in empty space outside one corner of the area occupied by the objects you want to select, then drag to draw a dotted box around them. When you release the mouse button, XP selects the objects.

◆ To select all the objects in an Explorer window, choose Edit ➤ Select All. To toggle the selection (selecting the objects that weren't selected and deselecting those that were), choose Edit ➤ Invert Selection. For example, to select all but three objects in an Explorer window, select those three objects and then choose Edit ➤ Invert Selection.

Drag-and-Drop

XP makes extensive use of functionality known as *drag-and-drop*, which lets you select an object on your Desktop or in a window, then drag it to a different location and drop it there.

Drag-and-drop has different effects depending on the object you're dragging, its source, and the location or object you drop it on. Here are some examples:

◆ Dragging a file and dropping it in a folder on the same drive moves the file from its source folder to the destination folder.

◆ Dragging a file and dropping it in a folder on a different drive copies the file from its source folder to the destination folder.

◆ Dragging a document and dropping it on the icon for a printer prints the document.

To use drag-and-drop, select an object by clicking it, keep holding down the mouse button, drag the object to its destination, and release the mouse button to drop it there.

Most drag-and-drop techniques use the primary mouse button, but some (usually less common) techniques use the secondary mouse button. The latter technique is referred to as *right drag-and-drop*.

Working with Windows and Dialog Boxes

When you're working in Windows, most of the action takes place in windows on-screen. A *window* is essentially a rectangular area on-screen. For example, when you run a program, it typically opens one or more windows for you to work in. Figure A.1 shows two program windows—a Notepad window and a My Computer window—open on the XP Desktop.

FIGURE A.1

Two program windows open on the XP Desktop

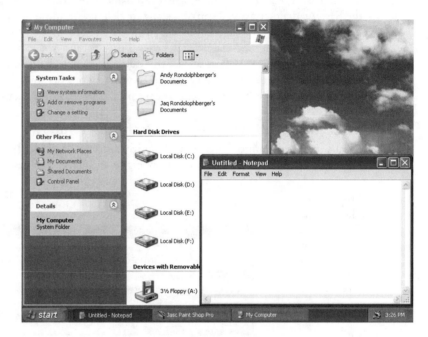

Most applications also use *dialog boxes*—fixed-size windows that typically contain controls but don't let you create documents.

The distinction between a window and a dialog box is somewhat flexible. Generally speaking, a window is resizable, whereas a dialog box is not. (Some dialog boxes display an extra section when you click a button such as More or Advanced, but this is different from being able to resize a window.)

Dialog Box Modality

In addition, most dialog boxes are *modal*. This means that when they are displayed, you cannot take any further action in the program that displayed them before dismissing the dialog box. Modality is intended to focus your attention on what the dialog box is expecting you to do.

NOTE   Technically, there are two types of modality: application modality *and* system modality. *When a dialog box is application modal, you can take no further action in its application until you dismiss the dialog box. When a dialog box is system modal, you can take no further action on your computer until you dismiss the dialog box. System modality is supposedly reserved for events of systemwide importance, such as Windows errors and crashes, but some applications display system-modal dialog boxes when they should display application-modal dialog boxes.*

The opposite of a modal dialog box is a *modeless* dialog box. A modeless dialog box does not prevent you from taking actions in its program while it's displayed. At this writing, modeless dialog boxes are relatively rare, but they're used in some applications. For instance, in Word for Windows, some dialog boxes are modeless. For example, when the Find and Replace dialog box is displayed, you can click in your document and continue working around the dialog box. But most dialog boxes in Word are modal. For example, when you display the Open dialog box, the Print dialog box, or the Save As dialog box, you can't take any further action in the program until you dismiss the dialog box.

The problem with modeless dialog boxes is that, because you can continue working while a modeless dialog box is displayed on-screen, you can in theory stack up an absurd number of modeless dialog boxes on-screen while you continue to work. In practice, most people get annoyed enough by modeless dialog boxes that they close them smartly, provided that they can see them.

Maximizing, Minimizing, and Restoring Windows

Most windows have three buttons: a Minimize button, a Maximize button that swaps places with a Restore Down button, and a Close button. Figure A.2 illustrates these buttons.

FIGURE A.2

Most windows have three buttons for minimizing, maximizing or restoring, or closing the window.

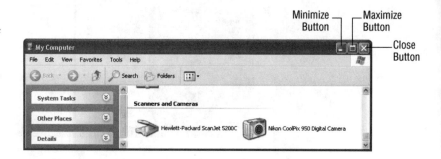

Minimize Button — Maximize Button — Close Button

These buttons are intuitive enough to use:

◆ Click the Maximize button to maximize its window. XP expands the window to take up all the Desktop and replaces the Maximize button with a Restore Down button.

◆ Click the Restore Down button to restore the window to its former size. As you'd expect, XP replaces the Restore Down button with the Maximize button again. The window is then said to be in a *normal* state—in other words, neither maximized nor minimized.

◆ Click the Minimize button to minimize its window down to a Taskbar button. Click the Taskbar button to restore the window to its preminimized size.

◆ Click the Close button to close its window.

You can also maximize, minimize, and restore windows by using the control menu (see the next section).

Using the Control Menu on Windows and Dialog Boxes

At the left end of its title bar, each window and dialog box has a *control menu* that contains commands for moving, resizing (windows only), and closing the window or dialog box.

When the control menu on a window is closed, it appears as a square bearing an icon representing the contents of the window. For example, the control-menu square for an Explorer window open to a hard drive displays a hard drive icon, and the control-menu square for a WordPad document bears the WordPad icon. By contrast, the control menu on a dialog box appears as part of the title bar—there's no visible indication that it's there.

To display the control menu on a window, click the square or press Alt+spacebar. To display the control menu on a dialog box, press Alt+spacebar (clicking doesn't work in a dialog box). Figure A.3 shows the control menu on a window.

FIGURE A.3

Use the control menu to move, resize, or close a window, or to move or close a dialog box.

The control menu for most dialog boxes offers just two commands: Move, and Close. The control menu for most windows offers these commands: Restore, Move, Size, Minimize, Maximize, and Close.

The Restore, Minimize, Maximize, and Close commands are self-explanatory. Only one of Restore and Maximize is available at any time: If the window is maximized, Restore is available; if the window is normal, Maximize is available.

Move is available if the window is in a normal state (because you cannot move a maximized window). To move the window by using the keyboard, select Move from the control menu, then use the arrow keys to move the window to where you want it, and press the Enter key. (You can also move the window with the mouse—but unless the window has somehow migrated to a position off your monitor, it's easier simply to drag the title bar of the window with the mouse rather than display the context menu and issue the Move command.)

Similarly, Size is available only if the window is in a normal state. Use the arrow keys to resize the window, and then press the Enter key.

TIP *Double-click the control-menu box to close a window.*

Dialog Box Controls

Figure A.4 shows the main controls that you'll find in dialog boxes in Windows. The following sections discuss these controls.

FIGURE A.4

A dialog box with the most-used controls in Windows

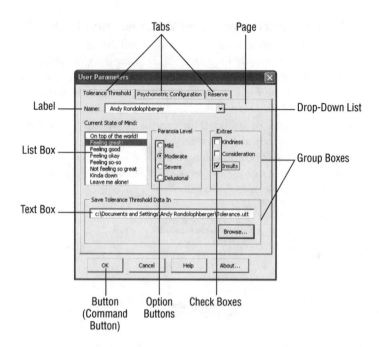

PAGE CONTROLS AND TABS

Some dialog boxes contain multiple *pages* of information. Each page typically contains a different set of controls. For example, in Figure A.4 (above), the Psychometric Configuration page and the Reserve page would contain a different set of controls than the Tolerance Threshold page.

To access one of the pages, you click its *tab*—the visible protrusion at the top of the page. Some people (including Microsoft, who should know better) refer to the pages as *tabs*, though this usage tends to be confusing.

The Windows convention is for the tab to be placed at the top of the page, though some programmers choose to place them at the bottom or at one of the sides of the pages for special effects (such as confusing the user).

LABEL CONTROLS

Labels are used to display text in dialog boxes. Typically, labels are static, though some dialog boxes use labels that you can change, either by clicking the label or by clicking a button associated with the label.

LIST BOX CONTROLS

A *list box* contains a number of items that typically are related. Most list boxes are configured so that you can choose only one of their items, but some list boxes are configured so that you can select multiple items.

DROP-DOWN LIST CONTROLS

A *drop-down list* control provides a number of preset values (presented via the list that you can access by clicking the down-arrow button). Some drop-down lists also let you enter a new value by typing into the text box.

The formal name for the latter type of drop-down list controls is *combo boxes* because they combine a text box and a list box.

GROUP BOX CONTROLS

The *group box* control is a visual aid for grouping other controls into logical sets. (The formal name for a group box control is *frame.*) For example, you'll find option buttons or check boxes arranged into group boxes to make clear that they belong together.

OPTION BUTTON CONTROLS

Option buttons (also called *radio buttons*) are groups of buttons of which only one can be chosen at any given time. (The name *radio button* comes from a physical radio with a number of preset stations. When you choose one preset button, it cancels the other buttons, because the radio can play only one station at a time.)

Selecting an option button clears all other option buttons in the set.

CHECK BOX CONTROLS

Check boxes are widely used controls for turning options on and off, or for indicating that (for multiple objects) the item specified by the check box is on for some and off for the others.

Most check boxes have two states: *selected* (with a check mark in them) and *cleared* (without a check mark in them). Clicking the check box toggles it from one state to the other. People use a variety of terms for describing what to do with check boxes, such as *put a check in the check box* or *click to remove the check from the check box*. For clarity, this book uses the phrases *select a check box* and *clear a check box*. If the check box in question is already in the state described, you don't need to do anything.

Some check boxes have a third state, in which the check box is selected but grayed out. This state, which technically is called a Null state and indicates that the check box contains no valid data, typically means that the option identified by the check box is on for part of the current selection. For example, in Microsoft Word, if you select three words, one of which has strikethrough formatting, and display the Font dialog box, the Strikethrough check box appears in a Null state, because it applies to part of the selection but not to all of it.

Some Windows applications use check boxes instead of option buttons. Their designers have wretched karma.

TEXT BOX CONTROLS

A *text box* is a control in which you can enter and edit text. Text boxes often contain a default value that you can change if necessary.

COMMAND BUTTON CONTROLS

A *command button* is a control that performs an action when you click it. For example, most dialog boxes contain a default action button (for example, a Print command button in a Print dialog box or an OK command button in many dialog boxes) to take the actions specified in the dialog box. Most dialog boxes contain a Cancel command button to cancel the actions specified in the dialog box and close the dialog box.

This book refers to command buttons as *buttons*.

CLOSING A DIALOG BOX

When you've made changes in a dialog box, you typically need to close it to apply them. To close a dialog box and apply the changes you've made, click the default command button (for example, an OK button, a Close button, or a Save button).

To close a dialog box without applying the changes you've made in it, click the Cancel button.

NOTE   *Some dialog boxes have an Apply button that you can click to apply your changes without closing the dialog box. This lets you make further changes before closing the dialog box.*

Appendix B

Faxing and Telephony

THIS APPENDIX DISCUSSES HOW to send faxes and make telephone calls in XP. XP Home provides strong fax features—not as strong as those in XP Professional (which lets you share faxing with other networked computers), but strong enough for most home or home-office use—and two programs for taking care of your telephony and dial-up needs.

This appendix covers the following topics:

◆ Installing and configuring the fax components

◆ Sending and receiving faxes in XP

◆ Annotating faxes you've received

◆ Using Phone Dialer

◆ Using HyperTerminal

Sending Faxes in XP

Despite the best efforts of Internet fax services that aim to take the telephone and the paper out of faxing, regular, station-to-station, paper faxing remains an essential part of daily office life, especially in home offices that need to share paper-based documents with their clients. But you can save time and effort (not to mention paper) by sending and receiving faxes directly from your computer—and you can keep incoming faxes away from inquisitive eyes around your house or office. If you have a scanner, you shouldn't even need to buy a fax machine if you don't have one already.

Sending faxes in XP isn't difficult, although XP's faxing components are annoyingly piecemeal instead of being integrated into a single, slick interface. This is because the components are borrowed from XP Professional and Windows .NET Server (which have a better excuse for needing multiple components to provide the flexibility for company-duty faxing and fax-management solutions) and then disguised a bit.

These are the XP faxing components and what they do:

◆ Fax Services is the umbrella term for XP's faxing components. The next four items are essentially manifestations of different aspects of Fax Services, which itself lurks mostly unseen in the background.

◆ The Fax Configuration Wizard is a user-friendly utility for configuring faxing. As long as you want to use the same settings for all your faxes, the Fax Configuration Wizard is pretty much a one-stop configuration solution.

◆ The Send Fax Wizard walks you through the steps of sending a fax. The most convenient way to invoke the Send Fax Wizard is by issuing a Print command for the document you want to fax.

◆ Fax Console is a program for manipulating the faxes you send and receive. It has an Inbox and an Outbox, an Incoming folder, and a Sent Items folder. It also offers features for configuring how Fax Services handles incoming and outgoing faxes.

◆ Fax Cover Page Editor is a program for creating custom cover pages for your faxes. It's not exciting (but then, neither are most cover pages), but it's effective.

To get faxing in XP, you'll probably want to take these steps in approximately this order:

1. Install Fax Services by running the Windows Component Wizard. (For reasons best known to Microsoft, Fax Services isn't included in default installations.)

2. Configure Fax Services.

3. Send a few faxes, and use Fax Console to see what happened to them.

4. Receive a fax or two.

Let's take it from the top.

Installing Fax Services

To install Fax Services, insert your XP CD in your CD drive (or make sure your installation source is available on your network) and that you're logged in as a Computer Administrator user. Then follow these steps:

1. Choose Start ➢ Control Panel. XP displays Control Panel.

2. Click the Printers and Other Hardware link. XP displays the Printers and Other Hardware page.

3. Click the Printers and Faxes link. XP displays the Printers and Faxes page.

4. Click the Set Up Faxing link in the Printer Tasks list (or choose File ➢ Set Up Faxing). XP launches the Windows Components Wizard, which installs Fax Services for you and then exits.

   ◆ If you didn't insert your XP CD, the Windows Components Wizard prompts you to install it or to specify your installation source.

   ◆ If you have Microsoft Office installed on your computer, the Windows Components Wizard may prompt you to install your Office CD.

NOTE   *You can also install Fax Services by selecting the Fax Services check box in the Windows Component Wizard, but clicking the Set Up Faxing link on the Printers and Faxes page is quicker and easier.*

That's the first step: You've got Fax Services installed. Now you need to configure it.

NOTE   *If XP won't let you add a fax printer, check that your modem supports faxing (some modems don't) and that you're logged in as a Computer Administrator user. Limited users and the Guest user can't add fax printers.*

Configuring Fax Services

XP provides a Fax Configuration Wizard to help you configure Fax Services. Take the following steps:

1. Choose Start ➢ All Programs ➢ Accessories ➢ Communications ➢ Fax ➢ Fax Console. The first time you run Fax Console, XP runs the Fax Configuration Wizard, which displays its Welcome screen.

   ◆ If your computer doesn't currently have a fax/modem installed, XP prompts you to install one. If you click the Yes button, it starts the Add New Hardware Wizard, which displays its Install New Modem page. Install the modem as described in Chapter 14.

   ◆ You can also run the Fax Configuration Wizard by double-clicking the newly installed fax on the Printers and Faxes page of Control Panel.

2. Click the Next button. The wizard displays the Sender Information page (shown in Figure B.1).

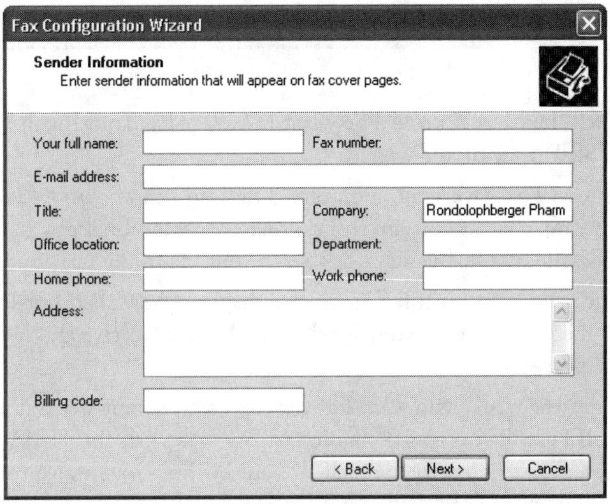

FIGURE B.1

The Fax Configuration Wizard walks you through configuring Fax Services and entering user information.

3. Enter your fax information: name, fax number, e-mail address, phone numbers, and so on.

4. Click the Next button. The wizard displays the Select Device for Sending or Receiving Faxes page of the wizard (shown in Figure B.2).

5. In the Please Select the Fax Device drop-down list, choose the fax device (for example, a modem) to use for sending faxes.

6. Leave the Enable Send check box selected (as it is by default) if you want to send faxes using this fax device.

7. If you want to receive faxes on this fax device, select the Enable Receive check box. Then select the Manual Answer option button or the Automatically Answer after *NN* Rings option button. If you select the latter, specify the number of rings in the text box.

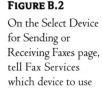

FIGURE B.2

On the Select Device for Sending or Receiving Faxes page, tell Fax Services which device to use for sending faxes.

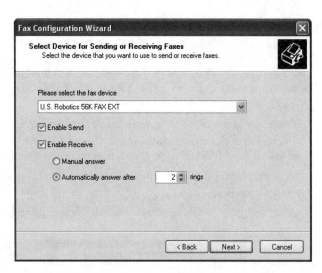

8. Click the Next button. The wizard displays the Transmitting Subscriber Identification (TSID) page of the wizard.

9. Enter a TSID for your computer. The TSID can be up to 20 characters long and can contain any information you can fit into them. Conventional practice is to use the TSID to identify yourself or your business, or to give your incoming fax phone number.

10. Click the Next button. The wizard displays the Called Subscriber Identification (CSID) page of the wizard. If you didn't select the Enable Receive check box, you get to skip this step and the next step.

11. Enter the CSID you want Fax Services to transmit when it answers a fax. Like the TSID, the CSID can be up to 20 characters long. As with the TSID, conventional practice is to use the CSID to identify yourself or your business, or to give your fax number so that the sender of the fax can see they've got the right number, business, or person.

12. Click the Next button. The wizard displays the Routing Options page of the wizard (shown in Figure B.3).

13. By default, Fax Services stores incoming faxes in Fax Console's Inbox. Specify if you want Fax Services to print the fax or save it to another folder as well as the Inbox:

   ◆ To print the fax, select the Print It On check box and select a printer in the drop-down list. (Remember that automatically printing every fax you receive on a shared printer removes the privacy advantages of receiving a fax via computer.) If you don't have a printer set up for this computer, the Print It On check box isn't available.

   ◆ To save the fax to a folder, select the Store a Copy in a Folder check box and use the Browse button and the resulting Browse for Folder dialog box to identify the folder.

FIGURE B.3

On the Routing Options page, specify whether Fax Services should print the fax or save it to a folder.

14. Click the Next button. The wizard displays the Completing the Fax Configuration Wizard page, which contains a summary of the options you chose. Check the configuration summary. To change anything, use the Back button to navigate to the appropriate page of the wizard. When all looks to be right, click the Finish button. The wizard closes itself, applies the settings you chose, and opens Fax Console.

Once you've used the Fax Configuration Wizard to configure faxing, you should be all set to send and receive faxes (as described in the next sections). You can rerun the Fax Configuration Wizard at any stage by choosing Tools ➢ Configure Fax from Fax Console. You can also change the fax settings more directly from Fax Console as described later in this appendix.

We'll examine Fax Console later in the appendix. First, here's how to send a fax.

Sending a Fax

To send a fax, follow these steps:

1. Create or open the document you want to fax. (If you need to fax a copy of printed material, use your scanner to create an image of the page.)

2. Issue a Print command as usual. (For example, press Ctrl+P.)

3. In the Print dialog box, select the Fax item for the fax you want to use.

4. If necessary, choose preferences for the fax. Click the Preferences button. XP displays the Fax Properties page of the Printing Preferences dialog box. In this dialog box, you can specify a different page size or orientation, but more often you'll want to change the setting in the Image Quality drop-down list. The standard setting is Normal (200×200 dpi). To send documents faster but with a more grainy effect, choose Draft (200×100 dpi).

5. Click the Print button in the Print dialog box. XP starts the Send Fax Wizard, which displays the Welcome to the Send Fax Wizard page.

6. Click the Next button. The wizard displays the Recipient Information page of the Send Fax Wizard (shown in Figure B.4).

FIGURE B.4

Specify the recipient or recipients of the fax on the Recipient Information page of the Send Fax Wizard.

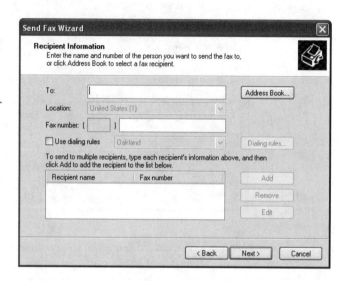

7. Enter the name of the recipient (or recipients) in the To text box.

♦ If the recipient doesn't have an entry in Address Book and you don't want to add them, enter their name or company in the To text box, and enter the fax number in the Fax Number text box. By default, Fax Services dials the number as you entered it. If you want to use dialing rules (having XP add any country, region, area, or long-distance codes the number needs based on your location), select the Use Dialing Rules check box and use the Location drop-down list to specify your location.

♦ To select a recipient from Address Book, click the Address Book button. In the Address Book dialog box, select the recipient from the appropriate contacts list. Click the To button to add the recipient to the Message Recipients list box. Click the OK button.

♦ If the recipient's Address Book entry contains no fax number, the wizard discards the recipient and displays a Send Fax Wizard message box telling you it has done so. If this happens, open Address Book and add the missing fax number, then select the recipient again from the Send Fax Wizard.

♦ If the recipient's Address Book entry contains both a business fax number and a home fax number, the wizard displays the Choose Fax Number dialog box (shown in Figure B.5). Select the Business Fax option button or the Home Fax option button (or, if it's available, the Other Fax option button) and click the OK button.

♦ To change the fax number for a recipient you've entered by using Address Book, select the recipient in the list box and click the Edit button. The wizard displays the Check Fax Number dialog box (shown in Figure B.6), in which you can change the information as necessary.

FIGURE B.5

If the recipient has both business and home fax numbers, the wizard displays the Choose Fax Number dialog box so that you can select the appropriate number.

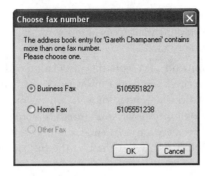

FIGURE B.6

Use the Check Fax Number dialog box to change a fax number you've entered from Address Book.

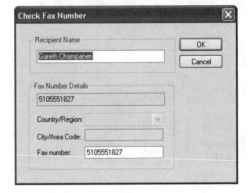

8. When you've finished adding recipients, click the Next button. The wizard displays the Preparing the Cover Page settings (shown in Figure B.7).

FIGURE B.7

Use the options on the Preparing the Cover Page page of the wizard to specify the type of cover page to include (if any).

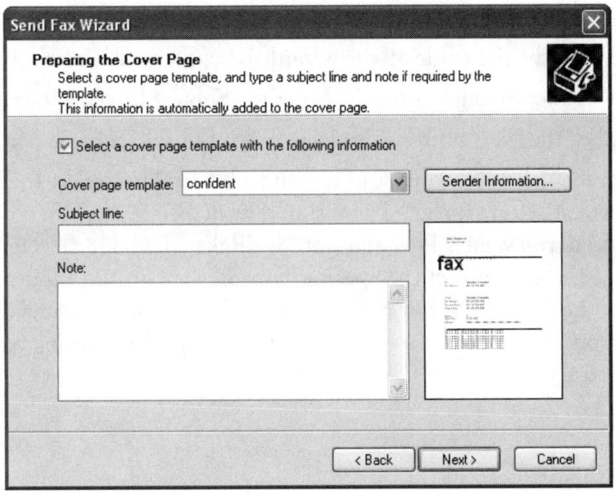

9. To include a cover page, select the Select a Cover Page Template with the Following Information check box. (If you don't want to include a cover page, leave this check box cleared.) Then specify the information to use:

◆ The first time you send a fax from this installation of Fax Services for this user identity, it's a good idea to check the sender information that Fax Services is planning to supply to the recipient. Click the Sender Information button. The wizard displays the Sender Information dialog box (shown in Figure B.8). Check that the information is appropriate. Modify it if necessary. To enter a temporary change for this fax but not store the change for future use, select the Use the Information for This Transmission Only check box.

FIGURE B.8

Check your sender information in the Sender Information dialog box before sending a fax.

◆ In the Cover Page Template drop-down list, choose the template to use. The preview box on the right side of the wizard shows an approximation of how the template looks.

◆ Enter the subject for the fax in the Subject Line text box and any note in the Note text box.

10. Click the Next button. The wizard displays its Schedule page (shown in Figure B.9).

11. In the When Do You Want to Send This Fax? list, select the appropriate option button. The default setting is the Now option button. Select the When Discount Rates Apply option button if you want XP to wait until it thinks telephone rates will be discounted (for example, in the evening). Select the Specific Time in the Next 24 Hours option button and enter a time in the text box if you want the fax to be sent at a particular time. (For example, you might choose to send a fax so that it arrived early in the morning but outside the recipient's sleeping hours.)

FIGURE B.9

On the Schedule page of the Send Fax Wizard, specify the fax priority and when you want to send the fax.

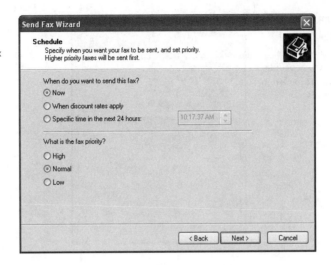

NOTE   *Looking at the Schedule page of the Send Fax Wizard, you may find yourself wondering where the wizard gets its knowledge of when discount rates apply. Does it (for example) have a hotline to the decision-makers at your local telco? Or does it apply some standardized information that might be wholly wrong for your location? In fact, it does neither. You specify the discount times in Fax Console, as discussed a little later in the appendix.*

12. In the What Is the Fax Priority? list, select the High option button, the Normal option button, or the Low option button as appropriate. High-priority faxes get sent before low-priority ones if they're due to be sent at the same time. Usually priorities become important only when you stack up faxes for later transmission.

13. Click the Next button. The Send Fax Wizard displays the Completing the Send Fax Wizard page, which lists the choices you've made.

14. Review the details of the fax. To look at how the fax will appear, click the Preview Fax button. Use the Back button to adjust any details. When you're ready, click the Finish button. The Send Fax Wizard closes and either starts sending the fax or queues it for transmission, depending on the options you chose.

If you chose to send the fax immediately, Fax Services displays the Fax Monitor dialog box (shown in Figure B.10 at its expanded size) so that you can see what's happening. Click the More button and the Less button (which replace each other as appropriate) to toggle between the small and expanded sizes of this dialog box. Click the Disconnect button to disconnect the current connection, the Answer Now button (not shown in the figure) to answer an incoming fax call manually, the Clear List button to clear the list of fax events, or the Hide button to hide the Fax Monitor dialog box.

FIGURE B.10

The Fax Monitor
dialog box lets you
see what's happening
on your fax modem.

If you're sending a lot of faxes, you may want to select the Keep This Dialog Visible at All Times check box to make Fax Services display the Fax Monitor dialog box all the time, whether it's sending faxes or not. You can also display the Fax Monitor dialog box at any time by choosing Tools ➤ Fax Monitor from Fax Console.

EXPERT KNOWLEDGE: FAXING AN EXISTING DOCUMENT FROM THE SEND TO MENU

When you're faxing a document you've just created, or that you've opened to review or edit before faxing it, starting the Send Fax Wizard from the Print dialog box is convenient. But if you want to fax an existing document, you can save time by faxing it from the Send To menu.

To create an entry for Fax Services on the Send To menu, follow these steps:

1. Open an Explorer window to the SendTo folder. You'll find it under \Documents and Settings *Username*\. If you haven't already turned on the display of hidden files in Explorer, you'll need to do so (choose Tools ➤ Folder Options, click the View tab, select the Show Hidden Files and Folders option button, and click the OK button).

2. Open Control Panel, click the Printers and Other Hardware link, and click the Printers and Faxes link.

3. Drag the Fax icon from the Printers and Faxes window to the SendTo folder. XP displays a Shortcut dialog box telling you that you cannot move or copy the Fax item and suggesting you create a shortcut instead. (Alternatively, right-drag the Fax icon to the folder and choose Create Shortcut from the context menu.)

4. Click the Yes button. XP creates the shortcut and names it Shortcut to Fax (or whatever your fax was named).

5. Rename the shortcut if you want. (For example, you might want to rename it **Fax**.)

Once you've done this, you'll be able to right-click a document and choose Send To ➤ Fax from the context menu to start the Send Fax Wizard.

Receiving a Fax

If you've set Fax Services to answer the phone automatically, it should collect any incoming faxes without your intervention. Once it successfully receives a fax, it converts it to a TIF file and places it in your Inbox so that you can investigate it at your leisure. TIF is a graphics format that you can edit in just about any image editor—including XP's built-in Windows Picture and Fax Viewer.

If you haven't set Fax Services to answer the phone automatically, you'll need to receive each fax manually. When the phone rings with the incoming fax call, open Fax Console and choose File ➤ Receive a Fax Now.

Managing Faxes from Fax Console

If you've been following along, you probably have Fax Console open by now. If not, choose Start ➤ All Programs ➤ Accessories ➤ Communications ➤ Fax ➤ Fax Console. XP opens Fax Console (shown in Figure B.11).

FIGURE B.11

Use Fax Console to monitor the state of your faxes and to pause or delete outgoing faxes.

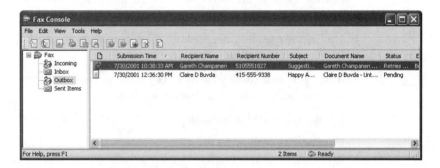

As you can see in the figure, Fax Console is a regular Microsoft Management Console snap-in. The left list box shows the fax printer (which may represent one fax device, two, or more), and under it four folders: an Incoming folder, an Inbox folder, an Outbox folder, and a Sent Items folder.

Fax Console supports a variety of actions, most of which you can take either from the context menu for a fax or from the toolbar. Figure B.12 shows the toolbar with labels.

FIGURE B.12

The Fax Console toolbar

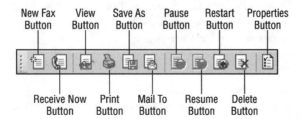

These are the key actions that you may want to take from Fax Console:

View a fax you've received   Display the Inbox and double-click the fax, select the fax and click the View button, or right-click the fax and choose View from the context menu. Fax Console opens the fax in Windows Picture and Fax Viewer.

Print a fax you've received   Display the Inbox, select the fax, and click the Print button, or right-click the fax and choose Print from the context menu.

Pause an outgoing fax   Display the Outbox, select the fax, and click the Pause button, or right-click the fax and choose Pause from the context menu.

Resume an outgoing fax   Display the Outbox, select the fax, and click the Resume button, or right-click the fax and choose Resume from the context menu.

Delete an outgoing fax   Display the Outbox, select the fax, and click the Delete button. Alternatively, select the fax and press the Delete key, or right-click the fax and choose Delete from the context menu.

Update your sender information   Choose Tools ➢ Sender Information and work in the Sender Information dialog box.

Add a personal cover page to a fax   Choose Tools ➢ Personal Cover Pages. Fax Console displays the Personal Cover Pages dialog box.

Display the Fax Monitor dialog box   Choose Tools ➢ Fax Monitor.

Configure your fax printer   Choose Tools ➢ Fax Printer Configuration and work in the resulting Properties dialog box for the fax printer, as discussed in the next section.

TIP   If you've used Personal Fax in Windows 9x, you can import your archived faxes by choosing File ➢ Import from Fax Console.

Configuring Your Fax Printer

By this time, you should already have configured your fax printer by using the Fax Configuration Wizard. As mentioned earlier, you can rerun the Fax Configuration Wizard at any time from Fax Console by choosing Tools ➢ Configure Fax. But you can also set the same properties, and others, by working directly in the Properties dialog box for the fax printer. To do so, choose Tools ➢ Fax Printer Configuration from Fax Console.

The following sections discuss the options in the Properties dialog box for a fax printer.

GENERAL PAGE OPTIONS

The General page of the Properties dialog box for a fax printer (shown on the left in Figure B.13) contains the following options:

Name text box   (Actually, *unnamed* text box would be more appropriate.) In this text box, enter the name by which you want to refer to the fax. The default name is *Fax*, which is succinct but uninformative.

Location text box If you feel the need, enter details of the location of the fax in this text box. (The location is more relevant with shared faxes, but XP Home doesn't support fax sharing.)

Comment text box Enter any comment about the fax printer in this text box. For example, you might note which phone line it uses.

Features group box This group box summarizes known information about the fax. This group box is mostly designed for printers, and for many fax modems the only relevant information is Maximum Resolution.

FIGURE B.13

The General page (left) and Devices page (right) of the Properties dialog box for a fax printer

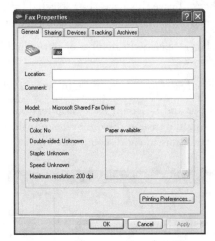
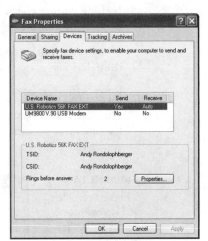

SHARING PAGE OPTIONS

The Sharing page actually has no options for XP Home, because XP Home doesn't support fax sharing. (XP Professional does.)

DEVICES PAGE OPTIONS

The Devices page of the Properties dialog box for a fax printer (shown on the right in Figure B.13) contains the following options:

Device Name list box This list box lists the fax devices installed on your computer and their current Send and Receive settings. To toggle the Send setting or the Receive setting, right-click the fax device and choose Send ➤ Enable, Send ➤ Disable, Receive ➤ Enable, or Receive ➤ Disable from the context menu.

Device **group box** This group box lists the TSID, CSID, and Rings before Answer setting for the fax device selected in the Device Name list box.

To change the properties for a device, select it in the Device Name list box and click the Properties button. Fax Console displays the Properties dialog box for the device. Then choose settings as discussed in the following sections.

Send Page Options

The Send page of the Properties dialog box for a fax device (shown on the left in Figure B.14) contains the following options:

Enable Device to Send check box   Select this check box to enable sending on the fax device. Clear this check box to disable sending. (For example, you might choose to use one fax device for outgoing faxes only and another for receiving faxes.)

TSID text box   You can change your TSID in this text box.

Include Banner check box   Leave this check box selected (as it is by default) to have Fax Services include a banner of information along the top edge of the faxes you send.

Number of Retries text box   Specify the number of retries in this text box. You can set any value from 0 to 99.

Retry After text box   Specify the retry interval (in minutes) in this text box.

Discount Rate Start text box and Discount Rate Stop text box   Use these text boxes to specify the times that Fax Services should treat as discount rates. (As mentioned earlier in this appendix, you can schedule faxes for transmission at discount-rate times.)

FIGURE B.14

The Send page (left) and Receive page (right) of the Properties dialog box for a fax device

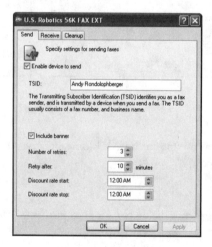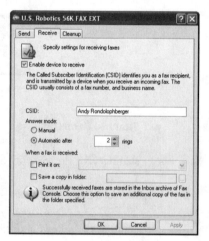

Receive Page Options

The Receive page of the Properties dialog box for a fax device (shown on the right in Figure B.14) contains the following options:

Enable Device to Receive check box   Select this check box to enable receiving on the fax device. Clear this check box to disable receiving.

CSID text box   You can change your CSID in this text box.

Answer Mode list   Use the Manual option button or the Automatic after *NN* Rings option button and text box to specify whether you want the fax device to answer incoming faxes automatically or to engage it manually yourself.

When a Fax Is Received group box   Use the Print It On check box and/or the Save a Copy in Folder check box to specify any action you want Fax Services to take with the fax apart from placing it in the Inbox. (See step 13 in "Configuring Fax Services" earlier in this appendix for more information.)

Cleanup Page Options

The Cleanup page of the Properties dialog box for a fax device contains the Automatically Delete Failed Faxes after *NN* Days check box and text box. If you want Fax Services to dispose of failed faxes, select this check box (which is cleared by default) and specify their stay of execution.

TRACKING PAGE OPTIONS

The Tracking page of the Properties dialog box for a fax printer (shown on the left in Figure B.15) contains the following options:

Please Select the Fax Device to Monitor drop-down list   Select the fax device for which you want to set tracking options.

Notification Area group box   Select or clear the Show Progress when Faxes Are Sent or Received check box, the Notify of Success and Failure for Incoming Faxes check box, and the Notify of Success and Failure for Outgoing Faxes check box to specify for which items Fax Services should display alerts in the notification area.

Fax Monitor group box   Select or clear the Sent check box and the Received check box to specify when you want Fax Services to display the Fax Monitor dialog box. Most people find it useful to see this dialog box whenever a fax is being sent or received.

FIGURE B.15

The Tracking page (left) and Archives page (right) of the Properties dialog box for a fax printer

To specify when Fax Services plays sounds, click the Configure Sound Settings button and work in the resulting Sound Settings dialog box (shown in Figure B.16).

FIGURE B.16

Use the Sound Settings dialog box to specify when Fax Services should play sounds.

ARCHIVES PAGE OPTIONS

The Archives page of the Properties dialog box for a fax printer (shown on the right in Figure B.15) lets you specify whether and where to archive incoming faxes and successfully sent faxes.

When you've finished choosing options, click the OK button. Fax Console closes the Properties dialog box and applies your choices.

Creating Custom Cover Pages with Fax Cover Page Editor

Instead of using Fax Services' canned cover pages, you can use custom cover pages that you create by using Fax Cover Page Editor. (You can also tweak the canned cover pages to suit your needs, or create new cover pages based on them.) Fax cover pages consist of text and graphics in your choice of layout (with some constraints) and use the COV extension.

Start Fax Cover Page Editor by choosing Start ➢ All Programs ➢ Accessories ➢ Communications ➢ Fax ➢ Fax Cover Page Editor. Alternatively, if you have Fax Console open, you can start Fax Cover Page Editor by choosing Tools ➢ Personal Cover Pages, then clicking the New button in the Personal Cover Pages dialog box that Fax Console displays.

When you launch Fax Cover Page Editor, it automatically creates a new, blank cover page. Figure B.17 shows Fax Cover Page Editor with a new cover page underway.

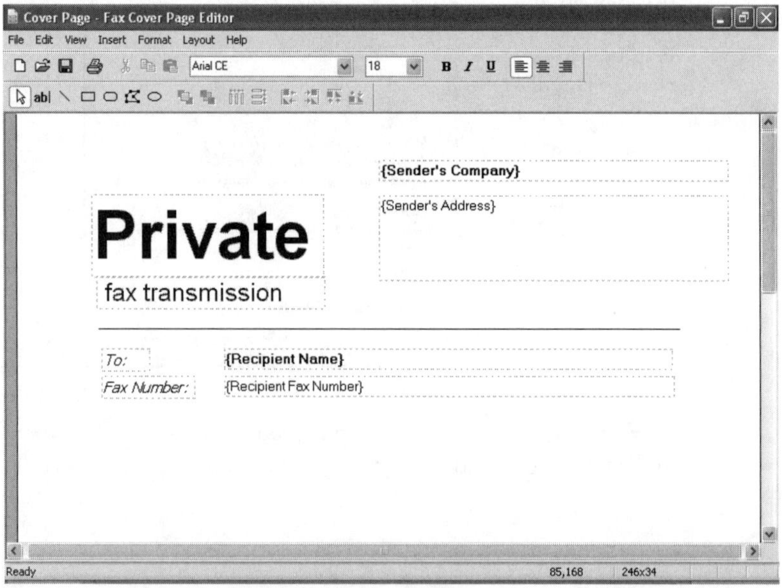

FIGURE B.17

Use Fax Cover Page Editor to create custom cover pages for your faxes.

Fax Cover Page Editor offers a lot of features that we don't have the space to cover in depth here. But these are the basic steps to follow to put together a cover page:

1. If necessary, create a new page: Press Ctrl+N or choose File ➤ New.

2. If necessary, adjust the paper size or orientation in the Page Setup dialog box (File ➤ Page Setup).

3. If you want to use the grid to help you position items more precisely and evenly, display it: Choose View ➤ Grid Lines.

4. Insert the fields for the text on the cover page by using the Insert menu. For example, choose Insert ➤ Recipient ➤ Name to insert the field for the recipient's name and Insert ➤ Sender ➤ Fax Number to insert the field for the sender's fax number.

5. Arrange the fields by using the commands on the Layout menu:

   ◆ To select one of the items on a cover page, click it. Alternatively, press the Tab key to move from the selected item to the next. Press Shift+Tab to select the previous item.

   ◆ You can select multiple items in a couple of ways. Either select the first item, hold down the Ctrl key, and then select the remaining items. Or click outside one corner of the group and drag the selection border until it extends around the items.

   ◆ To align selected objects, choose Layout ➤ Align Objects and choose Left, Right, Top, or Bottom from the submenu.

   ◆ To space selected objects evenly, choose Layout ➤ Space Evenly ➤ Across or Layout ➤ Space Evenly ➤ Down.

   ◆ To change the order in which items are stacked on top of each other, select an object and choose Layout ➤ Bring to Front or Layout ➤ Send to Back.

TIP To copy an item (except the Note field), select it, hold down the Ctrl key and the Shift key, and drag it to where you want the copy to appear.

6. Change the font of a selected field by choosing Format ➤ Font and working in the Font dialog box. Alternatively, use the toolbar buttons.

7. Change the alignment of text in a selected field by choosing Format ➤ Align Text and selecting Left, Center, or Right from the submenu.

8. Change lines and shading by choosing Format ➤ Line, Fill and Color and working in the Line, Fill and Color dialog box. (Before you ask—your color choices are limited to black, white, and shades of gray.)

9. Add any decorative elements (such as shapes or lines) by using the buttons on the Drawing toolbar.

10. Use Print Preview (File ➤ Print Preview) to make sure your cover page looks the way you want it to.

11. Save the cover page by choosing File ➤ Save and specifying the name and location in the Save As dialog box.

   ◆ If you want the cover page to be available to all users of this computer, save it in the `\Documents and Settings\All Users\Application Data\Microsoft\Windows NT\MSFax\Common CoverPages\` folder. (You'll need to have selected the Show Hidden Files and Folders option button on the View page of the Folder Options dialog box from Explorer to get to this folder.)

   ◆ If you want the Personal Cover Pages dialog box to list this cover page automatically, save it in the `\Fax\Personal Cover Pages\` folder under your `\My Documents\` folder.

   ◆ Otherwise, save the cover page in any folder that suits you and add it to the Personal Cover Pages list as described in the next section.

ADDING AN EXISTING COVER PAGE TO THE PERSONAL COVER PAGES DIALOG BOX

For most purposes, it's easiest to keep your personal cover pages where Microsoft wants you to keep them—in the `\Fax\Personal Cover Pages\` folder under your `\My Documents\` folder. But you can also keep them in other folders if you prefer.

If you do, you can add cover pages to the list in the Personal Cover Pages dialog box as follows:

1. From Fax Console, choose Tools ➤ Personal Cover Pages. XP displays the Personal Cover Pages dialog box (shown in Figure B.18).

FIGURE B.18

Use the Personal Cover Pages dialog box to manage your personal cover pages.

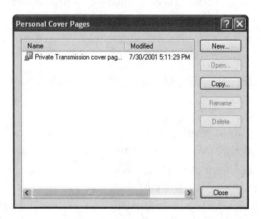

2. Click the Copy button. XP displays the Copy Cover Page to List of Personal Cover Pages dialog box, which is a common Open dialog box by another name.

3. Navigate to and select the cover page file.

4. Click the Open button. XP closes the dialog box and copies the cover page to the Personal Cover Pages dialog box.

Editing and Annotating a Fax

After you receive a fax, you may want to annotate it or censor it before passing it along to a family member or colleague (or, if you're brave or foolish, both). To do so, double-click the fax file to open it in a Windows Picture and Fax Viewer window. Then annotate it as described in the "Annotating an Image" section in Chapter 7. For example, you might want to draw a frame around a key section of the fax and attach a text box with commentary to it; you might want to draw a solid rectangle over a part of the fax that you want to keep secret; or you might want to add freehand doodles to the fax to convey a sense of freshness or informality. With Windows Picture and Fax Viewer's annotation features, the world is pretty much your lobster—at least, as far as annotating faxes goes.

Making and Receiving Calls with Phone Dialer

Phone Dialer is a telephony program with which you can make voice calls, video calls, and video-conference calls. You can make calls either via regular dial-up (station to station) or via the Internet.

Phone Dialer has been a part of Windows for several years now, and it's included in a standard XP Home installation (in other words, you don't need to install it separately the way you do Fax Services). But you could be forgiven for assuming that XP Home is somehow embarrassed by (or scared of) Phone Dialer, because it provides no shortcut for it on the Start menu. This is perhaps partly because Windows Messenger (discussed in the previous chapter) is muscling in on Phone Dialer's territory to some extent, and perhaps partly because Microsoft is so heavily committed to Internet telephony as to deprecate dial-up. But given that most people don't yet have always-on broadband connections, dial-up telephony remains important for many people, and Phone Dialer is a useful and capable if fundamentally unexciting program.

All of which is essentially a preamble to saying that you need to create your own shortcut to Phone Dialer. You'll find its executable, `DIALER.EXE`, in the `\Program Files\Windows NT\` folder.

EXPERT KNOWLEDGE: PHONE DIALER VERSUS NETMEETING

XP offers two separate programs for telephonic communication over regular phone lines and Internet connections: Phone Dialer (discussed in this section) and NetMeeting (discussed in Web Chapter 3). To get the most out of your calls, you need to understand the strengths and weaknesses of each program.

Both Phone Dialer and NetMeeting can make voice calls, video calls, and conference calls. With either program, each type of call can be dialed direct or made via an Internet connection.

That's about as far as the similarities go. The differences are significant and worth understanding. Phone Dialer is essentially a telephony program, while NetMeeting is essentially a collaboration and file-sharing program.

NetMeeting offers chat, whiteboarding, file sharing, and remote control of not only individual programs but also of the whole Windows Desktop. Phone Dialer offers none of these.

Phone Dialer can handle audio conferences and video conferences involving more than two people. (NetMeeting can handle audio and video for only two people at a time.) To compensate, Phone Dialer keeps each video window to a tiny size, while NetMeeting lets you adjust the size of the video you send.

To get the most out of Phone Dialer, you need a modem or an Internet connection; a sound card, microphone (or handset), and speakers; and a video camera (if you want to send video; you can receive video calls without a camera).

Obviously enough, you need to have Phone Dialer open to use it to place a call. Less obviously, you need to have Phone Dialer open to receive a call. So if you use Phone Dialer for telephony, it's a good candidate for adding to your Startup group so that XP starts it automatically when you log on.

To start Phone Dialer, double-click that shortcut you just created. Alternatively, choose Start ➤ Run, enter **dialer** in the Run dialog box, and click the OK button. Figure B.19 shows Phone Dialer. The left pane lists the directories and numbers available to you, broken down into these categories: Internet Directories, My Network Directory (a directory on the local network), Speed Dial (your list of Speed Dial entries), and Conference Room (any ongoing conferences).

FIGURE B.19

Phone Dialer lets you make voice and video calls over regular phone lines and over the Internet pages.

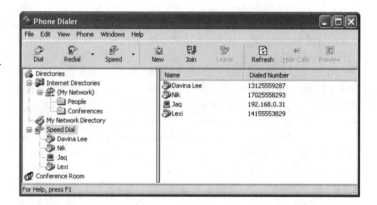

Configuring Phone Dialer

Before you start using Phone Dialer, perform some basic configuration. Take the following steps:

1. Choose Edit ➤ Options. Phone Dialer displays the Options dialog box.

2. On the Lines page (shown on the left in Figure B.20), make any necessary phone line choices:

   Preferred Line for Calling group box   Select the Phone option button or the Internet option button as appropriate. (You can specify phone or Internet for each call you make, but you'll save time by choosing your normal setting here.)

   Line Used For group box   In the Phone Calls drop-down list, the Internet Calls drop-down list, and the Internet Conferences drop-down list, you can specify the line you prefer to use. The default setting for each is Auto-Select, which lets Phone Dialer decide which line to use. The setting you're most likely to want to change is Phone Calls, which lists each modem you have. It also offers a choice called H323 Line, which is an Internet telephony line.

FIGURE B.20

On the Lines page (left) of the Options dialog box, choose which lines to use for which types of call. On the Audio/Video page (right), choose audio and video options.

3. On the Audio/Video page (shown on the right in Figure B.20), select options as appropriate:

Use the Telephone Handset Connected to This PC for All Calls check box   Select this check box to use a handset for all your calls. If XP doesn't detect a handset, this check box is not available.

Enable Acoustic Echo Cancellation check box   Select this check box to have Phone Dialer try to cancel out echoes.

Devices Used for Calling group box   In the Line drop-down list, select the Phone Calls item, the Internet Calls item, or the Internet Conferences item. Then make selections for this type of call in the Audio Record drop-down list, the Audio Playback drop-down list, and the Video Recording drop-down list. Select the Video Playback check box if you want to receive video playback on this type of call. For Internet conferences, the Devices Used for Calling group box also displays a Maximum Video Windows text box. In this, enter the maximum number of video windows you want to have open at any time. The default setting is 6, which is plenty for most people. You may want to reduce this number to get better video performance.

4. Click the OK button. Phone Dialer closes the Options dialog box.

Placing a Call

To place a call with Phone Dialer, follow these steps:

1. Click the Dial button or choose Phone ➢ Dial. Phone Dialer displays the Dial dialog box (shown in Figure B.21).

FIGURE B.21

Use the Dial dialog box to place a call.

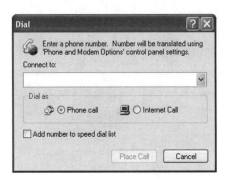

2. Enter the phone number, IP address, or DNS name in the text box. (Once you've used Phone Dialer, you can choose a recent number, address, or name from the drop-down list.)

3. In the Dial As group box, select the Phone Call option button for a regular (dialed) phone call. Select the Internet Call option button to call via the Internet.

4. If you want to create a Speed Dial entry for this number, address, or name, select the Add Number to Speed Dial List check box.

5. Click the Place Call button to place the call. Phone Dialer displays the active call window and the preview window (shown in Figure B.22).

FIGURE B.22

The active call window appears when you place a call.

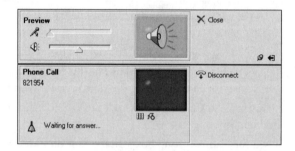

6. If the person you've called picks up the call, the active call window displays *Connected*.

7. Carry on the call as normal. Use the microphone and volume controls to adjust the microphone volume and speaker (or headphone) volume if necessary. If your telephony setup supports hold, the active call window displays a Hold button. Click this button to toggle the active call on and off hold.

8. Click the Disconnect button to end the call.

9. Click the Close button to close the active call window.

Receiving Incoming Calls

When someone calls you—either via the phone or via the Internet—Phone Dialer displays the active call window as shown in Figure B.23, flashing the message *Incoming call* and sounding a ringing tone. Click the Take Call button to accept the call or the Reject Call button to reject the call.

FIGURE B.23

When you get an incoming call, Phone Dialer displays the active call window and sounds a ringing tone.

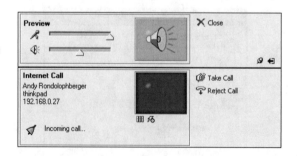

Keeping a Speed Dial List

Like most smart phones, Phone Dialer lets you create and maintain a Speed Dial list of numbers you call frequently.

ADDING AN ENTRY TO YOUR SPEED DIAL LIST

You can add entries to your Speed Dial list in several ways:

◆ This is the formal way:

1. Choose Edit ➢ Add to Speed Dial List. Phone Dialer displays the Speed Dial dialog box (shown on the left in Figure B.24).

2. In the Display Name text box, enter the name under which you want the Speed Dial listed.

3. In the Number or Address text box, enter the telephone number, the IP address, or the DNS name.

4. In the Dial As group box, select the Phone Call option button, the Internet Call option button, or the Internet Conference option button as appropriate.

5. Click the OK button. Phone Dialer closes the Speed Dial dialog box.

FIGURE B.24

Create Speed Dial entries for numbers you need to call frequently (left). Use the Edit Speed Dial List dialog box (right) to edit and rearrange Speed Dial entries.

◆ When you're using the Dial dialog box to place a call, select the Add Number to Speed Dial List check box.

◆ When you're on a call, click the Add to Speed Dial icon. Phone Dialer displays the Speed Dial dialog box with the telephone number, IP address, or DNS name entered in both the Display Name text box and the Number or Address text box. Change the contents of the Display Name text box if necessary, then click the OK button.

DIALING A SPEED DIAL NUMBER

You can dial a Speed Dial entry in several easy ways:

◆ Click the down-arrow on the Speed button and select the entry from the drop-down menu.

- Choose Phone ➢ Speed Dial and select the entry from the submenu.
- Expand the Speed Dial list in the left pane and double-click the entry.

EDITING YOUR SPEED DIAL LIST

You can edit your Speed Dial list to change the order in which the entries are listed, to change a particular entry, or to add or remove entries.

To edit your Speed Dial list, select Edit ➢ Speed Dial List or click the down-arrow on the Speed button and choose Edit Speed Dial List. Phone Dialer displays the Edit Speed Dial List dialog box (shown on the right in Figure B.24).

Edit your list as follows:

- Use the Move Up button and Move Down button to move a selected entry up or down the list.
- Click the Remove button to remove a selected entry.
- Click the Edit button to display the selected entry for editing in the Speed Dial dialog box.
- Click the Add button to display the Speed Dial dialog box. Specify the details for the entry and click the OK button.

When you've finished editing the list, click the OK button. Phone Dialer closes the Edit Speed Dial List dialog box.

Adding an Internet Directory to Phone Dialer

To add an Internet directory to Phone Dialer, follow these steps:

1. Choose Edit ➢ Add Directory. Phone Dialer displays the Add Directory Server dialog box.
2. Enter the name of the directory server in the text box.
3. Click the Add button. Phone Dialer closes the Add Directory Server dialog box and adds the directory server to your Internet Directories list.

NOTE *The My Network Directory list in Phone Dialer lets you access a directory of the network you're currently logged on to. This feature is primarily aimed at XP Professional users rather than XP Home users, because to use it, you need to be logged on to a network domain—which XP Home users cannot be.*

Closing Phone Dialer

When you close Phone Dialer, it displays the Confirm Phone Dialer Exit dialog box (shown in Figure B.25) to warn you that when you close it, you won't be able to accept Internet calls or receive notice of incoming calls. Click the Yes button to close Phone Dialer. If you don't want to see the Confirm Phone Dialer Exit dialog box again, select the Don't Ask Me Again check box before dismissing the dialog box.

FIGURE B.25

When you close
Phone Dialer, it displays the Confirm
Phone Dialer Exit
dialog box until you
tell it not to.

Using HyperTerminal

HyperTerminal is a dial-up communications program that you can use for connecting to other computers or bulletin board systems (BBSes) via terminal emulation. Because so much communication takes place via the Internet nowadays, you may need to use HyperTerminal only occasionally. But when you need it, it's straightforward and effective.

To use HyperTerminal, follow these steps:

1. Start HyperTerminal by choosing Start ➢ All Programs ➢ Accessories ➢ Communications ➢ HyperTerminal. When you start HyperTerminal, it assumes you want to create a new connection, and displays the Connection Description dialog box (shown on the left in Figure B.26). The first time you run HyperTerminal, it displays the Default Telnet Program? dialog box, asking whether you want to make HyperTerminal your default Telnet program. Choose the Yes button or the No button as appropriate. To prevent HyperTerminal from displaying this dialog box each time you start it, select the Don't Ask Me This Question Again check box before dismissing the dialog box.

FIGURE B.26

Name the new
connection in the
Connection Description dialog box
(left), and then
enter the connection
information in the
Connect To dialog
box (right).

2. Enter the name for the connection in the Name text box, select an icon in the Icon list box, and click the OK button. HyperTerminal displays the Connect To dialog box (shown on the right in Figure B.26).

3. Specify the country or region, enter the area code and phone number, and make sure the right dial-up device is selected in the Connect Using drop-down list. Then click the OK button. HyperTerminal displays the Connect dialog box (shown in Figure B.27).

FIGURE B.27

In the Connect dialog box, check the phone number and your current location. Then click the Dial button.

4. Check the phone number:

♦ To change the phone number, click the Modify button and change the country or region, area code, or phone number on the Connect To page of the Properties dialog box (shown in Figure B.28).

FIGURE B.28

Use the Connect To page of the Properties dialog box to change the phone number or to set redialing for a busy number.

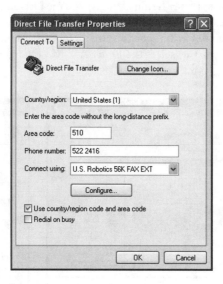

♦ To make HyperTerminal redial a busy connection automatically, click the Modify button. HyperTerminal displays the Properties dialog box for the connection. Then select the Redial on Busy check box on the Connect To page.

5. Check your location in the Your Location drop-down list. Change it if necessary. If you need to create a dialing rule, click the Dialing Properties button. XP displays the Phone and Modem Options dialog box.

6. Click the Dial button. HyperTerminal dials the number and, if it answers, establishes a connection.

What happens next depends on the computer you've dialed. For example, you may be prompted to enter a username and password to log in.

TIP   If you need to specify which type of terminal HyperTerminal should emulate for a connection, choose File ➤ Properties to display the Properties dialog box for the connection. (For example, most bulletin board systems use ANSI.) On the Settings page, choose the type of emulation you want. You can also specify the type of behavior you want for the function keys, arrow keys, Ctrl key, and Backspace key.

You may then want to take some of the following actions from the main HyperTerminal window:

◆ To upload a file, choose Transfer ➤ Send File. In the Send File dialog box, specify the filename and the protocol to use. (Use the default choice, Zmodem with Crash Recovery, unless you know you need to use another protocol.) Then click the Send button.

◆ To download a file, choose Transfer ➤ Receive File. In the Receive File dialog box, specify the folder in which to place the downloaded file and the protocol to use for receiving it. Then click the Receive button.

◆ To capture text in your HyperTerminal session, select Transfer ➤ Capture Text. In the Capture Text dialog box, specify the file in which to store the text. Then click the Start button. To pause capturing, choose Transfer ➤ Capture Text ➤ Pause. To resume paused capturing, choose Transfer ➤ Capture Text ➤ Resume. To stop capturing to this file, choose Transfer ➤ Capture Text ➤ Stop.

◆ To upload a text file, choose Transfer ➤ Send Text File. In the Send Text File dialog box, select the file to send and then click the Open button.

TIP   If you're transferring a large file, you may need to make sure that neither computer enters standby or hibernation during the transfer. If either computer does so, the file transfer fails.

When you've finished your session, log off the remote computer. Then hang up the connection by clicking the Disconnect button on the toolbar or by choosing Call ➤ Disconnect.

If you've made any changes to the connection, save them by choosing File ➤ Save.

Once you've created some connections, the Accessories menu off the Start menu displays a Hyper Terminal submenu as well as the HyperTerminal program item. This HyperTerminal submenu lists the connections you have created. To open one of them, and open HyperTerminal, select the connection from the submenu.

TIP   To make HyperTerminal listen for an incoming call, choose Call ➤ Wait for a Call. To stop HyperTerminal from listening, choose Call ➤ Stop Waiting.

Index

Note to the Reader: Throughout this index **boldfaced** page numbers indicate primary discussions of a topic. *Italicized* page numbers indicate illustrations.

Take It to the Next Level